ELEMENTS OF WRITING

Annotated Teacher's Edition

JAMES L. KINNEAVY
JOHN E. WARRINER

Fourth Course

Holt, Rinehart and Winston
Harcourt Brace Jovanovich HBJ

Austin • Orlando • San Diego • Chicago • Dallas • Toronto

Critical Readers

Bess Blunt
Hawthorne Brook Middle School
Townsend, Massachusetts

John J. Elias
Wilkes-Barre Area School District
Wilkes-Barre, Pennsylvania

Gayle Gaither
Durant High School
Durant, Oklahoma

Releah Hawks
A. Crawford Mosley High School
Lynn Haven, Florida

Sandra Strange
Springville High School
Springville, Utah

Herbert Welch
Cedar Springs High School
Cedar Springs, Michigan

Some material previously published in: ENGLISH COMPOSITION AND GRAM-MAR, FOURTH COURSE, Annotated Teacher's Edition, copyright © 1988 by Harcourt Brace Jovanovich, Inc.; WARRINER'S ENGLISH GRAMMAR AND COMPOSITION, FOURTH COURSE, Annotated Teacher's Edition, copyright © 1986 by Harcourt Brace Jovanovich, Inc.; WARRINER'S ENGLISH GRAMMAR AND COMPOSITION, FOURTH COURSE, Teacher's Manual, copyright © 1982, 1977, 1973, 1969, 1965, 1961 by Harcourt Brace Jovanovich, Inc. Copyright re-newed 1989 by Jean W. McLemore, Alison Warriner, Richard Treanor and John H. Treanor, Jr. All rights reserved.

Acknowledgments: See pages 1042–1051, which are an extension of the copyright page.

Printed in the United States of America

ISBN 0-03-047158-3   1 2 3 4 5 6   062   94 93 92

James L. Kinneavy, the Jane and Roland Blumberg Centennnial Professor of English at The University of Texas at Austin, directed the development and writing of the composition strand in the program. He is the author of *A Theory of Discourse* and coauthor of *Writing in the Liberal Arts Tradition*. Professor Kinneavy is a leader in the field of rhetoric and composition and a respected educator whose teaching experience spans all levels—elementary, secondary, and college. He has continually been concerned with teaching writing to high school students.

John E. Warriner developed the organizational structure for the Handbook of Grammar, Usage, and Mechanics in the book. He coauthored the *English Workshop* series, was general editor of the *Composition: Models and Exercises* series, and editor of *Short Stories: Characters in Conflict*. He taught English for thirty-two years in junior and senior high school and college.

Professional Essays

Donald M. Murray is Professor Emeritus of English at The University of New Hampshire, where he served as director of Freshman English and as English Department Chairperson. As a journalist, he won a number of awards including the Pulitzer Prize for editorial writing on the *Boston Herald* in 1954.

Lee Odell has a Ph.D. in English and Education from The University of Michigan. A former middle school and high school teacher of English, he now teaches writing at Rensselaer Polytechnic Institute. He has published frequently on the teaching of writing and is interested in the processes of writing, talking, and thinking.

Maxine C. Hairston has a Ph.D. in English from the The University of Texas at Austin, where she served as Director of Freshman English. She is the author of several texts on writing theory and the teaching of writing, including *A Contemporary Composition*.

Barbara J. Shade has a Ph.D. in Educational Psychology from The University of Wisconsin-Madison. She is a Professor and Dean of the School of Education at The University of Wisconsin-Parkside. She specializes in the social and psychological attributes of people with high academic achievement with an emphasis on African American. She has written extensively on culture and its impact on learning and achievement. She also served as consultant for this series.

Wanda B. Schindley has an Ed.D. in Composition and Rhetoric from East Texas State University. She teaches at Northeast Texas Community College and serves as coordinator and curriculum specialist for the Workplace Partnership program. She coauthored a teacher's resource series, *The English Teacher's Guide to the Essential Elements*.

Charles W. Leftwich has an Ed.D. in Educational Administration from Harvard University. He is a professor in the Department of Educational Administration at East Texas State University. He worked in public schools for over twenty-five years as a teacher, a vice-principal, a principal, and a superintendent.

Patricia G. Tweeddale has an Ed.D. in Educational Administration from East Texas State University. She has taught at-risk students in high school and has written about the impact of public education policy on such students. She is a partner in an educational consulting service that focuses on helping teachers to teach at-risk student populations.

Norbert Elliot has a Ph.D. in English from The University of Tennessee. A director of the writing program at New Jersey Institute of Technology, he is a specialist in test development and writing assessment.

Karen L. Greenberg has a Ph.D. in Linguistics from New York University. She is an Associate Professor of English at Hunter College of The City University of New York, where she directs the Developmental English Program and teaches courses in writing and linguistics. She is a director of the National Testing Network in Writing, and she has authored numerous books and essays on writing instruction and assessment.

David A. England has a Ph.D. in English from Indiana University. He is the Associate Dean of Teacher Education at Louisiana State University. A former high shool English teacher, he has served as a director for the National Council of Teachers of English and was active in the National Writing Project.

Acknowledgments

We wish to thank the following teachers who participated in field testing of pre-publication materials for this series:

Susan Almand-Myers
Meadow Park Intermediate
School
Beaverton, Oregon

Theresa L. Bagwell
Naylor Middle School
Tucson, Arizona

Ruth Bird
Freeport High School
Sarver, Pennsylvania

Joan M. Brooks
Central Junior High School
Guymon, Oklahoma

Candice C. Bush
J. D. Smith Junior High School
N. Las Vegas, Nevada

Mary Jane Childs
Moore West Junior High School
Oklahoma City, Oklahoma

Brian Christensen
Valley High School
West Des Moines, Iowa

Lenise Christopher
Western High School
Las Vegas, Nevada

Mary Ann Crawford
Ruskin Senior High School
Kansas City, Missouri

Linda Dancy
Greenwood Lakes Middle
School
Lake Mary, Florida

Elaine A. Espindle
Peabody Veterans Memorial
High School
Peabody, Massachusetts

Joan Justice
North Middle School
O'Fallon, Missouri

Beverly Kahwaty
Pueblo High School
Tucson, Arizona

Lamont Leon
Van Buren Junior High School
Tampa, Florida

Kathleen R. St. Clair
Western High School
Las Vegas, Nevada

Carla Sankovich
Billinghurst Middle School
Reno, Nevada

Sheila Shaffer
Cholla Middle School
Phoenix, Arizona

Joann Smith
Lehman Junior High School
Canton, Ohio

Margie Stevens
Raytown Middle School
Raytown, Missouri

Mary Webster
Central Junior High School
Guymon, Oklahoma

Susan M. Yentz
Oviedo High School
Oviedo, Florida

Susan Lusch
Fort Zumwalt South High
School
St. Peters, Missouri

Michele K. Lyall
Rhodes Junior High School
Mesa, Arizona

Belinda Manard
McKinley Senior High School
Canton, Ohio

Nathan Masterson
Peabody Veterans Memorial
High School
Peabody, Massachusetts

Marianne Mayer
Swope Middle School
Reno, Nevada

Penne Parker
Greenwood Lakes Middle
School
Lake Mary, Florida

Amy Ribble
Gretna Junior-Senior
High School
Gretna, Nebraska

Writers and Editors

H. Edward Deluzain has a Ph.D. in English Education from Florida State University. He teacher at A. Crawford Mosley High School in Panama City, Florida. He is a writer of educational material in literature and composition.

Patti Day-Miller has an M. A. with a Reading Endorsement from Indiana University. She has been the reading consultant for the Bartholomew Consolidated School Corporation of Columbus, Indiana and has written educational material for composition and literature textbooks.

Peter Harris has a Ph.D. in English literature from Texas Tech University. He is an Associate Professor of English at the West Virginia Institute of Technology in Montgomery, West Virginia.

Mary Elizabeth Podhaizer has an M. Ed. from The University of Vermont. She has been a writer of educational mate-

rials in literature and composition for fifteen years. She is currently engaged in research on secondary students' responses to literature.

Jim Skelton has an Ed.D. in Teaching Composition and Rhetoric from East Texas State University. He has been a newspaper reporter, a teacher of secondary English, and a writer of educational materials in composition and literature. He currently teaches English and Developmental Writing at Kingwood College near Houston, Texas.

Glenda A. Zumwalt has an Ed.D. in Teaching Composition and Rhetoric from East Texas State University. She teaches composition at Southeastern Oklahoma State University. She is a writer of educational material in composition and literature.

Contents in Brief

Table of Contents

PROFESSIONAL ESSAYS

▶ **A TEACHER'S GUIDE TO ELEMENTS OF WRITING**

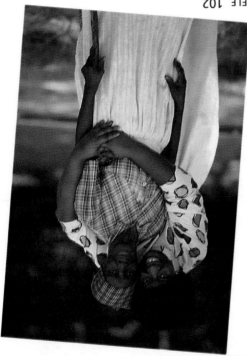

CHAPTER 2 UNDERSTANDING PARAGRAPH STRUCTURE

TEACHING CHAPTER 2 61A–61D

Reading a Model of Paragraph Form 64
from Nisei Daughter
Monica Sone

What Makes a Paragraph 67

CHAPTER 4 EXPRESSIVE WRITING

CHAPTER 6 CREATIVE WRITING

► CHAPTER 9 WRITING TO PERSUADE

▶ **CHAPTER 10** **WRITING ABOUT LITERATURE**

TEACHING CHAPTER 10 361A-361D

Reading a Model of Literary Analysis 364
from *The Best, Worst, and Most Unusual: Horror Films*
Darrell Moore

Writing a Critical Analysis 369

► CHAPTER 14 ENGLISH: ORIGINS AND USES

▶ CHAPTER **15** **THE PARTS OF SPEECH** 512

Their Identification and Function

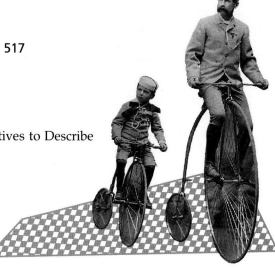

◀ CHAPTER **16** **THE SENTENCE**

Subjects, Predicates, Complements

▶ CHAPTER **19** AGREEMENT 616

Subject and Verb, Pronoun and Antecedent

► CHAPTER 29 Spelling 870

Improving Your Spelling

▶ CHAPTER **30** **SPEAKING**   898

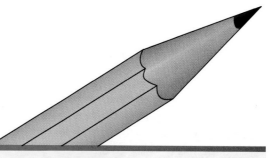

CHAPTER **36** STUDYING AND TEST TAKING 951

Fiction

Italo Calvino, "Mushrooms in the city," *Marcovaldo, or The seasons in the city*

Sandra Cisneros, "Eleven," *Woman Hollering Creek and Other Stories*

Harold Courlander with Ezekiel A. Eshugbayi, "Why No One Lends His Beauty," *Lode the Hunter and Other Tales from Nigeria*

Umberto Eco, *The Name of the Rose*

Edith Hamilton, *Mythology*

David Low, "Winterblossom Garden," *Ploughshares*

Lucy Maud Montgomery, *Anne of Green Gables*

R. K. Narayan, "An Astrologer's Day"

Tim O'Brien, "Where Have You Gone, Charming Billy?" *Going After Cacciato*

Ann Petry, *The Street*

John Steinbeck, *The Pearl*

Carl Stephenson, "Leiningen Versus the Ants"

Nonfiction

Emily R. Alling, "Letter to the Editor," *Newsweek*

Sandra R. Arbetter, "Introverts and Extroverts," *Current Health*

Sherry Baker, "Pioneers Underfoot," *Omni*

Robert D. Ballard, *Exploring the Titanic*

Althea Bass, "The Family Tipi," *The Arapaho Way: A Memoir of an Indian Boyhood*

Stanley Bing, "The Most Beautiful Girl in the World," *Esquire*

Jane Bosveld, "Can Bicycles Save the World?" *Omni*

Albert Britt, *Great Indian Chiefs*

Malcolm W. Browne, "3 Scientists Say Travel in Time Isn't So Far Out," *The New York Times*

Robert B. Carlson, "America's Ancient Skywatchers," *National Geographic*

James R. Chiles, "To break the unbreakable codes," *Smithsonian*

John Ciardi, "bits," *A Browser's Dictionary*

Michael D. Coe, "Olmec and Maya: A Study in Relationships," *The Origins of Maya Civilization*

"The Combi Player," *Consumer Reports*

Mason Crum, *Gullah*

Leonardo da Vinci, "Leonardo da Vinci to the Duke of Milan: 'certain of my secrets,'" *A Treasury of the World's Great Letters*

R. A. Deckert, "Quasi-Humans," *Omni*

Annie Dillard, *An American Childhood*

Timothy Egan, "School for Homeless Children: A Rare Experience," *The New York Times*

John Elkington, et al., *Going Green: A Kid's Handbook to Saving the Planet*

Betty Lou English, *Behind the Headlines at a Big City Paper*

Laurence M. Fisher, "A Thirsty California Is Trying Desalination," *The New York Times*

Lisa W. Foderaro, "At Rye High, Students Not Only Must Do Well, They Must Do Good," *The New York Times*

Roy A. Gallant, *Private Lives of the Stars*

John Steele Gordon, "Financial Folklore," *American Heritage*

Evan and Janet Hadingham, *Garbage! Where It Comes From, Where It Goes*

Helen Hayes, "Hayes: There Is So Much to Do"

Jesse L. Jackson, "We Need Power, Program, and Progress," *The Progressive*

Suzanne Jurmain, *Once Upon A Horse*

Pauline Kael, review—"Driving Miss Daisy," *The New Yorker*

Coretta Scott King, *My Life with Martin Luther King, Jr.*

Maxine Hong Kingston, "White Tigers," *The Woman Warrior*

Doris G. Kinney, "Reopening the Gateway to America," *Life*

Kwei-li, *Golden Lilies*

William Least Heat-Moon, *Blue Highways*

Aldo Leopold, "Sky Dance," *A Sand County Almanac*

Steve MacQueen, "Mo' Better Blues," *Tallahassee Democrat*

Charles Mann and Gwenda Blair, "Juan's Place," *Geo*

Milton Meltzer, ed., *Voices from the Civil War*

Sidney Moncrief, *Moncrief: My Journey to the NBA*

Darrell Moore, "Frankenstein," *The Best, Worst, and Most Unusual: Horror Films*

Rebecca Moore, "Why I choose to veg out," *Seventeen*

Daniel D. Morrison, "Date with Dracula," *American Way*

"Mourning Dove (Hum-ishu-ma)," *The Norton Anthology of Literature by Women*

John G. Neihardt, "Black Elk Speaks," *Black Elk Speaks: Being the Life Story of a Holy Man of the Oglala Sioux*

Lynn Norment, "The Fitness Craze," *Ebony*

Noel Petty, "A biography of Charles Spencer ('Charlie') Chaplin," *How to Become Absurdly Well-Informed About the Famous and Infamous*

George Plimpton, "Neil Armstrong's Famous First Words," *Esquire*

Joyce Pope, *Do Animals Dream?*

Ernie Pyle, "North Africa: November 1942–June 1943," *Ernie's War: The Best of Ernie Pyle's World War II Dispatches*

Boyce Rensberger, "Black Kings of Ancient America," *Science Digest*

Bob Secter, "Time out! Is baseball Finnished?" *Miami Herald*

Ellen Ruppel Shell, "Seeds in the bank could stave off disaster on the farm," *Smithsonian*

Monica Sone, *Nisei Daughter*

Gary Soto, "Foreword," *a fire in my hands*

Gary A. Taubes, "Boxer with a Future," *The Atlantic*

Kathleen Teltsch, "For Young and Old, A Pocket Paradise," *The New York Times*

Paul Theroux, *Riding the Iron Rooster*

Susan Allen Toth, "Nothing Happened," *Blooming: A Small Town Girlhood*

Ken Tucker, "New Dash for 'The Flash,'" *Entertainment Weekly*

Mark Twain, "A Genuine Mexican Plug"

"Two tornadoes damage airport, Miami school," *The Ledger*

Ed Ward, et al., *Rock of Ages: The "Rolling Stone" History of Rock & Roll*

H. G. Wells, *A Modern Utopia*

Tom Wolfe, "Clean Fun at Riverhead"

Rick Wolff, "A Yen for Baseball Cards," *Sports Illustrated*

Poetry

Gwendolyn Brooks, "The Bean Eaters," *Blacks*

N. Scott Momaday, "The Eagle-Feather Fan," *The Gourd Dancer*

Winfield Tounley Scott, "If All the Unplayed Pianos," *Some Haystacks Don't Even Have Any Needle and Other Complete Modern Poems*

David Wagoner, "Tumbleweed," *Collected Poems 1945–1976*

Drama

Bob Elliott and Ray Goulding, "Hard Luck Stories," *From Approximately Coast to Coast*

A Teacher's Guide to
ELEMENTS OF WRITING

CONTENTS

JAMES L.
KINNEAVY

DONALD MURRAY

KAREN
GREENBERG

BARBARA SHADE

LEE ODELL

MAXINE HAIRSTON

NORBERT ELLIOT

PATRICIA TWEEDDALE
CHARLES LEFTWICH

WANDA SCHINDLEY

... IN THE SPIRIT OF MAINTAINING THE LASTING VALUES AND STANDARDS OF THE ... SERIES

How Dare They?

Certainly when teachers saw a new name listed as a coauthor with John E. Warriner, some of you must have said, "How can the editors dare do this?" Like the editors, I am fully aware that Warriner has been a legendary name in high school English composition and grammar books since 1941, the year of the first edition of his series. His high school textbooks have changed somewhat through the decades, but they have stood the test of half a century—despite many educational trends and fashions—because they have incorporated important values and standards. I am aware of all of this, aware that Warriner's texts have almost a biblical authority.

But even the Bible is translated anew for different generations. So it is in the spirit of maintaining the lasting values and standards of the series while bringing a few further changes that this new edition of the series is published with a new name listed as coauthor. I was properly flattered when the company's editors asked me to be the consultant for the composition sections of the books in the new series. But I was also in awe of this long tradition of excellence and can only hope that this tradition can be upheld.

Like John E. Warriner, I have a long and varied experience as a teacher. He taught in junior high, high school, and college. I have taught in elementary school, high school, and college. He taught for many years; I have been teaching since 1941 and continue to teach today. For the past twenty-five years I have given workshops to high school students involved in statewide competitive contests in extemporaneous writing. Like Warriner, I have attempted to keep up with the profession and to reflect in my writings what we have learned and continue to learn about teaching the language arts. I have trained students to teach at all grade levels from elementary school through graduate school. I have also observed student teachers for years at the high school and college levels.

You will find in this series, therefore, an attempt to maintain the best values of the Warriner series and to add to it a few new features that teachers, administrators, scholars, and editors think will make it an even better set of books.

THE TEACHER'S EDITION IS A GREAT HELP

I know that teaching school combines the blue and white collar syndromes: You're there at 8:00 and leave at 4:00; then you take on extra-hour professional chores in the evening and on weekends of correcting papers, reading to keep up professionally (which you are doing right now), working on extracurricular activities, attending conventions, etc. You need all of the timesavers you can find.

You will find many of them in this edition. On each page you will find that your objectives, your lesson plan, and your resources are packed around the student text. Questions you can ask the students are provided (with answers). Vocabulary items are defined. Adaptations to more-advanced students, to less-advanced students, and to ESL students are suggested. Special exercises supplementing those in the textbook are provided. Student responses to questions are foreseen and reactions suggested. Applications to critical thinking and to cooperative learning are continually provided.

All in all these helps are a treasure trove. Before spending hours looking up supplementary materials for a class, look in your teacher's edition. Someone else may have done your work already and saved you hours. When I look at the wealth of all of these materials and contrast them to what I had to teach with in my early teaching years in both elementary and high school, I am green with envy.

Beginning teachers especially should exploit these materials, built upon the experiences of hundreds of their predecessors. These experiences can help new teachers avoid some all-too-common problems. Let me point out some of them.

RELATIONSHIP BETWEEN COMPOSITION AND GRAMMAR

You will find in the new series the same close relationship between composition and grammar that has characterized the series since its inception. You can see this by simply looking at the table of contents.

Such a look makes quite clear that the primacy and the preponderance of attention is given to writing, and that grammar is a handmaid to writing. But both are covered extensively.

Given the increasing importance of rhetoric in public schools and in college, you will find more depth in the composition section of this textbook. There is a more discernible structure to the various chapters on writing. These chapters reflect the concern for certain important kinds of writing—concerns that are reflected in many state writing tests. Thus, there is a chapter devoted to each of the major aims of writing: to inform, to persuade, to explain, to prove, to entertain, and to allow the students to express themselves. Each of the modes of writing usually gets a chapter at each grade level: narrating, describing, classifying and defining, and evaluating. This structure is more explicit in the new series than it was in the earlier ones.

In each of these chapters, however, the close relationship between composition and grammar

WHAT THIS TEXTBOOK DOES NOT WANT TO DO IS TO ENCOURAGE THE ISOLATED TEACHING OF GRAMMATICAL SKILLS IN A ROTE MANNER.

is maintained. There is a grammatical issue covered in each chapter, particularly relevant to the kind of writing being covered. Thus, a chapter on persuasion can consider the problem of fragments, often seen in advertisements. A chapter on description can consider the importance of adjectives and adverbs. Finally, nearly all of these chapters refer to the grammar chapters for coverage of issues that relate to the kind of writing under consideration.

This careful attempt to relate grammar to composition was explicit in the longtime title of this series, which has linked grammar to composition for years.

This linkage is confirmed by seventy years of *empirical research*. Studies at all levels, from elementary school through college, confirm that grammar is learned best when taught in conjunction with composition, as well as with speaking and with literature. These studies have been made in the United States, in Canada, in the British Isles, and in Australia. What this textbook does not want to do is to encourage the isolated teaching of grammatical skills in a rote manner. This is called the formal teaching of grammar. Sometimes, it has to be done. But most of the time, the grammar is linked to a writing assignment and even motivated by it. For instance, consistent fragments in a formal paper suggest a lesson in the sentence, emphasizing its elements and its completeness. This improves the composition and also teaches the grammar in a manner that gives it meaning.

THE PROCESSES OF COMPOSING

In keeping with the emphasis in the schools and in college writing courses, you will find a continuation of the unremitting concern with the processes of writing in every writing chapter of the series—a concern begun several years ago. The stress on process will be evident in the structuring of the chapters by the stages of the writing process; in the frequent use of support groups of students to react to each other's plans, drafts, and papers; and in teacher and peer interventions in the writing process. The idea that writing is a solitary, sedentary process, as a poet once said, is not at all adhered to in this textbook. Rather writing is viewed as a collaborative and cooperative action.

A COOPERATIVE ATMOSPHERE

The process view of writing that sees the writing place as a happy, cooperative workshop rather than a silent dungeon enables the students to get support and help from one another and from the teacher.

The students are usually divided into *peer support groups* of three or four, all working on similar projects, and all trying to help each other turn out better work. The members of the groups help one another plan the papers, critique each other's rough drafts, and provide a real audience for the final version. The members of the group are like a miniature research group working on a common project.

The teacher moves from group to group, helping in the planning, discussing problems, critiquing rough drafts, and grading the final drafts. Like the members of the peer support groups, the teacher fulfills different functions: at times the teacher is a motivator, a source of ideas, a theorist who has general ideas that apply to the current situation, a careful listener, a constructive critic of plans and rough drafts, a sympathetic reader and grader of the final version, and above all, a fellow writer.

With this view of the writing process, the teacher with a heavy *paper load* can find help from the students. The teacher isn't the only person who reads a student's paper. The other members of the support group can assist the teacher with useful feedback to the author at any level of the writer's concerns with mechanics, with word choice, with organization, with ideas, and with style. If the teacher trains support groups to be helpful and constructively critical, a good deal of the drudgery of grading papers can be avoided.

Finally, the writing process often results in some kind of *publication*, possibly in a public speech (or in a performance in the case of creative writing), sometimes in a class newspaper put out by desktop publishing on a computer, sometimes in a school newspaper, or maybe just in a permanent portfolio that the student keeps of his or her better work.

THE WHOLE AND THE PARTS

Another motif that you will see given more prominence from the very beginning and running through all of the writing chapters is the insistence on the relationship between the whole and the parts in the composing process. A theme is like a sentence: it is made up of parts that are uttered in a chronological sequence, but the whole is greater than the parts because it also includes the relationships among the parts and with the whole. We don't begin a sentence with no idea where it is going to end or what it is going to say; we begin with a whole and choose the parts to articulate it. We may change our minds halfway through a sentence and adjust to our new idea, the same phenomenon often happens with a whole theme.

This dominance of the whole *over the parts* explains the general structure of the book. The writing chapters come at the beginning of the book, and the grammar, usage, and mechanics make up the last section of the book.

✿✿✿✿✿

In other words, a theme begins with a vague but somewhat distinct idea of a whole and looks around for the parts that will embody that idea. The parts are single words, phrases, sentences, paragraphs, even large sections of the theme.

Consequently, in the writing chapters, each of these parts is treated as a part of a whole. A composition is not an expanded word or phrase or paragraph. An expanded paragraph is a big paragraph, just as an expanded wheel is just a big wheel, not suddenly a complete automobile. To use another metaphor, a student setting out to write a composition is like an architect who draws up a plan of the whole building; it's going to be a home or a department store or a restaurant or a sports coliseum or whatever. But the architect doesn't haphazardly gather bricks and steel and staircases and chimneys and just throw them together.

With this idea of the dominance of the whole over the parts, each of the writing chapters pursues the writing process through to the production of a complete theme. There are writing activities throughout addressing the parts, but they are all orchestrated to the final whole.

This *dominance of the whole over the parts* explains the general structure of the textbook. The writing chapters come at the beginning, and the grammar, usage, and mechanics make up the last section.

In fact, the suggested treatment for writing encourages the students to write rapidly and enthusiastically in their first plans, sketches, and drafts, without stopping to check spelling, word choice, or grammatical purity. The idea is to

> *T*HE IDEA IS TO SUPPORT THE WRITING PROCESS AS A CREATIVE SURGE IN THE BEGINNING. THE MECHANICAL MATTERS ARE OFTEN BETTER HANDLED IN THE REVISION.

support the writing process as a creative surge in the beginning. The mechanical matters are often better handled in revision.

AIMS AND MODES AS WAYS OF THINKING

The close connections among the aims and modes of writing and rather different ways of thinking have been emphasized in the introduction to the student's edition, so these will not be repeated here in any detail. But at the heart of the series is the notion that writing involves thinking all of the time; and different ways of writing involve different ways of thinking. Expressive writing is quite different from expository writing, and some students can do one type better than another. Nevertheless, a minimum competence in each aim and mode is necessary to the development of a full mental life. You are encouraged to reread the **"Introduction to Writing"** chapter to see the development of this notion.

THE AIMS OF WRITING AND DIFFERENT DIALECTS

You will undoubtedly notice that different levels of formality are suggested with the different aims of writing. In the chapters on expres-

sive writing, a casual, personal, and familiar style is suggested. At the other extreme, in the chapters on information and proof, a more formal sense of grammar and word choice is expected. This is true in real life and in the classroom. In between self-expression and these types of expository writing, there are various shades of formality in persuasive, creative, and exploratory writing.

The model adopted here is that of Martin Joos, whose book *The Five Clocks* distinguishes five different levels of formality that nearly all of us use, depending on the circumstances. Joos calls these the intimate, the colloquial, the consultative, the formal, and the ritual levels. We speak to our family members (and sometimes our pets) in the familiar dialect. We speak to our friends in an ordinary conversation on the colloquial level. We adopt the consultative tone usually when we are teaching class. We use our formal dialect when we are giving speeches at a convention. And we use the ritual level of formality when we are at church or are graduating or are being initiated into a society.

But teachers are not the only people who have their five levels of

formality. Teenagers also have their own dialects for intimacy—I say dialects because girls have a different intimate dialect than do boys. Teenagers also have their own colloquial, consultative, formal, and ritual dialects. Mature people have their own five levels. Finally, the elderly have their own five dialects, often quite different from the other age levels.

Being aware of the different purposes for writing and the various levels of formality also helps the teacher be more aware of *minority dialects*, such as those used by Hispanic, Asian, and African Americans. The use of these dialects in expressive and sometimes in creative writing is often to be encouraged. On the other hand, the dialect of the targeted audience is to be encouraged in persuasion. In expository writing, there is more emphasis on the standard dialect.

WRITING AND LITERATURE

While you are teaching this book on handling writing and grammar, you are also using a separate textbook for literature. But the necessity of putting the major readings in different literary genres covered in the ninth grade in a special book should not at all imply a separation of the study of literature from that of writing or grammar. All through the literature book, there are writing assignments that cover the same purposes that are taught in the writing book. Students are asked to react expressively, persuasively, creatively, and informatively to literary selections. Thus the literature textbook resonates the same tones and rhythms as the writing textbook.

Conversely, this series is permeated with reading and literature. Each writing chapter includes models of the type of writing that is being studied. Many samples are drawn from the literary canon. In one of the textbooks, for instance, to illustrate the aims of writing, there is an excellent poem by William Stafford. Nearly every chapter in the student's edition contains similar material. Of course, all of these selections are annotated.

Further, in this edition, in each chapter of the book there are **Literature Links,** which take common literary selections and relate them to the material being studied in the chapter. Besides the Literature Links, there is the **Quotation for the Day,** a writing prompt drawn from literature.

WRITING AND THE OTHER LANGUAGE ARTS

In addition to being highly integrated with literature, this writing textbook is also tightly integrated with reading, speaking, and listening.

Each chapter contains several reading samples of the type of writing being studied. These are carefully analyzed by the students by means of questions after each selection. These questions are usually answered in an oral forum. The oral emphasis continues throughout the chapter because each stage of the writing process is carried out by means of small support groups of three or four students helping each other in planning, organizing, writing, and revising, as explained above. Frequently the publication of the paper takes an oral form. Thus persuasive speeches are delivered in front of the class.

The support group is clearly as much of a listening group as it is a speaking group. Students learn to listen carefully to each other in order to make constructive suggestions for improvement.

Thus the four language arts are carefully interwoven into the structure of each chapter at each stage of the writing process.

WRITING AND NEW TECHNOLOGIES

Whenever possible, teachers should take advantage of the new technologies that are increasingly becoming available at the high school level. Consequently, throughout this edition, there are continual reminders of these possibilities. Let us mention a few of them.

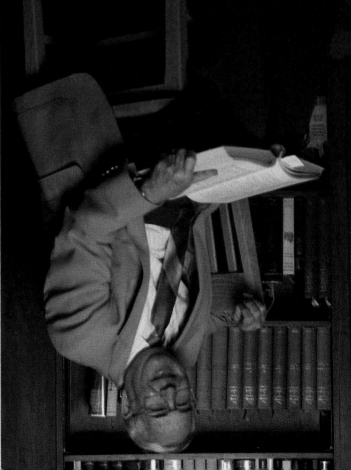

Networking with Computers

Some high schools have word processors available for use in teaching some writing classes. A few of these are even networked to allow student interactions with each other, either with the entire class or with selected support groups. The simultaneous writing reactions of all members of the class to a common reading assignment is one of the most effective methods to insure one hundred percent participation in group discussions, especially if the right questions are asked. And the use of computers to set up small support groups for the different stages of the writing process is also an exceptionally efficient technique of using small groups in teaching writing.

Revising and Word Processors

Even without networking, however, the use of word processors is to be commended whenever possible, particularly because of the manner in which revising is accomplished on computers. Students who formerly hated to revise now see revision as an easy and enjoyable manner to improve their work, not just at the level of vocabulary or mechanics, but even at the level of full discourse changes.

Spelling, Vocabulary, Grammar, and Word Processors

Word processors also bring substantial help to the poor speller and to the student having trouble finding the right word. Nearly all word-processing programs have some type of spell-check feature that shows students which words are incorrectly spelled. Thus each student can keep a list of his or her own problem words. This is acknowledged by nearly all spelling research as the single best way to improve spelling. Most spell-check programs are accompanied by programs that properly hyphenate words at the end of a line. This is an additional bonus for students who use word processors.

In addition, most word processors now come with a thesaurus of some size. This enables the students to look for options in vocabulary, even while working at the computer.

Thirdly, some word processors now have grammar programs that can check tense, case, subject-verb agreement, fragments, etc. These are not as common as spell-check features or thesauruses, but they are becoming available.

Publishing and Word Processors

Even if there is not a full classroom of word processors, it is possible to use a word processor as a desktop publisher to enable students to see some of their writings in elegant print and format. These can be put into portfolios for permanent records. Frequently throughout the annotated teacher's edition you are reminded of this option as one method of publishing the students' papers.

A FINAL WORD: USE YOUR OWN PERSONAL STAFF

Possibly after reading this essay, which brings together many of the rather complex tasks of the writing teacher, you may have been somewhat intimidated. But luckily you don't have to solve all of these problems overnight. The teaching of writing is a slow and cumulative process. Each chapter of this textbook focuses on a very specific issue and tries to teach just that particular skill. Following chapters build on the skill just learned. The student is slowly building up a range of abilities, not suddenly moving from barbarism to literacy.

Of course, in the preceding grades, your predecessors have worked with the students whom you now face, just as your colleagues will pick up where you leave off. And you are not alone at the present time: Your current colleagues are working with the same students in other classes.

In other words, just as writing is a cooperative endeavor among the students with each other and with you in your classroom, so also is it a cooperative endeavor among a sequence of teachers from year to year and among a group of teachers one year at a time. In many cases, parents are also willing cooperators.

Put Your Staff to Work

This textbook adds several more dimensions of helpmates. The authors are seasoned professionals who have faced many of the issues of these chapters before. These authors draw on other textbooks with which they are familiar. They also draw heavily on scholars that they have consulted. Thus, when I said earlier that the best way for a poor speller to improve spelling skills was to keep a journal list of personal mistakes, add to it when new mistakes are made, and consult this personal list regularly, this statement was drawing on ten years of research at two major universities with thousands of students. The marketing staff of this series is also made up of seasoned professionals who make it their business to find out what teachers want in a textbook. The teaching consultants who tried out the materials for these chapters were chosen because of their experience and knowledge. Finally, the editors of

this series are acknowledged masters in their field—they have marketed the best-selling series in writing and grammar for almost half of a century.

Thus, you the teacher are backed by a phalanx of authors, scholars, market experts, teacher consultants, and editors all trying to assist you as you work with your students and other teachers. They are really your own personal staff. Use this book intelligently and this staff springs to life at your command. Donne's statement particularly can be applied to teachers: "No teacher is an island."

This textbook tries to put you in touch with all of these other helpers in the business of education. It can take a good deal of the loneliness out of teaching.

No One Does A More Important Job

Finally, you should be assured that your task is at the top of educational priorities. No one does a more important job than the teacher of writing. Throughout history, people who can write have been considered educated. Writing, in fact, has been the hallmark of the educated person in antiquity, in the Middle Ages (they were called clerks at that time), and in the modern period as well. A person who teaches students how to write is at the forefront of the educational enterprise. Such a person is also teaching students how to think in ways that will enable them to cope with a complex modern society as full human beings. ❦

ELEMENTS OF WRITING addresses the *aims* and *modes* of writing and the *writing process* in the following ways:

Pupil's Edition
Demonstrates and teaches writing skills, focusing on the aims (the *why*) and the modes (the *how*) of writing
Provides an organized, easily understood approach that allows students to gain and sharpen writing skills

Annotated Teacher's Edition
Gives instructional strategies on how to teach the aims and modes
Offers lesson plans based on each stage of the writing process

Teacher's ResourceBank
Offers materials keyed to the writing process that assist students in achieving the aims and modes

USE GENRE AS LENS

BY DONALD M. MURRAY

"WE WRITE ABOUT WHAT WE DON'T KNOW ABOUT WHAT WE KNOW."

Students are usually introduced to each genre—essay, narrative, poem—in isolated units, as if one form of writing would contaminate another. But each genre is a lens, a way to observe, record, and examine the world. Students should be encouraged to use each genre to explore a single important experience.

Student writers and their teachers should begin the exploration with a personal experience—an event, a person, a place—that holds a significant mystery for them. Mystery is the starting place for most writing, what Grace Paley described when she said, "We write about what we don't know about what we know." Invite your students to explore a moment in their lives to which they keep returning in memory, the way the tongue seeks the missing tooth.

Encourage your students to play with the fragments of language connected with that experience in their minds and on paper to discover a line, a phrase, or a word that contains a tension or conflict within the experience. The "line" might be a word—*Christmas*—that might have special implications for a student with a Catholic mother and a Jewish father. It might be a phrase—*the debts of Christmas*—to a person whose family spends too much money to make up for their true family feelings. The "line" could be a sentence—"Each Christmas I remember my sister who will never grow old"—for someone who lost a sister years before. Each "line" has a tension and mystery the writer needs to understand by writing.

Before your students begin, it is important to remind them that all writing is experimental, that experimentation implies failure, and that failure is instructive. It is not possible they will fail; it is imperative that they fail. We do not improve our writing by avoiding failure, but by making use of it.

To guarantee failure, urge students to write the first draft fast. Velocity is as important in writing as it is in bicycle racing. Speed will produce the accidents of language, connection, and insight that will propel the draft forward towards meaning. And velocity allows students to escape, for the moment, the censor that demands premature correctness.

They should allow their drafts to instruct them. The evolving text will take its own course, exploring the experience as it is relived. If they are patient, receptive, and open to surprise, the text will tell them what they have to say. You may want to write two statements by E. M. Forster on the chalkboard:

Think before you speak is criticism's motto; speak before you think creation's.

and

How do I know what I think until I see what I say?

Students should write out loud, hearing the text as they write it. They may actually do this—it is your classroom—or read silently but *listen* to the text. As they tune their voices to the story being told, the voice—angry, nostalgic, humorous, sad, analytical, instructive, argumentative, poetic, even narrative—will reveal the meaning of the draft to the writer.

I invite you to stand beside me at my workbench and to observe me as I use genre to explore an experience of mine.

THE ESSAY

I prefer the term *reflective essay* to *personal essay* because the writer reflects on personal experience, or on a topic of personal interest. The essay is neither a simple narrative of experience nor of thought unanchored by experience, but a combination of thought and experience, an effort to discover and share meaning in experience. The essay is a demonstration of critical thinking.

Some notes on the craft of the essay.

• Narrow the territory to be explored so you can achieve depth.
• Be specific. The specific will instruct. The more specific you are, the more universal your audience will be.
• Work locally; the paragraph you have just written contains the seed of the next paragraph. For example, if you have said the experience was important, show how it was important in the next paragraph.
• Answer the reader's questions. Writing is a conversation between reader and writer.
• When the draft surprises you, pay attention. Develop the surprise to discover its meaning.

On April 21, while visiting a daughter and her husband in their new home, I got up early without the alarm, as is my habit, and ended up sitting at the top of the stairs waiting for my family to wake, and I found mystery in the experience. It was a moment full of emotion, and I needed—not wanted, but needed—to explore that moment through writing.

I made a few notes in my daybook:

I can remember myself as a small boy in Doctor Denton's trying to be quiet sitting at the head of the stairs (night) waiting for the family to get up

I can remember my own daughter's impatient waiting

Sunday morning I sit at the head of the stairs a good place to read, a good place legs waiting, wife, behind me in the room, my wife

THIS MORNING I DIDN'T GET UP UNTIL 5:45, BECAUSE I STAYED UP UNTIL 11:15 WATCHING THE NCAA BASKETBALL. BUT IN SUMMER I'LL BE UP AT 4:30, MAKE COFFEE, LET OUT THE DOG, GO PICK UP THE BOSTON GLOBE. THEN I WRITE.

John Hersey testified that ''To be a writer is to sit down at one's desk in the chill portion of every day, and to write.'' A few years ago poet Donald Hall said, ''I get up at 5 without an alarm. This morning I didn't get up until 5:45, because I stayed up until 11:15 watching the NCAA basketball. But in summer I'll be up at 4:30, make coffee, let out the dog, go pick up *The Boston Globe*. Then I write.''

In retirement I, like so many other over sixties, still get up early when there are no cows to milk, no commuter train to meet, no factory shift to join. It is habit, but for me a habit built not from compulsion but delight.

Sitting at the top of the stairs waiting for the young—and the not-so-young Minnie Mae—to wake, I try to define the strange emotion I feel. At last it comes to me. I am, after a lifetime of chasing the carrot, content.

I have another day to celebrate. Sitting here alone, I can enjoy the feeling of this house that is turning so quickly into a home. I am comfortable in this home and know that soon my wife will wake with a groan and a smile, and downstairs I will hear conversation and music, smell coffee and we will all make plans for the day not too far off when a grandchild will sit where I sit, perhaps beside me, waiting for another day to begin.

The grandchild has arrived. His name is Joshua. I have not yet sat beside him at the top of the stairs but I will.

The next day I wrote the column that was published in *The Boston Globe*, April 30, 1991:

> I am once again a small boy in Dr. Denton's sitting at the top of the stairs waiting for the snoring to stop and another day to begin. I am, at the same time, an old man sitting at the top of the stairs in the new home of a daughter and her husband, waiting once more for the snoring to stop and a new day to begin.
>
> Minnie Mae and I, on our first visit, have taken their bed, and they sleep on the hide-a-bed in the living room. They work in the theatre and have agreed to get up early—at 9 o'clock on Sunday morning—because the old folks are here.
>
> But I followed the custom of many old men and was up at 5:33 AM. I tiptoed downstairs, went out to the car, explored Mount Kisco, sipped a cup of coffee at Dunkin Donuts—yes, and had a dough-nut, and yes, juice to get down my six pills I take because of previous doughnuts—bought the Sunday ''New York Times,'' sat in the car reading it, and now, at eight AM sit at the head of the stairs where I can stretch my legs, flex my football knee, and read my book and wait.
>
> It has been a good morning, and I feel little guilt that I have not been able to sleep in. They will laugh at my compulsion to be up and doing, and I will tease them for their laziness, but they will not understand the joy I, like many over sixties, experience when I am up in the lonely hours of dawn.
>
> I ruminate—early morning is ideal for rumination—on the fact that as a child I was always up early when I could lose myself in a book—no TV then—explore the backyard or the vacant lot where the morning glories grew.
>
> Awake before the grown-ups, I could be what I needed to be:
>
> Lindbergh crossing the Atlantic alone, Admiral Byrd isolated in his tiny room under the Antarctic ice, the unnamed Indian scout watching the palefaces land on the Maine coast.
>
> As a teenager I bicycled my route for Gallagher's News Agency in Quincy finishing before the sun was up, drove Miller's grocery truck to market in Boston or cleaned the vegetables and laid them out in rows on the boxes balanced in front of the small store on Beach street.
>
> Only now I confess that when I nicked myself trimming the lettuce that was packed in ice, my hands numb and clumsy, I would turn that lettuce head so the blood did not show. I was apprentice to Miller's game: profit through deceit.
>
> I still remember playing grown-up early in the morning, the grocer's apron twice tucked so it did not sweep the sawdust strewn floor. The profit would be Miller's not mine, but I anticipated the customers who might, this Depression Saturday, pay cash. That anticipation would last until midnight when Mr. Miller would go out and scan the street right and left and reluctantly, when no one was on the street, give the command to close.
>
> In combat I preferred the early morning patrols, guard duty when I was alone to watch the theatre of morning's change from dark to light, the promise of a new day even when the landscape was littered with last night's dead.
>
> After college I worked for a morning newspaper and liked the mystery and companionship of the night worker, enjoyed the coming home at dawn. Eventually I returned to days, and morning became my best writing time as it is for most writers.
>
> Goethe advised, ''Use the day before the day. Early morning hours have gold in their mouth.''

It is 8 AM and they plan on rising 9 AM. I've been up at 5:33, explored town, coffee, read Sunday NY Times

✣ ✣ ✣ ✣ ✣

THE NARRATIVE

There are many wonderful ways to tell stories, but I suggest student fiction writers begin with the scene.

Conrad is supposed to have said that a novel is a series of scenes of confrontation. The writer experienced in nonfiction tells *about* the story; the fiction writer *reveals* the story. That is an enormous difference, and the writing of a scene is the best way to cross the divide. Students can draw on their experiences with TV and film. The reader observes a room with the fourth wall removed; the action within the room tells the story and the reader discovers its meaning. As the short-story writer Becky Rule points out, students think that fiction has no rules, but the rules come from the story, and they are established early; if Hamlet is an indecisive prince he can suddenly become a king but not a decisive one.

Some notes on the craft of narrative.

• Start with character, not theme. The story and its meaning are revealed through the interaction of the characters.

• Write in the third person. It gives you more room and detachment.

• Dialogue is action, what the characters do to each other. Joan Didion says, "I don't have a very clear idea of who the characters are until they start talking."

• Point of view is where the camera is positioned to record the scene. In the beginning, stick with one point of view, perhaps entering into one head but not jumping in and out of every head. If you are in one sister's head, you don't know Frank is in the freezer; in the other sister's head, you do.

• Kurt Vonnegut counsels, "Don't put anything in a story that does not reveal character or advance the action."

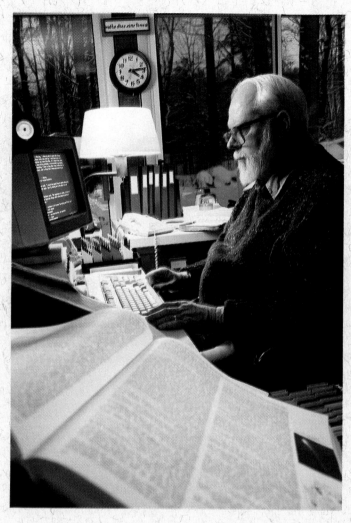

In writing a draft of my novel, I found myself stealing the experience from my own essay and began a scene:

Melissa found Iain sitting in the shadows at the top of the stairs, "It's 5:30 in the morning."

He nodded.

"On guard duty?"

"In a way. I often sit here in winter, watch the light just before dawn, the woods, the field that goes down to the lake."

She thought for a moment of what it would be like to be a spy to your life, always on guard and asked, "You said last night that wherever you are, you see a field of fire, are aware of where to dig in, put the machine guns, even after all there years?"

"I'm not proud of it, Melissa. It's just my geography, an infantryman's geography."

"Do you always see a geography of war?"

"Always first, then I can make it go away. Most times. It's natural, just the way I see things. The doctor sees you as kidney or a colon; I'm an old soldier, I see a field of fire, where the attack would come from."

"That's sad."

"Tedd's a soldier too, Melissa."

They hear the key probe for the lock, at last find it, and hurried down the stairs....

That is just a small fragment of narrative, and yet you can see how the story is revealing itself dramatically to the writer and the reader.

THE POEM

Poetry is the most disciplined and difficult form of writing. It is also the most fun. Experience is distilled by the writing of poetry. Poetry is always play—play with image and language so that meaning is revealed directly without rhetoric getting between the writer and reader or between experience and reader. Inexperienced poets often write with adjectives and adverbs, trying to describe their own feelings. The experienced poet writes with information, revealing specifics, provocative details, and compelling images that make the reader feel and think. The meaning is rarely stated but always there. In the poem, even more than fiction, the meaning is implied. The poem is the stimulus to the reader's thinking.

Some notes on the craft of poetry.

• Forget, for the moment, rhyme, meter, and traditional verse forms.

- Brainstorm images and other specifics, creating a list that may become a poem.
- Draft lines—not sentences but fragments of language—that capture an event, person, or place.
- Rearrange the lines until they reveal a meaningful pattern.
- Pay attention to the line breaks, trying to end on a strong word that causes the reader to read on.

The morning I wrote the column, I also wrote, on the computer, what might become a poem for my poetry group that was meeting that Thursday evening, I pasted this in my daybook:

Sitting at the top of the stairs
I listen to the silences
to understand Grandma's
war with Mother

Sitting at the top of the
stairs
I tune
train myself to I
illness

Later that day I made a handwritten note I also cut out and pasted in the daybook:

I lived at the top of the stairs, behind the living room couch, under the dining room table, the tent of tablecloth— in the apple tree, under the porch.

And still later I drafted a poem that went through one radical and three or four extensive revisions (periods of word play) until it became the following completed poem:

Childhood Espionage

Spy to my life, I lived at the top of the stairs, recorded silence, mapped how hurt was done. Under the porch, at the bedroom door, behind living room sofa, I filled notebooks with what was not said, not done. I escaped to the sidewalk, tried to read the shades drawn against my life. It must be Mother's shadow

light and shade, never let a secret fall out a window.

Sitting on the edge of the double bed, must be father's kneeling to pray, I cannot be sure, circle the block, listen to the neighbor's opera of argument, stand under an open window where conversation will pour over me Once I saw my friend's older sister. She never pulled the shade. The dogs learned my smell

and let me patrol back yard, alley, vacant lot, in silence. I found the room where the Beckers kept the boy with the enormous head, watched comfort flow

from a priest's dancing hands as he gave the last rites to Vinie's grandma, swayed to the rhythm of the Mitchells' bedroom dancing, lying down. Late, I returned to the home of closed doors where we passed each other without touching. We never raised our voices, never stood between

Students should be encouraged to take central experiences from their lives—Willa Cather said, "Most of the basic material a writer works with is acquired before the age of fifteen"—and explore them with an array of genre, using each lens—essay, narrative, poem— and then examining the subject through other genre, perhaps argument, report, screenplay, or news story, to discover the many meanings in their lives.

Sources quoted include Grace Paley, Joan Didion, and Kurt Vonnegut cited in the following work: Donald M. Murray, *Shoptalk: Learning to Write with Writers*, Boynton/ Cook Publishers, Inc. 1990.

ELEMENTS OF WRITING addresses the *aims* and *modes* of writing and the *writing process* in the following ways:

Pupil's Edition
Demonstrates and teaches writing skills, focusing on the aims (the *why*) and the modes (the *how*) of writing

Provides an organized, easily understood approach that allows students to gain and sharpen writing skills

Annotated Teacher's Edition
Gives instructional strategies on how to teach the aims and modes

Offers lesson plans based on each stage of the writing process

Teacher's ResourceBank™
Offers materials keyed to the writing process that assist students in achieving the aims and modes

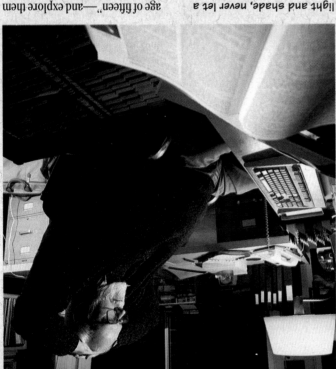

By James L. Kinneavy

Meet the Aims and Modes of Writing

THE PLACE TO START (AND END) THE TEACHING OF WRITING IS TO HAVE STUDENTS SEE WHAT WRITTEN LANGUAGE CAN DO FOR THEM.

WHY WRITE? WHERE DO I BEGIN?

Writing is a very complex activity, and so is the teaching of writing. I admit these facts, and I have been teaching writing for fifty years. You may be teaching your first class this year, and you probably have the same problem: In the face of this complex process, where do you start?

Some teachers recommend what may seem to be a very simple and logical approach: Start with the simple building blocks of writing and gradually work up to more complex blocks. In other words, teach students some elementary things about words, then move up to phrases, afterwards teach sentences, eventually work up to paragraphs, and finally, have students write full themes. Some say that this is how children learn to use language orally. At first blush this theory has a kind of plausible simplicity to it. Years of research, however, have shown that it doesn't work and that it isn't the way children learn language.

LANGUAGE GETS THINGS DONE

Babies see that family members around them accomplish things by using language, and they quickly learn to use it themselves to get food, drink, or attention. This is the motivation behind all language acquisition and usage, from cradle to grave—language gets things done.

Consequently, if we can keep this elementary driving force behind our attempts to teach writing (or any language art for that matter), we can draw on a basic incentive that even babies understand. But when language teaching is divorced from getting things done, students rightly find it boring and uninteresting.

For this reason, the place to start (and end) the teaching of writing is to have students see what written language can do for them. What can writing do? In one introductory chapter, we attempt to get students to look around and see what language is getting done. We call language-users the hidden agents behind many of the miracles of our age, we say that language is where the action is, and we call language-users the movers and shakers of the world.

We focus the student's attention on the different kinds of things that language accomplishes, using very concrete examples. But the principle is the same at every grade-level and on into the college educations, careers, and adult lives of our graduates: The central concept in the teaching of writing at every level is an awareness of the aims or purposes of writing.

THE FOUR MAJOR AIMS OF WRITING

Luckily for you, as well as for the students, these aims are not infinite, unpredictable, and unmanageable. They can be reduced to a few basic categories, and both you and the students have a good deal of practical experience with the categories in general. For example, one kind of language experience with which you are very familiar has to do with attempts to explain to or inform an audience about something of which it is partially

AS A TEACHER, YOU OFTEN TRY TO CONVINCE YOUR STUDENTS OF THE IMPORTANCE OF AN EDUCATION . . .

As a teacher, you often try to convince your students of the importance of an education and of their duties as citizens. As a matter of fact, in our culture we are bombarded with attempts to get read-ers to vote a certain way, to change attitudes or beliefs, to buy certain products, to switch allegiances, etc. Examples of such writing are ad-vertising, political speeches, legal oratory, editorials, and religious sermons. In all of these cases, the focus of the use of language is on the receiver of the message. Usu-ally, this kind of writing is called *rhetorical* or *persuasive writing*.

A fourth kind of writing, prob-ably your favorite, is literature. This type of writing is given an honored place in English classes. We read selections of literature. They are intended to delight us and some-times to teach us lessons. Examples of literature range from simple jokes, funny stories, ballads, small poems, and TV sitcoms to serious dramas, movies, novels, and epics. We try to get students to write this way when we teach creative writ-ing. Although all writing involves originality, we usually reserve the term *creative writing* for this kind of writing.

As a teacher, you are only too aware of a second kind of writing that places more emphasis on the writer. In this case, the writing reveals the feelings of the writer, allows the writer to voice his or her aspirations or reactions to some-thing in a quite personal way, or gives the writer a chance to articu-late important beliefs. Examples of this kind of writing are journals, diaries, myths, prayers, credos, and protests. Of course, some of this writing may also overlap with other kinds. The major emphasis in this kind of writing is on the writer. *This kind of writing is often called expressive writing.*

or totally ignorant. You do this daily in the classroom and the stu-dents are the targets of this use of language. Other examples of this kind of writing are news stories in newspapers and magazines, ency-clopedia articles, reports, text-books, discussions, proposed solutions to problems, research studies, etc. The emphasis is al-ways on the subject matter, con-sidered more or less objectively. *This kind of writing is generally referred to as expository writing.*

THE COMMUNICATION BASIS OF THE AIMS OF WRITING

As a perceptive reader, you may have noticed as we went through the four major aims of writing that each one emphasized a different element of the communication pro-cess. It is not accidental that the four major purposes of writing gener-ally can be reduced to four. The structure of the written communi-cation process is based on a writer, a reader, a language, and the sub-ject matter; you may have seen these elements presented in a graphic form, such as the commu-nication triangle shown below.

The major parts of the communication process.

You will find that students usu-ally recognize that these four ele-ments all play an important role in the writing process, but it is more difficult to get them to see that the role of each element changes in the different aims of writing.

CHANGING ROLES OF ELEMENTS IN DIFFERENT AIMS

In the expressive aim, as we pointed out above, the major focus of the attention is on the writer; the reader, language, and subject mat-ter take on secondary roles. In persuasion, on the other hand, the reader takes center stage; the writer, though present, wants to get the message acted upon and uses language and subject matter to achieve this end.

In expository writing, the sub-ject matter is given the lead role in the communication drama; the writer, reader, and language are subordinate to the explanation, proof, or communication of in-formation that is involved. In lit-erature, finally, the emphasis is on the beauty of the literary crafts-manship as an object of delight to the reader; the subject matter and the author, though present, are not as important as the literary object. When we are studying *Huck Finn,* the novel is more important than either Mark Twain or life on the Mississippi as expe-rienced by a young white boy and a black man.

To assist you to get students to see these differing roles, the rela-tionship between the elements of the communication process and those of the aims of discourse is expressed graphically below. (The major aims of writing and the main parts of the communication process).

The major aims of writing.

Consequently, from aim to aim there is a continual shifting of roles in the communication pro-cess. The lead role determines the major purpose of the writing and the other roles become subordi-nate. Many teachers have found that this simple diagram enables students to grasp the changing dynamics of language use.

DOMINANT AIMS
AND OVERLAP

As a teacher, you have probably written one or two of these different kinds of writing, but you may not have written all of them. In your own writing you are certainly aware that most writing does not attempt to achieve all of these aims at the same time. A specific piece of writing usually has a single dominant aim, subordinating the others to avoid conflicts and confusion. Though subordinate, the other aims are still present. Thus, movie ads in the newspaper contain important information about actors, actresses, directors, titles, show times, etc., but the information is there to persuade people to come to the movies.

Similarly, a scientific report proving that smelters of Sudbury, Ontario, affect the ecology of the area emphasizes in an objective way the evidence for this hypothesis. But there is clearly the implicit notion that something ought to be done about it (a persuasive strain). Indeed, all the aims overlap each other.

WHY ARE THE BASIC
AIMS IMPORTANT?

Despite overlaps, however, it is quite important to distinguish the various aims. It is crucial that both teachers and students understand why.

As a teacher, you are very aware that the criteria by which one kind of discourse is judged are different from the criteria by which another kind of discourse is judged. You know and try to impress upon your students that expository writing is judged on the basis of objective evidence; the appeal of the writer

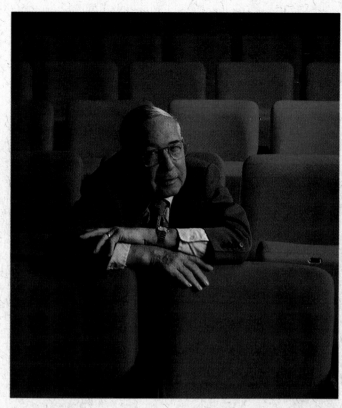

JAMES L. KINNEAVY
AUTHOR OF
*ELEMENTS OF
WRITING*

as such is not relevant to the final proof or explanation, nor is the use of emotion or humor. For this reason, you know that when you teach expository writing, it is important to discourage the use of these other kinds of appeal—they are, in fact, considered inappropriate in news stories, scientific reports, or textbooks. Thus the pedagogy of expository writing follows from the nature of this kind of writing.

But when you switch to teaching other kinds of writing, these other appeals are positive and important. In persuasion, for example, the emphasis is on the appeal of the writer and the appeal to the interests of the audience. The differences among exposition, persuasion, literature, and self-expression force you to emphasize different criteria when

teaching these different kinds of writing. There is no single criterion of aim which makes all writing good. That is why the different aims are taught separately.

THE MODES
OF WRITING

After all this talk about the aims of writing, you, as a teacher, might very well say to me, "Well, Mr. Kinneavy, all this may be very true. But are you maintaining that if I get students to pay attention to the aims of their writing, all other problems will disappear? There are many other facets of the process of writing to which we teachers have to pay attention. Grammar is clearly a persistent concern, as are spelling, vocabulary, sentence structure, paragraphing, genres of writing (letter, report, story, poem, speech, ad, etc.), subject matter,

and last but not least, the modes. What do you propose to do with all of these issues?"

I recognize all of these concerns and reply that they will be given close and continuous attention throughout the entire course, but in this introduction I would like to stress the last dimension, that of the modes of writing.

This dimension bridges the two mentioned just before it—genre and subject matter, and it implicates a major concern of all writing teachers—organization. More than any other aspect of writing, modes determine overall organization. This particular essay, for example, is a series of classifications and definitions.

At times in the history of writing, modes have been given almost as much attention as the aims, but most of the time they have been a serious second candidate. The modes are listed differently in various books. In this textbook we call narration, description, classification, and evaluation the modes. They could be called the genres of writing, and they could be called ways of looking at subject matter.

USE THE
NEWSPAPER TO
DISPLAY THE MODES

When I want to introduce students to the modes, I use a newspaper. I ask students to find examples of news stories (narratives). I ask them to find classifications, especially in the classifieds,

as they are called. I ask the students to examine individual items
within each section of the classifieds
and to tell me what the details are.
It becomes clear to them that there
are hundreds of specific descriptions of cars, houses, lost dogs,
jobs, etc., in the classifieds. Finally, I have the students check
reviews of books, movies, television programs, concerts, football
games, etc. These are all evaluations. Modes are as ubiquitous as
the aims of writing.

Like the aims, the modes have to
be taught separately. What makes a
good narrative is not what makes a
good evaluation or a good description or a good classification. The
rules of defining are not at all the
rules of narrating. As with the aims
of writing, the modes of writing
are different in nature and require
different pedagogies. Consequently, the modes are given careful consideration in the following
chapters.

**THE PHILOSOPHIC
BASIS OF THE MODES**

You are probably wondering if
there is a neat graphic structure
that you can use to help students
with the modes. Yes, there is. But,
before it can be presented, let us
ask the preliminary question,
''What is a mode?''

WHAT IS A MODE?

A mode is a different perspective
on a given subject matter. Take
George Washington or a razor, two
very different kinds of subject matter. I can write a history of George
Washington or a history of the development of a given razor. I can
describe the individuating characteristics of a given razor. I can
classify George Washington or a
razor. Finally, I can evaluate the
Washington, and I can evaluate the
razor. Each of these discourses is a
very different kind of writing.

What explains the differences? In
other words, what differentiates
narration from description, for example? Narration is always dynamic;
it is concerned with change,
whereas description is static. A narrator looks at the changing aspects
of something, whereas a describer
looks at the static aspects of the
same thing.

When you are trying to get students to see the difference between
description and classification, ask
them what a description of Washington entails and what a classification of Washington would require.
In description, the individuating
characteristics of his personality
are stressed (the father of our country, for example), but a classification of Washington pays attention
to the different roles he assumed
(president, general, husband, etc.).
Both pay attention to Washington
as static, and are therefore not like
narration.

When you are trying to get students to differentiate narration from
evaluation, first have someone tell
a little of the history of Washington
at Valley Forge. Then have someone evaluate Washington as a general. They will see that narration as
such, simply details change in something, whereas evaluation considers that thing's performance
against some norm and makes a
judgment of approval or disapproval. Both narration and evaluation are dynamic: Narration details
change, and evaluation considers
performance.

These differences are shown
above in The Modes as Four
Ways of Looking at Objects.

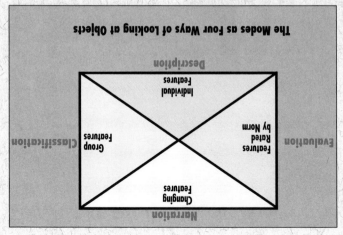

The Modes as Four Ways of Looking at Objects

In the textbook, these four
modes will be continuously related to the aims. Anything that is
written will always involve both
an aim and a mode. Together,
they solve nearly all of the organizational problems of writing, for
either the aim or the mode determines the way the theme is laid
out, as the following chapters will
show. The aim especially determines the style, as will be made
clear in each chapter. Thus, the
aim and the mode of a given piece
largely determine the main ideas,
the overall organization, and the
direction of the style.

ELEMENTS OF WRITING addresses the *aims* and *modes*
of writing in the following ways:

Pupil's Edition
Demonstrates and teaches writing skills, focusing on
the aims (the *why*) and the modes (the *how*) of
writing
Provides an organized, easily understood approach
that allows students to gain and sharpen writing
skills

Annotated Teacher's Edition
Gives instructional strategies on how to teach the aims
and modes

Teacher's ResourceBank™ Offers materials keyed to the writing process that
assist students in achieving the aims and modes

BY LEE ODELL

SHOWING VS. TELLING:
Using Models in Teaching Writing

MAKE US SEE WHAT YOU'RE TALKING ABOUT.

For some time now, teachers of writing have made a point of exhorting students to make their writing "show, not tell." Don't just tell us your reactions or opinions, we say to them. Make us see what you're talking about. If you're trying to describe a person, let us see facial expressions, details of clothing, mannerisms, actions; let us hear exactly what the person says. Or, if students are trying to write persuasively, we insist: Don't just give us your generalized conclusions. Give us some specific information that lets us see what you base your judgment on and that lets us decide for ourselves whether your judgment makes sense.

This advice is not an infallible, inflexible rule. Writers can't elaborate on everything. Furthermore, readers sometimes let a generali-zation pass unchallenged because it seems to ring true or because writers have sufficient authority for us simply to take their word on the matter. But if we are judicious in asking students to "show, not tell," the phrase constitutes good advice for writers and excellent advice for teachers. If we want students to make significant progress as writers, we will have to show them—not just tell them, *show*

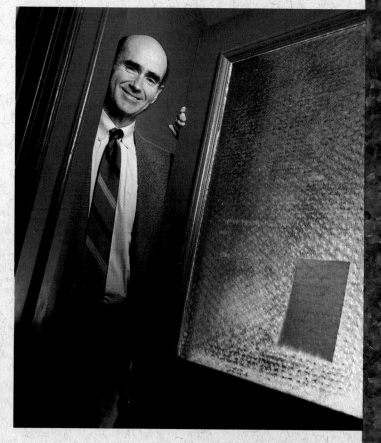

LEE ODELL OPENS HIS CLASSROOM DOOR AT RENSSELAER POLYTECHNIC INSTITUTE.

them—what we mean. In effect, we need to make sure they have models, not just of the kinds of writing they will do but of the writing processes.

There is, of course, a long history to the practice of working with models. For centuries, teachers of rhetoric and writing have required students to study the works of great writers, sometimes having students copy model texts word for word or asking students to imitate the sentence structures they found in these works. Indeed, a version of this practice persisted through the middle 1980s in the form of sentence combining. This system did not ask students to emulate one specific writer, but it did show them frequently used sentence patterns in the works of highly admired professional writ-ers so students could construct their own sentences based on a wide variety of these patterns.

Traditional approaches to us-ing models have their uses, but these approaches are not what I'm talking about here. I'm suggesting that we depart from traditional practice in several ways. For one thing, the model should come not solely from famous authors but rather from books and magazines students read willingly and have readily accessible. Also, teachers don't have to provide all the mod-els; students should be asked to bring in articles or excerpts from books that they personally find engaging and effective. Finally, these models should not be treated as though they are sacred; they are, instead, objects for analysis—for criticism as well as for praise. We and our students need to ex-amine entire models where writ-ers have used successful strategies that students might incorporate into their own writing, as the occasion warrants. But we and our students also need to identify things that don't work and maybe even to col-laborate on devising ways to im-prove the model.

There are several ways we might use models, but my favorite is to use them to help students solve their own writing difficulties. For example, a number of my students can't figure out how to begin a piece of writing, what Donald Murray would refer to as a "lead." When this is a problem, I ask stu-dents to bring in copies of the first pages of articles that they some-how found themselves reading, even though the topics might not normally have concerned them.

For example, one student brought in an article entitled "Hell on Wheels," which began this way:

Almost from the time the downtown No. 4 subway train began its 21-mile run below New York City at 11:38 p.m. on the night of Tuesday, Aug. 27, some-thing seemed amiss. Heading from the Bronx to Manhattan, the train overshot the platform at a couple of stations. At times it slowed to a crawl and then accelerated to breakneck speeds. The conductor contacted the mo-torman, Robert Ray, 38, several

I DON'T WANT STUDENTS TO THINK THERE IS JUST ONE WAY TO BEGIN A PIECE OF WRITING.

times on the intercom to find out if everything was all right. But Ray replied that he was fine. But that was clearly not the case....

This article begins, of course, with a claim about a specific event ("something seemed amiss.") and then illustrates this claim with a series of incidents. It mentions specific, troubling things that hap-pened (for example, the train "slowed to a crawl and then accel-erated to breakneck speeds"); it reports what people said to each other; and then it challenges what one of the people said ("But that clearly was not the case...."). In this last sentence, the author cre-ates a conflict that engages the reader and lets the reader know what the rest of the article will be about (i.e., it will show how the driver's claim was "not the case").

Other articles brought in by the students began quite differently—by citing troubling general statistics, for example, or by describing general trends in society that a reader was almost certain to know and be concerned about. These differ-ences are important. I don't want students to think there is just one way to begin a piece of writing. Consequently, I photocopied a va-riety of examples and asked stu-dents to talk them through to iden-tify the strategies writers had used to engage readers. My goal was to help students recognize some of the options that are open to them in doing their own writing.

In addition to bringing in mod-els written by professionals, it can be extremely useful for us to bring in copies of our own efforts to do the same kind of writing students are working on. And once we have developed an atmosphere of trust, it can be useful to bring in effective examples of student work, con-tinually asking such questions as these: What did the writer do here? How did he or she go about capturing our interest and letting us know what to expect in the rest of the text? Is there anything that this writer is doing that you might profitably do? Again, the goal is not to provide recipes or rules chiseled on tablets of stone but to get students to see what is pos-sible.

MODELING THE COMPOSING PROCESS

Thus far, I have been describing ways we might use written prod-ucts as models. In addition, we also need models of the compos-ing processes of writers. This modeling can be as sophisticated or as rudimentary as our students need. It can focus on the work of an individual writer as Donald Murray shows in his "Use Genre as Lens" essay or on the efforts of peers as they revise their initial drafts. That is, we need to let students see the processes profes-sional writers and students go through in doing their own writing and even in responding to class-mates' writing.

There are several activities teachers can use that allow stu-dents to observe their peers' writing processes. For example, a colleague was concerned that her tenth-graders would have difficulty passing the state basic competency test that is required for high school graduation. Knowing that one of the questions on that test was likely to require students to report information in a well-organized form, she could have concentrated on paragraph form and the proper use of transitions. But suspecting that her students' difficulties were more profound than that, she decided that her students weren't paragraphing because they did not understand that certain kinds of expository paragraphs require writers to group facts by setting up categories that the paragraphs would be about.

Consequently, she asked students to watch a videotape of a movie that she was fairly certain they would find moving, an account of the difficulties encountered by a child who had been classified as mentally retarded but who had, nonetheless, a number of good traits and who was personally likable. After students had watched the videotape, she asked them to write down every fact they could remember from the movie and to collaborate as a class to make the list as complete as possible. That night she typed a complete list of facts, made an overhead transparency of them, and then cut the transparency into strips, each strip containing one fact.

The next day, she asked students to collaborate on ways to group these facts. For instance, students noticed that many of the facts pertained to ways people reacted to the young boy, while others could be grouped under such headings

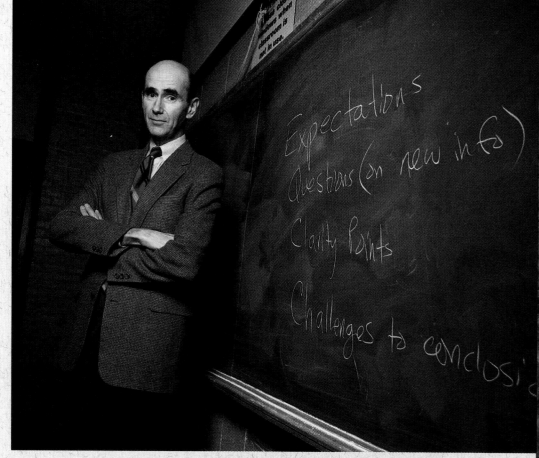

as the boy's reactions to other people or his abilities. As students discussed ways of grouping facts, the teacher reflected what they were saying by moving the transparency strips around on the overhead projector. She was showing, not telling, her students about the basic process they needed to create one type of organized paragraph.

Another approach to modeling the composing process comes from a ninth-grade teacher concerned that her students' descriptive writing was bland. She believed their real problem was not a lack of descriptive adjectives and adverbs but that students weren't really looking closely at the people or objects they were describing.

She also knew that television programs routinely provide excellent examples of the process of observing. That is, as a rule, television cameras do not stay in one

spot to observe everything from the same angle and distance. Instead, the cameras change position to vary the angles and the distances from which they view things. For example, one detective program began with a close-up shot of a ringing phone. Then the camera moved back so that the viewers could see a well-dressed man hurrying across an elegant apartment toward the phone. Next, the camera moved in to focus on the man's trembling hands as he nervously dried his sweaty palms on his handkerchief before picking up the phone. Finally, the camera shifted focus again, to show the head and shoulders of a burly, unshaven man speaking into a pay phone. These shifts in focus set the scene for the entire episode.

To help students understand this process of observing by shifting focus, the teacher asked students,

as part of their homework, to watch one of their favorite TV programs and to count the number of times the camera shifted its focus in a two-minute period. She also asked them to make notes about the different things they saw every time the camera shifted focus. The next day they discussed these episodes and concluded that a program in which the camera did not shift focus would almost certainly be dull.

To help students see how this process applied to writing, the teacher gave students the following description:

She probably has false teeth and wears glasses. She wears her hair up in a bun and wears dresses from the 1930s. She has a habit of tapping her pencil on her desk.

Students readily agreed that this passage was uninteresting. To help them see why, the teacher asked students to think of the grammatical subject of each sentence as the visual focus of each sentence. (In response to the predictable question, the teacher told students that, for this passage, they could think of the grammatical subject as "how the writer begins each sentence.") Students saw readily that this writer's "camera" was standing in one place, not shifting at all. So the teacher asked students to work in groups to revise the passage so that the grammatical focus reflected changes in visual focus. As one group collaborated on revising the passage, the following discussion took place:

"OK, let's start with her false teeth—yeah—write that down."

She has false teeth.

"No, dummy. We gotta start the sentence with 'her false teeth.'"

Her false teeth.

"OK, now what?"

"Oh, no. If we start with that we gotta add stuff. Like...'Her false teeth look funny.'"

"Yeah, put that down."

"No, you gotta tell what 'funny' means. She'll [the teacher] only ask 'What's funny mean?'"

"I got it." Her false teeth look yellow. "My grandma's are."

"Yeah, 'cause they're old, like her."

"Hey. Who's writing?"

"I am." "Her false teeth are yellow because they're old."

"That's good."

"OK, now the stuff on glasses. Oh, gosh. We're gonna have to add stuff to everything!"

Indeed, they would. And that was just the point. Their teacher wanted them to see that as they shifted visual focus, they would have to explore their subject further. Not only was their teacher showing these students a fundamental process of observing, but also she was showing them how the process of observing translated into the process of writing.

In addition to modeling the writing process, we also need to model the process of responding to writing. It is true that students can learn to make very helpful comments about their peers' writing. But the important phrase here is learn to. As Karen Spear has pointed out in her excellent book Sharing Writing, working in response groups is a complex process. It requires that students be able to go beyond uninformative, global comments ("Yeah, it's pretty good." "I guess it's OK.") and do two things: pay attention to specific words, phrases, or ideas and explain why and how they personally react to those things. The ninth-grade class I've just described illustrates one way to model the process of responding. When the teacher asked students to revise the bland description, she was showing them a process they could use in responding to each other's drafts. That is, she was helping them see that when they responded to a classmate's descriptive writing, they might consider whether the student had shifted focus and whether the shifts in focus helped give the reader a clearer visual picture of the person, object, or place being described. Indeed, the teacher made sure students worked as a class to give this sort of response to one or two students' subsequent drafts.

But modeling the response process may not be enough. It may also be necessary to model the processes of listening to and using those responses. Listening can be especially difficult when the response implies that a writer's work is unclear or in need of further effort. In such cases, any writer—and students are no exception—may well become defensive, more eager to prove that responses are invalid or irrelevant than to listen to those responses and consider the uses they might have. In other words, students may need to learn how to respond to responses. If so, teachers may need to model the way we want student writers to react to their classmates' comments. Specifically, we should bring in our own efforts to do some of the same writing students are doing and ask students to respond to it. Where is it clear or unclear? What sort of personality or attitude is in our writing conveying? At what points have we said things that seem appropriate or inappropriate for the audience we are addressing? My experience in doing this sort of work with students is that if they trust us, they can be very perceptive and painfully direct. If they don't get it, they can tell us so in no uncertain terms. In doing so, they give us a chance to show how a writer listens to readers, not by arguing but by attempting to find out why readers react as they do and then using that information to revise a subsequent draft.

The process of modeling is, like everything else about teaching writing, a slow business. One example rarely does the trick. But if we are persistent in showing students what is involved in producing good writing through the writing process, we can usually count on results. But if we don't model, we should expect our distinction between showing and telling to fall on deaf ears. If we don't follow our own advice, why should they?

ELEMENTS OF WRITING addresses the *writing process* and *cooperative learning* in the following ways:

Pupil's Edition

Provides students with detailed instruction for each stage of the writing process

Provides numerous activities and exercises in the writing chapters for students to work cooperatively

Annotated Teacher's Edition

Offers lesson plans based on each stage of the writing process

Offers *COOPERATIVE LEARNING* features that suggest activities for teaching writing and grammar

Teacher's ResourceBank

Furnishes materials that can be used for peer evaluation

BY MAXINE HAIRSTON

THE JOY OF WRITING

STUDENTS NEED TO GET SOME FUN OUT OF WHAT THEY'RE DOING.

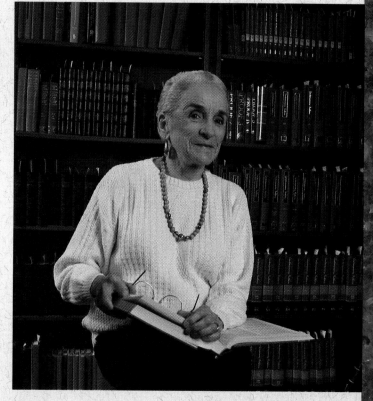

MAXINE HAIRSTON TAKES A BREAK FROM CLASSES.

In recent years I have come to believe that the most important job I can do as a writing teacher is to help my students enjoy writing. I say this because I'm convinced that unless students find some pleasure in their writing classes, most of them will not be willing to invest the time and energy required to turn out work that they—and we, as their teachers—can be proud of. Few adults are disciplined and determined enough to drudge away at some project—whether it's exercising or learning Spanish verbs—simply because someone else tells us that it will be good for us in the long run. We just won't stay with such projects unless there's some satisfaction in the process itself. How much harder it is, then, for youngsters to whom college or even next fall seems light years away to subject themselves to the hard work of learning to write if they get no pleasure from it at the time. Deficit motivation, working to avoid penalties or simply for a passing grade, isn't enough; students need to get some fun out of what they're doing. Fortunately, given what we now know about teaching the writing process, it's quite possible to create a writing classroom in which many students work from growth motivation; that is, they work at their writing because they enjoy doing it for its own sake.

Cognitive studies, ethnographic studies about writing, and the national projects argue that four characteristics define the congenial writing classroom, the kind in which students are likely to enjoy writing and to flourish as writers. First, teachers provide a low-risk environment that encourages students to write without fear. Second, teachers have students develop their papers through a series of drafts and revisions. Third, teachers honor the students' right to their own writing, allowing students to choose their own topics and encouraging them to write about their interests. Fourth, teachers create and support a collaborative learning environment.

ESTABLISHING A LOW-RISK CLASSROOM

Creating a low-risk environment in the writing classroom may seem like a formidable challenge, and indeed it can be at the beginning of a new term when many students are as wary as stray cats. They're nervous for fear someone is going to try to trap them. In the first week of a writing class sometimes I feel as if I want to wear a banner across my chest, emblazoned with '"Trust me! It's going to be all right!'" But I can understand students' anxiety. Students who have come from writing courses with a heavy emphasis on rules and form, courses in which they did badly, have good reason to see a composition course as a high-risk situation. No wonder they start out by trying to stay in the safety zone of rules and formulas.

The humanistic psychologist Abraham Maslow theorizes that all people have two sets of forces operating within them: a need for safety and a fear of risk on one hand and an urge toward growth

and autonomy on the other hand. Maslow also believes that every individual has an innate urge to create, to grow, to discover new abilities and talents. I agree; I think all children want to communicate, to write something that catches the interest and attention of others, but most will hesitate if they think they will be punished for

⁙⁙⁙⁙⁙

I N THE FIRST WEEK OF A WRITING CLASS SOMETIMES I FEEL AS IF I WANT TO WEAR A BANNER ACROSS MY CHEST, EMBLAZONED WITH '"TRUST ME! IT'S GOING TO BE ALL RIGHT!"

⁙⁙⁙⁙⁙

breaking rules. As Maslow points out, '"Safety needs are prepotent over growth needs....[and] in general, only a child who feels safe dares to grow forward health-ily'" (49). He adds, '"Only the [teacher] who respects fear and defense can teach. . . .'" (53).

The writing teacher's challenge is to foster the low-risk environment that will encourage creativity and expression but at the same time to work toward helping students master the writing conventions that they must know to be accepted as writers. There are several ways teachers can do this. First, of course, is to emphasize that we write in stages; we plan, we draft, we read and reread, and we revise. Final details matter when a writer gets ready to publish, but the most-productive writers learn how to suspend their error monitors in the early stages.

I have found it helps me to suspend my own error monitor when reading early drafts if I can put down my pencil and force myself to read strictly for content, good practice for trying to become a courteous reader. I ask myself, what is this writer trying to express? Why? How? Then I make only a large-scale response, focus-ing on being positive and on asking questions that could help the next draft. I emphasize that I hope to see substantial change and development in that draft. It would waste time even to mention error at this stage. When students realize that I really am not looking for mistakes in their drafts, they begin to relax and become more venturesome.

On second drafts, I still try to avoid writing on the paper, but focus on more specific suggestions for improvement. I also make checks in the margins to indicate potential trouble spots that the writers need to be aware of when they begin to polish their papers, sometimes adding a comment that the writer should be alert for problems with commas, subject-verb agreement, or whatever area seems most troublesome. This gives the writer specific areas to concen-

trate on at proofreading/editing time.

Probably one of the best ways to reduce risk in the writing class-room is to set up a portfolio system that allows students to draft a variety of papers over a period of time and then to choose a limited number to develop fully and submit for final evaluation. This method has become increasingly popular for a number of reasons. For one, student writers can work more as adult working writers do. They can attempt different kinds of writing, can stay with those projects that go well and, putting the others aside, they can invest as much as they like in them. It also gives students more control over the evaluation process. They decide which pieces they want evaluated; the teacher doesn't even have to see the others. There is considerable literature on the portfolio system if you find it an attractive option. (See also Elliot and Greenberg's essay ''The Direct Assessment of Writing,'' Notes for Teachers.'')

A final specific suggestion for reducing your students' anxieties is to establish a hierarchy of errors. We know from research that not all errors are created equal. Some are truly damaging, for instance, wrong verb forms, egregious sentence fragments, double negatives, and faulty parallelism. Errors like these set off alarms for most readers. Others, such as split infinitives, comparison of absolutes, or misusing *lie* and *lay* cause scarcely a ripple with most audiences. We should be lenient about such lapses and reduce the number of things our students have to worry about.

We should also remember that the more a writer attempts, the more mistakes he or she is likely to make. But if we are encouraging growth, we need to let student writers know that we regard such mistakes as the natural accompaniment of growth and as less important than the students' fresh ideas.

TEACHING THE WRITING PROCESS THROUGH A SYSTEM OF DRAFTS

Because this textbook so strongly emphasizes that drafting, evaluating, and revising are essential parts of the writing process, I don't feel I need to build an elaborate case for having students develop their papers in drafts. Fortunately, with most writing teachers and curriculum supervisors embracing the concept of writing as a process, students accept drafting as a routine practice. I hope so, because students write more freely and more confidently when they know that their readers view their drafts as "work in progress," not as finished products to be critiqued and judged. Under such a system, knowing they're not irrevocably committed to what they've written, writers can afford experiments. Writing tentatively, they can count on getting help from their readers to help them work out their ideas. That's very reassuring, particularly to students who haven't written much and aren't sure they have anything to say.

The less articulate, inexperienced writers are probably those who get the most out of numerous drafts because they have the opportunity to improve first attempts

WRITING CAN BECOME A GENUINE JOY FOR GOOD WRITERS WORKING AT THEIR PEAK.

❧❧❧❧❧

substantially before they must submit the papers for evaluation. They also have the chance to get feedback *during* the writing process, feedback that is far more valuable than comments on a paper that has already been graded. We know that many students, perhaps even most, pay scant attention to comments written on graded papers, especially negative comments. But when they get comments—both written and oral—on drafts, they are likely to pay attention because they use them to real advantage.

Good students also benefit from drafts, although sometimes they may resist doing them because the system requires more work than they've usually had to do in order to get good grades. But for some good writers, developing a paper through drafts can be a heady experience as they tap into talent they didn't know they had and then earn new recognition from their peers. Writing can become a genuine joy for good writers working at their peak.

In my opinion, the worse possible system for having students write papers is to give a fresh assignment each week, have everyone write the paper only once and turn it in for a grade, and then return the graded papers and repeat the process. Under such circumstances, the anxiety level skyrockets for all but the most able

students, writers get no help during the process (when they need it most), and teachers never learn what most students can really do. Even when students write in class, those papers should be drafts that they can work on again during the next class periods. Only then are students likely to develop their potential.

LETTING STUDENTS CHOOSE THEIR OWN TOPICS FOR WRITING

After several years of having students choose their own writing topics I am committed to the practice because it has several invaluable benefits. First, most students have never had an opportunity to write about matters they're genuinely interested in and can write about with authority. Too often they see traditional assignments that ask everyone to write on the same topic as meaningless exercises in which the teacher seems to be forgetting that students are individuals.

Second, students are more likely to put time and energy into their writing when they can explore topics that interest them. When students are writing on their own topics, they may also discover a potent truth: Writing is a powerful tool for learning, one that will serve them well.

Third, when students choose their own topics, a rich diversity

can develop as they write about their own special interests. Some students may write about family rituals that come from their ethnic heritages or about unusual people in their families; others may write about living in another country or on a military base; others may write about hobbies—bicycling or scuba diving or canoeing. The possibilities are almost endless. In many schools, a rich multicultural tapestry can emerge as students from diverse backgrounds and cultures read each other's work and share stories.

Fourth, students will become more-confident writers because they have more control over their writing. As they develop their expertise in some area, they begin to realize how much they know about something, whether it's car stereos or cooking hamburgers. They can take on a new identity in the class and find that people pay attention to what they have to say. That's good for all of us.

Finally, when students choose their own writing topics, the class simply becomes more interesting for everyone. Students may cover a remarkable range of subjects, and even those writing on similar topics bring different perspectives to them. Boredom drops quickly because everyone is constantly learning directly from other people's experiences. Perhaps the greatest bonus is to teachers, who not only garner a wealth of information about their students, but also over a period of years become mini-experts on numerous topics. Furthermore, they are spared trying to think up a good writing topic and then having to read fifty papers on that topic.

I BELIEVE STRONGLY IN PEER GROUPS AND COLLABORATIVE LEARNING IN WRITING CLASSES.

◆◆◆◆◆

It does take considerable class time to help select topics, since many students will protest that they have nothing to write about, but such obstacles can be overcome in a few days of brainstorming and group work in class. As teacher, you can come in with a list of possible topics and then work with the class to generate subtopics. Or ask everyone to bring in a list of fifteen things to write about, encouraging the concrete and specific rather than large, abstract categories.

I have had good success with asking students to choose a general topic to write on for the whole term and then to pick subtopics for individual papers. That way they get into their topics in some depth and eliminate the process of having to work through choosing a fresh topic for each paper. You may want to specify the kinds of papers students write within their topics—informative, expressive, persuasive, and so on—to focus the class within the formats they're learning from the textbook.

ESTABLISHING A COLLABORATIVE-LEARNING CLASSROOM

I believe strongly in peer groups and collaborative learning in writing classes. Perhaps their greatest advantage is that they give students an immediate sense of audience, something that's hard to achieve when the teacher is the only reader for the drafts. Usually they respect each other's opinions; in fact, they may take their peers' responses more seriously than they do the teacher's because they feel closer to peers and they genuinely want to communicate.

Students also begin to see how useful collaboration can be for generating ideas. Most students in writing groups readily admit how much their classmates have contributed to the final versions of their papers. Each class period when I hand back graded papers, I pick two or three of the best ones to read aloud and then ask the writer and the writer's group to comment on how the paper developed through drafts. Their accounts are revealing, and the investment they feel in each other's work is truly gratifying.

I favor randomly chosen groups of at least four students so if someone is absent, the discussion doesn't break down. I reorganize groups to allow working with as many writers as possible. This arrangement also enhances every student's exposure to diverse cultural experiences as they get to know other students more closely. Managing groups in the classroom may not be easy, although I suspect trained secondary teachers know considerably more about it than most college teachers do. For the teacher who doesn't feel comfortable with groups, there is considerable literature on the concept. (See the professional bibliography on p. 174.)

Ultimately, groups help to establish the whole class as a community of writers who work together, feel a common sense of purpose, and see writing as a shared enterprise that's important to everyone. We all know intuitively that the most important element for achieving a congenial writing classroom is the teacher's attitude, and for that reason it's important for the teacher to be a part of that community, not to be an outside authority and a judge. Teachers need to write with students during writing workshops and share writing with them—its joys and frustrations. With luck and time, I am convinced that both teachers and students will enjoy being in a writing classroom more than they might have thought possible. ✍

Work Cited

Maslow, Abraham. *Toward a Psychology of Being*, 2nd ed. New York: D. Van Nostrand Company, 1968.

ELEMENTS OF WRITING addresses students' understanding of the *writing process*, acceleration of learning through *cooperative group work*, and feedback to students through effective *assessment* in the following ways:

Pupil's Edition
Provides detailed instruction for each stage of the writing process
Provides numerous activities and exercises in the writing chapters for students to work cooperatively

Annotated Teacher's Edition
Provides students with detailed instruction for each stage of the writing process
Offers *COOPERATIVE LEARNING* features that suggest activities for teaching writing and grammar

Gives helpful assessment ideas in the *TIMESAVER*, *A DIFFERENT APPROACH*, and *ASSESSMENT* features

Teacher's ResourceBank™
Offers materials keyed to the writing process that assist students in achieving the aims and modes
Furnishes materials that can be used for peer evaluation
Provides an **Assessment Portfolio** section and **Holistically Graded Composition Models** for the writing chapters

By Barbara J. Shade

Teaching for Learning's Sake

THIS APPROACH TO TEACHING WILL EMPOWER STUDENTS AS LEARNERS.

Helping students incorporate ideas, skills, and concepts that will improve their ability to perform tasks and to solve problems is the ultimate goal of teaching. Teachers who achieve this goal effectively find ways to accommodate students' different learning styles so that the teaching-learning process works more efficiently.

What do we mean by *learning styles*? Over the years, researchers have identified three dimensions in which students have specific learning preferences: (1) their preferences for various environmental factors that influence the learning climate; (2) their preferences about the ways they choose to engage in the learning process (motivational style); and (3) their preferences for the various ways in which they process information (cognitive style).

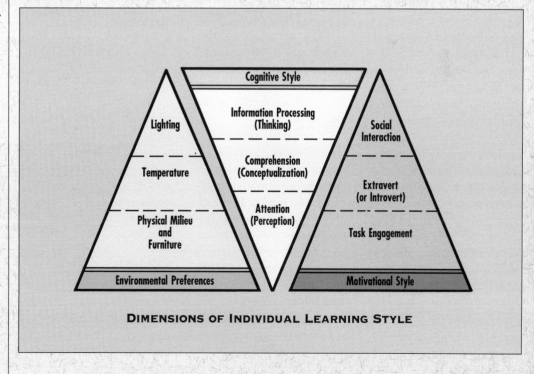

DIMENSIONS OF INDIVIDUAL LEARNING STYLE

ENVIRONMENTAL PREFERENCES

Individual environmental preferences focus on the lighting, temperature, and furniture used in the learning process. For example, some individuals might prefer bright light while others prefer it muted; some might prefer a warm room while others like it cool. A variation in studying postures has also been noted, with some individuals preferring to sit in a traditional classroom desk while others prefer to stand or recline when engaged in a learning task.[1]

MOTIVATIONAL STYLE

The second dimension of learning style focuses upon the extent to which students take responsibility for their own learning. Teachers often incorrectly assume that students' desire to engage in work is inherent. As with other aspects of learning, the extent to which individuals become involved in work depends upon how they have been socialized to respond to work. Some students, for example, have been taught to rely on others for assistance, to follow directions as given, and to perform the task as modeled. Others have been made more independent of others and have been taught to work alone, to find their own solutions, and to decide whether or not they can complete the work before asking for assistance. Corno and Mandinach refer to this stylistic dimension as

a preference for resource management, and students tend to use the approach that makes them feel the most comfortable and the most competent.

The teaching-learning process involves human interaction, and students prefer different levels of involvement with others, depending upon the social and personality development that emanates from their families and communities. Families stressing prosocial behavior encourage children to help, to share, and to work toward benefiting others.

These students are more likely to give and receive assistance in the learning process and to like cooperative-learning ventures.

Children trained to be highly individualistic and self-oriented are less likely to cooperate and offer help. Learners with this orientation function well in a competitive setting because they prefer to work alone and are less likely to enjoy cooperative-learning activities unless there is a reward or a method of accommodating their need for individuality.

COGNITIVE STYLE

The least discussed dimension of learning style—that of cognitive style—represents individually preferred ways of perceiving, organizing, and evaluating information so that it can be learned.

Three cognitive processes influence the way individuals acquire and produce knowledge. These are the perceptual, the conceptual, and the evaluative processes.

1. Perceptual Processes: The most recognized area in learning-style literature, this area focuses on the sensory modalities. Through cultural socialization, learners develop a preference for either the visual modality (photographs, graphs, art, texts); the aural modality (records, tapes, lectures); the haptic/kinesthetic modality (group discussions, interactive debates, drama); or some combination of these. Instruction delivered through the preferred modality establishes an instant rapport that allows students to process information more easily.

Different cultures socialize their children to attend to different cues in the environment; therefore, students have selective attention. Some students focus their attention on the task or idea being presented. For others, the people, their peers, their self-evaluation, or even the teacher's reaction to them are the most important elements on which to focus. How children choose to attend to cues is an important dimension of learning, and teachers who wish to ensure cognitive engagement find ways to influence the perceptive focus of the students.

[1] For a more detailed description of the social and physical environment preferences of students, the reader should examine the writings of Kenneth and Rita Dunn.

BARBARA SHADE AT UNIVERSITY OF WISCONSIN-PARKSIDE CAMPUS.

2. Conceptual Processes: Having focused on an idea that must be learned, students must then classify it based upon prior experiences. The techniques involved include assessing similarities and differences to prior knowledge, as well as determining how best to define or describe the concepts. Again, the extent to which students can manipulate various concepts depends upon whether or not the ideas can be communicated to them using a common language with commonly accepted images.

Some students prefer to have ideas presented in a hierarchical manner, beginning with the big picture followed by the details involved (whole to part). Other students prefer to have the information presented in a more sequential approach, beginning with the minute details and building toward the larger concept (part to whole). Regardless of the technique used, teachers must include methods of helping learners make connections with prior knowledge.

3. Evaluative Processes: The third aspect of cognitive style focuses on the processes of thinking about the information. *Thinking* is difficult to define, but many researchers define it as "comprehension monitoring." The major focus of thinking centers on the individual's ability to plan, monitor, and evaluate his or her learning and understanding about the information he or she is seeking to learn.

Again, teachers should look for variations in the way individuals approach thinking. On one hand, individuals may spend time using their imaginations to create ideas based upon personal views or beliefs. On the other hand, some individuals will engage in a more formal logic, which requires familiarity with the rules in order to select the correct problem-solving strategies. In the first type of information processing, individuals seem to arrive at their decisions rather intuitively, using a process that seems to be generated from an internalized logic. In the second type, the one most influenced by instruction, students learn to organize and review their approach to information or problems through an analytical process.

ACCOMMODATING VARIATIONS IN LEARNING STYLES

When teachers are first introduced to the concept of learning styles, they immediately conjure up visions of having to construct thirty different learning plans to accommodate their students. Learning styles is not another euphemism for individually guided education. Instead, it is an entreaty to teachers to provide different approaches and strategies that individuals can use as they work at learning.

In today's classrooms, there are basically *two distinct modes of learning*: the *traditional orientation*, the one to which most instruction is geared; and the *community orientation*, the one more likely to be displayed by African American, Hispanic American, Native American, and immigrant Asian students who identify closely with the culture of their ethnic communities.

Particular suggestions to enhance the instructional process for the community-oriented students who are often ignored in instructional delivery system include the following ones:

Environment Style Accommodation: For the community-oriented students, the classroom should become inviting and supportive as an experiential setting in which students can use various media to explore concepts that may be foreign to them because they are not prevalent in their communities or because their economic situation does not permit the type of travel or involvement in enrichment activities that is true of the more successful, economically affluent students. Being able to see an enlarged picture of the Eiffel Tower in the classroom can provide an important conceptual image that might be needed to foster comprehension. Because learning centers permit self-exploration, they should also become important aspects of the classroom design for all levels of students in all types of classes.

Motivational Style Accommodation: Having the opportunity to participate in a good class discussion on lesson content motivates community-oriented students, satisfying their needs to share information with others and to obtain feedback. Moreover, it provides them an opportunity to listen to different perspectives. Teachers should note, however, that group discussion is not the same as class recitation in which students are asked to recite facts and information to the teacher from a textbook. For example, it is not enough to discuss nouns as a part of speech without leading students through the concept of a complete sentence and of the purpose of using nouns within sentences and paragraphs. Moreover, students need to be able to identify nouns within the framework of their own speech and written narratives as well as to determine how and why they have used a particular word as a noun.

The key to a good group discussion is a teacher who is an excellent questioner, who is reflective, who can lead students to reflect and inquire, and who has an excellent understanding of the broad structure and relationships within the lesson content.

Information Processing Style Accommodation: Teachers can facilitate the processing of information by students through the use of some of the following techniques:

1. Present concepts with multimedia using a variety of modalities.

*T*HE KEY TO A GOOD GROUP DISCUSSION IS A TEACHER WHO IS AN EXCELLENT QUESTIONER, WHO IS REFLECTIVE, WHO CAN LEAD STUDENTS TO REFLECT AND INQUIRE, . . .

T EACHERS MUST REMEMBER THAT STUDENTS HAVE DIFFERENT PERCEPTIONS OF THE WORLD AND TEACH TO THESE PERCEPTIONS.

✦✦✦

2. Assist the students in identi-fying the relationships of concepts through cognitive mapping, brain-storming, or reciprocal teaching in which you ask them to predict possible answers in stories.

3. Take time to ensure there is a common understanding of words, concepts, or ideas. Bilin-gual students should be encour-aged to interpret the words in their languages. Students should also be encouraged to develop art projects as representations of the ideas and to use new words in their oral interactions with you.

4. Model the thinking processes that are needed to complete tasks successfully. Most importantly, provide students the time to think about a problem or to complete an assignment so that they grasp the underlying meaning. Students learn best when they can perform a task with the teacher available to provide feedback.

Teachers must remember that students have different perceptions of the world and teach to these perceptions. Assisting students in

---

The stylistic differences of these two preferences seem to lie along the following continuum:

School-Oriented Students	Community-Oriented Students
Environmental Preferences: Prefer less intense, perhaps earth-oriented colors or plain whites Seem able to work well in classrooms in which seats are in rows.	*Environmental Preferences:* Prefer warm, bright colors—blues and yellows are particularly soothing. Seem to prefer groupings of desks or tables, which perpetuate cooperation.
Motivational Style: Are individualistic and prefer to work alone on tasks. Are competitive and self-regulated in resource management.	*Motivational Style:* Are prosocial, more cooperative, and prefer to work with others on tasks. Are more dependent and like to have help from peers with constant reinforcement from the teacher or adult.
Cognitive Style: Learn well through auditory senses and function well with print media. Are able to focus attention on a specific task or object. Can focus on a single task for a sustained period of time. Understand American English used in textbooks, magazines, newspapers, and television, which facilitates comprehension. Backgrounds are closer to the writers of the curriculum materials, which facilitates meaning. Prefer or can handle material well when presented in a linear-sequential manner. Have been taught to use formal logic, algorithms, and analytical thinking. Are more likely to present written and spoken thoughts in a sequential manner. Are likely to function in a low-context fashion and to explain all variations of meanings because they assume the meaning is not shared.	*Cognitive Style:* Prefer visual material to emphasize oral presentation. Like group discussions, debates, and projects. Prefer to constantly scan room or object for new features, nonverbal cues, or contextual features. Prefer a variety of tasks in a relatively short time to maintain attention. Can focus on several tasks at one time. Likely to speak dialect or community-oriented language or are bilingual, which creates different orientation to words and meanings. Backgrounds usually differ from that of texts, requiring reinterpretation of the material within the context of the communities from which students come. Prefer to have material presented in a holistic, relational, or contextual manner, a presentation from whole to part. Are more intuitive and synergistic and may not have been taught to use formal logic to approach objects and problems. Have been exposed to more observational learning. Are more likely to present thoughts in a spiral or episodic fashion. Are likely to function in a high-context fashion and to assume that the meaning is shared by all individuals with whom they are communicating

learning requires lots of talking—talking between students and teachers and between students. Expressing ideas orally allows better processing and comprehension.

When considering the use of learning styles, teachers must confront three important perceptions. First, teachers should understand that the identified style preference should not and cannot be used as evidence of deficiencies. Being different does not mean that the child is deficient in ability. Second, teachers should not think that the community-oriented style reflects all members of a group. It is merely behavior that is most likely to be found within the community. Third, teachers who use the concept of learning styles should do so as indicators of approaches to lesson design and to the selection of methods of instruction, not as the basis for judging intellectual potential.

A FINAL CAVEAT

Developing a successful learner is the ultimate goal of a successful teacher, and ensuring that children become successful learners requires that teachers see themselves not as the ultimate purveyors of knowledge, but as guides through the learning process. This approach to teaching will empower students as learners. By incorporating various learning-style approaches in the classroom and in the curriculum, teachers will assist students to maximize the energy they spend in the learning process. This permits students to approach the learning process in their own words and to use the information as a bridge. When learners grasp the ideas and really know that they know, their sense of self-worth and confidence and their intellectual strength improve tremendously. It is at this point teachers know they, too, have been successful. What a great sense of accomplishment! ❧

Additional Readings

Grossman, Herbert. *Educating Hispanic Students.* Springfield, Illinois: Charles C. Thomas Publisher, 1984.

Henson, Kenneth T. *Theory Into Practice: Matching Teaching and Learning Styles.* Columbus, Ohio: Ohio State University, 1984.

Shade, Barbara J. *Culture, Style, and the Educative Process.* Springfield, Illinois: Charles C. Thomas Publisher, 1989.

Tharp, Roland and Ronald Gallimore. *Rousing Minds to Life.* New York: Cambridge University Press, 1988.

Trueba, Henry T., Lila Jacobs and Elizabeth Kirton. *Cultural Conflict and Adaptation: The Case of Hmong Children in American Society.* New York: Falmer Press, 1990.

ELEMENTS OF WRITING addresses the needs of America's diverse student populations and the range of students' *learning styles* in the following ways:

Pupil's Edition

Represents a wide range of ethnically diverse cultures in the literary models and a broad selection of topics in the exercises and examples

Accomodates a range of learning styles by providing a variety of student activities

Offers teachers a flexible program that can be easily adapted to suit a variety of situations

Annotated Teacher's Edition

Provides specific *MEETING INDIVIDUAL NEEDS* features such as *Learning Styles, Less-Advanced, Advanced, Students with Special Needs, LEP/ESL,* and *At-Risk*

Suggests ways for language teachers to address language diversity in the multicultural classroom

Teacher's ResourceBank

Meets individual needs of students with graphic organizers and reinforcement practice activities

INTEGRATING THE LANGUAGE ARTS

WANDA B. SCHINDLEY

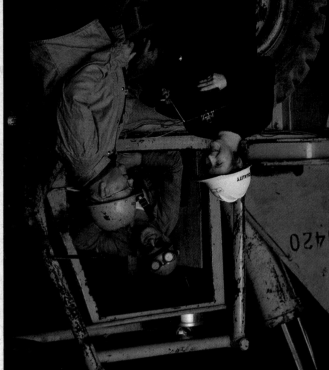

INTEGRATING THE TEACHING OF THE LANGUAGE ARTS CREATES THE MAGIC THAT HELPS STUDENTS LEARN.

Thirty-five years ago in a rural classroom, a creative woman integrated the teaching of reading, writing, speaking, listening, and even math. Her second-graders built a playhouse-size cardboard post office, made block-letter signs, wrote and read letters, counted tokens to buy and sell stamps, and spoke and listened as postmaster and customer. That teacher had not read research on the integration of skills or on using whole-language methodologies, but she knew intuitively what worked. I don't remember much about my experiences in kindergarten, first grade, third grade, or even fourth grade, but I remember well that second-grade classroom; I remember the magic of learning.

Integrating the teaching of the language arts creates the magic that helps students learn. It cre-

WANDA SCHINDLEY IS A SPECIALIST FOR THE WORKPLACE PARTNERSHIP.

ates a context for developing language proficiency and relevancy for reading, writing, speaking, and listening activities. Students grow through active participation in language activities. Although categorizing the language arts may be

necessary for describing curricula, in the classroom language skills are best learned through doing—through seeking meaning from texts, through writing and revising, and through sharing ideas and opinions.

SUGGESTIONS FOR INTEGRATING THE LANGUAGE ARTS

• Involve students in prereading activities such as discussion, writing, research, and sometimes, vocabulary development. Creating a context for reading involves discussing themes and related issues, making predictions, recalling prior knowledge and related experiences, and searching out related information.

• Involve students in prewriting activities such as discussion of possible topics and details, reading model essays, searching out and reading informative pieces, reading literary writing, interviewing others, and sentence-combining or sentence-revision activities. Like the writing process itself, development of language proficiency involves a recursive practice in reading, writing, thinking, speaking, and listening.

• Make writing assignments relevant by having students write for and share with real audiences for meaningful purposes. Have students share their writing with peers.

• Relate correctness—development of conventional usage, spelling, grammar, and punctuation—to the revising and proofreading stages of the writing process. Correctness becomes important to students when it helps them communicate their ideas clearly. Class review of grammar, usage, and mechanics can be done with sentences from student papers and with sentence-combining, sentence-manipulation, and vocabulary activities.

• Approach standard usage in speech as appropriate for use in business and academic situations, not as a replacement for all vernacular expression.

• Encourage student involvement in class discussion, team study groups, cooperative research projects and presentations, group creative writing, and role playing.

• Foster an atmosphere in which students feel free to respond to, to evaluate, and to critique literature.

• Act as facilitator in students' discovery processes through activities that encourage creative and critical thinking—decision making and problem solving—and allow students to take more responsibility for their own learning.

• Create an atmosphere of cooperation, caring, and high expectations.

USING THE TEXTBOOK IN AN INTEGRATED APPROACH

Literature selections are provided in each chapter to give students opportunities to read before writing. However, this book can be used in a literature-driven approach as the springboard to writing by incorporating into the study of each chapter ample readings from literature anthologies, magazines, and student papers. The features in each chapter of the *Teacher's Edition* contain suggestions for integrating additional literature selections (**Integrating the Language Arts: Literature Link**), using a

LIKE THE WRITING PROCESS ITSELF, DEVELOPMENT OF LANGUAGE PROFICIENCY INVOLVES A RECURSIVE PRACTICE IN READING, WRITING, THINKING, SPEAKING, AND LISTENING.

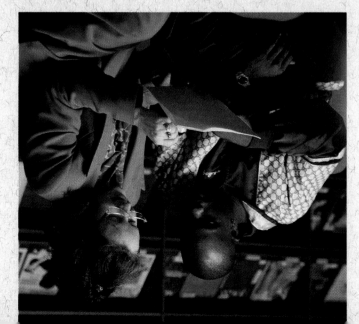

variety of group activities (**Cooperative Learning**), and encouraging students to use higher-level thinking skills to contribute to class discussion (**Critical Thinking**).

Throughout, the textbook guides students through the prewriting, writing, evaluating, revising, proofreading, and publishing phases of the writing process. It also instructs students in the dynamics and behavior involved in group work with ample opportunities for group writing, revising, speaking, and listening activities. The chapters on speaking and listening help students develop skills that will serve them throughout their school years and later as citizens.

The **Common Error** and **Integrating the Language Arts** features in each chapter of the *Teacher's Edition* contain suggestions for integrating the teaching of grammar, usage, and mechanics into the stages of the writing process, as do the suggestions for integrating the language arts in the introduction of each composition chapter.

Sample Integrated Lesson Plan

A lesson on creative writing might begin with a class discussion about stories and poems. Guiding questions encourage students to share attitudes (What kinds of stories/poems do you like?)
—in order to recall prior knowledge about the structure of stories (What happened toward the end of a favorite story? How did you feel as your read? What name do we use for the most exciting or scary part of the story?)

—and of poems (Can you think of a favorite poem? What do you like about the poem?)
—and to synthesize knowledge about fiction and poetry (What characteristics do stories and poems have in common? What other forms might a writer use to tell about an event or to express an idea?)

Students might then read the stories and poems and discuss their responses and evaluations of each. Volunteers might bring their favorite stories, poems, or lyrics to share with the class before beginning to write original stories and poems.

Teachers can use group stories and poems as guided practice and as a non-threatening introduction to creative writing. Students working in groups to create story lines and to describe characters and setting will quickly learn literary terminology to use within the group. A group activity in which students write noun poems might begin informal grammar instruction as the class brainstorms a list of words that name people, places, things, or ideas. Small groups can then choose from the list of topics for noun-metaphor poems.

Example: Dreams are
Envelopes of hope,
Fluffy clouds that
disappear in daylight,
Stars to reach for.

As groups begin to revise and proofread their poems for class presentation, teachers might focus on the use of commas and end marks.

When students begin the creative writing assignments, they are again given opportunities to write, discuss, read, think, talk, revise, and so on. Instruction in usage and mechanics can be provided to the class as the need arises, to partners as they debate an issue of correctness, and to individuals in one-on-one conferences.

Finally, students share their work with the class—perhaps anonymously at first, but eventually as accomplished and proud authors who share a firsthand knowledge of the creation of literature and a greater understanding of language. ✍

ELEMENTS OF WRITING addresses the *integration* of the various aspects of language in the following ways:

Pupil's Edition
Connects the study of writing to reading, speaking, listening, grammar, usage, and mechanics
Reinforces in the language-structure chapters the fundamentals of effective communication, stressing application and proficiency.

Annotated Teacher's Edition
Provides features that give a variety of strategies to link every aspect of language diversity instruction—*INTEGRATING THE LANGUAGE ARTS: Literature Link, Library Skills Link, Mechanics Link, Grammar Link, Usage Link, Technology Link*

Teacher's ResourceBank ™
Offers supplemental materials on every aspect of the language arts

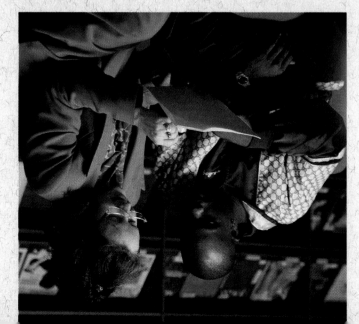

By Charles W. Leftwich & Patricia G. Tweeddale

ACCEPTING THE DIFFERENCES:

Teaching the At-Risk Student

...IT IS UNLIKELY THAT AT-RISK STUDENTS WILL LEAVE SCHOOL WITH THE BASIC SKILLS OUR EDUCATION SYSTEM SHOULD PROVIDE.

Teachers are facing a growing population of students for whom a minimal success such as completing high school is not probable. These students comprise the group known as at-risk, a label that can be acquired for reasons ranging from race and socioeconomic background to being a teenage parent or coming from a single-parent home, from having a parent or sibling incarcerated to being a latchkey child. Whatever the reason for the categorization, it is unlikely that at-risk students will leave school with the basic skills our education system should provide.

The task of teaching the at-risk student must begin with knowledge of individual student characteristics that are relevant to the instructional objective at hand. A focus upon stereotypical characteristics denies attention to the in-

PATRICIA TWEEDDALE AND CHARLES LEFTWICH IN THEIR OFFICE.

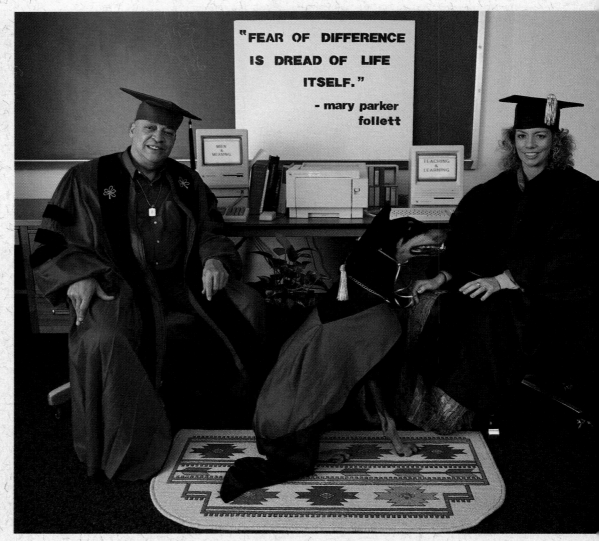

"FEAR OF DIFFERENCE
IS DREAD OF LIFE
ITSELF."
- mary parker
follett

dividual learner and what that student brings to the classroom. Because teaching and learning are highly interactive social encounters, the efficacy of any given encounter may be dependent upon the emotional response of both parties to their first contact.

The initial response by a teacher is often conditioned by previous exposure to learners similar to the one in question. Positive previous exposure leads to a sense of confidence in the ability to successfully foster and facilitate learning. However, if a teacher has had negative previous exposure, the quality of the initial encounter may be tainted by the teacher's lack of confidence in effecting learning or establishing a positive social interaction.

There are at least two sources for interference in the initial interaction between the teacher and the at-risk student, the vicarious and the real. Vicarious sources are grounded in images created by other teachers, the school organization, and community expectations, as well as portrayal in print and electronic media by editorial and entertainment entities.

The real source of interference in the initial interaction may well be so subtle as to escape recognition, and yet it seems to be pervasive. It is a fundamental rejection of differences. The nonverbal language exhibited by the at-risk stu-

dent is different or at least unfamiliar, and this may reinforce the teacher's sense of being called upon to do an impossible task. The student's verbal language may also be unfamiliar, and the clash between assumptions of what students ought to sound like and what the teacher actually hears further frustrates and impedes the teaching process.

Interaction between the teacher and the learner should focus upon the individual student's character-

istics with the intention of discovering what sets that individual apart from others. New learning is built upon old learning, and new knowledge is supported by old; therefore, the teacher of the at-risk student must concentrate on discovering what the student knows. Often this can be a difficult task since that knowledge may be communicated in a different mode. The teacher should be aware of some characteristics of the at-risk student: negative self-image, a

heavy dependence upon and rigid adherence to a distinct mode of concrete thinking, a unique dialect of spoken language, low motivation, and a lack of positive response to constructive criticism. Any at-risk student may exhibit one or all of these characteristics in varying degrees. What is important is to recognize and appreciate the student as an individual. Whatever the individual's characteristics, they are an integral part of the learner and as such must be taken

*F*OR THE TEACHER TO INTERACT SUCCESSFULLY WITH THE AT-RISK STUDENT, A SENSE OF TRUST AND ACCEPTANCE MUST BE ESTABLISHED.

into account in structuring interaction. And that structuring is solely the responsibility of the teacher; the structure must be the product of informed assessment rather than reactive judgment.

For the teacher to interact successfully with the at-risk student, a sense of trust and acceptance must be established. The student must suspend any suspicions of the teacher's intentions, which is no small accomplishment given the student's probable historical experience with schools. The teacher must overcome any negative preconceptions of the nature of the at-risk student that may stem from some students' appearance. In fact, teacher response to the appearance of the at-risk student may be a much larger barrier to a positive interaction than any of the student's other characteristics. The student cannot help but sense rejection by the teacher and will respond in kind. The student, being less sophisticated, frequently manifests inner anger and frustration by overt, socially unacceptable behavior. Administrators and teachers may deal with this behavior as if it were the real problem rather than a symptom. However, if the teacher is well aware of the differ-

ences that are brought to the classroom and can accept them, there can develop an interaction in which the teacher and the student are focused on, rather than distracted from, their respective tasks— teaching and learning.

Another difficulty in developing meaningful interaction is overcoming the sense of hopelessness that at-risk students feel. At-risk students know they are at-risk; they have been told this from the beginning. Innumerable sights and sounds reinforce an absence of control over their environment. Hopelessness often pervades the neighborhoods in which they live. Past experience has probably taught them that high hopes and effort more often than not lead to disappointment and heartbreak. The challenge for the teacher is to identify the students' strengths though they be disguised or denied beneath the protective facade of bravado and coolness, and to try to inspire and motivate students who have little or no expectation of success and who outwardly signal an intense desire to be left alone. To meet this challenge, the teacher more than ever before must be a thinker, a planner, and a decision maker. Then, drawing on

a rich professional knowledge base, the teacher can serve as a model and mediator.

It is one thing to understand intellectually that at-risk students bring to the classroom with them entirely different bents and behaviors. It is another, however, to confront these differences and to view them as starting points for teaching. If we are to succeed in teaching this segment of our student body, we have to understand and accept

these differences and to exercise our expertise as planners and implementers of instruction.

Successful teaching continues to hinge on the characteristics of the learner, the material to be learned, the specific tasks to be mastered, and the strategies utilized by the teacher. No one ever said it would be easy. Surprisingly though, many have found it to be professionally fulfilling and personally rewarding.

ELEMENTS OF WRITING addresses the needs of America's diverse student populations and the range of student *learning styles* in the following ways:

Pupil's Edition

Represents a wide range of ethnically diverse cultures in the literary models and a broad selection of topics in the exercises and examples

Accomodates a range of learning styles by providing a variety of student activities

Offers teachers a flexible program that can be easily adapted to a variety of situations

Annotated Teacher's Edition

Provides specific *MEETING INDIVIDUAL NEEDS* features such as *Learning Styles, Less-Advanced, Advanced, Students with Special Needs, LEP/ESL*, and *At-Risk*

Suggests ways for language teachers to address diversity in the multicultural classroom

Teacher's ResourceBank ™

Meets individual needs of students with graphic organizers and reinforcement practice activities

BY NORBERT ELLIOT & KAREN GREENBERG

THE DIRECT ASSESSMENT OF WRITING:

Notes For Teachers

HOW CAN ASSESSMENT STRATEGIES BE MODIFIED TO HELP BOTH TEACHERS AND STUDENTS?

Teachers spend a great deal of time assessing students' writing; they correct errors, offer suggestions, and assign grades. This process can be exhausting to teachers and discouraging for students. How can assessment strategies be modified to help both teachers and students?

Instruction and assessment can be aligned so that the two work together. To enable instruction and assessment to complement each other, teachers have turned to two relatively new methods of direct assessment: holistic scoring and portfolio assessment.

HOLISTIC SCORING

One of the most common methods of scoring writing samples is holistic scoring, a procedure based on the responses of con-cerned readers to a meaningful whole composition. Holistic scoring involves reading a writing sample for an overall impression of the writing and assigning the sample a score based on a set of consistent scoring criteria. Most holistic scoring systems use a scoring scale, or guide, that describes papers at six or eight different levels of competence.

Holistic scoring has many advantages:

1. It communicates to students that writing is a process leading to a unified, synergistic piece of writing.

2. Writing samples that have been holistically scored provide students with clear information about the quality of their writing, but they are less intimidating than grades or written critiques.

NORBERT ELLIOT, DIRECTOR OF THE WRITING PROGRAM AT THE NEW JERSEY INSTITUTE OF TECHNOLOGY.

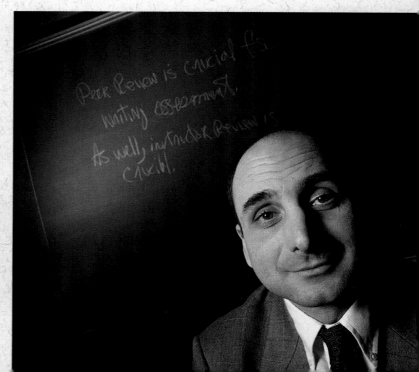

3. Holistic scoring is rapid. Readers spend only minutes judging the total effect of a paper.

4. The criteria on a holistic scoring scale give teachers a vocabulary to use in discussing essays with students and their parents.

5. The process of developing holistic scoring guides and scoring writing samples enables teachers to share their unique responses to writing, as well as their evaluative criteria. If an entire department uses the same scoring guide, students will realize that effective writing has definable features upon which all of their English teachers agree.

Nevertheless, there are weaknesses to this method. It alone cannot, for instance, provide diagnostic information about specific writing proficiencies and deficiencies. The score cannot substitute for a teacher's detailed responses to an essay—the provocative notes in the margin, the encouraging comments at the end, etc. This weakness, however, can be overcome if teachers review papers with their students in light of the scoring criteria.

Another weakness is more serious. Using holistic scoring, teachers often consider only one piece of writing during assessment. If only one sample of writing is evaluated, then teachers may not get a representative idea of students' writing ability, because this ability does not exist in a vacuum but varies from day to day and across the aims and modes of writing. In response to this concern, teachers have investigated a second method of direct assessment.

KAREN GREENBERG, DIRECTOR OF THE NATIONAL TESTING NETWORK IN WRITING.

PORTFOLIO ASSESSMENT

Portfolio assessment allows writing teachers to evaluate various samples of students' work, taken at various times under various conditions. Consequently, portfolio assessment can provide a fuller portrait of writing abilities.

To begin portfolio assessment, teachers develop a series of writing assignments that express the goals of a course. For instance, a group of teachers might require their students to write papers based on each of James Kinneavy's aims: expressive writing (a journal entry), informative writing (a summary of a news article), literary writing (a short story), and persuasive writing (an editorial). Over time, students work on these papers both at home and in class. Portfolios can include other forms of communication that students have produced, such as artwork, audio recordings, or videotapes.

Teachers need not assess everything that is included in a portfolio. In fact, it is often preferable not to evaluate every piece of a student's writing. This strategy allows teachers to separate instruction and response from formed evaluation. Portfolio assessment, therefore, can be based on samples that the teacher, the student, or both consider to be the student's best writing.

Clearly, there are advantages to this method:

1. Because multiple samples are assessed, portfolio assessment is a valid, authentic evaluation.

2. Because the authenticity of the assessment is increased, the curriculum becomes enriched.

As teachers plan tasks, they debate curricular values and strategies, devise workable instructional schemes for the classroom, and design thoughtful evaluative criteria for assignments.

With portfolio assessment, students gain a more positive attitude toward writing. Because they invest in their writing, students seek both teacher and peer response, create multiple drafts, and revise for their readers. Over time, a school's entire writing program can become an exciting adventure in communication and critical thinking.

CONCLUSION

There is still much to be investigated about the evaluation of writing. What kind of assessment best suits the multiple literacies on which our democratic society rests? What kind of local assessments will best supplement large-scale assessment? How can assessment reveal more about effective teaching? Answers will have to come from those who know students best: their teachers. 🍎

ELEMENTS OF WRITING addresses *holistic evaluation* and *portfolio assessment* in the following ways:

Annotated Teacher's Edition
Offers a wide variety of assessment ideas in the *TIMESAVER, A DIFFERENT APPROACH*, and *ASSESSMENT* features

Teacher's ResourceBank ™
Provides an **Assessment Portfolio** section and **Holistically Graded Composition Models** for the writing chapters

By David A. England

PROFESSIONAL BIBLIOGRAPHY

COMPOSING PROCESSES

Bellanoff, Pat, Peter Elbow, and Sheryl Fontaine I, eds. *Nothing Begins with N*. Carbondale and Edwardsville, IL: Southern Illinois University Press, 1991. An overview of what we know about the uses of freewriting in the classroom, with major sections on strategies and benefits for teachers and students.

Berthoff, Anne E. *The Making of Meaning*. Upper Montclair, NJ: Boynton/Cook Publishers, Inc., 1991. Suggesting that classrooms can become philosophical laboratories, Berthoff shows the way to practical approaches for thoughtful teachers.

Brannon, Lil, and C.H. Knoblauch. *Rhetorical Traditions and the Teaching of Writing*. Upper Montclair, NJ: Boynton/Cook Publishers, Inc., 1984. Staying with the theory and history provided in this book's early chapters rewards readers who come to understand better the basis and rewards of teaching in nontraditional ways.

Caplan, Rebekah. *Showing-Writing: A Training Program to Help Students to be Specific*. The University of California, Berkeley, CA: Bay Area Writing Project Publications. This nicely focused monograph is itself a good illustration of "showing, not telling," and it explains how the author tested her program for helping students learn to be more specific in their writing.

Dellinger, Dixie Gibbs. *Out of the Heart: How to Design Writing Assignments for High School Courses*. The University of California, Berkeley, CA: Bay Area Writing Project Publications. The author provides several examples of assignment sequences, each reflecting a solid discourse theory, for teachers who want to move beyond disconnected assignments in writing classes.

Kinneavy, James L., William J. McCleary, and Neil Nakadate. *Writing in the Liberal Arts Tradition* (2nd ed.). New York, NY: Harper & Row, 1990. This book is the basis for the writing chapters in the *Elements of Writing* series.

Kirby, Dan, and Tom Liner. *Inside Out: Developmental Strategies for Teaching Writing*. Upper Montclair, NJ: Boynton/Cook Publishers, Inc., 1981. *Developmental* aptly describes the authors' approach as they explain and demonstrate teaching strategies designed to help writers at all levels of sophistication improve their writing processes.

Kutz, Elanor, and Hephzibah Roskelly. *An Unquiet Pedagogy: Transforming Practice in the English Classroom*. Upper Montclair, NJ: Boynton/Cook Publishers, Inc., 1991. This seminal book will challenge traditional assumptions about learners and literacy as it explores how imagination and learner-constructed knowledge undergird any meaningful writing in classes where the development of true literacy is the goal.

Mohr, Marian M. *Revision: The Rhythm of Meaning*. Upper Montclair, NJ: Boynton/Cook Publishers, Inc., 1984. This book defines and exemplifies revision in terms that teachers will understand, adapt, and use as they help their students improve initial drafts.

Murray, Donald M. *Learning by Teaching*. Upper Montclair, NJ: Boynton/Cook Publishers, Inc., 1982. The author connects his process model for writing his thoughts on the processes of teaching writing in a readable text with useful examples and illustrations from the author's experiences as a teacher and writer.

———. *A Writer Teaches Writing* (2nd ed.). Boston, MA: Houghton-Mifflin, 1974. This early "writing process" work was designed to show how real writers write and to make that knowledge useful and powerful for teachers of writing.

Romano, Tom. *Clearing the Way: Working with Teenage Writers*. Portsmouth, NH: Heinemann, 1987. Especially helpful chapters on conferencing and evaluation distinguish this book, which is written in a lively style and which is supported with examples of students' writing and clear insights into a writing teachers' learning.

Willis, Meredith Sue. *Personal Fiction Writing: A Guide for Writing from Real Life for Teachers, Students, and Writers*. New York, NY: Teachers & Writers Collaborative. An experienced writer and teacher shares classroom-tested ideas on helping students to describe places, people, and action; to write dialogues and monologues; to create structure; and to revise what they have written.

Ziegler, Alan. *The Writing Workshop*, Vol. 1. New York, NY: Teachers & Writers Collaborative, 1981. This description of a workshop method for individualizing writing instruction includes ample references to students' work and sharp observations by the author.

———. Vol. 2. New York, NY: Teachers & Writers Collaborative, 1984. This is an excellent catalog of assignments exemplified by students' responses to them, along with the author's observations—a sequel to Vol. 1, which describes a writing environment conducive to such assignments and approaches.

Elbow, Peter. *Writing Without Teachers*. New York, NY: Oxford University Press, 1973. The title of the book should not suggest that teachers are not necessary, but rather that they assume different roles in nurturing students' group processes and peer-response activities.

Eubanks, Ilona M. "Nonstandard Dialect Speakers and Collaborative Learning." *The Writing Instructor* Vol. 10 (Spring 1991): 143-147. This article examines features of the traditional language-and-writing classroom that leads to difficulty, frustration, and often failure for speakers of nonstandard dialects.

Golub, Jeff, ed. *Focus on Collaborative Learning: Classroom Practices in the Teaching of English 1988*. Urbana, IL: National Council of Teachers of English, 1988. In compiling this collection of best practices, the editor includes pieces from teachers who describe general collaborative-learning skills before moving to others who discuss how these skills are applied in literature study and various writing activities, from prewriting through revision.

Healey, Mark K. *Using Students' Writing Response Groups in the Classroom*. The University of California, Berkeley, CA: Bay Area Writing Project Publications. In a monograph that realistically assesses problems often associated with response groups, the author provides practical suggestions on how to help students become more helpful in fostering growth in peers' writing.

Rabkin, Eric S., and Macklin Smith. *Teaching Writing That Works*. Ann Arbor, MI: The University of Michigan Press, 1990. In a step-by-step process for breaking the cycle of one individual student writing for a teacher, the authors move from the development of ideas in group settings through group editing and evaluation. Writing designed to help students accomplish "real work" is central to all group activities.

Spear, Karen. *Sharing Writing*. Upper Montclair, NJ: Boynton/Cook Publishers, Inc., 1988. This most practical guide to forming and nurturing response groups could only have been written with the benefit of this teacher's broad and thoughtful experience with response groups in writing courses. The book begins with an honest and promising appraisal of "challenges in peer response groups."

Brooks, Charlotte K., ed. *Tapping Potential: English and the Language Arts for the Black Learner*. Urbana, IL: National Council of Teachers of English, 1985. In addition to explaining why many African American children have not responded to the standard curriculum taught in traditional ways, contributors to this collection offer specific suggestions for classroom practices.

Cleary, Linda Miller. "A Profile of Carlos: Strengths of a Nonstandard Dialect Writer." *English Journal* 77 (September 1988): 59-64. A case study in which the language barriers and biases faced by one writer prove instructive for his teachers and for all teachers.

Connor, Ulla Maija, and Sara Allaei Kurtz. "Exploring the Dynamics of Cross-Cultural Collaboration in Writing Classrooms." *The Writing Instructor* 10 (Fall 1990): 19-28. After reviewing what is known about cross-cultural writing, the authors provide guidelines and recommendations for establishing collaborative groups in multicultural writing classes.

Daniels, Harvey, and Marcia Farr. *Language Diversity and Writing Instruction*. New York, NY: ERIC Clearinghouse on Reading and Communication Skills, National Council of Teachers of English: 1986. This book succeeds in providing just enough theory and background of teachers seeking to improve the writing of students who are native speakers of nonstandard dialects.

Gonzales, Roseann Duenas. "When Minority Becomes Majority: The Changing Face of English Classrooms." *English Journal* 79 (January 1990): 16-23. Even though the recommendations in this article are for all the language arts, applications to writing instruction will be easy and crucial to teachers in multicultural classes.

Marik, Ray. *Special Education Students Write: Classroom Activities and Assignments*. The University of California, Berkeley, CA: Bay Area Writing Project Publications. Case studies of students with special learning needs are the bases for the author's advocacy of well-sequenced, developmentally appropriate writing activities for all learners.

Rose, Mike. *Lives on the Boundary*. New York, NY: Penguin Books, 1989. The author's experiences as a remedial student contributed to his sensitive understanding of the educational underclass about which he writes so effectively.

Shade, Barbara J. Robinson, ed. *Culture, Style and the Educative Process*. Springfield, IL: Charles C. Thomas, 1989. This book provides insight into various cultures' learning styles as well as methods for enhancing students' retention by addressing their learning styles.

Shaughnbessy, M.P. *Errors and Expectations: A Guide for the Teacher of Basic Writing*. New York, NY: Oxford University Press, 1977. The author's strategies for unlocking expression and clarity for basic college writers are helpful to high school writers as well.

Sottlar, James, ed. *Teaching the Gifted*. Urbana, IL: National Council of Teachers of English, 1988. Ways to identify students with special talents in the language arts, to individualize instruction to meet their needs, and to encourage independent thinking in academically advanced students are among topics in this collection.

Urzua, Carole. "'You Stopped Too Soon': Second Language Children Composing and Revising." *TESOL Quarterly* 21 (June 1987): 279-304. This research report shares what six months of careful observations of Southeast Asian students' writing taught teachers about how second-language children learn to write.

ASSESSMENT

Belanoff, Pat, and Marcia Dickson. *Portfolio Grading: Process and Product*. Portsmouth, NH: Heinemann, 1991. In a good blending of theory and practice in how to use writing portfolios for assessment in many settings, this book allows teachers to plan strategies unique to their own purposes.

Clay, Marie M. "Research Currents: What Is and What Might Be in Education." *Language Arts* 67 (March 1990): 288-298. After discussing problems and limitations of standardized testing, the author makes recommendations toward more useful assessment models and philosophies across the language arts and into high school.

Holmes, Ken. *Perspectives on Teaching and Assessing the Language Arts*. Urbana, IL: National Council of Teachers of English, 1990. These essays include a rationale for multiculturalism in reading materials as well as a timely consideration of assessment in whole-language approaches.

Najimy, Norman C. *Measure to Measure: A Guidebook for Evaluating Students' Expository Writing*. Urbana, IL: National Council of Teachers of English, 1981. By using examples of students' writing, this guide suggests how teachers' responses can enhance instruction instead of threatening students.

Posner, Richard. "Life Without Scan-Tron: Tests as Thinking." *English Journal* 76 (February 1987): 35-38. This author demonstrates how six types of written, in-class tests improve his students' writing, thinking, and mastery of subject matter.

Robinson, Joy L., et al. *Creating Writers: Linking Assessment and Writing Instruction*. White Plains, NY: Longman, 1990. This book helps students and teachers agree on attributes of good writing and has scoring guides that help link instruction to assessment.

RESPONDING TO WRITING

Belanoff, Pat, and Peter Elbow. *Sharing and Responding*. New York, NY: Random House, 1989. This book provides useful examples of students' responses to peers' writing along with clear rationales and activities designed to increase the value of peer responses.

Freedman, Sarah Warhauer. Response to Student Writing. Urbana, IL: National Council of Teachers of English, 1987. This research report on the state of the art in response to writing not only indicates what teachers do and how students feel about it, but offers clear ideas on best practices in providing students with feedback.

Harris, Muriel. *Teaching One-to-One: The Writing Conference*. Urbana, IL: National Council of Teachers of English, 1986. The author provides a strong justification for one-on-one conferencing in the writing classroom and provides useful strategies and insights that can help writing teachers at all levels.

Sommers, Nancy. "Responding to Student Writing." *College Composition and Communication* 32 (May 1982): 148-56. The author encourages teachers to respond to the ideas, meanings, and purposes in students' papers before error hunting in order for students to engage in meaningful revision.

Sullivan, Patrick. "Responding to Student Writing: The Consequences of Some Common Remarks." *English Journal* 75 (February 1986). The author describes the hidden messages behind four types of comments teachers frequently make in responding to students' writing.

WHOLE LANGUAGE/INTEGRATION

Cronin, Hines, David Meadows, and Richard Sinatra. "Integrating Computers, Reading, and Writing Across the Curriculum." *Educational Leadership* 48 (September 1990): 57-60. Good illustrations suggest how visual maps can be constructed via computers to enhance students' thinking and organizational skills in all school subjects.

Kroll, Barry M., and Roberta J. Vann. *Exploring Speaking-Writing Relationships: Connections and Contracts*. Urbana, IL: National Council of Teachers of English, 1981. A precursor of many whole-language texts and approaches, these essays provide instructive analysis of how speaking and writing can be composed and contrasted toward better understanding and teaching of both.

Martin, Nancy, et al. *Writing Across the Curriculum*. Portsmouth, NH: Boynton/Cook Publishers, Inc., 1983. Each pamphlet in this series suggests ways to integrate the teaching of writing by "writing to learn" in various school subjects.

Newkirk, Thomas. *Only Connect: Uniting Reading and Writing*. Upper Montclair, NJ: Boynton/Cook Publishers, Inc., 1986. An excellent middle section on "Reading, Writing, and Interpreting" will help teachers see possibilities for reading in the writing classroom and vice versa.

Peterson, Bruce T, ed. *Convergences: Transactions in Reading and Writing*. Urbana, IL: National Council of Teachers of English, 1986. This collection of essays cuts across several fields in contemporary writing theory and research to explain the logic of integrating reading and writing in the classroom.

Schuman, Baird R., and Denny Wolfe. *Teaching English Through the Arts*. Urbana, IL: National Council of Teachers of English, 1990. In this "Theory and Research into Practice" (TRIP) booklet, the authors provide teachers with classroom-tested ways to connect reading and writing in English classes to popular culture and traditional art forms.

Self, Judith. *Plain Talk About Learning and Writing Across the Curriculum*. Urbana, IL: National Council of Teachers of English, 1987. Teachers of different subjects demonstrate how writing can provide a helpful way for students to think about content and experiences in all subjects.

WRITING ACROSS THE CURRICULUM

Fulwiler, Toby. *Teaching with Writing*. Upper Montclair, NJ: Boynton/Cook Publishers, Inc., 1987. An especially strong chapter on writing and testing helps make this treatment of process writing in the content areas valuable for teachers in all subject areas.

Gere, Anne Ruggles, ed. *Roots in the Sawdust: Writing to Learn Across the Disciplines*. Urbana, IL: National Council of Teachers of English, 1985. The editor has compiled essays on how writing can improve thinking and enhance learning in all the traditionally included subjects such as science and math with the added bonus of thoughtful essays on writing in art and foreign-language classes.

Kiniry, Malcolm, and Ellen Strenski. "Sequencing Expository Writing: A Recursive Approach." *College Composition and Communication* 36 (May 1985): 191-202. Though the model described here is based on a college program, the rhetorical strategies and discipline-specific approaches to writing are applicable to high school writers.

Talbot, Bill. "Writing for Learning in School: Is It Possible?" *Language Arts* 67 (January 1990): 47-57. The author describes his experiences in observing students who were learning how to use writing for learning and raises both concerns and hopes based on his observations. ❦

THIS WEEK
CENTRAL HIGH SCHOOL
JANUARY 10

Monday

　Swim Meet
　　Against Northside
　　Bus will leave　　　　　　4:00 pm

　Book Fair
　　Library
　　Every　　　　through Thursday　3:15 pm

　D　　　　　　　　　　　　　　　　　
　　　 club Tryouts
　　　uditorium

　　Fair　　　　　　　　　　　　3:15 pm
　　ibrary Annex

　Ecology Club
　　Room 126
　Plan for next Rec

Future Farmers
　chool Cafeteria
　egister for Spri

k Fair
　ary Annex

ling Team Tryou

ir
Annex

and -- State Competition
eave at 7:00 am. SHARP!　　3:15 pm

ANNUAL PLAY
PRESENTED BY
THE DRAMA CLUB
FRIDAY, JANUARY 21, 8:00 PM
CENTRAL HIGH SCHOOL
AUDITORIUM
ADMIT ONE

ELEMENTS OF

WRITING

JAMES L. KINNEAVY
JOHN E. WARRINER

Fourth Course

Holt, Rinehart and Winston

Harcourt Brace Jovanovich

Austin • Orlando • San Diego • Chicago • Dallas • Toronto

Critical Readers

Grateful acknowledgment is made to the following critical readers who reviewed pre-publication materials for this book:

John Algeo
University of Georgia
Athens, Georgia

Anthony Buckley
East Texas State University
Commerce, Texas

Norbert Elliot
New Jersey Institute of Technology
Newark, New Jersey

David England
Louisiana State University
Baton Rouge, Louisiana

Elaine A. Espindle
Peabody Veterans Memorial High
  School
Peabody, Massachusetts

William McCleary
Monroe Community College
Rochester, New York

Mary McFarland-McPherson
Chicago Public Schools
Chicago, Illinois

Linda E. Sanders
Jenks High School
Tulsa, Oklahoma

Ken Spurlock
Covington Independent Public
  Schools
Covington, Kentucky

Requests for permission to make copies of any part of the work should be mailed to: Permissions Department, Holt, Rinehart and Winston, Inc., Orlando, Florida 32887.

Some material previously published in: ENGLISH COMPOSITION AND GRAMMAR, FOURTH COURSE, Pupil's Edition, copyright © 1988 by Harcourt Brace Jovanovich, Inc.; WARRINER'S ENGLISH GRAMMAR AND COMPOSITION, FOURTH COURSE, Pupil's Edition, copyright © 1986, 1982, 1977, 1973, 1969, 1965, 1963, 1958 by Harcourt Brace Jovanovich, Inc. Copyright 1948 by Harcourt Brace Jovanovich, Inc. Copyright renewed 1991 by Alison Warriner, Jean W. McLemore and Kathryn Griffith. Copyright renewed 1986 by John E. Warriner and Francis Griffith. All rights reserved.

Acknowledgments: See pages 1042–1050, which are an extension of the copyright page.

Printed in the United States of America

ISBN 0–03–047147–8

1 2 3 4 5 6 7 8 9   062   95 94 93 92

ii

Authors

James L. Kinneavy, the Jane and Roland Blumberg Centennial Professor of English at The University of Texas at Austin, directed the development and writing of the composition strand in the program. He is the author of *A Theory of Discourse* and coauthor of *Writing in the Liberal Arts Tradition.* Professor Kinneavy is a leader in the field of rhetoric and composition and a respected educator whose teaching experience spans all levels—elementary, secondary, and college. He has continually been concerned with teaching writing to high school students.

John E. Warriner developed the organizational structure for the Handbook of Grammar, Usage, and Mechanics in the book. He coauthored the *English Workshop* series, was general editor of the *Composition: Models and Exercises* series, and editor of *Short Stories: Characters in Conflict.* He taught English for thirty-two years in junior and senior high school and college.

Writers and Editors

Ellen Ashdown has a Ph.D. in English from the University of Florida. She has taught composition and literature at the college level. She is a professional writer of educational materials and has published articles and reviews on education and art.

Phillis Goldenberg has an A.B. in English from the University of Chicago. She has been a writer and editor of educational materials in literature, grammar, composition, and critical thinking for over thirty years.

Elizabeth McCurnin majored in English at Valparaiso University. A professional writer and editor, she has over twenty years' experience in educational publishing.

John Roberts has an M.A. in English Education from the University of Kentucky. He has taught English in secondary school. He is an editor and a writer of educational materials in literature, grammar, and composition.

Alice M. Sohn has a Ph.D. in English Education from Florida State University. She has taught English in middle school, secondary school, and college. She has been a writer and editor of educational materials in language arts for twelve years.

Raymond Teague has an A.B. in English and journalism from Texas Christian University. He has been children's book editor for the *Fort Worth Star-Telegram* for more than ten years and has been a writer and editor of educational materials for seven years.

Carolyn Calhoun Walter has an M.A.T. in English Education from the University of Chicago. She has taught English in grades nine through twelve. She is a professional writer and editor of educational materials in composition and literature.

PART ONE

WRITING

SECRET FORCES *(pp. 2–15)*

OBJECTIVES

- To explore the ways that writers and writing affect the world
- To identify and analyze the aims of writing
- To compare and contrast the aims of writing

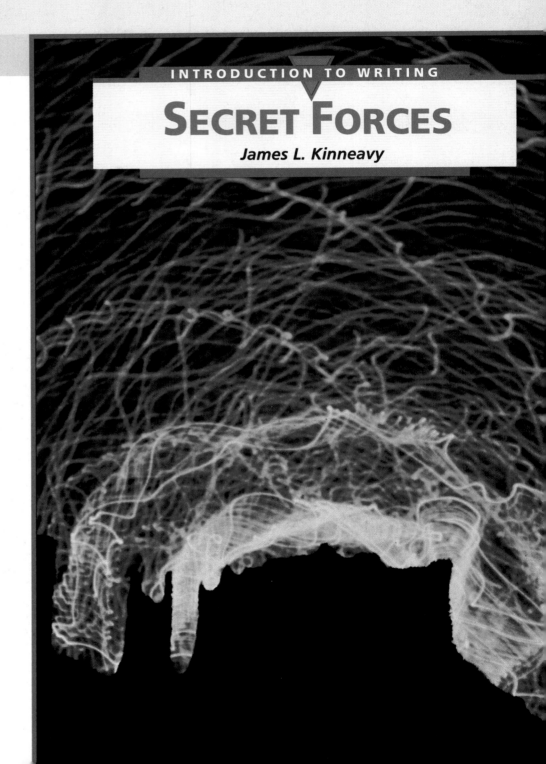

INTRODUCTION TO WRITING

SECRET FORCES
James L. Kinneavy

USING THE INTRODUCTION TO WRITING

This introduction to writing is just that—an introduction. It starts by talking briefly about the power of writing in peoples' lives to emphasize that writing is more than just schoolwork. Next, it touches upon the two central focuses of the writing chapters in the textbook—the "how" of writing (modes) and the "why" of writing (aims).

The communication triangle graphically reflects the four major aims of James Kinneavy's theory of discourse. For more information, refer to Dr. Kinneavy's essay in the front of this book entitled **"Meet the Aims and Modes of Writing,"** or to his two ☞

The world is not always what it seems. Even now you are surrounded by unseen forces. These powerful forces influence your life in many ways. They educate and entertain and connect. They make possible marvelous things like talking computers, telephones for people who are deaf, and manned space stations.

These forces are everywhere. You read about and see the results of them every day. In fact, you may become one of the **secret forces** yourself someday.

Have you guessed who these forces are? Do you know what gives them their power?

© P.R. Dunn

3

books, *A Theory of Discourse* and *Writing in the Liberal Arts Tradition.* ■

4

Who Are These Forces ?

These forces are often unseen, but they aren't really mysterious. In fact, the secret forces are all around you. They're the writers, planners, and communicators of the world. They're hard at work in every office, factory, museum, and laboratory.

They're political leaders, scientists, environmentalists, and city planners who determine what your world will be like someday. They're advertising people, song writers, and cartoonists who affect how you look at the world today. They're Nobel and Pulitzer Prize winners, dynamic public speakers, or famous generals. They're unknown speechwriters for government figures who change the world. They're script writers whose works delight you or move you or thrill you. They're newspaper or magazine writers who tell you about the world around you. The secret forces are people who see a need and set out to meet it.

Whether you see them or not, these forces are an important part of your life. They wield the power that shapes the world you live in.

What Is Their Power?

Whether they're in the spotlight or behind the scenes, all writers and planners have in common the power of communication. *Writers* have something to say (a *subject*), someone to say it to (an *audience*), and a way to say it (a *language*). You can think of these elements as a communications triangle with language—both written and spoken—at its very center.

How Do They Communicate?

The Writing Process

Powerful communication comes from presenting ideas effectively. Good writers use a general method for developing their ideas and communicating them clearly. The method is called the *writing process*. Different writers use the process differently—there's no right way or wrong way to go through it. But there are several steps, or stages, writers usually work through.

Prewriting	Thinking and planning; deciding what subject to write about and for what purpose and audience; gathering ideas and details; building a plan for presenting ideas
Writing	Writing a first draft; following some kind of plan to put ideas into sentences and paragraphs; including new ideas as they occur to you
Evaluating and Revising	Rereading the draft to decide about strengths and weaknesses; making changes to improve it
Proofreading and Publishing	Finding and fixing errors; making a final copy and sharing it with an audience

Why Do They Communicate ?

The Aims of Writing

Writers who are secret forces always have an *aim*—a purpose—in mind when they write. Sometimes they have more than one. But they know what they want to accomplish. There are four basic aims of writing: to inform, to persuade, to express oneself, and to create literature.

To Inform	Sometimes writers want to give information or to explain something to readers.
To Persuade	Writers may want to convince people to change their minds about something, or to stir people into action.
To Express Themselves	Sometimes writers want simply to explore their thoughts and feelings about something
To Create Literature	Writers may use their talents to create literature—stories, poems, songs, and plays.

On the following pages, you'll read four models. They all have the same topic—home loan foreclosures—but each model exemplifies a different aim for writing. Notice how the writing changes when the aim changes.

Mayor Asks for Federal Help

At a press conference earlier today, Mayor Jane Wing announced that she is asking for the federal government's help in dealing with the city's financial crisis.

Wing said that the closing of Resticon Corporation last fall caused the city's unemployment rate to triple. She added that sales tax revenues declined nearly fifty percent this quarter because the unemployed ex-Resticon workers had little or no money to spend. Property tax payments are late or unpaid for the same reason, adding to the city's financial crisis.

Wing said that her major concern is that many local homeowners can no longer meet their mortgage payments. She is requesting a federally backed program that will allow local banks to offer low-interest loans to people needing to refinance their homes.

"Such a loan program," she said, "will help prevent foreclosure and enable people to keep their homes while they seek other employment. By keeping our work force, we have a good chance of attracting another major employer like Resticon. The loan program will benefit the people now, and the city in the long run."

READER'S RESPONSE

1. If your family lived in Mayor Wing's city and were faced with foreclosure, would you be interested in the information in this article? What else might you want to know about the low-interest mortgage program?
2. What information does the article give about the reasons for the city's financial problems?

ANSWERS

Reader's Response

Responses will vary.

1. Many students will relate to the prospect of foreclosures in the community and will say they would be interested in the information in the article because it is presented to show the effect on the whole community. Students may want to know who would qualify for the loans, how much could be borrowed, where applications could be made, how soon the money could be loaned, and so on.

2. The economic conditions presented in the news story show the reader how one business's closing affects the entire community. The article states that the city's financial crisis began with the closing of Resticon Corporation. When this company failed, the unemployment rate tripled. Sales in the community dropped because workers couldn't afford to spend money; therefore, city sales tax revenues fell and property tax payments were uncollected. In addition, many homeowners could not meet their mortgage payments and were faced with foreclosure.

PERSUASIVE WRITING

Fellow Representatives, as you know, I represent the people of the fifth district of my state. It is an honor and a privilege. The people of the fifth district are a special group of people. Honest, hard-working, and self-reliant, they know the true value of the American life. They have dreamed the American dream and found it within their grasp. Now they are in danger of having it taken from them.

Recently, the fifth district has fallen on hard times. Resticon, the major employer, closed shop last fall, leaving more than 2,000 people unemployed. Such massive unemployment has affected the economic well-being of the entire area. Now, the people of my district are struggling to hang on. Their homes, the shining examples of their American dreams, are in danger of foreclosure.

Ladies and gentlemen, these good people are the backbone of America. Their dream is our dream. They work hard, they pay their taxes, they support their country in peace and war, they struggle to educate their children and pass on the dream to them. They need a chance to salvage that dream from the hard times surrounding them. They need our help.

Let's make it possible for them to hang on to their dreams. Please vote for this program that will allow these wonderful people to refinance their homes at low interest rates. Don't turn the best of America out into the street. I thank you, and the people of the fifth district thank you.

READER'S RESPONSE

1. If you were a member of Congress, would this speech persuade you to vote for the special legislation? Explain why or why not.
2. What ideas does this persuasive speech include that the informative article on page 8 does not?

ANSWERS
Reader's Response

Responses will vary.

1. Some students will say that this speech is persuasive because it plays on the emotions—the need for shelter and the dream of homeownership. Others will find that it is persuasive because it presents facts about the economic conditions in the fifth district—2,000 people are unemployed because the major employer closed. Encourage students to decide what is the most convincing to them.

2. This persuasive speech describes the people living in the district as honest, hardworking, and self-reliant. It compares the economic conditions of the community now with the American dream they are losing. It tells how the people in the fifth district live and explains what the speaker wants from the audience.

EXPRESSIVE WRITING

Dear Angie,
    I wanted to drop you a note t...

Dear Angie,

    I wanted to drop you a note to let you know I really miss you. The old neighborhood just isn't the same since you left. Since the plant closed, <u>For Sale</u> *signs have gone up all over town. Dino and his family just left and let their house go back to the bank. They couldn't make their mortgage payments any more. He didn't even say good-bye, but he left a school picture and a rose from his mama's garden on our front porch. I cried for a long time.*

    We don't know how long we can keep up the payments on our house. Dad says we may be able to refinance the house if the low-interest loan program goes through. He's working, and so is Mama, but they don't make near as much as they did at the plant. Our savings are almost gone. There's a rumor that a big company might start up in the old plant next spring. I'm scared that we won't be able to hang on till then.

    Write to me about life in sunny California. I can't imagine a year without winter. To tell the truth, it seems like winter all the time here since you and Dino left. Write me. Write me.

Love,
Celina

READER'S RESPONSE

1. Suppose you were Celina and watched your friends lose their homes. What would you think and feel?
2. In expressive writing, the writer explores or expresses thoughts and feelings. What thoughts and feelings does Celina express in this letter?

ANSWERS
Reader's Response

1. Students will respond in different ways to the letter. Many will say that if they were Celina, they would feel sad, dejected, lonely, or depressed. Others will say that watching friends lose their homes would make them angry, alienated, or resentful. Some may say they would be jealous of the friend who lives in a sunny community without economic problems.

2. Celina tells her friend that she really misses her and that the old neighborhood isn't the same since she left. She says she cried when Dino left, and since both friends are gone, it seems like winter all the time. She's afraid that her family won't be able to hang on financially until a new company opens up. She asks her friend to write to her about life in California.

HOME

by Gwendolyn Brooks

What had been wanted was this always, this always to last, the talking softly on this porch, with the snake plant in the jardiniere in the southwest corner, and the obstinate slip from Aunt Eppie's magnificent Michigan fern at the left side of the friendly door. Mama, Maud Martha, and Helen rocked slowly in their rocking chairs, and looked at the late afternoon light on the lawn and at the emphatic iron of the fence and at the poplar tree. These things might soon be theirs no longer. Those shafts and pools of light, the tree, the graceful iron, might soon be viewed possessively by different eyes.

Papa was to have gone that noon, during his lunch hour, to the office of the Home Owners' Loan. If he had not succeeded in getting another extension, they would be leaving this house in which they had lived for more than fourteen years. There was little hope. The Home Owners' Loan was hard. They sat, making their plans.

"We'll be moving into a nice flat somewhere," said Mama. "Somewhere on South Park, or Michigan, or in Washington Park Court." Those flats, as the girls and Mama knew well, were burdens on wages twice the size of Papa's. This was not mentioned now.

"They're much prettier than this old house," said Helen. "I have friends I'd just as soon not bring here. And I have other friends who wouldn't come down this far for anything, unless they were in a taxi."

Yesterday, Maud Martha would have attacked her. Tomorrow she might. Today she said nothing. She merely gazed at a little hopping robin in the tree, her tree, and tried to keep the fronts of her eyes dry.

"Well, I do know," said Mama, turning her hands over and over, "that I've been getting tireder and tireder of doing that firing. From October to April, there's firing to be done."

"But lately we've been helping, Harry and I," said Maud Martha. "And sometimes in March and April and in October, and even in November, we could build a little fire in the fireplace. Sometimes the weather was just right for that."

She knew, from the way they looked at her, that this had been a mistake. They did not want to cry.

But she felt that the little line of white, sometimes ridged with smoked purple, and all that cream-shot saffron would never drift across any western sky except that in back of this house. The rain would drum with as sweet a dullness nowhere but here. The birds on South Park were mechanical birds, no better than the poor caught canaries in those "rich" women's sun parlors.

"It's just going to kill Papa!" burst out Maud Martha. "He loves this house! He *lives* for this house!"

"He lives for us," said Helen. "It's us he loves. He wouldn't want this house, except for us."

"And he'll have us," added Mama, "wherever."

"You know," Helen sighed, "if you want to know the truth, this is a relief. If this hadn't come up, we would have gone on, just dragged on, hanging out here forever."

"It might," allowed Mama, "be an act of God. God may just have reached down and picked up the reins."

"Yes," Maud Martha cracked in, "that's what you always say—that God knows best."

Her mother looked at her quickly, decided that the statement was not suspect, looked away.

Helen saw Papa coming. "There's Papa," said Helen.

They could not tell a thing from the way Papa was walking. It was that same dear little staccato walk, one shoulder down, then the other, then repeat, and repeat. They watched his progress. He passed the Kennedys', he passed the vacant lot, he passed Mrs. Blakemore's. They wanted to hurl themselves over the fence, into the street, and shake the truth out of his collar. He opened his gate—the gate—and still his stride and face told them nothing.

"Hello," he said.

Mama got up and followed him through the front door. The girls knew better than to go in too.

Presently Mama's head emerged. Her eyes were lamps turned on.

"It's all right," she exclaimed. "He got it. It's all over. Everything is all right."

The door slammed shut. Mama's footsteps hurried away.

"I think," said Helen, rocking rapidly, "I think I'll give a party. I haven't given a party since I was eleven. I'd like some of my friends to just casually see that we're homeowners."

READER'S RESPONSE

1. How did you feel about the problems with home loan payments when you read the article on page 8? How are your feelings different now?
2. The basic aim of literary writing is to create a work of art. What other aims might Gwendolyn Brooks have had in writing this story? Explain.

ANSWERS
Reader's Response

Responses will vary.

1. Many students will notice that the newspaper article emphasizes how home loans will impact many people, while the short story shows the effect on just one family. Many will say that the emphasis on the feelings of one family is more powerful in affecting their views about home loans than the facts presented in the informative article.

2. In addition to the literary aim, Gwendolyn Brooks may also have intended to express her feelings about personal loss, to inform her readers how a family can persist in adversity, and to persuade her readers to empathize with her characters.

ANSWERS
Writing and Thinking Activities

1a. The representative's speech tries to persuade the audience by appealing to the listeners' emotions and by presenting facts about economic conditions.

b. The newspaper article explains the problems facing the city.

c. Responses will vary, but most students will agree that the story reveals the most about human emotions.

d. Responses will vary, but most students will find that the letter reveals the most about what the writer feels and thinks about the situation.

Questions 2 and 4 might be journal activities. Question 3 is a group activity. You might want to save these projects to work on at a later date.

Writing and Thinking Activities

1. Meet with two or three classmates to discuss the following questions about the four models you've read.
   a. Which model tries to convince people to do something? How?
   b. Which model explains the problems facing the city?
   c. Which model most dramatically shows the human emotions triggered by the financial crisis?
   d. Which model is mostly about what the writer feels and thinks about the situation?
2. Consider your own communication techniques. During a two-hour stretch of a typical day, make a list of all the different ways you communicate—writing, reading, speaking, and listening. Keep track of how much of your communication is informative, persuasive, self-expressive, or literary. Then, sit down with two or three classmates and discuss your communication patterns. Are they similar?

3. Notice how professional writers communicate. Bring a magazine or newspaper to class. Work with two or three classmates to find examples of these four kinds of writing: informative, persuasive, self-expressive, and creative writing. Which type of writing is used most often? Does each magazine and newspaper have about the same percentage of each type of writing?

4. When you hear the words *creative writing,* what do you think of—short stories? poems? novels? plays? What about other kinds of writing? Can letters to the editor, speeches, editorials, or journal entries also be creative? In what way? What other kinds of writing would you call original or creative?

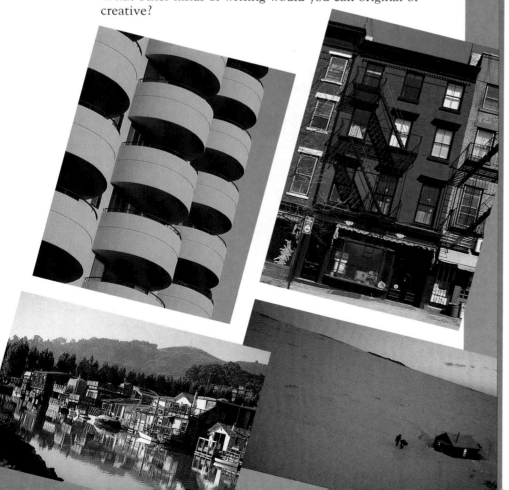

Chapter 1
WRITING AND THINKING

OBJECTIVES

- To identify obstacles that writers encounter
- To use the writing process as a means to overcome obstacles
- To analyze the writing process through an examination of its parts
- To use various prewriting techniques to develop writing ideas
- To analyze how writing is tailored to suit an intended purpose and audience
- To arrange information in an order that suits intended purpose and audience
- To plan and write a first draft
- To use self-evaluation as a basis for revising a first draft
- To use the techniques of peer evaluation in helping others revise writing
- To use proofreading guidelines and marks
- To create ideas for publishing written works

Motivation

Motivate students by asking them why the words *thinking* and *writing* are synonymous. Lead students to understand that when people write, ideas are discovered and released. Emphasize that writing reinforces learning and develops a greater level of maturity in communication. This chapter gives students strategies for generating ideas, planning, writing, and sharing.

Introduction

The purpose of this chapter is to introduce the writing process to students as a thinking and decision-making tool. As is shown, this process works for any aim or mode of writing.

The chapter explores and explains all the stages of the process for students—prewriting, writing, evaluating and revising, and proofreading and publishing. The chapter teaches students that writing is discovery and that it takes time to plan, write, rewrite, and publish.

The prewriting segment offers specific suggestions for generating ideas—writers' journals, brainstorming, clustering, selecting sensory details, focused reading and listening, and imagining. For writing, the chapter explains how to use existing plans to draft papers. And for evaluating, revising, proofreading, and publishing, students are given techniques, guidelines, and ideas.

Integration

Students can apply the concepts and strategies learned in this chapter to writing assignments in all of their classes.

The **Critical Thinking Exercises** help develop higher-level thinking skills that apply to any course that requires organization and interpretation of information.

Because the material in this chapter emphasizes clear, orderly development of ideas, organization of information, and analysis of the relationships between components in a process, this chapter can be integrated with computer studies.

The chart on the next page illustrates the strands of language arts as they are integrated into this chapter. For vocabulary study, glossary words are underlined in some writing models.

QUOTATIONS
All **Quotations for the Day** are chosen because of their relevance to instructional material presented in that segment of the chapter and for their usefulness in establishing student interest in writing.

INTEGRATING THE LANGUAGE ARTS

Selection	Reading and Literature	Writing and Critical Thinking	Language and Syntax	Speaking, Listening, and Other Expression Skills
from *a fire in my hands* by Gary Soto **18-20** Film review from the *Tallahassee Democrat* by Steve MacQueen **37** from *A Browser's Dictionary* by John Ciardi **40** from *The Norton Anthology of Literature by Women: The Tradition in English* by Sandra M. Gilbert and Susan Gubar **41** from **"We Need Power, Program, and Progress"** by Jesse L. Jackson **42** from *The Name of the Rose* by Umberto Eco **42** **"A biography of Charles Spencer ('Charlie') Chaplin (1889-1977)"** by Noel Petty **61**	Responding personally to literature **20** Applying interpretive and creative thinking **20, 49-50, 54** Drawing conclusions and making inferences **20, 44** Locating and interpreting information **30, 41-42, 44, 46** Analyzing a concrete biography **61**	Recording personal observations **20, 25-26, 27, 31, 33-34, 49-50** Writing a journal entry **25-26** Using freewriting and looping **27** Generating ideas by association **28, 29** Using brainstorming **28, 33, 34, 58, 61** Using clustering **29, 33** Finding information **30, 31, 32-34, 41-42, 58** Gathering sensory details **31** Taking notes **32-34** Drawing conclusions and making inferences **33-34, 41-42, 44** Applying interpretive and creative thinking **34, 38, 41-42, 46, 49-50, 54, 58, 61** Writing a persuasive piece **38** Writing an informative piece **38, 46** Analyzing the arrangement of information **41-42, 46, 54** Arranging ideas **44, 46** Classifying information **44, 46** Writing a first draft **46** Evaluating a paragraph **49-50, 54** Revising a paragraph **54** Writing a concrete biography **61**	Proofreading for errors in grammar, usage, and mechanics **54, 56-57**	Brainstorming with classmates **28, 34, 58, 61** Working in a team to find information **30** Listening with a focus **33-34** Working with classmates to organize information **44** Working with classmates to evaluate a paragraph **49-50** Working with classmates to evaluate and revise a paragraph **54**

SEGMENT PLANNING GUIDE

Whether you are planning for a quick review of a writing concept or preparing an extended lesson on composition, you can use the following Planning Guide to adapt the chapter material to the individual needs of your class.

SEGMENT	PAGES	CONTENT	RESOURCES
1 *Looking at the Process*	*17-21*		
Literary Model from *a fire in my hands*	18-20	Guided reading: a professional writer's discussion of ideas for writing	
Reader's Response	20	Model evaluation: responding to literature and finding ideas for writing	
2 *Aim and Process*	*22-23*		
3 *Prewriting*	*24-44*		Freewriting and Brainstorming
Finding Ideas for Writing	24	Introduction: finding ideas for writing	Clustering and Asking Questions
Chart: Prewriting Techniques	24	Guidelines: finding ideas for writing	
Keeping a Journal	25	Guidelines: starting a journal	Using Your Five Senses
Exercise 1	25-26	Applied practice: keeping a journal	
Freewriting	26	Guidelines: analyzing freewriting techniques	Reading and Listening with a Focus
Exercise 2	27	Applied practice: using freewriting techniques	
Brainstorming	27	Guidelines: analyzing brainstorming techniques	Imagining
Exercise 3	28	Applied practice: using brainstorming	Purpose, Audience, and Tone
Clustering	28-29	Guidelines: analyzing clustering techniques	
Exercise 4	29	Applied practice: using clustering	Arranging Ideas
Asking Questions	30	Guidelines: using the *5W-How?* and *What if?* questions	Arranging Ideas
Exercise 5	30	Cooperative learning: listing *5W-How?* questions	Using Charts
Using Your Five Senses	31	Guidelines: selecting sensory details	
Exercise 6	31	Applied practice: recording sensory details	
Reading with a Focus	32	Guidelines: reading critically	
Exercise 7	32-33	Applied practice: reading with a focus	
Listening with a Focus	33	Guidelines: listening critically	
Exercise 8	33-34	Applied practice: listening with a focus	
Exercise 9	34	Cooperative learning: brainstorming *What if?* questions	
Thinking About Purpose, Audience, and Tone	35-36	Guidelines: using criteria to analyze purpose, audience, and tone	
Critical Thinking: Analyzing Purpose and Audience	36-38	Guidelines: tailoring writing to situations	
Critical Thinking Exercise	38	Applied practice: writing for a different purpose and audience	
Chart: Arranging Ideas	39	Guidelines: examining methods of order	

All the resources listed in this chapter are located in the Teacher's ResourceBank™.

SEGMENT	PAGES	CONTENT	RESOURCES
Critical Thinking: Arranging Information	40	Guidelines: using appropriate order	
Critical Thinking Exercise	41-42	Applied practice: analyzing the order of details	
Using Charts	43	Guidelines: making charts for organization	
Critical Thinking: Classifying Information	43	Guidelines: using classification strategies	
Critical Thinking Exercise	44	Cooperative learning: making a chart	
4 *Writing*	*45-46*		The First Draft
Writing a First Draft	45-46	Guidelines: examining a writer's first draft	
Exercise 10	46	Applied practice: writing a first draft	
5 *Evaluating and Revising*	*47-54*		Peer Evaluation
Evaluating	47-48	Guidelines: analyzing strategies	Revising by Adding and Cutting
Critical Thinking: Evaluating	49	Guidelines: analyzing criteria for evaluating writing	
Critical Thinking Exercise	49-50	Cooperative learning: evaluating a paragraph	
Chart: Revising Techniques	51	Examples: learning revision techniques	
Chart: Guidelines for Evaluating and Revising	53	Guidelines: using evaluation and revision techniques	
Exercise 11	54	Cooperative learning: evaluating and revising	
6 *Proofreading and Publishing*	*55-59*		Proofreading
Proofreading	55	Guidelines: analyzing proofreading techniques	Manuscript Form
Chart: Proofreading	56	Guidelines: using criteria for proofreading	
Exercise 12	56-57	Applied practice: proofreading a paragraph	
Publishing	57-58	Publishing ideas: reaching a specific audience	
Chart: Manuscript Form	58	Guidelines: analyzing manuscript form	
Exercise 13	58	Cooperative learning: brainstorming ideas for publishing	
Chart: Symbols for Revising and Proofreading	59	Guidelines: examining proofreading symbols	
7 *Making Connections*	*60-61*		
Writing and Art: Concrete Biography	60-61	Applied practice: writing a concrete biography	
WHOLE-CHAPTER RESOURCE Chapter Review			

OBJECTIVES

- To write personal responses to literature
- To identify writing obstacles
- To explain the influence of poetry on a writer

TEACHING THE LESSON

As motivation, initiate a discussion by asking for students' opinions about greeting cards. Lead students to the idea that people choose cards that express what they would like to say. Ask students which they appreciate more, a card or a personal note. Ask why people send cards, as opposed to notes. Are

 VISUAL CONNECTIONS
Interior with Etruscan Vase

About the Artist. Henri Matisse was born in France in 1869. He studied law at the University of Paris and passed his first law exams before beginning his art studies in 1889.

During the first several years of his career, Matisse learned about composition and form by copying masterpieces from the Louvre and by doing landscapes and still-life paintings in the traditional, realistic style. By the late 1890s, Matisse had adopted Impressionist techniques. His style continued to develop, and in later works he uses bold, opposing colors to capture the essence of his subject. *Interior with Etruscan Vase,* painted in 1940, is an example of this style.

Matisse also sculpted figures in bronze and stone, and in the early 1950s, he started to cross the boundaries between sculpture and painting. Cutting forms directly out of colored paper, Matisse constructed artworks by pasting up the cutouts to form compositions. These pictures are characterized by their pure, bright colors and their abstract simplicity. Matisse died in 1954, but his artwork continues to inspire and influence artists today.

1 WRITING AND THINKING

people afraid they will not be able to express their feelings in writing?

Before reading the introductory paragraphs of the segment, ask students what they would prefer—discussing or writing. Some of the answers to the questions under **Writing and You** may help you identify the kinds of difficulties students encounter when trying to write. Tell students that many writers have the same problems with writing. In this unit, students will learn ways to make writing easier.

You may want to have a volunteer read the excerpt from *a fire in my hands*. Then guide students in finding and listing the parts of the writing process that Soto describes. Try to include discovery, getting started (his early attempts), finding

Looking at the Process

Being a good writer starts with being a good thinker and planner. The writing comes later, as part of the entire writing **process.**

Writing and You. Is writing easy for you? Or do you often find yourself sitting and staring at a blank sheet of paper? Do you enjoy writing or is it a pain that you'd rather live without? All writers, even professional writers, get frustrated. They have trouble getting started, finding information, thinking up ideas, and then putting their ideas on paper. Which of these parts of the writing process cause you the greatest trouble?

As You Read. As you read the following forward from Gary Soto's book of poems, think about the difficulties he faced and how he dealt with them.

Interior with Etruscan Vase, Henri Matisse (1940). Oil on canvas. 29″ × 39½″. Collection of The Cleveland Museum of Art, Gift of the Hanna Fund, 52.153. © 1993 Succession H. Matisse/ARS, N.Y.

17

ideas (reading other poets and looking at his own experience), and putting ideas on paper.

If possible, select a poem by Soto that you think will appeal to the class and show it on the overhead projector. Have students list in their journals details from the poem about the geography and culture of the San Joaquin Valley. Then have them list analogous details from their own environments beside Soto's descriptions.

Guide students through the first and second **Reader's Response** questions. Use the third question as independent practice by having students freewrite their opinions about using everyday objects as poetic subjects.

After discussing the three maxims in the box following the **Reader's Response**

USING THE SELECTION
from a fire in my hands

1

anthology: collection of literary pieces (such as poems and stories) printed in one book

2

What do you associate with the name "Frankenstein"? (Supplement students' knowledge as needed with information about films or Mary Shelley's novel.) Tell students to imagine what the subject of "Frankenstein's Daughter" might be. Ask, "What if Dr. Frankenstein had a daughter? What if the monster had daughter?" [Responses will vary, but encourage creativity.]

3

Gary Soto felt a strong commitment to poetry. What activities do you associate with the terms "seriousness" and "dedication"? [Responses will vary. Emphasize that most tasks require commitment and effort if success is to be achieved.]

18

F R O M

A FIRE IN MY HANDS

BY GARY SOTO

I began writing poems fifteen years ago while I was in college.
1 One day I was in the library, working on a term paper, when by chance I came across an anthology of contemporary poetry. I
2 don't remember the title of the book or any of the titles of the poems except one: "Frankenstein's Daughter." The poem was wild, almost rude, and nothing like the rhyme-and-meter poetry I had read in high school. I had always thought that poetry was flowery writing about sunsets and walks on the beach, but that library book contained a direct and sometimes shocking poetry about dogs, junked cars, rundown houses, and TVs. I checked the book out, curious to read more.

Soon afterward, I started filling a notebook with my own poems. At first I was scared, partly because my poetry teacher, to whom this book is dedicated, was a stern man who could see the
3 errors in my poems. Also, I realized the seriousness of my dedication. I gave up geography to study poetry, which a good many friends said offered no future. I ignored them because I liked working with words, using them to reconstruct the past, which has always been a source of poetry for me.

When I first studied poetry, I was single-minded. I woke to poetry and went to bed with poetry. I memorized poems, read English poets because I was told they would help shape my poems, and read classical Chinese poetry because I was told that questions, you could copy and display them in a prominent place in the classroom as a visual reminder for students.

Select students to identify troubles writers have and ways Soto or they might overcome these obstacles.

"...that library book contained a direct and sometimes shocking poetry about dogs, junked cars, rundown houses, and TVs."

VISUAL CONNECTIONS

Exploring the Subject. Gary Soto, a teacher of English and Chicano Studies at the University of California at Berkeley, is considered one of the most talented contemporary American poets. His first book of poetry, *The Elements of San Joaquin* (1977), won the U.S. Award of the International Poetry Forum. Most of Soto's poems reflect his memories of an impoverished youth and his experiences as a migrant worker. His poetry has helped enlighten others about the feelings and lifestyle of many Mexican Americans.

4

Pablo Neruda (1904–1973), a Chilean writer, is considered one of the best poets of the twentieth century. Neruda won the 1971 Nobel Prize for literature. His poetry celebrates love and nature and reflects his personal experiences from childhood to death.

5

How do you think Neruda's poetry influenced Soto? [Responses will vary. One possibility is that Soto's poetry also reflects personal experiences.]

it would add clarity to my work. But I was most taken by Spanish
4 and Latin American poets, particularly Pablo Neruda. My favorites of his were the <u>odes</u>—long, short-lined poems celebrating common things like tomatoes, socks, scissors, and artichokes. I
5 felt joyful when I read these odes; and when I began to write my own poems, I tried to remain faithful to the common things of my childhood—dogs, alleys, my baseball mitt, curbs, and the fruit of the valley, especially the orange. I wanted to give these things life, to write so well that my poems would express their simple beauty.

You might have students read and review some of Gary Soto's poetry and then share their reactions with the class. Some of Soto's works are *The Elements of San Joaquin, The Cat's Meow,* and *Where Sparrows Work Hard.*

ENRICHMENT

Although all students can appreciate Gary Soto's accomplishments, migrant students might be even more inspired because they can relate to problems and difficulties Soto faced and overcame. Discuss with students the problems they have faced, and then help set up realistic goals (schedule daily study periods, complete assignments

6

In 1980, Philip Levine won the National Book Critics Circle Award in poetry for *Seven Years from Somewhere* and *Ashes: Poems New and Old.* Some critics believe that Levine influenced Soto's writing style. Soto is a former student of Levine, who has been on the English faculty at Fresno State College since 1958.

7

Zen Buddhism: a religious movement introduced in Japan in the 12th century that stresses enlightenment through the most direct means possible

8

Sequoias: Coniferous trees of the pine family that reach a height of over 300 feet, found only in California

ANSWERS

Reader's Response

Students should give complete, honest answers. They should also give reasons for their opinions. For question 3, if students have read poetry about common objects, they should give titles or brief descriptions of the poems. To encourage students to respond freely, refrain from penalizing mechanical or grammatical errors.

20

I also admired our own country's poetry. I saw that our poets often wrote about places where they grew up or places that impressed them deeply. James Wright wrote about Ohio and **6** West Virginia, Philip Levine about Detroit, Gary Snyder about the Sierra Nevadas and about Japan, where for years he studied **7** Zen Buddhism. I decided to write about the San Joaquin Valley, where my hometown, Fresno, is located. Some of my poems are <u>stark</u> observations of human violence—burglaries, muggings, fistfights—while others are <u>spare</u> images of nature—the orange **8** groves and vineyards, the Kings River, the bogs, the Sequoias. I fell in love with the valley, both its ugliness and its beauty, and quietly wrote poems about it to share with others.

READER'S RESPONSE

1. Are you, like Soto, ever scared to write because you don't want others to criticize your writing? How can you overcome this fear?
2. When Soto became interested in writing poetry, he started reading more poetry. Do you agree that reading the writing of others can help a writer? Why?
3. Soto says that he wants to write about common things like dogs, fistfights, and orange groves. Have you ever read poetry about such everyday events and objects? Do you think such things make good subjects for poetry? Why?

SELECTION AMENDMENT
Description of change: excerpted
Rationale: to focus on the concept of the writing process presented in this chapter

on time) to help them become more successful in class. ■

LOOKING AHEAD

In this chapter, you'll learn a general approach to writing that you can apply to all types of writing. You'll go through the stages of the writing process from choosing a topic to publishing. As you work through the chapter, remember that

- writing and thinking are both part of the process
- the writing process is flexible: you can adapt it to your own writing style and situation
- your topic, audience, and purpose emerge together when you write for yourself

"I start at the beginning, go on to the end, then stop."

Anthony Burgess

• • • •

"I always know the ending; that's where I start."

Toni Morrison

AFRICAN AMERICAN

Because many African American students profit from sharing ideas in groups, you may want to introduce them to composition through group discussion. Ask students to share examples of writing in their daily environments and list these on the chalkboard. Examples might include textbooks, billboards, magazines, and newspapers. Through group interaction, encourage students to discuss the objectives of these forms using the following questions: What is the writer's motivation? Is the written form necessary? Why? Is it valuable? To whom? What kind of ideas are being communicated? Have students elaborate on their previous examples. Can they remember any advertisements verbatim?

SELECTION AMENDMENT
Description of change: excerpted
Rationale: to focus on the concept of writing presented in this chapter

THE "WHY" AND "HOW" OF WRITING

Discuss the meaning of the word *aim* with the class. Emphasize the importance of writers' knowing the aim of their writing. They must know the goal if they want to attain it. You may also want to explain that often the aims overlap, even though one aim is usually primary.

The two most important aspects of teaching the writing process are that it is recursive and that each person's process is individualized. Have students read the introductory paragraphs for aim and process, and then you can discuss the pie chart. ■

COOPERATIVE LEARNING

To help students understand how subject, audience, and purpose are related, have them work in groups of four to draw an analogy between these elements in writing and their use in television programs. Ask the groups to list the following prompts: Saturday morning network, prime time network, cable television, and public television. Have groups list at least two shows from each category and identify the subject, audience, and purpose. Each group member should be responsible for one category.

22

Aim—The "Why" of Writing

Why do people write?—usually for the same reason they talk. They have something to say, someone to say it to, and some purpose for saying it. Of course, that's a general *why*. But what are a few *why's*, or basic purposes, people have for writing?

WHY PEOPLE WRITE	
To express themselves	To get to know themselves, to discover meaning in their own lives
To share information	To give other people information they want or need; to share some special knowledge they have
To persuade	To convince other people to do something or believe something
To create literature	To be creative, to say something in a unique way

Process—The "How" of Writing

Anything people say or write has one of the four basic purposes you've just read about—sometimes even has more than one purpose at a time. For example, a writer may want to persuade as well as to share information. Like all the other speakers and writers in the world, you'll be writing for one or more of these four purposes.

As Gary Soto's experience shows, writing doesn't just happen. A great deal of thought goes into writing, using a whole *process* or series of stages. The process begins with a prewriting stage that is mostly thinking. It moves through other stages that focus more on writing and then on to more thinking after the writing occurs. That's why some sections of this chapter focus more on thinking and other sections focus more on writing.

The following diagram shows the stages that usually take place during the writing process. As the diagram shows, you can go back to an earlier stage, or even start over again, at any point in the process.

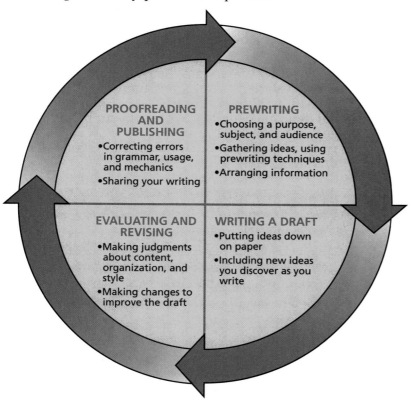

PROOFREADING AND PUBLISHING
•Correcting errors in grammar, usage, and mechanics
•Sharing your writing

PREWRITING
•Choosing a purpose, subject, and audience
•Gathering ideas, using prewriting techniques
•Arranging information

EVALUATING AND REVISING
•Making judgments about content, organization, and style
•Making changes to improve the draft

WRITING A DRAFT
•Putting ideas down on paper
•Including new ideas you discover as you write

For example, you're writing a report for art class on the life and work of artist Vincent van Gogh. You have gathered information from various books and have seen an exhibit featuring some of his works. You have your first draft almost finished. However, you see a newspaper story that a long-lost van Gogh painting has been found, and you find another book that contains some important facts about his life that you didn't have. You go back to the prewriting stage and take more notes. Then you start writing again by adding the new information to your first draft.

A DIFFERENT APPROACH

Have students work in teams of three or four to create original artistic presentations of this diagram. First, have teams review each stage and discuss the role each plays in the writing process. Then teams can brainstorm for original artistic approaches, for example, clay models, jigsaw puzzles, posters, and so forth. Encourage each team to create art that is unique. Allow time for teams to present their finished projects to the class.

PREWRITING

OBJECTIVES

- To use various prewriting techniques such as freewriting, brainstorming, clustering, the *5W-How* questions, and sensory details to find ideas for writing
- To keep a writer's journal
- To find ideas for writing by reading with a focus
- To find ideas for writing by listening for specific information
- To use "What if?" questions for prewriting

QUOTATION FOR THE DAY

"Writing is no trouble: you just jot down ideas as they occur to you. The jotting is simplicity itself — it is the occurring which is difficult." (Stephen Leacock, l869–l944, English-born Canadian humorist and economist)

You may wish to use the quotation to initiate a discussion of where and how writers get ideas.

MEETING
INDIVIDUAL
NEEDS

LEARNING STYLES

Auditory Learners. Students sometimes subvocalize when they read or write independently. Allow these students to quietly "think aloud" as they make entries in their journals.

 Prewriting

Finding Ideas for Writing

"Write about anything you want" and "write about one of the assigned topics" are opposite instructions—but you may have the same reaction to both: a big blank. Where *do* professional writers get their ideas for writing? How do they get started on an assignment? Every writer might say something different (even "I don't know—I just do it"), but there are definite ways to get your brain moving when you want (or need) to write. This section will give you practical help—summarized in the following chart—for finding ideas.

PREWRITING TECHNIQUES		
Writer's Journal	Recording personal experiences and observations	Page 25
Freewriting	Writing for a few minutes about whatever comes to mind	Page 26
Brainstorming	Listing ideas as quickly as they come	Page 27
Clustering	Using circles and lines to show connections between ideas	Pages 28–29
Asking Questions	Using the reporter's *5W–How?* questions	Page 30
Using Your Five Senses	Observing details of sight, hearing, smell, taste, touch	Page 31
Reading with a Focus	Reading to find specific information	Page 32
Listening with a Focus	Listening to find specific information	Page 33
Imagining	Imagining details for creative writing	Page 34

TEACHING THE LESSON

As you discuss the chart that summa-rizes the prewriting techniques, consider modeling each to help students visualize the application of the concepts. Where possible, base models on information from the excerpt from *a fire in my hands.* For example, com-pare Soto's notebook and his thinking about poetry each morning to **Keeping a Writer's** ☞

As the chart shows, you have many prewriting tech-niques to choose from and many ways to use them. You'll often use more than one technique at a time. You'll use some more than others because of your own thinking style. And you'll use different techniques for different writing situations. For example, if you're writing a per-sonal narrative about a hiking trip, you might use all five senses to recall vivid details about the adventure. But if you're searching for details about the subject "American railroads," you might use clustering or reading with a focus.

Keeping a Writer's Journal

If you aren't already doing so, start keeping a *writer's journal.* Use it to record thoughts, feelings, opinions, and great ideas—for example, things that bug you, song lyrics, and notes about famous people you wish you knew. Your journal can be small enough to carry around or big enough for drawing and pasting in cartoons and photos. Before you know it, you'll have a surprising source book of ideas for writing.

Here are some suggestions for getting started.

1. Make a habit of writing every day, and date your entries. Some people like to set a special time for writing—others like to be spontaneous and write when the mood (or an event) hits.
2. Write for yourself—which may mean messy and misspelled. Journals don't have "mistakes."
3. Be creative (even zany). Let your imagination go in songs, drawings, movie ideas, or poems.
4. React, reflect, explore random thoughts: Record some response to anything you include (like a quotation, an ad, a newspaper editorial). Why did you choose it?

EXERCISE 1 ▶ **Keeping a Writer's Journal**

If you're not already keeping a journal, start one now. And don't worry if nothing glamorous or dramatic hap-pened to you lately: Your personal thoughts, feelings, and

MEETING INDIVIDUAL NEEDS

LEP/ESL

Spanish. Although students may feel comfortable with their oral commu-nicative competence, many of them are probably anxious and uncomfortable about their writing abilities in English. Having them work with peers in small groups may ease their transition into this area of study. As an initial exercise, have them interview each other by asking questions such as, "What makes you happy?" or "What is the funniest thing that ever happened to you?" Ask each student to write a report of his or her classmate's responses.

ANSWERS
Exercise 1

In individualized notebooks (decorated spiral binders work well), students should record events or emotions experienced recently. Mechanical and grammatical errors should not be penalized.

Journal. Model his reading of other poets as **Reading with a Focus.** Use his finding ideas in the culture and environment of the San Joaquin Valley to model **Freewriting, Brainstorming, Clustering, Using your Five Senses,** and **Imagining.**

To illustrate how prewriting techniques are often used in combination, note the following examples: **Keeping a Writer's Journal** may at different times include every technique except **Reading With a Focus** and **Listening With a Focus,** but these two techniques could be combined by reading along while listening to a taped recording of the work.

To help students focus their efforts as they begin **Keeping a Writer's Journal,** suggest that each day they note the most

experiences are unique—and that's what makes journals fun and fascinating. To get started, try writing about one *event* or *emotion* that sticks in your mind from yesterday.

Freewriting

To *freewrite,* just let your mind go and write.

1. Use a watch or clock, set a time limit (three to five minutes is good), and keep writing until the time's up.
2. Start with a word, phrase, or topic that's important to you—like *gymnastics* or *animal rights.*
3. Write any ideas, images, or details that come to you, without stopping to think about grammar, spelling, or punctuation. Just let the words flow.
4. If the flow stops, copy the last word until something new appears, or talk to yourself: *I'm stuck—what can I say after "competition"—maybe maybe maybe "judges". . .*
5. To vary freewriting, choose one word or phrase from your freewriting, and use it as a starting point for more writing. This process is called *focused freewriting,* or *looping,* because it allows you to make a "loop" from what you've already written and then continue writing.

Here's a sample of a few minutes of freewriting on the word *recycling.*

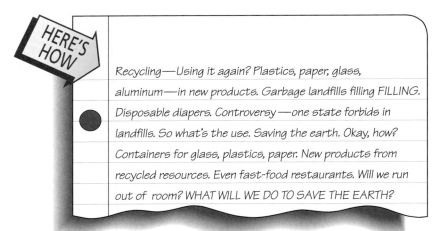

HERE'S HOW

Recycling—Using it again? Plastics, paper, glass, aluminum—in new products. Garbage landfills filling FILLING. Disposable diapers. Controversy—one state forbids in landfills. So what's the use. Saving the earth. Okay, how? Containers for glass, plastics, paper. New products from recycled resources. Even fast-food restaurants. Will we run out of room? WHAT WILL WE DO TO SAVE THE EARTH?

interesting things they have seen or heard in and outside class.

To help students understand **Free-writing**, have them write in their journals the name of a favorite book, song, film, or television program and then talk to partners for ten seconds about whatever comes to mind about their journal entries.

To illustrate focused freewriting, display the example from the textbook on an overhead projector and discuss the similarities between focused freewriting and clustering.

You may want to use **Exercise 2** as guided practice. Begin by assessing students' knowledge of the environmental dangers cited in the textbook. Ask volunteers to

EXERCISE 2 ▶ Using Freewriting

What's your concern about the environment? Write down a phrase that describes your thoughts and freewrite about it for three or four minutes. Then choose one phrase from your freewriting and do some focused freewriting or looping.

Brainstorming

Brainstorming generates ideas by free association. You can brainstorm alone, with a partner, or in a group.

1. Write any subject, word, or phrase at the top of a sheet of paper (or on the chalkboard).
2. Jot down *every* idea that comes to your mind. (In a group, brainstorm out loud and appoint one person to record all of the ideas.)
3. Don't stop to evaluate; just keep going until you run out of ideas.

Here are a group's brainstorming notes on electric cars. They're not all serious, but off-the-wall associations can always be cut or changed later.

HERE'S HOW

electric cars	speed? problems?
when first used?	probably dinky
need <u>long</u> cords	not dependent on gasoline
Who invented them?	high cost now, low later
car of the future	models: the Sparky,
no pollution	the Shocker
little pollution—	Who's building them?
what kind?	they're ready now—
how far on one charge?	just read <u>Road and Track</u>

ANSWERS
Exercise 2

Each student should create a phrase and use it as a starting point for freewriting. Remind students that they should write as many ideas as possible in the time allotted. Students should not be penalized for straying from the topic, as related concerns often surface during freewriting. For the second part of the assignment, students should pick their most interesting phrases, skip a few lines, and practice looping (focused freewriting) during the time you allot. Here students should stick to a subject. Mechanical and grammatical errors or incomplete sentences should not be penalized in either part of this exercise.

comment on each of these dangers. When you are satisfied that students have adequate background knowledge, tell them to free-write their thoughts on the assigned topic.

To introduce **Brainstorming**, you could have partners play an association game. Start by suggesting a broad subject such as a color, an animal, or a sport. Partners could then take five turns saying the first word that comes to mind after hearing the other prompt. Model the activity by exchanging associations with a volunteer.

Use **Exercise 3** as independent practice. Discuss the results in class as a way to assess students' comprehension. However, before class discussion, explain that as in journal entries, there are no mistakes in

ANSWERS
Exercise 3

Lists should include every idea the selected topic brings to mind, no matter how remotely related. Because the purpose here is quantity, groups might compete to see who can produce the most ideas in a given time.

A DIFFERENT APPROACH

Students might use a different color pen or pencil each time they divide a topic for clustering. Using colors will enable students to classify and locate topics more easily.

EXERCISE 3 ▶ **Using Brainstorming**

Practice brainstorming with a partner or a small group so that you'll hear ideas besides your own (which will probably spark more of your own). Together, list ideas about one of the following topics, or choose your own.

1. the funniest TV shows
2. compact discs
3. the American flag
4. slang
5. life in the year 2010
6. today's heroines

Clustering

Clustering is similar to brainstorming, but it is more visual and shows connections between ideas. Like brainstorming, clustering generally breaks a subject down into smaller parts, so it's good both for finding topics and gathering information.

1. Begin by writing a subject in the middle of your paper, and circle or box it.
2. Around the subject, write related ideas that you think of, circle them, and connect them with lines to your subject (and maybe to each other).
3. Let your new ideas lead to others. Just keep associating, circling, and connecting until you're ready to stop.

Clustering is also called *webbing*, a good name as the example shows. Even though your cluster or web may not make complete sense to someone else, you've made the connections and can follow your own thinking.

kinds of horses

brainstorming. Students should not feel inhibited while discussing their ideas by the fear that there is a pass/fail aspect to the exercise.

To explain clustering, draw an analogy to a paragraph. The cluster subject is like the main idea. The related ideas are similar to supporting information (sensory details, facts or statistics, and examples). Many of the related ideas can then be analyzed and, in turn, become the main ideas in other clusters with their parts as related ideas.

To help students visualize the concept, note that another term for clustering is webbing. You could draw the design of a simple spider web on the chalkboard and note that the central hub, where the spider lives, is like the cluster subject. The

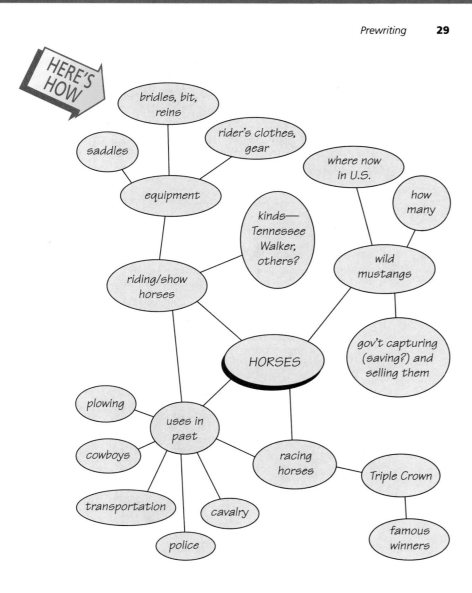

HERE'S HOW

- bridles, bit, reins
- saddles
- rider's clothes, gear
- equipment
- where now in U.S.
- how many
- kinds—Tennessee Walker, others?
- wild mustangs
- riding/show horses
- gov't capturing (saving?) and selling them
- **HORSES**
- plowing
- uses in past
- cowboys
- transportation
- cavalry
- police
- racing horses
- Triple Crown
- famous winners

 EXERCISE 4 **Using Clustering**

Create a cluster diagram using one of the topics you *didn't* use in Exercise 3 or another topic of your own choice. Use the clustering hints and Here's How diagram as guides.

INTEGRATING THE LANGUAGE ARTS

Literature Link. Have students read the poem "Richard Cory" by E. A. Robinson and use context clues to produce a cluster Robinson might have spun for the subject, "Richard Cory". Then play the song "Richard Cory" performed by Paul Simon and Art Garfunkel. Have partners produce clusters from Simon and Garfunkel's "Richard Cory" and then compare these with the clusters they created after reading the poem. Ask if Simon's details limit the reader's imagination. Note that Simon's full title was "Richard Cory, with apologies to E.A. Robinson."

ANSWERS
Exercise 4

Encourage students to use subjects that are fairly general—from which a second or third level of clustering can grow. Allow students to refer to the sample cluster diagram and the clustering hints when necessary. Students will probably not develop more than three or four main subheads in their diagrams.

foundation lines that radiate outward from the hub join it to different locations on a plant or other structure. These locations support and strengthen the hub much like details support the cluster subject. The foundation lines are like the relationships between the subject and the related ideas. If the relationship is strong, the line holds and the web is supported.

Prewriting webs or cluster designs vary among different writers, even changing with the same individual writing at different times. What is important is that no matter how far from the hub or subject the web is spun, the ideas should be related. As long as the ideas are related, the foundation lines will hold, and the hub (or main idea) will be supported.

Asking Questions

One to-the-point way of investigating a topic is asking the reporter's *5W-How?* questions: *Who? What? When? Where? Why? How?* You'll find, though, that every topic doesn't equal six questions. Sometimes a question word won't apply to your topic, and often you'll think of more than one good question for a word. Here are some questions you could ask for a paper about one group of Native Americans, the Creeks.

WHO?	Who were some famous Creek leaders or chiefs?
WHAT?	What was a Creek community like?
WHERE?	Where did the Creeks live?
WHEN?	When did they first encounter white people?
WHY?	Why are they called Creeks—an English word?
HOW?	How did Creeks govern themselves?

Tecumseh, Opothleyahola, Jerome Tiger, Angie Debo

EXERCISE 5   **Asking the *5W-How?* Questions**

You're a reporter covering a hot story for the school paper: the school board's proposal to require students to attend school year-round. Working in teams, list as many good *5W-How?* questions for digging out information about the proposal as you can, and then compare lists.

INTEGRATING THE LANGUAGE ARTS

Library Link. The **Here's How** examples for **Asking Questions** provide an opportunity for students to practice research skills. Before students begin, briefly review the use of the card catalogue and, if available, your library's computerized catalogue. You could explain that resource books on Native Americans might be necessary to answer all questions completely.

Ask the class to work in groups of four, with each member answering two questions. Assign each group a different Native American tribe (Creek, Iroquois, Sioux, Nez Percé, Navajo), having the group substitute only the tribe's name in the questions. The members should collaborate on finding resources and listing answers to make certain that the *5W-How?* questions are correctly answered. Have each group report its findings to the class.

ANSWERS
Exercise 5

Responses will vary.

Who on the board is in favor? *Who* is opposed?

What groups in the district favor year-round school? *What* groups oppose it?

Where did this idea come from?

When would year-round school begin?

Why would parents or teachers go along with this? *Why* not?

How would year-round school help students, parents, or teachers?

Note that the answers to any one of the *5W-How?* questions may frame the main idea of a particular work. In story telling, the answers to *Who?* and *What?* will often state the main idea. *Why?* explains cause and effect. *How?* explains a process. The answer to *Where?* may be the main idea in a geography report. *When?* is sometimes the main idea in a history report. It can also be the connection linking a work that has no main idea but describes a sequence of events.

Before starting **Exercise 5**, review informing and persuading as two purposes of writing. Note that the best questions for the purposes of the exercise will require informative answers. Based upon the answers to those questions, the reporter will

Using Your Five Senses

Wherever you are, whatever you're doing, sensations of hearing, touch, smell, and taste are zinging into your brain right along with visual images. Pay attention to them, and you can improve your writing with vivid sensory details.

For example, here are details you could record about an experience that's probably familiar: a night football game.

HERE'S HOW

TOUCH: cold air; sharp gusts of wind; cushiony bump of padded jackets on bleacher seats

SOUND: chants of cheerleaders and fans; deep roar and shrieks of fans; bands—sound fading in and out as they turn in formation; airplanes faint overhead

SMELL: hot dogs and mustard; popcorn; newly cut grass; cold fall air—leaf mold?

TASTE: greasy taste of salve on chapped lips; stale, too-salty popcorn; tangy mustard

SIGHT: greenish-yellow of grass; funny yellowish lights and dark sky; players in maroon, orange-gold, muddy uniforms; referees in crisp black and white; fans a sea of every color, with red jumping out—blankets, hats, gloves, coats

EXERCISE 6 ▶ Using Your Five Senses

If you really focus on your sensations, in any situation, you'll surprise yourself with life's sensory details—and your own sensitivity to them. Choose one of the following places, if possible *go to it* (if not, imagine it), and write down the sensory details you observe. You can make a column on your paper for each sense.

1. the lobby of a movie theater
2. inside your family's or a friend's car
3. the gymnasium during any kind of game or event
4. your school lunchroom at noon on a school day
5. a yogurt shop or any store

CRITICAL THINKING
Analysis

To analyze the role each sense plays in providing information, divide the students into groups of three or four and assign each group one sense. If possible, take the class outside or to the school cafeteria. Each student must concentrate on the designated sense and jot down experiences as they occur. Upon returning to the room, have groups convene to combine all members' notes. A member of each group should report its details to the class. Then discuss how the senses work independently and together to inform us of our surroundings.

ANSWERS
Exercise 6

Students should provide at least three relevant details for each sense when they visit or visualize one of the places suggested. You could test a good detail by evaluating its capacity to make the reader experience the place being described.

decide whether the article should inform (appear in the news section) or inform and persuade (an editorial or opinion column).

To begin the section **Using Your Five Senses**, note that beginning writers rely mostly on the sense of sight when describing. Suggest that students occasionally close their eyes for one minute in familiar surroundings and concentrate on using one of the other senses.

When covering **Reading with a Focus**, you may want to review the requirements for citing sources when using direct quotations and paraphrasing in writing.

Note that the stories to be covered on radio or television news programs are often

Reading with a Focus

How much do you know about the ancient Mayas of Central America? If you choose a topic you haven't experienced or can't observe firsthand, you'll probably use magazines and newspapers for ideas and information. Reading for a specific purpose—to find information about your topic—is very different from reading a novel for pleasure or browsing through a magazine. When you've found a possible source of information, follow these steps.

1. "Check out" the source first; don't start reading on page 1. Look for key words in the index (*Mayas, Central America*), study the table of contents, and in the text check headings, charts, and illustrations. Be on alert for your topic.
2. Skim until you're sure you've found information on your topic, and then slow down and read every word. Take notes on both main ideas and specific details, using your own words unless the exact quotation is important. Keep track of the sources you use.

 REFERENCE NOTE: For more on using library resources, see pages 920–925.

EXERCISE 7 ▶   **Reading with a Focus**

In Florida, the manatee, an aquatic mammal, is in danger of extinction. In California, the condor, a large vulture, faces similar problems. What animals in your state are on the endangered species list or may soon be put there? Find some information about an endangered animal, and read to find answers to the following questions. If you work in a group, each person could find a different source and compare your answers.

identified at the start of the program in the sequence in which they will be presented. When addressing **Listening with a Focus,** students should use the program introduction as a table of contents in a book. This will help them prepare to focus if a relevant item is to be included.

Suggest that for **Exercise 8,** students prepare *5W-How?* charts to assist them in answering the main questions.

To discuss **Imagining,** note that "What if?" questions can also be asked in familiar surroundings. Writers like Stephen King and filmmakers like Alfred Hitchcock have often based their creative works on unusual "What if?" twists to everyday situations.

You could use **Exercise 9** as independent practice. If students have difficulty

1. What are the animal's habitat and feeding habits?
2. Why is the animal in danger of becoming extinct? (Look for multiple reasons.)
3. How long has the animal been in trouble?
4. What efforts to date have been made to save the animal? How successful have these efforts been?

Listening with a Focus

Printed words aren't your only outside source of information. You can also listen—to radio and television programs, to video and audio tapes from the library, to people (anyone knowledgeable about your topic) in personal or telephone interviews. Good listening means focused listening, so prepare in advance.

1. Brainstorm or cluster what you already know about your topic, and reread any of your reading notes.
2. Make a list of the information you're looking for about your topic (in question form, if you want). Keep it by you as you listen.
3. Think ahead about note taking. You can't record every word, and you can't always "rewind" and rehear. Get the main points and supporting details by writing in phrases and using abbreviations.

☞ REFERENCE NOTE: For information on interviewing, see pages 913–914.

EXERCISE 8 ▶ **Listening for Specific Information**

Listen to an evening sportscast on your local television station. If there is more than one sportscast, divide the class so that some of you listen to each program. Listen for answers to the following questions.

1. What's the top sports story? Why is it ranked most important? Does it, for example, involve an outstanding sports performance, or does it involve the amount of money a player has signed for?
2. What sport is given the most time in the broadcast—football, baseball, soccer, or some other sport?

ANSWERS
Exercise 7

After locating sources, students should jot down answers as quickly as possible. The object here is for students to keep specific questions in mind as they consult no more than three sources each within a limited amount of time. At this point, no one should be penalized if sources do not provide all information. When groups compare individual answers, they can prepare a composite report with answers to all questions.

ANSWERS
Exercise 8

Although there are four main questions, this exercise calls for six answers. Be sure students have all questions in mind before they begin the listening assignment. Remind students to review questions just before the news and then to jot down notes for answers immediately after the news.

grasping the distinctions among different writing purposes, provide and discuss examples of different forms that illustrate the relationship between purpose and form. Note that in highly personal writing that others probably won't see, the purpose is often to sort out and understand feelings. Therefore, the writer is also the audience.

If you have shown examples of some literary forms listed in the textbook, you could have groups brainstorm and identify intended audience and tone in those examples. You could also have students discuss intended audience and suitable tones for the other forms of writing listed.

3. What's the most interesting story in the sportscast? What makes it interesting?
4. Based on the time devoted to each, whose sport seems more important—men's or women's?

Imagining

When you write creatively—stories, poems, plays, and so on—you usually write about people, places, and events that aren't real. You may begin with what you've observed, but many of the details have to come from your imagination. One way to spark your imagination for these kinds of details is to ask yourself "What if?" questions. Filmmakers and other creative people often use these kinds of questions to produce unusual ideas. The question *What if a family went on vacation and forgot to take one of the children along?* resulted in *Home Alone*—one of the biggest moneymaking movies of the early 1990s.

Here are some general questions that can help get you in a creative mode.

1. *What if I could change one thing in the past?* (What if my family had moved to a lighthouse off the coast of Maine? What if I had been born the greatest genius the world had ever seen?)
2. *What if something we take for granted were totally different?* (What if all the electricity all across the country went off at once and stayed off? What if everyone looked exactly alike?)
3. *What if I could create something new?* (What if I designed an invention that could move people through time as well as space? What if I could write music that would make everyone feel happy?)

A DIFFERENT APPROACH

Read aloud the first chapter of H. G. Wells's *The Time Machine.* Have students take notes about the characters, plot, and unfamiliar vocabulary words. When you have finished reading, write a list of student-suggested unfamiliar words on the chalkboard. Ask individual students to find and read definitions for each. Then initiate a discussion to lead the students in paraphrasing the plot and describing the characters.

After the discussion, tell students to imagine that they are time travelers who are about to create time machines. Explain that each student should imagine a design for the machine and then draw or describe it. Ask students to include brief explanations of how the machine works, where in time they will travel, and why they chose their destinations.

ANSWERS
Exercise 9

As students brainstorm, they should record ideas. Remind them to begin their questions with "What if?" When each group has ten or more ideas, students can make judgments about which idea is the best. The class might vote on the best movie idea from among group choices.

EXERCISE 9 ▶ **Using the "What if?" Questions**

The movie moguls are in trouble. They've got to come up with a dynamite movie idea, or the studio will go broke. Working with several of your classmates, brainstorm a series of "What if?" questions that might result in a movie idea for the studio. When you've finished, choose the idea you think would make the best movie.

Ask the class to list as many prewriting techniques as they can. Then ask for volunteers to share their answers and to explain the techniques. ■

 Prewriting

Thinking About Purpose, Audience, and Tone

Purpose.   Any piece of writing—even the most personal, that no one will ever see—has a *purpose,* a reason for being. You write in many different forms, but you always write for some end result: to express feelings, to be creative, to explain or inform, or to persuade. (You may even combine two or more purposes in a single piece of writing.) This chart shows the different forms you may use for each of the main purposes.

MAIN PURPOSE	FORMS OF WRITING
To express yourself	Journal, letter, personal essay
To be creative	Short story, poem, play, novel
To explain or inform	Science and history writing, newspaper and magazine articles, biography, autobiography, travel essay
To persuade	Persuasive essay, letter to editor, advertisement, political speech

Audience.   It's also true that your *audience*—your readers—affect what you say and how you say it. To consider the needs of your audience, you can use these questions.

- Why am I writing for this audience? Do I want to inform or persuade them? to share a personal experience, amuse them, or stir their emotions?
- What does my audience already know about my topic? (You want to help readers, not bore them!)
- What will this particular audience be looking for or find interesting?
- What level of language is appropriate for this audience? A simple or more complex vocabulary? Short sentences, long sentences, or both?

Tone. You can think of *tone* as the personality of your writing. You can sound outraged, sarcastic, serious, or funny. You can sound casual and personal or more distant and formal. How you sound—your tone—comes from the language you use. To create the tone you want, pay attention to

- choice of details (facts? sensory words? personal thoughts?)
- choice of words (slang? conversational style? figurative language? formal wording?)
- the rhythms and sounds of language (short, brisk sentences? long, leisurely ones?)

A word that's closely related to tone is voice. *Voice* simply means writing in a way that sounds like you. You can do this even when you're writing with a formal, serious tone by making your writing sound as natural as possible. Avoid using words or phrases just because they sound pretentious or knowledgeable. Use the precise word, but keep your writing as simple as possible. Let your own voice come through.

CRITICAL THINKING

Analyzing Purpose and Audience

You already tailor your writing to different situations even though you may not always stop and think about it. You don't write the same way in journal entries, reports, funny letters to friends, and thank-you letters to your aunt. Making that tailoring conscious simply makes your writing better.

Adjust your writing for both your purpose and your audience. To see how this works, read the following short review of *Mo' Better Blues*, a film by Spike Lee. The author's main purpose is to evaluate the film and thus to persuade others to see it.

Before starting the **Critical Thinking Exercise,** review with the class the definitions of informing and persuading on p. 22.

Before reading the film reviews, have volunteers share with the class, if possible, their knowledge of Spike Lee and *Mo' Better Blues.* Supplement the discussion as necessary.

Before students write the informative piece, you could show photographs illustrating changes in automotive design over the last four decades. Suggest that drawing pictures of the car of the future may help students get started.

Before students write the evaluation (ad), suggest that they think in terms of a sequence of events or reasons that will lead a

ADVANCED STUDENTS

Students might enjoy researching Spike Lee's career and accomplishments and then reporting their findings to the class. Using this information, the class could discuss possible audiences that Spike Lee attempts to reach and how he achieves his purpose.

LESS-ADVANCED STUDENTS

Students might have difficulty distinguishing informative from persuasive writing. Before beginning the **Critical Thinking Exercise,** guide students in examining and discussing automobile evaluations in magazines or newspapers. Work with them to look for examples of informative writing and car ads found in similar sources for examples of persuasive writing.

In *Mo' Better Blues,* one of America's most talented and intriguing filmmakers—Spike Lee—turns his eye to the jazz scene of New York. The film is alternately wonderful and trite, with Denzel Washington as a talented trumpet player who loves music more than the two women in his life. The ending feels false and tacked-on but can't dilute the pleasure of the film. The soundtrack has lots of wonderful music from Branford Marsalis and Bill Lee.

Steve MacQueen, *Tallahassee Democrat*

What guesses would you make about the audience for this review? Notice that, in addition to evaluating the film, the reviewer is careful to give enough information for readers who haven't seen the film. The audience consists of general readers, who may or may not have seen the film.

Now read a short passage that has a different purpose and a slightly different audience. These paragraphs are to inform readers who haven't seen the film about the movie and about Spike Lee's message in it.

SELECTION AMENDMENT
Description of change: excerpted
Rationale: to focus on the concept of purpose and audience presented in this chapter

buyer to want or need this particular car. Remind them of the current concerns about fuel efficiency and pollution. After students have completed the exercise, have them review their ads to identify their judgments and to label their supporting reasons. To conclude, have partners exchange ads and write evaluations by responding as parents with three young children. Ask, "What reasons would lead you to want or need this car?" and "What reasons would you have for not wanting or needing this car?"

LEARNING STYLES

Visual Learners. Students might find inspiration for their own ideas for future cars if you display colorful pictures or posters of various antique, classic, and late-model cars.

Kinetic Learners. Students might better organize their ideas for both informing and persuading if they are permitted to draw or make clay models of their cars of the future.

ANSWERS
Critical Thinking Exercise

Responses will vary. After brainstorming for ideas about new technology and visualizing a car's appearance, students should begin a straightforward paragraph of description with an explanation of how the car works. The tone should be authoritative, and the point of view should be third person. ("The twin jet exhaust overdrive conserves three gallons of potato-base fuel," etc.) For the persuasive paragraph, students may find further visualization and "What if?" scenarios useful. Such a tone excites and challenges. The point of view is second person, to address readers directly.

Spike Lee's *Mo' Better Blues* is a film celebration of black talent—not just of the trumpet player Bleek Gilliam, the movie's main character, but of Lee himself, his father, and his sister. Besides directing the film, Spike plays Gilliam's manager. Bill Lee—a jazz bassist and composer—wrote the score and provided much of the inspiration for the film. Joie Lee, who has appeared in all of Spike Lee's movies, plays a teacher in love with the music-obsessed Gilliam.

In the movie, which is set in contemporary New York, Gilliam is the classic committed artist who wants to do nothing but practice his art—purely—and finds that even those who love him and those who control his livelihood (manager, club owners) can stand in his way. He is left by his love, lied to, and cheated out of money (all the while packing in audiences) until finally a blow to his face leaves him unable to play.

Notice how, in this second piece, the writer gives much more information about the film than the reviewer whose purpose is to evaluate the film.

 CRITICAL THINKING EXERCISE:
Writing for a Different Purpose and Audience

What will the car of the future be like? Write a short, informative piece for readers who haven't seen the car that you plan to be driving in twenty years. Then, write an evaluation (an ad) of the same car. This time your purpose is to persuade readers to buy the car. These readers may or may not already have seen the car.

Prewriting

Arranging Ideas

By now you've gathered a ton of information. You could gather still more, but you really think you've had enough. Before writing, though, you need to think about arranging your prewriting ideas. This chart shows four common ways of ordering, or arranging, ideas.

ARRANGING IDEAS		
TYPE OF ORDER	**DEFINITION**	**EXAMPLES**
Chronological	Narration: Order that presents events as they happen in time	Story; narrative poem; explanation of a process; history
Spatial	Description: Order that describes objects according to location	Description (near to far; left to right; top to bottom; and so on)
Importance	Evaluation: Order that gives details from least to most important or the reverse	Persuasive writing; description; explanation (main idea and supporting details); evaluative writing
Logical	Classification: Order that relates items and groups	Definition; classifications; comparison and contrast

 REFERENCE NOTE: For more information on arranging ideas, see pages 82–85.

TEACHING *ARRANGING INFORMATION*

You may want to use the paragraph from *A Browser's Dictionary* as guided practice. Define terms with which students are not familiar. After displaying the text on an overhead projector and defining *analysis,* have students identify the main idea and bracket it in red. Then have students identify

LEP/ESL

General Strategies. You may want to help students focus more clearly on the purpose of sequencing. Offer the analogy of telling a joke. Ask students, "What happens if the punchline comes before instead of after the lead-in material? Is the joke still funny?" Solicit examples from real life (such as following recipes, or starting a car) in which sequence produces desired results.

COOPERATIVE LEARNING

You could use the excerpt from *The Norton Anthology of Literature by Women . . .* as a cooperative learning tool, by having partners find details in the paragraph. After students identify each detail, suggest that they use a time line like the one following to record major events in Mourning Dove's life, from birth to the publication of her novel.

Details
1st 2nd 3rd 4th 5th
Start ├──┼──┼──┼──┤ End

SELECTION AMENDMENT
Description of change: excerpted
Rationale: to focus on the concept of arranging information presented in this chapter

CRITICAL THINKING
Arranging Information

When you're deciding how to arrange ideas, once again think about purpose, audience, and subject. Sometimes purpose and audience lead to a particular arrangement. If you're writing about a typical school day in a letter to a foreign exchange student who'll soon be attending your school, you'll probably describe events in the order they happened (chronological order). But if you're writing about your own day in a journal entry, you might start with the highlights and move to the more insignificant incidents (order of importance).

Often the subject itself suggests the order of ideas. For example, this paragraph contrasts how American colonists paid for large items with how they made small transactions. It's natural for this writer to use logical order.

> Colonial America, lacking an official mint, suffered a constant shortage of small coins. Large transactions could be handled with letters of credit, but how did a traveler pay for a meal or for a drink? Coins of all nations were used in making change, the commonest being the Spanish silver piece of eight, very like the later U.S. silver dollar, and so called because it was stamped with a large Arabic 8 to signify a value of eight Spanish *reals*, a *real* having a value of about 12 1/2¢. (There was a Mexican *real* of that value (later a peso), but there is no evidence that the coin had a general circulation in the early colonies.) A whole piece of eight, however, was a coin of substantial value. To provide small change, these coins were regularly cut into halves and quarters called "bits."
>
> John Ciardi, *A Browser's Dictionary*

each example of comparison/contrast. As they do, number each in blue. Ask volunteers to apply the definition of analysis to this activity and to explain the process in their own words.

Using the paragraph on the next page from *The Name of the Rose* as independent practice, note that in descriptive writing, some paragraphs may not have a main idea. They may simply create an overall impression by depicting a setting. If students have difficulty analyzing the order of details, draw a schematic outline of a rectangular room with an opening for a door. As students identify individual features, use letters, simple drawings, or architectural notations to locate these features on the schematic. Then have students review order definitions.

CRITICAL THINKING EXERCISE:
Analyzing the Order of Details

Using the chart on page 39, decide which type of order each of these passages uses.

1.   The first native-American woman to write and publish a novel, Mourning Dove (a translation of Hum-ishu-ma) was a member of the Okanogan tribe, whose communities were located in British Columbia and north-central Washington state. Born near Bonner's Ferry, Idaho, she was given the English name Christal Quintasket but raised in part by a grandmother who taught her to respect the rapidly vanishing traditions of her people. Although she had little formal education—three years at the Sacred Heart Convent in Ward, Washington, and brief periods at government Indian schools—Mourning Dove began early to collect and transcribe Okanogan tribal legends. In 1912, she enrolled in a business school to study English and typing so that she could improve her work on Indian tales and on the novel-in-progress which was to become her *Cogewea the Half Blood: A Depiction of the Great Montana Cattle Range* (1927).

1. chronological   Sandra M. Gilbert and Susan Gubar, *The Norton Anthology of Literature by Women: The Tradition in English*

COOPERATIVE LEARNING
Create teams of three and assign each member one paragraph of the **Critical Thinking Exercise.** Allow the students to refer to the chart on p. 39. Remind groups that team members should collaborate on answers and help each other as needed. Ask students to initial their answers before the teams hand in their assignments.

INTEGRATING THE LANGUAGE ARTS
Vocabulary Link. You may want to discuss how transitions connect ideas and how certain transitions relate to certain types of writing. Brainstorm with the class for conjunctions and prepositions that can be used as transitional words or phrases that show chronological or spatial order. List these on a chalkboard or an overhead projector. Ask students to select from those that indicate spatial order to write five sentences describing the classroom. Then have them copy the lists in their journals for future reference.

SELECTION AMENDMENT
Description od change: excerpted *Rationale:* to focus on the concept of analyzing the order of details presented in this chapter.

⬆ A DIFFERENT APPROACH

If students have difficulty identifying the order of details in "We Need Power, Program, and Progress," write the terms *conservative, liberal,* and *progressive* on the chalkboard. Suggest that students think of them as related ideas in a cluster. Ask what the subject of this cluster is [attitudes toward change]. Then write "means/ends" as a cluster subject connected to three blank circles. Finally, decide what related ideas could be recorded in these cluster circles. The following diagram gives an illustration of this clustering:

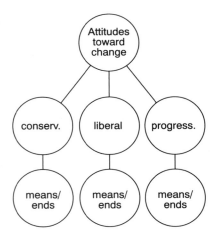

AMENDMENTS TO SELECTIONS
Description of change: excerpted
Rationale: to focus on the concept of arranging information presented in this chapter

42

2.   In the 1990s, as in the past, there will be conservatives, liberals, and progressives. Conservatives want to maintain the status quo or turn back the clock. Liberals want to change things a little, incrementally. Progressives want rapid, significant change. Too often, progressives focus almost exclusively on ends (programs) and not enough on means (power). We need power, program, and progress—in that order. Progressives need power in order to implement their program, in order to make progress.

2. logical   Jesse L. Jackson, "We Need Power, Program, and Progress"

3.   I said before that at this point you pushed a wooden door and found yourself in the kitchen, behind the fireplace, at the foot of the circular staircase that led to the scriptorium. And just as we were pushing that door, we heard to our left some muffled sounds within the wall. They came from the wall beside the door, where the row of niches with skulls and bones ended. Instead of a last niche, there was a stretch of blank wall of large squared blocks of stone, with an old plaque in the center that had some worn monograms carved on it. The sounds came, it seemed, from behind the plaque, or else from above the plaque, partly beyond the wall, and partly almost over our heads.

3. spatial   Umberto Eco, *The Name of the Rose* ⚡

TEACHING *CLASSIFYING INFORMATION*

You may want to provide students with a model or graphic representation of the solar system to show the size and comparative distance of each planet from the sun. Tell students that an easy way to remember the planets is to organize them in order of distance from the sun (Mercury,

Using Charts

As visual organizations of information, charts are often a helpful technique for arranging your prewriting notes. They help you see "blocks" of information, and their relationships, clearly. Here's a chart about two minerals and their effects on our health. The writer organizes the information into three categories: each mineral's sources, its function, and deficiency symptoms.

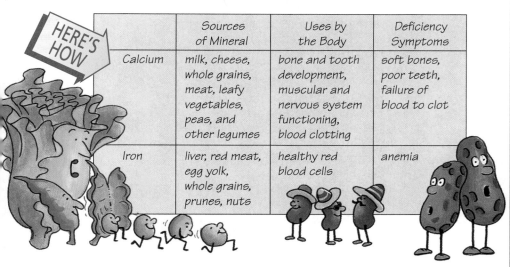

	Sources of Mineral	Uses by the Body	Deficiency Symptoms
Calcium	milk, cheese, whole grains, meat, leafy vegetables, peas, and other legumes	bone and tooth development, muscular and nervous system functioning, blood clotting	soft bones, poor teeth, failure of blood to clot
Iron	liver, red meat, egg yolk, whole grains, prunes, nuts	healthy red blood cells	anemia

CRITICAL THINKING

Classifying Information

When you make a chart, you're *classifying*, grouping together related information. And this takes thinking—deciding on the headings, or categories, to cover your information. Here's a way to approach the task.

1. Read through your notes. When you find items that seem to go together, rewrite them in a new list.
2. Look at each list, and decide what the items have in common. Why do they belong together? Your answer is a heading or category for the list.

MEETING INDIVIDUAL NEEDS

LEARNING STYLES

Kinetic Learners. Divide the class into two teams. Ask each team to make a list of all the ways they can group or classify their members. The group that comes up with the greatest number of ways and can demonstrate their means of classification, wins. You may want to explain that classifying is simply a way of showing how people, things, events, or ideas relate to each other.

Visual Learners. Students might benefit if you display a poster of the solar system before they begin to organize the information for their charts.

Venus, Earth, Mars, Jupiter, Saturn, Uranus, Neptune, Pluto).

For closure, have students refer to the charts they created for arranging ideas. Have them add a column head, "Graphic Aids" and insert "chart" and "timeline" in the appropriate places.

ANSWERS
Critical Thinking Exercise

Charts will vary. However information is arranged, charts should contain all the information in the example below.

PLANET	EARTH	SATURN
Proximity to Sun	3rd	6th
Characteristics	small dense warm	large not dense cold
Type	terrestrial	giant
Orbit	365 days	almost 30 years
Satellites	1	9

CRITICAL THINKING EXERCISE:
Making a Chart to Organize Information

With a small group, make a chart of the following information about the planets Saturn and Earth. Remember: first group similar information and then decide on headings. Compare your chart with another group's.

Earth—one of terrestrial planets
   (Mercury, Venus, Earth, and Mars)
Earth—third planet from sun
Earth's orbit (once around sun) 365 days
Saturn's almost 30 years
Saturn—one of giant planets
   (Jupiter, Saturn, Uranus, Neptune)
Saturn—sixth planet from sun
Giant planets—large, much less dense, and cold (because far from sun)
Terrestrial planets—small, dense, and warm
Earth—one moon
Saturn—at least twenty-two named satellites

A time line is a chart of chronological information. It helps you (and your readers) organize dated information by clearly showing the sequence of actions or events. Here is a time line of important events in American independence.

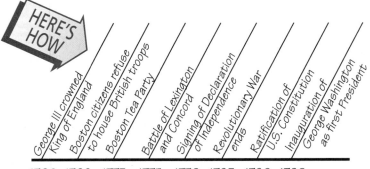

HERE'S HOW

George III crowned King of England
Boston citizens refuse to house British troops
Boston Tea Party
Battle of Lexington and Concord
Signing of Declaration of Independence
Revolutionary War ends
Ratification of U.S. Constitution
Inauguration of George Washington as first President

1760 1768 1773 1775 1776 1783 1788 1789

OBJECTIVE

- To plan and develop a first draft from existing prewriting notes

TEACHING THE LESSON

Tell students to find in the dictionary the meaning of *draft* as it is used in the text. Ask volunteers to share other definitions. Note that the ways to approach writing a first draft are as varied as the dictionary definitions of the word.

You may need to distinguish between freewriting and drafting—jotting down ideas

Writing a First Draft

Surprising, isn't it, how many pieces of paper you can fill in *pre*writing? Every idea is important (even the dead-end ones), and you could stretch planning out . . . until your paper's due. That's not the idea. At some point, you have to dive in and start a draft. (On the other hand, some of you may be itching to begin—it's possible to get impatient with prewriting!)

Just as there are perfectionists and "hurry up!" types in prewriting, there's no single, right way to write a draft. You may feel comfortable writing a first draft based on scribbled notes only you could interpret. Or you may need a detailed outline before you begin. You may write quickly, trying just to get your ideas down on paper. Or you may shape each sentence carefully, trying to connect ideas with exactly the right word. As you write your first draft, try these suggestions.

- Use your prewriting plans to guide your draft.
- Write freely, but try to express your ideas clearly.
- Don't hesitate to add new ideas and details. Writing *is* discovery.
- Don't worry about errors in grammar, usage, and mechanics. You can find and fix them later.

Here is the first draft of a brief paper on a sport called lacrosse. Notice how the writer makes a change (a revision) even while drafting and also writes personal notes and questions that will lead back to prewriting.

HERE'S HOW

Lacrosse is a team sport that Native Americans invented a long time ago. French explorers named it lacrosse because its long, curved playing stick looked like a bishop's staff, [what's French word?]. It's really a long-handled racket, with a mesh head like a pocket.

QUOTATION FOR THE DAY

"I have never started a poem yet whose end I knew. Writing a poem is discovering." (Robert Frost, 1874–1963, American poet, winner of the Pulitzer Prize for poetry)

After writing the quotation on the chalkboard, explain to students that starting an essay is similar to Frost's starting a poem. The writer discovers what he or she wants to say as the writing unfolds.

MEETING

INDIVIDUAL

NEEDS

LEP/ESL

General Strategies. Because students might not have had any exposure to the two sports mentioned in the text (lacrosse and in-line skating), you may want to suggest that they write first drafts about their favorite sports.

as fast as they occur, instead of using an existing prewriting plan. Refer to the example of a first draft as illustration.

You may want to use **Exercise 10** as guided practice, suggesting clustering or another prewriting technique as an alternative.

CLOSURE

Have a volunteer explain the difference between drafting and freewriting. ■

The ball is passed and received in this stick, and players score points by kicking or ~~throwing~~ hurling the ball into the goal.

Lacrosse is a rough game, but it's an ancient, formal sport. Since 18?? [check date] it's been the official national sport of Canada. Oren Lyons, on the Iroquois Nationals team [chief too—Onandagas?], has said, "We were playing team sports here when in Europe, they were still knocking people off horses, clubbing each other, fencing for keeps, all those so-called sports."

E X E R C I S E **10** ▶ **Writing a First Draft**

Here are some prewriting notes about a very modern sport, in-line skating. Work alone or with a partner to turn the notes into an interesting paragraph. You can add or drop details if you want. Then, arrange the information and start drafting.

In-line skates—roller skates similar to ice skates—four wheels in a single file down the middle of the skate

1980 first appeared—for professional ice hockey players to practice off-season

Can perform stunts—similar to skateboarding; most skaters just cruise

Expensive—$180 to $250 pair

Cheryl Rowars, Miami Beach, sells one to three pairs every day: "They sell because it's something fun to do. It's not replacing the skateboard, though."

Requires a strong sideways stroke—"A great workout" Sara Kendall, age 15

"It's a super athletic sport without contact"—Rick Carlson, South Miami

Beginning in 1981—bought by ordinary people

ANSWERS
Exercise 10

Responses will vary. Students should write a first draft using logical order. Starting with definition, they should group related ideas, add background, and include further information. Encourage students to combine related ideas into compound and complex sentences. Students may add or omit details but should include information and sources the audience needs. For example, the paragraph might begin, "In-line skates, skates with four wheels in a line, instead of a blade, first appeared in 1980. They were invented for ice hockey practice in the off-season, but by 1981, they had reached the general public."

OBJECTIVE

- To evaluate and revise the first draft of a given paragraph

MOTIVATION

Have students discuss planning a picnic—choosing a date, a site, a menu, and activities. Then have students evaluate the plan and revise it according to variables such as rain, cost, and effect of temperature on food. Afterward, relate their planning and changes to evaluating and revising.

Evaluating and Revising

Although they often occur at the same time, evaluating and revising are two separate steps in your writing.

> **Evaluating**—deciding on your paper's strengths and weaknesses
> **Revising**—making improvements

Evaluating

You have something to say about how good (or bad) things are every day. You evaluate your friend's new shirt and the food at a party. You evaluate your options for Thursday night: visiting your best friend or watching your favorite TV program. Evaluating your own writing, though, is more personal—and that means much harder.

Self-Evaluation.   Three strategies can help you evaluate your writing.

READING CAREFULLY. Read your paper several times, concentrating each time on something different. First, read for *content* (what you say), then for *organization* (how you've arranged your ideas), and then for *style* (how you've used words and sentences).

LISTENING CAREFULLY. Read your draft aloud to yourself and try to "hear" what you've written. Using a different sense—hearing instead of reading—may help you notice awkward sentences and foggy ideas.

TAKING TIME. Set your first draft aside for several hours or overnight. You usually see your writing more clearly—as if it's someone else's—if you put it out of your mind for a while.

Peer Evaluation.   All professional writers expect—and even rely on—other people to read their work: friends, family, editors. Other people are simply more objective, and, after all, writers write for *readers*.

Teacher's ResourceBank™
RESOURCES

> **EVALUATING AND REVISING**
> - Peer Evaluation
> - Revising by Adding and Cutting

QUOTATION FOR THE DAY

"The only impeccable writers are those who never wrote." (William Hazlitt, 1778–1830, English essayist and critic)

You may wish to write the word *impeccable* on the chalkboard and ask a volunteer to define the word. Then share the quotation with the class. As students begin evaluating and revising their first drafts, remind the class that although no writer is impeccable, it is still a goal to strive for.

Remind students that thinking and writing are part of the same process. Note that evaluating involves thinking and that revising is putting that thinking into practice through writing. Before beginning **Self-Evaluation**, p. 47, guide students toward the realization that objectivity is a critical element in personal evaluation. After reading **Self-Evaluation**, have students paraphrase the three strategies in their journals.

When discussing **Peer Evaluation**, note that even the wisest person makes mistakes. Good evaluators constructively criticize the work, not the person who wrote the work.

Cont. on p. 51

MEETING INDIVIDUAL NEEDS

LEP/ESL

General Strategies. The evaluating segment of the writing process could easily be one of the most critical stages for students. If at all possible, you may want to spend a short amount of time with each student, emphasizing the positive aspects of the draft and making comments that are purposefully encouraging. Your individual attention will probably prove to be the confidence-builder that each student requires.

ADVANCED STUDENTS

Have students research the lives and accomplishments of great musicians such as Mozart or Beethoven, write several paragraphs, and present their findings to the class. Tell students that you would like to use these paragraphs as examples for the evaluation process. Display one or two of these reports on an overhead projector. Using the criteria listed in the **Critical Thinking** section, guide the class in recognizing positive features as well as points for improvement.

48

You can have the help of outside readers by working with your classmates in peer-evaluation groups, which can be just two people or as many as four or five. Remember that in peer evaluation you have two roles: Sometimes you're the writer whose work is being evaluated, and sometimes you're the evaluator of other students' writing.

EVALUATING

Guidelines for the Writer

1. List some specific questions or concerns. What part of your paper do you think needs work?
2. Keep a positive attitude. Think of the evaluator's comments as real help for you. Don't get defensive or depressed about them.

Guidelines for the Peer Evaluator

1. Always look for strengths as well as weaknesses. Writers not only need encouragement, but they also need to know what's good in their writing and build on it.
2. Be serious and thorough about the evaluation, but also be sensitive. For example, ask the writer a question about a weakness instead of just pointing it out.
3. Make specific, positive suggestions for improvement. A criticism of a weakness without any ideas for fixing it is negative.
4. Look at content, organization, and style. Don't comment on mistakes in spelling, usage, and mechanics unless they make the meaning unclear. Proofreading comes later.

CRITICAL THINKING
(pp. 49–50)

OBJECTIVE

- To practice evaluation by applying given criteria to a model paragraph

TEACHING *EVALUATING*

Before starting the exercise, you may want to discuss the criteria by relating them to concepts that have been taught; for example, expression of a main idea through a topic sentence, kinds of supporting information, use of direct references and transitions, choosing an order of ideas, unity, and coherence.

 CRITICAL THINKING

Evaluating

You know that evaluating means making a judgment about whether something is good, bad, or somewhere in between. You evaluate things all the time—movies, CDs, the latest styles of jeans. When you evaluate anything, you measure it against a set of established criteria, or standards. Here are some criteria for evaluating effective writing.

1. The writing gets and holds your attention—it's interesting.
2. The meaning is clear.
3. There is a main idea.
4. There are enough supporting details for the main idea in the piece of writing.
5. The ideas are connected smoothly—no gaps or jumps to cause confusion.
6. The ideas are arranged well; their order makes sense.
7. The writing has no clichés (trite words or phrases) or unnecessary repetition and details.

 CRITICAL THINKING EXERCISE:
Evaluating a Paragraph

Try out your peer-evaluation skills, using the seven criteria given above. With a partner or small group, discuss the following paragraph and write at least three comments about what can be improved in the paragraph. As you work, keep in mind the Guidelines for the Peer Evaluator on page 48.

Ludwig van Beethoven lived from 1770 to 1827. He was born in Bonn, Germany. What's most amazing about Beethoven is that he composed some of his greatest music when he was totally deaf. Beethoven was from a musical family. He showed his genius early. Some of his music was published when he was twelve. When he was seventeen, he met Wolfgang Amadeus Mozart. Mozart

LEP/ESL

General Strategies. It may be helpful to begin with a class discussion differentiating the two terms *evaluating* and *criticizing*. Create two columns on the chalkboard and ask students to give examples from daily life that typify these behaviors. The idea is to emphasize that because evaluation is always based on set criteria, it is an objective rather than a subjective behavior. Reading food labels or checking one's heart rate after exercise is an example of evaluating facts.

TIMESAVER
Have group members initial individual comments before the group's evaluation is presented to you. You can then quickly assess student contributions and consider how well each group has collaborated.

If students appear to be having difficulty with the exercise, select volunteers to suggest a topic sentence. Ask others to find information that supports this main idea. Next, have volunteers identify persons who could be the subjects of direct references. Ask others to substitute references for their names. Then ask volunteers to suggest transitions that could be used to connect ideas. Ask others to suggest points at which these transitions could be substituted in the sample. Last, have partners work together to suggest an order that would make the main idea clear.

ANSWERS

Critical Thinking Exercise

Groups or partners should make at least three suggestions to solve problems with appeal, clarity, focus, supporting detail, transitions, arrangement, clichés, or unnecessary repetition. Suggestions will vary. Here are some possibilities:

1. No strong topic sentence to hold two main points (early genius and later deafness) together
2. Deafness mentioned in two places causing organizational problems
3. Many unnecessary repetitions and rough transitions because only one detail appears in each sentence
4. Unclear to reader at first that Beethoven was deaf when composing Ninth Symphony

said of Beethoven: "Keep your eyes on him. Someday, he will give the world something to talk about." Beethoven moved to Vienna. He stayed there for the rest of his life and is buried there too. He became deaf gradually but for the last seven years of his life was totally deaf. He completed his last symphony, the Ninth Symphony, in 1824. The Ninth Symphony is called the Choral Symphony because of its "Ode to Joy" chorus in the last movement. He was completely deaf then. He conducted the symphony when it was first performed. He couldn't hear the music or the applause.

Revising

After your classmates evaluate your paper, you'll need some time to think about their comments and suggestions and to combine them with your own ideas of what's wrong. Which comments about problems really seem on target? Which suggested changes seem like good solutions? (Remember your purpose and audience—they'll help you make decisions.)

Once you've decided what *needs* to be done, you move on to *doing* it: revising, or making the actual changes that will fix the problems you've found. There are four basic revision techniques—adding, cutting, replacing, and reordering—that you can use to make changes. In this

Have students evaluate their para-phrasing of the **Self-Evaluation** strategies. Select volunteers to read aloud what they have written and to share their specific questions and concerns. Model peer evaluation for the class by making comments that reflect the **Guidelines for the Peer Evaluator** on p. 48. Have partners take turns evaluating by using the guidelines in the textbook.

Before students begin revising, emphasize the chart of evaluating guidelines. When discussing the **Revising Techniques** chart, relate each technique to a concept that the students have already learned. New information should be added to make the meaning clear or to provide more support for the main idea. Cutting helps achieve 👉

---

stage, look at your first draft as just what it is—a begin-ning—and don't be shy about marking it up. Handwrite your corrections on the paper, using the revising and proofreading symbols on page 59, and then make a new copy by rewriting, retyping, or making the changes on the computer and printing the new version.

| REVISING TECHNIQUES ||
TECHNIQUE	EXAMPLE
1. **Add.** Add new information and details. Add words, phrases, sentences, whole paragraphs.	*↑ or chain of islands* The Japanese archipelago is made up of four large islands and many smaller ones.
2. **Cut.** Take out information, details, examples, or words. Cut repetition, wordiness, and details unrelated to the main idea.	From 1904 to 1914 the United States built the Panama Canal, ~~a canal~~ which connects ~~two bodies of water~~ the Atlantic and Pacific oceans.
3. **Replace.** Take out weak words, clichés, awkward-sounding sentences, unnecessary information or details. Replace with more precise words, more relevant details.	Sydney, Australia, was founded in 1788 and was the first place for British ~~troublemakers~~. *penal colony* *convicts*
4. **Reorder.** Move phrases, details, examples, or paragraphs for variety and an order that makes sense.	The Galapagos Islands are in the Pacific Ocean off South America, known for their giant tortoises and other unique species.

COOPERATIVE LEARNING

Give groups of three or four different sections of a recent newspaper and have them each evaluate one article. They should use the criteria for the **Critical Thinking Exercise.** Ask each group to decide what the intended audience and purpose of the selection is. Initiate a class discussion, with the groups presenting comments and conclusions. Have students give reasons for their ideas.

🔗 **INTEGRATING THE LANGUAGE ARTS**

Mechanics Link. When students revise, encourage them to add interest to their writing by varying sentence structure (simple, compound, complex). You may want to review comma placement for phrases, appositives, and conjunctions, as necessary. After brainstorming with the class for example sentences, write these on the chalkboard and discuss them with the class.

Partners might evaluate the first drafts they wrote for **Exercise 10** for correct comma placement.

unity and can add coherence. Replacing and reordering are directly related to coherence.

To help students visualize the relationship between the specific revisions and the concepts, have them make a chart with each of the revising techniques as a heading. Then have partners list each revision under the appropriate heading.

Use **Exercise 11** as cooperative learning. Before students begin, you could discuss the relationship between the characteristics and the criteria for effective writing in the **Guidelines for Evaluating and Revising**, p. 53. **Criteria 2, 3,** and **4** should be considered when evaluating content. **Criteria 5** and **6** should be considered when evaluating organization. **Criteria 1** and **7** should be

INTEGRATING THE LANGUAGE ARTS

Usage Link. Initiate a discussion about first, second, and third person points of view. Brainstorm with the class to identify specific examples of magazine and newspaper articles, stories, and books that have been written from each point of view. Note that a shift in point of view may occur in dialogue or direct quotations, but that the point of view remains consistent in a narrative.

Ask students to write two sentences from each point of view. Select students to write examples on the chalkboard and have the class evaluate and revise any point-of-view shifts found in a sentence. Remind students that they should always check for point-of-view consistency in their writing.

Here are the paragraphs on lacrosse (pages 45–46), revised by using the four revision techniques. To understand the changes, you may want to refer to the chart of symbols for revising and proofreading on page 59. Notice how the writer has answered the questions noted on the first draft.

HERE'S HOW

Lacrosse is a team sport that Native Americans invented a long time *(more than a thousand years)*	replace
ago. French explorers named it lacrosse because *(they thought)* its long, curved playing stick	add
looked like a bishop's staff, *a crosiero* what's French	replace
This stick is word? It's really a long-handled racket,	cut/replace
with a mesh head like a pocket. The ball is	
passed and received *carried* in this stick, and	reorder/add
players score points by kicking or throwing	cut
hurling the ball into the goal.	
Like hockey, Lacrosse is a rough game, but it's an *(with a lot of physical contact,)* *(that players are proud of.)*	add/cut/add
ancient, formal sport. Since 18??? [check *67*	add/replace
lacrosse has date] it's been the official national sport of	cut/replace
Canada. *Onandaga chief and a member of* Oren Lyons, on the Iroquois	replace
Nationals team [chief too—Onandagas?],	cut
has said, "We were playing team sports	
here when in Europe, they were still	
knocking people off horses, clubbing each	
other, fencing for keeps, all those so-called	
sports."	reorder

When you evaluate and revise, you're focusing on three different, important aspects of your paper—content, organization, and style—so plan to read through it at least three times. Some overall guidelines for evaluating and revising follow. In later chapters, you'll find similar charts that focus on a particular type of writing.

considered when evaluating style.

Emphasize that there is no single correct revision. Any two good writers will produce different revisions. What matters is that the students apply the criteria in the way each thinks best. After the students complete the exercise, you could have the revising teams find and note strengths in each other's revisions.

GUIDED PRACTICE

Have the students revise their paraphrasing of the **Self-Evaluation** strategies as guided practice in class.

☞

GUIDELINES FOR EVALUATING AND REVISING

EVALUATION GUIDE	REVISION TECHNIQUE
CONTENT	
1 Is the writing interesting?	**Add** examples, an anecdote (brief story), dialogue, and additional details. **Cut** or **replace** repetitious or boring details.
2 Does the writing say and do what you intended it to?	**Add** details that create pictures, express feelings, persuade, or inform or explain.
3 Are there enough details?	**Add** more details, facts, examples, or quotations to support the topic.
4 Are there unrelated ideas or details that distract the reader?	**Cut** irrelevant or distracting information.
5 Are unfamiliar terms explained or defined?	**Add** definitions or other explanations of unfamiliar terms. **Replace** unfamiliar terms with familiar ones.
ORGANIZATION	
6 Are ideas and details arranged in the best possible order?	**Reorder** ideas and details to make the meaning clear.
7 Are the logical connections between ideas and sentences clear?	**Add** transitional words and phrases (*therefore, for example, because*) to link ideas.
STYLE	
8 Is the meaning clear?	**Replace** vague or unclear wording. Use precise, easy-to-understand words and phrases.
9 Does the writing contain clichés or overworked phrases?	**Cut** or **replace** with specific details and fresh comparisons.
10 Is the level of language appropriate for the audience and purpose?	**Replace** formal words with more casual, conversational ones to create an informal tone. To create a more formal tone, **replace** slang and contractions.
11 Do sentences read smoothly?	**Reorder** to vary sentence beginnings and structure.

Literature Link. Have students read Edgar Allan Poe's "The Pit and the Pendulum" and identify the point of view [first person]. Briefly discuss and have students comment on Poe's use of first person for this work. [Comments will vary, but most students will probably agree that it makes the story more believable.] Ask students to work with partners to rewrite the first paragraph twice, once from the second and once from the third person points of view. When partners finish, create groups of four to evaluate and make suggestions for improvement. Ask the class to give reactions to this story from each different point of view. [Answers will vary, but students should give reasons for their opinions.]

INDEPENDENT PRACTICE

You may use **Exercise 11** as an independent assignment.

CLOSURE

Ask volunteers to help develop a profile of a good evaluator by having them suggest individual characteristics that would be a part of the profile. Some desirable characteristics might include tact, honesty, and good judgment. ■

54   *Writing and Thinking*

ANSWERS
Exercise 11

Revisions may vary. Here is a possibility:

Americans definitely have an odor phobia, but that's harmless; isn't it? All it means is deodorant and perfume producers are making money. However, two new products on the market are troubling. John Wright, president of Greenway Distributors, has decided children have odor problems. Of course that's not the way he puts it. He (and his company's ads) say the "younger set" should smell "fresh and clean." However, what he is really doing is selling scents for children seven to twelve years old — Autumn Wind for boys, Pink Spring for girls. His slogan is Never Too Young. Isn't this a little much? I mean, if adults want to spend money on perfume — well, they're adults. But what does this do to our children? They'll worry, something they don't need. They'll pester their parents to spend money on this foolishness, something parents don't need. But worst of all, they'll be pushed into growing up too soon. Why don't parents protest this just as they do violence on TV?

TIMESAVER

Ask students to highlight their revisions from **Exercise 11** before handing in the assignment.

EXERCISE 11 ▸ **Evaluating and Revising a Paragraph**

Work with a partner to evaluate and revise the following first draft of a paragraph. Be sure to focus on content, organization, and style for this activity, using the guidelines on page 53. (You may correct grammatical errors that you find, but that's not your main task.) Check with another revision team to see if they found similar problems and solutions.

Americans definitely have an odor phobia, but it's harmless, right? Just making money for deodorant and perfume makers. But two new products on the market are downright troubling to this writer. John Wright, president of Greenway Distributors, Inc., has decided that little kids smell bad. Of course that's not the way Mr. Wright puts it. He's selling perfume and cologne for children <u>seven</u> to twelve years old. He (and his company's ads) say that the "younger set" should smell fresh and clean. Specifically, "autumn wind" cologne for boys and "pink spring" for girls. If adults want to spend there money on such products, well--they're adults. And maybe they do smell bad. The slogan is "Never Too Young." What's wrong with the whole thing? Children will worry, something they don't need, bug their parents to make Mr. Wright rich, and--the real problem--be pushed into growing up too soon. Why don't parents protest this just like they do violence on TV?

OBJECTIVES

- To proofread a given paragraph
- To brainstorm ideas for publishing

MOTIVATION

Draw an analogy between revising a piece of writing and fine-tuning an automobile engine. Revising is making sure that all the parts of a piece of writing work together to ensure peak performance. Proofreading is like caring for the interior and exterior of a car. A person makes sure that all the details and the appearance are just right. ☞

Proofreading and Publishing

Just as you take one final look in the mirror before going out to fix whatever isn't "just right," you'll take a last look at your paper to be sure it's ready to face your readers. This final touching up—getting details and appearance just right—is called *proofreading*.

Proofreading

When you *proofread,* you carefully reread your revised draft to correct mistakes in grammar, usage, and mechanics (spelling, capitalization, and punctuation). Remember that your goal is to find and correct any errors. You've worked hard on your paper, and you don't want any mistakes to distract your audience from what you have to say.

To proofread, put your paper aside for a while. You've been reading it so much during revision that you're probably not noticing every word and comma. Distance can make mistakes jump out clearly.

When you proofread, slow down and read each word carefully. These techniques will make proofreading easier.

1. Focus on one line at a time. Use a sheet of paper to cover all the lines below the one you are proofreading. Some writers proofread backwards—beginning with the bottom line and moving to the top.
2. Try peer proofreading. Exchange papers with a classmate (or group of classmates) and check each other's paper for errors.
3. When in doubt, look it up. Use a college dictionary for spelling and a handbook like the one on pages 510–895 for grammar, usage, and punctuation.
4. Use the revising and proofreading symbols on page 59 to mark changes.

The following guidelines apply to almost all of the writing you'll do for school. Read them before proofreading. They'll remind you of typical errors you're looking for.

Teacher's ResourceBank™

RESOURCES

> **PROOFREADING AND PUBLISHING**
> - Proofreading
> - Manuscript Form

QUOTATION FOR THE DAY

"Publication is a self-invasion of privacy." (Marshall McLuhan, 1911–1980, Canadian author and educator)

After students have carefully proofread their writing, you may wish to write the quotation on the chalkboard and use it to initiate a discussion of publishing. Explain that publication allows the writer to share his or her final results with an audience.

LEP/ESL

General Strategies. Although proofreading is an integral part of the writing process, you may find that placing too much emphasis on perfect spelling, mechanics, and usage can block a student's ability to take risks with creative expression or to trust that he or she has something valuable to say.

Explain to students that proofreading backwards is especially helpful for checking spelling because it forces the reader to concentrate on individual words. It is less helpful for checking internal punctuation, agreement, and correct pronoun case because these sometimes require a sense of the meaning during proofreading.

To illustrate the concepts presented in the **Guidelines for Proofreading,** you could use an overhead projector to display sentences that contain examples of each problem discussed in the guidelines. Select students to identify the errors in the examples. Then using the appropriate proofreading symbols, you can show students how to correct the errors.

INTEGRATING THE LANGUAGE ARTS

Technology Link. You may want to ask students to proofread, correct errors, and then type the corrected copy on a word processor, using the spell-check feature. Tell students that proper names and technical terminology are often not written into general spell-check features of programs. Recommend that students consult a dictionary to verify the correct spelling of these words.

ANSWERS
Exercise 12

Correction	Reason
design	misspelled "desine"
sun's	apostrophe missing
universities	incorrect plural spelling
did	incorrect verb form used for past tense
were	incorrect subject-verb agreement
designed	misspelled "desinged"
students. They	run-on sentence
batteries	incorrect plural spelling
miles at speeds	sentence fragment
Unfortunately	misspelled "Unfortunatly"
Rains	first word of sentence should be capitalized

56   *Writing and Thinking*

GUIDELINES FOR PROOFREADING

1. Is every sentence a complete sentence? (See pages 446–457.)
2. Does every sentence end with the appropriate punctuation mark? Are other punctuation marks correct? (See pages 789–864.)
3. Does every sentence begin with a capital letter? Are all proper nouns and appropriate proper adjectives capitalized? (See pages 763–779.)
4. Does every verb agree in number with its subject? (See pages 619–634.)
5. Are verb forms and tenses used correctly? (See pages 678–704.)
6. Are subject and object forms of personal pronouns used correctly? (See pages 649–658.)
7. Does every pronoun agree with its antecedent in number and in gender? Are pronoun references clear? (See pages 637–639.)
8. Are frequently confused words (such as *lie* and *lay, fewer* and *less*) used correctly? (See pages 661–662, 697–704, 716–717, 738–756.)
9. Are all words spelled correctly? (See pages 870–895.)
10. Is the paper neat and in correct manuscript form? (See page 58.)

EXERCISE 12 ▶ **Proofreading a Paragraph**

See if you can find all ten mistakes in the following paragraph. Look for errors in grammar, usage, spelling, capitalization, and punctuation. Use the handbook at the back of the book or a dictionary to be sure you've found an error and to correct it.

How would you like to desine a car that runs only on the suns power? That's what college students from universitys done in a 1,600-mile car race from Florida to Michigan. The thirty-one cars was desinged by engineering students, they had solar batterys that could be recharged only twice a day. On the first day the cars

You could also distribute copies of a paragraph that needs proofreading. First, have the students read it individually. Next, display it on the overhead one line at a time. Then have students examine each line on the overhead and make the appropriate corrections on the handout.

As you discuss the **Guidelines for Manuscript Form** on p. 58, display a manuscript on the overhead projector to explain and point out an example in the model for each guideline. If other examples occur elsewhere in the manuscript, ask volunteers to find them and explain the applications of the guidelines.

☞

traveled 75 miles. At speeds up to 52 miles an hour.
Unfortunatly, heavy rains and cloudy
skies slowed the cars.
rains caused the
drivers' cockpits
to leak.

Publishing

Early in prewriting, your thoughts about an audience helped shape your writing. Now it's time to let some of these readers actually share the final result. Besides sharing your writing with your teacher, here are some other suggestions.

- Submit your writing for publication. Try the school newspaper or yearbook or magazine. Your local newspaper may be interested in publishing a letter to the editor or a feature article.
- Make a class anthology. Have each student contribute one piece of writing, a drawing, or a favorite cartoon. Exchange anthologies with other classes. You could donate your class anthology to a school library or children's floor in a hospital.
- Make an anthology of your best writing for your family and yourself. You can save it in a folder or notebook and add to it throughout high school.
- Enter a writing contest. Some of these have cash prizes; others award certificates. Ask your teacher or counselor for information.
- Make a video. If you can find a video camera (try your public or school library), work with a partner. While you take pictures to illustrate your writing, ask a good reader to read your writing aloud. Show your video to the class.
- Post movie and book reviews on a school bulletin board or in a library.

👥 COOPERATIVE LEARNING

Ask students to copy the paragraph in **Exercise 12** and to use proofreading symbols to proofread it. Then let them work in pairs to check each other's work and to note any errors they might have missed. Tell students that after proofreading, it is wise to have a partner double-check for possible missed errors. Students should present their proofread copies and final error-free copies for evaluation.

MEETING INDIVIDUAL NEEDS

LESS-ADVANCED STUDENTS

Students who are unfamiliar with proofreading symbols might be overwhelmed by the list in the textbook. For these students, you may wish to introduce the symbols a few at a time, giving students a chance to integrate a few symbols before introducing more.

AT-RISK STUDENTS

Seeing their papers displayed around the room can build students' confidence. You will probably want to help students make any necessary corrections so they can take pride in their work on display.

LEARNING STYLES

Kinetic Learners. Ask students to create a bulletin board or handouts of the proofreading symbols. Encourage originality, even humor, in their presentations, but reinforce that the symbols and meanings must be accurate.

ANSWERS
Exercise 13

As each group brainstorms, one member should record the publishing possibilities mentioned. Ask groups to use the suggestions in the textbook as a guide for developing more specific targets for publication.

---

58 *Writing and Thinking*

When someone else reads your paper (your teacher, another student, or some adult outside of school), appearance is important. If you follow these guidelines for your final copy, your papers will look better.

> ### GUIDELINES FOR MANUSCRIPT FORM
>
> 1. Use only one side of a sheet of paper.
> 2. Type, use a word processor, or write in blue or black ink.
> 3. If you type, double-space the lines. If you write, don't skip lines.
> 4. Leave margins of about one inch at the top, sides, and bottom of a page.
> 5. Indent the first line of each paragraph.
> 6. Number all pages (except the first page) in the upper right-hand corner.
> 7. All pages should be neat and clean. You may use correction fluid to make a few changes, but they should be barely noticeable.
> 8. Follow your teacher's instructions for placement of your name, the date, your class, and the title of your paper.

EXERCISE 13 ▶ **Publishing Your Writing**

Working with your classmates, brainstorm some other ideas for publishing your writing. Assign committees to follow up on all suggestions, including those listed above. Find out the specific information a writer would need to carry out each suggestion.

Reprinted by permission of NEA, Inc.

CLOSURE

Display a page from a local newspaper. Have volunteers find and explain proofreading errors or have them find examples of correct manuscript form and explain why they are correct. ■

SYMBOLS FOR REVISING AND PROOFREADING

SYMBOL	EXAMPLE	MEANING OF SYMBOL
≡	Maple High school	Capitalize a lowercase letter.
/	the First person	Lowercase a capital letter.
∧	the first ⟨of⟩ May	Insert a missing word, letter, or punctuation mark.
∧	sep⟨a⟩erate	Change a letter.
⌐	in the East ⟨South⟩	Replace a word.
⸜	Tell me the the plan.	Leave out a word, letter, or punctuation mark.
⸦	an unussal idea	Leave out and close up.
⌒	a water fall	Close up space.
∽	recieve	Change the order of the letters.
ⓣⓡ	the last Saturday of September in the month	Transfer the circled words. (Write ⓣⓡ in nearby margin.)
¶	¶ "Help!" someone cried.	Begin a new paragraph.
⊙	Please don't go⊙	Add a period.
⋏	Well what's new?	Add a comma.
#	birdcage	Add a space.
⊙	the following ideas⊙	Add a colon.
∧	Houston, Texas St. Louis, Missouri and Albany, New York	Add a semicolon.
=	two teen-agers	Add a hyphen.
⌄	Sallys new job	Add an apostrophe.
ⓢⓣⓔⓣ	An extremely urgent message	Keep the crossed-out material. (Write ⓢⓣⓔⓣ in nearby margin.)

A DIFFERENT APPROACH

You may want to invite local writers, newspaper reporters or editors, or television anchorpersons to speak individually or as a panel on their writing and publishing experiences. Prior to the guest experts' visit, students might collaborate in groups of three or four to brainstorm questions tailored to the visitors' occupations. The groups should take turns asking the guests questions.

The groups should also brainstorm and choose unique ways to publish what they learn. For example, one group might videotape the interview for other classes; others might write a synopsis to report to the school board or local newspaper, present a slide presentation at a school assembly, or take photos and write captions for a bulletin board display.

WRITING AND ART
Teaching Strategies

Before students plan their concrete autobiographies, you may want to discuss Chaplin's career and how the bowler hat became his trademark. You could also show other examples of concrete poetry such as Dorthi Charles's "Concrete Cat" or John Hollander's "Swan and Shadow." Then create groups of three or four and have them concentrate on a symbol for each member. Ask students to sketch silhouettes of their symbols and then write first drafts using their prewriting notes. Tell them to put this aside overnight.

Groups might reconvene to read and comment on members' first drafts. Have students experiment with different-colored paper and pens as they write their revisions.

For proofreading, have students exchange papers with partners to double-check for any errors. Ask students to sign the backs of their papers, and then you can display final copies on a bulletin board. Others might read and guess the author of each autobiography.

60

MAKING CONNECTIONS

WRITING AND ART

Concrete Biography

In this chapter, you've looked at the process of writing. For most people, writing usually means moving from left to right in straight lines. Sometimes, however, you can express your creativity by arranging words into shapes. (Why should words always make neat rectangles?) When poets arrange their words to form a shape, it's called *concrete poetry,* so you could call the biographical sketch that follows a concrete biography. It's about a famous comedian from silent movies, Charlie Chaplin, whose trademarks were a bowler hat and mustache.

Charles Spencer ("Charlie") Chaplin (1889–1977)
by Noel Petty

Born in 1889
Of an old theatric line,
Took his early curtain calls
In various East End music halls,
Then he thought he'd try his paces
In the New World's vaudeville places.
First, Fred Karno's tried to adopt him
Then, out West, the Keystones copped him.
But soon he left to strike out on his own
And silent films of his became well known
On movie screens from Shanghai to Madrid.
In *City Lights*, *The Gold Rush* and *The Kid*
His greatest character, the little tramp,
Left no throat lumpless and no eye undamp;
In *Modern Times* and in *The Great Dictator*
He found his voice as social commentator.
For pure balletic slapstick, his like we'll never see:

Charles
Spencer
Chaplin
R*I*P

What shape would you give your biography? A basketball, a trademark earring, a guitar, a ballet shoe, a car? Brainstorm with others about symbols, and then try writing a concrete biography for yourself. (You don't have to write in rhyme.) Just write in some shape that stands for you. You and your classmates might enjoy displaying your papers.

MEETING INDIVIDUAL NEEDS

LEP/ESL

General Strategies. You may want to allow students to write about famous people from their cultures. Encourage students to share their knowledge and experiences. You may need to allow library time for research.

GUIDELINES

Besides evaluating students' products, you may want to assign a process grade so that you can check to see that students are employing the writing process to complete this assignment.

Chapter 2

UNDERSTANDING PARAGRAPH STRUCTURE

Motivation

Begin by asking questions that will prompt students to analyze objects and organizations in their immediate environment, such as the class, the school, student government, or clubs. What is their overriding structure? What is the internal structure? What is the relationship between the strength of the parts to the strength of the whole? As students volunteer answers, emphasize that the strength of the whole is determined by the strength of its individual parts.

Introduction

Tell students that there are many aspects of paragraph structure that they will need to study and practice if they want to write effectively. They will learn that a good paragraph must have a main idea and often has a topic sentence. A good paragraph also needs unity and coherence.

The chapter will also help students to understand and use the four strategies for developing writing—description, narration, classification, and evaluation—in paragraphs and longer works.

Tell students that there are four aims or purposes for writing and that all four will be explained in this chapter. You may want to have students suggest topics appropriate for each of these aims: expressive, informative, persuasive, and creative.

Integration

As your students are studying literature, you may want to have them select paragraphs that exemplify characteristics and qualities studied in this chapter. The entire class will benefit from keeping a bulletin board of paragraphs that have unity; paragraphs that have coherence through the use of chronological order, spatial order, order of importance, and logical order; and paragraphs that have coherence through the use of direct references and transitional words and phrases. When appropriate, ask students to mark and annotate the paragraphs.

You may want to refer students to the sections on aims and modes for quick explanations as they work on **Chapters 4-10**.

In other disciplines, such as social studies, students can apply the use of proper paragraph structure to essay questions or to research papers.

The chart on the next page illustrates the strands of language arts as they are integrated into this chapter. For vocabulary study, glossary words are underlined in some writing models.

QUOTATIONS
All **Quotations for the Day** are chosen because of their relevance to instructional material presented in that segment of the chapter and for their usefulness in establishing student interest in writing.

INTEGRATING THE LANGUAGE ARTS

Selection	Reading and Literature	Writing and Critical Thinking	Language and Syntax	Speaking, Listening, and Other Expression Skills
FROM *Nisei Daughter* 64-65, 67 "Japanese Americans: Home at Last" 68 *Voices from the Civil War* 69 "Reopening the Gateway to America" 70 *Great Indian Chiefs* 70 *Riding the Iron Rooster* 71 *Going Green* 72 *Garbage! Where It Comes From...* 73 "Boxer with a Future" 74 "A Genuine Mexican Plug" 76 *Once Upon A Horse* 77-78 *Exploring the Titanic* 79 "Clean Fun at Riverhead" 79-80 *The Woman Warrior: Memoirs...* 82-83 *Anne of Green Gables* 83 "Hayes: 'There Is So Much to Do'" 84 *Rock of Ages: The Rolling Stone History...* 84-85 "Leiningen Versus the Ants" 88 *The Pearl* 90 *Gullah* 94 *Mythology* 95 "Winterblossom Garden" 96 "Nothing Happened" 96 *Behind the Headlines* 98 *Private Lives of the Stars* 98-99 *Do Animals Dream?* 99 "New Dash for 'The Flash'" 101	Responding personally to literature 66, 69-70 Finding main ideas 66, 69-70 Finding topic sentences 69-70 Identifying and analyzing order of ideas 86-87 Finding direct references 90-91 Finding transitional words and phrases 90-91	Writing a journal entry 66 Evaluating effectiveness of paragraphs 66 Comparing effectiveness of paragraphs 66 Analyzing main idea 66, 69-70 Responding personally to literature 66, 69-70 Identifying main ideas and topic sentences 66, 69-70 Collecting supporting details 75, 94, 101, 103-104, 104-105, 106-107 Identifying sentences that destroy unity 80-81, 103-104 Evaluating and making judgments 85, 86-87, 91-92 Synthesizing order of ideas 85, 86-87, 91-92 Identifying and analyzing order of ideas 86-87, 91-92 Rewriting a paragraph so the order of ideas makes sense 86-87, 91-92 Identifying direct references and transitions 90-91 Revising a paragraph by adding transitions 91-92 Using sensory details 94, 106-107 Applying interpretive and creative thinking 96-97, 102-103, 103-105, 106-107 Explaining a process 97 Using classification 100 Using evaluation 101 Revising, proofreading, and publishing 102-103, 104, 105, 107 Analyzing supporting sentences 103-104 Analyzing details and topic sentences 103-104, 104-105	Identifying transitional words and phrases 90-91 Proofreading for errors in grammar, usage, and mechanics 103, 104, 105, 107	Working with a classmate to share experiences 66 Explaining a process 97 Publishing writing by reading it aloud 107

SEGMENT PLANNING GUIDE

Whether you are planning for a quick review of a writing concept or preparing an extended lesson on composition, you can use the following Planning Guide to adapt the chapter material to the individual needs of your class.

	SEGMENT	PAGES	CONTENT	RESOURCES
1	*Looking at the Parts*	*64-66*		
	Literary Model from ***Nisei Daughter***	64-65	Guided reading: a model of paragraph form	
	Reader's Response/Writer's Craft	66	Model evaluation: responding to literature and analyzing paragraph structure	
2	*What Makes a Paragraph*	*67-76*		The Main Idea
	The Main Idea	67	Guidelines: analyzing location and importance of main idea in a model	The Topic Sentence
	Location of the Topic Sentence	68	Guidelines: examining a topic sentence in a model	Writing Supporting Sentences
	Importance of a Topic Sentence	69	Explanation: understanding purpose of a topic sentence	Writing Supporting Sentences
	Exercise 1	69-70	Applied practice: identifying main ideas and topic sentences	The Clincher Sentence
	Sensory Details	71	Guidelines: examining sensory details in a model	
	Facts and Statistics	71-73	Guidelines: examining facts and statistics in a model	
	Examples	73	Guidelines: analyzing use of examples in a model	
	Anecdotes	74	Guidelines: examining anecdotes in a model	
	Exercise 2	75	Applied practice: collecting supporting details	
	The Clincher Sentence	76	Guidelines: examining clincher sentence in a model	
3	*Unity*	*77-81*		Achieving Unity
	Unity	77	Introduction: examining literary models for ways to create unity	
	Topic Sentence	77-78	Guidelines: using topic sentence to create unity	
	Implied Main Idea	78-79	Guidelines: using implied main idea to create unity	
	Sequence of Events	79-80	Guidelines: using sequence of events to create unity	
	Exercise 3	80-81	Applied practice: identifying sentences that destroy unity	
4	*Coherence*	*82-92*		Achieving Coherence
	Order of Ideas	82-85	Guidelines: examining the use of various types of order in models	
	Exercise 4	85	Applied practice: choosing an order of ideas	
	Exercise 5	86-87	Applied practice: identifying order of ideas	
	Connections Between Ideas	88	Introduction: using direct references and transitions	

All the resources listed in this chapter are located in the Teacher's ResourceBank™.

SEGMENT	PAGES	CONTENT	RESOURCES
Direct References	88	Guidelines: examining models using direct references to link ideas	
Transitional Words and Phrases	89	Guidelines: examining models using transitional words and phrases to link ideas	
Chart: Transitions	89	Guidelines: examining transitional expressions	
Exercise 6	90-91	Applied practice: identifying direct references and transitions	
Exercise 7	91-92	Applied practice: using transitions	
5 *Strategies of Development*	*93-101*		Developing Paragraphs
Chart: Strategies	93	Guidelines: learning strategies to develop main ideas	Developing Paragraphs
Description	94	Guidelines: examining description in a model	Developing Paragraphs
Exercise 8	94	Applied practice: using description as a strategy	
Narration	95	Guidelines: using narration	
Telling a Story	95	Guidelines: examining narration in a model	
Explaining a Process	95-96	Guidelines: examining a process in a model	
Explaining Cause and Effect	96	Guidelines: examining cause and effect in a model	
Exercise 9	96-97	Applied practice: using narration as a strategy	
Exercise 10	97	Applied practice: explaining a process	
Classification	97-99	Guidelines: examining classification in models	
Exercise 11	100	Applied practice: using classification as a strategy	
Evaluation	100-101	Guidelines: examining evaluation in a model	
Exercise 12	101	Applied practice: using evaluation as a strategy	
6 *Making Connections*	*102-107*		
Writing Paragraphs for Different Purposes	102	Introduction: examining purposes for writing	
Writing a Paragraph to Express Yourself	102-103	Applied practice: writing about personal thoughts or feelings	
Writing a Paragraph to Inform	103-104	Applied practice: writing an informative paragraph	
Writing a Paragraph to Persuade	104-105	Applied practice: writing a persuasive letter	
Writing a Creative Paragraph	106-107	Applied practice: writing about a picture	
WHOLE-CHAPTER RESOURCE Chapter Review			

SEGMENT 1 *(pp. 62–66)*
LOOKING AT THE PARTS

OBJECTIVES
- To write and to share orally personal responses to literature
- To identify characteristics of paragraphs in a literary model

- To analyze paragraphs for main ideas and effectiveness

 VISUAL CONNECTIONS
Relative Realities #2

About the Artwork. The artist, Mark Hartman, achieves an intriguing effect in this painting by contrasting a flat, colorful surface with three-dimensional black-and-white objects. He used watercolors to paint the background before drawing the three-dimensional objects with charcoal. To ensure that the watercolors would not go into the white spaces, he covered those areas with masking tape. While using the charcoal, Hartman kept the lines smooth by using softer pencils for darker lines.

Exploring the Subject. This is an unusual type of self-portrait. The artist includes not only a sketch of himself, but several other images as well, such as an Egyptian face, a fish, and a screaming face adapted from Picasso's painting *Guernica.* The pointing fingers act as transitions by showing the relationships between objects. These images work together as sentences in a well-written paragraph would; they develop one main idea, a portrait of the artist.

2 UNDERSTANDING PARAGRAPH STRUCTURE

Before you have a volunteer read the introductory paragraphs of the chapter, point out to students that they already know a great deal about paragraphs because they have been studying them and reading them throughout their school years. You may want to have students discuss what they already know about paragraphs.

Explain that the excerpt by Monica Sone is from her autobiography. Sone grew up in a Japanese community in Seattle, Washington. Tell students to follow the instructions in **As You Read** to observe Sone's writing techniques as they read. To enrich class discussion, read the paragraphs by Sone aloud and discuss their structure. ☞

Looking at the Parts

Can you name all the parts in a computer? It has a processor, disc drives, a keyboard, and a monitor. But not all computers are alike. Some are faster or bigger or have more **parts** than others. The same is true of paragraphs. They all have certain things in common, but they are not all alike.

Writing and You. You see paragraphs all the time—in letters, books, and magazines. Some have only one word or sentence, but some go on for pages. Some paragraphs stand alone, but most of them work with others like links in a chain. What else have you noticed about paragraphs?

As You Read. As you read the following paragraphs from *Nisei Daughter*, notice how Monica Sone separates, yet links together, fond memories of her childhood.

Relative Realities #2, Mark Hartman (1989). Charcoal & watercolor on paper. 22" × 30". Collection of the artist.

QUOTATION FOR THE DAY

"All words are pegs to hang ideas on." (Henry Ward Beecher, 1813–1887, American preacher)

Write the quotation on the chalkboard and ask students to freewrite for a few minutes about what the quotation means. You may wish to ask a few volunteers to read aloud their responses. Explain that words, sentences, and paragraphs are vehicles for expressing ideas.

MEETING INDIVIDUAL NEEDS

LEP/ESL

General Strategies. Some students may be unaccustomed to the idea that a paragraph needs to have a single unifying idea. For example, in Arabic one main idea may span two or three paragraphs or one paragraph may have two or three main ideas. To help students focus on the concept of one main idea per paragraph, you may wish to have them read a paragraph and then ask what each sentence in it is about. Show students how each sentence deals with some aspect of the paragraph's main idea.

GUIDED PRACTICE

After you share your responses, have volunteers share their responses to the first **Reader's Response** question with the class. !nitiate the journal activity for question two by modeling with an experience of your own. Help students with the third question by using the annotations to analyze the first paragraph of the literary model with the class.

INDEPENDENT PRACTICE

Students can write their answers to the **Writer's Craft** questions on their own. You may want to suggest that students include reasons for their choices of main ideas.

MEETING INDIVIDUAL NEEDS

ADVANCED STUDENTS

While many writers follow the basic, standard structure of paragraphing, some writers don't. You may want to suggest that students study the paragraphing techniques of some of their favorite writers. Encourage students to share with the class examples of effective paragraphs written by their favorite authors.

Nisei Daughter

ASSESSMENT

Have students discuss their answers to the **Writer's Craft** questions. From this discussion and the sharing of responses to the **Reader's Response** section, you can assess students' understanding of the lesson concepts.

CLOSURE

Ask the class to discuss the importance of paragraphs in writing. You may want to have students refer to Monica Sone's paragraphs for details and examples.

☛

---

from

1

NISEI

DAUGHTER

by

MONICA

SONE

2 ***YES,*** life to us children was a wonderful treat—especially during hot summer nights when Father slipped out to a market stand down the block and surprised us with an enormous, ice-cold water-

3 melon. It was pure joy when we first bit into its crisp pink <u>succulence</u> and let the juice trickle and seeds fall on old newspapers spread on the round table in the parlor. Or sometimes on a wintry evening, we crowded around the kitchen table to watch Father, bath towel-apron draped around his waist, whip up a batch of raisin cookies for us. It wasn't everybody's father who could turn out thick, melting, golden cookies. We were especially proud that our father had once worked as a cook on romantic Alaska-bound freighters.

4 Life was hilarious whenever Mother played *Jan-ken-pon! Ai-kono-hoi!* with us. This was the game played by throwing out paper, scissors, and rock symbols with our hands, accompanied by the chant. The winner with the stronger symbol had the privilege of slapping the loser's wrist with two fingers. Mother pretended to cry whenever our small fingers came down on her wrist. With her oval face, lively almond-shaped eyes, and slender <u>aquiline</u> nose, Mother was a pretty, slender five feet of youth and fun.

I thought the whole world consisted of two or three old hotels on every block. And that its population consisted of families like mine who lived in a corner of the hotels. And its other inhabitants were customers—fading, balding, watery-eyed men, rough-tough bearded men, and good men like Sam, Joe, Peter, and Montana who worked for Father, all of whom lived in these hotels.

5 It was a very exciting world in which I lived.

USING THE SELECTION
from *Nisei Daughter*

1

The word *Nisei* means "second-generation." Sone's parents were referred to as *Issei* or "first generation."

2

This sentence is a generalization that all three paragraphs support.

3

Notice the sensory details Sone uses to support her idea of life as a wonderful treat.

4

This sentence serves as the topic sentence of the second paragraph.

5

How can one sentence be a paragraph? [This sentence functions as a conclusion and, set off by itself, adds emphasis to Sone's ideas.]

SELECTION AMENDMENT
Description of change: excerpted
Rationale: to focus on the concept of paragraph structure presented in this chapter

READER'S RESPONSE

1. Some of Monica Sone's fondest memories are connected with eating—watermelon juice trickling onto newspapers and her father making cookies. Get together with a partner and share the eating experiences (funny or serious) that stand out in your mind.
2. As a child, Sone thought the whole world was exactly like the neighborhood she lived in. In your journal, write about some of the impressions you had of the world when you were a young child.

WRITER'S CRAFT

3. Although all of Sone's paragraphs are about her memories from childhood, each paragraph makes a slightly different point. What is the main idea of each paragraph?
4. Sone's longest paragraph has five sentences, and the shortest has only one sentence. Is one paragraph more effective than the other? What do you think determines the length of the paragraphs?

> LOOKING AHEAD
>
> In this chapter, you'll study the form and structure of paragraphs. Keep in mind that
>
> ■ most paragraphs are a part of a longer piece of writing
> ■ most paragraphs have a main idea
> ■ a main idea may be supported or explained in several ways
> ■ there are four basic strategies for developing paragraphs

ANSWERS

Reader's Response

Answers will vary.

1. You may want to ask students to record their responses.
2. Be sure students give specific details to support their responses.

Writer's Craft

3. The main idea of the first paragraph is that Sone's father made summer nights grand. The main idea of the second paragraph is that Sone's mother made life fun by playing a game. The main idea of the third paragraph is that as a child Sone thought the whole world was made of old hotels like hers. The last paragraph emphasizes the first sentence and acts as a conclusion.
4. The paragraphs about Sone's father and mother are longer and more effective because they have more details and contain more information than the paragraph about the hotels and the last paragraph. Length is determined by function.

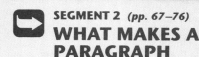
MOTIVATION

You could begin this lesson by drawing a comparison with a television series. Many half-hour programs, such as *The Cosby Show*, have features in common with paragraphs. A faithful viewer has a sense of the overall scheme of the program—the characters, the settings, and the typical problems. So, while one episode is a part of a larger ☛

What Makes a Paragraph

The Main Idea

Paragraphs, especially those that stand alone, usually are organized around one main idea. All the sentences in the paragraph make the *main idea* clear. For paragraphs that are part of longer pieces of writing, the other paragraphs help you understand the main idea.

Read the following paragraph from the selection by Monica Sone (page 65). What is its main idea?

> Life was hilarious whenever Mother played *Jan-ken-pon! Ai-kono-hoi!* with us. This was the game played by throwing out paper, scissors, and rock symbols with our hands, accompanied by the chant. The winner with the stronger symbol had the privilege of slapping the loser's wrist with two fingers. Mother pretended to cry whenever our small fingers came down on her wrist. With her oval face, lively almond-shaped eyes, and slender aquiline nose, Mother was a pretty, slender five feet of youth and fun.
>
> Monica Sone, *Nisei Daughter*

The first sentence of this paragraph states the main idea: that the author remembers her childhood as a time of great happiness. The other sentences support that idea by giving specific details about how the children played a game with their mother and how she looked and acted.

In the longer passage on page 65, you'll find that the other paragraphs help you understand this idea by giving details about other interesting experiences the author remembers from her childhood.

"IF IT SOUNDS LIKE WRITING, I REWRITE IT."

Elmore Leonard

Teacher's ResourceBank™
RESOURCES

WHAT MAKES A PARAGRAPH
- The Main Idea
- The Topic Sentence
- Supporting Sentences
- Supporting Sentences
- The Clincher Sentence

QUOTATION FOR THE DAY

"A sentence should read as if its author, had he held a plough instead of a pen, could have drawn a furrow deep and straight to the end." (Henry David Thoreau, 1817–1862, American poet, essayist, and transcendentalist)

Explain to the class that clear, straightforward sentences help create effective paragraphs. Encourage students to remember Thoreau's rule as they write topic sentences, supporting sentences, and clincher sentences.

SELECTION AMENDMENT
Description of change: excerpted
Rationale: to focus on the concept of main idea presented in this chapter

whole, it usually has a main idea. For example, Theo's girlfriend breaks up with him. This main idea has supporting details. For example, Theo becomes jealous of her new date. He takes out someone new, and then he begs his previous girlfriend to come back. And the program may end with a clincher—Theo swears undying devotion, but his girlfriend turns him down.

TEACHING THE LESSON

Guide students in their reading of the material about main ideas and topic sentences. Most students will already be familiar with these concepts. You may want to emphasize that paragraphs are usually part of longer pieces of writing and that there is an ongoing relationship among the parts that comprise the whole. Football players

LEP/ESL

General Strategies. Most students who have grown up in the United States will have already heard of the topics of the example paragraphs in this unit—Japanese internment, the United States Civil War, and European immigration to the United States. However, many students—especially recent arrivals—might have studied little, if anything, about these subjects and therefore might have trouble understanding what these paragraphs are about. You could help by providing a brief historical and cultural background of each article's subject matter. For example, you could explain when, where, and why the Civil War occurred and who fought in it.

SELECTION AMENDMENT
Description of change: excerpted
Rationale: to focus on the concept of main idea presented in this chapter

The Topic Sentence

The main idea of a paragraph is often expressed in a single sentence, called the *topic sentence.* In writing, you'll find that using a topic sentence helps the reader to identify your main idea.

Location of a Topic Sentence.   The topic sentence often appears as the first or second sentence of a paragraph. You'll recall that the first sentence of Sone's paragraph on page 67—the one about playing a game with her mother—states the main idea of the paragraph.

It's easier to understand what a paragraph is about if the topic sentence appears at the beginning. However, a topic sentence can occur at any place in a paragraph. In fact, you'll sometimes find topic sentences at or near the end of a paragraph. Writers sometimes place topic sentences there to create surprise or to summarize ideas.

Here's a paragraph about the success of Japanese Americans after they were released from camps where many of them were held during World War II. As you read, notice how the writer draws all the details together and sums up the information with a topic sentence at the end.

> Twenty-five years after the camps were closed, the average personal income of Japanese Americans was 11 percent above the national average; average family income was 32 percent higher. A higher proportion of Japanese Americans were engaged in professional occupations than were whites. By 1981, an astonishing 88 percent of Sansei (third generation) children were attending college, and of these, 92 percent planned professional careers. In California, where more than a third of the nation's 720,000 Japanese Americans reside (88 percent of them U.S. born), family income remains 15 percent above the statewide average. Wrote sociologist William Petersen: "Even in a country whose patron saint is Horatio Alger, there is no parallel to this success story."
>
> Arthur Zich, "Japanese Americans: Home at Last"

repeatedly practice throwing and receiving passes, but the activities are only elements of a complicated sport. Likewise, writers need to understand the elements of paragraphs and to practice writing them so that their essays and compositions will be stronger.

Have volunteers read **The Topic Sentence**, and then read the model paragraph from **"Japanese Americans: Home**

at Last" to the class. You may need to explain the reference to Horatio Alger.

Emphasize **Importance of a Topic Sentence**, p. 69. Some students misinterpret paragraph instruction in English class as prescribing rules that are not followed in real writing because many well-written paragraphs do not have topic sentences.

☞

Importance of a Topic Sentence.   Many paragraphs don't have a topic sentence. Some paragraphs, especially those that relate a sequence of events or actions, may not even seem to have a main idea. But topic sentences are useful, both to readers and to writers. They help readers know what they might find in the rest of the paragraph. And topic sentences help you as a writer to focus your paragraphs. They keep you from wandering off the main idea.

EXERCISE 1 ▶ **Identifying Main Ideas and Topic Sentences**

Each of the following paragraphs develops a main idea. Two of the paragraphs have topic sentences, and one does not. In your own words, state the main idea of each paragraph. Then identify the topic sentences of the two paragraphs that have them.

1.   Disease took more victims in the Civil War than the bullet did, and the toll from both was enormous. In the Federal forces four men died of sickness for every one killed in battle. In the early period almost one out of every four soldiers fell sick. It was just as bad or worse for the Confederates. At least half the men in a regiment could not fight for sickness, and often more. One authority on Confederate medicine estimated that on the average each Southern soldier was sick or wounded six times during the war. But five times as many fell sick as were injured.

Milton Meltzer, *Voices from the Civil War*

LESS-ADVANCED STUDENTS

To help students understand the typical structure of a paragraph, show them a visual representation of the relationship between the topic sentence, the supporting sentences, the specific details, and the clincher sentence. You could use the following example:

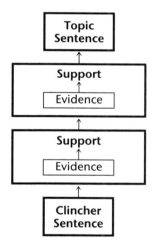

ANSWERS
Exercise 1

Statements of main ideas will vary.

1. Main Idea: In the Civil War, more people died of illness than were killed in battle.
   Topic Sentence: Disease took more victims in the Civil War than the bullet did, and the toll from both was enormous.

SELECTION AMENDMENT
Description of change: excerpted
Rationale: to focus on the concept of topic sentences presented in this chapter

It may be helpful to provide an analogy. For example, people learning a new dance step or technique focus on the structure—the way it's supposed to be done. Once they have mastered that, they add their own styles. Similarly, students need to master the basic structure of writing; then they can add their personal variations.

Guide students in their reading of **Supporting Sentences,** p. 71. After the first paragraph, remind students that the main idea of a paragraph is often expressed in a topic sentence, and even when that is not the case, the supporting sentences should always relate to a main idea.

2. Main Idea: Ellis Island, gateway for millions of Americans, has been restored and a new museum has been opened there.

3. Main Idea: The best chiefs of Indian tribes were great because of individual differences.
   Topic Sentence: These were all individual differences, basic differences in individual capacity, and it was these differences alone that set the Indian leaders off from the rest of their people.

INTEGRATING THE LANGUAGE ARTS

Test-Taking Link. Suggest to students that when they are answering essay questions on tests they introduce each paragraph with a clear topic sentence. Although this format isn't always the most effective in other types of writing, beginning each paragraph of a test essay with a topic sentence identifies the main idea of the students' answers for the reader. You may also want to suggest that students prewrite before they begin their essays.

2. The first step on American soil for 12 million immigrants was no patch of warm, welcoming earth but a wooden ramp at Ellis Island. More than 100 million living Americans trace their U.S. roots to a man, woman or child who came through Ellis Island between 1892 and 1954. America's gateway reopens this month with a new National Park Service museum commemorating four centuries of U.S. immigration. Privately funded, the $156 million restoration has been the work of the Statue of Liberty–Ellis Island Foundation, which also dressed up Miss Liberty for her 1986 birthday centennial.
Doris G. Kinney, "Reopening the Gateway to America"

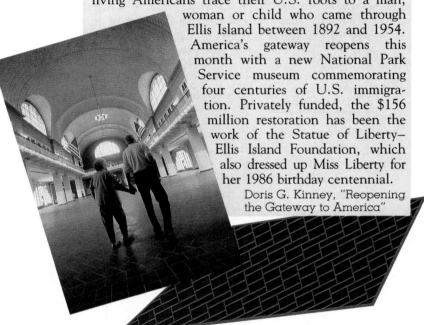

3. Pontiac had a great idea in his intertribal league against the whites. Tecumseh had a similar idea, backed by an unusual humanity toward captives and an exalted concept of a divine purpose embodied in him. Sitting Bull nourished an implacable hatred and suspicion of the whites and showed unusual power in intrigue. Chief Joseph exhibited an ability in the conduct of a losing war that Napoleon might have envied in his retreat from Moscow. . . . These were all individual differences, basic differences in individual capacity, and it was these differences alone that set the Indian leaders off from the rest of their people.
Albert Britt, *Great Indian Chiefs*

Supporting Sentences

The topic sentence of a paragraph states a general idea. To make that idea clear and interesting to the reader, you develop it with details in sentences that support the topic sentence. The kinds of details you'll use depends upon the subject. You might use *sensory details, facts or statistics, examples,* or an *anecdote.*

Sensory Details

Sensory details are details you observe through your five senses—sight, sound, smell, touch, taste. You use them to help create a picture or image in the reader's mind. If you describe the color of a snazzy new car, how the cold misty air feels, or how your favorite pizza tastes, you're using sensory details.

In this paragraph, notice how the writer uses details of sight, sound, smell, and touch to describe a train in China. In the first sentence, for example, the writer uses both sight and sound details to help you see and hear the train.

> The train pulled in, steaming and gasping, just as the sun came up. It had come from Dalian, 600 miles away, and it stopped everywhere. So it was sensationally littered with garbage—peanut shells, apple cores, chewed chicken bones, orange peels and greasy paper. It was very dirty and it was so cold inside the spit had frozen on the floor into misshapen yellow-green medallions of ice. The covering between coaches was a snow tunnel, the frost on the windows was an inch thick, the doors had no locks and so they banged and thumped as a freezing draft rushed through the carriages.
>
> Paul Theroux, *Riding the Iron Rooster*

Facts and Statistics

You can also support a main idea with facts and statistics. A *fact* is something that can be proven true by concrete information: in 1981, Sandra Day O'Connor became the first woman U.S. Supreme Court justice. A *statistic* is a fact based on numbers: according to the Motion Picture Association of America, more new films were released in

GUIDED PRACTICE

Explain the directions for **Exercises 1** and **2** to the class and guide them through an example for each.

INDEPENDENT PRACTICE

Students can complete **Exercises 1** and **2** as homework, or you could have students practice analyzing paragraphs from their own writing.

INTEGRATING THE LANGUAGE ARTS

Literature Link. Expressive writing, such as journals or travel literature, uses many sensory details to elicit for the reader the experiences being discussed. To illustrate this concept, have students read and analyze a work such as N. Scott Momaday's "Discovering the Land of Light" for its use of sensory details.

Ask students to identify the descriptive details that appeal to each of the senses and to explain how these details contribute to the picture of Momaday's boyhood in New Mexico.

Reading Link. You may want to have students find in magazines and newspapers examples of sensory details. Remind students that material must be appropriate for the classroom. Encourage them to use articles and stories but remind them that advertising uses some of the most effective sensory language.

Have students analyze the paragraphs to determine which senses are involved and how effective the descriptions are.

SELECTION AMENDMENT

Description of change: excerpted
Rationale: to focus on the concept of supporting a main idea presented in this chapter

the United States in 1920 (796) than in 1987 (478). You can look in reference materials to check that these facts and statistics are true.

In the following paragraph, facts and statistics support and prove the main idea that the enormous amount of trash Americans throw away today is a big problem: "2,460 pounds of paper," for example, is a statistic; "that we are running out of landfill space" is a fact.

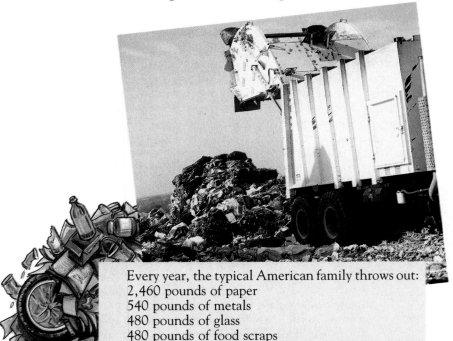

Every year, the typical American family throws out:
2,460 pounds of paper
540 pounds of metals
480 pounds of glass
480 pounds of food scraps
All told, each of us throws away more than 1,200 pounds of trash per year, far more than people in most other countries. About 80 percent of that garbage ends up in landfills—dumps, as they are more commonly known. (Of the remaining 20 percent, about half is recycled and half is incinerated.) One big problem is that we are running out of landfill space—more than half of the nation's landfills will be full within ten years.

John Elkington, Julia Hailes, Douglas Hill, and Joel Makower, *Going Green*

ASSESSMENT

You may want to have students go over their responses in class so you can evaluate their comprehension of the lesson concepts.

RETEACHING

If you find some students have not understood paragraph structure, you may want to have them work in groups on paragraphs you have highlighted from novels, stories, essays, or newspaper articles. Highlight topic sentences in red, support sentences in green, and clinchers in blue. Then have students identify and label each ☞

Supporting Sentences **73**

Examples

Another good way for you to support a main idea is to give *examples,* which are specific instances or illustrations of a general idea. An apartment is an example of a type of housing. Getting a scholarship is an example of what can happen if your grades are good.

This paragraph uses specific examples to show the extent of Japan's longtime recycling program. As you read, look for three specific examples the writer uses to support the main idea. The first example is about containers in city parks.

In Japan, recycling has been practiced for hundreds of years. In public places such as city parks, you'll see separate containers for paper and cans. Recycling centers are more than just the temporary storage places they are in the U.S.A. In Japan, retired or disabled people work in these centers, repairing old furniture or household appliances and then selling them again. And in Machida City, not far from Tokyo, they have a program called *chirigami kokan* ("tissue-paper exchange") in which you receive free recycled paper products, such as tissue paper, napkins, and toilet paper, in exchange for your old newspapers.

Evan and Janet Hadingham, *Garbage! Where It Comes From, Where It Goes*

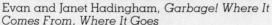
MEETING
INDIVIDUAL
NEEDS

ADVANCED STUDENTS

You may want to have students work in pairs to evaluate the use of facts and statistics in periodicals. Also ask each group to find examples in which the reader may become bogged down or overwhelmed by too many facts and statistics. Have students write notes that point out similarities and differences between the two paragraphs.

LEARNING STYLES

Auditory Learners. Explain to students that speaking and listening to oneself are skills that form the basis for writing. Most people have a ready supply of stories, experiences, images, or thoughts to relate to almost any point they are making. They just aren't aware of the supply of ideas they have. Emphasize that when students are writing, they need to remember to tap into this bank of ideas to support their main ideas. Encourage them to vocalize their thoughts aloud (even if in a whisper), to listen to themselves, and to transcribe whatever they say. Remind students that transcribing is more difficult than speaking and listening because people speak faster than they write.

AMENDMENTS TO SELECTIONS
Description of change: excerpted
Rationale: to focus on the concept of details in writing presented in this chapter

73

highlighted part. Students can share the examples they find with other groups.

CLOSURE

To summarize the lesson, make an outline of this segment on the chalkboard. As you write each topic or subtopic, have students explain or define it.

What Makes a Paragraph
I. The Main Idea
II. The Topic Sentence

INTEGRATING THE LANGUAGE ARTS

Literature Link. To compare paragraphing in an essay with paragraphing in poetry, you could have the class read and analyze a poem such as "Theme for English B" by Langston Hughes. Then show the text on an overhead projector. Explain that a stanza is like a poetic paragraph. In "Theme for English B", the first stanza is the introduction, and in each additional stanza Hughes states and supports an idea related to his introduction. Work with students to paraphrase each main idea and to find supporting details. [The second stanza of Hughes' poem gives his background. The third and fourth stanzas explain his likes, dislikes, and personality, and the last stanza discusses his being black. The last verse sums up the poem.]

Anecdotes

An *anecdote* is an extended example, or story, that can be used to support a main idea. In this paragraph, for example, the main idea is stated in the first sentence. An anecdote about Olympic boxer Mark Breland then supports the main idea about his ability to learn outside the ring.

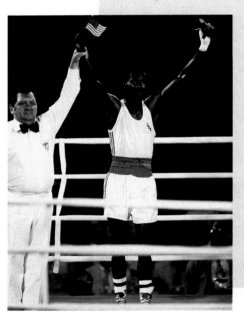

A little more than two years ago Breland proved that his ability to learn and adapt extends outside the ring. A casting director from Paramount saw his photograph in the newspaper and was struck by his stark good looks. She offered him a role in *The Lords of Discipline,* and he accepted with the alacrity of any eighteen-year-old discovered by Hollywood. In the film Breland plays Pearce, the first black cadet at a southern military academy that is unofficially bent on continuing as an all-white institution. Pearce is subjected to brutal hazing and then torture at the hands of his fellow cadets. The role of a strong, silent man-child who resolutely takes what the world dishes out and still triumphs was a familiar one to Breland after his youth in Bedford-Stuyvesant. Although the film role did not demand a broad range of emotion, he performed with dignity and little self-consciousness.

G. A. Taubes, "Boxer with a Future"

Notice the details that develop the anecdote, such as the type of role Breland undertakes and how he handles the role. These details help readers understand the main idea the anecdote supports.

SELECTION AMENDMENT
Description of change: excerpted
Rationale: to focus on the concept of anecdotes as support presented in this chapter

A. Location
B. Importance
III. Supporting Sentences
   A. Sensory Details
   B. Facts and Statistics
   C. Examples
   D. Anecdotes
IV. The Clincher Sentence

EXTENSION

You may want to have students create collections of example paragraphs from books, magazines, newspapers, and their own writings. Students can bracket the main ideas in the paragraphs and underline in red any topic sentences. ■

EXERCISE 2 ▶ **Collecting Supporting Details**

Here's your chance to write about a monument that has meaning for every American—the Statue of Liberty. Below are four main ideas that you might use in writing a paragraph about Miss Liberty. With each idea, a type of support—sensory details, facts or statistics, examples, or an anecdote—is suggested. Think up at least two ideas to support each main idea. You may have to do a little research to find support, especially facts or statistics.

EXAMPLE **1.** The Statue of Liberty, which itself is a symbol of liberty, is adorned with symbolism. (examples)

    1. *The crown on the Statue of Liberty has seven spikes, representing the world's seven seas and seven continents. A broken chain at the statue's feet and the statue's left foot thrust forward represent freedom from bondage.*

1. The dimensions of the Statue of Liberty are impressive. (facts and statistics)
2. The Statue of Liberty has special meaning for many American citizens. (examples)
3. I took a boat close to the statue one evening at sunset. (sensory details)
4. In America, we often take our liberty and the historic symbols that represent it for granted. (anecdote)

ANSWERS
Exercise 2

Responses will vary but each paragraph should include the support that is suggested.

👁 VISUAL CONNECTIONS
Exploring the Subject. The official name for this enormous copper statue is *Liberty Enlightening the World.* Liberty's face was modeled after the sculptor's mother, Auguste-Charlotte Bartholdi. Over one hundred years old, this statue is still a symbol of the freedom and opportunity available in the United States.

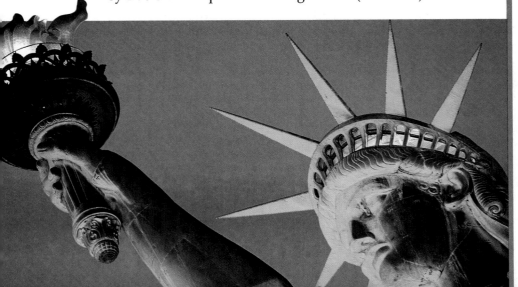

THE CLINCHER SENTENCE

You may want to explain to students that a clincher sentence is desirable in a paragraph that supports a topic sentence because it clarifies and emphasizes the main idea. A clincher gives a sense of completeness to the paragraph by restating the topic sentence. As the following diagram shows, a clincher sentence brings the discussion full circle.

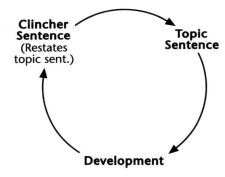

Clincher Sentence (Restates topic sent.)

Topic Sentence

Development

SELECTION AMENDMENT
Description of change: excerpted and italics added
Rationale: to focus on the concept of clincher sentences presented in this chapter

The Clincher Sentence

Novels and short stories have snappy endings that emphasize or summarize the authors' main ideas. You may want to add zing to the end of some of your paragraphs, especially long ones, by emphasizing or summarizing the main idea in your final sentence. This concluding sentence is called a *clincher sentence.* It pulls all your information together or emphasizes your main idea. The following paragraph uses a clincher to restate and emphasize the author's opening declaration of his determination to have a horse.

I resolved to have a horse to ride. I had never seen such wild, free, magnificent horsemanship outside of a circus as these picturesquely clad Mexicans, Californians, and Mexicanized Americans displayed in Carson streets every day. How they rode! Leaning just gently forward out of the perpendicular, easy and nonchalant, with broad slouch-hat brim blown square up in front, and long riata swinging above the head, they swept through the town like the wind! The next minute they were only a sailing puff of dust on the far desert. If they trotted, they sat up gallantly and gracefully, and seemed part of the horse; did not go jiggering up and down after the silly Miss Nancy fashion of the riding schools. I had quickly learned to tell a horse from a cow, and was full of anxiety to learn more. *I resolved to buy a horse.*

Mark Twain, "A Genuine Mexican Plug"

WRITING NOTE Clincher sentences shouldn't be overused. Be sure your clinchers emphasize or effectively restate the main idea. Don't use weak and unnecessary clinchers such as "Those are the reasons I dislike snow."

TEACHING THE LESSON

You may want to read aloud the opening paragraph in the **Unity** section and to emphasize the point that a paragraph needs a main idea but doesn't always have a topic sentence. Remind students that a paragraph has unity if all the sentences relate to one main idea or to a sequence of events or actions. ☞

Unity

A paragraph should have *unity;* that is, it should be about one main idea. Unity is created when all the sentences support the main idea, whether the main idea is stated in a topic sentence or is implied. (*Implied* means "understood but not directly stated.") In paragraphs that relate a series of actions or events, unity is achieved by the sequence of the actions or events. The unity is spoiled by any detail that doesn't relate to the main idea or to the sequence of events or actions.

All Sentences Relate to the Main Idea Stated in the Topic Sentence.   In the following paragraph, the topic sentence states the main idea—that horse-drawn chariots, though useful in battles, were a problem. As you read, notice how each of the supporting sentences includes a detail related to a problem involved in using the chariot. In the second sentence, for example, one problem is that a soldier driving alone had to wrap the reins around his waist to keep his arms free for fighting.

> By 1000 B.C. horse-drawn chariots were standard equipment in most armies, and soldiers had discovered that the world's greatest weapon was also the world's greatest nuisance. In the first place, the chariot was hard to use. A two-man chariot team could manage nicely if one man drove while the other bombarded the enemy with spears or arrows. But when a soldier

Teacher's ResourceBank™
RESOURCES

UNITY
- Achieving Unity

QUOTATION FOR THE DAY

"The discipline of the writer is to be still and listen to what his subject has to tell him." (Rachel Carson, 1907–1964, American marine biologist)

Write the quotation on the chalkboard, and ask students to explore the quotation in journal entries. Students might write about times when they learned something new by writing or reading. Explain that a paragraph that focuses on a main subject or idea is effective and unified.

Then ask volunteers to read aloud the rest of the information on unity and the three model paragraphs. Have the class discuss the strengths of each model.

GUIDED PRACTICE

Testing to see whether each sentence relates to the main idea, analyze the model paragraphs with students.

LEP/ESL

General Strategies. Because some students might have difficulty understanding some of the literary models in this section, they could have trouble identifying topic sentences and main ideas. Be sure that students understand the uncommon or abstract vocabulary used (such as *nuisance, spear,* or *chariot*), difficult sentence structures (such as past perfect tense and contrary-to-fact conditional clauses), and unfamiliar subject matter (such as the Titanic's sinking and demolition derbies).

AT-RISK STUDENTS

You may want to work with students to explain further the concept of unity. You could ask them to discuss styles of dressing. Many of them will have a distinct sense of what items go together and of what items would be out of place with a particular outfit. You can compare unity of appearance to the concept of unity in paragraphs.

drove alone, he had to tie the reins around his waist and control the horses with his body in order to keep his hands free for fighting. Since most chariots had no seats, the passengers and driver had to stand. They struggled to keep their balance as the little cart careened across country like a crazy roller coaster car and fought to keep their tempers when the chariot came to a sudden, unexpected halt. Such stops occurred frequently because chariots had to be carried across rivers and hoisted over hedges. They fell into ruts and wouldn't roll over rocks. They were too wide to squeeze through narrow mountain passes and so fragile that they broke down regularly.

Suzanne Jurmain, *Once Upon A Horse*

All Sentences Relate to an Implied Main Idea. The following paragraph doesn't have a topic sentence. But all the sentences work together to support an implied main idea—that the *Titanic's* two radio operators were too tired or busy to heed the last warnings before the luxury ship hit an iceberg in 1912. In the first sentence, for example, the fact that the radio operator was exhausted kept him from listening to the radio and hearing the warnings about the iceberg.

Students should be able to read the paragraphs in **Exercise 3** to find the offending sentences independently.

Assess students' mastery from their performance on **Exercise 3**, or have students identify details that spoil unity in their own writing.

In the radio room, Harold Bride was exhausted. The two operators were expected to keep the radio working twenty-four hours a day, and Bride lay down to take a much-needed nap. Phillips was so busy with the passenger messages that he actually brushed off the final ice warning of the night. It was from the *Californian*. Trapped in a field of ice, she had stopped for the night about nineteen miles north of the *Titanic*. She was so close that the message literally blasted in Phillips' ears. Annoyed by the loud interruption, he cut off the *Californian's* radio operator with the words, "Shut up, shut up. I'm busy."

Robert D. Ballard, *Exploring the Titanic*

All Sentences Relate to a Sequence of Events. Although the following paragraph doesn't actually state a main idea, it does have purpose and unity. The purpose is to narrate a series of events that happen at a demolition derby. The paragraph's unity comes from the sequence of events described. Each action detail is part of a sequence that begins when the second driver for the finals has to be selected. This paragraph, like all other narrative paragraphs, is actually a cause-and-effect paragraph. One action in the demolition derby (cause) results in the next action (effect), and so on.

After each trial or heat at a demolition derby, two drivers go into the finals. One is the driver whose car was still going at the end. The other is the driver the crowd selects from among the 24 vanquished on the basis of his courage, showmanship, or simply the awesomeness of his crashes. The numbers of the cars are read over loudspeakers, and the crowd chooses one with its cheers. By the same token, the crowd may force a driver out of competition if he appears cowardly or merely cunning. This is the sort of driver who drifts around the edge of the battle avoiding crashes with the hope that the other cars will eliminate one another. The umpire waves a yellow flag at him and

ADVANCED STUDENTS

The concept of unity applies to visual arts as well as to writing. You may want to have students research the principle of unity in art. They could discuss with the class examples of paintings that do or do not have unity.

AMENDMENT TO SELECTIONS
Description of change: excerpted
Rationale: to focus on the concept of topic sentence and main idea presented in this chapter

RETEACHING

If students are having difficulty with paragraph unity, give them sentences on strips of paper from two different paragraphs. Then help students to arrange the sentences in a logical order and to discard any sentences that detract from unity in either paragraph.

CLOSURE

Have students explain the meaning of *paragraph unity*. Then have them analyze one of the paragraphs by Monica Sone in the opening literary model to determine whether it has unity.

MEETING INDIVIDUAL NEEDS

LESS-ADVANCED STUDENTS

Form groups of three or four students. Have volunteers read both paragraphs of **Exercise 3** aloud, and then ask students to identify the main ideas of each paragraph. Have the students go through each paragraph sentence by sentence to decide whether each sentence relates to the main idea. In this way they should be able to locate the incorrect sentence in the first model.

SELECTION AMENDMENT
Description of change: excerpted
Rationale: to focus on the concept of paragraph unity presented in this chapter

he must crash into someone within 30 seconds or run the risk of being booed off the field in dishonor and disgrace.

Tom Wolfe, "Clean Fun at Riverhead"

EXERCISE 3 ▶ Identifying Sentences That Destroy Unity

One of the following paragraphs has unity, and the other doesn't. Try to figure out which <u>sentence destroys the unity</u> of that paragraph.   Paragraph 2 has unity.

1. A lot of wizardry went into the special effects in the 1939 MGM movie classic *The Wizard of Oz*. Perhaps the picture's most famous special effect is the tornado that carries Dorothy and her dog, Toto, to Oz. <u>Legend has it that L. Frank Baum got the idea for the name of Oz from a file cabinet drawer, labeled O-Z.</u> The tornado was created by using fans, a crane, and a canvas cone rotated by a motor. Another famous special effect is the melting of the Wicked Witch. She melted away by disappearing through the floor on a hydraulic lift. Her costume was fastened to the floor, and dry ice or liquid smoke created the melting effect. The Winged Monkeys "flew" by means of support wires. The Wicked Witch's skywriting was achieved by using black liquid released from a hypodermic needle to which was fastened a small profile of the witch.

Give the class copies of student paragraphs that lack unity (from previous years, if possible). Ask students to discuss what is wrong with the paragraphs and to determine how the writing should be revised. ■

81

2.   Gloria put her head farther down and pumped harder. The three leading competitors were not as far ahead as they had been only moments ago. Perhaps they were tiring. The last section of the race was five miles of steeply rising uphill. She geared down once and pushed herself, willing herself not to waste her time by checking positions. She passed one cyclist without even glancing at him, concentrating on keeping her pace smooth and strong. She had three miles left and two riders ahead of her. "Maybe I can go faster," she thought. Gritting her teeth, she forced the pace. "I can go faster. I can. I *will*," she persuaded herself. She pushed herself harder. With less than a mile left, she passed another rider. Concentrating, willing herself to victory, she passed the last competitor and pumped victoriously across the finish line, winner of the Annual 120-Mile Bike Marathon.

⇗ A DIFFERENT APPROACH

Another way to think of unity in a paragraph is to think of the topic sentence as having two parts, the subject and the viewpoint or opinion about that subject. The viewpoint governs the unity of the paragraph, not the subject. For example, if the topic sentence of a paragraph were "Forest fires have beneficial effects," only supporting details that prove beneficial effects can be used as support, not just anything relating to forest fires.

OBJECTIVES
- To determine the best order of ideas for paragraphs
- To identify the order of ideas in paragraphs
- To identify and revise a paragraph that is not coherent
- To identify direct references and transitions in a paragraph

Teacher's ResourceBank™

RESOURCES

COHERENCE
- Achieving Coherence

QUOTATION FOR THE DAY

"Today's poet has less trouble making himself heard than making himself plain." (Louis Untermeyer, 1885–1977, American author, poet, and editor)

Students might discuss the quotation and contribute to a list of ways writers can make their work clear. Lead the class to understand that using clearly connected ideas and arranging sentences in an order that makes sense are two ways to make paragraphs coherent.

MEETING

INDIVIDUAL

NEEDS

LEP/ESL

Spanish. The word *coherence* is similar to the Spanish *coherencia*. However, it's important not to assume that the concepts are familiar just because the words are cognates. Write a clear definition of coherence on the chalkboard. *Coherence* means "the connection of parts in a way that makes sense." When a person is incoherent, he or she is not easily understood; in fact, his or her speech doesn't make any sense to the listener.

---

82   *Understanding Paragraph Structure*

Coherence

A paragraph has *coherence* when the ideas are clearly connected and arranged in an order that makes sense to readers. This coherence helps readers follow your ideas easily.

Order of Ideas

You can help your readers follow your ideas by the way you arrange, or order, them. Often, the subject you're writing about will suggest the order of ideas.

Chronological Order.   In a story, the actions or events are usually arranged according to the order in which they occur. This is *chronological,* or time, *order.* (*Chrono-* means "time.") Chronological order works because it often shows the cause-and-effect relationship between events: one action (cause) results in another action (effect). You'll also use chronological order to explain a process, with steps in the process listed in the (time) order they are to be carried out. In the following paragraph, the writer uses chronological order to arrange the events in a story told by adults to young Chinese girls.

> When we Chinese girls listened to the adults talking-story, we learned that we failed if we grew up to be but wives or slaves. We could be heroines, swordswomen. Even if she had to rage across all China, a swordswoman got even with anybody who hurt her family. Perhaps women were once so dangerous that they had to have their feet bound. It was a woman who invented white crane boxing only two hundred years ago. She was already an expert pole fighter, daughter of a teacher trained at the Shao-lin temple, where there lived an order of fighting monks. She was combing her hair one morning when a white crane alighted outside her window. She teased it with her pole, which it pushed aside with a soft brush of its wing. Amazed, she dashed outside and tried to knock the crane off its perch. It snapped her pole in two. Recognizing the presence of great power, she asked the spirit of the white crane if it would teach her to fight. It answered with a cry that white crane

You may want to have a volunteer read the text and the model in **Chronological Order.** Help students with the unusual references in Kingston's paragraph. Tell students that *Woman Warrior: Memoirs of a Girlhood Among Ghosts* is classified as fiction though it is largely based on experience.

Have another volunteer read the section entitled **Spatial Order** and emphasize that spatial order is frequently used in descriptive writing.

After a volunteer reads **Order of Importance,** p. 84, have students discuss the various strengths of putting the most-important point first compared to putting it last.

Coherence **83**

boxers imitate today. Later the bird returned as an old man, and he guided her boxing for many years. Thus she gave the world a new martial art.

Maxine Hong Kingston, *The Woman Warrior: Memoirs of a Girlhood Among Ghosts*

Spatial Order. When you describe something, you usually arrange the details according to their location in space. *Spatial order* allows you to show where objects are in relation to each other (such as from left to right, from near to far, from front to back). In the following paragraph, spatial order helps you picture what a girl observes, from left to right and from near to far, during a buggy ride on Canada's Prince Edward Island. In the second sentence, for example, your attention is directed to "the right hand." What other words and phrases in the paragraph help you follow the girl's observations?

The shore road was "woodsy and wild and lonesome." On the right hand, scrub firs, their spirits quite unbroken by long years of tussle with the gulf winds, grew thickly. On the left were the steep red sandstone cliffs, so near the track in places that a mare of less steadiness than the sorrel might have tried the nerves of the people behind her. Down at the base of the cliffs were heaps of surf-worn rocks or little sandy coves inlaid with pebbles as with ocean jewels; beyond lay the sea, shimmering and blue, and over it soared the gulls, their pinions flashing silvery in the sunlight.

Lucy Maud Montgomery, *Anne of Green Gables*

ADVANCED STUDENTS

Some students will have mastered chronological order, so you may want to have them augment this section by doing research about the author, Maxine Hong Kingston, her book *Woman Warrior: Memoirs of a Girlhood Among Ghosts,* or other books she has written. Students could work in pairs and report to the larger group on their findings. Or, you may wish to have students research one of the martial arts, including its history, importance, or role in society today.

AMENDMENTS TO SELECTIONS
Description of change: excerpted
Rationale: to focus on the concept of chronological order presented in this chapter

Finally, tell students that many paragraphs they will study (and many that they write) will follow a logical order. Have a volunteer read the text and the model paragraph in **Logical Order** on p. 84. You may want to have a volunteer read the first page of the **Connections Between Ideas** section on p. 88. Emphasize that while this chapter deals with coherence within paragraphs, the same types of direct references and transitional words and phrases are very important for showing relationships between paragraphs in longer pieces of writing. Have a volunteer read Stephenson's paragraph and then discuss the types of references he uses. Point out that these types of references occur naturally in speech as well as in writing.

INTEGRATING THE LANGUAGE ARTS

Literature Link. Refer students to the Martin Luther King, Jr. speech "I Have a Dream" to discuss paragraphing in a speech. Tell them that because it is a speech, the paragraphs are shorter. The breaks indicate points when he pauses. Ask students to work in groups to analyze the type of order he uses in the speech. [He uses order of importance to build to his most important, final point.]

Order of Importance.   If your paragraph were to give information or persuade, you usually would arrange ideas or details in *order of importance.* You could begin with the least important idea or detail and move to the most important, or begin with the most important and move to the least important. Readers usually are more aware of what they read first or what they read last.

In this paragraph the actress Helen Hayes gives reasons why she thinks older people should write an "autobiography." She begins with the least important reason—the therapeutic value—and moves to the most important reason—the preservation of personal history.

> I also like to see older folks write an "autobiography." Writing is very therapeutic. In fact, experts say it promotes self esteem and personal integration. Personally, I think it also clears away the cobwebs and stimulates a fresh way of thinking and looking back at your life. Most important, perhaps, it leaves a private history of yourself and your family. Don't you wish your grandmother and her grandmother before her had done that?
>
> Helen Hayes, "Hayes: 'There Is So Much to Do'"

Logical Order.   *Logical order* simply means the grouping of related ideas together. If your paragraph classifies, divides, defines, compares, or contrasts, you might choose logical order to arrange your ideas. The writer of the following paragraph, for example, compares selling teenagers new singing idols with selling them other fads. Notice that details about the singing idols are grouped together, followed by the details about the other fads.

> It was the industry's consensus that Tin Pan Alley had missed the boat, and that if the traditional songwriting industry was to survive, rock and roll would have to be factored in. It wasn't enough for rockers to cut the occasional standard; they would have to be given well-crafted, professionally written pop songs that had a rock-and-roll feeling. And this, it

Have students examine the **Transitional Words and Phrases** chart on p. 89, and read the Steinbeck paragraph in its entirety to analyze its use of transitional words and phrases.

GUIDED PRACTICE

You may want to work with students to identify types of order used in sample paragraphs from a literature textbook. Possible choices for each type of ordering are "You Are Now Entering the Human Heart" by Janet Frame—chronological and logical order; "Waits" by Lewis Thomas—order of importance; and "The Mojave" by John ☛

Coherence   **85**

was beginning to occur to some of the brains on Tin Pan Alley, would mean that the kids would have to be fed some new pop idols—which didn't seem that hard, really. It was already a truism that kids would buy anything, and the Wham-O company had proved it. Late in 1958 they had started a craze for a length of plastic tubing stapled into a circle, marketed under the name Hula-Hoop. Millions sold, and then Hula-Hoops vanished as quickly as they came, but Wham-O had learned a valuable lesson to be applied to its other products, Silly Putty and the redoubtable Frisbee.

Ed Ward, Geoffrey Stokes, and Ken Tucker, *Rock of Ages: The Rolling Stone History of Rock & Roll*

EXERCISE 4 ▶ **Choosing an Order of Ideas**

Try to figure out what order—chronological order, spatial order, order of importance, or logical order—would be best to develop each of the following topics in a paragraph. (You might use more than one type of order for some of the topics.)

1. accomplishments of Dr. Martin Luther King, Jr.
2. description of the Oval Office in the White House
3. five health reasons in favor of a vegetarian diet
4. how to make your own camera
5. comparing blues and jazz music

VISUAL CONNECTIONS

Ideas for Writing. You may want to have students write informative/descriptive paragraphs about the photograph of the Hula-Hoopers. Before students write, have them reread the types of order of ideas to decide which one would be best. Have students work with partners to discuss their descriptions and to evaluate the types of order they have chosen.

ANSWERS

Exercise 4

Answers may vary. Here are some possibilities:

1. chronological order; order of importance
2. spatial order
3. order of importance; logical order
4. chronological order
5. logical order

AMENDMENTS TO SELECTIONS
Description of change: excerpted
Rationale: to focus on the concept of paragraph ordering presented in this chapter

Steinbeck—spatial order. If these works are not available, use corresponding choices from your literature textbook. Work through the example for **Exercise 6** as guided practice.

INDEPENDENT PRACTICE

Have students complete **Exercises 4–7** as homework, or have them create examples of the different types of ordering. You might also have them provide examples of ways to revise transitions, perhaps from their own compositions.

ANSWERS
Exercise 5

1. logical order

2. This paragraph uses chronological order, but the chronology needs revision. The sentences should be rearranged as follows:

> Sitting Bull was a mighty Sioux who distinguished himself early in life. He was born in 1831 in what is now South Dakota. At ten, he killed his first buffalo. At fourteen, he won his first honor in battle. He became known as a great warrior and in the 1860s was named chief of his nation. In 1866 he led raids against U.S. army troops moving into his people's land. The government agreed to peace talks by 1868, but Sitting Bull refused to participate. He helped lead the victorious Indian attack against Lieutenant Colonel George Armstrong Custer's regiment at the famous Battle of Little Bighorn on June 25, 1876.

3. spatial order

EXERCISE 5 ▶	**Identifying Order of Ideas**

Following are three paragraphs. Two of the paragraphs follow the types of order you've just studied, but in one paragraph the ideas have no sensible order. Identify that paragraph and rewrite it so that the flow of ideas makes sense. Then identify the type of order followed by each of the other paragraphs.

1.   W.E.B. Du Bois and Booker T. Washington were two of this century's most influential black writers. Washington wrote most of his works between 1900 and 1911. With a longer career, Du Bois wrote between 1900 and the 1950s. Their educations were not alike, although both had more education than was average for the time. Washington graduated from the Hampton Institute, a vocational school, almost twenty years before Du Bois received a Ph.D. from Harvard in 1895. Both writers were very interested in education, although they looked at it differently. Washington founded the Tuskegee Normal and Industrial Institute, which stressed vocational training as the first step in upward mobility. Du Bois believed in classical education, teaching for a time at Atlanta University. Their educational beliefs were revealed in their works, Washington's in *The Future of the American Negro* and *Up from Slavery* and Du Bois's in *The Education of Black People*.

Booker T. Washington

W.E.B. Du Bois

Have students discuss their answers for the exercises in class. Be sure students can logically justify their choices.

If some students still do not understand the various types of order that make paragraphs coherent, organize students into groups of four and have them label examples from magazines, newspapers, novels, and textbooks in which you have underlined and highlighted the supporting ideas and clues for each type of order. Each group ☛

Coherence　**87**

2.　Sitting Bull was a mighty Sioux who distinguished himself early in life. At fourteen, he won his first honor in battle. At ten, he killed his first buffalo. He was born in 1834 in what is now South Dakota. He became known as a brave warrior and was named a chief of his nation. He acted as the main medicine man before the victorious Native American attack against Lieutenant Colonel George Armstrong Custer's regiment at the famous Battle of Little Bighorn on June 25, 1876. In 1866 he led raids against U.S. army troops moving into his people's land. The government agreed to peace talks by 1868, but Sitting Bull refused to participate.

3.　The Sun Dance of the Plains Indians, also called the Medicine Dance or Thirst Lodge, is an annual event. This spring dance is held in a large circular open frame lodge representing the world's creation. A sacred cottonwood tree is placed in the center of the lodge. This tree acts as the focus of the dance and links sky and earth. On the tree is attached one or more sacred objects. A sacred object may be an eagle head or skull or a bison head or skull. The dancers move from the outside edge of the lodge to the tree at the center and back again. Each dancer always faces the tree. Each dancer concentrates on the tree or on one of the objects attached to the tree.

VISUAL CONNECTIONS
Exploring the Subject. In June of 1876, Sitting Bull and his followers were encamped on the Little Bighorn River searching for game. It was there later that month that Lieutenant Colonel George Armstrong Custer's regiment was defeated in a great battle. Sitting Bull was eventually killed at the age of 59 in an attempt by soldiers to arrest him on Grand River. The Sioux admired Sitting Bull for his leadership, his religious devotion, and his love for his people.

TIMESAVER
You may wish to have students work in small, mixed-ability groups to complete **Exercise 5** orally. This procedure will eliminate paper-grading time and will also allow students to learn by participating in group discussions. Each group will need to designate a member to record its revision of the second paragraph. Have one group read its corrected paragraph aloud and then lead a class discussion to analyze and possibly improve it.

should have two examples of each type of order—chronological order, spatial order, order of importance, and logical order.

Have the groups exchange their labeled findings so that the class can discuss the characteristics of the types of order.

CLOSURE

Ask students to summarize the four types of order for developing topics in paragraphs, to give examples of topics that would be appropriate for each of the four types, and to explain two methods to use for coherence.

Connections Between Ideas

To give a paragraph coherence, you should do more than arrange the ideas in an order that makes sense; you should also show how the ideas are connected. There are two ways to show connections: (1) make *direct references* to something else in the paragraph or (2) use words that make a *transition,* or bridge, from one idea to another.

Direct References.   A natural way to link ideas in a paragraph is to refer to a noun or pronoun that you've used earlier. You can make ***direct references*** in these three ways:

1. Use a noun or pronoun that refers to a noun or pronoun used earlier.
2. Repeat a word used earlier.
3. Use a word or phrase that means the same thing as one used earlier.

This paragraph, from a famous adventure story, has several direct references. The numbers above the references show you the type of reference.

> That same evening, however, Leiningen assembled *his*[1] workers. *He*[1] had no intention of waiting till the news reached *their*[1] ears from other sources. *Most*[1] of *them*[1] had been born in the district; the cry "The ants are coming!" was to *them*[1] an imperative signal for instant, panic-stricken flight, a spring for life itself. But so great was the *Indians'*[1] trust in *Leiningen,*[2] in *Leiningen's*[2] word, and in *Leiningen's*[2] wisdom, that *they*[1] received *his*[1] curt *tidings,*[3] and *his*[1] orders for the imminent struggle, with the calmness with which *they*[1] were given. *They*[1] waited, unafraid, alert, as if for the beginning of a new game or hunt which *he*[1] had just described to *them.*[1] The *ants*[2] were indeed mighty, but not so mighty as the *boss.*[1] Let *them*[1] come!
>
> Carl Stephenson, "Leiningen Versus the Ants"

MEETING

◆ **INDIVIDUAL** ◆

NEEDS

ADVANCED STUDENTS

Students who quickly grasp the concept of transitions could evaluate the coherence achieved by a professional writer in his or her writing. A good choice for an evaluation is A. M. Rosenthal's essay "No News from Auschwitz." Students can use the following questions:

1. Does the essay have clear transitions? Give at least three examples to support your opinion.
2. Do all sentences relate to the main idea? If so, explain how. If not, give specific examples that show unrelated sentences.
3. Rate this essay on a scale from one to four. How could the writer better his score? Give at least two suggestions for improvement.

LESS-ADVANCED STUDENTS

Students can practice using transitions by filling in the blanks in a paragraph. You can provide a paragraph with blanks left where transitions had been provided and then ask students to complete the paragraph.

SELECTION AMENDMENT
Description of change: excerpted
Rationale: to focus on the concept of coherence presented in this chapter

You may want to have students work
with the paragraphs they have put on the
bulletin board to add new examples. Have
the class analyze the paragraphs to determine the type of order used and then place
them in the appropriate categories. ■

Transitional Words and Phrases.   Words and phrases
that indicate the relationships between ideas are called
transitional expressions. Prepositions that show chronological or spatial order and conjunctions are also transitions. In the chart that follows, notice the relationships
shown by the different types of transitions and the types
of writing to which they're related.

TRANSITIONAL WORDS AND PHRASES		
Comparing Ideas/Classification and Definition		
also	besides	similarly
and	in addition	too
another	other	
Contrasting Ideas/Classification and Definition		
although	instead	otherwise
but	nevertheless	still
however	on the other	yet
in spite of	hand	
Showing Cause and Effect/Narration		
as a result	for	therefore
because	since	thus
consequently	so	
Showing Time/Narration		
after	eventually	meanwhile
at last	finally	then
at once	first	when
before	for a time	
Showing Place/Description		
above	from	on
across	here	over
around	in	there
before	nearby	to
beyond	next	under
Showing Importance/Evaluation		
first	mainly	then
last	more important	to begin with

COMMON ERROR

Problem. Although using pronouns in writing improves coherence by
referring to nouns in previous sentences,
many writers fail to have a clear antecedent for each pronoun. For example,
in the sentence "In our school, there are
scholars, athletes, artists, and leaders; they
make our school what it is today," the
reference is divided between four nouns.

Solution. Require students to
circle all the pronouns in their writing
and to draw arrows back to the correct
antecedents. The revision stage of the
writing process would be a good place
to incorporate this procedure.

INTEGRATING THE LANGUAGE ARTS

Technology Link. If possible, have students form groups of four to complete **Exercise 5** on computers. Have students number each sentence of the paragraphs as they enter them into their computers. As students reorganize the ideas, the numbers should accompany the appropriate sentences. Check each computer printout for the correct number sequence when evaluating.

In the following paragraph, transitional words, which are underlined, are used to strengthen the connections and show relationships in time and place.

> Then from the corner of the house came a sound so soft that it might have been simply a thought, a little furtive movement, a touch of a foot on earth, the almost inaudible purr of controlled breathing. Kino held his breath to listen, and he knew that whatever dark thing was in his house was holding its breath too, to listen. For a time no sound at all came from the corner of the brush house. Then Kino might have thought he had imagined the sound. But Juana's hand came creeping over to him in warning, and then the sound came again! the whisper of a foot on dry earth and the scratch of fingers in the soil.
>
> John Steinbeck, *The Pearl*

EXERCISE 6 ▶ **Identifying Direct References and Transitions**

The following paragraph uses both direct references and transitions to connect ideas. Label two columns "Direct References" and "Transitions." Then identify each <u>direct reference</u> and <u>transition</u> in the paragraph. Remember to refer to the chart of commonly used transitions on page 89, and to think about conjunctions and prepositions telling *when* and *where*.

EXAMPLE   Moreover, Mayor Mary Rodríguez made a promise to balance the city budget. When election day arrived, her pledge proved popular, and she won. Few people, however, realized how painful carrying out her commitment would be.

Direct References	Transitions
her	moreover
pledge	when
she	and
her	however
commitment	

SELECTION AMENDMENT

Description of change: excerpted
Rationale: to focus on the concept of transitions presented in this chapter

Although the popular cartoon *The Far Side*, by Gary Larson, is pretty far out, it has a fairly sane history. Larson says he always loved to draw, but he never took art lessons. Also, Larson says he always liked science. His famous panel, consequently, combines those two loves. In 1979, Larson started drawing a cartoon in the *Seattle Times* called *Nature's Way*. Before long, his drawings moved to the *San Francisco Chronicle* as *The Far Side*. Syndication began, and *The Far Side* became a household name. Larson says he frequently is asked, "Where do you get your ideas?" The artist answers that he doesn't know; the ideas mostly come from just thinking and doodling. Because people enjoy the cartoon so much, Larson decided to write a book about his work. That volume is *The PreHistory of The Far Side*.

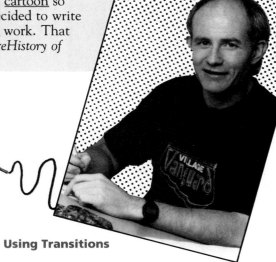

EXERCISE 7 ▶ **Using Transitions**

There's little wonder that the ideas in this paragraph are confusing—there are few transitions to make ideas clear to readers. Revise the paragraph by adding the transitions that help readers follow the order of ideas. (You may also decide to make other changes to improve the paragraph.)

> Angie was very interested in the Seven Wonders of the Ancient World. She decided to write a report on them. She went to Egypt last year. She saw the

ANSWERS
Exercise 7

Responses will vary. Here is a possibility:

Because Angie was very interested in the Seven Wonders of the Ancient World, she decided to write a report on them. Her interest began when she visited Egypt last year and saw the pyramids. To write her report, Angie first went to the library. There she checked out books on the ancient wonders and read about them in encyclopedias. Then Angie talked to her history teacher because she found conflicting information. For instance, most of the old books said that the Colossus of Rhodes stood over the harbor entrance on the Greek island of Rhodes. More modern research, however, indicates that the huge, bronze statue was not at the harbor. Before she wrote her report, Angie located pictures of all the seven wonders. Since she had seen the pyramids, Angie wrote most about them.

pyramids, the only existing wonder. To write her report, Angie went to the library. She checked out books on the ancient wonders. She read about them in encyclopedias. Angie talked to her history teacher. Angie found conflicting information. Most of the old books said that the Colossus of Rhodes stood over the harbor entrance on the Greek island of Rhodes. More modern research indicates that the huge bronze statue was not at the harbor. Angie located pictures of all the seven wonders. She wrote her report. She had seen the pyramids. That's why she wrote most about them.

STRATEGIES OF DEVELOPMENT

OBJECTIVES

- To use descriptive detail as a strategy
- To use narration as a strategy for developing paragraph outlines
- To explain a process to an audience
- To use classification to develop a main idea
- To evaluate subjects and to give reasons for the evaluations

Strategies of Development

Description, narration, classification, and evaluation are four strategies for developing a main idea. The strategy, or method, you choose to develop a paragraph depends upon your specific purpose and audience for writing. The strategy determines what kind of supporting details you will use, such as facts or examples, and affects the order of your ideas. These four strategies of development are basically different ways of looking at a topic or subject.

STRATEGIES OF DEVELOPMENT	
Description	Looking at individual features of a particular subject
Narration	Looking at changes in the subject over a period of time
Classification	Looking at a subject in relation to other subjects
Evaluation	Looking at the value of the subject (judging)

Each paragraph or each piece of longer writing you create should have a purpose and a strategy that develops that purpose. You may use description to write a friend about your dream car. Or you may use narration to write in your journal about what happened during the last football game. In school you might use classification to compare and contrast the sciences of biology and zoology. And you would choose evaluation to tell your theater teacher your opinion of a play you saw.

WRITING NOTE Frequently, paragraphs and longer pieces of writing have more than one purpose, so they use more than one strategy of development. For example, description and narration are often combined in reports, stories, and even poetry.

Teacher's ResourceBank™

RESOURCES

STRATEGIES OF DEVELOPMENT
- Developing Paragraphs
- Developing Paragraphs
- Developing Paragraphs

QUOTATION FOR THE DAY

"Talent alone cannot make a writer. There must be a man behind the book." (Ralph Waldo Emerson, 1803–1882, American essayist, poet, and philosopher)

Have students freewrite responses to the quotation. Explain that a good writer usually has a definite purpose for each piece of work he or she creates and a strategy that develops that purpose.

Have a volunteer read **Strategies of Development** through the **Writing Note** on p. 93. Compare studying these strategies independently to studying paragraphs independently. You could also compare studying these strategies to baseball players practicing batting in isolation repeatedly.

These skills are a small part of a complex game. Emphasize that writers often use a combination of strategies to achieve their purposes, especially in lengthy works.

Have a volunteer read **Description**, including the model by Mason Crum. Point out that writers often use description to promote an understanding of people, places, and objects.

MEETING INDIVIDUAL NEEDS

LEP/ESL

General Strategies. Some students might have difficulty with classification in English because the meanings of words in their native languages do not exactly match those of English words. For example, in Vietnamese, there is no single term for *cousin,* and the term for *green* includes part of English *blue.* Such small differences can lead students to feel uncertain about using English. You may wish to give some extra suggestions to your ESL students on how to define, compare, and contrast topics.

ANSWERS
Exercise 8

Be sure students appeal to all senses in their features. You may want to suggest that students use a prewriting strategy such as mapping to help them get started.

Description

What does your state flag look like? How will you recognize Gothic architecture?

To tell what something is like or what it looks like, you need to examine its particular features. Then you choose description as a strategy of development, using sensory details for support and spatial order. The following paragraph, for example, describes the brightly dressed Gullah women of the Carolina Sea Islands.

All day long they travel the highways in twos, threes, and dozens. Dressed in their best bibs and tuckers, they present a varicolored procession, moving leisurely over shell and sand roads. Every color of the rainbow is presented in their dresses, calicoes of blue, red, yellow, and green—garments simply made, and mostly homemade. They chat and laugh and enjoy the holiday spirit. Like the ancient Hebrews they have learned the happy art of combining religion and social life. A woman comes by with her large pocketbook balanced on her head—why, I do not know. A proud mother carries her baby in her arms, dressed in brilliant yellow.

Mason Crum, *Gullah*

EXERCISE 8 ▶ **Using Description as a Strategy**

"It's a really economical and smooth car," she says. "What kind is it? What does it look like?" her friend asks. Description adds information about a subject. Choose two of the following subjects and list at least five features—sensory details—to describe each one. Remember to use a technique like brainstorming or observing to think up sensory details (see pages 27 and 31).

1. a school dance
2. a favorite musician or musical group
3. your neighborhood on a winter's day
4. yourself when you have a bad cold
5. the busiest, most crowded place you've ever been

Narration

What happened when young Arthur tried to pull the sword from the stone? How does a video recorder work? What economic and political events caused the Berlin Wall to come down?

To answer these questions, you use the strategy of narration, looking at events or actions in time. And to find the answers to these questions, you have to look at changes over a period of time. Since you're looking at a subject from a time perspective, you usually use chronological (or time) order. You may use narration *to tell a story or incident* (what happened when Arthur tried the sword), *to explain a process* (how a video recorder works), or *to explain cause and effect* (why the Berlin Wall came down).

Telling a Story.   Storytellers use the strategy of narration to tell a story (what happened over time). The story may be either true or imaginary (fiction). In the following paragraph, the writer tells a story about a contest between the Greek gods Athena and Poseidon for the city of Athens.

> In one story of this contest between the two deities, woman's suffrage plays a part. In those early days, we are told, women voted as well as men. All the women voted for the goddess, and all the men for the god. There was one more woman than there were men, so Athena won. But the men, along with Poseidon, were greatly chagrined at this female triumph; and while Poseidon proceeded to flood the land the men decided to take the vote away from the women. Nevertheless, Athena kept Athens.
>
> Edith Hamilton, *Mythology*

Explaining a Process.   Telling how something works or how to do something is *explaining a process.* You use narration to explain a process because you look at your subject as it changes over time. In the following paragraph, the writer explains how he helps his mother close the family restaurant. (The steps in the process are the changes over time.)

Read and discuss **Evaluation**, p. 100. Then have students answer the lead-in questions about the model, **"The Flash,"** in their textbooks as a way of discussing the use of evaluation in the paragraph.

GUIDED PRACTICE

To model the process in **Exercise 8**, list sensory details on the chalkboard for a subject you select. Model the required skills in **Exercises 9–12** by using the first part of each of the exercises.

> At night I help my mother close the restaurant. I do what she and my father have done together for the past forty-three years. At ten o'clock I turn off the illuminated white sign above the front entrance. After all the customers leave and the last waiter says goodbye, I lock the front door and flip over the sign that says "Closed." Then I shut off the radio and the back lights.
>
> David Low, "Winterblossom Garden"

Explaining Cause and Effect. To explain what causes something or what the effects of something are, you also look at the way things have changed over the course of time. You use narration again. In this paragraph, the writer reveals the two effects of her realization that she was growing up and wouldn't always be at Ames High School. One effect is that she felt a sense of sadness. The other is that she "nestled" into familiar surroundings.

> As I grew older, I began to realize that this quiet was not going to last. Time was speeding up; at some sharply definable point I would grow up and leave Ames. At odd moments in those last years I would be surprised by sadness, a strange feeling that perhaps I had missed something, that maybe life was going to pass me by. At the same time I nestled securely in the familiar landscape of streets whose every bump and jog I knew, of people who smiled and greeted me by name wherever I went, of friends who appeared at every movie, store, or swimming pool.
>
> Susan Allen Toth, "Nothing Happened"

MEETING INDIVIDUAL NEEDS

LEP/ESL

General Strategies. Authors sometimes do not present events or steps in precisely the order in which they occurred, and they often use flashbacks. However, writers normally warn the reader of this condition by using transitional expressions such as *prior to that, in previous years,* or *we should consider.* You may find that some ESL students have not read many narratives in English; they may tend to write their points as they think of them and to omit needed transitions. You could advise students to be sure that they write events or steps in the same order in which they actually occurred or to be sure to use transitions to write about the events or steps.

ANSWERS

Exercise 9

Responses will vary.

1. telling a story

2. explaining a process

3. explaining cause-and-effect

AMENDMENTS TO SELECTIONS
Description of change: excerpted
Rationale: to focus on the concept of cause and effect presented in this chapter

---

EXERCISE 9   **Using Narration as a Strategy**

You've read about the different times you can use narration to develop a paragraph—to explain causes and effects, to explain a process, and to tell a story. Now, use the following instructions for using that strategy.

INDEPENDENT PRACTICE

Have students work in small groups to complete **Exercise 8**. Students could brainstorm long lists and then choose their five favorites to record as their own work. After you have modeled the activities, assign **Exercises 9–12** as independent practice.

ASSESSMENT

Ask students to share and discuss their answers to the exercises in class.

1. List the effects of poor nutrition and lack of exercise on your health as an adult.
2. List the steps in the process for getting a learner's driving permit in your state.
3. List the actions in a story about what might happen if an alien spacecraft landed on the White House lawn.

EXERCISE 10 ▶ **Speaking and Listening: Explaining a Process**

Think about a simple process that you could explain to the class or a smaller group—perhaps how to make tortillas or how to hook up a stereo system with tape deck, amplifier, receiver, and so on. Then make a list of the major steps in the process. Using your list as an outline, explain the process to your audience. If you like, use props or visual aids to make your process clearer.

Classification

What are the sizes and depths of the world's oceans? What is a laser? What are the differences between hurricanes and tornadoes?

To answer these questions, you need to *classify*, or look at a subject as it relates to other subjects in a group. There are three ways to classify: divide a subject into its

LEARNING STYLES

Visual Learners. Show students examples of graphic organizers to organize and focus information when they are writing classificatory papers. You can use the following examples:

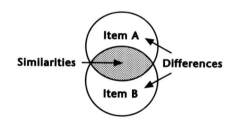

	Item A	Item B
Feature 1		
Feature 2		
Feature 3		

ANSWERS
Exercise 10

Responses will vary, but each presentation should include a clear, logical series of steps for the process being described. Details should clarify the process.

Give students several broad topics and have students suggest ways in which the topics could be approached by using each of the four writing strategies discussed here. For example, if you gave them the general topic *volleyball*, they might suggest the following approaches:

descriptive—the atmosphere in the locker room before a big game
narrative—a play-by-play report of a team winning a game
classification—how volleyball compares with other team sports
evaluation—the pros and cons of playing volleyball in high school

TIMESAVER

Both **Exercises 9** and **10** may require that students complete outside research. In order to save research time either in or out of class, have the appropriate research tools available in class. Your librarian or a history teacher may allow you to borrow tools for studying nutrition or facts on the White House, and a set of encyclopedias should be sufficient for researching **Exercise 10.**

parts (the oceans), define it (a laser), or compare and contrast it with something else (hurricanes and tornadoes).

Dividing.   With some subjects, the best way to explain them as a whole is to look at their parts. For example, to explain what the United Nations is, you may have to divide it into the parts that make up the overall organization known as the United Nations, such as the General Assembly, the Security Council, and the International Court of Justice. This paragraph uses the strategy of dividing in order to explain the makeup of the news department at the *New York Times.*

> In the news department at *The Times* there are some 570 people who assign, gather, and edit the news. Under the executive editor, A. M. Rosenthal, are managing editor Seymour Topping and his deputy and assistants, among them the news editor. There are nine news desks, and of these, the metropolitan, national, and foreign are the best-known. Each is headed by an editor who, with a deputy and assistants, supervises a staff of reporters or correspondents and oversees the flow of news to the respective copy desk and from there to the composing room. The other news desks—business and financial, culture, family/style, science, real estate, and sports—operate in much the same way.
>
> Betty Lou English, *Behind the Headlines*

Defining.   When you *define* a subject, you first identify it as a part of a larger group or class. Then you discuss features that make the subject unique in its class. In the following paragraph, the first sentence defines "stars" and identifies the larger group to which they belong (gas). The remaining sentences give details about stars that distinguish them from other types of gases.

> Stars are hot, glowing globes of gas that emit energy. Nearly all of a star's gas is hydrogen. Because the Sun is a hot ball of hydrogen that emits huge amounts of energy, it is a star, and the star

CLOSURE

You could have volunteers summarize the four strategies for writing and give details about each.

ENRICHMENT

You may want to expand **Exercise 8** into an actual writing assignment. Allow students to choose one of the five subjects. Students must then write clear, detailed descriptive paragraphs for each of the chosen topics. ■

closest to us. The next closest star is one called Alpha Centauri, more than 270,000 times farther away than the Sun.

Roy A. Gallant, *Private Lives of the Stars*

VISUAL CONNECTIONS

About the Artwork. This picture of stars was generated by a computer. Computers can be used to make paintings or drawings. They can also create fine art in the style of particular artists. The programmer determines the image.

CRITICAL THINKING
Analysis

You might want to have students analyze the structure of Joyce Pope's paragraph to see how she contrasts subjects. You could have students use a chart like the following one. After students have finished, you can have them compare their answers with the answers provided in the chart.

Feature	Spiders	Insects
wings	none	most have
bodies	2 main parts	3 main parts
legs	8 or more	6

Comparing and Contrasting. Another way to classify subjects is by comparing them (telling how they are alike), contrasting them (telling how they are different), or by both comparing and contrasting. The following paragraph contrasts the characteristics of spiders and insects.

Spiders are not insects. Although they are often confused with them, they differ from them in many ways. Most adult insects, for example, have wings; spiders never do. All insects have bodies divided into three major parts: head, thorax and abdomen, the latter two divided into smaller segments. The thorax carries four or six legs, never more. A spider's body is in two main parts. Attached to the front one of these are eight legs, never fewer.

Joyce Pope, *Do Animals Dream?*

AMENDMENTS TO SELECTIONS
Description of change: excerpted
Rationale: to focus on the concept of paragraph development presented in this chapter

ANSWERS
Exercise 11

Responses will vary.

1. Responses should be evaluated on whether or not the details support the particular types of individual tastes listed.
2. Responses should be evaluated on the basis of whether the features listed show schools to be different from other institutions in the larger group.
3. Responses should be evaluated on the basis of clarity and on whether or not the writer proves the main idea.

COOPERATIVE LEARNING
Organize students into groups of four or five and have them generate and discuss topics for evaluation. Write some broad topics of interest to students on the chalkboard. Possibilities include teenagers voting in elections or teenagers learning to drive. Have groups decide on a judgment for each of the topics and have them give two or three reasons to support each judgment. Be sure students can explain the criteria for their evaluations.

EXERCISE 11 Using Classification as a Strategy

How can you divide it, define it, compare it, or contrast it? Follow the directions to develop each of the main ideas given below.

Main Idea	Classification Strategy
1. There's a car on the market to appeal to every type of individual taste.	Examine the subject of cars by dividing them into types. List details for each type to support the main idea.
2. Take the teachers and books away, and would it still be a school?	Define the subject "school." What larger group does it belong to—political organization, an institution for learning, or some other group? Now, list some features that make it different from other groups.
3. If you're good at one computer game, will you be good at another?	Compare and contrast two computer games by listing their likenesses and differences.

Evaluation

Should our schools use suspension as a punishment for students who create discipline problems? Is Spike Lee's last movie any good?

To answer such questions, you look at the value of the subject, or make a judgment about it. There are two main reasons for evaluating a subject: to inform other people or to persuade them to think or act differently. Of course, an evaluation often has both purposes at once. For example, movie reviewers tell you their opinions in order to persuade you to see or to avoid movies. When you evaluate, it's important to give some reasons to support your evaluation (that is, tell *why* you have this judgment about the subject). The following paragraph is part of a review of the television series *The Flash*. What is the reviewer's evaluation of the program? Does he make you want to see it? Notice the supporting reasons the reviewer gives for his evaluation.

> *The Flash* (CBS) has sped over to Saturday nights—this week at 10 and thereafter at 8. If you haven't seen the show before, you really should check it out, because since its debut last fall, *The Flash* has shown the fastest improvement of any new show. This series, based on the DC Comics superhero who can run faster than the speed of light, has always had above-average special effects, but now it has something else: above-average stories and acting. John Wesley Shipp (as the Flash) and Amanda Pays (as the research scientist who helps keep the Flash's metabolism under control) have become a dreamy romantic couple—their banter is both heartfelt and clever.
>
> Ken Tucker, "New Dash for 'The Flash'"

E X E R C I S E 12▶ **Using Evaluation as a Strategy**

What's your evaluation? Why do you feel that way? Evaluate each of the following broad subjects by making a positive or negative judgment about it. Then give two or three reasons to support your judgment.

1. the latest movie you've seen
2. the latest book you've read
3. the most current fad around school (in clothes, hairstyles, or language)

INTEGRATING THE LANGUAGE ARTS

Literature Link. You may want to have students work in groups of three or four on this activity. If the selection is available in your literature textbook, have students read Psalm 1 from the Bible to analyze and discuss this Psalm as an example of evaluation. Circulate around the classroom to assess students' analyses. [In this evaluation, the writer gives his judgments about the happiness of the godly and the unhappiness of the ungodly. The purpose is to persuade the reader to live a godly life.]

ANSWERS
Exercise 12

Responses should be evaluated on the strength of the reasons given to support the opinions expressed. Would the reasons be sufficient to convince most readers?

SELECTION AMENDMENT
Description of change: excerpted
Rationale: to focus on the concept of evaluation presented in this chapter

101

MAKING CONNECTIONS

WRITING A PARAGRAPH TO EXPRESS YOURSELF
OBJECTIVE

- To write an expressive paragraph

WRITING A PARAGRAPH TO EXPRESS YOURSELF
Teaching Strategies

You may want to tell students that expressive writing is personal—it explores thoughts and feelings.

Explain that expressive writing is different from other writing in that its focus is on the writer and not on the audience (with the exception of personal letters). In general, expressive writing contains the same spontaneity that talking to a friend or singing in the shower has.

GUIDELINES

Students' writing should include at least two or more of the four characteristics of expressive writing:

1. use of first-person point of view
2. feelings
3. natural language
4. strong word connotations and associations

MAKING CONNECTIONS

WRITING PARAGRAPHS FOR DIFFERENT PURPOSES

In this chapter you studied the form and structure of paragraphs. Now you can apply that knowledge by writing paragraphs for different purposes: to express yourself, to inform, to persuade, and to create.

Writing a Paragraph to Express Yourself

Do you ever find yourself thinking about things that you want to understand more? Do you have feelings that you would like to explore? Writing about your thoughts and feelings can help you learn more about yourself, whether or not you share such writing with anyone else.

A diary or a writer's notebook—or any sheet of paper—is a good place to write an expressive paragraph. Use one of the following sentences to start an expressive paragraph.

Starter Sentences for Expressive Writing

It's so great that ____.
What really frustrates me is ____.
Happiness would be understanding ____.
The person I most admire is ____.
To improve the world, each person should ____.

Prewriting. Begin by identifying your thoughts and feelings about your topic, perhaps by simply listing them. Or make a cluster diagram to help you focus on the topic (see pages 28–29). You can also ask yourself a series of questions or review old journal entries for ideas.

Writing, Evaluating, and Revising. If you're writing only for yourself, write a first draft and leave it. If you'll share your paragraph, look more carefully at what you wrote and how you wrote it. Does the paragraph make sense and express what you want it to?

⊕ Proofreading and Publishing.   If you're sharing your writing, review your paragraph to correct errors in usage and mechanics. You could "publish" your paragraph by reading it aloud to the class. Or you and your classmates might make a booklet of your expressive paragraphs.

Writing a Paragraph to Inform

You live in a time when information of all sorts is constantly available—from other people, television, radio, newspapers, books, and many other sources. And people get information from you, too. When you write to inform, your purpose is to present clear, useful information.

The chart below gives some information about the sources of money for the United States Olympic Committee. Use the information in the chart and the following topic sentence to write an informative paragraph. If you want, research more information about the committee's funding. Assume that your audience (classmates) knows nothing about the committee's funding structure.

Topic Sentence: Money to run the United States Olympic Committee comes from different sources.

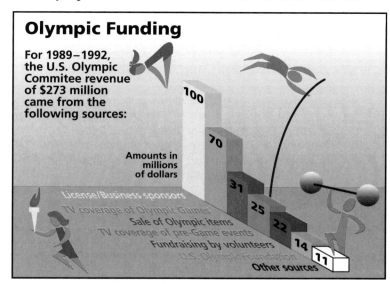

Olympic Funding

For 1989–1992, the U.S. Olympic Commitee revenue of $273 million came from the following sources:

Amounts in millions of dollars

100
70
License/Business sponsors
TV coverage of Olympic Games
Sale of Olympic items
TV coverage of pre-Game events
Fundraising by volunteers
U.S. Olympic Foundation
31
25
22
14
11
Other sources

Sources: U.S. Olympic Committee and *USA TODAY*

WRITING A PARAGRAPH TO PERSUADE

Teaching Strategies

Tell students that in persuasive writing they will focus on the audience—the opposite of the focus of expressive writing. Have the class discuss the reasons why the aims have different focuses. [Persuasive writing attempts to change the reader's mind or to get the reader to act in a certain way; expressive writing is primarily intended to put into words the feelings of the writer.]

Persuasive writing appeals to the reader's sense of trust, to feelings, and to reasoning. In this particular assignment, students will want to use logical appeals and probably emotional appeals as well. Point out that persuasive writing is a vital part of political campaigns and of advertising.

Prewriting and Writing. Study the chart carefully so that you understand the various sources of funding and the amounts given by the supporters. Next, write the topic sentence on your paper. Then, support the topic sentence with three or four sentences based on information from the chart or your own research. Be sure to arrange the information in order of importance. You may want to include a clincher sentence, too.

Evaluating and Revising. Does each supporting sentence give information (facts and statistics) about the topic sentence? If not, rewrite or cut any sentences that break the unity of your paragraph. Have you arranged the information in order of importance? If not, reorder the sentences.

Proofreading and Publishing. Review your paragraph to correct any errors in grammar, usage, and mechanics. Share your paragraph to inform someone about the Olympic Committee's funding.

Writing a Paragraph to Persuade

Even though you may not realize it, people are constantly trying to persuade you—to convince you to think or act in a particular way. Think about it. Every television or radio commercial and every magazine advertisement you see or hear tries to persuade you. Your friends, teachers, and parents frequently try to convince you to think or act differently.

You are taking sides in a controversy over whether whales should be moved from the ocean to the confinement of a local aquarium. Write a paragraph in which you try to convince people to support or not to support having a whale tank in the local aquarium paid for by local tax money. If you want, use one of the following topic sentences.

Topic Sentences:
Whales are an ecologically delicate species and should not be moved to a small, confining aquarium.

Whales should be brought to the local aquarium so that everyone can enjoy them.

GUIDELINES

Each paragraph should include three or four reasons to support the stand the writer has taken, with elaborations for each reason. Language should be appropriate to the audience—dignified and correct. Any or all of the three types of persuasive appeals can be used—personal appeal, logical appeal, or emotional appeal.

Prewriting. Which side of the controversy are you on? To help you decide, make two lists of reasons: one telling why you feel whales should be brought to the aquarium, and another telling why they should not be brought. Suggestions: How do you feel about animals' being taken from their natural habitats? about the amount of money and resources needed to provide for them in a large aquarium? After reviewing your own beliefs, decide which side to take. (You may want to do some research to gather support for your opinion.)

Writing, Evaluating, and Revising. For your paragraph, list three or four convincing reasons to back up your position. Be sure that your position is clearly stated in a topic sentence. After you write your draft, look at the reasons you have given. Do you have enough reasons? Are they convincing? Would they convince *you?* Revise your paragraph to make it more convincing.

Proofreading and Publishing. Correct any errors in grammar, usage, and mechanics. To see if someone else would be convinced, read your paragraph aloud to the class or to a small group.

WRITING A PARAGRAPH THAT IS CREATIVE

Teaching Strategies

Many students at this grade level read fantasy, science fiction, and other types of highly imaginative writing. You may want to have students choose especially effective paragraphs that illustrate setting and character description from their favorite books and have students read the passages aloud to the class. Discuss the ways in which the writing is effective. If necessary, review the concept of conflict.

VISUAL CONNECTIONS
High Tide: The Bathers

About the Artist. American artist Winslow Homer (1836–1910) is well known for his paintings of the sea—sail boats, sea captains, fishermen, and bathers—as well as for scenes of country and farm life. Both of his parents painted with watercolors, and he began to draw and paint as a child. During the Civil War he drew illustrations of battle scenes for *Harper's Weekly*.

High Tide: The Bathers is an oil which appeared in *Every Saturday* on August 6, 1870. A reviewer for *The Times* criticized it by saying that it was unpleasant to look at the "brick-dust" color of the young girl's legs.

Writing a Paragraph That Is Creative

"That's very creative!" or "You're so creative!" are always compliments. You're usually impressed when someone does something that you think is creative—something that is new, different, and original. Stories and poems are writers' attempts to use situations, characters, and/or language in their own special ways.

Look at the painting *High Tide: The Bathers,* by Winslow Homer. Write a paragraph that begins a story suggested by Homer's painting. In your paragraph, give your readers some idea about who the characters are, and describe the setting. Also, establish a conflict—a struggle of some kind—for the characters. These questions may help you imagine a scene that involves a conflict.

- Who are the bathers? What is their relationship to each other?
- Where are the bathers? What are they doing there? What do they plan to do next?
- What feelings do you get from the characters? Why do you see only one face clearly? What is the expression of the girl sitting on the beach?
- What part does the dog play in the bathers' story? Is the dog with them or with someone else, who is not seen?

Prewriting. Using the preceding questions, study the painting to see what details you want to imagine for your story. Jot down a list of the details, along with sensory descriptions such as the color of the sky and water, the sounds, and the smells.

Writing, Evaluating, and Revising. Write a paragraph that describes the scene at the beginning of your story, introduces the characters and situation, and prepares your readers for the conflict to come. Then exchange your paragraph with a classmate. Is the beginning of your story clear to your reader? Does your reader understand the situation and conflict? If not, add or change details.

Proofreading and Publishing. Review your paragraph to correct any errors in grammar, usage, and mechanics. Share your paragraph by reading it aloud to the class or to a small group. You may even want to finish writing the whole story.

GUIDELINES

Each paragraph should contain a setting, characters, and the beginning of a conflict. The emphasis of creative writing should be entertainment, so word choice is of major importance. This aspect is referred to as style, the special way a writer chooses words and phrases. Is the writing style of the paragraph unique?

"A sentence should contain no unnecessary words, a paragraph no unnecessary sentences, for the same reason that a drawing should have no unnecessary lines and a machine no unnecessary parts."

William Strunk, Jr.

Chapter 3

UNDERSTANDING COMPOSTION STRUCTURE

Motivation

You may want to introduce the chapter by leading a discussion about how people expect things to have definite beginnings, middles, and ends. You could start humorously by making a rough drawing of a dachshund on the chalkboard. Draw lines to indicate the beginning, middle, and end of this lengthy dog. Ask students to identify some other beginnings, middles, and ends. [Responses may include the plots of movies, television shows, plays, and books; terms of politicians; school years; and life itself.]

Be sure to relate the discussion to composition and point out that a composition also has a definite beginning, middle, and end. Explain that in a composition these are called the introduction, body, and conclusion, which students will learn more about in this chapter.

Introduction

Emphasize that a composition is a type of writing that covers a limited topic in several paragraphs, and usually consists of an introduction, a body, and a conclusion. You may want to write out the **Framework for a Composition** (p. 134) on the chalkboard and leave it there during your presentation of the chapter. That way, students will have a quick reference available at all times for the overall structure and the main points of the chapter.

Integration

This chapter provides students with a strong foundation for writing and reading activities in any course. While the chapter prepares students to write informative essays, the overall composition structure outlined in the chapter can guide them through almost any of the aims and modes in **Chapters 4-11**. A sense of composition structure will also help students write business letters (**Chapter 36: Studying and Test Taking**) and organized answers to essay questions (**Chapter 35: Letters and Forms**). The chapter can also supplement speaking and listening activities by helping students write effective speeches and by teaching them to listen for structure and organization.

The chart on the next page illustrates the strands of language arts as they are integrated into this chapter. For vocabulary study, glossary words are underlined in some writing models.

QUOTATIONS
All **Quotations for the Day** are chosen because of their relevance to instructional material presented in that segment of the chapter and for their usefulness in establishing student interest in writing.

INTEGRATING THE LANGUAGE ARTS

Selection	Reading and Literature	Writing and Critical Thinking	Language and Syntax	Speaking, Listening, and Other Expression Skills
FROM "Quasi-Humans" by R. A. Deckert **110** "A Thirsty California Is Trying Desalination" by Lawrence M. Fisher **113** "What's Your Type? Introverts and Extroverts" by Sandra R. Arbetter **123** "For Young and Old, a Pocket Paradise" by Kathleen Teltsch **123, 132** "Juan's Place" by Charles Mann and Gwenda Blair **124** "Financial Folklore" by John Steele Gordon **125** "Seeds in the bank could stave off disaster on the farm" by Ellen Ruppel Shell **125** "Pioneers Underfoot" by Sherry Baker **126** "3 Scientists Say Travel in Time Isn't So Far Out" by Malcolm W. Browne **127** "At Rye High, Students Not Only Must Do Well, They Must Do Good" by Lisa W. Foderaro **127** "A Yen for Baseball Cards" by Rick Wolff **129** "The Fitness Craze" by Lynn Norment **130-131** "School for Homeless Children: A Rare Experience" by Timothy Egan **131** "Neil Armstrong's Famous First Words" by George Plimpton **131-132**	Responding personally to literature **111, 127** Applying interpretive and creative thinking **111, 127, 133** Finding the main idea **111, 115, 129** Identifying supporting evidence **111, 129** Finding details **115, 127, 129** Analyzing thesis statements **115, 127, 129** Evaluating and making judgments **119, 127, 129, 133** Analyzing tone **127** Analyzing techniques for writing effective introductions **127** Analyzing a paragraph **129** Evaluating a conclusion **133**	Applying interpretive and creative thinking **111, 127, 133, 134, 137** Evaluating a writer's theory **111** Analyzing facts to arrive at a main idea **111, 115, 127, 129** Writing a thesis statement **115-116, 137** Constructing an early plan or an outline **119, 137** Improving a conclusion of a composition **133** Writing a conclusion **133, 134, 137** Writing an informative essay **135-137** Gathering ideas for writing **137** Writing an introduction to capture readers' attention **137** Writing paragraphs that clearly relate to the thesis **137** Writing body paragraphs that have unity and coherence **137** Proofreading and publishing an essay **137**	Using specific, clear, lively language in thesis statements **115** Identifying words that reveal tone **127** Identifying direct references **129** Identifying transitional words and phrases **129** Proofreading for errors in grammar, usage, and mechanics **137**	Working with classmates to develop a thesis statement **115-116** Working with a classmate to prepare an early plan or formal outline **119** Analyzing a paragraph with classmates **129** Working with a classmate to improve a conclusion **133**

SEGMENT PLANNING GUIDE

Whether you are planning for a quick review of a writing concept or preparing an extended lesson on composition, you can use the following Planning Guide to adapt the chapter material to the individual needs of your class.

SEGMENT	PAGES	CONTENT	RESOURCES
1 *Looking at the Whole*	*109–112*		
Literary Model from **"Quasi-Humans"**	110	Guided reading: a model of a composition form	
Reader's Response/ Writer's Craft	111	Model evaluation: responding to literature and analyzing composition form	
What Makes a Composition	112	Explanation: writing for enjoyment and information	
2 *The Thesis Statement*	*113–116*		Focusing on Thesis Statement
The Thesis Statement	113	Introduction: defining a thesis statement	
Hints for Writing	113–114	Guidelines: writing a thesis statement	
Writing Note	114	Writing suggestion: revising a thesis statement	
Exercise 1	115	Applied practice: analyzing thesis statements	
Exercise 2	115–116	Cooperative learning: writing a thesis statement	
3 *Early Plans and Formal Outlines*	*117–121*		Early Plans Formal Outlines
The Early Plan	117	Introduction: making an informal outline	
Grouping	117	Guidelines: using criteria to group details	
Ordering	117–118	Guidelines: learning types of ordering	
The Formal Outline	118	Example: analyzing a topic outline	
Exercise 3	119	Cooperative learning: making an early plan or outline	
Writer's Model	120–121	Guided reading: creating a title for a model composition	
4 *The Introduction*	*122–127*		The Introduction
Catching the Reader's Interest	122	Explanation: getting the reader's attention	
Setting the Tone	122	Explanation: expressing an attitude	
Presenting the Thesis Statement	122	Explanation: summarizing the main idea	
Techniques for Writing Introductions	123–126	Examples: examining introductions in models	
Exercise 4	127	Applied practice: analyzing introductions	

All the resources listed in this chapter are located in the Teacher's ResourceBank™.

	SEGMENT	PAGES	CONTENT	RESOURCES
5	*The Body*	*128-129*		The Body
	Unity	128	Explanation: using details to unify a composition	
	Coherence	128	Explanation: using order and transitions for coherence	
	Direct References	128	Explanation: using direct references to link ideas	
	Transitional Words and Phrases	129	Explanation: using transitional expressions to link ideas	
	Exercise 5	129	Cooperative learning: analyzing a paragraph	
6	*The Conclusion*	*130-134*		The Conclusion
	Techniques for Writing Conclusions	130-132	Guidelines: examining conclusions in models	
	Writing Note	133	Writing suggestion: creating titles	
	Exercise 6	133	Cooperative learning: improving a conclusion	
	Exercise 7	134	Applied practice: writing a conclusion	
	Writing Note	134	Writing suggestion: using appropriate point of view	
	Chart: Framework for a Composition	134	Guidelines: structuring a composition	
7	*Making Connections*	*135-137*		
	Writing an Informative Composition	135-137	Applied practice: writing an informative composition from given facts	
	WHOLE-CHAPTER RESOURCE Chapter Review			

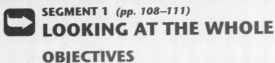

SEGMENT 1 *(pp. 108–111)*
LOOKING AT THE WHOLE

OBJECTIVES

- To respond to a composition
- To identify the thesis statement of a literary model and to analyze discussion that supports it

TEACHING THE LESSON

Ask students if they've heard the old saying, "Truth is stranger than fiction." Then introduce the article on cyborgs by stating that technology frequently and rapidly outdistances fiction. You may want to read the article aloud in class, or you could have students read the article independently. Either way, you will first want to define for students

VISUAL CONNECTIONS
Still Music

About the Artist. Ben Shahn was born in Lithuania in 1898, and his family moved to Brooklyn, New York, when he was eight. At the age of fifteen, Shahn became an apprentice at a lithography shop, where he developed techniques that he used in his later work. Shahn is known mainly for the posters and prints in which he expressed his views on social injustice. Ben Shahn died in 1969.

Exploring the Subject. Ask students to think about the meaning of the title *Still Music* as they look at this painting. Suggest that, although the stage in the picture is set for an orchestra, without the musicians and instruments there will be silence, or stillness. Relate this to writing: a writer may have some of the elements of a composition in place, but if any important part is missing, the composition will be incomplete and thus ineffective.

3 UNDERSTANDING COMPOSITION STRUCTURE

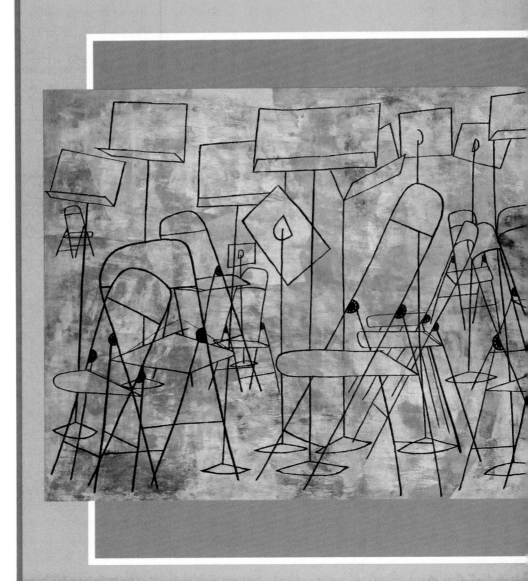

the terms *quasi* [in some degree] and *cyborg* [humans with mechanical enhancements]. The article probably will generate a lot of discussion, so allow adequate class time. The **Reader's Response** questions should help generate discussion.

Following a discussion of the article's subject, direct students' attention to the form of the article. Ask students to identify the article's introduction [first paragraph], body [rest of article until last paragraph], and conclusion [last paragraph]. When they have recognized these main parts of the composition, they should be ready for the **Writer's Craft** questions.

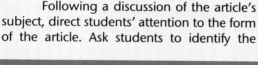

Looking at the Whole

Have you ever overheard just the punch line of a joke? Although everyone else is laughing, it doesn't seem funny to you—you didn't hear the whole joke. That's the way it is with a composition. All of the parts work together to make a **whole** composition.

Writing and You. A movie review in *Rolling Stone* . . . an article in *Life* magazine about space . . . a newspaper story about rising taxes. These are all compositions. If you look at them closely, you'll see that they have a certain form: an introduction, a body, and a conclusion. Besides magazines and newspapers, where else might you find compositions?

As You Read. As you read the following article from *Omni* magazine, notice how the writer uses composition form to tell about cyborgs.

Still Music, Ben Shahn (1948). Casein on fabric. 48" × 83½". Collection of The Phillips Collection, Washington, D.C. © 1993 Estate of Ben Shahn/VAGA, N.Y.

GUIDED PRACTICE

To find out how well students understand the article, ask the questions from **Reader's Response.** To extend the discussion, you could ask, "What other wonders do you think are 'within the range of today's computer chips'? of tomorrow's computer chips?"

INDEPENDENT PRACTICE

After you have discussed how the cyborg article reflects the general characteristics of composition form, have students answer the **Writer's Craft** questions on their own. Remind them to cite specific information from the article when answering the last question.

USING THE SELECTION
Quasi-Humans

1

bionic: having biological performance increased by electronic devices

2

cyborgs: humans with mechanical enhancements

3

Contact lenses have been around since the late 1800s. At first they were made of glass, and later glass and plastic. A big improvement came in 1938, when they were first made with lightweight molded plastic.

4

What does the author mean by "conscious technology"? [Responses will vary, but should suggest technology that can think and perceive.]

5

Isaac Asimov pursued dual careers that give him impressive credentials for such a statement—biochemistry and science fiction writing. He started teaching biochemistry at Boston University in 1955. He is noted for his writings about both science and science fiction.

110

QUASI-HUMANS

by R. A. Deckert

1
2
The Six Million Dollar Man and the Bionic Woman were TV's first cyborgs—part human, part technowizardry. We may soon live in a world populated by these beings, futurist Jerome Glenn believes, because we are evolving into them.

Cyborgs, says Glenn, are the inevitable result of two trends about to merge into one. The first trend—the increasing use of technology to correct physical disabilities—can be seen in the **3** progression from eyeglasses to contact lenses to surgically implanted lenses. The second trend—the tendency for technology to become more humanlike—is continuing to evolve rapidly. The ability to associate ideas as well as the ability to speak and to recognize voices are all within the range of today's computer chips.

Glenn says that the two trends will usher in an age of **4** "conscious technology" in which "robots will get biochips to become more human and humans will become cyborgs" within the first half of the twenty-first century.

By then technology won't be limited to simply correcting disabilities but will increasingly be used to enhance the human body's performance. "Contact lenses with zoom vision, miniature hearing aids to hear selected sounds at greater distances, or miniature transceivers to reach out and touch someone are just some of the ways future cyborgs will go beyond our inherited biology," Glenn says.

While he is confident that he has seen the future that lies ahead for humanity, Glenn acknowledges there is a certain amount of resistance to be overcome. "As **5** [Isaac] Asimov says, 'All new technology is rejected and then accepted.' I don't see any difference with this."

ASSESSMENT

Evaluate students' answers to the **Writer's Craft** questions to assess their understanding.

CLOSURE

Ask the class to define *composition* and identify the three parts [introduction, body, and conclusion]. ■

111

READER'S RESPONSE

1. What do you think of Jerome Glenn's theory? Do any of your own experiences and observations support his theory? Which ones?
2. Do you think it's true that people at first always reject new technology? If so, why?

WRITER'S CRAFT

3. What is the thesis statement—the sentence that tells the main idea—in this article?
4. In the body of the article, the author discusses two trends. What are they? How does this discussion reflect and support the main idea?

LOOKING AHEAD

In this chapter, you'll learn about the parts of a composition. You'll learn that

- most compositions have an introduction that attracts the reader's attention, sets the tone, and gives the thesis statement
- each body paragraph is unified and clearly connected to the surrounding paragraphs
- most compositions have a conclusion that reinforces the main idea and brings the composition to a definite close

ANSWERS

Reader's Response

1. Answers will vary. Students should support their responses with specific personal experiences and observations.
2. Answers will vary. If students answer "yes," their explanations will probably include that people are often afraid of new things. It is human nature to resist change.

Writer's Craft

3. The thesis statement is, "We may soon live in a world populated by these beings [cyborgs], futurist Jerome Glenn believes, because we are evolving into them."
4. The two trends are "the increasing use of technology to correct physical disabilities," and "the tendency for technology to become more humanlike." The discussion of these trends reflects and supports the main idea by giving concrete examples of how humans are evolving into cyborgs.

What Makes a Composition

Not only do you read compositions for information and enjoyment—you also write them yourself for the same purposes. For instance, in school you write compositions, also called *essays*, both for assigned papers and for tests. And you'll also write compositions when you apply for college admission and scholarships and for jobs. Many colleges and businesses often ask applicants to write compositions about themselves, their interests, and their goals.

In other chapters, you'll learn how to use the composition form when writing persuasive essays and research papers, when writing about literature, or when explaining a process. In this chapter you'll concentrate on the basic principles of composition form.

"Provoke the reader.

Astonish the reader.

Writing that has no surprises is as bland as oatmeal."

Anne Bernays

THE THESIS STATEMENT

OBJECTIVES

- To analyze the purpose and characteristics of a good thesis statement
- To write thesis statements that fit particular limited topics and lists of details

TEACHING THE LESSON

Begin the lesson by drawing a clear comparison between the topic sentence of a paragraph and the thesis statement of a composition. Be sure that students understand that a thesis statement may be one or two sentences. You could use the overhead projector to display some good examples of ☞

The Thesis Statement

A *thesis statement* gives the composition's main, or unifying, idea about a topic. It's a sentence or two in the introduction that "tells your readers what you're going to tell them." It announces your limited topic and your main idea about it, just as a topic sentence does in a paragraph.

Some thesis statements simply identify the limited topic, for example: "Californians are facing a water shortage resulting from several years of drought."

But most thesis statements, including the ones you'll be asked to write, do more. They identify a main idea the writer is actually trying to prove to the reader. Here's an example of this kind of thesis statement.

> Facing a possible fifth year of sustained drought, communities along the California coast are looking to desalinated ocean or bay water as a way to quench their thirst and water their lawns.
>
> Lawrence M. Fisher, "A Thirsty California Is Trying Desalination"

Hints for Writing and Using a Thesis Statement

1. **Develop your thesis statement from information you've gathered.** Review your prewriting material—the ton of facts and details you've gathered. Ask yourself: *What main, or unifying, idea do the facts and details suggest?*
2. **Include both a limited topic and your main idea about it.** Most thesis statements answer these two questions: *What's my topic? What am I saying about my topic?* To make sure you've included both parts, underline the limited topic and circle the main idea.

    For example, notice this thesis statement: "If you're interested in bicycle touring, you need to make some specific preparations involving your bike, yourself, your clothing, and your route." It's clear that this writer is going to discuss bicycle touring (topic) and specific preparations for your bike, yourself, your clothing, and your route (main idea).

QUOTATION FOR THE DAY

"The art of writing has for backbone some fierce attachment to an idea." (Virginia Woolf, 1882–1941, British novelist)

Write this quotation on the chalkboard, and explain that effective compositions require writers to present a strong main idea or thesis statement. You may wish to give students a few minutes to think of ideas, opinions, or beliefs to which they are fiercely attached. The resulting lists can supply thesis statements for future writings.

SELECTION AMENDMENT
Description of change: excerpted
Rationale: to focus on the concept of the thesis statement presented in this chapter

topic sentences in paragraphs and thesis statements in compositions.

It also may be helpful to discuss the word *thesis* to help students understand what a thesis statement is supposed to do. Tell them that a thesis is a position or proposition that the writer is putting forth for discussion. Tell them that the statement of that position (the thesis statement) should be clear and concise, but should also adequately cover the topic.

After students have read **Hints for Writing and Using a Thesis Statement,** you may want to discuss the hints. Consider each hint individually to be sure students understand them.

Use **Exercise 1** for guided practice by reading each thesis statement aloud and

LEP/ESL

General Strategies. Students are often told that thesis statements serve the purpose of capturing the reader's attention. However, those things that grab a reader's attention are often culturally specific. Students from other cultures might have problems developing thesis statements that the average U.S. reader would consider attention-getting.

If you work with students on improving their thesis statements, be aware that the cultural values that may make a thesis statement interesting for U.S. readers could be at odds with the cultural values of other students. Encourage students to explore and discuss any cultural difference that creates conflict. Remind students that any technique you introduce to them is suggested only to improve their writing and not to alter their cultural identity.

LEARNING STYLES

Visual Learners. As you go over the **Hints for Writing and Using a Thesis Statement** section with students, write the key words for each of the five hints on the chalkboard. Provide some examples of gathered information, limited topics, and clear and specific thesis statements.

3. **Be clear and specific.** Keep your language and ideas sharp and definite. Compare this vague and fuzzy thesis statement with the actual one you've just read: "So if you're interested in bicycle touring, you need to do some things before you leave."

4. **Keep your thesis statement in front of you as you plan and write.** It will help keep you on track. Every idea and detail should directly support your thesis statement, so be tough and get rid of any that don't.

WRITING NOTE

Your preliminary thesis statement, the one you develop before you actually write your composition, is probably direct and straightforward. You may even think it's a little dull. Later on, you can revise it to give it more punch and zing, as professional writers do. Here's an example of how one writer revised a thesis statement.

PRELIMINARY   The opening day of the baseball season marks the beginning of a long, dramatic conflict for the pennant for both individual players and teams.

REVISED   "Play ball!" For baseball fans everywhere, the umpire's opening-day cry begins another season of high drama for individual players and teams.

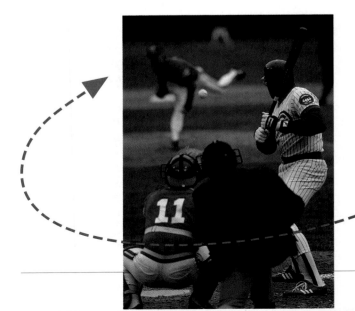

asking students to identify the topic and main idea of each statement. You can also have students rewrite the statements to illustrate that there is more than one way a thesis statement can be written.

Let students work independently with partners or in small groups for **Exercise 2.** Give students adequate class time to think about the limited topics and the details.

Then ask them to come up with their own thesis statements. You could have students read their thesis statements aloud and let them decide which ones are the best and why.

EXERCISE 1 ▶ Analyzing Thesis Statements

Do these thesis statements meet the two-part test? Does each one have a topic and a main idea? Identify the limited topic and the writer's main idea in each one.

EXAMPLE **1.** Hundreds of highly trained and motivated disabled athletes compete each year in the Paralympics, the World Championships, and Games for the Disabled.

 1. *Limited topic: athletes who have disabilities*
 Main idea: compete in the Paralympics, the World Championships, and Games for the Disabled

1. "No more helium-filled balloons!" Environmentalists and animal rights groups are boycotting balloons because they are concerned about wild animals that die from eating balloons.
2. If you call 911 in Darien, Connecticut, your ambulance crew will include at least one teenager, trained as a skilled volunteer emergency medical technician.
3. Mount McKinley is Denali, and Greenland has become Kalaallitt Nunaat. Dozens of geographical features and countries have had their names changed during the past decade.
4. The holiday of Kwanzaa, beginning on December 26 and lasting for seven days, is a celebration of African American history, culture, and values.
5. According to surveys of students, cheating is common in high school and college. Here are three suggested strategies for stopping widespread cheating.

EXERCISE 2 ▶ Writing a Thesis Statement

Work with a partner or small group to develop a thesis statement for each of the sets of prewriting details on the next page. Make your thesis statement interesting, specific, clear, and lively. Also check to see that your thesis statement meets the two-part test of stating both the topic and a main idea. Your group may want to compare these thesis statements with the ones other groups write.

ANSWERS
Exercise 1

1. Limited topic: environmentalists and animal rights groups
Main idea: are boycotting helium filled balloons

2. Limited topic: ambulance crews in Darien, Conn.
Main idea: include one highly trained teenager

3. Limited topic: geographical features and countries
Main idea: have had their names changed

4. Limited topic: the holiday of Kwanzaa
Main idea: is a seven-day celebration of African American history, culture, and values

5. Limited topic: strategies for stopping academic cheating
Main idea: there are three

ANSWERS
Exercise 2

Statements will vary but should be similar to the following examples:

1. Regulating public school clothing by banning certain items and possibly requiring uniforms might create an environment more supportive of learning.

2. The world's declining whale population is a result of whales being severely overhunted by nations who kill whales for money or scientific research.

Use the answers to **Exercise 2** as your assessment of students' understanding. You also could ask students these questions:

1. What two questions do most thesis statements answer? [What's the topic? What is being said about the topic?]
2. A thesis statement should always be what and what? [clear and specific]

CLOSURE

Ask students to define *thesis statement* and explain the criteria for good thesis statements. You could ask them to tell you their favorite thesis statements in the examples they've studied. ■

TIMESAVER

Depending upon how much practice you think students need, you could have each group work on only one of the two sets of prewriting details in **Exercise 2**.

CRITICAL THINKING
Synthesis

Writing a thesis statement requires students to synthesize their understanding of the topics in one or two concisely worded sentences. As you present this section, explain that a thesis statement serves both writer and audience by focusing attention on the composition's key aspects. Stress that a thesis statement can be explicitly or implicitly included in a composition's introductory paragraph.

116   *Understanding Composition Structure*

1. Limited topic: regulating public school clothing
   Ideas and details
   - goal—create an environment supportive of learning
     uniforms as option in public schools
     students and parents in favor
     ties for boys on Fridays
     sense of unity from wearing uniforms
   - banned items
     T-shirts
     cut-off or torn jeans
     shorts
     expensive jewelry

2. Limited topic: world's declining whale population
   Ideas and details
   - whales severely overhunted
   - 1930s estimated 500,000 fin whales living off Antarctica; 1989 estimated 2,000 blue, right, humpback, bowhead (kinds of whales) nearly extinct because of slaughter during last century
   - International Whaling Commission supposed to manage whaling, but whaling nations resist controls
   - Members of Greenpeace organization fight whaling—say that continued whaling threatens existence of whale
   - Iceland and Norway make money by selling whale meat to Japan
   - nations allowed to kill whales for scientific research

EARLY PLANS AND FORMAL OUTLINES

OBJECTIVE

- To prepare a formal outline from notes for a composition

TEACHING THE LESSON

Tell students that they should be aware of the procedures and forms for preparing both early plans—you may prefer to call them rough or informal outlines—and formal outlines. In presenting this section, follow the development of the composition on bicycle touring from grouping to formal outline to composition.

Early Plans and Formal Outlines

Some people are naturally neat and tidy—but most aren't. Here's your chance to clean house. Throw out every bit of information that doesn't directly support your thesis statement, and pull together every bit that does. *Early plans* and *formal outlines* help you do this.

The Early Plan

An *early plan* is also called a rough, or informal, outline. It looks like a set of orderly notes, with each group of details arranged under a heading. The first step in making an early plan is to group your ideas and information; the next step is to order, or arrange, them.

Grouping.   Use these three questions to sort and group information: *Which details belong together? What do they have in common? Which details don't fit in any group?* (Discard these details.) Also think of a heading—a word or phrase—that identifies what the details have in common. For example, here's how one writer grouped and labeled information for a composition on bicycle touring.

> *bicycle helmet, water bottle, tire repair kit—SAFETY ITEMS*
>
> *mountain bike, sport/touring bike, racing bike—TYPES OF BICYCLES*

Ordering.   You have two kinds of ordering to think about: (1) order of details within each group; (2) order of groups within the composition. In both cases, arrange your information in a way that will make sense to your readers.

Sometimes your topic suggests an order. For example, if you're explaining a step-by-step process, such as how to change an automobile's flat tire, you'd use *chronological (time) order*. You'd use *spatial order* to describe the layout of your school. You may use *classification* to describe three types of school athletes, or *order of importance* (from most important reason to least important, or vice versa) to persuade eighteen-year-olds to register to vote.

QUOTATION FOR THE DAY

"If you are a writer you locate yourself behind a wall of silence and no matter what you are doing, driving a car or walking or doing housework . . . you can still be writing, because you have that space." (Joyce Carol Oates, 1938–   , American author)

Ask students to freewrite for a few minutes about one of their favorite sports or competitive activities. Have a volunteer read his or her writing aloud. Ask the class to imagine what might happen if the student never thought about the activity until the day of the competition. Explain that successful writing also demands thinking ahead, planning strategies, and practicing.

Emphasize that all students should make rough outlines before they start writing because it's necessary to group information and to decide in what order to put it. Be sure that they understand the chapter discussions of grouping and ordering, and especially the discussion of different types of order.

Tell students that there are occasions (and assignments) when formal outlines are required, but that not all writers will make formal outlines before they start writing. Explain that some writers feel their information is sufficiently organized with a rough outline, and they work directly from that, while other writers feel they need formal outlines to help them organize and visualize their information. **Exercise 3** presents the kind of unorganized notes from which many

MEETING
INDIVIDUAL
NEEDS

LEP/ESL

Asian Cultures. Some students might have problems with formal outlines and tightly structured compositions because in their native cultures it is considered proper to develop discourse through digression—a technique that involves circling the main idea rather than being direct. The formality of compositional structure as taught in English classes is thought of as being almost disrespectful to the reader.

To help students with English composition structure, remind them that audience is an important aspect of writing and that an English-speaking audience will not be insulted by a direct treatment of the topic. However, readers can become confused by digressions in a discourse.

You may want to let students forgo a formal outline and use some other prewriting method of organization. Then, when students have written their first drafts, you can go over them with the students and help them recognize and edit any digressions that pull focus away from the topic.

But sometimes none of these orders apply. Then you just have to figure out an arrangement that will let your reader follow your ideas easily. "First things first" is a good rule for organizing information. For instance, if you're writing about unrest in the former Soviet republics, you'll first need to give a paragraph of background information about what led up to the problems.

 REFERENCE NOTE: For more on arranging ideas, see pages 82–85.

The Formal Outline

A *formal outline* has a format that shows the order and relationship of ideas, using letters and numbers to label headings. A *sentence outline* uses complete sentences for all main headings and subheadings, while a *topic outline* uses single words or phrases.

REFERENCE NOTE: For more information on formal outlines, see pages 424–425.

Here's the first part of a topic outline for the composition on pages 120–121. Notice that the outline lists the ideas in the paper's second and third paragraphs.

Title: Bicycle Touring
Thesis statement: If you're interested in bicycle touring, you need to make some specific preparations involving your bike, yourself, your clothing, and your route.

   I. Your bike
      A. Type of bike
      B. Condition of bike
      C. Equipment
         1. Map
         2. Light
         3. Kits
            a. Bicycle repair kit
            b. First-aid kit
         4. Saddlebags
         5. Water container
  II. Your physical condition
      A. Exercise program
         1. Muscles
         2. Endurance
      B. Goal: 10–15 miles

EXERCISE 3 ▶ **Making an Early Plan or an Outline**

Here are some notes for a composition about how to avoid getting hit by lightning. Work with a partner to organize this jumble of notes into an early plan or a formal outline for a composition. [Hint: The advice on what to do is different if you're indoors or outdoors.]

Surviving Lightning Storms
swimmers--get out of water immediately
in a small boat--get to shore
if you're inside, don't use telephone
before storm hits, unplug electric appliances
if outdoors, find shelter in a building, cave,
    canyon, thick growth of low trees
stay away from isolated trees, metal fences
if no shelter outdoors, keep low--away from high
    places, tall trees
if you're in car, stay there--a safe shelter
indoors, stay away from metal pipes, appliances,
    open doors, and windows
don't shower or take bath during electrical storm
number of deaths each year from lightning
people hit by lightning more frequently in summer
    and fall

belong together and what those details have in common. Then check to see that students understand the order of details within each group and the order of groups within the composition.

INDEPENDENT PRACTICE

Direct the students to use their early plans to prepare formal outlines for the topic in **Exercise 3.** Give students directions on whether to use a sentence outline or a topic outline.

COOPERATIVE LEARNING

Divide the class into four groups for practice in ordering information. Assign each group one of the four kinds of order (chronological, spatial, classification, order of importance). Then instruct each group to develop three different sets of details that would logically be arranged by the group's assigned type of order. Tell them that each set of details should consist of at least three items. To begin, students should look at the examples given in the chapter. Have the groups turn in their completed sets, and choose some to read to the class. Ask class members other than the ones in the group that originated the set to guess what kind of order is intended.

A WRITER'S MODEL

Following is the final draft of a composition based on the outline on page 118. As you read, try to think about a good title for the composition. (See the Writing Note on page 133.)

INTRODUCTION

Automobiles speed along highways about fifty-five miles an hour. Bullet trains rocket down their tracks at nearly two hundred miles an hour. And if that's not fast enough for you, the Concorde jet carries passengers faster than the speed of sound! Yet more and more people are choosing to take day trips, overnights, or extended tours the slow way--by bicycle. But don't pedal away yet. If you're interested in bicycle touring, you'll need to make some specific preparations involving your bike, yourself, your clothing, and your route.

Thesis statement

**BODY
Main topic:
Your bike**

The first thing to consider is your bicycle. With so many types to choose from--road bikes, off-road bikes, mountain bikes, and all-terrain bikes--you can pick one that's appropriate for the kind of terrain you'll be traveling on. Whichever bike you choose, it should be in excellent condition. Equip it with a map, a light, a bicycle-repair kit, a first-aid kit, saddlebags for food and clothing, and a water carrier.

**Main topic:
Your physical condition**

Your bike may be in good shape, but what about you? Whether your trip is a few miles to the next town or across country, you need to get yourself in good physical condition. Start an exercise program and build up your muscles and endurance gradually. You should be able to easily cycle ten to fifteen miles a day.

**Main topic:
Your clothing**

Now think about clothing. What you pack will depend on the season, but always prepare for possible bad weather. Pack rain gear and clothing that allows freedom of movement as it protects you from strong winds, wet, and cold. In general, avoid clothing that might interfere with

ASSESSMENT

Assess students' mastery of rough outlines and formal outlines through an evaluation of their performance on **Exercise 3**.

CLOSURE

Ask students to explain the differences between an early plan and a formal outline. ■

121

your mobility or comfort, and be sure to wear a helmet. Head injuries are a cyclist's biggest worry.

Main topic: Choosing your route

Finally, talk to experienced cyclists and read books and magazines to plan your route. You may want to join the American Youth Hostels (AYH), which offers its members inexpensive lodging and group rides. Bicycling magazine appears each month with information and special features about bicycle touring. And an organization called Bike-centennial publishes guidebooks, maps of the U.S. National Bicycle Trails Network, and a list of bicycle tour operators.

CONCLUSION

If you plan your trip well, you'll discover that bicycle touring--alone or with a group--is more fun than faster ways of travel. Before you go, give yourself enough time to get your bike, your body, your clothing, and your route in top condition. Careful advance planning practically guarantees a safe trip.

THE INTRODUCTION

OBJECTIVE

- To analyze the introductions of professional writers

TEACHING THE LESSON

You may want to stress that two important reasons for learning how to write effective introductions are to encourage readers to read what you've written and to tell the reader what you're writing about.

Ask students why the first reason is important. Lead a discussion about the many

---

Teacher's ResourceBank™

RESOURCES

THE INTRODUCTION
- The Introduction

QUOTATION FOR THE DAY

"Any writer overwhelmingly honest about pleasing himself is almost sure to please others." (Marianne Moore, 1887–1972, American poet)

Have students talk in small groups about how Moore's quotation relates to writing. You may wish to have volunteers share the results of their groups' discussions. Lead students to understand that what is entertaining to the writer is most often interesting to the reader; by composing an interesting introduction, the writer grabs the reader's attention and creates interest in the entire composition.

The Introduction

If you didn't have to, would you read a composition that begins like this: "In this composition I plan to tell you about some of the things I've learned about how scientists are studying human genes"? You probably wouldn't want to read it. It sounds too dull. An effective introduction will catch the reader's interest, set the tone of the composition, and present the thesis statement.

Catching the Reader's Interest. The introduction may be the most important paragraph in your composition. If the introduction isn't well written, your reader might not bother reading the rest of your paper. On pages 123–126 you'll find six strategies for grabbing the reader's attention.

Setting the Tone. As you introduce your topic, the words you choose and what you say set the composition's tone, the feeling you reveal about your topic. The tone of a composition may be serious, humorous, formal, informal, critical—even outraged.

For example, what can you tell about the writer's attitude from the two-sentence introduction to "Quasi-Humans" (page 110)? Its tone is definitely serious; there's nothing to indicate that this is a humorous piece. But it's also informal because a scholarly, technical discussion wouldn't refer to television shows or use the term *technowizardry*.

Presenting the Thesis Statement. You can be as clever as you want in order to catch the reader's interest, but somewhere you need to include a thesis statement that clearly summarizes the composition's main idea. Often, but not always, the thesis statement comes at the end of the introduction.

demands—including activities and reading selections—that compete for a reader's time. Introductions help readers make up their minds whether they want to take the time to read what you have written.

Be sure that students understand the three requirements of an effective introduction. They've studied the third requirement (the thesis statement) and are about to study the first (catching the reader's interest), so you may want to take a few extra minutes at this point to discuss tone. Define *tone* as an aspect of writing that shows a certain attitude on the part of the writer. Tell students that a writer's choice of words and details influences the tone of his or her writing. You may want to ask students why it's important to establish tone in the introduction. [The ☞

Techniques for Writing Introductions

Following are six techniques for writing effective introductions. You can also try combining techniques.

1. **Begin with a question.** Some introductions begin with a question that contradicts the thesis. Others use a rhetorical question, one with no answer expected. But any question that applies to the reader can be intriguing, as in this long introduction.

> If you could design your own personality, would you rather be lively, outgoing, and the center of attention, or quiet, thoughtful, and private?
>
> It would not be surprising if you opted for the first description. You would have lots of company. According to some estimates, there are three times as many lively extroverts in the United States as reflective introverts. Our society prefers fun-loving, friendly people with "good personalities" over quiet, private types.
>
> Is one style really better than the other? Do we have a choice?
>
> Sandra R. Arbetter, "What's Your Type? Introverts and Extroverts"

2. **Begin with an anecdote or example.** An anecdote is a little story, or incident, that may be humorous or just intriguing. This introduction begins with an example.

> The rhubarb is ready for picking in Julie Kirkpatrick's garden patch on East Fourth Street and Avenue C, and Francisco Ortiz is giving away snippets of sage and tarragon. This is El Jardin del Paraiso, a lofty name for a community garden that grows upon the rubble of long-gone tenements on the Lower East Side. The fenced space where tulips and fruit trees bloom had been a dump for garbage and old bedsprings. The neighborhood is dotted with boarded-up buildings.
>
> Kathleen Teltsch, "For Young and Old, a Pocket Paradise"

MEETING INDIVIDUAL NEEDS

LEP/ESL

General Strategies. Establishing tone might be difficult for some students because it involves a precise use of vocabulary. To help students learn to develop and control tone in their writing, introduce them to a thesaurus and refer them to the section in **Chapter 33: "The Dictionary"** that covers synonyms. A discussion of denotation and connotation might also prove helpful.

LESS-ADVANCED STUDENTS

You may want to help distinguish the attention-getting technique in an introduction from the thesis statement. Remind students that the thesis statement should be a clear statement of the main idea about the topic. You may want to have students identify the thesis statement in each of the models. You also could give them additional models. Some students might have trouble recognizing thesis statements when they are part of general introductions.

SELECTION AMENDMENT
Description of change: excerpted
Rationale: to focus on the concept of introductions presented in this chapter

tone gives the reader a clearer understanding of the purpose and meaning of the work.]

Next, adapt your coverage of the techniques for writing introductions to your students' interests. They might want to discuss some of the techniques and examples more thoroughly than others. You may want to present other models at various stages of your presentation. You should help students realize the importance of introductions, but you should also help them see that deciding upon effective introductions for their writings can be fun and challenging.

Use **Exercise 4** to give students the opportunity to analyze two introductions. You may want to have students bring in more examples of introductions for additional practice.

A DIFFERENT APPROACH

Give students copies of the following introductions about the growth of deserts:

1. A family gave up farming because the desert covered the garden.
2. "The sand is driving me away."
3. Deserts expand or shrink as the climate changes.
4. Did you know that some deserts are still growing?
5. Thousands of people have died and many more will die because of expanding deserts.
6. The growth of some deserts is having horrible effects on people and animals.
7. The sun was beating down on my head and the desert sand was inching its way toward my chair.

Have students identify which of the seven techniques for writing introductions is used for each one [**1.** example; **2.** quotation; **3.** background; **4.** question; **5.** startling fact; **6.** thesis statement; **7.** set scene].

3. **State a startling fact or an unusual opinion.** The article "Quasi-Humans" (page 110) uses this technique. Here's another example of an introduction designed to arouse the reader's curiosity.

> Juan de la Cruz Briceño may be the only man on earth to have an ancient Mayan city under construction in his backyard. Six days a week, a large open truck rumbles through the dawn fog behind Juan's home, scattering a flock of outraged chickens and disgorging a score of men. Behind them rise the ruins of Becan, a cluster of pyramids ringed by a destroyed canal, magnificent in their lonely desolation. The men from the truck quickly overrun the structures, swarming over rickety wooden scaffolding, working with stone and sweat to bring back the glories of this long vanished civilization. . . .
>
> Charles Mann and Gwenda Blair, "Juan's Place"

SELECTION AMENDMENT
Description of change: excerpted
Rationale: to focus on the concept of introductions presented in this chapter

4. **Begin with background information.** Facts and other specific details not only help your reader understand your main idea but may also create interest in your topic.

> Arising spontaneously from the people, folktales are little windows into the collective human psyche. Most people think of them as stories concerning the long ago and the faraway. In fact, all times and places have produced them, and modern times are no exception. Instead of dealing with dragons, wolves, and other menaces to the medieval world order, however, present-day folktales often revolve around modern technology and the attempts of human beings to come to terms with it.
>
> John Steele Gordon, "Financial Folklore"

5. **Set the scene.** Just as a short story may begin with a description of the setting (when and where the events take place), you might describe the setting of your topic. This introduction entices the reader with a vivid description of place that has little to do with the topic—storing seeds.

> It's barely 7 o'clock on a brisk spring morning, but the campus of Colorado State University in Fort Collins is already bustling with activity. On the track, joggers trot, runners sprint, while couples stroll and skateboarders glide nearby. Casting a feeble shadow over these proceedings is an undistinguished structure of tan-colored concrete and sandstone. This is the U.S. Department of Agriculture's National Seed Storage Laboratory (NSSL)—Fort Knox to our agricultural heritage. There are no bars on the windows, no security guards at the door, yet the billions of seeds stored here are beyond price—they are said to be our last line of defense against agricultural bankruptcy.
>
> Ellen Ruppel Shell, "Seeds in the bank could stave off disaster on the farm"

SELECTION AMENDMENT
Description of change: excerpted
Rationale: to focus on the concept of introductions presented in this chapter

Emphasize that the techniques for writing introductions are based on proven ways of getting readers' attention. Present them in their simplest forms: question, little story or example, fact or opinion, quotation, background, description, and thesis.

You could have each student write short examples of each of the techniques

Understanding Composition Structure

CRITICAL THINKING
Analysis

Tell students that sometimes writers don't directly state a thesis but imply or suggest one. Readers then have to use inference—a logical or reasonable conclusion based on known facts—to construct a formal thesis statement.

Refer students to the techniques used in models 3, 4, and 6, all of which have implied thesis statements. Ask students to write or state the main idea of each model in their own words.
[Statements will vary.

3. Workers are busily reconstructing the remains of an ancient Mayan city in a man's backyard.

4. The president of Little Big Horn College isn't interested in money or prestige, but in doing all she can to help the college.

6. The U.S. Department of Agriculture's National Seed Storage Laboratory is vital to our nation's future.]

SELECTION AMENDMENT
Description of change: excerpted
Rationale: to focus on the concept of introductions presented in this chapter

6. Begin with a simple statement of your thesis. You don't always have to be clever. You can be direct and straightforward and get right to your main ideas.

Chinatown is as much a San Francisco landmark as the Golden Gate Bridge. Little is known, however, about the people who originally settled that part of the city. Now Berkeley, California, archaeologist Allen Pastron thinks his recent discovery of one of Chinatown's original buildings reveals how the unsung Chinese pioneers lived.

Sherry Baker, "Pioneers Underfoot"

WRITING NOTE Professional writers often write two- or even three-paragraph introductions. But since you're writing a brief composition, limit your introduction to a single paragraph. A long-winded introduction—even if it's funny or fascinating—can get you way off track.

presented in the chapter. Tell them to concentrate only on the techniques at this point. Have them label the technique they are using for each example.

CLOSURE

Ask students to name the three requirements for an effective introduction [catches the reader's interest, sets the tone, presents the thesis], and ask them to list the seven techniques for writing effective introductions [question, anecdote or example, startling fact or opinion, quotation, background, scene, thesis]. ■

E X E R C I S E 4 ▶ **Analyzing Introductions**

Sharpen your skills by analyzing the introductions of professional writers. Read the two introductions below and answer the following questions about each one.

- What technique does the writer use in the introduction? (Look back over the techniques on pages 123–126.)
- How well do you think the technique works? (Would you read the article?)
- How would you describe the tone—the writer's attitude toward the topic? What words and details in the introduction reveal the tone?

1.   Could some advanced civilization devise a tunnel that would open shortcuts through space between distant regions of the universe or through time into the past?
      The traditional reaction of most scientists to such notions is to dismiss them as naïve science fiction. But three theoretical astrophysicists have published a suggestion that the laws of physics might not prohibit such "wormhole" travel through space and time.
      Malcolm W. Browne, "3 Scientists Say Travel in Time Isn't So Far Out"

2.   At Rye High School, only do-gooders get diplomas. And virtually everyone is a do-gooder. To graduate, students are required to perform 60 hours of community service over their four years.
      Lisa W. Foderaro, "At Rye High, Students Not Only Must Do Well, They Must Do Good"

ANSWERS

Exercise 4

First Introduction

1. The writer begins with a question.

2. Answers will vary, but most students should agree that the questions pique the reader's interest.

3. Answers may vary. The writer seems to favor the theoretical astrophysicists' view over that of other scientists. The tone could be described as formal. Words that reveal tone are *traditional*, *dismiss*, and *naïve*.

Second Introduction

1. The writer begins with what might be considered a startling fact.

2. Answers will vary. Students will probably agree that the technique is effective.

3. Answers may vary, but the tone seems to be positive. The term *do-gooder* helps reveal the tone.

SELECTION AMENDMENT
Description of change: excerpted
Rationale: to focus on the concept of introductions presented in this chapter

THE BODY

OBJECTIVE

- To analyze the unity and coherence of a paragraph by identifying the main idea, supporting details, direct references, and transitional words and phrases

TEACHING THE LESSON

Give students confidence about this stage of writing by helping them to understand and use unity and coherence. Help them see that everything in a composition relating to the main idea gives the composition unity. Explain that coherence is simply having related ideas logically arranged and clearly connected.

Teacher's ResourceBank™
RESOURCES

THE BODY
- The Body

QUOTATION FOR THE DAY

"Writing is the toughest thing I've ever done." (Richard Milhous Nixon, 1913–   , 37th president of the U.S.)

You may wish to write the quotation on the chalkboard and explain to students that many professional writers agree that writing is a difficult process. In their journals, students might write entries in which they describe their attitudes about writing by using the prompt "Writing is . . . ."

The Body

Your composition would read like a telegram if you simply stated your main ideas. And who would believe you? An effective composition consists mostly of a *body* of paragraphs. Each paragraph supports or proves a main point by developing it with supporting details.

 REFERENCE NOTE: See pages 93–101 for information on strategies of paragraph development.

Unity

It's a strain to try to follow someone whose thoughts leap illogically from topic to topic. When a composition has *unity,* the separate paragraphs work smoothly together to support a single main idea—your thesis. Drop all details and statements that detract from this sense of "oneness."

Coherence

Coherence means that ideas are woven together so they're strongly connected. In a coherent composition, the ideas are easy to follow and the writing seems to flow smoothly from beginning to end. The reader doesn't have to agonize over what something means; nothing sounds awkward or disjointed. You can make your composition coherent by arranging ideas in an order that makes sense and by using words and phrases—either direct references or transitional words and phrases—that show how ideas are connected.

Direct References.   One way to connect ideas is to make direct references to something you've already mentioned. Here are three ways to use direct references.

1. Use pronouns to refer to nouns or ideas. For example, by using *she, they,* or *this,* you can avoid awkwardly repeating nouns.
2. Repeat key words or phrases. Tie paragraphs together by reminding the reader of what's important. In "Quasi-Humans," page 110, for example, the key words *cyborgs, technology,* and *human* appear in almost every paragraph.
3. Use synonyms or slight rewordings of previous ideas and key words. Too much repetition sounds awkward.

For guided practice, review the body of **"Quasi-Humans"** with the class and discuss how the author achieves unity and coherence between paragraphs.

Assign **Exercise 5** as independent practice. Use students' responses to **Exercise 5** to determine how well they understand unity and coherence in a paragraph.

CLOSURE

Ask students to name three ways to use direct references [pronouns, repetition of key words and phrases, and synonyms or rewordings] and to tell what results from the proper use of references and transitions [unity and coherence]. ■

The Body **129**

Transitional Words and Phrases. *For example, therefore, of course, on the other hand*—these words and phrases connect ideas and make relationships clear.

 REFERENCE NOTE: See pages 89–90 for more about using direct references and transitional words and phrases.

EXERCISE 5 ▶ **Analyzing a Paragraph**

Do professional writers follow the rules? Here's a paragraph from *Sports Illustrated* magazine. With two or three classmates, look for direct references and transitional words and phrases. Find the key word(s) and pronouns, and explain what words or ideas the pronouns refer to. What's the main idea? Does every detail support it?

Japanese baseball cards were introduced in the '30s and '40s on a limited basis, and like the original U.S. cards, they continue to be used as a come-on for other products. For example, the country's leading card-maker, Calbee, attaches individually wrapped baseball cards to bags of potato chips. Because the card is on the outside of the package, someone could easily remove it without shelling out the 40 yen (31 cents) for the potato chips. "But that's not a problem in Japan," says Fuhrmann. "Kids just don't do that kind of thing."

Rick Wolff, "A Yen for Baseball Cards"

MEETING INDIVIDUAL NEEDS

STUDENTS WITH SPECIAL NEEDS

Learning and emotionally disabled students might feel overwhelmed by the prospect of writing a composition. In order to overcome their doubts, give students a great deal of positive reinforcement at this time. If students feel confident about their ability to complete the exercises in this chapter, they will feel more confident about their ability to write a composition. Each constructive criticism should be accompanied by much praise for those things students have done well. Praise even such things as completion of an exercise or neat handwriting.

ANSWERS
Exercise 5

The paragraph's main idea is that baseball cards are used to entice people to buy other products. The details provided seem to support this idea. Pronouns *they* and *it* both refer to Japanese baseball cards. Direct references are *cardmaker, country's,* and *baseball cards.*

SELECTION AMENDMENT
Description of change: excerpted
Rationale: to focus on the concept of the body of a composition presented in this chapter

THE CONCLUSION

OBJECTIVES

- To improve a poorly written conclusion
- To write an effective conclusion

MOTIVATION

Ask students if they know people who have a habit of not finishing their sentences or their work. Does such incompleteness bother them or others around them? Why? Most people appreciate a sense of completeness. Explain that a composition without a strong conclusion can produce an unsettling, unfinished feeling.

QUOTATION FOR THE DAY

"I always know the ending; that's where I start." (Tony Morrison, 1931– , American author)

You may wish to have several volunteers restate Morrison's quotation in their own words. Students might then answer the question, "What does Morrison's statement imply about the importance of endings?" Lead the class to understand that effective conclusions are essential to well-written compositions.

The Conclusion

Imagine seeing a movie that stops just before the ending or reading a novel with the last few pages missing. The conclusion of your composition is just as important as the introduction. A composition that lacks a strong conclusion leaves the reader feeling puzzled.

Techniques for Writing Conclusions

1. **Restate your main idea.** Say it again, but use different words. This is probably the easiest kind of conclusion to write. When you use this technique, it works well to put the thesis statement at the beginning of the last paragraph. (See the bicycle composition, pages 120–121.)
2. **Summarize the main points you've developed in the body.** Use different wording to sum up your main points. This type of conclusion emphasizes and reinforces your main points.

Some people start exercising to look good, but once they get into a fitness program they keep it up because they feel good. Regardless of the motivation, it is most important to embark upon a fitness program and stick with it. Schedule your workouts as you would any other important activity, for if exercise sessions aren't planned they usually don't happen. Many people find they are more successful with morning work-

The six techniques for writing conclusions are all that comprise this segment, so you'll want to cover them thoroughly. Because examples are not provided for each technique, you may want to give some of your own, or have the students write some for practice. Make sure students understand how each technique differs from the others.

You may want to use **Exercise 6** as a vehicle for guiding the students through the six techniques for writing conclusions. After the student pairs have had a chance to discuss the conclusion, lead them in a rewriting exercise to turn that conclusion into an example of each of the six techniques.

The Conclusion **131**

outs because, as the day progresses, other priorities often take priority over fitness. Discover your own limits and desires, and, most importantly, have fun. Exercise for the pleasure of it; before long, you'll be hooked on fitness.

Lynn Norment, "The Fitness Craze"

3. **End with a final comment or example.** Your last word may be a thoughtful observation, a personal reaction, or a look to the future or to larger issues. The writer of "Quasi-Humans" (page 110) ends by saying that a "certain amount of resistance" will have to be overcome before his vision of the future becomes a reality.
4. **End with a call to action.** Persuasive essays often end by asking the reader to take a specific action. This makes an effective ending for other kinds of compositions, too.

Alan Tiger, director of the Y.W.C.A. here, says he would like to see the program applied on a national level. "This school came up through the grass roots," he said. "It's a simple enough idea that any city can pull it off. You need the school district to get out front on it, but don't forget community support. People want to help."

Timothy Egan, "School for Homeless Children: A Rare Experience"

5. **Refer to the introduction.** Bring the reader back full circle by referring to something in your introduction. George Plimpton begins "Neil Armstrong's Famous First Words" by comparing Armstrong and Charles Lindbergh. He doesn't mention Lindbergh again until the conclusion:

Charles Lindbergh is supposed to have said, "Well, I made it!" when he touched down at Le Bourget. What he actually said, leaning out, with the crowd surging around his plane, was: "Are there any mechanics here?" And then, "Does anyone here speak

MEETING INDIVIDUAL NEEDS

LEP/ESL

General Strategies. In some cultures, bringing a discourse to an end entails a sense of finality not found in English composition. For example, a Korean conclusion might imply or state explicitly that there is no need for further discussion of the topic.

If your students write this type of conclusion, tell them that in English composition closure does not necessarily call for discontinued consideration. A conclusion that dismisses further consideration of the topic implies an arrogance in the author that most native English speakers would find distasteful.

LESS-ADVANCED STUDENTS

Some students might not grasp the differences among techniques 1, 2, and 5. Explain the difference between a restatement and a summary and compare a few examples of each. Tell students that referring to the introduction doesn't mean restating or summarizing the composition's main point. It means specifically mentioning something that was mentioned in the introduction.

SELECTION AMENDMENT
Description of change: excerpted
Rationale: to focus on the concept of conclusions presented in this chapter

As an alternate exercise, you could lead the students in rewriting the conclusion of **"Quasi-Humans"** (p. 110) to illustrate each of the six techniques. You could then use **Exercises 6** and **7** for independent practice.

INDEPENDENT PRACTICE

Students should do **Exercise 7** on their own. Remind them that the conclusions they write should not lessen the composition's unity and coherence.

VISUAL CONNECTIONS

Exploring the Subject. Charles Lindbergh and Neil Armstrong are two of the most famous Americans associated with the history of flight. Lindbergh, who was born in 1902 in Detroit, Michigan, flew the world's first solo, nonstop, transatlantic flight. He left in his plane *Spirit of St. Louis* on May 20, 1927, and landed near Paris thirty-three hours and twenty-nine minutes later. Armstrong, who was born in 1930 in Wapakoneta, Ohio, was the first human to walk on the moon, which he did on July 20, 1969.

English?" So it is apparent that however self-deprecatory Armstrong is about his own contributions, he is certainly a giant leap ahead of Lindbergh in the immortal-words department.

> George Plimpton, "Neil Armstrong's Famous First Words"

(By the way, Neil Armstrong's "famous first words"—delivered when he first stepped on the moon on July 20, 1969—were: "That's one small step for a man, one giant leap for mankind.")

6. **Use a quotation.** A quotation that's startling or moving works just as well to end a composition as it does to begin one.

> The gardeners still have nagging worries they could lose El Jardin to developers. "I don't think there is another place where our neighborhood people could go," said Ms. Kirkpatrick. "You need a ray of hope and you find it seeing what can grow out of rubble."
>
> Kathleen Teltsch, "For Young and Old, a Pocket Paradise"

SELECTION AMENDMENT
Description of change: excerpted
Rationale: to focus on the concept of conclusions presented in this chapter

ASSESSMENT

Use students' work on **Exercise 7** to evaluate their understanding of the six techniques for writing conclusions. Be sure to check the conclusions with the rest of the essay to verify that unity and coherence is maintained.

CLOSURE

Ask students to name the six techniques for writing conclusions [restate main idea, summarize main points, end with comment or example, end with call to action, refer to introduction, use a quotation]. ■

The Conclusion **133**

WRITING NOTE

You can wait until you've finished writing your composition before you worry about its title. Use your thesis statement—and your imagination—to think of a brief, catchy way to describe what your readers are about to encounter.

Try writing several titles until you find one you like. Here are some suggestions for the bicycle touring composition (pages 120–121). Which one do you like best? Can you think of others?

EXAMPLES Seeing the Country on Two Wheels
Advice for Beginning Bicycle Trippers
Bicycle Touring: Muscle, Sweat, and Gears

EXERCISE 6 **Improving a Conclusion**

Here's the first draft of a conclusion for a composition about uniforms in public schools. Get together with a partner to answer these questions: *What's wrong with this conclusion? How can it be improved?* Then, write a better conclusion. You can change it any way you like, make up details, or even start over completely. (For some ideas, refer to the techniques on pages 130–132.)

Someday all public school students--both boys and girls--may wear uniforms. Will uniforms make schools better or worse than the way things are today? No one knows.

ANSWERS
Exercise 6

The problem with the conclusion as written is that it raises a question that can't be answered. Revisions of the conclusion will vary. Here's an example:

Telling students what they cannot wear to school is not far removed from dictating what they do wear. While it is true that wearing the same things can create a sense of unity among the students, whether this creates an environment supportive of learning remains to be seen. However, if current trends of regulating public school clothing continues, all public school students may someday wear uniforms.

ANSWERS
Exercise 7

Conclusions will vary. Here's an example:

Bicycle touring can be an enjoyable and memorable experience. However, if you don't prepare for it properly, you could be in for your worst vacation ever. So choose those clothes and routes carefully and get that bike and body in shape! [call to action]

INTEGRATING THE LANGUAGE ARTS

Literature Link. If your students' literature book contains it, have students read "The Hawk Is Flying" by Harry Crews. Then ask students to tell which of the six techniques for writing conclusions Crews uses. [He ends with a final comment.] You then could have students use different techniques to write different conclusions for the essay. Ask for volunteers to read the new conclusions.

E X E R C I S E 7 ▶   **Writing a Conclusion**

Use your imagination to write a different conclusion for the composition about bicycle touring (pages 120–121). Use one technique or some combination of the techniques on pages 130–132. Feel free to make up quotations and additional details. (It's a good idea to read the composition again before you begin.)

WRITING NOTE

The two models of composition form you've read in this chapter are written in different points of view. The first one, "Quasi-Humans" (page 110), is written in the third-person point of view (*he, she, it, they*). Since a third-person point of view keeps the writer at a distance from the reader, it's the point of view you'll need to use when you're writing a formal composition. The second composition, the one on bicycle touring (pages 120–121), is written in the second-person point of view (*you, your*). Since the second-person point of view brings the writer closer to the reader, you'll usually use it when your composition is more informal.

FRAMEWORK FOR A COMPOSITION	
Introduction	■ Arouses the reader's interest ■ Sets the tone ■ Presents the thesis statement
Body	■ States the main points ■ Provides support for the main points
Conclusion	■ Reinforces the main idea ■ Leaves the reader with a final impression and a sense of completeness

SEGMENT 7 *(pp. 135–137)*
MAKING CONNECTIONS
WRITING AN INFORMATIVE
COMPOSITION
OBJECTIVE

• To use the composition form studied in
the chapter to write an informative essay

135

MAKING CONNECTIONS

WRITING AN INFORMATIVE COMPOSITION

A useful formula for writing an informative composition is *introduction + body + conclusion = composition*. Remember that to explain and inform is only one of the purposes for writing. Others are to express yourself, to be creative, and to persuade others. The composition form can also be adapted to these purposes.

In this assignment, you'll apply this three-part formula to write an informative essay about the President's Council on Physical Fitness and Sports. Since you are writing for a high school audience, your purpose will be to explain how students can qualify for awards. Imagine that the following list of facts and the following chart are the prewriting information that you've gathered so far.

Information About President's Council on Physical Fitness and Sports

1. Arnold Schwarzenegger, chairman: "Physical fitness must be made a priority in American schools."

WRITING AN INFORMATIVE COMPOSITION
Teaching Strategies

This assignment requires students to put together what they have learned in this chapter, so you will want to review what has been learned about the separate parts of a composition before students begin writing. Be sure to stress the importance of transitions when the students are ready to put the parts together into a unified whole.

Focus is another topic you will need to discuss with the students, since it determines which pieces of information are used and which are discarded. If students need more information, you may want to refer them to **Chapter 32: "The Library/Media Center"** for information on using the library.

Finally, be sure students understand each step of the writing process (prewriting, writing, evaluating and revising, and proofreading and publishing) and what each step involves.

GUIDELINES
Making Connections Activity

Student essays should contain the following items:

1. A one-paragraph introduction that catches the reader's interest, sets the tone, and presents the thesis statement

2. A body that gives supporting details about the main idea of the composition

3. A body that is coherent and makes proper use of direct references and transitional words and phrases

4. A conclusion that reinforces the main idea and gives a sense of completeness to the composition

The writing process in the assignment calls for the students to

1. Write a preliminary thesis statement

2. Make an early plan

3. Write an attention-getting introduction

4. Write a series of unified and coherent paragraphs

5. Write an effective conclusion

6. Submit a completed and proofread composition

2. A nation of young couch potatoes with flabby muscles; half don't get enough exercise; a third can't run a mile in less than 10 minutes

3. Council founded in 1966: awards program for boys and girls 6 through 17 based on ability to pass physical tests

4. More than 4 million students participated in recent years; 18,000 schools

5. Students in 85th percentile in all five events get emblem and Certificate of Achievement signed by president

6. Students in 50th percentile get National Physical Fitness Award emblems and certificates

7. Students who have disabilities also compete

8. Five events: curl-ups (sit-up with bent knees, arms crossed on chest, partner holding feet); shuttle run (30-foot run picking up and moving blocks); 1-mile combined run and walk; pull-ups; V-sit reach (reaching with hands through legs in sitting position)

9. Free booklet *Get Fit*—from President's Council on Physical Fitness and Sports, 450 Fifth Street, N.W., Washington, DC 20001

	AGE	CURL-UPS (Limited one min.)	SHUTTLE RUN (seconds)	V-SIT REACH (inches)	ONE-MILE RUN (min./sec.)	PULL-UPS
BOYS	6	33	12.1	+3.5	10:15	2
	7	36	11.5	+3.5	9:22	4
	8	40	11.1	+3.0	8:48	5
	9	41	10.9	+3.0	8:31	5
	10	45	10.3	+4.0	7:57	6
	11	47	10.0	+4.0	7:57	6
	12	50	9.8	+4.0	7:11	7
	13	53	9.5	+3.5	6:50	7
	14	56	9.1	+4.5	6:26	10
	15	57	9.0	+5.0	6:20	11
	16	56	8.7	+6.0	6:08	11
	17	55	8.7	+7.0	6:06	13
GIRLS	6	32	12.4	+5.5	11:20	2
	7	34	12.2	+5.0	10:36	2
	8	38	11.8	+4.5	10:02	2
	9	39	11.1	+5.5	9:30	2
	10	40	10.8	+6.0	9:19	3
	11	42	10.5	+6.5	9:02	3
	12	45	10.4	+7.0	8:23	2
	13	46	10.2	+7.0	8:13	2
	14	47	10.1	+8.0	7:59	2
	15	48	10.0	+8.0	7:59	2
	16	45	10.1	+9.0	8:23	1
	17	44	10.0	+8.0	8:15	1

Prewriting. Add or subtract from the data bank given above. You don't have to use all the information given, and you can do some research to find additional facts. (Suggestions: Find out which schools in your area participate in the program. If your school participates, what are the statistics? Interview a physical education teacher or a coach.)

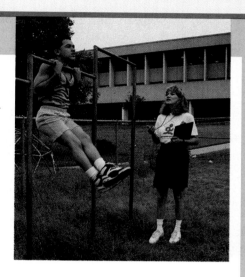

As you look over the facts, narrow your topic to one you can cover in a brief composition. Express your main idea in a preliminary thesis statement. Then group and order the information you'll use into an early plan. (Remember that you're supposed to be writing an informative paper; don't get waylaid into writing a persuasive essay.)

Writing, Evaluating, and Revising. Follow your early plan as you draft your composition, and try one of the introduction techniques suggested on pages 123–126. As you draft the body, concentrate on unity and coherence. Each paragraph should develop one main point directly related to your thesis statement. Watch out for unity within paragraphs, too. When you get to the conclusion, review the techniques for writing conclusions on pages 130–132. If you can, let your first draft sit awhile before you reread it carefully to see how you can improve it.

Proofreading and Publishing. When you're satisfied with your revisions, change your focus and search for errors in grammar, usage, and mechanics. Exchange papers with a partner and proofread each other's compositions. (See the proofreading guidelines on pages 55–56.) Find a way to share your composition with an audience. If your school isn't participating in the program of the President's Council on Physical Fitness and Sports, you might use your compositions to try to get the program underway.

Chapter 4

EXPRESSIVE WRITING

Motivation

To begin this unit, ask each student to bring an object to class that reminds him or her of an important time or event. For example, a student might bring a toy, a medal or trophy, a piece of jewelry, or a photograph. If the object is no longer available, the student might draw a picture of it or describe it in writing. Discuss with students why the items are important; what thoughts, feelings, images, or details the objects evoke; and the story that surrounds each object. You could even create a display of the objects during the course of this unit.

Introduction

Have students share reflections about memorable events. You may want to talk about the importance of auto-biographical writing to emphasize that writers can gain insight into their feelings and experiences by writing about themselves. Much of literature comes from authors' personal experiences and their desires to understand themselves and the world.

Guide students through an exploration of the differences between expressive writing and the other aims of discourse. Students can consider how they might write about childhood memories for each of the different aims. You may want to have students write down appropriate titles for each aim.

With this basic introduction to the expressive aim, students should be prepared to examine the literary model.

Integration

This chapter will integrate well with activities in the classroom that are related to study of literature. Students can compare novels or selections in their textbooks with the literary model for organization, details, purpose, audience, tone, and meaning. Then they can compare their personal narratives to a published one by analyzing and evaluating the effectiveness of their finished products.

It may be helpful to students if you teach verb usage and dialogue punctuation while working with this unit.

The chart on the next page illustrates the strands of language arts as they are integrated into this chapter. For vocabulary study, glossary words are underlined in some writing models.

QUOTATIONS
All **Quotations for the Day** are chosen because of their relevance to instructional material presented in that segment of the chapter and for their usefulness in establishing student interest in writing.

INTEGRATING THE LANGUAGE ARTS

Selection	Reading and Literature	Writing and Critical Thinking	Language and Syntax	Speaking, Listening, and Other Expression Skills
from *Black Elk Speaks* as told through John G. Neihardt (Flaming Rainbow) 140-142 from *An American Childhood* by Annie Dillard 156-158 Paragraph by Ernest Hemingway from *Writers on Writing* 163 from *A Modern Utopia* by H. G. Wells 168-170 "Sky Dance" from *A Sand County Almanac* by Aldo Leopold 172-173	Analyzing organization 143 Analyzing details 143, 158, 170 Responding personally to literature 143, 158, 170 Finding details 143, 158, 170 Finding main idea 158 Understanding metaphor in a personal narrative 158	Writing a journal entry 143 Evaluating meaning 143, 152, 153, 170 Applying interpretive and creative thinking 143, 152, 158, 165, 170, 171, 173 Analyzing details 143, 158, 165, 170 Choosing a topic 146 Recalling details 146, 151, 170 Creating a natural tone 148 Contrasting speaking style with writing style 148 Writing the meaning of a personal experience 153 Analyzing a personal narrative 158, 166 Writing a draft of a personal narrative 162 Organizing details 162, 173 Analyzing a writer's revisions 165 Revising a personal narrative 166, 167 Proofreading a personal narrative 167 Describing a personal utopia 170 Using symbolic elements in an expressive self-portrait 171 Writing a personal narrative 173	Identifying transitional words and phrases 143 Proofreading for errors in grammar, usage, and mechanics 167, 170	Talking and listening to others 148 Interpreting meaning in a group 152 Working with classmates to analyze a personal narrative 158, 166 Working with classmates in evaluation and revision 166 Creating an expressive self-portrait 171

SEGMENT PLANNING GUIDE

Whether you are planning for a quick review of a writing concept or preparing an extended lesson on composition, you can use the following Planning Guide to adapt the chapter material to the individual needs of your class.

SEGMENT	PAGES	CONTENT	RESOURCES
1 *Discovering Yourself*	*139-143*		
Literary Model from ***Black Elk Speaks***	140-142	Guided reading: a model of personal expression	
Reader's Response/Writer's Craft	143	Model evaluation: responding to literature and analyzing personal expression	
2 *Ways to Express Yourself*	*144*		
3 *Prewriting*	*145-154*		Gathering Specific Details
Choosing a Personal Experience	145-146	Guidelines: selecting suitable topics for personal narratives	
Exercise 1	146	Applied practice: exploring topics	
Writing Assignment: Part 1	146	Applied practice: choosing a topic	
Planning Your Personal Narrative	147	Introduction: planning your personal narrative	
Thinking About Purpose, Audience, and Tone	147	Guidelines: analyzing and selecting appropriate purpose, audience, and tone	
Exercise 2	148	Cooperative learning: creating a natural tone	
Recalling Details	148-150	Guidelines: gathering details	
Chart: Recording Details	150	Guidelines: assessing a chart	
Writing Assignment: Part 2	151	Applied practice: recalling details	
Reflecting on the Meaning of the Experience	151	Guidelines: using criteria to focus on experience	
Critical Thinking: Interpreting Meaning	152	Guielines: interpreting meaning	
Critical Thinking Exercise	152-153	Cooperative learning: interpreting meaning	
Writing Assignment: Part 3	153	Applied practice: stating the meaning of an experience	
Organizing Your Ideas	154	Guidelines: organizing events in chronological order	
4 *Writing*	*155-162*		Writing a Personal Narrative
The Structure of Your Personal Narrative	155	Guidelines: structuring a personal narrative	
Literary Model from ***An American Childhood***	156-158	Guided reading: analyzing basic elements of a personal narrative	
Exercise 3	158	Applied practice: analyzing a personal narrative	
Writer's Model	159-161	Sample: examining personal narrative in a student model	

All the resources listed in this chapter are located in the Teacher's ResourceBank™.

SEGMENT	PAGES	CONTENT	RESOURCES
Chart: Framework for a Personal Narrative	162	Guidelines: structuring a personal narrative	
Writing Assignment: Part 4	162	Applied practice: writing a first draft	
5 *Evaluating and Revising*	*163-166*		Writing a Personal Narrative
Literary Model from *Writers on Writing*	163	Guided reading: learning how one writer edits	
Chart: Evaluating and Revising a Personal Narrative	164	Guidelines: applying evaluation and revision techniques	
Exercise 4	165	Applied practice: analyzing a writer's revisions	
Exercise 5	166	Cooperative learning: evaluating and revising	
Grammar Hint	166	Writing suggestion: using action verbs	
Writing Assignment: Part 5	166	Applied practice: evaluating and revising	
6 *Proofreading and Publishing*	*167*		Writing a Personal Narrative
Publishing	167	Publishing ideas: reaching a specific audience	
Writing Assignment: Part 6	167	Applied practice: proofreading and publishing	
7 *Writing Workshop*	*168-170*		All the resources for this chapter may be used in this segment.
Imagining a Utopia	168	Introduction: creating a utopia	
Literary Model/Questions from *A Modern Utopia*	168-170	Examining techniques: creating a utopia for expressive writing	
Describing a Personal Utopia	170	Applied practice: writing about a personal utopia	
8 *Making Connections*	*171-173*		
Self-Expression and Art	171	Guidelines: creating a self-portrait Applied practice: creating a visual self-portrait	
Narratives Across the Curriculum: Science	171-173	Guidelines: writing about a personal experience Applied practice: writing a personal narrative about animals	
Literary Model from *A Sand County Almanac*	172-173	Guided reading: examining details in a personal narrative	

WHOLE-CHAPTER RESOURCES
A Writing Process Log, A Writing Prompt, Holistically Graded Models, Assessment Portfolio Materials

OBJECTIVES

- To identify and analyze the characteristics of personal expression
- To analyze the expressive qualities of a literary model

MOTIVATION

Before students open their books, put the first two lines of the literary model on the chalkboard or on a transparency. Do not identify the excerpt. After students have read the lines to themselves, begin a discussion of what concrete information students find in the lines. The discussion should evolve into an anticipation of what might follow the first

VISUAL CONNECTIONS
Kachina Dance

About the Author. James Humetewa, Jr., is a Hopi artist who was born near Tuba City, Arizona, in 1926. He later worked as a painter and assistant at the Museum of New Mexico in Santa Fe. During his years at the museum, Humetewa observed a wide variety of Native American art, and the subjects of his own paintings reflect some of those influences.

Humetewa's work is characterized by his unusual use of color and his careful attention to details that give the viewer an accurate portrayal of the Hopi culture. A notable stylistic element of Humetewa's paintings is the outlining around the figures. In some pictures the outlines are quite heavy; in others the lines are much lighter.

Exploring the Subject. This painting shows a mixed kachina dance, in which the dancers, who represent not only legendary characters but also the spirits of animals and plants, perform the sacred dances and sing the prayers of the Hopi people.

4 EXPRESSIVE WRITING

two lines. What do the students predict is going to happen? What mood do they sense? Have students explain their responses. You may also want to ask students to guess what kind of writing this excerpt represents.

Have a volunteer read the introductory material. Afterwards, explain that expressive writing is often private but that many writers choose to publish personal narratives; these are quite popular in literature today. Such is the case with Black Elk's story.

Have several students read the model aloud, and have them pause periodically to

Kachina Dance, James Humetawa (1944). Hopi, born 1926. Watercolor on paper. 22" × 30". Collection of The Philbrook Museum of Art, Tulsa, OK.

Discovering Yourself

What do you really know about yourself? What can you **discover** about **yourself?** One way you can find out more about your inner feelings is to write about them.

Writing and You. "I'll never forget the time when . . . " "I felt so good the day that . . . " You probably think or talk this way often. Many writers take these thoughts further by writing them down. Doing so helps us explore our deepest feelings, our fears, hopes, and dreams. You may want to write just for yourself. Or you might share your feelings with others in a personal narrative. Can you think of an emotional experience you would like to write about?

As You Read. As you read the following narrative, notice how Black Elk, an Oglala Sioux, looks inside himself to tell about the hardships of his people.

QUOTATION FOR THE DAY

"So when I was a little boy, I loved listening to my old people. The other little guys would go out and play around together, but I would go sit with the old people and listen to them." (Wallace H. Black Elk, 1921?–   , Lakota shaman)

Ask students to focus on the earliest memories they have of their "old people." Can they remember what they heard, felt, and saw? Ask students to write two or three sentences about their memories.

LEP/ESL

General Strategies. Have students share any personal experiences or stories they have heard about life in their native culture. Ask them to relate how their life today is different from their ancestors' ways of life.

discuss the details of the story. Before using the **Reader's Response** questions, allow students to draw conclusions about the ideas and predictions they generated before they read the selection.

GUIDED PRACTICE

Guide students through the **Reader's Response** questions. Have a volunteer write a list of images and a list of feelings on the chalkboard as you and the students reflect on the story.

USING THE SELECTION
from **Black Elk Speaks**

1

What is the reader's first impression as he or she reads the first sentence?
[Answers may vary, but the reader may experience curiosity as to why the wind is mentioned first, and why they, whoever they are, can see only a little way ahead. The reader might also sense apprehension in the tone of the narrator.]

2

Lakota: a tribe within the Sioux nation

COOPERATIVE LEARNING
Allow students to practice asking questions by pretending that Black Elk is coming to visit your classroom to be interviewed. Have students work in small groups to develop at least five good interview questions. Then have each group share and evaluate its questions. Write the questions on the chalkboard and have the groups speculate on how Black Elk might respond.

140

from

Black Elk Speaks

as told through

JOHN G. NEIHARDT

(Flaming Rainbow)

1 The wind came up again with the daylight, and we could see only a little way ahead when we started west in the morning. Before we came to the ridge, we saw two horses, dim in the blowing snow beside some bushes. They were huddled up with their tails to the wind and their heads hanging low. When we came closer, there was a bison robe shelter in the brush, and in it were an old man and a boy, very cold and hungry and discouraged. They were 2 Lakotas and were glad to see us, but they were feeling weak, because they had been out two days and had seen nothing but snow. We camped there with them in the brush, and then we went up on the ridge afoot. There was much timber up there. We got behind the hill in a sheltered place and waited, but we could see nothing. While we were waiting, we talked about the people starving at home, and we were all sad. Now and then the snow haze would open up for a little bit and you could see quite a distance, then it would close again. While we were talking about our hungry people, suddenly the snow haze opened a little, and we saw a shaggy bull's head coming out of the blowing snow up the <u>draw</u> that led past us below. Then seven more appeared, and the snow haze came back and shut us in there. They

INDEPENDENT PRACTICE

After students have discussed the **Reader's Response** questions, have them convey their feelings by writing in their journals. Then they can complete the **Writer's Craft** questions on their own. Encourage students to be thorough in their answers.

ASSESSMENT

You can evaluate student understanding during the **Reader's Response** discussion through observation. Have students turn in their answers to the **Writer's Craft** questions for further assessment.

141

could not see us, and they were drifting with the wind so that they could not smell us.

3 We four stood up and made vows to the four quarters of the world, saying: "Haho! haho!" Then we got our horses from the brush on the other side of the ridge and came around to the mouth of the draw where the bison would pass as they drifted with the wind.

4 The two old men were to shoot first and then we two boys would follow the others horseback. Soon we saw the bison coming. The old people crept up and shot, but they were so cold, and maybe excited, that they got only one bison. They cried "Hoka!" and we boys charged after the other bison. The snow was blowing hard in the wind that sucked down the draw, and when we came near them the bison were so excited that they backtracked and charged right past us bellowing. This broke

---

"...when we came near them the bison were so excited that they backtracked and charged right past us bellowing."

---

the deep snow for our horses and it was easier to catch them. Suddenly I saw the bison I was chasing go out in a big flurry of snow, and I knew they **5** had plunged into a snow-filled <u>gulch</u>, but it was too late to stop, and my

3

What do you suppose Black Elk means by "four quarters of the world"?
[north, south, east, and west]

4

Notice this is the first time the storyteller refers to himself. How old do you think Black Elk is at this time?
[He refers to himself as a boy; perhaps he is in his early teens.]

5

How do you feel as you read this passage?
[The word *plunged* suggests a comparison of the snow-filled gulch to a swimming pool or pond. The words *floundering and kicking* might elicit the feeling of fear or chaos.]

Ask students why they think Black Elk chose to tell about his experiences and then write their answers on the chalkboard [to entertain, to inform others]. Ask students to discuss reasons they might feel a need to publish a personal narrative. [They may be more interested in sharing what they have discovered rather than merely expressing themselves.]

ADVANCED STUDENTS

Students might benefit from seeing how the first-person point of view is important in a personal narrative. They could form in groups, choose a person other than the narrator in Black Elk's narrative, and rewrite one paragraph from that perspective. Each group could rewrite a different paragraph and then share its revision with the class. Students will observe in this activity how important the character of the narrator is in a personal narrative.

VISUAL CONNECTIONS

Exploring the Subject. Have students examine the picture of Black Elk on p. 41 and consider why his narrative is told through Neihardt. Then have students examine the painting of the Native Americans with the buffalo and discuss how this painting reflects the sensory details of the story.

SELECTION AMENDMENT
Description of change: excerpted
Rationale: to focus on the concept of expressive writing presented in this chapter

142

National Museum of American Art, Washington, D.C./Art Resource

horse plunged right in after them. There we were all together—four bison, my horse and I all floundering and kicking, but I managed to crawl out a little way. I had a repeating rifle that they gave me back at the camp, and I killed the four bison right there, but I had thrown my mittens away and the gun froze to my hands while I was shooting, so that I had to tear the skin to get it loose.

When I went back to the others, the other boy had killed three, so we had eight bison scattered around there in the snow. It was still morning, but it took till nearly dark for my father and the other old man to do the butchering. I could not help, because my hands were frozen. We finally got the meat all piled up in one place, and then we made a camp in a fine shelter behind a big rock with brush all around it and plenty of wood. We had a big fire, and we tied our tanned robes on our horses and fed them plenty of cottonwood bark from the woods by the stream. The raw robes we used for the shelter. Then we had a big feast and we sang and were very happy.

READER'S RESPONSE

1. What images in Black Elk's narrative are most vivid in your mind? Why do you think these details or mental pictures made a strong impression on you?
2. Black Elk's experience shows the physical hardships he faced. Can you imagine what it would be like to have to chase bison through the snow for food for your family? In your journal, write about your own life as compared with this experience of Black Elk.

WRITER'S CRAFT

3. Black Elk uses many details that help readers feel the bitter cold. How do the details about Black Elk's hands in the last two paragraphs help you feel the awful cold?
4. Black Elk uses many transitional words and phrases to help readers follow the order of events. In the first sentence, for example, he says, "The wind came up *again* . . . *when* we started west in the morning." What are some other transition words and phrases in the first paragraph?

> "**A** people without history
> is like the wind
> on the buffalo grass."
>
> *Sioux Saying*

ANSWERS
Reader's Response

Responses may vary.

1. Students should give specific details from the narrative and explain why the images made a strong impression.
2. Students should include specific details from their own lives and from Black Elk's narrative to support their responses. Journal entries should not be penalized for incomplete sentences or mechanical errors.

Writer's Craft

Responses may vary.

3. Students answers should include specific examples from the last two paragraphs.
4. "Before," "When," "but," "because," "there," "then," "behind," "While," "Now and then," "again," "While," "suddenly," "up," "below," "Then,"

 INTEGRATING THE LANGUAGE ARTS

Literature Link. A good example of a personal narrative is "The Tuft of Flowers" by Robert Frost. Students might read this poem and list the characteristics this poem shares with a personal prose narrative, such as sensory details, thoughts and feelings of the writer, first-person point of view, organization, and transitional words.

TEACHING THE MODES

This section presents students with the four methods of organization they can use to achieve the expressive aim or purpose. Read the information aloud to your students,

A DIFFERENT APPROACH

Ask students to bring their favorite magazines to class; teen magazines, sport magazines, beauty magazines, or car magazines would be appropriate. Ask them to find examples of the four different organizational methods. Point out that an entire article probably won't be confined to only one of the modes because most literature will employ a combination. When they think they have found at least one example of each mode, ask students to share and discuss their examples.

COOPERATIVE LEARNING

Students can practice applying the four methods of organization by working in small groups to create sentences that indicate how a particular topic might be expressed. Have them decide on a general topic for all groups to consider, and then have each group come up with four sentences. Have the groups share and compare their responses. For example, they might choose the topic, *School.* An expressive-narrative sentence might say, "I had an awful day at school yesterday." An expressive-descriptive sentence could be, "Drama is an exciting class." For expressive-classificatory, the sentence might be, "What is school spirit?" And an expressive-evaluative sentence could read, "Peer support groups are valuable programs in high school."

Ways to Express Yourself

Like anyone who does expressive writing, Black Elk wants to present his own thoughts and feelings. But he's also writing to inform readers about the terrible condition of the Oglala Sioux and to persuade readers that tragic changes are occurring in the lives of his people. Expressing yourself is your main reason for writing a personal narrative. Here are some examples of the ways you can develop an expressive message.

▶ **Narration:** writing in your journal about a funny event at school; writing a letter to a friend about getting lost on the subway.

Description: describing your fellow camp counselors in a letter; describing your dog's funny habits in a poem.

Classification: in a journal entry, comparing last year's soccer team with this year's; defining the word *enthusiasm* and explaining what it means to you.

Evaluation: in your school newspaper, evaluating your volunteer work at the animal shelter; writing a letter to discuss what you think of a company's product.

LOOKING
AHEAD

In the main assignment in this chapter, you'll use the strategy of narration to tell about an important personal experience. As you write, you'll explore and discover the meaning of your experience. Keep in mind that an effective personal narrative

- describes the important events, people, and places that were part of the experience
- includes your thoughts and feelings
- uses specific sensory details
- explains what the experience meant to you

SEGMENT 3 *(pp. 145–154)*
PREWRITING

OBJECTIVES

- To select an experience as a topic for a personal narrative
- To analyze with a group the differences in speaking and writing expressively

- To recall and organize details for a personal narrative
- To state the meaning of an experience in a personal narrative

Prewriting **145**

Writing a Personal Narrative

 Prewriting

Choosing a Personal Experience

Some experiences stand out in your memory—and not just the "big occasions." You may never forget the first time your band played in public (absolute terror and then relief when everybody danced).

But you may also remember—vividly—your first walk on a beach, when all that happened was watching sandpipers and gathering shells, but you decided you were *determined* never to live in the city.

Your experience for a personal narrative may be simple and ordinary instead of unusual or surprising, but if it passes these three tests, it's a good topic.

1. The experience seems important to you: it has personal meaning.
2. The experience is clear in your memory: you remember details.
3. The experience is not too private: you're willing to share it with others.

Teacher's ResourceBank™
RESOURCES

PREWRITING
- Gathering Specific Details

QUOTATION FOR THE DAY

"I remember the green coat that I wore in fifth and sixth grades when you either danced like a champ or pressed yourself against a greasy wall, bitter as a penny toward the happy couples." (Gary Soto, 1952–   , Mexican American poet, from "The Jacket")

Ask the students if they have read this story and if they remember any other details from it. Ask them to write a quick description of this or another "ugly coat similar to the one in "The Jacket".

VISUAL CONNECTIONS

Exploring the Subject. Sandpipers range from 5 to 15 inches in length, and most have long pointed wings and long legs in relation to their body size. The breeding distribution is mostly in the northern hemisphere. They usually nest on the ground, and the species which breed in marshlands hide their nests in vegetation near the water. They usually lay clutches of four eggs, and young sandpipers are often led away from their nests just a few hours after hatching.

145

Have students draw upon relatively recent memories and then work backward to earlier experiences. There are four steps to this activity: Begin by asking students to remember an incident from the day before and to record details about it, especially what they thought and how they felt. Then, have students record something they were doing on this day a week ago, and something that happened a year ago. They should concentrate on details, especially on their thoughts and feelings. Finally, ask students to record their earliest childhood memory. Have students share their responses.

MEETING INDIVIDUAL NEEDS

LEP/ESL

General Strategies. When some students write about personal experiences, they often settle for general adjectives such as *happy, sad, surprised,* and *scared.* As a remedy, you can have the class brainstorm for synonyms. Start them off with *elated, disheartened, amazed,* and *petrified.* Introducing students early to a thesaurus may be a great help in expanding their vocabularies.

ANSWERS
Exercise 1

Students should freewrite in journals or brainstorm in groups to find at least three important and memorable experiences that can be shared.

The first test is one to think about a bit. Unlike most other papers you write, the focus of a personal narrative is **you.** That's why the word *experience,* not *event,* is significant. You won't write about celebrations for the Chinese New Year just to describe what your neighborhood does, but because those celebrations made an impression on you. What counts is what you saw, heard, did, felt, and thought.

EXERCISE 1	**Tapping Your Memory for Personal Experiences**

How did you meet your best friend? Have you ever had to think fast in an emergency? Did your favorite aunt give you the world's ugliest sweater to wear to a party? All of these events could be topics for a personal narrative. The subjects and suggestions below can help trigger your memories. Choose two or three of the general topics below and try to remember specific, important experiences about them.

- **People:** family, coaches, friends, neighbors
- **Places:** a treehouse, the gym, a pool, a place to be alone
- **Experiences:** secrets, surprises, borrowing and lending, disappointments, graduations
- **Values:** loyalty, friendship, honesty, maturity

EXAMPLES   People: Neighbors
"I remember the time the baby in the apartment next door wandered off and I helped find her."
Places: The gym
"I remember the time when I shot the winning basket against our biggest rivals."

WRITING ASSIGNMENT

PART 1:
Choosing an Experience for a Personal Narrative

Now put the experiences you've remembered to the test. Ask yourself: Was this experience somehow significant to me? Can I recall details to bring it alive? Do I want to make it public? Choose one personal experience as a topic to write about.

TEACHING THE LESSON

Discuss the information with students. You may want to involve the memories they listed for **Motivation**. Have them consider how their memories fit the three tests. Students should be looking for one good idea that will be suitable for a personal narrative.

GUIDED PRACTICE

Model **Exercise 1** for your students by putting the first category on the chalkboard. Brainstorm aloud for experiences on one or two of the subjects.

For **Writing Assignment: Part 1**, have students choose an experience on which to focus by using the given questions.

Prewriting   **147**

Prewriting

Planning Your Personal Narrative

The narrative you'll write is personal, but it's not a diary or journal entry meant for you alone. It's an essay written for others—a way to share your experience. This means planning and shaping your narrative for maximum effect, to communicate what you want.

Thinking About Purpose, Audience, and Tone

Purpose.   Your purpose in this paper is to express yourself. You're telling about something that happened to you and exploring your thoughts and feelings about it. In this remembering and exploring, you'll make some discovery—about yourself, others, or the world around you—and share it with an audience.

Audience.   Making your experience real and alive to an audience—any audience—calls for details, details, details: solid descriptions of both events and feelings, so that your readers live through the experience with you.

But you'll also think about your particular audience: teacher and classmates? family? a trusted adult? a more distant audience? Sometimes these readers will need help, or background, to understand your topic. If you're writing for classmates about dropping your grandmother's ring down the school's bleachers, they'll understand the situation. But if you're telling about a chess competition, they'll probably want to know where and when it occurred, how it was organized, and some basic facts about the game.

Tone.   Since this is a personal expression paper, your voice should come through—as though you're talking right to readers. You may feel happy or angry or sad about the experience, but you'll sound honest to your readers. Personal expression is informal, which means using everyday vocabulary and sentence structure. And you'll write in the first person, using *I, me, our,* and *we.*

MEETING INDIVIDUAL NEEDS

AT-RISK STUDENTS

Expressive writing can build students' self-esteem because it makes them realize that their experiences are important. Encourage students to take themselves and their experiences seriously as subject matter for their writing. If students are having a hard time thinking of experiences on which to base their personal narratives, you may want to work with them individually by asking questions similar to the ones in the instruction lines of **Exercise 1**.

Use your chosen topic to model the speaking and listening process outlined in **Exercise 2.**

To help students with **Writing Assignment: Part 2,** demonstrate creating a model by using a detail chart or transparency. Use the topic chosen during **Writing Assignment: Part 1.**

Demonstrate **Writing Assignment: Part 3** by using your model detail chart. Circle the key ideas as you develop your statement of meaning.

ANSWERS
Exercise 2

1. Students should write the most important, vivid parts of an experience in their sentences.

2. Narrators should tell groups the same story but with more detail.

3. Listeners should have time between speakers to note conversational words, phrases, or sentence structure.

EXERCISE 2 ▶ Speaking and Listening: Creating a Natural Tone

You have a unique style of expressing yourself—a way of talking that is only yours. If you want your writing to sound more like talking, why not try talking it out—with good listeners? To improve tone, try this method with a small group.

1. Think about your topic, write down a few sentences about it, and give them to the group to read.
2. Now *tell* your partners the same information out loud. Just talk—but don't repeat your written words.
3. Ask the listeners to pinpoint differences in your speaking and writing (words, expressions, sentence length), and discuss how to make the written sentences more natural.

Recalling Details

Have you ever had the experience of a certain smell or sound suddenly exploding a whole memory in your head? One whiff of a strong, old-fashioned soap, and you're right back in your grandfather's workshop.

In a way, that's what you need to do in your narrative: provide concrete, sensory details that will *recreate* your experience for readers.

Lively, Specific Details.   Don't just state, for example, that you stood on a diving board. Say instead that your knees had turned to mashed potatoes and that noises from the pool were a blurred roar. Readers will share in your experience if you use details that are specific, not vague, and that appeal to all the senses. See what details you can come up with now, and then add others later when you're writing your first draft.

Helps to Memory.   While some details will leap out of your memory, as fresh as when they happened, others may be cloudy or lost. If so, you can use brainstorming or freewriting to uncover them. You can also talk to other people who were involved (use *their* memories as well as your own) and even revisit places for a firsthand refresher of details.

For **Exercise 1**, give students ten minutes to freewrite or brainstorm on their chosen subjects. Have students concentrate on details and feelings rather than the sequence of events.

Have students complete **Writing Assignment: Part 1** by applying the given questions to each of the experiences they remembered when deciding on a topic for their personal narratives.

Divide the class into groups of three or four to complete **Exercise 2**.

For **Writing Assignment: Part 2**, students might find it easier to recall more specific details if the activity is assigned as homework.

☞

Events, People, and Places.   Begin with exactly what happened—first, second, third. Events are the "bones" of your narrative, its framework. First you remember main events: (1) you watched divers at a pool, (2) the lifeguard taught you some dives, and so on. Then you reach back for details about each event: You watched other kids do swan dives but you would only try plain dives from the pool's edge.

Recalling events will lead you to people. Who—besides yourself—played a part in your experience? What did they look like? What did they say? Telling that your grandfather smelled of a certain after-shave puts your readers right beside him. Use all your senses to describe yourself, another person, even crowds or animals.

Give the same all-five-senses attention to describing place details in your narrative. After all, a place can be a key part of your experience—like a white-water river on a canoe trip. But even if everything takes place somewhere ordinary—like your bedroom—put readers there. Make them *see* your posters, *smell* a candle, *feel* the cold floor.

WRITING NOTE   You're telling a story, so use dialogue to add variety and bring people to life. You could write *My mother shouted at us to stop the rehearsal.* But her own words emphasize her mood: *Mother shouted, "Unplug those guitars now—or I will!"* Dialogue should fit the speaker and can be informal, including the use of slang and sentence fragments.

MEETING INDIVIDUAL NEEDS

LEARNING STYLES

Auditory Learners. Students might benefit from telling their stories to one or more students who could write down the key details. These details then can be given back to the speaker for use in his or her writing. Students can help the storyteller by asking questions that will provide many and varied details for the writer to use. If possible, allow every student to serve as both a storyteller and a listener.

👁 VISUAL CONNECTIONS
Ideas for Writing. In order to teach the importance of concrete details, have students consider this photograph of a diving coach and recall a time when they were taught a certain sport or skill. Ask students to gather in pairs and relate their experiences to their partners. Each student should list the abstract words their partner uses in one column and the concrete details in another. You may then want to challenge students to change their abstract remarks into concrete descriptions.

Have students complete **Writing Assignment: Part 3** by using the notes generated in **Writing Assignment: Part 2** as a resource in determining their statement of meaning.

ASSESSMENT

Have students turn in their charts from **Writing Assignment: Parts 2** and **3** to check for their understanding of gathering and organizing details and interpreting meaning. For **Exercises 1** and **2** and **Writing Assignment: Part 1**, you can use observation and conferencing.

COOPERATIVE LEARNING

Have students work in small groups to prepare their detail charts. Working with others on the details for their narratives might provide them with spontaneous questions and feedback for their charts.

Thoughts and Emotions. Don't forget yourself in this living picture you're creating. What's going on *inside* you? (Look inside other people, too, if their reactions make a difference.) Use specific words to record your feelings (*furious*, *delighted*), and use actions, appearance, and dialogue to tell readers how you feel. ("Mashed-potato" knees show fear.) Use a chart like this one to recall and record details.

HERE'S HOW

WHO OR WHAT?	DETAILS
Events	
1. Watching divers at swim center	Kids practicing jackknives, swan dives. I dive (plain ones) from side.
2. Brian offers to help me	He says, "Why not off the board?" Try—really scared—pull it off.
3. Practice and make team	Hard work—lots of bad "landings." Water in face. Keep it a secret.
4. In first meet	Mom, Dad, Gerald, Elizabeth having picnic. My name over loudspeaker. Me on high board (shock). Picture in paper, swan dive.
People	
Me	Shy (not like G. & E.), 12—athletic, always at pool.
Brian	College student, swims like a fish, friendly smile, called me "a natural."
Gerald and Elizabeth	Older, popular, good grades, in clubs ("Oh, you're E & G's sister!")
Mom and Dad	At center a lot with us. Running (terrified I'm drowned). Amazed then proud.
Places	
Center	Pool, activity room, picnic place—really <u>hot</u>.
Pool	Diving boards, lots of kids—noisy.
Thoughts and Feelings	
Envy divers	Imagine being graceful, cutting water cleanly. Afraid to use board.
Surprise and fear!	Don't remember going up on board. Knees soft, roar in head.
Relief	Praise great!
I am a diver!	On high board, seeing family, feeling confident. No medal—but their pride.

RETEACHING

Bring to class pictures from current magazines that depict people engaged in different activities. Distribute the pictures to the class and have students work individually or in small groups to prepare charts for the pictures, such as the **Here's How** chart.

CLOSURE

Ask students what insights they gained as they chose a topic for a personal narrative and gathered and organized their materials. Write their ideas on the chalkboard.

Prewriting   **151**

When recalling details about your experience

- look for specific details and sensory details
- use brainstorming or clustering, interviewing, and observing to help your memory
- focus on events, people, places, thoughts, and feelings

  PART 2:
Recalling Details

Sometimes relaxing is the best way to unlock memory. Make a chart like the one on page 150 to record details, and try closing your eyes and imagining yourself back in time, going through the experience again. Gather as many details as you can. "Replay" the experience in your mind as many times as you need to so you can gather the details you need.

Reflecting on the Meaning of the Experience

As you've recalled details, especially thoughts and feelings, the meaning of your experience has probably become clearer. Now is a good time to try to bring it into focus. Don't be surprised, however, if your understanding of your experience changes as you write your draft.

To reflect on (think about) why the experience was important to you, use these questions.

1. Were you somehow different at the end of the experience? If so, what were you like at the beginning? How exactly did you change?
2. Did you learn something new about yourself? What?
3. Did you learn something new about other people, human nature, or life in general? What was it?

Some unusual insight (never before thought or felt!) isn't what's necessary here. It can be as simple as "I realized that my grandfather would soon be gone. I should spend time with him *now*."

INTEGRATING THE LANGUAGE ARTS

Literature Link. If possible, have students read Harry Crews' "The Hawk Is Flying." Ask them to pay special attention to the way Crews uses sensory details and the way he ties past experiences to the experience he is describing in the composition. Ask them how they, as readers, know how Crews' feelings affect his actions.

Then ask students how this technique affects the composition.

OBJECTIVE

- To interpret the meaning of an experience for a personal narrative

TEACHING *INTERPRETING MEANING*

Read the explanation of interpreting meaning to the class. Then have students return to their groups from **Exercise 2** to work on the **Critical Thinking Exercise.** Students could use the charts they have created with their notes about main events, thoughts, and feelings for their narratives.

LEP/ESL

General Strategies. Students might benefit from a discussion about how people from other cultures feel when they first move to the United States. Perhaps they can transfer their thoughts, feelings, and experiences to the story about Jae Rhee and better understand how to come up with the meaning or interpretation of a narrative.

AT-RISK STUDENTS

Students are sometimes absent from school because they have emotional or even drug or alcohol problems. If this is the case, they might hesitate to delve into the meanings of certain thoughts, feelings, and experiences because they might be too painful. You may want to work closely with these students, giving them plenty of feedback and encouraging them to follow through with their writing.

 CRITICAL THINKING

Interpreting Meaning

When you *interpret,* you bring out meaning: you explain something, make it understandable. You're used to doing this in literature. For example, a character in a story competes fiercely for a scholarship but in the end turns it down to stay at home with her mother. It's up to you to interpret her action, and you decide the girl just can't bear to leave her mother alone in her last years.

An experience may have more than one interpretation (perhaps the girl also sees that she competed mainly to beat a rival), so—whether in literature or your narrative— you aren't trying to uncover the "correct" meaning. You're trying to state a meaning that makes the facts and details understandable.

 CRITICAL THINKING EXERCISE:
Interpreting the Meaning of an Experience

The following notes give the main events of an experience, along with a person's thoughts and feelings about it. With others, read and discuss the statements, put yourself in the person's place, and suggest a possible meaning for the experience. What could be its importance? Write the meaning in one or two sentences. (You can give more than one interpretation if you want.)

- A Korean boy, Jae Rhee, and his family moved to neighborhood (last year). Not in U.S. long, but Jae's English pretty good.
- Jae and I partners for science experiments so get to know him a little. Jae's shy but tries to do his part in everything. Like him, try to be friendly.
- The Rhees open small store. I go in, Jae's unpacking fruit, says hi. When I pay for milk, Jae's mother looks away (I'm smiling at her), puts change on counter, not in my hand. Feels odd, but forget it.

Members of the groups could help each other with **Writing Assignment: Part 3** as students interpret and state the meanings of their experiences.

EXTENSION

To encourage students to stretch their imaginations, have them do some fantasy writing. Have students pretend to be in a place where they have never been. Have them freewrite their experiences as they imagine the who, what, where, when, how, and why of this fantasy place. ☛

- Happens more (with Mr. Rhee too). Other people—kids *and* parents—start to talk. "Rhees unfriendly. Rude. Think they're better." Feel funny around Jae; just do experiments, don't talk.
- Rhees' store not doing well. One day Jae's not in school—they've moved, new people in store. Surprised, mixed-up feelings.
- Social studies class this year, unit on "cultural differences." Teacher talks about how gestures, feelings about personal space, and respectful behavior differ from one culture to another.

PART 3:
WRITING ASSIGNMENT
Stating the Meaning of Your Experience

What you've just done for the experience about Jae Rhee, now do for your own experience. Look closely at your notes about main events, thoughts, and feelings, and write one statement of meaning. You can use a simple framework like "I realized that _____," or "At first, I _____, but afterward I _____."

👁 VISUAL CONNECTIONS
Ideas for Writing. Have students write a dialogue between two students in which one student faces a problem about learning to live in a new environment. The other student should respond or react to the new student's problem. After your students have written their dialogues, they can role-play them or read them aloud.

ANSWERS
Critical Thinking Exercise

Answers may vary.

While the writer has learned something about other people from the experience (people from Asian cultures can mean something completely different by their gestures than westerners), the writer also has experienced inner change (the writer no longer presumes an understanding of external signals, but looks for deeper communication).

ENRICHMENT
Have students create a collage with magazine pictures that depict the topic of their personal narratives. They can find scenes that illustrate details from their charts and create captions for each scene. ■

Organizing Your Ideas

The natural order for the events of a narrative is *chronological:* what happened first, second, third, and so on. The notes you've made should already be in chronological order, but check to be sure. Do all the events follow in sequence, so that a reader can move easily from one to another?

 REFERENCE NOTE: For more help with chronological order, see pages 82–83.

 WRITING NOTE Are there exceptions to the rule of chronological order? Yes. You might start at the end of your experience and then "flash back" to its beginning. For example, in a narrative about losing your ring, you could first describe yourself on hands and knees, under the bleachers, searching for it. After painting that interesting scene for readers, you could explain—in chronological order—how you got there.

WRITING NOTE

As students consider flashbacks as a possible organization technique for their narratives, it may help them to see this technique used in a literary piece. A good subject for study would be "An Occurrence at Owl Creek Bridge" by Ambrose Bierce. Have them read the stormy and examine its sequence of events.

👁 VISUAL CONNECTIONS

Ideas for Writing. After discussing Gary Larson's cartoon, you may want to stress that order is important in composition; however, chronological order is not the only way to arrange narrative events. You may want to remind students that many successful writers and screenwriters use flashbacks to make their works less predictable and more interesting. Challenge students to attempt a flashback arrangement of their narrative events. Remind students to begin with the most important or striking event and then continue with the occurrences that led to the event.

154

"And so you just threw everything together? ... Mathews, a posse is something you have to *organize*."

OBJECTIVES

- To analyze the details and meaning of a personal narrative
- To organize and draft a personal narrative

MOTIVATION

Begin the drafting stage of the writing process by having students consider a good personal experience story that they have heard lately. Ask students to list the elements of the story that held their interest. [They might cite the language, the events, the way the teller told the story, the subject matter, who was involved, suspense, or humor.] ☞

Writing Your First Draft

The Structure of Your Personal Narrative

Like other essays, personal narratives have three parts: *introduction, body,* and *conclusion.* You use the introduction—one or two paragraphs—to grab your readers' attention (usually with specific details) and to supply background information: What do readers need to know about people, places, or events to understand your experience? Your introduction may also let your readers know the experience you're going to tell about has a certain importance. It's not just another story.

In the body, you present events in chronological order. To connect these events clearly for readers, you can use transitional words like *at first, then,* and *finally.*

In the conclusion (again, maybe only one paragraph), you bring your essay to a close by explaining the meaning of your experience. But that doesn't mean tacking on a moral—"I learned never to lie"—at the end. It means that the meaning should be obvious to the reader because of the way you've portrayed the experience.

 REFERENCE NOTE: For more help on writing the introduction, body, and conclusion, see pages 122–134.

As you write, remember that—to have a strong impact on readers—a personal narrative

- relates an experience that meant something to you
- describes in specific, sensory detail the events, people, and places important to the experience
- explores your thoughts and feelings
- explains the experience's meaning for you

These elements are basic, but in the hands of different writers, they still produce unique results. In the following narrative, Annie Dillard recalls a childhood incident that still moves her as an adult. As you read, remember that the writer wants you to live through the experience with her. Do you?

Teacher's ResourceBank™
RESOURCES

> **WRITING YOUR FIRST DRAFT**
> - Writing a Personal Narrative

QUOTATION FOR THE DAY

"Good writing is not the perfectly tailored garment of a Personage, perfectly pressed since last he wore it; it is the rumpled suit of a living person, still relaxing from the strain of his labors, its pockets stuffed with trash and with things worth getting at." (Martin Joos, 1907–1979, American philologist)

Even though the first draft of a writing assignment needs a structure, students should know that it cannot be perfect at this stage. Ask them to discuss the importance of details as related to this quotation. They might compare the "with trash and with things worth getting at" with the details that bring writing to life.

After students have compiled their lists, explain to them that a written narrative must focus on these same elements because the reader will not have the benefit of a story-teller's physical presence. The writer has to create that effect with written words.

TEACHING THE LESSON

Before students read the professional model, ask a student to read aloud the introductory material on p. 155. Then refer students to Black Elk's narrative and ask them to identify the beginning, middle, and end of that selection. Students will then need to consider their prewriting and how they might go about arranging their information

USING THE SELECTION
from An American Childhood

1

What kind of rhythmic device does Dillard use here to get our attention?
[Alliteration of the *s* sound and the repetition of the phrase "it turned."]

2

Polyphemus moth: a large, tan American silkworm moth that has an eyespot on each hind wing

3

What sensory details does Dillard use here? ["clawed"; "one leg at a time"; "the wet, mashed thing"; "green jar"]

VISUAL CONNECTIONS
Exploring the Subject. Annie Dillard, 1945–   , is an American columnist and poet. She is best known for *Pilgrim at Tinker Creek,* for which she won the 1974 Pulitzer Prize in nonfiction.

| A PASSAGE FROM AN AUTOBIOGRAPHY |

from An American Childhood
by Annie Dillard

INTRODUCTION
Feelings/
Meaning of
experience

Summary of
experience

BODY
Event 1
Sensory details

Thoughts and
feelings

Sensory details

Event 2

Background
details

1 At school I saw a <u>searing</u> sight. It turned me to books; it turned me to jelly; it turned me much later, I suppose, into an early version of a runaway, a <u>scapegrace</u>. It was only **2** a freshly hatched Polyphemus moth crippled because its mason jar was too small.

The mason jar sat on the teacher's desk; the big moth emerged inside it. The moth had **3** clawed a hole in its hot cocoon and crawled out, as if agonizingly, over the course of an hour, one leg at a time; we children watched around the desk, transfixed. After it emerged, the wet, mashed thing turned around walking on the green jar's bottom, then painstakingly climbed the twig with which the jar was furnished.

There, at the twig's top, the moth shook its <u>sodden</u> clumps of wings. When it spread those wings — those beautiful wings — blood would fill their veins, and the birth fluids on the wings' frail sheets would harden to make them tough as sails. But the moth could not spread

Writing Your First Draft **157**

Detail

its wide wings at all; the jar was too small. The wings could not fill, so they hardened while they were still crumpled from the cocoon. A smaller moth could have spread its wings to their utmost in that mason jar, but the Polyphemus moth was big. Its gold furred body was almost as big as a mouse. Its brown, yellow, pink, and blue wings would have extended six inches from tip to tip, if there had been no mason jar. It would have been big as a wren.

Sensory details

Event 3
Details

4

The teacher let the deformed creature go. We all left the classroom and paraded outside behind the teacher with pomp and circumstance. She bounced the moth from its jar and set it on the school's asphalt driveway. The moth set out walking. It could only heave the golden wrinkly clumps where its wings should have been; it could only crawl down the school driveway on its six frail legs. The moth crawled down the driveway toward the rest of Shadyside, an area of fine houses, expensive apartments, and fashionable shops. It crawled down the driveway because its shriveled wings were glued shut. It crawled down the driveway

Sensory details

5

Details

Sensory details

4

pomp and circumstance: ceremonial procession; showy display

5

Why does the writer repeat the word "crawl"? [Perhaps the repetition is used to emphasize the moth's struggle survive in the world.]

VISUAL CONNECTIONS
Exploring the Subject. The Polyphemus moth of North America has a wing spread of 12.5 cm. Although butterflies and moths are closely related, (they both belong to the lepidoptera order) they differ to an extent. Butterflies usually fly by day and rest with the wings raised over the back; however, moths usually fly by night and rest with their wings wrapped over their bodies or outspread.

Help students with **Writing Assignment: Part 4** by photocopying the beginnings of all the models in this chapter. Have students experiment with several beginnings of their own and share them with the class. This will give those students having difficulty getting started an opportunity to discuss ideas and receive feedback.

INDEPENDENT PRACTICE

Divide the class into pairs or groups of three to complete **Exercise 3**. Remind them to discuss not only the organization, details, feelings, and meaning of the narrative; but also how the figurative language adds to the story.

Background
details

toward Shadyside, one of several sections of town where people like me were expected to settle after college, renting an apartment until they married one of the boys and bought a house. I watched it go.

CONCLUSION
Thoughts
Details

Feelings

Event 4
Feelings
Meaning of
experience

6

I knew that this particular moth, the big walking moth, could not travel more than a few more yards before a bird or a cat began to eat it, or a car ran over it. Nevertheless, it was crawling with what seemed wonderful <u>vigor</u>, as if, I thought at the time, it was still excited from being born. I watched it go till the bell rang and I had to go in. I have told this story before, and may yet tell it again, to lay the moth's ghost, for I still see it crawl down the broad black driveway, and I still see its golden wing clumps heave.

6

How does Dillard figuratively describe the moth and why? [She uses a metaphor comparing the image of the moth to a ghost, perhaps to make the reader aware of how the image keeps coming back to the author, who learned at an early age how hard it must be for frail things to survive in a world that often doesn't care.]

ANSWERS
Exercise 3

Answer may vary.

1. The moth emerges from the cocoon, walks on a twig, and tries to open its wings. The jar keeps its wings closed. The teacher takes the moth outside. Unable to fly, the moth walks off down the driveway.

2. Students should include a detail such as "gold, furred body" and a feeling such as "excited from being born."

SELECTION AMENDMENT
Description of change: excerpted
Rationale: to focus on the concept of expressive writing presented in this chapter

EXERCISE 3 ▶   **Analyzing a Personal Narrative**

Read the essay about the crippled moth (pages 156–158), and then meet with two or three classmates to discuss these questions.

1. In this experience, the main actor is the moth, and the writer is an observer. What are the events that Annie Dillard describes?
2. Dillard is known for using precise, fresh words to describe both things and feelings. Find a sensory detail about the moth and a detail about feelings that you especially liked—or were surprised by.
3. Where does Dillard work background, or helpful explanations, into her essay? What do you learn?
4. Dillard tells us the importance of the experience in her first paragraph. What do you think the moth meant to her?
5. Dillard reveals the meaning of the experience again at the end of the narrative. How does she do that without tacking on a moral?

ASSESSMENT

Students should turn in their group answers from **Exercise 3**. Mastery of **Writing Assignment: Part 4** can be determined by observation and conferencing or by having students turn in the assignment for evaluation.

RETEACHING

To help students examine the importance of organization and details in a narrative, take a brief story and divide it into about ten or more sections, depending on the length of the story. Divide the class into small groups. Scramble the sections of the story so they are no longer in sequence, distribute the scrambled story to each group of students, and

A Basic Framework for a Personal Narrative

Annie Dillard is a professional writer, and as you saw, she's experienced enough to make her writing more than a little bit out of the ordinary. But when you're learning to write a personal narrative, a simpler model may help. The following narrative shows a good framework for your writing.

A WRITER'S MODEL

The Diving Lesson

INTRODUCTION

Without admitting it to myself, I always seemed to live in the shadows of my older brother and sister. After all, they were "A" students, popular leaders in every club. Whenever I met new people, they'd say, "Oh, you're Elizabeth and Gerald's younger sister!" I liked the attention, but it had a bad side, too. You see, I made average grades, had a few friends instead of hundreds, and was too shy even to join a club. Secretly, I always suspected people wondered how in the world we could be from the same family.

Background information

Feelings

Details

Thoughts

BODY
Event 1

But something magical happened when I turned twelve. That June, my parents began taking the family to a local community center. We could swim, play games, and visit with other families. Actually, though, I'm not sure what my brother and sister did during those hot summer days at the center, because for the first time in my life I was too busy doing my own thing.

Foreshadowing of meaning

Details

Sensory detail

Every day I watched three or four kids practice their dives: jackknives, swan dives, half gainers. I memorized all the names, studied all their moves, and imagined I was the one springing high in

Details

Thoughts

3. The explanation of the moth spreading its wings in the first part of the third paragraph and the description of the size of the jar in the latter part of that paragraph help explain what is happening physically to the moth during emergence. The moth's not being able to spread its wings is compared to young people not being able to spread their wings in a stifling community.

4. The experience made Dillard a reader and a "scapegrace." Students might answer that the moth in the jar is a metaphor for how Shadyside clips its youths' wings.

5. The meaning of the experience is revealed through symbolism which catches the reader's attention because of the subtle comparison of the writer's situation and the moth's situation in the last two paragraphs. The meaning of the experience is thus as clear as a tacked on moral could make it, and yet a lot more subtle than a moral would make it.

have them put the story back together. When they have done so, have each group read its story. Compare the results of each group's efforts, and then have students list the types of clues they looked for as their groups organized the stories.

CLOSURE

Allow students to discuss their concerns about this first draft. What difficulties have they encountered? What part of the writing has gone smoothly? What parts of their prewriting have they not used? Have they discovered other information they have now added? Be sure students are aware that these concerns are natural and that everyone

VISUAL CONNECTIONS
Exploring the Subject. The graceful swan dive is a dive that is made with the diver facing the water and arching her body backward when leaving the diving board. The diver leaves the board with arms and legs extended and eyes fixed on a point at the far end of the pool. As the diver's body rises, she lowers her arms at right angles to her body. As she descends, her eyes focus on a spot in the water that is 3 to 5 feet from the board. This is where the diver enters, arms overhead and body nearly vertical.

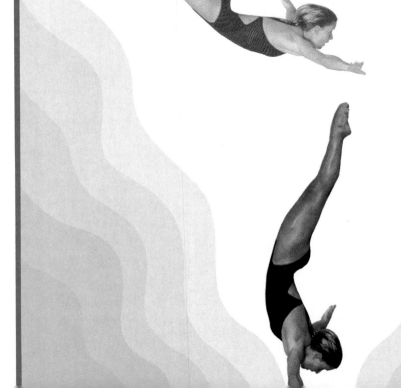

the air, twisting gracefully, cutting into the water without a splash. Instead I did plain dives from the pool's edge. The board was for pros.

Sensory details

Event 2 Then one day it happened. The lifeguard and diving coach, a college student who swam like he'd been born in the water, called to me just as I surfaced from a dive. "Why don't you do that off the board?" he asked. "I could teach you some others." If Brian hadn't been so friendly, I might have tried to escape. But instead I found myself on the board, knees like mashed potatoes, the pool noises just a roar in my head. There was no place to go but in--head first.

Details

Feelings
Sensory details

EXTENSION

To extend the idea of sensory details in expressive writing, ask students to find some details from their narratives, such as a specific place, person, or action. Have students take these details and describe them figuratively—either through personification, metaphor, or simile—and extend the description as completely as possible. ☞

Event 3	"See?" Brian said afterward. "You're a natural." That was the right thing to say, then, because I needed praise. But this "natural" never worked so hard in her life. At first, instead of perfect, splashless dives, I took a lot of water slaps in the face. Eventually, though, I was not just graceful but good enough for the center's team. Meanwhile my parents thought I was "playing at the pool."	Thoughts Feelings Sensory details Thoughts
Event 4	My mother still likes to tell the next part of this story. One Saturday, she and Dad and my brother and sister were eating lunch at the center's picnic area when they heard my name blared over a loudspeaker. Here Mother always says, "We thought you had drowned!" But by the time they ran to the pool, the announcements were about a diving and swimming meet. However, their shock wasn't over: There was their younger daughter, poised confidently on the board, waiting to execute her first competition dive.	Details Sensory detail Feelings Details
CONCLUSION **Meaning of experience**	And what a dive it was! I didn't win any medals in that meet, but I did get my picture in the newspaper (a clean swan dive from the <u>high</u> board) and had the reward of my parents' amazed and proud faces. Looking back, I realize now that my parents didn't need "proof" to think I was worth something. I did. I needed an accomplishment all my own, and diving was it. From then on, I felt like a person, not a shadow.	Details Feelings Thoughts

As you begin to write your first draft, you may find it helpful to model your essay on "The Diving Lesson." It uses the following pattern, or framework. (Notice how the framework allows you to add both events and details about these events according to what's most important in your experience.)

MEETING
INDIVIDUAL
NEEDS

LEP/ESL

General Strategies. Most stories written by Western authors employ the chronological pattern with an attention-grabbing introduction and a reflective conclusion. Students from cultures which may have very different patterns might find it helpful to realize that putting one's ideas on paper this way doesn't mean that one must think or create in such a linear, orderly fashion. Point out that it is acceptable to have a creative process that varies radically from the final product.

Students might then create a poem from their descriptions.

ENRICHMENT

Personal narratives are often similar to fables and parables, in that a character usually learns a lesson which illustrates the point of the story. Create a list of morals from Aesop's fables. Have each student choose one and write a fable or parable with that moral as the focus. ■

FRAMEWORK FOR A PERSONAL NARRATIVE

Introduction ● ● ● ● ● ▶	Attention grabber, Background information
Event 1 ● ● ● ● ● ● ● ▶	Details — event, people, places; Thoughts and feelings
Event 2 ● ● ● ● ● ● ▶	Details — event, people, places; Thoughts and feelings
Event 3 ● ● ● ● ● ● ▶	Details — event, people, places; Thoughts and feelings
Possibly more events ● ▶	More details about more events; Thoughts and feelings
Conclusion ● ● ● ● ● ▶	Meaning of the experience for narrator

WRITING ASSIGNMENT

PART 4:
Writing a Draft of Your Personal Narrative

You have events, you have details, you have a meaning. Now put them all together, sentence by sentence, so that readers can share your experience with you. Using your prewriting notes and following the framework above, write a rough draft.

"A writer's material is what he cares about."

John Gardner

SEGMENT 5 *(pp. 163–166)*
EVALUATING AND REVISING

OBJECTIVES

- To analyze the revisions of a model personal narrative
- To work collectively in evaluating and revising a personal narrative

- To evaluate and revise the content and organization of a personal narrative

Evaluating and Revising

You've just been the writer. Now you have to be a reader. A help in making this about-face is to set your draft aside for a while (to rest from your writer role). Doing this isn't so unusual. Many writers—including some famous ones—rely on reading their drafts as a start on revising them. Ernest Hemingway, for example, says this about rereading and revising (what he calls "editing") his work:

> I rise at first light and I start by rereading and editing everything I have written to the point I left off. That way I go through a book I'm writing several hundred times. Most writers slough off the toughest but most important part of their trade—editing their stuff, honing it and honing it until it gets an edge like a bullfighter's killing sword. One time my son Patrick brought me a story and asked me to edit it for him. I went over it carefully and changed one word. "But, Papa," he said, "you've only changed one word." I said: "If it's the right word, that's a lot."
>
> Ernest Hemingway, *Writers on Writing*

To evaluate and revise your own work, you can use the following chart. If you find a problem indicated in the left-hand column, use the revision technique suggested in the right-hand column.

Teacher's ResourceBank™
RESOURCES

EVALUATING AND REVISING
- Writing a Personal Narrative

QUOTATION FOR THE DAY

"The joy of life is variety." (Samuel Johnson, 1709–1784, English lexicographer, critic, and writer)

Lead students in a discussion of the areas of their narratives that could be varied (for example, vocabulary, sentence type, and sentence length).

VISUAL CONNECTIONS

Exploring the Subject. Ernest Hemingway (1899–1961) won both a Nobel and a Pulitzer prize for his writing. He developed a plain, forceful prose style characterized by crisp dialogue and vivid descriptions of places and things. Have students discuss Hemingway's description of his revising process, especially in light of their own narratives.

SELECTION AMENDMENT
Description of change: excerpted
Rationale: to focus on the concept of evaluating and revising presented in this chapter

MOTIVATION

Put an excerpt from a story or personal narrative on a transparency after you have deleted most of its sensory details, figurative language, and expressive elements, and added some stiff, formal wording. After students have read the story, ask them if they think the story lacks anything. List their responses on the chalkboard.

TEACHING THE LESSON

At this time, students should check the content of their drafts to make sure that they have provided enough information to interest the reader and that they have organized their story in such a way that the events are clear.

Work through the first question of **Exercise 4** with your students.

ADVANCED STUDENTS

Especially talented writers in a class sometimes feel they gain little from revision sessions. Point out that good writing depends on the writer's ability to make sound decisions and choices, and that good writers usually develop a sensitivity for details, word choices, and organization; therefore, they can identify and improve the weaknesses in their own work. Students should also become more adept at improving their own writing by helping to generate ideas, solutions, and possible alternatives for the problems they see in others' writing.

 ## INTEGRATING THE LANGUAGE ARTS

Vocabulary Link. Students might benefit from creating a class thesaurus poster on which they have listed synonyms for certain verbs that they tend to use repeatedly in a narrative, such as *go* and *said.* The poster could be displayed on the wall and whenever students come up with a new word or synonym, they can add it to the list.

---

164   *Expressive Writing*

EVALUATING AND REVISING PERSONAL NARRATIVES

EVALUATION GUIDE	REVISION TECHNIQUE
1 Is the tone friendly, honest, and informal?	**Replace** stiff and formal wording with conversational language.
2 Does the writer use first-person point of view?	**Replace** third-person pronouns with first-person pronouns.
3 Is there enough background information?	**Add** details that help readers understand events, people, or feelings.
4 Do details make the events, people, and places clear and real?	**Add** details that appeal to the five senses.
5 Are thoughts and feelings described?	**Add** details about important thoughts and feelings of people in the narrative.
6 Are the events in chronological order?	**Reorder** events in the order in which they happened.
7 Has the writer revealed the meaning of the experience?	**Add** a few sentences to the conclusion showing the experience's importance to you.

Reproduce a paragraph similar to the one in **Exercise 5.** Have students point out areas that need improvement.

Have students work independently on **Exercise 4.**

You may want to have students begin **Exercise 5** independently. Have them make their evaluations and highlight the areas they feel need improvement.

For **Writing Assignment: Part 5,** have students evaluate their narratives, highlighting in different colors words that indicate a friendly and informal tone, background details, sensory details, thoughts, and feelings. Then have them underline the sentences that express the meaning of their narratives.

Reminder

When you evaluate and improve your narrative, make sure it

- begins with an attention-grabbing introduction
- includes clear transitions between events and paragraphs
- uses a variety of sentences

EXERCISE 4   **Analyzing a Writer's Revisions**

Study the writer's revision of the fifth paragraph in "The Diving Lesson" (pages 159–161). Then answer the questions that follow the paragraph.

"See?" Brian said afterward. "You're a natural." That was the right thing to say,
[because I needed praise.]
then, but this "natural" never worked so   **add**

hard in her life. Eventually, though, she   **replace**

was not just graceful but good enough for   **reorder**

the center's team. At first instead of perfect   **add**
[took a lot of water slaps in the face.] [meanwhile]
dives, I did pretty bad ones. My parents   **replace/add**

thought I was "playing at the pool."

1. Why did the writer add *because I needed praise* in the third sentence? Do you think breaking this sentence into two sentences is a good idea? Why or why not?
2. Why did the writer move the sentence beginning *Eventually, though . . .*? How does this help the meaning?
3. In the same sentence, what's the reason for replacing *she* with *I*?
4. Why did the writer replace *did pretty bad ones* with *took a lot of water slaps in the face*? What's the effect of the change?
5. Why did the writer add *splashless* to the next-to-the-last sentence and *meanwhile* to the last sentence?

MEETING INDIVIDUAL NEEDS

LEP/ESL

General Strategies. Have students verbalize their analyses of the writer's revisions in **Exercise 4** before answering the questions.

ANSWERS

Exercise 4

Any answer that may vary is indicated by an asterisk (*).

1. The additional clause explains why Brian said the right thing. *Students should express their own opinions about the change. Some may like short, concise sentences; other might feel the long sentences sound more like real speech.

2. The sentence was out of chronological order; making the team should follow, not precede, practice.

3. This change corrects a problem in the point of view.

4. The writer has added specific sensory details so the reader can more clearly picture those first dives.

5. "Meanwhile" shows the parents' chronological relation to her diving practice.

ASSESSMENT

Have students turn in both their assignments and group notes from **Exercise 4**. For **Exercise 5**, have the groups turn in their revised paragraphs. To assess **Writing Assignment: Part 5**, have students turn in their highlighted drafts, peer evaluations, and revised drafts.

CLOSURE

Ask students to discuss ways of evaluating and revising drafts. List their suggestions on the chalkboard and have them contemplate how they might approach evaluating and revising in the future. Would they do anything differently? ■

ANSWERS

Exercise 5

Responses may vary. Students should correlate their revisions with the **Evaluating and Revising Personal Narratives** chart. They may make revisions to create more conversational language; replace the third-person pronouns with first-person pronouns; add details that help with thoughts and feelings; add sensory details; reorder events; or add sentences that depict the importance of the event.

GRAMMAR HINT

Students can improve their use of action verbs if they understand the difference between linking and action verbs and active and passive voice in writing. As students work on revising their drafts, they could circle all linking verbs and look for ways they can change them to more active constructions.

EXERCISE 5 ▶   **Evaluating a Personal Narrative**

The following paragraph ends a narrative about losing a ring—a gift from the writer's grandmother. In a small group, evaluate the paragraph and suggest changes to improve it. Use the guidelines on page 164.

> I thought seeing my grandmother's sorrowful face would be the hardest part of the whole experience. What the guilty girl learned was different. My grandmother, gentle and soft-voiced, wasn't upset about her nice ring. She got it when she was nineteen. What she said made a big impression on me. My fear was really hardest.

GRAMMAR HINT

Using Action Verbs

Action verbs express action, both physical and mental: *She **dances** like a pro and **knows** the new styles.* Action verbs are important in a personal narrative because your whole subject is action of one kind or another: events, thoughts, and feelings. Make them as precise and vivid as possible.

EXAMPLES   I **sprang** high in the air, **twisted** gracefully, and **cut** into the water without a splash.

 REFERENCE NOTE: For more information on action verbs, see pages 524–525.

WRITING ASSIGNMENT   PART 5:
Evaluating and Revising Your Personal Narrative

Now, judge and improve your own paper. Use the chart on page 164 to evaluate and revise your narrative.

OBJECTIVE

- To proofread and publish a personal narrative

TEACHING THE LESSON

After reviewing problem areas, students can begin **Writing Assignment: Part 6.** Students should inform you of the publishing method they have chosen and then proceed to publish their personal narratives. Ask students to compare their first and final drafts and to note changes that took place during the writing process. ■

Proofreading and Publishing **167**

Proofreading and Publishing

You'll probably need to recopy, retype, or reprint your revised essay. Then carefully proofread it for mistakes in grammar, punctuation, and spelling, and publish it in some way. Here are two suggestions.

- Have an "Unforgettable Experience Day" in class. Be ready to play the part of storyteller when it's your turn. Practice reading out loud beforehand, so that you can read with expression and look up from the page.
- Make a performing script from your narrative for a readers' theater, a class skit, or a video.

WRITING ASSIGNMENT

PART 6:
Proofreading and Publishing Your Personal Narrative

Read your paper with an eagle eye for errors, fix them, and then publish your essay, using the ideas listed above or your own.

"Most of the basic material a writer works with is acquired before the age of fifteen."

Willa Cather

Teacher's ResourceBank™

RESOURCES

PROOFREADING AND PUBLISHING
- Writing a Personal Narrative

QUOTATION FOR THE DAY

"Watch your use of the word *because*. You don't have to link sentences up and make reasons for them. The juxtaposition speaks for itself. It is a matter of grammar. Don't get bogged down in the need to explain." (Natalie Goldberg, American writer, poet, and teacher).

Goldberg advises the writer to make statements such as, "Rico sped over to the mall. He needed that belt he had seen yesterday," instead of linking them with *because*. Ask students to work in pairs to create such statements.

INTEGRATING THE LANGUAGE ARTS

Technology Link. To help students get started with the proofreading stage, let them try one of the computer software programs designed for that purpose. The programs highlight various errors, identify them, and offer the user various options for correction.

OBJECTIVES

- To analyze a description of a personal utopia
- To use the writing process to describe a personal utopia

MOTIVATION

Begin the writing workshop by asking students if there are things about the world they would like to change. Have them brainstorm what they would change and why and how they would change things. List their ideas on the chalkboard. Then have students freewrite on one of the changes and share their responses.

Teacher's ResourceBank™
RESOURCES

WRITING WORKSHOP

All the resources for this chapter may be used in this segment.

QUOTATION FOR THE DAY

"The Utopian is a poet who has gone astray." (William Ralph Inge, 1860–1954, Dean of St. Paul's Cathedral, London)

Lead students in a discussion of what "utopia" means [either an idealized place or situation or a visionary scheme for a perfect society]. Then ask students to agree or disagree with the quotation in a short paragraph.

USING THE SELECTION
from A Modern Utopia

1

tramway: British, a track for streetcars

2

reticulations: networks

3

draught horses: horses for pulling heavy loads

168

WRITING WORKSHOP

Imagining a Utopia

You've looked at the personal narrative as a form of expressive writing. Another form of expressive writing is creating a **utopia.** Long before Sir Thomas More coined the word *utopia* in 1516 (it means "no place" in Greek), people have imagined and expressed in writing their personal, perfect places or worlds. Sometimes they propose a model for the future, and sometimes their utopias are expressed in stories.

One early believer in a utopia was the writer H. G. Wells. (He also wrote *The War of the Worlds* that so terrified Americans when Orson Welles broadcast it on the radio in 1938.) In 1905, Wells described his version of utopia in the book *A Modern Utopia*. In this excerpt, Wells describes transportation in the ideal society. As you read, think about Wells's predictions of his future utopia. How right or wrong was he?

from A Modern Utopia
by H. G. Wells

1   Such great tramways as this will be used when the Utopians wish to travel fast and far; thereby you will glide all over the land surface of the planet; and feeding them and distributing from them, innumerable minor systems, clean little electric tramways I picture them, will

2   spread out over the land in finer reticulations, growing close and dense in the urban regions and thinning as the population thins. And running beside these lighter railways, and spreading beyond their range, will be the smooth minor high roads such as this one we now approach, upon which independent vehicles, motor cars, cycles, and what not, will go. I doubt if we shall see any horses upon this fine, smooth, clean road; I doubt if there will be many horses on the high

3   roads of Utopia, and, indeed, if they will use draught horses at all upon that planet. Why should they? Where the world gives turf or sand, or along special tracts, the horse will perhaps be ridden for exercise and pleasure, but that will be all the use for him; and as for

TEACHING THE LESSON

Discuss with students other ways they can express their emotions using narration [letters, conversation, journals, and diaries]. Then you can direct students to the selection. Once students understand about utopias and how they might describe one, they can write about their own. After students read the excerpt, have them discuss how they visualize the scene Wells depicts. Then they can discuss the questions that follow the excerpt.

Students can now proceed through the prewriting, writing, evaluating and revising, proofreading, and publishing steps on their own. They may need several days to complete their descriptions of a utopia.

☞

4   the other beasts of burthen, on the remoter mountain tracks the mule will no doubt still be a picturesque survival, in the desert men will still find a use for the camel, and the elephant may linger to play a part in the pageant of the East. But the burthen of the minor traffic, if not the whole of it, will certainly be mechanical. This is what we shall see even while the road is still remote, swift and shapely motor-cars going past, cyclists, and in these agreeable mountain regions there will also be pedestrians upon their way. Cycle tracks will abound in Utopia, sometimes following beside the great high roads, but oftener taking their own more agreeable line amidst woods and crops and pastures; and there will be a rich variety of footpaths and minor ways. There will be many footpaths in Utopia. There will be pleasant ways over the

5   scented needles of the mountain pinewoods, primrose-strewn tracks admidst the budding thickets of the lower country, paths running beside rushing streams, paths across the wide spaces of the corn land, and, above all, paths through the flowery garden spaces amidst which the houses in the towns will stand. And everywhere about the world, on road and path, by sea and land, the happy holiday Utopians will go.

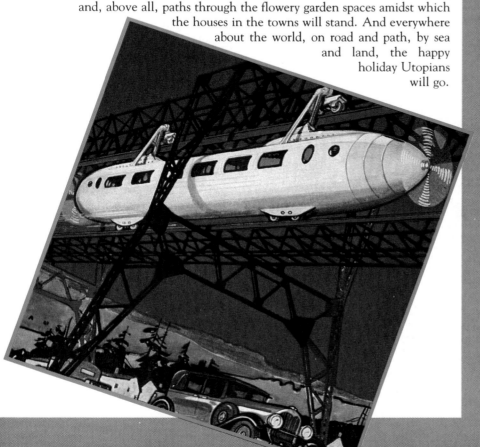

4

burthen: archaic for burden

5

What imagery do you notice in this passage?
["scented needles of mountain pinewoods"; "rushing streams"; "wide spaces of the corn land"; "flowery garden spaces"]

MEETING **INDIVIDUAL** NEEDS

LEP/ESL

General Strategies. Some students who are new to this country might see the United States as a utopia, or they might dream about going back home to make their native country better. Ask these students to write about the utopia their native country could be.

LEARNING STYLES

Visual Learners. Because the **Writing Workshop** is an imaginative writing activity, learners who rely on visual input might need to draw pictures of their utopia before writing about it. Or, they could look in books or magazines for pictures of what they imagine their utopia would include. Futuristic artwork might be stimulating to these students as they try to visualize what they will be writing about.

SELECTION AMENDMENT
Description of change: excerpted
Rationale: to focus on the concept of expressive writing presented in this chapter

You may want students to turn in all steps of the writing process to check for mastery and understanding. Assess each step individually before evaluating the final product.

CLOSURE

Ask students to summarize what they gained from creating and describing their personal utopias. Do they believe that they have the power to change the world around them for the better? If so, how do they plan to go about making those changes? ∎

ANSWERS
Writing Workshop Questions

1. Students will probably agree that Wells' prediction about electric tramways has only been fulfilled in large cities. Some might point to electric bullet trains being planned by some cities and might suggest Wells' predictions may yet come true.

2. Wells predicted horses would be used only for pleasure riding. This has proved correct. (Note: He does not mention racing because he is only discussing transportation, not sports.)

3. While this passage deals only with nature in terms of traffic in the future, students should find that Wells sees nature mostly as a decorative background. It isn't depicted as threatening danger, presenting engineering challenges, or even affording useful employment. Wells visualizes Utopians being more a part of nature than people are today as shown in the last four sentences of the excerpt.

⬛ COOPERATIVE LEARNING

Students could work in small groups to create their utopias and produce as a group descriptive writing with illustrations that could be used as a wall display.

1. How accurate was Wells's prediction about "clean little electric tramways" that would spread out over the country?
2. In 1905, most transportation was provided by the horse. What was Wells's prediction about the horse? How accurate was he?
3. What role does Wells visualize nature playing in Utopia? Would Utopians be more or less a part of nature than people are today?

Describing a Personal Utopia

Prewriting. Think of something that really matters to you about life in your community or city, the United States, or the world. (You may want to brainstorm from areas like education, environment, government, transportation, male/female roles, or art to find a specific focus. For example, if you brainstormed about male/female roles, you might think about females in the military.) Then, concentrating on your topic, imagine the utopia, or perfect world, you would want to see one hundred years from now. Use any comfortable prewriting technique (like freewriting, visualizing, or "What if?" questions) to generate details. (See pages 24–34 for more information on prewriting techniques to use.)

Writing, Evaluating, and Revising. There's no set form or length for a personal expression of a utopia. But in this exercise, write informally and describe the utopia in the present tense, as if it actually exists ("No cars clog the streets as electric monorails speed by high overhead.") If possible, have someone read your draft. Can the reader picture your world? make sense of how it works or what it contains? Look for changes that will make the utopia more "real."

Proofreading and Publishing. After you check for errors and correct them, you may want to see if you and your classmates can combine your utopias into a single society. Give it a name; find or draw pictures of places, vehicles, people and their clothes; write the music that people listen to. Then, through a skit or practiced readings of your papers, tell the whole class what life is like in your utopia.

SEGMENT 8 *(pp. 171–173)*
MAKING CONNECTIONS

SELF-EXPRESSION AND ART OBJECTIVE
- To create a visual self-portrait

PERSONAL NARRATIVES ACROSS THE CURRICULUM OBJECTIVE
- To write a personal narrative about an encounter with a special animal

MAKING CONNECTIONS

SELF-EXPRESSION AND ART

Words aren't the only way to express something about yourself. You could write your own theme song, design an outfit, or, like artist Pablo Picasso, paint a self-portrait.

Try your hand at making a visual portrait of yourself. You don't have to be an artist. You could make a collage or an abstract or symbolic portrait— anything that says, "This is me." (For example, Picasso— who also created collages—was very interested in African sculpture. What animal or object would you want in your self-portrait?)

SELF-EXPRESSION ACROSS THE CURRICULUM

Science

Animals fascinate people. Whether the setting is a swamp where scientists observe the rare Florida crocodile, or the backyard where your sister watches a nest of wrens, or even your living room where the whole family plays with a puppy, human beings spend some important moments with their furred, feathered, slippery, and hard-shelled friends.

Aldo Leopold was an observer of nature. In this narrative from *A Sand County Almanac*, he relates an experience of watching the performance of a male woodcock. As you read, notice the specific details that make the bird's flight seem real.

SELF-EXPRESSION AND ART
Teaching Strategies

Have students read the material and then brainstorm about all of the animals or objects they could include in their self-portraits. They might even create imaginary animals or objects.

GUIDELINES

Students should be able to tell how the animal or object in their self-portrait relates to their personality.

VISUAL CONNECTIONS
About the Artist. Pablo Ruiz y Picasso (1881–1973) was born in Malaga, Spain, the son of an art professor. Even as a young art student, he experimented with avant-garde styles. Picasso was also a successful sculptor, graphic artist, and ceramicist who explored many styles and themes throughout his long career.

PERSONAL NARRATIVES ACROSS THE CURRICULUM
Teaching Strategies

The selection by Aldo Leopold should be read aloud. Students might then examine the narrative for sensory details, the author's thoughts and feelings, and the meaning of the event. As students look at the suggested activity, you may want to review the steps of the writing process.

Students can now proceed on their own to write a personal narrative about their encounters with a special animal.

172

USING THE SELECTION
Sky Dance

1

What is the comparison here?
[The dance of the bird is metaphorically compared to a live theatrical performance.]

2

woodcock: a small game bird with short legs and a long, sensitive bill used to probe for worms; related to the snipe

3

What sensory details are used here? [hearing: "musical twitter," "soft liquid warble," "peenting"; sight: "wide spirals," "tumbles like a crippled plane"]

Sky Dance
by Aldo Leopold

I owned my farm for two years before learning that the sky dance is to be seen over my woods every evening in April and May. Since we discovered it, my family and I have been reluctant to miss even a single performance.

The show begins on the first warm evening in April at exactly 6:50 p.m. The curtain goes up one minute later each day until 1 June, when the time is 7:50. This sliding scale is dictated by vanity, the dancer demanding a romantic light intensity of exactly 0.05 foot-candles. Do not be late, and sit quietly, lest he fly away in a huff.

The stage props, like the opening hour, reflect the temperamental demands of the performer. The stage must be an open amphitheater in woods or brush, and in its center there must be a mossy spot, a streak of sterile sand, a bare outcrop of rock, or a bare roadway. Why the male woodcock should be such a stickler for a bare dance floor puzzled me at first, but I now think it is a matter of legs. The woodcock's legs are short, and his struttings cannot be executed to advantage in dense grass or weeds, nor could his lady see them there. I have more woodcocks than most farmers because I have more mossy sand, too poor to support grass.

Knowing the place and the hour, you seat yourself under a bush to the east of the dance floor and wait, watching against the sunset for the woodcock's arrival. He flies in low from some neighboring thicket, alights on the bare moss, and at once begins the overture: a series of queer throaty *peents* spaced about two seconds apart, and sounding much like the summer call of the nighthawk.

Suddenly the peenting ceases and the bird flutters skyward in a series of wide spirals, emitting a musical twitter. Up and up he goes, the spirals steeper and smaller, the twittering louder and louder, until the performer is only a speck in the sky. Then, without warning, he tumbles like a crippled plane, giving voice in a soft liquid warble that a March bluebird might envy. At a few feet from the ground he levels off and returns to his peenting ground, usually to the exact spot where the performance began, and there resumes his peenting.

It is soon too dark to see the bird on the ground, but you

can see his flights against the sky for an hour, which is the usual duration of the show. On moonlight nights, however, it may continue, at intervals, as long as the moon continues to shine.

At daybreak the whole show is repeated. In early April the final curtain falls at 5:15 a.m.; the time advances two minutes a day until June, when the performance closes for the year at 3:15. Why the disparity in sliding scale? Alas, I fear that even romance tires, for it takes only a fifth as much light to stop the sky dance at dawn as suffices to start it at sunset.

4
5
6

What animal—wild or tame, seen once or seen every day—has made a strong impression on you? It may be an animal that you have seen on a farm or even on a city sidewalk. Write a personal narrative about your encounter(s) with that special animal. What was the importance of what happened? What can you generalize from it? You can write one paragraph or more, but remember to use details to make this animal, what happened, and what you felt really come alive for readers.

4
disparity: lack of equality

5
What seems to be Leopold's meaning of his experience? [Perhaps he sees animals in their naturalistic setting acting out some of the very rituals that human go through, such as wooing and courting.]

6
suffices: satisfies

GUIDELINES

Students should record specific observations about the animal, noting the time and place of their observations and details of its behavior.

SELECTION AMENDMENT
Description of change: excerpted
Rationale: to focus on the concept of expressive writing presented in this chapter

Chapter 5

USING DESCRIPTION

OBJECTIVES

- To identify the descriptive mode and to analyze the characteristics of descriptive writing
- To select an appropriate topic for a descriptive essay
- To analyze the intended audience for a descriptive essay
- To select details to support a description
- To organize and draft a descriptive essay
- To evaluate and revise the content of a descriptive essay
- To proofread and prepare a descriptive essay for publication

Motivation

You may want to initiate a class discussion on the nature of description and its importance in writing. Begin by having students silently choose familiar locations and then give several details describing their chosen places to the class. Students should not be allowed to give any proper names or other give-away information. Instead, they might give details about a building's shape, size, or color. Allow other students to guess what locations are being described. Point out the importance of specific details. Finally, ask questions that will prompt students to evaluate which details were helpful in the descriptions and why those details were important. Also, students might have suggestions for details that would have been more relevant in the descriptions. Emphasize the importance of clear, meaningful details.

Introduction

Through a discussion, help students see that description not only is entertaining, but also is essential when sharing experiences and feelings. Further, help students realize that description must be written with a purpose in mind. To achieve that purpose the writer must use specific details, sensory details, and figurative language to make comparisons.

You may want to help students distinguish the descriptive mode from other modes of discourse. For example, if the student's purpose is to inform about a certain event that has occurred, the student might give a sequential listing of happenings (narrative); a comparison of that event with another (classificatory); a review of the event's impact on the people attending (evaluative); or a word picture showing the audience's reaction to the event (descriptive).

Integration

This chapter can easily enhance other activities in your classroom as well as in other disciplines. For example, if students are reading Shakespeare's *Tragedy of Julius Caesar* or Sophocles's *Antigone*, have them find words or phrases in the plays that describe characters such as Caesar or Antigone. Then have students analyze the way the characters' descriptions influence the audience's reaction to the characters.

If you are doing a research unit, you could use the material on pp. 210-211 to assist students in distinguishing objective information from subjective information.

You could incorporate a grammar study emphasizing parts of speech when students create word banks of their own. Use the resulting word lists for reference material for your students.

The chart on the next page illustrates the strands of language arts as they are integrated into this chapter. For vocabulary study, glossary words are underlined in some writing models.

QUOTATIONS
All **Quotations for the Day** are chosen because of their relevance to instructional material presented in that segment of the chapter and for their usefulness in establishing student interest in writing.

Integrating the Language Arts

Selection	Reading and Literature	Writing and Critical Thinking	Language and Syntax	Speaking, Listening, and Other Expression Skills
from **"Date with Dracula"** by Daniel D. Morrison **176-177** from **"The Most Beautiful Girl in the World"** by Stanley Bing **184-185** from *Blue Highways* by William Least Heat-Moon **193** from **"The Swan"** by Richard Zabel **194** from *The Street* by Ann Petry **196-198** **"If All the Unplayed Pianos"** by Winfield Townley Scott **207** from *Ernie's War: The Best of Ernie Pyle's World War II Dispatches* by Ernie Pyle **209-210**	Responding personally to literature **178, 198, 207** Finding details **178, 198, 207, 210** Analyzing connotation and description **178, 198** Identifying and analyzing personification **178, 198** Judging author's purpose, audience, and tone **184-185** Identifying point of view **184-185** Evaluating and making judgments **184-185, 198, 207** Recognizing figurative language **196-198, 210** Recognizing free verse poetry **207** Finding details in poetry **207**	Evaluating description **178, 198, 210** Analyzing personification **178, 198** Analyzing purpose, audience, and tone **184-185** Analyzing point of view **184-185** Differentiating objective and subjective details **185, 211** Choosing a subject for descriptive writing **185** Gathering and charting ideas **185, 188** Collecting details using observation, recall, research, and imagination **188, 189** Applying interpretive and creative thinking **188, 189, 195, 198, 207, 208** Listing details **189** Choosing emphasis **189** Organizing details **190** Making comparisons using metaphor and simile **195** Evaluating descriptive writing **198, 200, 202-203, 210** Writing a first draft of a description **199** Analyzing a writer's revisions **202-203** Evaluating and revising descriptive writing **203** Proofreading and publishing a descriptive essay **204** Analyzing poetry **207** Writing a free verse poem **208** Proofreading and publishing a free verse poem **208** Writing an objective description **211**	Recognizing connotations of words **178** Using metaphor and simile **195** Proofreading for errors in grammar, usage, and mechanics **204** Proofreading a free verse poem **207**	Interviewing for information **189** Working with classmates to evaluate a writer's revisions **202-203** Reading poetry aloud **207, 208** Presenting an oral report **210**

SEGMENT PLANNING GUIDE

Whether you are planning for a quick review of a writing concept or preparing an extended lesson on composition, you can use the following Planning Guide to adapt the chapter material to the individual needs of your class.

SEGMENT	PAGES	CONTENT	RESOURCES
1 Creating Pictures and Images	175-178		
Literary Model from **"Date with Dracula"**	176-177	Guided reading: responding to literature and analyzing descriptive writing	
Reader's Response/ Writer's Craft	178	Model evaluation: responding to literature and analyzing descriptive writing	
2 Uses of Description	179-180		
3 Prewriting	181-190		Listing Sensory Details
Focusing Your Description	181-184	Guidelines: choosing a subject and thinking about purpose and audience	
Deciding on Tone	183	Guidelines: choosing appropriate tone for purpose and audience	
Exercise 1	184-185	Applied practice: analyzing a model	
Literary Model from **"The Most Beautiful Girl in the World"**	184-185	Guided reading: analyzing purpose, audience, and tone	
Writing Assignment: Part 1	185	Applied practice: developing a subject	
Planning Your Description	186-187	Guidelines: collecting details, determining an emphasis, and organizing details	
Exercise 2	188	Applied practice: collecting details	
Exercise 3	189	Cooperative learning: collecting details	
Writing Assignment: Part 2	189	Applied practice: collecting details and finding an emphasis	
Organizing Details	189	Guidelines: using appropriate order	
Chart: Using Order	190	Guidelines: analyzing methods of order	
Writing Assignment: Part 3	190	Applied practice: organizing details	
4 Writing	191-199		Writing a Description
Using Descriptive Language	191-194	Guidelines: using sensory words and figurative language	
Chart: A Sensory Word Bank	192	Guidelines: using a word bank	
Literary Model from *Blue Highways*	193	Guided reading: examining sensory words	
Literary Model from **"The Swan"**	194	Guided reading: examining a figure of speech	
Chart: Figurative Language	194	Guidelines: examining types of figurative language	

All the resources listed in this chapter are located in the Teacher's ResourceBank™.

SEGMENT	PAGES	CONTENT	RESOURCES
Critical Thinking: Making Comparisons	195	Guidelines: using comparison for description	
Critical Thinking Exercise	195	Applied practice: making comparisons	
Literary Model from *The Street*	196-198	Guided reading: examining figurative language	
Exercise 4	198	Applied practice: analyzing a description	
A Writer's Model	198-199	Guided reading: examining description in an essay	
Writing Assignment: Part 4	199	Applied practice: writing a first draft	
5 *Evaluating and Revising*	*200-203*		Writing a Description
Chart: Evaluating and Revising Description	201	Guidelines: applying evaluation and revision techniques	
Grammar Hint	202	Writing suggestion: using participles	
Exercise 5	202-203	Cooperative learning: analyzing a writer's revisions	
Writing Assignment: Part 5	203	Applied practice: evaluating and revising	
6 *Proofreading and Publishing*	*204-206*		Writing a Description
Publishing	204	Publishing ideas: reaching a specific audience	
Writing Assignment: Part 6	204	Applied practice: proofreading and publishing	
A Student Model	205-206	Sample: examining a descriptive essay	
7 *Writing Workshop*	*207-208*		All the resources for this chapter may be used in this segment.
A Free Verse Poem	207	Guidelines: writing free verse poetry	
Literary Model/Questions "If All the Unplayed Pianos"	207	Guided reading: examining a free verse poem	
Writing a Free Verse Poem	208	Applied practice: writing a free verse poem	
8 *Making Connections*	*209-211*		
Combining Description with Narration	209	Introduction: using description in narration	
Literary Model from *Ernie's War: The Best of Ernie Pyle's World War II Dispatches*	209-210	Guided reading: recognizing description in narration	
Description Across the Curriculum: Objective Description in Science	210-211	Guidelines: writing an objective description Applied practice: writing an objective description	

WHOLE-CHAPTER RESOURCES
A Writing Process Log, A Writing Prompt, Holistically Graded Models, Assessment Portfolio Materials

CREATING PICTURES AND IMAGES

OBJECTIVES

- To write personal responses to literature
- To identify and analyze the characteristics of description in writing

TEACHING THE LESSON

You may want to initiate a class discussion about description before beginning the chapter. Begin by asking a student to describe his or her favorite food. Prompt the student with questions about taste, smell, or feel. Then use the resulting description to generate responses to these questions:

 VISUAL CONNECTIONS
The Bedroom

About the Artist. Vincent Van Gogh was born in the Netherlands in 1853. He did not begin painting until he was 27 years old, and until then he had trouble succeeding in other occupations. Van Gogh started his art studies in The Hague, but he left the school and painted independently until he moved to Paris at age 33. Van Gogh's brother Theo directed an art gallery there that dealt in impressionist paintings; Gauguin, who influenced Van Gogh greatly, was among the artists represented by Theo.

In 1889 Van Gogh was admitted to the hospital of Saint Pol at Saint-Rémy for treatment of his mental illness. There he developed the imaginative, visionary style that he is noted for. Although Van Gogh is considered an impressionist painter, his work differs from that of other impressionists. While his contemporaries were painting realistic subjects in an expressive style, Van Gogh adapted impressionist techniques to paint what he imagined and referred only indirectly to reality.

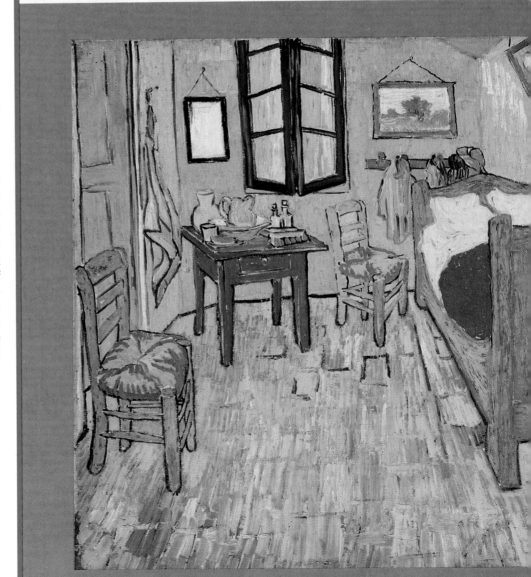

5 USING DESCRIPTION

1. What type of information helps to describe an object?
2. Why is detailed description necessary?

Have a volunteer read the introductory paragraphs of the chapter. Pointing out the sensory details, read aloud the literary model. Explain the importance of these details when describing. The model contains vocabulary that may be unfamiliar to some students; be certain they are able to understand the content.

You may want to guide students through the **Reader's Response** questions and allow a few students to share stories of their own. If students are hesitant to share, you may want to tell a short anecdote of

Creating Pictures and Images

One way to explain what something looks like is to show a picture of it. Another way is to **create a picture or image** with words.

Writing and You. When you read a novel, you feel closer to the main character when you picture what he or she looks like. When you read about the sea, a foreign land, or a mysterious setting, images begin to form in your head. Like painters—Van Gogh, for example—writers help you form these images by appealing to your senses. They bring them to life with their words. Have you ever tried to describe your room to someone who has never seen it?

As You Read. In the following selection, Daniel D. Morrison describes a castle in Romania. As you read, notice how he uses sensory details to bring the scene to life.

The Bedroom, (1888), Vincent Van Gogh, Dutch, 1853–1890. Oil on canvas. 29 ½″ × 37″. The Art Institute of Chicago, Helen Birch Bartlett Memorial Collection.

LESS-ADVANCED STUDENTS

Students might need help to understand connotations as discussed in **Writer's Craft.** Explain that words can have very close meanings (denotation) but have very different feelings (connotations). Give several examples to illustrate this concept, such as *curious* and *nosy* or *remind* and *nag.*

your own. Discuss the slide glosses of the model with your students to model analyzing literature.

Before asking students to answer the **Writer's Craft** questions on their own, make sure all students understand the words *personification* and *connotations*.

CLOSURE

Ask the class to give a brief explanation of description and to explain the importance of sensory detail. Have students think of at least three situations in which description would be important.

from
"DATE WITH DRACULA"

by Daniel D. Morrison

USING THE SELECTION
Date with Dracula

1

British author Bram Stoker's novel *Dracula* (1897) helped to popularize the legend of the vampire. In these legends that originated in Asia and Europe, the vampire is an unsettled soul, usually a criminal, who must suck human blood to survive. All of the evil-doing was done by night; the vampires must return to sleep in their coffins during daylight.

2

What kind of place is Morrison describing? How do the words he uses make you feel about the castle grounds? [It is a frightening place. The words are full of evil or danger.]

3

What does the character probably imagine is coming toward him? What do you think Morrison intends you to think is coming? [Answers may vary. A likely answer is Dracula.]

1 **D**racula once stood on the steps where I was now standing. I backed slowly away from the castle door and sat on a large rock overlooking the castle grounds. It was **2** nearly dark now. The trees glared silently but shook their branches with <u>malevolent</u> intent; the rocks all around me squatted like black <u>gnomes</u>. A mist began to fall down upon the valley, wrapping the mountains in a dirty gray shroud. Below me, on the hillside, the leaves rustled; someone, or something walked toward me. Then it stopped. Was it watching, waiting?

My fears now rising uncontrollably, I decided to return to the shop below to join Monique. But as I turned to walk down **3** the trail, I could hear someone coming up the trail toward me, so I called out, no more than a whisper. "Monique?" There was no answer, but the steps continued their steady advance on the gravel trail. I called again; again, no answer. I backed up to where the hilltop ended in a <u>precipice</u>. I could retreat no farther.

You might want to have students read the British novel *Dracula* by Bram Stoker. Published in 1897, this novel has been the basis for several film versions, including *Nosferatu* in 1922 and *Dracula* in 1931. ■

VISUAL CONNECTIONS

Exploring the Subject. The actor Bela Lugosi starred in Tod Browning's classic film *Dracula* (1931). Dozens of vampire movies followed throughout the twentieth century. Lugosi's Dracula, with his pallid face, protruding incisors, and dark hair helped to create the vampire stereotype known today.

"There was nothing I could do, nowhere to run, no one to help me."

Whoever it was—whatever it was—continued to approach, hidden from view by the boulders strewn among the trees. I stood waiting, the sound of my heart competing with the excited voices in the forest.

Slowly, steadily, a low dark form rounded a boulder and crested the

4 hill. A dog, all broad shoulders and massive muscles, walked toward me, its head hung low to the ground, its eyes staring directly at me. It had thick, black fur, with a wide muzzle, lips curled back just slightly with the hint of a snarl. It walked with purpose in its steps, the stare <u>malicious</u>. The animal blocked my only avenue of escape. There was nothing I could do, nowhere to run, no one to help me.

4

What senses does Morrison use in describing the dog? [sight, sound, touch]

As the dog neared, I could hear its labored breath, could see the drool on its jowls, the white of its pointed canine fangs. Its eyes locked onto mine and never blinked. This, I thought, has to be a nightmare. The voices in the trees grew louder, then hushed as if in anticipation of what was about to happen. The creature walked to within a few feet of where I stood, and it seemed I could feel the heat of its moist breath on my face, on my neck. Then it stopped.

READER'S RESPONSE

1. Do Morrison's descriptions seem real and believable to you? Why? How do they make you feel?
2. Like Morrison, have you ever been frightened by your own imagination? (Why not swap stories with your classmates?)

WRITER'S CRAFT

3. What are five specific details from the description that appeal to your senses of sight or hearing?
4. Descriptive writers sometimes use personification— giving human qualities to nonhuman objects—to help tell about a scene or an incident. How does Morrison use personification to describe trees and rocks?
5. Connotations—the emotional overtones—of words are often important in descriptions. In Morrison's description of the dog, what are some words that especially make you see and feel the author's terror?

ANSWERS

Reader's Response

Answers will vary.

1. Morrison's descriptions do seem real and believable because they are so detailed and concrete and because they play on a variety of senses. They make the reader feel as if he or she were present at the scene.
2. Each student should have a different story to tell.

Writer's Craft

Answers will vary.

3. nearly dark (sight), rocks . . . squatted (sight), mist began to fall (sight), leaves rustled (hearing), someone, or something walked toward me (hearing—he cannot see it yet)
4. Morrison writes that "the trees glared silently but shook their branches with malevolent intent," and "the rocks . . . squatted."
5. "lips curled . . . with the hint of a snarl," "the stare malicious," "drool on its jowls," "white of its pointed canine fangs." "never blinked," "creature"

SELECTION AMENDMENT
Description of change: excerpted and indention added
Rationale: to focus on the concept of descriptive writing presented in this chapter

SEGMENT 2 *(pp. 179–180)*
USES OF DESCRIPTION

TEACHING THE AIMS

This section is designed to give students a simple overview of the possible uses of the descriptive mode. Discuss the different aims of writing—informative, expressive, persuasive, and creative—and have students suggest examples for each. If possible, point out uses of the descriptive mode in suggested examples. You may also want to bring newspaper articles to class and to ask students to identify the use of description in different articles, as well as the purposes behind the articles.

Assess students' understanding of the aims by having individual students tell which ☞

179

Uses of Description

Description as a kind of writing always has a primary purpose. This is true whether the author is trying to present an accurate description of something real or a picture that reveals his or her feelings or beliefs. The author carefully chooses details that support the primary purpose. There are many uses of description. Here are some examples.

To Inform: writing a newspaper article in which you describe the opening of a new music store, including the modern interior, the displays of CDs and tapes, and the people who are workers or customers there; writing a report for science in which you describe the landscape and the workers at a dinosaur dig in Colorado.

▶ **To Express Yourself:**   in your journal, writing a description about a school or community event that particularly affected you; in a letter to the editor of your community newspaper, describing the success of a school fund-raising dinner.

To Persuade: describing the effects of pollution on a specific lake or river to persuade people to clean up the environment in the region; describing a neglected area of town to convince the city council to improve living conditions.

▶ **To Be Creative:**   creating the setting and describing the characters in a short story; re-creating in a poem the sights and sounds of a storm that causes a boat to break loose from its mooring and crash into the rocks as it is driven onto the shore.

If you pick up a brochure at a travel agency, you'll find a description of exotic, faraway lands. If you read the sports section of your local newspaper, you'll find descriptions of specific plays made by the players of various sports. If you look for them, you'll find descriptions around you everywhere—in novels, in encyclopedias, in news stories, in poems, in biographies, even in textbooks.

MEETING INDIVIDUAL NEEDS

LEP/ESL

General Strategies. In writing expressive descriptions, some of your students might use dialect, such as *let on* for *pretend, mighty* or *powerful* for *very,* and *victuals* for *food.* Explain that for this aim of writing, the use of words and phrases that resemble common speech is a necessity. In expressive writing, because the writer focuses on him- or herself, the emphasis is on the inner feelings and thoughts of the individual.

COOPERATIVE LEARNING

Divide the class into groups of four or five students. Give groups several old magazines and ask students to find examples of descriptive writing in articles or advertisements. You may also want students to create collages of the descriptions and to label the different aims of descriptive writing.

aim or purpose a specific use of description is
trying to achieve. ■

Descriptions, if they are effective, have one thing in common—they "paint a picture" in the mind of the reader.

LOOKING
AHEAD

In the main part of this chapter, you'll write a description that is subjective. Your primary purpose will be expressive or creative. Keep in mind that descriptive writing

■ uses precise words
■ provides sensory details that re-create in the mind of your reader a person, place, thing, or event
■ is organized in a manner that is easy to follow

"*Don't describe it. Show it. That's what I try to teach all young writers – take it out! Don't describe a purple sunset, make me see that it is purple.*"

James Baldwin

INTEGRATING THE LANGUAGE ARTS

Literature Link. If the work is available in your literature textbook, ask students to analyze the use of description in Mark Twain's "Genuine Mexican Plug." Have students label the purpose of different selections of descriptive writing from the story. For example, ask students if Twain's first-paragraph description of horse riding is mainly intended to be informative, expressive, persuasive, or creative. You may want to point out to students that although Twain's primary purpose is expressive, he also persuades, informs, and entertains.

OBJECTIVES

- To analyze purpose, audience, and tone in an expressive/descriptive passage
- To select an appropriate topic for expressive/descriptive writing
- To utilize observation, recall, research, and imagination to collect details
- To choose an impression for an expressive/descriptive essay
- To organize details for an expressive/descriptive essay

☞

Writing a Description

Focusing Your Description

Have you ever been in a movie audience when the picture became fuzzy, and the audience began to chant "Focus! Focus!"? Like a clear, sharp movie image, a good description also needs a focus. Before you write, bring your description into focus by thinking about your subject, your purpose and audience, and your attitude toward the subject.

Choosing a Subject

Many times outside circumstances decide the subject of your description for you. For example, if you were involved in an accident, you'd need to describe the damage for an insurance claim. Or, your history teacher might ask you to describe conditions that led up to the French Revolution.

But if the choice of a subject is yours, it's a good idea to think of a specific person, object, or place that you already know well or that you can observe directly.

Thinking About Purpose and Audience

At times, good description stands on its own. For instance, you may just want to recapture a specific moment for your journal. More often, however, good description is used for a specific *purpose*, as an important part of other types of writing. For example, if you're writing to inform your chemistry teacher about the results of your lab experiment, part of your report might be a description of the color, texture, and odor of the resulting solution. Or, if you're writing a letter to the editor urging an all-school, anti-litter campaign, your most convincing support might be a detailed description of the bleachers after last Saturday's game.

QUOTATION FOR THE DAY

"Every novel is an attempt to capture time, to weave something solid out of air." (David Beaty, 1919–   , British novelist)

You may wish to use the quotation to help students begin thinking about the subjects, purposes, and audiences for their descriptive writing. Ask students to recall novels or short stories they have read recently and to freewrite for a few minutes about some scenes or descriptive details they remember. Lead the class to understand that details help make descriptions more memorable and more realistic.

Begin by having students brainstorm a list of possible topics. As they make suggestions, have a student list the possibilities on the chalkboard. Urge students to give as many ideas as possible to show them the diversity of subjects they might choose to describe.

As you read over the material on audience, purpose, and tone, remind students that these considerations will eliminate some of the numerous ideas presented during the **Motivation** or that they have come up with on their own.

For each stage of the prewriting material, have student volunteers read the text

LEP/ESL

Asian Languages. The word *tone* has several meanings in English, such as "musical sound," "body condition," "aspect of writing," and "aspect of some languages." Chinese, Thai, Lao, and Vietnamese also have tone; in these languages the meaning of a word depends on the musical pitch at which it is spoken. For example, *bain* in Vietnamese may mean "three," "grandmother," or "cypress" depending on pitch.

LESS-ADVANCED STUDENTS

To aid students in gathering details and to help strengthen their powers of observation, have them use a cluster organizer like the following example:

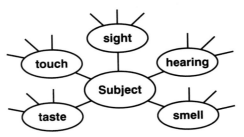

182   *Using Description*

Your *audience* for a description is usually very closely tied to your purpose. As you think about why you're writing your description, consider your readers by asking:

- Who is going to read this?
- Why are they reading it?
- What do I want my audience to think, feel, do, or know after reading my description?

Once you know why you're writing a description and who your audience is, you'll also know whether your description should be *objective* or *subjective*.

Objective Description.   An *objective description* creates an accurate, thorough picture without revealing a particular judgment or feeling about the subject. You write this kind of description when your purpose is to inform and sometimes to persuade. Objective description consists mostly of realistic, or factual, details, as this short description of a starfish shows.

A typical starfish has five arms, one of which is slightly bent. Its surface is etched with small nodules. Many starfishes are a uniform color, a pale mustard yellow.

Subjective Description.   A *subjective description* creates a selective picture that reveals the writer's thoughts and feelings about the subject. When your purpose is to express yourself, to be creative, and sometimes to persuade, you will probably write a subjective description. Subjective description consists mostly of sensory details and figurative language (see pages 191–194), as this second starfish description on the next page shows.

> When I look at the starfish skeleton on the table, it almost seems alive. It's like a little man, his head bent slightly as he looks at me and points with one hand back to the sea where I found him.

Deciding on Tone

You also focus your description by deciding on an appropriate tone. In an objective description, you usually use a more formal, impersonal tone. To remain more distant from your subject, you usually use the *third-person point of view*—pronouns such as *it, she, he,* and *they.* Like the writer of the objective description about the starfish, you aren't in the picture at all—you remain separate from it, never revealing your own thoughts and feelings.

In a subjective description, you often use an informal, personal tone to bring yourself close to the subject. Like the writer of the subjective starfish description, you put yourself in the picture by including your own thoughts and feelings. In this case, you use first-person pronouns such as *I* and *we*—the *first-person point of view.* (In some instances, such as writing a description to persuade an audience, you may choose a third-person point of view instead.)

Charting the decisions you make now can help you focus your description as you continue developing it. For example, if your subject is the black-necked crane of Asia, you might record your decisions this way.

HERE'S HOW

SUBJECT:	black-necked crane of Asia
PURPOSE:	for a news editorial; to persuade others to help save the crane
AUDIENCE:	students, teachers, general public
POINT OF VIEW:	third person
TONE:	personal
TYPE:	subjective

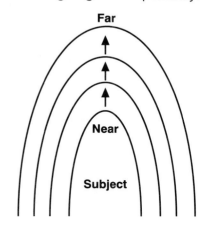

Work with students to describe another animal objectively or subjectively. Then students might speculate on the audience, purpose, and tone involved.

Use this class discussion to help guide students in their choices of a writing topic.

To help students with **Exercise 2**, practice gathering details with the class.

Divide the class into four groups and assign each group a collecting method: direct observation, recall, imagining, or researching. Have each group use one of the topics generated during **Motivation** to list all details about that topic that it can. (The research group might need some time in the library or with resource materials.) Then have each

INTEGRATING THE LANGUAGE ARTS

Reading Link. You may want to reinforce the importance of point of view in establishing the tone in writing. Present several magazine or newspaper articles with differing points of view to your students. Guide your students in a discussion of the differing effects of first-person point of view versus third-person point of view.

CRITICAL THINKING
Analysis

Have students rewrite an editorial from a current newspaper or magazine by using a point of view different from that used by the author. For instance, if the article were written in first-person, it should be rewritten in third-person. Divide the students into small groups to analyze the different effects of the original article and the rewrite. One student in each group should be designated as the reporter. This student will report the group's decisions to the entire class.

184

Saving the Black-necked Crane

EXERCISE 1   **Analyzing Purpose, Audience, and Tone**

Read this description about an unusual dog named Elizabeth. Then answer the questions that follow.

I named the dog Elizabeth. Height: about thirty inches. Weight: thirty-five pounds. Eyes: brown. Tongue: red. Tail: rich and plumy. A coat of pure china white, so thick and lustrous and profuse that people would later suggest that I shear her and turn the output into a serape. In the summer she shed badly. In the winter, worse. All my clothes and furniture were coated with a fine layer of white flax. When she was young, her tummy was as pink as a baby's bottom, and she had a marvelous, doggy smell, clean, pungent, yet sweet. Her personality? All I can say is that when the Lord made her, he forgot to add any malice, guile, or aggressiveness. Didn't chase squirrels, even. If another dog attacked her, she would roll over on her back immediately and expose her soft underbelly, clearly conveying the message: "Go ahead and kill me. I don't mind, but I think it would be a totally unnecessary waste of energy. But hey, just my opinion." Not once in her life was she hurt by any living creature.

group list its details on the chalkboard. Emphasize the large number and variety of details generated by these collection methods.

Before assigning **Exercise 3**, discuss possible interview questions with your class. Have students make lists of questions from the suggestions of other students.

Between assigning **Writing Assignment: Parts 2 and 3**, discuss with students possible organizational methods. Remember that some students will need extra time for research and to arrange interviews before completing these writing assignments.

Elizabeth was not smart, but she made the most of it. "She's the sweetest dog in the world," said a friend about her. "But she's got an IQ somewhere between a brick and a houseplant." . . . For all intents and purposes, she was mute: Not a bark, yelp, nor whimper escaped her. In fourteen years, I heard her voice maybe three times. It was always a shock.
Stanley Bing, "The Most Beautiful Girl in the World"

1. What is the author's purpose: to express himself, to inform, or to persuade the reader to do or believe something? How can you tell?
2. Who do you think is the writer's audience? Why would they be reading this description?
3. What is the writer's tone? How does he feel about his subject?
4. What point of view does the writer use?
5. Is the description objective or subjective? How can you tell?

PART 1:
Developing a Subject for Your Description

The writer of the description you've just read wrote about his dog. Now, choose a specific person, place, or object as the subject for your own subjective description. Then, fill out a chart like the one on page 183, recording your ideas about your subject, purpose, audience, point of view, tone, and type.

ANSWERS
Exercise 1

1. The writer is primarily expressing his own experience. It is written as a personal reminiscence. He is also informing and entertaining the reader.

2. The audience is probably other dog owners/lovers who are reading for pleasure.

3. The tone is informal and humorous. The writer is close to and fond of his subject.

4. The writer uses first-person point of view.

5. The description is subjective. It uses informal, conversational style and tone (for example, sentence fragments, imaginary speeches from the dog, and slang words like *tummy*) and first-person point of view to reveal the writer's feelings about the dog. Words and phrases such as "marvelous," "sweetest dog in the world," and the statement about Elizabeth's IQ clearly convey personal impressions.

SELECTION AMENDMENT
Description of change: excerpted
Rationale: to focus on the concept of purpose, audience, and tone presented in this chapter

COOPERATIVE LEARNING

You may want to have students exchange papers with partners to peer evaluate the feasibility of each other's chosen topics from **Writing Assignment: Part 1**. Students should be given a list of questions to address when looking over their partners' charts. For example, they may need to determine if information is available on a certain topic.

VISUAL CONNECTIONS

Exploring the Subject. The Indianapolis 500 is the most famous race on the Championship Trail. It is usually held on Memorial Day in Indianapolis, Indiana. There are thirty-three starting positions, and to qualify a driver must successfully compete in the trials on the two weekends prior to the race. If he wins the 500–mile race, he wins the richest purse in automobile racing.

186

---

186   *Using Description*

Prewriting

Planning Your Description

Have you ever arrived at the library without your library card or shown up for a test without a pencil? Anyone making an extra trip to retrieve the library card or to find a pencil probably has vowed to plan ahead next time. In writing a description, planning ahead means collecting details, determining an emphasis for your description, and organizing details. It will be time well spent.

Collecting Details

An effective description is made up of specific details. You can collect these details in several ways.

Observing Directly.   If you're writing about something you can observe firsthand, go directly to the source and study your subject carefully. For example, if you're describing your bicycle for a newspaper classified ad, look at the bike carefully. What is the exact color? Is the seat leather or vinyl—smooth or textured? How tall is it?

Recalling.   Sometimes your description may be about a subject you've seen before but can't observe directly now. Then, you have to tap into all the little details stored in your memory. Imagine yourself back in the time when

Assess students' mastery of audience, purpose, and tone through an evaluation of their performance on **Exercise 1**. For the development of an appropriate subject, you may use observation and conferencing. To evaluate students' abilities to collect and organize details, refer to their performance in **Exercises 2** and **3**.

For **Writing Assignment: Part 3**, have students exchange lists for peer evaluation. Encourage students to discuss and evaluate their ordering methods and choice of details with each other as you offer suggestions as needed.

you were actually observing your subject. For example, you might describe your experience last year at the Indianapolis 500 auto race. To re-create the scene, you would try to remember the sights (mobs of people), the sounds (loud roar of engines), and the smells (oil and grease).

Researching.   Sometimes you may have to describe a subject you haven't experienced directly. In this case, you can gather details from other sources: books, magazines, pictures, audiovisual materials, or interviews. For example, you might collect details about undersea sights and sounds by watching a Jacques Cousteau film. You might collect details on George Washington's life and appearance by reading an encyclopedia article, biography, or collection of letters and by observing his portraits.

Imagining.   Description can move beyond the boundaries of reality. To create a description of an imaginary person, place, or object, begin with what you know. For example, you know the features you'd identify in describing a real person. To create an imaginary one, just create the details in your mind—for a man, you'd decide on the color of his hair, the shape of his nose, the way he walks, stands, sits, talks, and so on.

Identifying an Emphasis

At times you may want to describe all parts of your subject. At other times you may want to create a special *emphasis,* or impression. For example, if you're trying to persuade your classmates to save the sandhill crane, you may want to emphasize its beauty. In this case, you would probably gather details about how the sandhill crane looks in majestic flight. However, you'd probably omit the loud penetrating noise that the crane makes. Or, in describing your dog, you may want to emphasize its friendliness. Details such as "sparkling eyes" and "thumping tail" would support this impression, but "muddy paws" or "matted fur" would not.

   Decide whether you want your description to convey a particular impression, and, if so, what it will be. Then evaluate the details you've gathered to decide which ones support that impression.

Write a brief description of a room on the chalkboard. Do not put the details in any specific order; rather, make the description convoluted and confusing. Work with students to rewrite the sentences in a new order that helps in understanding what the room really looks like.

Ask students to discuss the successes and difficulties they had while gathering details. Students should describe which collecting methods they found most helpful. Remind them that their descriptions are not written yet, and they may find more details to add in later.

ANSWERS

Exercise 2

Details will vary, but students should include details for senses other than just sight. For instance, the shoes might "click" or "whisper" as the wearer walks.

1. Each student should look carefully at the shoe and note its texture, color, shape, and odor. The student may also want to think about the way the shoe now feels on the foot. Observations should involve a variety of senses.

2. The student should at the same time compare the shoe with the way it once looked.

3. Each student should choose a specific kind of shoe for research.

4. It is very important that the student have a specific purpose in mind. Are the shoes for dress? For class? For running? For basketball? For hiking? Each purpose involves a different kind of shoe.

---

188   *Using Description*

EXERCISE 2 ▶ **Collecting Details**

Using the following steps, exercise your collecting skills on the subject of shoes.

1. Observe one of the shoes you're wearing now.
2. Recall how your shoe looked when it was new.
3. Research a shoe. Read up on high-button shoes or the latest trends in athletic shoes.
4. Imagine the "perfect" shoe: design and describe the "perfect" shoe for a specific purpose or for a special outfit.

On your paper, make a copy of the following chart. Use it as a guide for collecting as many kinds of details about shoes as you can. You probably won't fill in all the spaces.

	Sight	Hearing	Smell	Touch
Observing				
Recalling				
Researching				
Imagining				

HERE'S HOW

Have students extend their observational skills to write informative paragraphs using the narrative and descriptive modes. First, each student should choose a person to observe and then watch and record every detail of the person, the actions, and the setting. Then the writer will make a conclusion about the subject based on his or her observations and use this judgment as the topic sentence. Support should include sensory details and narrative details (actions). An example of a topic sentence might be, "It was obvious that the teacher wanted the day to end." ■

EXERCISE 3 ▶ **Speaking and Listening: Collecting Details**

Another way to gather details when you can't observe directly is to interview someone who has. To gather details about shoes teenagers once wore, interview a parent or an older friend or relative about their shoes when they were your age. Ask questions about style and appearance, but also ask for details related to other senses as well. For example, how did the shoes sound when the person walked down the sidewalk?

PART 2:
Collecting Details and Finding an Emphasis

Now that you're experienced in collecting details, concentrate on details for the subject you selected in Writing Assignment, Part 1 (page 185). List as many details about your subject as you can, using any of the techniques for gathering details: observing, recalling, researching, and imagining. If you feel it's appropriate, decide on an emphasis or impression you'd like to convey, too.

Organizing Details

You can create a vivid picture and highlight your emphasis by presenting details in a clear order. Spatial order, order of importance, and chronological order are three possibilities for doing this. The order that you actually use will depend on your purpose for writing and how you want your readers to feel or think.

INTEGRATING THE LANGUAGE ARTS

Listening Link. You may want to remind students that when conducting an interview, they should have a prepared list of questions. However, also point out the importance of listening in an interview. Many times the person being interviewed will bring up information or ideas that the interviewer did not plan to ask about. Listen for hints of further information and ask follow-up questions to get all the details.

Technology Link. If you have access to computers, consider having students use word-processing programs for their prewriting activities. For example, they could set up journals on their own word processing data disks. Each entry would be put in a different file on the disk, with students adding new thoughts to the files at any time.

TYPE OF ORDER	WHEN TO USE	EXAMPLE
spatial (from top to bottom, from side to side, from near to far)	primarily for sight details; to show how details are located in space	describe how a building looks from top to bottom or from left to right
importance (from least to most important, from most to least important)	for all types of details; to identify emphasis or to convey an idea or impression	describe sounds in the woods on a dark night, loudest to softest
chronological (time order)	for all types of details; to show the order in which events or actions occur	describe a crying child as she begins to cry and then gets louder and louder

 REFERENCE NOTE: For more information on the types of order, see pages 82–85.

Reminder

To plan your description

- observe, recall, research, or imagine your subject
- identify an emphasis or impression you want to convey
- arrange your details in a clear order

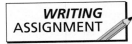
WRITING ASSIGNMENT

PART 3:
Organizing Details

Look carefully at the list of details you gathered in Writing Assignment, Part 2 (page 189). Thinking about your purpose, audience, and emphasis, decide on the best way to present your details. Add, subtract, or change any details that don't fit your plan. When you've finished, number the details in the order you think you'll be using them in your description.

WRITING YOUR FIRST DRAFT

OBJECTIVES

- To analyze the effectiveness of descriptive writing
- To write a first draft of a description

MOTIVATION

Give students one minute to look intently at a large poster or picture at the front of the room. Then have them freewrite a detailed description of the picture or poster. Allow students to share their descriptions with the class. Students who caught details not mentioned may want to point out these details. Bring the class to a consensus ☞

Writing Your First Draft

Now that you've collected and organized details for your description, it's time to write your first draft.

To create a clear image of your subject, you need to select specific words. For example, when the writer William Least Heat-Moon describes a room lighted by "three fifty-watt bulbs," you know exactly how much and what kind of light there was. When you describe how the sun reflects off a new car, *glinted* gives your readers a more specific picture than *shone*.

Good descriptions include specific adjectives, adverbs, nouns, and verbs that appeal to your senses. They may also include comparisons that help you understand the subject and give you new insights. When Virginia Wolfe describes sea anemones "stuck like lumps of jelly to the side of the rock," you understand how a sea anemone looks even if you haven't seen one firsthand.

Using Descriptive Language

Sensory Words. When you write, words and phrases that appeal to the senses make your observations come alive for your readers. Whenever possible, use the precise sound—*roared*, or *twittered*, or *cawed*; or touch—*icy* or *slimy*; or taste—*bitter* or *sour*; or smell—*rotten* or *sweet*. If you don't have a name for a smell, or a taste, or a touch, just name the source of the observation—"the scent of freshly baked bread."

QUOTATION FOR THE DAY

"You can get help from teachers, but you are going to have to learn a lot by yourself, sitting alone in a room." (Theodor Geisel, "Dr. Seuss," 1904–1991, American children's author and cartoonist)

As students begin writing their first drafts, share the quotation with the class. Explain that creating the first draft of a description is a part of the process that writers most often do by themselves. Tell students that they alone have access to the mental pictures they want to recreate on paper by using sensory words and figurative language.

VISUAL CONNECTIONS

Ideas for Writing. You may want students to locate pictures of various types of sea anemones in encyclopedias or other books and to write sensory descriptions of each type found. This collection of descriptive phrases and colorful pictures might make a pleasant display.

on the prominent details. Explain to students that this vivid description is what they want to capture in their own writing.

TEACHING THE LESSON

Have student volunteers read the opening paragraphs on p. 191. Be sure to discuss the importance of word choice with your students. Before reading **Using Descriptive Language** (p. 192), you may want to have students offer suggestions about ways they might improve the descriptiveness of words in their own writing.

LEP/ESL

General Strategies. You may find that some of your students produce their fresh, creative comparisons using figurative language by thinking of the appropriate words in their native languages and then looking the words up in bilingual dictionaries to find English equivalents. Often these comparisons fail to regard connotations. For example, instead of "The fist of loud music pounded all thought from my mind," a student might write "The hand of loud music pushed all thinking from my spirit." Some ESL students might need some extra time with you to work with additional examples of figurative speech.

ADVANCED STUDENTS

Ask students to try to include onomatopoetic words in their descriptions. You may need to remind your students that these are words whose sounds imitate the sounds they name, as in *sigh* or *murmur*.

Using a Word Bank. Sometimes writers keep lists of words, or word banks, to refer to when they're looking for just the right word. It's a little like having their own specialized thesaurus. Here's a word bank of sensory words you might refer to when you're writing descriptions.

A SENSORY WORD BANK		
SIGHT WORDS		
Appearance		
frail	glossy	flushed
sturdy	slender	muscular
pale	portly	angular
tapered	swollen	shapely
Color		
ivory	ebony	crimson
rose	hazel	canary
bronze	raven	pearl
milky	bleached	azure
SOUND WORDS		
boom	roar	rasp
whine	shriek	screech
hum	mutter	sigh
growl	snort	whimper
SMELL WORDS		
fragrant	earthy	spoiled
stench	piney	musty
flowery	stale	fresh
TOUCH WORDS		
cool	icy	fuzzy
oily	silky	velvety
gritty	sandy	slippery
TASTE WORDS		
sweet	tart	salty
tangy	sour	bittersweet
spicy	bitter	mellow

Have students attempt to add words to **A Sensory Word Bank** on p. 192. Also, some students may need to see or hear other examples of figurative language.

When reading the **Model for Description** (p. 196), occasionally point out the sensory details, similes, metaphors, and other devices used.

Stress that **A Writer's Model** on p. 199 is a model for students' own writing. Once again, you may want to pause while reading to have students point out especially descriptive details.

William Least Heat-Moon wrote a book about his travels on America's side roads. As you read this paragraph, notice how he re-creates what he observed through his senses.

> The old store, lighted only by three fifty-watt bulbs, smelled of coal oil and baking bread. In the middle of the rectangular room, where the oak floor sagged a little, stood an iron stove. To the right was a wooden table with an unfinished game of checkers and a stool made from an apple-tree stump. On shelves around the walls sat earthen jugs with corncob stoppers, a few canned goods, and some of the two thousand old clocks and clockworks Thurmond Watts owned. Only one was ticking; the others he just looked at.
>
> William Least Heat-Moon, *Blue Highways*

Although William Least Heat-Moon's description appeals most to his readers' sense of sight, it also includes details of sound ("ticking") and smell ("coal oil" and "baking bread"). The sensory words you use will vary depending upon your subject and emphasis. But remember that for both you and your readers, your five senses usually work together in creating an impression.

Figurative Language. To describe a person or object, you often make a comparison: "He acts just like his older brother." When you use *figurative language* (sometimes called figures of speech), you are also comparing. But, instead of comparing similar things, you're comparing

STUDENTS WITH SPECIAL NEEDS
Students with attention deficit disorder will probably have difficulty sitting still to write for long periods. You may want to provide other activities for students to break up their writing periods. By providing a peer-conference area or a teacher-student conference area, students will be able to get up and move around while continuing to improve their writing.

INTEGRATING THE LANGUAGE ARTS
Library Link. When trying to think of extra-descriptive words or phrases, students might need to use a thesaurus. To reinforce how a thesaurus is used, have students look up words in the word bank to add words to the bank.

SELECTION AMENDMENT
Description of change: excerpted
Rationale: to focus on the concept of sensory description presented in this chapter

Sometimes students have difficulty expanding details to make them more descriptive. You may want to give a list of descriptive words such as *red, loud, fast,* or *smooth* and work with students to write comparisons changing the words into more vivid phrases.

Have students answer the questions on **Exercise 4** as a class activity to reinforce the reasons one answer is correct or better than another.

Cont. on p. 196

COOPERATIVE LEARNING

As students add to the word bank, have five groups of students create a bulletin-board size chart to use as a reference throughout the unit. Each group of students could be given a different section to fill—sight words, sound words, smell words, touch words, or taste words. Students could have a week of competition to place as many words as they can on their section of the board.

INTEGRATING THE LANGUAGE ARTS

Literature Link. Anne Tyler, in her short story "With All Flags Flying," describes characters in many different ways, the least of which is by a physical description of their looks. As students read this short story, have them pay close attention to the character description. How is the old man described? What descriptions of other objects or places help the reader to see him clearly? What about Clara? Francie? Lead students in an analysis of the descriptions used. What was most effective? Least effective?

SELECTION AMENDMENT
Description of change: excerpted
Rationale: to focus on the concept of figurative language presented in this chapter

194

---

194   *Using Description*

unlike things that share one basic feature. Because the comparison is so unusual, it catches your audience's attention. Here's an example:

> "From the sky *South Dakota was a* perfectly flat *green-and-brown quilt.*"
>
> Richard Zabel, "The Swan"

The basic feature South Dakota and a quilt have in common is that they are flat and have alternating colors. Otherwise, they are very unlike things and make for an unusual comparison.

Used wisely, figurative language can help your readers' understanding by linking a familiar image with an unfamiliar one: *"Looking like a harmless drifting log, a crocodile* can float unnoticed toward its prey." As the following chart shows, figurative language may express comparisons in several ways.

TYPE OF FIGURATIVE LANGUAGE	EXAMPLE
A **simile** uses the words *like* or *as* to make the comparison.	The loud music shielded me like a crash helmet.
A **metaphor** makes a direct comparison.	The loud music was my crash helmet, protecting me from outside forces.
Personification gives human characteristics to things.	The fist of loud music pounded all thought from my mind.

OBJECTIVES

- To create descriptive metaphors and similes
- To create sentences that include metaphors and similes

TEACHING *MAKING COMPARISONS*

After reading the explanations and examples given in the textbook, work with students to use descriptions of classroom objects to create similes and metaphors. To assess students' understanding of these devices, evaluate students' performance on the **Critical Thinking Exercise.**

Writing Your First Draft   **195**

CRITICAL THINKING
Making Comparisons

If you're lucky, a fresh, creative comparison may occur to you as a sudden inspiration. Usually, though, you have to devote some effort to looking at reality in a new way.

To create a unique figure of speech, analyze the parts of your subject carefully. If you're describing a melting icicle, the drip may remind you of tears: *The dripping icicles were crying over their own departure.* Or, the icicle's shape may remind you of a sword: *The icicle is winter's sword.*

 CRITICAL THINKING EXERCISE:
Making Comparisons

Stretch your imagination. Create at least three original metaphors or similes by comparing an item from Column A with an item from Column B. Write a sentence expressing your comparison, adding descriptive words or phrases as you wish.

EXAMPLE   *The frightened child clung like a stamp to its mother.*

Column A	Column B
fog	sand
puppy	stamp
sailboat	leaf
bicycle	ball
child	tablecloth

MEETING INDIVIDUAL NEEDS

LEP/ESL

General Strategies. Being able to detect nuance of meaning is a skill that requires a broad and continuous exposure to English. You may want to present the **Critical Thinking Exercise** as a whole-class activity to offer support for ESL students. Ask the class to suggest sentences using the words in the columns, and write the suggestions on the chalkboard.

ANSWERS
Critical Thinking Exercise

Answers will vary. Possible comparisons include "The ball fled over the fence like an escaping puppy" and "The fog was a tablecloth completely covering the city." Additional possibilities include "The sailboat sailed over the water like a leaf on the wind," "The sleeping puppy was a ball that had rolled under the table," "The fog was thick as sand on a beach," "The bicycle coasted as effortlessly as a leaf falling from a tree," and "The tumbling child was a ball bouncing down the lawn."

Keep in mind that the first sentences are often the most difficult for the students to write. You may want to tell students they can worry about the best way to introduce their descriptions after most of the body has been written.

Students will need to write their first drafts independently. Student-teacher conferences during this stage of the writing process will help you to assess the students' progress while also allowing you to help students stay on task.

---

196   *Using Description*

WRITING NOTE

With overuse, figurative language loses all its freshness and originality and becomes stale and worn out. These worn-out expressions (for example, "cool as a cucumber" or "busy as a bee") are called *clichés.* Try to avoid them in your writing.

A Model for Description

Ann Petry created the following description for the opening of a novel. As you read, notice the specific words that appeal to various senses and emphasize a harsh, desolate feeling. Look for the writer's use of figurative language as she makes the wind seem human.

A PASSAGE FROM A NOVEL

from The Street
by Ann Petry

Personification

Sight detail

Specific details

There was a cold November wind blowing through 116th Street. It rattled the tops of garbage cans, sucked window shades out through the top of opened windows and set them flapping back against the windows; and it drove most of the people off the street in the block between Seventh and Eighth Avenues except for a few hurried pedestrians who bent double in an effort to offer the least possible exposed surface to its violent assault.

It found every scrap of paper along the street—theater throwaways, announcements of dances and lodge meetings, the heavy waxed paper that loaves of bread had been wrapped in, the thinner waxed paper that had enclosed sandwiches, old envelopes, newspapers. Fingering its way along the curb, the wind set the bits of paper

---

1

Ann Petry (1911–   ) is a graduate of the University of Connecticut. During her life she has been a pharmacist, salesperson, reporter, novelist, short-story writer, and biographer. Two of her better known novels include *The Narrows,* (1953) about racial conflict in a New England town, and *The Street,*(1946) which concerns poor people in a ghetto.

2

How does the description in the first paragraph of the selection make you feel? What kind of response do you think Petry wants to elicit from her readers? [The reader feels cold; she probably wants the reader to sense the harshness of the street.]

To assess students' mastery of the use of figurative language, evaluate their performance on **Exercise 4.** Student-teacher conferences during the writing stages will help you to evaluate the progress of students' writing.

Provide eight to ten relatively unfamiliar images (such as that of a wooly mammoth) and have students compare the unfamiliar image to a familiar one: for example, "A wooly mammoth lumbered across the horizon like a giant, slow army tank."

Writing Your First Draft **197**

3 | to dancing high in the air, so that a barrage of paper swirled into the faces of the people on the street. It even took time to rush into doorways and areaways and find chicken bones and pork-chop bones and pushed them along the curb.

It did everything it could to discourage the people walking along the street. It found all the dirt and dust and grime on the sidewalk and lifted it up so that the dirt got into their noses, making it difficult to breathe; the dust got into their eyes and blinded them; and the grit stung their skins. It wrapped newspaper around their feet entangling them until the people cursed deep in their throats, stamped their feet, kicked at the paper. The wind blew it back again and again until they were forced to stoop and dislodge the paper with their hands. And then the wind grabbed their hats, pried their scarves from around their necks, stuck its fingers inside their coat collars, blew their coats away from their bodies.

Touch detail

Sound details

3

barrage: a continuous attack of questions; a continuous firing of guns

MEETING
INDIVIDUAL
NEEDS

LEP/ESL

General Strategies. A Writer's Model includes words not used with their usual meanings, such as "cloud of pizza odors," in which *cloud* names something olfactory rather than visual as it usually does, or "head for" in which *head* means "go." Such word uses, as well as some words, such as *saucer* or *flicker,* may be unfamiliar to ESL students and may hinder their understanding of the passage. It is a good idea to check to see that students understand uncommon words and meanings.

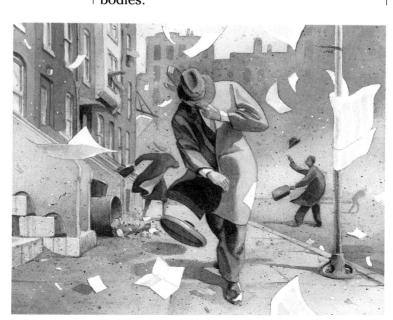

Ask students to share descriptive phrases from their own writing. What kinds of figurative language did they find most difficult to use? Easiest to use? Remind students that they will still have opportunities for revision if they come up with new ideas for description.

Have students bring in their science textbooks or scientific articles. Work with the class to compare the use of description in the scientific writing with that in the literature examples already read in class. List the similarities and differences on the chalkboard. ■

ANSWERS

Exercise 4

Answers for all except number 1 will vary. Here are some possibilities:

1. Petry announces her subject in her first sentence.

2. She writes of the wind's "sucking" window shades out of windows, "driving" people from the street, and of the wind's "violent assault"; she writes of it sending a "barrage" of paper into people's faces; it "blinds" people, "stings" them, and "entangles" them with paper.

3. The wind "sucked," "drove"; Petry's writing of the wind's "assault," its "finding" scraps of paper, "fingering" its way, "taking time" to rush into doorways and areaways, "finding" bones and "pushing" them, "trying to discourage" people.

4. Sound: the wind rattles tops of garbage cans; window shades flap; people curse and stamp their feet
Touch: cold November wind; dust got in eyes; grit stung skins; the wind's cold fingers went inside collars, touched the back of Lutie Johnson's neck

5. Some students might think Petry exaggerates. Others might suggest eliminating the material about the window shades.

SELECTION AMENDMENT
Description of change: excerpted
Rationale: to focus on the concept of specific description presented in this chapter

The wind lifted Lutie Johnson's hair away from the back of her neck so that she felt suddenly naked and bald, for her hair had been resting softly and warmly against her skin. She shivered as the cold fingers of the wind touched the back of her neck, explored the sides of her head. It even blew her eyelashes away from her eyes so that her eyeballs were bathed in a rush of coldness and she had to blink in order to read the words on the sign swaying back and forth over her head.

EXERCISE 4 ▶ **Analyzing a Description**

1. Where does Petry announce the subject of her description?
2. Petry uses many details that emphasize the wind's violent nature. What are some of these details?
3. From the second sentence on, Petry *personifies* the wind—making it seem human—when she says that "it rattled the tops of garbage cans." What are other examples where the writer personifies the wind?
4. Petry uses many sight details in this description. What are three or four sound details that she uses? Touch details?
5. Have you ever been in a heavy, violent wind like the one Petry describes? Do you think her description is accurate? Would you add or change anything in her description?

A Writer's Model for You

Ann Petry is a professional writer who imagines specific details right down to two different types of wax paper— "heavy" and "thinner." Most of the time you'll be observing or recalling details from experience. But like Ann Petry, you can also create a specific word picture by using figurative language and sensory details. As you write your own description, you might follow this shorter model—it describes a place like one you might know.

A WRITER'S MODEL

Subject
Emphasis

Sound detail
Sight detail

Simile

   Whenever I'm hungry for a snack, I head for Angela's Pizza Place, just around the corner from school. Angela's is quite a place. It looks as though it's been there forever. On the outside, there's an ancient neon sign that buzzes and flickers against the peeling white paint on the red brick wall. Inside, an antique espresso machine sits like a brass robot guarding the front door. And on the shiny dining room walls, bright colors reflect off the fake Tiffany lamps hanging over every booth.

Touch detail

Smell details

Sight details

Writer's
feeling

   Each time I turn the greasy doorknob to open Angela's front door, the first thing that greets me is a wonderful warm cloud of pizza odors. My mouth starts to water as the cheese and garlic aromas embrace me. While I wait for my order, I usually watch the chef in the kitchen, tossing dough, pouring sauces, putting pies in the oven, and cutting slices. As entertaining as the air-borne saucers of dough are, though, no one comes to Angela's for the sights alone. My first bite of hot melted cheese always reminds me of exactly why I come here.

 CRITICAL THINKING
Analysis

  Ask students to analyze the order in which details are arranged in **A Writer's Model** [spatial order]. Why is this order appropriate? [When you come upon any structure, you must start with the outside before moving inside; therefore, the outside is a natural starting place for arranging the details in this case.]

PART 4:
Writing Your First Draft

Remember that the two models you've just read have been revised and proofread. No one expects your first draft to be perfect. Just do your best to turn your prewriting notes into a draft. Write a paragraph or two on the subject you've been developing in Writing Assignment, Parts 1–3. Include the details you've gathered in the order you planned on, but don't hesitate to include any new details that occur to you as you write. Sometimes the act of writing stimulates the flow of new ideas.

EVALUATING AND REVISING

OBJECTIVES

- To analyze a description's strengths and weaknesses
- To evaluate and revise a descriptive paragraph to eliminate weaknesses

TEACHING THE LESSON

You may want to begin by passing around an extremely out-of-focus picture and asking students to identify the content. Students will likely have difficulty identifying it or will make quite different guesses. Point out the importance of clear focus and details in their descriptive writing.

Teacher's ResourceBank™
RESOURCES

EVALUATING AND REVISING
- Writing a Description

QUOTATION FOR THE DAY

"In all pointed sentences, some degree of accuracy must be sacrificed to conciseness." (Samuel Johnson, 1709–1784, English writer)

After sharing the quotation with students, explain that writers often describe scenes, people, or objects that are much too complex to be completely and accurately described in a brief paper. Instead, many writers include only those details that give the reader some insight into the real essence or character of the thing begin described. Encourage students to evaluate the quality of the details they have selected for their papers.

Evaluating and Revising

Evaluating. Now that you've drafted your description, it's time to evaluate it—to judge it for both strengths and weaknesses, to see what works and what doesn't.

Revising. If you identify any problems, revise by making the changes that will improve your paper. To do so, ask yourself the questions in the left-hand column in the chart on the next page. Then, if you identify a particular problem, use the suggestions in the right-hand column as a guide for revising.

Shoe, by Jeff MacNelly, reprinted by permission: Tribune Media Services

The **Evaluating and Revising Description** chart is designed to help students identify strengths and rectify weaknesses in their papers. You may find it helpful to provide a few examples to help students use the chart effectively. Remind students that they are revising content, not proofreading for grammatical or mechanical errors. Their papers are still first drafts that may not be ready to turn in. Use the **Grammar Hint** on p. 202 as a tool to improve the style of students' papers.

Exercise 5 provides an opportunity to model the skills required for revision. It especially focuses on improving clarity and detail.

Writing Assignment: Part 5 provides students the opportunity to evaluate

EVALUATING AND REVISING DESCRIPTION

EVALUATION GUIDE	REVISION TECHNIQUE
1 Does the description identify what or who is being described?	**Add** a sentence or a phrase that clearly identifies your subject.
2 Is the tone of the description consistent?	**Cut** or **replace** any words or remarks that don't accurately convey your attitude toward your subject.
3 Are the details of the description arranged in an order that makes sense to readers?	**Reorder** the details so that they support your purpose and emphasis.
4 Does the description contain realistic sensory details?	**Add** precise details about the person, place, or thing that appeal to the reader's senses.
5 Does the description present a clear emphasis or a main impression?	**Add** details that support the emphasis you want to present. **Cut** details that do not contribute to your intended main impression.
6 Are specific words and figurative language used effectively?	**Replace** general words with specific and vivid nouns, verbs, adjectives, and adverbs; **cut** any clichés; **add** fresh comparisons.

LEP/ESL

Asian Languages. Many languages (such as Chinese, Lao, Vietnamese, Malay, Tagalog, and Japanese) do not have participles. Because some students might not have a clear idea of what a participle is, they might avoid using participles and use the present tense instead. Explain participles and give the infinitive form, such as *see,* and have the students form their participles [*seeing* and *seen*] and make phrases and sentences using these participles ["seeing-eye dog" and "The article seen by me was on page 4 of the paper"].

ADVANCED STUDENTS

Because of the continual push for adequate detail in descriptive writing, some advanced students may tend to over-describe. You may need to work with these students on analyzing the necessity of individual details and on evaluating the importance of specific details. For example, tell students to use vivid nouns instead of an abundance of adjectives.

and revise their own work independently. You may want to have students who have not yet read each other's work exchange papers so that objective evaluations may be made.

ASSESSMENT

Have students fill in a chart like that on p. 201 when they are first evaluating their papers for **Writing Assignment: Part 5** and when they complete the assignment for another student. This way you will be better able to assess students' development in evaluation and revision.

GRAMMAR HINT

You may want students to check their drafts for the correct use of participles. Explain that writers sometimes create dangling modifiers or misplaced modifiers that obscure the meaning of their writing. To be sure that students have logical, clear references for all participles, have them circle any participles in their papers and draw arrows to the word or words modified.

MEETING INDIVIDUAL NEEDS

LEARNING STYLES

Visual Learners. Students might benefit from the opportunity to illustrate their descriptions. This activity will help them see the objects they are describing and lead them to notice details that are missing in the writing. The pictures might also make a nice display for the completed descriptive paragraphs.

202

GRAMMAR HINT

Using Participles

Do you get the most from your descriptive sentences? As an observer, you can take in a variety of sensory details at the same time. Good description offers readers the same opportunity. Look over your sentences. You can combine actions and concentrate images by using participles, verb forms that act as adjectives.

EXAMPLES

No Participle   The rain was pouring. It ran in rivulets down the gutter.

Participle   The *pouring* rain ran in rivulets down the gutter.

No Participle   The nervous coach watched the clock. She paced the sidelines.

Participle   *Watching* the clock, the nervous coach paced the sidelines.

No Participle   The clerk was startled when he was called by the customer.

Participle   *Called* by the customer, the *startled* clerk jumped up suddenly.

REFERENCE NOTE: For more help with participles, see pages 579–580.

EXERCISE 5   Analyzing a Writer's Revisions

Following is the first draft of a paragraph taken from the writer's model on page 199. Working with one or two classmates, try to decide why you think the writer made the changes that are shown in the revision. Use the evaluating and revising chart on page 201 to help you answer the questions that follow the paragraph.

Ask students the following questions:

1. Were you able to identify strengths in your writing?
2. What are some of the strengths?
3. Were you able to discover weaknesses in your writing?
4. What are some of the weaknesses?
5. How were you able to correct the weaknesses? ■

Whenever I'm hungry for a snack, I
head for Angela's Pizza Place, just around
the corner. It looks as though it's been   **add**
   (from school. Angela's is quite a place.)
there forever. Inside, an antique espresso   **reorder**
machine sits like a brass robot guarding
the front door. On the outside, there's an
   (that buzzes and flickers)
ancient neon sign against the peeling   **add**
white paint on the red brick wall. And on
the shiny dining room walls, bright colors
                    fake Tiffany lamps
reflect off the lights hanging over every   **replace**
booth. I've seen the place when it was dirty   **cut**
inside though, and it's not as appealing.

1. Why did the writer add the words *from school* to the first sentence?
2. Why did the writer rearrange the order of the third and fourth sentences? What type of order does the paragraph now have?
3. Why did the writer add the words *that buzzes and flickers* to the description of the neon sign?
4. Why did the writer replace the word *lights* with *fake Tiffany lamps* in the next-to-last sentence?
5. Why did the writer cut the last sentence? [Hint: Review page 187].

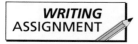

WRITING ASSIGNMENT

PART 5:
Evaluating and Revising Your Description

Now try evaluating and revising your own description. Exchange descriptions with a classmate and evaluate each other's work. Next, go over your own paper, using the chart on page 201 as a guide. Think carefully about your classmate's suggestions and your own evaluation. Then, make any changes that will improve your description.

ANSWERS
Exercise 5

Answers will vary. Here are some possibilities:

1. It gives a clearer identification of the subject and locates it more precisely.
2. Rearranging enhances spatial order: outside to inside. It shows things in the order in which one would see them.
3. The addition gives a specific sound detail and makes it easier for the reader to perceive the scene.
4. It adds fresh figurative language and is more concrete and thus easier to visualize.
5. Cutting makes the paragraph support the purpose: describing Angela's as a good place to go for a snack.

TIMESAVER

If you are planning to read the drafts as well as the final versions of the papers, you may want to have students underline or highlight sections in the drafts that were changed for the final copy. Not only will this help you to identify revisions quickly, but it will also help students see what improvements they have made in their writing.

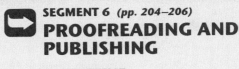
TEACHING THE LESSON

To demonstrate the importance of proper grammar and mechanics, have students attempt to correct the following sentence without changing the given order of the words:

pete said sarah may call tom.

QUOTATION FOR THE DAY

"We want the creative faculty to imagine that which we know." (Percy Bysshe Shelley, 1792–1822, British poet)

Write the quotation on the chalkboard and ask students in small groups to discuss the quotation and to devise a statement explaining how Shelley's quotation might relate to descriptive writing. Have a representative from each group share the statement with the class before students begin proofreading and publishing their descriptions.

MEETING INDIVIDUAL NEEDS

LEP/ESL

General Strategies. The word *polish* as used here might be unclear to some students, because they may think of polishing furniture or shoes. Once you have explained the ideas, students might still need guidance from you. Explain that polishing involves selecting the best choice from among various words, expressions, and grammatical structures.

---

204   *Using Description*

Proofreading and Publishing

Proofreading.   Polish your description by proofreading carefully so that your readers "see" your subject rather than any distracting errors.

Publishing.   When your polished description is ready for a wider audience, try these two suggestions to reach some readers.

- If your classmates are familiar with your subject, read your description aloud to them without naming your subject. Then ask classmates to identify your subject. If they guess correctly, ask them which details were most helpful in uncovering its identify.
- Submit your description to the school newspaper or literary magazine.

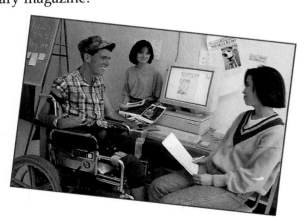

WRITING ASSIGNMENT

PART 6:
Proofreading and Publishing

Let your readers "see" your subject by proofreading your description carefully, one line at a time, and correcting any errors. Then use one of the suggestions you've just read or one of your own to share your work with an audience.

You may want to lead students in discussion of the links between punctuation, capitalization, and meaning.

After reading **A Student Model**, discuss the strengths and weaknesses of this essay. Next, assign **Writing Assignment: Part 6.** Remind students that careful proofreading takes time and concentration, but leads to a much-improved essay.

After students have carefully proofread their essays, you may want to discuss various methods of publication before students write their final versions. They will need to keep their audience in mind as they neatly rewrite the essays.

☞

A STUDENT MODEL

In talking about her description, Alissa Bird says what she found hardest to do was "to get all the grammar correct" and "to write in a certain form." Nevertheless, Alissa—a student at Crestwood High School in Roswell, Georgia—vividly describes a person and a place important to her.

The Wise Lady
by Alissa Bird

I saw my great-grandmother for the first time when I was about seven years old. She was sitting in her blue quilted armchair with a copy of <u>Reader's Digest</u> in her small, soft, wrinkly hands. Blue veins protruded from her transparent skin. When she heard the banging of the screen door, she got up and scooped me up into her arms and planted a big kiss on my cheek.

The one thing that sticks out in my mind is her pink bathroom where everything was always spotless. The entire bathroom was pink: the towels, the carpet, the walls, the bathtub, and even the bottle of bubble bath on the rim. I also remember the mysterious winding stairs that went up to the unknown rooms. When I got the chance to explore the upstairs, I remember how the stairs creaked like a haunted house.

I can still hear the chirp of the birds in the backyard by the huge vegetable garden she always kept weedless. The sound of an oven buzzer reminds me of the times when I was at her house and her buzzer would go off. When she opened the oven door, the delicious aroma of chocolate chip cookies would fill the air.

A STUDENT MODEL
Evaluation

1. In the first paragraph, Alissa clearly identifies her great-grandmother as the subject of her description.

2. Alissa's very positive attitude toward her great-grandmother is reflected with words such as "small," "soft," "delicious aroma," and "inspiration."

3. The details of this description are ordered to emphasize the importance of the lessons Alissa obtained from her great-grandmother.

4. Alissa includes numerous details to present a clear impression: for example, "scooped me up" and "mysterious winding stairs."

5. Specific color and concrete images are used effectively in sentences such as "The entire bathroom was pink" and "The stairs creaked like a haunted house."

INTEGRATING THE LANGUAGE ARTS

Mechanics Link. When students are checking the spelling in their papers, it helps if they read the paper from back to front. If they read the essay correctly, it is easy to get caught up in the content and to forget to check the spelling. By reading one word at a time backwards, they must concentrate on the words themselves.

CRITICAL THINKING
Evaluation

Often, it helps students better understand the grades they receive on papers if they have completed the grading process themselves. You may want to provide students with the grading scale or methods you will be using to evaluate their writing. Students should then evaluate **"The Wise Lady"** on p. 205. Discuss with students the results of their evaluations. Did results differ? What were similarities in the evaluations?

I will forever remember the long summers I spent with that wise old lady. I will always remember how we took walks around the town and to the grocery store just about every day I was there. My great-grandmother taught me about real life and that life is what you make it. She has been a real inspiration to me, and I hope that when I have grandchildren of my own I can inspire them just as much.

OBJECTIVES

- To analyze free verse
- To identify an appropriate topic for poetry
- To use the writing process to create free verse

TEACHING THE LESSON

You may want to begin by sharing several examples of free verse with your students. Initiate a discussion of the characteristics of free verse. The explanation at the beginning of this segment explains these characteristics well. After reading Wagoner's poem, ask students to respond orally to the questions. You may want to use these ☛

207

WRITING WORKSHOP

A Free Verse Poem

A good description captures and expresses an image, feeling, or idea by using specific sensory detail. Free verse poetry also does this—but in a condensed way. When you write free verse poetry, you usually don't have a regular pattern of rhythm and rhyme. Instead, you arrange words in each line according to your natural speech patterns. And, as in a good subjective description, you use sensory details and figurative language.

The following free verse poem is about a plant that grows in the American West. Its name comes from the way the plant breaks off near the ground and tumbles over and over as the wind blows it.

Tumbleweed
by David Wagoner

Here comes another, bumping over the sage
Among the greasewood, wobbling diagonally
Downhill, then skimming a moment on its edge,
Tilting lopsided, bouncing end over end
And springing from the puffs of its own dust
To catch at the barbed wire
And hang there, shaking, like a riddled prisoner.

Half the sharp seeds have fallen from this tumbler,
Knocked out for good by head-stands and pratfalls
Between here and wherever it grew up.
I carry it in the wind across the road
To the other fence. It jerks in my hands,
Butts backwards, corkscrews, lunges and swivels,
Then yaws away as soon as it's let go,
Hopping the scrub uphill like a kicked maverick.
The air goes hard and straight through the wires and weeds.
Here comes another, flopping among the sage.

QUOTATION FOR THE DAY

"Great poetry is always written by somebody straining to go beyond what he can do." (Stephen Spender, 1909–   , British poet)

Share the quotation with the class and ask students to respond by writing journal entries about personal accomplishments or goals they have reached.

MEETING INDIVIDUAL NEEDS

ADVANCED STUDENTS

Allow each student to write one poem based on the model and one following a different format. Let students read their poems to the class and have them discuss the power of the images created.

LEARNING STYLES

Auditory Learners. Arrange for students to talk-write their rough drafts to partners. One person could describe his or her subject aloud while the other person could write down words and phrases. Students can then trade roles.

responses to assess students' understanding of the poetry.

To help students develop their own topics for free verse, have them spend a few minutes brainstorming possibilities as a class activity.

Have students complete the requisite writing steps as indicated. You may wish to complete the assignment over several days.

CLOSURE

Ask students to explain the importance of descriptive writing in poetry. How does it differ from description in longer forms of writing? ■

ANSWERS
Writing Workshop Questions

Answers will vary. Here are some possibilities:

1. He uses, among others, "bumping," "wobbling," "swimming," "Tilting," "lopsided," "barbed," and "riddled."

2. The two similes are "like a riddled prisoner" and "like a kicked maverick." They encourage sympathy for the tumbleweed.

3. The poem has more of a sense of movement or flowing when it is read without the breaks.

4. It could represent people who are bounced around by life's circumstances.

INTEGRATING THE LANGUAGE ARTS

Technology Link. You may want to have students type their poetry for display. If students are using word processors, they could attempt to print their poems in the shape of the animal or plant being written about. They might also be able to use the computers to generate pictures.

1. What sensory words does the poet use to show the actions or behaviors of the tumbleweeds?
2. What two similes does the poet use? How do they affect your feelings about the tumbleweeds?
3. Read the poem once as it is written, recognizing the line breaks. Then read it again as though it were a paragraph, pausing for punctuation but ignoring the line breaks. What is the effect of the change?
4. If you read this poem on a symbolic level, what kinds of people might the tumbleweed represent?

Writing a Free Verse Poem

 Prewriting. Many plants and animals have characteristics that remind us of people in general or of particular people we know—bears, ostriches, squirrels, cabbages, pine trees. Brainstorm or freewrite to think of a plant or animal that has some interesting similarities to human beings. Then use these questions to gather details for your poem:

■ What are the most obvious characteristics, behaviors, or actions of the plant or animal you have identified?
■ What features of the plant or animal could be compared to someone you know or to people in general?
■ What sensory details could you include to highlight those features? visual details? details of sound?
■ What similes would give your subject human qualities?

Writing, Evaluating, and Revising. To write your description, try a pattern that is loosely like Wagoner's: Start your first sentence and your last sentence with the same two words—"Here comes . . ." or "There goes . . ." or "There stands . . ." Describe the features and the actions of the plant or animal in natural-sounding sentences, but break lines to emphasize important characteristics or behaviors.

Read your poem aloud and listen for whether your feelings and ideas come through clearly. Then ask someone else to read your poem to see if it's clear. Use your evaluation and your reader's feedback to revise your poem.

 Proofreading and Publishing. Check the final copy of your poem. Are you satisfied with its presentation on the page? If your school has a literary magazine, consider submitting your poem. Or, plan a poetry reading with classmates.

MAKING CONNECTIONS

COMBINING DESCRIPTION WITH NARRATION OBJECTIVE

- To read and report orally on the collection
Ernie's War: The Best of Ernie Pyle's World War II Dispatches

MAKING CONNECTIONS

COMBINING DESCRIPTION WITH NARRATION

Description is narrative's comfortable companion. In a narrative, the story's actions come alive through the descriptions of the people, places, objects, and feelings they involve.

Many people think Ernie Pyle was America's best war correspondent during World War II. Notice how he combines narration with description in the following dispatch from the front lines of Africa in 1943.

from Ernie's War: The Best of Ernie Pyle's World War II Dispatches
by Ernie Pyle

1   "A narrow path comes like a ribbon over a hill miles away, down a long slope, across a creek, up a slope and over another hill.

"All along the length of this ribbon there is now a thin line of men. For four days and nights they have fought hard, eaten little, washed none, and slept hardly at all. Their nights have been violent with attack, fright, butchery, and their days sleepless and miserable with the crash of artillery.

2   "The men are walking. They are 50 feet apart, for dispersal. Their walk is slow, for they are dead weary, as you can tell even when looking at them from behind. Every line and sag of their bodies speaks their inhuman exhaustion.

COMBINING DESCRIPTION WITH NARRATION
Teaching Strategies

You may want to have students write narratives of their own. Have each student choose an event such as a family gathering, a vacation, or a performance. Students should attempt to narrate the happenings as Ernie Pyle does. The narration is written in the present tense; he is describing something that is happening as he speaks. Students should duplicate this method to make their readers feel that the events are occurring as they read. Remind students to use plentiful, accurate, picture-forming details.

USING THE SELECTION
Ernie's War: The Best Of Ernie Pyle's World War II Dispatches

1

Why is this selection written in quotation marks? [It is quoted from Ernie Pyle; he is speaking the words that are written down.]

2

dispersal: placement at points along a line

- To analyze a scientific description
- To reword a subjective description into an objective description

3

Notice the metaphorical description of the men's movements.

GUIDELINES

If you have students present oral reports from their own reading, you may want to have peers evaluate the presentations. Reports will vary depending on the time given for preparation and the subject chosen.

"On their shoulders and backs they carry heavy steel tripods, machine-gun barrels, leaden boxes of ammunition. Their feet seem to sink into the ground from the overload they are bearing.

"They don't slouch. It is the terrible deliberation of each step that spells out their appalling tiredness. Their faces are black and unshaven. They are young men, but the grime and whiskers and exhaustion make them look middle-aged.

"In their eyes as they pass is not hatred, not excitement, not despair, not the tonic of their victory—there is just the simple expression of being here as though they had been here doing this forever, and nothing else.

3 "The line moves on, but it never ends. All afternoon men keep coming round the hill and vanishing eventually over the horizon. It is one long tired line of antlike men."

Pyle reported events as he saw them, but his descriptive details help you to "see" them too. What figure of speech does Pyle use when he describes the line of moving men? What is Pyle's overall emphasis in his description of the soldiers? What details in his writing support this impression?

Until he was killed by a sniper's bullet in 1945, Pyle filed six newspaper columns a week for his thirteen million readers. He rarely reported the war's events on a "grand scale." Instead, Pyle's subjects were usually individual soldiers and their stories. Some of his best columns are collected in books, including *Ernie's War: The Best of Ernie Pyle's World War II Dispatches.* You might like to find one of these books and read about the very human face of war. Then share your reading in an oral report to your classmates.

DESCRIPTION ACROSS THE CURRICULUM

Objective Description in Science

Description in the sciences informs its readers about exact observations. Notice the realistic, factual details and specific words in the following description of a crocodile.

A crocodile is an aquatic, meat-eating reptile that has lived in the warmer parts of this earth for about 135 million years. It is often called a "living fossil" because scientists believe that it looks pretty much the same now as it originally did. It has thick, tough, dark green skin stretched over an armor of bony plates. A crocodile's long triangular snout contains forty to sixty razor-sharp teeth set in sockets in each jawbone. When the snout is closed, these teeth interlock, with two very large ones sticking out from the lower jaw. With eyes and nostrils on top of its head, the crocodile can see, breathe, and smell, while hiding most of its body under the often cloudy swamp water.

Is this an objective or subjective description? How can you tell? Reread the subjective description of the collie Elizabeth on pages 184–185. Keeping the same subject, write a paragraph of objective description, as though you were describing the dog for a science report. (Remember that scientists take pride in using accurate, realistic details.)

DESCRIPTION ACROSS THE CURRICULUM
Teaching Strategies

You may want to have students bring other examples of objective and subjective description they find in magazines, science books, or encyclopedias.

Rather than have all students rewrite the collie description, you may want to have some students rewrite articles that they bring to class.

GUIDELINES

The description of the crocodile is objective. The details do not convey emotions. The description is straightforward and precise. The only opinion (as opposed to what seems to be fact) is presented in quotation marks and explained. The point of view is third person.

The paragraph written about the dog by the students would have to be unlike the one about Elizabeth in several ways: It could use no slang (tummy); it would have to be in third person (no use of *I*); it would use complete sentences; it would include no personal anecdotes, only anecdotes to illustrate recurrent activities; it would not make jokes about the dog's IQ.

Chapter 6

CREATIVE WRITING

OBJECTIVES
- To identify the aim and to analyze the characteristics of literary writing
- To select an appropriate idea to develop into a short story
- To determine a story's purpose, audience, and tone
- To select point of view, characters, setting, and plot for a story
- To write a draft of a story using selected story elements
- To evaluate and revise the content, organization, and style of a story
- To proofread a story and prepare it for publication

Motivation

Read your favorite narrative poem or short story to the class and then ask students what kinds of writing are creative. You can then explain how the literary aim differs from the other writing aims.

Introduction

You may want to help students distinguish the literary aim from the other aims of discourse. To illustrate the literary aim, you could introduce and summarize Shakespeare's *Tragedy of Julius Caesar*. Then explain that other pieces of discourse on the play may have quite different aims. For example, a scholarly article about Shakespeare's use of color imagery in *Tragedy of Julius Caesar* has an *informative* purpose; an editorial which quotes *Tragedy of Julius Caesar* and encourages public removal of city commissioners reflects a *persuasive* aim; and a journal entry about how social groups at school are similar to those in the play has an *expressive* aim.

This basic introduction to the literary aim should help students understand more fully the short stories in this chapter, **"Eleven"** and **"Mushrooms in the City."**

Integration

The material presented in this composition chapter has many applications to other concepts found in this textbook. **Writing Assignment: Part 2** could be used as a follow-up to **Chapter 5: "Using Description"** which focuses on descriptive writing. Additionally, the **Writing Workshop** could be linked to **Chapter 7: "Writing to Inform"** which covers informative writing. Because students will have to research the information used in their historical narratives, you could correlate this activity with the library information found in **Chapter 32: "The Library Media Center."**

Writing a short story will help prepare students for writing literary analyses in **Chapter 10: "Writing About Literature."** Focusing on literary elements in their own writing (such as characterization, setting, conflict and plot, mood, tone, purpose, and audience) will help students recognize and analyze these elements in all pieces of literature.

You may want to remind students that the four stages of the writing process occur for any writing assignment in any discipline.

The chart on the next page illustrates the strands of language arts as they are integrated into this chapter. For vocabulary study, glossary words are underlined in some writing models.

QUOTATIONS
All **Quotations for the Day** are chosen because of their relevance to instructional material presented in that segment of the chapter and for their usefulness in establishing student interest in writing.

INTEGRATING THE LANGUAGE ARTS

Selection	Reading and Literature	Writing and Critical Thinking	Language and Syntax	Speaking, Listening, and Other Expression Skills
"Eleven" by Sandra Cisneros **214-218** from **"Where Have You Gone, Charming Billy?"** by Tim O'Brien **224** **"Mushrooms in the City"** by Italo Calvino **231-235** **"Tornadoes Damage School"** from *The Ledger*, Lakeland, Florida **243-244**	Making and supporting inferences about characters **219, 236** Identifying conflict **219, 236** Analyzing characters **219, 236** Responding personally to literature **219, 236, 244** Applying interpretive and creative thinking **219, 236, 244** Recognizing the twist ending as a convention of the short story **236** Identifying facts and details in a news story **244** Comparing informative and literary paragraphs **244**	Writing a paragraph from a character's point of view **219, 224** Responding personally to literature **219, 230, 236, 244** Developing a story idea **222** Analyzing point of view by rewriting a passage from third to first person **224** Finding the main idea **224, 236** Developing characters and setting **226, 238** Gathering plot details by creating a chain-of-events outline **227** Organizing information on a story map **228** Writing and evaluating dialogue **230** Analyzing suspense, mood, setting, and characterization in a short story **236** Writing a first draft of a story **238** Analyzing a writer's revisions **241** Evaluating and revising a short story **241** Proofreading and publishing a short story **242** Analyzing a news story **244** Using the *5W-How?* questions to plan and analyze a news story **244-245** Writing a news story using the writing process **244-245** Writing a fable **246-247** Researching and writing a historical narrative **247**	Using pronouns consistent with the first person point of view **224** Proofreading for errors in grammar, usage, and mechanics **242, 245**	Discussing and rewriting a passage's point of view **224** Discussing character and setting descriptions **226, 236** Writing dialogue in a small group **230** Answering questions in a small group about a literary model **236** Working in a group to revise story drafts **241** Sharing stories with classmates **247**

SEGMENT PLANNING GUIDE

Whether you are planning for a quick review of a writing concept or preparing an extended lesson on composition, you can use the following Planning Guide to adapt the chapter material to the individual needs of your class.

SEGMENT	PAGES	CONTENT	RESOURCES
1 *Imagining Other Worlds*	*213-219*		
Literary Model **"Eleven"**	214-218	Guided reading: a model of creative writing	
Reader's Response/ Writer's Craft	219	Model evaluation: responding to literature and analyzing creative writing	
2 *Ways to Write Creatively*	*220*		
3 *Prewriting*	*221-228*		Asking "What if" Questions
Exploring Story Ideas	221-222	Guidelines: finding ideas for stories	Listing Character Traits
Writing Assignment: Part 1	222	Applied practice: developing a story idea	Collecting Details for Setting
Planning Your Story	223	Introduction: thinking about story elements	Planning a Plot
Thinking About Purpose, Audience, and Tone	223	Guidelines: determining purpose and audience	
Critical Thinking: Analyzing Point of View	223-224	Guidelines: using criteria to distinguish point of view	
Critical Thinking Exercise	224	Cooperative learning: rewriting a passage in a different point of view	
Literary Model from **"Where Have You Gone, Charming Billy?"**	224	Guided reading: analyzing a point of view in a model	
Thinking About Characters and Setting	225-226	Guidelines: developing characters and setting	
Writing Assignment: Part 2	226	Cooperative learning: describing character and setting for a story	
Developing the Plot	226	Introduction: analyzing conflict and plot	
Chart: Types of Conflict	227	Guidelines: distinguishing internal and external conflict	
Writing Assignment: Part 3	227	Applied practice: creating a chain-of-events outline	
Making a Story Map	228	Guidelines: examining a story map	
Writing Assignment: Part 4	228	Applied practice: developing a story map	
4 *Writing*	*229-238*		Writing a Short Story
The Basic Elements of Stories	229-230	Guidelines: creating effective characters and dialogue	
Exercise 1	230	Cooperative learning: writing and evaluating dialogue	
Looking at a Short Story	230	Introduction: using conflict in a story	

All the resources listed in this chapter are located in the Teacher's ResourceBank™.

SEGMENT	PAGES	CONTENT	RESOURCES
Literary Model **"Mushrooms in the City"**	231-235	Guided reading: examining conflict in a story	
Exercise 2	236	Cooperative learning: analyzing organization	
A Basic Framework for a Story	236	Introduction: analyzing a short story	
A Writer's Model	236-238	Sample: examining conflict in a student model	
Writing Assignment: Part 5	238	Applied practice: writing a first draft	
5 *Evaluating and Revising*	*239-241*		Writing a Short Story
Evaluating and Revising	239	Introduction: using a chart	
Chart: Evaluating and Revising	240	Guidelines: applying evaluation and revision techniques	
Exercise 3	241	Applied practice: analyzing a writer's revisions	
Writing Assignment: Part 6	241	Cooperative learning: evaluating and revising	
6 *Proofreading and Publishing*	*242*		Writing a Short Story
Publishing	242	Publishing ideas: reaching a specific audience	
Mechanics Hint	242	Writing suggestion: punctuating dialogue	
Writing Assignment: Part 7	242	Applied practice: proofreading and publishing	
7 *Writing Workshop*	*243-245*		All the resources for this chapter may be used in this segment.
A News Story	243	Guidelines: writing factual stories to inform	
Model/Questions **"Tornadoes Damage School"**	243-244	Examining techniques: analyzing a sample news story	
Writing a News Story	244-245	Applied practice: creating a news story	
8 *Making Connections*	*246-247*		
Speaking and Listening: Creating a Fable	246-247	Guidelines: writing a fable Cooperative learning: writing and listening to fables	
Short Story Writing Across the Curriculum: History	247	Guidelines: combining historical facts with fictional details Applied practice: writing a story about a historical person or event	

WHOLE-CHAPTER RESOURCE
A Writing Process Log, A Writing Prompt, Holistically Graded Models, Portfolio Assessment Materials

OBJECTIVES

- To evaluate a short story by analyzing its plot, conflict, and characters
- To write a new ending for a story

 VISUAL CONNECTIONS
Ships of the Long Range Pioneer Fleet

About the Artist. Julian Baum was introduced to astronomy when he was a child; his father, a section director for the British Astronomical Association, encouraged him to observe the moon and stars. Baum found the wonders of the night sky inspiring, and he attended the Cheshire School of Art and Design to learn techniques for producing science fiction and astronomical art. He studied photography, experimenting with scale models to create special effects like the effects in *Ships of the Long Range Pioneer Fleet.*

Ideas for Writing. Ask students what they know about the ships in this picture. After discussing the clues in the picture and in the title, have each student write an introduction for a short story about the voyage of the ships. Suggest to students that they write from the point of view of a character in the story.

6 CREATIVE WRITING

MOTIVATION

Have students name short stories they have read and reasons why they liked these stories. Then ask further questions about these stories. Tell students that they have learned something from the short stories without realizing it.

TEACHING THE LESSON

To focus on the important elements in **"Eleven,"** list the new concepts of imagination, purpose, and conflict, on the chalkboard and then have students define these concepts in their own words. Next, ask several students to take turns reading **"Eleven"** to the class.

Imagining Other Worlds

Think about what life would be like without **imagination**—how boring it would be. Imagination takes us where we can never go in real life. It propels us into **other worlds** where things are whatever we want them to be.

Writing and You. Using their imaginations, writers write stories we never tire of reading and hearing—novels, mysteries, science fiction, children's stories. Some writers write about things that never were and never will be, yet they seem real because they play on our imaginations. Other writers start with real events and use their imaginations—and ours—to make them into something entirely new. How much do you use your imagination?

As You Read. In the following story, Sandra Cisneros tells about an event that could have happened to anyone growing up. How is it real? How is it fiction?

Ships of the Long Range Pioneer Fleet, Julian Baum (1985). Mixed media. 12" × 16". Science Photo Library/ Photo Researchers, Inc.

QUOTATION FOR THE DAY

"Imagination, n. A warehouse of facts, with poet and liar in joint ownership." (Ambrose Bierce, 1842–1914, American journalist, short-story writer, and poet)

Ask students to apply this quotation to a piece of literature they have read in a previous chapter. Have volunteers discuss what elements of the poet and the liar they find in the piece.

MEETING INDIVIDUAL NEEDS

LEP/ESL

General Strategies. This is an opportunity for students to start writing daily journals. Writing a story can be a terrifying assignment for students who have limited English vocabularies. Keeping journals will allow students to practice expressing themselves without the fear of being graded. In their journals they can record dreams, family stories, and experiences. They can also use their journals to ask questions and, as this chapter specifies, try out ideas for short stories.

GUIDED PRACTICE

The **Reader's Response** and **Writer's Craft** questions provide an opportunity for guided practice. Before discussing the questions, answer the first question for the students to help stimulate class discussion. Then have volunteers discuss their answers to this question. You can continue with questions 3 and 4 in the same manner.

214

ELEVEN
BY
SANDRA
CISNEROS

USING THE SELECTION
Eleven

1

Who is the "they" to whom the author refers? [Students should say that the pronoun refers to adults in general.]

2

Why might the author include this and other references to her earlier years? [Students might say that she realizes that growing older doesn't necessarily mean that she is a new person, but that she still retains a part of all her earlier experiences.]

3

What purpose does the use of "you" serve? [Students might see that it makes the story more personal for the narrator to be speaking to the reader in this way.]

1   What they don't understand about birthdays and
2   what they never tell you is that when you're eleven, you're also ten, and nine, and eight, and seven, and six, and five, and four, and three, and two, and
3   one. And when you wake up on your eleventh birthday you expect to feel eleven, but you don't. You open your eyes and everything's just like yesterday, only it's today. And you don't feel eleven at all. You feel like you're still ten. And you are—underneath the year that makes you eleven.

Like some days you might say something stupid, and that's the part of you that's still ten. Or maybe some days you might need to sit on your mama's lap because you're scared, and that's the part of you that's five. And maybe one day when you're all grown up maybe you will need to cry like if you're

INDEPENDENT PRACTICE

Have students write their answers to the second question in **Reader's Response.** Working in groups of four, students can exchange papers and read each other's paragraphs. Then have each group pick one paragraph to read aloud to the class.

ASSESSMENT

If you choose to grade the paragraph written for the **Reader's Response** question, you may want to check to see that students maintain the style and the first person point of view established in the story.

three, and that's okay. That's what I tell Mama when she's sad and needs to cry. Maybe she's feeling three.

4   Because the way you grow old is kind of like an onion or like the rings inside a tree trunk or like my little wooden dolls that fit one inside the other, each year inside the next one. That's how being eleven years old is.

You don't feel eleven. Not right away. It takes a few days, weeks even, sometimes even months before you say Eleven when they ask you. And you don't feel smart eleven, not until you're almost twelve. That's the way it is.

Only today I wish I didn't have only eleven years rattling inside me like pennies in a tin Band-Aid box.

5   Today I wish I was one hundred and two instead of eleven because if I was

6   one hundred and two I'd have known what to say when Mrs. Price put the red sweater on my desk. I would've known how to tell her it wasn't mine instead of just sitting there with that look on my face and nothing coming out of my mouth.

"Whose is this?" Mrs. Price says, and she holds the red sweater up in the air for all the class to see. "Whose? It's been sitting in the coatroom for a month."

"Not mine," says everybody. "Not me."

"It has to belong to somebody," Mrs. Price keeps saying, but nobody can remember. It's an ugly sweater with red plastic buttons and a collar

"Because the way you grow old is kind of like...my little wooden dolls that fit one inside the other, each year inside the next one."

4

This is one of the examples of figurative language that the author uses. See if students can identify some others. [Students should indicate the other similes such as any of the images to which the red sweater is compared.]

5

The sentence beginning with "Today I wish . . ." is very long. Why would the author include this and other lengthy sentences? [You may need to indicate to students that the author chooses this style to mirror the thinking process of the character. One thought flows right after the other.]

6

This is the first appearance of one of the conflicts.

CLOSURE

Have students discuss examples from stories they have read in the categories of imagination, conflict, and purpose. Discuss the responses and end the lesson by telling students that all stories will include these main elements. ■

7

This sentence indicates the internal conflict that Rachel experiences. She feels uncomfortable with herself.

8

This dialogue expresses Rachel's frustration over the mistaken ownership of the sweater.

9

You may want to ask students if they have encountered a similar situation of an adult being allowed to make a mistake. Have them tell how the situation was resolved. This question could serve as a prewriting exercise for the second question in **Reader's Response.**

10

Why is Rachel trying to focus on the good things that are happening on her birthday? [Students might say that she is trying to deal with her anger and frustration by escaping into happy thoughts or that she's trying to live up to acting eleven even though she feels like acting younger.]

216

and sleeves all stretched out like you could use it for a jump rope. It's maybe a thousand years old and even if it belonged to me I wouldn't say so.

7   Maybe because I'm skinny, maybe because she doesn't like me, that stupid Sylvia Saldívar says, "I think it belongs to Rachel." An ugly sweater like that, all raggedy and old, but Mrs. Price believes her. Mrs. Price takes the sweater and puts it right on my desk, but when I open my mouth nothing comes out.

8   "That's not, I don't, you're not . . . Not mine," I finally say in a little voice that was maybe me when I was four.

"Of course it's yours," Mrs. Price says. "I remember you wearing it
9   once." Because she's older and the teacher, she's right and I'm not.

Not mine, not mine, not mine, but Mrs. Price is already turning to page thirty-two, and math problem number four. I don't know why but all of a sudden I'm feeling sick inside, like the part of me that's three wants to come out of my eyes, only I squeeze them shut tight and bite down on my teeth real hard and try to remember today I am eleven,
10   eleven. Mama is making a cake for me for tonight, and when Papa comes home everybody will sing Happy birthday, happy birthday to you.

But when the sick feeling goes away and I open my eyes, the red sweater's still sitting there like a big red mountain. I move the red sweater to the corner of my desk with my ruler. I move my pencil and books and eraser as far from it as possible. I even move my chair a little to the right. Not mine, not mine, not mine.

11   In my head I'm thinking how long till lunchtime, how long till I can take the red sweater and throw it over the schoolyard fence, or leave it hanging on a parking meter, or bunch it up into a little ball and toss it in the alley. Except when math period ends Mrs. Price says loud and in front of everybody, "Now, Rachel, that's enough," because she sees I've shoved the red sweater to the tippy-tip corner of my desk and it's hanging all over the edge like a waterfall, but I don't care.

"Rachel," Mrs. Price says. She says it like she's getting mad. "You put that sweater on right now and no more nonsense."

"But it's not—"

"Now!" Mrs. Price says.

This is when I wish I wasn't eleven, because all the years inside of me—ten, nine, eight, seven, six, five, four, three,
12 two, and one—are pushing at the back of my eyes when I put

11

Rachel thinks about the different things she can do with the sweater. What does this represent? [The ways of disposing of the sweater represent ways to handle problems—ignore them or throw them away.]

12

When Rachel puts the sweater on, which plot step occurs? [If students have not been exposed to plot structure, they might not see that this is the climax. You may have to indicate this.]

one arm through one sleeve of the sweater that smells like cottage cheese, and then the other arm through the other and stand there with my arms apart like if the sweater hurts me and it does, all itchy and full of germs that aren't even mine.

13 That's when everything I've been holding in since this morning, since when Mrs. Price put the sweater on my desk, finally lets go, and all of a sudden I'm crying in front of everybody. I wish I was invisible but I'm not. I'm eleven and it's my birthday today and I'm crying like I'm three in front of everybody. I put my head down on the desk and bury my face in my stupid clown-sweater arms. My face all hot and spit coming out of my mouth because I can't stop the little animal noises from coming out of me, until there aren't any more tears left in my eyes, and it's just my body shaking like when you have the hiccups, and my whole head hurts like when you drink milk too fast.

14 But the worst part is right before the bell rings for lunch. That stupid Phyllis Lopez, who is even dumber than Sylvia Saldívar, says she remembers the red sweater is hers! I take it off right away and give it to her, only Mrs. Price pretends like everything's okay.

15 Today I'm eleven. There's a cake Mama's making for tonight, and when Papa comes home from

---

13

When Rachel cries, how has the plot progressed? [This is the beginning of the resolution.]

14

"Mrs. Price pretends like everything's okay" resolves one conflict, although not very satisfactorily. Now Rachel doesn't have to deal with being branded as the owner of the sweater; however, she still wasn't able to convince Mrs. Price that she wasn't the owner, so her internal conflict has not been resolved.

15

The last two paragraphs of the story echo which earlier parts of the story? What effect do these paragraphs create? [The first sentence of the last paragraph echoes the first sentence of the first paragraph. The second to the last paragraph echoes the twelfth paragraph's last sentence. This achieves unity in the story.]

work we'll eat it. There'll be candles and presents and everybody will sing Happy birthday, happy birthday to you, Rachel, only it's too late.

I'm eleven today. I'm eleven, ten, nine, eight, seven, six, five, four, three, two, and one, but I wish I was one hundred and two. I wish I was anything but eleven, because I want today to be far away already, far away like a runaway balloon, like a tiny *o* in the sky, so tiny-tiny you have to close your eyes to see it.

READER'S RESPONSE

1. A good story, even though it's fiction (not true or factual), seems real. Does this story seem real to you? Is it easy to believe that this actually happened to a young girl on her eleventh birthday? Why?
2. Is there another way this story could have ended? Might the teacher have apologized? Could the girl have reacted differently to the sweater? Use your imagination and write a new ending for the story.

WRITER'S CRAFT

3. The author uses the narrator's thoughts and dialogue to bring her characters to life. What do you know about the girl who is telling the story? What do you know about the teacher?
4. Every story has some kind of conflict or problem. What is the conflict in this story?

ANSWERS

Reader's Response

Responses will vary.

1. Students might say that this story seems real to them because of Rachel's dialogue with herself. Most students will recall when a situation has upset them and they did not know how to deal with the situation. Students also might include something about how sometimes events happen which can keep a birthday from being entirely happy.
2. Some possible endings might be that the teacher could have believed Rachel when she said the sweater wasn't hers, or that Rachel might have marched out of the room rather than crying.

Writer's Craft

Answers may vary.

3. The text indicates that Rachel is insightful. She describes growing older as being "like an onion or like the rings inside a tree trunk or like my little wooden dolls that fit one inside the other. . . ." Students might say that she is unsure of herself and that her character has been developed more than that of the teacher.
4. Students should see the conflict that Rachel has with the teacher over ownership of the sweater. They might not see the internal conflict she has over her lack of self-confidence.

TEACHING THE MODES

This section applies Kinneavy's four modes of creative writing. Examples of each mode are presented, but no specific definitions are given. Thus, you may want to write the four modes on the chalkboard and then ask students to brainstorm definitions for each mode as each would be applied to short stories. You could also ask each student to bring to class one short example of one mode used in a literary work. ■

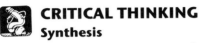
CRITICAL THINKING
Synthesis

The modes rarely occur alone in writing, and you may want to stress that any piece of literature will probably contain examples of all four modes, even if one mode, such as narration, predominates. Therefore, for students to synthesize the lesson, have them work in groups of four and ask each group to find a piece of literature embodying more than one aim. Then have each group prepare a short oral report on the use of the modes found in the chosen piece of literature.

Ways to Write Creatively

A story, like the one you just read and the one you'll write in this chapter, is one way to write creatively. When people write creatively, they produce literature—stories, poems, songs and ballads, plays, and movie and television scripts. The key elements of creative writing are the use of imagination and the use of language in special and unique ways. Here are four ways in which writers develop creative writing.

▶ **Narration:** telling a story about a girl who witnesses events of the American Revolution; in a movie script, telling the story of a Texas Ranger's life in a frontier settlement.

Description: describing the interior of a space station in a science fiction story; describing the smells of the food in a poem about a festival.

Classification: comparing and contrasting London and Paris in a novel that takes place in the two cities; in a poem about a fish, comparing its battered skin to strips of old wallpaper.

Evaluation: in a play, showing how power can corrupt a person who becomes king; creating a story that is a parody (an amusing imitation) of the fairy tale "Little Red Riding Hood."

LOOKING AHEAD

In the main assignment in this chapter, you'll use the strategy of narration to write a story. As you work through the chapter, keep in mind that a short story

- has a plot involving a problem or conflict
- may contain characters, settings, plots, and details based on real life
- is developed mostly through the author's own imagination

OBJECTIVES

- To discover an idea to develop into a short story
- To write and share a short paragraph describing the story's main character and a paragraph describing the setting
- To create a plot outline listing the story's main conflict and events
- To develop a story map detailing point of view, characters, setting, and plot

☞

Writing a Short Story

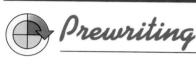

Exploring Story Ideas

Ideas for stories are everywhere. One way to find an idea is to ask yourself "What if?" questions, much as these writers may have.

- What if a ferocious shark terrorized a summer beach?
- What if a selfish Southern belle had to struggle through the Civil War and Reconstruction?
- What if a French nobleman escaped an unjust imprisonment, discovered a fabulous treasure, and sought revenge against his accusers?

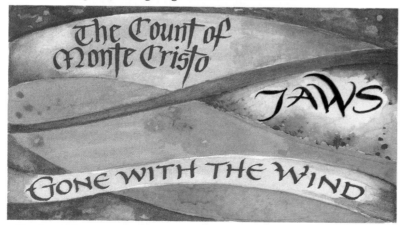

Each of these questions inspired a book and then a movie. That's all you need to get started—a spark of an idea that your imagination can nurture and transform into a story.

Where can you find ideas? First, look around you. Notice people, events, places that intrigue you. Recall vivid experiences, crazy dreams, interesting conversations. Anything that interests, horrifies, tickles, or angers you might be an idea just waiting to become a story.

Teacher's ResourceBank™
RESOURCES

PREWRITING
- Asking "What if" Questions
- Listing Character Traits
- Collecting Details for Setting
- Planning a Plot

QUOTATION FOR THE DAY

"He is so stupid you can't trust him with an idea./He is so clever he will catch you in the least error./He will not buy short books./He will not buy long books./He is part moron, part genius, and part ogre./There is some doubt as to whether he can read." (John Steinbeck, 1902–1968, American novelist and winner of the 1962 Nobel Prize for literature)

Steinbeck half-seriously describes his reader, someone he obviously considers during his writing process. Have students write a detailed description of their readers.

Cont. on p. 224

222 *Creative Writing*

To find story ideas, think about

- a journal entry about your first date, touchdown, or A+
- an early memory about a special family holiday
- a picture of your favorite place
- a top-ten list of your worst fears, biggest pet peeves, most embarrassing moments

WRITING ASSIGNMENT

PART 1:
Developing a Story Idea

Ignite your imagination to find a story idea. You might mull over your experiences, flip through photo albums, watch people, or talk to friends. "What if?" questions can jump-start your imagination if you're having a hard time getting started. Keep at it until you find an idea you'd like to develop into a story.

LEP/ESL

General Strategies. Students with a limited English vocabulary might need extra help choosing and developing a story topic. For this first story, you could allow students to use a topic that you present in class. You may also want to encourage students to brainstorm ideas in their journal entries.

"What I am trying to achieve is a voice sitting by a fireplace telling you a story on a winter's evening."

Truman Capote

TEACHING *ANALYZING POINT OF VIEW*

Use the four questions in the text as the basis for a class discussion of point of view and present an example from your literature textbook of each point of view. Ask students to analyze these examples. Then have students recall the favorite story they described before reading the chapter's

Prewriting

Planning Your Story

With just the spark of an idea, you're ready to start planning your story. Planning involves thinking about purpose, audience, and tone. You'll also be looking at point of view, characters, setting, and plot.

Thinking About Purpose, Audience, and Tone

Your main *purpose* in story writing is to be creative. And since you're the author, you have many opportunities to do so. Your characters, settings, and problems can be whatever you alone decide they should be. But another purpose in story writing is to entertain your *audience*— your readers. So you'll want to keep their interests and knowledge in mind as you plan. What will keep them entertained? Classmates, for example, might enjoy a detailed description of a teenage character's dress and hairstyle. But small children or adults might not care for the same details.

Writing stories also gives you flexibility in your tone. *Tone* is the attitude you take towards your characters and the events in your story. And you communicate that tone through the details and words you choose. The tone in your story can be serious, humorous, mysterious, or sarcastic. There are many other tones you can adopt as well.

CRITICAL THINKING

Analyzing Point of View

Point of view means who's telling the story. A story is always told by a narrator (who is not the author). Sometimes the narrator is a character in the story, and sometimes the narrator remains outside the story. You can use the following questions to analyze the point of view.

ADVANCED STUDENTS

To challenge advanced students to explore their interests, have them take a cross-curricular approach in developing their story ideas, characters, settings, and plots. For example, encourage students interested in computers to set their stories in a computer lab, computer class, or computer business and then to incorporate their knowledge of computers into the story.

introductory model. Ask volunteers to analyze their stories' narrator types and to provide specific examples and details for support. ⚡

Cont. from p. 222
TEACHING THE LESSON

This segment covers plot, setting, and characters. First, you may want to check to see that students understand what the text means by a "What if?" question. You can have students brainstorm "What if?" questions and write the best ones on the chalkboard. In addition, discuss the other ways

MEETING INDIVIDUAL NEEDS

LEP/ESL

General Strategies. When discussing point of view, it is helpful first to review pronoun forms. Explain that the first person point of view uses *I, me,* and *my,* while third person uses the pronouns *he, she, it.* As practice for the **Critical Thinking Exercise,** have students change a model sentence from third to first person.

🦅 TIMESAVER

After groups have rewritten O'Brien's passage, ask them to highlight all indicators of the first person, such as personal pronouns. These marks will help them check their work, and it will also make your grading easier.

ANSWERS
Critical Thinking Exercise

Revisions will vary. The following paragraph is an example:

Ahead of me other soldiers are flopped down in weeds beside the road. But I can't look. PFC Paul Berlin can't feel another thing. Just gritty pebbles on the road shoulder where I lie and the smooth plastic of the rifle stock against my forehead.

SELECTION AMENDMENT
Description of change: excerpted
Rationale: to focus on the concept of point of view as presented in this chapter

1. Is the narrator a character in the story? Does the narrator use first-person pronouns like *I* and *me*? Does the narrator express his or her own thoughts and feelings, but not those of other characters? If so, the story has a *first-person point of view.*
2. Is the narrator outside the story and not a character in the story? Does the narrator use third-person pronouns like *he* and *she*? If so, the story has a *third-person narrator.*
3. Does the third-person narrator look at the story through the eyes of *one character only*? This type of narrator can't tell what other characters are thinking or feeling. This is called a *limited narrator.*
4. Can the third-person narrator tell what *everyone* is thinking and feeling? This is called an *omniscient (all-knowing) narrator.*

⚡ CRITICAL THINKING EXERCISE:
Analyzing Point of View

What goes through a soldier's mind as he's facing battle? In this excerpt, the narrator describes the feelings of one soldier. The passage is written in the third-person point of view. You're Private Berlin. Working with some classmates, rewrite the passage from the first-person point of view. Use the pronouns *I* and *me*. Make up details if you wish. You might imagine, for example, what it is that Private Berlin is pretending about his camping trip.

> At the rear of the column, Private First Class Paul Berlin lay quietly with his forehead resting on the black plastic stock of his rifle, his eyes closed. He was pretending he was not in the war, pretending he had not watched Billy Boy Watkins die of a heart attack that afternoon. He was pretending he was a boy again, camping with his father in the midnight summer along the Des Moines River. In the dark, with his eyes pinched shut, he pretended.
>
> Tim O'Brien, "Where Have You Gone, Charming Billy?"

to brainstorm main ideas such as recalling experiences, dreams, and conversations.

You may want to suggest to students that finding one creative idea is analogous to formulating a thesis statement for an expository essay.

Review with students the material devoted to purpose, audience, and tone, and cite examples from familiar literature. Next, introduce one or two examples of character and setting from favorite stories of yours and discuss their strengths. You could give students copies of the descriptions to use as models.

You may also want to review the **Types of Conflict** chart on p. 227 with students. Ask volunteers to offer specific examples of other types of external and internal conflicts.

☛

MEETING INDIVIDUAL NEEDS

LESS-ADVANCED STUDENTS

Suggest that less-advanced students create character and setting collages from magazine pictures. These collages can be used as visual writing prompts. For example, instead of writing ideas about different characters and settings, suggest that students first create two collages, one containing ten pictures of characters and one containing ten pictures of settings.

Thinking About Characters and Setting

Characters.   Who will be the people in your story? And what will they be like? You can create a completely made-up character, maybe using traits from all different kinds of people. Perhaps you'll create a character who has the humor of Bill Cosby, the looks of Kevin Costner, and the brains of Albert Einstein. Or you might take a person you know and change a few details to fit the character your story needs. Just keep developing details about your characters until you feel you know them well.

Setting.   Stories are always set in a particular time and place. The time and place might be as unusual as nine hundred years ago in a medieval castle in Scotland. Or they can be as ordinary as your back yard last week. When the time and place aren't central to the story, the details of setting may not be very important. But if you want to create a mood—or feeling, such as mystery or suspense—setting can be very important. That's why a ghost story set in an overgrown graveyard on a dark and stormy night is scary. The setting helps the reader feel the mood of mystery and heightens the suspense.

In **Writing Assignment: Part 1**, you could help students by first choosing a familiar character, perhaps from a popular TV show. Create a "What If?" situation for this character. Then, for **Writing Assignments: Parts 2** and **3**, answer the review questions about this character and create a setting. Finally, to model **Writing Assignment: Part 4**, create a sample story map on the chalkboard.

INTEGRATING THE LANGUAGE ARTS

Literature Link. Available in some literature textbooks, "Mr. Parker" by Laurie Colwin is a model of character and setting (as well as plot conflict and development). Ask students to read the story and to mark all passages of particularly vivid character and setting descriptions. In a class discussion have students explain why the passages are successful descriptions.

Point out the contrasts in the descriptions of the two piano teachers and what the differences indicate about their characters.

COOPERATIVE LEARNING

Ask students to choose partners to help them brainstorm for story details. Students could first brainstorm ideas separately on paper and then discuss their ideas. Encourage students to finish the exercise by recording five details they might use for a story.

226

---

226   *Creative Writing*

Reminder

Ask yourself the following questions to get ideas for your characters and setting.

Characters:
- How do the characters look, walk, and talk?
- How do they dress?
- How do they stand, move, and sit?
- What do they think about?
- What kind of personality do they have? Are they absent-minded? shy? anxious? bubbly?
- What do other characters in the story think about them?

Setting:
- What's the time and place of the story?
- What kind of houses do people live in at this time?
- What kind of work do they do?
- How important is the time and place to the story?
- Do I want the setting to create a mood, or feeling? What sights, sounds, and smells should I describe?

WRITING ASSIGNMENT

PART 2:
Developing Your Characters and Setting

Can you see your characters in your mind? Do you feel the setting? Write a short paragraph describing your main character with as much detail as you can. Then write another paragraph about your setting. Share your paragraphs with a couple of classmates. Ask them if your character seems real. Can they imagine your setting? What mood does it suggest?

Developing the Plot

What will happen in your story? Does boy meet girl? Does boy lose girl? What happens in a story is called the *plot.* Most plots open with a *conflict,* or problem, that can be either *external* or *internal.*

Students should now be prepared to complete all of the **Writing Assignments** independently. You may want to have them work in pairs or groups of three to complete one or more of the parts.

You may want to try a credit/no credit system of evaluation for the **Writing Assignments**. Because students are only formulating ideas, they will benefit most from supportive comments.

TYPES OF CONFLICT

EXTERNAL CONFLICT	EXAMPLES
A character faces a conflict with another character or group.	John argues with his father over his curfew.
A character faces a conflict with nature.	As he is on his way home to make his curfew, a heavy rain causes Julio's car motor to die.
INTERNAL CONFLICT	**EXAMPLE**
A character struggles with opposite thoughts and feelings within himself or herself.	Sue wants to stay longer at the party—but she knows she'll be grounded if she breaks her curfew.

After the opening conflict, the plot unfolds in a series of events that build on and cause each other. Will Sally's speeding ticket cause her parents to take away the car? Will she lose her part-time job if she can't drive? *Suspense* builds when readers wonder about what will happen next. Event builds upon event until the main conflict is resolved at the end.

As you develop your plot, think about the order of events. Listing events in the order they happen (chronological order) can help you develop a quick plot outline. You'll also be able to see if the events lead logically to the ending. Maybe your ending is a surprise, but it should still flow naturally from the story's events and characters.

WRITING ASSIGNMENT

PART 3:
Gathering Plot Details

What will happen in your story? What conflict will set the chain of events in motion? What will be the order of events? How will the story end? Jot down your ideas, creating a chain of events that outlines your plot.

Write the following sentence on the chalkboard:

Zuni Littlefoot trudged beneath the broiling Arizona sun.

Ask students what information they have learned from this sentence [setting—Arizona; character—Native American]. Next, ask students what they don't know [details about plot, character, and conflict]. Explain to students that they determine basic elements during prewriting. ■

A DIFFERENT APPROACH

To help students generate story ideas, you could choose a large photo from a popular magazine and work with the class to create a story map based on this photo. The person pictured could be famous or totally unknown, or you could even choose a setting to work from.

Begin by showing the picture to the class and then asking questions such as "Who is this and what is he or she going to do next?" Then build on students' answers until you have a completed story map.

Making a Story Map. As you plot your story's course, you may find it helpful to create a story map. Then you can see how all your story elements fit together. Here's how one writer developed a story map.

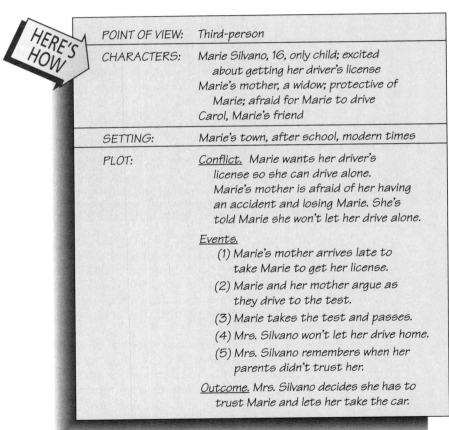

HERE'S HOW

POINT OF VIEW:	Third-person
CHARACTERS:	Marie Silvano, 16, only child; excited about getting her driver's license Marie's mother, a widow; protective of Marie; afraid for Marie to drive Carol, Marie's friend
SETTING:	Marie's town, after school, modern times
PLOT:	<u>Conflict.</u> Marie wants her driver's license so she can drive alone. Marie's mother is afraid of her having an accident and losing Marie. She's told Marie she won't let her drive alone. <u>Events.</u> (1) Marie's mother arrives late to take Marie to get her license. (2) Marie and her mother argue as they drive to the test. (3) Marie takes the test and passes. (4) Mrs. Silvano won't let her drive home. (5) Mrs. Silvano remembers when her parents didn't trust her. <u>Outcome.</u> Mrs. Silvano decides she has to trust Marie and lets her take the car.

WRITING ASSIGNMENT

PART 4:
Developing a Story Map

With the main landmarks for your story almost in place, you're ready to develop a story map. Using all the ideas you've developed so far, create a map for your story. Keep your plan handy as you write your story.

WRITING YOUR FIRST DRAFT

OBJECTIVES

- To work with others to add dialogue to a story paragraph
- To analyze a short story's character, setting, conflict, and ending
- To write a rough draft of a short story

MOTIVATION

Ask students to think about all the times they tell stories informally, such as recounting incidents to friends or explaining their behavior to parents. Tell students that writing a rough draft is very similar to telling someone a story.

Writing Your First Draft

The Basic Elements of Stories

If you've read many stories, you know they vary widely. Some stories, in fact, take place all in the mind of one character. Others are more traditional. Most stories, however, center on effective characters—people that seem so real they almost come off the pages—and their dialogue.

Writing stories gives you total creative control. You create characters, choose their hair color, decide their fate. While you're being creative, just remember your readers. Most of all, they want a good, suspenseful story that keeps them reading. Effective characters and dialogue are two elements that are sure to keep them reading.

Characters.   Think of the people in your story as real. How can your readers get to know them? The answer is simple: The same way they get to know people in real life! Writers can reveal characters by

- telling readers directly what the character is like
- describing how the character looks and dresses
- having the character speak
- revealing the character's thoughts and feelings
- showing how others feel about or behave toward the character
- showing the character's actions

Dialogue.   The dialogue, or talk, of the characters does two important things. First, it shows what kind of people the characters are. Second, it moves the plot along in a natural, interesting way. Following are some questions to ask yourself as you write dialogue.

- Do the words and sentences fit the characters? Do the children talk like children and the adults talk like adults?
- Do the characters sound natural? Do they use phrases, contractions, and slang?
- Does the dialogue show what characters are like and/or move the story along?

Teacher's ResourceBank™
RESOURCES

WRITING YOUR FIRST DRAFT
- Writing a Short Story

QUOTATION FOR THE DAY

"For me Calvino is one of the most wonderful writers, and the magic in his work is something that has been an influence . . . ." (Louise Erdrich, 1954–   , Native American poet, novelist, and short-story writer)

You may want to save this quotation to use after students have read the story **"Mushrooms in the City"** by Italo Calvino. Ask students to make a conjecture about the meaning of *magic* as Erdrich uses it and to decide whether they see magic in the Calvino story.

To introduce and discuss the ways to reveal characters, ask students to reexamine their character descriptions, looking for examples of each strategy. Then ask volunteers to read one example illustrating each strategy.

Read aloud the four questions in the text that concern dialogue. Then show students models of dialogue that might help them answer those questions. See if students can find examples of dialogue from other stories they have read in the textbook.

As an introduction to **A Writer's Model** on pp. 236–238, discuss what **"Mushrooms in the City"** says about human nature, emotions, and interactions, and how the conflict, plot, characters, and

230 *Creative Writing*

■ Do the dialogue tags—phrases like "they said," "he groaned," or "she screamed"—identify the speaker and add interest?

EXERCISE 1 ▶ **Speaking and Listening: Evaluating Dialogue**

Here's part of a story about two brothers who manage to argue about everything. The writer hasn't used much dialogue. Get together with three or four of your classmates. See if you can liven up the paragraph by writing convincing dialogue for the characters. Then take turns letting each group read its dialogue aloud. Listen to the different versions, and evaluate the dialogue. Make specific suggestions for improving the dialogue, using the questions on the previous page and above as a guide.

> World War III was just erupting when I walked into the kitchen. Jesse asked Tom if Tom was planning to ignore the full trash can. Tom said it wasn't his turn. After a few heated exchanges, Mom intervened. Then they tried to blame her for the argument. She silenced them both by banishing them to their rooms and taking away their car keys. Mom always was the world's greatest peacemaker.

Looking at a Short Story

The following story, by a professional writer, has been translated from Italian. It has a simple plot about a worker who discovers wild mushrooms growing in the city. The main conflict is only suggested, not directly presented. To discover it, think about what the mushrooms represent to the character Marcovaldo. [Hint: Remember that one type of conflict can be nature versus man or woman.]

setting convey these meanings. Ask students to keep these ideas in mind and then read **A Writer's Model** aloud. Point out the dialogue tags in the story and ask the class to suggest more descriptive verbs.

After examining these two models, students should now be ready to write the first rough drafts of their stories. Remind them to review their prewriting notes and story maps and to refer to this material while writing.

A SHORT STORY

Mushrooms in the City
by Italo Calvino

BEGINNING
Attention grabber

The wind, coming to the city from far away, brings it unusual gifts, noticed by only a few sensitive souls, such as hay-fever victims, who sneeze at the pollen from flowers of other lands.

Setting

One day, to the narrow strip of ground flanking a city avenue came a gust of spores from God knows where; and some mush-

Introduction of main character

1

rooms germinated. Nobody noticed them except Marcovaldo, the worker who caught his tram just there every morning.

2

This Marcovaldo possessed an eye ill-suited to city life: billboards, traffic-lights, shop-windows, neon signs, posters, no matter how carefully devised to catch the attention, never arrested his gaze, which might have been running over the desert sands. Instead,

Character development

he would never miss a leaf yellowing on a branch, a feather trapped by a roof-tile; there was no horsefly on a horse's back, no worm-hole in a plank, or fig-peel squashed on the sidewalk that Marcovaldo didn't remark and ponder over, discovering the changes of season, the yearnings of his heart, and the woes of his existence.

MIDDLE

Thus, one morning, as he was waiting for the tram that would take him to Sbav and Co., where he was employed as an unskilled laborer, he noticed something unusual near the stop, in the sterile, encrusted strip of earth beneath the avenue's line of trees; at certain points, near the tree trunks, some bumps seemed to rise and, here and there, they had opened, allowing roundish subterranean bodies to peep out.

USING THE SELECTION
Mushrooms in the City

1

You could point out that in short stories, the main character is introduced very early in the text. As an example, tell students to notice that Marcovaldo is first mentioned at the end of the second paragraph.

2

Ask students to list three things they are told about Marcovaldo. [Students might say the Marcovaldo is observant, unhappy in the city, and an unskilled laborer.]

3

Why might the author choose to use the description of Marcovaldo as "absent-minded?" [Calvino may be trying to indicate that the character is prone to make mistakes. This would serve as foreshadowing for future action.]

VISUAL CONNECTIONS

Exploring the Subject. The mushroom is actually a fungus that is producing fruit. *Mushroom* is the word used generally to identify the edible species, while *toadstool* is reserved for the poisonous species.

　　Mushrooms have been an important part of the folklore of many countries. The ancient Greeks and Romans considered them to be one of the foods of the gods. Because they appear unexpectedly and disappear quickly, mushrooms have inspired much speculation.

232

Character development/ thoughts

　　Bending to tie his shoes, he took a better look: they were mushrooms, real mushrooms, sprouting right in the heart of the city! To Marcovaldo the gray and wretched world surrounding him seemed suddenly generous with hidden riches; something could still be expected of life, beyond the hourly wage of his stipulated salary, with inflation index, family grant, and cost-of-living allowance.

3

　　On the job he was more absent-minded than usual; he kept thinking that while he was there unloading cases and boxes, in the darkness of the earth the slow, silent mushrooms, known only to him, were ripening their porous flesh, were assimilating underground humors, breaking the crust of clods. "One night's rain would be enough," he said to himself, "then they would be ready to pick." And he couldn't wait to share his discovery with his wife and his six children.

Suspense

Character development/ dialogue

　　"I'm telling you!" he announced during their scant supper. "In a week's time we'll be eating mushrooms! A great fry! That's a promise!"

　　And to the smaller children, who did not know what mushrooms were, he explained ecstatically the beauty of the numerous species, the delicacy of their flavor, the way they should be cooked; and so he also drew into the discussion his wife, Domitilla, who until then had appeared rather <u>incredulous</u> and <u>abstracted</u>.

"Where are these mushrooms?" the children asked. "Tell us where they grow!"

Conflict

At this question Marcovaldo's enthusiasm was <u>curbed</u> by a suspicious thought: Now if I tell them the place, they'll go and hunt for them with the usual gang of kids, word will spread through the neighborhood, and the mushrooms will end up in somebody else's pan! And so that discovery, which had promptly filled his heart with universal love, now made him wildly possessive, surrounded him with jealous and distrusting fear.

Character development/ thoughts

Dialogue— 4 suspense

"I know where the mushrooms are, and I'm the only one who knows," he said to his children, "and God help you if you breathe a word to anybody."

Suspense

The next morning, as he approached the tram stop, Marcovaldo was filled with apprehension. He bent to look at the ground and, to his relief, saw that the mushrooms had grown a little, but not much, and were still almost completely hidden by the earth.

He was bent in this position when he realized there was someone behind him. He straightened up at once and tried to act <u>indifferent</u>. It was the street-cleaner, leaning on his broom and looking at him.

Character 5 development/ description

This street-cleaner, whose jurisdiction included the place where the mushrooms grew, was a lanky youth with eyeglasses. His name was Amadigi, and Marcovaldo had long <u>harbored</u> a dislike of him, perhaps because of those eyeglasses that examined the pavement of the streets, seeking any trace of nature, to be <u>eradicated</u> by his broom.

Conflict

It was Saturday; and Marcovaldo spent his free half-day circling the bed of dirt with an absent air, keeping an eye on the street-cleaner in the distance and on the mushrooms,

4

What does the dialogue reveal about Marcovaldo's character? [Students might say that he is not a character who trusts others.]

5

How does Calvino develop the character of Amadigi? [He gives a brief physical description and he gives another character's opinion of Amadigi.]

234   *Creative Writing*

Suspense

and calculating how much time they needed to ripen.

That night it rained: like peasants who, after months of drought, wake up and leap with joy at the sound of the first drops, so Marcovaldo, alone in all the city, sat up in bed and called to his family: "It's raining! It's raining!" and breathed in the smell of moistened dust and fresh mold that came from outside.

At dawn—it was Sunday—with the children and a borrowed basket, he ran immediately to the patch. There were the mushrooms, erect on their stems, their caps high over the still-soaked earth. "Hurrah!"— and they fell to gathering them.

Conflict

"Papà! Look how many that man over there has found," Michelino said, and his father, raising his eyes, saw Amadigi standing beside them, also with a basket full of mushrooms under his arm.

Dialogue— suspense

"Ah, you're gathering them, too?" the street-cleaner said. "Then they're edible? I picked a few, but I wasn't sure . . . Farther down the avenue some others have sprouted, even bigger ones . . . Well, now that I know, I'll tell my relatives; they're down there arguing whether it's a good idea to pick them or not . . ." And he walked off in a hurry.

Marcovaldo was speechless: even bigger mushrooms, which he hadn't noticed, an unhoped-for harvest, being taken from him like this, before his very eyes. For a moment

Character 6 development

he was almost frozen with anger, fury, then— as sometimes happens—the collapse of individual passion led to a generous impulse. At that hour, many people were waiting for the tram, umbrellas over their arms, because the weather was still damp and uncertain. "Hey, you! Do you want to eat fried mushrooms tonight?" Marcovaldo shouted to the crowd of people at the stop. "Mushrooms are growing here by the street! Come along! There's

Dialogue— suspense

6

What emotions do the story's conflicts generate in Marcovaldo? [His conflict with himself about revealing the mushroom's location to his children causes him to feel first "universal love" and then "wildly possessive, surrounded . . . with jealous and distrusting fear." His conflict with Amadigi makes him feel "frozen with anger, fury" and then "a generous impulse."

CLOSURE

Ask students to discuss what they found easiest about writing their drafts and what they found most difficult. List responses in two columns on the chalkboard.

EXTENSION

Bring in a short example of dialogue written in formal English. In small groups, ask students to rewrite it using informal English. Then ask each group to read aloud their revised dialogue to the class.

Writing Your First Draft   **235**

plenty for all!" And he walked off after Amadigi, with a string of people behind him.

They all found plenty of mushrooms, and lacking baskets, they used their open umbrellas. Somebody said: "It would be nice to have a big feast, all of us together!" But, instead, each took his own share and went home.

OUTCOME

They saw one another again soon, however; that very evening, in fact, in the same ward of the hospital, after the stomach-pump had saved them all from poisoning. It was not serious, because the number of mushrooms eaten by each person was quite small.

Marcovaldo and Amadigi had <u>adjacent</u> beds; they glared at each other.

translated by William Weaver

WRITING NOTE

In this story, the writer doesn't present the conflict immediately. Instead, he begins with descriptions of the setting and of the main character, Marcovaldo. As you read the story, you realized that these descriptions are important to understanding the main conflict. It arises both from the city setting, where mushrooms are seldom found, and Marcovaldo's love of nature.

MEETING INDIVIDUAL NEEDS

LEARNING STYLES

Auditory Learners. To help students assess the completeness of their character descriptions, organize the class into pairs and ask each pair to introduce their fictional characters to one another. Use the following questions:

1. Who is the character?
2. Where does he or she live?
3. What does he or she do?
4. In what is he or she most interested?

Visual Learners. You may want to show a filmed version of a short story, preferably one students have read in class. Discuss how the film handles character and setting description. You could also discuss the dialogue, character motivation, and the plot's conflict and resolution.

ADVANCED STUDENTS

Ask advanced students as a group to find stories that contain an interesting opening or closing, a fully-described character, a realistic conflict and plot, and a creative dialogue. Ask the group to present the elements found in the stories as a dramatic reading.

Ask students to find an example of a poem containing character description, setting description, plot conflict, and resolution. Have them mark the passages in the poem or briefly describe the conflict and resolution. ■

ANSWERS

Exercise 2

Answers will vary. The following answers are possibilities:

1. The main conflict is that Marcovaldo is trying to get the mushrooms (man vs. nature). A minor conflict is that Marcovaldo feels he must protect the mushrooms from destruction by others.

2. Calvino shows Marcovaldo's feelings (in thoughts and words) as hope, fear, greed, possessiveness, generosity, and excitement. Two examples are his absentmindedness on the job as he thinks of growing mushrooms and his switch from expansive descriptions to guardedness when older children ask about where the mushrooms grow.

3. The setting is very important to the story. This story needed to be set in the city to make the conflicts plausible.

4. Students probably will have been surprised by the ending. One clue is Amadigi and the relatives' hesitation about whether mushrooms are safe.

COOPERATIVE LEARNING

Explain that although **A Writer's Model** is written in the third person, the narrator enters the mind of only one character—Marie. Ask students to think about how different the story would be if it were told from Mrs. Silvano's point of view. Then have students work in groups of three to rewrite the story from Mrs. Silvano's viewpoint.

> **EXERCISE 2** ▶ **Analyzing the Organization of a Short Story**

Meet with a small group of classmates to discuss the answers to the following questions about "Mushrooms in the City."

1. What is the main conflict in the story? What are some minor conflicts?
2. Marcovaldo might seem a little odd to you. How does Calvino make him seem real, despite his quirks? Point to specific examples in the story to explain your answer.
3. How important is the setting? Could the story have happened anywhere else?
4. Were you surprised by the ending? What clues in the story prepare you for the surprise ending?

A Basic Framework for a Story

"Mushrooms in the City" shows how a master of storytelling combines plot, characters, and setting to create several levels of meaning. The following story, which you might want to use as a model for your own, gives you a less complicated model to follow. The conflict in this story is revealed more through events and dialogue.

A WRITER'S MODEL

Licensed to Drive

BEGINNING
Event 1
Character development and conflict

"Where is she?" Marie sighed, checking her watch again. "It'd be just like her to forget--on purpose. You know she doesn't want me to do this."

"Calm down," Carol said. "Isn't that your mother's car?" She pointed to the old, blue car making a wide turn into the school parking lot.

Dialogue

"Finally. Let me drive," Marie said as her mother pulled up. Marie drove slowly out of the parking lot as Carol gave her the thumbs up sign.

Event 2

Character development/ dialogue Conflict

Background

Event 3

Event 4 Suspense MIDDLE

Character development/ thoughts

Dialogue

Event 5 Character development/ dialogue

"You're fifteen minutes late, Mom," complained Marie.

"I couldn't get out of work earlier," Mrs. Silvano said. "This is too early, if you ask me. You just turned 16! I hope you don't pass. And even if you do, I'm not sure I'll let you drive alone."

Marie shook her head and bit her tongue to keep from speaking back to her mother. She knew this speech; she'd heard it a million times. Her aunt had been hurt by a reckless teenage driver just three years before. Her mother couldn't stand the thought of her driving alone.

"I'd be more careful," Marie promised, as she turned into the test site. "You know you can trust me."

Marie was excited when she passed the test so easily, but her mother didn't say a word. When she asked to drive home, Mrs. Silvano snapped, "No, it's almost dark."

The ride home was silent and tense. Marie wanted desperately to take the car out, to show Carol, to drive with the windows down and the radio tuned to her favorite rock station. But she knew better than to push her mother now. Mrs. Silvano would only dig her heels in. She tried to think of something to say.

"Carol's brother's getting married."

"Who, Paul?" Mrs. Silvano asked, perking up just a bit.

"Yeah, and Carol's parents are furious. Said he's too young, it won't last, he should wait." Marie sighed, thinking of parents who don't understand their kids.

"Well, he's 20, isn't he? And he finished school? I was young when I married your papa." She smiled, thinking of the memory. "My parents didn't like it one bit, not one bit. But I knew better and I was right, too. Marriage lasted 22 years. We'd still be married if he was alive. And what about your aunt? She still can't walk without help."

 INTEGRATING THE LANGUAGE ARTS

Literature Link. If this story is available in your literature textbook, ask students to trace the plot structure in Isaac Bashevis Singer's "The Fatalist." Students should identify the two narrative voices [first person for both the frame and inner stories]. You could also have them note any interesting character and setting descriptions as well as words indicating tone and mood.

Vocabulary Link. Students might need help including interesting word choices in their drafts. To focus on vocabulary, hand out a sheet listing descriptive and dynamic words. Or list rather plain and simple words on the chalkboard and ask students to suggest more descriptive alternatives. Use a model paragraph which contains spaces for deleted words. Have students add descriptive words to this model.

CRITICAL THINKING
Analysis

Explain to students that what a character says and does should be clearly motivated. Ask students to use the following questions to analyze character motivation in **"Mushrooms in the City"**:

1. Why does the world suddenly seem "generous with hidden riches" to Marcovaldo when he discovers the mushrooms? [Marcovaldo is a "sensitive" soul who possesses "an eye ill-suited to city life." Thus, the mushrooms help him to connect with nature and to escape temporarily from his daily life.]

2. Why does Marcovaldo's enthusiasm turn to suspicion and "jealous and distrusting fear" when his children ask the location of the mushrooms? [He is afraid the children will tell their friends who will harvest the mushroom crop. Thus, his fear makes him overly possessive of his find.]

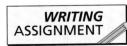
TIMESAVER

Before turning in their rough drafts, ask students to color-code character and setting descriptions with highlighters. Also ask them to underline all dialogue and dialogue tags. These marks will help you focus more quickly on these aspects of the drafts.

Dialogue

Suspense

OUTCOME

Dialogue

She choked up and fell silent. Even after three years she couldn't talk about her sister without crying.

"I know, Mom," Marie said. "But not all kids are bad drivers."

"Maybe," grunted Mrs. Silvano, clenching the steering wheel tighter.

Marie sighed and closed her eyes. It's hopeless. I'll be the only kid in school with a license who can't drive, she thought.

They arrived home and got out. As Mrs. Silvano unlocked the front door, she paused as if she had something to say. Then she suddenly jabbed the keys into Marie's hand.

"Don't you want to drive over to Carol's?" she said roughly.

"You mean it, Mom? Really?"

"Well, I guess I have to trust you sometime. Might as well be now. Hearing about Paul made me remember when my parents didn't trust me. But I want you to be careful. Night driving can be tricky. And be back in thirty minutes or no more driving."

Marie gave her a quick hug and jumped in the car. The headlights of the old car shone through the darkness as she drove away.

WRITING ASSIGNMENT

PART 5:
Writing a Draft of Your Story

By now you should have a good idea of how your story will develop. Use your prewriting ideas and story map to make your characters, setting, and plot come to life.

OBJECTIVES

- To analyze a writer's revisions
- To use peer feedback and an evaluating and revising chart to revise a rough draft of a story

TEACHING THE LESSON

Discuss and clarify each strategy in the **Evaluating and Revising Short Stories** chart. Then provide a copy of a poorly written short story and revise the story by using the chart's criteria as guided practice. Next, read **Exercise 3** in class and discuss the revisions by answering the questions. ☞

Evaluating and Revising

You may want to read your story to others in a small group and then listen to their feedback. You can also use the chart on the next page to help you analyze and improve each other's stories. Ask yourself each question in the left-hand column. If your answer is *no,* use the revision technique suggested in the right-hand column.

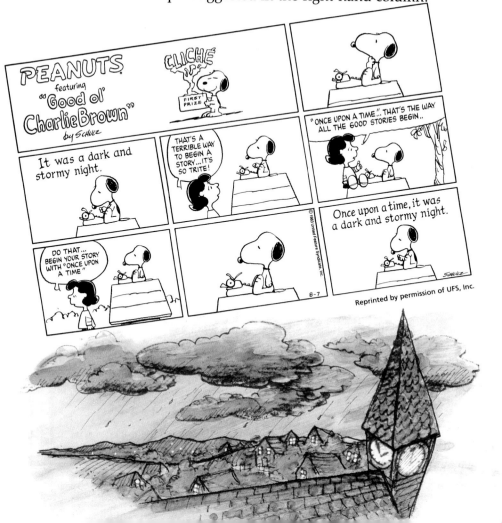

Reprinted by permission of UFS, Inc.

Teacher's ResourceBank™
RESOURCES

EVALUATING AND REVISING
- Writing a Short Story

QUOTATION FOR THE DAY

"Listen!/ All of you beauty-makers,/Give up beauty for a moment./ Look at harshness, look at pain,/Look at life again . . . ." (Langston Hughes, 1902–1967, African American poet)

Ask each student to choose a well-written sentence or paragraph in his or her story and to apply this quotation to that sentence or paragraph. Volunteers might then share their observations of whether this exercise led them to reevaluate or change their writing.

Place students in even-numbered groups. Ask each student to read a partner's story and discuss changes, using the **Evaluating and Revising Short Stories** chart as a guide. Next, tell students to switch partners and continue evaluating. After students have finished the groupwork, they are ready to evaluate and revise their own stories.

ASSESSMENT

Have students write their names on the evaluating and revising charts they complete for their partners' stories. You may want to grade students based upon their participation.

LEP/ESL

General Strategies. Encourage students to evaluate their story ideas first. Students often think of revising in terms of correcting grammar and spelling errors. Explain that most professional authors have editors to help point out mechanical errors. Tell students that you will help them with grammar and spelling (or pair them with another student) when they have finished working their way through the evaluation guide for revising their stories.

LESS-ADVANCED STUDENTS

To help students revise more effectively, tell them to read a passage or the whole story once to answer the first question, read it again to answer the second question, and to continue in this fashion until they are finished with all the evaluating questions.

ADVANCED STUDENTS

Ask advanced students to develop an alternate evaluating and revising chart for the class's peer editing groups. One of the students could read and explain the chart to the class.

EVALUATING AND REVISING SHORT STORIES

EVALUATION GUIDE	REVISION TECHNIQUE
1 Does a conflict set a chain of events in motion? Is the order of events clear?	**Add** a conflict between characters or within a character. **Reorder** events in the order they happen.
2 Do the events create suspense? Do the actions lead to a logical ending?	**Cut** events that slow the story down. **Add** details that build suspense. **Add** details that prepare for the ending.
3 Are the characters interesting and real?	**Add** details about what the characters do, feel, say, and think. **Add** realistic dialogue.
4 Is the point of view consistent? Is it either first-person or third-person?	**Cut** details that make the point of view inconsistent. **Add** first-person or third-person details as necessary.
5 Does the setting help readers picture the action or establish a mood?	**Add** specific sensory details. **Cut** details that detract from the mood.

When you revise your story, make sure you use

- transitions to show the order of events
- sentence variety to keep your readers interested

Evaluating and Revising **241**

EXERCISE 3 ▶ **Analyzing a Writer's Revisions**

Study the writer's revision of the first three paragraphs of the story on pages 236–238. Then answer the questions that follow the paragraph.

"It'd be just like her to forget--on

purpose. You know she doesn't want me to

do this." "Where is she?" Marie ~~said,~~ *sighed*   **replace/**

checking her watch again.   **reorder**

"Calm down," Carol said. "Isn't that

your mother's car?" She pointed to the car *old, blue* ∧   **add**

making a wide turn into the school

parking lot.

"Finally. Let me drive," ~~I~~ *Marie* said as ~~my~~ *her*   **replace**

mother pulled up. Marie drove slowly out

of the parking lot as Carol gave her an *the thumbs*   **replace**

∧ *up sign.* ~~encouraging look.~~

1. Why did the writer move the third sentence to the beginning of the paragraph?
2. In the third sentence, why did the writer replace *Marie said* with *Marie sighed*?
3. In the second paragraph, why did the writer add the words *old, blue* before the word *car*?
4. In the last paragraph, why did the writer change the word *I* to *Marie* and the word *my* to *her*?
5. In the last sentence, why did the writer replace *an encouraging look* with *the thumbs up sign*?

PART 6:
Evaluating and Revising Your Story

Use feedback from your classmates and the chart on page 240 to revise your story. Like a professional writer, make changes that will make readers want to keep reading.

PROOFREADING AND PUBLISHING

OBJECTIVES

- To proofread a short story
- To share a short story with an audience

TEACHING THE LESSON

Compose a proofreading checklist with students. Next, identify and correct the errors in a writing sample for the class. Then have each student proofread a partner's paper. To close, ask students to describe the errors they found in their papers. ■

Teacher's ResourceBank™
RESOURCES

PROOFREADING AND PUBLISHING
- Writing a Short Story

QUOTATION FOR THE DAY

"One has to dismount from an idea, and get into the saddle again, at every parenthesis." (Oliver Wendell Holmes, 1809–1894, American physician, professor, and man of letters)

Lead students in a discussion of their writing styles. Do they revise, rewrite, and proofread as they go along, or do they write rapidly and make changes later?

MEETING INDIVIDUAL NEEDS

LEP/ESL

General Strategies. To help students punctuate dialogues, first present part of a dialogue which has all the punctuation removed. Have students work alone or in pairs to insert the correct punctuation. Then check the dialogue with the class, and give students an opportunity to ask questions.

---

242 *Creative Writing*

Proofreading and Publishing

Your story is almost ready, but don't forget to proofread. Once your story is ready, use these ideas for sharing it.

- Publish your stories in a literary magazine.
- If the story involves friends or family members, consider giving or mailing it with a brief note.

MECHANICS HINT

Punctuating Dialogue

Remember these points when proofreading dialogue.

1. Begin a new paragraph when the speaker changes.
2. Use quotation marks around the speaker's words.
3. Separate dialogue tags from the rest of the sentence with a comma, a question mark, or an exclamation point. Begin a new sentence with a capital letter.
4. Do not capitalize the second half of a sentence that is separated by the dialogue tag.

EXAMPLES   "Watch out!" he screamed. "There's a car coming!"

"Don't go," he pleaded, "until we've finished reviewing for the test."

☞ REFERENCE NOTE: For more information on punctuating dialogue, see pages 834–838.

WRITING ASSIGNMENT

PART 7:
Proofreading and Publishing Your Story

You've worked hard on your story, so proofread it carefully. Then publish or share your story with others.

SEGMENT 7 *(pp. 243–245)*
WRITING WORKSHOP
OBJECTIVES
- To analyze the structure and techniques used in a news story
- To use the writing process to compose and publish a news story

TEACHING THE LESSON

Read the commentary on a news story to the class and then ask a student to read aloud **"Tornadoes Damage School."** Have volunteers provide answers for the four study questions.

Bring in copies of two well-written news stories, one from the local newspaper and one from the school paper. Use these ☞

WRITING WORKSHOP

243

A News Story

Did you notice the headline of today's newspaper? Maybe it said "Firefighter Rescues Baby" or "Jury Finds Defendant Not Guilty." These headlines summarize real-life stories that unfold every day. A news story is similar to a fictional story in that it usually tells about a conflict or problem. But it's different because it must rely only on facts, not on a writer's imagination, to tell its story.

News stories are usually short and follow a very tight structure. The opening paragraph is called the **lead.** It summarizes the important facts of the story by answering the *5W-How?* questions—*Who? What? When? Where? Why?* and *How?* The rest of the story then fills in the details, with the most important details first. See how the following news story follows this format.

Tornadoes Damage School

MIAMI—Tornadoes smashed windows and doors in an elementary school, injuring a teacher, and ripped through a small airport, damaged homes and tore off a warehouse roof Tuesday.

The first twister touched down near Sylvania Heights Elementary School in West Miami, injuring a teacher caught outside.

"It was a miracle only one person got hurt," Principal Lucy Williams said.

About 30 children under the supervision of the physical education teacher were outside waiting for parents to pick them up at dismissal time when the instructor spotted the oncoming tornado, she said.

Teacher's ResourceBank™
RESOURCES

WRITING WORKSHOP
All the resources for this chapter may be used in this segment.

QUOTATION FOR THE DAY

"A well-written lead makes commitments to the reader, and they have to be fulfilled. The lead makes a point, or perhaps several. The story proves them. Look at it that way, and the lead will provide a road map for the story that follows." (John Chancellor, 1927–   , and Walter R. Mears, 1935–   , American journalists)

As Chancellor and Mears explain in their book, *The News Business* (1983), a lead introduces the story, sets the tone of the piece, and summarizes its most important points. Have students spend time creating an interesting, well-written lead.

models, and identify how the *5W–How?* questions are answered in one story. Then have students find these elements in the other story.

Next, discuss any questions students might have about the writing process and assignment.

CLOSURE

In a class discussion, ask students to compare and contrast the writing process for a creative short story and a news story. Which process did they enjoy more? Why? ∎

Teachers and administrators rushed the children into a corridor moments before the storm hit, but a teacher was caught outside.

"It picked her up and dropped her down, and when she came in she was all covered in mud and had a cut on her forehead," said Williams.

The storm broke out the school's front doors and smashed windows, she said, and tore the tin covering off the roof.

A second tornado ripped through the Pembroke Pines area. Planes at North Perry Airport were overturned and torn apart.

The Ledger, Lakeland, Florida

ANSWERS
Writing Workshop Questions

1. Where — Miami; Why — tornadoes; What — elementary school, airport, homes, warehouse; Who — teacher; When — Tuesday; How — injured one and smashed windows and doors at school, ripped up airport, damaged homes, tore off roof of warehouse

2. One tornado hit the school at dismissal time (with children outside), picked up and dropped a teacher, and removed part of the roof. The second tornado hit a subdivision and an airport.

3. The principal's words are the eyewitness report of an authority — a spokesperson who knows what happened at the school.

4. The paragraphs are much longer in the short story.

1. Which *5W-How?* questions does the writer answer in the lead paragraph?
2. What facts do the other paragraphs give you about the tornadoes?
3. Why does the writer quote the principal?
4. Compare the average length of paragraphs in "Mushrooms in the City" (pages 231–235) to the average length of paragraphs in this news story. What is the difference?

Writing a News Story

Prewriting. To start your news story, look for a story that's important to your school or local community. Dig out all the facts of your story by asking *Who? What? When? Where? Why?* and *How?* Keep digging for facts and interviewing people until you know everything you possibly can about your story.

SELECTION AMENDMENT
Description of change: excerpted
Rationale: to focus on the concept of writing a news story as presented in this chapter

Writing, Evaluating, and Revising. Start your news story with a vivid lead that summarizes the story's important facts. Notice how the story about the tornado used active verbs like *smashed* and *ripped* in its lead to catch the reader's interest. Then use short, concise paragraphs to report the story's main facts. Be sure your story portrays the events and people accurately. Whenever possible, use quotes from the people involved. When you evaluate and revise, be sure to check the accuracy of your facts and quotes.

Proofreading and Publishing. Proofread your news story carefully for mistakes in grammar and usage. To publish it, consider submitting it to your school or local newspaper. Other media rely on news stories, too. What about a local radio or TV station? They might like the angle a student reporter can give.

LEP/ESL

General Strategies. The format of a news story is very unlike that of a short story. You may find that your students need to look at one or two more news stories to get a better idea of how these two types of writing differ. They might bring in news items of interest to them (which will help them get started on getting ideas for their own stories) and identify the lead paragraph and the *5W–How?* questions answered in the lead. Have students examine the paragraphs in the news story and identify how the format differs from that of a short story.

INTEGRATING THE LANGUAGE ARTS

Usage Link. This is an opportunity to discuss or review the difference between active and passive voice, since students will need to use the active voice in their news stories. Have students create a sentence in the passive voice, then revise it so that it is in the active voice. Then have volunteers put their examples on the chalkboard.

SPEAKING AND LISTENING OBJECTIVE

• To write a fable

SPEAKING AND LISTENING

Teaching Strategies

Bring to class one or two examples of short fables. Read them aloud but don't read the moral. Ask students if they can supply the moral.

Read through the description of the fable-writing process. Brainstorm with the class for possible morals, proverbs, mottos, and sayings that students can use in their fables. You may want to point out that a fable's moral is similar to an expository essay's thesis statement, except that a moral always comes at the end.

GUIDELINES

Fables must include morals, of course, and you may want students to underline the moral to make assessment easier. Students should also include two plot incidents, although you may want to specify more. You could have peer-editing groups evaluate different aspects of the fable.

MAKING CONNECTIONS

SPEAKING AND LISTENING

Creating a Fable

Do you ever hear sayings like "A bird in the hand is worth two in the bush"? Where do these sayings come from? Many of them started as the moral from a fable. A fable is a very short story that teaches a lesson about life. The characters in a fable are usually animals that speak and behave like humans. A very familiar fable is the one about the ant and the grasshopper. The moral from that fable is "He who idles when he's young will have nothing when he's old."

To create your own fable, first think of a proverb, motto, or saying that sums up an important truth about life. Think about popular sayings, or ask friends to recite their favorites. You might use as your motto "Too many cooks spoil the broth" or "Liars are not believed even when they tell the truth."

- To write a short story for children that explains an event in the life of a historical figure or an important historical event

247

Then, make up a simple plot that contains just one or two incidents. Remember, the outcome of the conflict must teach the moral you've chosen. Think of animal characters. It may help you to list some animals and the human quality connected with each one. For example, foxes are often considered sly and crafty, while dogs are portrayed as loyal and friendly.

After you write your first draft, read it to a small group of your classmates. Ask them to guess the moral of your fable. Then repeat the process as classmates read their fables to you.

SHORT STORY WRITING ACROSS THE CURRICULUM

History

You're writing a biography or history book for young children. Maybe you want to explain how Ponce de León arrived in what is now Florida or why Betsy Ross made a flag for the new nation. What will catch and keep your young readers' interest? You can always use a fast-moving plot, believable characters, and interesting settings—the elements of any good story.

To start, you'd rely on the basic historical facts of the story. Then you might create fictional details that would make the story more interesting. With Columbus, for example, you might invent details about how he loved the sea as a small boy and loved to sail boats. From there, you could tell the basic story of his historic trip.

Choose an important event in history or in the life of a hero whose life you can research in an encyclopedia. Before you write, make a story map. Be sure that all the historical details are factual. Then, write a short story—geared toward small children—that explains this event.

SHORT STORY WRITING ACROSS THE CURRICULUM
Teaching Strategies

You may want to coordinate the lesson with students' history classes.

Ask students for examples of historical narratives they have enjoyed. Ask them to specify, with examples and details, why they enjoyed the narratives.

Bring to class an example of a historical narrative. This could even be a literary example such as *The Iliad*, or *The Odyssey*, "Paul Revere's Ride," or an excerpt from a literary piece such as one of Shakespeare's histories. Ask students to read the selection, or if it is short, you may want to read it aloud. Then discuss its structure, characterizations, and setting. You may also want to discuss the author's use of language, details, examples, and historical facts.

GUIDELINES

Students will have to use proper language for a young audience. You may want to have them turn in their story maps. Assessment can also be limited to one feature such as character development or plot organization.

WRITING TO INFORM

- To identify the informative aim and to analyze the characteristics of a comparison/contrast informative essay
- To choose topics for a comparison/contrast essay
- To gather information for a comparison/contrast essay
- To develop a thesis statement for a comparison/contrast essay
- To classify objects and ideas
- To analyze the elements of a comparison/contrast informative essay
- To write the first draft of a comparison/contrast informative essay
- To understand how to evaluate and revise the comparison/contrast informative essay
- To revise the comparison/contrast informative essay
- To proofread a comparison/contrast essay to prepare it for publication

Motivation

Students often enjoy informing others about a new television show, a new student, or a new car. Begin this chapter by discussing the term *informative*. Have students list facts (information) about a television show and then make a comparison and contrast of two or more other television shows. Be sure to steer the students away from a persuasive aim. Have them remain in the informative aim.

NEWS UPDATE

Introduction

This chapter presents comparison and contrast essays for evaluation by students, beginning with the essay **"Moncrief: My Journey to the NBA."** The students will read the essays and determine their elements. Students will evaluate the opening sentence, the thesis statement, supporting paragraphs, and the conclusion in such essays as **"Time out! Is baseball Finnished?"** and **"Snorkeling and Scuba Diving."** Finally, students will write their own comparison/contrast informative essays using the writing process.

Integration

This chapter can serve as a resource for other activities. For example, students who are trying to explain the similarities and differences of the student clubs to incoming freshmen or transfer students could write a comparison/contrast informative essay. **Exercise 1** will assist students in understanding what kinds of information to compare and contrast.

Students who are in marketing or business courses might wish to pay special attention to **A Student Model: "Football and Cyberball."** This essay explains how a product can be presented in an informative comparison/contrast essay.

The block and point-by-point methods discussed in this chapter are useful in all types of comparison and contrast essays, including informative.

The **Making Connections: Test Taking** segment will be useful because students frequently are asked to write comparison/contrast informative essay answers to test questions.

The chart on the next page illustrates the strands of language arts as they are integrated into this chapter. For vocabulary study, glossary words are underlined in some writing models.

QUOTATIONS

All **Quotations for the Day** are chosen because of their relevance to instructional material presented in that segment of the chapter and for their usefulness in establishing student interest in writing.

Selection	Reading and Literature	Writing and Critical Thinking	Language and Syntax	Speaking, Listening, and Other Expression Skills
from *Moncrief: My Journey to the NBA* by Sidney Moncrief with Myra McLarey **250-253** "Time out! Is baseball Finnished?" from *The Miami Herald* by Bob Secter **267-270** "The Eagle-Feather Fan" by N. Scott Momaday **287**	Responding personally to literature **254, 270-271** Analyzing organization **254, 270, 271** Understanding comparison/ contrast **254, 257, 286-287** Finding main idea **257, 282-283** Locating and interpreting information **261, 270-271, 276-277, 283, 286-287** Finding details **270-271, 276-277, 282-283, 285-287** Identifying metaphor **286-287** Recognizing elements of style **286-287**	Writing a journal entry **254** Responding personally to literature **254** Applying interpretive and creative thinking **254, 270-271** Analyzing structure of a comparison/contrast essay **254, 276-277** Classifying objects and ideas **257** Determining purpose and audience **259, 270-271, 284** Choosing a subject for comparison/contrast **259** Gathering and arranging information **261-262, 264, 284** Developing thesis statement **265** Writing a draft of a composition in the informative aim **273** Recognizing a thesis statement **276-277** Evaluating the author's revisions **276-277** Evaluating and revising **277** Proofreading and publishing a revised draft **279** Using research to support a thesis **284** Writing an extended definition **284** Writing for an essay test **285-286** Writing comparison/contrast in another genre: poetry **287**	Proofreading for errors in grammar, usage, and mechanics **279, 284** Using reference materials **282-283**	Working with a classmate to classify objects and ideas **257** Making a chart to arrange information **264** Reading a poem aloud **268-287** Working with a classmate to analyze organization **270-271** Evaluating a classmate's revisions **277**

SEGMENT PLANNING GUIDE

Whether you are planning for a quick review of a writing concept or preparing an extended lesson on composition, you can use the following Planning Guide to adapt the chapter material to the individual needs of your class.

SEGMENT	PAGES	CONTENT	RESOURCES
1 *See Patterns*	*249-254*		
Literary Model from ***Moncrief: My Journey to the NBA***	250-253	Guided reading: a model of comparison and contrast	
Reader's Response/ Writer's Craft	254	Model evaluation: responding to literature and analyzing comparison and contrast writing	
2 *Uses of Comparison and Contrast*	*255*		
3 *Prewriting*	*256-265*		Analyzing Features
Choosing Subjects	256	Guidelines: selecting suitable topics	
Critical Thinking: Classifying Objects and Ideas	257	Guidelines: grouping objects or ideas	
Critical Thinking Exercise	257	Cooperative learning: classifying objects and ideas	
Thinking About Purpose and Audience	258	Guidelines: analyzing and selecting appropriate purpose and audience	
Writing Assignment: Part 1	259	Applied practice: choosing subjects for comparison and contrast	
Gathering and Arranging Information	260-264	Guidelines: gathering and arranging information	
Writing Assignment: Part 2	261-262	Applied practice: making a chart of gathered information	
Writing Assignment: Part 3	264	Applied practice: making a chart of arranged information	
Developing a Thesis	265	Guidelines: writing a thesis statement	
Writing Assignment: Part 4	265	Applied practice: developing a thesis statement	
4 *Writing*	*266-273*		Writing a Comparison/ Contrast Essay
The Elements of a Comparison/Contrast Essay	266-267	Guidelines: combining basic elements effectively	
Literary Model **"Time out! Is baseball Finnished?"**	267-270	Guided reading: examining a comparison/contrast essay	
Exercise 1	270-271	Cooperative learning: analyzing the organization of a comparison/contrast article	
A Basic Framework for a Comparison/Contrast Essay	271	Guidelines: organizing a comparison/contrast essay	
A Writer's Model	271-273	Guided reading: examining a sample essay	
Writing Assignment: Part 5	273	Applied practice: writing a first draft	

All the resources listed in this chapter are located in the Teacher's ResourceBank™.

SEGMENT	PAGES	CONTENT	RESOURCES
5 *Evaluating and Revising*	*274-277*		Writing a Comparison/ Contrast Essay
Charts: Evaluating and Revising	275	Guidelines: applying evaluation and revision techniques	
Exercise 2	276-277	Applied practice: analyzing a writer's revisions	
Writing Assignment: Part 6	277	Applied practice: evaluating and revising	
6 *Proofreading and Publishing*	*278-281*		Writing a Comparison/ Contrast Essay
Publishing	278	Publishing ideas: reaching a specific audience	
Grammar Hint	279	Writing suggestion: using the degrees of comparison	
Writing Assignment: Part 7	279	Applied practice: proofreading and publishing	
A Student Model	280-281	Sample: examining an informative essay	
7 *Writing Workshop*	*282-284*		All the resources for this chapter may be used in this segment.
An Extended Definition	282-283	Guidelines: classifying by definition	
Writing an Extended Definition	284	Applied practice: writing a short essay	
8 *Making Connections*	*285-287*		
Test Taking: Writing for an Essay Test Question	285-286	Guidelines: writing for an essay test question Applied practice: writing a comparison/contrast essay	
Comparison Across the Curriculum: Literature	286-287	Applied practice: writing a poem using metaphor	
Literary Model **"The Eagle-Feather Fan"**	287	Guided reading: analyzing the metaphors in a poem	

WHOLE-CHAPTER RESOURCES
A Writing Process Log, A Writing Prompt, Holistically Graded Models, Assessment Portfolio Materials

OBJECTIVES

- To analyze the construction of a comparison/contrast essay
- To write personal responses to a literary model

MOTIVATION

Letting students find comparisons and contrasts, discuss the opening picture of the segment.

 VISUAL CONNECTIONS
Still Life with Telephone and Flowers

About the Artist. Leigh Behnke is noted for her paintings of New York City, in which she often contrasts different views of the same image. Behnke focuses mainly on architectural subjects, and many of her paintings show how changing light affects a scene.

7 WRITING TO INFORM

TEACHING THE LESSON

Begin by having a student read the introductory paragraphs aloud. Then discuss how the quotation and the artwork are pertinent to the lesson.

Have a volunteer read the essay and note the structure of the introduction [a dynamic and intriguing opening sentence followed by a series of parallel examples of the players who will be compared and contrasted, and the thesis statement].

After reading the entire essay, discuss the essay's structure. [The paragraphs are ordered by the three players who are being compared and contrasted. Most of the paragraphs compare and contrast within

Seeing Patterns

Would you accept these challenges? Define *poetry* without saying the words *creative writing* or *literature*. Tell someone what Walt Disney's *Beauty and the Beast* is like without mentioning movie animation. Write a report on the Vietnam War without referring to any other U.S. war. No? No wonder. In life, nothing stands totally alone. **Seeing patterns and relationships** is one of the most natural ways to understand our world and to give information about it.

Writing and You. You use this strategy in different ways. You define *poetry* by how it's like and unlike other literature. You discuss *Beauty and the Beast* within the category of animated film. You understand the Vietnam War by contrasting it with World War II. Look at whatever interests you: Are there patterns or relationships to explore?

As You Read. In the following selection, Sidney Moncrief looks at patterns among three great basketball players. What does he see?

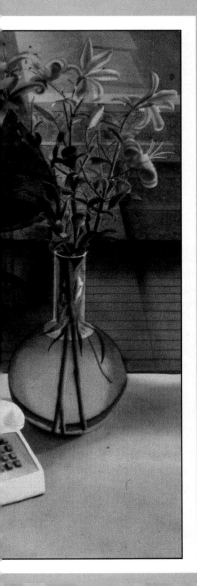

Still Life with Telephone and Flowers, Leigh Behnke (1983). Watercolor on paper. 40½" × 52¼". Collection of Glenn C. Janss. Courtesy of Fischbach Gallery, N.Y.

"So before writing, learn to think." (Nicolas Boileau-Despréaux, 1626–1711, French critic and poet)

Ask students to list five important experiences they remember. Then, with the help of a small group, have them look for patterns, similarities, and differences among the events. Finally, have each group write a brief statement about how the quotation relates to writing comparison and contrast papers.

MEETING **INDIVIDUAL** NEEDS

LEP/ESL

General Strategies. One technique to introduce classification to your ESL students would be through, clustering or webbing activity. This organizer helps students see how items or ideas are classified into categories. It can be further expanded to a comparison and contrast activity. For instance, students can proceed to compare the schools in their native countries to American schools.

GUIDED PRACTICE

After reviewing the essay, work with students to draw a line chart that analyzes the essay. The lines should be as follows: top line — the title; second line — the exciting opening sentence, beginning paragraph, and thesis statement; third line — paragraphs 3, 4, and 5, where Moncrief compares and contrasts himself with Larry Bird;

250

from
Moncrief: My Journey to the NBA

by Sidney Moncrief with Myra McLarey

1

Notice that the author uses first person point of view.

2

Paragraph 2 is a transition paragraph between the introduction and the first body paragraph.

1   My fear of being in the pros soon <u>dissipated</u>. It helped that I was never in awe of the talent of the big-name players—such as Larry Bird, Michael Jordan and Dr. J. I respected the stars and their talent, but I also knew I could compete.

2   Playing the best challenged me to be my best—to test my limits. It was also just plain fun to play against players with such skill. I found I could be playing very hard against a guy on another team and still be impressed with his play. If an opponent made a good shot or a great move or an impressive pass, in my mind I'd say, *What a play!* Sometimes I even complimented the player if I got the chance. I think you can play better if you allow yourself to respect your opponent.

I played against so many good players that it's impossible, really, to single out the best. Of course, Larry Bird would have to be high on anybody's list. He's intense, he works hard, he's versatile, and he's a real team player. With our difference in size I didn't guard Larry that much in the pros. I did go one-on-one with him the last game of my college career.

line—paragraphs 6 and 7, which compare Magic Johnson with Bird and Moncrief; and fifth line—the last two paragraphs that compare Dr. J and Moncrief.

Also, share your personal responses to **Reader's Response.**

INDEPENDENT PRACTICE

You can use both **Reader's Response** and **Writer's Craft** questions as independent practice.

"**Larry Bird [is]... intense, he works hard, he's versatile, and he's a real team player.**"

VISUAL CONNECTIONS

Exploring the Subject. Larry Bird, born in 1956 in French Lick, Indiana, is a forward for the Boston Celtics of the National Basketball Association. He played college basketball at Indiana State University before joining the Celtics in 1979. For 1979–1980 he was named the NBA Rookie of the Year. Larry Bird wrote his autobiography, *Drive*, in 1989.

No matter how great a college coach is, he doesn't have the time or the <u>expertise</u> to fully analyze an opponent. So when I played Bird in college, we didn't have any detailed <u>tendency</u> reports on him. When I guarded him the second half of the game, I had no idea of his specific moves. I had not seen him play before, and I was too busy the first half guarding someone else to watch him. I was simply playing defense the way I had always played it. His offensive skills were not nearly as refined as they are now, and he didn't have teammates who could get the ball to him like he does now, so my athletic ability allowed me to do a pretty good job on him. Sometimes I guarded Larry in the pros, but it was a different story then. I couldn't really play him in the pros—I'm too small.

3   If I were bigger and could play him, though, I'd push him to his right, because he likes to move to his left to shoot. I'd push him to his right, play him tight to force him to drive, and then I'd try to block him out on any shots. On post, I'd try to front him and not let him get the basketball.

3

Although this paragraph is still about Larry Bird, the author paragraphs for cosmetic purposes, to break the look of too much solid text.

CLOSURE

Ask students to discuss how this line-by-line layout of the essay can serve as an example for their essays.

EXTENSION

As with all essays, comparison/contrast essays rely on sentence structure to be effective. Take students back through this essay and discuss where the long sentences and short sentences occur and why. Longer sentences give information and carry a reader along with them. Short sentences, on

252

4

Moncrief achieves interest in the opening sentence by asking a rhetorical question.

4 **W**hat can I say about Magic Johnson except that he deserves his name? He controls the tempo of the game. He gets all the players involved and, like Bird, he plays an unselfish ball game. He's very right-handed, so he has a strong tendency to move to his right. Even though he's good enough to go left or right, you play him to go right. His outside shot is pretty good too, so you have to play him tight. If he's on the post, he's very difficult to guard because he's so big—he's 6'8"—and agile. You can't play behind him; if he gets the ball with his back to the basket, he's just going to hook it. You can't front him; he'll be able to catch a lob.

What you do with Magic is pick him up in the back court and make him turn. You don't want him coming at you face forward; you want him to come at you with his back turned and back you down the court. That way you can get help from your defense. Magic is not as difficult to keep from scoring as Jordan or Bird. But he's such a great all-around player, and like Bird, he can beat you so many different ways. If he can't beat you scoring, he'll beat you with his passing, and his play-making—he'll beat you by making things happen on the court.

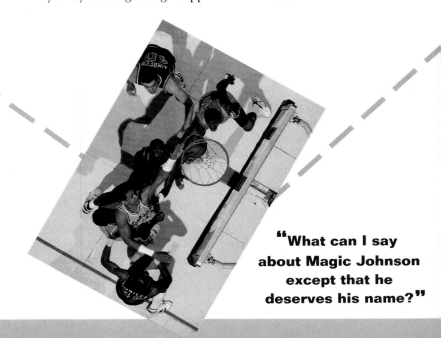

"What can I say about Magic Johnson except that he deserves his name?"

the other hand, are meant for emphasis, and they usually stop a reader to make a point.

ENRICHMENT

Students might be interested in reading the rest of Sidney Moncrief's book *Moncrief—My Journey to the NBA*. It was published by August House Publishers, Inc. in 1990. ■

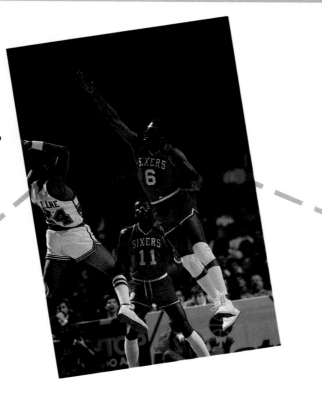

"Mostly, though, with Dr. J, you just had to yell for help."

5   **D**r. J was extremely difficult to guard. He is big. And he is good. Doc is right-handed and he likes his right. But if he wanted to shoot a jump shot, he liked to move to his left, take one dribble, then pull up and bank it off the glass. With Doc, I tried to take away his right hand and force him to take the jumper. On the post, you couldn't front him, you couldn't play behind him—you had to play him in-between. I used a move Eddie Sutton had taught me in college (we called it half-mooning): face him from the side and get a hand in front of his face. You also had to try to keep Doc out of the open court—he was one of the best open-court players in the history of the sport—by picking him up early and not letting him get the basketball.

Mostly, though, with Dr. J, you just had to yell for help.

5

Moncrief orders his paragraphs not only by the three players, but also by the expertise of each one; the abilities get stronger with each player discussed.

"Playing the best challenged me to be my best—to test my limits."

ANSWERS

Reader's Response

1. Each student should include a rationale for his or her opinions.

2. Be sure students give specific details.

Writer's Craft

3. He explains each man's best skills and the strategies needed to defend each.

4. The essay organizes the information by the difficulty level involved in guarding each man. Perhaps the author could have used the skills of each player as the categories of comparison and contrast. The organization makes it easy to follow.

READER'S RESPONSE

1. Do you know anything about the three basketball players Moncrief is giving information about? Do you think it is interesting to see what one great athlete thinks about the skills of other great athletes? Why?

2. What sport or entertainment medium are you interested in—football? auto racing? rock music? movies? In your journal write about two or three of the big names in that field. How are they alike? How are they different?

WRITER'S CRAFT

3. Moncrief lets readers know all three athletes better by *comparing* and *contrasting* them. He starts out with the obvious similarities among the men; they are all great basketball players. How does he contrast them?

4. How is the information about the three players organized? How could Moncrief have organized the information to make the differences among the men more obvious? What is the advantage of the organization he used?

SEGMENT 2 *(p. 255)*
STRATEGIES FOR WRITING TO INFORM
TEACHING THE MODES

The objective is to show students the four modes or strategies to use when writing to inform. Students need to be aware of these modes: narration, description, classifi-cation, and evaluation. They also need to know how to use them effectively.

This chapter focuses on informative writing. In this kind of writing no opinion is given, only facts. You could have students begin the class period by comparing and contrasting a suggested topic such as own-ing large dogs or small dogs. ■

255

Strategies for Writing to Inform

A quick glance at one general-interest magazine or a list of nonfiction best-sellers will show you that informative writing can use several strategies. Examining patterns and relationships, the strategy of *classification,* is just one of four basic strategies. Here are examples of how you might use each of the strategies to inform.

Narration: writing a travel essay about your visit to the Taos Pueblo; writing a biographical sketch of a Nobel Prize winner.

Description: in a paper for science class, describing the surface of Mars; in an article for your school newspaper, describing the features of the new gymnasium.

▶ **Classification:** in an essay for literature class, contrast-ing the hero and the villain in a short story; in an oral report for health class, defining *posttraumatic stress disorder.*

Evaluation: writing a letter to a friend about a new album you think she would enjoy; explaining to your boss why you think the store's merchandise should be rearranged.

LOOKING AHEAD

In the main assignment in this chapter, you'll use comparison and contrast in an informa-tive essay. You'll be using the strategy of clas-sification. As you work, keep in mind that a comparison/contrast essay

- looks at relationships or patterns
- focuses on two or more subjects
- discusses similarities, differences, or both

 INTEGRATING THE LANGUAGE ARTS

Literature Link. Show how comparison and contrast are used in lit-erature by referring students to Shake-speare's "Sonnet 18: Shall I Compare Thee to a Summer's Day." In this sonnet, Shakespeare is comparing and contrast-ing a woman to a summer's day. Have students list the comparisons and con-trasts. Because Shakespeare says the woman is even more excellent than a summer's day, be sure to point out that while the sonnet illustrates comparison and contrast, it is not informative. The informative aim does not offer an opin-ion; it states only the facts.

 CRITICAL THINKING
Synthesis

Have students create another type of comparison, an analogy. Explain that in an analogy two objects (or ideas) are not compared; instead, their relation-ship is.

Writers commonly use analogies to simplify complex relationships, such as equating the scattering of billiard balls on a pool table with what happens to atomic particles during nuclear bombardment.

Ask students to write their own analogies to show comparisons between relationships. Some possible examples are life and a ferris wheel, the writing process and building a house, and a football game plan and playing chess.

OBJECTIVES

- To choose subjects for a comparison/contrast essay
- To gather and arrange information for a comparison/contrast essay
- To develop a thesis statement for a comparison/contrast essay

Cont. on p. 258

QUOTATION FOR THE DAY

"He who does not expect a million readers should not write a line." (J. W. Goethe, 1794–1832, German poet, dramatist, and thinker)

Write the quotation on the chalkboard and ask students to freewrite about the importance of audience when choosing a subject for a paper.

MEETING
INDIVIDUAL
NEEDS

LEP/ESL

General Strategies. Some students might become easily frustrated by the vast amount of information being presented. To keep their interest, have students consider writing essays comparing and contrasting themselves with someone they know: a friend, a family member, or a role model.

Writing a Comparison/Contrast Essay

 Prewriting

Choosing Subjects

Sometimes a writing situation leads naturally to comparison/contrast subjects. For example, if you were interested in a new Civil War movie, you might naturally compare and contrast it with the classic film *Gone with the Wind*. In a newspaper article about a candidate for class president, you'd probably compare and contrast that candidate with others running for the same office.

When you write comparison/contrast essays, you have three choices:

1. You can write about the similarities only.
2. You can write about the differences only.
3. You can write about both similarities and differences.

If your teacher assigns a comparison/contrast essay, be sure to understand the assignment. Sometimes, *compare* is used as an "umbrella" term that means analyze *both* similarities and differences.

In choosing subjects for comparison and contrast, be sure of two things:

- the subjects have some basic similarities
- the subjects are different enough to be interesting

CRITICAL THINKING
(p. 257)

OBJECTIVE

• To classify objects and ideas

TEACHING *CLASSIFYING OBJECTS AND IDEAS*

The way the TV show *Jeopardy* sets up its categories is a perfect example of a way to classify objects and ideas. Another example is the binomial nomenclature used in biological sciences. For explanation, discuss the reasons that the mosquito is classified

Prewriting   **257**

 CRITICAL THINKING

Classifying Objects and Ideas

When you choose subjects to compare and contrast, you must understand (1) *if* they have anything in common, and (2) *what* it is they have in common. You're actually using the critical thinking skill of classifying: grouping objects or ideas into categories that show their similarities.

If you were playing a game that required you to identify categories, the questioner might ask you, "What is the category for algebra, history, physics?" One good answer, of course, would be "school courses"! After identifying the categories for "cars, buses, trains" (types of land transportation) and for "moon, sun, comet" (celestial bodies), you win!

 CRITICAL THINKING EXERCISE:
Classifying Objects and Ideas

Now make your own game. Work with a partner to figure out the category that tells what each of the following groups has in common. Be as specific as you can in stating the category. [Hint: One group can't be classified because the items have nothing in common.]

EXAMPLE   **1.** honesty, kindness, courage, dependability
   1. *Category: desirable character traits*

1. Classical period, Middle Ages, Renaissance
2. lions, tigers, elephants, gorillas
3. mumps, chickenpox, German measles
4. football, baseball, soccer
5. oxygen, television, spaghetti
6. Washington, D.C.; Paris, France; Tokyo, Japan; London, England
7. Himalayas, Alps, Rockies
8. a poem, a painting, an opera
9. democracy, monarchy, dictatorship
10. a sunset, a ballgame, a movie

LEP/ESL

Spanish. The **Critical Thinking Exercise** requires that students work with partners. Many of your Spanish-speaking students will not have the vocabulary or cultural background necessary to complete this exercise, especially if they choose fellow ESL students as partners. In contrast, if paired with native English speakers with strong cognitive and interpersonal abilities, ESL students are likely to assimilate valuable information beyond the targeted classification skill.

ANSWERS
Critical Thinking Exercise

1. historical eras
2. African animals
3. childhood diseases
4. team sports
5. no commonality

6. capitals of countries
7. mountain ranges
8. types of artistic works
9. types of governments
10. things to watch

differently than the spider. To assess, ask a volunteer to define the word *classify*. ⚡

Cont. from p. 256
MOTIVATION

Discuss other movies that might be compared to either *Glory* or *Gone with the Wind*. When students give their opinions about movies they like, use this interest to talk about the differences between the persuasive and informative aims.

258   *Writing to Inform*

Prewriting

Thinking About Purpose and Audience

Purpose. Your *purpose* in exploring subjects with comparison/contrast may be any one of the four basic purposes for writing: to inform, to persuade, to express yourself, or to be creative. In this chapter, however, you'll focus on informing. And within that basic purpose, you'll have a more narrow one. You may

- Show similarities between subjects

    EXAMPLE   Show how competitive in-line skating and ice skating are alike

- Show differences between subjects

    EXAMPLE   Show how factories in the United States and Japan are different

- Show both similarities and differences between the subjects

    EXAMPLE   Show how two types of weight training equipment available for home use have both similar and different features

Audience.   When you inform, you have to think about what your *audience* knows and doesn't know so that you can define unfamiliar terms and give background information. It's also important to think about what will interest your readers—remember that you want to hold your readers' attention while you inform them! This can mean a subject that will be new to many of them, as high-tech Japanese factories might be. But it can also mean your approach to your subject. Perhaps your audience knows something about weight-training equipment but would really like to know how two systems compare for developing certain muscles. Perhaps your readers would like to know how two systems compare in possible modifications as the user's ability increases. Try to make your comparison/contrast one that will bring a new subject to light or shed new light on a familiar one.

A DIFFERENT APPROACH

Ask students to find and analyze examples of classification in the letters to the editor of the local newspaper. Explain that most of these letters will have a persuasive aim.

Students should mount the letters on paper and analyze them for purpose, point of view, and points of comparison.

Have a student read the information under **Purpose.** Explain that classifying information allows a person to understand a subject better. In fact, many school assignments require students to make comparisons and contrasts.

Next, have another student read about audience. Then expand on the material in the textbook by discussing how important it is to have an audience other than just the teacher. The purpose of this paper is to inform someone besides the teacher about whatever subject the student chooses.

For **Gathering Information** (pp. 260–261), discuss who Michelangelo and Leonardo da Vinci were. Carefully discuss the six features listed in the chart and tell

Prewriting **259**

WRITING NOTE

As with other types of writing, remember to narrow your subjects. It's hard to write an interesting, detailed essay comparing the Middle Ages with today or even comparing New York with Miami. However, you could compare and contrast transportation in the Middle Ages with transportation today, or the architecture of New York and Miami.

◆ **MEETING** **INDIVIDUAL** **NEEDS**

LEARNING STYLES

Visual Learners. Students will benefit from seeing a Venn diagram that shows the relevant features and specifics for the comparison of *The Wonder Years* and *Life Goes On* given on p. 260. Have the class discuss possible details while you write them down.

PART 1:
Choosing Subjects for Comparison/Contrast

After digging around in your mind, select two subjects that interest you for your comparison/contrast essay. Test your subjects to make sure that they meet these two requirements: (1) they have some basic similarities, and (2) they have enough differences to make the comparison/contrast significant. Remember to consider the purpose and audience for your essay.

students that to collect this information one would have had to do some research. Then you can explain that to write good, informative, comparison/contrast essays, students might need to do some research. You should then call on students and have them explain why, for instance, the information under feature 2 is not under feature 5.

Arranging Information on p. 262 can be read silently by students in class. Then you can go back to the organization chart and discuss why the features about Michelangelo and da Vinci were ordered as they were. Ask students if the order could have been different. Then read the paragraphs at the bottom of p. 262 about the block and point-by-point methods.

LESS-ADVANCED STUDENTS

If students seem to be having trouble with this writing assignment, you may want to allow them to use the information on Michelangelo and Leonardo da Vinci as the basis of their papers. Tell students they can add or subtract details as needed.

 INTEGRATING THE LANGUAGE ARTS

Library Link. Because the third paragraph under **Gathering Information** indicates that students might need to do research first, be sure to take them to the library or allow for some library time. Assign the collecting of relevant features for independent study so that students can do the research on their own.

Gathering and Arranging Information

After you've chosen subjects and thought about your purpose and audience, you need to figure out the *relevant features* you'll compare and contrast. Then you can gather and organize information about these relevant features.

Gathering Information

On TV courtroom dramas, you'll hear lawyers saying things like, "That's not relevant, your honor." *Relevant* means "related to the main point." When you're exploring a subject by comparison/contrast, you look at the *relevant features* of both items. These are the features that will inform readers about your main idea.

Suppose your purpose is to inform readers about the TV programs *The Wonder Years* and *Life Goes On*. You think that both programs show families as they are in real life. That's the basic thing they have in common and it's also your main idea. How can you inform readers of this main idea? What details will you use to support it? You might compare and contrast the settings (time and place), the ages of the main characters, and typical situations in the shows. These would be the relevant features, about which you'd gather information for your paper. What is relevant may differ depending on your audience, however. For example, a teenage audience might be interested in the typical situations, while another audience might be more interested in the settings.

If you're familiar with your subjects (two television programs, for example), you can probably recall or observe all of the information you'll need for your paper. But if your subjects are unfamiliar (two historical periods or two places you've never been), you'll need to do some research to gather information.

The following chart shows how you could gather information about two famous artists: Michelangelo and Leonardo da Vinci. Notice that most of the relevant features are similarities.

Continue by reading and discussing the method chart on p. 263 carefully.

Finally, have a volunteer read aloud the material about developing a thesis statement. Draw students' attention to the **Reference Note** on p. 265 for more help.

GUIDED PRACTICE

Before having students do **Writing Assignment: Part 1,** brainstorm for topic ideas and talk about similarities and differences. A suggestion might be two types of bicycles—touring bikes and dirt bikes. To make sure students understand the informative aim, emphasize that many comparisons do not end in making a choice. If students ☞

HERE'S HOW

Relevant Features		
	Subject 1: *Michelangelo*	**Subject 2:** *Leonardo da Vinci*
Feature 1: accomplishments	*sculptor, painter, architect, writer of sonnets*	*painter, sculptor, architect, engineer, scientist*
Feature 2: commitment	*dedicated to art; often went days without sleeping or eating*	*dedicated to art; often went days without sleeping or eating*
Feature 3: innovations	*master of perspective; pioneered unpainted statuary*	*master of perspective; inventor of classic style of painting during Renaissance*
Feature 4: most famous work	*murals of Sistine Chapel*	*The Last Supper and Mona Lisa*
Feature 5: new information	*restoration of Sistine Chapel shows use of brilliant, not dark, colors*	*restoration of The Last Supper shows use of brilliant, not dark, colors*
Feature 6: fame	*famous in his lifetime and throughout history*	*famous in his lifetime and throughout history*

Literature Link. If available, have students read parts of Plutarch's *Life of Caesar* and Shakespeare's *The Tragedy of Julius Caesar.* Then have each student write a comparison/contrast essay about the comparable details in each. Students should organize their data in charts before writing.

MEETING INDIVIDUAL NEEDS

LEARNING STYLES

Visual Learners. A good way to model block and point-by-point methods is to show on the chalkboard or on the overhead projector how a coach can either explain a play by showing what each player will do from beginning to end or by showing what the entire team will do as a unit.

WRITING ASSIGNMENT

PART 2:
Gathering Information

Now it's your turn to gather information for your essay. As an aid in gathering information, make a chart like the one above for the two subjects you have chosen to compare and contrast. Decide what relevant features you will use, and write them in the chart. Don't forget your audi-state that touring bikes are more fun than dirt bikes, explain that writers are entitled to opinions, but that in this discussion, students need to state only the facts, not make choices.

Have the class take a few moments to compare the two shows mentioned in the textbook or two other shows with which the entire class is familiar. Have students write these similarities or differences in columns on the chalkboard.

ence. What features do they care about? (You may need to do some research first.) As you gather information, you may need to revise the chart.

© Grimmy Inc. Reprinted by permission.

Arranging Information

You need to make an important decision before you begin writing: how to organize your paper. There are two helpful ways to organize comparison/contrast writing: the *block method* and the *point-by-point method*.

With the **block method,** you discuss all the features of one subject and then all the features of the second subject. When you use this method, you discuss the same features for the second subject as you do for the first. With the **point-by-point method,** you discuss one feature of the first subject and the same feature of the second subject. Then you move to the second feature, and so on.

For example, in an essay about Leonardo da Vinci and Michelangelo, you might group information by discussing Leonardo first (his achievements, innovations, and major works.) Then you might discuss Michelangelo (his achievements, innovations, and major works). That's the block method.

After a short discussion, read the directions for **Writing Assignment: Part 1** aloud and give students time to think about their subjects independently.

Allow students to work in groups to help each other make charts for **Writing Assignment: Part 2.** You can monitor each student within the groups.

The paradox of independent practice in a group situation is appropriate. Students can, without direct monitoring by the teacher, arrange the information, but with confidence that a teammate can help them if necessary. Group members should read and evaluate thesis statements and make suggestions to team members who can then rework the theses.

Or you might start with the idea that both Michelangelo and Leonardo were geniuses in many fields. Then you could go on to the next features: their dedication, new contributions, most famous works, and fame in their lifetimes. This is the point-by-point method important.

Remember to treat the relevant features in the same order for both subjects. The order of the relevant features is often most to least or least to most important.

The following chart on two African American writers from the colonial period to the Civil War illustrates the two methods of arranging information in a comparison/contrast essay.

BLOCK METHOD	POINT-BY-POINT METHOD
Subject 1: Phillis Wheatley (1753?–1784) Feature 1: born a slave Feature 2: 1st black woman to publish volume of poetry in U.S. Feature 3: well read in the Bible and Latin classics Feature 4: dedicated her life to poetry *Subject 2: Jarena Lee* (1783–?) Feature 1: born a free woman Feature 2: 1st black woman to write her autobiography in U.S. Feature 3: well read in the Bible; wanted to become female preacher Feature 4: dedicated her life to evangelizing	*Feature 1: status at birth* Subject 1: Phillis Wheatley born a slave Subject 2: Jarena Lee born a free woman *Feature 2: accomplishment in writing* Subject 1: Phillis Wheatley 1st black woman to publish volume of poetry in U.S. Subject 2: Jarena Lee 1st black woman to write autobiography in U.S. *Feature 3: knowledge* Subject 1: Phillis Wheatley well read in the Bible and Latin classics Subject 2: Jarena Lee well read in Bible; wanted to become a female preacher *Feature 4: purpose in life* Subject 1: Phillis Wheatley dedicated her life to poetry Subject 2: Jarena Lee dedicated her life to evangelizing

MEETING INDIVIDUAL NEEDS

LEARNING STYLES

Visual and Kinetic Learners. Make copies of a blank chart for your class like this one with the **Block Method** and **Point-by-Point Method** columns. Students can manipulate their information within the chart to see which is the better format for their essay subjects.

ASSESSMENT

As students finish and share their organizational charts with teammates, you can move from student to student to make sure all charts are workable. Charts that are not workable can be referred back to the groups.

CLOSURE

Have students review the steps involved in the prewriting stage: **Choosing Topics, Gathering Information, Arranging Information,** and **Developing a Thesis Statement.**

VISUAL CONNECTIONS

Exploring the Subject. Phillis Wheatley's first poem to be published was "An Elegiac Poem on the Death of George Whitfield." This work acclaims the life of the famous English minister, George Whitfield. Another poem, "A Farewell to America," Wheatley dedicated to her mistress, Susanna Wheatley.

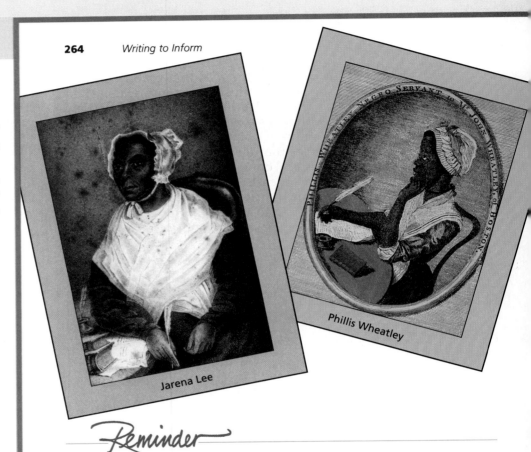

264   *Writing to Inform*

Jarena Lee

Phillis Wheatley

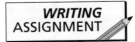

To gather and arrange information

■ decide on the relevant features of the subjects
■ make a chart showing similarities and/or differences
■ choose the point-by-point method or the block method

WRITING ASSIGNMENT

PART 3:
Arranging Information

You've done most of the hard work by gathering information. Now you need to decide on how to arrange that information. It's your decision. Choose the organization that you think you'll be more comfortable with. Using the block method or the point-by-point method, make a chart like the one shown on page 263.

EXTENSION
Have each student write an informative paper comparing a common idea in two or more pieces of literature. Explain to students that they can use another prewriting method for gathering their information—reading and taking notes. Good choices to use as the basis of this paper are the poems "The Courage That My Mother Had" by Edna St. Vincent Millay and "Mother to Son" by Langston Hughes. ■

 Prewriting

Developing a Thesis Statement

The thesis statement of a comparison/contrast paper should state your subjects and your approach. It must

- identify what people, things, or ideas you are comparing or contrasting
- identify whether you will emphasize comparisons, emphasize contrasts, or balance the two

Here is a thesis statement that will emphasize contrasts. First the writer identifies the two things she's going to write about—the American and the French revolutions. Then she shows that she'll concentrate on contrasts by saying that the two events had only one similarity.

> The American Revolution and the French Revolution both started out to give power to the common people, but the similarities stopped there.

 REFERENCE NOTE: For more information on writing thesis statements, see pages 113–114.

WRITING NOTE

Very often in an essay that explores differences, you begin with the one or two similarities the subjects have in common and then explore the differences. In the same way, to explore similarities, you may begin with the one or two differences between the subjects and then devote most of your paper to exploring similarities.

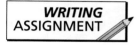
WRITING ASSIGNMENT

PART 4:
Developing a Thesis Statement

Are you going to compare your subjects? Contrast them? Or compare and contrast them? Write a thesis statement that announces to your reader what you plan to do in your paper. Use your prewriting chart on page 261 for ideas.

DEVELOPING A THESIS STATEMENT

Be sure to remind students that when using the point-by-point method, the order in which they discuss the categories in the bodies of their papers should follow the order that categories are listed in their thesis statements. For example, if a thesis statement comparing Michelangelo and Leonardo da Vinci is "Michelangelo and Leonardo da Vinci share many similarities in their achievements, innovations, and major works," the three body paragraphs will be about achievements, innovations, and major works, in that order.

TIMESAVER
Because the thesis statement controls the paper, writing it is a crucial step. Conduct individual conferences with students to be sure they have strong thesis statements. Spending an extra amount of time early will save time later when the essays are to be graded.

WRITING YOUR FIRST DRAFT

OBJECTIVES

- To analyze the organization of a comparison/contrast informative essay
- To write the first draft of a comparison/contrast informative essay

MOTIVATION

Ask students what the next step for builders is after they get all their materials gathered and organized. [Students will probably say that the next step is to start creating the structure.] Explain that students are also in the creation stage. They have gathered and organized their information and are now ready to build their drafts.

Teacher's ResourceBank™
RESOURCES

WRITING YOUR FIRST DRAFT
- Writing a Comparison/Contrast Essay

QUOTATION FOR THE DAY

"How many good books suffer neglect through the inefficiency of their beginnings!" (Edgar Allan Poe, 1809–1849, American story writer and poet)

Use the quotation to emphasize the importance of creating interesting beginning paragraphs. Ask students to write journal entries about times when they have made judgments about people or places based on first impressions. Explain that readers also make judgments based on first impressions, so good writers attempt to pique the readers' interests with their introductions.

Writing Your First Draft

You've completed much of the important work on your paper. All that's left to do is to put the information in your prewriting chart into sentences and paragraphs. You'll also have to think about an introduction, body, and conclusion.

The Elements of a Comparison/Contrast Essay

Introduction. As in any essay, the introductory paragraph should capture your reader's attention. You might begin the introduction of a paper about two Renaissance artists by saying "Leonardo and Michelangelo are not just names for Ninja Turtles; they were real people with real gifts." The introduction should also include the thesis statement, usually placed at the end.

Body. The body is the place to use the block method or the point-by-point method to present details about your subjects. Use transitions to connect and clarify ideas. Words and phrases like *also, similarly, both, in the same way,* and *just as* signal a comparison. *By contrast, however, unlike,* and *on the other hand* signal a contrast.

☞ REFERENCE NOTE: For more information about transitions, see pages 89–90.

In the body, you develop ideas with specific details, facts and examples, and quotations. In the paper about the two Renaissance artists, for example, you might discuss details about the artists' paintings: "Both Michelangelo and Leonardo recorded their ties to the church. Michelangelo painted the ceiling of the Sistine Chapel, and Leonardo painted a religious scene in *The Last Supper* on the wall of a monastery dining hall."

Conclusion. The ending of any essay must make the reader feel satisfied. A good, safe way to end is to summarize the information in the body and show how it sup-

Ask a volunteer to read aloud the information about the structure of the essay [introduction, body, and conclusion] and have the class discuss it. You may want to use a graphic organizer as a visual reinforcement of the structure; for example, an inverted triangle for the introduction, boxes for the body paragraphs, and a triangle for the conclusion.

The newspaper article about baseball can be introduced by talking about the origin of baseball, some great names associated with the game, and so forth. Discuss the vocabulary words before beginning. Then focus on why this is an informative essay [facts and information, not opinion] ☞

Writing Your First Draft   **267**

ports the thesis. Another way to end your essay is with an evaluation, a final comment that judges the relative worth of the two subjects. To end an essay comparing two sports cars, for example, you might say, "The Hawk and the Tornado are fairly evenly matched in terms of quality; but if you want to have fun, drive a Hawk."

Looking at a Comparison/Contrast Essay

The article that follows explains the similarities and differences (mostly the differences) between baseball in the United States and a Finnish sport called *pesapallo*. Notice how the writer inserts a reference to the comedy routine of Abbott and Costello, as well as background information on the game of *pesapallo,* to keep the reader interested.

A NEWSPAPER ARTICLE

1 | ## Time out! Is baseball Finnished?
by Bob Secter

INTRODUCTION

Attention grabber

HANCOCK, Mich.—There were lots of reasons why Jimmy Piersall was known as a flake back when he played major league baseball; but one of the best came the day he hit a home run as a New York Met and ran the bases backward.

GUIDED PRACTICE

Read and analyze the essay on snorkeling with the class for its organizational methods and structural elements. Asking students for examples from the essay, write these elements on a transparency. Follow with a short discussion of diction and placement of facts in an essay.

All of which has little to do with the subject of this story, except to illustrate the <u>maxim</u> that what may seem like <u>buffoonery</u> in one setting could make perfect sense in another. Had Piersall been playing in, say, Helsinki rather than New York, he might have fit right in.

Yes. Baseball has been Finlandized.

Background

The Finns call the game *pesapallo* and are so crazy about it that it is considered their national pastime. Of course they do it a little differently. They don't actually backpedal their way from base to base a la Piersall, but, looking at it from a <u>chauvinist</u> American perspective, they do take a backward route around the base paths.

Difference— Factual support

First base is where third base ought to be, second is sort of around where first should be and third is somewhere out in left field.

Difference— Factual support

That's right, Abbott. Who isn't on first. I Don't Know is. Sort of.

Background

Anyway, Finnish <u>emigres</u> have spread the game to Scandinavia, Canada and even Australia. And over the weekend, they took their first crack at the toughest market of all—the United States, the guarantor of all that is pure and noble about baseball.

Background

Here in Michigan's rugged upper peninsula, the heart of Finnish America, two Canadian *pesapallo* teams squared off Saturday in a demonstration game before thousands of slightly <u>befuddled</u> spectators at an ethnic festival. In a real slugfest, the Toronto Sisu eked out a 16–15 win over the archrival Thunder Bay Repais.

Organizers of the annual FinnFest say that they hope to field enough domestic talent to stage home-grown *pesapallo* matches at future gatherings. Already, the Hancock High School baseball coach is talking about teaching the Finnish version to his team.

2

This wording has the connotation of America's being too boastful about its game.

3

An allusion to Abbott and Costello's comedy routine.

4

guarantor: one who is responsible for something

5

eked out: barely managed

Writing Your First Draft **269**

Difference—Factual support

The main selling point of *pesapallo,* devotees say, is action. There are no long pauses between pitches, the ball is almost constantly in play and both fielders and runners are forever scampering all over the place.

Difference—Quotation

"In American baseball, a runner on second is in scoring position but in our game, he's just tired," winked Jari Lemonen, who plays for the Repais. "Usually when we get out there, we pack a lunch."

Background—History

6 The Abner Doubleday of Finland was Lauri Pihkala, a professor who apparently was <u>mesmerized</u> by baseball during early 20th century study tours in the United States. He combined the American game with some native ball-playing sports and *pesapallo* was born.

Similarities—Factual support/Statistics

Both baseball and *pesapallo* feature four bases, three outs an inning, nine innings, nine players on a side, a hard ball, mitts and a bat—although the Louisville Slugger of Finland is called a "Jarvinen Kanuuna."

Difference—Factual support

That's where the similarities end. The *pesapallo* pitcher, for instance, stands next to the plate and tosses the ball up in the air, varying his delivery not with curves or sliders but by the height the ball goes.

6

Abner Doubleday: a United States army officer who is noted as the traditional inventor of baseball

LESS-ADVANCED STUDENTS

If students are having trouble organizing their essays, you may want to offer them an alternative graphic organizer. The following example is one possibility:

Title:	Intro. Para.
	Thesis
Topic Sent.: (Feature 1) 1. Subject 1 2. Subject 2	Topic Sent.: (Feature 2) 1. Subject 1 2. Subject 2
Topic Sent.: (Feature 3) 1. Subject 1 2. Subject 2	Concl. Para.

Difference—Factual support

Instead of waiting in a dugout, teammates of the batter stand around what is roughly equivalent to the batter's box and scream out advice whether to swing or not at a pitch. The batter can hit as many as three fair balls before he has to run. And the route around the basepaths sort of zigzags first to the left, then the right, then the left again.

Difference—Factual support/ Statistics

Confused? Try this. A three-base hit is a *kunnari,* or home run. The batter scores, even though he is allowed to stay on third and score again if somebody knocks him in. But getting a *kunnari* is not easy because a ball that's knocked out of the park—about 300 feet from home to the farthest point of the *pesapallo* outfield—is considered a *laiton* (foul).

Difference

When an outfielder catches a fly ball, that doesn't necessarily mean the batter is out. He might just be *haava* (wounded), a sort of purgatory state for sluggers that requires them to forfeit the turn at bat but doesn't exactly count toward ending the inning. And when someone does make an out, he's not just out, he's *pallo* (killed). This is no game for wimps, that's for sure.

CONCLUSION Difference—Quotation

There's one other important difference. At the end of the game, American ballplayers hit the showers. "When we're done," said Thunder Bay shortstop Pavli Kaki, "we go off to the sauna."

The Miami Herald

EXERCISE 1 ▶ **Analyzing the Organization of a Comparison/Contrast Article**

Now it's your turn to analyze the professional's work. Meet with two or three classmates to answer the following questions about the *pesapallo* article.

1. Why do you think the writer doesn't give equal space to discussing the rules and history of baseball?
2. Besides discussing *pesapallo* rules, what background information does the article provide?
3. At the midpoint of the article (paragraph 13), the writer summarizes several similarities between baseball and *pesapallo*. Then he goes on to discuss another five features that apply only to *pesapallo*. Why is he able to do this without explaining each contrasting feature in baseball? [Hint: What does the audience know?]

A Basic Framework for a Comparison/Contrast Essay

The professional model on *pesapallo* does not use a simple block or point-by-point method of organization—it doesn't give the two subjects equal time. (It's also written by a professional who earns his living by writing.) But using a simple block or point-by-point method may help you write and organize your essay more effectively. The following writer's model illustrates the block method of organization. Notice that the writer discusses all of the features (equipment, training, and dangers) for snorkeling, and then deals with all the same features for scuba diving.

A WRITER'S MODEL

Snorkeling and Scuba Diving

INTRODUCTION   If you're out on the water and see a red and white flag on a boat or pole, beware of creatures beneath the sea. The flag signals that human beings are underwater. They may be snorkeling or scuba diving. Both sports let people glimpse the amazing underwater plants and animals, but snorkeling and scuba diving are worlds apart.

Attention grabber

Thesis statement

CRITICAL THINKING
Analysis

Each of the example essays in this chapter employs comparison/contrast. Discuss the transitions used between the paragraphs in these essays to help students synthesize all the examples. Here are some questions to ask the students:

1. What does the author do to make the paragraph transitions?
2. Does the author repeat an idea or does he or she perhaps repeat a word or a phrase?
3. Does the author make a reference to the thesis statement to maintain continuity?

INTEGRATING THE LANGUAGE ARTS

Technology Link. If students have access to computers, you might have them build bibliography or reference files for any research they do on their topics. Suggest that students use the hanging-indent (block indent) format for each entry and that they then add entries periodically. Finally, students should sort the files to obtain alphabetically arranged bibliographies.

272

BODY
Subject 1: Snorkeling

Snorkeling is easy. It doesn't take any special training and requires minimum equipment. You need a mask to keep the water out of your eyes and nose, and a snorkel, a short breathing tube that fits in your mouth and has an opening at the surface. The snorkel lets you keep your head underwater and breathe air at the same time. Many snorkelers use fins, but they're optional. Snorkelers can dive below the surface of the water for as long as they can hold their breath--probably about ten feet. The only real danger that snorkelers face is being run over by a boat; that's the point of the diving flag.

Feature 1: Training

Feature 2: Equipment

Feature 3: Time underwater

Feature 4: Dangers

Subject 2: Scuba diving

Scuba diving is a much more elaborate sport with far greater rewards. If snorkelers get a peek at underwater life, scuba divers get a long and leisurely look. You must take classes (three to five weeks' worth in a classroom, pool, and natural body of water) to become a certified diver. Besides the mask and fins that snorkelers wear, scuba divers also need a tank of air, a weight belt, a regulator, a buoyancy compensator, and a watch. The air that you carry lets you stay under for forty-five minutes or an hour at a depth of thirty feet. Scuba divers also need one other

Feature 1: Training

Feature 2: Equipment

Feature 3: Time underwater

essential thing: a buddy. Scuba diving can be dangerous; divers are told not to dive alone. The dangers that scuba divers face include overexpansion of the lungs, air embolism to the brain, the bends, running out of air, disorientation, and nitrogen narcosis. You should be in good physical condition. But it's a safe sport if you know what you're doing. According to scuba divers, what you experience near a reef is like nothing else.

Feature 4: Dangers

CONCLUSION   So if you're willing to spend more money (you need access to a boat) and get special training, scuba diving lets you get a better, close-up, longer look at underwater life. But snorkeling is a poor man's substitute, and still gives you a breathtaking view of life in another medium. It's like visiting another planet.

Evaluation

Final comment

A DIFFERENT APPROACH

Ask students to form two panels of two students each. One panel will tell about a sport or product, and another will tell about a sport or product to which the first will be compared. An example is football and soccer or classical music and country and western music. Be sure that the pairs maintain an informative dialogue, rather than argue about which is best. A panel monitor might set up a point-by-point method of delivering the information. First one side and then the other will cite a parallel fact. Or a block method could be used, in which the two students on one side could list all their facts first, followed by the other side.

INTEGRATING THE LANGUAGE ARTS

Usage Link. Using transitions correctly is often very difficult for students. Be sure to refer to the **Reference Note** on p. 266 if students need more help with transitions. Ask each student to create a list of transitions that can be referred to in the writing process. Words students might include are *alike, also, both, similarly, in contrast, however,* and *yet.*

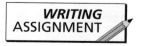 PART 5:
Writing a First Draft

Now is the time to use the information you developed in previous parts of your writing assignment to write a rough draft of your paper. Try to state your ideas as clearly as possible. Remember to give evidence in the form of facts, examples, and quotations to support each feature.

OBJECTIVES

- To analyze a writer's revisions of a comparison/contrast informative essay
- To revise a comparison/contrast informative essay

TEACHING THE LESSON

You may want to put the history of the word *revise* on the chalkboard and ask students how its original meaning ties in with its meaning within the writing process. [*re*, "again" + *vis*, "look"]

Have a volunteer read the six evaluation questions and discuss each one with the class. To provide practice, read through

QUOTATION FOR THE DAY

"Boredom, after all, is a form of criticism." (William Phillips, 1933–   , American writer and editor)

As students begin evaluating and revising their first drafts, share the quotation with the class. Encourage students to revise any sentences that might bore or confuse their readers.

MEETING
INDIVIDUAL
NEEDS

LEP/ESL

General Strategies. Many students will need individual attention at this stage of the writing process. If feasible, meet with each of them privately and have them read their essays aloud. Your immediate feedback will bolster their confidence and give them the information necessary to make effective revisions. Try to refrain from correction, but do call their attention to problem areas.

SELECTION AMENDMENT
Description of change: excerpted
Rationale: to focus on the concept of evaluation and revision presented in this chapter

---

 Evaluating and Revising

Cast a cold eye over your first draft as you look for ways to improve it. Use the following guidelines for both self-evaluation and peer evaluation (see page 48). First, ask yourself the questions in the left-hand column of the chart on the next page. If you identify a weakness, use the revision technique suggested in the right-hand column.

"In baseball you only get three strikes and you're out. In rewriting, you get almost as many swings as you want and you know, sooner or later, you'll hit the ball."

Neil Simon

Exercise 2 with the class and have volunteers answer questions 1–4. To provide independent practice, ask students to complete **Writing Assignment: Part 6.**

ASSESSMENT

You can have your students write their revisions on their first drafts in a different color ink than they used originally. You can also use the questions in the **Evaluating and Revising Comparison/Contrast Essays** chart to guide your assessment of students' revisions.

EVALUATING AND REVISING COMPARISON/CONTRAST ESSAYS

EVALUATION GUIDE	REVISION TECHNIQUE
1 Do the first one or two sentences grab the audience's attention?	**Add** an interesting statement or example, or **replace** existing sentences with one.
2 Are the subjects similar enough to compare and different enough to be interesting?	**Cut** subjects that aren't similar or different enough, and **replace** with new subjects.
3 Does the thesis statement clearly identify the subjects and main idea of the essay?	**Add** a sentence (or **replace** an existing one) that clearly identifies the subjects and main idea of the essay.
4 Is the essay body organized by the block method or the point-by-point method?	**Reorder** the organization by moving sentences to create the block method or the point-by-point method.
5 Are each of the features of the two subjects handled in the same order?	**Reorder** the arrangement of sentences so the features of the two subjects are handled in the same order.
6 Is the conclusion effective?	**Cut** the ineffective sentences, and **add** effective statements that summarize or evaluate.

COOPERATIVE LEARNING

Put students in groups of three and assign each student a specific evaluation task. One student (perhaps a less-advanced student) could evaluate all the opening sentences for effectiveness. Another student (perhaps an advanced student) could evaluate to see if the thesis statement is supported. A third student could evaluate transitions, while a fourth could examine the concluding paragraph.

INTEGRATING THE LANGUAGE ARTS

Vocabulary Link. Explain to students that other kinds of comparisons often used by writers are the simile and the metaphor. These figures of speech compare unfamiliar aspects of a subject with known and familiar things.

Have students find examples of at least two similes and two metaphors in poems from their literature textbooks.

Have students contribute to a quick review of the elements of the informative essay.

Besides evaluating and revising the content of their essays, students might also evaluate and revise the stylistic aspects of their papers. You could have students employ the following revision strategies to guide them as they assess their writing:

![icon] **COOPERATIVE LEARNING**

Have students meet in groups of three or four to complete peer evaluations. Use the following instructions to guide students as they evaluate:

1. Underline or highlight what you think is the thesis statement.
2. Share your essay with the group by passing it to each member to read.
3. Have the group suggest needed changes on the essay in pencil.
4. Each student should indicate one strong sentence or word choice the author has made.
5. Have students initial the top of the first page of the essay to indicate that they have read it.

| EXERCISE 2 ▶ | **Analyzing a Writer's Revisions** |

Here's a revision of the first two paragraphs of the writer's model on pages 271–272. See if you can figure out why these changes are improvements. Then answer the questions that follow.

If you're out on the water and see a red and white flag on a boat or pole, beware of creatures beneath the sea. The flag signals that human beings are underwater. They may be snorkeling or scuba diving. Both sports let people glimpse the amazing underwater plants and animals. ⟨↪ but snorkeling and scuba diving are worlds apart.⟩   **add**

Snorkeling is easy, ~~but scuba diving is harder.~~ It doesn't take any special training and requires minimum equipment. The snorkel lets you keep your head underwater and breathe air at the same time.   **cut**

You need a mask to keep the water out of your eyes and nose, and a snorkel, a short breathing tube that fits in your mouth and has an opening at the surface. Many   **reorder**

snorkelers
~~people use fins.~~ ⟨↪ but they're optional.⟩ Snorkelers can dive below   **replace/add**
the surface of the water for as long as they can hold their breath--probably about ten feet. The only real danger that snorkelers face is being run over by a boat; that's the point of the diving flag.

1. Bracket the first words of all sentences to check for sentence variety.
2. Highlight all verbs to check for active voice and vivid verbs. (not in quotations)
3. Circle all *who, which,* and *that* constructions to check for possible subordinations. ■

1. Why did the writer add the clause *but snorkeling and scuba diving are worlds apart* to the end of the first paragraph? [Hint: What is the thesis statement? Does the paper compare or contrast the two sports?]
2. In the first sentence of the second paragraph, why did the writer cut the clause *but scuba diving is harder*? [Hint: Is this paper developed by the block method or the point-by-point method?]
3. Why did the writer move the fourth sentence of the second paragraph?
4. In the fifth sentence of the second paragraph, why did the writer replace the word *people* with *snorkelers* and add the clause *but they're optional*?

ANSWERS
Exercise 2

1. The words are added to make the thesis reflect the fact that the essay both compares and contrasts the subjects.
2. Because the writer uses the block method, scuba diving shouldn't be discussed until later in the essay.
3. The fourth sentence is a specific detail that is introduced by the second sentence.
4. These changes make the sentence more specific and more factual.

WRITING ASSIGNMENT

PART 6:
Evaluating and Revising Your Comparison/Contrast Paper

It's hard to evaluate objectively the way your own hair looks before you leave for school in the morning. It's even harder to cast a cold, objective eye on your own writing. Use the questions from the chart on page 275 to evaluate your paper. Then exchange papers with a partner, and use the questions to evaluate each other's papers. Use your partner's comments and your own evaluations to revise your essay. Remember to be helpful in giving specific suggestions to your partner for improvements.

ARLO AND JANIS reprinted by permission of NEA, Inc.

PROOFREADING AND PUBLISHING

OBJECTIVES

- To proofread a comparison/contrast essay
- To publish a comparison/contrast essay

MOTIVATION

Ask students why people dress differently for different occasions. Elicit the idea that there are times when a person's appearance is very important in making a good impression. Tell students that proofreading helps writers find errors that would detract from the ideas they want to publish.

Teacher's ResourceBank™

RESOURCES

PROOFREADING AND PUBLISHING
- Writing a Comparison/Contrast Essay

QUOTATION FOR THE DAY

"Sloppily prepared pieces, peppered with mechanical glitches that could easily have been caught and corrected by the writer, are rarely going to sell—and the few that do are bound to be heavily edited." (David Peterson, American author and editor)

Copy this quotation on the chalkboard and ask students to discuss why they think writing with good content but with poor grammatical form might not sell.

LEP/ESL

General Strategies. ESL students will most certainly have problems with prepositions. Even when ESL students go to a dictionary, the multiple definitions for such words tend to be confusing. Therefore, you may want to scan students' essays to see that prepositions are used correctly. You may need to offer extra practice in this area.

278

Proofreading and Publishing

Proofreading. Put the finishing touches on your paper by checking the revised draft for mistakes in spelling, capitalization, punctuation, and usage. (See page 56 for Guidelines for Proofreading.) Try peer proofreading, too. Your classmates may be able to spot mistakes you've missed.

Publishing. Then try these ideas for publishing your finished paper.

- Your comparison/contrast paper may be of interest to the teacher and students in another course in your school. For example, a physical education teacher might distribute your comparisons of two sports. A history teacher might share your paper on two American presidents.
- Post your opinions. You can post papers that compare/contrast subjects of interest (books, movies, TV shows, restaurants, cars) on a bulletin board where everyone in the class can read them.

You may want to focus on two or three specific problems in the proofreading stage. For example, you may find students are having trouble with capitalization or pronoun usage. Remind students that because it is often difficult to see errors in one's own writing, they should each have at least one other person read their essays.

Tell students to use the **Guidelines for Proofreading** to guide them as they look for problems in their papers.

Use a sample paragraph you have created to model proofreading. Then have students complete **Writing Assignment: Part 7**.

☞

GRAMMAR HINT

Using the Degrees of Comparison

What's wrong with these statements?
a. *Pesapallo* is most exciting than baseball.
b. Of all the kinds of swimming, scuba diving is the better.

When you use adjectives and adverbs in a comparison/contrast paper, you need to be aware of the degrees of comparison. Most adjectives and adverbs have three degrees of comparison:

POSITIVE	COMPARATIVE	SUPERLATIVE
cold	colder	coldest
bad	worse	worst
ridiculous	more ridiculous	most ridiculous

1. When comparing two items, use the comparative degree.

   Pesapallo is **more exciting** than baseball.

2. When comparing three or more items, use the superlative degree.

   Many people consider *pesapallo,* soccer, and lacrosse the **most exciting** sports of all.

☞ REFERENCE NOTE: For more help with degrees of comparison, see pages 719–722.

GRAMMAR HINT

Instead of grading an extended exercise on degrees of comparison, check to see if students understand degrees of comparison by having each student follow these directions:

1. Look through the essay to find five adjectives or adverbs. At least one of each should be irregular. (Refer to **Chapter 22** for a quick explanation of irregular comparisons.)
2. Prepare three columns: "Positive," "Comparative," and "Superlative." Write the words in columns to compare them.
3. Share the lists of words with the class and show how each word was used within the sentence.

A DIFFERENT APPROACH

Students can make suggestions for ways to share their essays. One way is to display the essays in the school hallway, perhaps with hand-drawn illustrations, magazine photos, cartoons, or computer-generated graphics or pictures.

PART 7:
Proofreading and Publishing Your Essay

It's time to be picky. Proofread your essay carefully to correct all errors. Write your final version, and proofread it. Then decide how you will publish your essay or share it with others.

CLOSURE

For closure, have a volunteer give a quick definition of proofreading.

EXTENSION

The model essay can be used as the springboard for a review of all the essays presented in the chapter. Discuss the audience and purpose of the **"Football and Cyberball"** essay, the essay's structure, and where it could be published. Next, ask students about the audience, purpose, and structure of the other essays: **"Time out! Is baseball**

A STUDENT MODEL

Evaluation

1. To grab the audience's attention, Chris uses sensory details—"smell of hot popcorn and hot dogs"—in his description of a football game.
2. Cyberball and football are similar enough to compare but different enough to be interesting.
3. The thesis statement (the last sentence of the introduction) clearly identifies the topics and purposes of the essay.
4. Chris uses a modified block method to organize his essay.
5. He handles each of the features of cyberball and football in the same order.

280

A STUDENT MODEL

Things to compare and contrast are all around you, as Chris Chavis shows in the following essay. Chris, a student at Mid Central High School in Norman, Oklahoma, effectively compares two all-American pastimes—playing football and playing a video game. As you read, see if you agree with his ideas.

Football and Cyberball
by Chris Chavis

The smell of hot popcorn and hot dogs drifts through the stadium. On the field, the home team scores a touchdown and the crowd ignites into a wild cheer. This is another typical afternoon watching one of America's favorite pastimes, but now, thanks to modern technology, you can play football in the comfort of your own home, or anywhere else for that matter. Today, instead of sitting in the hot sun watching football, you can actually participate in electronic Cyberball, one of the best arcade football games ever made. Football and Cyberball have many similarities, but, as usual, the shift from old technology to new creates many changes--some better and some worse.

Cyberball is easier to play than football. Cyberball requires the machine, the program, and, if you're playing at the arcade, several quarters. Cyberball also requires a significant amount of physical coordination. Manual dexterity is not necessarily a must, but if you expect to do well, you'll have to possess some hand-eye coordination.

Football requires a considerable amount of equipment. In order to play, you have to have enough people to form two teams, protective gear for each team--padding and helmets,

Finnished?" and **"Snorkeling and Scuba Diving."** Discuss with students the importance of having a specific audience, purpose, and structure in mind when writing. ■

and a football. Generally, football is played in a field or a vacant lot outdoors somewhere. And, in order for your team to be successful, you need to have several players with extraordinary physical skill.

Cyberball develops several important, fundamental skills. By having to control your futuristic, robotic players by manipulating a joystick, you develop extraordinary hand-eye coordination. The computer's quick moves when it is on offense also demand that you develop even faster reflexes in order to dominate. You must learn problem-solving skills and develop your intellect.

Football also develops many important, though more physical, skills. Football builds many muscles and can greatly enhance your physical fitness. You can also develop stamina and quicker reflexes by running and dodging the opposing team. However, one of the greatest skills developed from football is strong leadership, which many football players keep the rest of their lives.

Football and Cyberball have several obvious similarities, and, in fact, Cyberball is strongly based on football. They are different in many ways, however. I believe that Cyberball has many advantages over football and is what I prefer to play.

 INTEGRATING THE LANGUAGE ARTS

Vocabulary Link. A discussion of strong verbs works well in exploring the opening sentences of the model essay. The author uses such vivid verbs as *drifts, scores,* and *ignites.* These verbs entice the reader to continue. Take a few minutes to discuss other strong verbs such as *demand, control,* and *whisper.* Talk about why *whisper* is a strong verb even though the meaning of the word is "to speak quietly." Next, let students brainstorm strong verbs they like to use in their own vocabulary. Discuss the appropriateness or inappropriateness of slang words.

TEACHING THE LESSON

Read the explanation and example of extended definition in class and answer any questions students have. After discussing the answers to questions 1 and 2 on p. 283, divide the class into cooperative-learning groups of three or four.

Allow groups to brainstorm for a list of possible topics. Then students can use this

Teacher's ResourceBank™
RESOURCES

WRITING WORKSHOP
All the resources of this chapter may be used in this segment.

QUOTATION FOR THE DAY

"From time to time I find myself terribly limited by the dictionary." (Marcel Ayme, 1902–1967, French author)

Allow students in small groups to discuss the quotation and to write statements about what the quotation means. Ask a representative from each group to share the results with the class. Then tell students that extended definitions give more information than dictionary definitions, which present only the category and distinguishing characteristics of a word.

282

WRITING WORKSHOP

An Extended Definition

Comparison/contrast is one way to use the strategy of *classification*. Definition is another. When you define, you reverse the process you use to compare and contrast. To compare and contrast, you start with a large group or class (artists or sports) and pull out individual members to examine. To **define,** you group individual things together in a common group or class. A **dictionary definition** is a brief explanation of a word's meaning. When the word being defined is a noun (an object, place, person, or idea), the definition does two things:

- names the general class or category to which the word belongs
- gives the characteristics that distinguish the word from all other words in its general class

In the following dictionary definition, the general class is underlined. The rest of the definition tells how the word differs from other members of its class.

> *Pesapallo* is a <u>sport</u> resembling baseball, generally played in Finland, having bases run in an order backward to U.S. baseball.

You can also write an extended definition that is anywhere from one paragraph to several pages long. Here are some ways to extend a definition.

- Give an example.
- Tell how it works.
- Describe its properties.
- Tell other facts about it.
- Use a quotation from an authority.

The following model gives an extended definition of an Athabascan Indian concept. As you read, think how the writer extends the definition.

prewriting to create their first drafts independently. Suggest to students that they follow the instructions in the textbook for each stage of the process.

ASSESSMENT

Ask students to volunteer to read their definitions. Pay attention to not only the definitions, but also to the sentence transitions that create coherence. Call on all students so that assessment can be total.

Instead of "goodbye," Athabascans say "Tlaa" when they leave each other. Tlaa means something like "See you" or "Until we meet again." An Athabascan would be puzzled by our idea of "goodbye." To say goodbye is so final. An Athabascan would say that people cannot really leave each other because they are always in each other's mind and heart. People cannot really be away from each other when each one is a part of the other. If the daughter goes away to school, the mother says "Tlaa." The mother thinks the daughter is coming back home. And, if she doesn't come home, then they will see each other at another place. The Athabascan language has no word for goodbye.

1. What is the word being defined? What is its simple, dictionary definition?
2. What examples or concepts does the author use to extend the definition?

MEETING INDIVIDUAL NEEDS

LEP/ESL

General Strategies. If there are several language groups represented in your classroom, use the definition model as a springboard to discuss how other languages and cultures say "goodbye." Be aware of vocabulary words in this segment (such as *properties, authority, concept,* and *philosophy*) with which your ESL students might be unfamiliar.

ANSWERS
Writing Workshop Questions

1. *Tlaa* is being defined. Its simple definition is "see you" or "until we meet again."

2. The author talks about how people can't really leave each other and gives an example of how this can be true.

Writing an Extended Definition

 Prewriting. Choose as your subject an object or idea that interests you. Make sure that your subject is complex enough so that there's more to say about it than one sentence.

EXAMPLES School: a slang term, summer vacation, a hard class

Sports: an athlete, a coach, a free agent

Society: a shopping mall, a great car, a strict parent

Philosophy: duty, freedom, wisdom

Think of examples, descriptive details, or facts, or find appropriate quotations to extend the definition. To get some ideas, consult several dictionaries or encyclopedias. Who is your audience? Make sure you include any necessary background information.

Writing, Evaluating, and Revising. To write a one- or two-paragraph definition, begin with a one-sentence definition similar to what a dictionary might give. (Don't copy a dictionary's definition. Reword it so that it is distinctly your own.) Then extend your definition by adding an example, descriptive details, facts, or quotations. Use peer editing for suggestions on improving your definition. Consider these questions: Does the paragraph begin with a precisely worded one-sentence definition? Does the extended definition include an attention-getting example, descriptive details, or a quotation from an author?

 Proofreading and Publishing. Proofread your definition to be sure it's free of careless errors before you give it to someone else to read. You could read your definition to a small group of classmates or to the whole class (withhold the word you are defining), and see if they can guess the subject.

MAKING CONNECTIONS

TEST TAKING

OBJECTIVE

- To write a response to an essay test question

MAKING CONNECTIONS

TEST TAKING

Writing for an Essay Test Question

In school, especially in civics and history classes, you'll often be faced with test questions that require comparison/contrast answers. You need to look carefully at each comparison/contrast question to decide whether to balance comparison and contrast, to emphasize comparison, or to emphasize contrast.

Here's some information on two women rulers you might study in a world history class. If your teacher gave you a test with an essay question asking you to compare and/or contrast them, what would you do? Do the two monarchs have more similarities or more differences? Would you base your paragraph on comparison or contrast? Write a paragraph about the two women in which you either emphasize their similarities or their differences.

WOMEN MONARCHS		
	ELIZABETH I	CATHERINE II
Position	absolute monarch	absolute monarch
Power	absolute	absolute
Title	Queen of England and Ireland	Empress of Russia
Birth-Death	1533–1603	1729–1796
Time of reign	1558–1603	1762–1796
Marital status	single	widow
Nickname	Good Queen Bess	Catherine the Great

(continued)

TEST TAKING

Teaching Strategies

Give students the following reminders:

1. Take time to plan and organize your essay, perhaps by using an outline or mapping technique.
2. Plan a thesis statement that explains what you intend to write.
3. Watch the time as an essay exam is taken. You should learn to finish the essay within the allotted time.

GUIDELINES

Be sure students' paragraphs each include a statement that gives the author's purpose—comparison or contrast—and the topics. Also, check for specific details for each feature given for the two topics.

WOMEN MONARCHS (continued)		
	ELIZABETH I	CATHERINE II
Occurrences during reign	encouraged trade and commerce court as artistic center influenced by Renaissance encouraged rise of serious drama (Shakespeare) commissioned portraits by famous painters established large naval force, defeated Spanish Armada planned governmental reforms established Church of England	encouraged trade and commerce court as artistic center influenced by Enlightenment patron for Russian dictionary of 285 words, 200 languages commissioned portraits by famous painters established large naval force planned reforms but peasants revolted so enslaved serfs granted freedom of worship

ELIZABETH I

CATHERINE II

COMPARISON ACROSS THE CURRICULUM

Literature

A *metaphor* is a figure of speech that makes a direct comparison between two basically unlike things without using the words *like* or *as*. The poet Anne Sexton, for example, creates a metaphor when she says "each spring will be a sword you'll sharpen. . . ." What is compared in the following poem about a fan? Can you find the metaphors?

COMPARISON ACROSS THE CURRICULUM

Teaching Strategies

Have students meet in groups to discuss metaphors and to read their poems to each other. Each group should choose one poem to share with the entire class. Add at least one metaphor from each student's poem to a metaphor bulletin board. Include on the board the name of the poet, the poem, and the student.

GUIDELINES

You may want to have each student write down the metaphors and an analysis of the two things compared.

The Eagle-Feather Fan
by N. Scott Momaday

The eagle is my power,
And my fan is an eagle.
1   It is strong and beautiful
In my hand. And it is real.
My fingers hold upon it
As if the beaded handle
2 Were the twist of bristlecone.
The bones of my hand are fine
And hollow; the fan bears them.
3 My hand veers in the thin air
Of the summits. All morning
4 It scuds on the cold currents;
All afternoon it circles
To the singing, to the drums.

Bring a poem (you may write your own) to class that has a metaphor comparing two unlike things. Read the poem aloud, and ask everyone to listen carefully to find the metaphor. Have them tell what two things are being compared and how they are alike.

If you write your own poem, think about comparing two things that are not generally considered alike. Remember that a poem is not always rhymed and that it can be about many subjects—baseball, concrete mixers, and even giraffes. (See pages 207–208 on writing poems.)

USING THE SELECTION
The Eagle-Feather Fan

1

This is a metaphor comparing the feathers and a hand. The feather fan gives the narrator power to fly with the eagle and to feel its strength.

2

bristlecone: the cone from the bristlecone pine tree, the needles of which grow in clusters of five

3

veers: changes direction

4

scuds: glides or skims along easily

INTEGRATING THE LANGUAGE ARTS

Vocabulary Link. Riddles, extremely popular in Anglo-Saxon England, often had kennings in them. A kenning is a two-word metaphor, such as "battle-flasher" for *sword*.

Discuss with the students riddles they know. Reinforce how words are used to describe something without saying the name of the object or concept itself.

Have students create their own riddles and tell each student to incorporate at least three kennings. Then ask students to read their riddles aloud to see if the class can guess the answers.

WRITING TO EXPLAIN

OBJECTIVES
- To identify and analyze cause-and-effect relationships
- To choose an appropriate topic for a cause-and-effect essay
- To gather facts and examples to support assertions of cause and effect
- To arrange causes and effects in logical order for prewriting
- To draft a cause-and-effect essay
- To evaluate and revise the structure and content of a cause-and-effect essay
- To proofread and publish a cause-and-effect essay

Motivation

You may want to initiate a class discussion on cause and effect by asking students for examples of cause and effect in their own lives. Has something happened to them recently that has had an effect on their lives? Or has something happened that has or will have an effect on their community? For example, a new factory might have been built (cause) that will create jobs but also will pollute the air and water (effects). Ask your class how the examples they mentioned are part of larger chains of causes and effects. What might have been the cause of the factory's being built? What might air and water pollution cause?

Introduction

The **Chapter Motivation** has explained how cause and effect works in the world. Now tell students that recognizing and using cause and effect is also an important part of the four aims of composition—expressive, literary, informative, and persuasive. In this chapter, students will learn how cause and effect work in an expository essay (informative), a process analysis essay (informative), and a folktale (literary).

Integration

Students will find an understanding of cause and effect useful to them throughout the language arts as well as across the curriculum. The segments concerning analysis of cause and effect will improve students' reading comprehension in all their classes. Learning how to use cause and effect in writing will help students not only in their language arts classes, but also in social science and science classes, where they are often required to write papers and answer essay questions that analyze cause and effect. Furthermore, the critical thinking segment will help students to detect fallacies of logic that they encounter every day outside the classroom.

The chart on the next page illustrates the strands of language arts as they are integrated into this chapter. For vocabulary study, glossary words are underlined in some writing models.

QUOTATIONS
All **Quotations for the Day** are chosen because of their relevance to instructional material presented in that segment of the chapter and for their usefulness in establishing student interest in writing.

Selection	Reading and Literature	Writing and Critical Thinking	Language and Syntax	Speaking, Listening, and Other Expression Skills
from **"Hard Luck Stories"** by Bob Elliott and Ray Goulding **290-292** **"Why I choose to veg out"** by Rebecca Moore **303-305** from *The Arapaho Way* by Althea Bass **317-318** **"Why No One Lends His Beauty"** by Harold Courlander with Ezekiel A. Eshugbayi **321-323**	Analyzing the author's purpose **292, 306** Responding personally to literature **292, 306, 318** Applying interpretive and creative thinking **292, 306, 323** Summarizing main ideas **306** Analyzing a cause-and-effect essay **306, 312** Identifying sequence of events **306, 318** Reading for details **318** Listing steps in a process **318** Discussing a folk tale **323** Finding a cause-and-effect folk tale or myth **323**	Analyzing cause-and-effect relationships **292, 306** Responding personally to literature **292, 306, 318** Brainstorming **296** Applying interpretive and creative thinking **296, 306, 323** Choosing a topic **296, 321** Gathering and organizing information for writing **299, 300, 321** Distinguishing between false cause and effect, oversimplification, and true cause and effect **301** Evaluating a cause-and-effect essay for content and structure **306, 312** Analyzing a cause-and-effect essay **306, 312** Writing a first draft of a cause-and-effect essay **309** Evaluating and revising a draft of a cause-and-effect essay **310** Analyzing a writer's revisions **312** Writing a process analysis essay using the writing process **318-319** Evaluating a process analysis essay **319** Analyzing a visual aid **320** Writing a cause-and-effect folk tale or myth **323**	Proofreading for errors in grammar, usage, and mechanics **314, 319**	Working with classmates to brainstorm topics for a cause-and-effect essay **296** Creating visuals to organize information **299** Discussing information shared in an oral presentation **300** Giving an oral presentation **300, 321** Working with classmates to identify fallacious reasoning **301** Working with classmates to analyze a cause-and-effect essay **306, 312** Working with classmates to analyze a writer's revisions **312** Sharing an essay with an audience in a panel presentation **314** Creating a visual to explain a process **321** Working with classmates to analyze, research, and write folk tales **323**

CHAPTER 8

SEGMENT PLANNING GUIDE

Whether you are planning for a quick review of a writing concept or preparing an extended lesson on composition, you can use the following Planning Guide to adapt the chapter material to the individual needs of your class.

SEGMENT	PAGES	CONTENT	RESOURCES
1 *Making Things Clear*	*289-292*		
Literary Model from **"Hard Luck Stories"**	290-292	Guided reading: a model of cause-and-effect writing	
Reader's Response/ Writer's Craft	292	Model evaluation: responding to literature and analyzing cause and effect	
2 *Strategies for Writing to Inform*	*293-294*		
3 *Prewriting*	*295-301*		Listing Causes and Effects
Choosing a Topic	295	Guidelines: selecting suitable topics for a cause-and-effect essay	
Thinking About Purpose and Audience	295-296	Guidelines: analyzing and selecting appropriate purpose and audience	
Exercise 1	296	Cooperative learning: exploring possible topics	
Writing Assignment: Part 1	296	Applied practice: choosing a topic	
Gathering and Organizing Information	297-299	Guidelines: analyzing and arranging information	
Writing Assignment: Part 2	299	Applied practice: gathering information	
Writing Assignment: Part 3	300	Applied practice: arranging information	
Exercise 2	300	Cooperative learning: making a presentation	
Critical Thinking: Understanding Causal Relationships	300-301	Guidelines: identifying fallacies	
Critical Thinking Exercise	301	Cooperative learning: identifying fallacies	
4 *Writing*	*302-309*		Writing a Cause-and-Effect Essay
Writing Your First Draft	302	Guidelines: writing the introduction, the body, and the conclusion	
Literary Model **"Why I choose to veg out"**	303-305	Guided reading: examining an essay for cause and effect	
Exercise 3	306	Cooperative learning: analyzing a cause-and-effect essay	
A Framework for a Cause-and-Effect Essay	306	Introduction: structuring an essay	
A Writer's Model	307-308	Guided reading: analyzing cause-and-effect in an essay	

All the resources listed in this chapter are located in the Teacher's ResourceBank™.

SEGMENT	PAGES	CONTENT	RESOURCES
Chart: Framework for a Cause-and-Effect Essay	308	Guidelines: structuring a cause-and-effect essay	
Writing Assignment: Part 4	309	Applied practice: writing a first draft	Writing a Cause-and-Effect Essay
5 *Evaluating and Revising*	*310-312*		
Evaluating and Revising	310	Introduction: using criteria to evaluate and revise	
Chart: Evaluating and Revising Cause-and-Effect Essays	311	Guidelines: applying evaluation and revision techniques	
Exercise 4	312	Cooperative learning: analyzing a writer's revisions	
Writing Assignment: Part 5	312	Applied practice: evaluating and revising	
6 *Proofreading and Publishing*	*313-315*		Writing a Cause-and-Effect Essay
Usage Hint	313	Writing suggestion: using clear pronoun antecedents	
Publishing	313-314	Publishing ideas: reaching an intended audience	
Writing Assignment: Part 6	314	Applied practice: proofreading and publishing	
A Student Model	314-315	Sample: examining cause and effect in a student essay	
7 *Writing Workshop*	*316-319*		All the resources for this chapter may be used in this segment.
Explaining a Process	316	Guidelines: writing to explain a process	
Literary Model/Questions from *The Arapaho Way*	317-318	Examining techniques: analyzing a sample essay	
Writing a Process Analysis Essay	318-319	Applied practice: applying skills to the writing process	
8 *Making Connections*	*320-323*		
Directions and Process Explanations: Visuals	320-321	Guidelines: using visuals Applied practice: using visuals in a presentation	
Cause and Effect in Literature: Folk Tales	321	Introduction: understanding cause and effect in folk tales	
Literary Model/Questions **"Why No One Lends His Beauty"**	321-323	Cooperative learning: answering questions about a folk tale	

WHOLE-CHAPTER RESOURCES
A Writing Process Log, A Writing Prompt, Holistically Graded Models, Assessment Portfolio Materials

MAKING THINGS CLEAR

OBJECTIVES

- To write personal responses to literature
- To analyze cause-and-effect relationships within a literary model

TEACHING THE LESSON

To motivate students for this lesson, tell them that they are about to hear how cause and effect works in a skit by the comedy duo of Bob and Ray. Ask students who their favorite comedy teams are and whether these teams use cause and effect in their acts.

You may want to make sure your students have understood the introductory

VISUAL CONNECTIONS
Bullet through Balloons

About the Artist. Dr. Harold Edgerton, an Institute Professor at M.I.T., invented the stroboscopic flash in the early 1930s. His invention was originally intended for use in testing high-speed motors, but the light is useful for many other scientific observations. It also revolutionized photography by making possible not only stop-motion photographs but also candid snapshots.

Dr. Edgerton has used the techniques he invented to produce many educational photographs. These pictures blend science and art, because although Edgerton is mainly interested in showing the unseen aspects of events objectively, many viewers are also impressed by the beauty of these images.

8 WRITING TO EXPLAIN

paragraphs, especially the second paragraph. If they are having trouble, go through each cause-and-effect example with them slowly and explain how each involves cause and effect.

Then have three students read aloud the roles of Bob, Ray, and Boatwright in *Hard Luck Stories*. Before students begin to read, alert your class to listen for cause and effect.

You could also point out to your students that because this is comedy, events are exaggerated for comic effect.

Making Things Clear

Remember exasperating your parents with *Why? Why? Why?* (Or being exasperated yourself by a young friend.) Actually, while adults can get weary of explaining, they really welcome a child's curiosity. They know that the world is a complex place, that wanting explanations is a way to learn, that **making things clear** is something we must do all our lives.

Writing and You. And it's true. You asked your mother what the bitter-tasting medicine would do. Now you look to a scientist for the effects of ocean pollution, to a reporter for the reasons behind new graduation requirements, to a biographer for the causes of your sports hero's triumph at the Olympics. What explanations would you like to explore—and make clear to others?

As You Read. In the following dialogue, comedians Bob and Ray explore causes of a man's hard luck. Yes, the explanation is a bit odd, but does it make sense? That's the test.

Bullet through Balloons, Dr. Harold E. Edgerton (1959). Photograph. © The Harold E. Edgerton 1992 Trust. Courtesy of Palm Press, Inc., Concord, MA.

MEETING INDIVIDUAL NEEDS

LEP/ESL

General Strategies. Students might be able to grasp the concept of cause and effect more readily through visual representation. On the chalkboard, write the following headings and examples; then ask students to give other examples that fit.

Cause	Situation	Effect
Poor eyesight	Wearing glasses	Improved vision

GUIDED PRACTICE

Guide your class through the **Reader's Response** questions. As students recount scenes from situation comedies, help them identify causes and effects. Point out that comedy relies on the fact that the effects of something are not anticipated. Use the annotations to model analysis.

INDEPENDENT PRACTICE

Let your students answer the two **Writer's Craft** questions as either homework or an in-class assignment. You may want to specify that students respond to these questions in two to four sentences to ensure that their answers are complete but not rambling.

290

USING THE SELECTION
Hard Luck Stories

1

Cause-and-effect relationships are ironic when the effects or results are the opposite of what might be expected. Can you locate any examples of this type of irony in Ray's speech? [It is ironic that people enjoy listening to tragic stories, and it is ironic that Ray wants to "start the fun" with a "sad specimen."]

2

Look for an ironic twist in connection with the meaning of Mr. Boatwright's name. A boatwright is someone who constructs and repairs boats.

FROM

BY **BOB** ELLIOT AND **RAY** GOULDING

RAY: Again today our scouts have been searching the railroad
1 and bus stations for victims of misfortune. We've found that you listeners enjoy hearing these pathetic people tell their tragic stories. And of course, we all get a warm feeling when our generous Bob and Ray organization steps forward with its lovely gifts to solve each and every problem. So Bob—let's start the fun with that sad specimen there beside you.

2 **BOB:** Sure thing, Ray. This is Mr. Morton Boatwright of Kansas City, Missouri. And according to your card, Mr. Boatwright—you became stranded in New York while you were attempting to begin a voyage to a <u>virtually</u> unexplored area of central Africa. I'm sure there must be quite a story that goes with that.

ASSESSMENT

Your evaluation of students' answers to both the **Reader's Response** and the **Writer's Craft** questions should help you assess your students' comprehension at this point.

RETEACHING

If students are having difficulty understanding cause and effect, try diagramming the cause-and-effect relationships in the model on the chalkboard. A diagram of the answer to **Writer's Craft** question number four might look like this:

☛

291

3 **BOATWRIGHT:** Well, no—at least not originally. I was just going to Africa because you can't buy a giraffe in Kansas City.

4 But then, the <u>tramp steamer</u> I was planning to take from New York to the Ivory Coast left without me. And I've run out of money waiting around here for some other form of transportation. So I guess it has gotten to be quite an interesting story by now.

BOB: Yes. And I imagine it might become even more fascinating if we knew why you need a giraffe so badly.

5 **BOATWRIGHT:** Well, that's easy enough to explain. You see, I don't live right in Kansas City. I live in a suburb about twenty miles out of town. It's like most of your upper-middle-class suburbs where the neighbors all try to keep up with each other. One of them gets a new car—and then the rest of us have

6 to. Next, one gets a boat—and then everybody else does. So I had to think of something that would really make the rest of them look shabby.

BOB: Like buying a giraffe, you mean.

BOATWRIGHT: That's right. It seemed like the ideal way to flaunt my wealth. A giraffe owner doesn't even have to mention

7 that he's got a new giraffe. You just put him in the front yard and act casual about it, while the neighbors turn green with envy.

3

Identify the cause and the effect in this sentence. [Cause: you can't buy a giraffe in Kansas City; effect: Mr. Boatwright decides to go to Africa.]

4

A tramp steamer is a ship that has no regular itinerary; instead, it acquires cargo, passengers, and destinations as it goes along.

5

It is ironic that the man sees his need for a giraffe as "easy enough to explain."

6

This phenomenon of trying to outdo one's neighbors is so prevalent that it has been given a name—"keeping up with the Joneses."

7

The image created of a giraffe grazing in a suburban front yard is absurd and very funny. Humor is created by combining two incongruous elements—a giraffe and a yard in the suburbs.

SELECTION AMENDMENT
Description of change: excerpted and sentence deleted
Rationale: to focus on the concept of cause and effect presented in this chapter

cause — wants giraffe

cause/effect — goes to N.Y., catches boat

cause/effect — becomes stranded

cause/effect — waits for steamer

effect — goes bankrupt

CLOSURE

Ask students to explain in a few sentences how something can be both a cause and an effect. Have them give an example from the model of a cause that is also an effect. ■

8

It is ironic that while Boatwright is trying to carry out a scheme to flaunt his wealth, he goes bankrupt.

9

Does Boatwright "truly merit our heartfelt sympathy"? [Answers may vary, but most students will say that Boatwright does not merit sympathy, because he acted so foolishly.]

ANSWERS

Reader's Response

1. Be sure students give reasons to support their opinions.

2. You may want students to label which are the causes and effects of the scenes they choose.

Writer's Craft

3. Mr. Boatwright's being stranded was caused by the boat leaving without him. The effect of being stranded is that he went bankrupt.

4. First he wanted a giraffe. This desire caused him to try to go to Africa to get one. He became stranded in New York when the boat to Africa left without him. His being stranded caused him to go bankrupt because he was waiting in New York for a tramp steamer.

BOB: But if you're only looking for a new way to flaunt your wealth—how do you happen to be appearing on our show as a hardship case?

8 BOATWRIGHT: My fried chicken <u>franchise</u> back home went bankrupt while I was hanging around here waiting for a tramp steamer to the Ivory Coast.

9 BOB: Well, then you truly merit our heartfelt sympathy, sir. But to help you get back on your feet, here's this lovely gift from our generous Bob and Ray organization. It's a gorgeous revolving lawn sprinkler complete with fifty yards of plastic garden hose.

BOATWRIGHT: Well, I can't flaunt this in front of the neighbors. They've already got sprinklers and garden hose.

READER'S RESPONSE

1. Comedians often turn the causes and effects of people's misfortunes, even their own, into comedy. Do you think this comedy routine is funny? Why?
2. Can you think of any funny scene from a TV situation comedy that focuses on some incident and its effects? Why do you think it's funny?

WRITER'S CRAFT

3. Even though this is a humorous dialogue, Mr. Boatwright does present an explanation—an explanation of causes and effects. In what way is his being stranded in New York City both a cause and an effect?
4. Mr. Boatwright's misfortune is brought about by a series of causes and effects. What is the chain of events—sequence of causes and effects—that led to his being stranded?

SEGMENT 2 *(pp. 293–294)*

STRATEGIES FOR WRITING TO INFORM

TEACHING THE MODES

Emphasize to students that they can use several strategies in compositions to achieve the informative aim. Discuss the examples given under each mode with students and be sure students understand that the two narration examples involve cause-and-effect explanations. Ask students to give further examples of how each mode might be used in developing an informative composition. ■

293

Strategies for Writing to Inform

The explanation of Mr. Boatwright's plight is a funny story, and in fact *narration* is the strategy writers use in a cause-and-effect explanation. Narration presents events that happen over time; it shows change. And of course an effect is a change that follows a cause in time. Writers can also use other strategies to explain. Here are some examples of how the four basic writing strategies can be used to explain.

▶ **Narration:** in an essay for history class, explaining the causes of American involvement in World War I; telling your younger brother about the effects of baking soda when it's used to put out electrical fires.

Description: in a field observation report for science class, explaining the environmental importance of wetlands by describing their physical composition, vegetation, and animal inhabitants; in a speech to your community council, describing the bike paths in your neighborhood to explain why more routes are needed.

Classification: in an article in the school newspaper, explaining and giving evidence of the differences between older coal-burning plants and those using new technology; in a student council report to the school board, explaining and giving evidence that a dance class should be classified as an athletic course.

Evaluation: evaluating a computer printer by explaining the different typefaces it has, its speed, and its controls; telling your friends a new album is mediocre by examining the lyrics, melodies, and musical performances.

COOPERATIVE LEARNING

Divide the class into groups of four, one person representing each of the four strategies. Instruct each group to work together to select topics that could be developed in compositions using the strategies. Then tell group members to work together to come up with at least five details that could be included in compositions on the chosen topics. Each group could share its work with the rest of the class. Finally, involve students in a discussion about the appropriateness and workability of the topics and details they have developed.

INTEGRATING THE LANGUAGE ARTS

Literature Link. Most people don't think of cause and effect when they think of poetry, but cause-and-effect relationships are everywhere, even in poetry. To demonstrate this concept, have your students read a poem such as Elizabeth Bishop's "The Fish." After students have read the poem, ask what they think causes the speaker of the poem to "let the fish go." You may want to let students discuss their opinions orally or to have them write informative paragraphs explaining their opinions. In either case, make sure students substantiate their opinions with specific evidence from the poem.

LOOKING AHEAD

In the main assignment in this chapter, you'll use the strategy of narration to develop a paper explaining causes and effects. Your purpose in writing will be to explain. As you work through the writing assignments, keep in mind that cause-and-effect writing

- focuses on a particular situation or event
- provides an answer to one or both of these questions: Why did it happen? What were the results?
- gives evidence that the explanation is sound

"Writing a story or a novel is one way of discovering <u>sequence</u> in experience, of stumbling upon cause and effect in the happenings of a writer's own life."

Eudora Welty

PREWRITING

OBJECTIVES

- To brainstorm and choose an appropriate topic for a cause-and-effect essay
- To create a graphic organizer for a cause-and-effect essay
- To arrange causes and effects in logical order
- To present information in a group
- To use feedback from classmates to improve a cause-and-effect essay

Writing a Cause-and-Effect Essay

Choosing a Topic

You've heard a great deal about the "greenhouse" effect. What, exactly, are its causes? What about high-definition television? How will it affect our entertainment habits over the next several years? These topics each lend themselves to a cause-and-effect analysis. If you can reasonably ask and answer one or both of these two questions about a topic, the topic is suitable for a cause-and-effect essay:

1. *Why did it happen?* [CAUSE]
2. *What is the result?* [EFFECT]

WRITING NOTE

Remember that you're writing a short essay, not a book. Choose a limited topic that you can discuss thoroughly in a brief essay.

TOO BROAD | Causes and effects of pollution
LIMITED | Effects of water pollution during the last two months at Lake Mohonk

Thinking About Purpose and Audience

You could explore causes and effects when you're writing for any of the basic purposes. But remember that the *purpose* of your cause-and-effect essay in this chapter will be to explain. You want to help an *audience* understand a situation by explaining its causes, effects, or both:

1. The causes of a situation or event (why the elephant is endangered, page 298)
2. The effects of a situation or event (the results of a high school's change to a double shift, page 307)
3. Both causes and effects of a situation or event (why someone chooses vegetarianism and what happens as a result, page 303)

Teacher's ResourceBank™

RESOURCES

PREWRITING
- Wiring a Cause-and-Effect Essay

QUOTATION FOR THE DAY

"As I see it, writing is applied psychology because it is the art of creating desired effects. It follows from this that our chief need is to know *what* effects are desirable and *how* to create them." (John R. Trimble, American writer and teacher)

Ask students to freewrite about the quotation. Encourage them to make connections between the quotation and cause-and-effect writing.

MOTIVATION

Ask students to name situations or events that are of interest to them. Write the responses on the chalkboard, and then tell students to answer the questions "Why did it happen?" or "What is the result?" with respect to the situations or events they have named.

TEACHING THE LESSON

You may want to break this segment into two parts when teaching it—**Choosing a Topic** and **Gathering and Organizing Information**. Pausing to emphasize important points, read **Choosing a Topic** on p. 295 to your class. Then take your students through the process of evaluating possible topics. First, test each topic generated in the

MEETING INDIVIDUAL NEEDS

LESS-ADVANCED STUDENTS

You may want to discuss what an essay is and does. Stated as simply as possible, an essay is a short piece of writing, usually presenting the view of the writer. An informative essay cannot contain just feelings and opinions; it must be built on a foundation of facts and evidence. Once the students choose their topics, ask them to write a one-sentence statement of purpose. For example, "I am writing to explain to my reader how . . . ." This statement can clarify the topic and objective in the student's mind and allow you to determine if the student is headed in the right direction.

ANSWERS
Exercise 1

Each small group should have generated at least five topics. Check topics by asking "Why did it happen?" and "What is the result?" You should be able to ask one or both of those questions. Each topic should have a tight focus.

Since you want your explanation to be clear to your readers, you have to think about them. What do they already know about your topic? What do they need to know as background? Most important: What information will show them that your explanation is sound and reasonable? If you explain that one result of a part-time job is learning to manage time better, you can't just expect readers to take your word for it. They'll want evidence, perhaps interviews with students and guidance counselors.

Reminder

When you're looking for a topic for a cause-and-effect essay

- brainstorm, talk to other people, read the newspaper, and watch the news to find a topic that interests you
- be sure that you can ask the questions *Why did it happen?* and *What are the results?* about the topic
- remember that your purpose is to explain to readers, with evidence

---

EXERCISE 1 ▶ **Exploring Possible Topics**

What puzzles you about the world? Think of some situations or events that make you wonder *Why?* or *Then what?* Working with a small group, brainstorm several topics suitable for short cause-and-effect essays. Include some topics that focus on your school and community.

PART 1:
Choosing a Topic

One benefit of writing cause-and-effect essays is learning something new in the process. Remember that although you have to be able to ask the questions *Why did it happen?* and *What are the results?* about your topic, you don't have to know the answers yet. Choose a topic to write about—either one your group identified in Exercise 1 or another topic that interests you.

Motivation by asking "Why did it happen?" and "What is the result?" Next, determine whether the topic is focused enough. Finally, decide who the audience will be and whether the topic will be interesting. Reinforce that students should choose topics that interests them.

Ask student volunteers to read the rest of the prewriting segment aloud to the

class. Stress the importance of facts in an informative essay.

Help students choose topics for their essays by dividing the class into small groups and having the groups do **Exercise 1.** Circulate from group to group to answer questions and to check students' progress.

To model organizing information for students, go through **Writing Assignment:** 👉

Prewriting

Gathering and Organizing Information

Remember that your purpose is to explain: to make the relationships between causes and effects *clear* to your audience. To do this, you'll need to back up your statements with evidence (facts, statistics, and examples) that is organized to make sense.

Gathering Information

You can gather information by brainstorming with other students, interviewing people who know something about your subject, or doing library research. Be sure to gather enough information. In a sense, you'll have to prove to your readers that what you say is true—and the more information you can select from, the better. For example:

> *Topic:* Littering around the high school
> *Cause:* Students litter because there aren't enough trash cans.
> *Evidence:* 1. Number of trash cans in school
>   2. Number overflowing by noon
>   3. Number of times they're emptied

👉 REFERENCE NOTE: See pages 337–338 for more information on using evidence to support a statement.

Thinking About Causes.   One kind of cause-and-effect essay explains the causes of a certain effect. If you've chosen this type of topic, begin by writing your topic on a piece of paper. Then ask yourself *Why did it happen?* and list *all* the likely causes you can think of. It's possible, of course, for an effect to result from only *one* cause. For example, if the television is unplugged (cause), it won't come on (effect). But most situations and events have several causes.

The following chart, for example, lists three causes that explain why the African elephant is in danger of becoming extinct. The writer gathered these facts by reading magazine and newspaper articles and by talking to her biology teacher.

Parts **2** and **3** on the chalkboard with a sample topic. Try different methods of organizing causes and effects (least-to-most important, most-to-least important, or chronological order) and ask students which methods would be appropriate for different topics.

Your students should be ready to do **Writing Assignment: Parts 2** and **3** independently. Students might need time for research, either to go to the library or to interview experts.

VISUAL CONNECTIONS

Exploring the Subject. Elephant tusks are the biggest teeth in the world. Elephants use them to dig up shrubs, to strip bark from trees, and to fight. Baby elephants have small milk-tusks that fall out before they are two years old. Milk-tusks are then replaced by the magnificent permanent tusks. Unfortunately, some people hunt elephants for their tusks to make ivory ornaments and jewelry. Each year, more than 100,000 elephants are slaughtered for their tusks.

MEETING INDIVIDUAL NEEDS

LESS-ADVANCED STUDENTS

Some students will have difficulty remembering to include a supporting fact for each cause and effect they use. To help them, you may want to have students list each cause and each effect, with supporting facts, on index cards.

Students can use the cards to help them organize their essays. They might want to lay the index cards out on their desks and to rearrange them to find the most effective order of causes and effects.

298   *Writing to Explain*

HERE'S HOW

TOPIC: The African elephant is in danger of becoming extinct.

CAUSES:
1. Poachers kill the elephants for their ivory.
2. Natives kill elephants for trampling their crops.
3. Elephants' habitats are being cleared for farming land, leaving them with little room for foraging.

AFRICA

WRITING NOTE   Sometimes, there is a chain of causes and effects. For example, you learn that the marching band's uniforms are in such poor condition because the money budgeted for uniforms was used to buy instruments. But that happened because school rules no longer allow an annual pretzel sale to raise money for instruments. The first cause was really the effect of an earlier cause: a chain led to the situation.

Thinking About Effects. Sometimes effects are obvious, especially if some time has passed since a situation or event occurred. It's easy to see the effects of abandoned silver mines in the Old West—the ghost town is there. But sometimes effects are not so clear.

Use **Exercise 2** as a means of assessing students' understanding. Circulate from group to group to be sure that students have chosen suitable topics, have identified causes and effects clearly, and have gathered supporting facts.

Write a topic on the chalkboard that would not work for a cause-and-effect essay such as "improving the cafeteria." Ask your class if it is a good topic and then have them explain why it is not a good topic. ■

When you focus on effects, state your topic clearly. Then ask yourself *What are the results?* List all the likely results of the situation or event. Notice that the results may be both negative and positive. In explanatory writing you want to be thorough and fair, so you'll explore both kinds of effects in your essay. (In persuasive writing, you might stress the effects that support your position.)

> TOPIC: A chemical factory is to be built on parkland on the outskirts of town.
>
> EFFECTS: 1. The factory will provide new jobs.
>   2. Business will improve for local shopkeepers.
>   3. Local citizens will have less space for recreation.
>   4. The animal and plant life of the area will be affected by loss of parkland and possible pollution from the factory.

Arranging Information

Most writers arrange causes or effects in the order of importance: They start with the most important one and move to the least important. Or they do the reverse and emphasize the most important one by saving it for last. (Usually, the last thing people read is what they remember best.) Causes and effects may also be presented in *chronological order* or in the order of *most familiar to least familiar*.

 REFERENCE NOTE: For more information on arranging information, see pages 82–85.

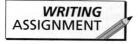 PART 2:
Gathering Information

Get yourself organized with a graphic aid. First, clearly state your topic (the situation or event you'll be writing about). Then, complete a chart in which you list each cause or effect that you plan to discuss. For each cause or effect, jot down at least one supporting fact, statistic, or example. You don't have to list the same number of causes and effects.

 TIMESAVER

Before students complete **Writing Assignment: Parts 2** and **3,** you may want to make sure they have chosen appropriate topics. Do this by passing around a sheet of paper so students can write their names and the topics they have chosen. This procedure should provide a quick and easy way for you to detect inappropriate topics.

INTEGRATING THE LANGUAGE ARTS

Library Link. Because many students have probably chosen to write about current events, you may want to encourage them to look for magazine and newspaper articles on their subjects. Remind students that the *Readers' Guide to Periodical Literature* indexes articles alphabetically by subject and by author. You may need to go over the information in the *Readers' Guide* with your class.

OBJECTIVE

• To identify false cause and effect and oversimplification of cause and effect

TEACHING *UNDERSTANDING CAUSAL RELATIONSHIPS*

When reading this critical thinking segment aloud to your class, stop to clarify each new idea. Give additional examples of both false cause and effect and over-simplification. After the lesson has been read, ask students if they can think of other examples of false cause and effect or over-

A DIFFERENT APPROACH

The relationship between cause and effect provides the action for many cartoons and comic strips. Students will probably have seen some Roadrunner cartoons. Tell the students to think about how many of those cartoons are based on the effects of Wile E. Coyote's attempts to catch Roadrunner. You might even want to clip a cartoon from a newspaper, reproduce it on a transparency, and ask students to identify the depicted cause and effect.

Then have each student draw a comic strip in which the action is based on cause and effect. Students could choose well-known cartoon characters or they could create their own.

ANSWERS
Exercise 2

Students' presentations should clearly state their topics and identify causes and effects as well as supporting facts.

---

300   *Writing to Explain*

PART 3:
Arranging Information

Now's the time to decide whether you'll focus on causes, effects, or both. Also think about how many causes and effects you can write about. Have you gathered enough evidence? Arrange your information by numbering the causes and/or effects in the order you'll present them.

EXERCISE 2 ▶ **Speaking and Listening: Presenting Your Information Orally**

Using your chart, present your information orally to a small group of classmates. Have them listen to see if they can follow your cause-and-effect analysis. Is your topic clear? Can they identify the causes and/or effects you plan to write about? What do they think of your supporting information for each cause or effect? Listen to your class-mates' questions and comments, and use their sugges-tions to improve your plans for your paper.

CRITICAL THINKING

Understanding Causal Relationships

When you are gathering information for a cause-and-effect explanation, you need to think critically about *causal relationships*—how causes and effects are connected. For example, someone who isn't thinking critically might jump to the conclusion that a slump in movie theater attendance is simply the effect of an economic recession. A more critical thinker, however, might look for other causes and determine that the current slump is part of a longer trend related to the availability of inexpensive videocassettes and VCRs. By thinking critically, you can avoid two common thinking errors, or *fallacies*, in cause-and-effect explanations.

simplification and have them discuss their answers as a class. When the class has a basic understanding of the lesson, have students proceed to the **Critical Thinking Exercise.** Then ask a representative from each group to explain the group's response to one of the three sentences.

To close the lesson, have volunteers give examples of false cause and effect.

1. **False Cause and Effect.** The relationship between a cause and an effect must be valid, or sound. An effect must be the *direct* result of a cause. Just because one event follows another, you can't assume that the first event causes the second. (See also page 340.)

False Cause and Effect	The year after the school cut special courses like Russian, painting, and computer programming, our Brain Bowl team dropped from first to third place. Fewer courses weakened our performance.
Cause and Effect	After Elisa graduated, our team had no one with a main strength in history. That lost us ten crucial questions.

2. **Oversimplifying.** Most (not all) events have more than one cause. When you identify a single cause and ignore all others, you're oversimplifying.

Oversimplification	Slavery was the cause of the Civil War.
Cause and Effect	The question of slavery was one of several issues that led directly to the Civil War.

 CRITICAL THINKING EXERCISE:
Identifying Fallacies

Does walking under a ladder result in bad luck? Does a four-leaf clover bring good luck? No, these are superstitions, not valid reasoning. With a small group of classmates, read the following statements carefully. Explain whether each statement is valid, or whether it illustrates one of the two errors in logic you've just read about.

EXAMPLE 1. Annie's lost her lucky charm, which made her fail a math test and lose a contact lens.
1. *False cause and effect: Not studying enough probably made Annie fail her math test. She probably lost her contact lens because she didn't put it away in its case.*

1. Bob was kicked off the team he missed six practices.
2. The airport was fogged in; all planes were grounded.
3. The only cause of homelessness is the drastic cut in government spending on low-income housing.

LEP/ESL

General Strategies. You may want to define the term *fallacies* as "false beliefs." As part of a group discussion, ask students to give examples of fallacies from history. [Early explorers believed the Earth was flat.] Then ask students to suggest fallacies occurring in their daily experiences. What false beliefs do people have today? Encourage students to enter into the group discussion.

ANSWERS
Critical Thinking

Explanations may vary. Here are some possibilities:

1. Valid: It seems reasonable to kick someone off a basketball team for missing six practices.
2. Valid: It is reasonable that planes be grounded when an airport is fogged in.
3. Oversimplification: Homelessness has many causes.

WRITING YOUR FIRST DRAFT

OBJECTIVES

- To analyze the basic elements of an effective cause-and-effect essay
- To write the first draft of a cause-and-effect essay

MOTIVATION

You may want to stress to your class that a first draft is like a base coat of paint—it should cover the subject, but it does not have to be perfect. Tell them that the most important thing will be just to start writing.

Teacher's ResourceBank™
RESOURCES

WRITING YOUR FIRST DRAFT
- Writing a Cause-and-Effect Essay

QUOTATION FOR THE DAY

"What . . . is the aim of literature and art if not to imbue the world with feeling and meaning, to broaden and deepen our understanding of ourselves and of the things around us." (Arthur Koestler, 1905–1983, British philosopher)

Write the quotation on the chalkboard and lead students to understand that writing cause-and-effect essays can broaden and deepen their understanding of themselves and the things around them.

MEETING INDIVIDUAL NEEDS

LEP/ESL

General Strategies. No matter how many times students have seen the expression "thesis statement," there is no guarantee that they have a solid understanding of how to create one. You may want to compare the thesis statement to the front door of a house. If it is missing or is not highly visible, the reader may not be able to find his way into the house or, in this case, into the essay.

---

302 *Writing to Explain*

Writing Your First Draft

Writing the Introduction. Entice your reader by beginning with a question, an anecdote (brief story), or an example that relates your topic to the reader's life or concerns. Your introduction should also include a *thesis statement*, which is often the paragraph's last sentence. A good thesis statement states your main idea and indicates the essay's focus (causes, effects, or both). For an example of an effective model, study the introduction to the Writer's Model on pages 307–308.

Writing the Body. Be sure to include any necessary background information or to define terms at the beginning of the body. Then draft a separate paragraph for each cause or effect. Remember that you need to provide accurate information (facts, examples, statistics) to back up your statements.

Writing the Conclusion. The conclusion should summarize your essay's main points. You can give the conclusion some punch by ending with a new thought: a final comment, question, prediction, or call to action. For a good example, study the sample conclusion in the Writer's Model on pages 307–308.

Patterns of Cause-and-Effect Essays

Writers may emphasize causes, effects, or both. The writer of the following magazine article focuses on both causes and effects. As you read, notice how she combines factual information with her personal story.

Calvin & Hobbes, copyright 1987 Universal Press Syndicate. Reprinted with permission of Universal Press Syndicate. All rights reserved.

After students have read the introductory paragraphs on p. 302, have a volunteer read **"Why I choose to veg out"** to the class. Ask students if they think the article meets all the criteria established in the lesson's introductory paragraphs. Students might point out that the author does not write a separate paragraph for each cause and each effect. Explain that experienced writers do not always adhere to the structural guidelines that are useful to beginning writers. Before going on, try to reach a consensus about whether the article meets the mentioned criteria.

You may then want to use **A Writer's Model,** p. 307, to discuss the framework for a cause-and-effect essay.

A MAGAZINE ARTICLE

Why I choose to veg out
by Rebecca Moore

INTRODUCTION—
Attention
grabber

1 At Christmastime last year I went out to dinner with a bunch of people from work. I sat studying the menu while the waitress took everyone's order. When she got to me, I asked if I could order the chef's salad without the meat. As soon as she left I faced a semicircle of icy glares. Immediately the attack began:

2 "Don't you wear leather shoes?" (No.) "Don't you eat eggs?" (Yes. As well as milk and cheese to make sure I get enough calcium.) "So you think you're healthier than we are?" (I hope!) "What about the poor little vegetables you're murdering?"

The sarcasm and defensiveness were unbelievable.

Background

3 I've been a vegetarian for more than eleven years, so I've run into this kind of hostility a lot. But I've never thought that being a vegetarian made me into some sort of higher being. Nor that it automatically made me healthier than everyone else—I still have to be careful to eat properly balanced meals. Not all of us vegetarians are "out to get" meat eaters. I and a lot of other vegetarians don't try to impose our views on others. I think it's about time <u>carnivores</u> out there stopped **4** getting on *our* case about our getting on *their* case.

Cause 1—

Evidence for
cause 1

I became a vegetarian when I was eight—because of camp food. The vegetarians at camp got special homemade dishes, while the rest of us ate gray sloppy joes that came straight from the can. I was never a huge vegetable fan, but I was raised with some respect

USING THE SELECTION
Why I Choose to Veg Out

1

This is figurative language. The people did not actually attack the author; they began to question her. Why is the word *attack* more effective than the word *questioning*?

2

The parenthetical remarks are the author's unspoken responses.

3

There are several words in this essay that classify people according to what they eat: *vegetarian*—someone who doesn't eat meat; *carnivore*—someone who eats only meat. Can you think of other words that classify people, or animals, according to what they eat? [*herbivore*—an animal that eats grasses and plants; *omnivore*—an animal that eats everything]

4

Italics are used for emphasis.

Students can use this framework in conjunction with the organizational patterns they worked out in **Writing Assignment: Part 3.**

GUIDED PRACTICE

Guide your students through **Exercise 3** by initiating a class discussion of the questions. To model the skills required for **Writing Assignment: Part 4,** begin a cause-and-effect essay of your own by writing it on a transparency while your class helps you.

304   *Writing to Explain*

Cause 2—

Evidence for
cause 2

Effect 1—

Evidence for
effect 1

Effect 2—
Evidence for
effect 2

for my stomach—and I'd have taken anything over those rubbery turkey sandwiches.

Then I started taking care of the chickens, rabbits, horses, goats, and salamanders that I was surrounded by for the first time. After only one week, the chickens ran up to me when I whistled. I could snuggle a little chick while I was reading a book, and it would fall asleep with its neck stretched out over my shoulder. I began to wonder why people dismissed animals as dumb—to me they were absolutely fascinating. . . .

Upon my arrival home at summer's end I announced my change to my family. My mother thought it was great, but she wasn't about to go out of her way to cook special vegetarian meals for me. I figured that I would just ignore the entrée and eat the side dishes. No problem. . . .

My mom tried to teach me about nutrition. Her trick was to eat as many different-colored foods as possible. If your plate is filled with a rainbow of foods—purple cabbage, green peppers, oranges, red tomatoes—you're sure to get a good dose of vitamins. Now, I realize this is not a foolproof method and shouldn't be relied upon in the long run, but for a few years it got me through those mealtimes when I was left to my own devices. . . .

5

The expression *dumb animals* actually refers to the fact that animals cannot speak.

6

Entrée is derived from the french word *entrer,* meaning "to enter." In this context *entrée* means "the main course of a meal."

Students should be ready to do **Writing Assignment: Part 4** independently. Use student-teacher conferences to help students who are having problems. At this point, focus on what students are doing well, rather than on what they are doing poorly.

You can probably get a good idea of how students are doing on their drafts from your student-teacher conferences.

Cause 3—Evidence for cause 3

Fact 1

Fact 2

Fact 3

For me vegetarianism had become a means of expressing my belief in animal rights. My mother and sister made the change to a meatless diet to avoid the 7 unhealthy chemicals and high cholesterol and also because of the faulty economic reasoning behind raising animals for food. A meat-centered diet contributes to such economic and geographic problems as world hunger, soil erosion, and high energy costs. Our food decisions affect nearly everything 8 around us. Almost *one half* of the United States' harvested acreage is used to feed livestock, and only a fraction of that is returned to us in the form of meat on our plates: It takes sixteen pounds of grain to make just 9 *one* pound of beef. Meat is *not* the only source of protein available to us; by combining certain plant foods, we can get plenty of protein. . . .

7

Many animals that are bred for slaughter are fed antibiotics and other chemicals to make them fat and robust. Some people believe that these chemicals are unhealthy for the people who eat the animals.

8

If the land used now to raise beef were used to grow grain, many more people could be fed.

9

The combination of legumes with whole grains provides a good source of protein.

CONCLUSION

10

Final comment

Call to action

Vegetarians are regular people who have made a conscious decision about their eating habits, people who haven't taken for granted the diet they were "assigned" at birth by their family or culture. Whether you're a vegetarian or not, becoming more knowledgeable about the foods you eat can't hurt. To all those nonvegetarians out there, don't take it personally that some of us don't eat meat. Educate yourselves, and *bon appétit!*

Seventeen

10

The main idea of the article is stated in the conclusion.

SELECTION AMENDMENT
Description of change: excerpted and indentions added
Rationale: to focus on the concept of drafting a cause-and-effect essay presented in this chapter

Find or create a student cause-and-effect essay and copy it onto a chalkboard or a transparency so the class can read it together. Tell students that they are going to grade the paper for (**1**) an attention-getting opener, (**2**) a thesis statement, (**3**) causes or effects developed with facts, (**4**) effective organization, and (**5**) a conclusion that summarizes main points. Give students a few minutes to read the essay and to rate it. If the paper has all five elements, it should receive an A. If it is missing one criterion, it should receive a B, and so on. Afterwards, discuss with students the ratings they have given the paper and why.

TIMESAVER

Rather than evaluating students' answers to the questions in **Exercise 3,** you may want just to discuss students' responses in class.

ANSWERS
Exercise 3

1. Students' reactions to the introduction will vary. However, using a revealing incident does grab the reader's attention.

2. Personal reasons mentioned in the order in which they happened are bad camp food, fascination with animals, and belief in animal rights.

3. Students' answers will vary. Here are some possibilities: She had to modify eating habits; she learned about nutrition.

4. Students' responses will vary but should be substantiated.

WRITING NOTE   You may have noticed that the article you've just read is written in an *informal style.* For example, Moore both refers to herself in the first person and uses contractions: "I've been a vegetarian for more than eleven years, so I've run into this kind of hostility a lot." Moore uses this style because her readers are teenagers (the article was first published in *Seventeen* magazine), and she wants them to feel comfortable. Keep in mind, though, that a more formal style would be appropriate for some subjects and audiences. (See Chapter 14 for more information on levels of language.)

EXERCISE 3   **Analyzing a Cause-and-Effect Essay**

After reading Rebecca Moore's article, meet with two or three classmates to discuss the following questions.

1. Describe your reactions to the introduction, where the writer captures the reader's attention—the attention grabber.
2. Which of the causes are personal reasons mentioned in the order in which they happened?
3. In your own words, summarize the effects of the author's becoming a vegetarian.
4. Do you think the writer's purpose is just to explain, or is she also trying to persuade? Why do you think so? How do you feel about this article? Would it cause you to become a vegetarian?

A Framework for a Cause-and-Effect Essay

How you organize your essay depends mostly on whether you emphasize causes or effects or both. The essay you've just read was written by a professional writer who discusses both causes and effects of her decision to become a vegetarian. The following essay focuses on effects. As you read, see what kinds of evidence the writer has included to support her statements. You might wish to use this writer's model as a framework for your own essay. Or, you might wish to focus on causes.

Writing Your First Draft **307**

A WRITER'S MODEL

**INTRODUCTION—
Attention
grabber**

Background

Cause

**Thesis
statement**

Last year finding a seat in a classroom was like playing musical chairs. We were packed forty and fifty to the classroom. The traffic around the high school at 8:30 A.M. and 3:30 P.M. was a police officer's nightmare, and lunch hour was always a stampede. In January the school board decided to try some creative scheduling to relieve the overcrowding. Now we go to school and eat lunch in two shifts, which has had some interesting effects on the students.

**Evidence for
effect 1**

Effect 1

Effect 2

**Evidence for
effect 2**

Since longtime buddies now come to school, go to lunch, and head for home at different times, new friendships are being formed. Meeting new people definitely makes life more interesting.

Except for when the shifts overlap a couple of times a day, the halls are not so crowded. You can actually get to your locker and get your books without being crushed. You can arrive at your next class on time.

VISUAL CONNECTIONS
Ideas for Writing. Have any changes been made at your school lately? You may want students to write letters or editorials to the school newspaper complaining about or praising changes that have taken place at your school. Or, if no changes have been made, can students think of any that need to be made? Have students write letters or editorials proposing changes they feel are necessary. Be sure they include causes and effects as they support their complaints, praises, or proposals.

INTEGRATING THE LANGUAGE ARTS
Technology Link. You may want to remind students that if they have access to word processors, this would be a good time to use them. Students can use printouts of the prewriting files or the split-screen capability of a word processor to view the prewriting file while composing in a draft file.

Explain to students that advertisements frequently use false cause and effect to promote products. For example, an ad might imply that you will have more dates if you use a certain product. Advertisements also use oversimplification of cause and effect. For example, an ad might promise that you will be healthy if you take a certain vitamin. (Vitamins alone cannot ensure good health.)

Have students evaluate ads to compile a scrapbook of such advertisements from newspapers and magazines, or have students make a collage or poster. ■

INTEGRATING THE LANGUAGE ARTS

Literature Link. There is a famous line in the Bible that comments on the cause-and-effect relationship between what people give or do and what they receive: "Whatsoever a man soweth, that shall he also reap." (Galatians 6:7). The poem "A Black Man Talks of Reaping" by Arna Bontemps alludes explicitly to this biblical line. If this poem is available in your literature textbook, have students read it and then have them write informative paragraphs analyzing the use of cause and effect in the poem.

---

308   *Writing to Explain*

Effect 3
Evidence for effect 3

But most important, the classrooms are no longer crowded. We actually have our own desks and aren't being bumped, jostled, scrunched, and flattened while the teacher tries to present the lesson. We can comfortably listen, and we can learn.

CONCLUSION— Summary of effects

Final comment

Reorganizing the high school into double shifts has resulted in many new friendships and a pleasanter school atmosphere. But the most important result may be better-educated students.

If your essay is mostly about the effects of a situation or event, you can follow the pattern of the writer's model, illustrated in the following chart.

FRAMEWORK FOR A CAUSE-AND-EFFECT ESSAY

Introduction • • • • • ▶ Attention grabber, Causes, Thesis statement

Body • • • • • • • ▶ Effect 1/Discussion, Effect 2/Discussion, More effects/Discussion

Conclusion • • • • • ▶ Summary of main points

Final comment • • • ▶ Specific details

An essay that focuses on causes will follow a similar pattern, but with these differences: The introduction will touch on the effects of a situation or event, and the body will be devoted to a discussion of the causes. An essay that deals with *both* causes and effects usually discusses the causes first. The magazine article "Why I choose to veg out" (see pages 303–305) follows this last pattern.

Reminder

A cause-and-effect essay should

- clearly answer at least one of these questions: *Why did it happen? What are the results?*
- include evidence to support cause-and-effect statements
- present information in an effective order
- have a direct, straightforward tone

WRITING ASSIGNMENT

PART 4:
Writing a First Draft

Your chart of causes, effects, and evidence (from Writing Assignment, Part 3, page 300) is all you need to write your first draft. These reminders will help you get started:

1. Write a thesis statement.
2. Think of an attention-getting opening, and write an introductory paragraph.
3. Write the body—one cause or effect to a paragraph. Make sure you develop each cause or effect with facts, examples, and so on.
4. Write a conclusion that summarizes your main points. End with something new (such as a comment, a question, or a prediction).
5. As you write your draft, keep in mind your purpose and audience.

EVALUATING AND REVISING

OBJECTIVES

- To analyze a writer's revisions
- To evaluate a classmate's first draft
- To use a classmate's evaluation to improve one's essay

TEACHING THE LESSON

You may want to analyze and discuss the **Evaluating and Revising Cause-and-Effect Essays** chart with your class. Ask students to provide examples of each criterion from their drafts. For instance, ask students to read aloud their attention-grabbing introductions or to explain how they have organized their causes and effects.

QUOTATION FOR THE DAY

"Blot out, correct, insert, refine,/ Enlarge, diminish, interline;/Be mindful, when invention fails,/To scratch your head, and bite your nails." (Jonathan Swift, 1667–1745, English satirist)

Ask students to brainstorm in small groups lists of actions associated with revision. Then share the quotation with the class and encourage students to remember the actions listed as they begin evaluating and revising their work.

VISUAL CONNECTIONS

Related Expression Skills. Ask students to create their own diagrams like Professor Butts's diagram for a simplified pencil sharpener.

Explain that they should plan their cause-and-effect sequences first to make sure they make a seemingly simple task as complicated as the task in the diagram shown here.

Evaluating and Revising

What have you done especially well in your draft? Where might you make improvements? Use the following chart to help you make changes in your draft. Begin by asking yourself a question in the left-hand column of the chart. If you identify a particular weakness, use the revision technique suggested in the right-hand column.

Pencil Sharpener

Professor Butts gets his think-tank working and evolves the simplified pencil sharpener. Open window (A) and fly kite (B). String (C) lifts small door (D), allowing moths (E) to escape and eat red flannel shirt (F). As weight of shirt becomes less, shoe (G) steps on switch (H) which heats electric iron (I) and burns hole in pants (J). Smoke (K) enters hole in tree (L), smoking out opossum (M) which jumps into basket (N), pulling rope (O) and lifting cage (P), allowing woodpecker (Q) to chew wood from pencil (R), exposing lead. Emergency knife (S) is always handy in case opossum or the woodpecker gets sick and can't work.

You may also want to remind students that at this stage they will probably be making substantial changes—reorganizing, adding to, or deleting from their first drafts. The fact that they are making big changes now probably means that they are doing a good job of evaluating and revising.

Go through **Exercise 4** orally with the class by asking for and discussing students' responses to each question.

Writing Assignment: Part 5 combines cooperative learning with independent practice. Ultimately, however, the changes students decide to make in their papers are up to them.

EVALUATING AND REVISING CAUSE-AND-EFFECT ESSAYS

EVALUATION GUIDE	REVISION TECHNIQUE
1 Does the introduction grab the reader's attention?	**Add** an anecdote, question, or example that connects the topic to the reader. **Replace** some of the wording to make your anecdote, question, or example clearer and more interesting.
2 Does the introduction contain an effective thesis statement?	**Add** a sentence (or **replace** an existing sentence) that clearly states the essay's main idea and indicates whether the essay will focus on causes, effects, or both.
3 Are statements of causes and effects adequately developed?	**Add** facts, statistics, examples, or quotations to support statements.
4 Are the cause-and-effect statements logical?	**Cut** any fallacies of false cause and effect and oversimplification. **Add** logical statements.
5 Is the information presented in an effective order?	**Reorder** causes and effects in order of importance or familiarity or in chronological order.
6 Does the essay have an effective conclusion?	**Add** a concluding paragraph that summarizes the main idea and adds a final comment.

MEETING INDIVIDUAL NEEDS

ADVANCED STUDENTS

Students might be interested in learning how professional writers have revised their works. Many libraries carry famous authors' biographies that show writers' works in various stages. Ask students to write informative paragraphs on their findings and to present them to the class.

AT-RISK STUDENTS

You may want to introduce evaluating and revising to students by providing copies of a puzzle that asks "What's wrong with this picture?" Explain that evaluating an essay is like asking "What's wrong with this picture?" When students revise their essays, they are correcting the things that are wrong with the picture.

Observing students' papers while the class is working on **Writing Assignment: Part 5** should give you an idea of how students they are doing at evaluating and revising their essays.

Ask students to tell you how evaluating and revising a cause-and-effect essay might be different from evaluating and revising other types of essays. [Order might be less important and might not require attentive avoidance of false cause and effect.] ∎

ANSWERS

Exercise 4

1. The revised sentence uses a simile to grab the reader's attention.
2. The words "forty and fifty" paint a more specific, vivid picture.
3. The writer moved the sentence to reflect the chronological order of the events described.
4. The metaphor describes the situation much more vividly.
5. The change creates a thesis sentence.

MEETING INDIVIDUAL NEEDS

LEARNING STYLES

Visual Learners. Have students use graphic organizers to check that they have included all the necessary evidence in their drafts. After putting the following chart on the chalkboard, ask students to copy it and to fill it in with the information in their drafts.

Cause/Effect	Evidence
Body Paragraph 1	
2	
3	

EXERCISE 4 ▶ **Analyzing a Writer's Revisions**

Here is the writer's revision of the first paragraph of the paper on page 307. With some classmates, discuss the writer's revisions. Then answer the questions that follow.

(4 Last year finding a seat in a classroom was like playing musical chairs.
forty and fifty to
ʌWe were packed ~~tightly in~~ the   **add/replace**

classroom. In January the school board   **reorder**

decided to try some creative scheduling to

relieve the overcrowding. The traffic

around the high school at 8:30 A.M. and
a police officer's nightmare
3:30 P.M. was ~~bad~~, and lunch hour was   **replace**

always a stampede. Now we go to school
which has had some
and eat lunch in two shifts, ~~That's a lot~~   **replace**
interesting effects on the students.
~~better.~~

1. Why did the writer add the sentence "Last year finding a seat in a classroom was like playing musical chairs"? [Hint: How does this sentence interest you?]
2. In the second sentence, why did the writer replace the words *tightly in* with the words *forty and fifty to*?
3. Why did the writer move the second sentence?
4. In the new third sentence, why did the writer replace *bad* with *a police officer's nightmare*?
5. Why did the writer replace the last sentence with the clause *which has had some interesting effects on the students*? [Hint: What is the thesis statement?]

PART 5:
Evaluating and Revising Your First Draft

It's usually much easier to spot weaknesses in someone else's writing than in your own. Exchange essays with another student, and apply the questions from the chart on page 311. Discuss your evaluations with your partner, and make changes to improve your essay.

OBJECTIVES

- To proofread and correct a cause-and-effect essay
- To share a cause-and-effect essay with an audience

MOTIVATION

Ask your students if they would leave their houses with their clothes in disarray. They probably wouldn't because they spend time each morning making sure they look just right. Tell students that they should also make sure that their essays look just right before they turn the essays in.

☞

Proofreading and Publishing

Proofreading. You've worked hard on your cause-and-effect essay. Now, give it the final touches. If you have even the slightest doubt about the spelling of a word, the placement of a comma, or the correct form of a verb, consult a dictionary or the handbook that begins on page 510.

USAGE HINT

Clear Pronoun Antecedents

When you're explaining causes and effects, you might decide to use a pronoun to refer to a word you've mentioned earlier. When you do that, you have to be sure that the antecedent is clear. The *antecedent* of a pronoun is the word or phrase it refers to, or replaces. Rewrite a sentence in which the antecedent is unclear.

CONFUSING	The glass and the bowl were sitting on the table. When *it* broke, no one could understand what happened. [What broke—the glass or the bowl?]
CLEAR	The glass and the bowl were sitting on the table. When **the glass** broke, no one could understand what happened.

 REFERENCE NOTE: For more information about clear pronoun antecedents, see pages 668–670.

Publishing. Remember that the purpose of your essay is to explain something to *somebody*. On the next page there are some suggestions for sharing your cause-and-effect essay with an audience:

Teacher's ResourceBank™
RESOURCES

PROOFREADING AND PUBLISHING
- Writing a Cause-and-Effect Essay

QUOTATION FOR THE DAY

"In a very real sense, the writer writes in order to teach himself, to understand himself, to satisfy himself; the publishing of his ideas, though it brings gratifications, is a curious anticlimax." (Alfred Kazin, 1915–   , American writer and university professor)

Ask students to respond to the quotation by writing journal entries that explore how they feel about publishing their work. Do they agree with Kazin?

USAGE HINT

You may want to remind students that every pronoun must also agree with its antecedent in number. Tell students to be careful because some pronouns appear to be plural but are actually singular:

1. *Everybody* brought *her* (or *his*) own lunch.
2. Did *everyone* proofread *his* (or *her*) essay?

You may want to give several more examples of clear and unclear pronoun antecedents on the chalkboard. (See **Usage Hint.**) Then remind your students of all the other things they could be looking for as they proofread their papers: spelling and capitalization errors, comma errors, and subject-verb agreement errors.

After students have proofread their papers, conduct a brainstorming session to come up with additional ideas for publishing students' essays. Finally, you could read the model aloud as an example of a student essay that did get published.

MEETING INDIVIDUAL NEEDS

LESS-ADVANCED STUDENTS

Students might need to be reminded that content is not usually changed during the proofreading process. Most all content should be in place by now. The objective of proofreading is to check for other problems: spelling, proper use of apostrophes and commas, subject-verb agreement, run-on sentences, and replacing passive voice with active voice (when possible). As a note of encouragement, emphasize that professional writers always have several people check their final drafts.

---

314 *Writing to Explain*

- Convert your essay to a letter to the editor and send it to your local newspaper.
- Work with a small group of classmates to prepare a panel presentation of your cause-and-effect essays on similar subjects.

WRITING ASSIGNMENT

PART 6:
Proofreading and Publishing Your Essay

Proofread your essay carefully and correct all errors. Try peer proofreading, too. When you've made your corrections, copy a final version (proofread it also) and use one of the suggestions you've just read or one of your own to share your essay with an audience.

A STUDENT MODEL

Cause and effect is all around you, even in your daily life. Arletha Johnson, a student at Peoria High School in Peoria, Illinois, explains how getting a job affected her life. Arletha's reason for getting a job might surprise you, but the final result of her decision will probably please you.

Get a Job
by Arletha Johnson

For someone like me, sitting around watching television sounded like fun. My Friday nights were spent staring at the television. After seeing reruns of a particular show five times,

If students are having difficulty with proofreading, you may want to have each of them create a sentence containing two deliberate errors. Then have students exchange sentences and challenge each other to find the errors in the sentences.

Ask students what mistakes they discovered in their essays. Write the responses on the chalkboard and call students' attention to the types of errors that are mentioned frequently. ■

I felt I needed to make a change. I finally decided to get a job and received my first employment at one of the local fast-food restaurants.

Before I received the job, all I knew how to do was tell time by what was on the television. Since I had a job, I had to learn "responsibility," something I never thought I would hear come out of my mouth. My avid television watching decreased as my responsibilities increased. Of course, being a frequent television watcher as I was, I didn't have many friends. That all changed as I was able to communicate with people. Many of the people I met changed from mere acquaintances to friends. Also, I actually considered doing something with my life, like going to college.

And of course, being the "couch potato" that I was, I didn't have such high self-esteem. I only felt better about myself when I was able to find the remote control on top of the refrigerator. Since I have been working, my self-esteem has come from a job well done. All in all, if getting a job could turn me into a successful working part of society, it was all worth it.

A STUDENT MODEL
Evaluation

1. Arletha uses an anecdote in her introduction to grab the reader's attention.
2. The effects of Arletha's new job are developed with specific examples, such as "My . . . television watching decreased . . ." and . . . "I was able to communicate with people."
3. The arrangement of the causes and effects is effectively presented in order of importance.
4. Arletha's conclusion summarizes the main idea and adds a final comment.

COOPERATIVE LEARNING
You may want to group students in pairs to proofread each other's papers. Try to pair students with comparable abilities so that they will each have about the same number of errors in their essays. You may want to hold each student accountable for how good a job she or he does proofreading by having students sign the papers that they proofread.

SEGMENT 7 *(pp. 316–319)*
WRITING WORKSHOP
OBJECTIVES
- To analyze a process essay
- To write an essay that explains a process

TEACHING THE LESSON

First, discuss with your class the two types of process analysis essays (how to perform a process and how something works or happens) and the three requirements (completeness, order, and tone). Next, ask for a volunteer to read the excerpt from **The Arapaho Way.** Discuss with the class the questions that follow the excerpt, or ask for

Teacher's ResourceBank™
RESOURCES

WRITING WORKSHOP
All the resources for this chapter may be used in this segment.

QUOTATION FOR THE DAY

"Knowledge is the foundation and source of good writing." (Horace, Quintus Horatius Flaccus, 65–8 B.C., Roman lyric poet and satirist)

Share the quotation with students and ask them to brainstorm lists of activities they perform well. Explain that each activity they listed could be the subject of a process-analysis essay.

LEP/ESL

General Strategies. You may want to focus on the first type of process-analysis essay (how to perform a process) with students. This type of essay allows students to draw upon familiar contexts and encourages them to bring personal experiences to the assignment.

316

316

WRITING WORKSHOP

A Process Explanation

How does a tadpole become a frog? How does a forward slam-dunk a basketball? How does a compact disk player work? Cause-and-effect explanations are very closely related to another kind of explanation—the *process explanation.* Both explanations are narrative; they explain events over the course of time. Cause-and-effect explanations focus on *why* something happens, and process explanations focus on *how* something happens. There are two basic types of process explanations.

1. **How to perform a process.** In this type of essay, you explain a process you know well or one you'd like to learn: how to make spinach lasagna, how to play a guitar, how to handpaint a T-shirt, or how to snorkel. By following your step-by-step directions, readers should be able to do the process.
2. **How something works or happens.** This type of essay explains a topic that's more abstract, one that readers can't "do" themselves. For example, you may explain how a bill becomes a law, how an automatic teller machine works, or how fluorocarbons destroy the ozone layer of the atmosphere.

Both types of process essays have three requirements: completeness, order, and tone.

- **Completeness.** Mention every step in the process; don't leave anything out. Depending on your audience, you may need to explain necessary materials and define unfamiliar terms.
- **Order.** In process essays, order is crucial. Discuss each step in chronological order, the order in which each step must be done.
- **Tone.** Use simple, straightforward language. An ideal process essay is not only clear but also lively and interesting.

volunteers to write answers on the chalkboard.

As guided practice, go through the prewriting process on the chalkboard with your class. Have students brainstorm together for a topic while a volunteer writes the ideas on the chalkboard. Then choose one example and write each of its steps in order. If you choose a "how to perform a process" topic, you may also want to make a list of all the things you will need to complete the process.

As independent practice, students should write their own process-analysis essays. As this assignment might take students several class periods, you may want to assign the essay as homework.

The following excerpt is from a book about the traditional Arapaho way of life. The writer, Althea Bass, put into book form her many hours of conversation with an elderly Arapaho named Carl Sweezy. What process does Sweezy describe in these paragraphs?

MEETING INDIVIDUAL NEEDS

LEARNING STYLES

Kinetic Learners. If you choose to assign the first type of process-analysis essay (how to perform a process), you may take this assignment one step further to improve students' understanding. Active involvement, particularly within a supportive social environment, often enhances learning. The suggestion to have students demonstrate for the class is an excellent strategy. A hands-on manipulation of materials allows students to approach the essay concept more holistically. You may want to offer extra credit to those students who are interested in giving demonstrations. Encourage the class to answer questions at the end of the presentation to ensure peer interaction.

An Arapaho woman, in putting up a tipi, started with three poles that she bound together about three feet from the small end. These she set up on the ground like a big tripod. Then she propped more poles on the ground and rested them above in the fork of the first three. These were spaced evenly in a circle and formed the framework of the tipi. Many buffalo skins sewed together had once made the cover for this

CLOSURE

To close this lesson, ask your class to give the three requirements for a process-analysis essay [completeness, order, and a simple, straightforward tone].

ENRICHMENT

Students might want to read more about the traditional Arapaho way of life. Althea Bass' book *The Arapaho Way: A Memoir of an Indian Boyhood* was published by Clarkson N. Potter, Inc. ∎

318

ANSWERS

Writing Workshop Questions

1. Students should include the following steps:
   a. Bind three poles together to set up as a tripod.
   b. Prop more poles evenly in a circle in the fork of the tripod.
   c. Cover poles with lodge cloth.
   d. Leave two flaps open at the top with two more poles thrust through them.
   e. Fasten the cone-shaped canvas above the entrance with wooden pegs.
   f. Cover the entrance with skin or canvas held down with wood.
   Sweezy uses chronological order.

2. Necessary materials were poles, lodge cloth, wooden pegs, and a strip of wood.

3. Answers will vary. Be sure students explain their responses.

frame, but the old lodge skins soon wore out after the buffalo were gone, and then a heavy cloth called lodge cloth or strouding was used. This cloth was cut and sewed in such a way that it formed a kind of cone stretched over the poles. Yet it was not exactly a cone, for two flaps, or ears, were left open at the top, with two more poles thrust through them in such a way that they made the smoke hole above the center of the lodge large or small, depending on how they were braced on the ground. These could be adjusted according to how much wind blew and in what direction.

Above the entrance, the cone-shaped canvas was fastened together with wooden pegs about the way an overcoat is fastened with big buttons. The opening that made the entrance was covered with a skin or a length of canvas held down by a strip of wood that weighted the bottom.

Althea Bass, *The Arapaho Way*

1. List the steps in putting up a tipi, or tepee, in the order in which Sweezy explains them. What order does he use?
2. What materials were necessary?
3. If you had the materials and this explanation, do you think you could put up a tipi? Why?

Writing a Process Analysis Essay

Prewriting. Choose a process that you're familiar with or one that you'd like to know about. Imagine that your audience is a group of fifth- and sixth-grade students. You can write an essay that explains how to perform a process or one that explains how something works. Here are some ideas to get you started:

HOW-TO:	How to make origami (Japanese paper flowers and animals)
	How to tie-dye a T-shirt
	How to jump-start a car
HOW SOMETHING WORKS:	How a microwave oven works
	How a telephone works
	How a compact disk player works

SELECTION AMENDMENT
Description of change: excerpted and paragraphs deleted
Rationale: to focus on the concept of explaining a process presented in this chapter

When you've chosen a topic, jot down each step in the process. Be complete; list every step. Arrange the steps in the order in which they occur (chronological order). You may need to do some library research to gather information.

 Writing, Evaluating, and Revising.   First, draft an introduction that introduces your topic and purpose. Try to think of a lively, attention-grabbing opening. Next, present the necessary background information (materials needed, terms to be defined); then, explain each step in chronological order. Include details—examples, facts, and so on—to explain the process thoroughly, and use transitions to guide your reader through the process. Ask two classmates to read your first draft and tell you if anything confuses them. Revise your essay for clarity and completeness. You may also want to include an explanatory diagram like the one below to present information on the process.

Proofreading and Publishing.   Proofread your revised version carefully (see the guidelines for proofreading on page 56). To share your writing, read your essay aloud to your class or do a class demonstration, explaining each step in the process.

Metal stirrer fan, spun by circulating air, reflects and scatters microwaves

Food heated from sides and above

False floor

Microwaves reflected from floor

Microwave beam

Magnetron

Controls

Blower circulates air, cools magnetron and spins stirrer

Food heated from below

MEETING INDIVIDUAL NEEDS

LEARNING STYLES

Kinetic Learners. Kinetic learners writing process essays will benefit from actually performing the processes as they do the prewriting for their essays. For example, a kinetic learner writing a process essay about how to make a kite should go through the actual process of making a kite while writing down each step in order. This suggestion will also work well for students who are having a hard time achieving completeness in their essays.

A DIFFERENT APPROACH

Another possible structure students could use to follow as they write is one that integrates materials with steps. Here is one possibility:

Step 1	Step 2	Step 3
Materials	Materials	Materials

DIRECTIONS AND PROCESS EXPLANATIONS

Teaching Strategies

After students have had a chance to study the visual aid, have them answer orally the questions that follow the diagrams. Discuss their answers and make sure the class has a good understanding of how the visual aid helps to explain the greenhouse effect. You can draw your own example of a visual aid on the chalkboard. Two examples should give students a good idea of how to create their own visual aids. Also, remind students to choose processes that will be well-suited to visual aids.

ANSWERS

1. The arrows show the direction in which heat is flowing at each stage in the process.

2. Answers will vary. Visual learners might say that the visual aid is more important.

3. Students' ideas will vary.

320

320

MAKING CONNECTIONS

DIRECTIONS AND PROCESS EXPLANATIONS

Visuals

Writing is only one way to explain. You can also explain by telling, showing, and drawing. *Visuals* (diagrams, drawings, charts) can make a complicated process or a set of directions much easier to understand. What complicated process does this visual explain?

How 'greenhouse effect' works

This year has been the USA's third-warmest on record, putting new focus on the debate about the "greenhouse effect." The current amount of greenhouse warming makes the Earth livable, but more could cause trouble.

1. Sun's energy warms the Earth . . .

2. . . . but the Earth radiates away heat.

3. Molecules of carbon dioxide, some other gases, radiate some heat back, keeping earth at an average of around 59 degrees. Without them, it would cool to around zero.

5. Scientists fear added gases will reflect too much heat back, warming the Earth and changing weather patterns.

4. Human activities, such as using fossil fuels, burning tropical rain forests, add carbon dioxide, other gases to the atmosphere.

USA Today, December 4, 1990. Copyright 1990, *USA Today*. Reprinted with permission.

1. This visual shows five steps. Notice the arrows. What do they show?

2. Can you understand the writing without the visual? Can you understand the visual without the writing? Which do you think is more important to you?

CAUSE AND EFFECT IN LITERATURE OBJECTIVES

- To analyze cause and effect in a folk tale
- To write a folk tale or a myth that explains the causes or effects of a human trait

3. Think of a process you can explain or a set of directions you can give to other students in your class. Here are some ideas:

- Explain how helicopters and hummingbirds are able to hover in the air.
- Explain how a pearl is formed in an oyster shell.
- Give directions for changing the oil in a car.
- Give directions on how to find the nearest shopping mall in your town or city.

After you choose your topic, plan an oral presentation to your class. Think through the steps in the process you're explaining or the directions you're giving, and create a visual that illustrates them. When you give your talk, use your visual to help your audience understand your explanation.

CAUSE AND EFFECT IN LITERATURE

Folk Tales

Our ancestors wondered why the world is the way it is: why animals are what they are, why people have certain characteristics. So our ancestors told folk tales to make connections between the causes and effects they saw, to explain the world of human and animal behavior. As you read the following Nigerian folk tale, ask yourself what it is trying to explain about beauty and character.

Why No One Lends His Beauty
by Harold Courlander with Ezekiel A. Eshugbayi

1   BEFORE, before, in the beginning of things, people wore their beauty as they wore clothes. It is said that there was a girl named Shoye who possessed beauty that was the pride of her village. Wherever she went, people said: "When before has anyone seen such beauty?"

There was another girl in the village named Tinuke. She did not have such beauty to wear. She envied Shoye. She went to her one day

CAUSE AND EFFECT IN LITERATURE
Teaching Strategies

You may want to read this folk tale to your class. Involve the class by asking students to follow along in their books and to read aloud what the people said whenever they see the words *people said*. For example, in the first paragraph they would read aloud, "When before has anyone seen such beauty?" (Or you might want to ask a group of volunteers to read the people's statements.)

If you wish, ask for a volunteer to read the chief's part as well.

USING THE SELECTION
Why No One Lends His Beauty

1

The word *before* is repeated to emphasize that this story took place a very long time ago.

2

What does this say about Shoye's character? [that she is generous and trusting]

3

Folk tales are tales that are handed down orally from generation to generation. Notice how important the voice of the people is throughout this folk tale.

4

Imagine beauty being a possession, like clothes. Do you think people would buy and sell it? What about plastic surgery? Can beauty be bought?

5

This is false cause and effect. Ugliness does not really cause bad luck.

6

What does this say about Tinuke's character? [Tinuke is ashamed of her behavior.]

7

Can you think of other stories in which someone who seemed ugly became beautiful? ["The Ugly Duckling," "The Frog Prince"]

8

This is personification. Beauty cannot really deceive — only people can deceive.

and said: "I must go on a journey for my family. I have no beauty.

2 Lend me your good looks until I return." Shoye did not hesitate. She gave her good looks to Tinuke. Tinuke took the beauty. Her face shone with it. She walked gracefully. She left the village and went on her journey.

3 People who saw her said: "Whenever has such a beautiful girl been seen?" She went to the town where a chief lived. His friends told him: "There is a girl in the town. She comes from another place. She has great beauty." The chief sent for Tinuke. He saw her beauty. He took her as a wife. She did not return to her own village.

Shoye waited. She was very ugly. When she went to the market, people said: "When before has anyone seen such ugliness?"

4 Tinuke did not return. Shoye's friends said: "Tinuke has surely stolen your beauty. You must find her." So Shoye went in search of Tinuke. She came to the town of the chief.

5 People said: "What ugliness! She has a hideous face! It will bring bad luck on us. Send her away!" But Shoye would not go away. She heard that Tinuke now lived in the house of the chief. She went

6 there. She asked for Tinuke. Tinuke would not come. She hid behind the walls of the chief's compound.

When the chief passed through his gate, he saw Shoye there. He said: "Who is the girl with the ugly face crouching before my estate?"

His guards said: "She asks for Tinuke. Tinuke will not see her."

The chief spoke to Shoye. He said: "Why do you wait here?"

Shoye answered: "I have a friend in my village. She borrowed my beauty. She came here. She now lives in your house. She does not return to her village. She does not return what she borrowed."

The chief said: "You mean that beautiful girl that I have taken as my wife? How could such beauty not belong to the one who wears it?" He sent for Tinuke. She came. She saw Shoye. She was ashamed. She

7 gave Shoye's beauty back to her. Shoye took it. Her face shone. She walked gracefully. Tinuke was now ugly.

People said: "Whenever has a chief had so ugly a wife?"

The chief said: "Beauty and good character are not the same thing. Because a woman wears beauty does not mean that she behaves well. This girl Tinuke came to me wearing beauty, but her character was faulty. Shoye, who was ugly because someone else borrowed her beauty, her behavior was good. One may borrow beauty but not good

8 character. Thus, beauty deceives. And, therefore, I order that henceforth one may not lend his beauty to another. Each person shall wear what is his own."

9   Thereafter, it was this way. One could neither lend nor borrow beauty. Each person wore what was his own. And there came to be a saying:

10   "Beauty is only worn; it is not the same as character."

Get together with two or three classmates and answer the following questions. You might want to divide up the questions among you and do some library research.

1. How is the problem between Tinuke and Shoye resolved? How does this folk tale explain the expression "beauty is only skin-deep"?

2. Many cultures (groups of people) have myths or folk tales that explain the causes or effects of human behavior. Find another cause-and-effect folk tale or myth, and share it with your class. (For example, in the story of Daedalus and Icarus, the ancient Greeks explained the dangers, or the effects, of being over-confident.)

3. Try writing a folk tale or myth that explains the causes or effects of a human trait or characteristic.

9

This story tells us the cause for the fact that, today, beauty is not something one can wear like clothes.

10

Stories from many cultures communicate the same message—that good character is more essential than beauty. Do you think that people have learned this lesson? Why or why not?

ANSWERS

1. Tinuke returns Shoye's beauty. This folk tale demonstrates the truth of the expression "beauty is only skin deep" by emphasizing the importance of good character over good looks.

2. If students have difficulty finding appropriate folk tales or myths, refer them to *World Tales* collected by Idries Shah, published by Harcourt Brace Jovanovich, Inc.

3. Students' folk tales or myths should explain the causes or the effects of some human trait.

SELECTION AMENDMENT
Description of change: excerpted
Rationale: to focus on the concept of cause and effect in literature presented in this chapter

WRITING TO PERSUADE

OBJECTIVES
- To choose a topic for a persuasive essay and to gather supporting details
- To write a draft of a persuasive essay
- To evaluate and revise a draft of a persuasive essay
- To proofread and publish a final draft of a persuasive essay

Motivation

A day or two before you begin this chapter, ask your students to look around their homes for examples of persuasive writing from sources other than newspapers or magazines. You may want to suggest that students look in the daily mail, especially if their households receive a lot of junk mail. On the day students bring their examples to class, choose three or four items and ask the class to give more detailed information about aspects of persuasive writing. For example, to explore audience analysis, ask students to tell why they think their families received the mailings. Are their families likely to be persuaded to do what the mailings ask? Are the statements mainly facts, or are they mainly opinions? Are opposing points of view considered? If they are, how are they presented?

Introduction

For many people, persuasion is one of the most important aims of writing. While attempts to persuade people coexist with literary, expressive, and informative writing, persuasive writing requires special attention as a separate category.

In the course of this chapter, each student will plan, write, revise, and publish a persuasive essay on a topic he or she chooses. You may want to emphasize at the start of the chapter that students need to make sure that their topics are suitable for persuasion and can be argued effectively. The best topics are those of immediate personal interest that students actually know something about or can learn about through research.

Integration

If you teach Shakespeare's *Tragedy of Julius Caesar,* you have at your disposal one of the best pieces of persuasive writing in the English language: Antony's "Friends, Romans, countrymen. . ." speech (Act III, Scene ii). You can have your students use the evaluation criteria on p. 352 to analyze why Antony's speech is effective.

You can also use Antony's speech to teach the critical-thinking skills of comparison and contrast by having your students compare Antony's funeral oration to Brutus' much less effective speech in the same scene ("Romans, countrymen, and lovers, hear me for my cause. . ."). Again, let students use the evaluation criteria presented in this chapter to analyze why Brutus fails where Antony succeeds. You can also use this chapter to teach your students how to organize and develop persuasive speeches.

If you want to teach critical reading skills, the **Critical Thinking** feature entitled **Evaluating Your Reasoning** on p. 340-341 offers five logical fallacies that students can look for in writing.

The chart on the next page illustrates the strands of language arts as they are integrated into this chapter. For vocabulary study, glossary words are underlined in some writing models.

QUOTATIONS
All **Quotations for the Day** are chosen because of their relevance to instructional material presented in that segment of the chapter and for their usefulness in establishing student interest in writing.

Selection	Reading and Literature	Writing and Critical Thinking	Language and Syntax	Speaking, Listening, and Other Expression Skills
"A Letter to the Duke of Milan" by Leonardo da Vinci 326-328 "Can Bicycles Save the World?" by Jane Bosveld 343-346 from *On Being a Writer* by Ellen Goodman 351 A letter to the editor by Emily R. Alling 357 from *My Life with Martin Luther King, Jr.* by Coretta Scott King 360-361	Finding details 329, 342, 346 Finding the main idea 329, 358 Evaluating a writer's opinion 329, 346, 358 Identifying tone 346 Interpreting a title 346 Analyzing a letter to the editor 358	Writing a journal entry 329 Applying interpretive and creative thinking 329, 334, 346, 350, 353-354, 358, 359 Evaluating a writer's effectiveness 329, 346, 353-354, 358 Responding personally to a piece of persuasive writing 329, 346, 358 Distinguishing fact from opinion 334 Writing an opinion statement 334, 358 Choosing a topic 334, 358, 361 Identifying opposing arguments 336, 350, 358 Analyzing illogical statements 341-342 Using prewriting techniques to find reasons and evidence 342, 358 Organizing support for an opinion 342, 358 Analyzing a persuasive essay 346, 351-352, 353-354 Writing a draft of a persuasive essay 350 Evaluating and revising a draft of a persuasive essay 351-352, 353-354 Analyzing a writer's revisions 353 Evaluating a persuasive essay 353-354 Proofreading and publishing a persuasive essay 355, 358 Identifying logical and emotional appeals 358 Writing a letter to the editor 358 Analyzing advertising for persuasive language 359 Writing a persuasive speech 362	Identifying connotations of words 346 Analyzing the relationship between connotation and tone 346, 353 Selecting appropriate tone 350 Analyzing the effects of specific words 353 Proofreading for errors in grammar, usage, and mechanics 355, 358 Analyzing loaded words, snob appeal, and testimonials 359-360	Working with classmates to distinguish fact from opinion 334 Identifying opposing arguments with classmates 336 Working with classmates to analyze a persuasive essay 346, 353-354 Making decisions in a small discussion group 353-354 Delivering a persuasive speech 361

CHAPTER 9

SEGMENT PLANNING GUIDE

Whether you are planning for a quick review of a writing concept or preparing an extended lesson on composition, you can use the following Planning Guide to adapt the chapter material to the individual needs of your class.

	SEGMENT	PAGES	CONTENT	RESOURCES
1	*Taking a Stand*	*325–329*		
	Literary Model **"A Letter to the Duke of Milan"**	326–328	Guided reading: a literary model of persuasive writing	
	Reader's Response/ Writer's Craft	329	Model evaluation: responding to literature and analyzing persuasive writing	
2	*Ways to Persuade*	*330–331*		
3	*Prewriting*	*332–342*		Supplying Reasons and Evidence
	Choosing a Topic	332	Guidelines: selecting topics for persuasive writing	
	Opinions	333	Guidelines: distinguishing fact from opinion	
	Exercise 1	334	Cooperative learning: distinguishing fact from opinion	
	Writing Assignment: Part 1	334	Applied practice: choosing a topic	
	Thinking About Purpose, Audience, and Tone	335	Guidelines: analyzing and selecting appropriate purpose, audience, and tone	
	Exercise 2	336	Cooperative learning: identifying opposing arguments	
	Supporting Your Opinion	337–338	Guidelines: examining persuasive methods	
	Emotional Appeals	339	Guidelines: using emotional appeals	
	Critical Thinking: Evaluating Your Reasoning	340–341	Guidelines: evaluating reasoning	
	Critical Thinking Exercise	341–342	Applied practice: evaluating illogical statements disguised as reasons	
	Writing Assignment: Part 2	342	Applied practice: supporting opinions	
4	*Writing*	*343–350*		Writing a Persuasive Essay
	The Basic Elements of Persuasive Essays	343	Introduction: analyzing basic elements in a persuasive essay	
	Literary Model **"Can Bicycles Save the World?"**	343–346	Guided reading: examining basic elements	
	Exercise 3	346	Cooperative learning: analyzing a persuasive essay	
	A Simple Framework for a Persuasive Essay	347	Introduction: analyzing basic elements in a model	
	A Writer's Model	347–350	Guided reading: examining an essay	

All the resources listed in this chapter are located in the Teacher's ResourceBank™.

SEGMENT	PAGES	CONTENT	RESOURCES
Chart: Framework for a Persuasive Essay	350	Guidelines: structuring a persuasive essay	
Writing Assignment: Part 3	350	Applied practice: writing a first draft	
5 *Evaluating and Revising*	*351-354*		Writing a Persuasive Essay
Literary Model from *On Being a Writer*	351	Guided reading: examining how a writer edits	
Chart: Evaluating and Revising Persuasive Essays	352	Guidelines: applying evaluation and revision techniques	
Exercise 4	353	Applied practice: analyzing a writer's revisions	
Exercise 5	353	Cooperative learning: evaluating a persuasive essay	
Grammar Hint	354	Writing suggestion: changing sentence length for emphasis	
Writing Assignment: Part 4	354	Applied practice: evaluating and revising	
6 *Proofreading and Publishing*	*355-356*		Writing a Persuasive Essay
Publishing	355	Publishing ideas: reaching a specific audience	
Writing Assignment: Part 5	355	Applied practice: proofreading and publishing	
A Student Model	355-356	Sample: deciding effectiveness of persuasion	
7 *Writing Workshop*	*357-358*		All the resources for this chapter may be used in this segment.
A Letter to the Editor	357	Guidelines: writing letters to express opinions	
Model/Questions	357-358	Examining techniques: analyzing a sample letter	
Writing a Letter to the Editor	358	Applied practice: applying skills to the writing process	
8 *Making Connections*	*359-361*		
Persuasion Across the Curriculum: Advertising and Persuasion	359-360	Guidelines: examining persuasive methods Cooperative learning: comparing and writing ads	
Speaking and Listening: Public Speaking and Persuasion	360-361	Guidelines: applying persuasive techniques to speeches	
LIterary Model from *My Life with Martin Luther King, Jr.*	360-361	Guided reading: examining a persuasive speech Applied practice: writing a persuasive speech	

WHOLE-CHAPTER RESOURCES
A Writing Process Log, A Writing Prompt, Holistically Graded Models, Assessment Portfolio Materials

OBJECTIVES

- To write responses to literature
- To identify and analyze the characteristics of persuasion
- To evaluate the persuasive qualities of a literary model

MOTIVATION

Initiate a class discussion on persuasion by using the following question:

When do you try to persuade someone to do something or to believe something?

Encourage varied responses and list them on the chalkboard.

 VISUAL CONNECTIONS
Welders

About the Artist. Ben Shahn (1898–1969) used art to express his opinions about issues important during his lifetime. Like a writer whose aim is to persuade readers to take action, Shahn sought to inspire his viewers to support the causes he believed in, such as antidiscrimination, workers' rights, and affordable health care. For viewers today, Shahn's prints offer a visual history of the major social issues of the first half of the twentieth century.

Exploring the Subject. This picture was intended to support antidiscrimination. It also served, with the added caption, to persuade workers to vote. The Congress of Industrial Organizations used the poster in its 1944 voter-registration campaign.

9 WRITING TO PERSUADE

for full employment after t
REGISTER

Have a volunteer read aloud the introductory paragraphs of the chapter. Point out that persuasive writing responds to the needs and values of the audience. Leonardo da Vinci's audience is a nobleman, Ludovico Sforza, for whom power and military superiority are of great importance.

The opening paragraph of the model on the next page might puzzle many of your students. Begin with a paraphrase of the paragraph to put the vocabulary difficulties aside and to prepare students for the list of reasons that Da Vinci presents to the duke. You may choose to read the entire letter to your class as they follow in the textbook and

Taking a Stand

Persuasion is the world of beliefs and opinions—the world where people **take a stand** and try to convince others to join them.

Writing and You. Like the artist whose work appears on these pages, we all take a stand at some time. Sometimes we use logical reasons to persuade others, but most of the time we use both logical reasons and emotional appeals. Politicians, for example, try to convince you to vote for them. Advertisers try to get you to buy their products. And you try to convince your parents to let you borrow the car on Saturday night. When was the last time you took a stand on something?

As You Read. Following is a letter written by Leonardo da Vinci in the fifteenth century. As you read, notice how he tries to persuade an Italian nobleman to give him a job.

Welders or *For Full Employment After the War*, Ben Shahn (1944). Lithograph in colors (poster). 27 3/8 " × 37 3/8 ". Collection of the New Jersey State Museum, Trenton, NJ. Gift of Circle F, FA1970.64.13. © 1993 Estate of Ben Shahn/VAGA, N.Y.

MEETING INDIVIDUAL NEEDS

LEP/ESL

General Strategies. You may want to allow students to work in small groups to answer the questions on p. 329 about Da Vinci's letter. Cooperation in group activities helps create a more relaxed classroom atmosphere, and students will be less afraid to ask questions and take risks in small groups.

to pause to determine if students are able to define unfamiliar words from context. If you have students read independently, you can prepare them by listing difficult vocabulary words on the chalkboard and explaining their meanings. Share your responses to questions 1 and 3 to model personal response and analysis.

ASSESSMENT

You can use students' answers to the **Reader's Response** and **Writer's Craft** questions to assess understanding of the material.

VISUAL CONNECTIONS
Exploring the Subject.
Leonardo da Vinci (1452-1519) was an artist, a scientist, and a scholar. He studied mathematics, physics, architecture, music, military engineering, anatomy, and biology. Ask students to explain the subject of each of these disciplines. Then have them discuss how the study of these subjects could help Da Vinci substantiate specific claims he makes in his letter.

USING THE SELECTION
A Letter to the Duke of Milan

1

Leonardo da Vinci is engaging in the age-old advertising trick of undercutting the competition. He implies that others only pretend ("pose") to be masters and suggests that their inventions are ordinary.

326

326

A Letter to the
Duke of Milan
by Leonardo da Vinci

Having, most illustrious lord, seen and considered the experiments of all those who pose as masters in the art of inventing instruments of war, and finding that their inventions differ in no way from those in common use, I am emboldened, without prejudice to anyone, to solicit an appointment of acquainting your Excellency with certain of my secrets.

RETEACHING

Give students copies of a short news story and of an editorial, preferably on the same subject. Work with the students to analyze and contrast both selections for their aims of writing [news story—informative; editorial—persuasive].

CLOSURE

Ask the class to give a brief definition of *persuasion*. Then ask student volunteers each to describe a situation that might call for persuasive speaking and one that might call for persuasive writing [speaking—asking to use the car; writing—applying for a scholarship].

☞

327

I I can construct bridges which are very light and strong and very portable, with which to pursue and defeat the enemy; and others more solid, which resist fire or assault, yet are easily removed and placed in position; and I can also burn and destroy those of the enemy.

II In case of a siege I can cut off water from the trenches and make <u>pontoons</u> and scaling ladders and other similar <u>contrivances</u>.

III
2
If by reason of the elevation or the strength of its position a place cannot be bombarded, I can demolish every fortress if its foundations have not been set on stone.

IV I can also make a kind of cannon which is light and easy of transport, with which to hurl small stones like hail, and of which the smoke causes great terror to the enemy, so that they suffer heavy loss and confusion.

2
Why doesn't Da Vinci explain his promises, such as how he would demolish fortresses? [Responses may vary. Perhaps he doesn't want to reveal his secrets; perhaps he is exaggerating.]

EXTENSION

Brainstorm with the class for examples of television or print advertisements. Then have students find examples of these advertisements. They can use the following questions to analyze the ads' techniques:

1. Which ads rely on famous people for promotion? Who are the people?

2. Which ads rely on appeals to emotions and needs? What are the emotions and needs?

3. Which ads appeal to the audience's logical side? Explain.

3

What would be the advantage of having Da Vinci "noiselessly construct" underground passages? [Noise might give away the troops' position.]

4

What does *ornamental* mean here? [beautiful, decorative] Why would Da Vinci say this about weapons? [Perhaps Da Vinci is aware that the duke wants his army to look good.]

V
3 I can noiselessly construct to any prescribed point subterranean passages either straight or winding, passing if necessary underneath trenches or a river.

VI I can make armored wagons carrying artillery, which shall break through the most serried ranks of the enemy, and so open a safe passage for his infantry.

VII
4 If occasion should arise, I can construct cannon and mortars and light ordnance in shape both ornamental and useful and different from those in common use.

VIII When it is impossible to use cannon I can supply in their stead catapults, mangonels, *trabocchi*, and other instruments of admirable efficiency not in general use—In short, as the occasion requires I can supply infinite means of attack and defense.

IX And if the fight should take place upon the sea I can construct many engines most suitable either for attack or defense and ships which can resist the fire of the heaviest cannon, and powders or weapons.

X In time of peace, I believe that I can give you as complete satisfaction as anyone else in the construction of buildings both public and private, and in conducting water from one place to another.

I can further <u>execute</u> sculpture in marble, bronze or clay, also in painting I can do as much as anyone else, whoever he may be.

Moreover, I would undertake the commission of the bronze horse, which shall <u>endue</u> with immortal glory and eternal honour the <u>auspicious</u> memory of your father and of the illustrious house of Sforza.——

And if any of the aforesaid things should seem to anyone impossible or impracticable, I offer myself as ready to make trial of them in your park or in whatever place shall please your Excellency, to whom I commend myself with all possible humility.

READER'S RESPONSE

1. Does this letter seem convincing to you? If you were the duke, would you hire Leonardo? Why?
2. Like Leonardo, have you ever tried to persuade someone to give you a job? What about the opposite—to persuade someone (probably a parent or a teacher) *not* to give you a job? In your journal, write a paragraph or two about your experience. Were you convincing?

WRITER'S CRAFT

3. What examples does Leonardo use to convince the duke that his inventions are different? Why does he include so many?
4. In the last paragraph, Leonardo uses a technique advertisers often use to persuade you to try something. What does he offer to do?
5. What picture of the writer comes through by the end of the letter?

5

To what emotions is Da Vinci appealing? [Responses may vary. He appeals to the duke's pride in his family.]

ANSWERS
Reader's Response

Responses will vary.

1. Most students will agree that Da Vinci presents a convincing case, although some might be skeptical of his claims. Students will likely say that they would hire him or at least accept his offer of a demonstration.

2. Students should provide specific details.

Writer's Craft

Responses will vary.

3a. Possible answers include his skill at building portable bridges, pontoons, ladders, light artillery, and armored weapons.

b. Da Vinci wants to show the duke that he has many valuable skills. If the duke can't use one of Da Vinci's talents, perhaps he can use another.

4. Da Vinci makes a "free trial offer."

5. He is confident, respectful, and humble.

TEACHING THE MODES

This segment gives students an overview of the four modes, or strategies, that writers have at their disposal. Persuasion is one of the aims, or purposes, of writing.

The others are the expressive, literary, and informative aims.

Some students might not immediately understand how evaluation is related to persuasion. Ordinarily, *evaluation* refers to making value judgments about something. When using the mode of evaluation as a means of persuading, writers concentrate on

COOPERATIVE LEARNING

Ask students to bring to class examples of persuasive material their families have received in the mail. Let students work in groups of three or four to analyze the modes used in the material. Point out that some writers use a combination of modes to develop their arguments, so students shouldn't be surprised to find more than one mode in a given document.

A DIFFERENT APPROACH

Show students a segment of a videotape of an extended commercial, and ask them to make a list of the modes that are used in the commercial. At the beginning of the activity, you may want to stop the video tape periodically to discuss how a particular mode is used to enable students to get used to looking for examples of the modes.

330

Ways to Persuade

Writers trying to persuade are like Leonardo—they want to get their readers to accept their opinion or move their readers to action.

Persuasive writing appears in many different forms and places—as newspaper editorials, as magazine articles, as speeches, and even as business memos. In each case, you as a writer or speaker are trying to convince others to accept your opinion. Here are some examples of the ways you can develop a persuasive message.

Narration: telling a story about a duck you found with a plastic ring around its neck to convince people not to litter our lakes and rivers; trying to convince your teacher that a hallway incident caused you to be late for class.

Description: describing your bicycle to someone you'd like to sell it to; describing a beach to convince your friends to go there with you.

Classification: defining the word *freedom* to convince people that they should register to vote; describing two shopping centers to convince your best friend that one is a better place to look for a new pair of jeans.

▶ **Evaluation:** deciding that the book you just read is worth reading and recommending it to the rest of your class; forming your own opinion about the importance of seat belts and writing a letter to the editor of your local paper, stressing their importance.

the good aspects of the idea or product to persuade others to accept the idea or product.

The textbook gives examples of the kinds of writing topics that can be approached through each mode. You may want to elaborate on this concept by having students work alone or in small groups to develop two or three more possible topics under each mode. You can then discuss these topics in class to make sure that everyone understands the four modes and their relation to persuasive writing.

To focus students more directly on evaluation, bring to class several ads from newspapers or magazines and ask students to analyze the ads by making a list of the good points about the products being emphasized. ■

LOOKING AHEAD

In the main assignment in this chapter, you'll use the strategy of evaluation to develop a persuasive essay. As you work through the writing assignments in the chapter, keep in mind that an effective piece of persuasive writing

- states the writer's opinion, or point of view, about the topic
- provides convincing support for the writer's opinion
- may use reasons and evidence as well as emotional appeals

MEETING INDIVIDUAL NEEDS

ADVANCED STUDENTS

Some students might enjoy the challenge of conducting original research to see which modes are used most often in editorial writing. Have students gather editorials from a variety of newspapers and magazines and analyze each one to find the primary mode used in each article, and the secondary mode(s) used in each article.

They can analyze the data they collect by calculating the percentage of use for each mode. You may want to have students work in pairs. In any case, all of the students involved in this research can pool their information to determine overall percentages. Ask students to explain why they think the numbers turned out the way they did.

This is Earth.

This is Earth without the ozone layer.

Don Wright, The Palm Beach Post

PREWRITING

OBJECTIVES

- To distinguish statements of fact from statements of opinion
- To select a topic for a persuasive essay and to create an opinion statement
- To use speaking and listening skills to identify and create support for opposing arguments
- To find and organize reasons and evidence to support an opinion

Teacher's ResourceBank™
RESOURCES

PREWRITING
- Supplying Reasons and Evidence

QUOTATION FOR THE DAY

"All men have a reason, but not all men can give a reason." (John Henry Cardinal Newman, 1801–1890, English theologian and writer)

Use the quotation as a springboard for discussion about using reasons to support a belief. Ask students if they can think of times when this quotation applied to them.

 VISUAL CONNECTIONS

Exploring the Subject. The baby seal in the photograph is a member of a species of seal that is hunted and brutally slaughtered every year for its fur. Hunters from Canada, the United States, Norway, and other countries round up large herds of pups and club them to death. The practice of hunting seal pups has been condemned by environmental and humanitarian organizations as cruel and inhumane and as a potential cause of extinction of the species.

Writing a Persuasive Essay

 Prewriting

Choosing a Topic

You have opinions on many different questions. For example, do you believe it's right or wrong to kill animals so that people can wear fur? Do you think that the government should ban the use of chemicals that may be changing the earth's climate? Or should the government wait for more evidence to come in?

Those particular questions may not matter much to you, but you may feel strongly about other issues that would be good topics for a persuasive essay. Before you choose a topic, think about these questions.

1. Is the topic important to you?
2. Do you have an opinion on the topic?
3. Do people have different opinions about the topic?
4. Is there an audience for you to convince?

An Important Topic. You may write about a topic of local interest, such as the need for a traffic signal at an intersection in your town. Or you may choose a topic of national interest, such as whether U.S. companies should sell advanced weapon systems to other countries.

Whatever topic you choose should matter to you, and it should be important enough to argue about. You won't change your readers' minds about a question of personal taste. For example, you can't persuade a cat owner that dogs are better pets than cats. Don't even try. But you

Lead students in a discussion of how they think advertisement writers prewrite. [They should mention very careful audience analysis, the product image the writers want to project, and the reasons that will be most convincing to the audience.] You may want to mention that the careers of many business people stand or fall on how persuasive their writing is. You could even invite a business professional, especially one in sales, to talk to the class about the role of persuasion in his or her career.

might want to argue for or against clearing the streets of all stray dogs and cats.

An Opinion, Not a Fact.   Remember the difference between an opinion and a fact. An *opinion* is a belief or a point of view. People can have different opinions about the same subject. For example, some people think that all teenagers are excellent drivers, but others believe that all teenagers are terrible drivers. You can't prove that either opinion is true—or untrue.

A *fact,* on the other hand, is a statement that can be checked. You can prove that a fact is true or false. It's a fact, for example, that insurance companies charge teenagers a higher premium than older drivers.

Opposing Opinions.   The saying "There are two sides to every question" applies especially to choosing a topic for a persuasive essay. A good topic has at least two conflicting sides. For instance, some people believe that students in public high schools should be required to wear uniforms. Others believe that such uniforms violate students' freedoms. And both sides offer sound arguments to support their opinion.

Finding Your Audience.   As you consider different topics, you need to think about who your audience will be. What group of people will most strongly object to what you have to say? And what are their reasons? As part of your essay, you'll have to refute (argue against) their reasons.

An Opinion Statement

Stating your opinion on the topic in one clear sentence will help you focus your thinking. Because this statement tells where you stand (your "position" on the topic), it's also called a position statement or proposition. Here are some examples.

> Our school should offer courses in an Asian language.
> Baseball stars deserve the high salaries they receive.
> Two years of community or military service should be required after graduation from high school.

MEETING INDIVIDUAL NEEDS

LEP/ESL

General Strategies. Students might be relatively unfamiliar with local and national issues that would ordinarily lend themselves to good persuasive topics. Emphasize that good persuasive writing doesn't have to deal with major public concerns. It can also concern very personal issues, including trying to persuade a friend to do something.

This segment is divided into three very closely related concerns that a writer must address before beginning a persuasive essay. You may want to approach the lesson with the idea that all three areas affect one another in a circular fashion. For example, the topic will appeal to a particular audience, but the audience will also affect how the writer's position is stated. The topic and audience will affect the reasons and evidence used in the essay, and the availability of reasons and evidence will in part determine how the topic is stated.

Have students survey the segment by skimming the pages and reading the boldface titles. List the sections in the segment on the chalkboard and explain how they are

 CRITICAL THINKING
Evaluation

It isn't always easy to judge whether a statement is fact or opinion because some statements are based on different interpretations of data. For example, the assertion by some scientists that global warming is taking place is based on one set of figures, but other scientists dispute that conclusion and say that those who believe in global warming aren't looking at the right set of numbers.

You can point out this problem to your students and discuss with them strategies for differentiating fact from opinion. [Some methods of analysis students might mention are investigating the credentials and possible self-interest of experts, learning about both sides of an issue before making a judgment, and maintaining a healthy skepticism.]

A DIFFERENT APPROACH

Point out to students that opinion statements usually contain the word *should* or can be easily rewritten to include *should*. They can test their opinion statements, as well as those of others, by including *should* with the verb.

When choosing a topic for a persuasive essay

- find a topic that's important to you by looking through magazines and newspapers, listening to television and radio, and brainstorming (see pages 27 and 32–33)
- know the opinions that conflict with yours on the issue
- identify the part of your audience that disagrees with you, the people that you want to convince
- write an opinion statement, a sentence that clearly states the topic and your opinion on it

EXERCISE 1 ▶ **Distinguishing Fact from Opinion**

In an argument, you can't let anyone pass off an opinion as if it were a fact. How good are you at telling them apart? Work with a partner or small group to decide whether each of the following statements is an *opinion* or a *fact*. Remember that an opinion is a point of view or a belief. A fact is a statement that can be checked or proved.

1. Earth is the most important planet in the solar system.
2. In 1609 Galileo aimed a telescope at the stars and discovered four of Jupiter's moons.   **1.** opinion   **2.** fact
3. When it re-enters the earth's atmosphere, the space shuttle orbiter is traveling more than 16,000 miles per hour.   **3.** fact
4. We know that there must be other intelligent beings in the universe.   **4.** opinion   **5.** fact
5. The Hubble space telescope cost 1.5 billion dollars.

 PART 1:
Choosing a Topic

Now you're ready to decide on a topic for your persuasive essay. Choose a topic that's important to you. For example, if you think that your community needs a youth center, who do you think should pay for it? When you have your topic clearly in mind, write an opinion statement.

interrelated. You may want to ask volunteers to read the material aloud so you can stop and comment on important areas of the lesson to make sure students understand the relevant concepts.

Some students might have trouble finding meaningful topics that are truly persuasive. You can help with this problem by encouraging students to review their journals and to think about events or situations at home or at school that they'd like to see changed. Review students' topics carefully to make sure they're appropriate for the assignment.

☛

Prewriting

Thinking About Purpose, Audience, and Tone

Your *purpose* in writing persuasion is to convince your readers (1) to follow the course of action you suggest or (2) to think differently about an issue.

To win your *audience* to your point of view, you must find out as much as you can about them. What do they already know about the issue? What concerns do they share with you? Why is their opinion different from yours? What's the strongest argument that they can come up with? For example, if you think that the food in the high school cafeteria should be improved, you may have to persuade several different groups. To analyze their concerns, you might make a chart like this one.

AUDIENCE	CONCERNS
Your classmates	More ethnic food; more variety; food that tastes better
Parents	Nutritious food that students will eat
Principal and teachers	Reasonable cost; no junk food
Cafeteria manager	Staying within budget; serving food that's easy to prepare, keep warm, and clean up

The *tone* of your essay is important because it reveals your attitude toward both your topic and your audience. (Remember that your attitude is conveyed by the language you use to write about your topic.) Describing the cafeteria food in a sarcastic tone may entertain your classmates, but it might turn off the people you most need to convince. A little humor might be effective, but your overall tone should be serious and formal.

COOPERATIVE LEARNING
The directions for **Exercise 1** ask students to work with a partner or a small group. When they've finished the items in the exercise, ask groups to analyze an editorial from a newspaper or magazine and to identify the statements of fact and opinion they find.

A DIFFERENT APPROACH
One way to help students understand the idea of audience for their essays is to have them visualize a person who they feel is representative of the type of people they are going to try to persuade and then to analyze how this person feels about the topic. This strategy can be especially effective if the audience is large and relatively diverse, such as the general public.

You can use the first two items in **Exercise 1** for guided practice. Work students through the items by talking about why the first item is an opinion and the second is a fact. You can do the same thing with **Exercise 2.**

You can provide guided practice for **Writing Assignment: Parts 1** and **2** in a

ANSWERS

Exercise 2

Responses will vary.
Every item should include a specific audience that is likely to object and logical reasons the audience might put forth in objection to the opinion. Here are some possibilities:

1. Some taxpayers might disagree, claiming that year-round school would increase taxes to pay for additional teachers, supplies, and so forth.

2. Some taxpayers might disagree because building the extra lanes would cost money that would have to come from higher taxes.

3. Toy manufacturers might disagree because it would cut back on the sale of their products and limit their right of free speech.

4. Physical education teachers might disagree because many students don't have time for physical exercise except during physical education classes.

5. High school athletes might disagree because this restriction isn't placed on any other school activity.

336   *Writing to Persuade*

EXERCISE 2 ▶ **Speaking and Listening: Identifying Opposing Arguments**

A good debater can argue either side of an issue. This exercise gives you practice in looking at issues from opposing points of view. Work in a small group to focus on these two questions:

  a. *What group might strongly disagree with this opinion?*
  b. *What might their reasons be for disagreeing?*

For each opinion statement, let one person identify an audience that might strongly disagree. Then have other group members pretend to be that opposing audience, thinking of their reasons for disagreeing with the opinion statement.

> EXAMPLE OPINION: Motorcyclists should be required to wear safety helmets.
>
> *What group might strongly disagree?* some motorcyclists
> *What reasons might they give for disagreeing?*
> 1. A helmet takes away much of the pleasure we get from riding a motorcycle. We like to feel the wind in our hair.
> 2. It's our right to make decisions about our own safety.

1. The school year should be extended year-round to twelve months.
2. Our community must create bicycle lanes on all major roads.
3. Commercials should be banned on children's television programs.
4. Physical education classes are unnecessary for high school students.
5. High school athletes should be required to have a 3.0 grade-point average to participate in school sports.

Let students work on the exercises and the writing assignments independently. If you have students generate topics as homework, you may want to spend some time the next day in class putting some of the topics on the chalkboard and talking about their strengths and weaknesses. You can do the same thing with students' reasons and evidence. After you've discussed several topics, give students an opportunity to rethink some of their topics before you collect assignments.

Prewriting

Supporting Your Opinion

Experience may have already taught you that most people won't change just because you tell them they should change. To persuade others, you have to present your reasons logically and back up each reason with evidence. Sometimes it helps to appeal to their emotions, too.

No matter what you write, you may be unable to persuade people who strongly oppose your opinion. But your essay will be successful if you can at least make them understand and respect your point of view.

Logical Appeals

Two kinds of logical appeals—*reasons* and *evidence*—are aimed at your audience's ability to think.

Reasons. *Reasons* tell why readers should accept an opinion. For example:

Opinion: A drivers' training course should be a requirement for high school graduation.
Reasons: 1. Teenagers who take drivers' training courses are better drivers.
2. Good driving is an essential skill for nearly every adult.

But reasons alone will persuade few readers. Most readers want proof that your reasons make sense.

Evidence. *Evidence* supplies proof for your reasons. There are two kinds of evidence:

■ *facts*—statements that can be checked by testing, personal observation, or reading a reliable reference source.

 a. Of the students who took drivers' training at our school last year, 93 percent passed the state licensing examination on the first try.
 b. Because teenagers who take drivers' training have fewer accidents, insurance companies charge them lower rates.

INTEGRATING THE LANGUAGE ARTS

Speaking Link. You may want to have your students stage a mock debate on one or more of the items in **Exercise 2.** One or two students can take the affirmative position and argue in favor of the idea stated in the topic, and one or two others can take the negative side and argue against the idea. Students should prepare their points ahead of time and support their statements with facts and statistics whenever possible. Refer to **Chapter 30** for more information on speaking.

A DIFFERENT APPROACH

You may want to use the format of **Exercise 2** and have students choose their own topics. Students can work in groups of four or five, and group members can offer opposing ideas as each person in the group presents his or her topic.

CRITICAL THINKING
Evaluation

Rarely are all the facts given in support of an opinion equally relevant. Lead your students in a discussion of the criteria they should use in judging whether a fact is useful or not. Some useful criteria include how old the fact or statistic is, how large a group the fact or statistic represents, and the relevance of the fact to the situation under discussion.

INTEGRATING THE LANGUAGE ARTS

Library Link. The school library can be a valuable resource for students who are writing persuasive essays. Ask your librarian to give an orientation talk to your class, with special emphasis on the library's vertical file and periodicals collection.

You can use performance on the exercises to assess students' understanding of the concepts. The topics should be statements of opinion that students are likely to know something about (or be able to find information about), and they should also be specific enough to be handled in essays of three to four body paragraphs. Reasons and evidence should be factual and should appeal to the audiences the students intend to persuade. Reasons should be organized in a logical pattern, probably least-to-most important, although other patterns are possible.

■ *expert opinion*—statements by a recognized authority on the subject.

Alida Shumway, state highway commissioner, has said, "Teenagers who have completed a driver training course are safe drivers. There's no substitute for quality instruction from professionals in a school setting."

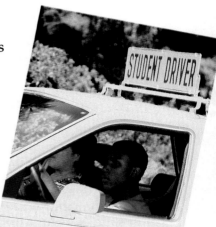

Finding Reasons and Evidence. For some opinions, you'll be able to use reasons and evidence that come from common knowledge and your own observations. For other issues, such as those having to do with national policy or science, for example, you may depend heavily on expert opinions and current information from reliable sources. You may also want to use nonprint sources—such as documentary and instructional videotapes and audiotapes—to gather support for your opinion. As you collect ideas and information, be sure to take notes. Don't try to sort out the stronger reasons and pieces of evidence from the weak ones until you've finished your research.

To find reasons and evidence to support your opinion

■ brainstorm, cluster, or freewrite to find out what you already know (see pages 26–29)
■ read books, magazine articles, or newspapers for information on your topic
■ talk with experts and others interested in the topic

RETEACHING

If students need help distinguishing between fact and opinion, give them index cards on which you have written facts and opinions. Have each student work in groups to take a turn reading a card aloud to identify the statement as fact or opinion.

CLOSURE

Lead students in a discussion of the most important pieces of persuasive writing they've ever seen. These could include TV commercials, printed ads, editorials, or any other type of persuasion. Ask students to identify the one feature of the writing that they found most effective.

Cont. on p. 342

Prewriting   **339**

Emotional Appeals

Which do you think are more powerful—appeals to logic or appeals to emotion (feelings)? Don't underestimate emotions. Advertisers rely almost entirely on emotional appeals to persuade you to buy their products. Emotional appeals can be convincing in a persuasive essay, too.

Think about how you want your audience to feel about your topic. Then tell about a personal experience or include an example that appeals to that emotion. For example, if you want to convince your audience to volunteer to read at a nursing home, you might use examples that awaken feelings of compassion. You could describe your visit with a stroke patient, a former teacher who helped many children learn to read, but can no longer read on her own.

Emotional appeals alone won't persuade people who strongly disagree with you. In fact, they are likely to become angry at this tactic. Use emotional appeals only when you think they might convince the audience.

WRITING NOTE

As you know, words have both denotative and connotative meanings. The *denotative* meaning is the dictionary definition. *Connotative* meanings are the feelings or attitudes that a word suggests. Words like *predator, slaughter, victim, home, family*, and *freedom* are just a few of the many words that are loaded with emotional meanings. Recognize the power of emotional words, and choose them carefully in an essay that emphasizes logical reasons and evidence.

PEANUTS reprinted by permission of UFS, Inc.

CRITICAL THINKING
Analysis

Ask students to work in pairs to analyze ads from magazines for emotional appeal. Students might focus on identifying the aspects of the ads that have emotional appeal and on recognizing the emotions to which they appeal. Is the emotional appeal justified? Does the emotional appeal divert readers from more serious questions about the product? Does the emotional appeal distort the truth about the product?

OBJECTIVE

- To evaluate and label faulty and illogical reasons

Begin the lesson by asking students how they react when they hear or read something that is obviously illogical. You can point out that sometimes people make illogical statements on purpose.

Ask students to read the first item, **Attacking the Person,** and to comment on

ADVANCED STUDENTS

Have students use the following questions to evaluate and analyze four television commercials:

1. What is the product's name?
2. What sales techniques are used?
3. What connotative language is used?
4. How would you evaluate the persuasive appeal of each commercial?

LESS-ADVANCED STUDENTS

You may want to rearrange the order of the **Critical Thinking** lesson slightly in working with students. Start with the second example of illogical reasoning, **False Cause and Effect,** because it is clearer than some of the others. After your students understand the concept of illogical reasoning, you can work with them on the other examples.

340

CRITICAL THINKING

Evaluating Your Reasoning

Your persuasive essay should be based on sound reasons and factual evidence. Here are five kinds of statements that look like reasons but really aren't because they're not logical. Study these five kinds of tricky statements carefully. When you're the person who's being persuaded, you should read and listen critically and be able to say, "Hey, wait a minute. *That's* not logical at all."

Statements Disguised as Reasons

1. **Attacking the Person.** Called "negative campaigning" in politics, this technique is also known as "name-calling." It weakens an argument because it doesn't deal with the real issues.

Attacking the Person	People who vote "no" on the school referendum don't care about children.
Facing the Issue	We need to hire more teachers. If we don't pass the school referendum, classes will have 35–40 students next year.

2. **False Cause and Effect.** Don't assume that one event caused the event that happened next. One event can follow another without having anything to do with the first event. What's wrong with the reasoning in this example?

First Event	A pharmaceutical company built a plant near the river this spring.
Second Event	Tests this summer show that the river is polluted.
False Cause-Effect	This plant is causing the river's pollution.

3. **Hasty Generalization.** Don't base a conclusion on inadequate evidence.

Inadequate Evidence	The first time I played baseball, I hit a home run.
Hasty Generalization	Baseball is an easy game that I can play well without having to practice.

why this reasoning is illogical. [It draws attention away from the main argument, and is therefore also misleading; in the example, for instance, the technique denies the fact that people who care about children may have good reasons for voting against the referendum.] Then ask students to give other examples of this kind of illogical reasoning. Handle each of the five types of illogical reasoning in this manner.

You can check students' understanding of illogical reasoning by examining how well they do on the **Critical Thinking Exercise** or how well they are able to eliminate illogical reasoning from their writing.

4. **Circular Reasoning.** When you restate your opinion in different words, don't try to pass off the restatement as a reason. In this example, both sentences say the same thing.

Statement of Opinion	Anna is the best choice for tenth-grade student council representative.
Circular Reasoning	She's the person who can do the finest job as tenth-grade student council representative.

5. **Either-Or.** The either-or thinker describes a situation in terms of two extreme alternatives and suggests that there is only one correct choice. Usually there are several choices between the two extremes.

Either-Or Reasoning	If you don't call me every night, you don't love me.

There may be several other reasons why someone doesn't call every night.

 CRITICAL THINKING EXERCISE:
Evaluating Reasons

Can you detect illogical statements disguised as reasons? Read the opinion and the statements that support it. Tell whether each statement is (a) attacking the person, (b) false cause and effect, (c) hasty generalization, (d) circular reasoning, or (e) either-or reasoning.

Opinion: Offering advanced placement (AP) classes is a waste of school time and money.

Supporting Statements:
1. Some AP students score poorly on the AP exam, which proves that AP classes don't get results.
2. Anyone who thinks that AP classes should be kept must be completely out of touch with reality.
3. We must cut the AP classes, or we won't be able to give an adequate education to our average students.

COOPERATIVE LEARNING
You may want to let your students work in groups of three or four to examine letters to the editor of a local newspaper to identify examples of faulty reasoning. You can also have them analyze newspaper and magazine headlines for examples of **false cause and effect**.

ANSWERS
Critical Thinking Exercise
1. hasty generalization
2. attacking the person
3. either-or reasoning
4. circular reasoning
5. false cause and effect

Cont. from p. 339
ENRICHMENT

Consumer Reports magazine regularly publishes a feature in which readers write in to point out misleading and false claims in advertising. Ask your school librarian for back issues to share with the class. Then ask students to give examples of their experiences with products or services they feel were misrepresented in advertising. Ask students what consumers can do to protect themselves from false advertising claims. [Suggestions might include researching publications like Consumer Reports, checking with friends who have tried the products, and reading disclaimers carefully.] ■

COOPERATIVE LEARNING

Students can work on **Writing Assignment: Part 2** in groups of three or four. The groups can brainstorm to find ideas for each group member and then the members can help each other to evaluate the usefulness of each reason or piece of evidence.

---

4. AP classes are the courses that are most easily dispensed with. Therefore, these are the courses that should be cut from the curriculum.
5. Before we had AP classes, our overall dropout rate at the high school was 10 percent. Now our overall dropout rate is 18 percent. It's obvious that our concentration of time and money on AP classes has increased the number of dropouts.

WRITING ASSIGNMENT   PART 2:
Supporting Your Opinion

Build your argument on a solid foundation of reasons and evidence to support your opinion. To organize your ideas, you can use a chart like the following one. As you list your reasons and evidence, decide what order you'll put them in. If you need more reasons, facts, and expert opinions, find them by reading and talking about your topic. Try to include an emotional appeal unless your teacher asks you to use only logical appeals.

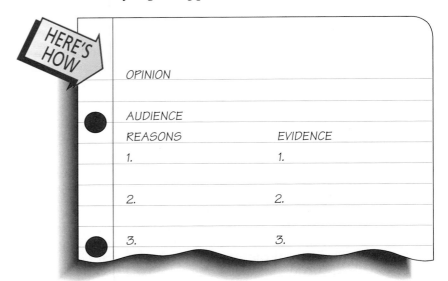

HERE'S HOW

OPINION	
AUDIENCE	
REASONS	EVIDENCE
1.	1.
2.	2.
3.	3.

WRITING YOUR FIRST DRAFT

OBJECTIVES

- To analyze a persuasive essay
- To write the first draft of a persuasive essay

MOTIVATION

Have students draw upon their experiences of watching television programs about lawyers and court trials. Ask what kinds of things lawyers say in their summation speeches to persuade the jury. Lead students to the realization that lawyers use the same techniques writers use to persuade—☞

Writing Your First Draft

The Basic Elements of Persuasive Essays

You've gathered your ideas for a persuasive essay. Now it's time to organize them into a composition that will convince your audience.

Keep in mind that a persuasive essay

- takes a stand on a topic that people disagree on
- tries to persuade an audience to think and perhaps act as the writer suggests
- uses reasons and evidence
- sometimes appeals to the audience's emotions

Professional writers combine these basic elements in different ways. As you read the following editorial, notice how the writer uses these basic elements to convince you.

A MAGAZINE EDITORIAL

Opinion

Can Bicycles Save the World?
by Jane Bosveld

Attention grabber

Background

Emotional appeal
Opposing opinion

Emotional appeal
Opinion

"Great Britain isn't as advanced as we are," wrote an American student in 1967. "Probably half the people still ride bicycles." The student was wrong about bicycle ridership in Britain—only about one in four Brits owns a bike, and most ride for leisure, not as alternative transport. But the American student's observation reflects the prevailing attitude in industrial nations that bicycles are somehow second-class vehicles, dwarfed by the power and convenience of automobiles. A bike, of course, won't win any contests of speed or long-distance commuting, but in an age when the <u>implications</u> of pollution threaten the health of the world, human power is looking better and better.

1

Teacher's ResourceBank™
RESOURCES

> **WRITING YOUR FIRST DRAFT**
> - Writing a Persuasive Essay

QUOTATION FOR THE DAY

"There is no rule on how to write. Sometimes it comes easily and perfectly; sometimes it's like drilling rock and then blasting it out with charges." (Ernest Hemingway, 1899–1961, American writer)

As students begin writing their first drafts, share the quotation with the class. You may wish to have students write journal entries telling whether or not they agree with Hemingway's comments about writing.

USING THE SELECTION
Can Bicycles Save the World?

1

Why does Bosveld use this slang term for the British? [It helps create an informal tone.] Would British people find this offensive? [They probably are not any more offended by this than Americans are offended by being called Yanks by the British.]

TEACHING THE LESSON

You may want to consider having student volunteers read this segment orally. The model essay on bicycles contains several vocabulary words and figures of speech that may be unfamiliar to students, and you can help them derive the meanings from context.

One of the questions in **Exercise 3** asks that students identify the tone of the

2

Why does Bosveld use the expression "horseless carriages" instead of "automobiles" or "cars"? [This suggests that it's been a long time since bicycles had much prestige as a means of transportation. It also supports the informal tone.]

Emotional appeals

Opinion

Reasons

2 Bicycle lovers have longed for the day when their machines would regain the respectability lost after horseless carriages took over the streets. They have <u>proselytized</u> about the joys of bike riding: the closeness one feels to nature when pedaling through the countryside; the <u>exhilaration</u> one feels at making it up a long hill or skillfully maneuvering through a busy intersection. Biking, they contend, is the one exercise suitable for just about everyone. When you ride a bike, the bike bears the weight of your body, allowing you to exercise your muscles without taxing your joints. Many an individual suffering from arthritis or knee trouble has turned to the bicycle for relief.

3

lobbying: attempting to influence, usually referring to pressure put on lawmakers to adopt, modify, or stop a particular bill

4

think tank: an informal name for an institution devoted to research and analysis of data

Background

Emotional appeal

3 Bicycle activists have mobilized in most North American and European cities, lobbying transportation departments for bike lanes and trying to rustle up support from nonbicycle riders. Despite these efforts, however, transportation planners have remained <u>notoriously</u> unsympathetic to the needs of bikers. It is a stance we may all come to regret. Consider these facts published in a recent article by the Worldwatch
4 Institute, a major think tank for environmental conservation:

model. Because tone is a concept that students often have difficulty with, you can help by suggesting that they imagine how the tone of voice of the writer, Jane Bosveld, would sound if she were reading the essay aloud. Then explain and illustrate how the connotations of words help create tone so that students will be attentive to informal words and expressions that denote tone.

You can model analyzing an essay for **Exercise 3** by discussing the first item in the exercise with the class. You can point out that a good title often deals with the implied theme or main idea of a piece of writing.

You can use the framework in the chart on p. 350 for guided practice in writing a first draft. Ask students to write the opening paragraphs of their drafts and then to ☞

Evidence/Facts   5
6
7

• Gasoline and diesel fuel emissions are major contributors to acid rain and the depletion of the ozone layer. They are also linked to about 30,000 deaths each year in the United States alone. Interestingly, the worst pollution comes from short car trips, because a cold engine is particularly inefficient, releasing a high percentage of unburned <u>hydrocarbons</u> into the atmosphere. Many of these short trips could easily be done on a bike.

Evidence/Facts

• If just 10 percent of the Americans who commute to work by car rode their bikes to work or to a train or bus that would take them to work, more than $1.3 billion could be cut from the U.S. oil import bill. Oil imports account for nearly a quarter of the country's $171 billion trade deficit. . . .

8

Expert opinion

    "In their enthusiasm for engine power," writes Marcia D. Lowe, author of the Worldwatch article, "transit planners have overlooked the value of human power. With congestion, pollution, and debt threatening both the industrial and developing worlds, the vehicle of the future clearly rides on two wheels. . . ."

Call to action

    But what would happen if we began to use bicycles more frequently? If, say, we hopped on a bike to go get a gallon of milk or to visit friends on the other side of town? What if we saved the car for big hauls and long trips? Before this can happen, of course, much must be done to make bicycle riding safe and pleasurable. Biking may be wonderful exercise and environmentally sound, but few individuals will be willing to pedal down roads where cars and trucks zoom past them with inches to spare, leaving the biker to wobble in a blast of air. Until roads are built with bike lanes or at least wide shoulders, few people are likely to get in the habit of biking. Even with those improvements, it will

Summary of reasons

Emotional appeal

Call to action   9

5

Notice how Bosveld persuades through evaluation. Here she points out the disadvantages of the types of vehicles that have replaced the bicycle.

6

Acid rain contains particles of toxic pollution that turn the rain from a neutral liquid into an acid that makes the water deadly to animals and kills vegetation.

7

Scientists studying the atmosphere of Venus in 1974 discovered that chlorine destroys ozone and that chlorine is being released into earth's atmosphere by industry and aerosol household products.

8

In an unfavorable trade deficit, more money is spent buying imported goods than is earned selling exported goods. When this happens, interest rates (the cost of borrowing money) rise and business growth slows down.

9

Notice that Bosveld states another opinion as though it were a fact. How are her arguments about transportation planning related to the bicycle? [Bike lanes must exist before people will start taking advantage of the bicycle for transportation.] Is this reason logically sound? [Bosveld comes close to committing the fallacy of false cause and effect.]

share these with the class. By discussing some of the better opening paragraphs with the whole group, you can guide students' work in this phase of their writing.

INDEPENDENT PRACTICE

Even if you work through one or two of the items in **Exercise 3** with the whole class, the other items in the exercise should provide students with ample practice in analyzing persuasive writing. You can let students work on their drafts independently either in class or at home.

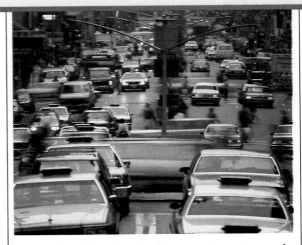

take a shifting of attitudes to get most people to take up two-wheel travel. People will need to believe that even one less trip in the car adds up to something, that riding a bicycle is, like recycling paper or conserving electricity, an endeavor worth pursuing. Deciding to ride a bike is taking on responsibility. Not everyone will choose to do so, but for everyone who does, the world, rest assured, will be at least a little better off.

Omni

Emotional appeal

Call to action

Emotional appeal

ANSWERS
Exercise 3

Responses will vary.

1. Bosveld's opinion statement seems to be "People can help save the environment by riding bicycles." Some students might be unconvinced, but most will probably be persuaded by Bosveld's arguments.

2. The essay's title is a statement of the main idea of the essay. Students' opinions of the title will vary.

3. Bosveld's main reason is that by cutting down the number of motorized vehicles people use, bicycle riding will help preserve the environment. She probably provides so much evidence to support this point because she knows that riding bicycles represents a radical departure from the lifestyles most Americans are used to. Her other reasons include the closeness to nature a person feels on a bike, the exhilaration that comes from a bike ride, and the exercise that bike riding provides.

4. Some strong connotative meanings are found in the words: *Brits, dwarfed, horseless carriages, proselytized, countryside, maneuvering, rustle up, notoriously,* and *hopped.* The tone is informal and hopeful.

EXERCISE 3 ▸ **Analyzing a Persuasive Essay**

Meet with two or three classmates to discuss the following questions.

1. What opinion statement do you think Jane Bosveld might have started with? Does she convince you?
2. What does the essay's title have to do with the writer's opinion? How do you like her title?
3. Which reason for her opinion does Bosveld emphasize? Why do you think she supplies so much evidence for this reason? What other reason(s) does she give?
4. Find some words that have strong connotative meanings. What would you say is the tone of this essay?

Evaluate students' responses to the questions in **Exercise 3** to determine how well they are able to analyze persuasive writing. Collect drafts of the essays to determine if students have the basic idea of how a persuasive essay should be organized and what elements it should contain. Do not make extensive comments on flaws in grammar, usage, and mechanics, because these problems can be addressed later. However, you will probably want to make sure that students have included the following items:

1. an appropriate topic for persuasive writing
2. a stated or clearly implied opinion
3. logical reasons and evidence to support the position
4. logically organized support

WRITING NOTE

Professional writers' persuasive essays aren't all alike. For instance, the statement of opinion may come right at the beginning of the essay, or it may appear much later. It may be stated directly in a sentence or two, or indirectly in a question or title. The number of reasons varies, and so does the order in which they're given. (The most important reason can be first or saved for last.) Some writers stick to logical appeals alone, but most include emotional appeals. A call to action—telling readers what action to take—may be present or left out entirely.

A Simple Framework for a Persuasive Essay

The essay "Can Bicycles Save the World?" shows you how one professional writer put together a persuasive essay. The following essay illustrates a framework or basic structure that you can use for your own essay.

A WRITER'S MODEL

Something Good for the Earth

INTRODUCTION

Garbage! It smells bad and looks disgusting. Most people prefer not to think about trash more than once a day when they "take it out." We in the United States get rid of a great deal of garbage. In fact, we throw away 40 percent of all the garbage in the world.

Attention grabber

Background

BODY

What's in that garbage that we toss out? Of the 200 million tons of garbage that U.S. citizens produce yearly, approximately 42 percent is paper (made from trees), 8 percent is glass, 9 percent is metal (from ore, a natural resource), 7 percent is plastic (from petroleum, a natural resource), 8 percent is rubber (from rain forests), 8 percent is food waste, and 18 percent is yard waste.

Facts and statistics

Try using **A Writer's Model** for reteaching. Work with students to answer the following questions:

1. Why does the writer give statistics in the second paragraph? [They help to establish the extent of the problem.]

2. How does the title reflect the writer's opinion? [The title is a restatement of the writer's feelings on the value of recycling.]

3. Has the writer chosen the best order in which to present reasons? [Yes, the statement of opinion follows an attention grabber and is supported by reasons and evidence.]

INTEGRATING THE LANGUAGE ARTS

Literature Link. If the work is available in your literature textbook, have students read the poem "The Forester" by Wilford Wilson Gibson, before they read **A Writer's Model.** Gibson's short poem is about a forester who is visited by the spirit of the wood, presumably come to punish him for having spent a lifetime cutting down trees. After students read the poem, ask them to address the following questions:

1. Why does the spirit of the wood take the forester with her? [The spirit wants to punish him for destroying the forest.]

2. How can this poem be considered a piece of persuasive writing in favor of recycling? [The spirit of the wood is striking back by punishing the forester for cutting down trees. The poet indirectly persuades readers to conserve natural resources by metaphorically showing the consequences of failing to conserve.]

Government officials estimate that 60 percent of our nation's trash could be recycled. Environmentalists suggest a much higher figure—as much as 70 to 90 percent. — **Statistics**

You can help do something good for the earth by recycling. Perhaps the most important reason for recycling is that it saves precious natural resources. Every week, for example, 50,000 trees are sacrificed to produce Sunday newspapers in the United States. Just by recycling newspapers, you can help to save a forest. — **Statement of opinion** / **Reason**

In addition to the direct savings of natural resources, recycling saves water and energy. Recycling paper instead of making paper from trees reduces water use by 60 percent and energy use by 70 percent. Aluminum cans show the biggest saving from recycling. It takes 95 percent less energy to produce a can from recycled aluminum than from ore. — **Reason** / **Explanation** / **Evidence/ Facts**

The third reason for recycling is that it reduces the mountains of garbage we produce. Garbage, unfortunately, doesn't disappear like magic after it's hauled away. For many years garbage was dumped into landfills, which also created — **Reason** / **Explanation**

CLOSURE

Ask for a volunteer to give the basic elements of a persuasive essay [takes a stand on an arguable topic, persuades reader to act or think as the writer, uses reasons and evidence, sometimes uses emotional appeals].

Writing Your First Draft **349**

monumental pollution problems. In older landfills, toxins leached into the soil and ground water, finding their way eventually into the food chain. And now we're running out of places that will accept garbage for landfill. The Environmental Protection Agency estimates that in the next ten years half of our cities will run out of landfill space.

Evidence/ Facts

Evidence/ Expert opinion

People object to recycling projects for two reasons. Recycling costs too much, they complain, adding to already over-burdened budgets. But taxpayers also overwhelmingly approve recycling fees, and recycling actually saves money because there's less solid waste disposal. Their second objection is that people are too lazy to separate trash and wash out cans and bottles. But that's not true. Across the nation, officials have been amazed at how willing residents pitch in and recycle.

Opposing argument

Facts against

Opposing argument

Facts against

CONCLUSION   Recycling is something each of us can do to help the earth. Trash makes our home, this planet, less livable for the children of today and tomorrow. We caused the problem, and we can solve it. Will you help?

Restatement of opinion

Emotional appeal

Call to action

 A DIFFERENT APPROACH
Some students who are familiar with outlining might find it a more convenient way to organize their essays. You can refer students to the material on outlining in **Chapter 3: "Understanding Composition Structure."**

INTEGRATING THE LANGUAGE ARTS

Literature Link. Have your students evaluate Brutus's funeral speech in Shakespeare's *The Tragedy of Julius Caesar* for its persuasive devices. Students can use the following chart to gather support in prewriting:

Devices	Examples
Logical Appeals (evidence)	
Personal Appeals (gaining audience's trust)	
Emotional Appeals (wants and needs of the audience)	

Have students find short persuasive essays in books or periodicals. Then have them identify the role each sentence plays in the essay—is it an opinion? a reason? supporting evidence? an appeal to the emotions? If possible, have students mount a copy of the essay on paper and color-code each category. Then you will be able to scan and grade quickly. ■

A DIFFERENT APPROACH

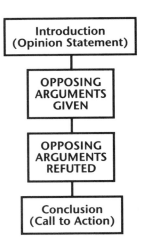

Another more complex structure for a persuasive essay is a framework called "straw man." In it the writer systematically presents and then refutes the arguments that would oppose his or her thesis. The following diagram shows the structure:

Introduction
(Opinion Statement)

OPPOSING
ARGUMENTS
GIVEN

OPPOSING
ARGUMENTS
REFUTED

Conclusion
(Call to Action)

You may find it helpful to model your own persuasive essay after the one on recycling. It follows the framework given below. The number of reasons and amount of evidence you use will depend on your topic and your audience.

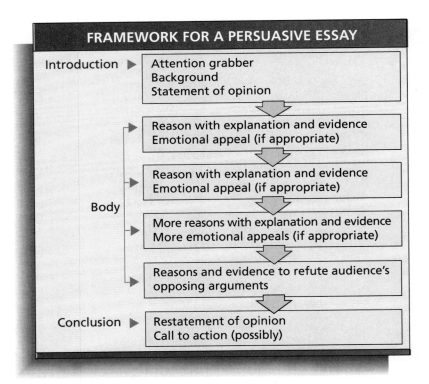

FRAMEWORK FOR A PERSUASIVE ESSAY

Introduction ▶
- Attention grabber
- Background
- Statement of opinion

Body
- Reason with explanation and evidence
  Emotional appeal (if appropriate)
- Reason with explanation and evidence
  Emotional appeal (if appropriate)
- More reasons with explanation and evidence
  More emotional appeals (if appropriate)
- Reasons and evidence to refute audience's opposing arguments

Conclusion ▶
- Restatement of opinion
- Call to action (possibly)

WRITING ASSIGNMENT

PART 3:
Writing a Draft of Your Persuasive Essay

You have everything you need to start writing. Using the basic framework as a model, write a first draft of your persuasive essay. Keep your audience in mind as you write. Think of the strongest objection opponents might have to your opinion. What reasons and evidence can you use to convince them to change their thinking?

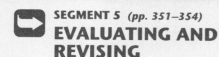

SEGMENT 5 *(pp. 351–354)*
EVALUATING AND REVISING
OBJECTIVES
- To analyze a writer's revisions
- To evaluate and revise a persuasive essay

TEACHING THE LESSON
The central focus of this segment is the chart on p. 352. You may want to read and analyze it with your students. After students have had a chance to ask questions, you can let them work on **Exercises 4** and **5** before they attempt to evaluate and revise their drafts.

☞

Evaluating and Revising

You have what looks like a whole essay, but you're not really finished yet. Now you need to take the time to think about your draft and decide what changes would make it better. As you do this, remember that you're not alone—most professional writers treat evaluating and revising as essential parts of the writing process. Perhaps you've read Ellen Goodman's column in your local newspaper. Goodman is a Pulitzer Prize winner and a nationally syndicated columnist—and here's what she has to say about making that extra effort in her writing.

> What makes me happy is rewriting. In the first draft, you get your ideas and your theme clear. If you're using some kind of metaphor you get that established, and certainly you have to know where you're coming out. But the next time through, it's like cleaning house, getting rid of all the junk, getting things in the right order, tightening things up. I like the process of making writing neat. When I read my column in the paper and I find I've used the same word twice close together or if I've got something dangling, I can't stand it.
>
> Ellen Goodman, from *On Being a Writer*

Use the chart on the next page to improve your first draft. Ask yourself each of the questions in the left-hand column. When you discover a weakness in your essay, use the revision technique suggested in the right-hand column.

QUOTATION FOR THE DAY
"Genius not only diagnoses the situation but supplies the answer." (Robert Graves, 1895–1985, British poet)
Write the quotation on the chalkboard and explain that being a good writer also involves diagnosing the situation and providing an answer; writers must evaluate their work and make revisions to improve their finished products.

MEETING
INDIVIDUAL
NEEDS

LEP/ESL

General Strategies. Students might need help with evaluating and revising their essays. If you have allowed them to write their drafts in their native languages, consider letting them evaluate and revise in those languages before they rewrite their essays in English.

SELECTION AMENDMENT
Description of change: excerpted
Rationale: to focus on the concept of evaluating and revising presented in this chapter

If you collect the drafts and comment on the revisions they require, you can probably let your students work independently. You may want to provide some time in class for them to start the evaluation and revision process so that they can ask questions and seek help from you or from peers.

You may also want to try using peer evaluation. After the class has been divided into peer evaluation groups, refer them to the segment in **Chapter 1: "Writing and Thinking"** that discusses peer evaluation. At this grade level, evaluation and revision are still difficult for many students, so many of them will need your help.

A DIFFERENT APPROACH

Students often need very specific directions when they are evaluating writing. It's a difficult task to respond to every element of an essay. To help students overcome this problem, ask them for specific examples of the strengths and weaknesses in the writing. You can use the following questions as a guide:

1. Which sentence states the opinion? Write it.
2. How many reasons has the writer given to support the opinion? Write them.
3. What words or phrases are the specific evidence? Write them.
4. What words or phrases are for emotional appeal? Write them.

EVALUATING AND REVISING PERSUASIVE ESSAYS

EVALUATION GUIDE	REVISION TECHNIQUE
1 Do the first one or two sentences grab the reader's attention?	**Add** an interesting example, fact, or observation, or **replace** existing sentences with one.
2 Does a clear statement of the writer's opinion appear early in the essay?	**Add** a sentence (or **replace** one) that clearly states the topic and your opinion.
3 Is background information given to help explain the topic?	**Add** examples or facts that will help your audience understand the topic.
4 Are there enough reasons and evidence to convince readers?	Research and **add** more reasons, facts, or expert opinions to your essay.
5 Are all of the reasons strong?	**Cut** statements that aren't real reasons at all (see pages 340–341). **Add** sound reasons that will make sense to your readers.
6 Does the essay respond to opposing arguments?	**Add** (or **replace**) reasons, explanations, and evidence to refute your opponents' strongest arguments.
7 If appropriate, does the essay contain emotional appeals?	**Add** sentences (or **replace** existing sentences) that clearly appeal to the emotions of your audience.
8 Is the conclusion effective?	Rewrite the conclusion. **Add** a sentence that uses different words but restates your opinion. **Add** a call to action.

GUIDED PRACTICE

You can provide guided practice on **Exercise 4** by conducting a class discussion on the first item in the exercise or by letting students work on the exercise in class while you circulate to offer help. You can give guided practice on **Exercise 5** by spending time working with each group.

INDEPENDENT PRACTICE

The exercises and the writing assignment should provide sufficient independent practice if you allow students to work on their own. You can assign both exercises for homework and then go over them in class the next day to answer any questions or to clear up any confusion students have.

Evaluating and Revising   **353**

EXERCISE 4   **Analyzing a Writer's Revisions**

Study the changes the writer made in her first draft of the fourth paragraph on page 348. Figure out why each change is an improvement by answering the questions.

do something good for the earth
You can help by recycling. Perhaps   **add**

the most important reason for recycling is

that it saves precious natural resources.

~~And the earth's natural resources are~~   **cut**

~~too precious to waste.~~ Every week, for

50,000   *sacrificed*
example, ~~many~~ trees are ~~used~~ to produce   **replace**

Sunday newspapers in the United States.

(newspapers)
Just by recycling, you can help *to save a forest*   **add**

1. Why did the writer change the first sentence? (Hint: Do the changes appeal to logic or feelings?)
2. Why did the writer cut the third sentence?
3. Which is more persuasive: *many trees* or *50,000 trees*? Why?
4. In the fourth sentence, what kind of appeal did the writer add by changing the word *used* to *sacrificed*?
5. Why did the writer add the word *newspapers* in the last sentence? What kind of appeal does the phrase "to save a forest" have?

EXERCISE 5   **Evaluating a Persuasive Essay**

Following is the first part of a brief essay. Work with others in a small group to decide what changes might improve this first draft. Be sure to refer to the evaluating and revising chart on page 352.

ANSWERS
Exercise 4

Answers may vary. Here are some possibilities:

1. The addition changes the appeal from logic to emotion.
2. The third sentence repeats the idea that natural resources are precious.
3. The exact figure of "50,000 trees" is more persuasive because it is more specific.
4. The writer added emotional appeal.
5. The word "newspapers" makes it clear that individuals can make a major contribution to the environmental effort by doing something as easy as recycling newspapers. The phrase has emotional appeal because it makes individuals feel responsible for something important.

ANSWERS
Exercise 5

Answers may vary. Here is a possible revision:

Nobody in this town should pay for swimming lessons because swimming is a skill that everybody needs. There are some poor families here who can't afford even a small fee. If kids from these families drown, we'll have nobody to blame but ourselves for being stingy.

A DIFFERENT APPROACH

If you have students conduct peer evaluations, make sure they understand that they need to be sensitive to the feelings of their classmates. They should be encouraged to point out strengths as well as weaknesses in the papers of the other members of the group.

You could use the following questions to guide students' responses:

1. What support is the strongest in the paper?
2. Which word choice is the best in the paper?
3. Which words grab your attention in the introduction?
4. What is the best part of the paper?
5. Would the paper persuade you? Why?

I guess pretty much everyone already has an opinion on this issue, but I want to tell you how I feel. First of all I think that nobody in this town should pay for swimming lessons. Swimming is a skill that everybody needs because it's important to everyone. There are some poor families here who can't afford even a small fee. If kids from these families drown, we'll have nobody to blame but ourselves for being stingy.

GRAMMAR HINT

Changing Sentence Length for Emphasis

To persuade others to your point of view, you need to be forceful. A short sentence gains force or emphasis if it's a change of pace from mostly longer sentences.

EXAMPLES   *Not emphatic*   There's a great deal of disunity on this issue, but we must work together.

   Emphatic   There's a great deal of disunity on this issue. We must work together.

☞ REFERENCE NOTE: For more information on sentence variety, see page 480.

PART 4:
Evaluating and Revising Your Persuasive Essay

Two heads are better than one, the saying goes. Borrow another head by exchanging essays with a classmate. Evaluate each other's essay by using the questions on page 352. After reading your partner's comments, evaluate your own essay, and revise any weaknesses you find.

PROOFREADING AND PUBLISHING

OBJECTIVE

- To proofread and publish a persuasive essay

TEACHING THE LESSON

You may want to focus your students' proofreading on a few common errors, especially if you've spent time reviewing material on these errors.

It isn't always easy to find realistic ways of publishing student work for a general audience, but you can encourage

Proofreading and Publishing

Proofreading and Publishing. To make sure your essay will make a good impression, proofread to correct errors in punctuation, spelling, usage, and capitalization. Then, think about publishing your essay or finding a way to share it with your audience.

- Send your essay to the school board, a local or national official, perhaps even the president. Be sure you include your name and address.
- With your classmates, evaluate and choose the strongest essays in the class. Send them to your newspaper and to radio or television stations.

PART 5:
Proofreading and Publishing Your Essay

Proofread your essay carefully, and correct any errors you find. To find spelling errors, try reading one line at a time. Recopy your essay and share it with others.

A STUDENT MODEL

Controversial issues touch everyone's life. Katie Baker, who attends Holmes High School in Covington, Kentucky, supports the opinion that public school students should wear uniforms. Does Katie's essay convince you to make the switch to a school uniform?

Teacher's ResourceBank™
RESOURCES

PROOFREADING AND PUBLISHING
- Writing a Persuasive Essay

QUOTATION FOR THE DAY

"Words are but the signs of ideas." (Samuel Johnson, 1709–1784, English writer)

As students begin proofreading and publishing their work, write the quotation on the chalkboard. Remind them that the purpose of this writing assignment has been to use words to persuade others to accept their ideas and that mechanical errors will distract the reader and make their work less persuasive.

STUDENTS WITH SPECIAL NEEDS

Some students may need help in physically writing their final versions. You can encourage them to type if they are able to do so, or you could let them dictate their final versions to you or to someone else who is willing to write for them.

students to submit their papers to the school newspaper.

You can use the framework on p. 350 and the questions for evaluation in the chart on p. 352 to direct your own evaluation of students' persuasive writing.

Conclude this phase of the chapter with a general discussion of what students have learned about persuasive writing. Are they better persuaders? Are they more alert to how others try to persuade them? Are they better able to evaluate persuasive arguments? ■

A STUDENT MODEL
Evaluation

1. Katie gives her opinion early in the essay, "Students enrolled in a public high school should be required to wear a school uniform."
2. Katie's second sentence gives background information to help explain her topic.
3. To support her opinion, Katie presents an expert's opinion (Mrs. Chung) and two strong reasons (lowering clothing expenses and reducing competition among students).
4. The essay addresses an opposing argument (loss of individual freedom).
5. Katie includes an emotional appeal with her choice of words such as *embarrassed* and *threat*.
6. Katie's conclusion restates in different words the statement of opinion.

INTEGRATING THE LANGUAGE ARTS

Technology Link. Students who use computers or word processors with spell-check features might need to be reminded to proofread their papers carefully themselves. The spell-check device can't tell, for example, when *than* should be *then*.

Uniforms Reduce Problems
by Katie Baker

Students enrolled in a public high school should be required to wear a school uniform. Many studies show improvement in both attitude and school work. Wearing uniforms would also reduce clothing costs and many problems related to competition in dress.

Mrs. Chung, a principal at a high school, conducted research on the results of wearing uniforms. She said, "In the past two or three years, several schools in the nation have begun to require a school uniform. All of these schools are reporting improved student grades and improved student behavior."

Uniforms are also less expensive than regular clothing. An outfit for a student can easily cost sixty dollars. A uniform would cost fifty-four dollars or less and would save money. This would be especially helpful to families on a low budget.

Last, uniforms would reduce the competition in dress among students. Students who don't have as much money as others wouldn't have to be embarrassed about their parents' income.

Uniforms wouldn't cause a threat to a student's individual freedom because there are lots of other things that make you "you" besides clothing. Wearing uniforms would reduce many problems and would improve grades and behavior. Therefore, students enrolled in a public high school should be required to wear a school uniform.

SEGMENT 7 (pp. 357–358)
WRITING WORKSHOP
OBJECTIVES
- To analyze a letter to the editor
- To write a letter to the editor on a topic of personal interest

TEACHING THE LESSON
You can use this segment as a follow-up to the persuasive essay as a way of linking classwork to the real world. If students aren't able to arrive at an appropriate topic for a local newspaper or a national magazine, encourage them to write for the school newspaper.

☞

357

WRITING WORKSHOP

A Letter to the Editor

Like a persuasive essay, a persuasive letter states an opinion, supports the opinion with reasons and evidence, and suggests a course of action. When you write a letter to persuade a friend to stay with your family during the summer, you expect an answer. When you write to a state or national official about an issue such as the minimum wage, you may get back a form letter.

One way to get people to respond to your ideas is to write a letter to the editor of a magazine or newspaper. Such letters reach not only the editor, but also a specific audience of readers concerned about the topic.

The following letter to the editor responds to an article printed in a previous issue of the magazine. As you read, decide whether you agree or disagree with the writer's opinion.

> To the Editor,
>
> Your attempt to help the "older generation" understand adolescents by packaging them into neat little bundles like "Malljammers" or "House Hoppers". . . unwittingly touched upon what is perhaps the greatest problem in high schools today: stereotyping. Rather than letting their own identities come out, many teens are assigning themselves to one of these groups and adopting a prescribed personality. Your promotion of these cliques as a means of expression for teens who need to feel accepted does nothing to encourage them to seek their own selves. I am about to enter my senior year in high school, and it appalls me to see people erect invisible barriers between themselves and other groups. In the future, please try to remind us all of the merits of individualism.
>
> Emily R. Alling
> Ledyard, Conn.
> *Newsweek*

Teacher's ResourceBank™
RESOURCES

WRITING WORKSHOP
All the resources for this chapter may be used in this segment.

QUOTATION FOR THE DAY
"By persuading others, we convince ourselves." (Junius, pseudonym of the author of a series of letters, The Letters of Junius, that were printed in the London *Public Advertiser* during the years 1769–1771)

Have students discuss what this quotation means. Also, have them consider whether this would apply to someone writing a letter to the editor. [Students might say that a person would probably have to feel strongly about an issue to write a letter to the editor, so they would already have been convinced.]

MEETING
INDIVIDUAL
NEEDS

LEP/ESL
General Strategies. You may want to point out that some students might have unique perspectives on local or national issues because of their backgrounds in different cultures. Ask students to share their views with the rest of the class.

Remind students that each letter should state an opinion early, use logical reasons and evidence in an orderly manner, and include a call to action, if appropriate. Each letter should also address opposing viewpoints.

CLOSURE

Ask a student to share his or her letter with the class. Let the class analyze it for the required elements. ■

ANSWERS
Writing Workshop Questions

Answers may vary.

1. *Newsweek* apparently published an article about adolescents that categorized adolescents into "neat little bundles."

2. Alling's topic is stereotyping. Her opinion is that stereotypes isolate people and squelch individualism.

3. In addition to the editor, Alling may be trying to address adults who foster stereotyping and adolescents who give in to the urge to stereotype themselves. Her opposing argument is that joining groups on the basis of stereotypes is a way for some people to feel accepted. She refutes this position by citing her personal experience that this type of grouping is harmful.

4. Alling's logical appeal is that adopting a "prescribed personality" discourages people from finding their true identities. Her emotional appeal is in favor of the American virtue of individualism. Many students will probably agree with Alling, but others will probably argue in favor of the comfort of their groups.

INTEGRATING THE LANGUAGE ARTS

Letter-Writing Link. Students might need to review the accepted form of a business letter and the proper way to address an envelope. You can refer them to **Chapter 35: "Writing Letters and Completing Forms"** if they need to review these matters.

1. What caused Emily Alling to write this letter?
2. What topic concerns the writer? What is her opinion?
3. In addition to the editor, what audience might the writer be trying to reach? What strong opposing argument does she mention? How does she try to refute it?
4. What logical and emotional appeals does the writer use to persuade her readers? Does she convince you?

Writing a Letter to the Editor

Prewriting. Think of a current topic you really care about. Have you heard some name-calling at school that makes you angry? Do you feel strongly that no child in the United States should go to bed hungry? Look through your favorite magazine or newspaper for topic ideas. Once you've found a topic, write a sentence that states your opinion. Then list the reasons and evidence you'll use to support your opinion. If you need more support, do some reading or talk to someone who knows something about your topic.

"Letters are expectation packaged in an envelope."

— Shana Alexander

Writing, Evaluating, and Revising. Before you begin writing, read some published letters to the editor. Notice that these letters are short and to the point. They immediately catch the reader's attention, often by stating the writer's opinion in an interesting way. After you've written a rough draft of your letter, ask a friend to read and evaluate it. Then revise your draft to make it more convincing.

Proofreading and Publishing. Proofread your letter carefully, and then send it to a newspaper or magazine whose readers will be interested in the topic. For example, if you're writing about teenagers and dating, you might send your letter to *Seventeen* magazine. Remember: Editors receive many more letters than they can print, so they choose only those that make the best impression.

SEGMENT 8 *(pp. 359–361)*

MAKING CONNECTIONS

PERSUASION ACROSS THE CURRICULUM

OBJECTIVES

- To analyze a 1931 advertisement for an automobile

- To compare a 1931 advertisement for a Pierce-Arrow car to a contemporary advertisement for a car

- To write and design an advertisement for a car of the future

☞

359

MAKING CONNECTIONS

PERSUASION ACROSS THE CURRICULUM

Advertising and Persuasion

Advertisers use a wide array of techniques to persuade people to buy products. In addition to logical reasoning, they rely heavily on these emotional appeals:

- *Loaded words* are words that carry strongly positive or negative connotations. (See page 505.) Advertisers appeal to your emotions by using words that suggest positive feelings. Who can resist a breakfast food, for instance, that's *delicious* and *crunchy*?
- *Snob appeal* uses words and pictures that appeal to your dreams of being rich and carefree. Ads that sell perfume and watches, for example, may show a woman driving an expensive car.
- *Testimonials* bring praise for the product from famous or wealthy people (not experts). Advertisers hope you'll transfer your admiration for the movie star to the cat food she recommends.

Study the following 1931 advertisement (page 360) for a Pierce-Arrow car. Analyze the ad to see what kinds of appeals it uses. Then find and bring to school a full-page car ad from a recent newspaper or magazine. Compare the modern ad to the 1931 ad. What similar and different techniques can you find? What emotional appeals do you notice? Are they convincing? You and your classmates might enjoy sharing your observations.

After you analyze the Pierce-Arrow ad, try this activity by yourself or with a partner. Write and design an ad for the car of the future, perhaps the year 2500. Be sure that the words and the picture work together to sell the product. Use emotional appeals to help convince your audience.

SPEAKING AND LISTENING
Teaching Strategies

You may want to have a volunteer who has a flair for interpretive reading recite King's speech as though King were delivering it. This student will have to practice to give the speech the emphasis it needs.

GUIDELINES

Students' speeches should follow the same guidelines as a persuasive essay for content and organization, and they should especially include an opening that grabs the attention of the audience. The speeches can be as short as three minutes.

USING THE SELECTION
from My Life with Martin Luther King, Jr.

360

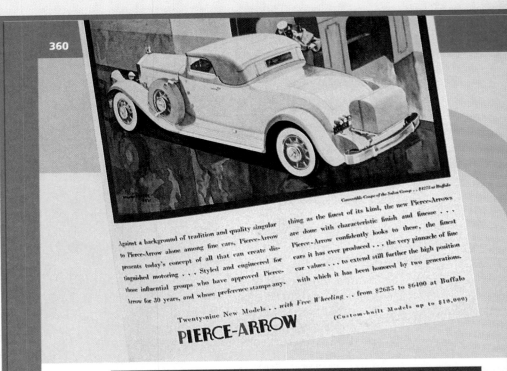

360

SPEAKING AND LISTENING

Public Speaking and Persuasion

Dr. Martin Luther King, Jr., one of the great speakers of the twentieth century, was awarded the Nobel Peace Prize in 1964. The following excerpt is from a persuasive speech given by Dr. King's wife, Coretta Scott King, on April 8, 1968, shortly after Dr. King was killed. This excerpt does not include Mrs. King's opinion statement. What do you think her opinion statement might be? Notice how Mrs. King skillfully combines logical and emotional appeals.

from **My Life with Martin Luther King, Jr.**
by Coretta Scott King

We must carry on because this is the way he would have wanted it to have been. We are not going to get bogged down.

I hope in this moment we are going to go forward; we are going to continue his work to make all people truly free and to make every person feel that he is a human being. His campaign for the poor must go on. . . .

We are concerned about not only the Negro poor, but the poor all over America and all over the world. Every man deserves a right to a job or an income so that he can pursue liberty, life, and happiness. Our great nation, as he often said, has the resources, but his question was: Do we have the will? Somehow I hope . . . the will will be created within the hearts, and minds, and the souls, and the spirits of those who have the power to make these changes come about. . . .

He often said, unearned suffering is redemptive, and if you give your life to a cause in which you believe, and which is right and just — and it is — and if your life comes to an end as a result of this, then your life could not have been lived in a more redemptive way. And I think that this is what my husband has done.

But then I ask the question: How many men must die before we can really have a free and true and peaceful society? How long will it take? If we can catch the spirit, and the true meaning of this experience, I believe that this nation can be transformed into a society of love, of justice, peace, and brotherhood where all men can really be brothers.

Think of someone whose actions you admire. Your hero may be an important historical figure such as Abraham Lincoln or Joan of Arc. Or it may be someone you know personally. Write and present a brief speech that you might give in tribute to this person. Try to persuade your audience to admire your hero.

1
Mrs. King uses the masculine pronouns to refer to all human beings. Do you think Mrs. King is sexist, or is she simply following an older rule about the use of pronouns? [She's probably following an older rule.]

2
redemptive: capable of saving people from some evil or harm

VISUAL CONNECTIONS
Exploring the Subject. Coretta Scott King, born in Marion, Alabama, on April 27, 1927, is the widow of the Rev. Dr. Martin Luther King, Jr. On April 4, 1968, Dr. King was assassinated in Memphis, Tennessee, while he was in that city to organize a strike by municipal sanitation workers. Dr. King, also an Alabamian, led the civil rights movement through his work with the Southern Christian Leadership Conference from the mid–1950s until his death. His work was at least partly responsible for passage of the 1964 Civil Rights Act and the 1965 Voting Rights Act. He won the Nobel Peace Prize in 1964. After he was assassinated, Mrs. King took over many of her husband's public responsibilities.

Chapter 10 WRITING ABOUT LITERATURE

Motivation

Bring a box to class and ask students to imagine that within it is a story so tremendous it would make *Robin Hood* seem boring. This tale would make them laugh, cry, and cringe with suspense. There is one catch. If anyone opens the box and glances at even one word, the entire text disappears.

Point out that all stories are like the story in the box—they have no value unless they are read. Stories exist for readers, not the other way around. Tell students that they, as readers, are the ultimate judges of what value a particular story has for them.

Introduction

Ask students to list the elements that make up a football game [players at different positions, touchdowns, penalties, running plays, and so forth]. Point out that a sportswriter might express complaints about the officials, persuade readers that the outcome was unfair, and even create a literary poem or ballad that sums up the game. Mainly, though, the writer's aim is informative, analyzing each of the important elements that occur in a particular game.

Ask students to list the main elements of a short story [plot, setting, character, point of view, foreshadowing, irony, theme]. A critic reviewing a story would use a sportswriter's approach, analyzing each important element that occurs in a particular story.

Integration

This chapter offers many opportunities for reading, writing, speaking, and listening activities. Learning how to analyze and respond personally to literature will help students understand and appreciate the poems, plays, and stories that they read during the year. Applying the suggestions for active reading will help them enjoy and benefit from everything they read, whether it is fiction or nonfiction.

Once students learn to write a literary analysis, they can use the framework shown in **Critical Analysis Across the Curriculum** (pp. 398-399) to write an analysis of almost anything. Once students can analyze, adding evaluation is a relatively simple step.

The chart on the next page illustrates the strands of language arts as they are integrated into this chapter. For vocabulary study, glossary words are underlined in some writing models.

QUOTATIONS
All **Quotations for the Day** are chosen because of their relevance to instructional material presented in that segment of the chapter and for their usefulness in establishing student interest in writing.

INTEGRATING THE LANGUAGE ARTS

Selection	Reading and Literature	Writing and Critical Thinking	Language and Syntax	Speaking, Listening, and Other Expression Skills
from *The Best, Worst, and Most Unusual: Horror Films* by Darrell Moore **364-366** "An Astrologer's Day" by R. K. Narayan **370-375** Movie review by Pauline Kael from *The New Yorker* **393-394** "The Bean Eaters" by Gwendolyn Brooks **396** "Audio and Video Come Together" from *Consumer Reports* **398**	Identifying supporting evidence **367** Finding details **367, 379** Responding personally to literature **367, 375, 379, 380, 393-394, 396-397** Applying interpretive and creative thinking **367, 375, 396-397** Identifying criteria used by professional critics **367, 393-394** Evaluating and making judgments **367, 375, 379, 380, 393-394, 396-397** Drawing conclusions and making inferences **367, 380, 393-394, 396-397** Identifying and discussing elements of fiction **379, 380**	Writing a personal response to literature **367, 375, 379, 380, 397** Thinking about literature from an author's or a character's point of view **375** Freewriting to generate ideas **375** Writing a critical analysis of a short story **379, 380** Writing a thesis statement **382** Gathering ideas for writing **383, 395** Using descriptive details to support the main idea **385-386, 395** Writing an initial draft **386** Analyzing a writer's revisions **388-389** Revising for main idea, support, organization, coherence, audience, and form **389** Writing a review of a movie or television program **395** Responding personally to poetry **396-397** Writing an analysis for a magazine **399**	Using quotation marks correctly **390, 391** Proofreading for errors in grammar, usage, and mechanics **390-391, 395**	Responding actively and imaginatively to literature **375, 380** Identifying and discussing elements of fiction **379, 380** Participating in peer evaluation **389, 395** Giving an informal explanation **399**

SEGMENT PLANNING GUIDE

Whether you are planning for a quick review of a writing concept or preparing an extended lesson on composition, you can use the following Planning Guide to adapt the chapter material to the individual needs of your class.

SEGMENT	PAGES	CONTENT	RESOURCES
1 *Reading and Responding*	*363-367*		
Literary Model from *The Best, Worst, and Most Unusual: Horror Films*	364-366	Guided reading: a model of a movie review	
Reader's Response/ Writer's Craft	367	Model evaluation: responding to literature and analyzing a movie review	
2 *Purposes for Writing About Literature*	*368*		
3 *Prewriting*	*369-383*		Analyzing a Plot Analyzing Story Elements
Reading and Responding to Stories	369	Introduction: reading actively	
Responding to Stories	369	Guidelines: using criteria for active reading	
Literary Model **"An Astrologer's Day"**	370-375	Guided reading: actively reading a short story	
Exercise 1	375	Cooperative learning: responding and reading actively	
Understanding and Using Literary Elements	376-379	Guidelines: examining plot, setting, character, point of view, foreshadowing, irony, and theme	
Exercise 2	379	Applied practice: exploring stories and literary elements	
Critical Thinking: Analyzing a Short Story	379-380	Guidelines: using criteria to analyze a short story	
Critical Thinking Exercise	380	Cooperative learning: using criteria to analyze a short story	
Writing Assignment: Part 1	380	Applied practice: choosing a story and analyzing its elements	
Thinking About Purpose and Audience	381	Explanation: writing for a specific audience	
Finding a Focus and Developing a Main Idea	381-382	Guidelines: finding a focus and developing a main idea	
Writing Assignment: Part 2	382	Applied practice: writing a thesis statement	
Collecting Support and Organizing Your Ideas	382-383	Guidelines: selecting details and arranging information	
Writing Assignment: Part 3	383	Applied practice: collecting support and organizing ideas	

All the resources listed in this chapter are located in the Teacher's ResourceBank™.

SEGMENT	PAGES	CONTENT	RESOURCES
4 *Writing*	*384-386*		Writing a Critical Analysis
Writing Your First Draft	384	Guidelines: analyzing the introduction, body, and conclusion of a literary analysis	
A Writer's Model	385-386	Guided reading: analyzing a literary analysis	
Writing Assignment: Part 4	386	Applied practice: writing a first draft	
5 *Evaluating and Revising*	*387-389*		Writing a Critical Analysis
Chart: Evaluating and Revising a Literary Analysis	387	Guidelines: applying revision and evaluation techniques	
Exercise 3	388-389	Applied practice: analyzing a writer's revisions	
Writing Assignment: Part 5	389	Cooperative learning: evaluating and revising	
6 *Proofreading and Publishing*	*390-392*		Writing a Critical Analysis
Mechanics Hint	390	Writing suggestion: using underlining	
Publishing	391	Publishing ideas: reaching a specific audience	
Writing Assignment: Part 6	391	Applied practice: proofreading and publishing	
A Student Model	391-392	Guided reading: examining a model	
7 *Writing Workshop*	*393-395*		All the resources for this chapter may be used in this segment.
A Critical Review	393	Guidelines: writing a critical analysis	
Literary Model from *The New Yorker*	393-394	Guided reading: examining a critical analysis	
Writing a Mini-Review	395	Applied practice: writing a movie or television review	
8 *Making Connections*	*396-399*		
Responding to Literature	396-397	Guidelines: writing a personal response Applied practice: writing a response to literature	
Literary Model "The Bean Eaters"	396	Guided reading: responding to a poem	
Critical Analysis Across the Curriculum	398-399	Applied practice: writing a critical analysis	
Literary Model "Audio and Video Come Together"	398-399	Guided reading: examining a critical analysis	

WHOLE-CHAPTER RESOURCES
A Writing Process Log, A Writing Prompt, Holistically Graded Models, Portfolio Assessment Materials

READING AND RESPONDING

OBJECTIVE

- To evaluate a critical analysis of a movie

TEACHING THE LESSON

Ask a volunteer to read aloud the opening paragraphs of the chapter. To familiarize students with establishing criteria, have them state the qualities of a great pizza. Then list on the chalkboard the criteria they think makes a great movie. [Students might list action, interesting characters and plot, good acting, directing, special effects, and so forth.]

VISUAL CONNECTIONS
Books on a Table

About the Artist. For years, John Peto's paintings were attributed to William Harnett, an acquaintance of Peto's who painted in a similar style. Although both artists were able to sell their work during the late 1800's, neither was well known before one of Harnett's paintings was discovered by an art dealer in the 1930s.

Harnett's work was then in demand and many paintings bearing his name entered the art market. But critics soon noticed that Harnett seemed to paint in two distinct styles: one nearing technical perfection, yet emotionally dry; the other somewhat less proficient but much more evocative. An art historian set out to unravel the mystery of Harnett's duality, and he found that the more subjective paintings were done by Peto, whose signature had been replaced by a forgery of Harnett's.

This trick once effectively raised the market value of the less-famous artist's work; today, however, both men are recognized as masters of the *trompe l'oeil* (fool the eye) style, in which objects are painted so realistically that they appear to be three-dimensional.

10 WRITING ABOUT LITERATURE

As a volunteer reads the analysis, have students identify each reference to the criteria on your list. Add any new ideas to the list.

Have students write replies to **Reader's Response/Writer's Craft** before sharing them in small groups or with the entire class. Assure students that any response is acceptable if supported by references from the model analysis.

Reading and Responding

We're all critics at heart. We **read** a book or see a movie, then **respond** by saying, "That was great!" or "That was awful!" Responding to what we read, see, or hear is a big part of our everyday lives.

Writing and You. Writers also respond to what they read, see, and hear. Professional critics write about the latest books or movies. In literature class, you write about the story you've just read. These written responses are more than casual reactions. The writer looks closely at plot and characters to see what makes a book or movie work. Do you ever read a review before you see a movie?

As You Read. Following is a review of the movie *Frankenstein*. As you read it, notice how the writer responds to all the various elements of the movie.

Books on a Table, John Frederick Peto (c. 1900). American, 1854–1908. Oil on canvas. 24 1/2" × 42 7/8". Collection of The Nelson-Atkins Museum of Art, Kansas City, MO. Gift of the Friends of Art (by exchange) 90–11.

ASSESSMENT

Class discussion of responses to **Reader's Response/Writer's Craft** will help you assess students' understanding of analysis. Close checking of questions 1 and 3 will show if students understand plot, theme, criteria, and evidence.

CLOSURE

Ask students to list the elements of a great movie used in the model critical analysis [great direction, great acting, great theme]. Also, have them recall why the evidence given by the analysis does or does not convince them that *Frankenstein* is a great film. [Answers may vary. Make sure students back up their opinions with examples.] ■

364

from The Best, Worst, and Most Unusual:

HORROR FILMS

by Darrell Moore

USING THE SELECTION
from *The Best, Worst, and Most Unusual: Horror Films*

1

phenomenon: a highly unusual or significant occurrence

2

Whale also directed *Bride of Frankenstein* (1935) and *The Invisible Man* (1933).

3

Karloff played the monster again in *Bride of Frankenstein, Son of Frankenstein* (1939), and *Frankenstein 1970* (1958).

4

What element of the movie is Moore analyzing in this paragraph?
[the story or plot]

5

tragedy: a noble character engages in a moral struggle that leads to his or her downfall

1
2
3
FRANKENSTEIN (1931) is a cultural phenomenon, the most famous horror film of all time. It was made by a great director, James Whale, and it featured a great actor, Boris Karloff. But there's more working here than the proper combination of great cinematic talents. The idea of the film, the portrayal of the film, the image and look of the film—even the timing of its release—are inseparable from its success.

4
This is, of course, the story of the scientist who created a monster from graverobbed parts. It is significant that Dr. Frankenstein is not mad. He is merely a brilliant scientist who wants to develop and test some equally brilliant theories. The basic plot is structured around the creation of the monster and the impact that creation has on a <u>parochial</u> and superstitious

5
society. And while the story plays out as tragedy—with the monster trapped and burned by the townspeople at the end— the film encourages the viewer to speculate: What would have happened if Dr. Frankenstein's assistant Fritz had <u>procured</u> a healthy, instead of a criminal, brain? Is the film tragic because the doctor dared too much, or simply because his experiment failed?

" *The horror of the creature is matched only by our desire that such a creature exist.*"

6   The movie takes a stand on the question: The doctor dared too much. That stand is made evident once the creature breathes life and the doctor must imbue that life with meaning. The doctor—or any mortal man—is fundamentally unable to give meaning to the creature's existence. Man is an insufficient God. This is the real tragedy of the film, and what sets it apart from an inspired mad-scientist film like *The Island of Lost Souls.*

     This theme is sounded without being spoken. But great films are not sermons; *Frankenstein* is exciting and physical. Through a scientific magic show (that we don't believe for a minute) of scrap iron and pure energy, Dr. Frankenstein (Colin Clive) gives life to a body made up of dead

6

What aspect of the movie is Moore analyzing in this paragraph?
[theme]

A MONSTER SCIENCE CREATED
But Could Not Destroy!

FRANKENSTEIN

THE WALKING NIGHTMARE THAT FRIGHTENED THE WORLD!

Starring BORIS KARLOFF as The MONSTER

👁 **VISUAL CONNECTIONS**
Exploring the Subject. The world of makeup man Jack Pierce was filled with creepy characters, but that was fine with him. His research into surgical techniques for *Frankenstein* provided realistic details that helped audiences accept the fantasy that a doctor gives life to an assortment of body parts. Pierce also created the creepy looks of three of the most famous monsters in movie history—Dracula, the wolfman, and the mummy.

7

The record time for applying makeup reportedly is 20 hours. Nine people applied tattoos to actor Rod Steiger for *The Illustrated Man* (1969). Such sacrifices are common in horror films. In *Bride of Frankenstein,* actress Elsa Lanchester kept monster makeup intact by eating food through a tube.

graverobbed parts. Suddenly, there is a living creature on the slab. The horror of the creature is matched only by our desire that such a creature exist. Fifty years of familiarity take away the shock—but not the marvel—of the creature's appearance.

7 The credit for the creature's enduring look goes to Universal make-up man Jack Pierce—who took five hours a day to build up Karloff's face. It was an image so striking that Universal was able to copyright it. But it was not created on a whim. Pierce had discovered—after research in several areas, including surgery, criminology, and <u>electrodynamics</u>—that there are "six ways a surgeon can cut the skull." Pierce went on to say that: "I figured Dr. Frankenstein, who was not a practicing surgeon, would take the easiest. That is, he would cut the top of the skull off, straight across like a pot lid, hinge it, pop the brain in, and clamp it tight. That's the reason I decided to make the Monster's

head square and flat like a box, and dig that big scar across his forehead, and have metal clamps hold it together."

Karloff was further fitted with a five-pound steel spine, eighteen-pound asphalt spreader's boots, and steel <u>struts</u> on his legs. The make-up of the monster was so critical to the success of the horror film that Karloff was led to and from the set with his head under a cloth (much like the Elephant Man in the steamboat scene) to conceal his appearance during production. He ate alone, and was totally isolated from everyone not connected with the film.

Ironically, Bela Lugosi was originally offered the role of the creature in Universal's *Frankenstein*. He refused the role, apparently because of the lack of a speaking part. The role went, of course, to Boris Karloff, who became more of a cultural <u>icon</u> as Frankenstein's monster than Lugosi did as Dracula.

READER'S RESPONSE

1. Does the author convince you that *Frankenstein* is a great film? Why or why not?
2. How would your feelings about the film have been different if Dr. Frankenstein had succeeded in his experiment?

WRITER'S CRAFT

3. In this review of *Frankenstein*, the writer focuses attention on plot and make up. What might a music review stress? a review of a novel?
4. Why do you think the author gives such a thorough description of Boris Karloff's makeup and costume?
5. The author's evaluation—judgment—of *Frankenstein* is that it is "exciting and physical." What evidence does he give to support this evaluation?

ANSWERS

Reader's Response

Responses will vary.

1. Proponents may stress acting, directing, makeup, or tragic theme. Opponents may mention lack of evidence for "great" acting and directing and claim that too much emphasis is put on makeup.

2. Most students will probably say they would feel less intrigued by the story if Frankenstein had succeeded.

Writer's Craft

3. Responses will vary. A music review might stress lyrics and bass playing. A review of a novel might stress plot and character.

4. The makeup and costume descriptions show the attention to detail and commitment to excellence that went into the film.

5. The author's evidence includes mentions of "graverobbed parts," being "trapped and burned," using a criminal's brain, the "magic show" of the creation, the horror of the creature, and the weight of the costume.

SELECTION AMENDMENT
Description of change: excerpted
Rationale: to focus on the concept of writing about literature presented in this chapter

PURPOSES FOR WRITING ABOUT LITERATURE

TEACHING THE MODES

Have students brainstorm ways they use the four purposes each day. Being aware of the purposes and how they relate to everyday life will help students recognize these methods in the works of others. Ask each student to write a brief synopsis of a movie script in which the earth is visited by creatures from outer space. The student should briefly tell about his or her favorite part of the movie, urge others to see the movie when it is released, give a brief summary of the movie, and write an alternative ending to the movie. ■

 INTEGRATING THE LANGUAGE ARTS

Literature Link. If possible, have students outline the plot of Finney's "Contents of the Dead Man's Pockets" and show how actions reveal character. They could also contrast how Chee and Old Man Fat feel about the land in "Chee's Daughter" by Platero and Miller or evaluate the ending of Jacobs' "The Monkey's Paw."

---

368   *Writing About Literature*

Purposes for Writing About Literature

The writer of the *Frankenstein* review had a specific purpose: to evaluate the movie and make a recommendation to readers. You might write about literature for the same reason, in book reviews and in some book reports. But there are other reasons to write about literature. Your purpose may be just to jot down a few notes that only you will ever see. Or your purpose may be to analyze the work in great detail and to share what you've learned with your readers. Here are some specific examples of the many purposes for writing about literature.

Self-Expression: writing in your journal about a book you read that made you feel especially good about yourself; writing a letter to a friend saying that you think Tolkien's hobbits are the greatest characters ever created.

Persuasion: writing a book review urging your readers to borrow or buy the book; writing a letter to the editor asking parents to read a particular story to their children.

▶ **Information:**   writing a critical analysis explaining the similarities between the characters in two different novels; writing a brief summary of a book for the school paper.

Creative Writing: writing a poem imitating the style of another poem; writing a sequel to a short story.

LOOKING AHEAD

In the main assignment in this chapter, you'll write a critical analysis. Your basic purpose will be to inform your readers of the results of your analysis. Keep in mind that an effective literary analysis

- has a thesis statement that presents at least one literary element and a main idea about it
- includes details from the work being analyzed
- is organized so it makes sense to the reader

PREWRITING

OBJECTIVES

- To freewrite a response to a story and to answer questions about the story while posing as the author or a character
- To write responses to stories by focusing specifically on their literary elements
- To analyze a story using a set of questions
- To write a one-sentence thesis statement for an analysis of a short story
- To collect support, arrange ideas and details, and create a rough outline

Writing a Critical Analysis

Reading and Responding to Stories

When you read a story, all sorts of thoughts and feelings buzz around in your head, thoughts like *Don't trust her— she's lying!* or *Boy, all this talking is boring.* Shouldn't serious readers shut off this mental activity? Absolutely not!

Responding to Stories as an Active Reader

The thoughts and feelings you have while you're reading mean you're reading actively—just like a lively conversation between you and the story. And the more you put into it, the more you'll get out of it. So tune in your inner thoughts, and use the following tips to expand them. (In parentheses you'll see active-reading thoughts about "An Astrologer's Day," a story you'll read on pages 370–375.)

- **Always respond personally** to what you read. (*I sort of like this phony stargazer and his funny sales lines.*)
- **Use your own experience and knowledge** to understand a character, action, or situation. (*This Town Hall Park sounds more like our flea market.*)
- **Question** anything that confuses, puzzles, or provokes you. (*"Honest" work? Should I buy this?*)
- **Predict** what will happen. If you're wrong (which is okay), figure out why you are. (*Something shadowy in this guy's past is going to haunt him.*)
- **React to the whole story,** and be definite about what you do and don't like. (Sorry, you'll have to supply your own example for that last hint.)

Looking at a Story

Following is a story about appearances. As you read, try to decide what kind of man the astrologer is. As always, "listen" to yourself read—pay attention to your own response.

Teacher's ResourceBank™
RESOURCES

PREWRITING
- Analyzing a Plot
- Analyzing Story Elements

QUOTATION FOR THE DAY

"The good critic is one who tells of his mind's adventures among masterpieces." (Anatole France, 1844–1924, French novelist and winner of the 1921 Nobel Prize for literature)

Ask students to name one of their favorite stories and to tell briefly why they like it.

MEETING INDIVIDUAL NEEDS

LEP/ESL

General Strategies. A multicultural audience may have responses that vary because of culturally based emotions. A character in a story who seems pathetic to one culture may seem laughable to another. Impress upon students that all viewpoints should be acknowledged and that being from a different culture may or may not affect how one responds to writing.

Write the following movie situation on the chalkboard and ask students how they might respond to such a scene:
The heroine, alone in a dark house, decides to investigate a noise in the attic. [Students might respond, "Don't open that door!"]
Tell students that this chapter will help them respond to stories the same way.

After a volunteer reads the tips preceding the story, you may want to model active reading using the first few lines of "An Astrologer's Day." (Example: "What are 'cowrie shells'? 'Obscure mystic charts' makes him sound like a fortune teller. His 'abnormal gleam' probably means he'll do

370 *Writing About Literature*

A SHORT STORY

An Astrologer's Day
by R. K. Narayan

Punctually at midday he opened his bag and spread out his professional equipment, which consisted of a dozen <u>cowrie shells</u>, a square piece of cloth with obscure mystic charts on it, a notebook, and a bundle of <u>palmyra writing</u>. His forehead was resplendent with sacred ash and <u>vermilion</u>, and his eyes sparkled with a sharp abnormal gleam which was really an outcome of a continual searching look for customers, but which his simple clients took to be a prophetic light and felt comforted. The power of his eyes was considerably enhanced by their position—placed as they were between the painted forehead and the dark whiskers which streamed down his cheeks: even a half-wit's eyes would sparkle in such a setting. To crown the effect he wound a <u>saffron</u>-colored turban around his head. This color scheme never failed. People were attracted to him as bees are attracted to cosmos or dahlia stalks. He sat under the boughs of a spreading tamarind tree which flanked a path running through the Town Hall Park. It was a remarkable place in many ways: a surging crowd was always moving up and down this narrow road morning till night. A variety of trades and occupations was represented all along its way: medicine sellers, sellers of stolen hardware and junk, magicians, and, above all, an auctioneer of cheap cloth, who created enough <u>din</u> all day to attract the whole town. Next to him in <u>vociferousness</u> came a vendor of fried groundnut, who gave his ware a fancy name each day, calling it "Bombay Ice Cream" one day, and on the next "Delhi Almond," and on the third "Raja's Delicacy," and so on and so forth, and people flocked to him. A considerable portion of this crowd dallied before the astrologer too. The astrologer transacted his business by the light of a flare which crackled and smoked up above the groundnut heap nearby. Half the enchantment of the place was due to the fact that it did not have the benefit of municipal lighting. The place was lit up by shop lights. One or two had hissing gaslights, some had naked flares stuck on poles, some were lit up by old cycle lamps, and one or two, like the astrologer's, managed without lights of their own. It was a bewil-

USING THE SELECTION
An Astrologer's Day

1

sacred ash and vermilion: ash and red-orange coloring imitate markings once used by Brahmans, the highest caste in Hindu society

2

How does the author use physical description to reveal character? [The narrator reveals that the sparkle in the man's eyes results not from knowing the future but from continually searching for customers.]

3

cosmos or dahlia stalks: brightly colored tropical American plants

4

What mood is created by the description of the gaslights, flares, cycle lamps, and moving shadows? [a dark, mysterious, enchanted mood]

As volunteers read the story, pause to see if students can define unfamiliar words from their contexts. If not, list words and definitions on the chalkboard. Also, encourage active reading by stopping to let students (1) respond to the reading; (2) discuss character, action, or situation; (3) ask questions; or (4) make predictions. Finally, let students react to the entire story.

You may want to model **Exercise 1** with a volunteer partner by using a brief role-playing activity. To keep students focused, tell them to imagine they are interviewing

dering crisscross of light rays and moving shadows. This suited the astrologer very well, for the simple reason that he had not in the least intended to be an astrologer when he began life; and he knew no more of what was going to happen to others than he knew what was going to happen to himself next minute. He was as much a stranger to the stars as were his innocent customers. Yet he said things which pleased and astonished everyone: that was more a matter of study, practice, and shrewd guesswork. All 5 the same, it was as much an honest man's labor as any other, and he deserved the wages he carried home at the end of a day.

He had left his village without any previous thought or plan. If he had continued there he would have carried on the work of his forefathers—namely, tilling the land, living, marrying, and ripening in his cornfield and ancestral home. But that was not to be. He had to leave home without telling anyone, and he could not rest till he left it behind a couple of hundred miles. To a villager it is a great deal, as if an ocean flowed between.

He had a working analysis of mankind's troubles: marriage, money, and the tangles of human ties. Long practice had sharpened his perception. Within five minutes he understood what was wrong. He charged three _pies_ per question, never opened his mouth till the other had spoken for at least ten minutes, which provided him enough stuff for a dozen answers and advices.

5

What is surprising (ironic) about claiming the astrologer's work is "as much an honest man's labor as any other"? [The astrologer is a fake; his work is dishonest.]

 VISUAL CONNECTIONS

Exploring the Subject. Indian street markets provide an array of sounds, sights, and smells. Peddlers loudly advertise their wares and haggle with customers over the price of firewood, jewelry, or boxes made of papier mâché. Bright, hand-woven carpets and silk saris (traditional garments for women) catch the eye. The aroma of vegetables, exotic fruits, Indian tea, and spices fills the air.

Emphasize that although terms such as *foreshadowing* and *irony* may be new, they have used these elements, perhaps without knowing what they were called, for most of their lives. Ask students for examples of each element from their favorite stories, movies, or TV shows.

GUIDED PRACTICE

Before students work on **Exercise 1**, you may want to guide them through the process. Ask the class to suggest responses and to choose one they want to tell the author or a character. Then have them create replies. (Example: "I find it hard to believe that Guru Nayak does not recognize a man who stabbed him." Reply: "Many years have

---

6

The astrologer may be a fake, but he understands human nature.

7

What mood is created by having the stranger blot out "the green shaft of light"? [an ominous, foreboding mood; the astrologer is placed in total darkness]

8

What is humorous (ironic) about the astrologer's comment? [The client would feel "good" if he knew he had found the enemy for whom he has searched.]

---

372   *Writing About Literature*

6 When he told the person before him, gazing at his palm, "In many ways you are not getting the fullest results for your efforts," nine out of ten were disposed to agree with him. Or he questioned: "Is there any woman in your family, maybe even a distant relative who is not well disposed toward you?" Or he gave an analysis of character: "Most of your troubles are due to your nature. How can you be otherwise with Saturn where he is? You have an <u>impetuous</u> nature and a rough exterior." This endeared him to their hearts immediately, for even the mildest of us loves to think that he has a forbidding exterior.

The nuts vendor blew out his flare and rose to go home. This was a signal for the astrologer to bundle up too, since it left him in darkness except for a little shaft of green light which strayed in from somewhere and touched the ground before him. He picked up his cowrie shells and <u>paraphernalia</u> and was putting
7 them back into his bag when the green shaft of light was blotted out; he looked up and saw a man standing before him. He sensed
8 a possible client and said: "You look so <u>careworn</u>. It will do you good to sit down for a while and chat with me." The other grumbled some reply vaguely. The astrologer pressed his invitation; whereupon the other thrust his palm under his nose, saying: "You call yourself an astrologer?" The astrologer felt challenged and said, tilting the other's palm toward the green shaft of light: "Yours is a nature . . ." "Oh, stop that," the other said. "Tell me something worthwhile. . . ."

Our friend felt <u>piqued</u>. "I charge only three pies per question, and what you get ought to be good enough for your money. . . ."

At this the other withdrew his arm, took out an anna, and flung
it out to him, saying: "I have some questions to ask. If I prove
you are bluffing, you must return that <u>anna</u> to me with interest."

9   "If you find my answers satisfactory, will you give me five
<u>rupees</u>?"

"No."

"Or will you give me eight annas?"

"All right, provided you give me twice as much if you are
wrong," said the stranger. This pact was accepted after a little
further argument. The astrologer sent up a prayer to heaven as
the other lit a <u>cheroot</u>. The astrologer caught a glimpse of his
face by the matchlight. There was a pause as cars hooted on the

10   road, *jutka* drivers swore at their horses, and the babble of the
crowd agitated the semidarkness of the park. The other sat
down, sucking his cheroot, puffing out, sat there ruthlessly. The
astrologer felt very uncomfortable. "Here, take your anna back.
I am not used to such challenges. It is late for me today. . . ." He

11   made preparations to bundle up. The other held his wrist and
said: "You can't get out of it now. You dragged me in while I was
passing." The astrologer shivered in his grip; and his voice shook
and became faint. "Leave me today. I will speak to you tomorrow." The other thrust his palm in his face and said: "Challenge
is challenge. Go on." The astrologer proceeded with his throat
drying up: "There is a woman . . ."

"Stop," said the other. "I don't want all that. Shall I succeed
in my present search or not? Answer this and go. Otherwise I
will not let you go till you disgorge all your coins." The
astrologer muttered a few incantations and replied: "All right. I
will speak. But will you give me a rupee if what I say is convincing? Otherwise I will not open my mouth, and you may do what
you like." After a good deal of haggling the other agreed. The
astrologer said: "You were left for dead. Am I right?"

"Ah, tell me more."

12   "A knife has passed through you once?" said the astrologer.

"Good fellow!" He bared his chest to show the scar. "What
else?"

"And then you were pushed into a well nearby in the field.
You were left for dead."

"I should have been dead if some passerby had not chanced
to peep into the well," exclaimed the other, overwhelmed by
enthusiasm.

9
How does negotiating the cost contribute
realism to the story? [Haggling over price
would be expected at such a bazaar.]

10
jutka: horse-drawn taxi

11
What do the stranger's actions suggest
about his character? [He will use physical
violence to get his way.]

12
Since the astrologer is a fake, what is the
only way he could know all this? [He was
the man with the knife.]

ASSESSMENT

You can assess whether students understand active reading and responding by watching them act out their freewriting responses as called for in **Exercise 1**. After two or three minutes, you could have the partners switch roles.

To see if students understand literary elements, grade their written comments in

374

13
Why might this be the story climax; the scene that determines how things turn out? [If Guru Nayak is not convinced the astrologer is genuine, he may realize the other's true identity.]

14
The astrologer wants to make sure Guru Nayak will not continue to search.

15
What is humorous (ironic) about the astrologer's claim? [He cannot know the future. Also, if Guru Nayak stays home, the astrologer has a chance to live to be a hundred.]

16
Guru Nayak, reflective and regretful, believes his enemy is dead. The astrologer is safe.

17
Why does the astrologer choose this death? [He knows that being crushed by a wagon will gratify Guru Nayak and help him accept the story.]

374

"When shall I get at him?" he asked, clenching his fist.

"In the next world," answered the astrologer. "He died four months ago in a far-off town. You will never see any more of him." The other groaned on hearing it. The astrologer proceeded:

"Guru Nayak—"

13 "You know my name!" the other said, taken aback.

"As I know all other things. Guru Nayak, listen carefully to what I have to say. Your village is two days' journey due north of **14** this town. Take the next train and be gone. I see once again great danger to your life if you go from home." He took out a pinch of sacred ash and held it to him. "Rub it on your forehead **15** and go home. Never travel southward again, and you will live to be a hundred."

16 "Why should I leave home again?" the other said reflectively. "I was only going away now and then to look for him and to choke out his life if I met him." He shook his head regretfully. "He has escaped my hands. I hope at least he died as he **17** deserved." "Yes," said the astrologer. "He was crushed under a lorry." The other looked gratified to hear it.

The place was deserted by the time the astrologer picked up his articles and put them into his bag. The green shaft was also gone, leaving the place in darkness and silence. The stranger had gone off into the night, after giving the astrologer a handful of coins.

It was nearly midnight when the astrologer reached home. His wife was waiting for him at the door and demanded an

RETEACHING

    People usually remember the outlandish and unusual. If students need a different approach to understand literary elements, divide the class into small groups to act out any elements that need reinforcing. One group might present skits that show each way to characterize—by speech, actions, appearance, or thoughts. Another ☞

explanation. He flung the coins at her and said: "Count them. One man gave all that."

    "Twelve and a half annas," she said, counting. She was overjoyed. "I can buy some jaggery and coconut tomorrow. The child has been asking for sweets for so many days now. I will prepare some nice stuff for her."

    "The swine has cheated me! He promised me a rupee," said the astrologer. She looked up at him. "You look worried. What is wrong?"

    "Nothing."

18   After dinner, sitting on the *pyol,* he told her: "Do you know a great load is gone from me today? I thought I had the blood of a man on my hands all these years. That was the reason why I ran away from home, settled here, and married you. He is alive."

    She gasped. "You tried to kill!"

    "Yes, in our village, when I was a silly youngster. We drank, gambled, and quarreled badly one day—why think of it now?

19 Time to sleep," he said, yawning, and stretched himself on the *pyol.*

EXERCISE 1 ▶   **Speaking and Listening: Responding and Reading Actively**

Did you ever wish you could talk to an author or a character? After reading "An Astrologer's Day," freewrite a response for one minute, *as if you're speaking directly to the writer or a character.* Here are some questions to get you started: Did you like the way the story ended? Or did you feel tricked? How do you feel about the astrologer? Then act out your freewriting response with a partner, following these pointers:

1. Look your partner in the eye; then read your response.
2. Your partner—taking the place of author or character—will listen carefully and "answer" you.
3. Keep the back-and-forth active responses going as long as you can.
4. Change places. Become the author or character, and answer your partner's freewriting response.

18

pyol: collected material for a person to sit or lie upon

19

Will the astrologer sleep well? [He may sleep better than before, knowing he is not a killer and that Guru Nayak will not seek him.]

ANSWERS
Exercise 1

Questions and answers will vary. Students might enjoy the irony of the ending, or they might feel tricked by a plot based on a coincidental meeting and Guru Nayak not recognizing his assailant. Some students will probably feel the astrologer is smart and resourceful; others might find him unethical and shallow.

You may want to model the freewriting and dialogue with a volunteer. Students who like to perform might want to share their dialogues with the entire class.

group might act out external or internal conflicts. A third group might enact scenes with verbal, dramatic, or situational irony. Each skit should be followed by a brief summary of the lesson to be learned.

CLOSURE

Ask students to name the hints for active reading and responding. Then ask volunteers to briefly summarize the seven literary elements.

AT-RISK STUDENTS

Students might write an "after" story to become familiar with plot, conflict, and climax. Beginning where **"An Astrologer's Day"** leaves off, ask students to imagine a scenario in which Guru Nayak guesses who the astrologer might be. What would Nayak do? How would the astrologer react (conflict)? What scene would settle it all (climax)?

Students who are inexperienced with dialogue, speaker tags, and so forth might summarize the ending.

Understanding and Using Literary Elements

Already you've been responding to some basic elements of a short story, perhaps the main character or the plot of "An Astrologer's Day." To write about a story, you need a good understanding—a working knowledge—of literary elements, and you need to keep them clearly in mind as you read.

You'll find that the elements below make your reading and writing more specific and sharp. They let you look *inside* a story—at its parts and the writer's techniques—and talk about it in clear, precise terms.

Plot. *Plot* is the story's "action," or series of events. Look closely, and you'll see that *conflict*—the problems the characters face—keeps the plot moving. Conflicts can be external (struggles with people, nature, or society) or internal (struggles with the character's own feelings or beliefs). The *climax* of a plot is the tense or exciting scene that settles the story's main conflict—that determines how things turn out.

Setting. *Setting* is the story's time and place; it may include weather, clothes, landscape, buildings, cars, rickshaws—many physical and social details. Setting provides important background for understanding people and events, and it may also create conflict (imagine a

To show how literary elements are related, let each student place the title of a favorite movie in a container and the main character of a favorite movie in another container. Have them pick slips from each and discuss changes that would occur from the new combination. If students happen to draw two slips that actually match, have them trade one slip with another student. How would plot, theme, irony, and setting be affected, for example, if Arnold Schwarzenegger in *Terminator 2* were replaced by Winnie the Pooh? What if Dorothy from *The Wizard of Oz* took the place of Indiana Jones? ■

destructive avalanche, for example) or set an emotional mood, or atmosphere (imagine a festive carnival).

Character.   Characters are the individuals in a story (animals or aliens, as well as people), and *characterization* is the way the writer reveals their qualities and traits. Writers can describe personality directly, but they can also show it indirectly through the characters' speech, appearance, thoughts, actions, and effects on others (what people say and feel about them). To understand a character, you may need to consider the motivation for actions and decide whether the character changes in the story.

Point of View.   *Point of view* is the angle from which a story is told: who tells it, how close this narrator is to the action, what *is* told, and what *isn't.*

In *first-person point of view,* the narrator is a character in the story and speaks as *I.* This narrator can only tell us what he or she sees and hears, is told, or *believes.* Maybe the character is reliable, but maybe not: Readers must decide.

In *third-person point of view,* the narrator is outside the story—not a character—and doesn't use the words *I, me,* and *mine,* but does use *he, her,* and *them* (third-person pronouns). A *third-person omniscient* narrator can tell the thoughts of any character (*omniscient* means "all-knowing"), relate any event, and even speak right to the reader or skip around in time.

In *third-person limited point of view,* the outside narrator reveals the thoughts of just one character. The story's events are filtered through the mind of one person.

Foreshadowing.   *Foreshadowing* is a hint or suggestion of coming events—a clue, in a way, that heightens our interest or prepares us for significant actions. Sometimes we recognize foreshadowing immediately: A jeweled bracelet shines "coldly" in its "padded coffin of a case," and we're instantly on alert for danger. But sometimes foreshadowing is less obvious: A character sees two dogs fight to exhaustion over a bone, but we don't learn

MEETING INDIVIDUAL NEEDS

STUDENTS WITH SPECIAL NEEDS

To provide motivation for writing, it may be effective to allow students to view a video-taped version of a piece of literature and allow them to write on aspects of this version. Place students in small discussion groups to help inspire them and to help them develop ideas.

It is also important to make sure students are not hindered by a limited vocabulary or background knowledge. Thus, discuss key concepts and vocabulary items before they read the selection.

INTEGRATING THE LANGUAGE ARTS

Literature Link. Students might analyze literary elements in a story such as Platero and Miller's "Chee's Daughter."

1. Plot: Chee argues with his in-laws over his daughter's return.
2. Setting: Chee's home (family compound blends into landscape of canyons and desert) contrasts with the trading post (barren land with ugly buildings along a highway).
3. Character: Love motivates Chee; greed motivates Old Man Fat.
4. Point of view: Third-person limited helps readers identify with Chee.
5. Foreshadowing: The cold wind suggests the winter that helps Chee.
6. Irony: The young man, not his elders, follows Navajo tradition.
7. Theme: A traditional lifestyle is superior to a modern lifestyle.

 TIMESAVER

If lack of time is a problem, you may choose to modify **Exercise 2.** Have students choose one story instead of two. The drawback is that one story is unlikely to include as many diverse elements. Also, students might choose a story they have read before and familiarity might diminish their reactions to some elements in the story. You may have to encourage them to admit negative reactions to a favorite story.

until later that he will battle his brother—for a girl who loves neither one.

Irony.   *Irony* is basically a contrast between appearance or expectation and reality. Writers use surprising, ironic twists to make us laugh but also to make us thoughtful or sad: Life and people don't always behave as we want. Writers use three kinds of irony. (All three examples come from a famous ironic story, Edgar Allan Poe's "The Cask of Amontillado." Read it if you haven't!)

- *verbal irony:* one thing is said but another is meant: A man who plans to kill his unsuspecting friend offers the toast "To your health!"
- *situational irony:* what is expected is not what happens: The friend attends a carnival expecting fun but instead meets his death.
- *dramatic irony:* the reader (or playgoer or moviegoer) knows something that a character does not: Readers know the man plans murder, but his friend does not.

Theme.   *Theme* is an important idea about life or human nature revealed in a story. It isn't just a subject (like "war"), but an insight ("War wounds are not just physical; they are carried inside forever"). Writers often don't state their themes directly, and you have to draw your own conclusions from characters, events, description, and dialogue. (Sometimes the title or the conflict may be clues.) You may find more than one theme in a story.

When you read a short story (or any other literary work)

- respond freely, by letting your thoughts and feelings flow naturally
- read actively, by responding personally, applying your own experience, questioning, predicting, and reacting to the whole
- think about the work's literary elements and how the writer uses them to get you to respond as you do

CRITICAL THINKING
(p. 379)

OBJECTIVE

- To analyze the literary elements of a short story by using a set of suggested questions

TEACHING *ANALYZING A SHORT STORY*

Read and discuss the questions to be sure students understand them. Emphasize that the questions address the literary elements they have already studied. You may want to model the **Critical Thinking Exercise** by answering question 4 (about setting) with specific details from the story. Stress that

Prewriting   **379**

EXERCISE 2 ▶ **Exploring Stories and Literary Elements**

What hooks you in a story? A shocking twist (heavy on the irony)? Weird settings in the future? Believable characters? Find out for yourself. Choose two stories (favorite or unknown ones), and respond to them actively, in writing, as you did in Exercise 1. This time, though, focus specifically on literary elements, using what you've just learned. Write out your comments to share with your classmates: "What I Like or Don't Like in Stories—and Why."

CRITICAL THINKING

Analyzing a Short Story

Analyzing means examining in detail: looking closely at the parts of a whole and their relationships. You're doing this naturally whenever you respond to different parts of stories—funny dialogue, a tragic ending—and you simply do it in a deeper, systematic way when you write a critical analysis.

Here are some questions that can help you analyze any short story. But remember: Literature is not a statement of scientific fact, but a creation in words of experience. Its readers vary, and so will its interpretations. In discussions, you'll naturally compare your answers with those of your classmates, but don't look for right or wrong answers.

1. What important conflicts or problems, external and internal, does the main character(s) face?
2. What is the story's climax, the outcome of the central conflict?
3. Where and when does the story take place?
4. Does the setting help explain characters and events, cause a conflict, or set a mood? (More than one may apply.) Explain.
5. What is the story's main character(s) like? (Use appearance, speech, thoughts, actions, and reactions of others.)

ANSWERS
Exercise 2

As students prepare to read two stories, suggest that they list the literary elements at the top of a sheet of paper to serve as reminders. As something in the stories affects them positively or negatively, they might put a plus (+) or minus sign (–) on their papers and freewrite their reactions. This can provide insight into what they like or do not like about stories.

ANSWERS
Critical Thinking Exercise

Responses may vary. Here are some possibilities:

1. Guru Nayak: find and punish his attacker (external); Astrologer: trick Nayak into leaving (external) and control his emotions and fears (internal)

2. Guru Nayak accepts the astrologer's story and leaves.

3. The setting is an Indian market in Town Hall Park, from midday until after midnight.

4. The city park, lively and filled with hucksters, suggests the unexpected. It sets a mood of enchantment, with strange lighting that makes people appear shadowy.

379

each question should involve both an answer and a reference to details from the story.

5. Appearance: dark whiskers, turban, sacred ash on his forehead, abnormal gleam of eyes.
   Speech: He first speaks clichés, but later skillfully convinces Nayak his enemy is dead.
   Thoughts: He senses a client, feels piqued when challenged, and feels uncomfortable at recognizing his foe.
   Actions: He presses Guru Nayak to have his fortune told; tricks him.
   Others' reactions: Guru Nayak shows the astrologer little respect until the story rings true.

6. The astrologer wants to hide, make money, and survive. Guru Nayak is motivated by hate. The astrologer feels relieved; Guru Nayak, disappointed, will no longer seek his attacker.

7. The point of view is third-person limited. The narrator does not reveal the astrologer's thoughts at the moment of recognition.

8. The setting foreshadows the strange events. "People were attracted to him . . ." suggests that someone will arrive. That "nine out of ten" usually agree with him implies a tenth who will not.

9. Dramatic irony occurs as the reader becomes aware that the astrologer is Guru Nayak's attacker. Verbal irony occurs when the astrologer says he can make Guru Nayak feel better. There is situational irony because the attacker becomes an astrologer to escape his past, which attracts his victim.

10. Good, bad, guilt, and punishment often are not clearly defined.

6. What motivates the main character(s) to act? Does the character(s) change in the story? If so, how?
7. Is the point of view first-person, omniscient, or third-person limited? Does the point of view affect what *you* know and feel? How?
8. Does foreshadowing help prepare for later events or situations? If so, give examples that you found effective.
9. Is irony—verbal, situational, or dramatic—at work in this story? Give examples, and discuss its effect.
10. What important idea about life or people do you find in this story?

 CRITICAL THINKING EXERCISE:
Analyzing a Short Story

Working with a partner or a small group, analyze "An Astrologer's Day" by asking the questions above and on page 379. Your group might enjoy exchanging interpretations with another group—and remember that it's okay for your viewpoints to differ. (In fact, discussing with your group *why* your individual interpretations are different can also be interesting.)

 PART 1:
Choosing a Story and Analyzing Its Elements

It's time to settle on a story that you'd like to think more about, feel and understand better, analyze closely, and tell others about in writing. Choose a story from your literature textbook or a favorite story of your own. Then use the questions above and on page 379 to analyze it.

Prewriting

Planning a Critical Analysis

Now it's time to turn your ideas about your short story into the raw material you'll use to write your essay.

Thinking About Purpose and Audience

You can write about literature for many purposes, but this chapter focuses on *critical analysis*. In your essay, you're taking on the role of "literary investigator": a close reader who knows, and can tell an audience, something about the literary elements in a short story.

For a critical analysis, you assume that your audience has read the story, which means that you don't need to retell the plot. Think of your audience as interested readers who want to know more.

Finding a Focus and Developing a Main Idea

You know now that your focus in an analysis paper is the story's literary elements, but how many and which ones?

In a short essay, you'll usually write about one element or two or three that fit together somehow. *Which* elements depends on two things: (1) your interest (What drew you to the story? A crazy character? A great historical setting?) and (2) the story itself (What did your analysis uncover? For what parts or aspects of the story do you have many notes or probing questions?). In short: Write about something that attracts you and seems important in the story.

With a topic (element) in mind, your next step—as in any informative essay—is to develop a main idea. What do you want to say *about* the element and the story? Then you can write a sentence—a thesis statement—that connects your topic and main idea about it.

Following are some thesis statements you might write about "An Astrologer's Day":

> Nayak's violent character is shown through his actions and speech.

 A DIFFERENT APPROACH
In the **Evaluating and Revising** segment, students will see exactly how to cut from their analysis sections where they have unnecessarily restated the plot. However, a more effective time to emphasize this might be during prewriting. You may want to highlight some of the phrasing used in the *Frankenstein* critique where the author showcased events in the movie without actually restating the plot.

CRITICAL THINKING
Classification

Have students classify the sample thesis statements on pp. 381–382 as emphasizing an element's function, effect, or development.

[Responses will vary. Here are some possibilities:

1. development (shows how Nayak's character is developed)
2. effect (helps reader understand the life of the people)
3. effect (mood reader feels) and function (how setting works to bring about conflict)
4. function (how irony works in the story)]

TIMESAVER

Before students begin their rough drafts, let them present to the class the evidence from their stories that supports their thesis statements. The class should judge whether the evidence is specific and sufficient enough to prove each thesis, and possibly suggest ways for the presenters to strengthen their arguments.

The setting of "An Astrologer's Day" gives us a good picture of what life is like for the city's people.

The setting of "An Astrologer's Day" creates a "bewildering" mood and also brings about the plot's main conflict.

In "An Astrologer's Day," verbal, dramatic, and situational irony are used to make us doubt the astrologer, build suspense, and develop theme.

Notice that the examples show you basic *kinds* of ideas used in literary analysis. You can write about an element's

- function (how it works in the story)
- effect (what you feel or understand because of it)
- development (how the writer builds or creates it)

The sample thesis statements also show how much flexibility you have in writing about elements. For example, you can write about one function of setting or two; you can write about one type of irony or about all three types plus theme. As long as you match the topic to the length of the assignment, the focus is yours.

WRITING ASSIGNMENT

PART 2:
Writing a Thesis Statement

It's a good bet that you already have a writing focus in mind. After all, you've both explored and analyzed your story. What made you choose it? What did you discover about it? Go over your thoughts and notes, pinpoint your focus, and decide the main idea you want a reader to understand. Write your thesis statement in one sentence.

Collecting Support and Organizing Your Ideas

Collecting Support. A critical analysis of literature has this in common with persuasive writing: it requires evidence to support your ideas. The "evidence" in this case, though, comes from the literature. In other words, you don't just tell readers that Nayak has a violent character; you *show* them with specific details from the story. Evidence may take the form of quotations, paraphrasing, summarizing, or quoting details.

 **REFERENCE NOTE:** For more information on using sources to support your ideas, see pages 414–415.

Organizing Your Ideas. With your main points listed and supporting details recorded, you can produce an early plan by arranging the information. Often your topic and ideas will suggest a natural way to do this.

For example, if you're analyzing a character and showing how he or she changes, chronological order (the plot order) makes sense. If a setting both sets a mood and causes a major plot problem, you'll probably want to begin with mood (which is background) and end with conflict. And you can also order ideas and supporting details by importance (most-to-least, least-to-most). Look for an arrangement that readers can easily follow.

"*Once upon a time, they lived happily ever after.*"

Drawing by H. Martin; c 1991 The New Yorker Magazine, Inc.

WRITING ASSIGNMENT

PART 3:
Collecting Support and Organizing Your Ideas

Remember: You want to *show* your readers, not just *tell* them. Now is the time to make notes of story details that led you to your ideas in the first place. (And you may also discover new evidence.) After collecting support, arrange both ideas and details, and create either a rough or a formal outline.

COOPERATIVE LEARNING
When planning their essays have students list main points and record supporting ideas in random order and share these with a classmate to generate and organize ideas. Have both students organize the ideas as they think best. Then have them compare and discuss differences.

OBJECTIVE

- To write a first draft of a critical analysis essay

TEACHING THE LESSON

As students read the model, point out labeled parts of the essay. Have students find topic sentences for the paragraphs and remind them that the topic sentence is followed by evidence that proves or illustrates it.

You may want to use the chalkboard to paraphrase, quote, and summarize passages as models for your students. Point out

QUOTATION FOR THE DAY

"Nothing is ended with honour which does not conclude better than it began." (Samuel Johnson, 1709–1784, English lexicographer, essayist, and poet)

Remind students that they might save a new idea or a new way of stating their theses for the conclusion.

LEP/ESL

General Strategies. Whereas active reading requires personal reactions to the literature, writing conventions require avoiding the words *I, me, my,* or *mine* when putting reactions on paper. Two techniques students can use to avoid these terms are rewording and the using of the pronoun *one.*

1. I questioned the motives of Dr. Frankenstein. [The motives of Dr. Frankenstein seemed questionable.]
2. I expected the ending to be happier. [One might have expected the ending to be happier.]

384

 ## Writing Your First Draft

Now that you've collected support and organized your ideas, you're ready to write your first draft. The *introduction* to your critical essay must include (1) the title and author of the short story and (2) your thesis statement. It can be simple, but it has the goal of all introductions: to interest readers. Why were you attracted to the story? Set down your own interest, and you'll catch the reader's.

The essay's *body* develops your main points, using the support you've gathered. Incorporating this support smoothly into your sentences is a special element of critical writing. You can paraphrase, quote, or summarize, but all references to the story must fit grammatically into your writing, as the following examples show.

HERE'S HOW

Because the narrator tells us that the astrologer doesn't know the future, calling his work "an honest man's labor" is irony with a sharp bite.	paraphrase / quotation
Just as ironically, Nayak might have passed on by, but the astrologer was insistent.	summary

The *conclusion* of an analysis is often a restatement of the thesis or summary of points. Other essay techniques are possible, such as echoing the introduction's ideas and details or ending with a larger observation about the story. Remember that the conclusion shouldn't be mechanical: "Now I will summarize my main points. . . ." It should be a satisfying finish for your readers.

The following Writer's Model shows you these basic essay parts for a critical analysis.

that the model has only a few words of direct quotation.

You also may want students to write their drafts in class so that you can give counsel as needed.

GUIDED PRACTICE

Help students get started by allowing them to write any paragraph they choose, regardless of its place in the final essay. Offer assistance as needed. If they can draft one paragraph, they can draft others step by step.

☞

A WRITER'S MODEL

An Analysis of Irony in
"An Astrologer's Day"

INTRODUCTION
Title and author

Thesis statement

"An Astrologer's Day," by R. K. Narayan, is ironic through and through. Almost nothing is what it seems to be, and one unexpected event follows another--for both readers and characters. This is a comic but thought-provoking story in which irony is used for several purposes: to make us doubt the astrologer, to build suspense, and to develop theme.

BODY
Support:
Quotation and details

From the first sentence, Narayan uses irony to make us doubt the astrologer. His "professional" equipment (the shells, the cloth with mysterious writing, and so on) is only for show. Ordinary listening skills, not the stars, help him astonish his "simple clients" with "shrewd guesswork."

Paraphrase and quotation

Because the narrator tells us that the astrologer doesn't know the future, calling his work "an honest man's labor" is irony with a sharp bite. The narrator's comments expose the astrologer as a greedy fake.

Support:
Summary/ Details

The narrator also uses irony to build suspense during the fortunetelling scene. From previous clues, we realize that the astrologer is the one who knifed and left Nayak--but Nayak doesn't know it. Will the astrologer pull off his risky trick? What will happen if he doesn't? The irony of knowing something Nayak doesn't makes the scene fascinating and tense.

Support:
Summary/ Details and quotation

The story's strongest irony, however, runs all through the plot and helps create theme. One important irony is that the astrologer has tried to escape his past but ends up, in a way, bringing it to himself. He's become an astrologer to get away from his crime, but his victim is attracted to an astrologer. As Nayak says, " 'I have some questions to ask.' " Just as ironically, Nayak might have passed on by, but the astrologer was insistent.

Ask students if these excerpts from **"An Astrologer's Day"** should be quoted or paraphrased in an analysis of irony. Have them discuss choices in groups. Probable responses are given.

1. "The place was lit up by shop lights." [paraphrase: seems unimportant]
2. "You will never see any more of him." [important quotation]
3. "The stranger had gone off into the night, after giving the astrologer a handful of coins." [paraphrase]
4. "The swine has cheated me!" [emotional quotation]

ASSESSMENT

As you assess students' first drafts, try to focus your comments on how well students have detailed and organized ideas rather than dwelling on mechanics.

CLOSURE

Have students list the parts of a critical analysis [introduction (including title, author, thesis statement); body (support, paraphrases, summaries, quotations); and conclusion (thesis restatement, final statement, summary, return to introduction)]. ■

CRITICAL THINKING
Classification

To help students understand irony, have small groups locate some examples in **"An Astrologer's Day"** and classify each as verbal, dramatic, or situational. Tell them to include one example of each. Answers may vary. Here are some possibilities:

1. verbal irony: "professional equipment" and "an honest man's labor"
2. dramatic irony: "knowing something Nayak doesn't"
3. situational irony: hiding as astrologer attracts Nayak, "insistence" that Nayak stop

---

Summary/ Details

Support: Interpretation of theme

Quotation

Quotations Summary/ Details

CONCLUSION

Return to introduction

But the story gets still more ironic: When the astrologer recognizes Nayak, he uses the truth to deceive him! For once, the astrologer really does know facts about a customer, and he uses them to save his own life. In the end, posing as an astrologer is an advantage.

Every situation in this story takes an unexpected twist, and we are left with the message that life never turns out as expected and that even good and bad aren't what they seem. For example, it is awful that the astrologer can say " 'why think of it now?' " about leaving a man for dead, but we certainly didn't want Nayak to shed more blood to punish him. It is dishonest to take money for fake prophecies, but the astrologer's customers are "comforted" and "pleased." It is the astrologer who is guilty of a violent crime, but Nayak was probably violent too--and still is.

The irony is so strong in "An Astrologer's Day" that good, bad, guilt, and punishment aren't clear-cut. What should we think? Obviously, R. K. Narayan doesn't want us to take this tale too seriously. Because no real harm is done, we can laugh at this upside-down world, not be shocked by it. We can simply enjoy all of the author's ironies.

PART 4:
Writing a First Draft of Your Critical Analysis

The writer's model you just read was a final draft. Don't panic: A polished, finished paper isn't expected of you now. Just let the model rest in your mind as you use your rough outline to get a first draft on paper. (But if the model gave you concrete ideas for your essay, use them!) Remember: Your goal is to support your thesis with evidence from the story so that your readers will understand your interpretation.

EVALUATING AND REVISING

OBJECTIVES

- To analyze and answer questions about a writer's revisions of a critical analysis
- To evaluate and revise a critical analysis

TEACHING THE LESSON

After discussing the evaluation and revision checklist, you may want to guide students through the answering of question 2 in **Exercise 2.** If students have trouble with the exercise, provide additional practice by having them use the checklist to evaluate paragraphs from the analysis of *Frankenstein* (pp. 364–367). ☞

Evaluating and Revising   **387**

Evaluating and Revising

The following checklist will help you to correct your paper's weaknesses. Ask yourself each question in the left-hand column. Then use the technique in the right-hand column to correct any problems.

EVALUATING AND REVISING A LITERARY ANALYSIS	
EVALUATION GUIDE	**REVISION TECHNIQUE**
1 Does the introduction include the title and the author?	**Add** the missing title or author.
2 Does the introduction identify the thesis, or focus, of the analysis?	**Add** a sentence or two (or replace an existing one) identifying a literary element and your main idea about it.
3 Is there enough support from the story for your ideas?	**Add** quotations, plot events, or other details.
4 Is support smoothly incorporated into the sentences?	**Add** or **replace** words and punctuation so that quotations and paraphrases are grammatically complete.
5 Have purpose and audience been considered in writing the critical analysis?	**Cut** informal expressions. **Cut** plot details that the audience may know or that are not related to your purpose.
6 Does the conclusion bring the essay to a definite close?	**Add** a sentence or two (or **replace** existing ones) that restate your main idea or summarize existing points.

Teacher's ResourceBank™
RESOURCES

EVALUATING AND REVISING
- Writing a Critical Analysis

QUOTATION FOR THE DAY

". . . the way to perfection is through a series of disgusts." (Walter Pater, 1839–1894, English essayist and critic)

Pater was referring to Leonardo da Vinci's attempts to perfect his painting style. Ask students how it could apply to evaluating and revising their written work.

LEP/ESL

General Strategies. Exchanging papers for evaluation is often a discomforting experience because some students view offering comments as criticism rather than constructive feedback. If students preface their comments with polite introductory statements, the criticisms will seem less negative. You may want to offer the following examples when students make suggestions to their classmates:

1. You might want to . . .
2. I wonder if this is the best way to put this . . .

CLOSURE

Ask students to recall the questions used to help them evaluate and revise their critical analyses. Also, ask them to list possible revision techniques. ■

![TIMESAVER icon] TIMESAVER

You may want to assign **Exercise 3** as homework. Have students briefly compare responses and discuss differences in small groups before discussing responses as a class.

Students might also make copies of their papers so that peer evaluation can also be assigned as homework.

![CRITICAL THINKING icon] CRITICAL THINKING
Synthesis

Revision may seem complicated to students. Emphasize that revising consists of only four techniques: replace, cut, reorder, or add. These can be used for evaluating and revising almost anything. Ask students to think of ways to redesign their school using the four revision choices. [They might replace buildings, cut unused lockers, reorder (rearrange) classrooms, or add parking space.]

ANSWERS
Exercise 3

1. Listing the author and title reveals quickly what story is being analyzed.
2. The original sentence states the plot. The writer changed it to a thesis statement that gives, in the order they will be discussed, three specific ways that the author uses irony in the story.

E X E R C I S E 3 ▶	**Analyzing a Writer's Revisions**

Study the writer's revisions of the first two paragraphs of the model analysis on page 385. Then answer the questions that follow the paragraphs.

("An Astrologer's Day," by R. K. Narayan)

This story is ironic through and   **replace**
through. Almost nothing is what it seems
to be, and one unexpected event follows
another--for both readers and characters.

This is a comic but thought-provoking
in which irony is used for several purposes:
story. In it, an astrologer meets the man   **replace**
to make us doubt the astrologer, to build suspense,
he once wounded with a knife, pushed in
and to develop theme.
a well, and left for dead.

Because the narrator tells us that the
astrologer doesn't know the future, calling
"an honest man's labor"
his work honest is irony with a sharp bite.   **replace**

From the first sentence, Narayan uses   **reorder**
irony to make us doubt the astrologer. His
"professional" equipment (the shells, the
cloth with mysterious writing, and so on)
is only for show. Ordinary listening skills,
not the stars, help him astonish his
"simple clients" with "shrewd guesswork."

The narrator's comments expose the
as a greedy fakeo
astrologer.   **add**

1. Why did the writer add the title and author of the story to the first line?
2. Why did the writer make such extensive changes in the last sentence of the first paragraph? [Hint: What is the thesis statement of the critical analysis?]

3. In the first sentence of the second paragraph, why did the writer replace the word *honest* with the quote *"an honest man's labor"*?

4. Why did the writer move the second, third, and fourth sentences of the second paragraph?

5. Why did the writer add the words *as a greedy fake* to the last sentence of the second paragraph?

3. The exact quote is striking. The writer probably felt the verbal irony should be shown word for word.

4. The writer wanted the original first sentence to be a conclusion drawn from the three sentences that follow it, therefore the three sentences are moved to precede it.

5. Many readers might wonder what he was exposed as.

WRITING NOTE As you evaluate and revise your paper, remember that all your support shouldn't be direct quotations. Too many quotations can have a choppy, unoriginal, and even irritating effect (do *you* like to read strung-together quotations?). Use quotations when the author's exact wording is especially striking, important to your point, or more precise than a paraphrase. The rest of the time you can paraphrase or summarize ideas and details from the literary work.

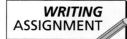

WRITING ASSIGNMENT

PART 5:
Evaluating and Revising Your Critical Analysis

Exchange papers with another student, and use the questions from the evaluating and revising chart on page 387 to evaluate each other's papers. Be prepared to explain to your partner where changes are needed to improve his or her essay. Then use your partner's comments and your own evaluation to revise your critical analysis.

"The answers you get from literature depend upon the questions you pose."

Margaret Atwood

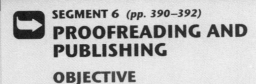
TEACHING THE LESSON

Ask students to share any proofreading methods they use. Stress multiple proofreadings with a different goal each time—to check quotation marks, correct spelling, and so forth.

Carefully review rules for using underlining. You may choose sentences from a

Teacher's ResourceBank™

RESOURCES

PROOFREADING AND PUBLISHING
- Analyzing a Story

QUOTATION FOR THE DAY

"Patience is not only a virtue, but it pays." (B. C. Forbes, 1880–1954, U.S. businessman and editor of *Forbes Magazine* from 1917–1954)

Lead students in a discussion of what they find most challenging about proofreading and urge them to focus on that area the next time they write.

LEP/ESL

General Strategies. Remind students to proofread for short sentences that could be combined with subordinating or coordinating conjunctions. With so much material in this chapter for students to learn and remember, they might forget to be careful about other skills.

390

---

390   *Writing About Literature*

Proofreading and Publishing

Proofreading. You probably have a proofreading method you're comfortable with—which is all the more reason to try a different one! Comfort lets errors creep in, and double-checking never hurts. Use your usual method, but then proofread again another way (perhaps backward). For this essay, also pay special attention to

- quotation marks (Do you have opening *and* closing marks?)
- punctuation used with quotation marks (See pages 835–836.)
- the story title (Is it enclosed in quotation marks?)

MECHANICS HINT

Using Underlining

When you write about literature or other art forms, you need to know how to indicate the title of the work. Sometimes you use quotation marks and sometimes you use underlining. (If you have a computer that does italics, it's the same as underlining.)

1. Use quotation marks to enclose the titles of stories, poems, songs, book chapters, and articles.

   One of Elizabeth Bishop's poems is called "The Fish."
   Alice Walker's short story "Everyday Use" is told in the first-person point of view.

2. Underline the titles of books, paintings, television programs, plays, and movies.

   The setting of Stephen Crane's novel *The Red Badge of Courage* is a battlefield during the Civil War.
   The movie *Dances with Wolves* won several Oscars.

 REFERENCE NOTE: See pages 831–840 for more information about quotation marks and underlining.

story and use them to model correct and incorrect use of underlining.

Suggest publication possibilities and ask students to add to your suggestions. Ask students for publication possibilities such as presenting on videotape, circulating writing in an exchange group, or adapting stories in the form of plays. Emphasize to students that writing is meant to be read. This last step reinforces the connection between reading and writing. You may want to reward them with praise or points for sharing their work.

Publishing. With your teacher's help, you might use the following ideas to share your paper with others.

- Get together with other students who wrote on the same general topic: character, conflict, point of view, and so on. Read each other's papers, and talk about what attracted you to the story and literary element you wrote about.
- Make a class file of essays as a reference tool for future assignments. You might arrange the papers alphabetically by author's name, and make a separate index that will let students look up essays by topic, story title, or story author.

  PART 6:
Proofreading and Publishing Your Critical Analysis

Proofread your paper (remember to try a new method as a double-check), and—whatever you do—don't let it sit in a folder unread. Use the suggestions above, take your essay home to your family, give it to your best friend, or surprise a former teacher by offering it (name removed, if you like) for his or her files.

A STUDENT MODEL

Matt Sanders, a student at East Mecklenburg High School in Charlotte, North Carolina, discusses Thomas Mann's "The Infant Prodigy." Matt has this advice for you: "It is very important to know the work of literature thoroughly and to understand it. Prewriting and planning are very important in getting your thoughts analyzed and your ideas organized. Once a suitable thesis is concocted, the paper should write itself."

INTEGRATING THE LANGUAGE ARTS

Mechanics Link. Students sometimes have trouble distinguishing ellipses and periods. You could use the chalkboard to emphasize the difference visually. For several days, place a period in the upper right corner of the chalkboard and place three ellipsis marks in the upper left corner. Remind students that four marks are used together only when ellipsis marks are followed by a period.

COOPERATIVE LEARNING

Some students might combine their critical analyses and create casebooks with artfully designed construction paper or cardboard covers. These might be kept on file for future students.

Casebooks might focus on a particular story or on a literary element such as plot or theme. Students might collaborate on a brief introduction that introduces the story or literary element and that gives a brief synopsis of each analysis in the collection.

The Big Picture
by Matt Sanders

A full portrait of a character cannot be created by revealing just his or her thoughts. The thoughts of others about that character play a crucial role in telling the complete story. By using the omniscient point of view, Thomas Mann creates a full portrait of Bibi, the main character in "The Infant Prodigy."

Many different pictures of Bibi are painted. One picture shows Bibi as an innocent, prodigious child who is full of talent. One character, the old man, sees Bibi's talent as being a gift from God. The business man, while analyzing the monetary aspects of the performance, says " 'Really he does not play so badly.' " The young girl sees Bibi as an innocent child with a talent of expressing passion. The critic also sees the innocence and talent in Bibi. " 'As an individual he still has to develop, but as a type he is already quite complete, the artist <u>par excellence</u>.' "

Another picture created by the omniscient narrator shows Bibi and his performance as a hoax used to play up to the audience. It sees through Bibi's dazzling performance. The piano teacher criticizes his performance as being unoriginal. Of his form she thinks, " 'And his hand position is entirely amateur. One must be able to lay a coin on the back of his hand--I would use a ruler on him.' " The critic also sees through Bibi's performance. He sees every move as a publicity stunt. The impresario's kiss is a " 'good old gag.' "

The third and final picture painted by the omniscient narrator is painted by Bibi himself. This is a picture of contempt for the audience. Bibi, on the outside, is a talented performer who loves pleasing the audience. However, by analyzing his thoughts, the true Bibi is seen. He thinks that the audience is unaware of true musical talent: "Now I will play the fantasy, it is a lot better than <u>Le Hibou</u>, of course, especially the C-sharp passage. But you idiots dote on the <u>Hibou</u>, though it is the first and silliest thing I wrote." When the princess talks to him about his music he thinks, " 'Oh, what a stupid old princess!' "

By using the omniscient point of view, the author can tell the complete story. By combining the thoughts of Bibi and the other characters in the story, Thomas Mann paints a full portrait of Bibi.

A STUDENT MODEL
Evaluation
1. Matt includes the title and author in the first paragraph.
2. Matt identifies the thesis of the analysis in the last sentence of the first paragraph.
3. Purpose and audience are considered in this critical analysis because it does not contain informal expressions and does not contain details of the plot that are unrelated to the purpose.
4. The conclusion brings the essay to a definite close restating the main idea.

SEGMENT 7 *(pp. 393–395)*
WRITING WORKSHOP

OBJECTIVE
- To plan, write, evaluate, revise, proofread, and publish a critical review of a movie or television program

TEACHING THE LESSON
Students probably understand the main literary elements by now, but you may need to review direction, acting, and other elements of film.

Students might analyze other brief reviews in magazines or in local newspapers. For practice, you could use the chalkboard to guide the class through planning and ☛

393

WRITING WORKSHOP

A Critical Review

Everyone is a movie and television reviewer once in a while. "Don't bother spending money on *Killer Cows III*," you tell a friend. "Even the cows are bored, not scary." Your reviews for friends are casual, but they have the same final purpose as published reviews: to judge whether the movie or program is worth watching.

Reviews (whether for films, television, or books) combine critical analysis of a work's elements with evaluation, or judgment. How good or effective is the movie—in its elements and as a whole? Judgments like this are opinions, but they're opinions based on standards (for example, the standard that a horror movie like *Killer Cows* should be scary). A reviewer who conveys only the message that "This was the stupidest excuse for a movie I've ever seen" without telling *why* won't convince anyone (or keep many readers).

Of course, reviews must tell you something of the work's subject, plot, or theme. Yet they have to strike a careful balance: enough information for understanding but not enough to spoil enjoyment. A special kind of review is the mini-review that newspapers and magazines often publish of movies they have reviewed at greater length in previous issues. The mini-review must combine information about the film for the reader who hasn't yet seen it and the reviewer's evaluation of it—the acting, directing, production values, and so on in a very short space. Following is a mini-review of the film *Driving Miss Daisy*. What do you learn about the content of the film itself? What is the reviewer's opinion of the film?

Alfred Uhry's adaptation of his much honored play is still full of manipulative bits—it's virtually all manipulative bits—but the director, Bruce Beresford, understands how to work them while cutting down on their obviousness. Set in Atlanta, starting in 1948,

Teacher's ResourceBank™

RESOURCES

WRITING WORKSHOP
All the resources for this chapter may be used in this segment.

QUOTATION FOR THE DAY

"It is in the hard, hard rock-pile labor of seeking to win, hold, or deserve a reader's interest that the pleasant agony of writing again comes in." (John Mason Brown, 1900–1969, U.S. drama critic, essayist, and lecturer)

Lead students in a discussion of the oxymoron "pleasant agony." You might ask them to cite examples from their own lives.

MEETING
INDIVIDUAL
NEEDS

LEP/ESL

General Strategies. Pauline Kael's review fits a lot into a small space. More than half her words are contained in just two sentences. Embedding relative clauses and adding many adjectives make for long but concise sentences. She uses parentheses three times and dashes twice. For her last sentence, she uses *and* as her first word, ignoring a convention but saving space and providing a sense of conclusion for the review. Discuss Kael's strategies.

writing a short review of a movie or program you have shown in class. Stress taking a stand by pointing out the many judgmental terms in Kael's review: "manipulative," "suspicious," "fine," and so forth.

As students work in groups to plan, write, and revise their reviews, you could circulate to answer questions. Remind students of their purpose: A positive review should make readers want to see the program; a negative review should make readers want to avoid it.

COOPERATIVE LEARNING
Put students in small groups to identify characteristics of successful television shows or movies (as they possibly did when discussing *Frankenstein*). After they have listed and shared positive and negative aspects of their movie or program, others who saw the production might add their own reactions for consideration.

VISUAL CONNECTIONS
Exploring the Subject. Until *Driving Miss Daisy*, Alfred Uhry had never written any plays except musicals. Based on real persons and originally scheduled to run only five weeks in a nonprofit theatre with 74 seats, the play won the 1988 Pulitzer Prize.

The movie, adapted by Uhry, won the Academy Award for Best Picture of 1989. Jessica Tandy won Best Actress for her portrayal of Miss Daisy.

the movie is the story of the companionship that develops between stubborn, suspicious Miss Daisy (Jessica Tandy), a wealthy Jewish widow of seventy-two, and her resilient chauffeur, Hoke (Morgan Freeman), a widower about a decade younger than she is. Essentially, it's about how he changes her. He's made upright, considerate, humane—he's made perfect—so that nothing will disturb our appreciation of the gentle, bittersweet reverie we're watching. But it's acted (and directed) eloquently. Tandy and Freeman achieve a beautiful equilibrium. And Dan Aykroyd comes through with a fine performance as Miss Daisy's good-old-boy son.

Pauline Kael, *The New Yorker*

SELECTION AMENDMENT
Description of change: excerpted
Rationale: to focus on the concept of critical reviews presented in this chapter

ASSESSMENT

A checklist may help you quickly assess students' critical reviews:
1. title and overall evaluation
2. concise plot statement
3. judgments and examples of important elements ["In her death scene" (example), "the giant lizard out-acts the rest of the cast" (judgment).]

CLOSURE

Ask students to list the purpose and the major features of a critical review. Have them recall criteria for evaluating plot, direction, acting, and other specific elements. ■

395

Writing a Mini-Review of a Movie or Television Program

Prewriting. Choose a movie or television show to review. (It can be one you've already seen *if* you remember it well.) Before anything else, think clearly about your standards: the elements and qualities you'll be looking for. If possible, do this groundwork with a group. Choose the most important story elements like characterization and plot, acting, and photography. Remember that a mini-review is a condensed review, and you won't have much space.

As you watch (or recall) the movie or program, make notes of specific details and your reactions. Then review your notes to focus your ideas. You can use a simple focusing tool like *The good things about the movie (program) are _____. The things that don't work well are _____.*

Writing, Evaluating, and Revising. Remember that the reader is looking to you for basic information in a very short space: title, director and writer (if possible), actors, and a one- or two-sentence plot summary. In your short review's body, use as many details as possible so readers can picture what you mean. When you have a draft, ask a partner to answer these questions: Is there enough plot information for people who haven't seen the movie? Are specific elements of the movie praised or criticized? Does the review bring the movie or show (good or bad) to life? Use your partner's evaluation as you revise. Try to keep your review as short as Pauline Kael's review of *Driving Miss Daisy*.

Proofreading and Publishing. Proofread your revised review, ask your partner to check it, and correct all errors. (Titles of films and television programs are underlined or italicized.) Then go on the air with your review: Stage it for your classmates in pairs as though you were Roger Ebert and Gene Siskel (above), or another pair of film reviewers.

MAKING CONNECTIONS

RESPONDING TO LITERATURE
OBJECTIVE

- To write a personal response that relates thoughts and feelings about a poem, a story, or a play

RESPONDING TO LITERATURE
Teaching Strategies

Point out that most people do not read literature or see films to marvel at the writer's craft or to closely analyze elements, but simply because they hope the story will make them laugh or cry or give some insight into their lives. Tell students that this lesson will let them respond more personally, emotionally, and informally to a poem, a story, or a play.

USING THE SELECTION
The Bean Eaters

1

Details of food and tableware suggest age and poverty.

2

Brooks knows that readers will identify with people who are "Mostly Good," and not seemingly perfect.

3

What is suggested by describing their memories as "twinklings/twinges"? ["Twinkling" suggests bright and shiny memories; "twinges" suggests pain or regret.]

MAKING CONNECTIONS

RESPONDING TO LITERATURE

Many times in life "Don't take it personally" is good advice. But not when you're reading literature. As you saw in this chapter, even for a formal critical essay the starting point is your individual reactions. Personal involvement is one of the pleasures and powers of art in any form: to feel that what you're reading, seeing, or hearing makes a direct connection.

Here's a poem you may have read and then one reader's response to it. As you read, think of your own thoughts and feelings about the poem. Does it remind you of anyone? What does it make you think of? What do you think of the poem?

The Bean Eaters
by Gwendolyn Brooks

They eat beans mostly, this old yellow pair.
Dinner is a casual affair.
1 Plain chipware on a plain and creaking wood,
Tin flatware.

2 Two who are Mostly Good.
Two who have lived their day,
But keep putting on their clothes
and putting things away.

And remembering . . .
3 Remembering, with twinklings and twinges,
As they lean over the beans in their rented back room that
    is full of beads and receipts and dolls and cloths.
    tobacco crumbs, vases and fringes.

HERE'S HOW

<u>Response</u>

I guess at first I just felt sort of sorry for these two old
people. What I thought was really sad was that they
seemed to be good people, but they just didn't have
anything—they must be very lonely. Then I thought
about this "remembering" and the things their room
seems to be full of. And I thought about all the times I
felt down and would get out my old scrapbook full of
stupid, little things like drawings and postcards from
friends and ribbons I won six years ago. And I would feel
sad that those times were past, but glad that I had
them to remember. And then I thought these people still
have their memories—their "twinklings." And I didn't feel
so sad about them anymore.

Now write your own response to the poem—or to any
poem, story, or play that you want to choose. Write it as if
you're talking to someone you feel comfortable with—
perhaps your best friend.

VISUAL CONNECTIONS
Related Expression Skills. Illustrations or photographs often accompany literary works. Guide students in a discussion of how the photograph of this elderly couple influences their response to the poem or how the poem influences their response to the photograph.

You may want to remind students to respond to the **"The Bean Eaters"** as active readers. Give them a few minutes to list their thoughts and feelings by clustering or freewriting. Ask for volunteers to share some of these responses with the class before reading the response in their textbooks.

To emphasize the informal and subjective nature of personal responses, have students read the textbook response and count the number of times the textbook uses *I* [12], *I thought* [4] and variations of *I felt* [4].

GUIDELINES

Responses will vary. Since the audience is supposed to be a friend, you may want to evaluate responses at the student's option, perhaps as extra credit.

CRITICAL ANALYSIS ACROSS THE CURRICULUM

OBJECTIVE

- To write or deliver a speech that is a critical analysis

CRITICAL ANALYSIS ACROSS THE CURRICULUM

Teaching Strategies

The purpose of a critical analysis is to provide information about how something works. Stress that students can be confident that subjects they find interesting and enjoyable will be interesting and enjoyable to someone else (school, hobbies, new products, and so forth).

Each student should list a subject, its purpose or value, its parts and features, and how it works before beginning a rough draft. Ask students to find or invent a magazine or a club that would be interested in their topics. Encourage them to publish or present their work in class or in a real magazine or club.

Give students an opportunity to react to each other's work before they finish their final drafts. A good approach is to have students read in small groups and have listeners ask questions at any point where they feel confused. They can stop at that point and discuss the problem.

CRITICAL ANALYSIS ACROSS THE CURRICULUM

In critical analysis, as you know by now, you use a knowledge of elements (component parts) to analyze something in detail. You can apply this skill not only to short stories but to cars, snow skis, scientific equipment, and political speeches—to anything whose parts and features you know well. Following is an analysis of a new type of audiovisual equipment, the "combi" player.

AUDIO AND VIDEO COME TOGETHER

Before there were CD players, there were laser-disc players, machines linked to a TV set to play very high quality video images. Initially, laser-disc players went nowhere. But a new variety of laser-disc player is now trying to piggyback on the CD's popularity.

The new machines, known as combination or "combi" players, can play 12-inch video discs with their digital soundtrack or five-inch CDs. The combi players also take three- and eight-inch discs, as well as the new CD-Vs (discs . . . with a five-minute music video plus 15 minutes of music only).

We examined two of the least expensive combi players, the *Pioneer CLD1070* . . . and the *Magnavox CDV484*. . . .

Their sound quality was as good as we've come to expect from CD players. The picture quality was also quite good: Both players delivered a picture with higher resolution than a VHS videotape can provide, approximately the quality of a Super-VHS tape. And, like conventional CD players, the combis let you move quickly from one track to another on a compact disc or speed to a particular scene on a video disc.

Laser discs haven't made it to the mom-and-pop video rental store yet, although large stores may have a small selection for rent. The biggest selection, however, is available for purchase from mail-order record and video clubs and major retailers for $25 to $35 per disc.

Consumer Reports

What are you interested in and fairly expert in (if you do say so yourself): maps? athletic equipment? telescopes? clarinets? Choose something that you would enjoy explaining clearly—either in writing or in an informal talk.

You can analyze, as in the example above, a certain *type* or *category* of your subject area. For example, if your subject area is "bicycles," you could analyze the recent "hybrid bikes." Or you can analyze a *particular example*, such as a specific new model of hybrid bicycle, whose features you'd like to scrutinize.

If you're writing your analysis, imagine that it's going to be published in a magazine specifically for lovers of your subject (and give the magazine a name: *Map Maniacs*, say, or *Clarinet Freaks*). If you're outlining and delivering a talk, imagine that it's for a club (like the Grand Order of Off-road Vehicle Owners).

Calvin & Hobbes, copyright 1987 Universal Press Syndicate. Reprinted with permission of Universal Press Syndicate. All rights reserved.

GUIDELINES

Analyses will vary but should contain the topic's purpose or value, how it works, and its features or parts.

VISUAL CONNECTIONS

About the Artist. *Calvin and Hobbes,* a comic strip of a young boy and his stuffed tiger, was created by Bill Watterson in 1985. It now appears in more than 1,800 newspapers. Watterson has allowed *Calvin and Hobbes* to be collected in books, which have sold millions.

Chapter 11 WRITING A RESEARCH PAPER

OBJECTIVES

- To analyze the structure and content of a research paper
- To select an appropriate topic for a research paper
- To write a list of research questions
- To collect and evaluate sources for a research paper and to prepare source cards
- To draft an early plan for a research paper and to take notes from sources
- To write an outline for a research paper
- To write a draft of a research paper and to prepare a Works Cited list
- To evaluate and revise the content and organization of a research paper
- To proofread a research paper and prepare it for publication

Motivation

Initiate a class discussion that will help students understand why they should learn how to write research papers. Have students name specific occasions in and out of school when the ability to do research might be useful. [You might suggest the following occasions for research: to find out about family history, to gather information to present to city council members to persuade them to vote against development in an environmentally sensitive area, to discover the voting record of someone running for office, and to learn about medicine that a doctor prescribes.]

Introduction

Tell students that the aim of a research paper is to inform. Tell them that when they are doing research they will be informing themselves and that when they write and publish their reports, they will be informing others.

To help students distinguish between the informative aim and other aims, focus students' attention on the examples of informative writing they encounter daily, such as newspapers, car manuals, lists of ingredients, and textbooks. You might also have students generate examples.

Point out that their aim—informative—dictates that they follow certain conventions, such as preparing a *Works Cited* page, when writing their reports.

Integration

Students can refer to this chapter when writing research papers for classes across the curriculum. Also, the chapter can be used as a reference when studying **Chapter 10: "Writing About Literature,"** in which students are required to draw on outside sources.

The chart on the next page illustrates the strands of language arts as they are integrated into this chapter. For vocabulary study, glossary words are underlined in some writing models.

QUOTATIONS
All **Quotations for the Day** are chosen because of their relevance to instructional material presented in that segment of the chapter and for their usefulness in establishing student interest in writing.

Selection	Reading and Literature	Writing and Critical Thinking	Language and Syntax	Speaking, Listening, and Other Expression Skills
from **"America's Ancient Skywatchers"** by Robert B. Carlson **402-404** from **"To Break the Unbreakable Codes"** by James R. Chiles **411**	Identifying facts and theories **405** Identifying supporting details **405, 440-442** Identifying sources of information **405** Reading for purpose, audience, and tone **411-412**	Writing a journal entry **405** Writing about personal experiences **405** Formulating an opinion **405, 440-442** Distinguishing fact from theory **405** Identifying supporting details **405, 440-442** Identifying information sources **405** Evaluating topics for research **409, 424** Choosing and developing a specific topic **409** Analyzing purpose, audience, and tone **411-412** Evaluating audience for a report **412** Thinking about purpose and audience **413, 444-445** Developing questions for research **413, 444-445** Using resources **419** Collecting and evaluating sources **419** Preparing source cards **419** Developing an early plan and taking notes **423, 442** Evaluating and making judgments **423, 424, 440-442, 444-445** Analyzing a topic **424** Writing thesis statements **424, 442** Preparing an outline **425** Writing a first draft **435** Preparing a *Works Cited* list **435** Analyzing a writer's revisions **436-437** Evaluating and revising a report **437** Analyzing a book report **440-442** Applying critical and interpretive thinking **440-442** Writing a book report **442** Writing objective questions **444-445** Presenting information in an objective manner **444-445**	Punctuating titles correctly **419, 423, 435** Proofreading for errors in grammar, usage, and mechanics **439, 442**	Discussing questions about purpose, audience, and tone **411-412** Interviewing classmates about a topic **412** Brainstorming with classmates about library and community resources **419** Evaluating and revising a classmate's report **437** Using visuals in an oral presentation **443-444** Conducting a public opinion poll **444-445** Sharing results of a public opinion poll **444-445**

SEGMENT PLANNING GUIDE

Whether you are planning for a quick review of a writing concept or preparing an extended lesson on composition, you can use the following Planning Guide to adapt the chapter material to the individual needs of your class.

SEGMENT	PAGES	CONTENT	RESOURCES
1 *Exploring Your World*	*401-405*		
Literary Model from **"America's Ancient Skywatchers"**	402-404	Guided reading: a model of a research report	
Reader's Response/ Writer's Craft	405	Model evaluation: responding to literature and analyzing a research report	
2 *Ways to Develop a Report*	*406*		
3 *Prewriting*	*407-425*		Asking Research Questions
Choosing a Subject	407	Guidelines: choosing a suitable topic	Using Sources of Information
Selecting a Suitable Topic	408-409	Guidelines: examining criteria to choose a topic	
Exercise 1	409	Applied practice: evaluating topics for research	
Writing Assignment: Part 1	409	Applied practice: developing a specific topic	
Thinking About Purpose, Audience, and Tone	410	Guidelines: analyzing and selecting appropriate purpose, audience, and tone	
Exercise 2	411-412	Cooperative learning: analyzing purpose, audience, and tone	
Literary Model from **"To Break the Unbreakable Codes"**	411	Guided reading: analyzing author's purpose, audience, and tone	
Exercise 3	412	Cooperative learning: analyzing audience	
Research Questions	412	Guidelines: using criteria to develop questions	
Writing Assignment: Part 2	413	Applied practice: beginning research	
Finding and Evaluating Sources of Information	414	Introduction: using library and community resources	
Charts: Resources	414-415	Guidelines: examining source possibilities	
Evaluating Sources	415	Guidelines: learning rules for evaluations	
Preparing Source Cards	416	Guidelines: recording information from sources	
Chart: Guidelines for Recording Source Information	416-418	Guidelines: recording sources	
Exercise 4	419	Cooperative learning: finding sources	
Writing Assignment: Part 3	419	Applied practice: collecting and evaluating sources	
Writing Assignment: Part 4	419	Applied practice: preparing source cards	
Drafting an Early Plan	420-421	Guidelines: deciding points to research	
Taking notes	421-422	Guidelines: quoting, summarizing, and paraphrasing	
Writing Assignment: Part 5	423	Applied practice: planning and note taking	

All the resources listed in this chapter are located in the Teacher's ResourceBank™.

SEGMENT	PAGES	CONTENT	RESOURCES
Developing a Thesis	423	Guidelines: expressing a main idea	
Critical Thinking: Analyzing Your Topic	423-424	Guidelines: analyzing a topic	
Critical Thinking Exercise	424	Applied practice: analyzing a topic	
Preparing the Final Outline	424-425	Guidelines: arranging note cards and ideas	
Writing Assignment: Part 6	425	Applied practice: preparing an outline	
4 *Writing*	*426-435*		Writing a Research Paper
Combining the Basic Elements	426	Guidelines: recalling parts of informative compositions	
Mechanics Hint	427	Writing suggestion: using quotations	
Giving Credit to Your Sources	428	Guidelines: documenting within a report and preparing *Works Cited* lists	
Charts: Guidelines for Giving Credit	428-429	Guidelines: crediting sources	
A Writer's Model	430-435	Guided reading: examining a research report	
Writing Assignment: Part 7	435	Applied practice: writing a first draft	
5 *Evaluating and Revising*	*436-438*		Writing a Research Paper
Exercise 5	436-437	Applied practice: analyzing a writer's revisions	
Writing Assignment: Part 8	437	Applied practice: evaluating and revising a report	
Evaluating and Revising Research Reports	438	Guidelines: applying evaluation and revision techniques	
6 *Proofreading and Publishing*	*439*		Writing a Research Paper
Writing Assignment: Part 9	439	Applied practice: proofreading and publishing	
7 *Writing Workshop*	*440-442*		All the resources for this chapter may be used in this segment.
A Book Report That Evaluates	440-442	Guidelines: using criteria for evaluating	
Model/Questions	440-442	Examining techniques: analyzing a book report	
Writing a Book Report	442	Applied practice: evaluating an autobiography	
8 *Making Connections*	*443-445*		
Research Across the Curriculum: Visual Arts	443-444	Explanation: learning the importance of research	
Speaking and Listening: Creating Research Sources	444-445	Applied practice: conducting a public opinion poll	
WHOLE-CHAPTER RESOURCES	Review Form A, Review Form B		

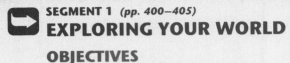
EXPLORING YOUR WORLD

OBJECTIVES

- To respond to a sample research report
- To analyze the structure and content of a sample research report

MOTIVATION

Bring copies of several high-interest, research-based articles to class for students to read.

VISUAL CONNECTIONS
Detail from *Cosmic Blink*

Exploring the Subject. This detail from the mural *Cosmic Blink* illustrates some of the achievements of science and commemorates the people who worked to expand humankind's understanding of the universe. The three large figures are, from left to right, Kepler, Einstein, and Newton.

Ideas for Writing. Students who are interested in science and history can use this picture as a springboard for possible research topics. Have students work together to discuss the people and things shown in the picture. Remind them to record their ideas and questions as their first prewriting notes.

11 WRITING A RESEARCH PAPER

You may want to read the excerpt from the article **"America's Ancient Sky-watchers"** aloud and to invite students to discuss the subject and the second **Reader's Response** question.

Then guide students through an analysis of the sample report and lead a discussion of possible sources of information for such a report.

After you and your students have discussed the article and various research sources, students can answer the **Writer's Craft** questions independently. Suggest that students re-read the article before answering the questions.

Exploring Your World

Research is a way of **exploring your world.** It's how we learn about the past and the present, and how we make decisions about the future.

Writing and You. Reports of research are everywhere—in books, magazines, and newspapers. Science writers report the latest findings on the environment, health, and astronomy. Historians and biographers dig up new information or give old information a new twist. Reporters turn their research into news stories. What other kinds of writers write research reports?

As You Read. Researchers have discovered that the ancient Incan and Mayan people knew a great deal about astronomy. As you read the following report, see if you can tell which information is factual and which is yet to be proved.

Detail of *Cosmic Blink,* Billy Morrow Jackson (1988–89). Oil on panel. Entire painting is 48" × 96". Collection of Parkland College, Champaign, IL.

QUOTATION FOR THE DAY

"We shall not cease from exploration and the end of all our exploring will be to arrive where we started and know the place for the first time." (T. S. Eliot, 1888–1965, English author)

You may wish to ask students to freewrite for a few minutes about what this quotation means to them. Then several volunteers might read their responses to the class. Lead students to understand that exploration plays an important part in researching and writing reports. Just as travelers explore new lands or astronauts explore space, writers explore by finding and considering information.

MEETING INDIVIDUAL NEEDS

LEP/ESL

General Strategies. One way to assist students in expanding their vocabularies is to offer practice in determining the meanings of words from their contexts. The excerpt from **"America's Ancient Skywatchers"** provides fertile ground for this activity. For example, point out that the statement "astronomy was not a science as we who are schooled in the Western tradition tend to think of it" reveals that astronomy is considered a science.

Have students use context clues to define *tapestry, discern, shamans, illuminate, celestial,* and *fanciful.*

401

Use an evaluation of students' answers to the **Writer's Craft** questions for assessment purposes.

RETEACHING

Give students copies of daily newspapers, and let each student choose an article of interest. Ask students if they can tell from the articles where the writers researched the information. Did the writers use interviews, print sources, or other media sources?

402

FROM

AMERICA'S ANCIENT SKYWATCHERS

by Robert B. Carlson

1 For many pre-Columbian Americans, whether Inca, Maya, Anasazi—or indeed many among their living descendants— astronomy was not a science as we who are schooled in the Western tradition

2 tend to think of it. Rather, the movements of sun and moon were the journeys of gods personified. In Mesoamerica the stars and the bright planets in their intricate wanderings were often conceived of as gods moving through the night sky en route to rebirth each

3 sunup. They wove an enormous celestial <u>tapestry</u> mirrored in the warp and weft of the lives of the people themselves.

USING THE SELECTION
from "America's Ancient Skywatchers"

1

The Incas established a great empire in Peru that lasted until the Spanish arrived in the 1500s. The Mayas lived in Guatemala and southern Mexico and flourished before the Spanish conquest. The Anasazi were cliff dwellers who lived before A.D. 1300 in the area where New Mexico, Arizona, Utah, and Colorado meet.

2

Why do you think people have often thought of celestial bodies as gods? [Responses will vary. One possibility is that celestial bodies are very impressive, and people tend to deify what impresses them.]

3

In weaving, the *warp* are the threads that run lengthwise in the loom, and the *weft* are the threads that go back and forth across the warp. Carlson is relating the events in people's lives to weaving and to the movements of the stars and planets.

CLOSURE

Ask the class to give a brief definition of *research*. Then ask students to name three places that they encounter research.

ENRICHMENT

Ask students to find examples of well-researched articles in textbooks for other courses, such as social studies or science. Have them analyze why the articles are interesting and what sources the writers may have used. ■

403

o observe and predict the recurrent paths of divine lights was to know the fates of kings and empires, to discern the proper day for rituals, to forecast animal migrations, the season of the life-giving rain, and the time for planting. The power to foretell required that observers, probably spe-

4 cially trained shamans or priests, make accurate records and preserve them. The information must have been accumulated over generations and generations, the observers

5 using naked-eye sighting techniques to discover the patterns of movement in the

6 universe. Their knowledge reached a level comparable to that of ancient cultures of the Old World.

> "...the movements of sun and moon were the journeys of gods personified."

Their records were preserved in calendars made of wood, string, and stone or, in Mesoamerica, written in accordion-fold books of animal hide or plaster-coated bark paper. Heavenly comings and goings were also recorded in the alignment of buildings and in city plans. These provided sight lines to mark significant risings and settings of celestial bodies. Such constructions often approached our own scientific astronomy in accuracy, but they had a sacred purpose.

7 We might compare this combination of technical knowledge and religious motive to a church window so placed that sunlight passing through it will illuminate a saint's statue on the saint's day.

Stone Calendar

4

In gathering research for this article, why would books or articles on Native American shamans be useful? [Stories of their experiences and observations might provide important and interesting details.]

5

The refracting telescope was invented in the early 1600s.

6

England's Stonehenge is a familiar example of an ancient alignment that may have traced the movements of celestial bodies.

7

Does the author's analogy help you understand the ancient architects' purpose? [Responses will vary.]

8

invested: endowed, thought of as having a quality

9

Note the transitional expressions that the author uses in this paragraph to lend clarity and coherence: *too* in the first sentence and *Just as* and *so* in the last sentence.

10

The Nazca were among the earliest settlers in Peru, arriving there in the first centuries A.D. They made colorful pottery, some of which was shaped like animals and vegetables.

11

Students might know another explanation sometimes offered for the Nazca Lines — that they were made by extraterrestrials as landing sites for spaceships. Are such explanations reasonable? [Responses will vary and could produce a lively discussion. Interested students might research this idea.]

12

mutually exclusive: incompatible

8
9   Earth too was invested with divinity. Many pre-Columbian American groups believed that their ancestors emerged from the underworld by way of a cave—the mouth of the earth. The earth's surface they divided into four quarters, often endowed

Nazca Lines (Hummingbird)

with distinctive trees, animals, deities, periods of time, and colors. Just as they arked the sky, so they set down paths of pilgrimage on the sacred landscape.

The most notable—and controversial—of these routes may be the ground drawings made on the bone-dry desert of southern Peru. The geometric figures of animals and plants; the spirals, zigzags, <u>trapezoids</u>, triangles; and the straight lines that stretch as far

10   as the eye can see—all these are called Nazca Lines for the culture that established itself in that forbidding terrain 2,000 years ago.

11   Many speculations, some reasonable, some fanciful, have been made about the significance of the lines. One explanation suggests that the straight lines were aligned to astronomical risings and settings. Another that at least some of the <u>effigy</u> figures represented constellations. Still

another idea, recently investigated in depth by astronomer-anthropologist Anthony Aveni and anthropologists Gary Urton and Persis Clarkson, maintains that the long, straight

Nazca Lines (Bird)

lines connected sacred sites and marked ritual pathways walked by celebrants to make offerings at

12   the far ends. These <u>hypotheses</u> are not mutually exclusive; all may have an element of truth.

Nazca Lines (Spider)

READER'S RESPONSE

1. When the ancient Americans looked up at the night sky, they saw more than just stars and planets—they saw stories in the sky. As a child (or even now), you may have done the same thing, perhaps at a summer camp-out. In a brief journal entry, tell about your own skywatching stories or experiences.
2. Like the ancient skywatchers, people who believe in astrology depend on the stars to plan their daily lives. What's your opinion of astrology?

WRITER'S CRAFT

3. What's the difference between a *fact* and a *theory*? Give two examples of facts in this report. Where does Carlson give some theories?
4. Writers of research reports must support their main ideas with specific examples and details. Give three details that Carlson uses to support his idea that Mesoamericans believed the movements of the sun and moon were related to the activities of their gods.
5. Carlson identifies some sources for some of the information he is sharing. What are those sources?

 VISUAL CONNECTIONS
Exploring the Subject. The Nazca Lines of Peru, some as long as five miles, are in the Atacama Desert. Among animal shapes formed by the lines are monkeys, spiders, birds, and lizards. While the Nazca Lines are well known, they aren't unique. Other such lines are found in Chile, England, and the United States (particularly in Iowa, Arizona, California, and Georgia).

ANSWERS
Reader's Response
Responses will vary.

1. Some students may not have had skywatching experiences. Allow such students to write fictional accounts.
2. Students should give reasons for their opinions.

Writer's Craft
Answers may vary.

3. A fact can be proven to be true; a theory is an unproven assumption about facts. Examples of facts include the location of Nazca Lines and their shapes. Examples of theories include ideas about the role of shamans and speculation about the significance of Nazca Lines.
4. Details include the fact that observers recorded the movements of celestial bodies in calenders and in the alignments of buildings, and that they used these movements to decide days for rituals.
5. Carlson mentions astronomer-anthropologist Anthony Aveni and anthropologists Gary Urton and Persis Clarkson as sources.

TEACHING THE MODES

To reinforce students' understanding of the modes in the context of a research report, work with students to generate examples of how each mode could be used in a report. Point out that the basic aim of these modes for a research paper is informative but that writing that includes research can incorporate other aims (persuasive, expressive, or literary). ■

INTEGRATING THE LANGUAGE ARTS

Literature Link. To make the point that authors often do research for all types of writing, have students read a short story such as "Trap of Gold" by Louis L'Amour or "Leiningen Versus the Ants" by Carl Stephenson. Tell students that, unlike a research report, the short story's primary aim is literary rather than informative. After students have read a short story, ask them to determine what information the author might have researched and what sources the author might have used. Ask students how the story would be different without the details that seem to have been researched.

Ways to Develop Research

You live at a time when you can find out more than you want to know about almost anything. Newspapers, magazines, and journals give the latest information about research results. Businesses, government agencies, speech-makers, and even advertisers turn out tons of reports.

Some of these research papers are informal, and some are formal. Robert Carlson's papers on ancient skywatch-ers is *informal* because it doesn't give a detailed list of sources. A *formal* report, on the other hand, like the ones in journals (periodicals that publish scientific reports) and the ones you write for school, always has a detailed list of sources. Readers of formal reports demand to know, "Where does this information come from?" Reports can be developed in various ways. Here are some examples:

▶ **Narration:** writing a biographical report about your favorite athlete; reporting on recent events in Africa.

Description: describing a Navajo sand painting from the Beauty Chant; describing a space-shuttle liftoff.

▶ **Classification:** reporting on the different parts of the human brain; comparing and contrasting two athletes.

Evaluation: supporting the thesis "All the best rock bands are British"; reporting scientific findings about the effects of food coloring on humans.

LOOKING AHEAD

In the main assignment in this chapter, you'll write a formal research paper. To report the results of your research, you'll use the strategy of either narration or classification. Keep in mind that a research paper

- presents factual information about the topic
- presents information from several sources
- tells readers the source of the information

OBJECTIVES

- To evaluate topics for research
- To choose a subject and limit it to a specific topic
- To analyze the purpose, audience, and tone of a paragraph from a report

- To analyze, through discussion, the audience of a report
- To develop research questions
- To identify and evaluate resources
- To prepare source cards for a report
- To record and organize information for a report
- To prepare a final outline for a report

Writing a Research Paper

Finding and Limiting a Subject

You've probably heard the expression "getting started on the right foot." In writing a research paper, the "right foot" is an interesting subject that you can develop into a suitable topic.

Choosing a Subject

A good research subject is one that's interesting to both you and your readers. To be interesting, however, your subject does not have to be exotic or far away. In looking for a subject, don't neglect what's available right in "your own back yard." After all, you may not be able to travel to the ruins in Peru, but you can discover the origins of your town or village just by visiting your library or historical society. Remember that some research captures our attention and imagination merely by shedding new light on familiar subjects.

To find possible research subjects, you can

- thumb through the subject cards in the card catalog
- look through the pamphlets and clippings in your library's vertical file
- browse through the nonfiction shelves in the library or along the documentary shelves in a videotape store
- skim articles of local and national interest in current newspapers and magazines
- watch television programs, such as *NOVA*, on scientific or historical topics
- talk with adult relatives or friends who have unusual or interesting jobs or backgrounds
- visit local museums and historical societies

QUOTATION FOR THE DAY

"Penetrating so many secrets, we cease to believe in the unknowable. But there it sits nevertheless, calmly licking its chops." (H. L. Mencken, 1880–1956, American writer, editor, and critic)

Lead students in a discussion of the seemingly infinite amount of information available today. Tell students that during their research they will probably discover that they are unable to include in their reports everything there is to know about their topics.

Ask students to talk about tasks that they've found overwhelming. Perhaps they've had to mow, rake, trim, and weed a whole yard. Maybe they've washed dishes at a busy restaurant. Point out that they probably made it through the tasks by taking one step at a time. And they probably were proud of their accomplishments afterward.

Tell students that writing a research report is similar. The task may seem overwhelming, but when taken one step at a time, it's not.

LEP/ESL

General Strategies. You may want to encourage foreign–born ESL students to write reports dealing with current events in their native countries. This strategy reinforces the links between students and their native cultures and offers them topics that are probably of personal interest to them.

AT-RISK STUDENTS

While most of the exercises call for partner or group participation, you may want to plan even more cooperative work. At-risk students can benefit greatly from discussing their progress on their reports with their classmates. In fact, you may want to pair each student with a research partner or to have students work in small groups throughout the study of this chapter.

Limiting Your Subject to a Specific Topic

You may already know that the key to good writing is using specific details. Even if your research paper were twenty pages long, you still wouldn't have space to discuss a broad subject in any detail. Suppose, for example, you chose the subject "the civil rights movement." You'd be faced with the impossible task of trying to cover dozens of subtopics, including "voting rights," "sit-ins," and "Montgomery bus boycott."

Maybe you chose the subject "the civil rights movement" because you vaguely remember an interesting magazine article about it. But at this point you have no specific information. Start by getting some general knowledge, an overview, of your subject. That will help you identify some smaller parts of the broad subject. Here are some ways to go about getting an overview.

- Read two or three general articles in reference books like encyclopedias. Notice headings and subheadings in the articles.
- Watch a videotape on your subject.
- Look up your subject in the *Readers' Guide to Periodical Literature* or in the library's card catalog or on-line computerized catalog. Note the topics that are listed under the subject headings, and read the descriptions of articles and books.
- Discuss your subject with someone (a teacher, neighbor, parent, and so on) who has expert knowledge about it.

Selecting a Suitable Topic

After getting an overview of your subject, you will probably have several possible topics in mind. But they may not all work well as topics for a research paper. To choose the best possible topic, ask yourself the following questions:

1. *Are there a variety of sources for this topic?* A highly personal topic such as "my experience on opening night of the class play" would not be a good choice because it has only one source: *you.* On the other hand, "favorite opening night experiences of three leading ladies" might have real possibilities. You

This segment provides information about the first stage of the writing process and starts students on writing assignments that lead to students' finished research reports. The prewriting stage of the writing process is divided into several steps, so it's natural to break your teaching into those steps. Allow plenty of time to discuss each step and focus on students' comprehension. Be sure that students understand how to apply each step to the preparation of their research reports before proceeding. Here are five divisions with textbook headings to use when teaching this segment:

Finding and Limiting a Subject. Have students generate suitable subjects, and write them on the chalkboard. Then for each

could read the autobiographies of several famous stage actresses and perhaps interview the "star" of a local theater group.

2. *Are sources of information readily available?* You may have trouble finding the information you need if a topic is too recent or too technical, or if the source material isn't available locally. For example, information about "legal precedents for *Brown v. Board of Education of Topeka*" would be too technical to appear in most popular publications.

EXERCISE 1 ▶   Evaluating Topics for Research

Which of the following topics could you use for a five-page research report? Some topics are too personal or technical, and some would be difficult to find information about. Which topics are too general to be covered in detail in a short paper? For each topic that seems unsuitable, first identify the problem, and then suggest a more limited or workable topic.

1. Chinese immigration to America
2. two successful experiments in a recent U.S. space mission
3. operations in the mechanical drive of the Jarvik-7 artificial heart
4. ancient art of Egyptian hieroglyphics
5. my favorite grade-B horror movies

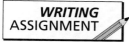

PART 1:
Developing a Specific Topic

Get off on the right foot by thinking about your own choice of a subject. Choose one subject that interests you, and use the techniques listed on page 408 to get an overview. Next, identify three or four possible topics related to your subject. After making certain that there are sources of information available, choose one of these topics for your report.

INTEGRATING THE LANGUAGE ARTS

Speaking Link. Stress that getting a good overview of a subject is very important when limiting the subject to a specific topic. To ensure that students take this step seriously, have them make short oral reports on the information they have learned in their overviews.

ANSWERS
Exercise 1

Suggestions for workable topics will vary.

1. too general; possible limited topic: Chinese immigration to America in the 1980s
2. appropriate
3. too technical; possible workable topic: two recent improvements in the artificial heart
4. appropriate
5. too personal; possible workable topic: recent trends in grade-B horror movies

WRITING NOTE   This chapter takes you step-by-step through the process of writing a research paper, but you'll find that you often move through the steps differently from your classmates. For example, if you are already very familiar with your subject, you may jump ahead to limiting your topic right away. Or, you may move "backward" if you realize that your topic isn't a good choice. If you do repeat a step, don't get discouraged. You'll make up for lost time and produce a much better report by changing direction when you need to.

Thinking About Purpose, Audience, and Tone

Purpose.   The basic purpose of a research paper is to inform. As you conduct your research, you will gather information and develop your own ideas about your topic. When you write your report, you'll inform readers about what you've learned.

Audience.   People who read a research report are looking for information. They want to come away from the report with a better understanding of the topic. As you explore your topic and write your report, consider your audience's interest level and information level.

- *Interest level.* Look for an unusual approach to the topic or surprising details about it.
- *Information level.* Take your readers beyond what they already know. But don't get so technical or complex that your readers will have difficulty understanding your report.

Tone.   TV documentaries, such as the Public Broadcasting System's *NOVA* or the National Geographic specials, often have a narrator who explains the images that you see on the screen. The narrator's tone of voice—usually calm, serious, and formal—lends authority to the information you're getting. If you use a serious, relatively formal tone in your report, your readers will be more likely to take it seriously.

EXERCISE 2 ▶ **Analyzing Purpose, Audience, and Tone**

What do you know about how secret codes work? Read the following paragraph from a report on secret codes. Then get together with a small group of classmates to discuss the questions that follow on page 412.

> A typical code takes ideas in the message—words or even whole phrases—and changes them into something else, usually groups of numbers taken out of a codebook resembling a small dictionary. To compose a coded message, the sender first writes what he intends to say ("Attack is imminent") and then looks up the words in his codebook. "Attack" is 1140, and "imminent" is 4539. And that's his message: 1140 4539. To further confound the enemy, the sender might scramble the signal by using a special key to encipher those numbers, by switching around the order, or both. The receiver must have an identical codebook and know anything extra the sender has done to scramble the number groups.
>
> James R. Chiles, "To Break the Unbreakable Codes"

Calvin & Hobbes, copyright 1986 Universal Press Syndicate. Reprinted with permission of Universal Press Syndicate. All rights reserved.

Then, if students have not had extensive note-taking experience, model various note-taking methods on the chalkboard.

Developing a Thesis Statement and **Preparing the Final Outline.** You can use the **Critical Thinking Exercise** to show students how to form thesis statements. Do either all or part of the exercise as a class.

INDEPENDENT PRACTICE

After you've discussed the various steps of the prewriting stage and let students work through the exercises in class, assign **Writing Assignment: Parts 1–6** as independent practice.

ANSWERS
Exercise 2

Responses will vary. Here are some possibilities:

1. The writer might have told an exciting story about secret agents and secret codes.

2. The writer describes the codebooks. The writer gives a specific example and explains it in simple, clear language.

3. The tone is formal.

ANSWERS
Exercise 3

Encourage students to give direct, helpful answers to their classmates' questions.

1. The writer's purpose is to inform readers about secret codes. How might the paragraph have been different if the subject stayed the same but the writer's purpose were to entertain readers?
2. How can you tell the writer assumed that most readers had never seen a codebook? What does the writer do to make the explanation of how a secret code works clear to readers?
3. How would you describe the tone of this paragraph?

EXERCISE 3 ▶ **Speaking and Listening: Analyzing the Audience for Your Report**

To help you get a better feeling for your audience, interview one or more of the classmates who will be the readers of your report. Start by telling your classmate briefly what you've learned about your topic and what you plan to find out. Then ask your classmate these questions.

1. How much do you already know about the topic? Have you ever read any articles or books about it? Do any television shows or tapes discuss it?
2. What seems interesting to you about the topic? What would you like to know about it?
3. Is anything about the topic confusing to you? What would help you understand the topic better?

Developing Research Questions

Your research will be much easier if you're searching for the answers to specific questions. Rely on your natural curiosity. Think about what you want to know about your topic, and jot down some questions to research. Here are some general questions that will help you think of specific questions about your topic.

- What is the topic? How can you define it?
- What groups, or classes, make up the topic?
- What are the topic's parts, and how do they work together?
- How has the topic changed over time?
- How is the topic similar to or different from related topics?
- What are the topic's advantages or disadvantages?

ASSESSMENT

The six parts of the writing assignment in this segment provide a good opportunity to measure students' prewriting skills.

RETEACHING

Give students copies of an article that includes research, perhaps an article from a magazine. Give students time to read the article. Then trace the author's logical prewriting steps with your students. Have students consider these questions:

1. What is the subject of the article?
2. What is the specific topic?

Prewriting **413**

To find a topic and begin your research

- use resource materials to find a general subject
- limit the general subject to a suitable topic
- stop to think about your purpose, audience, and tone
- develop a list of research questions about your topic

PART 2:
Beginning Your Research

Use your natural curiosity and what you already know about the topic to begin your research. Start by thinking about your purpose and audience. Then make a list of three or four research questions about your topic.

INTEGRATING THE LANGUAGE ARTS

Listening Link. Have several representatives from the community speak about the information available at their businesses or offices. If possible, have these speakers bring samples of the information they have available. For example, a representative from a local environmental agency could bring copies of the results of studies the agency has done recently.

3. What is the purpose of the article?
4. Who is the audience?
5. What is the tone of the article?
6. What are three research questions that the author might have asked about the topic?
7. What sources might the author have used?

8. What is the article's thesis statement?
9. What are three details that support that thesis statement?

INTEGRATING THE LANGUAGE ARTS

Library Link. You may want to have students review **Chapter 32: "The Library/Media Center."** You may also want to work with your school librarian to arrange an orientation session in your school library.

Give students a short list of topics and have them work in groups to locate information about one of the topics in at least three of the following library resources: card catalog or on-line catalog, *Readers' Guide to Periodical Literature,* microfilm or microfiche, general reference books, specialized reference books, videotapes and audiotapes, and vertical file.

Prewriting

Finding and Evaluating Sources of Information

We're bombarded daily with so much information that this has been called "the age of information." You may not even realize how many sources of information surround you. Here are some library and community sources you can use for your research.

LIBRARY RESOURCES	
SOURCE	**TYPE OF INFORMATION**
Card catalog or on-line catalog	Books listed by title, author, and subject; some libraries also list audiovisual materials—videotapes, records, CDs, audiotapes, and films
Readers' Guide to Periodical Literature or InfoTrac™	Magazine and journal articles, indexed by subject and author; InfoTrac™ also indexes five major newspapers
Microfilm or microfiche	Indexes to major newspapers such as *The New York Times* and *The Washington Post,* back issues of newspapers and magazines
General reference books	Encyclopedias, encyclopedia yearbooks, dictionaries
Specialized reference books	Biographical reference books, encyclopedias of special subjects (sports, art, etc.), atlases, almanacs (See pages 923–925 for more about reference books.)
Videotapes and audiotapes	Movies, documentaries, filmstrips, videotapes, audiotapes of books
Vertical file	Pamphlets listed by subject, clippings
The librarian	Help in finding and using sources

 REFERENCE NOTE: For more information on using the library, see pages 920–925.

CLOSURE

Ask students to summarize briefly the steps in the prewriting stage of the writing process.

EXTENSION

If students have problems limiting subjects, they might need instruction in moving from the general to the specific. To help students master this skill, put the following ladder of abstraction on the chalkboard:

I found an animal in the kitchen.
I found a reptile in the kitchen.

Prewriting **415**

COMMUNITY RESOURCES	
SOURCE	**TYPE OF INFORMATION**
Video stores	Documentary and instructional videotapes and audiotapes
Local government offices	Facts and statistics, information on local government policies, experts on local government
Local offices of state and federal officials	Voting records of government officials, recent or pending legislation, experts on state and federal government
Museums and historical societies	Special exhibits; libraries and book-stores; experts on history, science, art
Schools and colleges	Libraries, experts on various subjects
Local newspaper offices	Clippings files on local events and history

Evaluating Sources of Information

Some sources are more useful than others. Before you use a source, make sure that the 4 *R*'s apply.

1. *Relevant.* Does the source have information directly related to your topic? For a book, check the table of contents and the index. For a nonprint source, read a review or summary of the work.
2. *Reliable.* Can you trust your source to be accurate and objective? Well-respected magazines and newspapers such as *Smithsonian* or the *Christian Science Monitor* are usually reliable sources.
3. *Recent.* How up-to-date is the information? What is the copyright date? Even a historical topic, such as "women artists in the Middle Ages," should have some recent sources. New information is continually being researched and published.
4. *Representative.* If your topic is controversial, you need to find sources with opinions and information on both sides of the issue. For example, if some scientists say exercise adds to life span and others say it doesn't, you must report both theories.

ADVANCED STUDENTS

In addition to having students use both print and nonprint sources, you may also want to distinguish between primary and secondary sources and have students use both for their reports. Examples of primary sources include interviews, journals, letters, books of fiction, and works of art.

LEARNING STYLES

Kinetic Learners. Some students might especially benefit from a trip to the library to let them have hands-on experience with the card catalog, the *Readers' Guide to Periodical Literature,* microfilm or microfiche, videotapes and audiotapes, the vertical file, and other library resources.

I found a snake in the kitchen.
I found a python in the kitchen.
I found Peter, my pet python, in the kitchen.

Discuss the fact that an animal could be any of millions of creatures. As students move down the ladder, the possibilities becomes more limited until the reference is to one specific animal. Have students construct ladders of abstraction for their subjects, placing the general subject at the top as in the example.

Preparing Source Cards

You have this great quotation you want to use in your report, but you can't remember where you found it. If you've ever had anything like that happen, you know it's important to keep a record of your sources. That's where source cards come into the picture.

For each of your sources, write the author, title, and publication information on an index card. (These source cards are sometimes called *bibliography cards.*) Or, if you wish, you may list your sources on a piece of paper. Give each source a number. With good source information, you won't need to run back again and again to the card catalog or *Readers' Guide.* These source cards will also make it easier to prepare the final list of sources, or *Works Cited,* that accompanies your report.

The following guidelines tell you how to record the necessary information for different types of sources. As you fill out your cards, refer to these guidelines, and note the special uses of punctuation.

GUIDELINES FOR RECORDING SOURCE INFORMATION

1. **Book with One Author.** Write the author's name, last name first; the title of the book; the place of publication; the publishing company's name; and the year of publication. (To locate a book later, write its call number in the upper right-hand corner of the index card.)

   EXAMPLE   Chen, Román Piña. The Olmec: Mother Culture of Mesoamerica. New York: Rizzoli, 1989.

2. **Source with More Than One Author.** For the first listed author, write the last name first. For all other authors, write the first name first.

   EXAMPLE   Rust, William F., and Robert J. Sharer.

3. **Anthology or Compilation.** Write the name of the editor, last name first; the abbreviation *ed.;* the title of

(continued)

LEARNING STYLES

Visual and Kinetic Learners. Most tenth-graders have not had extensive experience with the research report format, so the mechanics of filling out source cards may pose some problems. Before students fill out their cards, try some whole-class practice. Have students bring information on their sources to class. They should include a mixture of books, articles, and nonprint sources. Then have kinetic learners write examples of source cards on the chalkboard. Visual learners can watch for errors as the other students work.

ENRICHMENT

Show a videotape, perhaps from public television, that you consider to be well researched. Have students analyze the possible sources used in the production; identify the subject, limited topic, and main idea (thesis statement) of the program; and evaluate the organization of the information presented in the program. ■

GUIDELINES FOR RECORDING SOURCE INFORMATION *(continued)*

the book; the place of publication; the publishing company's name; and the year of publication.

EXAMPLE   Benson, Elizabeth P., ed. The Olmec & Their Neighbors. Washington: Dumbarton Oaks Research Library and Collections, Trustees for Harvard University, 1981.

4. **Magazine Article.** Write the author's name, last name first; the title of the article; the name of the magazine; the day (if given), month (abbreviated), and year of publication; and the page numbers on which the article begins and ends. (If no author's name is given, begin with the title of the article.)

EXAMPLE   Rust, William F., and Robert J. Sharer. "Olmec Settlement Data from La Venta, Tabasco, Mexico." Science 7 Oct. 1988: 102-04.

5. **Newspaper Article.** Write the author's name, last name first; the title of the article; the name of the newspaper; the day, month, and year of publication; and the page number. If the newspaper has different editions and/or sections, write the edition (use *ed.*) and/or the section before giving the page number.

EXAMPLE   New York Times 1 Aug. 1991, early ed., sec. 1: 2.

6. **Encyclopedia Article.** Write the author's name, last name first (if given); the title of the article; the name of the encyclopedia; and the year of publication, followed by the abbreviation *ed.* for *edition*.

EXAMPLE   "Olmec." Encyclopedia Americana. 1990 ed.

7. **Radio or Television Program.** Write the title of the program; the local station call letters; the city of broadcast; and the day, month, and year of the broadcast.

EXAMPLE   NBC Nightly News. WNBC, New York. 8 July 1991.

(continued)

COOPERATIVE LEARNING
You could let students work in groups of three or four to write bogus source cards that break all the rules in the guidelines. For example, the cards could lack punctuation marks or list information in the wrong order. When each group has finished its bogus cards, ask groups to exchange the cards. Groups should then correct or redo the cards they receive in the exchange.

RADIO OR TELEVISION PROGRAM

If the network is not identified in the program title, students should list it before the affiliate call letters. If pertinent, students should list the narrator (Narr. Hugh Downs), producer (Prod. Tony Burden), or director (Dir. Sarah Marino) between the title and network.

INTEGRATING THE LANGUAGE ARTS

Mechanics Link. To give students practice using quotation marks to enclose a person's exact words, have students interview one another about the topics of their research reports and use quotation marks as they record responses. For example, a student might ask a classmate why she chose a particular topic. The student might then record the classmate's response: Margaret said, "I chose to research the history of comic books because I have always loved them."

GUIDELINES FOR RECORDING SOURCE INFORMATION *(continued)*

8. **Movie.** Write the title of the work; the director's name; the distributor's name; and the year of release. (Use *Dir.* for *director.*)

   EXAMPLE   Jivaro. Dir. Edward Ludwig. Paramount, 1953.

9. **Filmstrip, Slide Program, or Videotape.** Write the title of the work; the medium; the producer, director, or developer's name; the distributor's name; the year of release, and the running time or number of slides. (Use *Dir.* for *director* and *Prod.* for *producer.*)

   EXAMPLE   The Ancient New World. Videocassette. Prod. Churchill Films. Churchill Films, 1986. 16 min.

10. **Interview.** Write the interviewee's name; the type of interview (Personal or Telephone); and the day, month, and year of the interview.

    EXAMPLE   Sutphin, Andrea. Telephone interview. 17 Apr. 1991.

     REFERENCE NOTE: For help with capitalizing and punctuating titles, see pages 777–778, 831–832, and 840.

As you prepare your source cards, be sure to

- follow a specific format for recording source information
- record all information accurately, double-checking authors' names, titles, and page numbers
- indicate when you are citing an author's exact words by using quotation marks
- follow the rules for punctuating and capitalizing titles (pages 777–778, 831–832, and 840) and for using quotation marks to give an author's exact words (pages 834–836)

WRITING NOTE The format for identifying sources in this chapter is that of the Modern Language Association of America (MLA). You'll use it for preparing source cards, taking notes, and preparing your final list of sources. Your teacher may instead ask you to use a different format, such as that of the American Psychological Association (APA).

EXERCISE 4 ▶   **Using Library and Community Resources**

With a small group, brainstorm some sources for answering the two practical, everyday questions that follow. For each question, try to think of two library sources and two community sources. Check the 4 *R*'s: Are your sources relevant, reliable, recent, and representative?

1. What percentage of eligible people voted in the last election? are registered? How can we get more 18-year-olds to register and vote?
2. What approaches are your community and the nation taking to decrease the dropout rate?

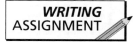

WRITING ASSIGNMENT   PART 3:
Collecting and Evaluating Sources

Explore your library and community sources to see what you can find out about your topic. (Find five or six sources of information.) Then evaluate each source by checking its 4 *R*'s (see page 415). You and a classmate might exchange your lists and evaluate each other's sources.

WRITING ASSIGNMENT   PART 4:
Preparing Source Cards

Prepare a source card for each source you've decided to use. Use the guidelines and examples on pages 416–418.

Prewriting

Planning, Recording, and Organizing Information

You've identified some sources that look promising. Now you need to collect information and find some way of organizing it.

Drafting an Early Plan

Faced with a stack of books or an interview date, you may be uncertain about where to begin. After all, you can't take notes or ask questions about *everything* concerning your topic. One way to get some idea about where to start is to make an *early plan*—a list of points that you plan to research. For example, suppose you read some new information about the Olmecs' form of government and learned that the Olmecs developed a calendar and a form of writing. Here's the way you could use this information in an early plan.

HERE'S
HOW

> The Olmecs
>
> Discovery of lost Olmec civilization
> Archaeologists
> Other scientists
> Government
> Villages and cities
> Powerful rulers
> Calendar
> Writing

A DIFFERENT APPROACH
Ask someone who has written and published research articles to speak to the class. Ask the writer to offer personal hints and suggestions to help students with their research and their writing.

Refer to your early plan as you take notes, and use its headings in deciding what information to record. But remember that your early plan can be changed. If you discover new information related to your topic, add a heading to your early plan. Or, if you decide not to develop a point in your early plan, delete the heading.

Taking Notes

As you take notes from a source, you can either quote, summarize, or paraphrase the material. Notice how these three techniques are used to take notes on Boyce Rensberger's article "Black Kings of Ancient America."

TECHNIQUE	EXAMPLE
Quote only when the author's exact words, as well as ideas, are important. To quote, copy the source material word for word, and put quotation marks around it.	"The great stone heads of Mexico are by far the most spectacular evidence that, as civilization was dawning in the New World more than 2,000 years before Columbus 'discovered' America, black people from Africa had already reached these shores. They came not as slaves but as free men and women, experienced mariners who had sailed across the Atlantic from one of the ancient advanced civilizations of Africa."
Summarize when you need to remember only the main idea. Read or listen to the material first. Then, without looking at the source, write your notes in your own words.	Boyce Rensberger believes that the features of the Olmecs' great stone heads show that Africans must have come to the New World long before Columbus arrived.
Paraphrase when you need to remember more detailed information. Restate the material by using your own vocabulary and sentence structure.	Boyce Rensberger believes that the African features of the Olmecs' great stone heads prove that Africans—free men and women, not slaves—reached the New World 2,000 years before Columbus. He believes that they sailed across the ocean from one of Africa's advanced civilizations.

Whichever method you use, always check your notes against the original to be certain that you have quoted, summarized, or paraphrased accurately.

Unless you attack note taking in an orderly way, you'll be faced with trying to untangle a jumble of notes. Experienced note-takers give this advice:

- Take notes on 4″ × 6″ note cards, using a separate card for each item of information and each source. If you use notebook paper instead, you'll need a separate sheet for each source.
- In the upper left-hand corner, write a key word or phrase (perhaps a heading from your early plan) so you can tell at a glance what the card is about.
- In the upper right-hand corner, write the source card number (see page 416). End each note with the page number where you found the information.

HERE'S HOW

importance	6

"The Olmec culture is generally considered to have given rise to all the other great civilizations that developed in Central America, including the Mayan and, much later, the Aztec."

p. 76

WRITING NOTE

Unless you're quoting a source directly, *always* take notes in your own words. Change the sentence structure, too. When you use someone else's words or ideas without giving proper credit, you're *plagiarizing*. No matter how you ultimately use your source (direct quotation, paraphrase, or summary), you must give credit for other people's ideas as well as their words.

CRITICAL THINKING
(pp. 423–424)

OBJECTIVE

• To write thesis statements that reflect four different approaches to one topic

TEACHING *ANALYZING YOUR TOPIC*

Discuss with students each of the four possible approaches to a topic and the accompanying sample thesis statements. Then work with students to use the four approaches to generate thesis statements for another topic.

PART 5:
Planning and Note Taking

Use what you've already learned about your topic to identify points you'd like to explore further. Make these the headings as you draft your early plan. Then start taking notes from your sources. You can't, of course, take notes about *everything*. Use the headings in your early plan to decide what information to record.

Developing a Thesis Statement

Your *thesis statement* is a signpost to guide both you and your reader. It expresses the main idea of your report and indicates what you plan to cover. Think about the ideas and conclusions you've drawn from your research so far, and write a preliminary thesis statement. (You can always revise it later.) Right now it will help focus your note taking, and later it will help you organize your report.

 REFERENCE NOTE: See pages 113–114 for more help with writing thesis statements.

CRITICAL THINKING

Analyzing Your Topic

When you *analyze* a topic, you break it down into its smaller parts and think about how the parts are related. For any topic it's possible to take several different approaches. Analyzing the possible approaches is an important first step in writing your thesis statement.

For example, following are four possible approaches and sample thesis statements for the topic "the role of women in the American military services." Notice that each approach emphasizes a different aspect of this topic.

■ **Exploring new information**

EXAMPLE   In the 1990s, women in the American military services have many varied roles.

Suggest that for students' research papers they consider several possible approaches to their topics and then choose the one that will make the best use of the information they have gathered. ⚡

⬧ A DIFFERENT APPROACH

Select an article from a newspaper or a magazine about a topic of interest to students. Read the article aloud or have a student read it aloud. Then ask students to tell you the main idea of the article. Lead a class discussion of the writer's approach to the topic. Ask students to tell you some details that are indicative of that approach. You could write the details on the chalkboard. Then ask students what other approaches the author might have taken with the same topic.

ANSWERS
Critical Thinking Exercise

Responses will vary. Here are some guidelines for evaluation:

1. This thesis statement should clearly reflect the fact that the report will give new information or new ideas about the topic.

2. References to time and change should be central to this thesis statement.

3. Be sure that this thesis statement mentions both cause and effect.

4. This thesis statement should clearly state what is being compared or contrasted.

- **Examining how the topic has changed over time**

  EXAMPLE   Women's roles in the American military services have changed drastically since women were first admitted to the armed services.

- **Demonstrating a cause-and-effect relationship**

  EXAMPLE   Past successes of American women in the military have resulted in their broader roles in the 1990s.

- **Demonstrating a comparison/contrast relationship**

  EXAMPLE   Roles for American women in the military services are much more limited than those for women in the armed services of many other countries.

⚡ CRITICAL THINKING EXERCISE:
Analyzing a Topic

Suppose you're planning to write a research report about some aspect of space exploration. You've done some research, and you're ready to develop a preliminary thesis statement. How will you approach your topic? Write four thesis statements to illustrate these different approaches: (1) exploring new information, (2) examining how the topic has changed over time, (3) demonstrating a cause/effect relationship, and (4) demonstrating a comparison/contrast relationship. To get some ideas, look back at the example thesis statements on women in the armed forces. Make up whatever details you need for your thesis statements. ⚡

Preparing an Outline

Your early plan helped you organize your research. But now that you've collected your information, you'll probably find you need to do more organizing. Although you may not know exactly how you want to organize your report until you have written and revised your first draft, it's helpful to begin organizing before you start writing.

One way to begin organizing is to create an outline. Start by arranging your note cards into stacks, according to the headings in your early plan. You can then create subheadings and divide a stack into smaller piles or group several small, related stacks together under a broader category.

Here's an outline the writer created after completing research on the Olmecs. Notice that it is a *formal* outline, with Roman numerals and capital letters. A formal outline like this is usually written after the report is written. The writer includes it with the research report where it serves as a kind of table of contents for the reader.

 REFERENCE NOTE: For help with writing a formal outline, see page 118.

The Olmecs: New Light on a Distant Past

I. Discovery of lost Olmecs
   A. Work of archaeologist Serran
   B. Theory about relics and unknown culture
   C. Excavations and scientific study
II. Olmec society and government
   A. Villages and cities
   B. Powerful rulers
      1. Evidence from cities
      2. Other evidence
III. Olmecs as advanced civilization
   A. Sophisticated calendar
   B. Knowledge of astronomy
   C. Hieroglyphic writing
IV. Disagreement about archaeological evidence
V. Importance of Olmecs

 PART 6:
Preparing an Outline

This is the time to organize your notes and create an outline. Use it as a guide as you write, but feel free to revise it if you find a better way to develop your paper.

SEGMENT 4 (pp. 426–435)
WRITING YOUR FIRST DRAFT
OBJECTIVE
- To write a first draft of a research report that includes parenthetical citations of sources and a Works Cited list

MOTIVATION

Tell students that the hardest stages of the writing process for a research report—the research and planning stages—are behind them. If they have laid good foundations in prewriting, actually writing their reports should not be too difficult.

QUOTATION FOR THE DAY

"According to [some] scholars, the Olmecs believed they were descended from a race of were-jaguars—the offspring of a male jaguar and a human female . . . ." (Richard A. Diehl, professor of Anthropology, University of Alabama)

You could use this quotation to spark students' interest in **A Writer's Model,** which is about the Olmecs. Ask students to speculate why a group of people might have believed they were descended from jaguars.

MEETING
INDIVIDUAL
NEEDS

LEARNING STYLES

Visual Learners. You may want to make a chart on poster board of the basic elements of a research report and display it in a prominent place in the classroom so that students can refer to it as needed.

SELECTION AMENDMENT
Description of change: excerpted
Rationale: to focus on the concept of writing presented in this chapter

426

Writing Your First Draft

All your careful preparations will finally pay off. Now that you've collected and organized your information, the actual writing will be easy.

Combining the Basic Elements of a Research Report

Keep these two goals in mind as you begin writing. You want to interest your readers and help them understand your topic. You also need to pull together, or synthesize, ideas and information from a variety of sources and state them in your own words. Like any informative composition, your research report should include all of these elements:

- an interesting opening that captures your reader's attention
- a thesis statement that presents your main idea
- a series of body paragraphs that develop and support the thesis statement
- a clear order for your ideas and information
- a conclusion that restates your main points

☞ REFERENCE NOTE: To review the basic elements of a composition, see pages 122–134.

As you write the first draft of your body paragraphs, be guided by your final outline. You'll develop each main heading into one or two paragraphs.

"I believe more in the scissors than I do in the pencil."

Truman Capote

Begin this section by leading a class review of the basic elements of a research report. Tell your students that a research paper includes the same basic elements as any informative composition.

Next go over the material on incorporating quotations and documenting sources. Stress that guidelines for documenting sources are to be understood and referred to rather than memorized. Before students begin their drafts, have them read **A Writer's Model.**

After students have read the model, you could use the side-margin annotations to focus a discussion on its organization and form. Be sure that students understand the basic elements of an informative composition 👉

MECHANICS HINT

Using Quotations

To give your paper credibility, sprinkle it lightly with direct quotations, following these guidelines:

1. Place a directly quoted phrase or clause into your own sentence, and enclose it in quotation marks.

   Researcher Michael D. Coe says experts are almost unanimous in their belief that **"**the Olmec civilization is older than any other in Mesoamerica**"** (183).

2. Run a short quotation (four lines or fewer) into your text. Introduce it in your own words, and enclose it in quotation marks.

   According to Coe**,** **"**There is now little or no dissent from the proposition that the Olmec civilization is older than any other in Mesoamerica, including the Classic Maya**"** (183).

3. Set off a longer quotation by indenting each line ten spaces from the left margin. Introduce the quotation in your own words, usually followed by a colon, but do not use quotation marks.

   Archaeologists have solved the mystery of when the Olmecs flourished:

   > There is now little or no dissent from the proposition that the Olmec civilization is older than any other in Mesoamerica, including the Classic Maya. Recent excavations in both lowland and highland Mexico have proved this beyond all doubt (Coe 183).

   (**Source:** Coe, Michael D. "Olmec and Maya: A Study in Relationships." <u>The Origins of Maya Civilization</u>. Ed. Richard E. W. Adams. Albuquerque: U of New Mexico P, 1977. 183-195.)

MECHANICS HINT

Have each student find three examples from printed sources (newspapers, magazines, books) that illustrate the three guidelines for using and punctuating direct quotations. Have students underline the examples. Then have students exchange examples and identify each as representing guideline 1, 2, or 3.

⚡ TIMESAVER

Instead of discussing individually the basic elements of a research paper, the use of quotations, and the documentation of sources, you may want to proceed straight to **A Writer's Model** and teach these items as you read through the report. You may find this an especially good alternative method if your class is advanced.

before they start writing their first drafts. Depending on the nature and capabilities of your class, you may want to give students a definite length requirement for their first drafts.

GUIDED PRACTICE

You could give students time in class to begin their first drafts (**Writing Assignment: Part 7**) so that you can assist them with any initial problems. Be sure that students have written clear thesis statements and that they are properly citing their sources and correctly using quotation marks.

MEETING INDIVIDUAL NEEDS

LEP/ESL

General Strategies. The guidelines for giving credit to sources may contain too much information for students to assimilate on their own. Before preparing a Works Cited page, students might need extra practice with the bibliographical form. Pair LEP/ESL students and give the pairs several incorrect versions of the Olmec report's Works Cited page. Have students correct the incorrect versions by comparing them to the original on p. 435.

LESS-ADVANCED STUDENTS

Deciding when to give credit to a source may be difficult for some students. To help them see the difference between general information that doesn't need to be credited and information that should be credited, locate ten bits of information that would need to be credited in a research report and mix them up with ten bits of information that can be found in general reference sources.

Read the mixed-up list to your class. As you read each fact, ask the class if it should be credited or not, and have students support their answers.

Giving Credit to Your Sources

In your report you'll document your sources throughout the paper itself and in a separate list at the end, labeled *Works Cited*.

Giving Credit Within the Body of Your Report.

Every researcher-writer faces two problems: (1) when to give credit, and (2) how to give credit.

1. *How do you decide when to give credit?* As a rule, it's not necessary to acknowledge general information you already know or can easily find in general reference sources. (*In Chinatown in San Francisco, signs are written in both Chinese and English.*) You also don't have to acknowledge general information from public sources like newspapers or TV. (*Smoking may cause cancer and heart disease.*)

2. *How do you show the credit?* There are several styles for giving credit. In this chapter, documentation follows the format recommended by the Modern Language Association of America (MLA), which uses parenthetical citations. Some teachers prefer footnotes, placed at the bottom of the page and corresponding to numbers in the text. Here's one example; but if you need to use footnotes, you'll have to follow another style guide.

[1] Román Piña Chen, The Olmec: Mother Culture of Mesoamerica (New York: Rizzoli, 1989) 25.

GUIDELINES FOR GIVING CREDIT WITHIN THE REPORT

Place the information in parentheses at the end of the sentence in which you've used someone else's words or ideas.

1. **Print Source with One Author.** Author's last name followed by the page number(s). (Chen 83)

2. **Print Sources by Authors with the Same Last Name.** First and last names of each author followed by the page number(s). (Mary Smith 21) (John Smith 102)

3. **Print Source with More Than One Author.** All authors' last names, followed by the page number(s). (Rust and Sharer 102)

After you think students have a good understanding of the basic elements of an informative composition and know how to document sources correctly, have them write the remainders of their first drafts on their own.

Use students' first drafts to assess their mastery of the skills involved in writing research reports, including the documentation of sources and the incorporation of direct quotations.

Writing Your First Draft **429**

GUIDELINES FOR GIVING CREDIT WITHIN THE REPORT *(continued)*

4. **Print Source with No Author Given.** Title, or a shortened form, and the page number(s). ("New Information" 34)

5. **One-Page Print Source.** Author's name, or the title if no author's name is given. (Bower)

6. **Nonprint Source.** The title, or a shortened form. (The Ancient New World)

7. **More Than One Print Source by the Same Author.** Author's last name and the title or a shortened form of it, followed by the page number(s). (Nissen, "Olmec Legacy" 21) (Nissen, "New Discoveries" 45)

8. **Author's Name Given in Paragraph.** Page number only. (76)

Preparing the List of Sources. The citations in the body of your report refer to a detailed list, the *Works Cited* page at the end of your report. (If you've used print sources only, you can call this a *Bibliography*.) Readers who want to know complete publication information can refer to this page as they read your paper.

GUIDELINES FOR PREPARING THE LIST OF WORKS CITED

1. On a separate sheet, center the words *Works Cited* (or the word *Bibliography*) one inch from the top.

2. For each entry on the list, follow the format you used for your source cards (pages 416–419).

3. List your sources by the author's last name. If no author is given, alphabetize by the first important word in the title. If you use two or more sources by the same author, write the author's name in the first entry only. For all other entries, write three hyphens where the author's name should be, followed by a period. Then give the title, publication information, and page number(s).

4. Begin each listing at the left margin. If a listing is longer than one line, indent all the following lines five spaces.

ADVANCED STUDENTS

Most students probably won't want to hear about any style for giving credit other than the one you want them to follow. However, you may want to introduce students to a few other crediting styles. You may also want to point out the footnoting capabilities of modern word processing programs, which can save time and reduce frustration.

INTEGRATING THE LANGUAGE ARTS

Vocabulary Link. Previously, what is called the Works Cited page today was referred to as the bibliography. You may want to explain to students why this shift occurred. The base word in *bibliography* is the Greek word for book, *biblion*. Hence, a bibliography has been associated with the citing of books and other printed publications. However, nonprint sources are often used today. *Works Cited* has developed as a general heading that more adequately covers all sources, print and nonprint.

If some students are still having difficulty mastering the basics of writing a research report, show your class a short, informative documentary film or video. Tell them to listen for an interesting opening, a thesis statement, supporting details, the organization of ideas, and a conclusion. Students should also listen for direct quotations and citations of sources. If you are using a VCR, you may want to pause during the videotape to discuss the various elements as they occur.

INTEGRATING THE LANGUAGE ARTS

Library Link. Remind students that one method of writing an effective introduction is to use a pertinent quotation. For example, a report might begin, "Shakespeare said that '. . . ,' but unfortunately that's not true today." To help students find quotations, identify the books of quotations frequently available in libraries. Bartlett's *Familiar Quotations* is one of the most widely known of these books.

MEETING
INDIVIDUAL
NEEDS

LEARNING STYLES

Auditory Learners. You may want to read aloud the writer's model and discuss its content and form as you go along.

Now read the following research report about the Olmecs. Notice how the report combines basic composition form with documentation of sources.

A WRITER'S MODEL

The Olmecs: New Light on a Dark Past

INTRODUCTION
Interest grabber

In old movies the determined explorers hack their way through tangled jungle vines, searching for the lost civilization. Suddenly, they stumble into a hole hidden by dense undergrowth. At the bottom of this dark pit, they discover a huge stone monument covered with mysterious carvings. Quite by lucky accident, the explorers have discovered a civilization that existed four thousand years ago.

Background information

Three or four thousand years ago, in the jungles of Mexico by the Gulf of Mexico, the people known as the Olmecs developed a complex, advanced civilization. About seventeen hundred years ago, the Olmecs disappeared. Today, thanks to the efforts of many archaeologists and other

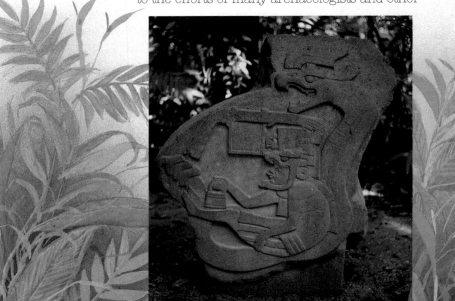

CLOSURE

Ask students to list the basic elements of a research report.

EXTENSION

Encourage students to provide visual aids for their research reports. Students could create original visual aids or find appropriate existing ones. ■

Writing Your First Draft **431**

Thesis statement

scientists, tourists can gaze at Olmec monuments and learn about the Olmec culture. Unlike the stereotyped movie version, however, no explorer found the Olmec culture accidentally. The "discovery" of the lost Olmec culture, like that of most "lost" cultures, has been the result of years of continuing exploration and scientific investigation.

BODY
Discovery of lost Olmecs

Paraphrase
Print source

The discovery of the lost Olmec culture began around 1869. That year an archaeologist named José Maria Melgar y Serran wrote an article about an enormous stone head that he discovered in the jungles of Mexico (Chen 25). Other archaeologists wrote and spoke about finding more stone heads, stone monuments, and smaller relics. Gradually, archaeologists realized that the objects must have come from the same culture, but they also knew that the objects did not come from any known cultures. They theorized that the objects came from an ancient, unknown culture that once existed in the area where the objects were found. The next step was to begin excavations of the area (Bernal 28).

Summary

Print source

Topic sentence— conclusion about information

Since excavations of the Olmec areas began in 1938, archaeologists have used many scientific methods to locate the Olmec ruins and learn about their culture. Some of the ruins, for example, were discovered or mapped by aerial

MEETING
INDIVIDUAL
NEEDS

LESS-ADVANCED STUDENTS

To help students visualize the organization of the report, you may want to write an outline of the writer's model on the chalkboard.

ADVANCED STUDENTS

You may want to have students write alternative introductions and conclusions for the writer's model. Students could review the seven techniques for writing effective introductions and the six techniques for writing conclusions in **Chapter 3: "Understanding Composition Structure."** You could ask volunteers to read their alternatives to the rest of the class.

A DIFFERENT APPROACH

Refer students to the section in **Chapter 2: "Understanding Paragraph Structure"** on connecting ideas within and between sentences in a paragraph. Explain that direct references and transitional expressions are also used to connect ideas between paragraphs in a longer composition. Work with students to find the direct references and transitional expressions that help link ideas between paragraphs in **A Writer's Model.**

Specific examples

photography from airplanes or, more recently, from satellites. Scientists used carbon-dating, or radioactive dating, to establish the age of bones and relics found at the sites. Specialists studied fossil remains of plants and animals (Grove 27).

Olmec society

Using these methods, scientists have learned much about how the Olmecs lived. From the earliest excavations, experts learned that the Olmec culture consisted mostly of farming villages grouped around large cities. At first they believed that the Olmecs used these cities only for religious ceremonies (Chen 83). However, excavations in 1986 convinced many experts that the Olmecs also lived in these cities (Bower; Rust and Sharer 102).

Two different sources

Early in their civilization, most of the Olmecs farmed in an effort to grow enough food to eat. Gradually, as they developed advanced farming methods such as irrigation, they grew a surplus of food. This surplus allowed some Olmecs to leave their farms to become religious and political leaders, or specialists such as artists or craftsmen. Some of the villages grew into the large, important cities that were discovered in early excavations (Chen 83).

Olmec rulers

Archaeologists believe that the Olmecs had very powerful rulers, probably priests. Scattered around the Olmec countryside are huge stone heads whose features are probably those of past rulers. Each of the heads is eight feet high, and some weigh up to forty tons (Rensberger 74). According to Andrea Sutphin of the Orlando Museum of Art, the stones weren't native to the area; they came from nearby mountains. It is possible that the Olmecs moved them down the river on a raft. Explorers have also found the remains of large monuments and pyramids that must have required the work of many men over many years. Archaeologists believe that only very powerful rulers could have planned such projects and commanded such large groups of men (Drucker 30).

Advanced civilization

Calendar

Direct quotation

Print source— author's name given in report

Astronomy

Writing

Background information/ Definition

Evidence indicates that the Olmecs were a highly advanced civilization. Dates carved on the fronts of small statues and other objects suggest that the Olmecs may have had the world's first sophisticated calendar, even before the Mayas (Bernal 95). Archaeologist Ignacio Bernal suggests that the Olmec calendar was "the most complete and nearly perfect system of calculating time conceived in America." (92). This calendar enabled the Olmecs to predict the best times for planting and harvesting (Grove 183). Knowledge of the calendar also indicates that the Olmecs knew astronomy. They knew, for example, about the movements of the sun and the moon (Bernal 96).

Archaeologists also now believe that the Olmecs may have been the first to use hieroglyphic writing. (In hieroglyphic writing, a picture or symbol represents a word, syllable, or sound.) Evidence includes an Olmec sculpture carved with the figure of a man who appears to be walking. Behind the man is the carving of a human foot, which experts believe is the hieroglyphic symbol for "walking" or "marching." Other sculptures have carvings that resemble stars and rain clouds, which also appear to be hieroglyphic symbols (Chen 184).

VISUAL CONNECTIONS
Related Expression Skills. A Writer's Model cites an expert, Boyce Rensberger, as proposing that the stone heads were probably made to represent past rulers. Have interested students create heads to represent past leaders that they admire. Students could model heads of papier mâché or clay or they could draw or paint heads. Display students' artwork along with a picture of one of the Olmecs' stone heads.

Related Expression Skills. Students who are intrigued by the Olmec calendar or the Olmec hieroglyphs might want to prepare brief oral reports about these subjects. They also might want to compare Olmec calendars or hieroglyphs with those of other ancient civilizations. Other students might want to research and use maps to trace possible routes between Africa and Mexico.

CRITICAL THINKING
Analysis

Remind students that informative writing should be as objective as possible. Point out how the author of **A Writer's Model** introduces various opinions about the Olmecs without seeming to show a bias toward one opinion. Because students might have difficulty identifying bias, bring some examples of biased writing to class to show them. Discuss how each example is biased and how the bias is evident. Discuss how tone and the connotations of words can contribute to biased writing.

Tell students that if they are writing about topics that are controversial and that they have strong opinions about, they might want to reveal their biases to readers at the beginnings of their reports.

434

Disagreement

Archaeologists do not always agree about clues to Olmec history and culture. For example, some archaeologists believe that the features of the huge stone heads indicate that the Olmec rulers originally came from Africa. Boyce Rensberger describes this theory:

Longer direct quotation

> The great stone heads of Mexico are by far the most spectacular evidence that, as civilization was dawning in the New World more than 2,000 years before Columbus "discovered" America, black people from Africa had already reached these shores. They came not as slaves but as free men and women, experienced mariners who had sailed across the Atlantic from one of the ancient advanced civilizations of Africa. (75)

Print source— author's name mentioned in paragraph

Other archaeologists disagree with this theory. For example, archaeologist Michael Coe believes these features appear as they do because of the nature of the Olmec tools (Rensberger 76).

Almost seventeen hundred years ago, the Olmec culture disappeared. Archaeologists disagree about the cause. Some believe that the peasants resented the great power of the priests and revolted against them, bringing down the civilization in the process. Others believe that other nearby cultures may have been responsible (Chen 208).

Importance

Most archaeologists, however, agree about the importance of the Olmecs to world history. One archaeologist summarizes the feelings of most social scientists when he writes that "the Olmec culture is generally considered to have given rise to all the other great civilizations that developed in Central America, including the Mayan and, much later, the Aztec" (Rensberger 76). For many years, not much was known about this important civilization. Today, however, thanks to years of research and analysis, scientists are bringing light to a distant past.

Direct quotation

Print source— Direct quotation

CONCLUSION
Summary statement

Works Cited

Bernal, Ignacio. <u>The Olmec World</u>. Trans. Doris
    Heyden and Fernando Horcasitas. Berkeley:
    U of California P, 1969.
Bower, B. "Domesticating an Ancient 'Temple
    Town.'" <u>Science News</u> 15 Oct. 1988: 246.
Chen, Román Piña. <u>The Olmec: Mother Culture</u>
    <u>of Mesoamerica</u>. New York: Rizzoli, 1989.
Drucker, Philip. "On the Nature of Olmec
    Polity." <u>The Olmec & Their Neighbors</u>.
    Ed. Elizabeth P. Benson. Washington:
    Dumbarton Oaks Research Library and
    Collections, Trustees for Harvard University.
    1981. 29-47.
Grove, David C. <u>Chalcatzingo: Excavations on the</u>
    <u>Olmec Frontier</u>. New York: Thames, 1984.
Rensberger, Boyce. "Black Kings of Ancient
    America." <u>Science Digest</u> Sept. 1981: 74+.
Rust, William F., and Robert J. Sharer. "Olmec
    Settlement Data from La Venta, Tabasco,
    Mexico." <u>Science</u> 7 Oct. 1988: 102-04.
Sutphin, Andrea. Telephone interview. 17
    Apr. 1991.

PART 7:
Writing Your First Draft

Now you're ready to write! Using your final outline and
note cards as a guide, write the first draft of your report.
Give credit to your sources by using parenthetical citations following the MLA format in this chapter. Then prepare your Works Cited list. Be sure to list only the sources
you actually used in your report.

EVALUATING AND REVISING

OBJECTIVES

- To analyze a writer's revisions
- To apply evaluating and revising guidelines to a research report

TEACHING THE LESSON

Be sure that students understand how to use the chart, **Evaluating and Revising Research Reports.** You may want to call attention to the three verbs most often emphasized under **Revision Technique** [*add, replace, cut*]. As guided practice, go over **Exercise 5** with students in class. Then, as independent practice, have students work

---

Teacher's ResourceBank™
RESOURCES

EVALUATING AND REVISING
- Writing a Research Paper

QUOTATION FOR THE DAY

"The only sure weapon against bad ideas is better ideas." (Whitney Griswold, 1909–1963, American educator)

This quotation could serve as a reminder to students that the ideas in their writing must be logical and based on facts. Tell students to keep the quotation in mind as they evaluate the ideas in their reports.

---

436 *Writing a Research Paper*

Evaluating and Revising

The presentation of your ideas is the heart of your report. Use the chart on page 438 to evaluate and revise content and organization. Ask yourself the questions in the left-hand column. Then use the revision techniques in the right-hand column to correct any problems.

EXERCISE 5 ▶ **Analyzing a Writer's Revisions**

The following paragraph shows how the writer revised the first draft of the eighth paragraph in the sample report (page 433). Study the paragraph, and then answer the questions about the revisions that follow.

 # Evidence indicates that the Olmecs were a highly advanced civilization.

Archaeologist Ignacio Bernal suggests that the Olmec calendar was "the most complete and nearly perfect system of calculating time conceived in America" (92). Dates carved on the fronts of small statues and other objects suggest that the Olmecs may have had the world's first sophisticated calendar, even before the Mayas (Bernal 95). This calendar enabled ~~these people~~ *the Olmecs* to predict the best times for planting and harvesting *Grove* (183). Knowledge of the calendar also indicates that the Olmecs knew astronomy. ~~Astronomy is the science dealing with the sun, moon, and other heavenly bodies.~~ They knew, for example, about the movements of the sun and the moon (Bernal, 96).

add/reorder

replace

add

cut

cut

RETEACHING

Write three headings on the chalkboard: *Add*, *Replace*, and *Cut*. Then give examples from graded student papers of sentences that need something added, replaced, and cut.

1. Why does the writer move the first sentence and then add a new sentence to the beginning of the paragraph?
2. Why does the writer replace the phrase *these people* with the phrase *the Olmecs*?
3. Why does the writer change the citation in the second sentence of the paragraph?
4. Why does the writer delete the sentence that begins *Astronomy is . . .*?
5. Why does the writer change the citation in the paragraph's last sentence?

PART 8:
Evaluating and Revising Your Report

Get some help by exchanging your report with a classmate. Use the evaluating and revising guidelines in the chart on page 438 to give each other friendly advice. Apply the guidelines to your own report also, and make changes to improve your first draft.

ANSWERS
Exercise 5

1. In the first draft, the first sentence is a detail rather than a topic sentence. The writer replaces that sentence with a topic sentence that expresses the main idea.
2. The writer replaces the phrase for clarity. *These people* might refer to the Mayas.
3. According to MLA format, when the author's name is not mentioned in the text, it should be part of the citation.
4. Most high school students already know the definition of *astronomy*.
5. According to MLA format, no comma separates an author's name and the page number(s).

INTEGRATING THE LANGUAGE ARTS

Grammar Link. You might need to remind your students to use a variety of compound, complex, and compound-complex sentences in their writing. Using a variety of sentence structures will improve students' writing style and will help their readers see the connections between ideas and pieces of information. Review the sentence structures with students, and then have students read through their reports specifically for sentence structures. Tell students to revise and combine sentences if they have too many sentences with the same type of sentence structure in their reports.

CLOSURE

Refer students to the cartoon on p. 437 and ask them what advice they would give Calvin to help him revise his essay. [Possible answers include reminding Calvin that something "made up" is not a fact and telling him that he should probably include several facts in his essay.] ■

MEETING INDIVIDUAL NEEDS

LEP/ESL

General Strategies. If possible, guide each student individually through the **Evaluating and Revising Research Reports** chart. You may need to clarify guidelines such as "Is the report suitable for its audience?" and "Is the tone of the report appropriate?" Words such as *suitable* and *appropriate* may hold little meaning for students. Try using specific examples from their reports to help them understand if they are meeting the necessary criteria.

EVALUATING AND REVISING RESEARCH REPORTS

EVALUATION GUIDE	REVISION TECHNIQUE
1 Does a thesis statement appear early in the report?	**Add** a thesis statement to the first or second paragraph of your report.
2 Is the report suitable for its audience? Is it interesting, informative, and clear?	**Add** interesting, unusual, or surprising details. **Add** necessary definitions, background information, and explanations.
3 Is the tone of the report appropriate?	**Replace** words or phrases that give your report a casual or informal tone.
4 Are sources relevant, reliable, recent, and representative?	**Cut** information that is irrelevant or out-of-date. **Replace** with information from better sources.
5 Are ideas and information pulled together (synthesized) and stated in the writer's own words?	Check that each topic sentence expresses your ideas in your own words. **Add** or **replace** topic sentences as necessary.
6 Are ideas developed and supported with adequate information? Will readers find the information complete?	**Add** facts and figures, theories, and expert opinions about your topic where necessary.
7 Does all the information relate directly to the topic and approach?	**Cut** unnecessary information.
8 Is proper credit given for each source of information?	**Add** documentation for any information that isn't common knowledge. Check format guidelines.
9 Does documentation follow the format recommended by your teacher?	**Replace** as necessary to follow the MLA format or other format recommended by your teacher.

PROOFREADING AND PUBLISHING

OBJECTIVE

- To proofread and share a research report

TEACHING THE LESSON

Ask students what they will be checking for as they proofread their reports. Write appropriate responses on the chalkboard. Afterward, write on the chalkboard anything that students failed to mention. ■

Proofreading and Publishing

Take another look at your report, and clean up all spelling, mechanical, and usage errors. Make a final check of your documentation as well. Then find a way to share what you've learned.

- If you're applying for a part-time job or for a special award or honor, submit your report as an example of your ability to plan and carry out a long-term project.
- Plan a bulletin board that features research as a theme. Select one in a location where all students can stop and look—maybe the front hall of your school. Post examples of research reports from your English class as well as from history and science classes.

WRITING ASSIGNMENT

PART 9:
Proofreading and Publishing Your Report

Proofread your report carefully and correct any errors. Be extra careful to get your documentation (citations and *Works Cited* page) just right. Publish or share your report with others.

Teacher's ResourceBank™

RESOURCES

PROOFREADING AND PUBLISHING
- Writing a Research Paper

QUOTATION FOR THE DAY

"Good swimmers are oftenest drowned." (Thomas Fuller, M.D., 1654–1734, English physician, writer, and compiler)

Lead students in a discussion of the relationship of this quotation to the proofreading part of the writing process. Suggest that those most confident about their spelling and usage may not be as careful as they should be in proofreading their reports.

MEETING INDIVIDUAL NEEDS

LEP/ESL

General Strategies. Ask students to identify their areas of weakness, such as spelling, verb usage, or comma usage, and to focus first on those areas. You could also have students exchange reports and help one another with the task of proofreading.

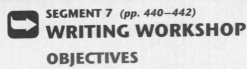

WRITING WORKSHOP

OBJECTIVES

- To analyze a book report on an autobiography
- To write a book report on an autobiography

MOTIVATION

Ask students to name some famous people who have written autobiographies recently or whose autobiographies they would like to read. Ask students what autobiographies they've enjoyed in the past and why they enjoyed them.

Teacher's ResourceBank™
RESOURCES

WRITING WORKSHOP
All the resources for this chapter may be used in this segment.

QUOTATION FOR THE DAY

"Okay, as weird as *this* is, *this* is truly how I feel. Therefore, if I write anything else, it would be a lie." (Ntozake Shange, 1948–   , African American playwright, poet, and novelist)

Lead students in a discussion of whether they would be totally honest if they wrote an autobiography. If students say they would not be completely honest, ask them why.

MEETING
INDIVIDUAL
NEEDS

LEP/ESL

General Strategies. Because this assignment requires a very thorough understanding of a book, you may want to allow ESL students to read autobiographies written in their native languages. Then have students write their book reports in English.

WRITING WORKSHOP

A Book Report That Evaluates

When you watch a TV movie, you usually *evaluate* it. You may talk excitedly about the story or decide that watching it was a waste of time—you make a *judgment* about its value to you. You can also evaluate a book by judging it against certain *criteria*, or guidelines. Here are some guidelines for evaluating a book about the writer's own life.

GUIDELINES FOR EVALUATING AUTOBIOGRAPHY

1. Is the author honest? Does he or she write about details that make the author's life seem less than perfect?
2. Does the author present details of places, people, and events that we otherwise wouldn't have known about?
3. Does the author use fresh and natural-sounding language?
4. Does the author write about his or her thoughts and feelings, as well as events?

Here is the beginning of a book report on an autobiography titled *Golden Lilies* by Kwei-li. As you read, see if the writer measures the book against the guidelines above.

The Voice of Kwei-li

Golden Lilies by Kwei-li is a series of letters by a Chinese woman who was born in 1867. In the first half of the book, eighteen-year-old Kwei-li writes letters to her husband. He has been appointed to a distant political post, and has left his young wife in the home of her mother-in-law. Twenty-five years later, in the book's second half, Kwei-li writes letters to her mother-in-law. She now lives in Kiang-su with her politically powerful husband. Throughout this superior autobiography, the voice of a woman who lived more than a hundred years ago shines through.

Start by tying the **Writing Workshop** in with writing research reports. Point out the similarities and differences between book reports and research reports. Then read, or have a student volunteer read, the sample book report, **"The Voice of Kwei-li."** You may want to lead a class discussion that applies the **Guidelines for Evaluating Autobiography** to the sample book report.

Discuss with students the answers to the four questions that follow the sample book report. Then instruct students to follow the stages of the writing process to write book reports on autobiographies independently.

In her letters Kwei-li writes of both her joys and sorrows. Early in the book she speaks of her love for her husband: "Few women have the joy I feel when I look into my loved one's face and know that I am his and he is mine, and that our lives are twined together for all the days to come" (34-35). She writes also of her great joy at the birth of her first son and her almost unbearable sorrow at his death even before his father has seen him. In the second half, she mourns the passing of the old Chinese ways: Her daughter wants to be a doctor; and her son, accused of being a traitor, is saved only at the last moment.

Kwei-li's details help the reader to understand the old and new China. We see the endless labor of peasants doomed to spend the rest of their lives grinding herbs. They are "harnessed to great stones" and go "round and round all day, like buffalo at the waterwheel" (40). Throughout the book, Kwei-li paints in words China's great beauty. She watches "the mists cling lovingly to the hilltops, while leaves from giant banyan trees sway idly in the morning wind . . ." (171).

1. In the first paragraph, the writer provides some background information. Why is this information important?
2. In the second paragraph, why do you think the writer quoted some of Kwei-li's words from the book? What do the numbers *34–35* in parentheses tell the reader?

CRITICAL THINKING
Evaluation

The third guideline for evaluating autobiographies calls for a sophisticated evaluation of diction. Work with students to develop criteria by which to evaluate diction. Criteria might include avoidance of clichés and tired adjectives and adverbs and avoidance of stilted or pompous-sounding language. You may want to bring to class examples of boring, contrived writing and examples of fresh and natural-sounding language.

ANSWERS
Writing Workshop Questions

Responses may vary. Here are some possibilities:

1. The information is important to help the reader understand the people involved and the basic situation of their lives.

2. The writer uses a quotation from the book to better show Kwei-li's personality and the strength of her feelings. The quotation also shows her natural-sounding language. The numbers are the numbers of the pages on which the quotation appears in the book.

CLOSURE

Ask students to repeat the four items from **Guidelines for Evaluating Autobiography** and to tell why each of these guidelines is important to consider when writing a book report. ∎

442

3. The writer clearly states that the details help the reader's understanding.
4. The writer's evaluation is positive. In the first paragraph, the writer states that the work is a "superior autobiography" and that Kwei-li's voice "shines through." In the second paragraph, the writer seems pleased that Kwei-li writes of both her joys and sorrows. In the third paragraph, the writer states that the author has provided helpful details and has successfully used words to paint China's beauty.

INTEGRATING THE LANGUAGE ARTS

Speaking and Listening Link. Have students prepare oral presentations based on their book reports. After all students have delivered their presentations, have each student name at least one autobiography discussed during the presentations that he or she would like to read.

3. The third paragraph evaluates Kwei-li's use of details. What do you think is the writer's evaluation on this point?
4. Even though you don't have the entire book report, you may be able to tell what the writer thinks of *Golden Lilies*. Do you think the writer's evaluation is positive or negative? Why?

Writing a Book Report

Prewriting. For your report, choose an autobiography (make sure it's not a biography) of someone you admire. If you have enough time, read it once just for pleasure. Then go back over it to evaluate it. You can insert slips of paper between pages with important information you want to refer to later. Jot down some notes that will help you explain the book and your opinion about it. Copy quotes exactly, noting the page where the quote appears.

Writing, Evaluating, and Revising. In the first paragraph, give readers the background they'll need to understand your report. End the first paragraph with a thesis statement stating your overall evaluation. Each body paragraph should discuss one of the criteria listed in the guidelines on page 440. Use specific details from the book, including quotations, to support your points. End your report with an overall summary of your evaluation.

Proofreading and Publishing. Polish your report by checking carefully for errors in spelling, punctuation, and usage. Then you might check with your school librarian to see whether you could put your report in the library along with a copy of the book that students can borrow.

443

MAKING CONNECTIONS

RESEARCH ACROSS THE CURRICULUM

The Visual Arts

Research is playing an important role in the preservation of two of the world's greatest art masterpieces which might otherwise be someday lost forever. Leonardo da Vinci's *Last Supper*, painted on a wall of a monastery in Milan, Italy, and Michelangelo's frescoes, painted on the ceiling of the Sistine Chapel in Rome, are about five hundred years old. Over the years, heat, humidity, dirt, pollution, and wars have badly damaged both works. Previous attempts at restoration damaged them even further when layers of paint, glue, and varnish were added to the originals.

During the 1970s restorers began extensive projects to clean, preserve, and restore both works as nearly as possible to their original condition. Research has been an important part of both projects. Restorers need to know as much as possible about how da Vinci and Michelangelo actually painted—what kinds of brush strokes they used and how they mixed their colors, for example. In earlier restorations, painters often added new layers of colors

RESEARCH ACROSS THE CURRICULUM

Teaching Strategies

If possible, show students a videotape of the *NOVA* episode that documents the restoration of the Sistine Chapel. Afterward, discuss how research was used in the restoration project. Challenge students to find more information about these or other restoration projects.

👁 VISUAL CONNECTIONS

Exploring the Subject. Although most art critics feel that the bright colors uncovered in the restoration reveal Michelangelo's true style, some experts believe that Michelangelo added a dark coat of varnish to his work as a finishing touch. These critics feel that the restoration actually damages the frescoes and gives us a false idea of Michelangelo's style. The controversy, which is explored in the *NOVA* videotape, illustrates that even experts may disagree about their findings.

GUIDELINES

Each student should be able to tell you at least one way that research played a role in the restorations.

SPEAKING AND LISTENING

Teaching Strategies

If your class is very big, individual pollsters might wear out their welcome fast. Have the class conduct one public opinion poll, or divide the class into four or five groups and have each group conduct a different poll. You could invite students to suggest some other topics about which they would like to conduct polls. Write appropriate ideas on the chalkboard and let the class or groups vote on the ideas for their polls.

Students might need some help in formulating questions that are objective and neutral. Tell students to avoid loaded words, words with connotations that might affect answers.

and even beards or clothes to the figures. Understanding the techniques of da Vinci and Michelangelo helps restorers decide what is original and what was added later.

A *NOVA* episode, available on videotape, documents the restoration of the Sistine Chapel. Popular magazines, such as *Time, Newsweek,* and *National Geographic,* gave the restorations extensive coverage including photographs. You might want to view the videotape (it's available at many video stores). Or use the *Readers' Guide* to find articles about both restoration projects. Bring the articles to class to share with your classmates. As you view the videotape or read the articles, look for ways that research has played a role in the restorations.

SPEAKING AND LISTENING

Creating Research Sources: Public Opinion Polls

You've probably been met in shopping malls by people conducting public opinion polls about your shopping habits and product preferences. The results of these polls are used to help businesses increase their sales.

Consider taking some public opinion polls in your own school. If you want the poll to represent the opinions of all students, you need to poll students from all grade levels. Or, you might restrict the poll to your own grade level. Try to poll ten percent of the population. If there are three hundred students in your grade, for instance, talk to thirty of them. Also try to select students who represent the entire group. You might, for example, select every tenth person from an alphabetical listing of the class.

Write some objective questions with answers that you can easily tally. For example, if you want to find out about favorite and least favorite lunchroom foods, have students rank five foods from 1 to 5 (with 5 being the favorite). To find out students' opinions on an issue, give them a neutral statement and then ask whether they agree or disagree. Such a statement might be "A constitutional amendment should be passed prohibiting the burning of the American flag."

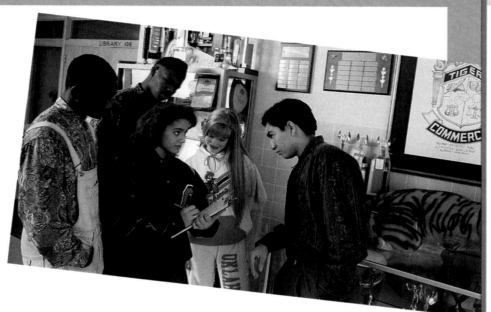

Try one of the ideas on the following list, and conduct a public opinion poll in your school. (You may also have ideas about different topics.)

- Favorite/least favorite foods served in the lunchroom
- Favorite/least favorite musicians, actors, television shows, movies, and so on
- Ideas to improve education in your community
- Opinions on national/foreign policy issues

When you finish your poll, tally your findings and present the results to your class. Consider using the results in an article for your school newspaper or a letter to the editor of your local newspaper.

WRITING COMPLETE SENTENCES

OBJECTIVES

- To identify and correct sentence fragments and run-on sentences
- To create complete sentences from phrases and clauses
- To write paragraphs with correct sentence structures

Motivation

Initiate a class discussion on the importance of communication. Try to lead students to discover that this importance has two aspects: a basic human aspect and a practical aspect.

The basic human aspect of the importance of communication is derived from people's need as individuals to express themselves in ways unique to their separate identities and still be understood. Expression without understanding can be very frustrating and can inhibit an individual's ability to function as a productive member of society.

The practical aspect of the importance of communication is derived from the need to relay information clearly and accurately. At times, this need can be urgent, depending upon the information involved. Directions for taking or administering medication, for example, demand clarity and precision to insure the safety of the patient. Ask your students if they can think of other examples when concise communication is necessary for safety reasons. [The use of electrical appliances is potentially dangerous without proper instructions.]

Introduction

This chapter contains information that will help students identify sentence fragments and run-on sentences and eliminate these problems from their writing. There are examples of both types of problems and how to correct them. The **Writing Note** features offer additional information on usage and provide tips on identifying and correcting problems in sentence structure.

The section on sentence fragments describes the three-part test to determine if a sentence is complete and defines and illustrates the two kinds of sentence fragments: phrase fragments and subordinate clause fragments. The section on phrase fragments discusses verbal phrase, appositive phrase, and prepositional phrase fragments.

The section on run-on sentences defines and illustrates the two kinds of run-on sentences (the fused sentence and the comma splice) and describes the methods of revising them.

Integration

Using the material in this chapter in conjunction with **Chapter 13: "Writing Effective Sentences"** may help students avoid sentence fragments and run-ons without discouraging them from experimentation with more complex structures. Let them know that mistakes will be made, but this too is part of learning to write well.

The material in this chapter can also be used with any of the composition chapters of the textbook, particularly with the sections of those chapters dealing with the proofreading and revision stages of the writing process.

The chart on the next page illustrates the strands of language arts as they are integrated into this chapter. For vocabulary study, glossary words are underlined in some writing models.

QUOTATIONS
All **Quotations for the Day** are chosen because of their relevance to instructional material presented in that segment of the chapter and for their usefulness in establishing student interest in writing.

Selection	Reading and Literature	Writing and Critical Thinking	Language and Syntax	Speaking, Listening, and Other Expression Skills
from *I Know Why the Caged Bird Sings* by Maya Angelou **448**	Contrasting sentence fragments and complete sentences **448-449** Identifying the missing parts of incomplete sentences **448-449** Identifying subordinate clause fragments **453** Identifying sentence fragments in a paragraph **453, 455, 459, 460** Identifying and revising sentence fragments and run-on sentences **453, 455, 459, 460**	Analyzing sentence fragments **448-449** Applying interpretive and creative thinking **451, 454** Creating complete sentences from phrase fragments **451** Combining subordinate clauses with independent clauses to form complete sentences **453** Evaluating and revising sentence fragments in a paragraph **453, 455, 459, 460** Creating complete sentences from subordinate clauses **454** Evaluating and revising run-on sentences **458** Evaluating and revising fragments and run-on sentences **459** Creating a paragraph with complete sentences **460** Evaluating and revising a paragraph with phrase and clause fragments **460**	Proofreading for errors in grammar, usage, and mechanics **451, 454, 460** Correcting fragments and run-on sentences by changing punctuation and capitalization **453, 455, 458, 459, 460**	Working with classmates to write and analyze paragraphs **460**

SEGMENT PLANNING GUIDE

Whether you are planning for a quick review of a writing concept or preparing an extended lesson on composition, you can use the following Planning Guide to adapt the chapter material to the individual needs of your class.

SEGMENT	PAGES	CONTENT	RESOURCES
Sentence Fragments	*446-455*		Types of Sentence Fragments A
Sentence Fragments	446-447	Guidelines: identifying and revising sentence fragments	Types of Sentence Fragments B
Style Note	448	Writing suggestion: using fragments for effect	
Exercise 1	448-449	Applied practice: identifying sentence fragments	
Phrase Fragments	449	Introduction: identifying and correcting verbal, appositive, and prepositional phrases	
Verbal Phrases	449-450	Guidelines: identifying and correcting verbal phrases	
Appositive Phrases	450	Guidelines: identifying and correcting appositive phrases	
Prepositional Phrases	450	Guidelines: identifying and correcting prepositional phrases	
Writing Note	450	Writing suggestion: placing verbal phrases clearly	
Exercise 2	451	Applied practice: revising phrase fragments	
Subordinate Clause Fragments	451-452	Guidelines: identifying subordinate clauses	
Writing Note	452	Writing suggestion: using adverb clauses	
Exercise 3	453	Applied practice: revising subordinate clause fragments	
Exercise 4	454	Applied practice: using subordinate clauses in sentences	
Writing Note	454	Writing suggestion: including a series of items in a sentence	
Exercise 5	455	Applied practice: identifying and revising fragments	
Run-On Sentences	*456-459*		Identifying Run-on Sentences
Run-On Sentences	456	Guidelines: identifying and correcting run-on sentences	
Writing Note	456	Writing suggestion: reading aloud to identify run-on sentences	
Revising Run-on Sentences	456-458	Guidelines: examining ways to correct run-on sentences	
Exercise 6	458	Applied practice: revising by correcting run-ons	
Review	459	Applied practice: revising fragments and run-on sentences	

All the resources listed in this chapter are located in the Teacher's ResourceBank™.

SEGMENT	PAGES	CONTENT	RESOURCES
3 *Making Connections*	*460*		
Fill in the Missing Pieces	460	Guidelines: examining the effects of sentence fragments Cooperative learning: writing paragraphs that contain sentence fragments and using peer evaluating and revising	
WHOLE-CHAPTER RESOURCES Review Form A, Review Form B			

SEGMENT 1 *(pp. 446–455)*
SENTENCE FRAGMENTS
OBJECTIVES
- To use the three-part test to identify the sentence parts missing in fragments
- To create complete sentences from phrase fragments
- To identify and correct subordinate clause fragments in a paragraph
- To create complete sentences from subordinate clause fragments
- To identify and correct fragments in a paragraph

QUOTATION FOR THE DAY

"Whate'er is well conceived is clearly said, and the words to say it flow with ease." (Nicolas Boileau-Despreaux, 1636–1711, French poet and literary critic)

To help students see how thinking carefully before they write leads to better writing, have them freewrite a few sentences about a particular topic. Ask them to write quickly, perhaps giving them only a minute. When the time is up, give them another topic and give them time to think about it before they write. When the new sentences are written, ask the students to compare the two groups of sentences. Most should find the second group more coherent and meaningful.

446

12 WRITING COMPLETE SENTENCES

LOOKING AHEAD

Sentences are the building blocks of your writing. That's why it's important to check your sentences for clarity and completeness. As you work through this chapter, you will learn how to

- identify and correct sentence fragments
- identify and correct run-on sentences

Sentence Fragments

A *sentence fragment* is a group of words that is only a part of a sentence. Since a fragment of something is not the whole thing, it won't be as useful to you as it could be. Just as a fragment of a bowl can't hold much food, a fragment of a sentence may not communicate what you want to say.

You may want to introduce this section by writing *Before we begin class* and *Your writing assignment* on the chalkboard. This should get the students' attention and cause some consternation among them. If you then act like the students are supposed to do something, their nervousness might increase until one of them asks for more instructions. You could then act surprised and ask, "What's wrong with my instructions? Aren't they clear?" The ensuing discussion should provide adequate opportunity for you to begin the mini-lesson on fragments.

Sentence Fragments   **447**

To be complete, a sentence must (1) have a subject, (2) have a verb, and (3) express a complete thought. If any of these pieces are missing, the group of words is a fragment rather than a complete sentence.

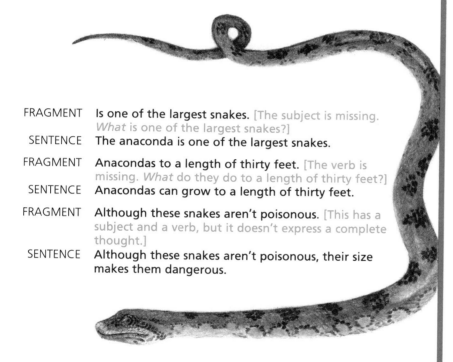

FRAGMENT	Is one of the largest snakes. [The subject is missing. *What* is one of the largest snakes?]
SENTENCE	The anaconda is one of the largest snakes.
FRAGMENT	Anacondas to a length of thirty feet. [The verb is missing. *What* do they do to a length of thirty feet?]
SENTENCE	Anacondas can grow to a length of thirty feet.
FRAGMENT	Although these snakes aren't poisonous. [This has a subject and a verb, but it doesn't express a complete thought.]
SENTENCE	Although these snakes aren't poisonous, their size makes them dangerous.

Fragments usually occur when you're writing in a hurry or are a little careless. For example, you might create a fragment by leaving out an important word or two. Or you might chop off part of a sentence by putting in a period too soon.

To find out if what you've written is a fragment, you can use this simple three-part test:

1. Does the group of words have a subject?
2. Does it have a verb?
3. Does it express a complete thought?

If even one of your answers is "no," then you have a fragment.

The **Motivation** activity will help get students involved in this lesson by illustrating how sentence fragments represent incomplete thoughts and how this problem in communication can affect the students. The discussion that follows the activity should center on how sentence fragments are confusing because they lack important information. Try to lead students to discover how the missing information in sentence fragments can be supplied by asking and then answering the appropriate questions. For example, if the fragment *Before we begin class* is to be made into a complete sentence the questions "What will happen?" or "What are we supposed to do?" would help students supply the missing information.

INTEGRATING THE LANGUAGE ARTS

Literature Link. If your students' literature book has Sandra Cisneros' short story "The House on Mango Street," have the students read and discuss the story. Then ask them to identify the sentence fragments. (There are at least thirteen.) Ask the students to identify the types of fragments used and to tell why they think Cisneros used fragments at all. [Basically, the use of fragments gives the story a more conversational tone, which strengthens the connection between narrator and audience.] You may want to have students rewrite the fragments as complete sentences to see how this would change the story.

STYLE NOTE

By itself, a sentence fragment doesn't express a complete thought. But a fragment can make sense in writing if it is clearly related to a sentence that comes before or after it.

Read the following groups of words from Maya Angelou's autobiography *I Know Why the Caged Bird Sings:*

> The birthday girl. The center.

By themselves, these fragments don't make sense because we don't know what they relate to. But now read them along with the sentence that the writer placed before them:

> In the Store I was the person of the moment.
> The birthday girl. The center.

As you can see, the sentence gives the fragments meaning. It fills in the missing parts.

Experienced writers like Maya Angelou sometimes use sentence fragments for effect. As a beginning writer, however, you should avoid using fragments. Eventually you'll feel comfortable enough to experiment, but it's important to master the basics first.

EXERCISE 1 ▶ **Identifying Sentence Fragments**

Try the three-part test on each of the following groups of words. In each case, identify what, if anything, is missing. If the group of words is missing a subject, write <u>S</u>. If it is missing a verb, write <u>V</u>. If the group of words has both a subject and a verb but doesn't express a complete thought, write <u>I</u>. Write <u>C</u> if the words form a complete sentence.

1. Vampire bats only in the tropics of North and South America. **1. V**
2. Most horror tales about vampire bats aren't true. **2. C**
3. Vampire bats very small mammals. **3. V**
4. Although they do bite other animals. **4. I**
5. Don't drain their victims of blood. **5. S**

One way to help students learn about fragments and how to correct them would be to have each student write a verbal phrase, an appositive phrase, a prepositional phrase, and a subordinate clause. Then, one at a time, have the students copy their fragments on the chalkboard so that you can determine whether they understand the differences between the types of fragments.

Next, ask volunteers to form complete sentences using the fragments. You may want to occasionally suggest alternative structures so the class can see the variety of ways fragments can be made into complete sentences.

Because this activity could take lots of time, you may want to spread it out over a few days, or you could choose a few volunteers and use their fragments for examples. ☛

6. Their small teeth are as sharp as needles.   **6.** C
7. While animals are sleeping.   **7.** I
8. But can be dangerous.   **8.** S
9. The greatest danger to victims is infection.   **9.** C
10. Vampire bats carriers of rabies.   **10.** V

"What was it like back in the days when people talked and wrote in complete sentences?"

Berry's World, by Jim Berry. Reprinted by permission of NEA, Inc.

Phrase Fragments

A *phrase* is a group of words that does not contain a subject and a verb. Because it doesn't have all the basic parts of a sentence, a phrase by itself is a fragment. Three kinds of phrases are often mistaken for sentences: *verbal phrases, appositive phrases,* and *prepositional phrases.*

Verbal Phrases

A *verbal* is a word that is formed from a verb but is used as another part of speech. Because verbs and verbals are look-alikes, it is sometimes hard to tell the difference between them. That's why *verbal phrases*—phrases that contain verbals—are easily mistaken for sentences. They can appear to have verbs in them when they really don't.

Watch for two kinds of verbals in phrases. The first kind of verbal has an ending such as *–ing, –d,* or *–ed* and doesn't have a helping verb (like *is, were,* or *have*). The second kind of verbal has the word *to* in front of it (*to run, to look*).

Another possibility is to divide the class into groups once the students have written their fragments and let the groups form sample sentences and check each other's work while you eavesdrop. This activity can also be used in simplified form for each type of phrase and clause.

Exercise 1 can be used to assess students' ability to recognize fragments and can be covered orally as guided practice or used as a diagnostic test. You may want to have students identify the missing information as you suggest questions that would lead them to supply that information. Conversely, leading students to discover what kind of

FRAGMENT	To see Devils Tower National Monument.
SENTENCE	We stopped in northeastern Wyoming to see Devils Tower National Monument.
FRAGMENT	Established in 1906.
SENTENCE	Established in 1906, Devils Tower was the first national monument in the United States.
FRAGMENT	Seeing the movie *Close Encounters of the Third Kind.*
SENTENCE	Seeing the movie *Close Encounters of the Third Kind* made me interested in Devils Tower.

Appositive Phrases

An *appositive* is a word that identifies or explains a nearby word in the sentence. An *appositive phrase* is an appositive and its modifiers. Because an appositive phrase does not have a verb and does not express a complete thought, it cannot stand alone as a complete sentence.

| FRAGMENT | A strange rock formation. |
| SENTENCE | Devils Tower, a strange rock formation, has special significance in the movie. |

Prepositional Phrases

A *prepositional phrase* is a group of words that begins with a preposition and ends with a noun or pronoun.

| FRAGMENT | Of volcanic rock. |
| SENTENCE | Devils Tower is an 865-foot-tall tower of volcanic rock. |

WRITING NOTE   When a verbal phrase modifies, or describes, another word in the sentence, it's usually best to place the phrase as close as possible to the word it modifies. For instance, in the example at the top of this page, the verbal phrase *established in 1906* needs to stay close to *Devils Tower.* But some verbal phrases, such as the phrase *to see Devils Tower National Monument,* make sense either at the beginning or at the end of the sentence.

☞ REFERENCE NOTE: For more help with phrase placement in sentences, see pages 464–465 and 728–730.

COOPERATIVE LEARNING

Divide the class into groups of three students each and have them write paragraphs composed of fragments— two fragments from each student in the group. Then have the groups trade paragraphs to revise the fragments into complete sentences. Finally, have one representative from each group read the revised paragraphs to the class.

You may want to allow discussions between the groups that wrote the paragraphs and the groups that revised them. How were the fragments revised and why were they revised in that manner? What other revisions are possible? How might other revisions change the effect or focus of the sentences?

INDEPENDENT PRACTICE

Exercises 2, 3, 4, and **5** can be used as independent practice, although you may also use some of them as guided practice. If, for example, students don't do well on **Exercise 2**, you may want to work with them on **Exercise 4.** The same principle applies with **Exercises 3** and **5.**

Sentence Fragments **451**

EXERCISE 2 ▶ Revising Phrase Fragments

Using the photograph to help spark your imagination, create a sentence from each of the following phrase fragments. You may (1) add the fragment to a complete sentence or (2) develop the fragment into a complete sentence by adding a subject, a verb, or both.

EXAMPLE **1.** climbing up the cliff
   1. *Climbing up the cliff, I tried not to look down.*
      or
      I was climbing up the cliff.

1. in the jungle
2. watching for wild animals
3. to swing on huge vines
4. on the way
5. scratched and bruised
6. the fearless explorer
7. led by experienced guides
8. at the top of the cliff
9. surprised by a loud noise
10. to write about the experience

ANSWERS
Exercise 2

Sentences will vary. Here are some possibilities:

1. The photographers were hired to take pictures in the jungle.
2. They spent many hours watching for wild animals.
3. Chimpanzees like to swing on huge vines.
4. On the way to the water hole, the photographers saw an elephant.
5. The photographers were scratched and bruised when they fell off the cliff.
6. The fearless explorer saved them from the hungry lion.
7. They were led by experienced guides to the elephant graveyard.
8. At the top of the cliff, the photographers admired the view.
9. They were suddenly surprised by a loud noise.
10. After they returned, the photographers decided to write about the experience.

TIMESAVER
To save yourself some time, tell students to underline the fragments they use to make sentences in **Exercises 2** and **4** and to circle the places in **Exercises 3** and **5** where fragments have been joined to each other or to independent clauses. This procedure will allow you to check the students' work quickly and accurately.

Subordinate Clause Fragments

A *clause* is a group of words that has a subject and a verb. One kind of clause, an *independent clause,* expresses a complete thought and can stand alone as a sentence. For example, the independent clause *I missed the bus* is a com-

ASSESSMENT

To determine how well students have mastered the material on sentence fragments, carefully check students' answers to **Exercises 2–5. Exercises 2** and **4** should show how well the students have learned to revise fragments, while **Exercises 3** and **5** should reveal how good students are at recognizing and revising fragments.

CLOSURE

Ask the class to recite the questions that make up the three-part test for sentence fragments. [Does the group of words have a subject? Does it have a verb? Does it express a complete thought?] ■

452   *Writing Complete Sentences*

plete sentence. But another kind of clause, a ***subordinate clause,*** doesn't express a complete thought and can't stand alone as a sentence. A subordinate clause fragment is easy to identify because it suggests a question that it doesn't answer.

FRAGMENT   Because the weather often changed several times a day. [*What* was the result of the weather changing?]

SENTENCE   Because the weather often changed several times a day, filming *White Fang* in Alaska was very difficult.

FRAGMENT   Who directed *White Fang*. [Note that this group of words would be a complete sentence if it ended with a question mark. But as a statement, it doesn't express a complete thought. It doesn't tell *who* directed the movie.]

SENTENCE   Randal Kleiser, who directed *White Fang*, thought it was worth the trouble to film the movie in Alaska.

FRAGMENT   That needed constant care. [*What* needed constant care?]

SENTENCE   The cast of *White Fang* included many animals that needed constant care.

☞ **REFERENCE NOTE:** For more about independent and subordinate clauses, see pages 595–615.

WRITING NOTE

A subordinate clause telling *why, where, when,* or *how* (an adverb clause) may be placed before or after the independent clause. When you combine sentences by inserting an adverb clause, try the clause in both positions to see which sounds best to you.

EXAMPLES   Because the setting added to the beauty of the film, everyone was glad *White Fang* had been filmed in Alaska.

or

Everyone was glad *White Fang* had been filmed in Alaska because the setting added to the beauty of the film.

When the subordinate clause comes first, remember to separate it from the independent clause with a comma.

EXERCISE 3 ▶ Revising Subordinate Clause Fragments

Use what you've learned about subordinate clause fragments to correct the following paragraph. First, find the clause fragments. Then, revise the paragraph, combining the subordinate clauses with independent clauses. (There may be more than one way to do this.) Change the punctuation and capitalization as necessary.

Before and during the Civil War, the Underground Railroad helped hundreds of slaves to escape to the North. The Underground Railroad was a system of travel. That moved the slaves from one house to another. Until they reached the North and freedom. "Conductors" on the Underground Railroad would plan the slaves' journey to the next "station." One conductor on the Underground Railroad was Harriet Tubman. Who was born a slave in 1821. She escaped from the South in 1849. Which was a very dangerous thing for a female slave to do alone. Because of Harriet Tubman. More than three hundred people were able to reach freedom.

ANSWERS
Exercise 3

Paragraphs will vary. Here is an example:

Before and during the Civil War, the Underground Railroad helped hundreds of slaves to escape to the north. The Underground Railroad was a system of travel that moved the slaves from one house to another until they reached the North and freedom. "Conductors" on the Underground Railroad would plan the slave's journey to the next "station." One conductor on the Underground Railroad was Harriet Tubman, who was born a slave in 1821. She escaped from the South in 1849, which was a very dangerous thing for a female slave to do alone. Because of Harriet Tubman, more than three hundred people were able to reach freedom.

👁 VISUAL CONNECTIONS
Exploring the Subject. Harriet Tubman was born a slave in Bucktown, Maryland and escaped from a plantation on Maryland's eastern shore when she was in her late twenties. A year later, she returned to Maryland to guide members of her family to freedom. After that, she became one of the Underground Railroad's most active conductors, making nineteen successful trips into slave territory despite huge rewards offered for her capture.

ANSWERS
Exercise 4

Sentences will vary. Here are some possibilities:

1. I am going to see Elton John, who is a popular singer.
2. I first heard him when you played your new record album.
3. Because the concert is next Friday, I'm going to buy tickets today.
4. I'll get you one if the tickets aren't sold out.
5. I hope he sings "Tiny Dancer," which is my favorite song.

EXERCISE 4 ▶ **Using Subordinate Clauses in Sentences**

You've had some practice at revising subordinate clause fragments. Now use your skills and your imagination to make a complete sentence from each of the following subordinate clauses. To make a complete sentence, add an independent clause at the beginning or at the end of the subordinate clause. Add capitalization and punctuation wherever you need to.

EXAMPLE   1. because her family came from Mexico
          1. *Because her family came from Mexico, Linda Ronstadt heard many Mexican folk songs while she was growing up.*

1. who is a popular singer
2. when you played your new record album
3. because the concert is next Friday
4. if the tickets aren't sold out
5. which is my favorite song

WRITING NOTE   You've seen that it's easy to mistake phrases and subordinate clauses for complete sentences. It's also easy to mistake a series of items for a complete sentence. In the following example, the series of items in dark type is a fragment. It may make sense along with the sentence that comes before it, but it can't stand on its own because it doesn't express a complete thought.

FRAGMENT   I tried out for different positions on the team. **Pitcher, shortstop, and catcher.**

To correct the series fragment, you can
- make it into a complete sentence
- link it to the previous sentence with a colon

SENTENCE   I tried out for different positions on the team. **I tried out for** pitcher, shortstop, and catcher.

or

I tried out for different positions on the team: pitcher, shortstop, and catcher.

E X E R C I S E 5 ▶   **Identifying and Revising Fragments**

The writer of the following paragraph wants to describe the high point of her summer—a white-water rafting trip. But the sentence fragments in the paragraph make the meaning unclear. Help make the paragraph clearer by finding and revising the fragments. To correct each fragment, you can (1) link it to an independent clause or (2) develop it into a complete sentence.

Whenever I look at photographs of white-water rafting, I remember what a great time I had on my first raft trip. The first mile or so of the raft trip was easy. As we paddled slowly in the moving current. The guide pointed out the strange rock formations along the banks of the river. Once we got used to paddling, we were ready for adventure. Wanted to experience the thrill of the white water. The guide helped us navigate "the eye of the needle." Which was a difficult stretch of the rapids. Paddling through the rapids, I almost hit a rock. Lost my balance and almost fell overboard. The white water was scary. But was exhilarating too. I hope I can take another raft trip next summer!

SEGMENT 2 *(pp. 456–459)*
RUN-ON SENTENCES
OBJECTIVES
- To identify and revise run-on sentences
- To identify sentence fragments and run-on sentences in a paragraph

MOTIVATION
Write the following passage on the chalkboard and invite students to decipher it: that that is is that that is not is not.

Without proper punctuation, this sentence will probably seem to be nothing more than a list of repeated words. When supplied with punctuation, it becomes "That that is, is. That that is not, is not." Use this example as a

QUOTATION FOR THE DAY
"Talking and eloquence are not the same: to speak, and to speak well, are two things. A fool may talk, but a wise man speaks." (Ben Jonson, 1573–1637, English dramatist and poet)

If talking and eloquence are not the same, neither then are writing and writing eloquently. The run-on sentence is one type of mistake that keeps writing from becoming eloquent. Remind students that in the real world, as well as in school, people are often judged by their ability (or inability) to write well. In school, grades depend on this ability. After graduation, being successful in a chosen career field may depend upon being able to write well. Lead students in a discussion of how writing well is important to different careers.

---

456   *Writing Complete Sentences*

Run-on Sentences

A *run-on sentence* is two or more complete sentences that are written as one sentence. Because run-on sentences don't show where one idea ends and another begins, they are confusing to the reader. There are two kinds of run-on sentences: the *fused sentence* and the *comma splice.*

In a *fused sentence,* the writer has joined two or more sentences with no punctuation between them.

RUN-ON   Measurements originally were related to the sizes of people's hands, arms, and feet an inch was the width of a thumb.

CORRECT   Measurements originally were related to the sizes of people's hands, arms, and feet. An inch was the width of a thumb.

In a *comma splice,* the writer has joined two or more sentences with only a comma to separate them.

RUN-ON   A foot was the length of a person's foot, a yard was the distance from a man's nose to the end of his thumb when his arm was outstretched.

CORRECT   A foot was the length of a person's foot. A yard was the distance from a man's nose to the end of his thumb when his arm was outstretched.

WRITING NOTE   To identify run-on sentences, try reading your writing aloud. A natural, distinct pause in your voice usually means that you've come to the end of a thought. If your voice pauses but your sentence keeps going, you may have a run-on.

Another way to spot run-ons is to look for subjects and verbs. This will help you see where one complete thought ends and another one begins.

Revising Run-on Sentences

There are several ways to revise a run-on sentence. As shown in the examples on this page, you can always make

TEACHING THE LESSON

The problem with run-on sentences is primarily one of punctuation, so you may want to review the appropriate rules in **Chapters 25** and **26** with your students. The gist of this lesson will center on the four ways to correctly punctuate connected independent clauses as discussed under **Revising Run-on Sentences. Exercise 6** provides

Run-on Sentences   **457**

two separate sentences. But you can also make a compound sentence if the independent clauses in the run-on are closely related.

1. You can make a compound sentence by adding a comma and a coordinating conjunction (*and, but, or, yet,* or *nor*).

    RUN-ON   Spanish is the official language of Guatemala many Guatemalans speak Maya Indian languages.
    REVISED Spanish is the official language of Guatemala, **but** many Guatemalans speak Maya Indian languages.

2. You can make a compound sentence by adding a semicolon.

    RUN-ON   About half the people in Guatemala are descended from Maya Indians about half have mixed Spanish and Indian ancestry.
    REVISED About half the people in Guatemala are descended from Maya Indians; about half have mixed Spanish and Indian ancestry.

3. You can make a compound sentence by adding a semicolon and a *conjunctive adverb*—a word such as *therefore, instead, meanwhile, still, also, nevertheless,* or *however.* A conjunctive adverb needs to be followed by a comma.

    RUN-ON   Guatemala's rich soil is its greatest natural resource, agriculture is one of the country's main industries.
    REVISED Guatemala's rich soil is its greatest natural resource; **therefore,** agriculture is one of the country's main industries.

LEP/ESL

Spanish. Have students write some sentences in Spanish that are run together and then have the students rewrite the sentences in English so you can help punctuate the sentences correctly. This activity should help the students learn some of the differences in syntax and punctuation between Spanish and English. Spanish-speaking students might have trouble recognizing run-on sentences in English because it is often acceptable to run sentences together in Spanish.

LEARNING STYLES

Auditory Learners. Reading the run-on sentences in **Exercise 6** aloud may help students understand the problems with run-ons. You may want to exaggerate the confusing effect of run-ons by reading them faster than normal. Then read the sentences again with proper punctuation. You may want to exaggerate the pauses a little so the students can see how punctuation works as an organizer to help make sentences clear and understandable.

practice in revising run-ons by using all four methods. You may want to help students construct their own sentences by using the four methods of punctuating as guided practice before students begin revising, or you can use some of the items in **Exercise 6**. Familiarizing the students with the proper procedures should improve their ability to recognize and correct run-on sentences. Use the rest of the items in **Exercise 6** and the **Review** on p. 459 as independent practice.

INTEGRATING THE LANGUAGE ARTS

Mechanics Link. To show students that correcting run-on sentences includes adding the proper punctuation, write the following sentence on the chalkboard:

> I went to the grocery store the jars on the shelves were empty.

Read the sentence aloud to the class and emphasize the lack of pauses by reading at a steady pace. Ask the students to tell what is wrong with the sentence. [It is two separate ideas punctuated as a single sentence.] Then ask them what is confusing about the sentence. [The word *store* can be both a noun and a verb, and it is unclear exactly how the word is to be used.] Now correct the sentence for the students. Use each of the four methods for correcting run-ons. [(1) I went to the grocery store. The jars on the shelves were empty. (2) I went to the grocery store, but the jars on the shelves were empty. (3) I went to the grocery store; the jars on the shelves were empty. (4) I went to the grocery store; however, the jars on the shelves were empty.]

 REFERENCE NOTE: For more information about how to form compound sentences, see pages 467–468 and 610–611.

EXERCISE 6 ▶ **Revising by Correcting Run-ons**

The following items are confusing because they're run-on sentences. Clear up the confusion by correcting them. To correct each run-on, use the method of revision that is given in parentheses.

1. Knights in the Middle Ages were bound by a code of honor, it was called the code of chivalry. (two sentences)
2. Knights were supposed to be brave and loyal, they were supposed to protect defenseless people. (comma and coordinating conjunction) **2.** , and
3. Some knights were true to the code of chivalry, many fell short of the ideal. (semicolon and conjunctive adverb) **3.** ; however,
4. A knight could be punished for showing cowardice; his sword would be broken in half to show his disgrace. (semicolon)
5. A knight depended on his horse for transportation and in battle, his horse was very valuable to him. (semicolon and conjunctive adverb) **5.** ; therefore,
6. Many knights belonged to strict religious orders, they were monks who fought as soldiers. (two sentences)
7. Originally, knighthood wasn't a mark of distinction; the first knights were ordinary mounted soldiers. (semicolon)
8. Eventually knighthood became a sign of nobility, the knights were considered part of the upper class. (comma and coordinating conjunction) **8.** , and
9. Orders of knighthood still exist in Great Britain, knighthood doesn't have the same meaning that it did in the Middle Ages. (comma and coordinating conjunction) **9.** , but
10. Knighthood is now an honorary order, it is bestowed on people to recognize great achievements. (semicolon)

ASSESSMENT

To evaluate students' understanding of the methods to correct run-on sentences, check students' responses to **Exercise 6** and the **Review.** Make sure that the method the students used for correcting each sentence in **Exercise 6** is the one called for in the directions.

CLOSURE

Ask the class to recite the methods of correcting run-ons [(1) making two sentences (2) separating independent clauses with a semicolon (3) separating independent clauses with a comma and a coordinating conjunction (4) separating independent clauses with a semicolon and a conjunctive adverb followed by a comma] ■

Run-on Sentences   **459**

> **R E V I E W** ▶ **Revising Fragments and Run-on Sentences**

When you read the following paragraphs, you'll notice several sentence fragments and run-on sentences. First identify each fragment and run-on. Then rewrite the passage correctly. Change the punctuation and capitalization wherever necessary.   **Revisions may vary.**

Today, the pyramids of Egypt are fascinating to
F tourists, archaeologists, and historians. Who travel to
Africa to see them. The pyramids symbolize a great
R/F ancient civilization⌃ Egypt was a powerful influence. For ⌃;
thousands of years in the ancient world.
F The main purpose of the pyramids. Was to entomb the
pharaohs. Sometimes a pharaoh's wife was buried with
F him in the pyramid. All his worldly possessions⌃also **were**
R buried⌃ food, clothing, and water were provided for the ⊙
F journey. To the other world.
Although many pyramids have been emptied of their
F treasures⌃ The pyramids themselves continue to interest ⌃
R people⌃they are the only one of the Seven Wonders of the
F Ancient World. That is still standing.

⛓ **INTEGRATING THE LANGUAGE ARTS**

Technology Link. Word processors have insert functions that allow revisions without rewriting (or retyping) the entire sentence. The insert function works well with revising run-ons because the proper punctuation and coordinating conjunction or conjunctive adverb can be easily placed where they need to be. If your class has access to word processors, you may want to demonstrate this function to the class.

SEGMENT 3 *(p. 460)*

MAKING CONNECTIONS

FILL IN THE MISSING PIECES
OBJECTIVES

- To write a paragraph by using correct sentences
- To revise sentence fragments in a paragraph

FILL IN THE MISSING PIECES
Teaching Strategies

Although this activity is designed to get students to revise paragraphs back to their original forms, it is more important for students to be able to recognize and correct fragments and run-ons. Reassure the students that if their revisions do not match the original paragraphs this does not mean they have failed. There are many ways to revise fragments and run-ons, any of which can be as valid as the original sentences.

When the students are through revising and begin comparing the revisions and originals, any differences can be used as prompts for discussion of the revision process. However, evaluations of which versions are better should be kept to a minimum as long as the revisions are appropriate. The main point of concern is whether the revisions are grammatically correct.

GUIDELINES

You may want to caution students not to take out too much from their paragraphs. It should not be impossible for the students revising the paragraphs to come close to the originals.

460

MAKING CONNECTIONS

Fill in the Missing Pieces

You've learned that sentence fragments are confusing because they are missing some important parts. Here's a chance to see just how confusing fragments can be.

First, team up with one of your classmates. Working together, write a paragraph in response to the photograph that follows. Use complete sentences, and make your paragraph as clear as possible.

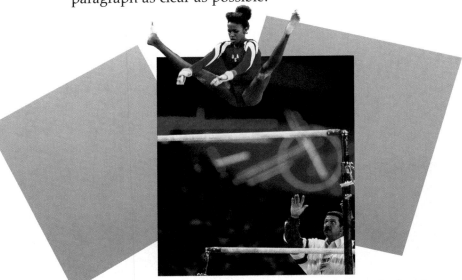

Next, write a second version of the paragraph, leaving out several subjects and verbs and creating phrase and clause fragments. Then, trade your second version with that of another team. Try to fill in the missing pieces of each other's paragraphs to reconstruct the original, complete sentences.

Compare your final versions to the original paragraphs. How well did you do in supplying the missing parts? How has the meaning of each paragraph changed?

Chapter 13 WRITING EFFECTIVE SENTENCES

OBJECTIVES

- To combine sentences by inserting words and phrases and by using compound subjects and compound verbs
- To combine pairs of sentences into compound sentences
- To combine pairs of sentences into complex sentences with subordinate clauses
- To revise a paragraph by combining sentences
- To revise sentences to create parallelism
- To revise stringy and wordy sentences
- To revise sentences to vary their beginnings
- To revise a paragraph to create a variety of sentence structures
- To write a composition using a variety of sentence structures

Motivation

Ask students what they would think if they heard a rock song in which the guitarist repeated one chord over and over again. Would they like the song? Would it hold their attention? Why or why not?

Point out that writing is comparable to music in that words can be combined in different ways to have varying rhythms to flow like musical notes. Tell students that if writers combine words in only one way, their writing will be as dull as a song in which one chord is repeated over and over again.

Tell students that in this chapter they will learn techniques to help them increase the variety of sentence structures in their writing, thereby making their writing more effective.

Introduction

Tell students that regardless of their aim for writing—expressive, persuasive, literary, or informative—they will need to be able to write effective sentences. Point out that even though they might have excellent ideas for their compositions, it is crucial that students communicate their ideas effectively in the form of well-written sentences.

Integration

You will probably want to refer to this chapter throughout the year as students write compositions and particularly as students revise their compositions. You may also want to point out examples of effective sentence structure as students study selections in their literature textbooks. Encourage students to analyze the sentence styles of their favorite authors and to be conscious of how professional writers use sentence variety to create memorable prose.

You may want to integrate the teaching of **Chapter 32: "End Marks and Commas"** with the study of effective sentences because it is often the fear of committing comma errors that keeps students from attempting to use varied sentence patterns.

The chart on the next page illustrates the strands of language arts as they are integrated into this chapter. For vocabulary study, glossary words are underlined in some writing models.

BEST SENTENCE

QUOTATIONS

All **Quotations for the Day** are chosen because of their relevance to instructional material presented in that segment of the chapter and for their usefulness in establishing student interest in writing.

Selection	Reading and Literature	Writing and Critical Thinking	Language and Syntax	Speaking, Listening, and Other Expression Skills
	Recognizing sentences that need revisions in a paragraph **473, 482** Identifying faulty parallelism in sentences **474-475** Reading and evaluating sentences for wordiness **478**	Combining sentences by inserting words **463-464** Combining sentences by inserting phrases **466-467** Combining sentences by using compound subjects and verbs **468** Combining sentences into compound sentences **469-470** Combining sentences into complex sentences **472-473** Revising a paragraph by combining sentences **473** Revising sentences to create parallelism **474-475** Revising stringy sentences **476-477** Revising wordy sentences **478** Revising sentences to vary sentence beginnings **479-480** Revising a paragraph to create a variety of sentence structures **482** Writing a composition using a variety of sentence structures **482** Writing and revising awkward and confusing sentences **483**	Using commas to separate nonessential phrases and clauses **466** Using commas after introductory words, phrases, or clauses **466, 472-473** Using commas and coordinating conjunctions, semicolons, or semicolons and conjunctive adverbs to form compound sentences **469-470**	Choosing a creative name for a class contest **483** Voting for winning contest entries **483**

SEGMENT PLANNING GUIDE

Whether you are planning for a quick review of a writing concept or preparing an extended lesson on composition, you can use the following Planning Guide to adapt the chapter material to the individual needs of your class.

SEGMENT	PAGES	CONTENT	RESOURCES
1 *Combining Sentences*	*461-473*		Inserting Words and Phrases
Combining Sentences	461-462	Guidelines: examining sentences in a model	Using Compound Subjects and Verbs
Inserting Words	462-463	Guidelines: combining sentences by inserting a key word from one sentence into another	Creating a Compound Sentence
Chart: Using the Same Form/Changing the Form	463	Example: combining two sentences into one	Creating a Complex Sentence
Writing Note	463	Writing suggestion: forming adjectives and adverbs	
Exercise 1	463-464	Applied practice: combining sentences by inserting words	
Exercise 2	464	Applied practice: combing sentences by choosing and inserting words	
Inserting Phrases	465-466	Guidelines: combining sentences by inserting prepositional, participial, and appositive phrases	
Exercise 3	466-467	Applied practice: combining sentences by inserting phrases	
Using Compound Subjects and Verbs	467	Guidelines: combining sentences by using coordinating conjunctions	
Grammar Hint	468	Writing suggestion: checking for subject-verb agreement	
Exercise 4	468	Applied practice: combining sentences by using compound subjects and verbs	
Creating a Compound Sentence	468-469	Guidelines: combining sentences by creating a compound sentence	
Writing Note	469	Writing suggestion: using the coordinating conjunction "so" sparingly	
Exercise 5	469-470	Guidelines: combining sentences into compound sentences	
Creating a Complex Sentence	470	Introduction: using subordinate and independent clauses	
Adjective Clauses	470	Guidelines: making an adjective clause by replacing the subject with *who, which* or *that*	
Mechanics Hint	471	Writing suggestion: punctuating adjective clauses	
Adverb Clauses	471	Guidelines: making an adverb clause by using *although, after, because, if, when,* and *while*	
Noun Clauses	472	Guidelines: making a noun clause by adding *that, how, what, whatever, who,* or *whoever*	

All the resources listed in this chapter are located in the Teacher's ResourceBank™.

SEGMENT	PAGES	CONTENT	RESOURCES
Exercise 6	472-473	Applied practice: combining sentences into a complex sentence	
Review A	473	Applied practice: revising a paragraph by combining sentences	
2 *Improving Sentence Style*	*474-482*		Using Parallel Structure
Using Parallel Structure	474	Guidelines: examining parallel and unparallel structure	Stringy and Wordy Sentences
Exercise 7	474-475	Apple practice: revising sentences to create parallel structure	Varying Sentence Structure
Revising Stringy Sentences	475-476	Guidelines: examining a stringy sentence	
Exercise 8	476-477	Applied practice: revising stringy sentences	
Revising Wordy Sentences	477	Guidelines: examining wordy and revised sentences	
Exercise 9	478	Applied practice: revising wordy sentences	
Varying Sentence Beginnings	478-479	Guidelines: varying sentence beginnings	
Chart: Varying Sentence Beginnings	479	Guidelines: beginning sentences with single-word modifiers, phrases, and subordinate clauses	
Exercise 10	479-480	Applied practice: varying sentence beginnings	
Varying Sentence Structure	481	Guideline: varying sentence structure to create a better writing style	
Exercise 11	482	Applied practice: revising a paragraph to create a variety of sentence structures	
Review B	482	Applied practice: writing a composition using a variety of sentence structures	
3 *Making Connections*	*483*		
Enter a Contest	483	Applied practice: writing and revising an awkward and confusing sentence	

WHOLE-CHAPTER RESOURCES Review Form A, Review Form B

OBJECTIVES

- To combine sentences by inserting words and phrases
- To combine sentences by using compound subjects and compound verbs
- To combine pairs of sentences into compound sentences
- To combine pairs of sentences into complex sentences

13 WRITING EFFECTIVE SENTENCES

Teacher's ResourceBank™

RESOURCES

COMBINING SENTENCES

- Inserting Words and Phrases
- Using Compound Subjects and Verbs
- Creating a Compound Sentence
- Creating a Complex Sentence

QUOTATION FOR THE DAY

"You never want to bore your readers. It's the biggest sin, next to misleading them and lying. One way to stay interesting is to change the length of your sentences, so that the rhythm is interesting." (Ethel Grodzins Romm, American writer)

Ask students if they've ever felt sleepy when listening to a repetitive sound such as the lapping of waves or the tick of a clock. Point out that just as certain repetitive sounds often lull people to sleep, repetitive sentences often bore readers.

> **LOOKING AHEAD**
>
> You've heard that "variety is the spice of life." In this chapter, you will learn how to add spice, or variety, to your sentences by
>
> - using sentence-combining techniques
> - improving your sentence style

Combining Sentences

Short sentences can be effective, but too many of them make writing sound choppy. For example, notice how the many short sentences in the following paragraph make it boring to read.

MEETING INDIVIDUAL NEEDS

STUDENTS WITH SPECIAL NEEDS

Students with learning disabilities may not understand or retain terms such as *prepositional phrase, participial phrase,* and *appositive phrase,* yet they may be able to use the sentence-combining techniques correctly. When explaining these techniques, use simple language. For example, you could say, "move this group of words from one sentence to another" rather than "insert a participial phrase."

VISUAL CONNECTIONS

Ideas for Writing. Protective coloration is common among animals. Many animals have coloring that helps them to blend in with their habitats, thus concealing them from predators. Some are even capable of changing color dramatically as they move from place to place.

Have interested students write informative paragraphs about the protective coloring of one or more animals. Remind students to avoid using too many short, choppy sentences in their paragraphs.

462

---

462 *Writing Effective Sentences*

Penguins have black backs. Penguins have white fronts. These colors act as camouflage. Some of a penguin's enemies fly. Some of a penguin's enemies swim. From above, a penguin's black back doesn't show in the water. From below, its white front just looks like sunlight on the water.

Sentence combining is a way to improve choppy writing. See how the paragraph about penguins can be improved by combining the short sentences into longer, smoother sentences.

Notice that even though the sentences are longer, the revised paragraph is shorter and more precise. That's because sentence combining has helped to eliminate repeated words and ideas.

Penguins have black backs and white fronts that act as camouflage. Some of a penguin's enemies fly and some swim. From above, a penguin's black back doesn't show in the water, and from below, its white front just looks like sunlight on the water.

Inserting Words

You can combine short sentences by taking a key word from one sentence and inserting it into another sentence. When you do this, you may need to delete one or more words. You may also need to change the form of the word you insert.

As you lead students through the various methods for combining sentences, ask for volunteers to read aloud the original sample sentences and then to read the revised ones. Discuss with students how each revision was achieved. You may also want to give students additional examples of each technique for combining sentences.

As you teach each of the sentence-combining techniques in this segment, you may want to integrate some grammar review from **Chapters 15–19** to help students understand the terminology used. You may also want to review some of the rules of punctuation presented in **Chapters 25** and **26**.

USING THE SAME FORM	
ORIGINAL	James Thurber wrote many short stories. His stories are amusing.
COMBINED	James Thurber wrote many **amusing** short stories.
CHANGING THE FORM	
ORIGINAL	Thurber's illustrated stories are especially fun to read. The illustrations are humorous.
REVISED	Thurber's **humorously** illustrated stories are especially fun to read.

WRITING NOTE

When you change the form of a word before inserting it into a sentence, you often add an ending that makes the word an adjective or an adverb. The endings you'll use most frequently are *–ed, –ful, –ing,* and *–ly.*

E X E R C I S E 1 ▶ **Combining Sentences by Inserting Words**

Here are five sets of sentences about the many uses of common plants. Combine each set into one sentence by inserting the italicized word(s) into the first sentence. The directions in parentheses will tell you how to change the form of a word if it is necessary to do so. **Answers may vary.**

EXAMPLE   **1.** You can find books that describe the uses of herbs. These books describe the *many* uses that herbs have.
         1. *You can find books that describe the many uses of herbs.*

1. Plants have always been valued for their ᴧproperties. ~~These properties are *medicinal.*~~   **1.** medicinal
2. Digitalis,ᴧa medicine for heart failure, is extracted from the foxglove plant. ~~Digitalis is an *effective* medicine.~~   **2.** an effective
3. ᴧ𝒯he recipes for many old-fashioned herbal remedies have been lost. ~~The loss of these recipes is *unfortunate.*~~ (Add an *–ly.*)   **3.** Unfortunately,

CRITICAL THINKING
Analysis

Direct students' attention to the example of sentence combining given under **Changing the Form.** Ask students whether or not the sentences could have been combined to read "Thurber's humorous, illustrated stories are especially fun to read." [No.] Why not? [The meaning of the sentences is changed. In the original pair of sentences, the word *humorous* describes *illustrations.* In this combination, *humorous* describes *stories.*]

GUIDED PRACTICE

On the chalkboard, model the first sentence combination from each exercise in this segment. Enlist students' participation and guide them through the sentence-combining process dictated by each exercise.

INDEPENDENT PRACTICE

Exercises 1–6 and **Review A** can provide students with independent practice in combining sentences. You may also want to ask students to write original paragraphs on topics of their choice. In their paragraphs, students should use the sentence-combining techniques presented in this segment.

464   *Writing Effective Sentences*

INTEGRATING THE LANGUAGE ARTS

Literature   Link. Sometimes writers use short, choppy sentences to create certain effects. If the story is accessible to your students, have them read "The Pit and the Pendulum," by Edgar Allan Poe. When they have finished, direct their attention to the story's last paragraph and have a volunteer read the paragraph aloud. Ask students what impression its short, choppy sentences convey. [Responses will vary. The succession of short sentences conveys the rapidity of the sequence of events described and helps to create a breathless quality. The narrator of the story seems unable to breathe due to extreme excitement.]

4. Some herbal remedies have been passed down through many generations of families. ~~The families~~ *trust* ~~these remedies.~~ (Add an *–ed*.) **4.** trusted
5. Plants are still used to make products such as shampoos and hair dyes. ~~These products are *beauty* products.~~ **5.** beauty

EXERCISE 2 ▶ **Combining Sentences by Inserting Words**

In Exercise 1, the key words were italicized for you. Now it's up to you to decide which words to insert. There may be more than one way to combine each set of sentences; choose the combination you think is best. Change the forms of words wherever you need to.   Revisions will vary.

1. Isak Dinesen's book *Out of Africa* tells about her experiences on a plantation in Africa. ~~It was a coffee plantation.~~ **1.** coffee
2. Dinesen managed the plantation for ten years. ~~She managed it single-handedly.~~ **2.** single-handedly
3. One year, a swarm of locusts descended on her farm. ~~The swarm was huge.~~ **3.** huge   **4.** detailed
4. Dinesen's descriptions paint a vivid picture of her life in Africa. ~~Her descriptions have a lot of detail.~~
5. *Out of Africa* was made into a movie. ~~The movie was a success.~~ **5.** successful

ASSESSMENT

You could use **Review A** in conjunction with samples of students' writing to evaluate students' mastery of the variety of sentence-combining techniques discussed in this segment.

RETEACHING

Provide copies of a paragraph consisting of short, choppy sentences and have students use the sentence-combining techniques described in this segment to revise the paragraph. You could use an old student paper or create an appropriate paragraph.

Or provide copies of well-written paragraphs and have students revise the ☞

Combining Sentences **465**

Inserting Phrases

You also can combine closely related sentences by reducing one sentence to a phrase and inserting it into the other sentence. When it is inserted, the phrase gives additional information about an idea expressed in the sentence.

Prepositional Phrases

A *prepositional phrase* contains a preposition and its object. Usually, you can insert a prepositional phrase into another sentence without changing it in any way.

ORIGINAL   My sister loaned me a copy of *The Martian Chronicles.* It is by Ray Bradbury.
REVISED   My sister loaned me a copy of *The Martian Chronicles* **by Ray Bradbury.**

Participial Phrases

A *participle* is a word that is formed from a verb but is used as an adjective. A participle usually ends in *–ing* or *–ed*. A *participial phrase* contains a participle and words related to it. The whole participial phrase acts as an adjective in a sentence.

Sometimes you can combine sentences by reducing one sentence to a participial phrase. When you insert the participial phrase into the other sentence, place it close to the noun or pronoun it modifies. Otherwise you may confuse your reader.

ORIGINAL   Juanita Platero describes the conflict between old and new ideas. She does this as she writes about Navajo culture.
REVISED   **Writing about Navajo culture,** Juanita Platero describes the conflict between old and new ideas.

Appositive Phrases

An *appositive phrase* is made up of an appositive and its modifiers. It identifies or explains a noun or pronoun in a sentence. Sometimes you can change one sentence into an appositive phrase and insert it into another sentence. Like a participial phrase, an appositive phrase needs to be placed directly before or after the noun or pronoun it modifies. The phrase should be separated from the rest of

INTEGRATING THE LANGUAGE ARTS

Usage Link. Remind students that modifying phrases should be placed as closely as possible to the words they modify. To give students practice placing modifying phrases correctly, write the following sentences on the chalkboard and have students revise them to eliminate misplaced modifiers:

1. Growing in my garden, she loved the snapdragons.
2. He read about her scientific achievements in the journal.
3. Ignacio found his sister's doll mowing the lawn.
4. Leaping gracefully, we watched the dancers.
5. Isabelle described hang gliding in class.

465

paragraphs so that they include only short choppy sentences. You could then discuss with students which versions of the paragraphs are more effective and why.

Ask students to identify the different methods for combining sentences.

the sentence by a comma (or two commas if you place the phrase in the middle of the sentence).

ORIGINAL   Ray Bradbury is best known for his science fiction stories. Ray Bradbury is an American writer.

REVISED   Ray Bradbury**, an American writer,** is best known for his science fiction stories.

☞ **REFERENCE NOTE:** For more information about the different kinds of phrases, see pages 572–594.

| EXERCISE 3 ▶ | **Combining Sentences by Inserting Phrases** |

Insert phrases to combine each of the following sets of sentences into one sentence. (There may be more than one way to combine each set.) For each sentence set, the hints in parentheses will tell you when to change the forms of words and when to add commas. To help you get started, the words you need to insert are italicized in the first five sentence sets.

EXAMPLE   1. Migrant farm workers move from region to region. They follow the seasonal crop harvests. (Change *follow* to *following*.)

1. *Following the seasonal crop harvests,* migrant farm workers move from region to region.

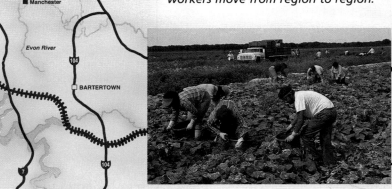

1. Migrant laborers move constantly. They *search for work.* (Change *search* to *searching* and add a comma.)
2. Many live in extreme poverty. They live *without adequate food, shelter, and medical care.*

ANSWERS

Exercise 3

Revisions will vary. Here are some possibilities:

1. Migrant laborers move constantly, searching for work.
2. Many live in extreme poverty, without adequate food, shelter, and medical care.

Write a paragraph composed of short, choppy sentences on the chalkboard and have students independently revise the paragraph by combining sentences. Then have students exchange their revised paragraphs and evaluate one another's revisions. You could provide the following criteria for evaluation:

1. Is the revision more interesting than the original paragraph?
2. Does the revision retain the meaning of the original paragraph?
3. Are several of the sentence-combining techniques used in the revision? ■

3. Many migrant laborers are unable to find other kinds of work. They *lack education*. (Change *lack* to *lacking* and add a comma.)
4. César Chávez champions the rights of migrant farm workers. He is *a labor union organizer*. (Add two commas.)
5. Chávez was born in Arizona. He was born *on a farm*.
6. His family became migrant workers. They became migrant workers after losing their farm.
7. Chávez helped make the voices of farm workers heard. He organized grape pickers in the 1960s. (Change *organized* to *organizing* and add a comma.)
8. He established a union. It was called the National Farm Workers Association. (Add a comma.)
9. Chávez has organized strikes and boycotts. He is committed to nonviolent protest. (Add a comma.)
10. He has helped to improve working conditions for migrant laborers. He has done this through his organizing efforts.

3. Lacking education, many migrant laborers are unable to find other kinds of work.
4. César Chávez, a labor union organizer, champions the rights of migrant farm workers.
5. Chávez was born on a farm in Arizona.
6. His family became migrant workers after losing their farm.
7. Organizing grape pickers in the 1960s, Chávez helped make the voices of farm workers heard.
8. He established a union, the National Farm Workers Association.
9. Committed to nonviolent protest, Chávez has organized strikes and boycotts.
10. Through his organizing efforts, he has helped to improve working conditions for migrant laborers.

Using Compound Subjects and Verbs

You can also combine sentences by using compound subjects and verbs. Just look for sentences that have the same subject or the same verb. Then use coordinating conjunctions (such as *and, but, or, nor, for,* and *yet*) to make a compound subject, a compound verb, or both.

ORIGINAL   Jaguars are large, spotted cats. Leopards are large, spotted cats.
REVISED   **Jaguars and leopards** are large, spotted cats.
[compound subject with the same verb]

ORIGINAL   Jaguars live in the Americas. Jaguars hunt in the Americas.
REVISED   Jaguars **live and hunt** in the Americas.
[compound verb with same subject]

ORIGINAL   Jaguars hunt and attack other animals. Leopards hunt and attack other animals. These cats rarely attack humans.
REVISED   **Jaguars and leopards hunt and attack** other animals **but rarely attack** humans. [compound subject and compound verb]

GRAMMAR HINT

Point out to students that when a compound subject is joined by *or* or *nor,* the verb should agree in number with the part of the subject that is closest to the verb. For example, in the sentence "Neither the cake nor the cookies are done " the verb (*are*) agrees with the closest half of the compound subject (*cookies*).

GRAMMAR HINT

Checking for Subject–Verb Agreement

When you combine sentences by using compound subjects and compound verbs, check to make sure your subjects and verbs agree in number.

ORIGINAL Asia is home to the leopard. Africa is home to the leopard.

REVISED Asia and Africa **are** home to the leopard.

☞ **REFERENCE NOTE:** For more information on agreement of subjects and verbs, see pages 619–634.

EXERCISE 4 ▶ **Combining Sentences by Using Compound Subjects and Verbs**

Here are five sets of short, choppy sentences. Combine each set into one sentence by using a compound subject, a compound verb, or both. **Answers may vary.**

1. Glaciers˄shape landforms. ~~Volcanoes also shape landforms.~~ **1. and volcanoes**
2. Antarctica˄is mostly covered by glaciers. ~~Greenland is mostly covered by glaciers.~~ **2. and Greenland are**
3. ~~Glaciers move slowly.~~ Glaciers˄shape the land as they flow across it. **3. move slowly and**
4. A volcano begins as molten rock beneath the earth's surface˄.~~It~~ gradually rises upward. **4. and**
5. Volcanoes˄can create˄land area. ~~Glaciers can also create land area. They both can destroy land area.~~ **5. and glaciers/and destroy**

Creating a Compound Sentence

If the thoughts in two sentences are related to one another and are equal in importance, you can combine the sentences to form a *compound sentence.* A compound sentence is two or more simple sentences joined by

- a comma and a coordinating conjunction
  or
- a semicolon
  or
- a semicolon and a conjunctive adverb

ORIGINAL	Lions and tigers are the largest cats. Cheetahs are the fastest.
REVISED	Lions and tigers are the largest cats**, but** cheetahs are the fastest. [comma and coordinating conjunction]

or

Lions and tigers are the largest cats**;** cheetahs are the fastest. [semicolon]

or

Lions and tigers are the largest cats**;** **however,** cheetahs are the fastest.
[semicolon and conjunctive adverb]

☞ **REFERENCE NOTE:** For more information about how to create compound sentences, see pages 610–611.

WRITING NOTE
You can use the coordinating conjunctions *and, but, or, nor, for, so,* and *yet* to form compound sentences. However, because *so* is often overworked in writing, you should think twice before using it.

EXERCISE 5 ▶ **Combining Sentences into Compound Sentences**

The following sentences are fine by themselves, but together they would make a choppy paragraph. Using the three methods you've learned, combine each pair of sentences into a compound sentence. Try to use each method at least once. Add commas as necessary.

Revisions will vary.

1. Amy Tan grew up in the United States‿ ~~H~~er parents were born in China. **1. , but**

2. She began her writing career as a business writer‿ ~~S~~he eventually turned to fiction. **2. ; however,**

3. Her first novel‿~~was~~ published in 1989‿ ~~I~~t became a best-seller almost immediately.

4. Tan's Chinese heritage is important to her. Much of her writing focuses on relationships in Chinese American families.   **4. , and**
5. Her fiction often explores the positive aspects of being a second-generation American. It also explores the difficulties.   **5. , but**

Book Signing
Thursday, 2:30
Amy Tan, author of
The Joy Luck Club

Creating a Complex Sentence

If two sentences are unequal in importance, you can combine them by forming a *complex sentence.* Just turn the less-important idea into a subordinate clause and attach it to the other sentence (the independent clause).

👉 REFERENCE NOTE: For information about independent and subordinate clauses, see pages 598–606.

Adjective Clauses

You can make a sentence into an adjective clause by replacing its subject with *who, which,* or *that.* Then you can use the adjective clause to give information about a noun or pronoun in another sentence.

ORIGINAL   The Sargasso Sea is a strange, still area. It is part of the Atlantic Ocean.

REVISED   The Sargasso Sea is a strange, still area **that is part of the Atlantic Ocean.**

ORIGINAL   Christopher Columbus noted the unusual quantity of floating seaweed. He crossed the Sargasso Sea.

REVISED   Christopher Columbus, **who crossed the Sargasso Sea,** noted the unusual quantity of floating seaweed.

MECHANICS HINT

Punctuating Adjective Clauses

If an adjective clause is not essential to the meaning of the sentence, set it off with commas. If it is essential to the meaning, no commas are necessary.

NONESSENTIAL   That poster**,** **which was a birthday present,** is one of my favorites.

ESSENTIAL   The poster **that I got for my birthday** is hanging on the wall.

👉 REFERENCE NOTE: For more about essential and nonessential clauses, see pages 797–799.

Adverb Clauses

You can also combine sentences by turning one sentence into an adverb clause. The adverb clause modifies a verb, an adjective, or another adverb in the sentence you attach it to.

To make a sentence into an adverb clause, add a subordinating conjunction (*although, after, because, if, when, while*) at the beginning. The conjunction shows the relationship between the ideas in the adverb clause and the independent clause. If the adverb clause comes first, set it off from the independent clause with a comma.

👉 REFERENCE NOTE: For a complete list of subordinating conjunctions, see page 604.

ORIGINAL   Sailing ships were sometimes trapped in the Sargasso Sea. There wasn't enough wind to sail by.

REVISED   Sailing ships were sometimes trapped in the Sargasso Sea **when there wasn't enough wind to sail by.**

ORIGINAL   Sailors used to fear the Sargasso Sea. They heard strange tales about it.

REVISED   **Because they heard strange tales about it,** sailors used to fear the Sargasso Sea.

MEETING INDIVIDUAL NEEDS

LEARNING STYLES

Kinetic Learners. For students who learn best from a hands-on activity, write simple sentences on strips of paper. Then write modifiers, phrases, and clauses on separate strips of paper. Have students use scissors and tape to create compound and complex sentences from the strips. Remind students to insert punctuation marks where necessary.

Noun Clauses

You can make a sentence into a noun clause by adding a word like *that, how, what, whatever, who,* or *whoever.* Then you can insert it into another sentence just like an ordinary noun. When you combine the sentences, you may need to change or delete some words.

ORIGINAL Someone ate my lunch. That person had better confess.
REVISED **Whoever ate my lunch** had better confess.

ORIGINAL Jerome hasn't heard. Hockey practice is canceled.
REVISED Jerome hasn't heard **that hockey practice is canceled.**

E X E R C I S E 6 ▶ **Combining Sentences into a Complex Sentence**

Here are ten pairs of sentences about Greek mythology. Combine each pair by turning the second sentence into a subordinate clause and inserting it into the first sentence. For the first six pairs, you are given hints about how to create the subordinate clauses. For the last four, you'll need to use your own judgment. You may have to add or delete some words in the sentences. Add commas where necessary. [Hint: Before you begin, review the words that can be used to introduce subordinate clauses. These words are included in the explanations on pages 603–604.]

OBJECTIVE

- To revise a paragraph by combining sentences in a variety of ways

1. Hercules was a brave hero of Greek mythology. He was given twelve difficult tasks. (Use *who*.)
2. The Parthenon was once a temple for the goddess Athena. The Parthenon is located in Athens. (Use *which*.)
3. Perseus was able to kill the Gorgon Medusa. The god Hermes and the goddess Athena helped him. (Use *because*.)
4. Cassandra had the power to predict the future. No one believed her prophecies, though. (Use *although*.)
5. Helios lived on the Greek island of Rhodes. Helios was the sun god of the Greeks. (Use *who*.)
6. The Greeks believed something about Hestia. Hestia protected the homes of faithful worshipers. (Use *that*.)
7. Hercules accidentally killed Linus. At the time, Linus was trying to teach him how to play the lyre.
8. Scylla was a dangerous sea monster. She lived in a cave.
9. Odysseus had many adventures. He was trying to get home to his wife and son.
10. King Midas wanted everything he touched to turn to gold. He was greedy.

REVIEW A ▶ Revising a Paragraph by Combining Sentences

Using all the sentence-combining skills you have learned, revise and rewrite the following paragraph. Use your judgment about which sentences to combine and how to combine them. Try for smooth, varied sentences that are easy to understand, but don't change the original meaning of the paragraph.   Revisions will vary.

People have always been fascinated by dreams. No one knows for certain why we dream. Scientists have ∧ , but found out something about when we dream. Scientists try to find out about dreaming. ̷S̷c̷i̷e̷n̷t̷i̷s̷t̷s̷ ̷d̷o̷ ̷t̷h̷i̷s̷ by studying people as they sleep. They've learned that dreaming takes place during a particular phase of sleep. ̷T̷h̷e̷ ̷p̷h̷a̷s̷e̷ ̷i̷s̷ called REM ∧ s̷l̷e̷e̷p̷.̷ ̷R̷E̷M̷ ̷s̷t̷a̷n̷d̷s̷ ̷f̷o̷r̷ ̷s̷o̷m̷e̷t̷h̷i̷n̷g̷.̷ ̷I̷t̷ ̷s̷t̷a̷n̷d̷s̷ ̷f̷o̷r̷ , or "rapid eye movement." ∧ REM sleep occurs each night. ∧ I̷t̷   sleep. lasts for about ninety minutes.   and

SEGMENT 2 *(pp. 474–482)*
IMPROVING SENTENCE STYLE

- To revise sentences to vary sentence beginnings
- To revise a paragraph to create a variety of sentence structures

OBJECTIVES

- To revise sentences to create parallelism
- To revise stringy and wordy sentences

QUOTATION FOR THE DAY

"A sentence should read as if its author, had he held a plow instead of a pen, could have drawn a furrow deep and straight to the end." (Henry David Thoreau, 1817–1862, American philosopher and writer)

With this analogy, Thoreau seems to be saying that a good sentence gets straight to the point, rather than twisting and meandering. Ask students to formulate analogies that describe effective sentences, and have volunteers read their analogies to the class.

ADVANCED STUDENTS

Select well-written sentences from literary selections and have students write sentences that imitate the structural elements used in these sentences. You could also make it a practice to call attention to matters of style in the literature the class is reading and to read aloud well-written passages.

474

Improving Sentence Style

In the first part of this chapter, you learned how to reduce choppiness in your writing by combining sentences. Now you'll learn several more ways to polish your sentence style and make your writing more effective.

Using Parallel Structure

When you join several equal or related ideas in a sentence, it's important that you express these ideas in a similar way. You do this by balancing the structure of your sentence parts. For example, you balance an adjective with an adjective, a phrase with a phrase, and a clause with a clause. This kind of balance in writing is called ***parallel structure.*** Begin to look for parallel structure in sentences when you combine words, phrases, and clauses by using the coordinating conjunction *and.*

NOT PARALLEL	A successful athlete is three things: healthy, alert, and showing consideration. [two adjectives and a phrase]
PARALLEL	A successful athlete is three things: **healthy, alert, and considerate.** [three adjectives]
NOT PARALLEL	It takes a careful use of time to play a sport, to keep up with schoolwork, and social life. [two phrases and a noun]
PARALLEL	It takes a careful use of time **to play a sport, to keep up with schoolwork,** and **to have a social life.** [three phrases]
NOT PARALLEL	I promised that I would spend more time studying and to help out more around the house. [a clause and a phrase]
PARALLEL	I promised **that I would spend more time studying** and **that I would help out more around the house.** [two clauses]

 E X E R C I S E 7 **Revising Sentences to Create Parallelism**

Some of the following sentences are out of balance. Bring balance to them by putting the ideas in parallel form. You

MOTIVATION

To introduce students to this segment, write the words *parallel, stringy,* and *wordy* on the chalkboard. Ask students to define the words and to guess how they are related to writing.

TEACHING THE LESSON

As you teach the segment, work with students to generate additional examples of each type of weak sentence discussed—unparallel, stringy, and wordy. Write examples on the chalkboard and then work with students to revise the weak sentences. For **Varying Sentence Beginnings** on p. 478, work with students to write several sentences

Improving Sentence Style **475**

may need to delete or add some words. If a sentence is already correct, write *C*. Revisions will vary.

INTEGRATING THE LANGUAGE ARTS

Speaking and Listening. A good example of parallel sentence structure can be provided by Martin Luther King, Jr.'s speech "I Have a Dream." Ask a student volunteer to prepare and read aloud all or part of this speech. Afterward, discuss with students where King uses parallel structure and how it contributes to the power of his speech.

1. Athens, the capital of Greece, is known for its ancient ruins, busy lifestyle, and ~~enjoying~~ fine Greek food.
2. Because it is nearly three thousand years old and ∧~~having~~ a rich history, Athens attracts many visitors. **2. has**
3. Athens attracts artists~~, and~~ historians, and ~~is attractive to~~ tourists.
4. People drive very fast in Athens and scare the pedestrians. **4. C**
5. Athens is fun to visit if you watch out for traffic and ~~to~~ learn to jump out of the way of cars.

Revising Stringy Sentences

What's a *stringy sentence*? Read this one.

> I woke up early so that I could get ready to catch the school bus, and I was going to the state band championships, and I hoped I would play well, and I pretended I wasn't excited, but I could barely eat my breakfast.

You've learned to combine sentences, but someone overdid this one! A **stringy sentence** has too many independent clauses strung together with coordinating conjunctions like *and* or *but*. Because the ideas are all treated equally, it's difficult to see how they are related to one another.

that begin with single-word modifiers, several that begin with prepositional and participial phrases, and several that begin with subordinate clauses.

Finally, to teach **Varying Sentence Structure** on p. 481, write a sentence on the chalkboard that can serve as the first sentence of a collaborative paragraph. Have students come to the chalkboard and add various types of sentences until the paragraph is complete. The paragraph should include at least one compound and one complex sentence and sentences with varied beginnings. Afterward, evaluate the paragraph as a class. Does it include varied sentence structures? Are there any unparallel, stringy, or wordy sentences?

To fix a stringy sentence, you can

- break the sentence into two or more shorter sentences
- turn some of the independent clauses into subordinate clauses or phrases

Now read the following sentences aloud and hear the difference. Notice how the writer has broken up the stringy sentence into three shorter sentences and turned an independent clause into a subordinate clause.

> I woke up early so that I could get ready to catch the school bus. I was going to the state band championships, and I hoped I would play well. Although I pretended I wasn't excited, I could barely eat my breakfast.

There are usually several ways to revise a stringy sentence. The important thing is to make the meaning clear for your reader.

EXERCISE 8 ▶ **Revising Stringy Sentences**

Revise each of the following stringy sentences to make the meaning clear. For some items, you can just break the stringy sentence into two or more shorter sentences. For others, you'll need to turn an independent clause into a subordinate clause or a phrase to show the relationship between the ideas. Change the punctuation wherever necessary.

1. Music is used for entertainment, relaxation, and self-expression, and it is used in every culture, and it is an important part of our lives.
2. Music is an ancient art, and people learned to make flutes around 10,000 B.C., and they began to write music around 2,500 B.C.
3. Today, much popular music is electronically produced, and many musicians play electric guitars and synthesizers, and some even play electric violins.
4. Different countries have different kinds of music, but some kinds of music are internationally popular, and those kinds include rock music.

ANSWERS

Exercise 8

Revisions will vary. Here are some possibilities:

1. In every culture, people use music for entertainment, relaxation, and self-expression. It is an important part of our lives.
2. Music is an ancient art. People learned to make flutes around 10,000 B.C., and they began to write music around 2500 B.C.
3. Today, much popular music is electronically produced. Many musicians play electric guitars and synthesizers, and some even play electric violins.
4. Different countries have different kinds of music, but some kinds of music, such as rock music, are internationally popular.
5. Rock music first became popular in the 1950s. Although it was inspired by blues and jazz music, its sound was different from anything people had heard.

GUIDED PRACTICE

Before students begin the exercises in this segment, model a revision of at least one sentence from each exercise on the chalkboard.

INDEPENDENT PRACTICE

Students should complete **Exercises 7–11** and **Review B** as independent practice. Suggest that students refer to the example sentences as they work.

Improving Sentence Style   **477**

5. Rock music first became popular in the 1950s, and it was inspired by blues and jazz music, but its sound was different from anything people had heard.

Revising Wordy Sentences

When you read sentences like the following one, you probably wonder what language the writer is using: "Anticipating that tomorrow's forthcoming examination may be perplexing, I have made the astute conclusion that we should diligently scrutinize our scholarly tomes at the decline of day." How much easier and clearer to say "The test tomorrow may be hard, so let's study tonight."

Bloom County, © 1984, Washington Post Writers Group. Reprinted with permission.

Here are three tips for creating sentences that aren't too wordy.

- Don't use more words than you need to.
- Don't use fancy, difficult words where plain, simple ones will do.
- Don't repeat words or ideas unless it's absolutely necessary.

WORDY   My brother's room has a lot of mess in it.
IMPROVED   My brother's room is messy.

WORDY   The reason I am undertaking the pursuit of ballet study is that I want to be a professional dancer someday.
IMPROVED   I am taking ballet lessons because I want to be a professional dancer someday.

WORDY   Makana has trained as a singer for years and is a well-trained, talented singer.
IMPROVED   Makana is a well-trained, talented singer.

A DIFFERENT APPROACH

Let students use thesauruses to rewrite maxims in a difficult, wordy style. For example, "Everything that coruscates is not necessarily synonymous with or in anyway identical to bullion" is a possible rephrasing of "All that glitters is not gold." Students might want to challenge their classmates to guess the original maxims.

ASSESSMENT

Assess students' grasp of the concepts in this segment by their responses in **Review B**. Use students' performances on **Exercises 7–11** to determine whether or not they need more work on specific techniques.

RETEACHING

You could supply your class with photocopies of compositions that include unparallel, stringy, and wordy sentences. Work with students to revise the compositions to eliminate weak sentences and to include a variety of sentence structures.

INTEGRATING THE LANGUAGE ARTS

Literature Link. Have students look at the first sentences of stories in the short-story section of their literature textbooks. Students will probably discover that many short stories begin with short, simple sentences. Stories that begin with short, simple sentences include "The Cold Equations" by Tom Godwin, "The Fatalist" by Isaac Bashevis Singer, "Mr. Parker" by Laurie Colwin, "With All Flags Flying" by Anne Tyler, and "Boys and Girls" by Alice Munro. Ask students why authors might choose to begin stories with short, simple sentences. [Short, simple sentences serve to capture the reader's attention. First sentences often give just enough information to intrigue readers and engage their interest.]

---

478 *Writing Effective Sentences*

EXERCISE 9 ▶ **Revising Wordy Sentences**

Some of the following sentences are wordy and need improving. For each sentence, ask: Does it have any unnecessary words? Does it have any fancy words that can be replaced with simple ones? Does it repeat any ideas? If you answer "yes" to any of these questions, revise the sentence to reduce the wordiness. If a sentence doesn't need improving, write C.   Revisions will vary.

1. Caves are dark, damp areas~~, that don't have any light.~~
2. Many caves have beautiful, icicle-like mineral formations called speleothems.   **2.** C
3. Luray Caverns, ~~which is~~ a cave system, ~~situated in the area of~~ Northern Virginia, is famous for its colorful speleothems.   **3.** in
4. Lascaux Cave, a famous cave in Southwestern France, has many ~~ancient,~~ prehistoric wall paintings.
5. Cavefish are small, cave-dwelling fish that ~~are not equipped with optical organs.~~   **5.** don't have eyes.

Varying Sentence Beginnings

You would probably get bored if you ate the same food at every meal. Variety is as important in your writing as it is in your diet. The basic subject-verb sentence pattern is fine sometimes, but if it's all you ever use, your writing will be monotonous.

Read the following paragraph. Notice that, while the paragraph is correct, it is boring because every sentence follows the same subject-verb pattern.

> The pool was nearly empty on an early weekend morning. Dedicated swimmers swam multiple laps. A few sunbathers and parents with small children sat on the grass at the edge of the pool and watched. The day grew hotter, and the sun rose higher. The pool became more crowded. The pool was soon filled with young people. They laughed as they played games and splashed each other.

Now read a revised version of the paragraph. Notice how the varied sentence beginnings break the monotony of the subject-verb pattern.

CLOSURE

Ask a volunteer to describe the methods of improving sentence style discussed in this segment. [Answers should include using parallelism, revising stringy and wordy sentences, and varying sentence beginnings and structures.]

ENRICHMENT

An effective method of teaching sentence style is to use example sentences from students' papers to demonstrate different kinds of weak sentences. Without naming their authors, write sentences on the chalkboard and have the class discuss needed revisions. You may also want to give examples of good sentences from students' papers. ■

Improving Sentence Style **479**

On an early weekend morning, the pool was nearly empty. Dedicated swimmers swam multiple laps. A few sunbathers and parents with small children sat on the grass at the edge of the pool and watched. As the day grew hotter and the sun rose higher, the pool became more crowded. Soon the pool was filled with young people. Laughing, they played games and splashed each other.

Instead of starting all your sentences with subjects, try opening sentences in a variety of ways. Begin with single-word modifiers, with phrases, and with subordinate clauses. Remember to add commas as necessary after introductory words, phrases, or clauses.

VARYING SENTENCE BEGINNINGS
SINGLE-WORD MODIFIERS
Grotesquely, Dr. Frankenstein's monster began to rise from the table. [adverb]
Frightened, Dr. Frankenstein jumped back. [participle]
Cackling, Igor ran from the room. [participle]
PHRASES
With little hope Sam entered the writing contest. [prepositional phrase]
Excited that he won, Sam accepted the award. [participial phrase]
SUBORDINATE CLAUSES
Because Manuel was tall, people expected him to play basketball.
Although Manuel wasn't interested in playing basketball, he always went to the games.

INTEGRATING THE LANGUAGE ARTS

Grammar Link. Have students work in pairs to write sentences that begin with each of the following grammatical forms:

1. adverb clause [When Sam arrived at the park, he was ready to play.]
2. noun clause [How he could catch the big fish puzzled Sean.]
3. participial phrase [Pleased by the present, the child grinned broadly.]
4. prepositional phrase [In the morning we will start our journey.]
5. single-word modifier [First, we must read the instructions.]

EXERCISE 10 ▶ **Varying Sentence Beginnings**

Using what you've learned about varying sentence beginnings, revise each of the following sentences. The hint in parentheses will tell you whether to begin with a phrase, a clause, or a single-word modifier.

ANSWERS
Exercise 10

Revisions will vary. Here are some possibilities:

1. Established in 1945, the United Nations was designed to promote world peace and human rights.
2. When the organization was founded, fifty nations joined the United Nations.
3. Today, over 150 nations belong to the United Nations.
4. After World War II, the United Nations tried to keep peace by getting countries to discuss their problems.
5. Although the United Nations is not always successful in its efforts, it has helped many nations to resolve their conflicts peacefully.
6. Located in New York City, the headquarters of the United Nations include several large buildings.
7. By providing food, shelter, and legal protection, the United Nations helps many refugees.
8. Because it supplies food to famine-stricken countries, the World Food Council is an important part of the United Nations' relief efforts.
9. Initially, the United Nations Children's Fund (UNICEF) provided aid for children who were victims of World War II.
10. In 1965, UNICEF was awarded the Nobel Peace Prize.

480

EXAMPLE 1. The United Nations is a worldwide organization, and it includes delegates from many nations. (phrase)
  1. *Including delegates from many nations, the United Nations is a worldwide organization.*

1. The United Nations was established in 1945, and it was designed to promote world peace and human rights. (phrase)
2. Fifty nations joined the United Nations when the organization was founded. (clause)
3. Over 150 nations belong to the United Nations today. (single-word modifier)
4. The United Nations tried to keep peace after World War II by getting countries to discuss their problems. (phrase)
5. The United Nations is not always successful in its efforts, but it has helped many nations to resolve their conflicts peacefully. (clause)
6. The headquarters of the United Nations are located in New York City and include several large buildings. (phrase)
7. The United Nations helps many refugees by providing food, shelter, and legal protection. (phrase)
8. The World Food Council is an important part of the United Nations' relief efforts because it supplies food to famine-stricken countries. (clause)
9. The United Nations Children's Fund (UNICEF) initially provided aid for children who were victims of World War II. (single-word modifier)
10. UNICEF was awarded the Nobel Peace Prize in 1965. (phrase)

Varying Sentence Structure

You've learned to create different kinds of sentences by combining and rearranging ideas. Now you can use this skill to create a better writing style. For varied, interesting paragraphs, it sometimes isn't enough just to create sentences of different lengths. You also need to use a variety of sentence structures. That means using a mix of simple, compound, complex (and sometimes even compound-complex) sentences in your writing.

☞ REFERENCE NOTE: For a discussion of how simple, compound, complex, and compound-complex sentences differ, see pages 610–611.

Read the following short paragraph, which is made up of only simple sentences.

> I visited a friend on her grandparents' farm. I was about ten years old at the time. There wasn't much room in the farmhouse. My friend and I begged hard. We got to sleep in the hayloft in the barn. It was wonderful. We lay awake at night. We counted shooting stars. We told each other our dreams and our hopes for the future.

Now read the revised version of the paragraph. The writer has included a variety of sentence structures to break the monotony of the first version.

> When I was about ten years old, I visited a friend on her grandparents' farm. Because there wasn't much room in the farmhouse and because we begged hard, my friend and I got to sleep in the hayloft in the barn. It was wonderful. We counted shooting stars as we lay awake at night, and we told each other our dreams and our hopes for the future.

In particular, notice how the use of subordinate clauses improved some sentences and made the paragraph clearer. Besides adding variety to your sentences, subordinate clauses help show how the ideas in a sentence are related.

☞ REFERENCE NOTE: For more information about using subordinate clauses in sentences, see pages 469–470 and 598–611.

 CRITICAL THINKING
Analysis

Tell students to look through their favorite magazines for well-written articles. Then have them analyze the sentences in at least three paragraphs of the articles to determine the sentences' structures. Have students answer the following questions about the paragraphs that they analyzed:

1. Do all the sentences have the same structure?
2. Is one sentence structure predominant?
3. Can you detect any patterns in the structures of the sentences? For example, do all the paragraphs begin or end with the same types of sentences?
4. Do the structures of the sentences seem to correspond with their contents? For example, if the sentences are describing an exciting rock concert, do their structures convey a sense of excitement?

ANSWERS
Exercise 11

Paragraphs will vary. Here is a possibility:

My friends and I had lunch at the food court on the second floor of the mall. About twenty restaurants are there, serving food from different countries. Lin had soup and salad, I had a delicious burrito, and Joe and Debbie split a pizza. Then we walked around and looked at the people, who we all thought looked pretty funny. There was a fashion show on the main floor. Debbie and I admired the clothes, but Lin and Joe liked watching the models. Then we looked at a display of new cars and talked about the kinds of cars we'd like to have.

REVIEW B

Teaching Note. Review B calls on students to write persuasively. For an example of persuasive writing, refer students to **A Student Model** on p. 356.

ANSWERS
Review B

Paragraphs should include a variety of sentence structures and should avoid unparallel, wordy, and stringy sentences.

EXERCISE 11 ▶ **Revising a Paragraph to Create a Variety of Sentence Structures**

Using what you've learned about combining sentences and varying structure, revise the following paragraph to make it smoother and more varied. A combination of different kinds of sentences will make the paragraph much more fun to read.

My friends and I had lunch. We ate at a food court on the second floor of a mall. The food court has food from different countries. About twenty restaurants are there. Lin had soup and salad. I had a burrito. It was delicious. Joe and Debbie split a pizza. Then we walked around and looked at the people. We all thought they looked pretty funny. There was a fashion show on the main floor. Debbie and I admired the clothes. Lin and Joe liked watching the models. We looked at a display of new cars. We talked about the kinds of cars we'd like to have.

REVIEW B ▶ **Writing a Composition Using a Variety of Sentence Structures**

It's Academy Award time, and your school newspaper is publishing students' nominations for the awards. Write a paragraph nominating your favorite movie, actor, or actress. If you want your reader to be convinced that your choice is the best one, you'll need to make your paragraph lively and clear. Capture your reader's attention by using a variety of interesting sentence structures. Avoid wordy and stringy sentences, and be sure to check for parallel structure as you revise.

SEGMENT 3 *(p. 483)*
MAKING CONNECTIONS

• To revise a poorly written sentence into an effective sentence

ENTER A CONTEST
OBJECTIVES

• To write a very awkward, poorly constructed sentence and to enter the sentence in a bad-sentence contest

483

MAKING CONNECTIONS

Enter a Contest

You know there are many contests that give awards for good writing. But did you know that there are also contests for *bad* writing? The most famous of these is the Bulwer-Lytton Contest, which awards prizes for the worst first sentence of an imaginary novel. The first year the contest was held, over 10,000 people entered their worst sentences.

Have your own classwide sentence contest. The rules are given here. Be creative and think of a good name for the contest.

Part I

1. Each contestant submits the most awkward, boring, and confusing sentence he or she can develop. (Reviewing the examples of stringy and wordy sentences on pages 475–477 will help you get started.)
2. After all entries are submitted, the class votes on which entry should be awarded the prize for worst sentence.

Part II

1. Each contestant now revises the winning worst sentence, making it clear, straightforward, and interesting.
2. The class votes on the second set of entries, selecting which entry has turned the worst sentence into the best sentence.

ENTER A CONTEST
Teaching Strategies

You may want to schedule the first part of this activity for the last ten or fifteen minutes of a class period and schedule the voting and revising for the following day. Such a schedule will give you a chance to type students' sentences on a ballot.

GUIDELINES

Sentences will vary. Have students identify their bad sentences as wordy, stringy, unparallel, short and choppy, or a combination of these. Then have them describe how they revised the poorly written sentence into an effective sentence.

ENGLISH: ORIGINS AND USES

- To trace the development of the English language, explaining why and how English has changed and continues to change
- To use an advanced dictionary to discover word origins and changing meanings of words
- To identify and use formal and informal English
- To recognize different dialects and what shapes them
- To define and recognize examples of colloquialism, slang, idiom, and jargon
- To use precise word choice in writing, with awareness of the possibility of false synonyms, the connotations of words, and the ridiculousness of unnecessary jargon
- To recognize the misleading use of language in advertisements
- To recognize mixed figures of speech, tired words, and clichés and to revise these weaknesses in writing
- To evaluate the language of a piece of writing for clarity, word choice, and intended audience

Motivation

You may wish to connect this study of the history and uses of language to the students' reading of *Tragedy of Julius Caesar*. Ask them what is most difficult about reading Shakespeare. If the students mention the language, ask what is difficult about it. To refresh their memories, place a short excerpt from the play on an overhead projector (or on the chalkboard or on a handout). Ask students why Shakespeare's works are so difficult to read since he wrote in English. Guide the discussion to include words no longer used, words with different meanings, and different pronunciations of words (most obvious when lines are sup-

posed to rhyme). Point out that studying English's origins is important because much of modern English-speaking culture would be lost without an understanding of the language that produced it.

Introduction

Continuing the reference to Shakespeare, you may want to point out that English never stops changing. Suggest that a large part of the generation gap between students and their parents results from problems in communication. For example, if a teenager tells his or her parent that something is "bad," the parent may not understand that "bad" has come to mean "good." It helps to understand that language changes with society. In this way, you can introduce this chapter on the development of the English language.

Integration

This chapter can foster an awareness of the importance of language. The last part of the chapter, on how English is used, can be especially useful as a reference for writing as well as for understanding literature written before the twentieth century.

For future writing assignments, you may want to focus on diction (word choice), especially during the revision stage of the writing process. Encourage students to pay attention to their language and to craft the structure of their writing carefully.

The chart on the next page illustrates the strands of language arts as they are integrated into this chapter. For vocabulary study, glossary words are underlined in some writing models.

QUOTATIONS

All **Quotations for the Day** are chosen because of their relevance to instructional material presented in that segment of the chapter and for their usefulness in establishing student interest in writing.

INTEGRATING THE LANGUAGE ARTS

Selection	Reading and Literature	Writing and Critical Thinking	Language and Syntax	Speaking, Listening, and Other Expression Skills
"Blues Ain't No Mockin Bird" by Toni Cade Bambara **498**	Using reference materials **489** Applying interpretive and creative thinking **489, 506-507** Responding personally to literature **498**	Making inferences and drawing conclusions **489, 506-507** Identifying and revising nonstandard English **499** Analyzing loaded words and euphemisms **506** Revising jargon **506-507** Writing an advertisement **509**	Understanding the development and history of English **486, 491, 495** Identifying word origins **493** Identifying features of dialect **498** Explaining the meanings of colloquialisms **502** Identifying slang words **502** Choosing appropriate synonyms **503-504** Responding to the connotations of words **504** Revising sentences by replacing clichés **508**	Finding new words in nonprint sources **495** Discussing connotations with classmates **504**

SEGMENT PLANNING GUIDE

Whether you are planning for a quick review of a writing concept or preparing an extended lesson on composition, you can use the following Planning Guide to adapt the chapter material to the individual needs of your class.

SEGMENT	PAGES	CONTENT	RESOURCES
1 *Where English Comes From*	*484-495*		The Tree of Language Old and Middle English Modern English
Where English Comes From	484-485	Introduction: learning the roots of English	
Old English	486	Explanation: comparing Old English to Modern English	
Exercise 1	486	Applied practice: matching Old English and Modern English words	
Old English Gains New Words	487	Explanation: recognizing words borrowed from Latin and Vikings	
Middle English	487	Explanation: recognizing words borrowed from French	
Looking at Language	488	Example: examining loan words	
English Triumphs	489	Explanation: understanding how English regained popularity	
Exercise 2	489	Applied practice: researching the Hundred Years' War	
Modern English	490	Explanation: recognizing changes that led to Modern English	
The Great Vowel Shift	490	Explanation: comparing Old English pronunciation to modern-day pronunciation	
Exercise 3	491	Applied practice: evaluating contributions to early Modern English	
London Sets the Standard	491-492	Explanation: understanding how English became standardized	
Loanwords from English	492	Explanation: examining English words used in other languages	
Exercise 4	493	Applied practice: identifying the origins of loanwords	
American English	493-494	Guidelines: understanding the beginning of American English	
English Around the World	494-495	Explanation: examining the increasing use of English	
A Changing Language	495	Explanation: understanding that languages change	
Exercise 5	495	Applied practice: identifying new words in English	
2 *How English is Used*	*496-502*		Formal and Informal English
Dialects of American English	496-497	Explanation: learning about dialects	
Regional Dialects	497	Explanation: examining regional dialects	
Ethnic Dialects	498	Explanation: examining ethnic dialects	
Exercise 6	498	Applied practice: identifying features of a dialect	

All the resources listed in this chapter are located in the Teacher's ResourceBank™.

SEGMENT	PAGES	CONTENT	RESOURCES
Standard American English	498-499	Guidelines: distinguishing standard and nonstandard English	
Exercise 7	499	Applied practice: revising nonstandard English	
Standard English—Formal to Informal	500	Guidelines: using formal and informal English	
Charts: Formal and Informal English	500	Guidelines: examining levels of usage	
Uses of Informal English	501	Introduction: defining and identifying informal English	
Colloquialisms	501	Explanation: examining colloquialisms	
Exercise 8	502	Applied practice: explaining the meanings of colloquialisms	
Slang	502	Explanation: examining slang	
Exercise 9	502	Applied practice: identifying slang words	
3 *How to Say What You Mean*	*503-508*		Choosing the Right Synonym
Synonyms	503	Guidelines: choosing the right word	Denotation and Connotation
Exercise 10	503-504	Applied practice: choosing appropriate synonyms	
Denotation and Connotation	504	Guidelines: considering emotional effects of words	Jargon and Gobbledygook
Exercise 11	504	Applied practice: responding to the connotations of words	Mixed Figures of Speech and Clichés
Loaded Words	505	Guidelines: recognizing loaded words	
Euphemisms	505	Guidelines: recognizing euphemisms	
Exercise 12	505	Applied practice: analyzing loaded words	
Jargon	506	Explanation: recognizing kinds of jargon	
Exercise 13	506-507	Applied practice: revising jargon	
Mixed Figures of Speech	507	Explanation: defining mixed figures of speech	
Tired Words	507	Explanation: defining tired words	
Clichés	508	Explanation: defining clichés	
Exercise 14	508	Applied practice: revising sentences by replacing clichés	
4 *Making Connections*	*509*		
Writing a Travel Ad	509	Applied practice: writing an advertisement	
WHOLE-CHAPTER RESOURCES Review Form A, Review Form B			

WHERE ENGLISH COMES FROM

OBJECTIVES

- To match Old English and present-day English words
- To research the Hundred Years' War
- To evaluate contributions to early Modern English
- To research the origins of loanwords
- To record new English words

QUOTATION FOR THE DAY

"Remember that you are a human being with the divine gift of articulate speech; that your native language is the language of Shakespeare and Milton . . ." (George Bernard Shaw, 1856–1950, Irish dramatist)

Share the quotation with students and remind them that just as people learn about themselves by researching the history of their families, students can learn about a language by studying its history.

MEETING
INDIVIDUAL
NEEDS

LESS-ADVANCED STUDENTS

To help students succeed as cooperative learners in the activity discussed in **Teaching the Lesson** have all the students preparing the same notes (on Old English, for example) meet to prepare their teaching notes. The advanced students can help the less-advanced students with the preparation of their notes.

14 ENGLISH: ORIGINS AND USES

> **LOOKING AHEAD**
>
> In this chapter, you will take a close look at the English language. You will learn
> - where English comes from
> - how English continues to grow and change
> - how to choose among the many varieties of English when you speak and write

Where English Comes From

Have you ever wanted to trace your ancestry through the centuries—to discover your roots? You would find that your family tree goes back farther than recorded history. Its roots may even be in a land you never heard of.

MOTIVATION

To interest students in tracing the evolution of Modern American English, draw this diagram on either the chalkboard or the overhead projector. The nationalities follow roughly the developmental stages of the blending process that produced Modern American English.

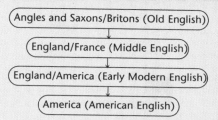

Lead a discussion of the diagram to show that American English is the result ☞

The English language also has a family tree. It is one of dozens of languages that branched off from a single source, an original parent language. We call this original language ***Proto-Indo-European.*** Proto-Indo-European was spoken so long ago that we have no records of its beginnings. But we do know that it was being spoken in Eastern Europe at least six thousand years ago.

The people who spoke Proto-Indo-European were wanderers. Gradually, they split up into tribes and migrated all across Europe and as far east as India. As the tribes branched off in different directions, so did their language. Each tribe developed its own *dialect*, or separate version, of Proto-Indo-European. Soon the dialects developed into distinct languages.

English, French, German, Spanish, and Italian are just a few of the languages that began as offshoots of Proto-Indo-European. These languages still bear a family resemblance. For example, notice how similar the words for *north* are in several Indo-European languages.

ENGLISH	FRENCH	GERMAN	SPANISH	ITALIAN
north	nord	norden	norte	nord

LEP/ESL

Spanish. Because the Great Vowel Shift did not occur in Spanish, Spanish speakers will probably have trouble pronouncing and spelling any word with a single stressed *a, e,* or *i.* For example, they might pronounce *came* as *kam, serene* as *sa—ran',* and *time* as *tem.* You could help students by playing a game in which you spell words aloud as students write them. (Be sure to include many words with stressed *a*'s, *e*'s, and *i*'s.) Then each student in turn should pronounce one of the words and spell it. You could give one point for each correct pronunciation and one for each correct spelling.

ADVANCED STUDENTS

Ask advanced students to look up the histories of words in the *Oxford English Dictionary* and to report their findings to the class. They could choose a general category and research ten words related to that category. For example, a student could choose gems as a subject and then research the histories of the names *amethyst, diamond, sapphire, emerald, opal, ruby, garnet, lapis lazuli, jade* and *amber.*

of English and American influences; English is the result of English and French. Ask students what traits might be a result of this blending of people. Elicit answers such as physical build, coloring, temperament. Then point out that just as people are products of their heritage, so are languages. Explain that this lesson will help them to understand how American English came about.

Divide the class into groups of four. Have the groups outline the influences that produced Old English, Middle English, Modern English, and American English. Each student will be responsible for one of the four influences. After reading the textbook carefully and making notes, he or she will then teach the other students in the group about

LEARNING STYLES

Visual and Kinetic Learners. You can encourage visual and kinetic learners by asking them to create posters illustrating the development of English.

A DIFFERENT APPROACH
You may want to reinforce students' learning by asking them to create a quiz on the development of Modern English. Students could work in groups and then exchange quizzes. This activity could be either review, reinforcement, or assessment.

486

Old English (450–1100)

The first speakers of English were tribes known as the Angles and Saxons. In about A.D. 450, the Angles and Saxons migrated to the pleasant, fertile island of Britain, which was already inhabited by a Celtic tribe known as the Britons. The island looked like a good place to call home, and the Anglo-Saxons settled down—after killing or driving off many of the Britons. The Anglo-Saxons named their new home "land of the Angles," or *Englalond*—which eventually became *England*. We call their language *Old English*.

Old English was similar to Modern English in many ways. In fact, the Anglo-Saxons used many of the same words we do, in somewhat different forms.

OLD ENGLISH	etan	drincan	dæg	niht
MODERN ENGLISH	eat	drink	day	night

However, Old English had a very different structure from Modern English. While Modern English mostly uses word order to show the roles of words in a sentence, Old English used many different word endings to show gender, number, case, and person. For example, the noun *hund* (*hound*) had to be written *hund, hundes, hunde, hundas, hunda,* or *hundum* depending on its use in a sentence.

EXERCISE 1 ▶ **Matching Old English and Present-Day English Words**

See if you can match each present-day English word in the first column with its Old English ancestor in the second column. [Hint: Use the process of elimination.]

1. calf	1. c	**a.** fot
2. cow	2. j	**b.** eage
3. foot	3. a	**c.** cealf
4. snow	4. e	**d.** geong
5. nose	5. i	**e.** snaw
6. eye	6. b	**f.** sealt
7. heart	7. g	**g.** heorte
8. young	8. d	**h.** niwe
9. new	9. h	**i.** nosu
10. salt	10. f	**j.** cu

that phase of the development of English. You may want to add structure to the task by providing students with a list of the kinds of information that should be included in each student's report: the sources of new words, examples of new words, and the historical context.

After the peer teaching is completed, each student should have a complete set of notes on the development of English.

Old English Gains New Words

In about A.D. 600, missionaries began a vigorous conversion of the English to Christianity. The missionaries introduced a new language as well as a new religion. Educated English people began to learn Latin, the language of the Church. They borrowed many Latin words and made them part of English. For example, the words *school, altar, candle,* and *paper* are all **loanwords,** or borrowed words, from Latin.

The English also learned new words from another—at first unwelcome—source. Around 790, Vikings from Scandinavia began to raid Britain, launching savage attacks over the next several centuries. Many Vikings ended up settling in England. Eventually, about nine hundred loanwords from their language, Old Norse, entered Old English. Many of the English words that come from Old Norse begin with *sc* or *sk.*

OLD NORSE	skalpr	skrap	skith	sky
MODERN ENGLISH	scalp	scrap	ski	sky

"Egad! Vikings! And they mean business!"

Middle English (1100–1500)

In 1066, England was attacked again—this time by the Normans from France. The army led by William of Normandy defeated the English at the Battle of Hastings and took control of the country. For the next 150 years, a few

---

MEETING INDIVIDUAL NEEDS

ADVANCED STUDENTS

Select a passage in Middle English from Chaucer's *Canterbury Tales,* perhaps the first few lines of the "Prologue" or the first part of one of the tales. Ask students to write a paraphrase of the passage. Allow them to use the *Oxford English Dictionary* to look up meanings of words. Then have students compare their paraphrases with a Modern English translation and write informative paragraphs comparing Modern English and Middle English.

LEARNING STYLES

Visual and Auditory Learners. To teach the effects of the Great Vowel Shift, ask one or two students to create a chart or poster showing the sound changes the shift caused. After reading aloud an excerpt from Chaucer, use the chart to show how the Great Vowel Shift changed the pronunciation of the words in the excerpt.

GUIDED PRACTICE

Go over **Exercises 1, 3,** and **4** as a class. (Each student will need a dictionary for **Exercise 4.**) Ask for a volunteer to report on the Hundred Years' War. Then the class can discuss **Exercise 2.**

INDEPENDENT PRACTICE

Assign **Exercise 5** to be done independently.

A DIFFERENT APPROACH

Show the class how language grows by asking each student to choose two words and to make a small poster illustrating the different meanings the words have had, the dates the meanings changed, and, if available, the circumstances that produced the changes in the words. You could display these posters to reinforce the point that English is a growing language.

MEETING INDIVIDUAL NEEDS

AT-RISK STUDENTS

You may want to concentrate on the backgrounds of Modern American English with students. Have them look up words they use every day to find the origins of those words. They can use any dictionary, but if they use the *Oxford English Dictionary* they will likely need your help.

---

488   *English: Origins and Uses*

thousand French-speaking people governed English life. French became the language of government, law, business, and literature. Latin remained the language of religion. The few English people who received schooling were educated in these languages. Not surprisingly, many English words that are linked to wealth and power were borrowed from French after the Norman Conquest.

| OLD FRENCH | jurer | leisir | taxer |
| MODERN ENGLISH | jury | leisure | tax |

A Feast of Loanwords

Some of our everyday words give clues to what English life was like after the Norman Conquest. For example, the words *hog, calf,* and *sheep* came to us from Old English; but the words *bacon, veal,* and *mutton* were borrowed from French before the fifteenth century. These word origins reflect the social structure of the times. The English peasants raised the livestock, while the French nobles got to *feast* (another French word!) on the meats.

French, the language of the educated, was used for almost all written communication. But English didn't die. It was still the spoken language of the common people—the farmers, herders, servants, and craftspeople. As these people spoke it, however, the language changed into a form we call **Middle English.** English grammar became more regular. For example, as shown on page 486, the Old English word *hund* originally had six different forms. Speakers of Middle English kept only two forms—*hund* and *hundes.*

English Triumphs

For a few hundred years, it seemed that French might prevail as the national language of England. But several factors weighed in favor of English. For one thing, the English-speaking people outnumbered the French rulers. For another, the Normans in England gradually lost contact with France.

By the mid-1300s, educated people were again using English for writing as well as for speaking. As you can see from the following passage by the fourteenth-century poet Geoffrey Chaucer, Middle English wasn't far removed from the English we use.

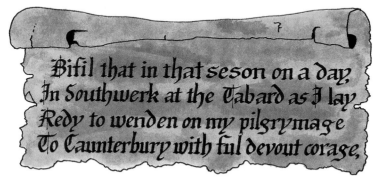

Bifil that in that seson on a day,
In Southwerk at the Tabard as I lay
Redy to wenden on my pilgrymage
To Caunterbury with ful devout corage,

EXERCISE 2 ▶ **Researching the Hundred Years' War**

The fate of English hung in the balance after the French conquered England. However, several factors, including the Hundred Years' War, helped English survive. Read about the Hundred Years' War in an encyclopedia or another reference source. How did the war affect English people's attitude toward the French? Why do you think the French language lost popularity in England as a result of the war?

INTEGRATING THE LANGUAGE ARTS

Vocabulary Link. Begin a vocabulary-building activity by asking students to name new terms in English as a result of the widespread use of computers. Continue to brainstorm with the class to list new words from several fields, such as science, technology, medicine, and warfare.

ANSWERS
Exercise 2

Answers may vary. Here are some possibilities:

Protracted fighting between the British and the French during the Hundred Years' War (1337–1453) began a lasting enmity between the people. British victories at Crécy (1346) and Agincourt (1415) fueled British nationalism and made French the language of a conquered enemy. Students might also find that although the war was begun by the English to protest French seizure of ancestral Norman-British lands in France, British nobility was decisively separated from France, and their grip on the French language began to slip. Their children became native English speakers.

RETEACHING

You may want to ask groups to make posters showing the family tree of the English language. Ask the students to include developmental influences on the language and changes that each influence caused. Encourage students to include as much information as possible on the posters.

A DIFFERENT APPROACH

Help students realize how quickly language changes by asking them to create a dictionary for a foreign student who has studied English from textbooks written ten to fifteen years ago. Ask the class to think of words the student would need in order to understand everyday conversation. Students might want to illustrate some words. This activity is suited to group work.

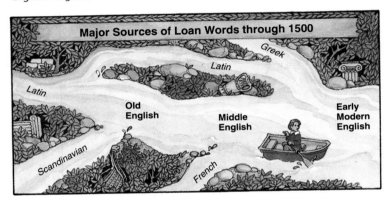

Major Sources of Loan Words through 1500

Modern English (1500—Present)

Several different things happened to English as it moved into the modern period. It underwent changes in pronunciation, grammar, and spelling; it became standardized; and it expanded into an international language.

The Great Vowel Shift

Middle English sounded very different from the English we speak. For example, in Chaucer's time, *care* would have sounded like *car*, *meek* like *make*, and *bite* like *beet*. The changes in pronunciation happened gradually. By the late 1400s, they were just about complete. We call this shift in pronunciation the ***Great Vowel Shift.***

LOOKING AT Language

Is't Modern English?

If you've ever read *Romeo and Juliet* or another of Shakespeare's plays, you know that you have to get used to Shakespeare's English. For example, he used words like *sooth* ("truth") and *thence* ("from there") that we hardly ever hear in present-day English. He also used unfamiliar contractions such as *ne'er* ("never") and *is't* ("is it").

However, Shakespeare's writing looks much more familiar to us than Chaucer's does. That's because Shakespeare used an early form of Modern English.

EXERCISE 3 ▶ **Evaluating Contributions to Early Modern English**

Listed below are five very ordinary words in our language. These words—along with many others—were added to the language during early Modern English times. Try to write the thought expressed by the word without using the word. How important to the language are these contributions to the Modern English vocabulary?

1. leapfrog
2. lonely
3. dislocate
4. laughable
5. critical

London Sets the Standard

By 1500, almost everyone in England spoke English. But for a long time there was no standard version of the language, and different regions used completely different dialects. Scribes wrote in the dialects of their areas and spelled words whatever way they chose. However, the dialect of London eventually became the most widely used dialect, since London was the center of English culture, business, and trade.

When William Caxton brought the first printing press to England in 1476, he set up his print shop in London and began printing books in the London dialect. Printed books—which could be made faster and more cheaply than hand-copied ones—began to spread across England. As the spellings of many words were "fixed" in print, the London dialect became a national standard.

VISUAL CONNECTIONS
Exploring the Subject. William Caxton set up his printing business in Westminster Abbey in London. He was born in the Weald of Kent and lived abroad for thirty years. Ironically, the first book to be printed in English, *The Recuyell of the Historyes of Troye*, was produced in Flanders.

You may want to reinforce the point that English continues to grow. Let the class brainstorm to think of new words in categories such as politics, sports, music, school, shopping, and informal conversation. It may be better to let students choose the categories so they can control this discovery activity.

Students also need to be familiar with the *Oxford English Dictionary*. Duplicate several pages and show students what information is available. Choose the pages for especially interesting entries such as *bonfire* or *tragedy*.

Soon handbooks of "proper" English usage, spelling, and pronunciation appeared on the market. People also compiled lists of "hard words" and their definitions. Some of the lists grew long enough to be called dictionaries.

English had become standardized, but it didn't stop changing. Even as the first printers were setting up shop, the Renaissance was sweeping England, sparking a renewed interest in the classical languages. As a result, thousands of Greek and Latin loanwords entered English.

English Travels Abroad

In about 1600, English merchants and adventurers began to seek out riches in foreign lands across the sea. As they explored, traded with, and colonized other places, they helped to make English an international language. They also enriched English with a rich crop of loanwords from other languages. Here are just a few examples.

NATIVE AMERICAN	moccasin, raccoon
AFRICAN	chigger, marimba
HINDI	jungle, bandanna

LOOKING AT *Language*

Loanwords from English

Words are like people: when they move to a foreign country, they often take on the accent of the native speakers. For example, Japanese speakers adopted the English term *personal computer* but shortened it to *paso-kon*. The Polish word *ajskrym* is a respelling of *ice cream*. And the Italian word *schiacchenze* is actually *shake hands* spelled as Italian speakers pronounce it.

Sometimes English loanwords become the basis for new words. For instance, after borrowing the English word *teens*, people in Germany went a step further and coined the word *twens*. German people also use the term *steadyseller* for a book that isn't quite a "best-seller."

Every time someone uses English in a new way, the language becomes richer and more complex. How do you think English loanwords will affect the growth of other languages?

LOANWORDS FROM ENGLISH

Discussion should establish that loanwords cause language and cultural vocabulary to grow and that through loanwords English speakers and speakers of other languages will be able to understand each other better. You may want to explain that one of the reasons English is so easy for many to understand is the number of loanwords it contains.

Provide students with two brief written passages, one from a formal piece of writing and one from an expressive piece. Ask students to look up the source of each word. Then ask them to list observations about the sources of the words used in each selection. They might make observations about the parts of speech that come from each source and the predomination of one source in each selection. Students will probably discover that many everyday words are of Anglo-Saxon origin, while many of our adjectives and words dealing with emotions come from other sources. They should write their observations in an informative paragraph comparing the passages. ■

| EXERCISE 4 ▶ | **Identifying the Origins of Loanwords** |

Each of the following English words was borrowed from another language. Look up each word in a dictionary that gives etymologies (word histories). What language was it borrowed from? What word was it derived from?

1. geology
2. geyser
3. cigar
4. studio
5. psychology

6. violin
7. complex
8. desperado
9. boom
10. machine

American English

American English was born when English colonists brought the English language to the Western Hemisphere. They borrowed words from Native American languages, invented new words of their own, and changed the pronunciations and uses of some old words. At the same time, they kept some older pronunciations and grammatical uses that the British back in England began to change. By 1776, the American dialect was distinct enough to be called American English.

ANSWERS
Exercise 4

1. Greek: *gea*—earth + *logos*—study, thought, reason
2. Icelandic: *Geysir*—hot spring, *gjosa*—gush
3. Spanish: *cigarro,* from Mayan: *sigar*—to smoke rolled tobacco leaves
4. Italian: *studio*—room for study, from Latin: *studium*—enthusiasm, study, literary work
5. Greek: *psyche*—soul, breath + *logos*—study, thought, reason
6. Italian: *violina*—little *viola*
7. Latin: *complexio*—dilemma, from *cum*—with, extra + *plexus*—interwoven, plaited
8. Spanish, from Latin: *de*—without + *spero*—to hope
9. Middle English from Dutch, or imitation of noise: *boom*—tree, boom of ship
10. French, from Latin: *machinatio*—machine (*machinor*—devise or plot)

INTEGRATING THE LANGUAGE ARTS

Library Link. To give students an idea of the diversity within the Indo-European family of languages and to introduce them to some other language families, have them consult an encyclopedia to determine which language family each of the following languages is part of:

Arabic	Hawaiian	Russian
Arapaho	Hebrew	Sanskrit
Bantu	Hopi	Spanish
Chinese	Hungarian	Tibetan

[Answers may vary slightly according to how recently the reference work was published, but possible answers are Hebrew and Arabic—Afroasiatic; Bantu—Niger-Congo; Hungarian—Ural-Altaic; Chinese and Tibetan—Sino-Tibetan; Hawaiian Austronesian; Arapaho—Algonquian; Hopi—Uto-Aztecan; Russian, Sanskrit, and Spanish—Indo-European.]

Native Americans, Africans who came as slaves, and immigrants from most countries around the world have left their mark on American English. Following are just a few of the loanwords that took an American route into English.

NATIVE AMERICAN	coyote, toboggan
GERMAN	kindergarten, frankfurter
AFRICAN	gumbo, okra
CHINESE	yen, chop suey
SPANISH	canyon, patio

Just as America has emerged as a world power, American English has quickly become the standard for English in the twentieth century. American television, radio, movies, books, and newspapers have spread American English to even the most remote corners of the globe.

English Around the World

English has come a long way from its humble beginnings. From a dialect spoken by a few Anglo-Saxons, it has become the most widely used language in the world. About one-fourth of the world's population speaks English, and by 1990 it was the official language in eighty-seven nations and territories. This graph shows how the number of speakers of English has grown since the beginning of the Modern English period.

Speakers of English (in millions)

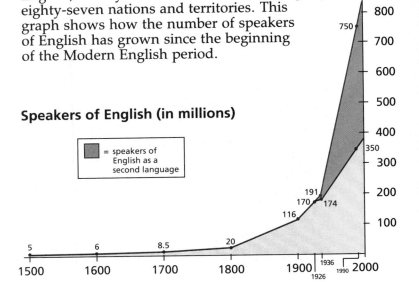

= speakers of English as a second language

In many fields, English is the common language that allows people from different cultures to communicate. It is the world language of

- commerce
- science
- teaching
- computers
- air traffic control

A Changing Language

The history of English is a history of growth and change. Today, English is growing and changing at an even faster rate than ever.

One source of growth is English-speaking people's constant interaction with the world's many cultures and languages. This interaction brings a steady flow of new words—and new uses of old words—into the language.

Another major source of growth is the vocabulary of science and technology. At last count, over 500,000 scientific and technical terms had become part of the English language. That's about equal to the number of words in our general vocabulary!

Will English ever stop changing? The answer is probably not. Four hundred years from now, English may have changed so much that our descendants will need a translator to decode our language. Twentieth-century English will probably look as strange to them as Old English looks to us.

EXERCISE 5 ▶ **Identifying New Words in English**

Spend a week watching and listening for words that you think are new to English (invented within the past year). Pay attention to new slang words and technical terms that you read in magazines, that you hear on television, and that you and your friends invent. Jot down any that you find. Then look up each in a current dictionary to see if it is a new word or an old word that has been given a new meaning.

ANSWERS
Exercise 5

The purpose of the exercise is to encourage students to listen to the language around them. They should each pick a minimum of five words to look up and should record alternative meanings they find. You may remind them that not finding a word can mean several things: It was invented after the date the dictionary was published; it is so old-fashioned that it was left out; or it is slang. Encourage students to look for the word in a dictionary of slang. You may also remind the class that some new-sounding words are loanwords (like *ninja*—Japanese hired killer), combinations from Greek or Latin (as with most new drugs), or acronyms (like HUD for *Housing and Urban Development Office*).

SEGMENT 2 *(pp. 496–502)*

HOW ENGLISH IS USED

OBJECTIVES

- To write features of a dialect
- To revise nonstandard English in a paragraph
- To explain the meanings of colloquialisms
- To list and evaluate slang words

TEACHING THE LESSON

Try asking students about the English they have heard spoken by people from other places. What was different about the English? Lead students to understand that they have been describing dialects.

Because, whether they are aware of it or not, all of your students constantly adjust to different dialects, you may want to teach

---

QUOTATION FOR THE DAY

"I hate false words, and seek with care, difficulty, and moroseness, those that fit the thing." (Walter Savage Landor, 1775–1864, English writer)

Using the quotation as the basis for discussion, explain to the class that there are many ways to express an idea. Encourage students to select appropriate words, to be aware of words' denotations and connotations, and to avoid tired words and mixed figures of speech.

How English Is Used

How many ways can you think of to say "hello" to someone? If you made a list of these words, you would have just a glimpse of the choices you make when you use English. There are many different ways of saying the same thing, and each word or expression has its appropriate use.

The words you use fall into two basic categories. They depend on

- background—where you come from and what your cultural heritage is
- circumstances—who you are talking or writing to, what your purpose is, and what the situation is

Becoming familiar with the different forms, uses, and meanings of English will help you become a better writer. The more you know about your language, the more precise and effective your word choices will be.

Dialects of American English

English is spoken in many different places by many different groups of people. Because each group of English-speakers is unique, it's natural that each would develop its own special form of the language. These special forms are called *dialects.*

It's important to know that the words "right" and "wrong" don't apply to varieties of English. Different varieties can be correct for different groups of people. For people in Great Britain, British English is the correct form of English; for people in the United States, American English is the accepted form. They are simply different versions of the language.

Regional Dialects

If you live in Texas, you may think people from New York talk "funny." They may think you talk "funny" as well. Your English sounds different from theirs because you and they speak different *regional dialects.*

There are three major regional dialects in the United States: *Northern, Midland,* and *Southern.* People in one region often pronounce words differently from people in another region. Some Northerners tend to drop the *r* from a word and lengthen the /a/ sound, so that *barn* sounds like "bahn." Some Midlanders and Southerners tend to add an *r* sound, so that *wash* sounds like "warsh."

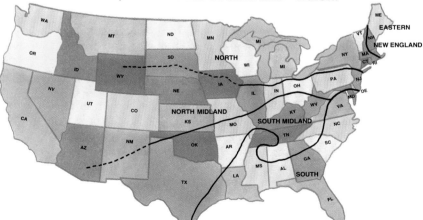

Regional dialects also differ from one another in vocabulary and grammar. For example, someone from New England might call a soft drink *tonic,* while people in other parts of the country might call it *soda* or *pop.* Someone from the South might say "sick *at* my stomach," while someone from the North might say "sick *to* my stomach."

After these activities, each student should have written a definition of each major term in this segment and listed examples of each.

GUIDED PRACTICE

You may want to use the first one or two words or sentences from **Exercises 6–9** for guided practice. Working with the whole class, go over these items to see whether or not students understand the new concepts. Because answers may vary, allow as many students as possible to give their solutions.

TIMESAVER

Most of the exercises in this segment require revision of sentences or paragraphs. To help you see changes more readily, have students label the revisions they have made.

ANSWERS

Exercise 6

Most important in this exercise are students' attempts to describe the way they—not others—really talk. They should retain in their revisions the dialectical features that they actually use orally. Nonstandard English should be encouraged rather than penalized (though students might point out the following dialect variations in the given paragraph: *frozen over, me and Cathy, stompin, next door, waitin our turn on the tire, tapdancin, splinterin, every which way, kinda spooky, a sort of weird spider, back porch, making cakes drunk*).

Ethnic Dialects

An ***ethnic dialect*** is a dialect used by people who share the same cultural heritage. Because the United States is made up of many cultures, American English is also made up of many ethnic dialects. These dialects include the Irish English brought by Irish immigrants, the Yiddish English spoken by many Jews, and the Spanish-influenced English of people from Cuba, Mexico, and Puerto Rico. Black English, one of the largest ethnic dialects, has elements of African languages as well as of Southern dialect.

EXERCISE 6 ▶ **Identifying Features of a Dialect**

The following passage is told from the point of view of a young African American girl. The writer has written the narrative in a special way to capture the sounds of the narrator's language. Is the narrator's way of talking different from yours? How would you express the same thoughts in your own words?

> The puddle had frozen over, and me and Cathy went stompin in it. The twins from next door, Tyrone and Terry, were swingin so high out of sight we forgot we were waitin our turn on the tire. Cathy jumped up and came down hard on her heels and started tapdancin. And the frozen patch splinterin every which way underneath kinda spooky. "Looks like a plastic spider web," she said. "A sort of weird spider, I guess, with many mental problems." But really it looked like the crystal paperweight Granny kept in the parlor. She was on the back porch, Granny was, making the cakes drunk.
>
> Toni Cade Bambara, "Blues Ain't No Mockin Bird"

Standard American English

Every variety of English has its own set of rules and guidelines. No variety is the best or the most correct. However, one kind of English is more widely used and

SELECTION AMENDMENT
Description of change: excerpted
Rationale: to focus on the concept of dialect presented in this chapter

ASSESSMENT

When independent practice has been completed, have students hand in papers for evaluation. You can use students' writing to evaluate the appropriateness of their use of the different forms and varieties of English.

accepted than others in the United States. This variety is called *standard American English.*

Standard American English is the one variety that belongs to all of us. Because it's commonly understood, it allows people from many different regions and cultures to communicate with one another clearly. It is the variety of English you read and hear most often in books and magazines, on radio and television. It is the kind of English that people are expected to use in most school and business situations.

The **Handbook** in this textbook gives you some of the rules and guidelines for using standard American English. To identify the differences between standard American English and other varieties of English, the **Handbook** uses the labels *standard* and *nonstandard*. *Nonstandard* doesn't mean wrong language. It means language that is inappropriate in situations where standard English is expected.

☞ **REFERENCE NOTE:** For more about standard English, see page 738.

A DIFFERENT APPROACH

You may want to have students bring advertisements to class and rewrite the advertisements in formal English. Students might also make lists of examples of colloquialisms and slang found in current advertisements. Lead a discussion about the effectiveness of informal English for advertising.

E X E R C I S E 7 ▶ **Revising Nonstandard English**

The following paragraph is a speech that the writer plans to give to the members of a drama club. The writer has a worthwhile message, but the inappropriate use of nonstandard English is likely to distract his audience. First, identify the nonstandard features in the paragraph. Then, revise the paragraph to make it standard throughout.

This here club isn't going to get nowhere unless we members cooperate. For one thing, we gotta start getting more enthusiastic about coming to the meetings. There's been too many absences, with too many excuses like "I would of come, but I had to feed my dog." Everybody knows about the meetings ahead of time, so you don't have no excuse for not showing up. Another thing is that the members should all take equal responsibility for the club. The same people hadn't ought to always take care of refreshments, plan the program, and books the meeting room. I'm not saying that you're all lazy, but we got a long way to go toward getting this club organized good.

ANSWERS
Exercise 7

This club
anywhere
There *have*
I would *have* come
there is no excuse
Also the members
should take equal
same people *shouldn't* always take care
book the meeting room
we *have* a long way to go
organized *well*

For students who haven't mastered the segment's concepts through the various kinds of practice already completed, you may want to try activities that are more visual and kinesthetic. Work with students to plan posters illustrating different uses of English, including terms, definitions, and examples.

Ask students to list the characteristics of each type of English—informal, dialect, and formal—and to give one example of each.

MEETING
INDIVIDUAL
NEEDS

ADVANCED STUDENTS

Ask students to select a passage in informal English from their writing (about one hundred words long) and to rewrite it twice: first in their local dialect, and then in standard formal English. Then students should underline and identify colloquialisms and slang in the passages written in informal English and in dialect.

500 *English: Origins and Uses*

Standard English—Formal to Informal

The flexibility of English lets you adapt your language to almost any situation. The kinds of language that you use in different situations are called *levels of usage.* The levels of usage in standard English reach from the very formal to the very informal, with a wide range in between. No level of usage is "higher" or better than another; each has its appropriate use.

The following chart lists some of the uses of formal and informal English.

USES OF FORMAL AND INFORMAL ENGLISH		
	FORMAL	INFORMAL
SPEAKING	formal, dignified occasions, such as banquets and dedication ceremonies	everyday conversation at home, school, work, and recreation
WRITING	serious papers and reports	personal letters, journal entries, and many newspaper and magazine articles

Formal and informal English differ from one another in several ways. The main differences between them are in sentence structure, word choice, and tone.

FEATURES OF FORMAL AND INFORMAL ENGLISH		
	FORMAL	INFORMAL
SENTENCE STRUCTURE	long and complex	short and simple
WORD CHOICE	precise; often technical or scientific	simple and ordinary; often including contractions, colloquialisms, and slang
TONE	serious and dignified	conversational

ENRICHMENT

Have students find examples of dialect in literature that reinforce characterization or theme. A good source is Bernard Malamud's short story "The First Seven Years" or Langston Hughes' poem "Mother to Son."

EXTENSION

You may want to ask students to create new colloquialisms or slang words for common situations. Have students work in groups to create between three and five new terms. Ask each group to present its terms to the class. Let the class guess what the terms mean. ■

Uses of Informal English

In using language, people constantly make up new words and attach new meanings to old ones. Some of the most colorful and inventive uses of English occur in informal speaking and writing. The informal words and expressions that we use fall into two categories: *colloquialisms* and *slang.*

Colloquialisms

The word *colloquial* comes from a Latin word that means "conversation." **Colloquialisms** are the colorful expressions of conversational language. They add a friendly, informal tone to speaking and writing.

EXAMPLES   Carlota was **on top of the world** after she **aced** her
history exam.
The teacher knew you were trying to **put one over on**
her when you said the dog ate your homework.
What's the matter? You look **down in the mouth.**

Many colloquialisms are also idioms. An **idiom** is a word or phrase that means something different from the literal meanings of the words. For example, *to put one over on* somebody has the colloquial meaning "to deceive or trick" somebody. But the literal meaning of the phrase is something quite different.

INTEGRATING THE LANGUAGE ARTS

Literature Link. Ask students to analyze the use of colloquial language in poetry. Have students read a poem such as John Updike's "Ex-Basketball Player" for examples of colloquialisms. Then ask students to write an informative paragraph explaining how these colloquialisms (*hanging loose, hang back, hang together*) make Updike's portrait of the basketball player seem more real.

ANSWERS
Exercise 8

1. explain it to me
2. I don't understand
3. don't give up
4. improvise
5. take advantage of someone

ANSWERS
Exercise 9

Students might brainstorm in groups for at least five words for *disgusting* and five for *amazing,* with extra points for additional examples. Class discussion about which terms will last and which will be out of fashion next year can be based on comparison or on other good reasoning. For example, a student might reason, "*Gross* is going to last. People have been using it for years." For extra credit, students might look up their expressions in a slang dictionary to see where the phrases came from and what they meant originally. For example, *cute* originally meant *curvy,* sometimes even *bowlegged.*

502

EXERCISE 8 ▶ **Explaining the Meanings of Colloquialisms**

A pen pal from another country wants to learn some American colloquialisms. She has asked you to explain the following expressions, which are confusing to her because they can't be taken literally. Explain the meaning of each expression in simple, straightforward language. Use a dictionary to find the meanings of any expressions you can't explain.

1. clue me in
2. (I don't) get it
3. hang in there
4. play it by ear
5. slip one over on (someone)

Slang

Slang is highly informal English. It consists of made-up words or of old words used in new ways. Slang is usually clever and colorful, and it can make the user seem up-to-date. The following words are all considered slang when used with the given meanings.

> *bad:* good, excellent
> *dude:* man or boy
> *humongous:* huge, enormous
> *make like:* imitate
> *scarf down:* eat greedily

Slang words are often a special vocabulary for close-knit groups, such as students, musicians, sailors, and surfers. For example, in the 1980s the word *tubular* was surfers' slang for "pleasing, fine." Like *tubular,* most slang words live a short life.

EXERCISE 9 ▶ **Identifying Slang Words**

What slang words do you and your classmates use to mean "disgusting" and "amazing"? List as many as you can think of. Which ones do you think will become a lasting part of the language? Which will likely live a short life?

HOW TO SAY WHAT YOU MEAN

- To analyze loaded words and euphemisms used in a magazine
- To revise jargon in a given passage
- To revise sentences by replacing clichés

OBJECTIVES

- To choose appropriate synonyms
- To analyze responses to the connotations of words

☛

How to Say What You Mean

A word can have many layers of meaning. It can also have different meanings depending on where and how it is used. To use words well, you need to understand some of the meanings and associations they may have. You want to be sure that your words will say what you want them to say.

"It states quite clearly . . . 'evening dress.'"

© 1991 Jim Unger distributed by Universal Press Syndicate

Synonyms

Using **synonyms**—different words that have similar meanings—is a way to bring variety to your writing. But it's important to remember that no two words are exactly alike. Each word has its own shade of meaning, and some words have more precise meanings than others. For example, read the following sentences:

> The child on the bus **looked** at me.
> The child on the bus **stared** at me.

Look and *stare* are synonyms, but they can suggest quite different things. *Look* is a very general word; *stare* is a specific word that describes a particular way of looking at something. Since the first synonym that occurs to you might not be the best one, use a thesaurus (a book of synonyms) along with a dictionary to find just the right word.

EXERCISE 10 ▶   **Choosing Appropriate Synonyms**

For each sentence, decide which of the words in parentheses is <u>the better replacement for the italicized word</u>. Keep in mind the overall meaning of the sentence. Use a dictionary to check any words you're not sure about.

1. She wrinkled her nose slightly at the *unpleasant* smell of burned oatmeal. (*revolting, distasteful*)

QUOTATION FOR THE DAY

"Men ever had, and ever will have, leave/To coin new words well suited to the age./Words are like leaves, some wither ev'ry year,/And ev'ry year a younger race succeeds." (Horace, Quintus Horatius Flaccus, 65–8 B.C., Roman poet and satirist)

After writing the quotation on the chalkboard, ask students to restate it in their own words. Explain that the English language changes and grows over time.

To demonstrate to students that word choice is important in writing and speaking, pose a problem for them at the beginning of the lesson:

"Suppose you have been working at a local fast food place. You have been working about forty hours a week in addition to going to school. How can you make it clear

to us that you are working too hard? Tell me without using the word *work*."

A student might use the word *labor* to mean "working very hard," or *slave* to mean "working overly hard." Make the point that revisions in word choice can make fuzzy writing clearer.

LEP/ESL

General Strategies. In presenting new vocabulary items, you will need to mention the connotations of words, connotations such as *formal, polite, technical,* or *offensive,* along with examples of their use. Speakers of other languages often have had little experience with the connotations of English words, and they are sometimes too easily satisfied to know just the denotation they can find in a bilingual dictionary.

ANSWERS

Exercise 11

Group discussion can establish whether student reactions result from personal associations or generally accepted differences. Generally accepted connotations are noted here. Any answer that may vary is indicated by an asterisk (*).

1. duty * (honor, drudgery)
2. propaganda (negative)
3. proud * (noble, haughty)
4. fake (negative)
5. puppy * (cute, not housebroken)
6. creeping (negative)
7. smile (favorable)
8. serious* (resolute, dangerous)
9. laughter * (with one, at one)
10. rain * (to cool a hot day, to spoil a picnic)

---

504 *English: Origins and Uses*

2. Marcia was furious at Carl for *telling* her most guarded secret. (*uttering, divulging*)
3. *Laughing* happily, the two children showered each other with crisp fall leaves. (*giggling, snickering*)
4. Each *symmetrical* snowflake glistened as it melted. (*equal-sided, well-balanced*)
5. Emphasizing the importance of the upcoming election, the senator *urged* everyone to vote. (*nagged, pressed*)

Denotation and Connotation

Compare the meanings of the following sentences:

Nan's persistence surprised everyone.
Nan's stubbornness surprised everyone.

The two sentences mean basically the same thing. *Stubbornness* is another word for *persistence,* "the quality of not giving up easily." This is the **denotation** of the words. But the effect of the words on the reader or listener can be quite different. *Stubbornness* suggests that Nan is unreasonable, narrow-minded, and unwilling to listen to others. This is the **connotation** of the word *stubborn.*

It is especially important to consider the connotations of words when you are choosing synonyms. Otherwise, you may replace a word with one that has an unintended effect on your reader.

EXERCISE 11 ▶ **Responding to the Connotations of Words**

Which of the following words have favorable connotations for you? Which have unpleasant connotations? Which don't stir any feeling at all? Compare your reactions with those of your classmates. Note which words have the same effect on everyone and which bring different responses from different people.

1. duty
2. propaganda
3. proud
4. fake
5. puppy
6. creeping
7. smile
8. serious
9. laughter
10. rain

The word choices dealt with in this lesson require students to have an awareness of the exact meaning of words. Encourage students to use a dictionary when they are unsure about the full meaning of a word.

To teach the lesson on precise selection of synonyms, you can use the example given in the text on p. 503 to show why some words may be almost the same in meaning and still have quite different connotations.

Follow the same procedure to teach denotation and connotation, loaded words, jargon, euphemisms, mixed figures of speech, tired words, and clichés.

Loaded Words

A word that has very strong connotations, either positive or negative, is said to be **loaded.** Loaded words appeal to our emotions. They can bias us for or against something because of the feelings they arouse.

EXAMPLES The local diner serves cheap, greasy chicken.
The local diner serves inexpensive, home-fried food.

The mob of protesters shouted their demands.
The group of protesters made their voices heard.

A writer or speaker who wants to influence your opinion may use loaded words. For example, politicians, advertisers, and writers of editorials tend to use loaded language.

Euphemisms

Sometimes a word or phrase may be considered offensive because it is too direct. You may choose to replace it with a *euphemism*—an agreeable term that stands for a more direct, less pleasing one.

EUPHEMISM	MORE DIRECT TERM
dentures	false teeth
memorial park	cemetery
substandard housing	slum
washroom	toilet

Sometimes euphemisms are used to misrepresent facts or to cover up the truth. For example, a salesperson may tell you a car is "experienced" when it is actually used. And a politician may say he "misspoke" when he actually lied.

STYLE NOTE Keep in mind the emotional effect your words are likely to have. Loaded words and euphemisms can be effective in writing, but you need to choose them carefully. Avoid words that may mislead your readers.

MEETING INDIVIDUAL NEEDS

LEP/ESL

General Strategies. You may want to point out to students trite expressions and clichés whenever they arise in class, even when they are not being explicitly studied; in this way, ESL students will get used to them. Native speakers of English will have heard many English clichés and trite expressions since they were children and will know many of them. Students from other language backgrounds might not recognize how common and trite these expressions are. They will likely find *fit as a fiddle* and *in good shape* equally fresh and satisfactory as expressions for an idea which in their language may not be expressed by a cliché.

After you teach each section, work the first problem of each exercise to be sure students understand these special concerns with word choice. Because there is only one sentence in **Exercise 13**, you may want to reword only the first two lines as a class.

Ask students to complete each exercise in writing. Be sure they give a brief explanation of each answer. When students have finished, go over the exercises orally by calling on different students to give their answers and the explanations of those answers.

INTEGRATING THE LANGUAGE ARTS

Literature Link. You may want to tie this lesson in with a nonfiction literature unit. If selections from the book are available, have students read a chapter from *The Right Stuff* by Tom Wolfe and ask them to list examples of pilot's jargon. Using their lists, students can discuss how this language creates a feeling of authenticity.

A DIFFERENT APPROACH

Another misuse of language students could research and report on is *doublespeak*. Coined from George Orwell's novel *1984*, this term refers to ambiguous language that is purposefully deceptive. In other words, doublespeak is more negative than jargon or gobbledygook because it attempts to use nonfactual, evasive, or self-contradictory language to hide the truth.

You could show students the following examples to explain what to look for:

DOUBLESPEAK	TRANSLATION
1. nervous wetness	sweat
2. encore telecast	rerun
3. terminal living	dying
4. discomfort	pain
5. civil disorder	riot
6. dehired	fired

Sources students might use to find more examples are *Doublespeak Dictionary* by William Lambdin and *The Language of Oppression* by Haig Bosmajian.

506   *English: Origins and Uses*

EXERCISE 12 ▶   **Analyzing Loaded Words and Euphemisms**

Look through a popular magazine, and pick an ad or an article that you find especially convincing. What makes the writing effective? What loaded words or euphemisms does the advertiser use, and how do the words influence your emotions?   Responses will vary. You may want students to include copies of their ads or articles with their answers.

Jargon

Jargon can refer to language that has a special meaning for a particular group of people, such as people who share the same profession, occupation, or hobby. For example, publishers and printers use the word *bleed* as jargon for "run an illustration off the edge of a page." This kind of jargon can be practical because it reduces many words to just one or two.

The second kind of jargon, also called *gobbledygook*, is wordy, puffed-up language. Users of gobbledygook choose big words over short ones, difficult words over simple ones. They confuse their readers with vague, pretentious language. For example, in the following cartoon, the senator uses puffed-up language to make his statement sound impressive. See how his "translator" sums up the unimpressive truth.

Shoe, by Jeff MacNelly, reprinted by permission: Tribune Media Services.

EXERCISE 13 ▶   **Revising Jargon**

The following passage is confusing because it is written in jargon. First, figure out what the writer was trying to say. Then, rewrite the passage in clear language, using only as many words as you need.

RETEACHING

You may want to have students look in newspapers or magazines for examples of exact synonyms, words with connotative meanings, loaded words, euphemisms, jargon, and clichés. You could pair each student that needs help with a student that has already mastered the concept. Ask the pairs of ☞

In spite of the fact that government aviation agencies were not in agreement with respect to the question of the cause of the accident at Kennedy Airport, the court has decided that one of the factors contributing to the crash was a propeller that had been structurally weakened.

Handle with Care

Some words can get in the way of your meaning. They can confuse your audience or make your topic seem dull. There are three kinds of expressions you should handle with care: *mixed figures of speech, tired words,* and *clichés.*

Mixed Figures of Speech

A *figure of speech* describes one thing by comparing it to another thing. A figure of speech is not meant to be taken literally. For example, if your sister calls your room a *pig-pen,* she doesn't mean that you keep pigs there. She means that your room looks rather dirty, like a pigpen.

It's important to use figures of speech in a consistent way. If you begin with one comparison and switch to another, you create a *mixed figure of speech.*

MIXED	Great waves of embarrassment broke over her, all but drying up the little confidence she had. [*Great waves* suggest water, which would hardly *dry up* anything.]
BETTER	Great waves of embarrassment broke over her, all but **washing away** the little confidence she had.

Tired Words

A *tired word* is a word that was once clear and forceful. But it has been used so often and so carelessly that it has become vague and weak. For example, overuse has watered down the original, clear meaning of *wonderful,* "causing wonder and amazement." Similar tired words are *good, nice, fine,* and *great.* These words may be acceptable in conversation, but they are too vague to be effective in writing.

ANSWERS
Exercise 13

Revisions may vary. Here is a possibility: Although federal and city aviation investigators did not agree about the reason for the accident at Kennedy Airport, the court decided one cause was that a propeller had broken.

INTEGRATING THE LANGUAGE ARTS

Writing Link. You may want to have students evaluate an editorial or other piece of persuasive writing for emotive language. First, ask students to analyze the writing. They should draw a circle around each word that has emotional connotations, draw a triangle around any euphemisms, and draw a wavy line below any loaded words. Next, ask students to evaluate the effectiveness of the word choice in the writing. Then, ask students to write their evaluations of the word choice and to give examples to support their conclusions.

508 *English: Origins and Uses*

Clichés

A tired expression is called a *cliché.* Like tired words, many clichés were once fresh and original. For example, *butterflies in my stomach* was probably a striking turn of phrase the first time it was used to describe stage fright. But it has become stale through constant use. Some clichés are overused figures of speech: *blanket of snow, busy as a bee, white as a sheet.* Others are overused phrases such as *easier said than done, fair and square, last but not least.*

E X E R C I S E **14** ▶ **Revising Sentences by Replacing Clichés**

The clichés in each of the following sentences are italicized. Rewrite each sentence, substituting simple, straightforward language for the clichés.

1. After *a meal fit for a king,* we agreed that *a good time had been had by all.*
2. *In this day and age,* political figures who remain *on the fence* when *burning questions* are argued will be *doomed to disappointment* on election day.

3. Although warned not to *bite off more than I could chew,* I signed up for six courses.
4. *To make a long story short,* I failed two courses, and *to add insult to injury,* I had to go to summer school.
5. The novel's main character wandered from *the straight and narrow path* and was eventually *embraced by the long arm of the law.*

509

MAKING CONNECTIONS

Writing a Travel Ad

A beach resort has decided to advertise in a travel magazine to attract more customers. You've been hired to create their new ad. As the ad writer, your job is to convince people that the resort is a beautiful, fun, exciting place to spend their vacation. You've decided to use this collage of photographs to catch your reader's eye, but you also need to write some convincing copy.

Write an ad that will convince readers to send off for more information about the resort. Remember that ad writers don't have much space to work with. You'll need to make every word count.

WRITING A TRAVEL AD
Teaching Strategies

To get students started, brainstorm about what will best attract tourists. Then ask each student to write at least one line that might appear in the advertisement. After each student has written an idea, expand this lesson into a group activity with three or four students in each group. Ask students to share their ideas with the group and then to agree on the best ideas for the ad. Give groups sheets of typing paper and ask them to sketch their proposed ads, including a simple drawing of the beach scenes and the advertising copy lettered in the desired size. Display finished ads in front of the room and allow a representative from each group to explain the reasoning behind that group's advertisement. Ask for responses from the rest of the class about the persuasiveness of the ads.

GUIDELINES

The travel ads should be succinct and should include persuasive language. You may want to refer to **Chapter 9: "Writing to Persuade"** for help with persuasion.

PART TWO

HANDBOOK

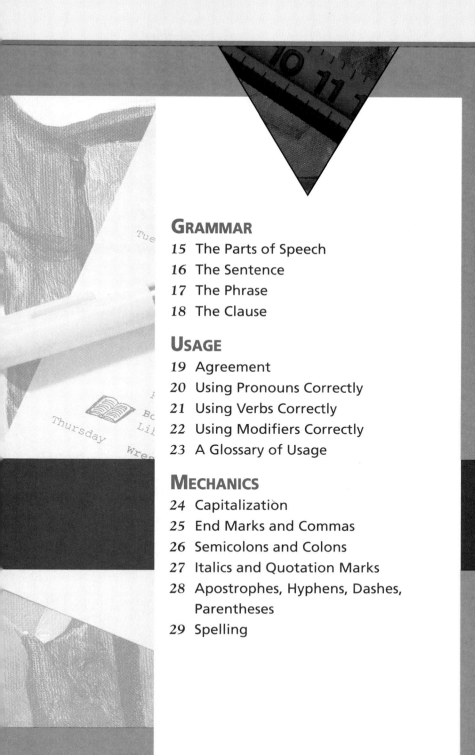

OBJECTIVE

• To identify the parts of speech of words in sentences and in a paragraph

GRAMMAR

CHAPTER OVERVIEW

This chapter discusses the eight parts of speech and how they are used. A **Writing Application** feature has each student use adjectives to describe an imagined self. A **Picture This** feature asks students to use adverbs in stage directions for a scene from *Romeo and Juliet*. A section on determing parts of speech is included before **Review: Post-tests 1** and **2**.

USING THE DIAGNOSTIC TEST

The first section of the **Diagnostic Test** asks students to identify the parts of speech for twenty italicized words in ten sentences.

Part B of the **Diagnostic Test** gives an additional twenty italicized words to classify in sentences appearing in a paragraph. Together, the two parts of the test make a good indicator of how much instruction will be needed on parts of speech. For most students, **Part A** will be easier than **Part B**.

If only a few students are unable to demonstrate mastery, you might have them work independently to review definitions and do exercises.

GRAMMAR

15 THE PARTS OF SPEECH

Their Identification and Function

Diagnostic Test

A. Identifying the Parts of Speech in Sentences

Identify the part of speech of each <u>italicized word</u> in the following sentences. n. = noun   adj. = adjective   prep. = preposition
                                        v. = verb   adv. = adverb   pro. = pronoun

EXAMPLE   **1.** In the nineteenth century, many men *worked* as
              cowboys on *cattle* drives.   conj. = conjunction
          1. *worked—verb; cattle—adjective*   itj. = interjection

1. When the drive was <u>*over*</u>, the cattle were shipped to northern cities to meet the <u>*need*</u> for hides, meat, and tallow.   **1.** adj./n.
2. There <u>*were*</u> <u>*few*</u> comforts on the trail.   **2.** v./adj.
3. Some <u>*improvement*</u> came after <u>*Charles Goodnight*</u> put together the first chuck wagon.   **3.** n./n.
4. A hinged lid swung <u>*down*</u> from the wagon to reveal a simple <u>*but*</u> complete kitchen.   **4.** adv./conj.

5. The *first* chuck wagons were pulled *by* oxen. **5.** adj./prep.
6. *These* were later replaced by mules *or* horses. **6.** pro./conj.
7. *Most* of the cowhands who took part in the historic cattle drives remain *nameless*. **7.** pro./adj.
8. Cowboys were *instrumental* in opening trails used by the men and women who *settled* the frontier. **8.** adj./v.
9. *Railroads soon* began to crisscross the country; the cowboy was no longer needed to drive cattle. **9.** n./adv.
10. *Hey!* Did you know that ranchers still hire *cowboys* to brand and herd cattle, repair fences, and do many other jobs? **10.** itj./n.

B. Identifying the Parts of Speech in a Paragraph

Identify the part of speech of the <u>italicized word or words</u> in each sentence in the following paragraph.

For abbreviation key, see Diagnostic Test: Part A.

EXAMPLE **[1]** *Neither* the cowboys *nor* the cattle had an *easy* life on the trail.

　　1. *Neither-nor—conjunction; easy—adjective*

[11] In the *thirty* years following the Civil War, millions of longhorn cattle were driven *over* long trails from ranches in Texas to railroads in Kansas. **[12]** During this *period*, the cowboy *became* an American hero. **[13]** Novels *and* magazine articles *glorified* life on the range. **[14]** The men *who* rode this rugged land, however, had to endure *many* hardships. **[15]** Cowboys spent most of their *time* in the saddle, rounding up strays and moving the herd *along*. **[16]** Caring for sick animals, repairing fences, and, *well*, doing what needed to be done were *all* part of a normal working day. **[17]** At the end of such a day, each cowboy *not only* had to look after his horse *but also* had to cook dinner for *himself* and do a host of other chores. **[18]** The quiet *evenings* gave cowboys a chance to relax by telling stories and singing *campfire* songs. **[19]** Such details of trail life are *realistically* portrayed in the *popular* paintings of Charles M. Russell. **[20]** *Because of* these images and our need for a *truly* American hero, cowboys have become a colorful part of our history.

11. adj./prep.
12. n./v.
13. conj./v.
14. pro./adj.
15. n./adv.
16. itj./adj.
17. conj./conj./pro.
18. n./adj.
19. adv./adj.
20. prep./adv.

GRAMMAR

OBJECTIVES
- To identify nouns in sentences
- To replace common nouns with proper nouns

GRAMMAR

514

GRAMMAR

514 *The Parts of Speech*

THE EIGHT PARTS OF SPEECH		
noun	pronoun	adjective
verb	adverb	preposition
conjunction	interjection	

Nouns

15a. A *noun* is a word used to name a person, place, thing, or idea.

Your name is a noun, and so is the name of your state. *Tree* is a noun. The names of things that you cannot see or touch are nouns: *sympathy, fairness, generosity, truth.* These words name qualities or ideas.

▷ EXERCISE 1 **Identifying Nouns in Sentences**

Identify the twenty-five <u>nouns</u> that appear in the following paragraph. Treat as single nouns all capitalized names containing more than one word. Do not include years, such as *1815.*

EXAMPLE [1] Elizabeth Cady Stanton was born in Johnstown, New York, in 1815.
1. *Elizabeth Cady Stanton, Johnstown, New York*

[1] As a young <u>woman</u>, <u>Elizabeth Cady Stanton</u> studied the <u>classics</u> and <u>mathematics</u> both at <u>home</u> and at <u>Troy Female Seminary</u>, from which she graduated in 1832. [2] Beginning at an early <u>age</u>, she recognized the <u>injustices</u> suffered by <u>women</u>, especially in <u>education</u> and <u>politics</u>. [3] In 1840 she married <u>Henry Stanton</u>, a prominent <u>abolitionist</u>. [4] At an antislavery <u>convention</u> in <u>London</u>, <u>Mrs. Stanton</u> was outraged at the <u>treatment</u> of the female <u>delegates</u>. [5] She later helped to organize the first <u>meeting</u> addressed to women's <u>rights</u>. [6] At that <u>convention</u>, she read her <u>"Declaration of Sentiments,"</u> outlining the inferior <u>status</u> of <u>women</u> and calling for <u>reforms</u>.

Proper Nouns and Common Nouns

A *proper noun* names a *particular* person, place, or thing.
A *common noun* names a *class* of things.

PROPER NOUNS	COMMON NOUNS
Atlanta, Nantucket, Mount McKinley	city, island, mountain
Louisa May Alcott, General Powell	novelist, general
Museum of Fine Arts, World Trade Center	museum, building
Queen Elizabeth 2, Spirit of St. Louis	ship, airplane

NOTE: Compound nouns are made up of two or more words put together to form a single noun. Some compound nouns are written as one word, some as two or more words, and some with hyphens.

ONE WORD	TWO OR MORE WORDS	HYPHENATED WORD
basketball newspaper	car pool Arts and Crafts Club	passer-by sister-in-law

EXERCISE 2 **Replacing Common Nouns with Proper Nouns**

For each of the following common nouns, give a proper noun.

EXAMPLE **1.** river
1. *Mississippi River*

1. play **3.** street **5.** president **7.** ocean **9.** poem
2. state **4.** song **6.** newspaper **8.** writer **10.** car

Concrete Nouns and Abstract Nouns

Concrete nouns name objects that can be perceived by the senses. *Abstract nouns* name a quality or an idea.

CONCRETE NOUNS dog, sunset, thunder, silk, apple
ABSTRACT NOUNS liberty, beauty, kindness, success

ANSWERS
Exercise 2

Answers will vary. Here are some possibilities:

1. *A Raisin in the Sun, A Doll's House, Romeo and Juliet*
2. California, Ohio, Hawaii
3. Rodeo Drive, Main Street, Pennsylvania Avenue
4. "Home on the Range," "The Star-Spangled Banner," "Yesterday"
5. George Bush, George Washington, Abraham Lincoln
6. *The New York Times, USA Today, Washington Post*
7. Atlantic Ocean, Pacific Ocean, Indian Ocean
8. Sylvia Sanchez, Charles Dickens, S.E. Hinton
9. "The Raven," "Stopping By Woods on a Snowy Evening," "Jabberwocky"
10. Ford Mustang, Toyota Celica, Pontiac Firebird

REVIEW A

OBJECTIVE

• To identify common and proper nouns, abstract and concrete nouns, and compound nouns

REVIEW A   **Classifying Nouns**

Identify each of the italicized nouns in the following paragraph as *proper* or *common*, and *concrete* or *abstract*. Also, tell if a noun is compound.

1. con.

2. con.— cd.

3. abs.

4. con.

5. con.— cd.

6. con.

7. con.

8. con.

9. abs.

10. con.— cd.

[1] *Cajuns* are descended from French settlers who were expelled from Acadia (Nova Scotia) by the British in 1755. When some of these displaced people settled in the [2] *Atchafalaya Swamp* in southeastern Louisiana, they had to invent [3] *ways* to use local foods in their traditional French recipes. If you've never tried Cajun food, the [4] *crawfish* and gumbo in these pictures may be unfamiliar to you. In addition to the plentiful crawfish, shrimp, oysters and other [5] *seafood*, freshwater fish, alligator meat, rice, and many [6] *spices* find their way into Cajun cooking. Gumbos, like this one, are soups thickened with [7] *filé*, which is powdered sassafras leaves. [8] *Gumbos* often contain okra and a meat such as sausage, chicken, or seafood. The [9] *popularity* of these and other Cajun dishes has spread throughout the [10] *United States* in recent years.

Pronouns

15b. A *pronoun* is a word used in place of a noun or of more than one noun.

EXAMPLE   Susan watched the monkey make faces at her little brother and sister. **She** laughed at **it** more than **they** did. [*She* is used in place of *Susan*, *it* in place of *monkey*, and *they* in place of *brother and sister*.]

Teacher's ResourceBank™

RESOURCES

PRONOUNS
• Types of Pronouns A
• Types of Pronouns B

PRONOUNS Rule 15b

OBJECTIVE

• To identify pronouns in sentences

15b

GRAMMAR

Personal Pronouns

	SINGULAR	PLURAL
First person	I, my, mine, me	we, our, ours, us
Second person	you, your, yours	you, your, yours
Third person	he, his, him she, her, hers it, its	they, their, theirs, them

Other Commonly Used Pronouns

RELATIVE PRONOUNS *(used to introduce adjective and noun clauses)*
who   whom   whose   which   that

INTERROGATIVE PRONOUNS *(used to begin questions)*
Who . . . ?   Whose . . . ?   What . . ? Whom . . . ?   Which . . . ?

DEMONSTRATIVE PRONOUNS *(used to point out a specific person or thing)*
this   that   these   those

INDEFINITE PRONOUNS *(used to refer to an indefinite person or thing)*
all   each   more   one another   either   most   other any   everybody much   several anybody   everyone neither   some anyone   everything nobody   somebody anything few   none   someone both   many   no one   such

REFLEXIVE PRONOUNS *(used to refer back to or to intensify a personal pronoun)*
myself   ourselves yourself   yourselves himself, herself, itself themselves

QUICK REMINDER

Write the following sentences on the chalkboard:

1. Tom wanted to take <u>Tom's</u> car to the car wash and clean <u>Tom's</u> car.
2. Shani tried to study for <u>Shani's</u> test, but <u>Shani</u> was constantly interrupted by <u>Shani's</u> friends.
3. All the people worked hard at <u>all the people's</u> company until <u>all the people</u> went home.

Have students replace the underlined words and phrases with appropriate pronouns. [**(1)** his, it; **(2)** her, she, her; **(3)** Everybody, their, they]

You may want to point out that pronouns can shorten sentences and make them more efficient.

MEETING INDIVIDUAL NEEDS

LEP/ESL

General Strategies. Some students will have difficulty in knowing when to use possessive pronouns in English. For example, because their language does not regard a body part as something to be possessed, Spanish speakers may say, "I have broken the arm" instead of ". . . my arm."

Explain that possessive pronouns can help writing be more specific. Ask students to think of other instances in which constructions in their native languages could be made more specific in English through the use of possessive pronouns.

GRAMMAR

SEGMENT 4 *(pp. 518–524)*
ADJECTIVES Rule 15c

OBJECTIVES
- To identify the words adjectives modify
- To differentiate between adjectives and pronouns

518 *The Parts of Speech*

NOTE: The words *my, your, his, her, ours,* and *their* are considered possessive pronouns in this book, rather than adjectives. Follow your teacher's instructions in referring to such words.

EXERCISE 3 Identifying Pronouns in Sentences

Identify the <u>pronouns</u> in each sentence in the following paragraph. If a pronoun is used more than once, note it each time it appears. [Note: The paragraph contains a total of twenty-five pronouns.]

[1] <u>Everybody</u> in <u>my</u> family likes to go camping, but <u>few</u> of <u>us</u> enjoy the outdoors more than <u>I</u> do. [2] Last summer <u>several</u> of <u>my</u> cousins and <u>I</u> stayed at a rustic camp in the Rocky Mountains, <u>which</u> are not far from <u>our</u> hometown. [3] At camp <u>we</u> all learned how to build a campfire and how to keep <u>it</u> going. [4] A group of <u>us</u> even went beyond <u>that</u>—<u>we</u> learned to cook meals over the open fire. [5] <u>One</u> of <u>our</u> counselors showed <u>those</u> <u>who</u> were interested how to cook simple meals. [6] <u>Each</u> of <u>his</u> recipes was easy to follow, and <u>everyone</u> ate <u>everything</u> in sight. [7] <u>We</u> all agree that <u>anything</u> cooked over an open fire tastes good.

Adjectives

15c. An *adjective* is a word used to modify a noun or pronoun.

Adjectives make the meaning of a noun or a pronoun more definite. Words used in this way are called *modifiers.*

An adjective may modify a noun or pronoun by telling *what kind, which one,* or *how many.*

WHAT KIND?	WHICH ONE?	HOW MANY?
blue ink	**this** park	**twenty** miles
old friends	**these** papers	**two** men
strong winds	**that** house	**several** apples

🦉 QUICK REMINDER

Write the following sentences on the chalkboard and ask students to make them more meaningful by adding adjectives:

1. The violinist played a piece of music.
2. The woman won the race.
3. The men watched the fires blaze.

An adjective may be separated from the word it modifies by other words.

EXAMPLES   She is **clever.**
The sky, which had been clear all day, became **cloudy.**

Articles

The most frequently used adjectives are *a, an,* and *the.* These words are usually called ***articles.***

A and *an* are ***indefinite articles.*** They indicate that a noun refers to one of a general group. *A* is used before words beginning with a consonant sound; *an* is used before words beginning with a vowel sound. *An* is also used before words beginning with the consonant *h* when the *h* is not pronounced.

EXAMPLES   **A** ranger helped us.
They planted **an** acre with corn.
We kept watch for **an** hour.

The is the ***definite article.*** It indicates that a noun refers to someone or something in particular.

EXAMPLES   **The** ranger helped us.
The hour dragged by.
They planted **the** acre with corn.

EXERCISE 4   **Identifying the Words That Adjectives Modify**

For each italicized <u>adjective</u> in the following sentences, identify the <u>word the adjective modifies</u>.

[1] By the 1890s, an *extraordinary* <u>craze</u> for bicycling had swept the United States. [2] Though <u>bicycles</u> had been *available* for years, the *early* <u>versions</u> made for an *awkward* <u>ride</u>. [3] *Ungainly* <u>cycles</u> like the ones shown on the next page had a very *large* <u>wheel</u> in the front and a *small* <u>wheel</u> in the back. [4] In 1885, however, a more *sensible* <u>model</u> was introduced, one that resembled the *modern* <u>cycle</u>. [5] *Energetic* <u>people</u> everywhere took to *this* <u>kind</u> of bicycle. [6] Bicycling quickly became a *national* <u>sport</u>. [7] Cyclists joined *special* <u>clubs</u>, which took *vigorous* <u>tours</u> through the countryside. [8] A *typical* <u>ride</u> might cover *twenty* <u>miles</u>,

INTEGRATING THE LANGUAGE ARTS

Literature Link. If students' literature book contains "The Fish" by Elizabeth Bishop, have different students read parts of the poem aloud. Then ask the class which adjectives best convey the personality of the fish, as Bishop depicts it. What makes those adjectives effective?

[The description of a "grunting" weight gives sound to the fish. "Battered," "venerable," and "homely" all make the fish seem less than grand. Yet the narrator speaks of, "the frightening gills, fresh and crisp with blood." The poet combines adjectives and figurative language to create the picture of a noble warrior, a fish that deserves to live.]

with a *welcome* stop along the way for refreshments. [9] Races were also *popular* with *enthusiastic* spectators, who often outnumbered those at ball games. [10] The fans enjoyed watching *these* tests of endurance, which sometimes lasted *six* days.

Pronoun or Adjective?

Some words may be used either as adjectives or as pronouns. To tell them apart, keep in mind what they do.

Adjectives *modify* nouns; pronouns *take the place of* nouns.

ADJECTIVE **Those** fans are excited.
PRONOUN **Those** are excited fans.

ADJECTIVE He is taller than **most** other players.
PRONOUN He is taller than **most** of the other players.

Notice that if the word is used as an adjective, a noun must closely follow it.

EXERCISE 5 **Identifying Words as Adjectives or Pronouns**

Identify each italicized word in the following paragraph as a *pronoun* or an *adjective*. For each adjective, give the word it modifies.

Although ants are related to wasps, [1] *these* two kinds of insects differ greatly from [2] *each* other. [3] *All* ants are social insects. They live together in colonies, [4] *each* made up of three castes: a queen, males, and workers. Unlike ants, [5] *most* wasps are solitary insects. Of [6] *these*

[7]⟨_many_⟩ are hunting wasps [8]⟨_that_⟩ make individual nests in soil or in decaying wood. However, not all wasps are antisocial; [9]⟨_some_⟩ behave more like their cousins the ants. [10] _These_ <u>wasps</u> live in permanent colonies of adults and young.

Nouns Used as Adjectives

When a noun is used as an adjective, call it an adjective.

EXAMPLES   **salad** bowl   **chicken** dinner
            grocery store   **gold** chain

NOTE: Sometimes pairs of nouns are used together so often that the first noun is no longer considered an adjective and the pair becomes a compound noun.

      EXAMPLES   city hall   sun deck   Brazil nut

WRITING APPLICATION

Using Adjectives to Describe an Imagined Self

When you use adjectives to describe a person or thing, you help your readers to understand something about the nature of that person or thing. Adjectives describe by telling _what kind_, _which one_, or _how many_.

WITHOUT ADJECTIVES   I sang at the wedding.
  WITH ADJECTIVES   **Happy** but **nervous,** I sang at the **large, formal** wedding.

The sentence without adjectives tells you nothing about the nature of "I" or "the wedding." Substitute totally different adjectives, and you'll see how quickly the natures of both change.

▶ **WRITING ACTIVITY**
Some outstanding writers have imagined themselves as an object or an animal. In the story "Metamorphosis," Franz

---

WRITING APPLICATION
   This exercise will give students practice in choosing appropriate adjectives. These adjectives will depend to a large extent on the images the students choose to use. Tell students that adjectives that draw attention to themselves can detract from the writer's intent. Simple, specific words transmit the clearest images to the reader.

WRITING APPLICATION

OBJECTIVE
- To write a descriptive paragraph or poem that features at least ten adjectives

GRAMMAR

GRAMMAR

CRITICAL THINKING
Analysis

Whatever they choose as subjects, students will need to immerse themselves in their subjects, and this will require careful consideration of the proper perspective. Encourage the students to recall specific incidents in their lives that might help them see the world through their chosen perspectives. For instance, if a student chooses to take on the identity of a bird, that student might recall a time when he or she flew in an airplane, climbed a tree, or was in some other way off the ground.

EVALUATING AND REVISING

Have students look over their writing. Is it concise? Are the adjectives interesting? Is there variation? Tell students that the best time to revise a paper is after it has had a chance to sit for a while. Then the writer can look at the words more objectively with the distance of a day or so. If such a wait is not possible, another person should look over the paper to decide what seems most and least effective.

REVIEWS B and C

OBJECTIVE

- To identify nouns, pronouns, and adjectives used in a sentence and to identify the words the adjectives modify

Kafka writes about a man who becomes an insect! Imagine that you are changed into an animal or an object. Using at least ten carefully chosen adjectives, write a paragraph or a poem describing yourself.

Prewriting Select an object or an animal that you think you would like to be. Next, freewrite descriptive words about the object or animal. You may want to consult an article in an encyclopedia for additional details or pictures of your chosen topic.

Writing As you write your first draft, concentrate on using the most vivid adjectives that you have listed.

Evaluating and Revising Read through your first draft and underline each adjective. For each one, ask yourself whether any other word more precisely describes your topic. Be sure that you have used at least ten different adjectives. Remember to count nouns used as adjectives.

Proofreading Check your paragraph or poem to be sure that all words are spelled correctly, especially any adjectives that you use infrequently in writing.

REVIEW B | **Identifying Nouns, Pronouns, and Adjectives**

Identify the <u>nouns</u>, <u>pronouns</u>, and adjectives used in the following sentences. For each adjective, give the word that it modifies. (Do not include the articles *a*, *an*, and *the*.) The words that adjectives modify are listed after each sentence.

1. <u>Our</u> <u>teacher</u>, <u>Mr. López</u>, identified the various <u>trees</u> along the nature <u>trail</u>. **1. trees/trail**
2. The bird <u>feeder</u> in the elm <u>tree</u> in <u>my</u> <u>yard</u> attracts <u>cardinals</u> and <u>chickadees</u>. **2. feeder/tree**
3. The <u>flag</u> over the <u>hotel</u> was a welcome <u>sight</u> to the two <u>travelers</u>. **3. sight/travelers**
4. The antique <u>doll</u> was dressed in a sailor <u>hat</u> and a blue <u>suit</u>. **4. doll/hat/suit**
5. A large <u>cake</u> sat in the <u>center</u> of the kitchen <u>table</u>. **5. cake/table**

6. Along <u>miles</u> of the <u>Hudson River</u>, (autumn) leaves colored the <u>highway</u> with (bright) splashes of <u>orange</u> and <u>red</u>. **6.** leaves/splashes

7. <u>Someone</u> has filled the (fruit) <u>bowl</u> with <u>dates</u> and <u>walnuts</u>. **7.** bowl

8. As a (young) girl, <u>Susan B. Anthony</u> was taught the (religious) tenets of the <u>Quakers</u>, <u>which</u> include the <u>belief</u> in the <u>equality</u> of (all) people. **8.** girl/tenets/people

9. (Many) people are working to <u>clean</u> up (polluted) rivers and <u>streams</u> to make <u>them</u> (livable) environments for <u>wildlife</u> again. **9.** people/rivers/streams/environments

10. The <u>dust jacket</u> of (that) anthology has certainly seen (better) days. **10.** anthology/days

▶ REVIEW C **Identifying Nouns, Pronouns, and Adjectives**

Identify each numbered, italicized word in the following paragraph as a <u>*noun*</u>, a <u>*pronoun*</u>, or an (*adjective*).

EXAMPLE   The Spanish built the first *ranchos*, or ranches, in the [1] *United States*.
1. *noun*

The [1] <u>*man*</u> in this picture is a *vaquero*, but it's okay if you call [2] <u>*him*</u> a cowboy—he is. *Vaqueros* got their name from the [3] (*Spanish*) word *vaca*, which means "cow." In fact, cowboys were at [4] <u>*home*</u> on the range in Mexico long

Californians Catching Wild Horses with Riata by Hugo Wilhelm Arthur Nahl (1833–1889) Collection of The Oakland Museum, The Oakland Museum Kahn Collection

SEGMENT 5 *(pp. 524–528)*

VERBS Rule 15d

OBJECTIVES

- To identify verbs as transitive or intransitive
- To write sentences using linking and helping verbs properly
- To identify action verbs and linking verbs
- To identify verbs and verb phrases

---

524   *The Parts of Speech*

before they gained [5]⟨*legendary*⟩status in the United States. Notice that this *vaquero* wears [6]⟨*leather*⟩chaps (*chaparejos*) to protect his legs and uses a [7]*lariat* (*la reata*) to rope the steer. [8]⟨*Many*⟩ other words that we associate with cowboys came into the English language from [9] *Spanish*. [10] *These* include *rodeo, stampede,* and *bronco.*

Verbs

15d.   A *verb* is a word that expresses action or a state of being.

Action Verbs

Words such as *bring, say, shout,* and *jump* are **action verbs.** Some action verbs express actions that cannot be seen— for example, *ponder, trust, evaluate,* and *review.*

Transitive Verbs

A *transitive verb* expresses an action directed toward a person or a thing named in the sentence. The action passes from the doer—the subject—to the receiver of the action, called the *object.*

EXAMPLES   **She trusts her friend.** [The action of the verb *trusts* is directed toward *friend.*]
Zora Neale Hurston wrote novels. [The action of the verb *wrote* is directed toward *novels.*]

Intransitive Verbs

An *intransitive verb* expresses action or a state of being without reference to an object.

EXAMPLES   **The audience applauded.**
The train stops here.

The same verb may be transitive in one sentence and intransitive in another. An intransitive verb is often used when the emphasis is on the action rather than on the person or thing affected by it.

QUICK REMINDER

Write the following incomplete sentences on the chalkboard:

1. The automobile ____ the telephone pole.
2. The package ____ on time.
3. The skier ____ also a doctor.
4. He ____.
5. I ____ the door.

Ask students to fill in the blanks with appropriate verbs. Have the students indicate whether the verbs are linking or action, transitive or intransitive. [Possible answers: **(1)** hit—action, transitive; **(2)** arrived—action, intransitive; **(3)** was—linking; **(4)** yawned— action, intransitive; **(5)** opened—action, transitive]

15d

EXAMPLES   Elsa **swam** the channel. [transitive]
Elsa **swam** for many hours. [intransitive]

Miss Castillo **weeds** the garden every day. [transitive]
Miss Castillo **weeds** every day. [intransitive]

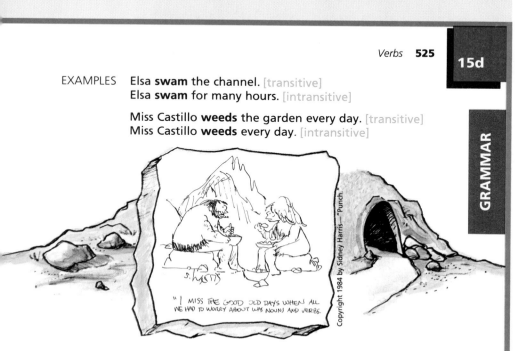

"I MISS THE GOOD OLD DAYS WHEN ALL
WE HAD TO WORRY ABOUT WAS NOUNS AND VERBS."

Copyright 1984 by Sidney Harris—"Punch."

EXERCISE 6   **Identifying Verbs as Transitive or Intransitive**

Identify the verb in each of the following sentences, and tell whether it is *transitive* or *intransitive*.

1. The strong winds <u>died</u> down.
2. We quickly <u>packed</u> lunch for a trip to the seashore.
3. The whitecaps on the ocean <u>had disappeared</u>.
4. The sunlight <u>sparkled</u> on the splashing surf.
5. At low tide, Rosita suddenly <u>spotted</u> a starfish.
6. She <u>noticed</u> its five purplish arms.
7. She <u>touched</u> a soft, brown sponge floating nearby.
8. She <u>added</u> it to her collection of seashells, dried seaweed, and driftwood.
9. Her collection <u>includes</u> several conch shells.
10. Three horseshoe crabs <u>swam</u> in the tidal pool.

Linking Verbs

Linking verbs (also called *state-of-being verbs*) help to make a statement by serving as a link between two words.

The most commonly used linking verbs are forms of the verb *be*.

MEETING INDIVIDUAL NEEDS

LEP/ESL

General Strategies. Some students may be confused by verbs that can be either transitive or intransitive. To help students understand when a verb is transitive, explain that when verbs are transitive, they connect subjects and objects through some action. This means that sentences with transitive verbs must have two nouns (or pronouns)—a subject and an object. Sentences without objects do not have transitive verbs.

LEARNING STYLES

Visual Learners. To give students extra practice with verbs, have students create comic strips that illustrate the difference between transitive and intransitive verbs.

COMMON ERROR

Problem. Students often overuse forms of the verb *be*. Instead of searching for precisely the right action verb to describe a situation, students too often settle for *is*.

Solution. Tell students to read through their papers and to look particularly for forms of the verb *be* or *have*. Can the paper be improved by replacing a verb with a more exact one? If not, can a verb phrase be made more concise?

Have student volunteers read papers aloud before and after revision.

ANSWERS

Exercise 7

Responses will vary. Examples of sentences with action (A) and linking (L) verbs are provided:

1. (L) The sea gulls appear calm. (A) The sea gulls appear every morning.

2. (L) The guards sound excited. (A) The guards sound the alarm.

3. (L) The rooms smell musty. (A) The girls smell smoke.

4. (L) We grow older by the minute. (A) Oranges grow in Florida.

5. (L) Trudy looks lovely today. (A) Trudy looks both ways before crossing the street.

526

be	were	shall have been	should be
being	shall be	will have been	would be
am	will be	can be	could be
is	has been	may be	should have been
are	have been	might be	would have been
was	had been	must be	could have been

Other Commonly Used Linking Verbs

| appear | feel | look | seem | sound | taste |
| become | grow | remain | smell | stay | turn |

In the following sentences, each noun or adjective that follows the linking verb refers to the subject of the verb.

Kelp **is** the scientific name for seaweed. [*Kelp* = name]
Kelp **tastes** good in a salad. [good kelp]
Like most seaweed, kelp **becomes** brown as it ages. [brown kelp]
Kelp **can be** a basic source of iodine. [Kelp = source]

Many linking verbs can be used as action (nonlinking) verbs as well.

EXAMPLES Emilia **felt** calm at the seashore. [linking verb: calm Emilia]
Emilia **felt** the waving strands of the ribbon kelp. [action verb]

Some kelps **grow** long. [linking verb: long kelps]
Some kelps **grow** large bulbs. [action verb]

Even *be* is not always a linking verb. It may be followed by only an adverb. In the sentence *They are here*, the word *here* is an adverb. It does not refer to the subject, *They*. To be a linking verb, the verb must be followed by a noun, a pronoun, or an adjective that refers to the subject.

EXERCISE 7 **Writing Sentences Using Verbs as Both Linking and Action Verbs**

For each of the following verbs, write two sentences. In the first sentence, use the verb as a linking verb; in the second sentence, use it as an action verb.

1. appear   2. sound   3. smell   4. grow   5. look

The Verb Phrase

A ***verb phrase*** consists of the main verb and its *helping verbs* (also called *auxiliary verbs*).

Commonly Used Helping Verbs				
have	do	may	can	could
has	does	might	will	would
had	did	must	shall	should

The forms of the verb *be* are also helping verbs.

EXAMPLES   **Did** she **paint** the house?
You **might have helped** with the trim.
Sally **will be launching** the canoe.
This year's budget **has** not **been approved.**

NOTE: The word *not* in a phrase such as *could not go* is not a helping verb. Both *not* and the contraction *–n't* are adverbs.

☞ REFERENCE NOTE: For more about helping verbs, see page 548.

▶ EXERCISE 8   **Identifying Verbs as Action Verbs or Linking Verbs**

Identify each italicized verb in the numbered sentences in the following paragraph as an *action verb* or a *linking verb*.

[1] Situated on the banks of the Nile River in Egypt, these ruins at Karnak *are* some of the most impressive sights in the world. [2] The largest structure there *is* the

INTEGRATING THE LANGUAGE ARTS

Literature Link. Have students read and discuss the Emily Dickinson poem "I Like to See It Lap the Miles." Have them list the verbs that describe the train's actions [*lap, lick, stop to feed, step, peer, pare, crawl, complaining, chase, neigh,* and *stop*]. What kind of verbs are these? [They are action verbs.] Is there anything strange about them? [With the exception of *stop,* they are not verbs that might typically be used to describe a train.] What effect do they give to the poem? [They give life to an inanimate object by describing its actions as though it were a living animal.]

VISUAL CONNECTIONS

Exploring the Subject. The temple of Amon-Re at Karnak is the largest of all Egyptian temples and one of the largest in the world. Its most striking feature is the vast pillared hall, with 140 pillars covering an area of 5800 square yards.

Amon or Amon-Re was the Egyptian sun god hailed as king of the gods by his followers. He was represented in human form, sometimes with a ram's head. The Greeks identified him with Zeus.

INTEGRATING THE LANGUAGE ARTS

Grammar and Speaking. Divide the class into groups and have each group make a presentation on a particular verb. Each presentation should contain the verb's origin, describe the action it involves, explain whether it is transitive or intransitive, and—if transitive—it should list possible objects.

---

528   *The Parts of Speech*

Great Temple of Amon. [3] As you can see, its immense size *dwarfs* people who come to view this architectural marvel. [4] When visitors follow the avenue of sphinxes that leads to the entrance, they *are amazed* at the 42-meter-high gateway. [5] The ceiling of the temple *rests* more than 23 meters above the floor. [6] Of course, the central columns that support the stone roof *are* enormous. [7] The surfaces of these huge columns *are decorated* with carvings. [8] Even an amateur engineer or artist *can appreciate* the tremendous efforts that must have gone into the completion of this temple. [9] We now *know* that inclined planes, combined with levers and blocking, enabled the ancient Egyptians to raise the large stones. [10] A remarkable technical achievement, the Great Temple of Amon *remains* a monument to the ancient builders' skills.

> EXERCISE 9   **Identifying Verbs and Verb Phrases**

Identify the <u>verbs and verb phrases</u> in each numbered sentence in the following paragraph. Be sure to include all helping verbs.

[1] Because of the cold weather, the members of the marching band <u>were worried</u> about their first performance. [2] Marcia and the other saxophone players <u>were clapping</u> their hands vigorously so that their fingers <u>wouldn't</u> <u>become</u> even number in the raw, icy air. [3] They <u>imagined</u> what <u>would happen</u> if their fingers <u>froze</u> to the keys of their instruments. [4] Instead of music, harsh noise <u>would blare</u> out and likely <u>startle</u> the spectators. [5] The other band members <u>would</u> likely <u>skip</u> a beat, and chaos <u>would</u> soon <u>spread</u> across the field. [6] Out of step, the flute players <u>might stumble</u> into the clarinet players, <u>collide</u> with the trombone players, or even <u>trip</u> over the drummers. [7] When half time <u>was called</u>, Marcia and her friends <u>rolled</u> their eyes and <u>laughed</u> about the dreadful scene they <u>had</u> just <u>pictured</u>. [8] Such a disaster <u>couldn't</u> possibly <u>happen</u>, <u>could</u> it? [9] As the band <u>marched</u> onto the field, large, white snowflakes <u>swirled</u> in the air and <u>settled</u> on the brand-new uniforms and shiny instruments. [10] People <u>were</u> already <u>leaving</u> the stands when the principal <u>announced</u> over the loudspeaker: "Ladies and gentlemen, the band <u>will</u> now <u>play</u> 'Jingle Bells.'"

OBJECTIVES

- To identify adverbs and the verbs, adjectives, and adverbs they modify in sentences
- To use adverbs correctly in sentences
- To use words as adverbs and adjectives in sentences

Adverbs **529**

15e

GRAMMAR

Adverbs

15e. An *adverb* is a word used to modify a verb, an adjective, or another adverb.

Adverbs modify by telling *how, when, where,* or *to what extent.*

Adverbs Modifying Verbs

Just as adjectives modify nouns and pronouns, adverbs modify verbs. An adverb makes the meaning of the verb clearer and more definite.

EXAMPLES   **The bird was chirping outside.** [*where*]
The bird chirped today. [*when*]
The bird chirped loudly. [*how*]
The bird chirped constantly. [*to what extent*]

 EXERCISE 10   **Identifying Adverbs and the Verbs They Modify**

Identify the <u>adverbs</u> in each numbered sentence in the following paragraph. For each adverb, give the <u>verb that it modifies</u>.

[1] The first balloonists <u>floated</u> gently above Paris in a hot-air balloon that <u>had been</u> cleverly <u>designed</u> by the Montgolfier brothers. [2] Although their earlier attempts

Teacher's ResourceBank™
RESOURCES

ADVERBS
- The Adverb

GRAMMAR

 QUICK REMINDER

Write the following sentences on the chalkboard. Have students identify the adverbs and the words they modify:

1. Janet plays her silver flute beautifully.
2. Henry has become most skilled at carpentry.
3. I can type really well.
4. Kenesha's dress was too small.
5. Desperately, he ran after the train.

Remind students that adverbs can modify verbs, adjectives, or other adverbs. [Answers: (1) *beautifully* modifies *plays;* (2) *most* modifies *skilled;* (3) *well* modifies *can type; really* modifies *well;* (4) *too* modifies *small;* (5) *Desperately* modifies *ran.*]

LEP/ESL

General Strategies. Students may have difficulty with the placement of adverbs that tell how often something occurs. For example, they may write, "Peter comes always late to breakfast," instead of "Peter always comes late to breakfast."

Tell students that most of the time, such adverbs should come before the verb.

Have students write paragraphs in which they describe activities they participate in with different frequency. Adverbs they can use to describe these activities include *always, sometimes, frequently, often, rarely,* and *never.* Let students work in pairs to help each other with revisions. Be sure to pair ESL students with native English-speakers.

LEARNING STYLES

Auditory Learners. Students might benefit by hearing adverbs used in different positions in a sentence to illustrate an adverb's different uses. Read the following sentences aloud and have students discuss what each sentence means:

1. Really, I want to go.
2. I really want to go.
3. I want to really go.

[**(1)** Puts emphasis on *really,* as if to convince a disbeliever; **(2)** places emphasis on *want;* **(3)** puts emphasis on *go,* as in "to go fast in a car."]

had failed, the Montgolfiers kept trying and <u>finally</u> <u>settled</u> on a balloon made of paper and linen. [3] Early balloons <u>differed</u> <u>significantly</u> from modern balloons like those on the previous page, which are <u>sturdily</u> <u>constructed</u> of coated nylon. [4] Despite their ingenuity, the Montgolfiers <u>originally</u> <u>thought</u> that smoke, rather than hot air, would <u>effectively</u> <u>push</u> a balloon <u>skyward</u>. [5] In their first experiments, they <u>bravely</u> <u>prepared</u> a smoky fuel from rotten meat and old shoes.

Adverbs Modifying Adjectives

EXAMPLES   It was a **fiercely** competitive game. [The adverb *fiercely* modifies the adjective *competitive*.]
The **exceptionally** brave police officer was given an award. [The adverb *exceptionally* modifies the adjective *brave*.]

NOTE: The most frequently used adverbs are *too, so,* and *very.* Try to avoid these overused words in your writing. Instead, think of more precise adverbs to make your meaning clearer.

EXERCISE 11   **Identifying Adverbs and the Adjectives They Modify**

In each of the following sentences, an adverb modifies an adjective. Identify the <u>adverb</u> and the <u>adjective it modifies</u>.

1. An <u>immensely</u> <u>long</u> wagon train started out from Denver, Colorado.
2. Both oxen and mules were used to pull <u>unusually large</u> wagons.
3. Even in good weather, the trail through the mountains was <u>fairly</u> <u>hazardous</u>.
4. A <u>moderately</u> <u>hard</u> rain could turn the trail into a swamp.
5. When the trail was <u>too</u> <u>muddy</u>, the heavier wagons became mired.
6. Wagons that were <u>extremely</u> <u>heavy</u> then had to be unloaded before they could be moved.
7. Stopping for the night along the trail was a <u>consistently</u> <u>welcome</u> experience.

8. It offered relief to <u>thoroughly</u> <u>tired</u> bones and muscles.
9. Nights in the mountains could be <u>quite</u> <u>cold</u>.
10. On <u>terribly</u> <u>cold</u> nights, the travelers would roll in blankets and sleep close to their campfires.

Adverbs Modifying Other Adverbs

EXAMPLES   The guide spoke **extremely** slowly. [The adverb *extremely* modifies the adverb *slowly,* telling *how* slowly.]
           We will go **later** today. [The adverb *later* modifies the adverb *today,* telling *when* today.]

NOTE: Many adverbs end in *–ly.* However, not all words ending in *–ly* are adverbs. For instance, the following words are adjectives: *homely, kindly, lovely, deadly.* To determine a word's part of speech, look at how the word is used in the sentence. Do not rely on spelling alone.

EXERCISE 12   **Identifying Adverbs and the Words They Modify**

The following paragraphs contain twenty adverbs. Identify the adverb or adverbs in each sentence. After each adverb, give the word it modifies and the part of speech of that word.

[1] A couple of months ago, my sister Juana and I finally decided to buy a houseplant. [2] The large ones we saw were too expensive for us. [3] In addition, they are almost always raised in hothouses, and, as a result, they do not adjust easily to living in cold climates. [4] Suddenly Juana had a brainstorm. [5] "Let's buy some seeds and grow them indoors. [6] That way, the seedlings will automatically adapt themselves to the climate in our house."

[7] At the seed store, the owner, Mrs. Miller, greeted us cheerfully. [8] We explained that we wanted to grow a large plant but that our room hardly ever gets bright sunlight and in the winter it can be especially chilly and dark. [9] We also mentioned that we wanted seeds for a plant seldom sold in local shops. [10] "I know what you need," Mrs. Miller promptly replied. [11] "These are seeds of the

GRAMMAR

COMMON ERROR

Problem. Many students overuse adverbs such as *really, very, certainly, definitely,* and *actually.*

Solution. Advise students to think about choosing just the right adverb for a situation instead of automatically writing the same one every time. Chosen with originality and care, adverbs can add to writing effectiveness.

Have students go over their papers to circle all the adverbs. You may want to remind them that most adverbs end in *–ly* and always answer one of these questions: When? Where? How? To what extent? How long? How much?

GRAMMAR

ANSWERS
Exercise 12

1. finally—decided, verb
2. too—expensive, adjective
3. almost—always, adverb; always—raised, verb; not—do adjust, verb; easily—do adjust, verb
4. Suddenly—had, verb
5. indoors—grow, verb
6. automatically—will adapt, verb
7. cheerfully—greeted, verb
8. hardly—ever, adverb; ever—gets, verb; especially—chilly, dark, adjectives
9. also—mentioned, verb; seldom—sold, verb
10. promptly—replied, verb
11. unusually—hardy, adjective
12. There—is, verb
13. back—got, verb
14. now—have, verb; perfectly—suited, adjective

532   *The Parts of Speech*

bo tree, an unusually hardy member of the fig family native to India. [12] There this tree is sacred to Buddhists because it is said that the Buddha received enlightenment under a bo tree." [13] When we got back to our house, we planted the seeds. [14] In a short time, they sprouted, and we now have an unusual houseplant that is perfectly suited to our cold environment.

PICTURE THIS

Remind students that Romeo has just fallen in love with Juliet and now overhears her confession to the stars that she loves him, too. One way to decide on accurate stage directions is by analyzing the characters. How do they feel? What are their goals? What are their fears? What challenges do they face? What threatens them?

PICTURE THIS

You are directing this production of Shakespeare's play *Romeo and Juliet*. The actors are in position and are waiting for your instructions on how to play the famous balcony scene in which the young lovers proclaim their feelings for each other. Shakespeare provided little direction, so it's up to you. Write five sentences of stage directions that you think would be appropriate for the scene. In each sentence, use at least one adverb to tell the actors how, when, where, or to what extent to do something.

Subject: stage directions for *Romeo and Juliet*
Audience: actors playing Romeo and Juliet
Purpose: to instruct actors how to play a scene

REVIEW D

OBJECTIVE

- To identify parts of speech within a paragraph and to identify the words adjectives and adverbs modify

▶ EXERCISE 13 **Using Words as Adjectives and Adverbs**

Write a pair of sentences for each word. In the first sentence, use the word as an *adjective;* in the second, use it as an *adverb.*

EXAMPLE   **1.** kindly
          1. *She had a kindly manner—adjective.*
             She spoke kindly—adverb.

1. daily   **2.** fast   **3.** late   **4.** more   **5.** far

▶ REVIEW D   **Identifying Parts of Speech**

Identify the part of speech of each italicized word in the following paragraphs. If the word is an adjective or an adverb, be able to tell <u>what it modifies</u>.

n. = noun
pro. = pronoun
v. = verb   adv. = adverb
adj. = adjective

With a [1] *thunderous* <u>roar</u>, a mighty avalanche [2] *crashes* [3] *headlong* down a mountainside. [4] *Some* of these slides travel at speeds of more than 200 miles an hour and pose a [5] *deadly* <u>threat</u> to skiers, mountain climbers, and the people [6] *who* live and work in the mountains.

One [7] *common* <u>suggestion</u> for surviving an avalanche is to make swimming motions to remain on top of the snow. However, people caught in avalanches [8] *rarely* <u>can save</u> [9] *themselves*. They are [10] *usually* [11] *immobilized*, and the slide forces snow into their nose and mouth.

Avalanche workers in the [12] *United States* and abroad have [13] *long* <u>realized</u> the [14] *potential* [15] *destructiveness* of selected slide paths. They [16] *have concluded* that an avalanche <u>can be</u> [17] *greatly* <u>reduced</u> if [18] *explosives* [19] *are* used to trigger a [20] *series* of [21] *smaller* <u>slides</u> before [22] *one* large <u>mass</u> of snow can build up. [23] *Today*, the detonation of explosives <u>has become</u> a standard [24] *practice* for controlling avalanches in [25] *this* <u>country</u>.

1. adj.   6. pro.
2. v.   7. adj.
3. adv.   8. adv.
4. pro.   9. pro.
5. adj.   10. adv.
    11. v.   12. n.
13. adv.
14. adj.
15. n.
16. v.
17. adv.
18. n.
19. v.
20. n.

21. adj.   **22.** adj.   **23.** adv.   **24.** n.   **25.** adj.

▶ EXERCISE 14   **Using Parts of Speech to Write a Description**

In the painting on the next page, folk artist Mattie Lou O'Kelley recorded her impressions of a circus parade that came through her town when she was growing up in the early 1900s. Imagine that you were with O'Kelley, watching

---

GRAMMAR

ANSWERS
Exercise 13

Responses will vary. Here are some possibilities:

1. She has not completed her daily exercises.
His father bakes bread daily.

2. Fast cars are often not fuel efficient.
They all run fast.

3. I enjoy the late movie.
We don't like to stay up late.

4. He ate more donuts than you.
They work more with new tools.

5. She threw the shot put a far distance.
The space ship flew far away.

ANSWERS
Exercise 14

One constant in the different sentences students write should be powerful action verbs. Adverbs can be used to unify the scene as the viewer looks first at one part of the parade and then at another.

GRAMMAR

OBJECTIVE

- To write sentences using words as prepositions and as adverbs and to identify the prepositional phrases and the words the adverbs modify

GRAMMAR

 VISUAL CONNECTIONS
The Circus Parade

About the Artist. The American folk artist Mattie Lou O'Kelley was born in Maysville, Georgia, in 1906. A self-taught artist, O'Kelley worked in both oils and watercolor and used pointillism and realism in her paintings. She received the Governor's Award for Outstanding Contribution to American Art from the governor of Georgia in 1976.

Teacher's ResourceBank™
RESOURCES

PREPOSITIONS
- The Preposition

 QUICK REMINDER

Write the following sentences on the chalkboard:

1. The riders went across.
2. The riders rode across the river.

Ask students what part of speech the word *across* is used as in each sentence. [In the first sentence, it is an adverb; in the second sentence, it is a preposition.] Then ask students why it is a different part of speech in each sentence. [In the first sentence, it tells where the riders went; in the second sentence, it shows the relationship between the verb *rode* and *river*.] Remind students that prepositional phrases can serve as adverbs or adjectives.

534

---

534 *The Parts of Speech*

the parade, and write ten sentences giving your impressions of that day. Use action verbs and vivid adjectives and adverbs to capture the excitement of this spectacle. Be prepared to identify the nouns, pronouns, adjectives, verbs, and adverbs in your sentences.

EXAMPLE **1.** *The beautiful acrobat skips lightly on the elephant's back.*

The Circus Parade by Mattie Lou O'Kelley. Photograph courtesy of the Museum of American Folk Art, NY. From the book "Circus" by Mattie Lou O'Kelley. Used with permission of Atlantic Monthly Press.

Prepositions

15f. A *preposition* is a word that shows the relationship of a noun or a pronoun to some other word in the sentence.

Notice in the following examples how the prepositions show six different relationships between *village* and *rode*.

I rode **past** the village.	I rode **near** the village.
I rode **through** the village.	I rode **around** the village.
I rode **toward** the village.	I rode **beyond** the village.

A preposition always introduces a *phrase*. The noun or pronoun that ends a prepositional phrase is the *object of the preposition*. In the previous examples, the object of the prepositions is *village*.

☞ REFERENCE NOTE: For more about prepositional phrases, see pages 574–576.

15f

Commonly Used Prepositions

aboard	below	for	past
about	beneath	from	since
above	beside	in	through
across	besides	inside	to
after	between	into	toward
against	beyond	like	under
along	but (meaning	near	underneath
amid	*except*)	of	until
among	by	off	up
around	concerning	on	upon
at	down	onto	with
before	during	outside	within
behind	except	over	without

Compound Prepositions

according to	in addition to	instead of
because of	in front of	on account of
by means of	in spite of	prior to

NOTE: The same word may be either an adverb or a preposition, depending on its use in a sentence.

EXAMPLES   Marge climbed **down**. [adverb]
Marge climbed **down** the ladder. [preposition]

Above, buzzards circled lazily. [adverb]
Above the dry riverbed, buzzards circled lazily. [preposition]

EXERCISE 15   Writing Sentences Using Words as Prepositions and as Adverbs

For each of the following words, write two sentences. In the first sentence, use the word as a preposition and underline the prepositional phrase. In the second sentence, use the word as an adverb. Be able to tell which word the adverb modifies.

EXAMPLE   **1.** In
    1. *We are going <u>in the house</u> now.*
        We are going in now.

1. around   **3.** inside   **5.** up
2. behind   **4.** on

GRAMMAR

535

CONJUNCTIONS Rule 15g

OBJECTIVE

• To identify coordinating and correlative conjunctions in sentences

Teacher's ResourceBank™
RESOURCES

THE CONJUNCTION
• The Conjunction

QUICK REMINDER

Write the following pairs of sentences on the chalkboard:

1. Maria likes milk. Milk is good for her.
2. Frank likes salt. Salt doesn't like Frank.
3. Sako will graduate. She will not get a good job.

Ask students to combine each pair of sentences with a conjunction. [Maria likes milk, and it is good for her. Frank likes salt, but it doesn't like Frank. Sako will graduate, or she will not get a good job.]

Remind students that conjunctions join related ideas, but the nature of their relationship dictates which conjunction is to be used.

MEETING
INDIVIDUAL
NEEDS

STUDENTS WITH SPECIAL NEEDS

It is important to vary the activities of students with attention-deficit disorder. Have the students make charts with the various parts of speech as headings. Then have students find pictures in magazines to illustrate linguistically by filling in their charts with nouns, verbs, adjectives, and adverbs that describe what is happening in their pictures. Finally, have the students combine these parts of speech into sentences with conjunctions, prepositions, and pronouns.

---

536 *The Parts of Speech*

Conjunctions

15g. A *conjunction* is a word used to join words or groups of words.

Conjunctions join parts of a sentence that function in the same way. The parts that are joined may be words, phrases, or clauses.

👉 REFERENCE NOTE: For a discussion on using conjunctions in sentence combining, see pages 466–470. For the rules governing the use of punctuation with conjunctions, see pages 467–468, 794–796, and 816–819.

Coordinating Conjunctions

Conjunctions that join equal parts of a sentence are called *coordinating conjunctions.*

and	for	but	so
or	yet	nor	

EXAMPLES   The orchestra played one waltz **and** two polkas.
We can walk to the mall **or** take a bus.
I looked for Hal, **but** he had already left.

Correlative Conjunctions

Conjunctions that are used in pairs are called *correlative conjunctions.* Like coordinating conjunctions, correlative conjunctions join equal parts of a sentence.

both . . . and	neither . . . nor
not only . . . but also	whether . . . or
either . . . or	

EXAMPLES   **Neither** the baseball team **nor** the soccer team has practice today.
Both the track team **and** the volleyball team enjoyed a winning season.
Their victories sparked the enthusiasm **not only** of students **but also** of teachers and townspeople.

👉 REFERENCE NOTE: **Subordinating conjunctions** are discussed with subordinate clauses on pages 603–604.

INTERJECTIONS Rule 15h

OBJECTIVE

- To write sentences using interjections properly

GRAMMAR

 EXERCISE 16 **Identifying Coordinating and Correlative Conjunctions**

Identify the <u>coordinating</u> and <u>correlative</u> conjunctions in the sentences in the following paragraph.

[1] Once Nantucket <u>and</u> New Bedford, Massachusetts, were home ports of huge whaling fleets. [2] Whaling brought tremendous profits into these ports, <u>but</u> the golden days of whaling ended about the time of the American Civil War. [3] Even when it was successful, a whaling trip was no pleasure cruise for <u>either</u> the captain <u>or</u> the crew. [4] Maintaining order was no easy task on a long voyage because the food <u>and</u> living conditions were often dreadful. [5] Inevitably, the sailors had time on their hands, <u>for</u> they didn't encounter a whale every day. [6] To relieve the monotony <u>and</u> resulting boredom, whaling ships often would exchange visits. [7] <u>Not only</u> the captain <u>but also</u> the whole crew looked forward to such visits. [8] Everyone enjoyed the chance to chat <u>and</u> exchange news. [9] The decline of whaling <u>and</u> of the whaling industry was signaled by the development of a new fuel. [10] By 1860, our country no longer needed large quantities of whale oil because kerosene, a cheaper <u>and</u> better fuel, had replaced it.

Interjections

15h. An *interjection* is a word that expresses emotion and has no grammatical relation to other words in the sentence.

EXAMPLES **Ouch! Ugh! Wow! Oops! Oh!**

These words are usually followed by an exclamation mark. An interjection that shows only mild emotion is set off from the sentence by a comma.

EXAMPLES **Well,** I'm just not sure.
When I'm having a bad week, **gosh,** I can hardly wait for the weekend.

 QUICK REMINDER

Write the following sentences on the chalkboard:

1. Wow I got an A on my paper.
2. I hate worms! Ugh
3. Well I saw her last week.

Ask students to identify the interjections and to supply the missing punctuation. [(1) Wow! (2) Ugh! (3) Well,]

OBJECTIVES
- To identify parts of speech in sentences
- To use words as different parts of speech in sentences

EXERCISE 17 Using Interjections

You just took your driver's license test. Wanting to share your feelings about the test and your results, you call your best friend. Write your conversation, using at least five interjections. You may choose interjections from the list below or use ones of your own. Be sure to use the words as interjections and not as adjectives or adverbs. Check to see that you have punctuated your interjections with exclamation points or commas as needed.

ah	cool	hey	wow	ugh
aw	great	no	yes	excellent

Determining Parts of Speech

15i. What part of speech a word is depends on how the word is used.

EXAMPLES Rich heard the **light** patter of raindrops. [adjective]
The room was filled with **light**. [noun]
Let's **light** some candles this evening. [verb]

EXERCISE 18 Determining the Parts of Speech of Words

Determine the part of speech of the <u>italicized word</u> in each of the following sentences. Be prepared to explain your answers. n. = noun   v. = verb   adj. = adjective

1. They decided that the hedge needed a *trim*. **1.** n.
2. Their hedges always look *trim* and neat. **2.** adj.   **3.** v.
3. We usually *trim* the tree with homemade ornaments.
4. Mom always *shears* a couple of inches off the top of the tree. **4.** v.
5. Later, she uses *shears* to cut straggling branches. **5.** n.
6. My brother *spices* peach preserves with nutmeg and allspice. **6.** v.
7. These *spices* are available in most stores. **7.** n.
8. Sage adds a tangy *flavor* to stew. **8.** n.
9. Many chefs also *flavor* stew with basil. **9.** v.
10. In their family, a *cross* word is rarely spoken. **10.** adj.

ANSWERS
Exercise 17

Responses will vary. Here is a possibility:

Hey, I finally did it. The bus goes by the Highway Department office, and I'd told you I was thinking about taking the written test before our Driver's Ed course is over. Wednesday the bus stopped for the light there, and, well, I, got off and went and took the test.

Aw! the written test was easy! When the officer saw I'd passed it, he wanted me to take the driving test, too. Well, I didn't have a vehicle, but he said he was driving his son's car and would let me use it. It was a 1979 Chevrolet, just like my grandmother's. Cool! I passed that test, too.

Teacher's ResourceBank™
RESOURCES

DETERMINING PARTS OF SPEECH
- Determining Parts of Speech

QUICK REMINDER

Write the following sentences on the chalkboard. Have students put in the part of speech called for.

1. (proper noun) ran to the window and (verb) (preposition) the street.
2. (interjection) (pronoun) shouted (conjunction) screamed (adverb).
3. A (adjective) monster (verb).

[Possible answers: **(1)** Jan ran to the window and looked at the street. **(2)** "Aiiii!" She shouted and screamed loudly. **(3)** A green monster appeared.]

REVIEWS E and F

OBJECTIVES

- To write sentences with words used as different parts of speech
- To identify the parts of speech of various words in a paragraph

15i

GRAMMAR

▶ REVIEW E

Writing Sentences Using Words as Different Parts of Speech

Write three sentences for each of the following words, using the word as a different part of speech in each sentence. At the end of the sentence, write what part of speech the word is in that sentence.

1. long   **2.** cut   **3.** back   **4.** fast   **5.** iron

▶ REVIEW F

Determining the Parts of Speech of Words

Identify the part of speech of each italicized word or expression in the following paragraph. n. = noun pro. = pronoun
v. = verb adj. = adjective adv. = adverb prep. = preposition conj. = conjunction

[1] *Early* farmers on the [2] *Great Plains* eked out a rough existence, [3] *for* there were few towns, stores, [4] *or* other hallmarks of civilization. Many farm homes were constructed with sod bricks, [5] *which* were cut out of the prairie. Trees were in short supply on these wind-swept lands, [6] *but* the resourceful settler might find a few [7] *cottonwoods* growing [8] *along* a stream. [9] *These* [10] *could be used* to build a frame for the roof, which was then covered [11] *lightly* with grassy earth. Grass, both [12] *on* the roof [13] *and* in the sod, helped to hold the house together. Some of [14] *these* rugged homes had a door made of timber, [15] *but* usually a cowhide [16] *was draped* across the entrance. [17] *Inside* was a dirt floor covered with a bearskin [18] *or* a buffalo hide. As more settlers moved [19] *west* bringing furnishings and [20] *building* materials, farmers eventually abandoned these first, primitive dwellings and built more conventional homes.

1. adj.
2. n.
3. conj.
4. conj.
5. pro.
6. conj.
7. n.
8. prep.
9. pro.
10. v.
11. adv.
12. prep.
13. conj.
14. adj.
15. conj.
16. v.
17. adv. **18.** conj. **19.** adv. **20.** adj.

▶ EXERCISE 19

Using Words as Different Parts of Speech

Your friend has just returned from a vacation in Europe. During her trip, she made the collage shown on the following page, picturing different types of transportation she used while traveling. After flying from the United States, she rode a bike in France, a train through the Swiss Alps, and a bus in Italy. She also went by ship to a Greek island, where she rode a donkey. Write your comments and

ANSWERS
Review E

Answers will vary. Here are some possibilities:

1. We all long for the lazy days of summer. (verb) We took the long way home. (adjective) We did not work long enough. (adverb)

2. Erris cut the cake into twenty-four neat pieces. (verb) The burglary suspect has a suspicious cut on his back. (noun) Nothing sparkles like cut glass. (adjective)

3. Please back the car into the garage carefully. (verb) She turned her back and walked away. (noun) The back door slammed. (adjective)

4. Some people still fast to purify their minds and bodies. (verb) In ancient times this was the main purpose of a fast. (noun) Now, some people who go without eating are usually looking for a fast way to lose weight. (adjective)

5. I asked my sister to iron my new shirt. (verb) She had to wait until the iron was hot. (noun) Her iron will and determination will see her through the audition. (adjective)

🕊 TIMESAVER

Have students underline the words they are to use in sentences in **Exercise 19** for easy checking.

GRAMMAR

OBJECTIVES
- To determine the parts of speech of words
- To write sentences with words used as different parts of speech

GRAMMAR

ANSWERS
Exercise 19

Answers will vary. Here are some possibilities:

1. noun: Where did you buy your bike?
verb: How far did you bike each day you were in France?

2. preposition: Aren't you glad you didn't have to pedal up the Alps on a bicycle?
adverb: Was your bicycle easy to pick up?

3. adjective: I like to ride my bicycle in the cool fall evenings.
interjection: You rode your bike all the way to the capitol? Cool!

4. conjunction: I can hardly believe you went that far, for you were only gone a month.
preposition: Were you used to riding a bicycle for exercise?

5. pronoun: That sounds like the trip of a lifetime.
adjective: That trip is something you will remember all your life.

GRAMMAR

540 *The Parts of Speech*

questions about her travels, using the following words as the parts of speech indicated. Each word will be used as two different parts of speech.

bike [noun, verb]
up [preposition, adverb]
cool [adjective, interjection]
for [conjunction, preposition]
that [pronoun, adjective]

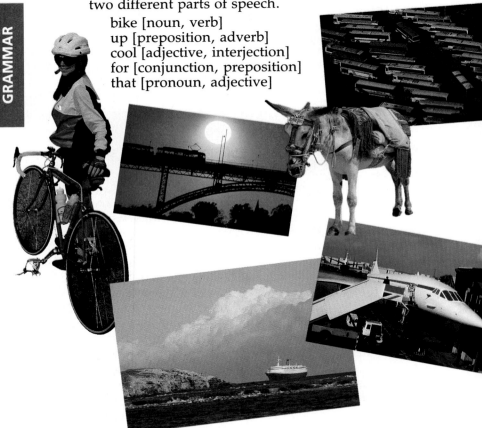

Review: Posttest 1

Determining the Parts of Speech of Words

Identify the part of speech of each italicized word in the following paragraphs. n. = noun   pro. = pronoun   v. = verb
adj. = adjective   adv. = adverb   prep. = preposition   conj. = conjunction

1. n.   Since the [1] *condition* of the roads prevented [2] *extensive*

2. adj.   use of wheeled vehicles, the most reliable means of trans-

3. n.   portation in colonial times was the [3] *saddle horse*. Some

[4]*exceptionally* wealthy people kept carriages, but [5]*these* were usually heavy vehicles [6]*that* were pulled by two or more horses. Such carriages were [7]*satisfactory* for short trips, [8]*but* they were not practical for long journeys.

Stagecoaches were introduced in [9]*America* about 1750. By this time, roads ran [10]*between* such major cities as New York and Boston. Although these roads [11]*were* little more than muddy tracks, [12]*most* were wide enough for a four-wheeled coach. [13]*Three* or four pairs of horses [14]*were harnessed* to a coach. However, the vehicles were so heavy that [15]*coach* horses tired [16]*quite* [17]*rapidly* [18]*and* either had to be rested frequently [19]*or* changed at post houses along the route. The design of horse-drawn vehicles soon improved, and until the early years of the twentieth century, buggies and wagons remained a common [20]*form* of transportation.

4. adv.
5. pro.
6. pro.
7. adj.
8. conj.
9. n.
10. prep.
11. v.
12. pro.
13. adj.
14. v.
15. adj.
16. adv.
17. adv. 18. conj. 19. conj. 20. n.

GRAMMAR

Review: Posttest 2

Writing Sentences with Words Used as Different Parts of Speech

Use each of the following words or groups of words in a sentence. Then indicate what part of speech the word or word group is.

EXAMPLE **1.** gold
   1. *Tamisha bought a gold bracelet. (adjective)*

1. novel
2. Park Avenue
3. this
4. are laughing
5. yesterday
6. tomorrow
7. or
8. but
9. both . . . and
10. silver

11. hiked
12. appeared
13. tasted
14. quietly
15. often
16. inside
17. underneath
18. oh
19. whew
20. in

ANSWERS
Posttest 2

Responses will vary.

1. Enrique checked out a novel to read this weekend. (noun) He is taking a novel approach to studying for a test. (adjective)

2. Park Avenue glittered like a jewel in the New York dusk. (noun) Linda caught the Park Avenue bus. (adjective)

3. This is the way home. (pronoun) This way is easiest. (adjective)

4. All the people in this room are laughing. (verb)

5. Yesterday seems as if it happened a hundred years ago. (noun) I can remember everything that happened yesterday. (adverb)

6. Tomorrow is a big day. (noun); Tomorrow I am flying to San Francisco. (adverb)

7. He had always kept his watch on his wrist or on the dresser. (coordinating conjunction)

8. She went to see the film but she did not stay for the ending. (coordinating conjunction) We had finished all of the problems but one. (preposition)

9. Both Juanita and Pedro read five books this month! (correlative conjunctions)

10. Iris likes to wear silver jewelry. (adjective) Tom invested his money in silver. (noun)

11. The entire biology class hiked for fifteen miles. (verb) She wore her skirt hiked up above her boots. (adjective)

12. Her face appeared in the mirror. (action verb) Her face appeared tired. (linking verb)

13. Ramiro tasted the soup carefully. (action verb) The soup tasted bland. (linking verb)

GRAMMAR

14. He listened quietly to the speech. (adverb)

15. She would often see the old man taking an afternoon nap on his porch. (adverb)

16. He looked inside. (adverb) He put his passport inside his jacket. (preposition) He kept valuable papers in an inside pocket. (adjective)

17. He got out of the car and looked underneath it. (preposition)

18. Oh, I forgot the ice cream. (interjection)

19. Whew! This has been a long exercise. (interjection)

20. Let me in. (adverb) The new boys arrived in town. (preposition)

SUMMARY OF PARTS OF SPEECH

Rule	Part of Speech	Use	Examples
15a	noun	names	**Larry** picks **grapefruit.**
15b	pronoun	takes the place of a noun	**Who** said **that these** are the **ones we** need?
15c	adjective	modifies a noun or a pronoun	That was a **happy** sight. They were very **noisy.**
15d	verb	shows action or a state of being	He **jumps** and **spins.** She **is** the winner.
15e	adverb	modifies a verb, an adjective, or another adverb	He learns **quickly.** She is **always** right. It flies **quite** high.
15f	preposition	relates a noun or a pronoun to another word	The cat was **by** itself **under** the oak tree **next to** the garage.
15g	conjunction	joins words or groups of words	Kyoko **and** Sheila passed the test. We can **either** go hiking **or** go swimming.
15h	interjection	expresses emotion	**My goodness! Hey,** stop that!

◘ DIAGNOSTIC TEST

OBJECTIVES

- To identify subjects, verbs, predicate adjectives, predicate nominatives, direct objects, and indirect objects
- To classify sentences as declarative, interrogative, imperative, or exclamatory and to provide the correct end punctuation for each sentence

16 THE SENTENCE

Subjects, Predicates, Complements

Diagnostic Test

A. Identifying Subjects, Verbs, and Complements

Identify the <u>italicized word or word group</u> in each of the following sentences as a *subject*, a *verb*, a *predicate adjective*, a *predicate nominative*, a *direct object*, or an *indirect object*.

1. Native *cactuses* in the Southwest are in trouble. **1.** s.
2. Some species are already *vulnerable* to extinction. **2.** p.a.
3. Cactuses *are being threatened* by landscapers, tourists, and collectors. **3.** v.
4. Many people illegally harvest these wild *plants*. **4.** d.o.
5. There are many unique *species* in Arizona. **5.** s.
6. Arizona is, therefore, an active *battlefield* in the war against the removal of endangered cactuses. **6.** p.n.
7. "Cactus cops" *patrol* the streets of Phoenix on the lookout for places with illegally acquired cactuses. **7.** v.
8. Authorized dealers must give *purchasers* permit tags as proof of legal sale. **8.** i.o.

GRAMMAR

Teacher's ResourceBank™
▼ **RESOURCES** ▼

FOR THE WHOLE CHAPTER
- Chapter Review Form A
- Chapter Review Form B
- Assessment Portfolio
  Grammar Pretests
  Grammar Mastery Tests

CHAPTER OVERVIEW

This chapter discusses sentence fragments, complete and simple subjects and predicates, subject complements, and objects. The chapter also teaches students how to classify sentences by purpose as declarative, imperative, interrogative, or exclamatory. The **Writing Application** then challenges students to use appropriately varied sentences in their writing.

Knowledge of the parts of sentences will help students to write varied sentences, to revise sentences for improved style, and to proofread for subject-verb agreement.

USING THE DIAGNOSTIC TEST

You may want to use the **Diagnostic Test** in conjunction with your assessments of students' writing to evaluate their understanding of sentences.

The **Diagnostic Test** does not test students' ability to distinguish fragments from sentences; therefore, you may wish to use **Exercise 1** to diagnose students' abilities in this area.

SEGMENT 2 *(pp. 544–546)*
SENTENCES AND SENTENCE FRAGMENTS Rule 16a

OBJECTIVE
• To identify groups of words as either sentences or fragments

---

544 *The Sentence*

9. First violations are *punishable* by a minimum fine of five hundred dollars. **9.** p.a.
10. Illegally owned cactuses *may be confiscated* by the police. **10.** v.
11. What a thorny problem cactus *rustling* has become! **11.** s.   **12.** p.a.
12. Why are illegal harvesters so *hard* to keep track of?
13. Many work at night and sometimes use permit *tags* over and over. **13.** d.o.
14. Always *examine* a large cactus for bruises. **14.** v.
15. Legally harvested cacti *should* not *show* any damage. **15.** v.

B. Classifying Sentences as Declarative, Interrogative, Imperative, or Exclamatory

Classify each of the following sentences as *declarative*, *interrogative*, *imperative*, or *exclamatory*. Then give the proper end punctuation.

16. Read this article about imperiled cactuses. **16.** imp.
17. The author describes a trip into the desert with a legal hauler. **17.** decl.
18. Can you imagine a saguaro worth three hundred dollars? **18.** int.
19. A crested saguaro is even rarer and can sell for thousands of dollars. **19.** decl.
20. No wonder illegal harvesting is booming! **20.** excl.

Sentences and Sentence Fragments

In conversation, you may leave out part of a sentence without confusing your listeners. In writing, though, it's better to use complete sentences because readers rely on them for help in understanding your meaning.

16a. A *sentence* is a group of words that contains a subject and a verb and expresses a complete thought.

Teacher's ResourceBank™
RESOURCES

SENTENCES AND SENTENCE FRAGMENTS
• The Sentence

🦉 QUICK REMINDER
Focus students' attention on sentences and sentence fragments by having each student write two fragments and two sentences about a favorite book, movie, or song. Tell students to be prepared to explain why the groups of words are sentences or fragments.

16a

GRAMMAR

To express a complete thought, a sentence must say something that makes sense by itself. A group of words that does not express a complete thought is a *fragment,* or a piece of a sentence, not a sentence.

SENTENCE   Cara won the essay contest sponsored by the magazine.

FRAGMENT   the essay contest sponsored by the magazine

SENTENCE   Her essay was chosen as the best one from over two thousand entries.

FRAGMENT   was chosen as the best one from over two thousand entries

SENTENCE   When the judges announced the winner, everyone applauded.

FRAGMENT   when the judges announced the winner

☞ REFERENCE NOTE: Fragments can be confusing when they are written as sentences, beginning with a capital letter and ending with an end mark of punctuation. See pages 446–447 for information on how to correct sentence fragments.

▶ EXERCISE 1   **Identifying Sentences and Fragments**

Identify each of the following word groups as a <u>sentence</u> or a *fragment*.

1. Willa Cather was born in Back Creek Valley in northern Virginia.   **1.** sent.
2. In 1883, when she was ten years old.   **2.** frag.
3. Her family moved to the treeless prairie of Nebraska.   **3.** sent.
4. Fascinated by the wild and rolling plains.   **4.** frag.
5. She tracked buffalo and collected prairie flowers.   **5.** sent.
6. Listening to the stories of neighboring settlers.   **6.** frag.
7. They told memorable tales about the harsh struggles of the homesteaders.   **7.** sent.
8. After she graduated from high school in the village of Red Cloud, Nebraska.   **8.** frag.
9. The picture of Red Cloud on the next page shows shops and people that would have been familiar to Willa Cather.   **9.** sent.
10. And the Opera House at the end of the street where Cather and her class graduated in 1890.   **10.** frag.

Teacher's ResourceBank™
RESOURCES

SUBJECT AND PREDICATE
• Subject and Predicate
• Subjects in Unusual Positions
• Compound Subjects and Verbs

QUICK REMINDER

Write the following sentences on the chalkboard and have students identify the simple subject and simple predicate in each.

1. My gold chain is missing!
2. Lira, my sister, remembered seeing it on my dresser.
3. We could not find it anywhere.
4. I looked in my cat's bed and found my gold chain.
5. Lira and I laughed.

546

SEGMENT 3 *(pp. 546–557)*

SUBJECT AND PREDICATE   Rules 16b–16g

OBJECTIVES

• To identify complete subjects and complete predicates in sentences
• To identify verbs and verb phrases in a paragraph
• To identify subjects and verbs in sentences
• To complete sentences by adding predicates

EXERCISE 2   **Identifying Sentences and Fragments**

Identify each of the numbered word groups in the following paragraph as either a *sentence* or a *fragment*. Be prepared to explain your answers.

1. sent.
2. frag.
3. sent.
4. frag.
5. sent.
6. frag.
7. sent.
8. frag.
9. sent.
10. sent.

[1] In college, Willa Cather discovered her talent for writing. [2] Contributing stories and reviews to local newspapers in Lincoln, Nebraska. [3] At first, her writing failed to reach a wider audience outside her region. [4] After some years as a schoolteacher and a magazine editor in New York City. [5] She succeeded in establishing herself as a writer. [6] Although Cather enjoyed living in New York. [7] She never lost touch with the sights and sounds of her childhood. [8] In her first novel, *O Pioneers!* [9] She describes how farmers turned the unruly plains into orderly fields of wheat and corn. [10] In a later novel, *My Ántonia*, the immigrant neighbors of her childhood play prominent roles.

Subject and Predicate

16b.   A sentence consists of two parts: the *subject* and the *predicate.*

The *subject* is the part that names the person or thing spoken about in the rest of the sentence. The **predicate** is the part that says something about the subject.

16b

The subject may come at the beginning, the end, or even the middle of a sentence.

EXAMPLES

SUBJECT
Some residents of the desert

PREDICATE
can survive a long drought.

PREDICATE
Noteworthy is

SUBJECT
the Australian frog.

PREDICATE
For up to three years

SUBJECT
these frogs

PREDICATE
can live without rainfall.

PREDICATE
How can

SUBJECT
an animal

PREDICATE
survive that long?

In these examples, the words labeled *subject* make up the **complete subject.** The words labeled *predicate* make up the **complete predicate.** Notice in the third example that parts of the complete predicate can come before and after the subject.

▶ EXERCISE 3   **Identifying Subjects and Predicates**

Identify the <u>complete subject</u> and the <u>complete predicate</u> in each of the following sentences. Keep in mind that the subject may come after the predicate.

1. The discovery of platinum <u>has been credited to people from a variety of countries</u>.
2. <u>Spanish explorers in search of gold</u> <u>supposedly discovered this precious metal in the rivers of South America</u>.
3. However, <u>they</u> <u>considered it a worthless, inferior form of silver</u>.
4. <u>Their name for platinum</u> <u>was *platina*, meaning "little silver."</u>
5. <u>Back into the river went</u> <u>the little balls of platinum</u>!
6. <u>The platinum</u> <u>might then become gold, according to one theory</u>.
7. <u>Europeans</u> <u>later mixed platinum with gold</u>.
8. <u>This mixture</u> <u>encouraged the production of counterfeit gold bars and coins</u>.
9. <u>Platinum</u> <u>commands a high price today because of its resistance to corrosion</u>.
10. <u>Such diverse products as jet planes and jewelry</u> <u>require platinum in some form</u>.

GRAMMAR

- To write an informative paragraph and to identify the subject and verb in each sentence
- To write a friendly letter that describes a work of art

LEARNING STYLES

Visual Learners. Look in books and magazines to find pictures of people performing actions, such as a baseball player hitting a ball or a parent reading to a child. Ask students to describe the subject in each picture and to tell what the subject is doing. Write on the chalkboard a complete sentence based on each description and ask the students to name the subject and the verb in each sentence.

GRAMMAR

The Simple Subject

16c. The *simple subject* is the main word or group of words in the complete subject.

EXAMPLES   **A dog with this pedigree is usually nervous.**
Complete subject   **A dog with this pedigree**
Simple subject   **dog**

The Taj Mahal in India is one of the most beautiful buildings in the world.
Complete subject   **The Taj Mahal in India**
Simple subject   **Taj Mahal**

☞ REFERENCE NOTE: Compound nouns, such as *Taj Mahal,* are considered one noun. For more about compound nouns, see page 515.

NOTE: In this book, the term *subject* refers to the simple subject unless otherwise indicated.

The Simple Predicate

16d. The *simple predicate,* or *verb,* is the main word or group of words in the complete predicate.

EXAMPLE   **Spiders snare their prey in intricate webs.**
Complete predicate   **snare their prey in intricate webs**
Simple predicate   **snare**

The simple predicate may be a single verb or a *verb phrase* (a verb and one or more helping verbs).

EXAMPLES   **walks   has been walking   might have walked**

When you identify the simple predicate, be sure to find all parts of a verb phrase.

EXAMPLES   **Did Rosa find you?**
Complete predicate   **did find you**
Simple predicate   **did find**

She has been looking for you all morning.
Complete predicate   **has been looking for you all morning**
Simple predicate   **has been looking**

GRAMMAR

NOTE: In this book, the term *verb* refers to the simple predicate unless otherwise indicated.

EXERCISE 4   **Identifying Verbs and Verb Phrases in Sentences**

Identify the <u>verb</u> in each sentence in the following paragraph. Be sure to include all parts of a verb phrase.

[1] Scientists throughout the world <u>have expressed</u> concern about the fate of the giant panda of China. [2] In recent years, this animal's natural habitat <u>has</u> slowly <u>become</u> smaller. [3] Many forests of bamboo, the panda's favorite food, <u>have died</u>. [4] A panda like the one pictured here <u>may devour</u> as much as forty pounds of bamboo daily. [5] However, each tender green shoot of bamboo <u>contains</u> only a small amount of nutrients. [6] In addition, the large but sluggish panda <u>is</u> not <u>known</u> as a successful hunter. [7] In their concern for the panda's survival, scientists <u>are</u> now <u>studying</u> the habits of this animal. [8] A captured panda <u>is held</u> in a log trap for several hours. [9] During this time, scientists <u>attach</u> a radio to the panda's neck. [10] The radio <u>sends</u> the scientists valuable information about the freed animal's behavior.

VISUAL CONNECTIONS
Related Expression Skills. The Chinese word for a panda is a compound word made up of the Chinese words for cat and bear—*catbear*. Ask students if they think the compound word *catbear* accurately describes the panda. Why or why not? Have students brainstorm for other compound words that could be used to describe the panda.

How to Find the Subject of a Sentence

Finding the subject of a sentence is easier if you pick out the verb first. Then ask "Who?" or "What?" followed by the verb.

EXAMPLES   **My cousin from Finland will arrive this afternoon.**
[The verb is *will arrive*. Who will arrive? *My cousin*
will arrive; therefore, *cousin* is the subject.]
On the other side of the brook stands a cabin. [The
verb is *stands*. What stands? *A cabin* stands; *cabin* is
the subject.]

▶ EXERCISE 5   **Identifying Subjects and Verbs**

Identify the <u>subject</u> and the <u>verb</u> in each sentence in the
following paragraph.

[1] Despite their fragile appearance, <u>butterflies</u> <u>have</u> a
lot of stamina. [2] <u>They</u> often <u>fly</u> more than one thousand
miles during migration. [3] The painted lady <u>butterfly</u>, for
example, <u>has been seen</u> in the middle of the Atlantic
Ocean. [4] In fact, this <u>species</u> <u>was</u> once <u>spotted</u> over the
Arctic Circle. [5] During the spring, <u>millions</u> of these
insects <u>flutter</u> across North America. [6] Huge <u>flocks</u> of
these colorful butterflies <u>fly</u> from their winter home in
New Mexico to places as far north as Newfoundland,
Canada. [7] Another long-distance <u>traveler</u>, the brilliant
orange-and-black monarch butterfly, <u>flies</u> south each September from Canada toward Florida, Texas, and California. [8] The migratory <u>flight</u> of the monarch <u>may cover</u> a
distance of close to two thousand miles. [9] Every winter
for the past several decades, <u>monarchs</u> <u>have gathered</u> in a
small forest not far from San Francisco. [10] The thick <u>clus-
ters</u> of their blazing orange wings <u>make</u> this forest very
popular with tourists.

16e.   The subject is never in a prepositional phrase.

A *prepositional phrase* is a group of words that begins
with a preposition and ends with a noun or pronoun.

EXAMPLES   through the years   of mine   on the team

☞ REFERENCE NOTE: For more about prepositional phrases, see
pages 574–576.

The noun or pronoun that ends a prepositional phrase
cannot be the subject of a sentence.

COMMON ERROR

Problem. Students often identify the nouns in prepositional phrases as
the subjects of sentences.

Solution. Suggest that students
bracket all prepositional phrases before
they attempt to find the subjects in sentences.

GRAMMAR

GRAMMAR

GRAMMAR

EXAMPLES   **One of my cousins has visited Ghana.** [Who has visited? *One* has visited, not *cousins,* which is part of the prepositional phrase *of my cousins.*]
On top of the building is an observatory. [What is? *Observatory* is, not *top* or *building,* which are parts of prepositional phrases.]

In many sentences you can easily isolate the subject and verb simply by crossing out all prepositional phrases.

EXAMPLE   The team ~~with the best record~~ will play ~~in the state tournament.~~
Subject   **team**
Verb   **will play**

▶ EXERCISE 6   **Identifying Subjects and Verbs**

Identify the <u>subject</u> and the <u>verb</u> of each sentence in the following paragraph. Remember that the subject won't be in a prepositional phrase.

[1] The <u>people</u> in this picture <u>are celebrating</u> an ancient Chinese tradition—heralding the arrival of the New Year. [2] These <u>festivities</u>, however, <u>are occurring</u> in the United States. [3] The Chinese New Year <u>celebration</u>, with its dragon parades and colorful decorations, <u>has added</u> another dimension to American culture. [4] In the 1850s, the earliest Chinese <u>immigrants</u> <u>came</u> to the United States for jobs in the gold mines and on the railroads. [5] At first, only <u>men</u> <u>were allowed</u> to immigrate. [6] Not until much

VISUAL CONNECTIONS
Ideas for Writing. Have students write expressive/descriptive paragraphs about this photograph. You could ask students to imagine that they are watching the parade with someone who cannot see and that they are trying to describe the scene to that person.

Tie this writing activity to the material in this chapter by having students label subjects and verbs in their completed paragraphs.

ANSWERS

Exercise 7

Predicates will vary. Here are some possibilities:

1. Last <u>month</u> <u>was</u> warm.
2. A white <u>fence</u> <u>surrounded</u> the yard.
3. The <u>surf</u> <u>was pounding</u> the shore.
4. The <u>road</u> by my house <u>is</u> bumpy.
5. The <u>students</u> in our school <u>held</u> a dance.

ANSWERS

Review A

1. complete subject: <u>Benjamin Banneker</u> (1731–1806)/ complete predicate: <u>was born</u> in Baltimore, Maryland, of a free mother and an enslaved father
2. complete subject: Considered free, <u>Banneker</u>/ complete predicate: <u>was</u> able to attend an integrated private school
3. complete subject: <u>he</u>/ complete predicate: There . . . <u>began</u> his lifelong study of science and math
4. complete subject: this young <u>man</u>/ complete predicate: Despite having only an eighth-grade education, . . . <u>became</u> a noteworthy American astronomer and mathematician
5. complete subject: His astronomical <u>research</u>/ complete predicate: <u>led</u> to his acclaimed prediction of the solar eclipse of 1789
6. complete subject: the <u>first</u> of his almanacs/ complete predicate: A few years later, . . . <u>was published</u>
7. complete subject: Banneker's <u>almanacs</u>/ complete predicate: <u>contained</u> tide tables and data on future eclipses

---

REVIEW A

OBJECTIVE

- To identify complete and simple subjects and predicates in sentences

later <u>were</u> <u>they</u> able to send home to China for their wives and sweethearts. [7] As a result, not until the 1920s <u>did</u> the close-knit <u>society</u> of America's Chinatowns <u>develop</u>. [8] <u>Do</u> <u>you</u> <u>want</u> to know more about the Chinese experience in America? [9] <u>I</u> <u>recommend</u> the book *Longtime Californ': A Documentary Study of an American Chinatown*. [10] In this book, <u>Victor G. Nee</u> and <u>Brett de Bary Nee</u> <u>trace</u> the history of Chinese immigration to the United States and the development of the Chinese American community in San Francisco.

▶ EXERCISE 7 **Completing Sentences by Supplying Predicates**

Complete each of the following sentences by adding a predicate to the complete subject. Then, underline the subject once and the verb twice.

EXAMPLE 1. One of the horses ____.
1. *One of the horses <u>has escaped</u> from the corral.*

1. Last month ____.
2. A white fence ____.
3. The surf ____.
4. The road by my house ____.
5. The students in our school ____.

▶ REVIEW A **Identifying Complete Subjects and Complete Predicates**

Identify the complete subject and the complete predicate in each sentence in the following paragraph. Then underline the subject once and the verb twice.

[1] Benjamin Banneker (1731–1806) was born in Baltimore, Maryland, of a free mother and an enslaved father. [2] Considered free, Banneker was able to attend an integrated private school. [3] There he began his lifelong study of science and math. [4] Despite having only an eighth-grade education, this young man became a noteworthy American astronomer and mathematician. [5] His astronomical research led to his acclaimed prediction of the solar eclipse of 1789. [6] A few years later, the first of his almanacs was published. [7] Banneker's almanacs contained tide tables and data on future eclipses. [8] Some

famous sayings and bits of practical advice were also included. [9] These popular almanacs came out every year for more than a decade. [10] In addition to his scientific discoveries, Banneker is known for his work as a surveyor during the planning of Washington, D.C.

Sentences Beginning with *There* or *Here*

The word *there* or *here* may begin a sentence, but it is usually not the subject.

EXAMPLE   **There are two apples left.** [What are left? *Apples.* Therefore, *apples* is the subject.]

> NOTE: In this use, *there* is an *expletive,* a word that fills out the structure of a sentence but doesn't add to the meaning.

There and *here* may be used as adverbs telling where.

EXAMPLES   **There are your gloves.** [What are there? *Gloves.*]
Here is my idea. [What is here? *Idea.*]

Sentences That Ask Questions

Questions usually begin with a verb, a helping verb, or a word such as *what, when, where, how,* or *why.* In most cases, the subject follows the verb or helping verb.

EXAMPLES   **Did you make the team?**
Why is he running?

In a question that begins with a helping verb, the subject always comes between the helping verb and the main verb. One way to find the subject in any question is to turn the question into a statement and find the verb. Then ask "Who?" or "What?" in front of the verb.

EXAMPLES   **Were your friends early?**
becomes
Your friends were early.
[Who were early? *Friends* were.]

Where did the horses cross the river?
becomes
The horses did cross the river where.
[What did cross the river? *Horses* did.]

8. complete subject: Some famous sayings and bits of practical advice/ complete predicate: were also included

9. complete subject: These popular almanacs/ complete predicate: came out every year for more than a decade

10. complete subject: Banneker/ complete predicate: In addition to his scientific discoveries, . . . is known for his work as a surveyor during the planning of Washington, D.C.

MEETING INDIVIDUAL NEEDS

AT-RISK STUDENTS

To engage students' interest in identifying parts of sentences, try incorporating a topic that interests many students—movies. First, have students help you to generate movie titles that are complete sentences. Write the titles on the chalkboard. [Possible titles include *The Empire Strikes Back, One Flew Over the Cuckoo's Nest, Heaven Can Wait, Guess Who's Coming to Dinner, Diamonds Are Forever,* and *Do the Right Thing.*] Then work with students to identify the subjects and verbs in the titles. After the class has studied **Sentences Classified by Purpose** you may also want to have students classify each title as declarative, imperative, exclamatory, or interrogative.

A DIFFERENT APPROACH

Students could play a game with commonly used pairs of subjects and verbs. Write sets of nouns and verbs on index cards. Here are some sets you could use:

Subject sets—Jack and Jill, salt and pepper, meat and potatoes, shoes and socks, cat and mouse

Verb sets—give and take, eat and run, touch and go, twist and shout, rock and roll

Group students in pairs, ask one pair to come to the front of the class and give an index card to one of the students in the pair. Tell the student with the index card to give the first half of the set as a clue; tell the second student to try to guess the word that completes the set. Then have each player that completes a set make up a sentence that includes the set as a compound subject or verb.

554 *The Sentence*

 EXERCISE 8   **Identifying Subjects and Verbs**

Identify the <u>verb</u> and the <u>subject</u> in each of the following sentences. Select the verb first.

1. There <u>were</u> three <u>questions</u> on the final exam.
2. Here <u>is</u> my <u>topic</u> for the term paper.
3. What <u>did</u> <u>you</u> <u>choose</u> for a topic?
4. <u>Will</u> <u>everyone</u> <u>be</u> ready on time?
5. There <u>will be</u> a study-group <u>meeting</u> tomorrow.
6. When <u>should</u> <u>we</u> <u>go</u> to the library?
7. There <u>were</u> very few <u>books</u> on the subject.
8. <u>Are</u> there many magazine <u>articles</u> about Nelson Mandela?
9. Where <u>will</u> our <u>conference</u> <u>be held</u>?
10. <u>Have</u> <u>you</u> <u>begun</u> the next chapter?

The Understood Subject

In requests and commands, the subject is usually not stated. In such sentences, *you* is the understood subject.

REQUEST   (You) Please rake the yard.
COMMAND   (You) Pick up the fallen branches.

When a request or command includes a person's name, the name is not the subject. The name is called a ***noun of direct address.*** *You* is still the understood subject.

EXAMPLE   (You) Wash the dishes, Jason.

Compound Subjects and Verbs

16f.   A *compound subject* consists of two or more subjects that are joined by a conjunction and have the same verb. The conjunctions most often used to link the parts of a compound subject are *and* and *or.*

EXAMPLES   **Mr. Olivero** and his **daughter** planted the garden.
[Who planted the garden? *Mr. Olivero, daughter.*]
Either **Mr. Olivero** or his **daughter** planted the **garden.** [Again, the two parts of the compound subject are *Mr. Olivero* and *daughter*.]

16g. A *compound verb* consists of two or more verbs that are joined by a conjunction and have the same subject.

EXAMPLES   At the street festival, we **danced** the rumba and **sampled** the meat pies.
I **have written** the letter but **have** not **addressed** the envelope.

NOTE: If the helping verb is the same for the two verbs in a compound verb, it may or may not be repeated. Both the subject and the verb may be compound.

EXAMPLE   My **aunt** and her **children will arrive** tomorrow and **stay** with us for the holidays.

EXERCISE 9   Identifying Subjects and Verbs

Identify the <u>subject</u> and the <u>verb</u> in each of the following sentences. If the subject is understood, write *(You)*.

1. <u>Jackets</u> and <u>ties</u> <u>are required</u> in that restaurant.
2. <u>Are</u> there <u>bears</u> <u>living</u> in these woods?
3. There <u>are</u> five new <u>students</u> in our class this term.
4. <u>Bring</u> both a pencil and a pen to the history exam.   **4.** *(You)*
5. <u>Miguel</u> neither <u>sings</u> nor <u>plays</u> an instrument.
6. Where <u>do</u> <u>you</u> and <u>Liz</u> <u>buy</u> your cassettes?
7. <u>Both</u> of the math problems <u>were</u> difficult.
8. <u>Play</u> ball!   **8.** *(You)*
9. There <u>is</u> much <u>wisdom</u> in folk sayings and proverbs.
10. <u>Is</u> <u>one</u> of the kittens sick?

EXERCISE 10   Using Subjects and Verbs

In preparing a report on the history of the typewriter, you've gathered the following notes and the pictures shown on the next page. Using information from these sources, write a paragraph about the development of typewriters. Underline the subject of each sentence once and the verb twice.

First typewriter designed by C. L. Sholes, 1867.
Had only capital letters—keys hard to press down.
Typed onto underside of paper, so typist couldn't see what was being typed.

ANSWERS
Exercise 10

Paragraphs will vary. Here is a possibility:

The first <u>typewriter</u> <u>was designed</u> by C. L. Sholes in 1867. <u>It</u> <u>had</u> only capital letters. The <u>keys</u> <u>were</u> difficult to press. This <u>typewriter</u> <u>typed</u> onto the underside of a piece of paper. Consequently, the <u>typist</u> <u>couldn't see</u> what was being typed. The odd <u>arrangement</u> of the letters on the first typewriter <u>is</u> still <u>used</u> on today's keyboards. In 1878, the <u>typewriter</u> <u>had</u> a shift key and lowercase letters. Then, in 1904, <u>Royal</u> <u>introduced</u> the first modern typewriter. Its <u>keys</u> <u>were</u> easier to press. In 1912, the first portable <u>typewriter</u> <u>was marketed</u>. Electric <u>typewriters</u> <u>were invented</u> in 1930. Modern <u>typewriters</u> with computer features eventually <u>replaced</u> older models.

GRAMMAR

GRAMMAR

OBJECTIVE

• To identify subjects, understood subjects, and verbs in sentences

Odd arrangement of letters on first typewriter still used today.
1878—typewriter had shift key and lowercase letters.
1904—Royal was first modern typewriter, keys easier to press.
First portable typewriter, 1912.
Electric typewriters invented 1930.
Modern typewriters have computer features.

▶ REVIEW B   **Identifying Subjects and Verbs**

Identify the <u>subject</u> and the <u>verb</u> in each of the following sentences. If the subject is understood, write *(You)*. Then underline the subject once and the verb twice.

1. <u>Bats</u>, most <u>birds</u>, and many <u>insects</u> <u>can fly</u>.
2. Other <u>animals</u> <u>can move</u> through the air without flying.
3. The <u>flying fish</u> <u>swims</u> fast and then <u>leaps</u> out of the water.
4. How <u>does</u> the <u>flying squirrel</u> <u>glide</u> from tree to tree?
5. There <u>are</u> <u>flaps</u> of skin between its legs.
6. How <u>do</u> <u>birds</u> <u>fly</u>?
7. Their <u>wings</u> <u>lift</u> and <u>push</u> them through the air.
8. <u>Look</u> carefully at an insect's wings.   **8. (You)**
9. <u>Most</u> <u>have</u> two sets of wings.
10. The <u>pair</u> in front <u>covers</u> the pair in back.

COMPLEMENTS Rules 16h–16k

OBJECTIVES

- To construct sentences from subjects, verbs, and complements
- To identify subjects, verbs, and complements
- To identify predicate nominatives and predicate adjectives ☞

16h

GRAMMAR

PICTURE THIS

While on a tour at the Delphi Museum in Greece, you enter a large room and see this life-size bronze statue of a young charioteer. A museum guide tells you that this statue, created in about 470 B.C., was originally part of a larger work that included a bronze chariot and four bronze horses. Write a postcard to a friend back home telling him or her about this statue and your reactions to it. Begin one sentence with *there* or *here*, include one question, and have at least one sentence in which the subject is understood.

Subject: *The Charioteer*, a
                  famous Greek
                  statue
Audience: a friend
Purpose: to comment on
                  a work of art

Complements

16h.   A *complement* is a word or group of words that completes the meaning of a predicate.

A group of words may have a subject and a verb and still not express a complete thought. Notice how the boldfaced words complete the meanings of the following sentences.

       S   V   C
That book is an **autobiography.**

PICTURE THIS

You may want to have students work in pairs during the evaluation and revision stage of this writing assignment. Have students use the following criteria for peer evaluation:

1. Did the writer use a warm, friendly tone?
2. Did the writer include his or her reactions to the statue?
3. Did the writer include at least one sentence beginning with *there* or *here*?
4. Did the writer ask one question?
5. Did the writer include a sentence with an understood subject?

       Remind students to offer positive suggestions to help the writer make any appropriate changes.

👁 VISUAL CONNECTIONS

Exploring the Subject. This life-size statue was once part of a larger work featuring the victor of a chariot race as he stood in his four-horse chariot. The proportions of the statue are exaggerated because it was designed to be viewed from below, with the chariot concealing the lower half of the statue. This is one of the earliest known statues of a charioteer.

GRAMMAR

Teacher's ResourceBank™
RESOURCES

COMPLEMENTS
- Subject Complements
- Direct Objects
- Indirect Objects

QUICK REMINDER

Write the following sentences on the chalkboard. Then ask students to identify the complement in each sentence.

1. Mary Ellen is a veterinarian.
2. She is ambitious.
3. She opened a clinic for small animals.
4. She gave us a tour of her animal hospital.

INTEGRATING THE LANGUAGE ARTS

Literature Link. Poets sometimes invert the usual subject-verb-complement order to maintain a poem's rhyme scheme or to emphasize a particular word by placing it at the end of a line. Have students read a poem that includes at least one such inversion. Possible poems include "The Forester" by Wilfrid Wilson Gibson, "I Wandered Lonely as a Cloud" by William Wordsworth, and "Ozymandias" by Percy Bysshe Shelley.

After students have read the poem, have them find any inversions of the usual subject-verb-complement order and discuss as a class what effect the poet achieves by inverting the word order.

   S   S   V   C
Both Eric and Bob felt **confident.**

   S   V   C   C
Sandra Cisneros writes **poetry** and **fiction.**

As you can see in the last example above, a complement may be a compound.

> **NOTE:** Every sentence has a basic framework called a *base.* In a sentence with no complement, the base is simply the subject and verb. In a sentence with a complement, the base includes the complement.

Complements can be found in both independent clauses and dependent clauses.

EXAMPLES   S   V   C
          Although he appeared **sluggish** at the start,

            S   V   C
          Ricardo won the **race.**

          S V   C   S   V
          Josie is an **engineer** who designs computer

          C
          hardware.

> ☞ REFERENCE NOTE: For a discussion of independent and dependent clauses, see Chapter 18.

> **NOTE:** Complements are never in prepositional phrases.

> EXAMPLES   Li Hua quoted the **poem.** [*Poem* is the complement.]
> Li Hua quoted from the **poem.** [*Poem* is part of the prepositional phrase *from the poem.*]

An adverb modifying a verb is not a complement. Only nouns, pronouns, and adjectives serve as complements.

EXAMPLES   **Lucy plays hard.** [*Hard* is an adverb, not a complement.]
                These pears are hard. [*Hard,* an adjective, is a complement.]

EXERCISE 11   **Writing Sentences with Subjects, Verbs, and Complements**

Construct sentences from the following sentence parts. Try to add more than only a word or two.

SUBJECT	VERB	COMPLEMENT
1. cyclists	planned	trip
2. musicians	performed	duet
3. speaker	looked	enthusiastic
4. dancer	tapped	rhythm
5. novel	is	suspenseful

GRAMMAR

EXERCISE 12 — Identifying Subjects, Verbs, and Complements

Identify the <u>subject</u> and the <u>verb</u> in each sentence in the following paragraph. Then identify the (complement) if there is one.

[1] A <u>hurricane</u> <u>is</u> a powerful (storm) that <u>can measure</u> two or three hundred (miles) in diameter. [2] Such <u>storms</u> <u>are</u> (notorious) for causing death and destruction. [3] To be classified as a hurricane, a <u>storm</u> <u>must have</u> (winds) of at least seventy-five miles per hour. [4] These <u>winds</u> <u>swirl</u> around the *eye*, an area of calm in the center of the storm. [5] *Wall clouds* <u>surround</u> the (eye) of a hurricane. [6] <u>It</u> <u>is</u> within these clouds that the strongest <u>winds</u> and heaviest <u>rain</u> <u>occur</u>. [7] The <u>winds</u> and <u>rain</u>, along with the force of the sea, often <u>produce</u> enormous (waves), called a *storm surge.* [8] In a surge like the one pictured here, <u>tides</u> <u>rise</u> several feet above normal. [9] Huge <u>waves</u> <u>produce</u> (floods) that <u>destroy</u> (life) and (property). [10] In fact, <u>90 percent</u> of hurricane-related deaths <u>result</u> from drowning in floods.

United States of America

Gulf of Mexico

Cuba

Hispaniola

Puerto Rico

Yucatan Peninsula

GRAMMAR

VISUAL CONNECTIONS
Ideas for Writing. Ask students to write poems or prose paragraphs that use extended metaphors to compare a storm to something else. Students' first sentences or lines should use the linking verb *be* and a predicate nominative to make a comparison. For example, "A storm is a child" or "The storm was an angry god." Encourage students to include vivid, unexpected, and expressive verbs, nouns, and adjectives to strengthen their comparisons.

LESS-ADVANCED STUDENTS

   Rule 16i in this segment states that a subject complement follows a linking verb. Some students, however, may not be able to identify linking verbs easily. You may want to give students the following list of commonly used linking verbs as a reference: *appear, be, become, feel, grow, look, remain, seem, smell, sound, stay, taste.*

⇄ A DIFFERENT APPROACH

Have students write paragraphs describing themselves to a foreign pen pal who has never met them. When they have finished their paragraphs, have students find all the subject complements in their writing and label them as predicate nominatives or predicate adjectives.

The Subject Complement

16i.   A *subject complement* is a noun, a pronoun, or an adjective that follows a linking verb. A subject complement identifies, describes, or explains the subject.

EXAMPLES   Lani is a soccer **player.** [*Player* identifies Lani.]
This could be **it.** [*It* identifies this.]
Roscoe seems **worried.** [*Worried* describes Roscoe.]

☞ REFERENCE NOTE: For more information about linking verbs, see pages 525–526.

   Remember that subject complements can appear in dependent clauses.

EXAMPLES   Although the watch is an **antique,** my aunt says that it is always **accurate.** [*Antique* identifies *watch* in the introductory adverb clause. *Accurate* describes *it* in the noun clause beginning with *that.*]

(1) A *predicate nominative* is a noun or a pronoun in the predicate that identifies or renames the subject of a sentence or a clause.

EXAMPLES   Some caterpillars become **butterflies.**
The winners should have been **they.**

(2) A *predicate adjective* is an adjective in the predicate that describes the subject of a sentence or a clause.

EXAMPLES   You look **happy.**
Norma appeared **calm.**

   Subject complements may be compound.

EXAMPLES   Our cats' names are **Wimpy** and **Henry.** [compound predicate nominative]
The yogurt tasted **sweet** and **creamy.** [compound predicate adjective]

NOTE: The subject complement may come before the subject of a sentence or a clause.

EXAMPLES   How **silly** that commercial is! [*Silly* is a predicate adjective describing *commercial.*]
Now we know what a fine **speaker** you are. [*Speaker* is a predicate nominative identifying *you.*]

GRAMMAR

EXERCISE 13 **Identifying Predicate Nominatives and Predicate Adjectives**

Identify the subject complement in each of the following sentences. Then, tell whether the complement is a <u>predicate nominative</u> or a <u>predicate adjective</u>. [Note: a sentence may have more than one subject complement.]

1. The last scene of the play is very <u>intense</u>.
2. Those two small birds are <u>finches</u>.
3. The music sounded <u>lively</u>.
4. It is <u>difficult</u> to choose a winner when each contestant's costume looks so <u>elegant</u>.
5. My goldfish Alonzo grows <u>larger</u> every day.
6. Andrea's report on digital recording is a highly detailed and technical <u>one</u>.
7. The setting of the story is a Spanish <u>castle</u> that looks <u>old</u> and <u>deserted</u>.
8. Your solution to this algebra problem is <u>clever</u>.
9. We felt <u>full</u> after we had eaten Thanksgiving dinner.
10. His entire story seems almost <u>unbelievable</u>.

EXERCISE 14 **Identifying Subjects, Verbs, and Subject Complements**

Each sentence in the following paragraph contains at least one subject complement. Identify each subject, verb, and subject complement. Make a chart like the following one, and fill in the correct words.

EXAMPLE [1] Although jazz is now popular all over the world, it was originally the music of African Americans.

	SUBJECT	VERB	SUBJECT COMPLEMENT
1.	*jazz*	*is*	*popular*
	it	*was*	*music*

[1] A typically American musical form, jazz was the sound of Louis Armstrong, "Count" Basie, Scott Joplin, and Ella Fitzgerald. [2] Created in the early twentieth century, jazz is a blend of elements from African and European music, but its irregular, or syncopated, rhythms are strictly African. [3] Early jazz was a combination of the cakewalk, a dance that was popular with many African Americans in the 1800s, and ragtime, which was mainly

GRAMMAR

LEP/ESL

General Strategies. English uses a subject-verb-object sentence structure. Other languages use subject-object-verb and verb-subject-object structures. For example, if you ask native Japanese, Korean, or Persian speakers "Whom did Tom call?" and they answer, "His friend called," they are probably trying to tell you that Tom called his friend. Consequently, some of your ESL students will need extra practice using the subject-verb-object sentence structure. Write subjects, verbs, and objects on separate strips of paper and have students tape the strips together to form sentences.

instrumental music. [4] After 1917, the future of jazz appeared bright when jazz phonograph records became popular. [5] People remain fascinated by jazz, perhaps because it sounds new each time it's played.

Objects

Objects are complements that do not refer to the subject. They follow action verbs rather than linking verbs.

EXAMPLES   The cat was chasing a **moth.**
Jeff's mother gave **him** some **grapes.**

☞ REFERENCE NOTE: For more information about action verbs, see pages 524–525.

Like subject complements, objects can be found in dependent clauses.

EXAMPLE   After we read the **story,** the teacher said that she would give **us** a **quiz** on it.

16j. A *direct object* is a noun or pronoun that directly receives the action of a verb or shows the result of the action. A direct object answers the question "What?" or "Whom?" after an action verb.

EXAMPLES   The mechanic fixed their **car.** [Fixed what? *Car.*]
She asked **them** to wait in the lobby. [Asked whom? *Them.*]

Verbs that express mental action, such as *study, dream,* and *understand,* are just as much action verbs as are verbs that express physical action, such as *push, leap,* and *stumble.*

EXAMPLE   Paco still **remembers** his first day of school. [Remembers what? *Day.*]

NOTE: Direct objects are never found in prepositional phrases.

EXAMPLES   Mom and I painted the **porch.** [*Porch* is the direct object.]
Mom and I painted on the **porch.** [*Porch* is part of the prepositional phrase *on the porch.*]

▶ EXERCISE 15 **Identifying Verbs and Their Direct Objects**

Identify the <u>verbs</u> and the <u>direct objects</u> in the following sentences.

1. I <u>borrowed</u> my parents' new <u>camera</u> recently.
2. First I <u>loaded</u> the <u>film</u> into the camera.
3. Then I <u>set</u> the shutter <u>speed</u>.
4. I <u>focused</u> the <u>camera</u> on a distant object.
5. I <u>could read</u> the shutter <u>speed</u> in the viewfinder.
6. A flashing red light <u>signals</u> an incorrect <u>setting</u>.
7. Slowly and carefully, I <u>pressed</u> the <u>button</u>.
8. I then <u>moved</u> the <u>film</u> forward for the next shot.
9. By the end of the day, I <u>had snapped</u> more than thirty-six <u>pictures</u>.
10. Unfortunately, the film processor <u>lost</u> my <u>roll</u> of film.

16k. An **_indirect object_** is a noun or pronoun that precedes the direct object and tells *to whom* or *for whom* (or *to what* or *for what*) the action of the verb is done.

DIRECT OBJECT   **Meli read her report.** [Read what? *Report.*]
INDIRECT OBJECT   **Meli read us her report.** [Read to whom? *Us.*]

If the word *to* or *for* is used in the sentence, the noun or pronoun following it is part of a prepositional phrase, not an indirect object.

EXAMPLES   **Jeff wrote me a note.** [*Me* is the indirect object.]
              Jeff wrote a note to me. [*Me* is part of the prepositional phrase *to me.*]

Both direct and indirect objects may be compound.

EXAMPLES   **Our family recycles glass and aluminum.** [compound direct object]
              The ski trip had given Lucia and me a wonderful vacation. [compound indirect object]

NOTE: Don't confuse adverbs in the predicate with complements.

EXAMPLES   **They turned right.** [*Right* is an adverb telling where.]
              You have the right to remain silent. [*Right* is a noun used as a direct object.]

MEETING
INDIVIDUAL
NEEDS

LESS-ADVANCED STUDENTS

     Write the following incomplete sentences on the chalkboard:

1. Baseball players throw ____.
2. The young artist painted a ____ on a building downtown.
3. Mario gives his ____ gifts on their birthdays.
4. A runner passes a ____ to another runner during a relay race.
5. Kim wrote the ____ to complain about air pollution in her city.

     Have students fill in each blank. Point out that the words they supply will serve as objects in the sentences. When students have filled in the blanks, you may also want to have them identify each object as either direct or indirect.

REVIEW C

OBJECTIVE

- To distinguish fragments from sentences and to identify the subjects, verbs, and complements of sentences

564 *The Sentence*

▶ EXERCISE 16 **Identifying Direct and Indirect Objects**

Identify the <u>direct objects</u> and <u>indirect objects</u> in the sentences in the following paragraph. Not all sentences contain both kinds of objects.

[1] Last summer, Leroy told <u>us</u> his <u>plans</u> for the future. [2] He wants a <u>place</u> on the U.S. swim team in the next Olympic games. [3] Of course, this goal demands <u>hours</u> of hard practice. [4] Every day, Leroy swims one hundred <u>laps</u> in the college pool and works out with weights for an hour. [5] Such intense training could have cost <u>him</u> his social <u>life</u>. [6] With his rigorous schedule, Leroy doesn't have much <u>time</u> to spend with friends. [7] However, we all understand and give <u>him</u> lots of <u>encouragement</u> and <u>support</u>. [8] But we can't teach <u>him</u> the fine <u>points</u> of competitive swimming. [9] His coach does <u>that</u>. [10] Working together, they can make Leroy's <u>dream</u> come true.

▶ EXERCISE 17 **Using Direct and Indirect Objects**

It's your first day working at a restaurant, and you've just taken this family's order. Because you want to be sure to get the order right, you take a minute in the kitchen to go over what each person wanted. Write five sentences that you might say to yourself to remember who should get what. In your sentences, use five direct objects and at least two indirect objects. For indirect objects, you could use pronouns or general terms such as *man* or *children*, or imagine that you know the people and use their names.

EXAMPLE **1. *Give Margot the squid and spinach appetizer.***

ANSWERS

Exercise 17

Sentences will vary. Here are some possibilities:

1. Mother ordered a hamburger without onions.
2. Emily needs extra dressing for her salad.
3. Give Dad the squash casserole.
4. Everyone ordered frozen yogurt after dinner.
5. Bring Peter an order of spaghetti.

SEGMENT 5 (pp. 565–569)
SENTENCES CLASSIFIED BY PURPOSE
Rule 16l

OBJECTIVES

- To classify sentences as declarative, imperative, interrogative, or exclamatory ☞

Sentences Classified by Purpose **565**

16l

 REVIEW C

Identifying Sentences and Fragments; Identifying Complements

Identify each of the following word groups as a *sentence* or a *fragment*. If a word group is a complete sentence, identify its <u>subject</u> and <u>verb</u>. If a sentence has a complement, label it as a *predicate adjective*, a *predicate nominative*, a *direct object*, or an *indirect object*.

1. <u>Has</u> the planning <u>committee</u> <u>announced</u> the date of the school carnival? **1.** sent.—d.o.
2. Perhaps next week. **2.** frag.   **3.** sent.—i.o./d.o.
3. <u>Linda</u> <u>gave</u> us a summary of her science project.
4. <u>It</u> <u>was</u> long and interesting. **4.** sent.—p.a./p.a.
5. Although it was well written. **5.** frag.
6. <u>Books</u> and <u>papers</u> <u>covered</u> the desk and <u>spilled</u> onto the floor. **6.** sent.—d.o.
7. <u>One</u> of those dogs <u>is</u> not very well trained. **7.** sent.—p.a.
8. <u>Ming Chin</u> <u>gave</u> the children a handful of oatmeal cookies. **8.** sent.—i.o./d.o.
9. <u>Kim</u>, <u>Juan</u>, and <u>Tracey</u> <u>were</u> winners at the track meet last Saturday. **9.** sent.—p.n.
10. How happy <u>they</u> <u>were</u>! **10.** sent.—p.a.

Sentences Classified by Purpose

16l. Sentences may be classified as *declarative, imperative, interrogative,* or *exclamatory.*

(1) A **declarative** sentence makes a statement. All declarative sentences are followed by periods.

EXAMPLES   Gwendolyn Brooks is the poet laureate of Chicago.
Although we were tired after working all day, we still wanted to go dancing.

(2) An **imperative** sentence gives a command or makes a request. Imperative sentences usually end with periods, but strong commands may end with exclamation points.

EXAMPLES   Pass the salt, please.
Speak softly.
Wait!

Teacher's ResourceBank™
RESOURCES

SENTENCES CLASSIFIED BY PURPOSE
- Classifying Sentences by Purpose

🦉 **QUICK REMINDER**
Write the names of the four types of sentences—*declarative, imperative, interrogative,* and *exclamatory*—on the chalkboard and have each student write one sentence of each type. You could then ask volunteers to read their sentences to the class.

565

• To write five expressive sentences that include at least one of each kind of sentence: declarative, imperative, interrogative, and exclamatory

LEP/ESL

Spanish. In written Spanish, interrogative and exclamatory sentences are introduced by inverted question marks and inverted exclamation points, respectively. Consequently, Spanish speakers might have trouble recognizing these types of sentences without the introductory marks. You may want to remind students that in English such marks are found only at the ends of sentences.

LEARNING STYLES

Auditory and Kinetic Learners. Have students practice dramatic readings of the four types of sentences. You could have students use the sentences in **Exercise 18** for their readings, or you may want to have them work in groups to create skits that include the four types of sentences.

566   *The Sentence*

(3) An ***interrogative*** sentence asks a question. Interrogative sentences are followed by question marks.

EXAMPLES   **Can you speak Spanish?**
What did you say?

(4) An ***exclamatory*** sentence expresses strong feeling. Exclamatory sentences are followed by exclamation points.

EXAMPLES   **What a beautiful day this is!**
How I enjoy autumn!

NOTE: Any sentence may be spoken in such a way that it is exclamatory. In this case, it should be followed by an exclamation point.

EXAMPLES   **This is inexcusable!** [Declarative becomes exclamatory.]
Stop the car! [Imperative becomes exclamatory.]
How could you say that! [Interrogative becomes exclamatory.]

REFERENCE NOTE: For a discussion of how sentences are classified by structure, see pages 610–611. For more on end marks of punctuation, see pages 789–792.

Classifying Sentences as Declarative, Imperative, Interrogative, or Exclamatory

EXERCISE 18

Classify each of the following sentences as *declarative*, *imperative*, *interrogative*, or *exclamatory*.

1. The loudspeakers in our living room are small yet powerful.   **1.** decl.
2. Turn down the sound!   **2.** imp. [*or* excl.]
3. Is that music or noise, Ramona?   **3.** int.
4. Listening to loud music every day can damage a person's hearing.   **4.** decl.   **5.** int.   **6.** decl.
5. How many watts does your amplifier produce?
6. Sound levels are measured in units called decibels.
7. Do you know that an increase of ten decibels represents a doubling in the sound level?   **7.** int.
8. Do not blast your sound system.   **8.** imp.
9. Keep it quiet!   **9.** imp. [*or* excl.]
10. Music played softly is relaxing.   **10.** decl.

Sentences Classified by Purpose **567**

 EXERCISE 19 **Using the Four Kinds of Sentences**

These colorful Tlingit totem poles stand in Saxman Indian Village in Ketchikan, Alaska. The Tlingits, who have lived in Alaska for hundreds of years, are well known for their carving skills, as well as their sense of humor. Yes, that's a short-legged Abraham Lincoln atop one of the poles! Write five sentences expressing your reactions to these poles. Use at least one of each kind of sentence: *declarative, imperative, interrogative,* and *exclamatory.*

EXAMPLE **1.** *What a surprise to see Abraham Lincoln on a totem pole!*

GRAMMAR

ANSWERS
Exercise 19

Sentences will vary. Here are some sample sentences:

1. What a surprise to see Abraham Lincoln on a totem pole! (exclamatory)

2. Go to Alaska to see these fascinating totem poles. (imperative)

3. Have you ever seen this type of artwork before? (interrogative)

4. I am impressed by the craftsmanship it takes to create them. (declarative)

5. Which is your favorite? (interrogative)

 WRITING APPLICATION
Ask students to brainstorm possible opening lines that will catch their readers' attention. Remind students that the flow of ideas is the most important element of brainstorming. Students should generate as many ideas as possible and wait until later to evaluate their work. For an example of persuasive writing, refer students to **A Student Model** on page 356.

CRITICAL THINKING
Evaluation
Work with students to develop criteria for evaluating their opening lines. Then model the process of evaluating an opening line using the criteria the class has developed. You could evaluate the opening line of **A Student Model** on page 356.

 WRITING APPLICATION

Catching a Reader's Interest with Appropriately Varied Sentences

In fishing, you need the right bait to catch the kind of fish you want. In writing, you need the right bait to catch your reader's interest. Your opening sentence is this bait.

OPENER 1: I think we should have a party.
OPENER 2: Shouldn't we have a party?
OPENER 3: Let's party!

These opening sentences contain similar information. Which of them would interest you to read further? Why?

567

REVIEWS D and E

OBJECTIVES

- To define the parts of a sentence and to give an example of each
- To identify subjects, verbs, predicate adjectives, predicate nominatives, direct objects, and indirect objects in a passage

ANSWERS
Review D

Responses will vary. Each response should include an example and the following information:

1. A sentence is a group of words that contains a subject and a verb and expresses a complete thought.

2. A complete subject names the person or thing spoken about in the rest of a sentence.

3. A verb is the main word or group of words in a complete predicate.

4. A verb phrase consists of a verb and one or more helping verbs.

5. A complete predicate is the part of a sentence that says something about the subject.

6. A simple subject is the main word or group of words in a complete subject.

7. A subject complement is a noun, a pronoun, or an adjective that follows a linking verb. It identifies, describes, or explains the subject.

8. A direct object is a noun or pronoun that directly receives the action of a verb or shows the result of the action.

9. An understood subject is the unstated subject, *you,* of a request or command.

10. An indirect object is a noun or a pronoun that precedes the direct object and tells to whom or for whom (or to what or for what) the action of the verb is done.

568

▶ WRITING ACTIVITY

Your neighborhood Residents' Council would like to sponsor a dance for the teenagers on your block. However, the council is not sure what kind of dances teens would like. You've decided to write a short letter to the council to give your opinion. Write some different opening sentences for your letter. Select the one that is the best "bait" for your audience, and then write a short letter.

Prewriting Decide how you feel about this issue. Then, jot down a few notes about why having the dance would or would not be a good idea. Next, write some different opening sentences. Choose the opener that you think will be the most interesting and effective.

Writing As you write your letter, be sure to refer often to your prewriting notes.

Evaluating and Revising Ask an adult you know to listen to your letter. Does he or she think your opening sentence is interesting? Does he or she find your letter persuasive? Revise any sentences or sections that aren't clear.

Proofreading Imagine that you are a council member, and read through your letter. Are there any grammar, punctuation, or spelling errors? Does the letter follow the proper business letter form? (See pages 941–943 for the correct forms of business letters.) Make all needed corrections, and then write a clean, final copy of your letter.

▶ REVIEW D   **Understanding the Parts of a Sentence**

In your own words, define each of the following terms, and give an example to illustrate it.

1. a sentence
2. a complete subject
3. a verb (simple predicate)
4. a verb phrase
5. a complete predicate
6. a simple subject
7. a subject complement
8. a direct object
9. an understood subject
10. an indirect object

REVIEW E

Identifying Subjects, Verbs, and Complements

Identify each of the italicized words in the following passage as a _subject_, a _verb_, a _predicate adjective_, a _predicate nominative_, a _direct object_, or an _indirect object_.

The Great Pyramid of Khufu (Cheops) is [1] *one* of the wonders of the ancient world. [2] *It* was once encased with blocks of polished limestone. However, [3] *weather and thievery* [4] *have combined* to destroy the original structure. As you [5] *can see*, the pyramid [6] *looks* [7] *weather-beaten*. Still, it is an impressive [8] *sight*.

Hundreds of years ago, one invading Arab [9] *ruler* decided to rob the tomb of Khufu. With many workers at his disposal, he gave the [10] *men* his [11] *instructions*. The workers [12] *hacked* through the incredibly hard solid blocks of granite. Unexpectedly, [13] *they* broke into a tunnel. Imagine their [14] *excitement*! All too soon, however, they [15] *discovered* an enormous [16] *plug* of granite blocking their way. They cut around the plug and finally reached the inner [17] *chamber*.

Strangely enough, there was no [18] *gold*. No vast treasures [19] *sparkled* under the light of the torches. The tomb [20] *had* probably *been robbed* many centuries earlier by Egyptians familiar with its secret entrances.

1. p.n.
2. s.
3. s.
4. v.
5. v.
6. v. 7. p.a. 8. p.n.
9. s.
10. i.o.
11. d.o.
12. v.
13. s.
14. d.o.
15. v.
16. d.o.
17. d.o.
18. s.
19. v.
20. v.

GRAMMAR

GRAMMAR

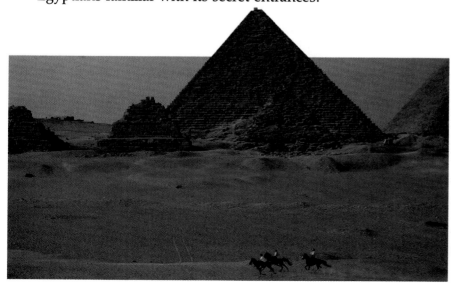

VISUAL CONNECTIONS
Exploring the Subject. The Great Pyramid of Khufu is said to be the largest building ever built. It covers over thirteen acres and contains approximately 2,300,000 blocks of stone that weigh an average of two and one-half tons each. It is estimated that it would have taken 100,000 people working constantly for twenty years to build the pyramid.

OBJECTIVES

- To identify subjects, verbs, predicate adjectives, predicate nominatives, direct objects, and indirect objects in sentences

Review: Posttest 1

A. Identifying Subjects, Verbs, and Complements

Identify each of the <u>italicized words</u> in the following sentences as a <u>subject</u>, a <u>verb</u>, a <u>predicate adjective</u>, a <u>predicate nominative</u>, a <u>direct object</u>, or an <u>indirect object</u>.

1. Have *you* ever met a robot?   **1.** s.
2. In the field of robotics, scientists have built vastly complex *robots*.   **2.** d.o.
3. Today these machines *are put* to work in factories, laboratories, and outer space.   **3.** v.
4. How were these complex *machines* first used?   **4.** s.
5. There are a *number* of interesting early examples of robots at work.   **5.** s.
6. One of the first robots was a mechanical *figure* in a clock tower.   **6.** p.n.
7. It raised a hammer and struck a *bell* every hour.   **7.** d.o.
8. At the 1939 New York World's Fair, Elektro and Sparko were popular *attractions*.   **8.** p.n.
9. Elektro was *tall*, more than seven feet high.   **9.** p.a.
10. Electric motors gave *Elektro* power for a variety of amazing tricks.   **10.** i.o.
11. Sparko was Elektro's *dog*.   **11.** p.n.
12. Sparko *could bark* and even *wag* his tail.   **12.** v.
13. Today, *some* of the simplest robots are drones in research laboratories.   **13.** s.
14. Basically, drones are *extensions* of the human arm.   **14.** p.n.
15. They can be *useful* in many different ways.   **15.** p.a.

B. Classifying Sentences as Declarative, Interrogative, Imperative, or Exclamatory

Classify each of the following sentences as *declarative*, *interrogative*, *imperative*, or *exclamatory*. Then give the proper end punctuation.

16. Can you picture a robot twenty-five feet tall**?**   **16.** int.
17. Step up and say hello to Beetle⊙   **17.** imp.

18. Perhaps you have already heard of CAM, an even more advanced robot. **18.** decl.
19. It can travel on long legs across rough terrain as rapidly as thirty-five miles per hour. **19.** decl.
20. How much it looks like a science fiction creature! **20.** excl.

Review: Posttest 2

Writing Sentences

Write sentences according to the following guidelines. Underline the subject once and the verb twice in each sentence. If the subject is understood, write *(You)*.

EXAMPLE   **1.** a sentence with a direct object
               1. *(You) Have another glass of milk.*

1. a declarative sentence with a verb phrase
2. a sentence beginning with *There*
3. an interrogative sentence
4. an exclamatory sentence
5. an imperative sentence
6. a sentence with a compound subject
7. a sentence with a predicate nominative
8. a sentence with a compound direct object and an indirect object
9. a sentence with a predicate adjective
10. a sentence with a compound verb

GRAMMAR

GRAMMAR

ANSWERS
Review: Posttest 2

Sentences will vary. Here are some possibilities:

1. I would have planted more trees on Earth Day if I had planned ahead.
2. There are many types of plants.
3. Have you studied about the plant life on our planet?
4. Plants are incredibly interesting!
5. (You) Go to the library and read about what types of plants grow in the world.
6. Eucalyptuses and tree ferns can be found in abundance in Australia's forests.
7. The mula mula is a plant.
8. The forest provides scientists fascinating plants and ecosystems to study.
9. The forest vegetation is lush in tropical regions.
10. The vegetation grows quickly and forms a series of distinct layers of trees of differing heights.

GRAMMAR

CHAPTER OVERVIEW

This chapter begins with a definition of prepositional phrases and a description of how these phrases are used. Then the different verbals are presented. The final segment of information concerns appositives and appositive phrases.

Including phrases to improve writing occurs most often during the revising stage of the writing process. In this chapter, students are given an opportunity to practice using prepositional phrases in the **Writing Application.**

USING THE DIAGNOSTIC TEST

The **Diagnostic Test** contains two parts. **Part A** focuses on identifying prepositional, participial, gerund, infinitive, and appositive phrases in sentences. **Part B** asks students to identify these types of phrases in a paragraph.

You may want to use the results of this test to determine whether your students have already mastered prepositional phrases or whether they need to study the related material in this chapter.

GRAMMAR

17 THE PHRASE

Prepositional, Verbal, and Appositive Phrases

Diagnostic Test

A. Identifying Phrases in Sentences

Identify each <u>italicized phrase</u> in the following sentences as *prepositional, participial, gerund, infinitive,* or *appositive.*

1. The sundial was one of the first instruments used for *telling time*.   **1.** ger.
2. *Regarded chiefly as garden ornaments,* sundials are still used in some areas *to tell time*.   **2.** part./inf.
3. The shadow-casting object *on a sundial* is called a gnomon.   **3.** prep.
4. Forerunners of the sundial include poles or upright stones *used as gnomons by early humans*.   **4.** part.
5. *To improve the accuracy of the sundial,* the gnomon was set directly parallel to the earth's axis.   **5.** inf.
6. The development of trigonometry permitted more precise calculations *in the construction* of sundials.   **6.** prep.
7. For everyday use, *owning a watch* has obvious advantages over *using a sundial*.   **7.** ger./ger.

8. *In the past*, sundials were used *to set and check the accuracy of watches*.   **8.** prep./inf.
9. The heliochronometer, *a sundial of great precision*, was used until 1900 *to set the watches of French railway workers*.   **9.** app./inf.
10. The difference *between solar time and clock time* is correlated by the use of tables *showing daily variations in sun time*.   **10.** prep./part.

B. Identifying Phrases in a Paragraph

Identify each <u>italicized phrase</u> in the following paragraph as *prepositional, participial, gerund, infinitive,* or *appositive.*

[11] A sundial is not difficult *to make with simple materials*. **[12]** First find a stick *to use as a gnomon*. **[13]** At high noon, put the stick in the ground, *tilting it slightly northward*. **[14]** *To mark the first hour*, place a pebble at the tip of the shadow made by the stick. **[15]** An hour later put another pebble at the tip *of the shadow*. **[16]** Continue this process *throughout the afternoon*. **[17]** *Starting the next morning*, repeat the hourly process. **[18]** Be sure *to place the last pebble at high noon*. **[19]** Observing the completed sundial, you will note that the hour markers, *the pebbles*, are not equidistant. **[20]** The *uneven spacing of the markers* demonstrates that shadows move faster in the morning and the evening than during the middle of the day.

11. inf.
12. inf.
13. part.
14. inf.
15. prep.
16. prep.
17. part.
18. inf.
19. app.
20. ger.

17a. A *phrase* is a group of related words that is used as a single part of speech and does not contain both a verb and its subject.

EXAMPLES   **should have waited** [verb phrase; no subject]
for you and her [prepositional phrase; no subject or verb]

A group of words that has both a subject and a verb is not a phrase.

EXAMPLES   **They will be here soon.** [*They* is the subject of *will be*.]
after she leaves [*She* is the subject of *leaves*.]

SEGMENT 2 *(pp. 574–579)*

PREPOSITIONAL PHRASES Rules 17a–17e

OBJECTIVES

- To identify prepositional phrases used as adjectives and the words they modify
- To identify prepositional phrases used as adverbs, the words they modify, and the parts of speech of the words modified

GRAMMAR

GRAMMAR

QUICK REMINDER

Write the following sentences on the chalkboard. Then have students identify the prepositional phrases and the words they modify.

1. The softball team travels by bus. [by bus — travels]
2. The boy with the football is Carlos. [with the football — boy]
3. She baby-sits for spending money. [for spending money — baby-sits]

Tell students that a prepositional phrase begins with a preposition, ends with a noun or pronoun that is the object of the preposition, modifies one or more other words in the sentence, and does not contain a verb or subject.

---

574   *The Phrase*

👉 **REFERENCE NOTE:** A group of words that has both a subject and a verb is called a *clause.* Clauses are discussed in Chapter 18.

Prepositional Phrases

17b.   A *prepositional phrase* is a group of words beginning with a preposition and ending with a noun or a pronoun.

EXAMPLES   The woman **with the helmet** is a motorcyclist.
The cashier gave the change **to me.**

NOTE: Don't confuse the common preposition *to* with the *to* that is the sign of the infinitive form of a verb: *to watch, to learn, to drive.* For more on infinitives, see pages 586–588.

17c.   The noun or pronoun that ends a prepositional phrase is the *object* of the preposition that begins the phrase.

PREPOSITIONAL PHRASE	PREPOSITION	OBJECT
before the second stoplight	before	stoplight
along the highway	along	highway
according to him	according to	him

👉 **REFERENCE NOTE:** For a list of commonly used prepositions, see page 535.

A preposition may have a compound object.

EXAMPLES   near **forests** and **rivers**
despite the **rain, snow,** and **ice**

Adjective Phrases

17d.   A prepositional phrase that modifies a noun or a pronoun is an *adjective phrase.*

**17
b–d**

EXAMPLES **The cottages by the lake are quite picturesque.** [The adjective phrase *by the lake* modifies the noun *cottages.*]

No one in the class has seen the movie yet. [The adjective phrase *in the class* modifies the pronoun *no one.*]

Two or more adjective phrases may modify the same noun or pronoun.

EXAMPLE **The picture of their candidate in today's newspaper is not at all flattering.** [The two adjective phrases *of their candidate* and *in today's newspaper* both modify the same noun, *picture.*]

An adjective phrase may also modify the object of another prepositional phrase.

EXAMPLE **The coconut palms in the park near the bay were planted a long time ago.** [*Near the bay* modifies *park,* the object of the preposition *in.*]

NOTE: Unlike single-word adjectives, adjective phrases always follow the noun or pronoun they modify.

EXERCISE 1 **Identifying Adjective Phrases**

Identify the <u>adjective phrases</u> in each of the following sentences. After each phrase, give the <u>word that the phrase modifies</u>.

EXAMPLE **1. Julius Caesar was one of the most successful generals in ancient Rome.**
     1. *of the most successful generals—one*
        in ancient Rome—generals

1. Roman roads were one <u>reason</u> <u>for Caesar's military successes</u>.
2. The <u>roads</u> <u>of ancient Rome</u> linked the far <u>corners</u> <u>of the empire</u>.
3. Large <u>blocks</u> <u>of hard stone</u> provided a sound <u>foundation</u> <u>for most major routes</u>.
4. Caesar's <u>interest</u> <u>in military roads</u> showed his <u>understanding</u> <u>of the importance</u> <u>of communication</u>.
5. Close <u>communication</u> <u>among the empire's provinces</u> strengthened the <u>power</u> <u>of the Roman rulers</u>.

**MEETING
INDIVIDUAL
NEEDS**

LEP/ESL

Spanish. English prepositions are often difficult to understand because they do not correspond to Spanish usage. To reinforce the correct use of prepositional phrases, place students in pairs and give each student a set of pictures, such as cartoons. Tell students not to look at each other's pictures. Each set (the number of pictures can vary) should have only one picture that exactly matches one in the partner's set. Tell students to ask and answer questions by using prepositions that describe their pictures. [Where are Snoopy and Charlie Brown? Snoopy is lying on his doghouse, and Charlie Brown is standing in front of it.] Have students continue until they decide which picture is the same in both sets.

LESS-ADVANCED STUDENTS

Try having students find prepositional phrases in sources that they find enjoyable to read, such as their journals, books, or magazines.

First, you may want to set a time limit or require a specified number of phrases to be found. Then students can write these phrases and also be prepared to tell how they are used.

INTEGRATING THE LANGUAGE ARTS

Literature Link. Refer to a story such as Bernard Malamud's "The First Seven Years" and direct students' attention to the paragraphs of dialogue that contain dialect. Identify any unusual sentences and explain that these sentences are examples of using prepositional phrases in an unfamiliar syntactical order. Have students rewrite these sentences as they might say them. Ask students how many of their revisions required the use of a preposition.

ANSWERS
Exercise 2

1. On Halloween — heard — verb; from the abandoned house next door — come — verb

2. inside the house — searched — verb; from the attic — searched — verb; to the basement — searched — verb

3. In the basement — found — verb

4. for food — were crying — verb

5. by them — had been made — verb

6. in the corner — found — verb; in it — placed — verb

7. with their temporary home — happy — adjective

8. to our house — took — verb

9. with an old towel — lined — verb; in the kitchen — set — verb

10. from our house — come — verb; at all hours — come — verb; of the night and day — hours — adverb

576

Adverb Phrases

17e. A prepositional phrase that modifies a verb, an adjective, or another adverb is an *adverb phrase.*

EXAMPLES   The mole burrowed **under the lawn.** [The adverb phrase *under the lawn* modifies the verb *burrowed.*]

Althea Gibson was graceful **on the tennis court.** [The adverb phrase *on the tennis court* modifies the adjective *graceful.*]

The storm lasted late **into the night.** [The adverb phrase *into the night* modifies the adverb *late.*]

Adverb phrases tell *when, where, why, how,* or *to what extent.*

EXAMPLES   The town grew quiet **after the storm.** [*when*]
He glanced **out the window.** [*where*]
Most street musicians play **for tips.** [*why*]
This summer we're going **by car.** [*how*]
She won the game **by two points.** [*to what extent*]

Adverb phrases may come before or after the words they modify, and more than one adverb phrase may modify the same word.

EXAMPLE   **In the first inning** she pitched **with great control.** [*In the first inning* tells *when* she pitched, and *with great control* tells *how* she pitched.]

 EXERCISE 2   **Identifying Adverb Phrases**

Identify each adverb phrase in the following sentences. Then give the word it modifies and the part of speech of that word.

[1] On Halloween, Dad and I heard eerie sounds come from the abandoned house next door. [2] We searched inside the house from the attic to the basement. [3] In the basement we found two stray kittens. [4] They were crying for food. [5] The strange noises we'd heard had been made by them. [6] I found an empty box in the corner and gently placed the kittens in it. [7] They seemed happy

REVIEW A

OBJECTIVES

- To complete sentences by adding adverb or adjective phrases
- To classify, as adjective or adverb phrases, the prepositional phrases used to complete sentences

with their temporary home. [8] Then we took the kittens back to our house. [9] We lined the box with an old towel and set it in the kitchen. [10] Now the eerie sounds come from our house at all hours of the night and day.

REVIEW A   **Completing Sentences by Inserting Prepositional Phrases**

Provide a prepositional phrase for the blank in each sentence. After the sentence, identify each phrase as an *adjective phrase* or an *adverb phrase*.

EXAMPLE   **1.** _____ Mrs. Bowen reads the newspaper.
   1. *In the evening Mrs. Bowen reads the newspaper.—adverb phrase*

1. _____ the children played hopscotch.
2. I saw a spider _____.
3. We planned a drive _____.
4. Her team played _____.
5. The sky divers jumped fearlessly _____.
6. Hundreds _____ stared.
7. _____ the cyclists unpacked their lunch.
8. There _____ winds a narrow road.
9. This movie runs _____.
10. _____ the dancers swayed with the music.

EXERCISE 3   **Using Prepositional Phrases**

You are the guest director for an episode of *The Cosby Show*. It's your chance to tell Bill Cosby and the other

ANSWERS
Review A

Answers may vary. Here are some possibilities:

1. During recess—adverb phrase; For fun—adverb phrase
2. with yellow spots—adjective phrase; in science class—adverb phrase
3. for Saturday—adverb phrase; along the riverfront—adjective phrase
4. by the rules—adverb phrase; after school—adverb phrase
5. out of the plane—adverb phrase; toward the earth—adverb phrase
6. of people—adjective phrase; within view—adjective phrase
7. On the picnic tables—adverb phrase; Without a word—adverb phrase
8. along the lake—adverb phrase; behind the barn—adverb phrase
9. past two hours—adverb phrase; until noon—adverb phrase
10. Around the dance floor—adverb phrase; During the waltz—adverb phrase

ANSWERS
Exercise 3

Responses will vary, but all responses should relate to the scene shown and should include at least two adjective phrases and three adverb phrases.

GRAMMAR

GRAMMAR

WRITING APPLICATION
The writing assignment offers students a chance to share their knowledge of performing a useful task, while learning the importance of clear directions. It also gives practice in sequencing.

CRITICAL THINKING
Analysis
Remind students that they will have to analyze their intended audiences when writing directions. For instance, if the directions are about how to change a tire, they cannot assume that the reader is familiar with lug nuts, and they will need to define the term to help the reader understand.

PREWRITING
To help your students get started, try brainstorming topics together and write these on the chalkboard. Then think of as many prepositional phrases as possible that relate to a chosen topic. A good subject to use is preparing a favorite food. For example, some phrases that might accompany making lasagna would be *in the water, on the noodles,* and *under the mushrooms.*

WRITING APPLICATION
OBJECTIVE
• To write directions that use prepositional phrases

578 *The Phrase*

actors in his television family what to do. Write five sentences giving directions for what should happen next in the scene on the previous page. If you are unfamiliar with *The Cosby Show,* imagine that these actors are characters in one of your favorite TV shows. Make up names and roles for them. In your sentences, use at least two adjective phrases and three adverb phrases, and underline each of these phrases.

EXAMPLE **1.** *Theo should run into the kitchen and start stacking the dishes in the sink.*

WRITING APPLICATION

Using Prepositional Phrases to Write Clear Directions

It's useful to be able to explain how to do something. By giving readers a detailed and accurate explanation, you help them duplicate your method and results. Information given in prepositional phrases can make your instructions clearer and more helpful.

HELPFUL To set the dye, rinse your new red shirt thoroughly.
MORE HELPFUL To set the dye, rinse your new red shirt thoroughly in a basin of cool water with one quarter cup vinegar.

▶ **WRITING ACTIVITY**
A friend has asked you to explain how to perform a useful task that you are good at. Write a paragraph explaining exactly how to accomplish the task. Use at least five prepositional phrases in explaining the process.

Prewriting First, think of something that you know how to do and can explain. Examples are how to change a tire, how to make gift-wrapping paper, and how to serve a tennis ball. When you have chosen a topic, make a simple outline of the necessary steps in the process.

SEGMENT 3 *(pp. 579–584)*

THE PARTICIPLE AND PARTICIPIAL PHRASE Rules 17f, 17g

OBJECTIVES

- To identify present and past participles and the words they modify
- To revise sentences by adding participles
- To identify participial phrases and the words they modify

 Writing Remember to refer frequently to your outline as you write your first draft.

 Evaluating and Revising Read your directions to a classmate to find out if the information is clear and detailed enough. Revise any steps that your listener finds confusing. Be sure that you have used a combination of adverb and adjective phrases in your directions.

 Proofreading and Publishing Read your directions carefully, step by step. Pay special attention to the correct placement of prepositional phrases and to the clear use of verb tenses to show when each step should occur. Members of your class may want to share their knowledge and abilities by putting together a how-to book to share with other students in your school.

Verbals and Verbal Phrases

Verbals are forms of verbs that are used as adjectives, nouns, or adverbs. They may be modified by adverbs and adjectives and may have complements.

The three kinds of verbals are *participles, gerunds,* and *infinitives.*

 REFERENCE NOTE: For a discussion of verbal phrases as sentence fragments, see pages 449–450. For more on verbals as dangling modifiers, see page 728.

The Participle

17f. A *participle* is a verb form that can be used as an adjective.

EXAMPLES The **simmering** soup smelled delicious. [*Simmering,* formed from the verb *simmer,* modifies the noun *soup.*]

 INTEGRATING THE LANGUAGE ARTS

Technology Link. If available, have students use a computer to write the paragraph. After a classmate evaluates the work, as described in the **Writing Activity,** students might identify all the prepositional phrases by making them either italic or boldfaced. This will make your assessment of the assignment less time-consuming, and it will show that students can identify prepositional phrases.

Teacher's ResourceBank™

RESOURCES

THE PARTICIPLE AND PARTICIPIAL PHRASE
- Participles and Participial Phrases

QUICK REMINDER
Write the following pair of sentences on the chalkboard:

1. The roses were blooming and looked beautiful.
2. The blooming roses looked beautiful.

Ask students how the use of *blooming* differs in the two sentences. [In the first sentence, it acts as a verb; in the second, it acts as an adjective.] Challenge the class to create another pair of sentences that illustrates this difference.

LEP/ESL

General Strategies. Students often have problems using participles ending in *–ing* and *–ed* as adjectives, especially those formed from the emotive verbs such as *amuse, bother, interest,* or *surprise.* This results in sentences such as "I am interesting in computers." Tell students that the *–ed* form acts as a verb, as in "I am interested in computers." The *–ing* form acts as an adjective, as in "Computers are interesting." You may want to follow up with a cloze passage where students can choose the *–ed* or the *–ing* form.

LESS-ADVANCED STUDENTS

Verbals and verbal phrases may be too difficult for some students. To give students extra practice on participles, hand out pages from a newspaper and have students circle the participles on the pages. Ask students to identify the participles and have them draw a box around the modified words.

A **chipped** fingernail can be annoying. [*Chipped,* formed from the verb *chip,* modifies the noun *fingernail.*]

There are two kinds of participles: *present participles* and *past participles.*

(1) *Present participles* end in *–ing.*

EXAMPLES   **The smiling graduates posed for the photographer.** [The present participle *smiling* modifies the noun *graduates.*]

  Checking the weather forecast, the captain changed course. [The present participle *checking* modifies the noun *captain.*]

A present participle can't be used alone as a verb, but it can be combined with a helping verb to form a verb phrase.

EXAMPLES   **The graduates were smiling.**
  The captain is checking the weather forecast.

When a present participle is used in a verb phrase, it is part of the verb and is not a verbal used as an adjective.

(2) Most *past participles* end in *–d* or *–ed.* A few are formed irregularly.

EXAMPLES   **Discovered by the guard, the startled burglar was led away.** [The past participles *discovered* and *startled* modify the noun *burglar.*]

  Hidden under the front porch, the toy truck was safely out of the rain. [The past participle *hidden* modifies the noun *truck.*]

Like a present participle, a past participle can be part of a verb phrase. When used in a verb phrase, a past participle is part of the verb and is not a verbal used as an adjective.

EXAMPLES   **The burglar was startled when he was discovered by the guard.**
  Why has Jonathan hidden his toy truck under the front porch?

☞ REFERENCE NOTE: For more on verb phrases, see pages 527 and 548.

▶ EXERCISE 4   Identifying Participles

Identify the present participles and past participles used as adjectives in the following sentences. (Some sentences contain more than one participle.) Give the noun or pronoun each participle modifies. Remember not to confuse participles used as verbals with participles used as part of a verb phrase.

EXAMPLE   **1.** We have been studying one of the most feared
            animals in the sea—the killer whale.
          1. *feared—animals*

1. Killer whales, long known as wolves of the sea, are not nearly as vicious as many people have thought.
2. Seeking to test the supposedly ferocious nature of the killer whale, scientists studied the whales' behavior.
3. After extensive study, scientists discovered that there is no proven case of an attack on a human by a killer whale.
4. In fact, scientists working with killer whales have confirmed that their charges are intelligent and gentle.
5. Gathered together in Johnstone Strait, a narrow channel between Vancouver Island and British Columbia in Canada, killer whales spend the summer and fall in large family groups.
6. Choosing this spot to observe the mammals, researchers were able to identify more than one hundred whales.
7. The team of scientists, noting the unique shape of each whale's dorsal fin, named each whale in order to keep more accurate records.
8. Impressed by the long life span of killer whales, scientists have estimated that males may live fifty years and females may survive a century.
9. Cruising in groups called pods, killer whales are highly social animals.
10. During the summer and fall in Johnstone Strait, many pods gather, splashing and playing in "superpods."

GRAMMAR

COMMON ERROR

Problem. Misplaced modifiers, or dangling participles, as they are also called, often appear in writing.

Solution. Suggest that students circle the modified word and place the participial phrase next to it. They can then break down these sentences and ask questions such as "What word does this phrase describe?"

A DIFFERENT APPROACH

An oral game can reinforce knowledge of participles and give students practice in speaking before the class in an informal atmosphere. Divide the class into two teams, having a person on each team keep score. Give a verb and tell the player to use it either as a participle or in a verb phrase. The player should repeat the participle and use it correctly in a sentence.

If a player succeeds, that student's team scores a point; if the participle is not used as you directed, a member of the opposing team takes a turn.

GRAMMAR

CRITICAL THINKING
Evaluation

Try having your students evaluate each other's participial phrases.

First, students should use **Exercise 5** and replace the suggested word with a synonym that is a participle. Next, have them exchange their sentences with a partner, who will then determine whether the new participle is a better choice than the original word. This can be done on a separate sheet of paper if necessary. The partners should be prepared to discuss their reasoning with the author of the sentences.

By altering this exercise, students will have further practice in revision, while also continuing their work with participles.

 EXERCISE 5

Revising Sentences by Adding Participles

Each of the following sentences has a participle in parentheses after it. Revise each sentence by inserting the participle next to the noun it best modifies.

EXAMPLE   1. We collected funds for the restoration of the building. (*damaged*)
            1. *We collected funds for the restoration of the damaged building.*

1. The space shuttle was greeted with loud cheers. (*returning*)
2. The committee selected three television shows for their educational value. (*nominating*)
3. My sister was in the kitchen and did not hear the doorbell. (*ringing*)
4. The carpenter is supposed to show us how to fix this chair. (*broken*)
5. In 1949, Luis Muñoz Marín became Puerto Rico's first governor. (*elected*)
6. The stream crosses the farmer's land at three places. (*winding*)
7. We handed the envelope to the mail carrier. (*crumpled*)
8. This book includes many interesting facts about dinosaurs. (*illustrated*)
9. The Douglas fir behind our house has become a haven for several small creatures. (*fallen*)
10. The plane narrowly missed a radio antenna. (*circling*)

The Participial Phrase

 17g. A *participial phrase* consists of a participle and any complements or modifiers it may have. The entire participial phrase acts as an adjective.

In each of the following sentences, an arrow connects the participial phrase with the noun or pronoun the phrase modifies.

EXAMPLES **Climbing the tree,** the monkey disappeared into the branches. [participle *climbing* with object *tree*]

I heard him **whispering to his friend.** [participle *whispering* with prepositional phrase modifier *to his friend*]

We watched the storm **blowing eastward.** [participle *blowing* with adverb modifier *eastward*]

Voted back into office, the mayor thanked her supporters. [participle *Voted* with adverb modifier *back* and prepositional phrase modifier *into office.*]

The concert **scheduled for tomorrow at the park** has been postponed until next week. [participle *scheduled* with two prepositional phrase modifiers: *for tomorrow* and *at the park*]

 REFERENCE NOTE: For information on the correct placement of participial phrases near the words they modify, see pages 464 and 728–730. See pages 797–800 for the punctuation of participial phrases.

EXERCISE 6 **Identifying Participial Phrases**

Identify each <u>participial phrase</u> in the following sentences. Then give the <u>noun or pronoun modified by the phrase</u>.

[1] <u>Hoping to be the first to reach the South Pole</u>, the British <u>explorer</u> Robert Scott (back row, center, in the photograph) took these four men with him on his final dash to

 TIMESAVER
Try concentrating on just the second part of **Exercise 6** to make your grading simpler. Have the students list the phrases in one numbered column and the noun or pronoun in a second numbered column. You can scan the noun or pronoun list, since it is easier to check one word.

VISUAL CONNECTIONS
Exploring the Subject. Students might be interested in knowing that it was late in 1910 when Robert Scott first left New Zealand for the South Pole in the ship *Terra Nova*. The party reached Cape Evans on Ross Island, set up headquarters, and started out over the ice in October, 1911.

Their bodies were found in a tent, along with all the records and diaries the men had kept. Scott's journal ended with an appeal for help for his family and for the families of his companions, knowing that he and his men would not survive the journey.

Ideas for Writing. You may wish to use this photograph to inspire a research project, perhaps in conjunction with a social studies class, in which students research and report on famous explorers or expeditions.

SEGMENT 4 *(pp. 584–586)*

THE GERUND AND GERUND PHRASE

Rules 17h, 17i

OBJECTIVES

- To identify gerunds and to tell how they are used in a sentence
- To identify participles and the words they modify in a sentence

---

584 *The Phrase*

the pole on January 4, 1912. [2] <u>Leading Scott by sixty miles</u>, however, a Norwegian <u>expedition</u>, <u>commanded by Roald Amundsen</u>, was moving swiftly. [3] <u>Having learned about Amundsen</u>, <u>Scott</u> realized a race to the pole was on. [4] <u>Plagued by bad weather and bad luck</u>, <u>Scott</u> fell farther behind Amundsen. [5] <u>Reaching the pole on January 17</u>, the <u>British</u> found that the Norwegians had already been there. [6] <u>Weakened by scurvy, frostbite, and exhaustion</u>, as is evident in the photograph, the five <u>explorers</u> set out on the eight-hundred-mile journey back to their base ship. [7] One <u>member</u> of the party, <u>overcome by exhaustion and injuries</u>, died before half the journey had been completed. [8] On March 15, another <u>member</u>, <u>leaving the camp at night</u>, walked deliberately to his death in a violent blizzard. [9] Eight months later, a rescue <u>mission</u>, <u>sent to find out what had happened</u>, found the bodies of Scott and his companions. [10] Today, the ill-fated Scott <u>expedition</u>, <u>acclaimed for its heroism</u>, is better known than the successful Amundsen expedition.

The Gerund

17h. A *gerund* is a verb form ending in *—ing* that is used as a noun.

Like nouns, gerunds can be subjects, predicate nominatives, direct objects, or objects of prepositions.

EXAMPLES **Reading** will increase your vocabulary. [subject]
One popular winter sport is **tobogganing.** [predicate nominative]
I enjoyed **seeing** you again. [direct object]
She cleared a path by **shoveling** the snow. [object of a preposition]

▶ EXERCISE 7 **Identifying Gerunds and Participles**

Identify the verbal in each of the following sentences and tell whether it is a <u>gerund</u> or a <u>participle</u>. If the verbal is a gerund, tell how it is used: as *subject, predicate nominative, direct object,* or *object of a preposition.* If the verbal is a participle, tell what (word it modifies).

Teacher's ResourceBank™

▼ RESOURCES

THE GERUND AND GERUND PHRASE

- Gerunds and Gerund Phrases

 QUICK REMINDER

Write the following sentences on the chalkboard:

1. Studying will improve your grades.
2. His favorite pastime is running.
3. I loved hearing the concert last night.
4. She relaxed by whistling songs.

Ask students what the marked words have in common. [All are verb forms ending in *—ing* and are used as nouns.] Explain that they have just described a gerund.

- To write a group story that uses gerund phrases
- To label the use of gerunds in a group story

GRAMMAR

EXAMPLES **1.** Sleeping on the job is foolish.
    1. *Sleeping, gerund—subject*
    2. Let sleeping dogs lie.
    2. *sleeping, participle—dogs*

1. Their <u>giggling</u> annoyed the other viewers. **1.** s.
2. Virginia looks forward to <u>fishing</u>. **2.** o.p.
3. After <u>studying</u>, how do you relax? **3.** o.p.
4. I am reading a <u>fascinating</u> mystery (nove<u>l</u>).
5. <u>Making</u> friends in a new school can be difficult. **5.** s.
6. The highlight of the season was <u>watching</u> our team win the regional tournament. **6.** p.n.
7. <u>Spinning</u> one full turn, (she) performed a pirouette.
8. Carlota makes money by <u>walking</u> dogs. **8.** o.p.
9. My grandmother and I enjoy <u>digging</u> for clams. **9.** d.o.
10. <u>Sensing</u> the danger nearby, (he) shouted for help.

The Gerund Phrase

17i. A *gerund phrase* consists of a gerund and any modifiers and complements it may have. The entire gerund phrase acts as a noun.

Because gerunds act as nouns, they may be modified by adjectives and adjective phrases.

EXAMPLE **The sudden shattering of glass** broke the silence. [The article *the,* the adjective *sudden,* and the adjective phrase *of glass* modify the gerund *shattering.* The gerund *shattering* is the subject of the sentence.]

Because gerunds are verb forms, they may also be modified by adverbs and adverb phrases.

EXAMPLE She enjoys **hiking in the mountains occasionally.** [The adverb phrase *in the mountains* and the adverb *occasionally* modify the gerund *hiking.* The gerund *hiking* is the direct object of the verb *enjoys.*]

NOTE: When a noun or pronoun comes before a gerund, it should be in the possessive form.

    EXAMPLES **Eli's** dancing won him first prize in the contest.
                   His dancing has greatly improved since last year.

MEETING INDIVIDUAL NEEDS

GRAMMAR

LESS-ADVANCED STUDENTS

You could share with students the following clue for identifying gerunds: If a pronoun can be substituted for the word or phrase in question, the word is a gerund, or the phrase is a gerund phrase.

Write the following sentences on the chalkboard and have students test the clue:

1. *Studying* often makes me hungry.
2. Ana likes *walking in the rain.*
3. *Howling loudly,* the wind frightened me.

The first two sentences contain gerunds because pronouns can be substituted: *It* often makes me hungry; Ana likes *it.* A pronoun cannot be substituted for *howling loudly,* which is a participial phrase.

ADVANCED STUDENTS

For an additional practice exercise in using gerunds, have students identify idiomatic expressions that require gerunds to complete them. Some examples are *look forward to, complain about,* and *interested in.* [One example is "I look forward to eating at the restaurant."] You may want to brainstorm with your class and make a list of the expressions on the chalkboard. Students can then write a specified number of sentences that incorporate these idioms.

ANSWERS

Exercise 8

Responses will vary. All responses should contain a gerund, and students should be able to tell how each gerund is used.

Teacher's ResourceBank™

RESOURCES

THE INFINITIVE AND INFINITIVE PHRASE

• Infinitives and Infinitive Phrases

QUICK REMINDER

Write the following phrases on the chalkboard and ask the students to tell whether each is a prepositional phrase or an infinitive:

1. to me   [prepositional]
2. to walk   [infinitive]
3. to laugh   [infinitive]
4. to race   [infinitive]
5. to the race   [prepositional]

   Explain that *to* followed by a noun or pronoun is a prepositional phrase, and *to* followed by a verb is an infinitive.

586

SEGMENT 5 *(pp. 586–590)*

THE INFINITIVE AND INFINITIVE PHRASE   Rules 17j, 17k

OBJECTIVE

• To identify infinitives and infinitive phrases and to classify their uses in sentences

---

586   *The Phrase*

▶ EXERCISE 8   **Writing Sentences with Gerund Phrases**

Have you ever played Build a Story? The first player writes the story opener, and then the next player adds another sentence. The players take turns adding sentences to make up a story. With a friend or classmate, try your hand at building a story. A special requirement for this version of the game is that each sentence must contain a gerund. Use gerunds as subjects, objects of the verb, predicate nominatives, or objects of prepositions. Be able to tell how each gerund is used. [Note: Make sure that each player goes five rounds.]

EXAMPLES   Player 1: *At first we enjoyed walking in the forest.*
(direct object)
Player 2: *Seeing the grizzly bear, however, gave us a scare. (subject)*

The Infinitive

17j.   An *infinitive* is a verb form, usually preceded by *to*, that can be used as a noun, an adjective, or an adverb.

INFINITIVES	
USED AS	**EXAMPLES**
Nouns	**To err** is human. [*To err* is the subject.] His dream is **to travel**. [*To travel* is the predicate nominative.] Betty wants **to act**. [*To act* is the direct object of the verb *wants*.]
Adjectives	The candidate **to believe** is Villegas. [*To believe* modifies the noun *candidate*.] She is the one **to ask**. [*To ask* modifies the pronoun *one*.]
Adverbs	Grandmother has come **to stay**. [*To stay* modifies the verb *has come*.] The favored team was slow **to score**. [*To score* modifies the adjective *slow*.]

NOTE: The word *to* plus a noun or a pronoun (*to bed, to the movies, to her*) is a prepositional phrase, not an infinitive.

▶ EXERCISE 9　　**Identifying and Classifying Infinitives**

Identify the <u>infinitives</u> in the following sentences and tell how each is used: as *subject, predicate <u>n</u>ominative, direct <u>o</u>bject, <u>a</u>djective,* or *<u>a</u>dverb.*

1. Do you want <u>to meet</u> at the corner?　**1.** d.o.
2. We are eager <u>to go</u>.　**2.** adv.
3. One way <u>to relax</u> is <u>to listen</u> to classical music.　**3.** adj./p.n.
4. I am ready <u>to leave</u>.　**4.** adv.
5. We are waiting <u>to talk</u> with the principal.　**5.** adv.
6. The soup is still too hot <u>to eat</u>.　**6.** adv.
7. <u>To excel</u>, one must practice.　**7.** adv.
8. This summer she hopes <u>to travel</u> in the West.　**8.** d.o.
9. <u>To hike</u> through the woods is fun.　**9.** s.
10. <u>To forgive</u> is sometimes difficult.　**10.** s.

The Infinitive Phrase

17k.　An *infinitive phrase* consists of an infinitive together with its modifiers and complements. The entire infinitive phrase can be used as a noun, an adjective, or an adverb.

EXAMPLES　**To hit a curve ball solidly** is very difficult. [The infinitive phrase, used as a noun, is the subject of the sentence. The infinitive *to hit* has an object, *ball*, and is modified by the adverb *solidly.*]

She wants **to be a truck driver.** [The infinitive phrase, used as a noun, is the direct object of the verb *wants*. The infinitive *to be* is followed by the predicate nominative *truck driver.*]

It is sometimes difficult **to listen attentively.** [The infinitive phrase, used as an adverb, modifies the adjective *difficult*. The infinitive *to listen* is modified by the adverb *attentively.*]

NOTE:　An infinitive may have a subject.

EXAMPLE　I asked **him to come** to my party. [*Him* is the subject of the infinitive *to come.*]

The infinitive, together with its subject, complements, and modifiers, is sometimes called an **infinitive clause.**

GRAMMAR

LEP/ESL

　　Spanish. Students might need extra practice in reviewing gerund and infinitive forms. The present participle in Spanish is called *gerundio,* but unlike the English gerund, it cannot be used as a noun or adjective. The Spanish infinitive form is normally used where English uses the gerund form. For practice, you may want to give students sentences such as "(To see/Seeing) is believing" and have them choose between the gerund or infinitive form. [Seeing]

GRAMMAR

LESS-ADVANCED STUDENTS

To give extra practice identifying how infinitives are used in sentences, give students magazines and have them find five sentences containing infinitives. One infinitive should be used as a subject, one as a predicate nominative, one as a direct object, one as an adjective, and one as an adverb.

Have students take turns putting these sentences on the chalkboard and have other students mark the infinitives and tell how they are used.

COOPERATIVE LEARNING

Have students work in pairs to write sentences with infinitive phrases. One student in each pair should write a sentence using an infinitive phrase. The other student should circle the infinitive and indicate how it is used. You may want to collect this assignment, as it has already been evaluated by one of the students in each pair.

The Infinitive Without *to*

Sometimes the *to* that is the sign of the infinitive is omitted in a sentence.

EXAMPLES   Did you watch her (to) **play** volleyball?
He will help us (to) **paddle** the canoe.
We don't dare (to) **go** outside during the storm.

EXERCISE 10 **Identifying and Classifying Infinitive Phrases**

Identify the <u>infinitive phrases</u> in the following sentences and tell how each is used: as *subject*, *predicate <u>n</u>ominative*, *direct <u>o</u>bject*, *<u>adjective</u>*, or *<u>adverb</u>*.

1. Our assignment was <u>to read *I Know Why the Caged Bird Sings*</u>. **1.** p.n.
2. We were asked <u>to examine Maya Angelou's descriptions of her childhood</u>. **2.** d.o.
3. <u>To grow up in Stamps, Arkansas, in the 1930s</u> was <u>to know great hardship</u>. **3.** s./p.n.
4. Maya Angelou tried <u>to show the everyday lives of African Americans during the Great Depression</u>. **4.** d.o.
5. <u>To accomplish this purpose</u> meant including many descriptions; one such passage told about the process for curing pork sausage. **5.** s.
6. Angelou has an extraordinary ability <u>to capture vivid details in her writing</u>. **6.** adj.
7. She helps <u>us see her grandmother's store through the eyes of a fascinated child</u>. **7.** (to) d.o.
8. Angelou was eager <u>to experience life beyond her hometown</u>. **8.** adv.
9. Her talents and ambition enabled <u>her to gain success as a writer, a dancer, and an actress</u>. **9.** d.o.
10. <u>To dramatize her African American heritage</u> was a dream she realized by writing a television series. **10.** s.

REVIEW B **Identifying Types of Verbals and Verbal Phrases**

Identify the ten <u>verbals or verbal phrases</u> in the following paragraph. Then tell whether each verbal or verbal phrase is a *<u>participle</u>*, a *<u>gerund</u>*, or an *<u>infinitive</u>*.

OBJECTIVE

- To identify and classify verbals and verbal phrases in a paragraph

EXAMPLE   [1] **Looking at these control panels in the flight deck of a jumbo passenger jet**, most of us feel completely lost.

1. *Looking at these control panels in the flight deck of a jumbo passenger jet—participle*

[1] Fortunately, there are <u>trained</u> people in the flight deck who know how <u>to use these controls and instruments</u>. [2] <u>Sitting in front of identical control panels</u>, both the captain and the first officer can fly the plane. [3] The captain, who uses the left-hand panel, operates a lever <u>called a yoke</u>, which controls the wing flaps and helps in <u>steering the plane</u>. [4] <u>Operating the brake panels</u> is another one of the captain's jobs. [5] To the captain's right is the first officer, whose job is <u>to help the captain</u>. [6] The throttle, which governs the engines' ability <u>to move the plane forward</u>, is located between the captain and the first officer. [7] Some of the <u>bewildering</u> instruments that you see are parts of the plane's navigation, autopilot, and communication systems. [8] At another station in the flight deck, the flight engineer monitors gauges and operates switches <u>to control the plane's generators and the pressure and temperature in the cabin</u>.

1. part./ inf.
2. part.
3. part./ ger.
4. ger.
5. inf.
6. inf.
7. part.
8. inf.

GRAMMAR

GRAMMAR

A DIFFERENT APPROACH

To give students practice in identifying and classifying infinitive phrases, divide the class into two teams. Choose a student on each team to be scorekeeper. Have a student from each team go to the chalkboard and use an infinitive phrase in a sentence as a subject, a predicate nominative, a direct object, an adjective, or an adverb.

Ask students in the audience to identify the infinitive and tell if it is used as you directed. If the player has succeeded, his or her team scores a point.

▶ REVIEW C   **Identifying Verbal Phrases**

Identify the twenty <u>verbal phrases</u> in the following paragraph. Then, tell what kind each phrase is: *participial*, *gerund*, or *infinitive*.

APPOSITIVES AND APPOSITIVE PHRASES Rules 17l, 17m

OBJECTIVES

- To identify appositives and appositive phrases and the words they identify or explain
- To write a news article, using appositives and appositive phrases

1. ger.
2. inf./ part.
3. ger./ ger.
4. ger./ ger./part.
5. inf./inf./ ger.
6. inf./inf./ inf./inf.
7. inf./ ger./ger.
8. ger./inf.

[1] <u>Finding a summer job</u> can be a difficult task. [2] The first step is <u>to scan the classified ads listed</u> in <u>your local newspaper</u>. [3] After <u>discovering available opportunities</u>, you can embark on the second step, which is <u>matching your skills with the requirements of a specific job</u>. [4] In most cases you can then contact a prospective employer by <u>making a phone call</u> or by <u>writing a letter requesting an interview</u>. [5] If you are asked <u>to interview for a job</u>, be sure <u>to take care</u> in <u>preparing for the interview</u>. [6] <u>To make a good impression</u>, be sure <u>to arrive on time</u>, <u>to dress neatly</u>, and <u>to speak courteously</u>. [7] Remember <u>to avoid such nervous habits</u> as constantly <u>checking your watch</u> or <u>shuffling your feet</u>. [8] By <u>presenting yourself as calm, confident, and courteous</u>, you may hear the magic words "We'd like you <u>to work for us</u>."

Appositives and Appositive Phrases

17l. An *appositive* is a noun or pronoun placed beside another noun or pronoun to identify or explain it.

EXAMPLES   My cousin **Bryan** is my best friend. [The noun *Bryan* is an appositive that identifies the noun *cousin.*]
Soledad, an excellent **driver,** has never had an accident. [The noun *driver* is an appositive that explains the noun *Soledad.*]

17m. An *appositive phrase* is made up of an appositive and its modifiers.

EXAMPLES   We saw three birds, **two robins and a cardinal.**
His grandparents, **the Vescuzos,** live on Miller Road, **a wide street lined with beech trees.**

An appositive phrase usually follows the noun or pronoun it refers to. Sometimes, though, it comes before the noun or pronoun.

EXAMPLE   **A diligent and quick-witted student,** Mark always gets good grades.

QUICK REMINDER

Write the following sentences on the chalkboard and ask students to name the noun that identifies or explains the subject:

1. My brother Ed loves track meets. [Ed]
2. Chris, a speedy runner, wins many races. [runner]
3. A dutiful and disciplined athlete, Mary trains three hours daily. [athlete]

Explain that these nouns are appositives and that an appositive usually comes after the word it modifies, but sometimes, as in the third sentence, precedes it.

17 l–m

Appositives and appositive phrases are usually set off by commas unless the appositive is a single word closely related to the preceding noun or pronoun. Commas are always used with appositives that refer to proper nouns.

EXAMPLES   My sister **Karen** is a tennis player.
Dr. Rosen, **our family dentist,** is a marathon runner.

 EXERCISE 11   **Identifying Appositives and Appositive Phrases**

Identify the <u>appositives and appositive phrases</u> in each of the following sentences. Be prepared to tell which <u>word each one identifies or explains</u>.

1. <u>Soccer</u>, <u>my favorite sport</u>, is very popular in South America and Europe.
2. The internationally famous soccer <u>star Pelé</u> is from Brazil.
3. <u>Hausa</u>, <u>a Sudanese language</u>, is widely used in western Africa.
4. Have you met my <u>teacher Mr. Zolo</u>?
5. My youngest <u>sister</u>, <u>Susan</u>, speaks fluent Spanish.

GRAMMAR

PICTURE THIS

You are looking at some real winners. As a reporter for the local newspaper, you just saw these contestants win

LEP/ESL

General Strategies. Students should not have many problems with appositives, but for additional practice you may want to find a newspaper article that uses appositives. Have students identify the appositives and the words or phrases defined by them. After doing this, the students might be more confident and better prepared to write an article on their own, as required in the **PICTURE THIS** assignment.

GRAMMAR

PICTURE THIS

Students might need to consult reference books about dogs. They might also need to read about the basic temperament of each breed, in order to discuss the dogs' personalities. You may want to write *who, what, when, where, why,* and *how* on the chalkboard and remind students that these questions are always answered in a well-written news article.

Students can read their news articles aloud to the class, and the class can listen for the appositives used.

591

A DIFFERENT APPROACH

Have several students go to the chalkboard and write sentences containing appositives that are used to modify subjects and direct objects. Have other students identify each appositive, identify the word it modifies, and tell how the modified word is used.

Next, have students write two sentences with appositive phrases. One appositive phrase should follow the noun it modifies, and the other should precede the modified noun. Have other students analyze the sentences as before.

REVIEW D

OBJECTIVE

- To identify participial, gerund, infinitive, and appositive phrases in a paragraph

at the annual dog show. Now you have to write a short news article on the show. Tell about the winners—their names, their breeds, their owners, their personalities. Describe how the winners were chosen, and tell why each winner was judged to be the best in its class. You may also want to describe other features of the show, such as the setting, the size and enthusiasm of the crowd, or the owners' preshow grooming of the contestants. In your article, use at least five appositives and appositive phrases. Newspaper articles usually present the most important information first, so be sure to include the *who, what, when,* and *where* of the dog show in the beginning of your article.

Subject: a dog show
Audience: local newspaper readers
Purpose: to inform

▷ REVIEW D   Identifying Verbal and Appositive Phrases

The following paragraph contains ten <u>phrases</u>. Identify each phrase as a *participial phrase*, a *gerund phrase*, an *infinitive phrase*, or an *appositive phrase*.

1. app.

2. part.

3. part.

4. inf./ app./ part.

5. ger.

6. inf.

7. ger./ ger.

[1] The Brooklyn Bridge, <u>a remarkable feat of design,</u> spans the East River in New York City. [2] <u>Linking the boroughs of Brooklyn and Manhattan,</u> it was once the longest suspension bridge in the world. [3] Pedestrians <u>walking across the bridge</u> are impressed by the grandeur of its graceful cables—a sensation the postcard on the next page cannot fully evoke. [4] <u>To support the twin towers on the bridge,</u> the brilliant John A. Roebling, <u>its engineer,</u> designed airtight caissons <u>filled with concrete</u>. [5] <u>Working underwater on the caissons</u> was painstakingly slow and extremely dangerous. [6] The workers also faced great danger when they had <u>to spin the cables from one side of the river to the other</u>. [7] Because of these hazards, the bridge is remembered not only for <u>being a masterpiece of engineering</u> but also for <u>having cost the lives of many of its builders.</u>

REVIEW: POSTTESTS 1 and 2

OBJECTIVES

- To identify prepositional, participial, gerund, infinitive, and appositive phrases in a paragraph
- To write sentences, using and labeling prepositional, participial, gerund, infinitive, and appositive phrases

GRAMMAR

Review: Posttest 1

Identifying Prepositional, Verbal, and Appositive Phrases

Identify each italicized phrase in the following paragraphs as a *prepositional phrase*, a *participial phrase*, a *gerund phrase*, an *infinitive phrase*, or an *appositive phrase*.

EXAMPLE   An interesting profession [1] *to consider as a career* is [2] *practicing law.*
1. *to consider as a career*—inf.
2. *practicing law*—ger.

Susana, [1] *our next-door neighbor*, wanted [2] *to become an attorney.* After she earned a degree [3] *from a four-year college,* she took the Law School Admissions Test [4] *to gain acceptance at an approved law school.* [5] *Having completed three full years of law school,* Susana was then awarded a J.D. degree. Before [6] *practicing law,* however, she took an exam [7] *required by the state board of bar examiners.* Only after [8] *passing this exam* was she ready [9] *to be admitted to the bar* and [10] *to practice law.*

[11] *Working as an attorney,* Susana provides service and advice [12] *relating to legal rights.* Although some attorneys try hard [13] *to keep cases out of court,* Susana enjoys the challenge [14] *of presenting cases to a jury.* [15] *Representing a*

1. app.
2. inf.
3. prep.
4. inf.
5. part.
6. ger.
7. part.
8. ger.
9. inf.   10. inf.
11. part.
12. part.
13. inf.
14. prep.
15. ger.

593

ANSWERS
Review: Posttest 2

Responses will vary. However, all responses should contain the requested prepositional or verbal phrase.

594 *The Phrase*

16. prep.

17. ger.

18. inf.

19. prep.

20. inf.

client in court, however, is only part [16] *of Susana's job.* She devotes hours to [17] *gathering enough evidence* [18] *to defend a client.* She also spends time [19] *on research* and is required [20] *to write numerous reports.*

Review: Posttest 2

Writing Sentences with Phrases

Write ten sentences, following the directions below for each sentence. Underline the phrase in each sentence.

EXAMPLE   **1.** Use *to get there from here* as an adjective phrase.
1. *What is the fastest way to get there from here?*

1. Use *in the garage* as an adjective phrase.
2. Use *for our English class* as an adverb phrase.
3. Use *from an encyclopedia* as an adverb phrase.
4. Use *by train* as an adverb phrase.
5. Use *walking by the lake* as a participial phrase.
6. Use *playing the piano* as a gerund phrase that is the subject of the sentence.
7. Use *to get a home run* as an infinitive phrase that is the direct object of the verb.
8. Use *to find the answer to that question* as an adverb phrase.
9. Use *the new student in our class* as an appositive phrase.
10. Use *my favorite writer* as an appositive phrase.

DIAGNOSTIC TEST

OBJECTIVES

- To identify independent and subordinate clauses
- To classify sentences according to structure

Teacher's ResourceBank™

RESOURCES

FOR THE WHOLE CHAPTER
- Chapter Review Form A
- Chapter Review Form B
- Assessment Portfolio
    Grammar Pretests
    Grammar Mastery Tests

18 THE CLAUSE

Independent and Subordinate Clauses

CHAPTER OVERVIEW

Students will be better motivated to study clauses if they understand why they are studying the clauses and how the clauses relate to writing. Explain that an understanding of clauses is essential to writing complete, correctly punctuated sentences.

Instead of assigning the entire chapter, you may want to refer to specific sections in regard to problems, questions about writing, or ways of punctuating sentences or clauses. This chapter may be useful when students are revising and proofreading the writing assignments for **Chapters 7** and **8**.

You may decide that some of the individualized activities will be of interest to the entire class and that your less-advanced students can learn from group participation with advanced students.

Diagnostic Test

A. Identifying and Classifying Clauses

Identify the italicized clause in each of the following sentences as an *independent clause* or a *subordinate clause*. Also, identify each subordinate clause as an *adjective clause*, an *adverb clause*, or a *noun clause*.

EXAMPLES **1.** A soccer field measures 115 yards by 75 yards, and *the netted goals at each end of the field are 8 yards wide by 8 feet high.*
1. *independent clause*

2. Soccer, *which is the national sport of many European and Latin American countries*, has enjoyed only limited success in the United States.
2. *subordinate clause—adjective clause*

USING THE DIAGNOSTIC TEST

The **Diagnostic Test** contains two parts: **Part A** asks students to identify clauses as independent or subordinate and then to determine how subordinate clauses are used; **Part B** requires students to classify sentences according to structure. To prevent needless reteaching, you may want to analyze the results of students' tests. For example, you may want to assign the section on adjective clauses to students who miss items 1, 3, and 6. If students miss items 4, 5, and 8, assign adverb clauses; if they miss 7 and 10, assign noun clauses.

After students have classified the sentences in **Part B**, help them to understand the importance of sentence variety by discussing whether the paragraph would have been as effective without a variety of sentence types.

1. adj. cl.

1. During a career _that spanned twenty years_, Pelé was probably the most popular athlete in the world.

2. He was named Edson Arantes do Nascimento, but _hardly anyone recognizes that name_.

3. adj. cl.

3. Soccer fans the world over, however, knew Pelé, _who was considered the world's best soccer player_.

4. adv. cl.

4. _While he was still a teenager_, he led his Brazilian teammates to the first of their three World Cup titles.

5. adv. cl.

5. _Whenever he played_, his skill and agility awed fans.

6. adj. cl.

6. Once, he juggled the ball on his foot for fifty yards, eluding four opponents _who were trying to take the ball away from him_.

7. n. cl.

7. _That he soon became a superstar_ is not surprising.

8. adv. cl.

8. _Even though soccer has never become as popular as baseball or football in the United States_, Pelé managed to spark considerable interest in the game.

9. After he signed with the New York Cosmos, _people flocked to the stands to watch him play_.

10. n. cl.

10. They soon recognized _that Pelé was an entertainer as well as an athlete_.

B. Classifying Sentences According to Structure

Classify each sentence in the following paragraph as _simple_, _compound_, _complex_, or _compound-complex_.

11. cx.
12. simp.

13. cx.

14. cd.

15. cd.-cx.

16. cx.

17. cd.

[11] Because tennis is so physically demanding, it's a sport in which strong young players can really shine. [12] Steffi Graf of Germany began playing tennis professionally at the age of thirteen. [13] Graf was still a teenager when she won the four Grand Slam tennis championships and an Olympic gold medal in 1988. [14] Another Olympic winner, Zina Garrison, began playing tennis in Houston at the age of ten, and at seventeen, she won the junior singles titles at Wimbledon and the U.S. Open. [15] The German tennis star Boris Becker won his first tournament competitions at the age of nine, but he didn't become a professional player until he graduated from high school. [16] Jennifer Capriati, who was born on Long Island, New York, won many national and international tennis competitions and earned more than eighty thousand dollars by the age of fourteen. [17] Another American player, Andre

OBJECTIVES

- To identify independent clauses and subordinate clauses
- To identify subjects, verbs, and complements in subordinate clauses

18. cx. **19.** cd.-cx.

Agassi, started serving on a tennis court at the age of two, and he, too, excelled at an early age. **[18]** Agassi won six major tournaments when he was only eighteen. **[19]** Tracy Austin and Chris Evert also started young, and each was sixteen years old when she made headlines by winning the women's title at the U.S. Open. **[20]** In tennis, young players really can become big winners. **20.** simp.

GRAMMAR

Teacher's ResourceBank™
RESOURCES

KINDS OF CLAUSES
- Independent and Subordinate Clauses
- Complements and Modifiers in Clauses

GRAMMAR

Kinds of Clauses

18a. A *clause* is a group of words that contains a verb and its subject and is used as part of a sentence.

Every clause has a subject and a verb, but not all clauses express a complete thought. Those that do are called *independent clauses*. Those that do not make complete sense by themselves are called *subordinate clauses*.

Independent Clauses

18b. An *independent* (or *main*) *clause* expresses a complete thought and can stand by itself as a sentence.

EXAMPLES The outfielders were missing easy fly balls.
The infielders were throwing wildly.

Independent clauses that express related ideas can be joined together in a single sentence. Often, the clauses are linked by one of the coordinating conjunctions (*and, but, or, nor, for, so, yet*).

EXAMPLE The outfielders were missing easy fly balls, **and** the infielders were throwing wildly.

Independent clauses can also be joined by a semicolon.

EXAMPLE The outfielders were missing easy fly balls; the infielders were throwing wildly.

 QUICK REMINDER
Write the following clauses on the chalkboard:

1. Alberto got an A on his examination.
2. Because he had studied carefully.

Ask students which clause makes sense by itself [the first]. Explain that this clause is independent because it does not depend on another clause to complete it. Explain also that the second clause is subordinate because it does not express a complete thought and cannot stand alone.

MEETING
INDIVIDUAL
NEEDS

LEP/ESL

General Strategies. Describing a subordinate clause by using expressions such as "does not express a complete thought and cannot stand alone" will not help your ESL speakers. It is better to describe this clause structurally as having a subject and a verb as well as a subordinating conjunction that links it to another clause.

LEARNING STYLES

Auditory Learners. To help auditory learners understand how independent and subordinate clauses function in writing, read aloud the paragraph from **Exercise 1**. As you read, emphasize each italicized clause. Then ask students whether the clause could stand alone as a complete thought.

 COMMON ERROR

Problem. Students often have trouble punctuating two independent clauses within the same sentence.

Solution. Ask students to study carefully the correct combinations of independent clauses shown on pp. 597–598. Summarize the three methods of linking independent clauses: a comma and a coordinating conjunction, a semicolon, or a semicolon and a conjunctive adverb.

A conjunctive adverb can be used after the semicolon to express the relationship between the independent clauses.

EXAMPLE   The outfielders were missing easy fly balls; **moreover,** the infielders were throwing wildly.

☞ REFERENCE NOTE: See pages 816–819 for more information on using semicolons between independent clauses.

Subordinate Clauses

18c. A *subordinate* (or *dependent*) *clause* does not express a complete thought and cannot stand alone.

Subordinate means "less important." Words such as *who, that, because, if, when, although,* and *since* signal that the clause they introduce is subordinate and must be joined to an independent clause to make a complete sentence.

SUBORDINATE   who spoke to our class yesterday
CLAUSES   that many students are eligible for scholarships
because no students have applied for them

SENTENCES   The woman **who spoke to our class yesterday** told us about sources of financial aid for college applicants.
She said **that many students are eligible for scholarships.**
Some scholarships are still available **because no students have applied for them.**

▶ EXERCISE 1   **Identifying Independent and Subordinate Clauses**

For each sentence in the following paragraph, identify the italicized clause as *independent* or *subordinate*.

[1] *Whenever I think of Barbara Jordan,* I remember her as she looks in this picture, delivering the commencement address at my sister's graduation in 1986. [2] In front of a huge audience, *Jordan spoke eloquently about the importance of values in our society.* [3] *Of course, her choice of subject matter*

surprised no one since Jordan has long been known as an important ethical force in American politics. [4]*When Jordan began her public service career in 1966*, she became the first African American woman to serve in the Texas Legislature. [5] In 1972, she won a seat in the U.S. House of Representatives, *where only one other black woman— Shirley Chisolm—had ever been a member*. [6] However, Jordan was still not widely recognized *until she gave the*

keynote speech at the 1976 Democratic National Convention. [7] Seen on television by millions of people, *Jordan immediately gained national attention*. [8] Two years later, Jordan decided *that she would retire from national politics.* [9] *After she returned to Texas in 1978*, Jordan taught at the University of Texas in Austin. [10] In 1991, she became the governor's special counsel on ethics and used *what she had learned in her many years of public service* to fight corruption in politics.

Complements and Modifiers in Subordinate Clauses

A subordinate clause may contain complements and modifiers.

EXAMPLES **Since she told us the truth** . . . [*Us* is the indirect object of *told; truth* is the direct object of *told.*]
When I am busy . . . [*Busy* is a predicate adjective modifying *I*.]
After he had cooked for us . . . [*For us* is an adverb phrase modifying *had cooked.*]
The portrait that he painted . . . [*That* is the direct object of *painted.*]
We couldn't tell who they were. [*Who* is a predicate nominative: They were *who.*]

 CRITICAL THINKING
Analysis

The paragraph in **Exercise 1** presents both facts and opinions about the life of Barbara Jordan. Explain to students that a fact can be proved true or false, but an opinion cannot be proved. Then ask students to find five facts and five opinions used in the paragraph. For example, the statement that the photograph was "taken when she delivered the keynote speech at the 1976 Democratic National Convention" is a fact because it can be tested; however, the statement that "she was used to being in the spotlight" is an opinion because Ms. Jordan's feelings cannot be proved. When students complete their lists, have them compare and discuss their findings. You might use this exercise in conjunction with **Chapter 9**.

VISUAL CONNECTIONS
Ideas for Writing. The paragraph in **Exercise 1** records relevant and interesting facts about the life of Barbara Jordan, who is pictured in the photograph. Have each student select a photograph of a public figure from a current newspaper or magazine and have the student write a paragraph about the person's life. Ask each student to include at least five independent clauses and five subordinate clauses.

SEGMENT 3 *(pp. 600–602)*

THE ADJECTIVE CLAUSE Rule 18d

OBJECTIVES

- To identify adjective clauses and the words they modify
- To identify relative pronouns and relative adverbs

600 *The Clause*

EXERCISE 2 | **Identifying Subjects, Verbs, and Complements in Subordinate Clauses**

Identify the <u>subject</u> and the <u>verb</u> in each italicized subordinate clause in the following sentences. Then identify any (complements) in the clause as *direct object*, *predicate nominative*, or *indirect object*.

EXAMPLE | **1.** *After he shows us his new boat,* we will go swimming.
1. *he—subject; shows—verb; us—indirect object; boat—direct object*

1. We couldn't see *who had won the* (race). **1.** d.o.
2. They couldn't tell (who) *the winner was.* **2.** p.n. **3.** d.o.
3. She is the celebrity (whom) *we saw at the restaurant.*
4. Look for the mouse (that) *you heard last night.* **4.** d.o.
5. He spotted a horse *that galloped away.*
6. *After we passed the* (test) we celebrated. **6.** d.o.
7. Do you know *which* (country) *she is from?* **7.** o.p.
8. *Because you had not given* (us) *the right* (address) we missed the party. **8.** i.o./d.o. **9.** d.o.
9. The package will arrive on time *if you ship* (it) *today.*
10. *Until Mike lent* (me) *this* (book) I had never heard of John Steinbeck. **10.** i.o./d.o.

The Uses of Subordinate Clauses

Subordinate clauses can be used in sentences as either adjectives, adverbs, or nouns.

The Adjective Clause

18d. An *adjective clause* is a subordinate clause that modifies a noun or a pronoun.

An adjective clause always follows the word it modifies. If the clause is necessary, or *essential*, to the meaning of the sentence, it is not set off with commas. If the clause simply adds information and is *nonessential* to the meaning of the sentence, commas are used to set it off.

QUICK REMINDER

Write the following sentences on the chalkboard:

1. The student who wrote the best essay won a $100 prize.
2. The ostrich, which was seven feet tall and quite mean, guarded the car lot.

Ask students whether the underlined clauses are independent or subordinate [subordinate]. Then ask students to identify the word that each subordinate clause modifies and to explain what the clauses in these sentences have in common. [*Student* and *ostrich* are the modified words. Both clauses are adjective clauses.]

EXAMPLES   The novel **that I'm reading now** is about the Irish revolt of 1798. [The clause is necessary to identify the novel, so it is not set off by commas.]
Our town's civic center, **which was renovated last year,** has been declared a landmark. [The clause adds nonessential information, so it is set off by commas.]

☞ **REFERENCE NOTE:** See pages 797–799, rule 25i, for help in deciding whether a clause is essential or nonessential.

Relative Pronouns

Adjective clauses are usually introduced by *relative pronouns*.

		Relative Pronouns		
who	whom	whose	which	that

These pronouns are called *relative pronouns* because they *relate* an adjective clause to the word the clause modifies—the antecedent of the relative pronoun. Each relative pronoun also has a function within the adjective clause.

EXAMPLES   Isabella Baumfree was an abolitionist **who is better known as Sojourner Truth.** [The relative pronoun *who* relates the adjective clause to *abolitionist. Who* also is the subject of the adjective clause.]

She is the person **whom I trust most.** [*Whom* relates the adjective clause to *person. Whom* is also the direct object of the verb *trust* in the adjective clause.]

The topic **about which he is writing** is controversial. [*Which* relates the adjective clause to *topic* and is the object of the preposition *about* in the adjective clause.]

Do you know the name of the group **whose recording is number one on the charts?** [*Whose* relates the adjective clause to *group. Whose* is also a possessive pronoun modifying *recording* in the adjective clause.]

Sometimes the relative pronoun is left out of a sentence. In such cases, the pronoun is understood, and it still has a function in the adjective clause.

MEETING INDIVIDUAL NEEDS

LESS-ADVANCED STUDENTS
Provide practice for less-advanced students by asking them to fill in the missing adjective clauses in the following sentences:

1. The swimmer (*who*) ____ won the race. [who came from my high school]
2. The dog (*that*) ____ woke up the neighborhood. [that barked so loudly]
3. The singer (*whose*) ____ stayed in our hotel. [whose record was just released]

Students might work together in pairs or in small groups and then share their sentences.

✏ COMMON ERROR
Problem. Students often have trouble in punctuating adjective clauses.
Solution. Write the following sentences on the chalkboard:

1. The writer who won the Pulitzer Prize for fiction in 1983 is also a renowned poet.
2. Alice Walker who won the Pulitzer Prize for fiction in 1983 is also a renowned poet.

Ask students which adjective clause should be set off with commas and why. [In the first example, the clause *who won the Pulitzer Prize for fiction in 1983* is necessary to identify the writer, but this clause is simply additional information in the second example and therefore should be set off with commas.]

INTEGRATING THE LANGUAGE ARTS

Literature Link. Have students read Christina Rosetti's poem "A Birthday." Then read the first stanza aloud. Ask students to listen for descriptive adjective clauses. Then have students examine the written stanza to see where the adjective clauses are placed and how effective the placement makes those clauses. [Lines a, c, and e contain independent clauses ending in predicate nominatives that are modified by the adjective clauses in lines b, d, and f. The repetition of adjective clauses sets up a pattern that is reversed in lines g and h, which contain predicate adjectives modified by adverb clauses. While the first three comparisons link the speaker's heart to a bird, a tree, and a shell, the final two lines emphasize her feelings for her love. The poem's grammatical repetition and variation show how such techniques contribute to meaning.]

602 *The Clause*

EXAMPLE   **Ms. Chung is the legislator** *[that* or *whom]* **we met.**
[The relative pronoun *that* or *whom* is understood. It relates the adjective clause to *legislator* and is the direct object of the verb *met* in the adjective clause.]

The relative adverbs *where* and *when* are sometimes used to introduce adjective clauses.

EXAMPLES   **Here is the spot *where* we will have lunch.**
This is the season *when* it rains almost every day.

EXERCISE 3   Identifying Adjective Clauses

Identify the <u>adjective clauses</u> in the following sentences, and give the <u>relative pronoun or relative adverb in each clause</u>. Then, tell what word the relative pronoun or relative adverb refers to.

EXAMPLE   **1. The topic that Melissa chose for her paper was a difficult one.**
1. *that Melissa chose for her paper—topic*

1. A speech community is a group of people who speak the same language.
2. There are speech communities that contain millions of people and some that have only a few.
3. The first language that you learn is called your native language.
4. People who master another language are bilingual.
5. People who conduct business internationally often need to know more than one language.
6. English, French, and Spanish, which many diplomats can speak, are among the six official languages of the United Nations.
7. Russian, Chinese, and Arabic are the other three languages that are used officially at the UN.
8. People for whom language study is important include telephone operators, hotel managers, and police officers.
9. Tourists who travel to other countries may need to know a language that is understood in different parts of the world.
10. French, for example, is a language that is widely understood in parts of Europe, Africa, and Southeast Asia.

THE ADVERB CLAUSE Rule 18e

OBJECTIVES

- To identify adverb clauses and the subordinating conjunctions that introduce them
- To write sentences with adverb clauses

The Adverb Clause

18e. An *adverb clause* is a subordinate clause that modifies a verb, an adjective, or an adverb.

An adverb clause tells

how	when
where	why
to what extent	under what condition

An adverb clause may modify the action of the *main verb* (the verb in the sentence's independent clause).

EXAMPLES   Donna sounds **as if she has caught a cold.** [*As if she has caught a cold* tells how Donna sounds.]
Before we left, we turned off the lights. [*Before we left* tells when we turned off the lights.]
You will see our house **where the road turns right.** [*Where the road turns right* tells where you will see our house.]
As long as he starts early, he will arrive on time. [*As long as he starts early* tells under what condition he will arrive on time.]
Will you move over **so that I can see?** [*So that I can see* tells why I want you to move over.]

☞ **REFERENCE NOTE:** Introductory adverb clauses are usually set off with commas. See page 801.

An adverb clause may also modify an adjective or an adverb in the independent clause.

EXAMPLES   Your stereo is louder **than it should be.** [The adverb clause modifies the adjective *louder,* telling to what extent the stereo is louder.]
The rice pudding tasted better **after we added the raisins.** [The adverb clause modifies the adverb *better,* telling when the rice pudding tasted better.]

Subordinating Conjunctions

Adverb clauses are introduced by *subordinating conjunctions.* Unlike relative pronouns, which introduce adjective clauses, subordinating conjunctions do not serve a function in the clause they introduce.

Teacher's ResourceBank™
RESOURCES

THE ADVERB CLAUSE
- The Adverb Clause

🦉 **QUICK REMINDER**
Write the following sentences on the chalkboard:

1. We decided to come home early because . . . .
2. Although . . ., he won the race.
3. I will prepare the salad if . . . .

   Ask students to complete each sentence with an adverb clause. Remind them that the subordinating conjunctions *because, although,* and *if* show relationships between the verbs and adverb clauses.

MEETING
INDIVIDUAL
NEEDS

LEP/ESL

   General Strategies. Ask students to reserve pages in their notebooks for collecting sentences that contain subordinating conjunctions ending with the word *that: now that, in view of the fact that, to the extent that, with the result that, provided that, so that,* and so forth. *That,* a word with a variety of functions in English, is often mistakenly omitted by students. Keeping a notebook of sentences, which students can review periodically, may help them master these connectors more easily.

CRITICAL THINKING
Analysis

Students sometimes have trouble analyzing relationships among the ideas presented in written material. This difficulty is particularly apparent when student writers use inappropriate connecting words—*and* for *but* or *since* for *although,* for example. Provide practice in making correct word choices by asking students to insert appropriate subordinating connections in the following sentences:

1. We will not pay the repair bill ____ the television is fixed. [until, unless]
2. ____ it rained, the baseball game was postponed. [Because, Since]
3. Mother served dinner early ____ we could get to the concert on time. [so that, in order that]

ANSWERS
Exercise 5

Answers will vary, but make sure that each first line uses a different subordinating conjunction. Here are some possible answers:

1. Title: "Daniel's Song"
   First line: Until I met you, Daniel, it rained on me every day.

2. Title: "Call Me"
   First line: Unless you call me, I just can't go on.

3. Title: "Student's Song"
   First line: Before I take this little test, I'd like back all the time I killed.

Common Subordinating Conjunctions		
after	before	unless
although	even though	until
as	if	when
as if	in order that	whenever
as long as	since	where
as soon as	so that	wherever
as though	than	whether
because	though	while

NOTE: Many of the words in this list can be used as other parts of speech, such as adverbs and prepositions.

▶ EXERCISE 4 **Identifying Adverb Clauses and Subordinating Conjunctions**

Identify the <u>adverb clause</u> in <u>each sentence of the following paragraph</u>, and circle the (subordinating conjunction).

[1] (Because) the house had been vacant for so long, we had to clean up the lawn and gardens. [2] The grass looked (as if) it hadn't been cut in months. [3] Ruth began mowing the lawn (while) Lou and I weeded the flower beds. [4] We had to borrow some tools (because) the weeds were so thick. [5] We hadn't been able to cut through the heavy undergrowth (until) we started using a machete. [6] (Before) we pulled out the weeds, we couldn't even see the roses. [7] We stacked the debris in a mound (so that) it could be hauled away later. [8] (After) Ruth had mowed the lawn, she was exhausted. [9] We all stretched out in the shade (when) we stopped for a rest. [10] Long hours in the sun had made us feel (as though) the day would never end.

▶ EXERCISE 5 **Writing Sentences with Adverb Clauses**

Have you written any good songs lately? What? You say you don't write songs! Then here's your chance to give it a try. You don't have to write the whole song. Instead, think of ten song titles and a first line for each song. In each first line, use a different subordinating conjunction from the list given at the top of this page.

The Uses of Subordinate Clauses **605**

EXAMPLE   Title: *Baby Sitters' Blues*
           First Line: *If only you'd eat your carrots, I'd let you watch TV.*

  REVIEW A

Identifying Adjective and Adverb Clauses

Identify the subordinate clauses in the following paragraph. Then, tell whether each is an *adjective clause* or an *adverb clause*.

[1] In 1978, the aeronauts Ben Abruzzo, Max Anderson, and Larry Newman, <u>whose home was Albuquerque, New Mexico</u>, became the first people to pilot a balloon across the Atlantic Ocean. [2] <u>Although Abruzzo and Anderson had been forced to land in the ocean in an earlier attempt in *Double Eagle*</u>, they didn't give up. [3] Instead, they acquired a new balloon, <u>which they named *Double Eagle II*</u>. [4] Newman joined them <u>because experience had shown the need for a third crew member</u>. [5] On its journey from Maine to France, *Double Eagle II* was airborne for 137 hours, <u>which is a little less than six days</u>. [6] The aeronauts stressed the fact <u>that *Double Eagle II* didn't just drift across the Atlantic</u>; they flew it across. [7] Abruzzo, Anderson, and Newman had to understand meteorology <u>so that they could take advantage of favorable winds</u>. [8] They also had to regulate their altitude constantly by adjusting their supply of helium and by losing ballast, <u>as the balloonists shown here are doing</u>. [9] <u>When the balloon gained too much altitude</u>, the crew lowered it by releasing some of the gas. [10] <u>If the balloon lost altitude</u>, the crew raised it by discarding ballast.

GRAMMAR

GRAMMAR

VISUAL CONNECTIONS
Exploring the Subject. Have your students explore, in various ways, the subject of ballooning. For example, one group of students could look up ballooning in an encyclopedia, while another group could visit a local travel agent to find out about balloon outings. Give student groups additional speaking practice by asking them to report their findings to the rest of the class.

605

OBJECTIVE

• To identify and classify noun clauses

Teacher's ResourceBank™

RESOURCES

THE NOUN CLAUSE
• The Noun Clause

QUICK REMINDER

Write the following noun clauses on the chalkboard:

1. that the game was lost
2. whoever reaches the finish line first
3. what classes she wanted to take

Then ask students to use the clauses to complete the following sentences:

1. The winner will be . . . .
2. The new student didn't know . . . .
3. . . . became obvious.

Remind students that noun clauses work as nouns.

MEETING

INDIVIDUAL

NEEDS

LEP/ESL

General Strategies. Point out to students that in English, whenever a noun clause is used as the subject of a sentence, it takes a singular verb. In the example, "The fact that you say it doesn't make it true," *the fact that you say it* is the noun clause and *does make* is the verb of the sentence. Sentences 6 and 8 in **Exercise 6** provide additional examples of this rule. Oral dialogues and writing dictations containing the standard forms can help students use noun clauses correctly.

The Noun Clause

18f. A *noun clause* is a subordinate clause used as a noun.

A noun clause may be used as a subject, a predicate nominative, a direct object, an indirect object, or the object of a preposition.

SUBJECT	**What I need** is my own room.
DIRECT OBJECT	She believes **that lost time is never found again.**
INDIRECT OBJECT	The store owner will give **whoever wins the contest** a valuable prize.
OBJECT OF PREPOSITION	She has written an article about **how she was elected to the Senate.**
PREDICATE NOMINATIVE	The happiest time in my life was **when we went to Colombia for the summer.**

Noun clauses are usually introduced by

that	where	whoever	whose
what	whether	whom	why
when	who	whomever	

☞ REFERENCE NOTE: Many of these words can be used to introduce adjective clauses. See page 469.

Sometimes the introductory word has a function in the clause and sometimes it doesn't.

EXAMPLES Do you know **what the problem is?** [The introductory word *what* is a predicate nominative—*the problem is what.*]

I know **that she is worried.** [The introductory word *that* has no function in the clause.]

In some sentences, the word that introduces a noun clause can be omitted.

EXAMPLE He told us **attendance is improving.** [The introductory word *that* is understood.]

She is the judge **we interviewed.** [The introductory word *whom* is understood.]

REVIEW B

OBJECTIVE

- To identify subordinate clauses and determine whether they are used as adjectives, adverbs, or nouns

18f

GRAMMAR

 EXERCISE 6

Identifying and Classifying Noun Clauses

Identify the <u>noun clauses</u> in the following sentences. Then, tell how each clause is used: as *subject, predicate nominative, direct object, indirect object,* or *object of a preposition.* [Note: A sentence may have more than one noun clause.]

1. Mr. Perkins, the band director, announced <u>that we would play at half time this week</u>. **1.** d.o.
2. We can never predict <u>whether he will choose a march or a show tune</u>. **2.** d.o.
3. He always gives <u>whoever will play each selection</u> a chance to express an opinion of it. **3.** i.o.
4. He is genuinely interested in <u>what we think of his choices</u>. **4.** o.p.
5. A drummer once told Mr. Perkins <u>she did not like most show tunes</u>. **5.** d.o.
6. <u>How she could say that</u> was a mystery to me. **6.** s.
7. Mr. Perkins told us <u>we would play a medley of marches</u>. **7.** d.o.
8. What everyone wanted to know was <u>who would play the solos</u>. **8.** p.n.   **9.** d.o.
9. He understands <u>why that was our first question</u>.
10. The crowd always applauds enthusiastically for <u>whoever plays a solo</u>. **10.** o.p.

 REVIEW B

Identifying Adjective, Adverb, and Noun Clauses

Each sentence in the following paragraph has at least one <u>subordinate clause</u>. Identify each subordinate clause, and tell whether it is an *adjective clause, adverb clause,* or *noun clause.*

[1] What's so special about the Blue Grotto, or *Grotta Azzurra,* <u>as the Italians say</u>? [2] In the painting on the next page, you can see <u>that the color and the hidden location of the Blue Grotto have made it famous</u>. [3] The grotto is a cavern <u>that can be entered only from the sea</u>. [4] It is located on the west side of the Italian island of Capri, <u>which stands at the entrance to the Bay of Naples</u>. [5] The opening to the cavern is only about three feet high, <u>so that visitors must lie down in a rowboat to enter it</u>. [6] The sap-

1. adj. cl.
2. n. cl.

3. adj. cl.

4. adj. cl.

5. adv. cl.

LESS-ADVANCED STUDENTS

Remind students that an introductory word usually gives a clue to the beginning of a noun clause. Sometimes, introductory words are implied rather than stated. Have students find the introductory words for each noun clause in **Exercise 6.** Ask students what introductory words are omitted in sentences 5 and 7. [Here are the introductory words for **Exercise 6:** (1) that (2) whether (3) whoever (4) what (5) that (6) how (7) that (8) what, who (9) why (10) whoever]

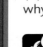 ## INTEGRATING THE LANGUAGE ARTS

Grammar and Writing. The paragraph in **Review B** describes the scene in Sandro Chia's painting *The Blue Grotto.* Ask each student to select a painting and to write a story about it. The painting could be one they have seen in a museum, an art book, an encyclopedia, or another illustrated book.

Encourage students not only to describe the scene that is shown in the painting, but also to narrate the events that might have led up to the scene, or the events that might take place afterward.

This assignment can be used in conjunction with **Chapter 5** or **Chapter 6.** Integrate the story-writing with grammar by asking students to include two adjective clauses, two adverb clauses, and two noun clauses.

GRAMMAR

WRITING APPLICATION

OBJECTIVE

- To describe works of art in paragraphs containing details and subordinate clauses

6. adj. cl.

phire blue of the water inside the spacious, oval-shaped cavern is caused by light <u>that is refracted through the deep pool</u>. [7] <u>Although the calm, blue water looks inviting</u>, the grotto is no longer a swimming hole. [8] In the past, however, people <u>who lived in the area</u> greatly enjoyed swimming there. [9] Tour guides tell <u>whoever goes there</u> <u>that centuries ago Tiberius, the Roman emperor, used the Blue Grotto as his private swimming pool</u>. [10] Seeing it today, you would agree <u>that it's a pool fit for an emperor</u>.

7. adv. cl.

8. adj. cl.

9. n. cl./ n. cl.

10. n. cl.

Courtesy Galerie Bruno Bischofberger, Zürich, Switzerland

VISUAL CONNECTIONS

About the Artist. Sandro Chia is one of several Italian-born artists known as postmodernists. In the 1980s, these artists rejected the modern pop style and began showing paintings that ironically combine the traditional and the modern.

As illustrated in *Blue Grotto*, Chia's art often combines the abstract and the representational. Chia specializes in plump figures that look inflated or bloated—thus producing an ironic, barren sensuality.

WRITING APPLICATION

This assignment allows students to form opinions of visual art and to articulate those opinions in written paragraphs. The assignment further encourages students to develop maturity and variety in their writing by having each student include at least five subordinate clauses in the paragraphs.

608

WRITING APPLICATION

Using Subordination to Reflect Your Thoughts

When you were a child, you probably used short, choppy sentences to express your thoughts. Almost all children do. But as you got older, your thoughts became more complex, and so did your sentences.

IMMATURE   Mary Cassatt was an American painter. I enjoy her works. She was an impressionist.

MATURE   I enjoy the works of Mary Cassatt, who was an American impressionist painter.

How was subordination used to make the second example sound more mature than the first?

▶ WRITING ACTIVITY

The student council has decided to decorate your school with prints of popular artworks. To decide which prints to get, the council has asked for recommendations, along with brief descriptions, for artworks that students would like to see. Write two paragraphs about two works that you would like to recommend. Use specific details and include at least five subordinate clauses.

Prewriting   Think of two paintings or prints that are your favorites. If you do not know their titles, try looking in books or asking a librarian or art teacher to find out what they are titled. Think about why you particularly like these works, and jot down your reasons.

Writing   As you write, you may think of additional details and reasons. If you do, pause for a moment and consider how they fit in with the rest of your notes. Add to your rough draft any of this new information that fits in smoothly.

Evaluating and Revising   Read through your paragraphs to be sure they each have a topic sentence supported by your reasons for recommending a specific artwork. Check to see that you have used a total of at least five subordinate clauses in the two paragraphs. If you have not, try combining sentences by creating adjective, adverb, or noun clauses.

Proofreading   Put your paragraphs aside for a while, and then read them again, looking for errors in grammar, punctuation, and spelling. Pay special attention to the proper use of the relative pronouns *which, that, who,* and *whom.* (See pages 751 and 661–662). Also, be sure that you have punctuated all subordinate clauses correctly (see pages 797–801).

CRITICAL THINKING
Analysis

Remind students that as they select their paintings or prints and write their paragraphs, they should keep in mind their purpose and audience. For example, by thinking of reasons why other students would like those paintings, they could choose paintings that the student council would want to use.

PREWRITING

If you choose to send students to the school library, you may want to have them first brainstorm what scenes or subjects they like in art. Then the librarian can guide them to landscapes or seascapes, portraits, or historic genre paintings. Having students explain why they like the paintings they chose may help students prepare to write.

EVALUATING AND REVISING

Have students evaluate each of their paragraphs for unity by turning the topic sentence into a question and then reading each supporting sentence in the paragraph to see if it answers the question.

GRAMMAR

GRAMMAR

OBJECTIVES

- To classify sentences as simple, compound, complex, or compound-complex
- To use the four kinds of sentences in descriptions
- To use the four kinds of sentences in a journal entry

Teacher's ResourceBank™

RESOURCES

SENTENCES CLASSIFIED ACCORDING TO STRUCTURE

- Classifying Sentences by Structure

QUICK REMINDER

Write the following sentence constructions on a transparency or on the chalkboard:

      S   V

1. The boaters rowed smoothly.

      S   V =   S

2. The swimmers swam; the boaters

      V

rowed.

      S   V

3. The boaters rowed

           S   V

while the fish watched.

      S   V =

4. The boaters rowed and the

      S   V

swimmers swam

         S   V

while the fish watched.

Ask students to identify each sentence as simple, compound, complex, or compound-complex. Explain that the clauses in a compound sentence are equal (the semicolon, comma and coordinating conjunction, or semicolon and conjunctive adverb can be visualized as an equals sign). However, the clauses in a complex sentence are not equal because one clause is subordinate to—or a part of—the other, independent clause.

GRAMMAR

610 *The Clause*

Sentences Classified According to Structure

The *structure* of a sentence is determined by the number and types of clauses it has.

18g. Sentences are classified according to their structure as *simple, compound, complex,* or *compound-complex.*

(1) A *simple sentence* has one independent clause and no subordinate clauses. It may have a compound subject, a compound verb, and any number of phrases.

EXAMPLES
          S   S   V

Cora and **Kareem bought** party supplies at the mall.

          S   V   V

Later, **they drove** to school and **decorated** the cafeteria for the Latin Club's annual banquet.

(2) A *compound sentence* has two or more independent clauses but no subordinate clauses.

A compound sentence is actually two or more simple sentences joined together either by a comma and a coordinating conjunction, by a semicolon, or by a semicolon and a conjunctive adverb such as *therefore, however,* or *consequently.*

EXAMPLES
          S   V

Cora hung colorful streamers from the ceiling, and

        S   V

Kareem set party favors on the tables.

               S   V   S

After an hour, **they took** a short break; then **they**

      V

went back to work.

          S   V

They agreed not to take any more breaks; otherwise,

          S   V

they would be late getting home.

☞ REFERENCE NOTE: See pages 796 and 816–819 for more information on punctuating compound sentences.

18g

GRAMMAR

NOTE: Don't confuse a compound predicate in a simple sentence with the two subjects and two predicates in a compound sentence.

COMPOUND PREDICATE

To pass the time, **they talked** about school and **told** stories about their families.

COMPOUND SENTENCE

To pass the time, **they talked** about school, and **they told** stories about their families.

(3) A *complex sentence* has one independent clause and *at least* one subordinate clause.

EXAMPLE When **they had finished** their work, **they complimented** each other on the results.

(4) A *compound-complex sentence* has two or more independent clauses and *at least* one subordinate clause.

EXAMPLE **Cora waited** for just the right moment to ask Kareem to go to the banquet with her, and **he** promptly **accepted** her invitation, adding that **he had been planning** to ask her the same thing.

☞ REFERENCE NOTE: For information on how sentences are classified according to purpose, see pages 565–566.

EXERCISE 7 **Classifying Sentences According to Structure**

Classify each of the sentences in the following paragraph as *simple*, *compound*, *complex*, or *compound-complex*.

[1] Our club, the Key Club, sponsored a rummage sale and requested donations from everyone at school. [2] We accepted whatever was donated, but we welcomed housewares most. [3] The principal donated a vacuum cleaner; the coach contributed a set of dishes; and several of the teachers provided towels and sheets. [4] We sold

1. simp.
2. cd.-cx.
3. cd.
4. cd.-cx.

LEP/ESL

General Strategies. It may be necessary to allow some students more time to complete **Exercise 8.** Encourage them to describe the fruits of their native countries, as well as those they recognize in the picture of the luau. It also may benefit the students to write without restrictions as to the number of compound or complex sentences.

INTEGRATING THE LANGUAGE ARTS

Literature Link. James Weldon Johnson's poem "The Creation" includes a variety of sentence types. Have students read the poem carefully and ask them why Johnson uses so few simple sentences. Then ask how Johnson uses compound and complex sentences effectively. [Johnson creates a powerful, rhythmic, melodic effect with the parallel structure of repeated independent clauses introduced by *And,* as in lines 10–12, and with the parallel structure of repeated adjective clauses introduced by *Who,* as in lines 81–83.]

LEARNING STYLES

Visual Learners. Divide your class into small groups and instruct students to read and evaluate one another's descriptions of the luau in **Exercise 8.** Have the students highlight the simple sentences in yellow, the compound sentences in blue, the complex sentences in red, and the compound-complex sentences in green. Tell them that a rainbow of colors indicates good sentence variety.

ANSWERS
Exercise 8

Answers will vary. Here are some possibilities:

1. Traditionally, roasting a pig for a luau was an event for men only, and each guest knew which piece of the pig he should be served, wherever he was seated. (compound-complex)

2. Our luau had fewer taboos. (simple)

3. The pig was cooked in an oven that was a hole in the ground. (complex)

4. The first dish was fish wrapped in ti leaves, and the second was salmon with poi, a tangy, purplish paste. (compound)

5. Hula dancers and fire jugglers performed in an atmosphere of frangipani trees and ginger blossoms. (simple)

---

612 *The Clause*

almost everything that had been donated, and we celebrated our success with pitchers of lemonade. [5] Afterward, we gave all the profits that we had made from the sale to the city's homeless shelter.

5. cx.

▶ EXERCISE 8 **Using the Four Kinds of Sentences**

You and your family won a vacation to Hawaii. While you were there, you attended this luau. *Luau* is a Hawaiian word meaning "feast," and that's exactly what it was! There were different kinds of meats and fruits to eat, and, for entertainment, hula dancers and fire jugglers performed. Write five sentences describing the luau. If you have ever eaten any of the foods that are shown, give your impressions of them. Use at least one of each of the four kinds of sentences—simple, compound, complex, and compound-complex. Be prepared to identify the kinds of sentences that you use.

EXAMPLE **1.** *The fresh pineapple at the luau wasn't as sweet as pineapple that comes in a can.* (complex)

You are an adventurer in a strange land and have just wandered into the mysterious place shown on the next page. Before going one step farther, you decide to make some notes about what you see. Write down your impressions of this scene. Think of reasons for the distinctive mood of the place and theorize about who may live here.

REVIEW: POSTTESTS 1 and 2

OBJECTIVES

- To identify independent and subordinate clauses, and to classify the subordinate clauses as adjective clauses, adverb clauses, or noun clauses

What should you explore first? Why? In your journal entries, include at least one simple sentence, one compound sentence, one complex sentence, and two compound-complex sentences.

Subject: thoughts at *The Rose Tower*
Audience: yourself and whoever may read your journal in the future
Purpose: to help you decide what to do next

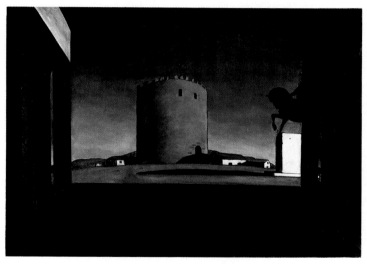

The Rose Tower by Giorgio de Chirico, Peggy Guggenheim Collection

PICTURE THIS

Before students begin writing their journal entries, have them discuss *The Rose Tower* in small groups. Ask them these questions: How does this painting make you feel? Does it put you in a particular kind of mood? How do the lighting and simple architecture contribute to the feeling? This group discussion should give students plenty of material for their notes.

👁 VISUAL CONNECTIONS

About the Artist. Giorgio de Chirico was born in Volos, Greece, on July 10, 1888. Influences on his art include the writing of Friedrich Nietzsche and the architecture of Paris, France, where he lived between 1911 and 1915. Chirico uses dim lighting and stark, isolated objects to create the tone of melancholy and nostalgia that he must have felt when he produced his first masterpieces shortly before and during World War I.

GRAMMAR

Review: Posttest 1

A. Identifying Independent and Subordinate Clauses; Classifying Subordinate Clauses

Identify each italicized clause in the following sentences as an *independent clause* or a *subordinate clause*. Then, classify each italicized subordinate clause as an *adjective clause*, an *adverb clause*, or a *noun clause*.

- To classify sentences according to structure as simple, compound, complex, or compound-complex
- To write sentences with varied structures

EXAMPLE **1.** The Brooklyn Bridge, *which was built in the latter half of the nineteenth century,* was the world's first steel-wire suspension bridge.
  1. *subordinate clause—adjective clause*

1. The Brooklyn Bridge, <u>*which spans the East River between Brooklyn and Manhattan in New York City*</u>, is one of the engineering wonders of the world. **1.** adj. cl.
2. Massive granite towers <u>*that are supported by concrete-filled shafts*</u> are among its remarkable features. **2.** adj. cl.
3. <u>*The bridge was designed and built by John and Washington Roebling, a father-and-son engineering team*</u> who were pioneers in the use of steel-wire cables.
4. The steel-wire cables give the bridge a graceful appearance <u>*that resembles a spider's web*</u>. **4.** adj. cl.
5. <u>*That the bridge combines strength with beauty*</u> remains a tribute to the Roebling family. **5.** n. cl.
6. The Roeblings discovered <u>*that construction work could be both slow and dangerous*</u>. **6.** n. cl.
7. <u>*Although she was not an engineer*</u>, Nora Roebling assisted in the efforts to complete the bridge. **7.** adv. cl.
8. <u>*Because they were required at times to work underwater in airtight chambers called caissons*</u>, many workers, including Washington Roebling, suffered from caisson disease, or decompression sickness. **8.** adv. cl.
9. Sailors, <u>*who were used to working at great heights*</u>, were hired to string the miles of cable. **9.** adj. cl.
10. <u>*John Roebling injured his foot at the work site*</u>, and as a result, he died of tetanus shortly after construction was begun.

B. Classifying Sentences According to Structure

Classify each of the following sentences as <u>*simple*</u>, <u>*compound*</u>, <u>*complex*</u>, or <u>*compound-complex*</u>.

11. cd.

[11] After being stricken with caisson disease, Washington Roebling succeeded his father on the project; however, he was confined to bed. [12] The Roeblings lived in a house that was near the construction site, and Washington supervised the work through a telescope. [13] He dictated instructions to Nora, and she relayed them to the work crew. [14] Whether the work on the bridge could

12. cd.-cx.

13. cd.

14. cx.

have continued without her assistance is doubtful.
[15] When the bridge was finally completed in 1883, President Chester A. Arthur attended the dedication ceremonies. **[16]** Because of his illness, Washington Roebling was unable to attend the ceremonies. **[17]** Instead, the president visited Roebling's home to honor the man who had struggled so valiantly to complete the bridge. **[18]** The bridge took fourteen years to build. **[19]** At the time of its completion, it was the world's longest suspension bridge. **[20]** The bridge is now more than a century old, and it still stands as a monument to the artistry, sacrifice, and determination of all the people who planned and built it.

15. cx.
16. simp.
17. cx.
18. simp.
19. simp.
20. cd.-cx.

GRAMMAR

Review: Posttest 2

Writing Sentences with Varied Structures

Write your own sentences according to the following guidelines.

EXAMPLE **1.** a simple sentence with a compound subject
1. *My aunt and uncle live nearby.*

1. a simple sentence with a compound verb
2. a compound sentence with two independent clauses joined by the conjunction *but*
3. a compound sentence with two independent clauses joined by a semicolon and a conjunctive adverb
4. a complex sentence with an adjective clause
5. a complex sentence beginning with an adverb clause
6. a complex sentence ending with an adverb clause
7. a complex sentence with a noun clause used as a direct object
8. a complex sentence with a noun clause used as the subject
9. a complex sentence with a noun clause used as the object of a preposition
10. a compound-complex sentence

ANSWERS
Review: Posttest 2

Answers may vary. Here are some possibilities:

1. My sister lives and works in Brooklyn.
2. Many people came to the party, but most of them left early.
3. I missed the bus; however, I was only a few minutes late.
4. The ones whose projects are selected will attend the regional contest.
5. If I study one more hour, I should be able to finish my homework.
6. They met with the company managers as soon as they could do so.
7. The families liked what they heard about the new health plan.
8. That thousands of children die of hunger every day is becoming known.
9. It is hard to agree about what we should do.
10. We told them that their plan wouldn't work, but they wouldn't listen to us.

GRAMMAR

OBJECTIVES

- To select verbs that agree with their subjects
- To identify verbs that agree with their subjects and to identify pronouns that agree with their antecedents

USAGE

Teacher's ResourceBank™

RESOURCES

FOR THE WHOLE CHAPTER

- Chapter Review Form A
- Chapter Review Form B
- Assessment Portfolio
    - Usage Pretests
    - Usage Mastery Tests

CHAPTER OVERVIEW

Two of the usage errors students most frequently commit are subject-verb disagreement and pronoun-antecedent disagreement. This chapter offers ways to help students master agreement through a number of activities. The activities involve goals well within the students' reach and lead students into learning material they might think they already know. The **Writing Application** demonstrates the importance of agreement for clarity in writing.

To reinforce learning, when students revise compositions, refer them to specific exercises that cover particularly troublesome areas.

USAGE

19 AGREEMENT

Subject and Verb, Pronoun and Antecedent

Diagnostic Test

A. Selecting Verbs That Agree with Their Subjects

For each sentence, choose the <u>verb</u> in parentheses <u>that agrees with the subject</u>.

EXAMPLE   **1.** Both coats *(is, are)* on sale this week.
          1. *are*

1. The jury (*has*, *have*) been paying close attention to the evidence in this case.
2. There (*is*, *are*) four herbs that almost any gardener can grow: basil, thyme, marjoram, and oregano.
3. All of these old letters (*was*, *were*) tied with ribbon and stored in a trunk in the attic.
4. Each of them (*is*, *are*) penned in bold, flowing handwriting, embellished with many flourishes.
5. Both Alicia and Isabel (*thinks*, *think*) that the former owner of the house put the letters in the attic.

6. Neither of them (<u>*knows*</u>, *know*) for sure who wrote that message.
7. The two songs we played in the Martin Luther King Day concert (*was*, <u>*were*</u>) written by Keneisha Watson.
8. Did you know that *archy & mehitabel* (<u>*is*</u>, *are*) a series of poems supposedly written by a cockroach that lives in a newspaper office with his friend, a cat?
9. Here (*is*, <u>*are*</u>) the latest scores of today's basketball games.
10. Neither potatoes nor peanuts (*is*, <u>*are*</u>) grown on this farm anymore.

B. Identifying Verbs That Agree with Their Subjects and Pronouns That Agree with Their Antecedents

In many of the following sentences, either a verb does not agree with its subject, or a pronoun does not agree with its antecedent. Identify each incorrect verb or pronoun, and give the correct form. If a sentence is correct, write C.

EXAMPLES
1. The flock of birds, almost blackening the sky, were an awe-inspiring sight.
1. *were—was*

2. Only a decade ago their number was declining.
2. *C*

11. The meeting got out of hand when the discussion period began since everyone tried to express~~their~~ opinion at the same time. **11.** his or her
12. There on the corner of your desk~~is~~ the books that I returned and that you claimed you never received. **12.** are
13. Two students from each class~~is~~ going to the state capital to attend a special conference on education. **13.** are
14. Each of them~~are~~ expected to bring back a report on the conference so that classmates can get firsthand information. **14.** is
15. Since they will be on vacation next month, neither Miguel nor his sister~~are~~ going to enter the mixed-doubles tennis tournament. **15.** is
16. The audience expressed~~their~~ admiration for the dancer's grace and skill by applauding wildly. **16.** its

USING THE DIAGNOSTIC TEST

The **Diagnostic Test** deals with the constructions that cause students the most problems. **Part A** tests for the ability to evaluate whether the subject of a sentence should have a singular or plural verb. The sentences in **Part A** contain collective nouns, singular and plural subjects, singular subjects that end in –s, and subjects separated from their verbs by phrases. **Part B** tests the same ability, but it also tests the ability to identify pronouns and their correct antecedents.

Through this test you will be able to determine where individual students need to focus their attention and where the whole class needs practice.

If only a few students miss questions involving subjects and verbs separated by phrases, you may want to have them look up the rules of subject and verb agreement, then drill them on exercises before having them write a few original sentences with intervening phrases.

OBJECTIVES

- To identify words as singular or plural
- To identify verbs that agree in number with their subjects

---

618 *Agreement*

17. After the senator had read the proposed amendment, anyone who disagreed with the ruling was allowed to state ~~their~~ reason.   **17.** his or her
18. This collection of old African American folk tales ~~demonstrate~~ the wisdom, humor, and creativity of my ancestors.   **18.** demonstrates
19. She is one of those competitive people who perform best under pressure.   **19.** C
20. Since neither of you ~~have~~ ever tasted fried plantains, my mother would like you to eat a Cuban meal at our house tonight.   **20.** has

---

Number

19a. When a word refers to one person or thing, it is *singular* in number. When a word refers to more than one, it is *plural* in number.

SINGULAR	video	child	I	thief	herself
PLURAL	videos	children	we	thieves	themselves

In general, nouns ending in *–s* are plural (*aunts, uncles, towns, crimes*); verbs ending in *–s* are singular (*gives, takes, does, has, is*).

👉 **REFERENCE NOTE:** For more information on the plural forms of nouns, see pages 877–880.

▶ EXERCISE 1   **Identifying Words as Singular or Plural in Number**

Identify each of the words listed below as either *plural* or *singular*.

1. stories
2. one
3. several
4. applies
5. people
6. mouse
7. genius
8. civics
9. ability
10. says
11. data
12. admire
13. both
14. mumps
15. woman
16. some
17. donates
18. donation
19. mathematics
20. many

Teacher's ResourceBank™

RESOURCES

NUMBER
- Number: Singular or Plural?
- Agreement of Subject and Verb
- Agreement and Prepositional Phrases

🦉 **QUICK REMINDER**

Ask each student to list five singular words with plurals that are formed in different ways. Then have them write the plural forms of the words. Write some of the singular and plural words on the chalkboard, and review briefly with the students how the plurals were formed.

ANSWERS
Exercise 1

1. plural
2. singular
3. plural
4. singular
5. plural
6. singular
7. singular
8. singular
9. singular
10. singular
11. plural
12. plural
13. plural
14. singular
15. singular
16. singular/plural
17. singular
18. singular
19. singular
20. plural

Agreement of Subject and Verb

19b. A verb should agree with its subject in number.

(1) Singular subjects take singular verbs.

EXAMPLES Earline **attends** college. [The singular verb *attends* agrees with the singular subject *Earline.*]
That boy **delivers** newspapers. [The singular verb *delivers* agrees with the singular subject *boy.*]

(2) Plural subjects take plural verbs.

EXAMPLES They **attend** college. [The plural verb *attend* agrees with the plural subject *they.*]
Those boys **deliver** newspapers. [The plural verb *deliver* agrees with the plural subject *boys.*]

Verb phrases also agree in number with their subjects. In a verb phrase, only the first auxiliary (helping) verb changes form to agree with the subject.

EXAMPLES Earline **is attending** college.
They **are attending** college.
A boy in my class **has been delivering** newspapers.
Two boys in my class **have been delivering** newspapers.

The form *were* is plural except when used with the singular *you* and in sentences that are contrary to fact.

EXAMPLES **You were** right. [*You* used as subject]
If I were in charge, I would make some changes. [contrary to fact]

EXERCISE 2 **Selecting Verbs That Agree with Their Subjects**

Choose the <u>verb</u> in parentheses <u>that agrees with the subject given</u>.

1. people (*walks*, <u>*walk*</u>)
2. you (*is*, <u>*are*</u>)
3. cattle (*runs*, <u>*run*</u>)
4. we (*talks*, <u>*talk*</u>)
5. Joan (<u>*was*</u>, *were*)
6. house (<u>*stands*</u>, *stand*)
7. result (<u>*is*</u>, *are*)
8. they (*believes*, <u>*believe*</u>)
9. crews (*sails*, <u>*sail*</u>)
10. women (*seems*, <u>*seem*</u>)

MEETING INDIVIDUAL NEEDS

LEP/ESL

General Strategies. Textbooks give rules of standard usage. However, even well-educated native speakers' speech varies from textbook English. This is because living languages constantly change. The first instances of change show up in spoken forms that through common use begin to sound correct. The textbook can be perplexing to second-language learners who put great trust in the informal speech of native speakers. You may want to discuss the fact that although a variety of forms are acceptable in casual speech, students who follow the textbook's rules will always be using standard English.

ADVANCED STUDENTS

You may wish to have some students work in groups of three or four to identify and analyze instances in which subject-verb agreement errors occur. A good place to look might be **Exercise 5** on p. 624, but any group of sentences with agreement errors will suffice. Lead students to discover that agreement errors occur only in the simple present tense with regular verbs, and in the tenses requiring present-tense or past-tense forms of irregular verbs such as *be, do,* or *have* (present and past progressive, present perfect, and present perfect progressive).

USAGE

USAGE

COOPERATIVE LEARNING

You may wish to hold a scavenger hunt for words. Divide the class into teams of two or three to search through their dictionaries for words with irregular plurals. Allow twenty minutes at first and add time if students are enjoying the hunt.

For each word, the team should record the correct spelling of the singular and plural. When time is up, let teams trade lists and check each other's work.

The students might wish to compile a class list of irregular plurals to be copied and shared with your other classes.

MEETING INDIVIDUAL NEEDS

STUDENTS WITH SPECIAL NEEDS

Students with learning disabilities may have difficulty in distinguishing relevant material. In order to learn agreement, they must be able to focus on the subject of a verb. To direct students' attention to the subjects of sentences, have them place parentheses around any prepositional phrases in the exercises. Also, you may want to pair auditory learners with good readers so that limited reading abilities do not interfere with students' understanding of the lesson.

As an additional activity, choose an article of high interest from a newspaper or magazine and make incorrect changes in the noun-verb agreement. Inform students of the number of errors in the article and have them correct these errors.

Intervening Phrases

19c. The number of the subject is not changed by a phrase following the subject.

The subject is never part of a prepositional phrase.

EXAMPLES   The **woman** on the stairs **is** Senator Reyes. [*woman is*]
The **women** in the front row **are** Cabinet officers. [*women are*]

Remember that prepositional phrases may begin with compound prepositions such as *together with, in addition to, as well as,* and *along with.* These phrases do not affect the number of the verb.

EXAMPLES   **Tammy,** along with her mother and aunt, **is** going to the concert. [Tammy is going.]
The **wind,** together with the rain and fog, **was** making navigation difficult. [wind was making]
Jack's **imagination,** as well as his sense of humor, **was** delightful. [imagination was]

A negative construction following the subject does not change the number of the subject.

EXAMPLE   **Carl,** not Juan and I, **is** doing the artwork.

 EXERCISE 3   **Selecting Verbs That Agree with Their Subjects**

Identify the <u>subject</u> of each of the following sentences. Then, choose the <u>verb</u> in parentheses <u>that agrees in number with the subject</u>.

EXAMPLE   **1.** The price of haircuts (*has, have*) gone up.
1. *price—has*

1. A heaping <u>basket</u> of turnip greens (<u>*was*</u>, *were*) sitting on the counter.
2. <u>Displaying</u> disregard for the rights and comforts of others (<u>*is*</u>, *are*) rude.
3. The community college <u>course</u> on collecting stamps (*attract*, <u>*attracts*</u>) many people.
4. The <u>members</u> of the Pak family (*meets*, <u>*meet*</u>) for a reunion every year.

OBJECTIVES

- To write sentences in which verbs agree with their subjects and pronouns agree with their antecedents
- To identify the subjects of sentences

5. The <u>carpeting</u> in the upstairs and downstairs rooms (*is, are*) getting worn.
6. The turquoise <u>stones</u> in this Navajo ring certainly (*is, <u>are</u>*) pretty.
7. One <u>friend</u> of my brothers (<u>*says*</u>, *say*) that I look like Whitney Houston.
8. The <u>package</u> of radio parts (<u>*was*</u>, *were*) smashed in the mail.
9. The <u>cost</u> of two new snow tires (<u>*was*</u>, *were*) more than I expected.
10. <u>Burt</u>, not Anne and Laura, (<u>*has*</u>, *have*) borrowed the bicycle pump.

REVIEW A   **Completing Sentences That Demonstrate Agreement**

Anna Mary Robertson Moses (1860–1961), better known as "Grandma Moses," became famous in old age for her paintings of rural America. Add words to the word groups on the following page to complete ten sentences about this Grandma Moses painting, titled *The Barn Dance*. Make sure that all verbs agree with their subjects and all pronouns agree with their antecedents. Be prepared to identify the subject of each sentence.

EXAMPLE   **1.** barn are
   1. *The doors of the barn are wide open.*

USAGE

Grandma Moses (1860–1961): *The Barn Dance*. Copyright © 1989 Grandma Moses Properties Co., New York.

Review A

Students' sentences will vary. Here are some possible sentences:

1. The <u>clouds</u> look like fluffy elephants.
2. A <u>musician</u> is playing to warm up for the dance.
3. A <u>pair</u> of horses pulls each of the wagons.
4. <u>All</u> of the people at the barn dance are enjoying the music.
5. <u>One</u> of the buildings in the distance is my house.
6. The <u>people</u> on the green wagon are waving.
7. Fiddle <u>music</u>, along with laughter and conversation, fills the air as the band begins a new dance.
8. The <u>guests</u> have noticed the cloudy sky.
9. If I were at this barn dance alone, <u>I</u>'d try to meet some new friends.
10. A <u>horse</u> is drinking from the trough.

VISUAL CONNECTIONS
About the Artist. Born Anna Mary Robertson, Grandma Moses grew up in rural New York. She began painting in 1938 at the age of seventy-eight. Her scenes of farm life in Virginia and New York were an overnight sensation, and she was famous by 1940. When she died in 1961 at the age of one hundred and one, some considered her the most famous American primitive painter.

USAGE

CRITICAL THINKING
Synthesis

When students have completed **Review A**, you may wish to let them work in groups of three or four to create a brief story about the picture. They might begin with the sentences they created for their individual exercises. Have them evaluate the additions they made to the word groups, discussing particularly the groups that require additional subjects. After students have compared the subjects they have added, have the group members combine their ideas about the painting to create a story.

Teacher's ResourceBank™
RESOURCES

INDEFINITE PRONOUNS
• Agreement with Indefinite Pronouns

QUICK REMINDER

Write the basic definition of indefinite pronouns on the chalkboard:

indefinite pronouns—pronouns that do not refer to a specific person or thing

Ask students each to write five indefinite pronouns and to identify them as singular or plural.

OBJECTIVES
• To write sentences with verbs that agree with their indefinite-pronoun subjects
• To identify subject-verb agreement in sentences
• To use given words as subjects to write a log entry

1. clouds look
2. musician is playing
3. horses pulls
4. barn dance are enjoying
5. buildings in the distance is
6. green wagon are waving
7. along with laughter and conversation, fills
8. guests have noticed the cloudy
9. I were at this barn dance
10. horse is drinking

Indefinite Pronouns

19d. The following indefinite pronouns are singular: *each, either, neither, one, everyone, everybody, no one, nobody, anyone, anybody, someone, somebody.*

Indefinite pronouns are pronouns that do not refer to a specific person or thing.

EXAMPLES   **No one leaves** early.
            One of the guitar strings **was** broken. [One was broken.]
            Neither of them **knew** the answer.
            Someone who likes apple juice **raids** the refrigerator at night.

Notice that a phrase or a clause following one of these pronouns does not affect the verb.

EXAMPLES   **Everybody likes** my uncle.
            Everybody in my neighborhood **likes** my uncle.
            Everybody who meets my uncle **likes** him.

19e. The following indefinite pronouns are plural: *several, few, both, many.*

EXAMPLES   **Several** of the women **are** pilots.
            A **few** in the crowd **were** rowdy.
            Have **both** tried harder?
            Many of the students **write** and **edit** on word processors.

19f. The indefinite pronouns *some, all, any, most,* and *none* may be either singular or plural, depending on the word they refer to.

These pronouns are singular when they refer to a singular word and plural when they refer to a plural word.

SINGULAR **Most** of the day **was** gone. [*Most* refers to singular *day.*]

PLURAL **Most** of the steers **were** grazing. [*Most* refers to plural *steers.*]

SINGULAR **Has any** of the shipment arrived? [*Any* refers to singular *shipment.*]

PLURAL **Are any** of the coins new? [*Any* refers to plural *coins.*]

SINGULAR **None** of the damage **was** serious. [*None* refers to singular *damage.*]

PLURAL **None** of the students **have** finished. [*None* refers to plural *students.*]

In each of the examples above, the prepositional phrase following the subject provides a clue to the number of the pronoun. When these pronouns are used alone, their number depends on the number of the item the speaker or writer has in mind.

EXAMPLES **Most were** interesting. [a number of books, photographs, ideas, etc.]

Most was interesting. [a portion of a book, movie, conversation, etc.]

 ORAL PRACTICE 1 **Using Verbs That Agree with Indefinite Pronouns**

Read the following sentences aloud, stressing the italicized words.

1. *One* of those cups *is* broken.
2. *Either* of the bikes *is* ready to go.
3. A *few* of the girls *are* experienced riders.
4. *Each* of the mariachi bands *has* performed one number.
5. *Some* of the mice *were* eating the cheese.
6. *Most* of the milk *is* gone.
7. *Neither* of the cars *has* a radio.
8. *None* of the apples *were* ripe.

 COMMON ERROR
Problem. The list of singular indefinite pronouns given in **Rule 19d** might be difficult for students to remember.

Solution. Simplify the lists by emphasizing that all compound indefinite pronouns require singular verbs. Regardless of whether the word being combined is *one* or *body,* every compound indefinite pronoun is singular.

LEARNING STYLES

Visual Learners. Students might more quickly master indefinite pronouns that may be either singular or plural by underlining both the subject of the sentence and the word that refers to the subject—usually, the object in the prepositional phrase after the subject pronoun.

Auditory Learners. In learning about pronouns of indefinite number, students will benefit from oral drills on both **Oral Practice 1** and **Exercise 5.** They should listen for cues such as prepositions (*of, on,* or *in*) that begin a phrase. If the indefinite pronoun is one that may be either singular or plural, the object of the preposition in the phrase gives its number to the indefinite-pronoun subject.

COMMON ERROR

Problem. Students often use plural verb forms with *either* and *neither*. Because each word suggests two alternatives, students may mistake the two choices (or a plural object in a prepositional phrase) for a plural subject.

Solution. To show that a choice between two singular alternatives always takes a singular verb, ask the students to imagine two doors: one red, one blue. Behind one door is what they most want; behind the other, what they most fear. They may choose either door, or neither, but they cannot walk through both doors at once.

Remind the students that *either* means "one or the other," but that *neither* means "not one and not the other." Students have less trouble with *either*; they might remember the meaning of *neither* by thinking of it as a contraction of *not* and *either*.

USAGE

► EXERCISE 4 **Writing Sentences with Verbs That Agree with Their Subjects**

Rewrite each of the following sentences according to the directions in parentheses. If necessary, change the number of the verb to agree with the new subject.

1. ~Everyone~ easily~understands~ the rules of this game. (Change *everyone* to *most people*.) **1.** Most people/understand
2. ~Neither~ of the actresses~was~ nominated. (Change *neither* to *both*.) **2.** Both/were
3. ~Has each~ of your cousins had a turn? (Change *each* to *both*.) **3.** Have both
4. Some of the~trees were~ destroyed. (Change *trees* to *crop*.) **4.** crop was
5. ~Have~ any of the~apples~ been harvested? (Change *apples* to *wheat*.) **5.** Has/wheat
6. ~Nobody visits~ that haunted house. (Change *nobody* to *many of our neighbors*.) **6.** Many of our neighbors visit
7. ~Each is~ well trained. (Change *each* to *several*.) **7.** Several are
8. ~One~ of the tires~needs~ air. (Change *one* to *all*.) **8.** All/need
9. All of the~fruit was~ eaten. (Change *fruit* to *pears*.) **9.** pears were
10. There~is~ baked~chicken~ for everybody. (Change *chicken* to *potatoes*.) **10.** are/potatoes

► EXERCISE 5 **Identifying Subject-Verb Agreement in Sentences**

The subjects and verbs in some of the following sentences do not agree. If a sentence is incorrect, write the correct form of the verb. If the sentence is correct, write *C*.

1. Several of the crew~was~ commended by the captain. **1.** were
2. Neither of the coaches~were~ happy with the decision. **2.** was
3. Each of us~are~ going to make a large poster for the upcoming election. **3.** is
4. Some of the frozen yogurt has started to melt. **4.** C
5. ~Does~ both of those games require special gear? **5.** Do
6. Either of the assistants usually gets the mail. **6.** C
7. None of the buildings were damaged by the hail. **7.** C
8. None of the food has been frozen. **8.** C
9. Neither of the book reports~were~ finished on time. **9.** was
10. Anyone who wants to can help me make gefilte fish for the Passover feast. **10.** C

▶ REVIEW B

Selecting Verbs That Agree with Their Subjects

For each of the following sentences, choose the <u>verb</u> in parentheses <u>that agrees with the subject</u>.

1. (*Has*, <u>*Have*</u>) any of you ever wondered how meals are served to space shuttle astronauts?
2. Each item for the day's menu (*come*, <u>*comes*</u>) sealed in its own container.
3. To help reduce weight on the spacecraft, many of the foods (*is*, <u>*are*</u>) dehydrated.
4. At mealtime, someone in the crew (*add*, <u>*adds*</u>) water to the scrambled eggs, vegetables, and puddings.
5. All of the water mixed with these foods (<u>*is*</u>, *are*) a byproduct of the fuel cells that provide the spacecraft's electricity.
6. Of course, not one of the beverages (<u>*is*</u>, *are*) pourable because there is no gravity.
7. As you can see, uncovered liquid (*bounce*, <u>*bounces*</u>) into the air like a ball if its container is accidentally jolted.
8. Much of the food (<u>*is*</u>, *are*) covered in sauce so that surface tension will help to keep the food in dishes.
9. Amazingly, most of the foods (<u>*taste*</u>, *tastes*) delicious.
10. The menu for the astronauts even (<u>*includes*</u>, *include*) steaks and strawberries.

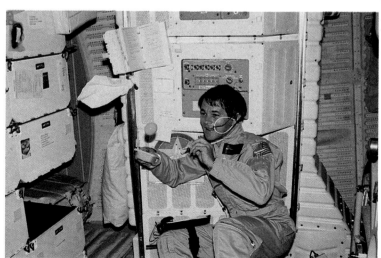

VISUAL CONNECTIONS

Ideas for Writing. Students who would enjoy imagining themselves as astronauts or in other challenging jobs might write brief narratives of their first morning in orbit or of the first day of a job. They could choose to focus on the first tasks of their morning or to describe what they see as they orbit the earth or complete an essential procedure in the space shuttle.

When students have finished their compositions, have groups of three or four identify the indefinite pronouns they used, check their use, and share the narratives and descriptions with one another.

PICTURE THIS

Before students write, lead them in a discussion of what a visitor from outer space might want to know about human life, beliefs, and social customs. Would visitors from Zan Dor understand suntanning, swimsuits, and beach games? Remind students that a log is intended to be read by others, so the language of the entries should be standard written English.

PICTURE THIS

You are the captain of the first spacecraft sent from the planet Zan Dor to explore Earth. As your invisible ship skims above the edge of a land mass, you look down and see this strange assembly of alien beings near a large body of water. You order your crew to cruise slowly above this scene while you try to figure out what the aliens are doing. Write a brief entry in the spacecraft's daily log, recording what you see below and speculating on what it means. As you write your log entry, use at least five of the following words as subjects: *aliens, everybody, inhabitants, we, many, most, all, none, any, some*. Be sure your subjects and verbs agree.

Subject: earthling behavior
Audience: yourself and future space travelers
Purpose: to inform

COMPOUND SUBJECTS Rules 19g–19i

OBJECTIVE

- To select verbs that agree with their subjects

Compound Subjects

A *compound subject* consists of two or more nouns or pronouns that are joined by a conjunction and have the same verb.

19g. Subjects joined by *and* usually take a plural verb.

EXAMPLES **Ramón** and **she like** hiking.
Her **brother,** her **uncle,** and her **cousin are** teachers.

NOTE: Subjects joined by *and* that name only one person or thing take a singular verb.

EXAMPLES Pork and beans **goes** well with barbecued chicken.
[One dish goes.]
Rock-and-roll **is** here to stay. [One kind of music is.]

19h. Singular subjects joined by *or* or *nor* take a singular verb.

EXAMPLES Marcelo or Donya **knows** the address.
Does either Dad or Mom have the key?
Neither our phone nor our doorbell **was** working.

NOTE: Singular subjects that are joined by the correlative conjunction *both . . . and* take a plural verb.

EXAMPLE Both the scout and the counselor **were** helpful guides.

19i. When a singular subject and a plural subject are joined by *or* or *nor,* the verb agrees with the subject nearer the verb.

EXAMPLES Either Harry or his **aunts are** planning the activities for the beach party.
Neither the potatoes nor the **roast is** done.

You can usually avoid such awkward constructions by rewording the sentence so that each subject has its own verb.

EXAMPLES Either **Harry is** planning the activities for the beach party, or his **aunts are.**
The **potatoes are** not done, and neither **is** the **roast.**

USAGE

QUICK REMINDER
Write these four sentences on the chalkboard and ask students to identify and correct any agreement errors:

1. Bacon and eggs are my favorite breakfast. [are — is]
2. Bacon and eggs is not available at the supermarket today. [is — are]
3. Either broccoli or cauliflower are available as a side dish. [are — is]
4. Neither John nor his parents is able to find a ripe melon. [is — are]

Discuss with students why the verb form supplied does not agree with the subject.

MEETING INDIVIDUAL NEEDS

LEP/ESL

General Strategies. Try an oral drill with the following sentences or create similar sentences by using names of students in the class.

1. Ramón and Teresa have new shoes.
2. Vanessa or Jason has braces.
3. Louis and Joanna have freckles.
4. Anil or Maria has straight A's.
5. Tanya or Tai has a job.

USAGE

USAGE

MEETING INDIVIDUAL NEEDS

LESS-ADVANCED STUDENTS

Many students have a highly speech-based concept of grammar and will benefit from **Oral Practice 2**. Repetition of sentences will help students to develop better speech patterns.

In **Oral Practice 2,** five sentences have intervening phrases. Encourage students to notice these phrases and to remember that they affect verb number only for indefinite pronouns that can be either singular or plural in number, such as *most, some,* and *all.* As students repeat these sentences, ask them to concentrate only on the subjects and the verbs, as an aid in making agreement decisions.

Teacher's ResourceBank™
RESOURCES

OTHER PROBLEMS IN AGREEMENT
• Other Problems in Agreement

628

OBJECTIVES
• To use collective nouns in sentences
• To write and revise sentences so that the verbs agree with their subjects

---

628 *Agreement*

 ORAL PRACTICE 2 | **Using Verbs That Agree with Compound Subjects**

Read the following sentences aloud, stressing the italicized words.

1. Every *one* of the kittens *has* been given away.
2. A *few* of us *are* going to Chicago.
3. *Each* of the photographs *was* in black and white.
4. *Neither* Sam *nor* Miguel *likes* sports.
5. *Either* Judy *or* Claudia *does* the dishes tonight.
6. Not *one* of the stations *is* coming in clearly.
7. *Several* of the plates *were* cracked.
8. *Both* Marilyn *and* Marge *have* summer jobs.

EXERCISE 6 | **Selecting Verbs That Agree with Their Subjects**

For each of the following sentences, choose the verb in parentheses that agrees with the subject of the sentence.

1. Neither my brother nor I (*has, have*) a car.
2. Marlon and she (*is, are*) the dance champions.
3. Our relatives and theirs (*is, are*) having a barbecue together.
4. Both Michael Chang and Zina Garrison (*plays, play*) a good game of tennis.
5. Either the director or the actors (*is, are*) going to have to compromise.
6. Neither the grapes nor the cantaloupe (*was, were*) ripe enough to eat.
7. Both Magic Johnson and Michael Jordan (*is, are*) popular with fans.
8. Our class or theirs (*is, are*) going to sponsor the dance.
9. Either the faucet or the shower head (*leaks, leak*).
10. Either a transistor or a capacitor (*has, have*) burned out in this receiver.

Other Problems in Agreement

19j. Collective nouns may be either singular or plural.

19j

A **collective noun** is singular in form, but it names a *group* of persons or things.

Collective Nouns			
army	club	group	series
assembly	committee	herd	squad
audience	crowd	jury	staff
band	faculty	majority	swarm
choir	family	number	team
class	flock	public	troop

Use a singular verb with a collective noun when you mean the group as a unit. Use a plural verb when you mean the members of the group as individuals.

EXAMPLES   The class **has** met its substitute teacher. [the class as a unit]
The class **were** disagreeing with one another about the answers. [the class as individuals]

The team **is** on the field. [the team as a unit]
The team **are** working together. [the team as individuals]

NOTE: A pronoun that refers to the collective noun should agree in number with the noun, as in the examples above.

EXERCISE 7   **Using Collective Nouns in Sentences**

You are at the soccer game shown on the following page. During the game, you see many different groups of people on the field, in the bleachers, and on the bench. You notice that sometimes the members of a group act separately and sometimes a group acts together as a whole. Think of five collective nouns that name the groups you see. (See the top of this page for a list of collective nouns.) Use each noun as the subject in two sentences. After each sentence, identify the collective noun as *singular* or *plural* in that sentence.

EXAMPLE   **1.** crowd
     1. *The crowd seem to be enjoying themselves.—plural*
       The crowd has nearly filled the bleachers.—singular

USAGE

QUICK REMINDER

You may want to remind students that the principle behind the rules in this section is that the correct form of a verb is the one that conveys the intended meaning most clearly.

Write the following sentence on the chalkboard:

The choir were late.

Then ask your students whether the subject and the verb agree. Some students will probably argue that the verb should be *was*: a choir is a single group, and its verb should be singular. *The choir were late* is correct if its members arrived late and at different times, but if the members arrived together as a unit, the verb should be *was*. This example shows that common sense is the basis of grammatical rules.

MEETING
INDIVIDUAL
NEEDS

LEP/ESL

General Strategies. An error frequently made by students who have studied English in foreign schools is to always attribute plurality to collective nouns such as *crew*, *company*, or *bunch*. The result is mistakes like "The company are important." This is a situation where many examples can illustrate the point. A quick brainstorming session to supplement the list of collective nouns should help.

USAGE

USAGE

ANSWERS
Exercise 7

Sentences will vary. Possible collective nouns include *team, coaching staff, squad, band, class, crowd, family, faculty, pep club,* and *audience.*

⚡ TIMESAVER
After students have finished **Exercise 7,** have volunteers read their sentences aloud, identify the collective nouns as singular or plural, and explain the intended meaning of each sentence. Errors will point out what reteaching is needed.

🔧 COMMON ERROR
Problem. Students sometimes use a singular verb to specify a collective-noun subject and then use a plural pronoun to refer to the subject.

Solution. Write the following sentence on the chalkboard and ask the class to discuss what is wrong with it:

The team was beaten badly last week; now they are out to win big. [The words *they are* should be changed to *it is.*]

After students decide what is wrong, have them think of two or three other examples of this error to write on the chalkboard. Help students through the correction process. If they can identify an error and correct it, they are less likely to commit it.

USAGE

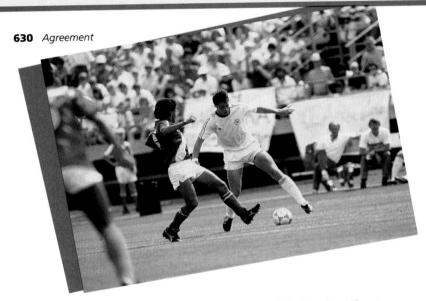

▶ EXERCISE 8   **Writing Sentences with Verbs That Agree with Their Subjects**

Rewrite the following sentences according to the instructions in parentheses, changing the number of the verb if necessary.

1. ₍Both of the records ₍are in the top forty. (Change *both* to *neither.*)   **1. Neither/is**
2. The Harlem Boys Choir ₍has been rehearsing ₍with the conductor. (Change *with the conductor* to *in small groups.*)   **2. have/in small groups.**
3. Either ₍my cousins or ₍Adrienne is bringing the pizza. (Reverse the order of the subjects.)   **3. Adrienne/my cousins are**
4. ₍Neither Carrie ₍nor Jana ₍is in the Pep Club. (Change *neither . . . nor* to *both . . . and.*)   **4. Both/and/are**
5. Gabriel García Márquez ₍and Octavio Paz ₍have won prizes in literature. (Change *and* to *or.*)   **5. or/has**   **6. each/**
6. ₍All of your papers ₍were graded. (Change *all* to *each.*)   **was**
7. Some of the ₍wood burns. (Change *wood* to *logs.*)   **7. logs bur**
8. The delighted team ₍was waving and grinning widely. (Change *waving and grinning widely* to *assembling to accept their medals.*)   **8. were assembling to accept their medals.**
9. ₍Everybody in the chorus is trying out for the play. (Change *everybody* to *no one.*)   **9. No one**
10. Macaroni ₍and cheese always tastes good. (Change *and* to *or.*)   **10. or**

19k. A verb agrees with its subject, not with its predicate nominative.

EXAMPLES The main **ingredient** in my hot sauce

is jalapeño **peppers.**

Jalapeño **peppers are** the main **ingredient** in my hot sauce.

When such a construction seems awkward to you, revise the sentence to avoid using a predicate nominative.

EXAMPLE **I use** jalapeño **peppers** as the main ingredient in my hot sauce.

19l. When the subject follows the verb, make sure that the verb agrees with it.

In sentences beginning with *here* or *there* and in questions, the subject follows the verb.

EXAMPLES Here **is** a **set** of keys.
Here **are** the **keys.**
Where **is** my **jacket?** Where **is** my **scarf?**
Where **are** my **jacket** and my **scarf?**

NOTE: Remember that contractions such as *here's, how's, what's,* and *where's* include the singular verb *is.* Use one of these contractions only if a singular subject follows it.

INCORRECT There's several photos of the oil spill in an article in this month's *Smithsonian.*
CORRECT There **are** several **photos** of the oil spill in an article in this month's *Smithsonian.*
CORRECT In this month's *Smithsonian,* there**'s** an **article** with several photos of the oil spill.

 EXERCISE 9 **Identifying Sentences with Subject-Verb Agreement**

For each of the following sentences, if the verb agrees with the subject, write C. If the subject and verb do not agree, write the correct form of the verb. Be ready to explain your correction.

 INTEGRATING THE LANGUAGE ARTS

Usage and Writing. Students are sometimes confused by terms that go outside their normal vocabulary. The term *predicate nominative* is an example. Remind students that a predicate nominative is located in the predicate and that it renames the subject (the nominative).

As students write, they might check for predicate nominatives by substituting an equal sign (=) for a linking verb such as *is* or *was.* If the noun or pronoun that follows the equal sign renames the subject, it is a predicate nominative. In the example, "My hobby is cars," *hobby = cars,* so *cars* is a predicate nominative. Students should make the verb agree with the subject, not with the word that renames it.

USAGE

USAGE

LESS-ADVANCED STUDENTS

If students make many errors in **Exercise 9**, you may wish to have them work in pairs to look up and study the rules that apply to the errors they made. Then have each pair write two or three sentences for the rules they missed.

1. Soap and water is the best cleanser for my face. **1.** C
2. ~~There's~~ the boats I told you about. **2.** There are
3. Both my father and sister ∧~~wants~~ to see the Dodgers game on Saturday. **3.** want   **4.** is   **5.** were
4. Either the twins or Jamie ∧~~are~~ playing a practical joke.
5. How ∧~~was~~ the swimming and sailing at the beach?
6. Each of these old photos ∧~~show~~ your Uncle Ahmad wearing a colorful, flowing dashiki. **6.** shows
7. Neither the windows nor the door is locked. **7.** C
8. Contemporary rock-and-roll ∧~~are~~ rooted in the ancient rhythms of African music. **8.** is
9. ∧~~There's~~ always a number of football games on television on New Year's Day. **9.** There are
10. ∧~~Where's~~ my socks? **10.** Where are

19m. Words stating an amount are usually singular.

When a weight, a measurement, or an amount of time or money is thought of as a unit, it takes a singular verb.

EXAMPLES   Two years **is** a long time.
                 Fifteen dollars **was** the price.
                 Ninety percent of the student body **is** present.

When the amount is thought of as individual pieces or parts, a plural verb is used.

EXAMPLES   **Two** of the years **were** especially rainy.
                 Fifteen of the dollars **were** torn.
                 Ninety percent of the students **are** present today.

NOTE: The expression *the number* takes a singular verb. The expression *a number* takes a plural verb.

        EXAMPLES   **The number** of female athletes **is** growing.
                         A number of girls **like** strenuous sports.

19n. The verb in a clause following *one of those* should be plural.

EXAMPLE   Melba is one of those **students** who always **try** their best.

19o. *Every* or *many a* before a subject takes a singular verb.

USAGE

USAGE

EXAMPLES **Every** mother, father, and grandparent **is** looking on proudly.
Many a hopeful performer **has** gone to Broadway in search of fame.

19p. The title of a work of art, literature, or music, even when plural in form, takes a singular verb.

EXAMPLES Paul Laurence Dunbar's *Majors and Minors* **is** a collection of his poetry. [one book]
Jean-François Millet's *The Gleaners* **is** a famous nineteenth-century painting. [one work of art]
Four Saints in Three Acts, with music by Virgil Thomson and words by Gertrude Stein, **was** first produced in 1934, with an African American cast. [one musical work]

19q. *Don't* and *doesn't* must agree with their subjects.

Use *don't* (the contraction for *do not*) with the subjects *I* and *you* and with plural subjects.

EXAMPLES **I don't** have any paper.
You don't need special permission.
The **players don't** seem nervous.

Use *doesn't* with singular subjects.

EXAMPLES **It [he, she] doesn't** show up in this picture.
The **tire doesn't** have enough air.

19r. Some nouns, although plural in form, take singular verbs.

EXAMPLES **Linguistics is** the science of language.
News of the concert's cancellation **was** disappointing to the band members.

A few nouns ending in *–ics* may be singular or plural.

EXAMPLES **Acoustics deals** with the transmission of sound.
The **acoustics** in the new auditorium **are** excellent.

Does politics interest you?
Your **politics are** distasteful to me.

 INTEGRATING THE LANGUAGE ARTS

Usage and Vocabulary. Rule 19r deals with nouns that may be singular or plural and nouns that seem plural in form but take singular verbs. Students can apply a simple test to decide whether such a noun is plural or singular. A word that ends in *–ics* is singular if it means the science or study of something. For example, *acoustics* means "the science that deals with the way sound behaves in an enclosed area." The same word is used in a plural sense to refer to the individual kinds of sound behavior within an area.

In the sentence "The acoustics in the new auditorium are excellent," it is clear that something other than a science is being described as "excellent." In this use, *acoustics* must be plural.

NOTE: Check a dictionary when you're not sure whether to use a singular verb or a plural verb with a noun that ends in *–ics.*

Some nouns that end in *–s* always take a plural verb even though they name a single item.

EXAMPLES **Are** the **scissors** sharp enough?
Your gray **slacks are** in the laundry.
The **pliers seem** to be missing.

▶ EXERCISE 10 **Using *Don't* and *Doesn't* Correctly in Sentences**

Choose the correct form (*don't* or *doesn't*) for each of the following sentences.

1. The calf ____ look very strong.   **1.** doesn't
2. It ____ matter if the weather is bad.   **2.** doesn't
3. She ____ play racquetball.   **3.** doesn't
4. ____ these piñatas look colorful?   **4.** Don't
5. I ____ mind helping out.   **5.** don't
6. You ____ have to watch the program.   **6.** don't
7. Loretta ____ enjoy cleaning house.   **7.** doesn't
8. A few of the contests ____ award cash prizes.   **8.** don't
9. ____ it arrive soon?   **9.** Doesn't
10. ____ he tinker with cars?   **10.** Doesn't

▶ EXERCISE 11 **Selecting Verbs That Agree with Their Subjects**

Choose the correct form of the verb given in parentheses in each of the following sentences.

1. Nguyen, along with her family, (*have, has*) invited me to the Vietnamese National Day celebration in the park.
2. They (*wasn't, weren't*) interested in learning how to play the accordion.
3. Carlos, not Martha or Jan, (*was, were*) answering all the letters.
4. Many of them (*has, have*) already read the novel.
5. *The Birds* (*was, were*) one of Alfred Hitchcock's great movies.
6. (*Doesn't, Don't*) Chuck intend to join the air force when he graduates?

CRITICAL THINKING
Evaluation

You may want to have students look carefully at **Exercises 11** and **12** to identify the intervening phrases in the sentences that contain them and to evaluate which of the phrases are important in determining the number of the verb.

7. Caroline, like most of her classmates, (*wishes*, *wish*) vacation could last forever.
8. There (*is*, *are*) some good programs on educational television.
9. Neither of those books by Naguib Mahfouz (*is*, *are*) on our reading list.
10. It (*doesn't*, *don't*) look good for our baseball league this season.

EXERCISE 12 — Selecting Verbs That Agree with Their Subjects

For each of the sentences following the picture below, choose the correct form of the verb in parentheses.

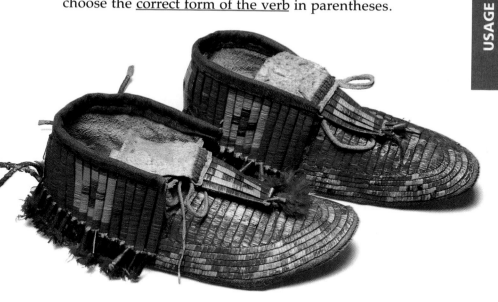

1. (*Doesn't*, *Don't*) these quilled moccasins look as if they are beaded?
2. Quillwork, one of the traditional Plains Indians handicrafts, (*is*, *are*) an ancient and sophisticated art form.
3. The number of quills that grow on one porcupine (*is*, *are*) higher than you might think—about thirty thousand!

REVIEW C

OBJECTIVES
- To identify sentences in which subjects and verbs agree in number
- To identify and correctly revise sentences in which subjects and verbs do not agree in number

636 *Agreement*

4. Five inches (*is*, *are*) the maximum length of these tubular spines.
5. Before being used in quillwork, every porcupine quill (*is*, *are*) dyed a bright color, softened in water, and flattened in an unusual way.
6. The quillworker, usually a woman, (*squeezes*, *squeeze*) each quill flat by pulling it between her teeth.
7. Among the Sioux, worn teeth were considered a badge of great honor because items decorated with colorful quillwork (*was*, *were*) so important in tribal life.
8. Working the quills into complex geometric patterns (*require*, *requires*) great skill and coordination.
9. In quill weaving, each of the ribbonlike quills (*is*, *are*) passed tightly over and under threads of fiber or leather.
10. The finished quillwork (*is*, *are*) sewn onto clothing, saddlebags, or cradleboards as a decoration.

▶ REVIEW C **Making Verbs Agree with Their Subjects**

For each of the following sentences, if the verb and subject agree, write *C*. If the verb and the subject do not agree, supply the correct form of the verb.

1. There ˄are one strain of measles that lasts only three days.   **1.** is
2. Few objections, besides the one about chartering the bus, ˄was raised.   **2.** were
3. *Six Characters in Search of an Author* is a modern play that raises many interesting questions about art and reality.   **3.** C   **4.** C
4. Some of this land is far too hilly to farm.   **5.** there are
5. In Maine, ˄there's many miles of rocky coastline.
6. Four minutes ˄were his record time in that race.   **6.** was
7. Performing in front of a thousand people ˄don't seem to bother the cellist Yo-Yo Ma.   **7.** doesn't   **8.** C
8. Two thirds of a cup of milk is needed for this recipe.
9. Every three years my family ˄visit Sierra Leone, the land our ancestors came from.   **9.** visits
10. Every student, teacher, and administrator ˄are contributing to the fund-raising drive.   **10.** is

USAGE

USAGE

636

AGREEMENT OF PRONOUN AND ANTECEDENT Rule 19s

OBJECTIVES

- To select pronouns that agree with their antecedents
- To identify and write sentences in which pronouns agree with their antecedents in gender and number

Agreement of Pronoun and Antecedent **637**

19s

▶ EXERCISE 13

Using Subject-Verb Agreement in Sentences

Butterflies come in many shapes and sizes—and in every color of the rainbow! Make up ten sentences about the butterflies shown here. Use one of the words listed below as the subject of each sentence. Do not use the same word as the subject of more than one sentence. Be sure that each verb you use agrees with its subject.

a few	each	neither	one
all	either	none	several
both	everyone	not one	some

EXAMPLE   **1.** *All of these butterflies look like flying flowers!*

Agreement of Pronoun and Antecedent

The word that a pronoun refers to is called its *antecedent*.

19s.   A pronoun should agree with its antecedent in gender and number.

Most personal pronouns can refer to antecedents that are masculine or feminine or both or neither.

EXAMPLES   **I** am **your** coach.
You are **my** friend.
We are with **them**.
They are **our** cousins.

USAGE

ANSWERS
Exercise 13

Sentences will vary. The singular subjects *each, either, everyone, neither, none, not one,* and *one* should have singular verbs. The plural subjects *a few, all, both,* and *several* should have plural verbs. *Some* may be either singular or plural, depending on context.

🦉 QUICK REMINDER

To emphasize the importance of clear pronoun reference, read this account to students:

> When Jennifer and Ruth got there, she called home and told her mom where they'd gone after he left the mall. Her mom said they'd invite them over if he could come too.

After reading the account, ask students to identify all the people referred to by pronouns:

1. Who had to call home?
2. Whose mom is it?
3. Who left the mall?
4. Who would be invited over?
[No certain answers are possible.]

Ask students to explain what makes the story confusing. [Some pronouns have no antecedents. Others do not have clear antecedents or do not agree with their antecedents.]

USAGE

637

LEP/ESL

General Strategies. It takes an ESL student about two years to learn to use third-person singular pronouns correctly in speech. Most speakers do not want to take the time while speaking to determine the correct words, so they might make many mistakes at first. In the meantime, it is more productive to respond to the content of their messages than to correct their speech in midsentence. Alternatively, in response to a student saying, "Pedro found her wallet," you might say, "Oh, he found his wallet! That's great."

LESS-ADVANCED STUDENTS

Students might be confused by grammatical terms that they do not use in everyday life, words such as *person, antecedent, gender,* and *neuter.* Even when they have learned these terms, they may forget what the terms mean.

Before students read further in this chapter, you may want to ask them to explain in their own words, and with examples, what each of the terms means. If students cannot explain them satisfactorily, review sample sentences on an overhead transparency or on the chalkboard to illustrate the terms.

Only the third-person singular pronouns indicate the gender of their antecedents. Masculine pronouns refer to males, feminine pronouns to females, and neuter pronouns to things and, often, animals.

MASCULINE	he	him	his
FEMININE	she	her	hers
NEUTER	it	it	its

EXAMPLES Does **Margaret** like **her** dance class?
Arturo is doing **his** homework.
Because the **car** wouldn't start, **it** had to be towed.

When the antecedent of a personal pronoun is another kind of pronoun, determine the gender to use by looking in a phrase following the antecedent.

EXAMPLES **Neither** of the **girls** brought **her** own lunch.
One of the **men** lost **his** keys.

When the antecedent could be either masculine or feminine, use both the masculine and feminine forms.

EXAMPLES **One** of the students left **his or her** pen behind.
Everybody in the club has paid **his or her** dues.

NOTE: You can often avoid the *his or her* construction by revising the sentence and using the plural form of the pronoun.

EXAMPLE **All** of the club members have paid **their** dues.

In conversation, plural personal pronouns are often used to refer to singular antecedents that could be either masculine or feminine. This form is being used more often in writing, too, and it may eventually be considered acceptable in written standard English.

EXAMPLES **Nobody** rode **their** bikes.
Everybody brought **their** fishing rods.

(1) Use a singular pronoun to refer to *each, either, neither, one, everyone, everybody, no one, nobody, anyone, anybody, someone,* or *somebody.* The use of a phrase or a clause after the antecedent does not change the number of the antecedent.

EXAMPLES **Each** of the teams had **its** mascot at the game.
One of the boys left **his** pen behind.
Everybody in the women's league has paid **her** dues.

NOTE: When the meaning of *everyone* or *everybody* is *clearly* plural, use the plural pronoun or, better, revise the sentence.

> CONFUSING   When **everybody** has arrived, explain the situation to **him.**
>
> CLEAR   When **everybody** has arrived, explain the situation to **them.**
>
> BETTER   When **all** the people have arrived, explain the situation to **them.**

(2) Use a singular pronoun to refer to two or more singular antecedents joined by *or* or *nor*.

EXAMPLE   Neither Heidi nor Beth took **her** umbrella with **her.**

(3) Use a plural pronoun to refer to two or more antecedents joined by *and*.

EXAMPLE   The guide and the ranger wrapped **their** rain ponchos in **their** saddle rolls.

NOTE: The number of a relative pronoun (*who, which,* and *that*) is determined by the number of the word to which it refers—its antecedent.

> EXAMPLES   Jessica is one **person who** has faith in **herself.** [*Who* is singular because it refers to *person.* Therefore, the singular forms *has* and *herself* are used to agree with *who.*]
>
> **All who want** to volunteer should raise **their** hands. [*Who* is plural because *all* is plural. Therefore, the plural forms *want* and *their* are used to agree with *who.*]

▶ EXERCISE 14   **Selecting Pronouns That Agree with Their Antecedents**

For each blank in the following sentences, select a pronoun that will agree with its antecedent.

1. his or her

1. Each of the players had ____ own odd superstition.
2. Someone on the boy's swimming team has parked ____ car in my space. **2.** his
3. Neither of the sweaters had ____ price tag removed. **3.** its

USAGE

COMMON ERROR

Problem. Students often do not realize that a relative pronoun takes the number of its antecedent. In a sentence such as "Books that are checked out have to be returned on Thursday," the antecedent for *that* is *books* (plural), so the verb (*have*) must be plural. A student who ignores the antecedent and thinks *that* is always singular will commit agreement errors.

Solution. Use a transparency on an overhead projector to show how the chain of reference works. Ask students to copy several sample sentences on a worksheet and to circle the antecedents and the relative pronouns. Then have them underline the words that must have the number of the antecedent.

USAGE

4. Did everybody at the press conference change ____ mind as soon as Mayor Bradley stated the facts? **4.** his or her

5. Many of the crew got ____ first case of seasickness in the storm. **5.** their

6. One of the houses had ____ windows broken by the hail last night. **6.** its

7. All of the art students buy ____ own paper. **7.** their **8.** their

8. Anyone who needs a pencil should raise ____ hand.

9. Either Stu or Mike will lend me ____ fishing gear. **9.** his

10. Each of the characters in Chinese calligraphy has ____ own beauty, mystery, and grace. **10.** its

▶ EXERCISE 15   **Making Pronouns Agree with Their Antecedents**

Most of the following sentences contain pronouns that do not agree with their antecedents. If all of the pronouns in a sentence agree with their antecedents, write C. If any pronoun does not agree with its antecedent, supply the correct pronoun.

1. All of these students at the Royal School of Dance in College Park, Florida, are learning traditional dances that **1.** their come from ~~her~~ African heritage.

2. Some of the African and Caribbean dances have **2.** their ~~its~~ roots in African folk tales.

3. At performances, the audience are often seen **3.** their clapping ~~its~~ hands and swaying along with the music.

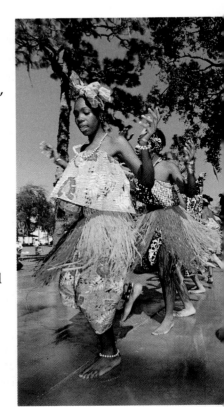

A DIFFERENT APPROACH
Allow students to work in groups of two or three on **Exercise 15.** Ask them to revise the sentences a second time by making the singular subjects plural and the plural subjects singular. These revisions will require changes in subjects and verbs or pronouns and antecedents.

Each student should then work alone to decide on changes and to proofread the revised sentences.

VISUAL CONNECTIONS
Related Expression Skills. Students who have taken dancing lessons or who just enjoy dancing might want to give an oral narration of an interesting or amusing experience they had while dancing, or they might describe a particular type of dance. They should make sure that their pronouns and antecedents agree.

OBJECTIVES

- To identify sentences in which subjects and verbs and pronouns and antecedents agree
- To identify and correctly revise sentences in which subjects and verbs or pronouns and antecedents do not agree
- To select verbs that agree with their subjects and pronouns that agree with their antecedents

4. Before the last dance recital, I noticed either Carla or Shana practicing ~~their~~ steps.   **4.** her
5. Carla is one of those students who always know their steps ahead of time.   **5.** C
6. Angelique and Pamela waved ~~her~~ cowtails gracefully during the first dance.   **6.** their
7. Every authentic costume adds ~~their~~ color and movement to the dramatic spectacle.   **7.** its
8. Everyone in the class brings ~~their~~ own personal style to the dances.   **8.** his or her
9. M. C. Hammer and other rap singers give a great deal of credit to the traditional sources of their art form.   **9.** C
10. Both their hip-hop dancing and their clothing style have ~~its~~ origins in ancient African culture.   **10.** their

▷ REVIEW D

Identifying Subject-Verb Agreement and Pronoun-Antecedent Agreement in Sentences

In some of the following sentences, either a verb does not agree with its subject or a pronoun does not agree with its antecedent. If a verb or pronoun is wrong, correct it. If the sentence is correct, write C.

1. Both Sid and Nikki like their new neighborhood.   **1.** C
2. ~~Are~~ either of you a member of the African American Cultural Society?   **2.** Is
3. Anthony, in addition to the other contestants, ~~were~~ ready for the competition to start.   **3.** was
4. One of the local police officers was the top scorer on the rifle range.   **4.** C
5. Neither Fernando nor Bruce has brought all of ~~their~~ camping gear.   **5.** his
6. *The Three Little Pigs* ~~are~~ my young nephews' all-time favorite animated feature.   **6.** is
7. Which pair of these Navajo earrings ~~were~~ made by Narciso?   **7.** was
8. Where is the Athletics Department?   **8.** C
9. Just before the parade started, each of the eight men inside the gigantic dragon costume got ~~their~~ final instructions from Mr. Yee.   **9.** his

USAGE

USAGE

10. A few of the crowd⌃~~was~~ murmuring impatiently. **10.** were
11. ⌃~~Is~~ there any of those peanuts left? **11.** Are
12. Either Chi Chi Rodriguez or Nancy Lopez is my golf hero. **12.** C
13. Every one of those stray cattle⌃~~are~~ going to have to be rounded up. **13.** is
14. An additional feature of these models is the built-in stereo speakers. **14.** C
15. Somebody has gone off and left⌃~~their~~ car running. **15.** his or her
16. If anybody calls, tell⌃~~them~~ I'll be back by six o'clock this evening. **16.** him or her
17. Each team has its own colors and symbol. **17.** C
18. One of the goats⌃~~were~~ nibbling on a discarded popcorn box. **18.** was
19. Here's the pair of gloves that you forgot. **19.** C
20. ⌃~~Are~~ there no end to these questions? **20.** Is

 REVIEW E

Selecting Verbs That Agree with Their Subjects and Pronouns That Agree with Their Antecedents

In each sentence, choose the <u>correct one of the two forms</u> given in parentheses.

1. Neither the manager nor the two salespeople (*was,* <u>*were*</u>) prepared for the number of customers.
2. Neither of the sets of barbells (<u>*was,*</u> *were*) easy to lift.
3. Where (<u>*is,*</u> *are*) the box of nails that came with this bookshelf kit?
4. A few of our classmates (*was,* <u>*were*</u>) invited.
5. The Harlem Globetrotters (<u>*is,*</u> *are*) surely one of the best-loved basketball teams in the world.
6. There (<u>*is,*</u> *are*) leftover macaroni and cheese in the refrigerator.
7. If anybody likes a spectacle, (<u>*he or she,*</u> *they*) will love seeing a drum corps competition.
8. Several of the audience (*was,* <u>*were*</u>) waving wildly, hoping that Martin Yan would wave back.
9. Where (<u>*has,*</u> *have*) the sports section of today's newspaper gone?
10. Anyone who wants to get (<u>*his or her,*</u> *their*) program autographed by Edward James Olmos had better hurry.

EXERCISE 16

Using Subject-Verb Agreement Correctly in Sentences

The same thought can almost always be expressed in more than one way. Read each of the following sentences, and then express the same thought in two more sentences. For each new sentence, use one of the two subjects given in parentheses. Be sure that your subjects and verbs agree.

EXAMPLE **1.** The boys desperately want to go to the circus. (*Both, Each*)

    1. *Both of the boys desperately want to go to the circus.*

    Each of the boys desperately wants to go to the circus.

1. Their father, as well as their mother, has agreed to the idea. (*Both of their parents, One of their parents*)
2. Not one of the townspeople wants to miss tonight's performance. (*Nobody, None*)
3. Each person has earned a lighthearted evening of watching clowns, tigers, and elephants shown in these posters. (*Everybody, All*)
4. But because the Great Depression has begun, not all of the families in town have money for tickets. (*not every one, a few*)
5. Forty-nine of the fifty free tickets to the circus have been spoken for. (*All but one, Only one*)

USAGE

ANSWERS
Exercise 16

Students' sentences may vary. Here are some possibilities:

1. Both of their parents have agreed to the idea.
   One of their parents has already agreed to the idea.
2. Nobody in town wants to miss tonight's performance.
   None of the townspeople want to miss tonight's performance.
3. Everybody has earned a lighthearted evening of watching clowns, tigers, and elephants.
   All have earned a lighthearted evening of watching clowns, tigers, and elephants.
4. But because the Great Depression has begun, not every one of the families in town has money for tickets.
   But because the Great Depression has begun, only a few families in town have money for tickets.
5. All but one of the fifty free tickets to the circus have been spoken for.
   Only one of the fifty free tickets to the circus has not been spoken for.

USAGE

VISUAL CONNECTIONS

Ideas for Writing. Most people have had friends with whom they really enjoyed going places or doing things. Sometimes those places and activities leave vivid memories.

You may want to have each student write a character sketch of a close friend. Each student should include a brief narration of an incident that demonstrates an important point about the friend's personality. When the compositions are completed, have students work in pairs to check for agreement.

WRITING APPLICATION
Prewriting

As students brainstorm lists of ideas, you may wish to remind them not to decide immediately whether an idea is important. They can be selective after they have finished brainstorming. Otherwise, they might be too choosy and have little to write about.

CRITICAL THINKING
Analysis

During prewriting, students should analyze and evaluate possible subjects in relation to the interests of their audience. From among the possible subjects on their prewriting lists, students will want to select the people, places, and events that will most interest the friend. You may wish to remind them to be sure that the events they write about have occurred since the friend moved away.

USAGE

WRITING APPLICATION

Using Agreement to Make Meaning Clear

If you want your reader to know exactly what you mean, your pronouns must clearly refer to their antecedents and agree with them. Suppose you are telling a friend about what happened at the movies last night. You say, "Melba said that Jo Ann ate all of the popcorn Bill bought for her." Whose popcorn did Jo Ann eat? The sentence should be revised to make the meaning clear.

CLEAR Melba said that Bill bought popcorn for her, but Jo Ann ate all of it.

CLEAR Melba said that Bill bought popcorn for Jo Ann, who ate all of it.

 WRITING ACTIVITY

Your best friend moved away two months ago. You have just received a postcard from him or her, asking what's been happening recently in the old neighborhood. You answer the postcard by writing a short letter that brings your friend up to date. In your letter, include at least five pronouns that agree with their antecedents.

Prewriting Make a list of several interesting things to tell your friend. You may write about your real neighborhood or about one you have made up. Decide on the order in which you will tell about the items on your list. You may want to use time order (telling when things happened) or spatial order (telling where things happened).

Writing As you write, think about how to make your letter interesting to your friend. Use details that will help him or her picture the neighborhood and its people.

Evaluating and Revising Ask a classmate to read your letter. Are the events you tell about interesting? Is it absolutely clear who did what and what belongs to whom? Use your helper's suggestions to revise your letter so that nothing in it is confusing.

OBJECTIVES
- To select verbs that agree with their subjects and pronouns that agree with their antecedents
- To identify and revise sentences in which pronouns do not agree with their antecedents and verbs do not agree with their subjects

PROOFREADING

Students should check to make sure that they have incorporated the basic items for a friendly letter: a return address, the date, a salutation, and a friendly closing. The friend's first name in the salutation should be followed by a comma.

Urge students to check carefully for pronoun-antecedent agreement and to have a classmate double-check their work.

Review: Posttest **645**

 Proofreading   Check over the grammar, punctuation, and form of your letter. Use a dictionary to look up the spelling of any word you are not sure of. Be sure each pronoun agrees with its antecedent and each verb agrees with its subject.

Review: Posttest

A. Selecting Verbs That Agree with Their Subjects and Pronouns That Agree with Their Antecedents

In the following sentences, write the correct form of each incorrect verb or pronoun. If a sentence is correct, write *C*.

EXAMPLES   **1.** Each leaf, flower, and seedpod were glimmering with frost.
1. *was*

2. Were any tickets left at the box office for me?
2. *C*

1. There ˄was̶ women, as well as men, who set out on the perilous journey into new territory.   **1.** were
2. The test results showed that about 80 percent of the class ˄was̶ in the average group.   **2.** were
3. A hostile crowd gathered outside the courtroom to show ˄their̶ disapproval of the verdict.   **3.** its
4. *Bronzeville Boys and Girls* ˄are̶ a collection of poems by Gwendolyn Brooks.   **4.** is   **5.** his or her
5. Neither of the candidates has prepared ˄their̶ speech.
6. Mr. Ortega, along with other members of his firm, ˄have̶ established a scholarship fund for art students.   **6.** has
7. To apply for the scholarship, a student must submit at least four samples of ˄their̶ work.   **7.** his or her
8. Chester or Nina, I think, ˄have̶ the best chance of winning.   **8.** has
9. Senator Hayakawa's committee ˄was̶ preparing their speeches for the meeting.   **9.** were
10. All of the bread ˄are̶ on the table.   **10.** is

B. Selecting Verbs That Agree with Their Subjects and Pronouns That Agree with Their Antecedents

For each sentence in the following paragraph, write the correct form of each incorrect verb or pronoun. A sentence may contain more than one error. If a sentence is correct, write C.

11. was

12. gather

13. is

14. his or her

15. leave

16. gets

17. are

18. doesn't

19. C

20. his or her/ says

[11] Neither my brothers nor my dad were surprised to hear that Aunt Bonnie is going to Africa next month as a Peace Corps volunteer. [12] First, she and the other members of the Kenya group gathers in Philadelphia for a few days of orientation. [13] Their focus at this point are to meet one another and get acquainted. [14] Then the whole group travels together to Nairobi, Kenya, where everyone will have their last chance for months to enjoy hot running water! [15] After one night in Nairobi, half of them leaves for the town of Naivasha for eleven weeks of cultural sensitivity training. [16] Each of the volunteers get to live with a Kenyan family during this period of training. [17] The close daily contact will help them learn to converse in Swahili, one of the languages that is spoken in Kenya. [18] Bonnie don't know yet where exactly in Kenya she is going to be posted. [19] She, as well as the other members of her group, expects to be assigned to the area of greatest need. [20] No one in the group has been told their specific job assignment, but Bonnie say she will probably be helping Kenyans develop small businesses.

USAGE

OBJECTIVES

- To identify the correct forms of pronouns in sentences
- To proofread a paragraph for correct pronoun forms

20 USING PRONOUNS CORRECTLY

Nominative and Objective Case

Diagnostic Test

A. Using Pronouns Correctly in Sentences

Choose the <u>correct word</u> in parentheses in the following sentences.

EXAMPLE **1.** Was it (*he, him*) driving the car when the accident occurred?
1. *he*

1. Francis said that in a few years he would give his stamp collection to his brother and (*I*, <u>*me*</u>).
2. Everyone was waiting impatiently to find out (<u>*who*</u>, *whom*) the new cheerleader would be.
3. My little sister is a much better basketball player than (<u>*I*</u>, *me*).
4. Rep. Ben Nighthorse Campbell is one congressman (<u>*who*</u>, *whom*) thinks Native Americans should be consulted more often about legislation that concerns them.

Teacher's ResourceBank™
RESOURCES

FOR THE WHOLE CHAPTER
- Chapter Review Form A
- Chapter Review Form B
- Assessment Portfolio
    Usage Pretests
    Usage Mastery Tests

CHAPTER OVERVIEW

Even accomplished writers and speakers of English have occasional difficulty with pronoun usage. In trying to be correct, speakers and writers sometimes get confused because the test of "what sounds right" won't work. Pronoun usage is a tricky instruction matter that warrants close study.

Less-advanced and LEP/ESL students will need to concentrate on **The Objective Case** and **The Nominative Case** segments, while advanced students could study these as review.

Advanced students should work to master **Special Problems in Pronoun Usage** and **Pronouns in Incomplete Constructions**. Material is provided that could help these students solve all questions regarding the use of *who* and *whom*.

The **Writing Application** and **Picture This** activities lead students to focus on the correct use of pronouns. These assignments may be adapted to your students' needs and abilities.

USAGE

Part A of the Diagnostic Test asks students to use pronouns correctly in sentences, and Part B asks students to identify correct pronoun forms in a paragraph. This test will tell you how much your students already know about the nominative and objective cases of pronouns. The results will help you to determine which material to present as new and which to present as review to the various groups of students in your classes.

5. We found that it was (*she, her*) who called twice while we were out of town.
6. The teacher said that (*whoever, whomever*) was ready could give a speech first.
7. Speaking of Ken Griffey, Jr., (*he, him*) and his dad are the first father and son ever to play professional baseball together on the same team.
8. Seeing a car with an out-of-state license plate in my driveway, I ran inside, and (*who, whom*) do you think was there?
9. Mrs. Martin and (*she, her*) have been friends since childhood.
10. As you swim, you use nearly all of your major muscles, which makes (*it, swimming*) one of the best forms of exercise.

B. Identifying Correct Pronoun Forms in a Paragraph

In each sentence in the following paragraph, choose the correct form from each pair in parentheses.

I recently read that anyone **[11]** (*who, whom*) comes from a large family grows up with a desire to be surrounded by people all the time. Well, just between you and **[12]** (*I, me*), that isn't always true! There aren't many teenagers who enjoy their privacy as much as **[13]** (*I, me*). Because I'm the oldest child, I've spent years settling squabbles between my brothers and sisters, helping with homework, and feeding **[14]** (*whoever, whomever*) was hungry. When my brothers got into trouble, I always smoothed things over between **[15]** (*they, them*) and Dad. And when **[16]** (*he, him*) and Mom were busy in the evening, I read to **[17]** (*whoever, whomever*) had an earlier bedtime than **[18]** (*I, me*). Even now that we're all older, the laughing, yelling, bickering, and commotion always let you know exactly **[19]** (*who, whom*) is home at any moment. You'd better believe that **[20]** (*this, this hectic upbringing*) has given me a deep craving for privacy, not for company!

CASE FORMS OF PERSONAL PRONOUNS

OBJECTIVE

- To identify and analyze personal pronouns in a paragraph

Case Forms of Personal Pronouns

Case is the form of a noun or pronoun that shows how it is used in a sentence. In English, there are three cases: *nominative, objective,* and *possessive.* Nouns have the same form in both the nominative and the objective case. They usually add an apostrophe and an *s* to form the possessive case.

☞ REFERENCE NOTE: See pages 848–849 and 851 for information on forming the possessives of nouns.

Personal pronouns change form in the different cases.

CASE FORMS OF PERSONAL PRONOUNS			
SINGULAR			
	NOMINATIVE CASE	OBJECTIVE CASE	POSSESSIVE CASE
First Person	I	me	my, mine
Second Person	you	you	your, yours
Third Person	he, she, it	him, her, it	his, her, hers, its
PLURAL			
	NOMINATIVE CASE	OBJECTIVE CASE	POSSESSIVE CASE
First Person	we	us	our, ours
Second Person	you	you	your, yours
Third Person	they	them	their, theirs

Notice that only *you* and *it* have the same form in the nominative and the objective case.

☞ REFERENCE NOTE: For more information on possessive personal pronouns, see page 850.

▶ EXERCISE 1 **Identifying Personal Pronouns in a Paragraph**

Each sentence in the following paragraph contains at least one pronoun. Identify each pronoun. Then, give its person, number, and case; also give its gender if applicable.

Teacher's ResourceBank™

RESOURCES

CASE FORMS OF PERSONAL PRONOUNS
- Case Forms of Personal Pronouns

🦉 QUICK REMINDER

Tell students that the English language lacks a distinct second-person plural pronoun form. Ask volunteers to explain what this means. [English uses the word *you* for the second-person singular and second-person plural forms.]

Ask students to list second-person plural forms commonly used in conversation [*you guys, you all, y'all*]. You may wish to encourage students to discuss and evaluate the various substitute forms in use.

MEETING
INDIVIDUAL
NEEDS

LEP/ESL

General Strategies. Because English has a relatively simple personal pronoun system, intermediate-level students have few problems with understanding which form to use if they are able to identify the nominative, objective, and possessive cases in sentences. Beginning students might need a more gradual introduction to the forms than the textbook provides, so spreading practice and review over a longer period of time may help them.

USAGE

USAGE

ANSWERS
Exercise 1

1. your — second person singular or plural, possessive case

2. you — second person singular or plural, nominative case
she — third person singular, nominative case, feminine

3. I — first person singular, nominative case

4. he — third person singular, nominative case, masculine
his — third person singular, possessive case, masculine

5. he — third person singular, nominative case, masculine
them — third person plural, objective case

6. they — third person plural, nominative case

7. I — first person singular, nominative case
his — third person singular, possessive case, masculine
mine — first person singular, possessive case

8. me — first person singular, objective case
he — third person singular, nominative case, masculine

9. their — third person plural, possessive case

10. we — first person plural, nominative case

EXAMPLE   **[1]**   Jeffrey and I were chatting in front of his locker before the Art Club meeting.

1.   *I—first person singular, nominative case; his—third person singular, possessive case, masculine*

[1] Jeffrey mentioned your interest in African art and Francine's interest in modern art. [2] Did you and she know that African tribal masks like the one below in the middle influenced the development of the Modernist movement in art? [3] I've learned that African carvings inspired such twentieth-century artists as Pablo Picasso, who created the painting on the left. [4] The year 1905 was probably when he and his friends first saw African masks exhibited in Paris. [5] Amedeo Modigliani was especially affected by the stark masks, and he and Picasso created many works based on them. [6] Notice that the eyes in Modigliani's carving on the right are very close together and that they and the lips often look like small knobs. [7] I used to think that Modigliani made his faces too long by mistake, but the error was mine. [8] Ms. Keller told me that he was copying the exaggerated shapes of Ivory Coast masks. [9] Picasso and Modigliani were only two of many European artists who got their inspiration from African art. [10] Obviously, we students weren't giving credit where credit was due!

THE NOMINATIVE CASE Rules 20a, 20b

OBJECTIVES

- To complete sentences by using personal pronouns in the nominative case ☞

20a

The Nominative Case

20a. The subject of a verb is in the nominative case.

EXAMPLES **I solved the problem.** [*I* is the subject of *solved.*]
Al and **she** cleaned the house. [*Al* and *she* is the compound subject of *cleaned.*]
They know that **we** are going. [*They* is the subject of *know,* and *we* is the subject of *are going.*]

When both parts of a compound subject are pronouns, you may not be sure which form to use.

EXAMPLE (*She, Her*) and (*I, me*) studied for the test.

To choose the correct form, try each pronoun separately with the verb.

SEPARATELY *She* studied for the test. *I* studied for the test. [*Her studied for the test* and *me studied for the test* sound strange.]

TOGETHER **She** and **I** studied for the test.

Using *we* and *they* as the parts of a compound subject may sound awkward to you, even though doing so is correct. If so, revise the sentence.

ORIGINAL **We** and **they** will go to the movie.
REVISED **We** will go to the movie with **them**.

ORAL
PRACTICE 1 **Using Pronouns as Subjects**

Read each of the following sentences aloud, stressing the italicized words.

1. *She* and *I* gave the dog a bath.
2. Terry and *he* plan to try out for the soccer team.
3. *We* sophomores organized the drive.
4. James Earl Jones and *she* are excellent role models for young actors.
5. Are *you* and *he* doing the report?
6. Either *we* or *they* may go to the championship finals.
7. The drill team and *we* band members took the bus.
8. The twins and *they* go everywhere together.

USAGE

Teacher's ResourceBank™
RESOURCES

THE NOMINATIVE CASE
- The Nominative Case

QUICK REMINDER

Tell students that one way to determine the correct pronoun form for compound subjects is by using each form separately.

Write on the chalkboard:
(*He, Him*) and (*I, me*) arrived early for the test Saturday morning.

Have students pair each pronoun with the verb. [He arrived. I arrived.] Tell them that when they are selecting pronoun forms, it is often helpful to work with as few words as possible, eliminating prepositional phrases and adverbs.

MEETING INDIVIDUAL NEEDS

LESS-ADVANCED STUDENTS

As students complete **Oral Practice 1,** you may want to have volunteers reduce the words in each sentence to make it easier to determine the correct pronoun form. For example, sentence 1 would be "She gave the dog a bath" and "I gave the dog a bath."

Remind students that the verb forms may change when the subjects change from plural to singular. For example, in sentence 2 the verb changes from *plan* to *plans.*

Before students begin **Exercise 3,** tell them that the subjects should be used to begin their sentences.

USAGE

- To compose sentences with pronouns in the nominative case as subjects
- To complete sentences by using pronouns as predicate nominatives

ANSWERS
Exercise 3

Answers may vary. Here are some possible sentences:

1. We teenagers go through many changes.
2. The other shoppers and I missed the sale.
3. He and his friends never have much money.
4. Liz, Michelle, and she are the best dancers.
5. They and their classmates have part-time jobs.

ANSWERS
Exercise 4

Answers may vary. Here are some sample sentences:

1. If my parents were in that soldier's shoes, <u>they</u> would worry and so would <u>I</u>.
2. <u>We</u> remember when the Iraqis invaded Kuwait and how <u>they</u> began a reign of terror.
3. <u>It</u> was even frightening secondhand, so <u>we</u> tuned out the newscasters, including Peter Arnett.
4. <u>He</u> was in Iraq, broadcasting as bombs fell on Baghdad.
5. With our Patriot missiles, <u>we</u> intercepted most of the Iraqi attacks on Israel.
6. Later <u>we</u> saw the great pain of Arab families, which <u>they</u> experienced in Iraq as well as in Kuwait.

▶ EXERCISE 2 Using Personal Pronouns in the Nominative Case to Complete Sentences

Pronouns will vary.

Supply a personal pronoun for each blank in the following sentences. Vary your pronouns. Do not use *you* or *it*.

1. The judge and ___ studied the evidence. **1.** she
2. Ted and ___ took the wrong train. **2.** he
3. Linda and ___ are planning a party. **3.** they
4. ___ students are having a science fair. **4.** We
5. Either Julius or ___ will give you a ride. **5.** she
6. ___ and ___ have been rivals for years. **6.** We/they
7. I'm sure ___ knew about the meeting. **7.** he
8. Soon ___ and ___ will be graduating. **8.** she/I
9. Did you know that ___ and ___ saw Chita Rivera in a Broadway production of *West Side Story*? **9.** he/I
10. ___ and ___ love those little Chinese dumplings served at dim sum restaurants. **10.** She/they

▶ EXERCISE 3 Writing Sentences with Pronouns in the Nominative Case

Use the following subjects in sentences of your own.

1. we teenagers
2. the other shoppers and I
3. he and his friends
4. Liz, Michelle, and she
5. they and their classmates

▶ EXERCISE 4 Writing Sentences Using Personal Pronouns

Your cousin was too young to understand what happened during Operation Desert Storm, but now that she is older, she is curious. You show her the map and pictures appearing on the next page, and explain in simple terms what happened before, during, and after the Persian Gulf Conflict. Write at least five sentences that include ten personal pronouns in the nominative case. Underline the nominative case pronouns you use.

EXAMPLE **1.** *When <u>I</u> saw the photos in a magazine, <u>they</u> made me very sad and very proud.*

USAGE

USAGE

20b

20b. A predicate nominative is in the nominative case.

A *predicate nominative* is a noun or pronoun that follows a linking verb and explains or identifies the subject of the sentence. A pronoun used as a predicate nominative always follows a form of the verb *be* or a verb phrase ending in *be* or *been*.

👉 REFERENCE NOTE: See page 560 for more information on predicate nominatives.

COMMON FORMS OF *BE*		PREDICATE NOMINATIVE
am is, are was, were may be, can be, will be, etc. has been, have been, had been, may have been, etc. should be, could be, would be	*are followed by*	I he she we you they

EXAMPLES   It was **I** who took the message.
The winner might be **he**.
Could the caller have been **she**?

NOTE: In casual conversation, expressions such as *It's me* and *That's her*, are acceptable. Avoid them in more formal speaking situations such as job interviews. In your written work, don't use them unless you're creating casual conversation in dialogue.

USAGE

✦ INTEGRATING THE LANGUAGE ARTS

Literature Link. Have students read William Stafford's poem, "Fifteen," and ask them to pay special attention to Stafford's use of pronouns in the nominative case. Ask the students why the narrator switches from *I* to *we* in the third stanza. [This indicates that the boy and the motorcycle have become one in the boy's fantasy.] Then ask them why they think Stafford used the first-person pronoun instead of a name. [The use of the first person creates a closer relationship between the narrator and the audience.] Explain to the students that this poem is an example of how the proper use of pronouns can relay meaning beyond that of the words themselves.

✦ COOPERATIVE LEARNING

As students study the material on **Rule 20b** regarding the use of the nominative case for predicate nominatives, you may want to point out that this construction is rare in casual speaking or writing. To demonstrate this, have students bring in newspaper articles or sports magazines. Have them work in groups of four or five to scan articles for the use of pronouns as predicate nominatives. They could circle each use and then trade materials with other groups to observe what they have found.

USAGE

653

EXERCISE 5 **Using Predicate Nominatives in Sentences**

Complete each of the following sentences by supplying the personal pronoun called for in parentheses.

1. Do you think it was ____? (*third person singular, masculine*)   **1.** he   **2.** she
2. It must have been ____. (*third person singular, feminine*)
3. Good friends are ____. (*third person plural*)   **3.** they
4. The pranksters were ____. (*first person plural*)   **4.** we
5. It was ____ at the door. (*third person plural*)   **5.** they

REVIEW A **Using Pronouns in the Nominative Case Correctly in Sentences**

Supply a personal pronoun for each blank in the following sentences. Use as many different pronouns as you can. Do not use *you* or *it*. Be ready to explain the reasons for your choice.

Pronouns will vary.

1. When I saw Dame Kiri te Kanawa in front of Lincoln Center, I couldn't believe it was ____.   **1.** she
2. Everyone applauded when Patty and ____ took a bow.   **2.** he
3. Where did Barry and ____ go after school?   **3.** they
4. Jimmy and ____ caught the runaway piglets.   **4.** I
5. It is ____ that you need to see.   **5.** we
6. Skip argued that it was Lana and ____ who made the error.   **6.** they
7. Was it Teresa or ____ who hit the home run?   **7.** he
8. Either David or ____ might be able to do it.   **8.** I
9. My sister and ____ love the South African musical group Ladysmith Black Mombazo.   **9.** I   **10.** she
10. I believe that the Masked Marvel has to be ____.

REVIEW B **Using Pronouns in the Nominative Case Correctly in a Paragraph**

For each numbered blank in the following paragraph, supply an appropriate personal pronoun. Do not use *you* or *it*.

1. We

[1] ____ tenth-grade students are determined to win this year's "Save the Earth" trophy at our school. The two

THE OBJECTIVE CASE Rules 20c, 20d

OBJECTIVES

- To use pronouns in the objective case as direct objects, indirect objects, and objects of prepositions
- To identify the correct pronoun form for objects of prepositions ☞

---

most enthusiastic people in our class are probably Pilar and [2] ____. I guess that's why Mrs. Nakamura asked if [3] ____ and [4] ____ would organize the paper drive by ourselves. Pilar explained to the class that if [5] ____ Americans recycled only our Sunday newspapers, half a million trees would be saved every Sunday! To illustrate her point, she showed this photo. That's [6] ____ standing next to 580 pounds of paper—the amount an average American uses in one year. [7] ____ have gathered some other facts to inspire our classmates to recycle. Our friend Ben said that [8] ____ and his mother heard on the radio that the average American uses 1,500 aluminum drink cans every year. [9] ____ were amazed to learn that the energy saved from recycling just one aluminum can could keep a TV set running for three hours! No matter who wins the trophy, it will definitely be [10] ____ who share the prize of a cleaner, healthier planet.

2. I
3. she
4. I
5. we
6. she
7. We
8. he
9. We
10. we

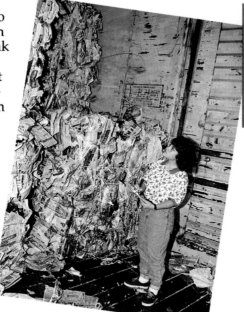

The Objective Case

Pronouns in the objective case are used as direct objects, indirect objects, and objects of prepositions.

☞ REFERENCE NOTE: See pages 562–563 and 574–576 for more information about the three kinds of objects.

20c. Direct objects and indirect objects are in the objective case.

A *direct object* is a noun or pronoun that receives the action of the verb or shows the result of the action.

USAGE

USAGE

Teacher's ResourceBank™
RESOURCES

THE OBJECTIVE CASE
- The Objective Case

🦉 QUICK REMINDER

You may want to write the following sentences on the chalkboard to remind students that objective-case pronouns may simply replace nouns that receive, directly or indirectly, the action of a verb. They may also be objects of prepositions.

Use the following sentences to discuss the basic parts of a sentence.

1. Liza gave Bao her car keys.
[subject, verb, indirect object, direct object]
2. He smiled at her.
[subject, verb, prepositional phrase]

- To write sentences using pronouns as objects of prepositions
- To write a fable that includes ten personal pronouns

LEP/ESL

General Strategies. If students make errors in this section, you will need to determine whether they are confusing the case forms or need a review in identifying direct and indirect objects. Not all languages follow the subject-verb-object pattern, so you may want to give additional review in identifying objects if you suspect this is a problem.

LESS-ADVANCED STUDENTS

Rather than ask these students to analyze grammatical structure by differentiating direct and indirect objects from objects of prepositions, you may want to combine the different kinds of objects. Explain that an object is generally a word that describes a person or a thing that an action is done to or for. You may want to write examples on the chalkboard.

LEARNING STYLES

Visual Learners. Familiarity with placement may help students identify correct pronouns. Have students work together as a group to design cards indicating likely placement for pronouns in the nominative and objective case. [Pronouns in the nominative case come before a verb or follow a form of the verb *be*; objective-case pronouns follow an action verb or a preposition.]

USAGE *(vertical label)*

656 *Using Pronouns Correctly*

EXAMPLES   Coach Johnson has been training **us.**
The coach has turned **them** into the best team in the state.

An *indirect object* is a noun or pronoun that tells *to whom* or *for whom* the action of the verb is done.

EXAMPLES   Serena paid **him** a compliment.
Carlos saved **me** a seat in the first row.

When a direct object or an indirect object is compound, try each pronoun separately with the verb. For the sentence to be correct, all parts of the compound must be correct.

EXAMPLE: The news surprised them and we.
The news surprised them is correct.
The news surprised we is incorrect.
ANSWER: The news surprised **them** and **us.**

EXAMPLE: Bao showed her and I pictures of Vietnam.
Bao showed her pictures of Vietnam is correct.
Bao showed I pictures of Vietnam is incorrect.
ANSWER: Bao showed **her** and **me** pictures of Vietnam.

▶ EXERCISE 6   **Using Pronouns in the Objective Case to Complete Sentences**

Supply a personal pronoun for each blank in the following sentences. Use a variety of pronouns. Do not use *you* or *it.*
Pronouns will vary.

1. The old sailor warned ____ about the danger.   **1.** us
2. The city awarded ____ its highest honor for their bravery in rescuing earthquake victims.   **2.** them
3. You could ask Deborah or ____.   **3.** him
4. The crowd cheered ____ heartily.   **4.** us
5. Make sure that you ask ____ what her Social Security number is.   **5.** her
6. The shark in that movie didn't scare ____ at all.   **6.** me
7. How can I recognize ____?   **7.** him
8. We saw Norman and ____ in their horse costume at the party.   **8.** her   **9.** them
9. Did you give Paula and ____ their assignments?
10. I bought my father and ____ identical birthday presents this year.   **10.** her

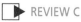 REVIEW C

Using Pronouns in the Nominative and Objective Cases in Sentences

The cheerleading squad is learning a new pyramid routine. To help get everyone organized, the coach has assigned each cheerleader a number. In each of the following sentences, replace the cheerleader's number with a correct personal pronoun. If *Number 1* is specified, use *I, we, me,* or *us.*

EXAMPLES **1.** Coach Welber told Cara and *Number 5* where to position themselves.
 1. *her*

2. I asked if *Number 8 and Number 1* could be in the pyramid next time.
 2. *we*

1. The three people forming the base of the pyramid were Harley, Michael, and *Number 5*. **1.** she
2. Kimiko is the smallest, so it was *Number 6* who got to be at the top first. **2.** she
3. The coach asked *Number 8 and Number 1* to give *Number 6* a boost. **3.** us/her
4. After *Number 4* and Emilio had been in the middle row awhile, Rosie and *Number 1* asked for a turn. **4.** she/I
5. Please tell Luisa and *Number 6 and Number 3* to stop laughing and pay attention. **5.** them
6. Give Rosie or *Number 1* a signal when you want to jump down, Kimiko. **6.** me

REVIEW C

Teaching Note. Students might not realize that when two numbers are joined by an italicized *and,* a plural pronoun should be used.

Direct students' attention to the second example in **Review C.** Explain that when two numbers are joined by an italicized *and,* the students should use a plural pronoun to replace the two numbers.

 VISUAL CONNECTIONS
Related Expression Skills. Before working on **Review C,** students may find it helpful to pretend to be the various characters in the picture. Allow students to work in groups of six. Each student should assume the role of one cheerleader (possibly wearing a name tag). Once they have enacted the scene, they might better understand the review exercise.

USAGE

USAGE

7. Next time, the ones in the middle row will be Harley and *Number 8*.   **7.** she
8. If anyone can support the person on top well, it's *Number 3*.   **8.** he
9. The winners of the next cheerleading meet will surely be *Numbers 1 through 8*.   **9.** we
10. Come here and I'll tell you and *Number 4* about the next new formation.   **10.** her

20d. The object of a preposition is in the objective case.

A prepositional phrase begins with a preposition and ends with a noun or pronoun called the *object of the preposition.*

EXAMPLES   to **them**   for **her** and **us**   with **him**

When the object of a preposition is compound, try each pronoun separately in the prepositional phrase.

NONSTANDARD   **Gwen wrote to her and I.** [*Gwen wrote to her* is correct. *Gwen wrote to I* is incorrect.]

STANDARD   **Gwen wrote to her and me.**

NOTE: Using incorrect pronoun forms after the prepositions *between* and *for* is a common error. The pronouns should be in the objective case.

INCORRECT   between *you* and *I,* for *she* and *they*
CORRECT   between you and **me,** for **her** and **them**

ORAL PRACTICE 2   **Using Pronouns as Objects of Prepositions**

Read each of the following sentences aloud, stressing the italicized words.

1. There were calls *for* Walker and *us.*
2. This message is *from* Dolores and *her.*
3. We sat *with* Arnie and *them.*
4. Margo looked *toward* Francine and *me.*
5. They gave copies *to him* and *me.*
6. This drawing is *by* either Hector or *him.*
7. Don't hold this *against* Cho and *her.*
8. I walked *between* Vince and *him.*

USAGE

20d

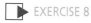 EXERCISE 7

Identifying the Correct Pronoun Forms for Objects of Prepositions

Identify the <u>correct pronoun</u> in parentheses in the following sentences.

1. The referee called fouls on (*he*, <u>*him*</u>) and (*I*, <u>*me*</u>).
2. Maggie is off fishing with Grandpa and (*he*, <u>*him*</u>).
3. We didn't want to leave without you and (*she*, <u>*her*</u>).
4. They assigned the same lab equipment to (*they*, <u>*them*</u>) and (*we*, <u>*us*</u>).
5. The duke directed a haughty sneer at the jester and (*he*, <u>*him*</u>).
6. After Carmen rolled the corn husks around the tamales, she handed them to Arturo and (*I*, <u>*me*</u>).
7. Everyone but Kevin and (*she*, <u>*her*</u>) thinks Ed Bradley is the best news commentator on television.
8. The player tried to dodge between Sherrie and (*I*, <u>*me*</u>).
9. The wary skunk circled around (*she*, <u>*her*</u>) and (*I*, <u>*me*</u>).
10. Uncle Vic will get the details from you and (*she*, <u>*her*</u>).

EXERCISE 8

Writing Sentences Using Pronouns as Objects of Prepositions

Write sentences of your own, using each of the following prepositions with a compound object. Use a personal pronoun for at least one of the objects in each sentence.

1. against   2. for   3. except   4. without   5. by

PICTURE THIS

You are a helper at a day-care center. The teacher wants you to entertain the group of children shown on the next page and, at the same time, teach them something about getting along with people who look different. She asks you to write a short fable with animal characters and read it to the children. In your fable, use at least ten personal pronouns. Use some of them as compound subjects, some

USAGE

TIMESAVER

To reduce paper-grading time and to increase students' exposure to correct oral usage, have students read their sentences for **Exercise 7** aloud. You will probably want to do this as a spot-check before having them exchange and grade the papers. You may want to collect the papers to check for mastery.

ANSWERS

Exercise 8

Sentences will vary. Responses should include pronouns in the objective case. Here are some sample sentences:

1. He turned Julie against John and her.
2. Mom bought new clothes for him and me.
3. Everyone's going except Colleen and him.
4. How could he do that without my parents and us?
5. The game was won by Max and me.

PICTURE THIS

You may want to further review the characteristics of fables with your students by reminding them that in most fables animals act and talk like people. Most fables also teach a lesson that is often summarized at the end.

Have students share a favorite fable with the class and encourage class discussion of the morals at the end of the stories.

USAGE

as compound direct or indirect objects, and some as compound objects of prepositions. Be sure to use the correct case for your pronouns. However, in the animals' dialogue, you may include such informal expressions as "It's me."

Subject: a fable about getting along well together
Audience: a group of four- to six-year-olds
Purpose: to entertain and to teach

> REVIEW D   **Identifying Correct Forms of Pronouns**

Choose the <u>correct pronoun</u> in parentheses in each numbered sentence in the following paragraph.

[1] Last fall, Tina talked Susan and (*I*, <u>*me*</u>) into going on a canoe trip with the Wilderness Club. [2] She warned (*we*, <u>*us*</u>) that we might get a good dunking before we were through. [3] When we set out, Susan and (<u>*I*</u>, *me*) could barely steer our canoe. [4] We watched another canoeist and saw how (<u>*she*</u>, *her*) and her partner maneuvered their craft. [5] They and (<u>*we*</u>, *us*) both did well until we hit the rapids or, rather, the rapids hit (*we*, <u>*us*</u>). [6] Susan grabbed for our sleeping bags, and (<u>*she*</u>, *her*) and (<u>*I*</u>, *me*) both scrambled for our food cooler. [7] All of (*we*, <u>*us*</u>) would-be

VISUAL CONNECTIONS
Ideas for Writing. Have students write about their impressions of day-care centers. For prewriting, organize students into groups of four or five. Have them discuss facts, feelings, or beliefs about day-care centers, and any experience they might have had with day-care centers. Then have each student write a draft of a paragraph that is either informative, expressive, or persuasive.

Divide the class into new groups and have students within each group read their paragraphs and discuss them.

INTEGRATING THE LANGUAGE ARTS
Literature Link. Have students read Emily Dickinson's "I Like to See It Lap the Miles" and have them discuss Dickinson's use of pronouns.

Although the referent for the pronoun *it* in the title and the first line of the poem is never explicitly identified, a close reading of the poem should reveal what *it* refers to [a train]. Tell students that such use of pronouns can be a powerful device but that if they use it they must be sure to supply the reader with enough clues to clearly define the missing referent.

SPECIAL PROBLEMS IN PRONOUN USAGE Rules 20e, 20f

OBJECTIVES

- To use *who* and *whom* correctly in subordinate clauses, and to identify the use of the pronoun
- To write sentences using phrases containing pronouns, and to identify how each phrase is used

20e

campers were drenched, but no quitters were (*we, us*). [8] Tina's warning haunted all of (*we, us*) as (*we, us*) hungry adventurers contemplated waterlogged sandwiches, soggy salads, and banana muffins with tadpoles in them. [9] Later, Susan and (*I, me*) discovered that our bedrolls had become portable water beds. [10] After a cold, squishy night, (*I, me*) concluded that wise are (*they, them*) who heed the voice of experience.

Special Problems in Pronoun Usage

Who and *Whom*

NOMINATIVE CASE	who, whoever
OBJECTIVE CASE	whom, whomever

NOTE: In spoken English, the use of *whom* is gradually dying out. Nowadays, it's acceptable to begin any spoken question with *who* regardless of whether the nominative or objective form is grammatically correct. In writing, though, it's still important to distinguish between *who* and *whom*.

20e. The use of *who* and *whom* in a subordinate clause depends on how the pronoun functions in the clause.

☞ REFERENCE NOTE: See pages 598–606 for information on subordinate clauses.

Follow these steps to decide whether to use *who* or *whom* in a subordinate clause.

STEP 1: Find the subordinate clause.
STEP 2: Decide how the pronoun is used in the clause—as subject, predicate nominative, direct object, indirect object, or object of a preposition.
STEP 3: Determine the case of the pronoun according to the rules of standard English.
STEP 4: Select the correct form of the pronoun.

USAGE

Teacher's ResourceBank™

RESOURCES

SPECIAL PROBLEMS IN PRONOUN USAGE
- *Who* or *Whom*?
- Pronouns Used as Appositives

🦉 QUICK REMINDER

Write the following sentences on the chalkboard and have students combine them, using the pronoun in parentheses. Ask students to explain why the pronoun usage is correct.

1. Juana is the baby sitter. Juana saved the child's life. (who) [Juana is the baby sitter who saved the child's life. The pronoun referring to Juana is the subject of the subordinate clause *saved the child's life,* so it should be in the nominative case.]
2. I voted for Quay. I know Quay from the soccer team. (whom) [I voted for Quay, whom I know from the soccer team. The pronoun referring to Quay is the direct object of *I know,* so it should be in the objective case.]

MEETING INDIVIDUAL NEEDS

LEP/ESL

Spanish. Most languages do not have an equivalent to the *who/whom* distinction. Thus, students may not have a first-language context to which they can relate this concept. It may be helpful to simply point out the lack in the Spanish language of a parallel to the *who/whom* distinction.

USAGE

COMMON ERROR

Problem. In an attempt to write more formally, students might use *whom* in their writing when *who* is correct.

Solution. One simple trick that might help students determine the correct form of the pronoun is to substitute other nominative-case pronouns (such as *I, she, they*) for the word *who* or *whom*. If a nominative-case pronoun is grammatically correct, the form *who* is needed. If a nominative-case pronoun is not correct, the objective form *whom* is correct.

**MEETING
INDIVIDUAL
NEEDS**

LESS-ADVANCED STUDENTS

The section on *who and whom* may be particularly difficult for students to master. The process of determining whether to use *who* or *whom* often requires more knowledge of English grammar than students possess. However, if they frequently use *whom* incorrectly in their speech and writing, you may want to give them the rule "When in doubt, use *who.*" You could also point out that *who* is acceptable in almost any informal construction.

---

662 *Using Pronouns Correctly*

EXAMPLE:	Roscoe is the only student (*who, whom*) got a perfect score.
STEP 1:	The subordinate clause is (*who, whom*) *got a perfect score.*
STEP 2:	In this clause, the pronoun is the subject of the verb *got.*
STEP 3:	As a subject, the pronoun should be in the nominative case.
STEP 4:	The nominative form is *who.*
ANSWER:	Roscoe is the only student **who** got a perfect score.

EXAMPLE:	Do you know (*who, whom*) she is?
STEP 1:	The subordinate clause is (*who, whom*) *she is.*
STEP 2:	In this clause, the pronoun (*who, whom*) is the predicate nominative: *she is (who, whom).*
STEP 3:	A pronoun used as a predicate nominative should be in the nominative case.
STEP 4:	The nominative form is *who.*
ANSWER:	Do you know **who** she is?

EXAMPLE:	I saw Sabrina, (*who, whom*) I know from school.
STEP 1:	The subordinate clause is (*who, whom*) *I know from school.*
STEP 2:	In this clause, the pronoun is the direct object of the verb *know: I know (who, whom).*
STEP 3:	As a direct object, the pronoun should be in the objective case.
STEP 4:	The objective form is *whom.*
ANSWER:	I saw Sabrina, **whom** I know from school.

Remember that no words outside the subordinate clause affect the case of the pronoun. In the second example above, the whole clause *who she is* is the direct object of the verb in the independent clause, *do know.* In the subordinate clause, though, *who* is used as a predicate nominative, which takes the nominative case.

NOTE: *Whom* is often left out of a subordinate clause, but its function is understood.

EXAMPLES   The actor (whom) I wrote to sent these photos. [*Whom* is understood to be the object of the preposition *to.*]
The man (whom) we saw on the elevator looked familiar. [*Whom* is understood to be the direct object of *saw.*]

PEANUTS Reprinted by permission of UFS, Inc.

▶ EXERCISE 9 **Determining the Use of *Who* and *Whom* in Subordinate Clauses**

Identify the <u>subordinate clause containing *who* or *whom*</u> in each of the following sentences. Then, tell how the relative pronoun (*who* or *whom*) is used in its own clause—as <u>*s*</u>*ubject*, *predicate* <u>*n*</u>*ominative*, <u>*d*</u>*irect* <u>*o*</u>*bject*, or <u>*o*</u>*bject of a preposition*.

EXAMPLE **1.** She is someone whom we all admire.
1. *whom we all admire—direct object*

1. The people <u>who are born in Puerto Rico</u> live in a commonwealth, with its own Senate, Supreme Court, and governor's Cabinet. **1.** s.
2. In 1969, the governor needed a secretary of labor <u>on whom he could depend</u>. **2.** o.p. **3.** d.o.
3. The person <u>whom he appointed</u> would occupy the most difficult and sensitive position in the Cabinet.
4. Do you know <u>who the choice was</u>? **4.** p.n.
5. The choice fell to Mrs. Julia Rivera De Vincenti, <u>who became the first woman to occupy a Cabinet post in Puerto Rico</u>. **5.** s. **6.** s.
6. De Vincenti, <u>who had completed the requirements for a Ph.D. degree in management and collective bargaining at Cornell University</u>, was a good choice.
7. De Vincenti, <u>who was later appointed to the U.S. Mission to the United Nations</u>, was the first Puerto Rican to serve in that capacity. **7.** s.
8. She addressed the General Assembly and showed that she was a person <u>who knew her job well</u>. **8.** s.
9. She praised her compatriots, <u>from whom new advances in agriculture had recently come</u>. **9.** o.p.
10. And De Vincenti made history again, for she was the first woman <u>who ever wore a pantsuit to address the General Assembly</u>! **10.** s.

USAGE

ADVANCED STUDENTS

You may wish to challenge students to write sentences of their own, using **Exercise 9** as a model. They can try them out working with partners.

LEARNING STYLES

Auditory Learners. Students might benefit from hearing the sentences in **Exercise 9** read aloud. Organize students into groups of four or five and have them take turns reading the sentences aloud. Remind students that while they might often hear *who* used in speech when the objective case is needed (because *who* sounds correct), in writing they will need to analyze the way the word is used in the sentence.

COOPERATIVE LEARNING

A team race will help students become more familiar with the correct use of *who* and *whom* in sentences. Put the following clauses on the chalkboard:

1. whom we adore
2. who believed in us
3. who wandered by
4. who asked directions
5. whom we helped

Have each team write as many sentences as possible in five minutes, using each clause at least once. Award a point for each correct sentence.

You may continue the game by having each team write clauses beginning with *who* and *whom* and then having them exchange clauses with another team. Again, give the teams a time limit to write sentences using the clauses correctly.

USAGE

INTEGRATING THE LANGUAGE ARTS

Grammar and the Library. You may wish to integrate the study of appositives with a review of the library. Have students familiarize themselves with biographies by locating the biography/autobiography section and any biographical encyclopedias.

Divide the class into pairs, and have each student write the name of a person who is unfamiliar to his or her partner. Have partners exchange names, find information in the library, and write short paragraphs about the person. The paragraph should contain at least two sentences with compound subjects or objects containing personal pronouns.

Have partners exchange paragraphs and evaluate them.

CRITICAL THINKING
Synthesis

After students read the examples in the **Appositives** section, have them go back over the example sentences to reduce the sentences to their essential elements. Tell students to determine whether or not the pronoun in question would be correct if it stood alone.

Tell students that reducing a sentence to its essential elements is a key to determining correct usage.

Appositives

 20f. Pronouns used as appositives should be in the same case as the word they refer to.

An ***appositive*** is a noun or pronoun given with another noun or pronoun to identify or explain it.

EXAMPLES   The late arrivals, **she, he,** and **I,** missed the first act. [The pronouns are in the nominative case because they are in apposition with the subject *arrivals.*]

The co-captains should be the best bowlers, **he and she.** [The pronouns are in the nominative case because they are in apposition with the predicate nominative *bowlers.*]

The article mentions the winners, **her** and **me.** [The pronouns are in the objective case because they are in apposition with the direct object *winners.*]

Ms. Lee gave the debaters, **them** and **us,** name tags. [The pronouns are in the objective case because they are in apposition with the indirect object *debaters.*]

The finalists were narrowed to two, **him** and **her.** [The pronouns are in the objective case because they are in apposition with the object of the preposition *two.*]

The pronouns *we* and *us* are sometimes used with noun appositives.

EXAMPLES   **We** sophomores raised the most money for charity. [The pronoun is in the nominative case because it is the subject of the sentence.]

The judges awarded **us** members of the jazz band a superior rating. [The pronoun is in the objective case because it is the indirect object of the verb *awarded.*]

To decide which form is correct for a pronoun used as an appositive or with an appositive, read the sentence with only the pronoun.

EXAMPLES   Coach Karas congratulated the two starting forwards, Angela and (*I, me*). [Omit the direct object *forwards*: Coach Karas congratulated Angela and **me.**]

(*We, Us*) girls made the playoffs! [Omit the appositive *girls*: **We** made the playoffs!]

OBJECTIVES

- To choose correct pronouns and describe how they are used in sentences
- To proofread a paragraph and identify correct pronoun forms
- To determine the proper case of pronouns used in sentences

MEETING
INDIVIDUAL
NEEDS

Special Problems in Pronoun Usage **665**

20f

 REFERENCE NOTE: See pages 590–591 for more information on appositives.

USAGE

 REVIEW E

Selecting Pronouns to Complete Sentences Correctly

Choose the <u>correct pronoun</u> in parentheses in each of the following sentences. Then, tell whether each is used as a <u>subject</u>, a <u>predicate nominative</u>, a <u>direct object</u>, an <u>indirect object</u>, an <u>object of a preposition</u>, or an <u>appositive</u>.

1. The two winners, Sean and (<u>*she*</u>, *her*), received huge green ribbons decorated with shamrocks. **1.** app.
2. Will Meg and (<u>*she*</u>, *her*) run the concession stand? **2.** s.
3. The coach asked you and (*I*, <u>*me*</u>) for help with the equipment. **3.** d.o.
4. Becky and (<u>*she*</u>, *her*) rode their bikes to the meeting. **4.** s.
5. The lighting crew for the play was Manuel and (<u>*I*</u>, *me*). **5.** p.n.
6. They treat (*whoever*, <u>*whomever*</u>) they hire very well. **6.** d.o.
7. I think it was Denzel Washington and (<u>*he*</u>, *him*) who starred in *Glory*. **7.** p.n.
8. They met Jennie and (*she*, <u>*her*</u>) at the airport. **8.** d.o.
9. Joe Leaphorn and Jim Chee are the Navajo detectives (*who*, <u>*whom*</u>) Tony Hillerman writes about in his crime stories. **9.** o.p.
10. I think that the people who were costumed as pirates are (<u>*they*</u>, *them*). **10.** p.n.

 REVIEW F

Proofreading a Paragraph for Correct Pronoun Forms

Some of the sentences in the following paragraph contain one or more pronouns that are used incorrectly. If a pronoun is incorrect, write the correct form. If the sentence is correct, write *C*.

[1] ~~Us~~ cousins were getting so confused at the family reunion that Rochelle, Darla, and ~~me~~ made the Family Relationship Chart shown on the next page. [2] Before long, the busiest people at the picnic were they and ~~me~~! [3] Aunts and uncles consulted us to find out ~~who~~ they were related to and just how they were related. [4] It all started when Jules wanted to know the connection

1. We/ I

2. I

3. whom

4. C

Many television sitcoms revolve around traditional or extended families. These shows are a rich source of examples of personal pronoun usage. Have students choose one or two favorite sitcoms to view with pencil in hand. Ask them to write down phrases and sentences in which characters are using personal pronouns. Warn students not to recreate the script; they just need to capture some statements to analyze later.

Have students share their findings and categorize their examples of pronoun usage as appropriate for informal dialogue or appropriate for writing.

USAGE

---

between him and Vicky. [5] We figured out that Vicky is the great-granddaughter of Jules's grandmother's brother, so ∧~~her~~ and Jules are second cousins once removed. [6] Looking at our chart, we could see that Vicky and Jules are in different generations, even though ∧~~him~~ and ∧~~her~~ are the same age. [7] All afternoon, curious relatives besieged Rochelle, Darla, and ∧~~I~~ with questions. [8] We helped ~~whomever~~ asked us. [9] Grandmother said she didn't know ∧~~who~~ to be prouder of, ∧~~we~~ or our cousins who made the refreshments. [10] Everyone learned something new about our family ties that day and gave the two other girls and ∧~~I~~ a big round of applause.

5. she
6. he/she
7. me
8. whoever
9. whom/us
10. me

Family Relationship Chart

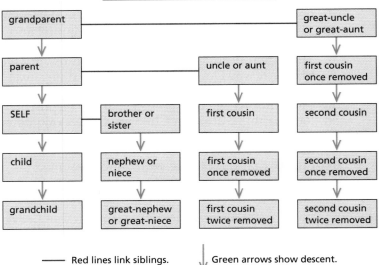

—— Red lines link siblings.   ↓ Green arrows show descent.

▶ REVIEW G

Determining the Proper Case of Pronouns in Sentences

For each of the following sentences, write *C* if the pronouns are all in the proper case. If a pronoun is incorrect, write the correct form.

1. Be careful ∧~~who~~ you tell.   **1.** whom
2. May Marie and I cut a few pictures out of this old copy of *Ebony*?   **2.** C

3. My family goes to the dentist, ~~who~~ Ms. Calhoun recommended. **3.** whom
4. Coretta said there would be other flag bearers in addition to Hugh and ~~I~~. **4.** me
5. At the head of the parade were ~~us~~ Girl Scouts. **5.** we
6. The treaty gave them and the Ojibwa people the right to harvest wild rice there. **6.** C **7.** C
7. Nobody except Josh and him finished the marathon.
8. We wish we had neighbors like Sylvia and him. **8.** C
9. Did your father and ~~them~~ reach an agreement about the boundary dispute? **9.** they
10. Joanne and ~~us~~ found a great beach. **10.** we

▶ EXERCISE 10 **Composing Sentences Using Pronouns**

Last month you joined the Climbing Club, and today you have just completed your first full day's climb. The club's advisor, Mr. Kraslow, has asked you to prepare a short report sharing your impressions of your first big climb. Use these pictures you took to help you write ten sentences for your report. Include one of the following phrases in each sentence. Be prepared to tell how each phrase is used.

1. Mr. Kraslow and us
2. Thomas and her
3. him and us
4. whoever
5. we newer climbers
6. they and Mr. Kraslow
7. he and they
8. Terri and me
9. Thomas and them
10. he and the Climbing Club

USAGE

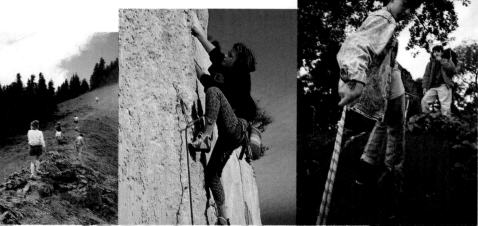

ANSWERS
Exercise 10

Answers may vary. Here are some possibilities:

1. That's a good picture of Mr. Kraslow and us. (object of a preposition)
2. The going was hard for Thomas and her. (object of a preposition)
3. The heaviest packs were given to him and us. (object of a preposition)
4. Whoever was last had to shout to be heard by everyone. (subject)
5. We newer climbers tried too hard at first. (subject)
6. They and Mr. Kraslow paced themselves better. (subject)
7. He and they had a good time. (subject)
8. Mr. Kraslow joked with Terri and me. (object of a preposition)
9. He encouraged Thomas and them. (direct object)
10. He and the Climbing Club plan to tackle Mt. Rainier. (subject)

USAGE

667

PRONOUNS IN INCOMPLETE CONSTRUCTIONS Rules 20g, 20h

OBJECTIVES

- To identify the correct pronouns for incomplete sentence constructions and describe how the pronouns are used
- To revise sentences correcting inexact pronoun references

Teacher's ResourceBank™

RESOURCES

PRONOUNS IN INCOMPLETE CONSTRUCTIONS

- Pronouns in Incomplete Constructions

USAGE

QUICK REMINDER

It is common to use incomplete constructions, but one way to determine correct pronoun usage is to finish sentences mentally. Write the following sentence on the chalkboard:

Dad loaned Tom more than me.

Ask students what the sentence means. [Students will probably say that it means the father made a larger loan to Tom than to the speaker.] Ask students how the sentence should be changed to mean that the speaker loaned less money to Tom than the father. [Dad loaned Tom more than I.] Tell students that they can check this construction by completing the sentence:

Dad loaned Tom more than I (loaned him).

ANSWERS
Exercise 11

1. they (played defense) — subject
2. I (was pleased) — subject
3. she (tried) — subject
4. he (is) — subject
5. she (knows her) — subject
   (I know) her — direct object
6. I (got) — subject
7. we (wanted tickets) — subject
8. we (live) — subject
9. I (visited Lisa) — subject
   (she visited) me — direct object
10. he (plays) — subject

668

Pronouns in Incomplete Constructions

20g. After *than* or *as* introducing an incomplete construction, use the pronoun form that would be used if the construction were completed.

> I know Mac better than **he** (knows Mac).
> I know Mac better than (I know) **him**.
> Do you visit Aunt Bessie as often as **we** (visit Aunt Bessie)?
> Do you visit Aunt Bessie as often as (you visit) **us**?

 EXERCISE 11 **Selecting Pronouns to Complete Incomplete Constructions in Sentences**

For each of the following sentences, choose the <u>correct form of the pronoun</u> in parentheses. Also supply in parentheses the missing part of the incomplete construction. Then, give the use of the pronoun in its clause. If a sentence may be completed in two different ways, provide both completions.

EXAMPLE   1. I like Arsenio Hall better than (*she, her*).
            1. *she (likes Arsenio Hall)—subject; (I like) her—direct object*

1. We played defense better than (<u>*they*</u>, *them*).
2. When Michael Chang won the men's singles title at the French Open, nobody was as pleased as (<u>*I*</u>, *me*).
3. Nobody tried harder than (<u>*she*</u>, *her*).
4. You are a month younger than (<u>*he*</u>, *him*).
5. I know Millie better than (<u>*she*</u>, <u>*her*</u>).
6. Did you get as far in that book as (<u>*I*</u>, *me*)?
7. Richard wanted more tickets than (<u>*we*</u>, *us*).
8. Bianca lives farther away than (<u>*we*</u>, *us*).
9. She visited Lisa more often than (<u>*I*</u>, <u>*me*</u>).
10. Carlos plays classical guitar in the style of Andrés Segovia but, of course, not as well as (<u>*he*</u>, *him*).

Inexact Pronoun Reference

20h. A pronoun should always refer clearly to its antecedent.

**20
g–h**

(1) Avoid an ambiguous reference.

In an ***ambiguous reference,*** a pronoun can refer to either of two antecedents.

AMBIGUOUS   Marissa called Yolanda while she was at the library.
             [Who was at the library, Marissa or Yolanda?]
    CLEAR   While **Marissa** was at the library, **she** called Yolanda.
                                    or
    CLEAR   While **Yolanda** was at the library, Marissa called **her.**

AMBIGUOUS   After viewing Roy's paintings and Elton's sculpture,
             the judges awarded his work the blue ribbon.
             [Whose work won the blue ribbon?]
    CLEAR   The judges awarded **Elton** the blue ribbon after
             viewing **his** sculpture and Roy's paintings.
                                    or
    CLEAR   The judges awarded **Roy** the blue ribbon after
             viewing **his** paintings and Elton's sculpture.

(2) Be sure that each pronoun you use has a specific, stated antecedent.

The pronouns *it, this, that, which,* and *such* are often used to refer to a general idea rather than to a specific noun. Using these pronouns in this way can lead to ***general reference*** errors.

GENERAL   Paul has a job interview after school today. That
           explains why Paul is all dressed up. [no specific
           antecedent for *That*]
  CLEAR   Paul is all dressed up because he has a job interview
           after school today.
                                  or
  CLEAR   The reason that Paul is all dressed up is that he has a job
           interview after school today.

GENERAL   My biology class is going on a field trip to the coast
           this week, which should be fun. [no specific antecedent
           for *which*]
  CLEAR   My biology class is going on a field trip to the coast
           this week. The trip should be fun.
                                  or
  CLEAR   Going on a field trip to the coast with my biology
           class this week should be fun.

USAGE

COMMON ERROR

Problem. Finding inexact pronoun references is a difficult task for students during the revision process. Because students know their intended meaning, they might not recognize points at which their writing is confusing.

Solution. One approach students could take is circling each *it, this, that, which,* and *such* in their writing. They could then draw a line to the word or words the pronoun refers to. If a student runs into a problem, he or she will need to revise the sentence to provide a clear reference.

Another approach is peer evaluation. A classmate might be more apt to spot any inexact references, and the writer can revise the unclear sentences.

INTEGRATING THE LANGUAGE ARTS

Usage and Writing. You may want to assign a writing topic that lends itself to pronoun use so that students can practice what they have learned. Give them the choice of writing a sports column, a music video review, or a dance review. During prewriting, you may want to approve topics in conferences.

Tell students that their aims can be expressive, literary, informative, or persuasive, and that they should include ten to fifteen personal pronouns in their essays. As students revise, ask them to check particularly for the correct use of personal pronouns.

Blondie, reprinted with special permission of King Features

Sometimes a writer will suggest a particular word or idea without stating it. A pronoun that refers to this unstated word or idea is said to have a *weak reference* to the antecedent.

WEAK When I listen in the car, I turn it up loud. [*It* may refer to a radio, tape player, or CD player. The writer suggests one of these devices but does not state which one.]

CLEAR When I listen to the **radio** in the car, I turn **it** up loud.

WEAK Royale writes stories, and she hopes to make it her career. [*It* most likely refers to the unstated noun *writing;* consequently, the writer has not made the pronoun-antecedent relationship clear.]

CLEAR Royale writes stories, and she hopes to make **writing** her career.

In conversation, people often use the pronouns *it, they,* and *you* unnecessarily. In writing, be sure to avoid such *indefinite reference* errors.

INDEFINITE In the newspaper, it reported that the robbers had been caught. [The pronoun *it* is not necessary to the meaning of the sentence. Revise the sentence to eliminate the wordiness caused by the indefinite reference.]

CLEAR **The newspaper reported that the robbers had been caught.**

INDEFINITE In the article, they include a toll-free number to call for more information. [The pronoun *they* is not necessary to the meaning of the sentence.]

CLEAR **The article includes a toll-free number to call for more information.**

NOTE: Familiar expressions such as *it is raining, it's early,* and *it seems like* are correct even though they contain inexact pronoun references. The antecedents to these pronouns are commonly understood to be the weather, time, and so forth.

Special Problems in Pronoun Usage **671**

 EXERCISE 12 **Correcting Inexact Pronoun References**

Revise each sentence in the following paragraph, correcting the inexact pronoun reference. If a sentence is correct, write *C*.

EXAMPLE **[1]** In a brochure recently published by the Environmental Protection Agency (EPA), it promotes recycling to reduce waste.

1. *A brochure recently published by the Environmental Protection Agency (EPA) promotes recycling to reduce waste.*

[1] The newest twist in recycling is *precycling*—cutting it off at its source. [2] Last month, after reading the EPA's brochure, my family decided to put its ideas into practice. [3] We now choose products that have less packaging; we carry groceries home in cloth bags instead of paper or plastic ones; and we buy containers that can be refilled, which is easy. [4] We even wrote to the Mail Preference Service, Direct Marketing Association, and asked that our names not be sold to mailing-list companies. [5] That greatly reduced the amount of junk mail we get. [6] When we do have waste products, inventing new ways to use them becomes a challenge in creative thinking; one of them was mine. [7] Now, we pack fragile objects in bits of plastic foam and other nonrecyclable materials so that they don't get broken in shipping. [8] We use plastic produce bags as sandwich wrappers or as liners for small trash cans, and it works just fine. [9] We also convert cottage cheese cartons and margarine tubs into food-storage containers, and we plan to make a habit of it. [10] In just a few short weeks, we've learned that in the 1990s, you recycle by remembering the three *r*'s: *r*educe, *r*euse, and *r*ecycle.

WRITING APPLICATION

Using Pronouns Correctly in a Letter

When you are writing about a complex event involving several people doing and saying things, your meaning can be lost if an antecedent is unclear.

USAGE

USAGE

WRITING APPLICATION
The writing assignment provides practice in writing a letter of explanation. The assignment requires that students use pronoun references correctly. You may wish to review the proper form for letters in **Chapter 35.**

CRITICAL THINKING
Analysis

Students may create extensive, informed lists of ideas in the prewriting stage. Tell them that they must narrow their lists to fit into one video. They might need to watch several successful videos and observe how many scenes and how many performers are included in the videos. Remind students that they must keep their audience and purpose in mind when narrowing their topic.

PREWRITING

If you assign this activity as homework, you may wish to suggest that students review several music videos for ideas about scenes, performers, and action. Such a review may also help them decide on the video they want to redirect.

WRITING

Encourage students to write freely. Remind them that they need not be overly concerned with errors at this stage.

UNCLEAR	Howard slipped, and Kiley recovered the ball and made a basket. **This** caused pandemonium among the fans. [What is the *this* that caused the pandemonium?]
CLEAR	**The quick recovery** caused pandemonium among the fans.

How else could you revise the unclear sentence to make its meaning clear?

▶ WRITING ACTIVITY

Your favorite musical group isn't happy with the director of their latest video. As a result, they are sponsoring a "Be a Music Video Director" contest. To enter, you have to write a letter explaining your idea for a different video of the same song. Tell which singers, dancers, and musicians you would cast in your video. Include at least ten pronouns in your sentences. Be sure that no pronoun has an unclear antecedent.

Prewriting Start by choosing the song you want to create a video for. Then, list some ideas for three or four scenes in your video. Next to each scene idea, list the performers you would use in that scene and describe the action. In addition to actual people, you may want to have cartoon characters or other animated figures in your video.

Writing As you write sentences about your music video, make the sequence of events clear. Make the spatial relationships clear, too, telling where the cast members are located.

Evaluating and Revising Check your rough draft to be sure that your explanation is clear. If you have included too many performers or too many details, eliminate the least interesting ones now. Have a classmate read your letter, looking for inexact uses of the pronouns *it, this, that,* and *which.* If he or she is confused by any sentences with inexact pronoun references, revise those sentences.

Proofreading Carefully read your letter again to be sure that all pronouns are in the correct case.

OBJECTIVES

- To choose the correct pronouns in sentences and explain their use
- To compose sentences using pronouns and pronoun phrases correctly

Special Problems in Pronoun Usage **673**

 REVIEW H

Selecting Pronouns to Complete Sentences

Choose the <u>correct pronoun</u> in parentheses in each of the following sentences. Be prepared to give reasons for your answers. s. = subject d.o. = direct object
p.n. = predicate nominative o.p. = object of a preposition

1. Heather and (*he*, *him*) live on a blueberry farm. **1.** s.
2. Did the teacher give that assignment to (*whoever*, *whomever*) was absent yesterday? **2.** s.
3. We wondered (*who*, *whom*) started the rumor. **3.** s.
4. Do you intercept passes as well as (*she*, *her*)? **4.** s.
5. The supporting players were Dina, Janelle, and (*she*, *her*). **5.** p.n.
6. I was standing in line behind Dave and (*he*, *him*). **6.** o.p.
7. You and (*I*, *me*) could write our biographical sketches on General Colin L. Powell, chairman of the Joint Chiefs of Staff. **7.** s.
8. The skit was written by Cy and (*he*, *him*). **8.** o.p.
9. The electrician warned (*he*, *him*) and (*I*, *me*) about the frayed wires. **9.** d.o./d.o.
10. Amy Tan, (*who*, *whom*) the critics had praised, autographed a copy of her novel *The Joy Luck Club* for me. **10.** d.o.

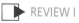 REVIEW I

Using Pronouns Correctly in Original Sentences

Outdoor murals like the one on the next page give artists a chance to express themselves on a grand scale! The owners of an enormous warehouse have made one long wall available to your class. Each team of students can paint whatever they wish on a thirty-foot section. The artwork can be serious or humorous, or it can just be a colorful design. Write ten sentences about the teams and their paintings. In each sentence, use a different pronoun or phrase from the following list. Be sure all pronouns are used in the way indicated in the exercise.

Francisco and I	me and my team	he
Matthew, Talbot, and us	Trenice and she	whoever
	who	them and you
her and them	whom	whomever
they and Luann		

ANSWERS
Review I

Answers may vary. Here are some example sentences:

1. To whom should these brushes be offered?
2. Whoever is best in art should get one.
3. The teacher gave her and them a bucket of paint.
4. The two artists, Trenice and she, dived right in with their brushes.
5. Francisco and I had the ideas.
6. It was he who suggested painting a red tree.
7. He encouraged me and my team.
8. The teacher applauded the creative students — Matthew, Talbot, and us.
9. I liked "Red Trees" better than they and Luann.
10. She rewarded Kim more than them and you.

USAGE

USAGE

REVIEW: POSTTESTS A and B

OBJECTIVES
- To determine the proper case of pronouns in sentences
- To proofread sentences and to supply correct pronoun forms

674 *Using Pronouns Correctly*

EXAMPLE   **1.** predicate nominative
          1. *The painters outlining the black unicorn are Trenice and she.*

1. object of a preposition
2. subject of a clause
3. indirect object
4. subject appositive
5. subject of the sentence
6. predicate nominative
7. direct object
8. object appositive
9. subject of an incomplete construction
10. direct object of an incomplete construction

Review: Posttest

A. Determining the Proper Case of Pronouns in Sentences

If a pronoun is used incorrectly in the following sentences, write the correct form of the pronoun. If a sentence is correct, write *C*.

1. Del can't do math any better than ~~her~~. **1.** she
2. There was some misunderstanding between him and his brother. **2.** C
3. To ~~who~~ was the letter addressed? **3.** whom
4. I showed the negatives to Cecilia and ~~she~~. **4.** her
5. It can't be they; that's not their car. **5.** C

 VISUAL CONNECTIONS
Related Expression Skills.
You may want to have students work in pairs to design or sketch a plan for a wall mural that reflects their interests or values. The mural sketch can be serious or funny. Have students consider what type of building they would use for a wall mural. After they have completed their sketches, you may want to have students write a paragraph describing their murals and explaining what their murals represent. Have students underline each pronoun that appears in their paragraphs.

6. Ben and you can come with them and me. 6. C
7. Leontyne Price's accomplishments were familiar to everyone in the class except him and I. 7. me
8. We band members have to be at school early to practice marching. 8. C
9. He's the sportscaster who irritates me with his pretentious talk. 9. C
10. In front of the school stood two drenched children, Charlene and he. 10. C

B. Proofreading Sentences for the Proper Case of Pronouns

Most of the following sentences have one or more incorrect pronouns. For each incorrect pronoun, write the correct form. If all of the pronouns in a sentence are correct, write C.

11. There's nothing like an action-packed all-star basketball game to give Dad and I a thrill! 11. me
12. The score was tied and the game almost over when Barkley's shot bounced off the rim, and him and Robinson rushed for the rebound. 12. he
13. As gravity pulled him and Robinson toward the floor, Barkley managed to tip the ball to Thomas. 13. C
14. Thomas saw Stockton coming and dribbled behind his back to elude he and Olajuwon. 14. him
15. When Stockton and Olajuwon collided, nobody was more surprised than them. 15. they
16. "If we make this basket, they and us will be tied," thought Thomas. 16. we
17. Thomas looked for Jordan, and realized that the blur streaking upcourt on the left was him. 17. he
18. "Five seconds to go—I have to pass to whomever is open, and Bird's the one." 18. whoever
19. Bird took a shot and missed, four players struggled for the ball, the ball went in, and all Thomas knew was that whomever had scored, it wasn't he. 19. whoever
20. In the whirlwind action during the last couple of seconds, the frantic referee couldn't see whom had fouled who. 20. who/whom

OBJECTIVES

- To write past or past participle forms of verbs to complete sentences
- To revise verb tense and voice in a paragraph
- To identify and correct errors in the usage of *lie* and *lay, sit* and *set,* and *rise* and *raise*

Teacher's ResourceBank™
RESOURCES

FOR THE WHOLE CHAPTER
- Chapter Review Form A
- Chapter Review Form B
- Assessment Portfolio
    Usage Pretests
    Usage Mastery Tests

USAGE

CHAPTER OVERVIEW

The material in this chapter will clarify for students the sometimes confusing nature of verbs. Principal parts of regular and irregular verbs, verb tense, and active and passive voice are all thoroughly discussed. Additional explanation for troublesome verbs such as *lie* and *lay, sit* and *set,* and *rise* and *raise* is provided and is reinforced by multiple exercises.

You may want to refer to this chapter when teaching writing. A quick review of the usage of verbs before the revision stage can provide students with the help they need to make their papers clear and effective.

USING THE DIAGNOSTIC TEST

The **Diagnostic Test** can be used in conjunction with an assessment of students' writing to identify students' strengths and weaknesses. Test results may also be used to determine grouping for cooperative-learning activities, as it is often helpful to group together students with varying levels of proficiency.

21 USING VERBS CORRECTLY

Principal Parts, Tense, Voice

Diagnostic Test

A. Writing the Past or Past Participle Form of Verbs

Write the correct past or past participle form of the verb given before each of the following sentences.

EXAMPLE   **1.** *do* Because he ____ his work so well, he got a raise.
                1. *did*

1. *write*   Although Emily Dickinson ____ poetry most of her life, very little of her work was published until after her death.   **1.** wrote
2. *drink*   When he saw that the animals had ____ all the water, he gave them more.   **2.** drunk
3. *throw*   Regarding weeds as unwanted intruders, she pulled them from the ground and ____ them over the fence.   **3.** threw
4. *swim*   The water was cold and daylight was fading, so he ____ only a short distance before turning back to shore.   **4.** swam

5. *freeze* The dew ____ during the night, covering each twig and blade of grass with a crisp, silvery coating. **5.** froze **6.** given

6. *give* After my brother had ____ his new puppy a bath, he seemed to be wetter than the dog.

7. *speak* She ____ in such a low, hushed voice that the people in the audience had to strain to hear her remarks. **7.** spoke

8. *run* Frightened by the traffic, the deer ____ back into the forest. **8.** ran

9. *ride* Leading the parade was an officer who ____ a prancing black horse. **9.** rode

10. *ring* When the church bell ____ on Tuesday evening, the villagers became alarmed. **10.** rang

B. Revising Verb Tense or Voice

Revise the following paragraph, correcting verbs that are in the wrong tense or that use an awkward passive voice. If a sentence is correct, write *C*.

[11] Katherine Davalos Ortega is born in 1934 in Tularosa, New Mexico, and worked in her family's restaurant and other businesses since she has been a small child. [12] Early in life a teaching career was chosen by her, but she was told that being Hispanic might prevent her from getting a teaching position. [13] As a result, she decided to pursue a business career instead, and by 1975, she has become the first woman president of a California bank. [14] In recognition of her professional abilities, Ms. Ortega was nominated by President Reagan to be Treasurer of the United States and was sworn in on October 3, 1983. [15] Her signature may be familiar to you, because it is appearing on more than twenty billion dollar bills and other types of U.S. currency.

C. Determining Correct Use of *Lie* and *Lay*, *Sit* and *Set*, and *Rise* and *Raise* in Sentences

Most of the following sentences contain at least one error in the use of *lie* or *lay*, *sit* or *set*, or *rise* or *raise*. Identify each

USAGE

ANSWERS

Diagnostic Test: Part B

Corrections are underlined.

11. Katherine Davalos Ortega <u>was</u> born in 1934 in Tularosa, New Mexico, and <u>has worked</u> in her family's restaurant and other businesses since she <u>was</u> a small child.

12. Early in life <u>she chose a teaching career</u>, but she was told that being Hispanic might prevent her from getting a teaching position.

13. As a result, she decided to pursue a business career instead, and by 1975, she <u>had</u> become the first woman president of a California bank.

14. C

15. Her signature may be familiar to you, because it <u>appears</u> on more than twenty billion dollar bills and other types of U. S. currency.

USAGE

incorrect verb, and give the correct verb. If a sentence is correct, write C.

16. The landlord asked us not to leave our lawn furniture ∧setting in the hallway.   **16.** sitting
17. They ∧lain the bricks in a pile next to where we ∧sat the wood.   **17.** laid/set
18. When the dough has risen for fifteen minutes, turn it out onto the floured board.   **18.** C
19. When we are rising from bed in the morning, the Chinese are ∧laying down to sleep.   **19.** lying   **20.** lay
20. The escaping slaves ∧laid quietly in the undergrowth.

The Principal Parts of Verbs

Every verb has four basic forms called *principal parts.* All of a verb's other forms come from its principal parts.

21a. The principal parts of a verb are the *infinitive,* the *present participle,* the *past,* and the *past participle.*

PRINCIPAL PARTS OF *WALK* AND *DO*			
INFINITIVE	**PRESENT PARTICIPLE**	**PAST**	**PAST PARTICIPLE**
walk	(is) walking	walked	(have) walked
do	(is) doing	did	(have) done

NOTE: The words *is* and *have* are included to remind you that when the present participle and past participle are used to form verb tenses, they're preceded by forms of these two helping verbs.

EXAMPLES   I **do** my homework after school.
   I **am doing** my homework now.
   I **did** my homework earlier.
   I **have done** all my homework already.

☞ REFERENCE NOTE: See page 527 for more information on using helping verbs with present participles and past participles.

USAGE

USAGE

REGULAR AND IRREGULAR VERBS
Rules 21a–21c

OBJECTIVES

- To read aloud sentences that include correctly used regular and irregular verbs
- To write past and past participle forms of irregular verbs to complete sentences ☞

Regular Verbs

21b. A *regular verb* is one that forms its past and past participle by adding *–d* or *–ed* to the infinitive.

INFINITIVE	PRESENT PARTICIPLE	PAST	PAST PARTICIPLE
work	(is) working	worked	(have) worked
receive	(is) receiving	received	(have) received
blame	(is) blaming	blamed	(have) blamed

 REFERENCE NOTE: For guidelines on spelling verbs when adding *–ed* or *–ing*, see pages 874–875.

A few regular verbs have an alternate past and past participle form ending in *–t*.

INFINITIVE	PRESENT PARTICIPLE	PAST	PAST PARTICIPLE
burn	(is) burning	burned *or* burnt	(have) burned *or* burnt
leap	(is) leaping	leaped *or* leapt	(have) leaped *or* leapt

Irregular Verbs

21c. An *irregular verb* is one that forms its past and past participle in some way other than by adding *–d* or *–ed* to the infinitive.

Irregular verbs form the past and past participle in one of the following ways:

- changing vowels
- changing consonants
- changing vowels *and* consonants
- adding *–en*
- making no change

USAGE

 QUICK REMINDER

Write the following sentences on the chalkboard and ask students to identify the verb in each sentence. Then have students write the present participle, past, and past participle forms of the verbs.

1. Gina and Laurie ride their bicycles to school.
2. Jim teaches me tall tales about the Old West.
3. My cat leaps onto the table.

MEETING INDIVIDUAL NEEDS

LEP/ESL

General Strategies. Point out to students that when they have questions about the principal parts of verbs, they can often find the answers in the dictionary. Tell them that the infinitive forms of verbs are listed as entry words and that the past, past participle, and present participle forms of irregular verbs are usually given in the entries. For example, if students look up *draw*, they will find *drew*, *drawn*, and *drawing*. As practice, have each student look up three irregular verbs and find the verbs' principal parts in the dictionary entry.

USAGE

• To use the correct past and past participle forms of irregular verbs in a letter

680 *Using Verbs Correctly*

EXAMPLES

INFINITIVE	PAST	PAST PARTICIPLE
fly	flew	(have) flown
bend	bent	(have) bent
sell	sold	(have) sold
beat	beat	(have) beaten
let	let	(have) let

NOTE: When you're not sure whether a verb is regular or irregular, check a dictionary that lists the principal parts of irregular verbs.

PRINCIPAL PARTS OF COMMON IRREGULAR VERBS			
INFINITIVE	PRESENT PARTICIPLE	PAST	PAST PARTICIPLE
begin	(is) beginning	began	(have) begun
blow	(is) blowing	blew	(have) blown
break	(is) breaking	broke	(have) broken
bring	(is) bringing	brought	(have) brought
burst	(is) bursting	burst	(have) burst
choose	(is) choosing	chose	(have) chosen
come	(is) coming	came	(have) come
dive	(is) diving	dove (*or* dived)	(have) dived
do	(is) doing	did	(have) done
draw	(is) drawing	drew	(have) drawn
drink	(is) drinking	drank	(have) drunk
drive	(is) driving	drove	(have) driven
eat	(is) eating	ate	(have) eaten
fall	(is) falling	fell	(have) fallen
freeze	(is) freezing	froze	(have) frozen
give	(is) giving	gave	(have) given
go	(is) going	went	(have) gone
hear	(is) hearing	heard	(have) heard
know	(is) knowing	knew	(have) known
leave	(is) leaving	left	(have) left
ride	(is) riding	rode	(have) ridden
ring	(is) ringing	rang	(have) rung
run	(is) running	ran	(have) run

MEETING INDIVIDUAL NEEDS

LESS-ADVANCED STUDENTS

Students might take one look at the **Principal Parts of Common Irregular Verbs** chart and feel overwhelmed. Ask them to choose five of these verbs and to write autobiographical sentences that incorporate the past or past participle form of each verb. For example, a student might incorporate the past participle form of *dive* into the autobiographical sentence "I have dived off the highest diving board at the public pool." Because this activity requires students to master a manageable number of verbs and to use the verbs in context, it will make the material more meaningful and less intimidating to students.

PRINCIPAL PARTS OF COMMON IRREGULAR VERBS *(continued)*			
INFINITIVE	**PRESENT PARTICIPLE**	**PAST**	**PAST PARTICIPLE**
see	(is) seeing	saw	(have) seen
sing	(is) singing	sang (*or* sung)	(have) sung
sleep	(is) sleeping	slept	(have) slept
speak	(is) speaking	spoke	(have) spoken
steal	(is) stealing	stole	(have) stolen
swim	(is) swimming	swam	(have) swum
take	(is) taking	took	(have) taken
teach	(is) teaching	taught	(have) taught
think	(is) thinking	thought	(have) thought
throw	(is) throwing	threw	(have) thrown
write	(is) writing	wrote	(have) written

 ORAL PRACTICE 1 **Using Regular and Irregular Verbs**

Read each sentence aloud, stressing each italicized verb.

1. Keisha *is braiding* Tiffany's hair in cornrows.
2. Bob *read* the want ads today, just as he *has read* them each day this week.
3. Mom, I *am bringing* you breakfast in bed, but I *have burned* your toast!
4. Warren *designed* the posters for the fall program.
5. Paloma Picasso, the jewelry designer, *has chosen* an artistic career different from her famous father's.
6. Carrie *went* to Penn State; Hector *is going* to Boston College.
7. Someone *ate* all the leftover spaghetti, but nobody *has touched* the baked beans.
8. If you *have* never *seen* a meteor shower, *run* outside right now!

EXERCISE 1 **Writing the Past or Past Participle Form of Irregular Verbs to Complete Sentences**

Give the correct past or past participle form of the verb given before each of the following sentences.

 INTEGRATING THE LANGUAGE ARTS

Usage and Vocabulary. After students have done **Oral Practice 1**, call on individual students to offer synonyms for the italicized verbs in the sentences. The synonyms should be in the same tenses and forms as the original verbs. For example, a student might substitute *is plaiting* for *is braiding* in the first sentence. Encourage students to be creative in their choices of synonyms.

USAGE

USAGE

USAGE

1. *sing*   The first drops of rain began to fall just after we had ____ the national anthem.   **1.** sung
2. *begin*   I had already ____ my homework.   **2.** begun
3. *freeze*   The sub-zero winds nearly ____ the Pawnee hunters as they tracked the herd of bison.
4. *fly*   Last summer we ____ in a lighter-than-air balloon.   **3.** froze   **4.** flew   **5.** saw
5. *see*   During our visit to Hawaii, we ____ a group of performers do a traditional hula dance.
6. *take*   My sister has ____ that course.   **6.** taken
7. *fall*   By the time Rolando finished carving the little figure of a saint, hundreds of tiny wood shavings had ____ to the floor.   **7.** fallen
8. *throw*   The horse had ____ its shoe.   **8.** thrown   **9.** broken
9. *break*   We hoped we hadn't ____ the machine.
10. *speak*   Harley's grandmother ____ to our class about her parents' life as sharecroppers in the early 1900s.   **10.** spoke

▶ EXERCISE 2   **Using the Correct Past or Past Participle Form of Verbs**

Give the correct form of each italicized verb in the following paragraph.

1. saw
2. chosen
3. come
4. wrote
5. brought
6. taught
7. went
8. fell
9. drawn
10. gave

We recently [1] (*see*) paintings by the African American artist Henry Ossawa Tanner. Tanner had [2] (*choose*) his lifelong career in art by the time he was thirteen years old. While walking in a park one day with his father, they had [3] (*come*) upon a landscape artist at work. Years later, Tanner [4] (*write*), "It was this simple event that set me on fire." Young Henry [5] (*bring*) such eagerness to his work that, before long, he [6] (*teach*) himself to draw well enough to be admitted to the finest art school in the country. His paintings were beautiful, but they did not sell, so Tanner [7] (*go*) abroad. He [8] (*fall*) in love with the city of Paris, and lived and worked there successfully for the rest of his life, winning many important painting awards. Shown on the next page is his best-known work, *The Banjo Lesson*, which he painted in Paris from sketches he had [9] (*draw*) years earlier in North Carolina. In 1991, long after Tanner's death, a touring exhibit finally [10] (*give*) Americans a look at the work of this gifted artist.

683

 VISUAL CONNECTIONS
Ideas for Writing. Have students think of someone who taught them to do something special. Perhaps a girl's aunt taught her to fish or a boy's older sister taught him to ride a bike. You may want to discuss some of your own experiences to help students generate ideas. Then ask students to write expressive paragraphs about their experiences. Have students include the past or past participle forms of at least three irregular verbs in their paragraphs.

USAGE

USAGE

▶ EXERCISE 3   **Selecting the Past or Past Participle Form of Verbs**

Choose the <u>correct form of the verb</u> in parentheses.

1. We (*did*, *done*) everything we could to help him.
2. Who has (*drank*, *drunk*) the rest of the orange juice?
3. Someone has already (*tore*, *torn*) out the coupon.
4. I wish you had (*spoke*, *spoken*) to me about it sooner.
5. I dived off the high board and (*swam*, *swum*) the length of the pool.
6. You must have (*rang*, *rung*) the doorbell while I was out.
7. Nancy had never (*ate*, *eaten*) a tamale before.
8. Lois (*blowed*, *blew*) up the balloon.
9. Suddenly the balloon (*burst*, *bursted*).
10. We were (*drove*, *driven*) to the train station in a taxi.

▶ EXERCISE 4   **Using the Past and Past Participle Forms of Verbs**

You have just joined a traveling circus, and you are in an acrobatic troupe with the performers shown on the next page. You work hard—not only perfecting your act but also helping with daily chores. Animals must be cared for,

ANSWERS
Exercise 4

Be sure students have correctly used at least five past and five past participle forms of verbs from the list. Assess students' work on the basis of whether or not they followed the directions. Give extra points for creativity.

683

OBJECTIVES

- To identify tenses of verbs in sentences and to explain the effect of different verb tenses on meanings of sentences
- To change the tenses of verbs in sentences

tents set up and taken down, and costumes made ready. You must also attend classes with a tutor! However, there's still time for fun. Write a short letter to your family, telling about your circus adventure. Use at least five past and five past participle forms of the irregular verbs listed on pages 680–681, and underline each one.

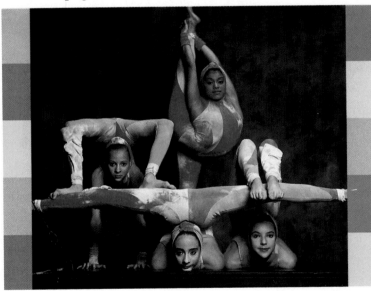

Tense

Teacher's ResourceBank™
RESOURCES

TENSE
- Verb Tense

QUICK REMINDER

Write the following sentences on the chalkboard. Have students correct the tenses of the underlined verbs.

1. I <u>talk</u> yesterday to the football coach about my position. [talked]
2. He already <u>leaves</u> when he called. [had already left]
3. Tomorrow we <u>have thought</u> about everything. [will think; will have thought]

21d. Learn the names of the six tenses and how each tense is formed.

Verbs change form to show the time of the action or the idea they express. The time indicated by the form of a verb is called its *tense.* In English, every verb has six tenses:

present	present perfect
past	past perfect
future	future perfect

The following charts show all six tenses of a regular verb (*talk*) and of an irregular verb (*throw*). Listing the verb forms in this way is called *conjugating* the verb.

- To write a fictional journal entry that includes at least five different verb tenses
- To proofread and revise a passage for correct verb forms

CONJUGATION OF THE VERB *TALK*			
Present infinitive: *to talk* Perfect infinitive: *to have talked*			
PRINCIPAL PARTS OF *TALK*			
INFINITIVE	**PRESENT PARTICIPLE**	**PAST**	**PAST PARTICIPLE**
talk	(is) talking	talked	(have) talked

PRESENT TENSE

SINGULAR	PLURAL
I talk	we talk
you talk	you talk
he, she, it talks	they talk

PAST TENSE

SINGULAR	PLURAL
I talked	we talked
you talked	you talked
he, she, it talked	they talked

FUTURE TENSE
(*will* or *shall* + the infinitive)

SINGULAR	PLURAL
I will (shall) talk	we will (shall) talk
you will talk	you will talk
he, she, it will talk	they will talk

PRESENT PERFECT TENSE
(*have* or *has* + the past participle)

SINGULAR	PLURAL
I have talked	we have talked
you have talked	you have talked
he, she, it has talked	they have talked

PAST PERFECT TENSE
(*had* + the past participle)

SINGULAR	PLURAL
I had talked	we had talked
you had talked	you had talked
he, she, it had talked	they had talked

(continued)

MEETING INDIVIDUAL NEEDS

USAGE

LEP/ESL

General Strategies. You may discover that some students neither write nor pronounce the *-es* ending for present tense, third person singular verbs, as in "She miss the bus almost every day." Similarly, they might have a tendency to omit the *–ed* ending for past tense, as in "She miss the bus yesterday." You may want to give students sentences containing these forms. Ask your students to underline all the *-es* and *-ed* endings for the third person, to circle the past-tense markers, and to read the sentences aloud. Listen carefully and model standard pronunciation when necessary.

STUDENTS WITH SPECIAL NEEDS

Learning disabled students have difficulty with abstract concepts. To illustrate verb tenses in a concrete way, read aloud a story with a chronologically ordered plot. Have students make a time line of the events in the story. Then have them write sentences that use verb tenses correctly to show the sequence of events in the story.

USAGE

CONJUGATION OF THE VERB *TALK* (continued)	
FUTURE PERFECT TENSE (*will have* or *shall have* + the past participle)	
SINGULAR I will (shall) have talked you will have talked he, she, it have talked	**PLURAL** we will (shall) have talked you will have talked they will have talked

 REFERENCE NOTE: For the conjugation of a verb in the passive voice, see pages 694–695.

In each tense another form, called the ***progressive form,*** may be used to show continuing action. The progressive form is made up of a form of *be* plus the verb's present participle.

Present Progressive	am, are, is talking
Past Progressive	was, were talking
Future Progressive	will (shall) be talking
Present Perfect Progressive	has, have been talking
Past Perfect Progressive	had been talking
Future Perfect Progressive	will (shall) have been talking

CONJUGATION OF THE VERB *THROW*			
Present infinitive: *to throw*		Perfect infinitive: *to have thrown*	
PRINCIPAL PARTS OF *THROW*			
INFINITIVE	**PRESENT PARTICIPLE**	**PAST**	**PAST PARTICIPLE**
throw	(is) throwing	threw	(have) thrown
PRESENT TENSE			
SINGULAR I throw you throw he, she, it throws		**PLURAL** we throw you throw they throw	
Present progressive: *am, are, is throwing*			

(continued)

USAGE

CONJUGATION OF THE VERB *THROW (continued)*

PAST TENSE

SINGULAR	PLURAL
I threw	we threw
you threw	you threw
he, she, it threw	they threw

Past progressive: *was, were throwing*

FUTURE TENSE
(*will* or *shall* + the infinitive)

SINGULAR	PLURAL
I will (shall) throw	we will (shall) throw
you will throw	you will throw
he, she, it will throw	they will throw

Future progressive: *will (shall) be throwing*

PRESENT PERFECT TENSE
(*has* or *have* + the past participle)

SINGULAR	PLURAL
I have thrown	we have thrown
you have thrown	you have thrown
he, she, it has thrown	they have thrown

Present perfect progressive: *has, have been throwing*

PAST PERFECT TENSE
(*had* + the past participle)

SINGULAR	PLURAL
I had thrown	we had thrown
you had thrown	you had thrown
he, she, it had thrown	they had thrown

Past perfect progressive: *had been throwing*

FUTURE PERFECT TENSE
(*will have* or *shall have* + the past participle)

SINGULAR	PLURAL
I will (shall) have thrown	we will (shall) have thrown
you will have thrown	you will have thrown
he, she, it will have thrown	they will have thrown

Future perfect progressive: *will (shall) have been throwing*

USAGE

USAGE

COMMON ERROR

Problem. Students might have difficulty in distinguishing among the past perfect tense, the present perfect tense, and the future perfect tense.

Solution. Remind students to look at the tense of the verb *have. Had* is in the past tense; it is combined with the past participle of a verb to create the past perfect tense. *Have* and *has* are in the present tense. Coupling either of these verbs with a past participle will form the present perfect tense. Likewise, *will have* is in the future tense, and it is combined with the past participle of a verb to create the future perfect tense.

INTEGRATING THE LANGUAGE ARTS

Literature Link. Students are often told to stick to one verb tense in their writing and are confused when they read a short story that incorporates several tenses. Tell students to read a short story and to identify the various tenses it incorporates. "The Doll's House" by Katherine Mansfield would be a good choice. Ask students why they think short stories often include so many different verb tenses. [A short story is a fictional narrative that relates a series of events. In order to show the sequence of events, several tenses must often be used.]

21e. Learn the uses of the six tenses.

(1) The ***present tense*** is used to express an action or a state of being occurring now, at the present time.

EXAMPLES   Sonja **owns** a calculator.
Larry **is** in the Chess Club.
We **are rehearsing** the play. [progressive form]

The present tense may be used to indicate habitual action.

EXAMPLE   He **runs** two miles a day.

The present tense is also used to express a general truth—something that is true at all times.

EXAMPLE   Haste **makes** waste.

The present tense is often used in discussing literary works, particularly in summarizing the plot or subject of a work. This use of the present tense is called the ***literary present.***

EXAMPLES   In Act III of Julius Caesar, the conspirators **gather** around Caesar. Casca **is** the first to stab him; then the others **plunge** their knives into Caesar.

Sometimes the present tense is used to relate past events in order to make them seem vivid. This use is called the ***historical present.***

EXAMPLES   During the unstable years following the 1910 Mexican Revolution, Emiliano Zapata **commands** a large army of revolutionaries and **occupies** Mexico City three different times.

(2) The ***past tense*** is used to express an action or a state of being that occurred in the past but did not continue into the present.

EXAMPLES   I **ran** toward the door.
I **was running** toward the door. [progressive form]

(3) The ***future tense*** is used to express an action or a state of being that will occur in the future. It is formed with *will* or *shall.*

EXAMPLES I **will leave** this week.
I **will be leaving** this week. [progressive form]

There are several other ways to indicate future time.

EXAMPLES I **am going to leave** this week.
I **leave later** this week. [present tense with a word or phrase clearly indicating future time]

(4) The ***present perfect tense*** is used to express an action or a state of being that occurred at some indefinite time in the past. It is formed with *have* or *has.*

EXAMPLE She **has visited** Chicago.

The present perfect tense is also used to express an action (or a state of being) that occurred in the past and continues into the present.

EXAMPLES She **has worked** there several years.
I **have been playing** guitar for nearly six months. [progressive form]

(5) The ***past perfect tense*** is used to express an action or a state of being that was completed before some other past action or event took place. It is formed with *had.*

EXAMPLES After she **had revised** her essay, she handed it in. [The action of revising was completed before the action of handing in.]
When he **had washed** the dishes, he sat down to rest. [The action of washing was completed before the action of resting.]

(6) The ***future perfect tense*** is used to express an action or a state of being that will be completed before some future action or event takes place. It is formed with *shall have* or *will have.*

EXAMPLES By the time I leave, I **will have packed** all my clothes. [The action of packing will be completed before the action of leaving.]
At the end of next year, I **will have been attending** school for eleven years. [progressive form]

ANSWERS
Exercise 5

1. The first sentence expresses an action that will occur in the future (future tense). The second sentence expresses an action that will be completed before some future action or event takes place (future perfect tense).

2. The first sentence expresses an action that occurred in the past but did not continue into the present (past tense). The second sentence expresses an action that occurred in the past and continues into the present (present perfect progressive tense).

3. The first sentence expresses an action that occurred in the past but did not continue into the present (past tense). The second sentence expresses an action that occurred in the past and continues into the present (present perfect tense).

4. The first sentence expresses an action that will occur in the future (future tense). The second sentence expresses an action that will be completed before some future action takes place (future perfect tense).

5. The first sentence expresses a continuing action that occurred in the past but did not continue into the present (past progressive tense). The second sentence expresses an action that occurred in the past and continues into the present (present perfect progressive tense).

690

EXERCISE 5 **Explaining the Uses of the Tenses of Verbs in Sentences**

Explain the difference in meaning between the sentences in the following pairs. Both sentences in each pair are correct. Identify the tense of the verb in each sentence.

1. I will start working by this afternoon.
   I will have started working by this afternoon.
2. What happened at the game?
   What has been happening at the game?
3. She lived in Cleveland for four years.
   She has lived in Cleveland for four years.
4. Before next year I will get a driver's license.
   Before next year I will have gotten a driver's license.
5. Some Green Berets were practicing tae kwon do during their lunch break.
   Some Green Berets have been practicing tae kwon do during their lunch break.

EXERCISE 6 **Using the Different Tenses of Verbs in Sentences**

Change the tense of the verb in each of the following sentences, according to the directions given after the sentence.

1. Otto lived here for a year. (Change to past perfect.) **1. had**
2. When the alarm goes off, I will get up. (Change *will get* to future perfect.) **2. have gotten**
3. Have you read Thomas Sowell's excellent how-to book *Choosing a College*? (Change *have read* to present perfect progressive.) **3. been reading**
4. When I get back, will you go? (Change *will go* to future perfect.) **4. have gone**   **5. Had/been**   **6. Have/been**
5. Were they at the party? (Change to past perfect.)
6. Were you invited? (Change to present perfect.) **7. has**
7. The soloist sings well. (Change to present perfect.) **sung**
8. The bus arrives on time. (Change to future.) **8. will arrive**
9. By the time you get here, Cammi will find out. (Change *will find* to future perfect.) **9. have found**
10. At ten o'clock, the klezmer band will play for an hour without a break. (Change to future perfect progressive.) **10. have been playing**

PICTURE THIS

Recently, you visited your cousins who live on this ranch. While you were there, heavy rains caused a nearby river to flood. You and your aunt and uncle and cousins managed to save their home from the rising water by quickly building a dike. After returning home, you decide you want your future children and grandchildren to know what your experience was like. You write a short account of what you did and how you felt as the waters rose and you and your family fought to hold them back. Use at least five different verb tenses in your journal entry. Be prepared to tell the tense of each verb you use.

Subject: your experiences during a flood
Audience: your descendants
Purpose: to inform

USAGE

PICTURE THIS

As prewriting, suggest that students jot down an outline of events in chronological order. What happened first, second, third, and so on? Once they have a clear idea of the sequence of events, students will be better able to use verb tenses correctly. You may want to ask students to underline the verbs in their accounts and to identify the tense of each verb.

USAGE

Consistency of Tense

21f. Do not change needlessly from one tense to another.

NONSTANDARD **Roy raised his binoculars and sees a large bear as it raced back to the woods.** [All the verbs refer to actions that happened at approximately the same time. However, the verbs are a mixture of past and present tenses.]

STANDARD **Roy raised his binoculars and saw a large bear as it raced back to the woods.** [The verbs are all in the past tense.]

STANDARD **Roy raises his binoculars and sees a large bear as it races back to the woods.** [The verbs are all in the present tense.]

NOTE: Sometimes, to show a sequence of events, you will need to mix verb tenses.

EXAMPLE **Before we had gone five miles, the car started making funny noises, and now it won't run at all.**

▶ EXERCISE 7 **Proofreading Paragraphs for Correct Verb Forms**

Some of the sentences in the following passage have at least one incorrect verb form. If a verb form is incorrect, write the correct form. If a sentence is correct, write C.

[1] The painting on the next page depicts the outcome of one of the most important battles of the Revolutionary War, a battle that took place in September and October 1777 at Saratoga, New York. [2] The leader of the British troops, General John Burgoyne, had set up camp near Saratoga and is planning to march south to Albany. [3] Burgoyne's army has been weakened by a recent attack from an American militia, which had ambushed some of his troops at Bennington, Vermont. [4] Although the march to Albany is dangerous, Burgoyne decided to take the risk because he feels bound by orders from London.

[5] Meanwhile, also near Saratoga, the American troops under General Horatio Gates and General Philip Schuyler gather reinforcements and supplies. [6] The American forces outnumbered their British enemies by a margin of

ANSWERS
Exercise 7

1. C
2. is — was
3. has — had
4. is — was; feels — felt
5. gather — had gathered (or *were gathering* or *gathered*)
6. C
7. are — were; are — were
8. launch — launched
9. withdraw — withdrew
10. have — had
11. sends — sent
12. is — was
13. C
14. leads — led
15. endure — endured; prepares — prepared
16. surround — surrounded
17. had surrendered — surrendered
18. is — was
19. becomes — became
20. C

USAGE

two to one. [7] The Americans are much better equipped than the British, whose provisions are badly depleted.

[8] In spite of these disadvantages, the British launch an attack on the Americans on September 19, 1777. [9] After four hours of fierce fighting, the Americans, led by Major General Benedict Arnold (who later became an infamous traitor to the American cause), withdraw. [10] The British, however, have suffered serious losses, including many officers. [11] Burgoyne quickly sends a message to the British command in New York and asked for new orders. [12] He never received a response from his superiors, possibly because the message is intercepted. [13] Burgoyne's tactics became desperate. [14] He boldly leads a fresh attack against the Americans on October 7. [15] This time, however, his troops endure even worse casualties, and the next day Burgoyne prepares to retreat.

[16] The Americans surround Burgoyne's army before it could leave Saratoga. [17] As the painting shows, Burgoyne had surrendered to Benedict Arnold. [18] The Convention of Saratoga, by which Burgoyne gave up his entire force of six thousand troops, is signed on October 17. [19] Saratoga becomes a turning point in the Revolutionary War. [20] Six years later, in 1783, the British signed a peace treaty with the Americans, and the Revolutionary War ended.

 VISUAL CONNECTIONS
The Surrender of Burgoyne

About the Artist. John Trumbull, born in 1756 in Lebanon, Connecticut, was left nearly blind in one eye by a boyhood injury. Nevertheless, Trumbull went on to become a colonel by the age of twenty-one, an amateur architect, an author, and a well-respected artist. Trumbull is best known for his paintings depicting momentous occasions in American history, his most famous painting being *The Declaration of Independence.* In 1843, John Trumbull died and, according to his wishes, was buried under the Yale Art Gallery.

USAGE

ACTIVE VOICE AND PASSIVE VOICE Rule 21g

OBJECTIVES

- To identify verbs in sentences as being in the active or the passive voice
- To rewrite passive voice verbs in the active voice

QUICK REMINDER

Write the verbs *terminate, build,* and *persuade* on the chalkboard. For each verb, ask your students to compose one sentence in the active voice and one sentence in the passive voice.

MEETING
INDIVIDUAL
NEEDS

ADVANCED STUDENTS

Tell students that although as a general rule they should avoid using the passive voice, there are times when it is effective. For example, the passive voice can be used to neutralize the sense of action, to create a sense of evasiveness, or to create suspense in writing. Have students look for examples of effective use of the passive voice in literature and in magazines and newspapers. You may want to ask students to share their examples of passive voice with the class and to explain why they are effective.

---

694 *Using Verbs Correctly*

Active Voice and Passive Voice

21g. A verb in the *active voice* expresses an action performed *by* its subject. A verb in the *passive voice* expresses an action done *to* its subject.

ACTIVE VOICE The blazing fire **destroyed** the outside walls. [The subject (*fire*) performs the action.]

PASSIVE VOICE The outside walls **were destroyed** by the blazing fire. [The subject (*walls*) receives the action.]

Notice that the object of the active sentence becomes the subject of the passive sentence. The subject of the active sentence is now given only in a prepositional phrase, which could even be omitted.

PASSIVE VOICE The outside walls were destroyed.

Notice, too, that the verb has been changed from *destroyed* to the verb phrase *were destroyed*. In a passive sentence, the verb phrase always includes a form of *be* (*is, was,* etc.) plus the past participle. Other helping verbs may also be included, depending on the tense.

ACTIVE VOICE She **grows** corn on her farm.

PASSIVE VOICE Corn **is grown** on her farm.

ACTIVE VOICE She **will plant** the corn in two weeks.

PASSIVE VOICE The corn **will be planted** in two weeks.

CONJUGATION OF THE VERB *PAID* IN THE PASSIVE VOICE	
PRESENT TENSE	
SINGULAR	**PLURAL**
I am paid	we are paid
you are paid	you are paid
he, she, it is paid	they are paid
Present progressive: *am, are, is being paid*	

(continued)

CONJUGATION OF THE VERB *PAID* IN THE PASSIVE VOICE *(continued)*	
PAST TENSE	
SINGULAR	*PLURAL*
I was paid	we were paid
you were paid	you were paid
he, she, it was paid	they were paid
Past progressive: *was, were being paid*	
FUTURE TENSE	
SINGULAR	*PLURAL*
I will (shall) be paid	we will (shall) be paid
you will be paid	you will be paid
he, she, it will be paid	they will be paid
Future progressive: *will (shall) be being paid*	
PRESENT PERFECT TENSE	
SINGULAR	*PLURAL*
I have been paid	we have been paid
you have been paid	you have been paid
he, she, it has been paid	they have been paid
Present perfect progressive: *has, have been being paid*	
PAST PERFECT TENSE	
SINGULAR	*PLURAL*
I had been paid	we had been paid
you had been paid	you had been paid
he, she, it had been paid	they had been paid
Past perfect progressive: *had been being paid*	
FUTURE PERFECT TENSE	
SINGULAR	*PLURAL*
I will (shall) have been paid	we will (shall) have been paid
you will have been paid	you will have been paid
he, she, it will have been paid	they will have been paid
Future perfect progressive: *will (shall) have been being paid*	

NOTE: Because the use of *be* or *been* with *being* is awkward, the progressive form is usually used only in the present tense and past tense.

INTEGRATING THE LANGUAGE ARTS

Grammar and Writing. Ask your students to write in the passive voice brief narratives about experiences they have had. Ask volunteers to read their papers aloud. The class should listen carefully to the readers, noting examples of writing that meet the objective. Then have students change their narratives to the active voice; have volunteers read the revised narratives aloud. Discuss the differences that the use of the active voice makes.

Technology Link. There are now computer programs available that can check writing for overuse of passive voice. If your school's computer department has such a program, you may want to encourage students to use it.

USAGE

USAGE

CRITICAL THINKING
Analysis

The chapter gives three situations in which the passive voice is useful:

1. when the performer is difficult to specify
2. when the performer is unknown
3. when the writer or speaker doesn't want to name the performer

As a week-long project, have students listen for and note use of the passive voice in their own speech and the speech of others. Tell students to analyze why the passive voice was used in each instance.

ANSWERS
Exercise 8

Revisions may vary.

1. passive — Many artists around the world admired the art of Lucia Wilcox.

2. active

3. passive — Raoul Dufy, Fernand Léger, Robert Motherwell, and Jackson Pollock befriended and taught her.

4. passive — Galleries all over the art world showed exhibits of her paintings.

5. active

6. passive — A tumor near the optic nerve caused it.

7. active

8. passive — She described her vision and her mind as "free of static" and "distractions."

9. passive — Because of her blindness, she altered her style from energetic silhouettes to larger canvases in lush colors.

10. passive — Many well-known artists imitated this style.

696

Using the Passive Voice

The passive voice emphasizes the person or thing receiving the action rather than the one performing the action. The passive voice is useful

- when the performer is difficult to specify
- when you don't know who performed an action
- when you don't want to give away the performer's identity

EXAMPLES   The mayor **was reelected** by a landslide. [performer difficult to specify]

My brother's bicycle **was stolen** yesterday. [performer unknown]

Vicious rumors **have been spread** about him. [performer deliberately concealed]

In general, though, it's a good idea to avoid the passive voice. The active voice makes your writing much more direct and forceful.

 EXERCISE 8   **Identifying Sentences in the Active or Passive Voice**

Label the verb in each of the following sentences as *active* or *passive*. Then rewrite each passive voice sentence in the active voice.

1. The art of Lucia Wilcox was admired by many artists around the world.
2. Her blindness during her last years made her final works particularly interesting.
3. She was befriended and taught by Raoul Dufy, Fernand Léger, Robert Motherwell, and Jackson Pollock.
4. Exhibits of her paintings were shown in galleries all over the art world.
5. Her blindness occurred suddenly, though not unexpectedly.
6. It was caused by a tumor near the optic nerve.
7. After becoming blind, she claimed she had better sight than anyone else.
8. Her vision and her mind were described by her as "free of static" and "distractions."

SIX TROUBLESOME VERBS

OBJECTIVES

- To read aloud and to stress the correct forms of *lie* and *lay*, *sit* and *set*, and *rise* and *raise* in sentences
- To select the correct forms of *lie* and *lay* and *sit* and *set* to complete sentences ☞

9. Because of her blindness, her style was altered from energetic silhouettes to larger canvases in lush colors.
10. This style was imitated by many well-known artists.

Shoe, by Jeff MacNelly, reprinted by permission: Tribune Media Services.

Six Troublesome Verbs

Lie and *Lay*

The verb *lie* means "to rest" or "to recline." It never takes an object.

The verb *lay* means "to put" or "to place" (something). It usually takes an object.

Teacher's ResourceBank™
RESOURCES

┌─────────────────────────────┐
│ **SIX TROUBLESOME VERBS** │
│ • Troublesome Verbs │
└─────────────────────────────┘

QUICK REMINDER
Write the verbs *lie, lay, sit, set, rise,* and *raise* on the chalkboard and ask students to compose one sentence for each verb. When students finish writing, give a brief definition of each word. Then ask volunteers to read their sentences aloud.

- To proofread and revise for correct forms of *lie* and *lay* in sentences and in a passage
- To write the correct forms of *sit* and *set* to complete a paragraph
- To write the correct forms of *rise* and *raise* to complete sentences

USAGE

USAGE

698 *Using Verbs Correctly*

PRINCIPAL PARTS OF *LIE* AND *LAY*			
INFINITIVE	**PRESENT PARTICIPLE**	**PAST**	**PAST PARTICIPLE**
lie (to rest)	(is) lying	lay	(have) lain
lay (to put)	(is) laying	laid	(have) laid

EXAMPLES The cat often **lies** on the porch, sunning itself.
It is **lying** there now.
A thick fog **lay** over the city.
The old papers **had lain** on the desk for months.

Lay your packages here.
I am **laying** your packages here.
The mason **laid** the bricks.
He **had laid** his keys on the ledge.

To decide whether to use *lie* or *lay,* ask yourself two questions:

QUESTION 1: What do I mean? (Is the meaning "to be in a lying position," or is it "to put something down"?)
QUESTION 2: What time does the verb express, and which principal part accurately shows this time?

EXAMPLE: Feeling drowsy, I (lay, laid) on the couch.
QUESTION 1: *Meaning*? Here the meaning is "to rest." Therefore, the verb should be *lie.*
QUESTION 2: *Principal part*? The time is past. Therefore, the principal part should be *lay.*
ANSWER: Feeling drowsy, I **lay** on the couch.

EXAMPLE: The teacher (lay, laid) the cards on the desk.
QUESTION 1: *Meaning*? Here the meaning is "to put." Therefore, the verb should be *lay.*
QUESTION 2: *Principal part*? The time is past. Therefore, the principal part should be *laid.*
ANSWER: The teacher **laid** the cards on the desk.

ORAL
PRACTICE 2   **Stressing the Correct Forms of *Lie* and *Lay* in Sentences**

Read each of the following sentences aloud, stressing the italicized verbs.

1. The ketchup bottle should *lie* on its side.
2. A light haze *lay* over the hills.
3. The cat *laid* its toy on the doorsill.
4. Someone's books are *lying* in the hall.
5. She had *lain* down for a nap.
6. Where could I have *laid* the recipe?
7. *Lay* the material on the counter.
8. You could *lie* down and relax.

EXERCISE 9 **Selecting the Correct Form of *Lie* and *Lay* to Complete Sentences**

In each of the following sentences, choose the correct verb in parentheses.

1. He (*lay*, *laid*) out the silverware.
2. Eduardo (*laid*, *lay*) the strips of grilled meat on the tortilla.
3. The pasture (*lies*, *lays*) in the valley.
4. A sheet (*lay*, *laid*) over the rug to catch the paint.
5. The clothing had (*lain*, *laid*) on the floor all week.
6. Kitty (*lay*, *laid*) the book down.
7. Mrs. Nakamoto was (*lying*, *laying*) out everything necessary for the tea ceremony.
8. The theories developed by Albert Einstein (*lay*, *laid*) the groundwork for many later scientific discoveries.
9. The cat has been (*lying*, *laying*) on my coat.
10. (*Lying*, *Laying*) the tip by my plate, I rose to leave the restaurant.

EXERCISE 10 **Determining the Correct Use of *Lie* and *Lay* in Sentences**

For each of the following sentences, write *C* if the verb is correct. If the verb is incorrect, write the correct form.

1. The towels ~~laying~~ in the corner all need to be washed. **1.** lying
2. After I had tripped, I sat there feeling embarrassed, my groceries lying all around me. **2.** C
3. Jackie Joyner-Kersee crossed the finish line and, exhausted, ~~laid~~ down in the grass. **3.** lay
4. The fox was lying hidden in the thicket. **4.** C

USAGE

COOPERATIVE LEARNING
Working on a group project will provide an opportunity for students to clarify their confusion over the verbs *lie* and *lay, set* and *sit,* and *rise* and *raise.* Divide the class into groups of four or five. Assign each group the task of writing a short skit that includes the six troublesome verbs. Then have the groups perform their skits for the class.

USAGE

INTEGRATING THE LANGUAGE ARTS

Literature Link. As a means of stressing to students that incorrect use of these verbs will affect the meaning of what they write, have students read a poem in which *lie, lay, sit, set, rise,* or *raise* is used correctly. Students might read "Miss Rosie" by Lucille Clifton (*sit*), "The Road Not Taken" by Robert Frost (*lie*), or "The Meadow Mouse" by Theodore Roethke (*lie*). After students have read the poem, have them analyze how the poem would be different if the wrong verb had been used (*set* for *sit,* or *lay* for *lie*). Would the meaning of the poem be clear to students? Would they be distracted by the incorrect usage? What might incorrect usage tell them about the speaker of the poem? Discuss these questions with your class.

5. C
5. Yesterday, all we did was lie around and play CDs.
6. He was lying under the car, tinkering with the muffler. 6. C
7. The workers had ˄lain down their tools and gone to lunch. 7. laid   8. lying   9. laid
8. My gym bag was ˄laying right where I had left it.
9. In his speech, César Chávez ˄lay the responsibility for social change on the shoulders of all citizens.
10. She sighed and ˄lay down the phone receiver. 10. laid

> EXERCISE 11
Proofreading a Paragraph for the Correct Use of *Lie* and *Lay*

In each sentence of the following paragraph, a form of *lie* or *lay* is used. If the wrong form is used, write the correct form. If a sentence is correct, write *C*.

1. C
2. laid
3. laid
4. lay
5. lying
6. lie
7. C
8. C
9. lying
10. lie

[1] Brent had planned to spend all day Saturday laying new tile in the kitchen. [2] Before he started, he ˄lay out all his materials and read the directions on the can of adhesive carefully. [3] At first, he made good progress and had ˄lain sixteen rows of tile by lunchtime. [4] Then he ate a sandwich and ˄laid down on the sofa for a few minutes. [5] When he returned to the kitchen, Brent found that his dog, Stanley, was ˄laying where the next row of tiles was supposed to go. [6] Brent had forgotten that Stanley liked to ˄lay in that particular place on the kitchen floor. [7] Unfortunately, Stanley weighed almost as much as Brent, and laying down the law to the dog had never worked. [8] Brent got a juicy meat scrap out of the refrigerator and laid it on the floor just beyond Stanley's snoring nose. [9] But the wily Stanley had been ˄laying in wait and, in a flash, grabbed the meat. [10] To Brent's dismay, Stanley resumed his nap with a satisfied sigh, and Brent learned that the worker isn't the only one who can ˄lay down on the job!

Sit and *Set*

The verb *sit* means "to rest in a seated position." It almost never takes an object.

The verb *set* means "to put," "to place" (something). It usually takes an object. Notice that *set* does not change form in the past or the past participle.

NOTE: In a few uses, *set* does not mean "to put" or "to place."

EXAMPLES   the sun sets, setting hens, set your watch, set a record, set out to accomplish something

PRINCIPAL PARTS OF *SIT* AND *SET*			
INFINITIVE	**PRESENT PARTICIPLE**	**PAST**	**PAST PARTICIPLE**
sit (to rest)	(is) sitting	sat	(have) sat
set (to put)	(is) setting	set	(have) set

EXAMPLES   You may **sit.**   The car **sat** in the driveway.
          Set your books here.   We **set** the books there.

ORAL
PRACTICE 3   **Stressing the Correct Forms of *Sit* and *Set* in Sentences**

Read each of the following sentences aloud, stressing the italicized verb.

1. *Set* the groceries on the counter.
2. *Sit* down anywhere you like.
3. Would you please *set* the lawn chairs under the tree in the front yard?
4. The bird *sat* on the wire.
5. During Hanukkah, we always *set* the menorah in a place of honor.
6. We had *sat* in the lobby for an hour.
7. They have been *sitting* on the porch.
8. Rosa Parks made history when she chose to *sit* rather than to give up her seat to a white passenger.

EXERCISE 12   **Selecting the Correct Form of *Sit* and *Set* to Complete Sentences**

In each of the following sentences, choose the correct verb in parentheses.

USAGE

A DIFFERENT APPROACH

Tell students they'll be competing in a Sentence Bee in which they will be able to practice correct usage of the verbs *lie, lay, sit, set, rise,* and *raise.* Divide the class into two teams. Give a student from one team instructions such as "Compose a sentence using the past perfect tense of *lay.*" The student will then compose a sentence fitting your description. If the sentence is correct, the student stays in the game. If it is incorrect, he or she is out, and the same challenge is offered to a student from the other team. Continue in this fashion until everyone has been eliminated except a winner, or until you run out of time. You may find it helpful to prepare the instructions ahead of time.

USAGE

1. A few of us were (*sitting*, *setting*) at our desks.
2. He (*sat*, *set*) in the rocker, reading.
3. He (*sat*, *set*) the package on the doorstep.
4. Ida was (*sitting*, *setting*) out the chips and dip for the guests.
5. We had been (*sitting*, *setting*) on a freshly painted bench.
6. They (*set*, *sat*) the seedlings in the window boxes.
7. She (*sits*, *sets*) in front of me.
8. (*Set*, *Sit*) this Pueblo pottery in the display case.
9. I could (*sit*, *set*) and watch the sunset every evening.
10. Bowls of Cuban black bean soup were (*sat*, *set*) in front of the hungry travelers.

▶ EXERCISE 13 **Writing the Forms of *Sit* and *Set***

For each numbered blank in the following paragraph, write the correct form of *sit* or *set*.

To gain a view of the surrounding land, Lewis and Clark's group climbed to an outcropping of gray rocks that [1] _____ atop the bluff. It was late afternoon, and the Shoshone guide Sacagawea [2] _____ her pack down beside the rocks and [3] _____ down in their shade to rest. Meriwether Lewis saw her from where he was [4] _____ nearby and approached with a friendly "May I [5] _____ here with

1. sat
2. set
3. sat
4. sitting
5. sit

USAGE

USAGE

REVIEW A

OBJECTIVE

• To select the correct forms of *lie* and *lay* and *sit* and *set* to complete sentences

you?" Several other members of the expedition saw them [6] _____ together and wondered what they were discussing. In fact, Lewis was asking her in what direction she thought the party should [7] _____ out in the morning. Gazing westward from the bluff, Sacagawea saw that she was in familiar territory and soon [8] _____ her mind on heading down the mountainside toward the northwest. By the time the sun had [9] _____, Lewis agreed that the route she had chosen would be the easiest to follow. A wise leader, he realized that he had never [10] _____ foot in these lands, while she had passed this way before.

6. sitting

7. set

8. set

9. set

10. set

 REVIEW A

Selecting the Correct Form of *Lie* and *Lay* and *Sit* and *Set* to Complete Sentences

In each of the following sentences, choose the <u>correct verb</u> in parentheses.

1. (*Sitting*, *Setting*) on the table was a pair of scissors.
2. Please (*sit*, <u>*set*</u>) the carton down carefully.
3. Sakura folded her kimono and (<u>*lay*</u>, *laid*) down on the soft, padded futon to sleep.
4. (<u>*Sit*</u>, *Set*) all the way back in your seat.
5. The dirty dishes had (<u>*lain*</u>, *laid*) in the sink for hours.
6. Yesterday Tom (*lay*, <u>*laid*</u>) the blame for his lateness on his alarm clock.
7. The cat always (<u>*sits*</u>, *sets*) on the couch.
8. If only we could have (*lain*, <u>*laid*</u>) our hands on that buried treasure!
9. The tickets to the Wynton Marsalis concert were (<u>*sitting*</u>, *setting*) right where I left them.
10. King Tut's tomb (<u>*lay*</u>, *laid*) undisturbed for centuries.
11. Have you ever (<u>*sat*</u>, *set*) around with nothing to do?
12. She (<u>*sat*</u>, *set*) down at her desk with her checkbook and calculator in front of her.
13. Santa Anna, (<u>*sitting*</u>, *setting*) on his horse, ordered his troops to attack the Alamo.
14. The beached rowboat (<u>*lay*</u>, *laid*) on its side.
15. She (<u>*sat*</u>, *set*) looking toward the horizon.
16. Laura had just (<u>*sat*</u>, *set*) down when the phone rang.
17. Julie (*lay*, <u>*laid*</u>) her handbag on the counter.

USAGE

USAGE

LEARNING STYLES

    Visual Learners. Have students make collages of pictures from magazines that illustrate the verbs *lie, lay, sit, set, rise,* and *raise.* Students should label their collages so that it is clear which verbs are being illustrated. You could display the completed collages in your classroom.

18. Pieces of the jigsaw puzzle were (*laying, lying*) on the floor.
19. Jack was (*sitting, setting*) outside on the top step.
20. Were you (*laying, lying*) down for a while before dinner?

Rise and Raise

The verb *rise* means "to go upward." It never takes an object.

    The verb *raise* means "to move (something) upward" or "to bring up." It usually takes an object.

PRINCIPAL PARTS OF *RISE* AND *RAISE*			
INFINITIVE	**PRESENT PARTICIPLE**	**PAST**	**PAST PARTICIPLE**
rise (to go upward)	(is) rising	rose	(have) risen
raise (to move [something] upward)	(is) raising	raised	(have) raised

EXAMPLES   I usually **rise** at 6:00 A.M.
                 Prices **rose** rapidly in the early 1980s.

                 Raise your hand if you know the answer.
                 The coach **raised** the bar on the high jump.

ORAL PRACTICE 4   **Stressing the Correct Form of *Rise* and *Raise* in Sentences**

Read each of the following sentences aloud, stressing the italicized verb.

1. *Has* the moon *risen* yet?
2. The tower *rose* high into the darkening air.
3. The temperature *rose* as the sun climbed higher.
4. Listening to "I Have a Dream," a speech by Martin Luther King, Jr., always *raises* my spirits.
5. Trails of mist were *rising* from the lake.
6. How much did the river *rise* during the flood?
7. The butterfly *rose* from the leaf and flitted away.
8. The dough was *rising* in the bowl.

EXERCISE 14

Writing the Correct Form of *Rise* and *Raise* to Complete Sentences

For each blank in the following sentences, write the correct form of *rise* or *raise*. The tenses of the verbs in sentences 4, 5, 6, 8, and 9 may vary.

1. ____ the flags higher, please. **1.** Raise
2. The gigantic Kodiak bear ____ on its hind legs and looked around. **2.** rose
3. The tide ____ and falls because of the moon. **3.** rises
4. Carlos and Pilar ____ the piñata above the heads of the children. **4.** raised
5. Up toward the clouds ____ the jet. **5.** rose
6. Many Native American peoples ____ corn as a staple food crop. **6.** raise
7. Prices have ____ in the last few years. **7.** risen
8. The traffic officer ____ his hand to signal us. **8.** raised
9. My sister and I ____ before the sun came up this morning. **9.** rose
10. César Chávez ____ to fame in the 1960s. **10.** rose

REVIEW B

Determining Correct or Incorrect Use of *Lie* and *Lay*, *Sit* and *Set*, and *Rise* and *Raise* in Sentences

If a sentence is correct, write *C*. If it is incorrect, revise the incorrect word or words.

1. Set the eggs down carefully. **1.** C
2. The frog was ~~setting~~ on the lily pad and croaking loudly. **2.** sitting
3. The judge studied the papers, then ~~lay~~ them beside her gavel. **3.** laid
4. The cattle were lying in the shade by the stream. **4.** C
5. Do you think the temperature will ~~raise~~ much higher? **5.** rise
6. Wanda ~~sat~~ out the equipment for the experiment. **6.** set
7. Why don't you ~~lie~~ those things down? **7.** lay
8. Instead of ~~laying~~ down, you should be getting some type of strenuous exercise. **8.** lying
9. Let's sit where we can get a good view of the Juneteenth parade. **9.** C
10. ~~Set~~ down for a while and relax. **10.** Sit

LESS-ADVANCED STUDENTS

Students might benefit from doing **Review B** in small groups. Assign the exercise to groups of two or three. You may want to group less-advanced students with those who better understand the material. Encourage students to talk about the sentences and to help one another with any problems. You may want to circulate through the room to make sure that less-advanced students are receiving the help they require.

USAGE

USAGE

WRITING APPLICATION

OBJECTIVE

- To write an informative essay that describes the order of events by using appropriate verb tenses

WRITING APPLICATION

This writing assignment provides each student with the opportunity to express pride in a personal heritage. Because there may be many students in your class who have moved frequently, you may want to allow students to broaden the scopes of their essays to include contributions to the nation rather than to the community. If there are students in your class who do not possess a strong sense of cultural identity, allow them to write on alternate topics.

CRITICAL THINKING
Synthesis

This activity asks students to project, based on what they know about the present contributions of a certain cultural or ethnic group, what can be expected from that group in the future. Because this requires a high level of critical thinking, you may want to model this thought process for students.

For example, you might note that the Greek Americans in your community are active in city government and have organized an annual festival that showcases Greek culture. Ask students what they can predict, based on this information, about the contributions of Greek Americans in the future. [Students might say that in the future Greek Americans in the community might hold important offices in city government and that their annual festival might attract tourists from other communities, thereby bringing revenue to the city.]

USAGE

706

---

706 *Using Verbs Correctly*

WRITING APPLICATION

Using Verb Tense to Establish Time of Action

To show the precise order of events, a writer sometimes needs to use several different tenses in a paragraph—or even in the same sentence.

EXAMPLE   The Japanese students *had planned* a tea ceremony, but because another group *was using* the activity room, they *will reschedule* the ceremony.

Each verb in the preceding sentence is in a different tense. If the verbs were all in the same tense, a reader would be confused about the order of the events.

 WRITING ACTIVITY
It's Cultural Appreciation Week at your school. Your teacher has asked you to write a short essay about your own cultural or ethnic group. In your essay, you should explore several ways in which people from your heritage have enriched life in your community. Use correct verb tenses to describe some of the contributions these people have made in the past, some activities they are currently involved in, and what you think they might offer in the future. Use at least five different verb tenses in your essay.

🌐 **Prewriting** Brainstorm a list of your ethnic or cultural group's outstanding leaders, scholars, athletes, and artists, as well as activities, events, clubs, and community service projects. Select three or four of the group's main contributions to mention in your essay. Many people can claim more than one ethnic or cultural heritage. If you can, you may want to write about the group you know the best or the one you are most interested in.

 Writing While you are writing your first draft, try to add details that show the uniqueness of your cultural heritage. Consider how you can control verb tenses to make the sequence of events in your essay clear.

USAGE

OBJECTIVES

- To select the correct forms of verbs to complete sentences
- To supply the correct forms of verbs to complete a paragraph

 Evaluating and Revising   Read through your essay to be sure you have included at least one contribution from each different time period: the past, the present, and the future. Check to see that you have used at least five different tenses.

 Proofreading and Publishing   Using your textbook, make sure that you have formed all verbs correctly. Pay special attention when checking the forms of irregular verbs. With your classmates, you might create a bulletin board display of all the essays your class has written. Or your class may wish to prepare a cultural-appreciation presentation for another class or for the whole school.

PROOFREADING AND PUBLISHING

To assist students in verifying that they have included at least five different verb tenses, ask them to label the tenses of all the verbs in their essays. This strategy will also save time for you when you are grading their papers.

ADVANCED STUDENTS

Ask advanced students to generate a synonym for each verb in **Review C**. Then have them create an exercise similar to **Review C** with the synonyms they have generated. The synonyms should be in the same forms as their counterparts in the exercise.

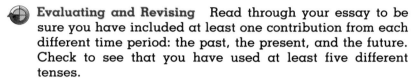

▶ REVIEW C   **Choosing the Correct Forms of Verbs to Complete Sentences**

In each of the following sentences, choose the <u>correct verb or form of the verb</u> given in parentheses.

1. Little Billy was (*lying*, *laying*) in wait for us.
2. He had accidentally (*thrown*, *throwed*) his homework away.
3. The spilled laundry (*lay*, *laid*) in a wet heap.
4. We ate until we almost (*burst*, *bursted*).
5. The kitten (*shrank*, *shrunk*) from the barking dog.
6. Haven't you ever (*swam*, *swum*) in a lake before?
7. When Chief Dan George walked to the podium, a cheer (*rang*, *rung*) out.
8. Have you ever (*rode*, *ridden*) a roller coaster?
9. I knew I should have (*brought*, *brung*) my camera.
10. Uh-oh, I think this phone is (*broke*, *broken*).

▶ REVIEW D   **Choosing the Correct Forms of Irregular Verbs**

Supply the correct form of each italicized verb in the following paragraph.

USAGE

1. seen
2. drawn
3. took
4. set
5. left
6. come
7. gone
8. run
9. began
10. threw

Have you ever [1] (*see*) this fascinating picture of an impossible structure? It is called *Waterfall*, and it was [2] (*draw*) by the Dutch artist M. C. Escher. He [3] (*take*) the basic idea for this artwork from the optical illusion shown beside it. As you can see, a two-story waterfall has [4] (*set*) a miller's wheel in motion. Then, after the water has [5] (*leave*) the wheel, it zigzags along a channel until it has [6] (*come*) to the top of the waterfall again. But wait—has the water [7] (*go*) uphill on its way back to the top of the waterfall? No, obviously the stream has [8] (*run*) away from the fall on the same level as the bottom of the fall. But then how can the water now be back at the top where it [9] (*begin*)? Escher never said, but he once wrote that if the miller simply [10] (*throw*) in a bucket of water now and then to replace water that had evaporated, he would have a "perpetual motion" machine!

© 1961 M.C. Escher/Gordon Art-Baarn-Holland

▷ EXERCISE 15   **Using Verbs to Express Time Relationships Clearly**

The time line on the next page shows several key events from American history. Make up five sentences that establish time relationships between two or more of the events named. In each sentence, use more than one verb and make each verb a different tense. Vary your sentence structure. Be prepared to tell how the tenses you used help explain the sequence of events.

EXAMPLE   *As De Soto was finishing his exploration of the Southeast, Cabrillo started to investigate the Pacific coast.*

REVIEW: POSTTEST

OBJECTIVES

- To write past or past participle forms of verbs to complete sentences
- To revise sentences to correct awkward use of voice as well as incorrect verb tenses ☞

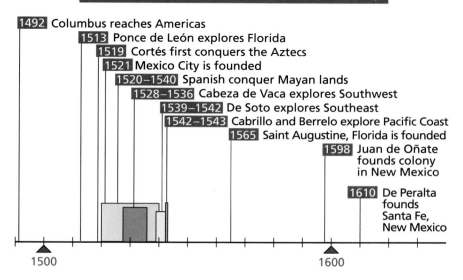

Some Important Events in American History

1492 Columbus reaches Americas
1513 Ponce de León explores Florida
1519 Cortés first conquers the Aztecs
1521 Mexico City is founded
1520–1540 Spanish conquer Mayan lands
1528–1536 Cabeza de Vaca explores Southwest
1539–1542 De Soto explores Southeast
1542–1543 Cabrillo and Berrelo explore Pacific Coast
1565 Saint Augustine, Florida is founded
1598 Juan de Oñate founds colony in New Mexico
1610 De Peralta founds Santa Fe, New Mexico

1500   1600

USAGE

Review: Posttest

A. Writing the Past or Past Participle Form of Verbs

For each of the following sentences, write the correct past or past participle of the verb given before the sentence.

1. *ride*   Jeffrey and Lee have ____ their bikes fifty miles today.   **1.** ridden
2. *write* I read the letters Grandpa ____ to Grandma in 1930.   **2.** wrote
3. *take*   Dad, I know that you've ____ us to two rap concerts this year, but please take us to just one more.   **3.** taken
4. *fall*   All that winter day the snow ____, blanketing everything.   **4.** fell
5. *see*   Rebecca soon ____ why the old house had sold so cheaply.   **5.** saw

6. *drink* The gerbil has ____ most of its water. **6.** drunk
7. *begin* As darkness fell and the children still did not return, I ____ to worry. **7.** began
8. *bring* Margot has ____ popcorn and apples for the party. **8.** brought
9. *speak* Police Sergeant Liakos ____ about responsible driving at the assembly yesterday. **9.** spoke
10. *give* The Nez Percé people had ____ the starving fur traders food and helped them repair their canoes. **10.** given

B. Revising Verb Tense or Voice

Rewrite the following sentences, correcting verbs that are in the wrong tense or that use an awkward voice. If a sentence is correct, write *C*.

EXAMPLES **1.** Genna gave her report on Captain James Cook and shows us some maps and pictures of the areas he explored.
  1. *Genna gave her report on Captain James Cook and showed us some maps and pictures of the areas he explored.*

  2. We were surprised to learn how many places were explored by him.
  2. *We were surprised to learn how many places he explored.*

11. Captain Cook, one of the greatest explorers of all time, sailed large areas of the Pacific Ocean and ~~makes~~ accurate maps of the region. **11.** made
12. Cook ~~joins~~ the navy as a seaman in 1755, and many promotions ~~were received by him~~ before he became the master of a ship in 1759. **12.** joined/he received
13. Because of his knowledge of geography, astronomy, and mathematics, he ~~is~~ selected to lead a scientific expedition to the Pacific. **13.** was
14. The purpose of Cook's expedition ~~is~~ to observe the passage of Venus between Earth and the sun, a very rare occurrence. **14.** was
15. On the voyage, Cook ~~wins~~ a battle against scurvy, a serious disease caused by lack of vitamin C. **15.** won

USAGE

USAGE

16. ∧Raw cabbage, which∧~~was~~ rich in vitamin C, ~~was eaten by the sailors~~ to prevent scurvy. **16.** The sailors ate/is
17. By the time the voyage∧~~is~~ over, the ship∧traveled around Cape Horn to Tahiti in the Pacific Ocean. **17.** was/had
18. After∧~~he observes~~ the passage of Venus, Cook∧~~sails~~ off to explore the east coast of New Zealand, which ∧~~was~~ claimed ~~by him~~ for England. **18.** observing/sailed/he
19. ∧The Hawaiian Islands ~~were later explored by~~ Cook on his final voyage to the Pacific and ~~were~~ named∧ the Sandwich Islands∧~~by him.~~ **19.** Cook explored/them
20. In a dispute over a canoe, Cook was killed by island inhabitants and in naval tradition was buried at sea in 1779. **20.** C

C. Determining Correct Use of *Lie* and *Lay*, *Sit* and *Set*, and *Rise* and *Raise* in Sentences

If a verb in one of the following sentences is incorrect, write the correct form. If a sentence is correct, write C.

21. You can∧~~sit~~ the wastebasket in the corner and then set up the chairs. **21.** set
22. Everyone rose when the judge entered the court-room and sat when she was seated. **22.** C
23. The mysterious shape suddenly∧~~raised~~ from the shadows. **23.** rose
24. I like to∧~~lay~~ out under the stars and just think. **24.** lie
25. The servant had∧~~lain~~ out the emperor's silken robes of yellow, the color that only members of Chinese royalty were permitted to wear. **25.** laid

OBJECTIVES
- To correct errors in the use of comparative and superlative forms
- To revise sentences by correcting dangling and misplaced modifiers

Teacher's ResourceBank™
▼ **RESOURCES** ▼

FOR THE WHOLE CHAPTER
- Chapter Review Form A
- Chapter Review Form B
- Assessment Portfolio
  Usage Pretests
  Usage Mastery Tests

USAGE

CHAPTER OVERVIEW

The first part of this chapter helps students to identify adjective and adverb modifiers and to correctly use the troublesome pairs *bad* and *badly, well* and *good,* and *slow* and *slowly.* The second part focuses on showing comparisons by correctly using comparative and superlative forms. The third part of the chapter shows how to recognize and correct dangling and misplaced modifiers.

USING THE DIAGNOSTIC TEST

You may want to use the **Diagnostic Test** to gauge whether students can correct errors in the use of comparative and superlative forms and whether students can revise sentences by correcting dangling and misplaced modifiers. You could supplement the test by having students write paragraphs in which they use comparative and superlative forms and correctly place phrases or clauses used as modifiers.

USAGE

22 USING MODIFIERS CORRECTLY

Forms, Comparison, and Placement

Diagnostic Test

A. Correcting Errors in the Use of the Comparative and Superlative Forms

Write the incorrect word or words from each sentence. Then write the correct form, adding or deleting words if necessary.

EXAMPLES
1. I was more hungrier than I had thought, so I ordered three sandwiches.
   1. *more hungrier—hungrier*

   2. This storm was even badder than the last one.
   2. *badder—worse*

1. During the 1960s, Ralph Abernathy and Medgar Evers were among the ~~most~~ best-known civil rights activists.
2. He was the ₌~~more~~ able and intelligent of the three job applicants.   **2.** most   **3.** more famous
3. Is Pocahontas ₌~~famouser~~ than Sacagawea?

4. John, Richard's twin brother, was the ~~oldest~~ by three and a half minutes.   **4.** older

5. After Diego had started lifting weights, he bragged that he was stronger than anyone₍in town.   **5.** else

6. People who live along this road complain because it is the ~~worstest~~ in the entire township.   **6.** worst

7. Floyd and his brother are landscape designers who are in demand throughout the state, but Floyd is the ~~best~~ known in this area.   **7.** better

8. After the band had practiced, their music sounded ~~more~~ better.

9. When I had a choice of strawberry or vanilla, I took vanilla because I like it ~~best~~.   **9.** better

10. Looking across the water at sunset, you can see the ~~beautifullest~~ view you can imagine.   **10.** most beautiful

B. Revising Sentences by Correcting Dangling and Misplaced Modifiers

Each of the following sentences contains either a dangling or a misplaced modifier. Revise each sentence, arranging the words so that the meaning is logical and clear. You may have to add or delete some words. Be sure to use commas where they are needed to set off introductory and interrupting modifiers.

EXAMPLE   **1.** The class sent a get-well message to their teacher on a balloon.
   1. *The class sent their teacher a get-well message on a balloon.*

11. Running in circles, they saw that the dogs could herd the sheep into the pen.

12. The winners marched onto the platform carrying ribbons and trophies.

13. A police officer warned students who drive too fast about accidents during the defensive-driving class.

14. After escaping from slavery, the importance of education was often stressed by Frederick Douglass.

15. A brightly colored watercolor was hanging on her wall depicting the four seasons.

16. Mother found a package outside our house tied with ribbons.

ANSWERS
Diagnostic Test: Part B

Answers may vary. Here are some possibilities:

11. They saw that the dogs, running in circles, could herd the sheep into the pen.

12. Carrying ribbons and trophies, the winners marched onto the platform.

13. During the defensive-driving class, a police officer warned students who drive too fast about accidents.

14. Frederick Douglass, after escaping from slavery, often stressed the importance of education.

15. A brightly colored watercolor depicting the four seasons was hanging on her wall.

16. Outside our house, Mother found a package tied with ribbons.

17. With a telephoto lens, Maria took a close-up photograph of a lion.
18. Sitting in a tree outside my window a small bird is apparently building a nest on one of the limbs.
19. A young woman wearing a suit and a hat knocked on the door.
20. Walking in the sunshine, we felt warm.

USAGE

QUICK REMINDER

Remind students that adverbs tell *where, when, how,* and *to what extent.* Adjectives tell *what kind, which one,* and *how many.*

Write the following sentences on the chalkboard. Have students classify each underlined word as an adjective or an adverb; then have them identify the question it answers.

1. The storm was fierce. [adjective; tells what kind of storm]
2. Josh bathed his dog yesterday. [adverb; tells when he bathed the dog]
3. Felipe baked the winning dessert. [adjective; tells which dessert he baked]
4. The star appeared surprisingly bright in the sky. [adverb; tells to what extent it appeared bright]

714

ADJECTIVE AND ADVERB FORMS Rule 22a

OBJECTIVES
• To identify adjectives and adverbs
• To select adjectives or adverbs to complete sentences
• To use adjective and adverb forms correctly in a paragraph

---

17. Maria took a close-up photograph of a lion with a telephoto lens.
18. Sitting in a tree outside my window, I see a small bird, apparently building a nest on one of the limbs.
19. A young woman knocked on the door wearing a suit and a hat.
20. Walking in the sunshine, it felt warm to us.

Adjective and Adverb Forms

A *modifier* is a word or a group of words that makes the meaning of another word more definite. Two parts of speech are used as modifiers: *adjectives* and *adverbs.* Adjectives modify nouns and pronouns. Adverbs modify verbs, adjectives, and other adverbs.

ADJECTIVE Lisa does **strenuous** exercise.
ADVERB Lisa exercises **strenuously.**

NOTE: Many adverbs end in *–ly,* but not all of them do. A few common adjectives also end in *–ly.*

EXAMPLES **costly** repairs **daily** schedule
lively discussion **lonely** scene

Some words have the same form whether they're used as adjectives or as adverbs. Therefore, you can't tell whether a word is an adjective or an adverb just by looking for the *–ly* ending. Instead, you have to determine how the word is being used.

ADJECTIVES	ADVERBS
We took an **early** flight.	We left **early** this morning.
She asked a **hard** question.	She tried **hard.**
They took the **first** step.	They went **first.**

22a. If a word in the predicate modifies the subject of the verb, use the adjective form. If it modifies the verb, use the adverb form.

ADJECTIVE   The swimmer was **careful.** [careful swimmer]
ADVERB   He swims **carefully.** [swims carefully]

In many cases, linking verbs are followed by a predicate adjective.

Common Linking Verbs		
appear	grow	smell
be (am, is, are, etc.)	look	sound
become	remain	stay
feel	seem	taste

Many linking verbs can also be used as action verbs. To tell whether a verb is a linking verb or an action verb, try a form of *seem* in its place.

LINKING   She **felt** happy. [*She seemed happy* makes sense. Therefore, *felt* is a linking verb in this sentence.]

ACTION   She **felt** the fabric. [*She seemed the fabric* doesn't make sense. Therefore, *felt* is an action verb in this sentence.]

LINKING   The old car **appeared** abandoned. [*The old car seemed abandoned* makes sense.]

ACTION   The car **appeared** suddenly. [*The car seemed suddenly* doesn't make sense.]

 REFERENCE NOTE: See pages 524–526 and 560–563 for more information on linking verbs and action verbs.

EXERCISE 1   **Identifying Adjectives and Adverbs**

The following paragraph contains fifteen adjectives and ten adverbs. For each sentence, identify each adjective and adverb and give the word it modifies. [Note: Do not include the articles *a, an,* and *the.*]

EXAMPLE   [1] First get a craft knife and some stiff black paper.
          1. *First—adverb—get; craft—adjective—knife; some—adjective—paper; stiff—adjective—paper; black—adjective—paper*

[1] In many cultures, cutting paper to make pictures is a traditional art. [2] For example, Mexican artisans use a small, very sharp knife to cut designs in pieces of colored paper. [3] As the oddly shaped scraps fall away, an image

LEP/ESL

Spanish. Because adjectives in Spanish generally follow the nouns they modify, you may want to have students pay special attention to adjective placement. In **Exercise 1,** have students identify where the adjective is located in relation to the noun it modifies—after a linking verb or before the noun. The students should see a pattern emerging (nouns usually preceded by adjectives) that is generally different from that of their native language.

INTEGRATING THE LANGUAGE ARTS

Literature Link. Have students read the paragraphs in Doris Lessing's "Through the Tunnel" that describe Jerry's successful dive. Let students try a form of *seem* in place of each verb to see if the verb is a linking verb or an action verb. Ask the class to discuss the difference in purpose between sentences that use action verbs and those that use linking verbs.

ANSWERS
Exercise 1

1. many—adjective—cultures; traditional—adjective—art

2. Mexican—adjective—artisans; small—adjective—knife; very—adverb—sharp; sharp—adjective—knife; colored—adjective—paper

3. oddly—adverb—shaped; shaped—adjective—scraps; away—adverb—fall; slowly—adverb—is revealed

4. each — adjective — part;
   somehow — adverb — must connect;
   another — adjective — part

5. these — adjective — designs;
   sometimes — adverb — leaves;
   background — adjective — pattern;
   main — adjective — subject

6. not — adverb — must be;
   even — adverb — slightly;
   slightly — adverb — dull;
   dull — adjective — knife;
   accidentally — adverb — might tear;
   tiny — adjective — bridges;
   paper — adjective — bridges

VISUAL CONNECTIONS
Exploring the Subject. Paper-cutting, which is known as *papel picado* in Mexico, is an intricate art that is popular throughout the world. The tissue-paper cuttings shown here are reproductions from *Family Pictures* by Carmen Lomas Garza.

Paper cutting began in China almost 2000 years ago. In Turkey, artists use knives to carve their designs, and in Poland, they use sheep shears to carve nature scenes into folded paper.

COOPERATIVE LEARNING
After initial discussion of the three troublesome pairs, let students teach each other the material. Set up six-member teams. Two members will teach *bad* and *badly,* two will teach *well* and *good,* and two will teach *slow* and *slowly.* Each pair of students is also responsible for writing a six-sentence practice exercise on the material for the other members of the team.

is slowly revealed. [4] Planning the work is a challenge because each part of the picture must connect somehow to the border or to another part of the design. [5] As you can see in these designs, the artist sometimes leaves a background pattern of stripes or lines to support the main subject. [6] The knife must not be even slightly dull, or the artist might accidentally tear one of the tiny paper bridges!

Three Troublesome Pairs

Bad and *Badly*

Bad is an adjective. In most uses, *badly* is an adverb.

EXAMPLES

ADJECTIVES	ADVERBS
The dog was **bad**.	The dog behaved **badly**.
The milk smelled **bad**.	The roof leaked **badly**.

Remember that a linking verb calls for an adjective form.

NONSTANDARD	The medicine tasted badly.
STANDARD	The medicine tasted **bad**.

☞ REFERENCE NOTE: See pages 498–499 for a discussion of standard and nonstandard English.

NOTE: In conversations, either *bad* or *badly* is acceptable after *feel.*

ACCEPTABLE IN CONVERSATION	He feels **bad** about the accident.
	He feels **badly** about the accident.

In writing, though, use *bad* after *feel.*

CORRECT IN WRITING	He feels **bad** about the accident.

Well and *Good*

Well may be used either as an adjective or as an adverb. As an adjective, *well* has three meanings:

(1) "in good health"

EXAMPLE   Fran is **well**.

(2) "well dressed or well groomed"

EXAMPLE   She looks **well** in red.

(3) "satisfactory"

EXAMPLE   Everything is **well**.

As an adverb, *well* means "capably."

EXAMPLE   We did **well** on the test.

Good is always an adjective. It should not be used to modify a verb.

NONSTANDARD   She sings good.
STANDARD   She sings **well**.

NONSTANDARD   The car runs good.
STANDARD   The car runs **well**.

STANDARD   That color looks **good** on you. [adjective following linking verb]

NOTE: *Well* is also acceptable in sentences such as the last example above.

EXAMPLE   That color looks **well** on you.

Slow and *Slowly*

Slow is used as both an adjective and an adverb.

EXAMPLES   We took a **slow** walk through the park. [*Slow* is an adjective modifying *walk*.]
Go **slow**. [*Slow* is an adverb modifying *go*.]

Slowly is always an adverb. In most adverb uses (other than *go slow* or *drive slow*), it is better to use *slowly*.

EXAMPLES   The tiger **slowly** crept forward.
Proceed **slowly** through each step.

USAGE

COMMON ERROR

Problem. Students often are unsure of how to choose between *good* and *well*.

Solution. Tell students that when they choose between *good* and *well*, they should always use *well* if the sentence calls for an adverb. For example, "Marta reads well." If an adjective form is needed, have students try the words *healthy, well groomed,* or *satisfactory* in place of *well* or *good*. If any of those three replacements maintains the meaning, students should choose *well* as the adjective. If not, *good* should be the choice.

INTEGRATING THE LANGUAGE ARTS

Usage and Writing. You may want to teach the troublesome pairs as students revise a writing assignment. Point out that nonstandard English is acceptable in informal conversation and in friendly letters. Standard English is generally used in formal situations. Ask students to label the following sentences as nonstandard or standard English:

1. Raphael hit the ball good in spring training. [nonstandard]
2. Edna could never eat her ice cream slow. [nonstandard]
3. Carl wanted an A very badly. [standard]

USAGE

COOPERATIVE LEARNING

You may want students to practice before they work on **Exercises 2** and **3**. Divide the class into two teams and have each team create sentences that call for a choice between *well* and *good*, *bad* and *badly*, and *slow* and *slowly* (six sentences per word-pair, eighteen sentences per team).

Alternating between teams, read one of a team's sentences and give the opposing team thirty seconds to choose the correct modifier and to explain the reasoning behind the choice. An incorrect explanation gives the other team a chance to respond. Teams receive a point for each correct answer and lose a point for each incorrect answer.

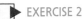 EXERCISE 2 **Selecting Adjectives or Adverbs to Complete Sentences**

Choose the <u>correct word</u> in parentheses in each of the following sentences.

1. I can't hear you (<u>*well*</u>, *good*) when the water is running.
2. The opening paragraph is written (<u>*well*</u>, *good*).
3. The situation looks (<u>*bad*</u>, *badly*).
4. Why does ketchup come out of the bottle so (*slow*, <u>*slowly*</u>)?
5. She certainly plays the marimba (<u>*well*</u>, *good*).
6. Can you dance as (<u>*well*</u>, *good*) as you sing?
7. These shoes don't fit (*bad*, <u>*badly*</u>) at all.
8. Our coach told us to do the exercise (*slow*, <u>*slowly*</u>).
9. Did you do (<u>*well*</u>, *good*) on the last algebra test?
10. The chef at the corner cafe cooks very (*bad*, <u>*badly*</u>).

EXERCISE 3 **Using Adjective and Adverb Forms Correctly in a Paragraph**

Each sentence in the following paragraph contains at least one italicized adjective or adverb. If an italicized word is incorrect, give the correct form. If the sentence is correct, write C.

1. C

[1] My brother opened Skipper's Skate City last April 1, and as the graph on the next page shows, the shop did not do *well* at first. [2] Skipper wondered whether business

2. slowly

had started ^*slow* because he wasn't advertising enough or because his window wasn't drawing people in. [3] He'd

3. slowly

see people walking ^*slow* past the shop and pointing at the gear on display, but hardly anyone came in. [4] By the end

4. badly

of May, Skipper even thought about giving up, because

5. C

he was doing so ^*bad*. [5] He would have felt really *bad* about failing, especially because my dad had loaned him money

6. well

to help get started. [6] Then school let out, and within days, business was going ^*good*. [7] In-line skates started

7. C

selling like crazy, and all summer, Skipper did so *well* that he was able to pay Dad back. [8] When school started,

8. well

skateboards kept selling ^*good*, but total sales fell some-

9. bad

what. [9] Skipper's receipts looked pretty ^*badly* during the fall, but thanks to Christmas and Hanukkah, all went

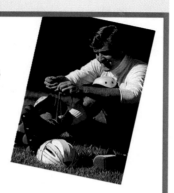

9. well **10.** good

~~good~~ in December. [10] By then, Skipper was a veteran of seasonal business cycles, so it didn't faze him a bit when January's receipts weren't as ~~well~~ as expected.

Skipper's Skate City
Cash Register Receipts, First Ten Months

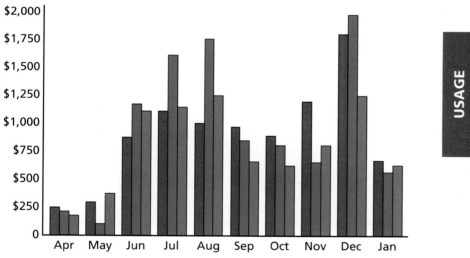

■ Skateboards, parts
■ In-line skates
■ Protective gear, clothes, magazines

Comparison of Modifiers

Adjectives state qualities of nouns or pronouns.

EXAMPLES **expensive** jacket **fluffy** clouds
shiny metal **original** one

You can show the degree or extent to which a noun or pronoun has a quality by comparing it with another noun or pronoun that has the same quality.

EXAMPLES This jacket is **larger** than that jacket.
Does it look **better** than the other one?

USAGE

Teacher's ResourceBank™
▼ **RESOURCES** ▼

> **COMPARISON OF MODIFIERS**
> • Regular Comparison
> • Irregular Comparison

 QUICK REMINDER
Write these examples on the chalkboard:

1. I am happy. He is happier. She is happiest of all.
2. I am successful. He is more successful. She is the most successful of all.

Ask students to give the comparative and superlative forms of *pretty, awkward, friendly,* and *ridiculous.* Then have the class check a dictionary for the correct answers [prettier, prettiest; more awkward, most awkward; friendlier, friendliest; more ridiculous, most ridiculous].

USAGE

USAGE

USAGE

Similarly, you can show degree or extent by using adverbs to make comparisons.

EXAMPLES **I ran well, but you ran better.** [The adverb *better* modifies the verb *ran*.]
The other clerk will be better able to help you. [The adverb *better* modifies the adjective *able*.]

22b. Modifiers change form to show comparison.

The three degrees of comparison are *positive, comparative,* and *superlative.*

POSITIVE	COMPARATIVE	SUPERLATIVE
low	lower	lowest
fearful	more fearful	most fearful
bad	worse	worst
good	better	best
promptly	more promptly	most promptly

Regular Comparison

Most modifiers follow these regular methods of forming their comparative and superlative degrees.

(1) One-syllable modifiers form their comparative and superlative degrees by adding *–er* and *–est.*

POSITIVE	COMPARATIVE	SUPERLATIVE
thin	thinner	thinnest
safe	safer	safest
dry	drier	driest

☞ **REFERENCE NOTE:** See pages 873–875 for guidelines on spelling words with suffixes.

(2) Some two-syllable modifiers form their comparative and superlative degrees by adding *–er* and *–est.* Other

22b

two-syllable modifiers form their comparative and superlative degrees with *more* and *most.*

POSITIVE	COMPARATIVE	SUPERLATIVE
lovely	lovelier	loveliest
tricky	trickier	trickiest
awkward	more awkward	most awkward
quickly	more quickly	most quickly

NOTE: A few two-syllable modifiers may use either *–er, –est* or *more, most: able, abler, ablest,* or *able, more able, most able.*

When you're not sure about the comparative or superlative form of a two-syllable modifier, look up the positive form in an unabridged dictionary.

(3) Modifiers that have more than two syllables form their comparative and superlative degrees with *more* and *most.*

POSITIVE	COMPARATIVE	SUPERLATIVE
catastrophic	more catastrophic	most catastrophic
predictably	more predictably	most predictably

(4) Modifiers indicate less or least of a quality with the words *less* and *least.*

POSITIVE	COMPARATIVE	SUPERLATIVE
frequent	less frequent	least frequent
carefully	less carefully	least carefully

Irregular Comparison

Some adjectives and adverbs do not follow the regular methods of forming their comparative and superlative degrees.

USAGE

INTEGRATING THE LANGUAGE ARTS

Usage and Proofreading. The correct spellings of comparative and superlative forms are often arrived at by using three spelling rules for adding suffixes. As students proofread their writing, remind them of the following rules:

1. With words ending in *–y* preceded by a consonant, change *–y* to *i* before any suffix not beginning with *i.* [For example, *dry* becomes *drier* or *driest.*]
2. When an adjective ends in a single consonant following a single vowel, double the final consonant before adding the ending. [For example, *thin* becomes *thinner* or *thinnest.*]
3. Drop the final *e* before a suffix beginning with a vowel. [For example, *safe* becomes *safer* or *safest.*]

Technology Link. Some word-processing programs include electronic dictionaries that students might use to check comparative and superlative forms. For example, if students are unsure whether *righter* or *more right* is the correct comparative form, they might see whether *righter* is listed in their spell-check program. If *righter* is listed, that is the correct choice. If not, *more right* is correct.

USAGE

USE OF COMPARATIVE AND SUPERLATIVE FORMS Rules 22c–22f

OBJECTIVES

- To write sentences that use comparative and superlative forms of modifiers
- To identify whether modifiers are used correctly in a series of sentences and to revise modifiers that are incorrect

---

722 *Using Modifiers Correctly*

POSITIVE	COMPARATIVE	SUPERLATIVE
bad	worse	worst
good well	better	best
little	less	least
many much	more	most

NOTE: Do not add –*er*, –*est* or *more, most* to irregularly compared forms: *worse*, not *worser* or *more worse*.

 EXERCISE 4 **Writing the Comparative and Superlative Forms of Modifiers**

Write the comparative and superlative forms of the following modifiers.

1. little
2. bad
3. humid
4. smart
5. silly
6. good
7. likely
8. well
9. fundamental
10. congenial

Use of Comparative and Superlative Forms

22c. Use the comparative degree when comparing two things. Use the superlative degree when comparing more than two.

COMPARATIVE   Omaha is **larger** than Lincoln.
Roberto is a **better** student than I am.
Which of these two shirts is **less** expensive?

SUPERLATIVE   Omaha is the **largest** city in Nebraska.
Roberto is the **best** student in the class.
Which of these four shirts is **least** expensive?

NOTE: In conversation, the superlative degree is commonly used to compare two things.

EXAMPLES   May the **best** team [of two] win.
Put your **best** foot forward.

In writing, however, the comparative degree should always be used when two things are being compared.

USAGE

22c

Writing Sentences Using the Comparative and Superlative Forms of Modifiers

EXERCISE 5

At the beginning of the twentieth century, teenagers thought a ride on an elaborate, hand-carved carousel was exciting. Today, as we approach the year 2000, young people are more likely to be interested in a wild roller-coaster ride! Write five sentences using adverbs and adjectives to compare the two rides shown below. Then write five sentences comparing three rides—the carousel, the rollercoaster, and a ride you imagine will be a favorite at the turn of the twenty-second century. In your sentences, use ten or more modifiers from the boxes below. After you use at least two modifiers from each box, you may use any of the others that you wish.

bright	happy	good	many	intense	exciting
simple	high			colorful	stressful
young	pretty	little	much	expensive	thrilling
scary	fast		bad	compelling	mature
safe	long			enjoyable	romantic

USAGE

ANSWERS

Exercise 5

The first five sentences should contain comparative forms of modifiers. The second five sentences should contain superlative forms of modifiers. Students should use at least ten modifiers from the boxes in their textbooks.

MEETING INDIVIDUAL NEEDS

LEP/ESL

General Strategies. A double comparison occurs when *–er* or *–est* is used with *more* or *most.* To help students avoid the use of double comparisons, such as *more better* or *most smartest,* suggest that they look for the words *more* or *most* in a sentence. Then have them check for *–er* or *–est.* Remind the class that both forms of comparison should not be used in the same sentence to modify a single word.

ADVANCED STUDENTS

Ask students why the comparative degree is used in the sentence "Stan is taller than everyone else in his class." They will probably agree that *taller* sounds correct, but they might mention that Stan is being compared with more than one student.

Point out that the collective pronouns *no one, anyone, each, everybody, anybody, someone,* and *somebody* are treated as singular.

USAGE

LESS-ADVANCED STUDENTS

To help students remember when to use comparative or superlative forms of modifiers, remind them that the suffix *–er* has two letters and is used to compare two things. [Basketball is rougher than baseball.] The suffix *–est* has three letters and is used to compare three or more things. [Compared with basketball and baseball, football is roughest.]

To transfer this key to comparative and superlative forms that do not use *–er* or *–est,* point out that comparisons of three or more must include a sound similar to that of the three-letter *–est,* as in *most awkward* or *least painful.*

 COOPERATIVE LEARNING

Have students work in small groups. Direct each group to create three sentences in which the comparisons are unclear. Then have the groups exchange sentences for correction. With votes for their own groups not allowed, let students select the funniest entries. The following sentences are examples:

1. The cannibals enjoyed boiling lobsters even more than their neighboring tribe.

2. I would enjoy going to a movie premiere with Madonna more than Arnold Schwarzenegger.

22d. Include the word *other* or *else* when comparing one thing with others in the same group.

NONSTANDARD | Stan is taller than anyone in his class. [Stan is a member of the class, and he cannot be taller than himself. The word *else* should be added.]

STANDARD | Stan is taller than anyone **else** in his class.

NONSTANDARD | Rhode Island is smaller than any state in the Union. [Rhode Island is a state, and it cannot be smaller than itself. The word *other* should be added.]

STANDARD | Rhode Island is smaller than any **other** state in the Union.

22e. Avoid double comparisons.

A *double comparison* is one that uses both *–er* and *more* (or *less*) or *–est* and *most* (or *least*).

NONSTANDARD | The second movie was more funnier than the first one.

STANDARD | The second movie was **funnier** than the first one.

NONSTANDARD | What is the most deadliest snake?

STANDARD | What is the **most deadly** [or deadliest] snake?

22f. Be sure your comparisons are clear.

In making comparisons, always state clearly what things are being compared.

UNCLEAR | The climate of Arizona is drier than South Carolina. [The sentence incorrectly compares a climate to a state.]

CLEAR | The climate of Arizona is drier than **the climate** of South Carolina.

CLEAR | The climate of Arizona is drier than **that** of South Carolina.

UNCLEAR | The Millers would rather grow their own vegetables than canned ones.

CLEAR | The Millers would rather grow their own vegetables than **buy** canned ones.

Use a complete comparison if there is any chance that an incomplete one could be misunderstood.

REVIEW A

OBJECTIVE

- To identify and correct errors in the use of modifiers

UNCLEAR	We know her better than Dena.
CLEAR	We know her better than **we know** Dena.
CLEAR	We know her better than Dena **does**.

EXERCISE 6 **Using Modifiers Correctly in Sentences**

In each of the following sentences, if a modifier is used incorrectly, write the correct form. If the sentence is correct, write C.

1. Laurie is ~~more~~ friendlier than she used to be.
2. Which of the four seasons do you like ∧better? **2. best**
3. I never saw a tribal leader ~~more~~ stronger than Chief Billie of the Seminoles.
4. Margaret Mead was one of the world's most famous anthropologists. **4. C**
5. Of the two colleges that I am considering, Spelman College in Atlanta looks the more interesting. **5. C**
6. The cheetah is the ~~most~~ fastest running animal in the world. **7. those in**
7. Muscles in the leg are stronger than ∧the arm. **8. other**
8. Denver has a higher elevation than any ∧major city in the United States. **9. than I wrote to Carlos. [*or* than Carlos**
9. I wrote to Sally more often ∧~~than Carlos~~. **wrote to Sally.]**
10. This year's drought was much ∧~~worser~~ than last ∧~~year~~. **10. worse/year's.**

REVIEW A **Identifying and Correcting Errors in the Use of Modifiers**

The following paragraph contains ten errors in the use of adjectives and adverbs. Find each error and supply the necessary correction.

1. most famous

[1] Among Pueblo potters of the Southwest, perhaps the ∧~~famousest~~ are the four women who made the coiled pots shown on the next page, using techniques handed down for more than 2,000 years. [2] Lucy Lewis's Acoma pottery is more delicate than any ∧Southwest pottery. **2. other** [3] She used the ~~most~~ whitest clay. [4] Because this clay is **4.** scarce, the walls of her pots are the ∧~~most thin~~. **thinnest** [5] Maria Martinez' San Ildefonso pottery is ~~more~~ thicker and heavier than Lewis's. [6] Of all the Southwest pottery styles, Martinez' black-on-black pottery may be the ∧~~wellest~~ **6. best** known. [7] No color is used, but the background areas of

AT-RISK STUDENTS

As you evaluate exercises, try to encourage success by at-risk students. Call on them to give exercise answers that draw on their strengths, or ask them to tutor people who have problems in these areas to help enhance the students' self-esteem.

WRITING APPLICATION

OBJECTIVE

- To use comparative and superlative degrees to write a comparison paragraph

USAGE

USAGE

the black pot are burnished slowly with a small smooth stone, until they become quite a bit ~~more~~ shinier than the main design. [8] Many of Margaret Tafoya's Santa Clara pots are also solid black, but of these two kinds of black pottery, the Santa Clara pots are the ~~heaviest~~. [9] The bold, colorful Hopi pots of Fannie Nampeyo may be the ~~more~~ impressive achievement of all, because Nampeyo's family had to re-create the technique by studying shards of ancient pots found in 1895.

8. heavier
9. most

LUCY LEWIS

MARIA MARTINEZ

MARGARET TAFOYA

FANNIE NAMPEYO

WRITING APPLICATION

Using Comparative and Superlative Degrees to Make Comparison Clear

Have you ever read a "buyer's guide" article before deciding which brand of a product to buy? People who write such articles must be especially precise in using comparatives and superlatives so that consumers can be sure which brand best suits their needs and budgets.

COMPARING TWO	Of these models, the Matsuo 2000 is less expensive.
COMPARING THREE OR MORE	Of these models, the Matsuo 2000 is least expensive.

▶ **WRITING ACTIVITY**
You and your sister Charlotte plan to buy a piece of audio equipment together. You have found a magazine article

WRITING APPLICATION
To help students write this comparison paragraph, have them refer to **Chapter 7: "Writing to Inform"** and **Chapter 8: "Writing to Explain."**

CRITICAL THINKING
Evaluation

Have students list the features of some imaginary equipment that would increase the listening pleasure of a visually impaired person. Comparing the three brands mentioned in the comparison paragraph to this equipment will help students evaluate the features of each. Students need not refer to the imaginary equipment when writing their paragraphs.

comparing several brands and showing the information in a big table. However, because Charlotte is blind, the table can't help her decide. She asks you to narrow the choices to four brands, and then to write and tape on a cassette for her a short comparison of their prices and features so that the two of you can make a decision.

Find a magazine article at home or in the library that has a table comparing different brands of a piece of audio equipment that interests you. You might choose a CD player, speakers, or a portable cassette player. Choose three products that seem acceptable. Write a clear comparison that you would tape for Charlotte, giving the most important information listed in the table about these three products. As you write, include each of the degrees of comparison: positive, comparative, and superlative.

Prewriting Study the table. List the features that you think would be most important to you and to Charlotte. Then, write down several comparisons you want to explain in your paragraph.

Writing As you write your first draft, carefully select comparative and superlative modifiers so that your explanation is not confusing. Tell why you would eliminate certain models from consideration. Remember, though, you are not deciding *for* Charlotte. You must present the information objectively to help her make her own decision.

Evaluating and Revising Exchange paragraphs, along with the magazine article you used, with a classmate. Ask him or her to evaluate the information you decided to include and the clarity of your presentation. Rephrase any confusing comparisons.

Proofreading and Publishing Using your textbook, check to be sure you have correctly used adjectives to modify nouns and pronouns and used adverbs to modify verbs, adjectives, and other adverbs. Pay special attention to the "troublesome pairs" section on pages 716–717 of this chapter. Your class may wish to collect all the paragraphs and bind them in a booklet titled *An Audio Equipment Consumer Guide.*

USAGE

PREWRITING

Remind students to consider their audience as they list important features of the equipment. Some students might enjoy numerous knobs and intricate tuning devices. Other students might prefer ease of operation over complexity.

WRITING

The following sentence shows how students might incorporate the degrees of comparison into their writing: "The maximum volume of this cassette player is dangerously loud, but the Sonic Boomer's volume is louder, and the Sound Blaster's volume is loudest of all."

EVALUATING AND REVISING

Because Charlotte would be listening to a tape of the comparison, students might read paragraphs aloud to each other to ensure that the comparisons are clear. Listeners should point out where they are confused or have questions about the comparisons.

PROOFREADING AND PUBLISHING

Listeners might also serve as additional proofreaders. A way to publish would be for students to make tapes of their paragraphs and to present them to the class.

USAGE

OBJECTIVE

- To revise sentences by correcting dangling modifiers

Teacher's ResourceBank™

RESOURCES

DANGLING MODIFIERS
- Dangling Modifiers

 QUICK REMINDER

Ask students to rewrite the following descriptions so that each modifier clearly and sensibly modifies a word in the sentence:

1. Lifting the trophy high over her head, the photographer snapped pictures of Kari. [Lifting the trophy high over her head, Kari waited as the photographer snapped pictures.]

2. Grazing peacefully, we saw a herd of buffalo in the distance. [We saw a herd of buffalo grazing peacefully in the distance.]

LEP/ESL

General Strategies. To reinforce the rule that the modifier has to have a logical association with a word in the sentence, provide modifiers such as *walking to school* or *to earn extra money* and have students add independent clauses. [While walking to school, I saw a beautiful rainbow. To earn extra money, Neal fixed his neighbor's car.] Have students check each other's work to see if there is a clear association between the two parts of the sentence.

USAGE

728

---

728 *Using Modifiers Correctly*

Dangling Modifiers

22g. A modifying phrase or clause that does not clearly and sensibly modify a word in the same sentence is a *dangling modifier.*

When a sentence begins with a verbal phrase, the phrase is followed by a comma. The word that the phrase modifies should come immediately after that comma.

UNCLEAR	Looking back over my shoulder, the team went into a huddle. [The participial phrase seems to modify *team*.]
CLEAR	Looking back over my shoulder, I saw the team go into a huddle.
UNCLEAR	Towed away by the wrecker, I just stood there and watched. [The participial phrase seems to modify *I*.]
CLEAR	I just stood there and watched my car being towed away by the wrecker.

NOTE: When *you* is the understood subject of a sentence, an introductory verbal phrase is not dangling. The phrase modifies the understood subject.

EXAMPLE   To get to Amy's house, (you) go south on First Street.

Correcting Dangling Modifiers

You can correct a dangling modifier by adding words that make the meaning clear and logical.

DANGLING	Going to the store, my bicycle tire went flat.
CORRECTED	Going to the store, I got a flat tire on my bicycle.
DANGLING	While filling the fuel tank, some of the gas spilled on the runway.
CORRECTED	While filling the fuel tank, the mechanic spilled some of the gas on the runway.
CORRECTED	While the mechanic was filling the fuel tank, some of the gas spilled on the runway.
DANGLING	To qualify for the Olympics, many trial heats must be won.
CORRECTED	To qualify for the Olympics, a runner must win many trial heats.
CORRECTED	Before a runner may qualify for the Olympics, he or she must win many trial heats.

22g

▶ EXERCISE 7 **Revising Sentences by Correcting Dangling Modifiers**

Revise each sentence so that the modifier *clearly* and *sensibly* modifies a word in the sentence. You will have to supply some words to fill out the sentence properly.

1. Caught in the net, escape was impossible.
2. Looking through the telescope, the moon seemed enormous.
3. While out running, his mouth got dry.
4. Going around the bend, the ocean came into view.
5. Doing a few tap dance steps, the floor got scratched.
6. Rushing to class, my books slipped from under my arm and fell down the stairs.
7. To grow plants successfully, light, temperature, and humidity must be carefully controlled.
8. After finishing the housework, the room almost sparkled.
9. To make manicotti, pasta is stuffed with ricotta cheese.
10. Concluding her opening speech, the jury looked at her in awe.

Shoe, by Jeff MacNelly, reprinted by permission: Tribune Media Services

USAGE

USAGE

OBJECTIVES

- To revise sentences by correcting misplaced phrase modifiers
- To revise sentences by correcting misplaced clause modifiers
- To write a descriptive paragraph

USAGE

Teacher's ResourceBank™

▼ RESOURCES ▼

MISPLACED MODIFIERS
- Misplaced Modifiers

🦉 QUICK REMINDER

Ask students to correct the misplaced modifiers in the following thesis statements:

1. I see too many fast-food restaurants driving through our city. [Driving through our city, I see too many fast-food restaurants.]

2. Athletes should go to physicians who have taken illegal steroids. [Athletes who have taken illegal steroids should go to physicians.]

ANSWERS
Exercise 8

Answers may vary. Here are some possibilities:

1. Mrs. Barry drove downtown to do some shopping after her husband had left for the factory.

2. Taking a shortcut through the woods, I found a huge boulder. ´

3. Pruning his fruit tree, Mr. Tate noticed some caterpillars.

4. The ragtime composer Scott Joplin wrote the opera *Treemonisha,* which was performed only once.

5. Driving over the bridge, Missie saw a heron.

6. Riding down the highway, we noticed several signs.

7. From our car window, we could see corn growing.

8. Barking wildly and straining at the chain, the dog forced the letter carrier to retreat.

730

USAGE

730   *Using Modifiers Correctly*

Misplaced Modifiers

22h. A modifying phrase or clause that makes a sentence awkward or unclear because it seems to modify the wrong word or group of words is a *misplaced modifier.*

Modifying phrases and clauses should be placed as near as possible to the words they modify.

Misplaced Phrase Modifiers

MISPLACED   I'm lucky because I feel that I can always talk about my problems with my dad.

CORRECTED   I'm lucky because I feel that I can always talk with my dad about my problems.

MISPLACED   We learned that Luis Valdez wrote *La Bamba* in our English class.

CORRECTED   In our English class we learned that Luis Valdez wrote *La Bamba.*

📄 EXERCISE 8   **Revising Sentences by Correcting Misplaced Phrase Modifiers**

In each of the following sentences, pick out the misplaced phrase and revise the sentence, placing the phrase near the word it should modify.

1. Mrs. Barry drove downtown after her husband had left for the factory to do some shopping.
2. I found a huge boulder taking a shortcut through the woods.
3. Mr. Tate noticed some caterpillars pruning his fruit tree.
4. Performed only once, the ragtime composer Scott Joplin wrote the opera *Treemonisha.*
5. Missie saw a heron driving over the bridge.
6. We noticed several signs riding down the highway.
7. We could see corn growing from our car window.
8. Barking wildly and straining at the chain, the letter carrier was forced to retreat from the dog.

22h

9. Rosa Parks calmly refused to move with quiet dignity to the back of the bus.
10. He recounted an incident about a nuclear chain reaction during his chemistry lecture.

PICTURE THIS

You are a famous business tycoon, now retired and writing your autobiography. You are working on the chapter about your preteen years. One of your most treasured memories is of this treehouse you built with your best friend when you were twelve. Write a paragraph about your treehouse. You may use comparative and superlative modifiers to compare it to two other rooms or places—for example, your business office and the inside of your executive jet. Or you may use linking verbs with adjectives to tell about how you felt while you were up in your treehouse and about what the treehouse meant to you.
(A list of linking verbs is on page 715.)

Subject:	the treehouse you built as a child
Audience:	the reading public
Purpose:	to inform and entertain

USAGE

---

9. With quiet dignity, Rosa Parks calmly refused to move to the back of the bus.
10. During his chemistry lecture, he recounted an incident about a nuclear chain reaction.

PICTURE THIS

As a prewriting activity, ask your students to close their eyes and to imagine that they are standing in a treehouse similar to the one shown in the textbook. What do they see? What do they hear? Are there any smells? Are they eating anything? How does it feel to be there? After a few moments, students might jot down thoughts and details that come to them.

MEETING INDIVIDUAL NEEDS

LEP/ESL

General Strategies. Emphasize to students that a misplaced modifier can be corrected by moving the phrase or clause closer to the word it modifies. Have students work in pairs to read the following sentences and to suggest ways to correct the misplaced modifiers:

1. At the age of eight, my parents sent me to camp. [At the age of eight, I was sent to camp by my parents.]
2. There is a car in the garage that has only one door and no windshield. [In the garage, there is a car that has only one door and no windshield.]
3. I bought a seat for my bicycle that is made of vinyl. [I bought a seat that is made of vinyl for my bicycle.]

USAGE

INTEGRATING THE LANGUAGE ARTS

Literature Link. Have students read and discuss Guy de Maupassant's "The Piece of Yarn," and ask them to examine the first paragraph to see how the author uses numerous modifiers to describe the farmers.

After students have identified as many adjectives, adverbs, and clause and phrase modifiers as they can, ask them if they are always sure exactly which word de Maupassant intends to modify. Read the paragraph aloud. Ask students if they can vividly imagine the farmers, or if so many modifiers weaken the description. Have them give reasons for their responses.

REVIEW B

OBJECTIVE

- To identify and correct errors in the use of modifiers

Misplaced Clause Modifiers

MISPLACED	We saw a building in the city that was being demolished.
CORRECTED	In the city we saw a building that was being demolished.
MISPLACED	The bowl fell on the floor which was full of gravy and broke.
CORRECTED	The bowl, which was full of gravy, fell on the floor and broke.
MISPLACED	Lynn got a package from one of the stores we had visited that she hadn't ordered.
CORRECTED	From one of the stores we had visited, Lynn got a package that she hadn't ordered.

 REFERENCE NOTE: See pages 797–801 and 804–806 for information on when to use commas to set off modifying phrases and clauses.

> **EXERCISE 9**

Revising Sentences by Correcting Misplaced Clause Modifiers

Revise each of the following sentences by placing the misplaced clause near the word it modifies. If you find a misplaced phrase, correct it, also.   Answers may vary.

1. I gave ˬfour olives ~~to my friend~~ that I had stabbed with my fork.   **1.** my friend
2. The plane ˬlanded safely on the runway. ~~that had the engine trouble.~~   **2.** that had the engine trouble
3. The picture ˬwas hanging on the wall. ~~that we bought in Canada.~~   **3.** that we bought in Canada
4. They took the kitten ˬto the manager's office. ~~that appeared to be lost.~~   **4.** that appeared to be lost
5. Jan showed the rooms ~~to her visitors~~ that she had painted ˬ   **5.** to her visitors.

> **REVIEW B**

Identifying and Correcting Errors in the Use of Modifiers

Most of the sentences in the following paragraph contain at least one error in the use of modifiers. If a modifier is incorrect, write the sentence correctly. You may need to rearrange words or add words to make the meaning clear. If a sentence is correct, write *C*.

[1] Much about life in ancient Egypt before the 1800s was unknown because nobody could read Egyptian hieroglyphics. [2] Then this black stone found in the Nile delta gave Egyptology the most publicity than it had ever had before. [3] Found in 1799 near a village called Rosetta, archaeologists called the slab the Rosetta Stone. [4] The slab was inscribed with three bands across its polished surface of writing, each in a different language: hieroglyphics on the top, another unknown language in the middle, and Greek on the bottom. [5] Scholars could read the Greek writing, which stated that each of the three bands contained the same decree in honor of Ptolemy V. [6] Full of excitement, it was hoped by archaeologists that they could use the Greek part to figure out the hieroglyphics. [7] But progress in translating the individual hieroglyphics went very slow. [8] It had been thought that each of the symbols stood for a whole word until this time. [9] However, a French scholar working on the Rosetta Stone named Jean François Champollion wondered why it took more hieroglyphic symbols than Greek words to write the same message. [10] He correctly guessed that certain symbols stand for parts of words, and after working hard for twenty years, many of the signs were proved to stand for sounds.

USAGE

ANSWERS
Review B

Answers may vary.

1. Because nobody could read Egyptian hieroglyphics before the 1800s, much about life in ancient Egypt was an unknown.

2. Then this black stone found in the Nile delta gave Egyptology more publicity than it had ever had before.

3. The stone, found in 1799 near a village called Rosetta, was called by archaeologists the Rosetta Stone.

4. The slab was inscribed across its polished surface with three bands of writing, each in a different language: hieroglyphics on the top, another unknown language in the middle, and Greek on the bottom.

5. C

6. Full of excitement, the archaeologists hoped that they could use the Greek part to figure out the hieroglyphics.

7. But progress in translating the individual hieroglyphics went very slowly.

8. Until this time, it had been thought that each symbol stood for a whole word.

9. However, Jean François Champollion, a French scholar working on the Rosetta Stone, wondered why it took more hieroglyphic symbols than Greek words to write the same message.

10. He correctly guessed that certain symbols must stand for parts of words, and after working hard for twenty years, he proved that many of the signs stood for sounds.

USAGE

734 *Using Modifiers Correctly*

Review: Posttest

A. Revising Sentences by Correcting Errors in the Use of Modifiers

Answers may vary.

Most of the following sentences contain errors in the use of modifiers. Revise such sentences, correcting the faulty modifiers. If a sentence is correct, write *C*.

1. Manaba was/her
1. While building a fire in front of the hogan, ~~Manaba's~~ dog began to tug at the hem of her doeskin dress.
2. I bought these clothes with my birthday money ~~that I'm wearing.~~   2. that I'm wearing
3. Adrianne knows more about chemistry than anybody in her class.   3. else
4. Hank worked rather ~~hasty~~ so he could catch up with Clay and Nina.   4. hastily
5. Although Marian felt bad about losing the game, she knew things could be ~~worser.~~   5. worse.
6. Millie can sing as well as Scott, but of the two, he's the ~~best~~ dancer.   6. better   7. the team won   8. a person needs
7. By playing carefully, the game ~~was won.~~
8. To build bridges as confidently as Mohawk iron-workers do, a good sense of balance ~~is important.~~
9. Because one carton of chemicals smelled ~~badly,~~ it was examined for contamination before being used in the laboratory.   9. bad
10. Although Helen is the better actress, Wenona will probably get the leading part because she is more reliable.   10. C

B. Revising a Paragraph by Correcting Errors in the Use of Modifiers

Some sentences in the following paragraph contain errors in the use of modifiers. If you find an error, write the sentence correctly. You may need to add or rearrange words for clarity. If a sentence is correct, write *C*.

[11] Hailed by many critics as one of today's greatest male vocalists, my Aunt Penny took me on my birthday to

see Bobby McFerrin. **[12]** Waiting for the concert to start, the auditorium was filled with eager fans. **[13]** Wondering where the band was, I kept my eyes on the empty stage. **[14]** When it was time for the show to start, a slender, barefoot man walked out from the wings, carrying a cordless microphone dressed only in blue jeans. **[15]** Assuming he was a stagehand, he began to sing, and then I realized that this was Bobby McFerrin! **[16]** Instantly, the complex rhythm of the music fascinated the audience that he made up as he went along. **[17]** I suddenly understood why one of his popularest albums is called *Spontaneous Inventions*! **[18]** Alone in the spotlight with only his voice and no band at all, two thousand people sat spellbound until he took his final bow. **[19]** All his life, Bobby McFerrin has enjoyed listening to and performing jazz, pop, rock, soul, African, and classical music. **[20]** Bobby's parents are both classical musicians, and he thanks them for giving him this rich musical environment on the back of every album he makes.

USAGE

ANSWERS

Review: Posttest Part B

Answers may vary. Here are some possibilities:

11. My Aunt Penny took me on my birthday to see Bobby McFerrin, hailed by many critics as one of today's greatest male vocalists.

12. The auditorium was filled with eager fans waiting for the concert to start.

13. C

14. When it was time for the show to start, a slender, barefoot man, dressed only in blue jeans and carrying a cordless microphone, walked out from the wings.

15. I assumed he was a stagehand until he began to sing, and then I realized that this was Bobby McFerrin!

16. Instantly the audience was fascinated by the complex rhythm of the music that he made up as he went along.

17. I suddenly understood why one of his most popular albums is called *Spontaneous Inventions*!

18. Alone in the spotlight with only his voice and no band at all, he kept two thousand people spellbound until he took his final bow.

19. C

20. Bobby's parents are both classical musicians, and on the back of every album he makes he thanks them for giving him this rich musical environment.

USAGE

Teacher's ResourceBank™
RESOURCES

FOR THE WHOLE CHAPTER
• Chapter Review Form A
• Chapter Review Form B
• Assessment Portfolio
      Usage Pretests
      Usage Mastery Tests

USAGE

CHAPTER OVERVIEW

This chapter is designed to help students identify and correct certain usage errors. It contains an abridged alphabetical glossary of common usage problems. The chapter begins with a brief discussion of the differences between standard and nonstandard English and explains most usage problems in terms of these two types.

The contents of this chapter can be useful during the evaluation and revision stage of the writing process. It can be referred to when teaching **Chapter 1,** which covers writing and thinking, **Chapter 4,** which deals with expressive writing, and **Chapter 14,** which explores the origins and uses of English.

USING THE DIAGNOSTIC TEST

The **Diagnostic Test** will help gauge students' ability to identify and correct common errors in usage. You may wish to use this test to determine whether any students rely strongly on nonstandard English in their writing. Note that some students will be able to identify errors in usage but will find it difficult to revise an expression appropriately.

USAGE

23 A GLOSSARY OF USAGE

Common Usage Problems

Diagnostic Test

Revising Expressions by Correcting Errors in Usage

In each of the following sets of expressions, one <u>expression contains an error in usage</u>. Rewrite this expression correctly, using standard formal usage.

EXAMPLE   **1. a.** She taught me to sing.
       b. fewer letters in the box
       c. Set down in the shade and rest.
     1. *c. Sit down in the shade and rest.*

   1. a. ~~anywheres~~ you travel   **1.** anywhere
     b. as fast as sound travels
     c. Learn French cooking from him.
   2. a. affect the outcome
     b. candidate implied in his speech
     c. ~~among~~ his two opponents   **2.** between
   3. a. made ~~illusions~~ to the Bible   **3.** allusions
     b. fewer participants in the contest
     c. What kind of car is that?

4. **a.** family emigrated from Germany
    b. should ~~of~~ gone yesterday   **4.** have
    c. discovered a new planet
5. **a.** Try ~~and~~ win the game.   **5.** to
    b. draw as well as her mother
    c. that kind of car
6. **a.** Let the dog out.
    b. an effect of cold weather
    c. books, pencils, papers, ~~and~~ etc.
7. **a.** ate everything ~~accept~~ the peas   **7.** except
    b. older than you
    c. Bring your records with you.
8. **a.** I heard nothing.
    b. ~~can't hardly~~ tell the difference   **8.** can hardly [*or* can't]
    c. Lay the book on the shelf.
9. **a.** picture fell off the wall
    b. What kind of ~~a~~ dog is that?
    c. larger than he
10. **a.** sitting beside the tree
    b. going a little ~~ways~~   **10.** way
    c. not reality but illusion
11. **a.** coat doesn't fit well
    b. Fewer people learned how to read back then.
    c. inside ~~of~~ the cabinet
12. **a.** car looks ~~like~~ it had been wrecked   **12.** as if
    b. chair that was blue
    c. water jug that burst
13. **a.** She effected an improvement.
    b. a problem that must be resolved
    c. ~~Less~~ students joined the club this year.   **13.** Fewer
14. **a.** Take the package to the mailroom.
    b. Apples fell off ~~of~~ the tree.
    c. will scarcely be enough food for all of them
15. **a.** invented a better safety device
    b. No one ~~beside~~ my aunt knows.   **15.** besides
    c. played well in the tournament
16. **a.** Funds were allotted among six counties.
    b. Where is my hammer ~~at~~?
    c. This is as far as the fence extends.
17. **a.** going nowhere
    b. Doesn't he know the way?
    c. She finished reading; ~~than~~ she wrote her essay.   **17.** then

USAGE

OBJECTIVES
- To distinguish correct expressions from errors in usage
- To correct usage errors in a paragraph

18. a. We were gone for a hour.   **18.** an
    b. Try to learn this poem.
    c. Leave the green grapes on the vine.
19. a. Set the brake on the car.
    b. The fog will rise from the lake.
    c. One of them glasses broke.   **19.** those
20. a. It was an illusion caused by light on the surface.
    b. Their report implies a need for funds.
    c. That dog he limps.
21. a. no exception to this rule
    b. being that she is the oldest   **21.** because [*or* since]
    c. Bring your own tools with you.
22. a. Set that down there.
    b. looked like it had been burned   **22.** as if
    c. They ought to study before the test.
23. a. The ice busted a pipe.   **23.** burst
    b. He lay on the couch and rested.
    c. emigrate from their birthplace
24. a. Leave me have my turn.   **24.** Let
    b. the mechanic that worked on our car
    c. somewhat cold for swimming
25. a. haven't only three days of vacation   **25.** have
    b. the effect of smoking on the lungs
    c. learned that the winner had been announced

This chapter contains a short glossary of common usage problems. You will notice that some examples are labeled *standard* and *nonstandard*. **Standard English** is the most widely accepted variety of English. It's used in most books, newspapers, and magazines. **Nonstandard English** is language that doesn't follow the rules and conventions of standard English.

☞ REFERENCE NOTE: For more information on the features of standard English and nonstandard English, see pages 498–499.

a, an These words, called *indefinite articles,* refer to one of the members of a general group.

> EXAMPLES   In ancient Greece and Rome, **an** oracle was **a** place where people consulted gods.
> The tourists searched for **a** hotel for more than **an** hour.

Teacher's ResourceBank™
RESOURCES

A, AN–BUST, BUSTED
- Common Usage Problems A

🦉 QUICK REMINDER
Tell students that the first step toward proper usage is to identify potential problems. Write the following sentence on the chalkboard:

He affected people anywheres he traveled, being that he was an hotel bellboy who could not accept tips.

Have students copy the sentence and correct any words or expressions that are used incorrectly [anywheres— anywhere; being that—because; an hotel—a hotel]

Use *a* before words beginning with a consonant sound; use *an* before words beginning with a vowel sound. In the second example, *a* is used before *hotel* because the *h* in *hotel* is pronounced. *An* is used before *hour* because the *h* in *hour* is not pronounced.

accept, except   *Accept* is a verb that means "to receive." *Except* may be either a verb or a preposition. As a verb, it means "to leave out." As a preposition, *except* means "excluding."

EXAMPLES   Gary could not **accept** defeat.
Students who were absent last week will be **excepted** from today's test.
Everybody **except** me knew the answer.

affect, effect   *Affect* is usually a verb meaning "to influence." *Effect* used as a verb means "to accomplish" or "to bring about." Used as a noun, *effect* means "the result of some action."

EXAMPLES   The heat did not seem to **affect** the team.
Did the medicine **effect** a cure?
The heat had no **effect** on the team.

all the farther, all the faster   These expressions are used informally in some parts of the country to mean "as far as, as fast as."

DIALECT   This is all the farther we can go.
STANDARD   This is **as far as** we can go.

allusion, illusion   An *allusion* is a reference to something. An *illusion* is a mistaken idea or a misleading appearance.

EXAMPLES   The poem's title is an **allusion** to a Hopi folk tale.
The documentary shattered viewers' **illusions** about migrant workers.
The magician was a master of **illusion**.

among   See **between, among.**

and etc.   *Etc.* is an abbreviation of the Latin *et cetera,* which means "and other things." Thus, *etc.* already includes *and.*

EXAMPLE   I earn money by baby-sitting, running errands, mowing lawns, **etc.** [not *and etc.*]

USAGE

MEETING INDIVIDUAL NEEDS

LEP/ESL

General Strategies. For the section on the usage of *a* and *an,* you may want to point out that not all words that start with vowels are preceded by *an.* These words begin with a *y* sound (as in *yes*) even though they are spelled with a vowel. Some examples are *European, university,* and *utility.* To show the importance of the first sound, you could say a phrase like ". . . understanding teacher" and have students decide whether to use *an* or *a.* This could be followed by a fill-in-the-blank exercise.

STUDENTS WITH SPECIAL NEEDS

This chapter may present problems for students with visual dyslexia because they often have trouble distinguishing between words that are similar in shape. For example, they may have trouble distinguishing between *affect* and *effect.* They may also invert or reverse letters. These characteristics also may be found in their writing.

To help with this exercise, highlight the differences between similar words. You could also have a peer tutor read aloud while the students with dyslexia read along.

USAGE

USAGE

anywheres, everywheres, nowheres, somewheres Use these words without the *s* at the end.

> EXAMPLE   **Anywhere** [not *anywheres*] you travel, you see the same hotel chains.

as See **like, as.**

as if See **like, as if.**

at Do not use *at* after *where*.

> NONSTANDARD   Where did you see them at?
> STANDARD   Where did you see them?

being as, being that Avoid using these expressions. Use *because* or *since* instead.

> NONSTANDARD   Being as her grades were so good, she got a scholarship.
> STANDARD   **Because** her grades were so good, she got a scholarship.

> NONSTANDARD   Being that he was late, he had to stand.
> STANDARD   **Since** he was late, he had to stand.

beside, besides *Beside* means "by the side of." *Besides* as a preposition means "in addition to." As an adverb, *besides* means "moreover."

> EXAMPLES   He glanced at the person **beside** him.
> Did anybody **besides** you see what happened?
> I liked the sweater, and it didn't cost much; **besides,** I needed a new one.

between, among Use *between* when you are referring to two things at a time, even if they are part of a larger group.

> EXAMPLES   A strong bond exists **between** the twins.
> The survey reveals many differences **between** the New England states. [Although there are more than two New England states, each one is being compared with each of the others separately.]

Use *among* when referring to all members of a group rather than to separate individuals in the group.

> EXAMPLES   We distributed the pamphlets **among** the crowd.
> There was some disagreement **among** the editorial staff about the lead story.

740

bring, take *Bring* means "to come carrying something."
Take means "to go away carrying something." Think of
bring as related to *come* and *take* as related to *go.*

EXAMPLES **Bring** your radio when you come.
Don't forget to **take** your coat when you go.

bust, busted Avoid using these words as verbs. Instead,
use a form of *break* or *burst.*

EXAMPLES I **broke** [not *busted*] the switch on the stereo.
The water main **burst.** [not *busted*]

▶ EXERCISE 1 **Identifying Correct Expressions**

For each sentence, choose the <u>correct word</u> from the pair
given in parentheses.

1. The tasks were divided evenly (*among,* <u>*between*</u>) the
   two scouts.
2. The audience was deeply (<u>*affected*</u>, *effected*) by Simon
   Estes' powerful baritone voice.
3. We were afraid the bull had (*busted,* <u>*broken*</u>) loose.
4. No one (*accept,* <u>*except*</u>) the sophomores is supposed
   to attend.
5. Please (*bring,* <u>*take*</u>) these papers when you leave.
6. Penicillin has (*affected,* <u>*effected*</u>) some remarkable
   recoveries.
7. I couldn't find the cat (<u>*anywhere,*</u> *anywheres*).
8. The crosslike rays radiating from the moon were an
   (*allusion,* <u>*illusion*</u>) caused by the screen door.
9. Somebody (*beside,* <u>*besides*</u>) Julie must have picked up
   the tickets.
10. In his remarks about Dr. King, the speaker made an
    (<u>*allusion,*</u> *illusion*) to Gandhi, whose nonviolent pro-
    tests paved the way for the civil rights movement in
    the United States.

▶ EXERCISE 2 **Proofreading a Paragraph to Correct
Usage Errors**

Correct all the usage errors you find in each sentence
in the following paragraph. Give the incorrect usage,
followed by the correct usage. If a sentence is correct,
write *C.*

 **INTEGRATING THE
LANGUAGE ARTS**

Usage and Writing. Have students compose two paragraphs that
include the usage pairs identified in
Exercise 1. Encourage students to show
the different meanings that occur within
the same sentence. This will test their
knowledge of the terms and emphasize
the differences in meaning. [Possible
sentences include "The team accepted
everyone except me" and "Take the coat
with you, but bring it back the next time
you visit."]

USAGE

USAGE

SEGMENT 3 *(pp. 742–746)*
CAN'T HARDLY, CAN'T SCARCELY—INVENT

OBJECTIVES

- To identify errors in usage
- To proofread a paragraph to correct errors in usage

742 *Glossary of Usage*

1. C

2. as far as

3. an/ brought

4. accepted

5. C

6. everywhere

7. C

8. Because/ among

9. C

[1] In 1903, this young Japanese artist, Frank Matsura, arrived in the backwoods settlement of Conconully, Washington. [2] This was ~~all the farther~~ he would go, for he lived in this rough frontier area for the remaining ten years of his life. [3] When he came to town, Matsura was wearing a elegant formal suit and was carrying bulky camera equipment he had ~~taken~~ with him. [4] Back in Seattle, Matsura had ~~excepted~~ a job in Conconully as a helper and laundryman at the Elliott Hotel. [5] Soon he was living in a tiny room behind the kitchen and bringing energy and cheer to his menial job. [6] When he was off duty, he brought his camera ~~everywheres~~ he went, photographing the area's people, scenery, events, ~~and~~ etc. [7] Later, he settled in nearby Okanogan and opened this small studio. [8] ~~Being that~~ Matsura was a warm, extroverted person, he made many friends ~~between~~ settlers and Native Americans alike. [9] Oddly, though, he never told anyone about his past. [10] To this day, nobody knows who he really was, where he was born ~~at~~, or why he chose to live and die so far from his home.

can't hardly, can't scarcely See **The Double Negative** (page 756).

could of Do not use *of* with the helping verb *could*. Use *could have* instead. Also avoid *had of, ought to of, should of, would of, might of,* and *must of.*

EXAMPLE   Muriel could **have** [not *of*] gone with us.

USAGE

Teacher's ResourceBank™
RESOURCES

CAN'T HARDLY, CAN'T SCARCELY—INVENT
- Common Usage Problems B

🦉 QUICK REMINDER

Write the following sentence on the chalkboard:

My sister she lives in New York, but she don't write often.

Have students copy the sentence and tell them to circle the subjects and place a square around the verbs in each independent clause [subjects— *Sister, she;* verbs— *lives, do write*].

Have students discuss why neither clause has proper subject-verb agreement. [The first clause has a double subject; the second has a plural verb with a singular subject.]

discover, invent *Discover* means "to find, see, or learn about something that already exists." *Invent* means "to be the first to make or do something."

> EXAMPLES Luis W. Alvarez **discovered** many subatomic particles.
> Sarah Boone **invented** the ironing board.

don't, doesn't *Don't* is the contraction of *do not. Doesn't* is the contraction of *does not.* Use *doesn't,* not *don't,* with *he, she, it, this, that,* and singular nouns.

> EXAMPLES It **doesn't** [not *don't*] matter to me.
> The poem **doesn't** [not *don't*] rhyme.

effect See **affect, effect.**

emigrate, immigrate *Emigrate* means "to leave a country to settle elsewhere." *Immigrate* means "to come into a country to settle there."

> EXAMPLES My great-grandfather **emigrated** from Mexico.
> Much of Australia's population is composed of people who **immigrated** there.

everywheres See **anywheres,** etc.

except See **accept, except.**

fewer, less *Fewer* is used with plural nouns. It tells "how many." *Less* is used with singular words. It tells "how much."

> EXAMPLES There are **fewer** whales than there once were.
> We should have bought **less** meat [but: fewer eggs].

good, well *Good* is an adjective. Do not use it to modify a verb. Instead, use *well.*

> NONSTANDARD They skate **good.**
> STANDARD They skate **well.**

Although it is usually an adverb, *well* is used as an adjective to mean "healthy," "well dressed or well groomed," or "satisfactory."

> EXAMPLES I didn't feel **well.**
> He looked **well** in his uniform.
> All seems **well.**

MEETING INDIVIDUAL NEEDS

LEP/ESL

General Strategies. ESL students learn much English by communicating with classmates who often misuse *good* and *well.* You may want to give them more examples of the correct use of *well* and *good.* A fill-in-the-blank exercise composed by the students might make the lesson seem more relevant to them.

LEARNING STYLES

Auditory Learners. Some students might tend to confuse *of* with *have* in such expressions as *could have, should have, must have* and so on. You may want to have each group compose a tongue twister or a catchy rhyme using these words to challenge themselves. Have each group read its selection to the rest of the class.

COMMON ERROR

Problem. Students often confuse *immigrate* with *emigrate.*

Solution. Tell students that an easy way to remember the difference between these words is by using the initial letters to create a mnemonic device. Explain that the *e* in *emigrate* can stand for *exit* and the *i* in *immigrate* can stand for *in.* Then have students create their own examples [*exile* and *exodus,* or *integrate* and *initiate* are possibilities].

INTEGRATING THE LANGUAGE ARTS

Technology Link. Have students check for proper grammar and usage within their writing by using a computer program. Grammar programs will readily catch a number of mistakes, including double subjects, double negatives, and nonstandard usage such as *anywheres* and *being that.* Emphasize that such programs are not foolproof. Often a program will do no more than note the potential for an error and ask the user, "Is this word used correctly?" It is up to the user of the program to understand the rules of grammar and usage.

TIMESAVER

Group students in pairs and have them complete **Exercises 3** and **4.** One student could be responsible for answering the questions in **Exercise 3,** and the other for the questions in **Exercise 4.** Have students exchange papers; correct these exercises with the class. In this way, students will be exposed to all the questions in both exercises.

744

NOTE: *Feel good* and *feel well* mean different things. *Feel good* means "to feel happy or pleased." *Feel well* means "to feel healthy."

EXAMPLES   The victory made us feel **good.**
If you don't feel **well,** lie down.

Using *good* as an adverb is acceptable in conversation but not in writing.

had of See **could of.**

had ought, hadn't ought Do not use *had* or *hadn't* with *ought.*

NONSTANDARD   You hadn't ought to say such things.
STANDARD   You **ought** not to say such things.
or
You **shouldn't** say such things.

NONSTANDARD   They had ought to have left earlier.
STANDARD   They **ought** to have left earlier.
or
They **should** have left earlier.

hardly See **The Double Negative** (page 756).

he, she, they Do not use unnecessary pronouns after nouns. This error is called the *double subject.*

NONSTANDARD   My father he works downtown.
STANDARD   My **father works** downtown.

illusion See **allusion, illusion.**

immigrate See **emigrate, immigrate.**

imply, infer *Imply* means "to suggest something." *Infer* means "to interpret" or "to get a certain meaning from a remark or an action."

EXAMPLES   In her speech, the candidate **implied** that she is for tax reform.
From the candidate's speeches, I **inferred** that she is for tax reform.

invent See **discover, invent.**

EXERCISE 3   Identifying Correct Expressions

For each sentence, choose the <u>correct word</u> from the pair given in parentheses.

1. Was it George Washington Carver or Thomas Edison who (*invented*, *discovered*) all those uses for peanuts?
2. From his letter I (*implied*, *inferred*) he would be away all summer.
3. He (*don't*, *doesn't*) always say what he means.
4. (*Emigration*, *Immigration*) to Alaska was spurred by the gold rush.
5. The heat has affected the growing season; we'll harvest (*fewer*, *less*) crops this year.
6. Many French Canadians (*emigrated*, *immigrated*) from Quebec to work in the industries of New England.
7. As beasts of burden, dogs served the Comanches (*good*, *well*), often pulling a travois laden with more than forty pounds of baggage.
8. Mary Beth Stearns (*discovered*, *invented*) a device to study electrons.
9. You could (*have*, *of*) borrowed some paper and a pencil from me.
10. Audrey must (*have*, *of*) taken my jacket by mistake.

EXERCISE 4   **Proofreading a Paragraph to Correct Usage Errors**

Correct all the usage errors you find in each sentence in the following paragraph. Give the incorrect usage, followed by the correct usage. If a sentence is correct, write *C*.

[1] The scientist/philosopher/writer Douglas R. Hofstadter ~~he~~ enjoys writing words so that they form perfectly symmetrical designs. [2] He and a friend ~~discovered~~ a new pastime; the resulting designs are called *ambigrams*. [3] Every word ~~don't~~ lend itself ~~good~~ to this method, but you'd be surprised how often a word can be made into an ambigram. [4] As you might ~~of~~ known already, a *palindrome* is a word or expression that has the same letters in the same sequence both forward and backward—for example, *toot* or *Madam, I'm Adam*. [5] I don't mean to ~~infer~~, though, that an ambigram has to be a palindrome— an ambigram simply has to *look* symmetrical. [6] Usually, ambigrams ~~can't~~ hardly be formed unless you tinker with the letter shapes and connect them in new ways. [7] You ~~had~~ ought to start with a word that has six letters or ~~less~~.

2. invented
3. doesn't/ well
4. have
5. imply
6. can
7. fewer

KIND, SORT, TYPE—WOULD OF

OBJECTIVES

- To identify errors in usage
- To proofread a paragraph to correct errors in usage
- To revise expressions by correcting errors in usage

QUICK REMINDER

Write the following sentence on the chalkboard and have students correct any errors:

Mark is the kind of person who believes that it takes all kind of people to make the world the kind of place in which we can kind of find our own kind of a peace.

Next, have students discuss the uses for *kind* and have them practice using the word in sentences.

MEETING INDIVIDUAL NEEDS

LEP/ESL

General Strategies. To give students more practice in using relative pronouns, have them combine sentences by using the correct relative pronouns (including *who, whom, where, that,* and *which*). For example, you could provide the following set of sentences:

The teacher asked me a question. I had difficulty answering it. [The teacher asked me a question that I had difficulty answering.]

For students who are having problems with these forms, you may want them to start with a sentence-completion exercise. Provide examples, such as "I talked to the man who. . . ."

746

---

746 *Glossary of Usage*

8. C
9. effects
10. have

[8] For some good ideas, look below at the ambigrams for the words *Jamal, Steve, Chris, Felix, Wendy, Mexico,* and *dance.* [9] Don't forget that you can mix cursive, printed, capital, and lowercase letters to create ~~affects~~ like the ones in these ambigrams. [10] If you become stumped, you might find that you could ~~of~~ succeeded by adding some decorative flourishes.

Jamal · Steve · Chris · dance · Mexico · Wendy · Felix

kind, sort, type These words should always agree in number with the words *this* and *that* (singular) or *these* and *those* (plural).

> EXAMPLE   I know more about **that kind** of music than about any of **those** other **kinds**.

kind of, sort of These expressions, widely used in conversation, mean "rather" or "somewhat." Avoid them in writing.

> ACCEPTABLE IN CONVERSATION   She seemed kind of bored.
> The waves were sort of rough.
>
> CORRECT IN WRITING   She seemed **rather** bored.
> The waves were **rather** [or *somewhat*] rough.

kind of a, sort of a The *a* (or *an*) is unnecessary. Omit it.

> EXAMPLE   This bolt takes a special **kind of** [not *kind of a*] nut.

learn, teach *Learn* means "to acquire information." *Teach* means "to instruct" or "to show how."

> EXAMPLES   She **learned** how to saddle a horse.
> The stable owner **taught** her how.

leave, let *Leave* means "to go away." *Let* means "to allow" or "to permit."

NONSTANDARD	Leave them go first.
STANDARD	**Let** them go first.
STANDARD	We **let** [not *left*] the trapped bird go free.

less See **fewer, less.**

lie, lay See pages 697–699.

like, as *Like* is usually a preposition. In informal English, *like* is often used in place of the conjunction *as.* Formal English calls for *as* to introduce a subordinate clause.

EXAMPLES The animal looked **like** a snake. [The preposition *like* introduces a prepositional phrase.]
It shed its skin **as** a snake does. [The conjunction *as* introduces a subordinate adverb clause.]

☞ REFERENCE NOTE: Phrases are discussed in Chapter 17, and clauses are covered in Chapter 18. For more on informal and formal English, see pages 500–501.

like, as if In informal speech, *like* is often used in place of the subordinating conjunction *as if* or *as though* to introduce a subordinate clause. When writing, avoid using *like* in place of these two conjunctions.

INFORMAL	This looks like it might be the right place.
FORMAL	This looks **as if** [or *as though*] it might be the right place.

might of, must of See **could of.**

no, none, nothing See **The Double Negative** (page 756).

nowheres See **anywheres,** etc.

of Do not use *of* with prepositions such as *inside, off,* and *outside.*

EXAMPLES The diver jumped **off** [not *off of*] the board.
Outside [not *outside of*] the building was a patio.

☞ REFERENCE NOTE: For information on using *of* with helping verbs (*had of* and *must of,* for example), see the listing for **could of.** For information on using *of* in the expressions *kind of* and *sort of,* see the listings for **kind of, sort of** and **kind of a, sort of a.**

off of See **of.**

ought to of See **could of.**

USAGE

COMMON ERROR

Problem. Students often confuse *like* and *as* because they do not understand clauses or prepositional phrases.

Solution. Give students three short rules and provide examples to support the rules.

1. Use *as* with a clause. A clause has both a subject and a verb.
   John Madden talks in commercials as he does during football games.
2. Use *like* with a phrase when showing resemblance. A phrase does not have both a subject and a verb.
   He walked like a football player.
3. Use *as* with a phrase when showing equivalency.
   He addressed the class as a man of merit.

INTEGRATING THE LANGUAGE ARTS

Literature Link. You may want to have students read a poem such as Lawrence Ferlinghetti's "Constantly Risking Absurdity . . ." or any other poem that includes an extended metaphor, to discover a use of *like* that shows resemblance.

Have students discuss why the author uses *like* rather than *as.* [Students might say that the poet was simply showing resemblance and not implying that a poet is always an acrobat.]

As a continuation of the activity, you may want to have students write poems that include extended similes or metaphors.

USAGE

EXERCISE 5 **Identifying Correct Expressions**

For each sentence, choose the <u>correct word or words</u> from the choices given in parentheses.

1. The total length of the Great Wall of China is about 4,000 miles, if branches (*off*, *off of*) the main wall are included.
2. Carlos was (*nowhere*, *nowheres*) in sight.
3. We went to the hardware store for a special (*kind of*, *kind of a*) wrench.
4. Rachel Carson's books (*learned*, *taught*) me to care about ecology.
5. (*Leave*, *Let*) us listen without any interruptions.
6. We could (*of*, *have*) left earlier, I suppose.
7. Why did she feel (*like*, *as if*) she'd said something wrong?
8. T. J. (*ought*, *had ought*) to see this program.
9. Why didn't the U.S. government (*leave*, *let*) the Cherokee people stay in their Southeast homelands?
10. They didn't want to take the boat out because the waves looked (*kind of*, *rather*) choppy.

 EXERCISE 6 **Proofreading a Paragraph to Correct Usage Errors**

Correct all the usage errors you find in each sentence in the following paragraph. Give the incorrect usage, followed by the correct usage. If a sentence is correct, write C.

1. C
2. rather [*or* somewhat]/ teach

4. let
5. as if
6. lie
7. C

[1] Until recent times, young girls had to master fancy needlework. [2] Beginning when a girl was ~~kind of~~ young, her mother or another woman would ~~learn~~ her many embroidery stitches. [3] Then, at the age of eight or ten, the girl would be given the task of making a sampler like the one shown on the next page, using every kind of ~~a~~ stitch she knew. [4] Usually, the girl's parents wouldn't ~~leave~~ her be idle. [5] She had to work on the sampler every day ~~like~~ her life depended on it! [6] When the sampler was finished, it didn't ~~lay~~ inside ~~of~~ a drawer either. [7] Instead, it was displayed to prove that the girl was industrious and well educated in the homemaking skills. [8] Many people

think that samplers must~~of~~ been popular in America and
~~nowheres~~ else. [9]However, these ~~kind~~ of needlework
exercises have been practiced in Europe, Asia, and Africa
for centuries. [10]Today, girls aren't judged by their stitch-
ery ~~like~~ they once were, and some never learn anything
about needlework.

8. have/
nowhere

9. kinds

10. as

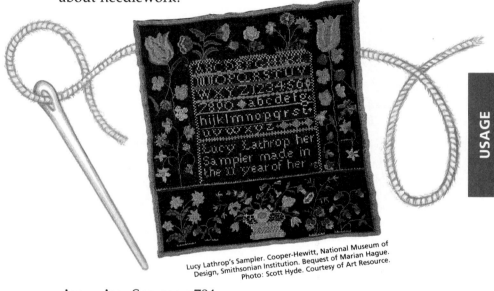

Lucy Lathrop's Sampler. Cooper-Hewitt, National Museum of
Design, Smithsonian Institution. Bequest of Marian Hague.
Photo: Scott Hyde. Courtesy of Art Resource.

rise, raise See page 704.

scarcely See **The Double Negative** (page 756).

she See **he, she, they.**

should of See **could of.**

sit, set See pages 700–701.

some, somewhat In writing, do not use *some* as an adverb
in place of *somewhat*.

> EXAMPLE   This medicine should help your cough **somewhat**
> [not *some*]

somewheres See **anywheres,** etc.

sort See **kind, sort, type.**

sort of See **kind of, sort of.**

take, bring See **bring, take.**

ADVANCED STUDENTS

Some students will benefit from
exposure to errors in usage not covered
in this chapter. Have students review
manuals of style such as Strunk and
White's *The Elements of Style*. Encourage
students to identify additional rules concerning errors in usage that might help
them or their classmates.

Students can then present the
rules they discover by providing examples or explanations of them. These rules
and the explanations students have
provided could be displayed in the
classroom.

USAGE

USAGE

COMMON ERROR

Problem. Students often confuse the conjunction *than* with the adverb *then*.

Solution. Explain to students that they should use *then* only when an expression answers the question *when*. Write the following reminder on the chalkboard:

then = when

At all other times, students should use *than,* which functions to compare or contrast. The following reminder can illustrate this:

than = comp*a*rison/contr*a*st.

teach See **learn, teach.**

than, then *Than* is a conjunction used in comparisons. *Then* is an adverb telling "when."

> EXAMPLES   She is younger **than** you.
> I swept the floor; **then** I emptied the trash.

that See **which, that, who.**

them Do not use *them* as an adjective. Use *those* instead.

> EXAMPLE   It's one of **those** [not *them*] fancy show dogs.

they See **he, she, they.**

this here, that there *Here* and *there* are unnecessary after *this* and *that.*

> EXAMPLE   Let's rent **this** [not *this here*] movie instead of **that** [not *that there*] **one.**

try and The correct expression is *try to.*

> EXAMPLE   When you're at bat, you must **try to** [not *try and*] concentrate.

type See **kind, sort, type.**

unless See **without, unless.**

way, ways Use *way,* not *ways,* in referring to a distance.

> EXAMPLE   She lives quite a **way** [not *ways*] from here.

well See **good, well.**

what Do not use *what* in place of *that* to introduce a subordinate clause.

> EXAMPLE   This is the book **that** [not *what*] I told you about.

when, where Do not use *when* or *where* incorrectly in writing a definition.

> NONSTANDARD   *S.R.O.* is when tickets for all the seats have been sold, leaving standing room only.
> STANDARD   *S.R.O.* means that tickets for all the seats have been sold, leaving standing room only.
>
> *or*
>
> *S.R.O.* is the abbreviation for *standing room only,* meaning that tickets for all the seats have been sold.

where Do not use *where* for *that*.

> EXAMPLE I read **that** [not *where*] the word *bayou* comes from the Choctaw word *bayuk,* meaning "small stream."

where . . . at See **at.**

which, that, who *Which* refers only to things. *That* refers to either people or things. *Who* refers only to people.

> EXAMPLES The running shoes **which** I want are on sale now.
> This is the bulb **that** needs replacing.
> Is she the runner **that** won the medal?
> Is she the runner **who** won the medal?

who, whom See pages 661–662.

without, unless Do not use the preposition *without* in place of the conjunction *unless.*

> EXAMPLE I can't use the car **unless** [not *without*] I ask Mom.

would of See **could of.**

▶ EXERCISE 7 **Revising Sentences by Correcting Errors in Usage**

Revise each sentence, correcting errors in usage.

1. A solar eclipse is when the moon comes between the earth and the sun.
2. The workers which put up that office building were certainly fast.
3. Ronald E. McNair was the only African American astronaut aboard the space shuttle what exploded in January 1986.
4. I really like them science fiction movies.
5. A run-on sentence is where two sentences are erroneously joined as one.
6. As soon as the rain lets up some, we'll leave.
7. Them mosquitoes can drive a person nearly crazy.
8. Jerry Rice carried the ball a long ways down the field before he was tackled.
9. I read in the paper where Amy Tan has a new novel coming out soon.
10. I'm tired of trying to cut the grass with this here old lawn mower that should be in an antique exhibit.

USAGE

USAGE

WRITING APPLICATION

The writing assignment gives students practice in following rules of usage within a persuasive writing activity.

If there is sufficient time, have students bring in actual fliers created by an organization or have them write to request fliers. Remind students that the fliers they create for this assignment will certainly be different. Have students discuss what information the professional fliers contain that theirs should also mention.

CRITICAL THINKING
Analysis

Remind students that many people will not immediately read an unsolicited advertisement. Encourage students to examine their prewriting lists and determine which services would be most interesting and applicable to the general public.

Tell students that a flier that fully explains a few services will be more persuasive than one that says little about a lot of services.

WRITING APPLICATION

OBJECTIVES
- To create a descriptive flier that uses standard English
- To provide and identify five examples of standard usage within a writing sample

WRITING APPLICATION

Using Standard English to Make a Good Impression

How you present yourself affects the way other people respond to you. When you appear to be intelligent and well-spoken, others usually have a higher regard for what you say. Like individuals, most businesses and organizations try hard to present themselves at their best. One of the ways they do so is by creating advertisements or public relations fliers. The use of correct standard English in such ads and fliers makes a good impression. Notice what different impressions you get from these two examples.

NONSTANDARD   Leave me tell you about some of the accomplishments of our association. You may of already heard about our very successful Thanksgiving food drive. Well, we also rose money for the new mobile clinic. This here clinic brings affordable, high-quality health care to people living in remote areas of our county.

STANDARD   Let me tell you about some of the accomplishments of our association. You may have already heard about our very successful Thanksgiving food drive. Well, we also raised money for the new mobile clinic. This clinic brings affordable, high-quality health care to people living in remote areas of our county.

Which of these statements would make a better impression on a potential volunteer or contributor?

 WRITING ACTIVITY

Create a flier for an organization that will soon be providing a public service in your community. The organization you choose might provide health, recreation, or housing services, or it might do something else. In a one-page flier, describe the organization's achievements and goals, and tell about some of the services it offers. Include at least five examples of the standard usage guidelines covered in this chapter, and underline each example.

USAGE

Prewriting Begin by listing services that your community needs and noting what kinds of organizations supply these services. You may write about a real service group, such as the American Heart Association, or you may wish to write about a group that you make up. Also, list some of the positive effects the group will likely have on your community. Organize your notes so that you can present your information in several coherent paragraphs.

Writing As you write your first draft, you may think of points you'd like to add or changes you'd like to make in the presentation of your information. If so, look back over your prewriting notes, and figure out where your additions and changes will best fit.

Evaluating and Revising Exchange papers with a classmate, and as the two of you read each other's ads or fliers, ask the following questions:

- What does this group or organization do?
- Why should I trust this organization to provide the services it promises?
- How will these services benefit the people in my community?
- What other services could this organization provide that would be more useful to my community?
- What is my overall impression of this organization or group?

Use your partner's responses to these questions to help you revise your draft for clarity and audience appeal. You may also want to get pamphlets or fliers from some local public service groups to see how information is presented in these publications.

Proofreading Now that you've worked so hard on creating a good impression, don't spoil the effect with incorrect punctuation. See Chapters 25–28 for guidelines on using marks of punctuation. Read over your paper again, checking for errors in grammar, spelling, and usage. Be sure that you have included five correct expressions from this chapter.

PREWRITING

Since students are attempting to write a persuasive flier, you may want to have students also generate a list of reasons why people may not want to use the organization's services. Then they can take the list of provided services and better focus on those to be addressed in the flier.

WRITING

Encourage students to approach the flier as if it were advertising. Tell students that catchy slogans and attention-getting headlines are often the quickest way to get a flier read.

A DIFFERENT APPROACH

When students publish the fliers, have them create a drawing or provide a picture to be used on the cover.

USAGE

USAGE

754 *Glossary of Usage*

▶ REVIEW A   **Identifying Correct Expressions**

For each sentence, choose the <u>correct word or words</u> from the choices given in parentheses.

1. Thanks to modern medicine, there are (*<u>fewer</u>, less*) cases of tetanus and diphtheria nowadays.
2. I tried to (*learn, <u>teach</u>*) my dog to do tricks, but he just sat and stared at me.
3. I see (*where, <u>that</u>*) pandas are an endangered species.
4. Cape Porpoise is (*<u>somewhere</u>, somewheres*) near Portsmouth.
5. Priscilla wrote a longer paper (*<u>than</u>, then*) Tammy did.
6. To make Native American fry bread, you need flour, baking powder, salt, (*and etc., <u>etc.</u>*)
7. We (*hadn't ought, <u>ought not</u>*) to decide until we know more facts.
8. It (*don't, <u>doesn't</u>*) make any difference when we finish.
9. Someone must (*of, <u>have</u>*) left the door unlocked.
10. Lewis Latimer (*discovered, <u>invented</u>*) and patented the first electric light bulb.

▶ REVIEW B   **Selecting Appropriate Expressions**

For each sentence, choose the <u>correct word or words</u> from the choices given in parentheses.

1. Stevie Wonder has written a number of hit songs since the 1960s, and it (*don't, <u>doesn't</u>*) look (*<u>as if</u>, like*) he's ever going to stop.
2. (*<u>Inside</u>, Inside of*) the box was (*<u>a</u>, an*) heap of glittering gems.
3. May I (*imply, <u>infer</u>*) from your yawns that you are bored?
4. My great-grandmother (*<u>emigrated</u>, immigrated*) from Italy when she was a young woman.
5. (*Beside, <u>Besides</u>*) speaking Spanish, Vera can speak a little Portuguese, and she reads both very (*good, <u>well</u>*).
6. Linda (*<u>doesn't</u>, don't*) enjoy doing (*them, those, <u>that</u>*) sort of exercise.
7. Ahead of us on the desert, a lake seemed to sparkle, but it was only an (*allusion, <u>illusion</u>*).
8. This water shortage will (*<u>affect</u>, effect*) the whole state (*accept, <u>except</u>*) for two counties.

9. I don't think my parents will (*leave*, *let*) me borrow the car in this kind of weather.
10. Because of the indiscriminate slaughter, each year there were (*fewer*, *less*) bison.

▶ REVIEW C   **Proofreading a Paragraph to Correct Usage Errors**

Correct each usage error you find in each sentence in the following paragraph. Give the incorrect usage, then the correct usage. If a sentence is correct, write *C*.

[1] Imagine single-handedly discovering a system for writing a language that had never before been written! [2] In about 1809, the Cherokee scholar Sequoyah became aware of "talking leaves," the written pages used by whites to communicate with one another. [3] Being that Sequoyah he felt that the ability to write had greatly helped whites, he decided he had ought to create a similar system for his people. [4] Instead of making up an alphabet like the one used in English, he chose to create this here *syllabary*. [5] Each character in Sequoyah's syllabary stands for one of the eighty-five syllables what are used in speaking Cherokee. [6] Sequoyah copied some letters from a English book, but in his system they have different meanings. [7] During the twelve years that it took Sequoyah to complete his writing system, he was ridiculed by many Cherokees who thought his efforts were kind of foolish. [8] But after the syllabary was finished and accepted by most Cherokees, they realized they should not of scoffed. [9] Within a few months' time, thousands learned

CHEROKEE SYLLABARY
Invented by SEQUOYAH

Dₐ	Rₑ	Tᵢ	Δₒ	Oᵤ	iᵥ
Sga Øka	Ϝge	ygi	Ago	Jgu	Egv
Ϙha	Ƥhe	Əhi	Ϝʰho	Γhu	Ϭhv
Wla	Ϭle	Ƥli	Ϭlo	Mlu	ϥlv
Ɣma	Ɑlme	Hmi	ʒmo	ɣmu	
Θna ƚhna Gnah	Λne	ɦni	Zno	ɘnu	Onv
Ƭqua	Əque	ƥqui	Ѵquo	Øquu	Ɛquv
Usa Ɑs	4se	bsi	ǂso	Ϭsu	Rsv
Lda Wta	Ϭde Ƭte	Jdi Jti	Vdo	Sdu	Ϭdv
Ϭdla ℂtla	Ltle	Ctli	ϥtlo	Ϙtlu	Ptlv
Ϭtsa	Vtse	Ƙtsi	Ktso	Jtsu	Ctsv
Ϭwa	Ϭwe	Owi	Owo	Ɉwu	6wv
Ϭya	ßye	Ayi	ɦyo	Gyu	Byv

PRONUNCIATION GUIDE
(In words the pronunciation may be different)

a, as in ah   o, as in oh   g, as in go
e, as in they u, as in true ts, as j in joy
i, as in ski   v, as uh in huh

d, h, k, l, m, n, qu, s, t, w, y, as in English
NOTE: The character 'nah' is not in use.

Adapted from "Cherokee Alphabet" created by Harry A. Moneyhun, 1991.

ANSWERS
Review C

1. discovering a system — inventing a system
2. C
3. Being that Sequoyah he felt — Because Sequoyah felt; he had ought to — he ought to
4. this here *syllabary* — this *syllabary*
5. what are used — that are used
6. a English book — an English book
7. were kind of foolish — were rather foolish
8. should not of scoffed — should not have scoffed
9. C
10. learning them — teaching them

THE DOUBLE NEGATIVE

OBJECTIVES

- To revise sentences that contain too many negative words
- To write a descriptive paragraph that uses five expressions from the glossary of usage

USAGE

USAGE

🦉 QUICK REMINDER

Write the following sentences on the chalkboard and ask students to identify the negative words in them:

Nathaniel didn't have no shoes to wear. [didn't, no]

Layla doesn't want neither dress. [not, neither]

Explain to students that in terms of usage, only one negative word per sentence is necessary.

MEETING
INDIVIDUAL
NEEDS

LEP/ESL

Spanish. You may find that some students use the double negative quite often, especially with words such as *nothing, none,* or *nobody.* The double negative is perfectly acceptable in Spanish. Oral practice will identify those students who are transferring this usage to English. Begin by asking questions that call for the negative form. You could ask "Did you see anyone sleeping in class today?" or "Did you go anywhere last weekend?" Give additional written practice to those students who are having trouble.

756

---

756 *Glossary of Usage*

how to read and write, and soon books and newspapers were being printed in Cherokee. [10] Sequoyah was honored by his people for learning them to read and write, and his writing method is still used today.

The Double Negative

A *double negative* is the use of two negative words when one is enough. Before the 1700s, two or more negatives were often used in the same sentence for emphasis. Today this usage is no longer considered correct, and a double negative is regarded as nonstandard. Avoid using double negatives in your writing and speaking.

hardly, scarcely Do not use the words *hardly* and *scarcely* with another negative word.

EXAMPLES   You **can** [not *can't*] **hardly** see ten feet in this fog.
We **had** [not *hadn't*] **scarcely** enough time to finish the test.

no, none, nothing Do not use any of these negative words with another negative word.

NONSTANDARD	There isn't no reason to be nervous.
STANDARD	There **is no** reason to be nervous.
STANDARD	There **isn't any** reason to be nervous.

NONSTANDARD	We searched for clues but didn't find none.
STANDARD	We searched for clues but **found none.**
STANDARD	We searched for clues but **didn't find any.**

NONSTANDARD	I didn't hear nothing.
STANDARD	**I heard nothing.**
STANDARD	**I didn't hear anything.**

OBJECTIVE

- To revise expressions by correcting errors in usage

The Double Negative **757**

 EXERCISE 8

Revising Sentences That Contain Too Many Negative Words

Each of the following sentences contains too many negative words. Revise each sentence in two correct ways. Be careful not to change the intended meaning.

EXAMPLE **1.** Before Sequoyah's syllabary, the Cherokee language hadn't never been written down.
1. *Before Sequoyah's syllabary, the Cherokee language had never been written down.*
Before Sequoyah's syllabary, the Cherokee language hadn't ever been written down.

1. As a young man, Sequoyah didn't have scarcely no contact with whites.
2. Before Sequoyah, not no person in history hadn't never single-handedly created no written language!
3. Some Cherokees didn't want no part of Sequoyah's system of writing.
4. It didn't take hardly no time at all for thousands of Cherokees to learn Sequoyah's symbols.
5. The Cherokees had a rich oral tradition, but they hadn't never been able to put none of it on paper.

 REVIEW D

Revising Sentences by Correcting Errors in Usage

Rewrite each sentence, correcting its error or errors in usage. Practice saying aloud the correct sentences.
Revisions will vary.

1. They ~~don't~~ have hardly any chance to score before the buzzer sounds; the situation looks ˄~~sort of~~ hopeless to me. **1.** rather
2. You ought to have seen how beautiful Santa Fe was at Christmas, with nearly every house surrounded by flickering *feralitos* —paper-bag lanterns that have candles inside ~~of~~ them.
3. I might˄~~of~~ gone to the concert if I'd ~~of~~ heard about it earlier. **3.** have   **4.** can/between
4. Pam and her sister Stacey look so much alike that you˄~~can't~~ hardly see much difference ~~among~~ them.
5. My cousins ~~didn't~~ hardly ˄~~know~~ how to swim, but they wouldn't˄~~of~~ missed going to the lake. **5.** knew/have

ANSWERS

Exercise 8

Revisions will vary. The following sentences are possibilities:

1. As a young man, Sequoyah didn't have much contact with whites.
   As a young man, Sequoyah had scarcely any contact with whites.
2. Before Sequoyah, no person in history had ever single-handedly created a written language!
   Before Sequoyah, not one person in history had ever single-handedly created a written language!
3. Some Cherokees didn't want any part of Sequoyah's system of writing.
   Some Cherokees wanted no part of Sequoyah's system of writing.
4. It didn't take much time at all for thousands of Cherokees to learn Sequoyah's symbols.
   It took hardly any time at all for thousands of Cherokees to learn Sequoyah's symbols.
5. The Cherokees had a rich oral tradition, but they had never been able to put any of it on paper.
   The Cherokees had a rich oral tradition, but they hadn't ever been able to put any of it on paper.

6. ~~Them~~ reference books in the library are kept in some kind of ~~a~~ special section. **6.** Those

7. This ~~here~~ is the car ~~what~~ I told you about. **7.** that

8. ~~Hadn't~~ you ~~ought to~~ try ~~and~~ help them? **8.** Shouldn't/to

9. Many of the Native American leaders ~~which~~ visited Washington, D.C., in the late 1800s proudly wore their traditional clothing rather than dress like their white hosts. **9.** who **10.** those

10. I wonder where ~~them~~ fishing poles are ~~at~~. **11.** anymore

11. We don't live in that ~~there~~ neighborhood ~~no more~~.

12. We might ~~of~~ gone on the tour, but we wouldn't ~~of~~ had ~~no~~ camera to take pictures. **12.** have/have/a/with which

13. A foot fault in tennis ~~is when~~ the server steps over the base line before hitting the ball. **13.** occurs

14. Since there ~~wasn't~~ scarcely any rainfall last spring, there are ~~less~~ mosquitoes this summer. **14.** was/fewer

15. When the play was over, the audience seemed ~~sort of~~ subdued. **15.** somewhat

16. Shing searched for *lomein* noodles in the grocery store, but didn't find ~~none~~. **16.** any

17. I saw on the news ~~where~~ manufacturers will start putting ~~them~~ air bags into all the new cars. **17.** that/those

18. Miss Kim ~~she~~ likes to give those ~~kind~~ of surprise quizzes. **18.** kinds

19. Let's try ~~and~~ finish early so we can relax ~~some~~. **19.** to/ somewhat

20. In the early 1500s, Ponce de León searched for the Fountain of Youth ~~somewheres~~ on the island of Bimini. **20.** somewhere

PICTURE THIS

You are a professional artist looking for a fresh medium in which to work. You've just seen an unusual exhibit of painted chifforobes—pieces of furniture that combine a wardrobe with a chest of drawers. The second-hand chifforobes were decorated, inside and out, by New Orleans high school students. You admire how these young artists have presented scenes from their lives to

---

PICTURE THIS

You may want to have students form groups and discuss what they would include in their descriptions. Tell students first to use headings such as *reactions* and *ideas*. Encourage students to generate lists containing things they would like, dislike, imagine, and so on.

illustrate their dreams and fears. You have so many thoughts and impressions that you decide to write some notes to yourself to remind you of your reactions to the exhibit. Describe in detail one of the chifforobes shown here. (You can describe an imaginary one if none of these three interests you.) Tell whether you were inspired by the exhibit and how you might use the chifforobe art to enrich your own work. In your paragraph, use correctly at least five expressions covered in this chapter.

Subject: an exhibit of chifforobes painted by high school students
Audience: yourself, a professional painter
Purpose: to inform, to remind, to inspire

OBJECTIVES

- To revise expressions by correcting errors in usage
- To proofread a paragraph to correct errors in usage

CRITICAL THINKING
Synthesis

Analyze and discuss the use of nonstandard grammar in dialogue. A good example would be either Langston Hughes's poem "Mother to Son" or Marjorie Kinnan Rawlings's short story "My Friend Moe." Emphasize that nonstandard grammar is included as a literary device to help reinforce realistic characters.

Next, tell students that they will work in groups of three to create scenes involving characters who will speak in either standard or nonstandard English.

In the groups, one student will write brief character descriptions of two different characters. The other two students then will compose dialogue for the invented characters. Students can practice speaking their dialogue and then present their scenes to the class.

USAGE

USAGE

760   *Glossary of Usage*

Review: Posttest

A. Revising Expressions by Correcting Errors in Usage

In each set of expressions, one <u>expression contains an error in usage</u>. Write the expression correctly, using standard formal usage.

EXAMPLE **1. a.** Her speech implies that a change is needed.
    b. Leave me have some oranges, too.
    c. This house is somewhat larger than our old one.
    1. *b. Let me have some oranges, too.*

1. **a.** ~~wasn't no~~ reason   **1.** was no [*or* wasn't any]
    b. words had no effect
    c. can hardly wait
2. **a.** families that ~~emigrated~~ to new lands   **2.** immigrated
    b. sail as far as the channel marker
    c. made allusions to classical literature
3. **a.** ~~being that~~ he was alone   **3.** because [*or* since]
    b. The people accepted new ways.
    c. the woman who was elected
4. **a.** what kind of gloves
    b. There is overtime besides the regular work.
    c. ~~an~~ historic moment   **4.** a
5. **a.** saw on TV that our team had won
    b. Lee Haney proudly ~~excepted~~ his seventh straight Mr. Olympia trophy.   **5.** accepted
    c. the house beside the highway
6. **a.** those lockers beside the gym
    b. ~~Leave~~ him have his own way.   **6.** Let
    c. Leave the door open when you go.
7. **a.** Teach your dog this trick.
    b. I'm feeling ~~kind of~~ ill.   **7.** rather [*or* somewhat]
    c. might have been too late
8. **a.** taller than her sister
    b. Dough will rise in a warm place.
    c. We read ~~where~~ the damage was extensive.   **8.** that
9. **a.** Try to be on time.
    b. They walked a long way.
    c. ~~Them~~ stairs are dangerous and need repairs.   **9.** Those

10. **a.** The bag burst, spilling the rice.
     b. The Polynesian alphabet has twelve characters,
        fewer than half the letters in the English
        alphabet.
     c. <u>Take those books off ~~of~~ that shelf.</u>

B. Proofreading Paragraphs to Correct Usage Errors

Correct each usage error you find in each sentence in the
following paragraphs. Give the incorrect usage, followed
by the correct usage. [Note: A sentence may contain more
than one error.] Revisions of double negatives will vary.

[11] After the Civil War ended, Joseph E. Clark decided
that African Americans ~~had~~ ought to start a town of their
own. **[12]** He wanted to build such a town, but no one
would sell or donate land for this kind of ~~an~~ endeavor.
[13] But Joe Clark was a man who had great determination,
and he ~~wasn't~~ hardly going to give up hope. **[14]** Finally in
1877, with money ~~what~~ was donated by a New York phi-
lanthropist and land offered by a Floridian named Josiah
Eaton, Clark obtained the first twelve acres of what would
become Eatonville, Florida.

[15] Eatonville, located just ~~besides~~ Orlando, is recognized as the oldest incorporated African American town
~~anywheres~~ in the United States. **[16]** This ~~here~~ community
has always been populated and governed entirely by
blacks. **[17]** The African Americans ~~which~~ flocked to
Eatonville built homes, churches, and schools, and they
cultivated gardens and orange groves. **[18]** The residents
didn't lose ~~no~~ time in establishing a library, a post office,
and a newspaper. **[19]** Today, after more than a hundred
years of self-government, the citizens of Eatonville continue to feel the ~~affects~~ of Joe Clark's courage and vision.
[20] With its light industry, new businesses, and booming
real estate development, Eatonville enjoys economic
growth just ~~like~~ the rest of Central Florida does.

13. was
14. that
15. beside/anywhere
17. who
18. any
19. effects
20. as

USAGE

CHAPTER OVERVIEW

Students can use this chapter as a reference for specific usage problems. A quick review early in the year may help your students avoid capitalization problems later.

The examples on the **Summary Style Review** at the end of the chapter can often teach students about correct capitalization faster than rules can. Exceptions and special problems are discussed to help students avoid confusion.

This chapter can be helpful with usage problems that may arise during the teaching of any composition chapter and **Chapter 15: "The Parts of Speech."**

MECHANICS

MECHANICS

24 CAPITALIZATION

Standard Uses of Capitalization

Diagnostic Test

Correcting Sentences by Using Capitalization Correctly

For each of the following sentences, identify the word or words containing an error in capitalization. If a sentence is correct, write C.

EXAMPLE   **1.** In the Fall the trees along Main street are lovely.
          1. *fall; Street*

1. This year my easiest classes are geometry, spanish, and American history.
2. Mexico city is built on the site of tenochtitlán, the capital of the aztec empire.
3. We rent videotapes from the Grand Video company.
4. Colorado is located West of the Great Plains.
5. Lansing, Michigan, is in Ingham county.
6. She lives at 321 Maple boulevard, which is south of here.

7. My RCA <u>Stereo</u> is ten years old and still works well.
8. Carla entered her Saint Bernard in the Centerville Dog <u>club's</u> show.
9. They live half a block north of Twenty-<u>First</u> Street.
10. Our neighbors are alumni of Howard <u>university</u> in Washington, <u>d.c.</u>
11. Last <u>Spring</u> my step-sister Lisa joined the National Audubon <u>society</u>.
12. While we were in San Juan, <u>puerto rico</u>, we toured El Morro <u>Fortress</u>.
13. The club members celebrated <u>bastille day</u> by having dinner at a French restaurant.
14. Has Ms. Davis written to the U.S. <u>department</u> of Agriculture for information on soybean cultivation in the Midwest?
15. Mars was the Roman <u>God</u> of war.
16. We're holding a car wash next Saturday to raise money for the <u>junior</u> Prom.
17. The <u>Islands</u> that make up the <u>west indies</u> separate the Atlantic <u>ocean</u> from the <u>gulf</u> of <u>mexico</u> and the Caribbean <u>sea</u>.
18. Would you like to be the first student to ride in a <u>Space Shuttle</u> that orbits the earth?
19. The post-Civil <u>war</u> period known as <u>reconstruction</u> officially ended in 1877, when federal troops were withdrawn from the <u>south</u>.
20. Erica wants to be <u>Secretary</u> of the Shutterbug <u>club</u>.

In your reading, you'll notice that some writers do not always follow the rules presented in this chapter. However, you will see that most writers do follow these rules most of the time. In your own writing, following these rules will help you communicate clearly with the widest possible audience.

NOTE: Some modern writers, for reasons of style, do not follow the rules governing capitalization. When you quote from a writer's work, always use capital letters exactly as the writer uses them.

👉 REFERENCE NOTE: See pages 834–835 for more about using capital letters in quotations.

MECHANICS

USING THE DIAGNOSTIC TEST

You may want to gauge your students' general knowledge of basic capitalization rules with the **Diagnostic Test**, which consists of twenty sentences containing errors in capitalization.

With some students, the simplest approach to problem areas may be to read the rules and examples with them and assign the exercises at the end of each set. Other students might not need to spend time reviewing all of the chapter, so you can concentrate on the rules and exceptions, or simply have students use this chapter as a reference tool.

MECHANICS

Teacher's ResourceBank™

RESOURCES

FIRST WORDS, THE PRONOUN *I*, THE INTERJECTION *O*, PROPER NOUNS AND PROPER ADJECTIVES

• First Words, *I*, and *O*
• Proper Nouns and Adjectives A
• Proper Nouns and Adjectives B
• Proper Nouns and Adjectives C

QUICK REMINDER

Write the following proper nouns on the chalkboard and ask students to correct capitalization errors:

1. Atlantic ocean [Ocean]
2. rotary club [Rotary Club]
3. Main street [Street]
4. Spanish armada [Armada]
5. a South Sea Island [island]
6. senator Lewis [Senator]
7. aunt Yolanda [Aunt]
8. her Aunt [aunt]
9. a committee Chairman [chairman]
10. a Congressional representative [congressional]

INTEGRATING THE LANGUAGE ARTS

Literature Link. Ask students to look at examples of common nouns that are capitalized in an Emily Dickinson poem. Ask students for ideas on the poetic purpose of nonstandard capitalization. [Students might say that nonstandard capitalization is used to personify animals, nature, or things; to exalt an idea; or to make an abstract idea concrete.]

---

764 *Capitalization*

24a. Capitalize the first word in every sentence.

EXAMPLES **The** Second Seminole War lasted nearly eight years. **After** the war many Seminoles remained in the Everglades and never officially made peace with the U.S. government.
After studying reports on new cars, my mom said, "**The** models with front-wheel drive have been improved."

Traditionally, the first word in a line of poetry is capitalized.

EXAMPLES **S**torm, blow me from here
With your fiercest wind
Let me float across the sky
'**T**ill I can rest again.

Maya Angelou, "Woman Work"

24b. Capitalize the pronoun *I* and the interjection *O*.

The interjection *O*, usually used only for invocations, is followed by the name of the person or thing being addressed. Don't confuse *O* with the common interjection *oh*, which is capitalized only when it begins a sentence or is part of a title.

EXAMPLES The first line **I** read in the poem was "Hear us, **O** Zeus."
I finished the race, but **oh,** was **I** exhausted.

24c. Capitalize proper nouns and proper adjectives.

A ***common noun*** names one member of a group of people, places, or things. A ***proper noun*** names a particular person, place, or thing. ***Proper adjectives*** are formed from proper nouns.

 REFERENCE NOTE: See page 515 for more about common nouns and proper nouns.

Common nouns are not capitalized unless they

- begin a sentence
- begin a direct quotation
- are part of a title

- To proofread a paragraph to correct capitalization
- To write a paragraph using capitalization correctly

COMMON NOUNS	PROPER NOUNS	PROPER ADJECTIVES
a writer	Shakespeare	Shakespearean sonnet
a country	France	French bread
a queen	Victoria	Victorian era
a planet	Venus	Venusian terrain

In proper nouns that have more than one word, all articles and short prepositions (those with fewer than five letters) are not capitalized.

EXAMPLES   Prince **of** Wales
National Association **for the** Advancement **of** Colored People

In a compound adjective, the proper noun or proper adjective is usually the only part capitalized.

EXAMPLES   **Spanish**-speaking countries   northern **Italian** cuisine

NOTE: Proper nouns and proper adjectives may lose their capitals after long use.

EXAMPLES   diesel   bologna   braille

When you're not sure whether to capitalize a word, check a dictionary to see in which uses (if any) it is capitalized.

(1) Capitalize the names of persons.

Given names	Matthew	Jennifer	Latrice	Nguyen
Surnames	Bowman	Cruz	Kantor	Ryan

NOTE: Some names contain more than one capital letter. Always verify the spelling with the person, or check it in a reference source.

EXAMPLES   **De La Cruz**   **La Porte**   **McEnroe**   **O'Shea**
Red Cloud   **Wells-Barnett**   **St. John**   **Van Gogh**

The abbreviations *Jr.* (*junior*) and *Sr.* (*senior*) should always be capitalized.

EXAMPLES   Jerome W. Wilson, **Jr.**   Simon L. Snyder, **Sr.**

MECHANICS

LEARNING STYLES

Auditory Learners. Some students might benefit from an oral exercise that gives them practice in forming proper nouns from common nouns. Begin with a general category and ask a volunteer to name a specific example in that category. If you were to say "building," for example, a student might say "Empire State Building." Repeat this exercise until you think students are comfortable with the concept.

MECHANICS

LESS-ADVANCED STUDENTS

You may want to read aloud the rules and examples in this segment with a focus on special problems and exceptions to the rules. After you assess **Exercise 1**, ask students to make charts showing any specific error patterns. Students can add errors to their charts as they proceed through the chapter and can refer to the applicable rules when necessary.

✎ COMMON ERROR

Problem. Students who fail to capitalize first words might be writing run-on sentences or sentence fragments.

Solution. Have students who are having trouble with first-word capitalization review the material in **Chapter 12: "Writing Complete Sentences."** Remind students to proofread for these errors.

👁 VISUAL CONNECTIONS

Ideas for Writing. The photograph of Lucy Jefferson by Gordon Parks captures wisdom gained from life-long experience. His autobiographical works translate his flair for visual detail into verbal detail. Ask each student to bring a photograph from a personal collection or from a magazine to class and to write a profile of the subject. The profile should include at least five proper nouns and five proper adjectives.

MECHANICS

 EXERCISE 1 **Correcting Paragraphs by Using Capitalization**

If the capitalization of a sentence is correct, write C. If not, write the correct form of each incorrect word.

Words that should be capitalized or lowercased are underscored.

EXAMPLE   [1] These pictures capture only a few of the many sides of Gordon parks, renowned Photographer, film director, writer, and composer.

    1. *Parks; photographer*

[1] A <u>Self</u>-taught photographer, <u>gordon</u> Parks grew up in Fort Scott, Kansas. [2] <u>after</u> winning a <u>rosenwald</u> Fellowship for a series of pictures about life in Chicago's <u>Slums</u>, <u>He</u> got his first full-time photography job with the Farm Security Administration in Washington, D.C. [3] In 1949, he joined the staff of *Life* <u>Magazine</u>. [4] During his nearly twenty years with *Life*, Parks covered assignments ranging from <u>Junior</u> <u>High</u> <u>School</u> science conventions to Paris <u>Fashion</u> <u>Shows</u>. [5] He also wrote many of the essays that accompanied his photographs, as well as <u>Two Volumes</u> of autobiography, *The Learning Tree* and *A Choice of Weapons*.

[6] Turning to a career in the movie industry in 1968, Parks moved to Hollywood, where his son Gordon Parks, <u>jr.</u>, took this photograph of him preparing to direct a scene from the film version of *The Learning Tree.* [7] Parks   7. C
also wrote the film's screenplay and, working at the grand piano in his Hollywood apartment, its musical score. [8] His success with the film led to other writing and directing projects, including *Shaft, Shaft's Big Score,* and *Leadbelly,* the story of blues musician Huddie <u>ledbetter</u>.

[9] In August 1988, in a White House <u>Ceremony</u>, <u>parks</u> was awarded the National Medal of Arts, and the following year he was inducted into the National Association of Black Journalists Hall of Fame. [10] His most recent projects include another <u>Autobiographical</u> volume, *Voices in The Mirror,* and the words and music for *Martin,* a classical <u>Ballet</u> honoring the late <u>martin luther king</u>, jr.

(2) Capitalize geographical names.

TYPE OF NAME	EXAMPLES	
Countries	Mexico Ghana	the United States of America
Towns, Cities	Chicago Berlin San Diego	Laredo Stratford-on-Avon St. Petersburg
Counties, Townships, Parishes	Orange County Franklin Township Manhattan	Caddo Parish Yorkshire Third Precinct
States	Oregon New York	Texas South Carolina
Regions	the South the West the Northeast	New England Yukon Sun Belt

NOTE: Words such as *south, east,* and *northwest* are not capitalized when they indicate direction.

EXAMPLES   **west** of the bridge   heading **north**

MEETING INDIVIDUAL NEEDS

LEP/ESL

General Strategies. You can make **Exercise 1** more equitable for ESL students by pairing them with native English-speakers. The latter can act as cultural informants by telling the ESL students exactly how many words in each sentence should be capitalized and how many should be lowercased.

Distinguishing common from proper nouns can be problematic if students don't know all the words in a sentence or passage. For example, in **Exercise 1,** the second line reads, ". . . a series of pictures in Chicago's Slums, ... If students don't know what *slums* means, they might think it is a part of a name of a Chicago park, zoo, or building. Then they would be wrong, both for meaning and for capitalization.

COMMON ERROR

Problem. When the name of a particular place includes several words, students may be confused about which words to capitalize.

Solution. List on the chalkboard articles and prepositions that are likely to occur in names of particular places—*a, an, by, for, of, on,* and *the.* Remind students that an article or short preposition is capitalized only if it is the first word of a proper noun.

MECHANICS

MECHANICS

COOPERATIVE LEARNING

Divide the class into groups of three or four students. Ask each group to write a tourist brochure for a specific geographical region. The brochure should include information about at least one town or city and should refer to geographical features—lakes, rivers, mountains or ranges, and caves. The brochure should mention specific historical sites and figures as well as recreational and entertainment facilities. You could also have students provide directions to each attraction. Remind students to capitalize geographical names correctly. Have the groups present their brochures to the class.

TYPE OF NAME	EXAMPLES	
Continents	South America Asia	Europe Africa
Islands	Galveston Island the Lesser Antilles	the Isle of Wight Key West
Mountains	Allegheny Mountains Sierra Madre	Mount St. Helens Pikes Peak
Bodies of Water	Atlantic Ocean Red Sea Persian Gulf	Suwanee River Rio Grande Lake of the Ozarks
Parks	Redwood State Park Central Park	Stone Mountain Memorial Park
Roads, Highways, Streets	Route 41 Interstate 10 Sunshine State Parkway	Central Avenue South Fiftieth Street Pleasant Hill Road

The second word in a hyphenated number begins with a small letter: *Fifty-third Street.* Words such as *city, island, river, street,* and *park* are capitalized when they are part of a name. Otherwise, they are common nouns and are not capitalized.

PROPER NOUNS	COMMON NOUNS
traffic in Mexico City visiting Captiva Island bridging the Ohio River across Delancy Street	traffic in a large city visiting a barrier island bridging the river across a congested street

EXERCISE 2

Correcting Phrases by Capitalizing Words

If a phrase is correct, write *C.* If a word or words should be capitalized, write the entire phrase correctly.
Words that should be capitalized are underscored.
EXAMPLE **1.** atop granite peak
1. *atop Granite Peak*

1. zion national park
2. gulf of tonkin
3. explored Mount ararat
4. the hiking trails in a nearby state park 4. C
5. at moon lake
6. a house on starve island
7. beside the ohio river
8. in lancaster county
9. the illinois oil fields
10. across baffin bay
11. ventura boulevard
12. the tides in the bay 12. C
13. new york skyline
14. forty-fifth street
15. near the isle of man
16. the west side of the river 16. C
17. the north
18. near dundee mountain
19. coffee from brazil
20. coast of australia

▶ EXERCISE 3   **Proofreading a Paragraph to Correct Capitalization**

Capitalize the words that should begin with a capital letter in each sentence in the following paragraph. Do not include the words already capitalized. If a sentence is correct, write *C*.

EXAMPLE   [1] Until last year I'd never been farther from lawrenceburg, tennessee, than pulaski, which is only seventeen miles east.
    1. *Lawrenceburg, Tennessee, Pulaski*

[1] Naturally, I was excited when our choir decided to have an international arts and crafts fair to raise money for a trip to washington, d.c. [2] Colleen O'Roark suggested that the fair feature crafts and food from countries in europe, africa, and asia. [3] Juana Santiago, whose family is from venezuela, pointed out that we should also include items from central america and south america. [4] Julian 4. C Moore, who recently returned from visiting his aunt in Monrovia, said he'd bring a display of Liberian baskets. [5] Karen Cohen offered items from quebec, our neighbor to the north. [6] Erin McCall, whose family moved to lexington avenue from phoenix, arizona, volunteered to bring rocks from petrified forest national park. [7] Since Maxine Hirano was born in tokyo, japan, she promised to demonstrate paper-folding. [8] Some of us met later at Paula Bowen's house, on the northeast corner of columbus street and hickory lane, to choose items to represent the united states. [9] We selected Native American artifacts

TIMESAVER
You may want to assign **Exercise 3** for homework and go over the answers with students in class. Survey the class for error patterns and review those rules that seem to be giving students problems.

INTEGRATING THE LANGUAGE ARTS

Mechanics and Writing. Have students pretend to be pioneers traveling during the 1800s to their new homes in the West. Have them write diary entries describing their trip. Students should each include at least ten proper nouns or proper adjectives.

from the <u>southwest</u>, country crafts from the <u>appalachian mountains</u>, and shell gifts from the southern states along the <u>gulf</u> of <u>mexico</u>. [10] When the fair was over, we had raised enough money to include on our trip to the nation's capital a tour of <u>mammoth</u> <u>cave</u> <u>national</u> <u>park</u> in <u>kentucky</u>.

(3) Capitalize the names of organizations, teams, business firms, institutions, buildings, and government bodies.

TYPE OF NAME	EXAMPLES	
Organizations	American Medical Association National Honor Society Organization of American States	
Teams	New York Rangers Houston Oilers Eastside Jets	Harlem Globetrotters Portsmouth Chess Masters
Business Firms	Eastern Airlines International Business Machines	Xerox Corporation National Broadcasting Company
Institutions, Buildings	Stanford University Sears Tower Fox Theater	Good Samaritan Hospital Ridgemont High School
Government Bodies	the Senate Parliament Congress Tampa City Council	Department of the Interior the Nuclear Regulatory Commission

NOTE: Do not capitalize words such as *democratic, republican,* and *socialist* when they refer to principles or forms of government. Capitalize these words only when they refer to a specific political party.

EXAMPLES   Voting is part of the **d**emocratic process.
           George Bush was the **R**epublican nominee.

The word *party* in the name of a political party may be capitalized or not; either way is correct.

EXAMPLE   Republican **party**
              or
            Republican **Party**

MECHANICS

MECHANICS

REFERENCE NOTE: Do not capitalize words such as *building, hotel, theater, college, high school, post office,* and *courthouse* unless they are part of a proper name. For more discussion about the differences between common and proper nouns, see pages 764–765 and 515.

(4) Capitalize the names of historical events and periods, special events, and holidays and other calendar items.

TYPE OF NAME	EXAMPLES	
Historical Events and Periods	the **Dark Ages** **Great Depression** **Paleolithic Period** **Children's Crusade**	the **Battle of Gettysburg** the **Yalta Conference**
Special Events	the **Iowa State Fair** the **Boston Marathon**	the **All-Star Game** the **National Minority Job Expo**
Holidays and Other Calendar Items	**Friday** **March**	**Valentine's Day** **Earth Day**

NOTE: Do not capitalize the name of a season unless the season is being personified or is part of a proper name.

EXAMPLES We looked forward to **s**pring after the long **w**inter.
Are you going to the **W**inter Wonderland Dance?

"**W**inter slumbering in the open air,
Wears on his smiling face a dream of **S**pring!"

Samuel Taylor Coleridge, "Work Without Hope"

 EXERCISE 4 **Writing a Paragraph Using Capitalization Correctly**

Your family recently inherited the abandoned town shown on the next page. Write a paragraph explaining how you would go about revitalizing the town. What would you name the town? What names would you give to streets and avenues? What organizations, business firms, institutions, government offices, and special events would you set up? Include in your paragraph a combined total of at least twenty proper nouns and proper adjectives. Use a variety of names, not just your family name.

MECHANICS

MECHANICS

MECHANICS

772 *Capitalization*

EXAMPLE   *I'd name the town New Century City, and the first business I'd open would be a teenagers-only club called Syncopation.*

(5) Capitalize the names of nationalities, races, and peoples.

EXAMPLES   Italian, Canadian, Caucasian, Asian, Jewish, Hispanic, Navajo, Micronesian, Indo-Iranian

(6) Capitalize the brand names of business products.

EXAMPLES   Sealtest frozen yogurt, Kraft cheese, Kodak camera

Notice that the noun that often follows a brand name is not capitalized: an Apple computer.

(7) Capitalize the names of ships, monuments, awards, planets, and any other particular places, things, or events.

TYPE OF NAME	EXAMPLES	
Ships, Trains	the *Titanic*	the *Orient Express*
Aircraft, Spacecraft, Missiles	the *Spirit of St. Louis*	*Apollo* *Patriot*
Monuments, Memorials	Aztec Ruins National Monument Vietnam Veterans National Memorial	
Awards	Nobel Prizes Bronze Star Medal	Academy Award Stanley Cup
Planets, Stars, Constellations	Pluto Ursa Major	Betelgeuse Big Dipper

LANGUAGES, SPECIFIC COURSE NAMES, AND TITLES Rules 24d, 24e

OBJECTIVE

• To use proper nouns and proper adjectives in a descriptive letter

24d

> **NOTE:** Do not capitalize the word *earth* unless it is being used along with other astronomical names that are capitalized. The words *sun* and *moon* are never capitalized.

24d. Do *not* capitalize the names of school subjects, except for names of languages and course names followed by a number.

EXAMPLES **English, Latin, German, g**eography, **a**lgebra, **c**hemistry, **m**usic, **A**lgebra II, **C**hemistry I

> **NOTE:** Do not capitalize the class names *senior, junior, sophomore,* and *freshman* unless they are part of a proper noun.
>
> EXAMPLES   A number of **s**ophomores attended the **J**unior Prom.
> The **S**ophomore Singers performed for the **f**reshmen.

▶ REVIEW A

Correcting Sentences by Capitalizing Words

Identify the <u>words that should be capitalized</u> in each of the following sentences. Do not include the words already capitalized.

EXAMPLE   **1.** The spanish explorer juan ponce de león landed in florida in 1513.
    1. *Spanish, Juan, Ponce de León, Florida*

1. The area now known as <u>florida</u> was originally inhabited by <u>native</u> <u>american</u> peoples, including the <u>apalachees</u>, the <u>creeks</u>, and the <u>seminoles</u>.
2. The state is bounded on the north by <u>alabama</u> and <u>georgia</u>, on the east by the <u>atlantic</u> <u>ocean</u>, on the south by the <u>strait</u> of <u>florida</u> and the <u>gulf</u> of <u>mexico</u>, and on the west by <u>alabama</u> and the <u>gulf</u> of <u>mexico</u>.
3. The <u>spanish</u> founded <u>st</u>. <u>augustine</u>, the state's first permanent <u>european</u> settlement, in 1565, making it the oldest colonial city in the <u>united</u> <u>states</u>.
4. When <u>spain</u> ceded <u>florida</u> to the <u>united</u> <u>states</u> in 1819, the <u>u.s</u>. government demanded that the native peoples move west.
5. The strength and dignity of the <u>seminole</u> leader <u>osceola</u>, who led his people in the fight to retain

---

Teacher's ResourceBank™

▼ RESOURCES ▼

> **LANGUAGES, SPECIFIC COURSE NAMES, AND TITLES**
> • Titles

🦉 QUICK REMINDER

Write the following sentences on the chalkboard and ask volunteers to correct the capitalization errors:

1. Dr. Velez will be teaching spanish and a course in American History this year. [Spanish, history]
2. Angela is the best student in our psychology 101 class. [Psychology]
3. After struggling with algebra last year, I will take geometry 305 this year. [Geometry]
4. I saw the president addressing the press outside the white house. [President, White House]
5. My Uncle Ed is coming for sunday dinner. [uncle, Sunday]

MECHANICS

MECHANICS

OBJECTIVES
- To correct sentences by capitalizing words
- To proofread a paragraph for correct capitalization

VISUAL CONNECTIONS

Exploring the Subject. Osceola, the Seminole leader, became a victim of treachery when he was taken prisoner by an American general during a peace conference. He died in a prison near Charleston, South Carolina, in 1838.

COOPERATIVE LEARNING

Divide the class into groups of four or five students and have each group construct four compound-complex sentences that contain errors involving capitalization rules. Encourage students to refer to the exceptions and special problems for ideas. Have students select two of their sentences for you to write on the chalkboard for the class to correct. Award five points for each sentence that stumps the class. [Here is a sample sentence with errors yet to be added: Henry David Thoreau was an advocate of civil disobedience, and his ideas in the essay "On the Duty of Civil Disobedience" have been followed by important philosophers and statesmen such as Mohandas Gandhi, Leo Tolstoy, and Martin Luther King, Jr.]

MECHANICS

MECHANICS

774 *Capitalization*

George Catlin. "Osceola." Courtesy of the American Museum of National History, New York, 33771.

their lands, are evident in this 1838 painting by <u>george</u> <u>catlin</u>.

6. Most of the <u>seminoles</u> were eventually deported to present-day <u>oklahoma</u>, but a few hundred fled to the <u>everglades</u>, a huge wilderness area in south <u>florida</u> that now includes <u>everglades</u> <u>national</u> <u>park</u>.

7. Founded in 1886, <u>eatonville</u>, <u>florida</u>, is the oldest incorporated <u>african</u> <u>american</u> town in the <u>united</u> <u>states</u>.

8. After the <u>cuban</u> <u>revolution</u> in the late 1950s, and again in the early 1980s, many <u>cubans</u> fled to <u>miami</u>.

9. Miami has also served as a major point of entry for <u>haitian</u> refugees who've braved the <u>atlantic</u> <u>ocean</u> in search of a better life.

10. Among the <u>asians</u> who've settled in the state are refugees from <u>vietnam</u>, many of whom make their living fishing along the northern coast of <u>florida</u>.

REVIEW B   **Proofreading Paragraphs for Correct Capitalization**

Identify the <u>words that should be capitalized</u> in each sentence in the following paragraphs. Do not include the words already capitalized.

EXAMPLE   [1] Trivia games test your knowledge of subjects as diverse as american inventors, the korean war, and popular music.

1. *American, Korean War*

[1] Last <u>saturday</u>, <u>may</u> 18, my brother Ted and <u>i</u> finally won our first trivia match against our parents. [2] Some of the courses Ted is taking this semester are history, political science, and <u>french</u>; mine include <u>world</u> <u>literature</u> I and <u>geography</u> II. [3] We surged into the lead when our parents couldn't remember that the first <u>u.s.</u> satellite, *<u>explorer</u> I,* followed the <u>u.s.s.r.</u>'s *<u>sputnik</u> I* into space. [4] From geography class I remembered that <u>mount mckinley</u> is the highest point and <u>death</u> <u>valley</u> is the lowest point on the <u>north</u> <u>american</u> continent.   **4. McKinley**

[5] Our parents rallied for the lead by knowing that the boy on the <u>cracker</u> <u>jack</u> box is named <u>jack</u> and that his dog's name is <u>bingo</u>. [6] Then Ted came up with the fact that the steel framework of the <u>statue</u> of <u>liberty</u> was designed by the <u>frenchman</u> <u>alexandre</u> <u>gustave</u> <u>eiffel</u>, who also designed the <u>eiffel</u> <u>tower</u> in <u>paris</u>. [7] None of us knew that <u>john</u> <u>wilkes</u> <u>booth</u> was only twenty-six years old when he shot <u>president</u> <u>lincoln</u> at <u>ford's</u> <u>theater</u> on <u>good</u> <u>friday</u> in 1865. [8] Mom, who's a loyal <u>democrat</u>, knew that *<u>engine</u> 1401*—the <u>southern</u> <u>railways</u> locomotive that carried <u>franklin</u> <u>d.</u> <u>roosevelt's</u> body from <u>warm</u> <u>springs</u>, <u>georgia</u>, to <u>washington</u>, <u>d.c.</u>—can now be seen in the <u>smithsonian</u> <u>institution</u>.

[9] Ted and I lost some points because I didn't know that <u>kleenex</u> tissues were first used as gas-mask filters during <u>world</u> <u>war</u> I. [10] But Ted won the game for us by remembering that the <u>white</u> <u>house</u> was called the <u>executive</u> <u>mansion</u> before it was burned by the <u>british</u> during the <u>war</u> of 1812.

PICTURE THIS

The year is 1850. After seeing this handbill, you and a friend decided to sign on as deckhands on the Mississippi River steamboat. Your friend, however, backed out at the

NOW HIRING
★Deck Hands★
★Roustabouts★
Wages Paid In
$ CASH $
STEAMER
ROB'T E. LEE
Leave St. Louis for New Orleans
Friday, July 9th at 8:30 A.M.
See Mr. Armstrong at Longyman's Wharf

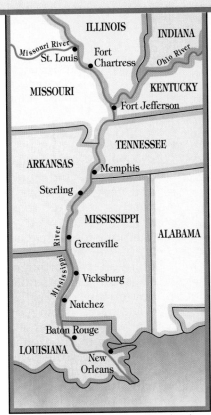

last minute. You've just completed your first trip down the river from St. Louis to New Orleans. Using this map, write a letter to your friend describing your experiences on the trip. Give reasons why your friend should (or should not) sign on for the next trip. In your letter, use a combined total of at least ten proper nouns and proper adjectives.

Subject: working as a deckhand on a nineteenth-century steamship
Audience: a friend
Purpose: to persuade

24e. Capitalize titles.

(1) Capitalize the title of a person when it comes before a name.

EXAMPLES **General** Powell **Dr.** Sakamoto **President** Kennedy

Do not capitalize a title used alone or following a name, especially if the title is preceded by *a, an,* or *the.*

EXAMPLES In 1987, Wilma Mankiller became the first woman elected **p**rincipal **c**hief of the Cherokee Nation of Oklahoma.
Who was **p**resident during World War II?
Ann Richards became the **g**overnor of Texas in 1991.

MECHANICS

LEP/ESL

General Strategies. You may need to explain the term *title* to students. Before you begin your explanation, be sure students understand that this word is used for both people and documents. Students might get a clearer picture if you draw a stick figure, a book, and a painting on the chalkboard and show how each has a title. For example, you may write *Dr. Nguyen* under the stick figure, *Don Quixote* under the book, and *Mona Lisa* under the painting.

When a title is used without a person's name in direct address, it is usually capitalized.

EXAMPLES   Ms. **M**ayor, will you please test the microphone?
Do you intend to visit the disaster area, **G**overnor?
Please be seated, **S**ir [or sir].

NOTE: For special emphasis or clarity, writers sometimes capitalize a title used alone or following a person's name.

      EXAMPLES   The **G**overnor firmly stated her opinion on the issue.
                    According to the **P**resident, America needs to strengthen its industrial base.
                    Her predecessor called the new **P**rincipal **C**hief "the absolute best person for the job."

(2) Capitalize words showing family relationship when used with a person's name but *not* when preceded by a possessive.

EXAMPLES   **A**unt Edith, **U**ncle Fred, **G**randmother Bechtel, my **b**rother, your **c**ousin, Maria's **n**iece

(3) Capitalize the first and last words and all important words in titles of books, periodicals, poems, stories, plays, historical documents, movies, radio and television programs, works of art, and musical compositions.

Unimportant words in a title include

- articles: *a, an, the*
- short prepositions (fewer than five letters): *of, to, in, for, from, with*
- coordinating conjunctions: *and, but, so, nor, or, yet, for*

TYPE OF TITLE	EXAMPLES
Books	*Songs of the Tewa* *One of the Lucky Ones* *Poetry Is Alive and Well and Living in America*
Periodicals	*U.S. News & World Report* *Chicago Sun-Times*

(continued)

MECHANICS

MECHANICS

INTEGRATING THE LANGUAGE ARTS

Literature Link. Contrast the traditional capitalization pattern of a Gwendolyn Brooks poem with that of an E. E. Cummings poem that does not conform to capitalization rules.

Ask students for ideas about the effects of capitalization patterns in poetry. [A possible response is that a humorous or whimsical tone is heightened by using lowercase letters at the beginning of lines of poetry.]

TYPE OF TITLE	EXAMPLES
Poems	"Love Without Love" "I Like to See It Lap the Miles"
Stories	"The Man to Send Rain Clouds" "The Woman Who Had No Eye for Small Details"
Plays	*A Raisin in the Sun* *Life with Father* *Sunday in the Park with George*
Historical Documents	**Treaty of Versailles** **Emancipation Proclamation** **Charter of the United Nations**
Movies	*Lean on Me* *North by Northwest* *The Corn Is Green*
Radio and Television Programs	*War of the Worlds* *Face the Nation* *You Can't Do That on Television*
Works of Art	*Crossing the Brook* *Two Mexican Women and Child*
Musical Compositions	"Ebony and Ivory" *Pictures at an Exhibition* *Amahl and the Night Visitors*

NOTE: The words *a, an,* and *the* written before a title are capitalized only when they are the first word of the title. They are usually not capitalized, however, at the beginning of the names of most magazines and newspapers.

EXAMPLES   Last summer, Joan read *The Outsiders* and *A Day in the Life of President Kennedy.*
Joan reads the *Atlantic Monthly* and the *Rocky Mountain News.*

 REFERENCE NOTE: For information about which titles should be italicized and which should be placed in quotation marks, see pages 831–832 and 840.

(4) Capitalize names of religions and their followers, holy days and celebrations, holy writings, and specific deities.

MECHANICS

MECHANICS

REVIEWS C and D

OBJECTIVES

- To correct sentences by capitalizing words
- To proofread paragraphs for correct capitalization

TYPE OF NAME	EXAMPLES	
Religions and Followers	Judaism Buddhism Christianity	Moslem Taoist Mormon
Holy Days and Celebrations	Ash Wednesday Ramadan Yom Kippur	Hanukkah Potlatch Pentecost
Holy Writings	the Bible the Talmud the Koran	Rig-Veda Exodus Dead Sea Scrolls
Specific Deities	Allah God	Vishnu the Holy Spirit

The words *god* and *goddess* are not capitalized when they refer to the deities of ancient mythology. The names of specific mythological deities are capitalized, however.

EXAMPLE   **Ceres** was the Roman **goddess** of grain.

NOTE: Some writers capitalize all pronouns that refer to the Deity. Other writers capitalize such pronouns only to prevent confusion.

EXAMPLE   Job wondered why the Lord allowed His servant to suffer.

REVIEW C   **Correcting Sentences by Capitalizing Words**

If the capitalization of a sentence is correct, write C. If not, write the correct form of each word that needs correcting. Words that should be capitalized or lowercased are underscored.

1. At the <u>hirshhorn museum</u> in <u>washington</u>, <u>d.c.</u>, we saw one of <u>georgia o'keeffe's</u> finest paintings, <u>cow's skull</u>, <u>red</u>, <u>white</u> and <u>blue</u>.
2. Kim read about <u>bill cosby's</u> television series <u>the cosby show</u> in <u>people</u> magazine.
3. When I visited <u>grandma</u> Sánchez at <u>white sparrow</u> Hospital, I read to her from <u>jimmy santiago baca's</u> <u>martín</u> and <u>meditations</u> on the <u>south valley</u>.
4. In 1908, <u>mary baker eddy</u> founded the <u>christian science monitor</u>.

COOPERATIVE LEARNING
Divide the class into groups of no more than five students. Ask them to write skits with roles for gods and goddesses from Greek, Roman, Norse, Asian, Egyptian, or Native American mythologies. Each student should be responsible for creating dialogue for at least one character. Ask groups to hand in copies of the skits so that you can check for understanding of the appropriate capitalization rules.

You may want to have the groups perform their skits for the class.

MECHANICS

MECHANICS

5. My cousin Judy's favorite statue is *indian hunter* by <u>paul</u> manship.
6. I enjoyed reading <u>annie</u> <u>dillard's</u> *pilgrim at tinker creek*, particularly the chapter "<u>the</u> <u>horns</u> of the <u>altar</u>."
7. Prize-winning journalist <u>carl</u> <u>t</u>. <u>rowan</u> was the first <u>african</u> <u>american</u> to serve on the National Security <u>council</u>.
8. The <u>president</u> addressed the <u>american</u> people in a television news broadcast after he had met with the president of France.
9. Last week <u>mayor</u> <u>johnson</u> and the county commissioners attended the groundbreaking ceremony for the new hospital.
10. Jane White, president of our <u>latin</u> <u>club</u>, showed us a videotape of *julius caesar*.

▶ REVIEW D **Proofreading Paragraphs for Correct Capitalization**

If the capitalization in a sentence is correct, write *C*. If not, write the correct form of each word that needs correcting.
Words that should be capitalized or lowercased are underscored.

EXAMPLE [1] The energetic personality of montana's state Senator from the Fiftieth District really comes through in this painting by Christopher Magadini.

1. *Montana's, senator*

[1] Bill Yellowtail, <u>jr</u>., the first member of the <u>crows</u> to serve in the <u>State</u> <u>Senate</u>, represents an area hit hard by drought and a decline in the demand for beef. [2] Yellowtail, a <u>democrat</u>, ran for office to help save the <u>Area's</u> remaining small family farms and ranches. [3] A <u>Rancher</u> himself, he raises cattle in the Lodge Grass <u>valley</u> in <u>Southeastern</u> Montana with his <u>Mother</u>, his brother, and his sister.

[4] Between <u>Legislative</u> sessions, Yellowtail supplements his income from ranching by outfitting fly-fishing trips on the Bighorn <u>river</u>. [5] He also works as a <u>Tour</u> <u>Guide</u> on the Crow reservation and at the Custer <u>battlefield</u> <u>national</u> <u>monument</u>. [6] In addition, he's a consultant for the Montana-<u>wyoming</u> Agriculture-Tourist Project,

which is helping ranchers diversify into tourism, and he's on the <u>Board</u> of <u>Directors</u> of the Nature Conservancy.

[7] After graduating from Lodge Grass <u>high</u> <u>school</u> at the head of his class, Yellowtail attended <u>dartmouth</u> College in <u>hanover</u>, New Hampshire. [8] Although Dartmouth was founded to educate <u>american</u> Indians, Yellowtail was the first <u>native</u> <u>american</u> to enroll there in twenty years. [9] At first he felt unprepared academically, but when he graduated in 1971, he was on the <u>Dean's</u> list. [10] Yellowtail majored in <u>Geography</u> because, he says, "<u>the</u> relationship between humanity and the environment is little understood; it's a <u>Discipline</u> we very much need today."

 VISUAL CONNECTIONS
Related Expression Skills. Ask students to create a montage or a collage of an individual they know. They should combine a photograph with other illustrations that connect the person's image to a wider environment. Then you may want students to write a paragraph that explains the collage, with details that include proper nouns and proper adjectives.

MECHANICS

MECHANICS

WRITING APPLICATION

Writing guidebooks will require students to use proper nouns and adjectives as they describe features and attractions in their town. You may wish to refer your students to **Chapters 5** and **7** for information about using descriptive detail and writing to inform.

CRITICAL THINKING
Analysis

Remind students that their audience will probably not be familiar with American slang or jargon. Directions must be stated with absolute precision. Students should analyze their material to correct ambiguities.

PREWRITING

Remind students that their Japanese audience will probably be interested in aspects of American life that Americans take for granted. Tell students to check community calendars for special events and exhibits that illustrate regional American culture and history. An arts-and-crafts fair or a regional foods festival could provide a central theme for the guidebook.

EVALUATING AND REVISING

If available, word processors allow students a great deal of flexibility in revising their work. However, students should be reminded that spell-check and grammar-check options are not foolproof. Most systems are not capable of recognizing proper nouns or capitalization errors.

WRITING APPLICATION

Using Capital Letters Correctly

Capital letters are signals. They let your readers know that you're starting a new sentence or that you're referring to a specific person, place, or thing. Notice how the use of capital letters affects the meaning in the following examples:

> To reach the old pioneer settlement, cross the little Yellow River and turn right at the sandy road exit.
> To reach the Old Pioneer Settlement, cross the Little Yellow River and turn right at the Sandy Road exit.

▶ WRITING ACTIVITY

You've been asked to write a guidebook for a group of visitors from your town's sister city in Japan. Write an informative booklet that helps your visitors take a brief walking or driving tour through your town.

Prewriting List the sights you'll include in your guidebook. (If you live in a small town, you may want to include some nearby points of interest. If yours is a large city, you'll have to limit the tour to only one part of town or only main sights.) For information on the town's history, you may want to check the local library.

Writing As you write your first draft, keep in mind that this is your guests' first visit. Try to anticipate their questions without overloading them with details. If you'd like to, sketch a map of your tour with the various stops labeled.

Evaluating and Revising Take a friend on a trial run of the tour. Is the route you've chosen a sensible one? Have you included enough information about each point of interest, and is the information correct? If you made a map, be sure to check it, too. Then add, delete, change, or rearrange items to make your guide book clearer and more interesting.

Proofreading and Publishing Proofread your guidebook carefully, paying special attention to the correct use of capital letters. Remember to proofread your map if you included

OBJECTIVES

- To capitalize sentences correctly
- To capitalize sentences in a paragraph correctly

one. Naturally, you'll also want to make sure that your grammar and usage are faultless for the visitors. After sharing your guidebook with your classmates, you could compile a larger guide to your town or city and give it to new students. You could also offer copies to the local chamber of commerce or historical society.

Review: Posttest

A. Capitalizing Sentences Correctly

For each of the following sentences, write the <u>words that should be capitalized</u>.

EXAMPLE   **1.** Renée searched everywhere in freeport, maine, until she found a gift at I. I. bean for her grandparents.
1. *Freeport, Maine, L. L. Bean*

1. The title of her new television special, which airs next fall, is <u>*one* in a *million*</u>.
2. Both <u>ernest</u> <u>hemingway</u> and <u>walt</u> <u>disney</u> once worked for the <u>*kansas* *city* *star*</u>.
3. Every <u>thanksgiving</u> <u>day</u> before dinner, <u>grandma</u> <u>penny</u> sings "<u>we</u> <u>praise</u> <u>thee</u>, <u>o</u> <u>god</u>, <u>our</u> <u>redeemer</u>, <u>creator</u>," which was translated from the <u>german</u> by <u>julia</u> <u>b.</u> <u>cady</u> <u>cory</u>.
4. In 1982, <u>colombian</u> writer <u>gabriel</u> <u>garcía</u> <u>márquez</u> was awarded the <u>nobel</u> <u>prize</u> in literature.
5. The winner of the first <u>kentucky</u> <u>derby</u>, the annual race at <u>churchill</u> <u>downs</u> in <u>louisville</u>, was a horse named <u>aristides</u>.
6. In 1983, <u>sally</u> <u>ride</u> became the first <u>american</u> woman in space when the space shuttle <u>*challenger*</u> was launched from <u>cape</u> <u>canaveral</u>, <u>florida</u>.
7. One of the cities of the <u>incas</u>, <u>machu</u> <u>picchu</u>, lay hidden among the <u>andes</u> <u>mountains</u> in southern <u>peru</u> and was never discovered by the <u>spanish</u> conquerors.

8. Frederick <u>douglass</u> was the first <u>african</u> <u>american</u> member of the <u>department</u> of <u>justice's</u> <u>u</u>.<u>s</u>. <u>marshals</u> <u>service</u>.
9. If Beth passes <u>english</u> and <u>history</u> II, her parents will let her apply for a job at the 7-<u>eleven</u> store on <u>forty</u>-third <u>street</u>.
10. Our debate team argued in favor of pro-<u>american</u> economic policies as the best way to foster democracy in the developing countries of <u>africa</u>, <u>asia</u>, and <u>south</u> <u>america</u>.

B. Capitalizing a Paragraph Correctly

For each sentence in the following paragraph, write the <u>words that should be capitalized</u>.

EXAMPLE　[1] Last summer we visited my uncle carlos, who lives in new york city.
　　　　1. *Uncle Carlos, New York City*

[11] One of <u>new</u> <u>york</u> <u>city's</u> most popular tourist attractions is the <u>empire</u> <u>state</u> <u>building</u>. [12] The building, at <u>fifth</u> <u>avenue</u> and <u>thirty</u>-fourth <u>street</u>, attracts 2,500,000 visitors a year. [13] Among them are troops of <u>boy</u> <u>scouts</u> and <u>girl</u> <u>scouts</u>, who camp out on the eighty-sixth floor. [14] The building was financed by <u>john</u> <u>jacob</u> <u>raskob</u>, the founder of <u>general</u> <u>motors</u>. [15] It opened in 1931, during the <u>great</u> <u>depression</u>. [16] At the time, it was the tallest building on earth (1,250 feet), but it's since been overshadowed by the <u>world</u> <u>trade</u> <u>center</u> (1,350 feet) and by <u>chicago's</u> <u>sears</u> <u>tower</u> (1,450 feet). [17] The observatory on the one hundred and second floor accounts for much of the <u>empire</u> <u>state</u> <u>building's</u> continuing appeal; when the weather is clear, it provides a view of five states: <u>new</u> <u>york</u>, <u>new</u> <u>jersey</u>, <u>connecticut</u>, <u>pennsylvania</u>, and <u>massachusetts</u>. [18] On <u>may</u> 1, 1991, publicists threw a party to mark the building's sixtieth birthday. [19] One of those who attended was actress <u>fay</u> <u>wray</u>, who starred in the 1933 movie *king kong*, in which the building was featured. [20] Another attendee was <u>jack</u> <u>brod</u>, one of the original tenants, who proclaimed of the building, "<u>it's</u> got history woven into it."

SUMMARY STYLE REVIEW

Names of Persons

Mrs. Andrew D. McCall, Jr.	a family friend
Sean Jackson	the boy next door
Mr. Hank Bluehouse	a guidance counselor

Geographical Names

Kansas City	a city in Missouri
Cook County	a county in Illinois
Diego Garcia Island	an island in the Indian Ocean
Rocky Mountains	a mountain range
Arctic Ocean	on the ocean floor
Seventy-first Street	a busy street
Torreya State Park	a state park
in the West, South, Midwest	turning west, south, north

Organizations, Business Firms, Institutions, Government Bodies

Perfect Harmony Glee Club	a choral club
Head over Heels, Inc.	a gymnastics training center
Lane High School	an inner-city high school
Supreme Court	a federal court
Department of the Treasury	a department of government

Historical Events and Periods, Special Events, Calendar Items

the Vietnam War	a long war
the Ice Age	a prehistoric age
the World Series	a series of baseball games
Memorial Day	a national holiday
March, June, September, December	spring, summer, autumn, winter

Nationalities, Races, Religions

Australian	a nationality
Caucasian	a race
Christianity	a religion
God	myths about the Greek gods

(continued)

MECHANICS

MECHANICS

SUMMARY STYLE REVIEW *(continued)*

Brand Names

Chevrolet Blazer	an **automobile**
Amana	a **refrigerator**

Other Particular Places, Things, Events, Awards

Enterprise	an aircraft **carrier**
Silver Streak	a train
Discovery	a spacecraft
Bancroft Prize in History	an award
the **Milky Way**	a galaxy
Earth, Mercury, Neptune	here on **earth**
the **Lincoln Memorial**	a **memorial** in Washington
Junior Prom	a **junior** in high school
Medal of Freedom	a cherished **medal**

Specific Courses, Languages

Carpentry I	after **carpentry** class
Japanese	a foreign **language**
World History II	a history test

Titles

Mayor Feinstein	a **mayor**
the **President of the** **United States**	the **president** of the club
the **Prince of Wales**	a **prince's** hobby
Uncle Jim	her **uncle**
The Color Purple	a novel
the *Sacramento Bee*	a daily **newspaper**
Holy Bible	a religious **book**

DIAGNOSTIC TEST

OBJECTIVE

- To correct sentences by adding end marks and commas

25 PUNCTUATION

End Marks and Commas

Diagnostic Test

Correcting Sentences by Adding End Marks and Commas

Add end marks and commas where they are needed in the following sentences.   Optional commas are circled.

EXAMPLE   **1.** Well what do you want me to say
             1. *Well, what do you want me to say?*

1. Although scholars aren't certain about who was the first European printer to use movable type⊙Johann Gutenberg is usually credited⊙

2. The students who have signed up for the field trip may leave at noon⊙but all others must attend classes⊙

3. Gloria⊙did you notice where I left my bowling ball and bowling shoes **?**

4. Miriam Colón⊙who was born in Puerto Rico⊙founded the Puerto Rican Traveling Theatre.

Teacher's ResourceBank™
RESOURCES

FOR THE WHOLE CHAPTER
- Chapter Review Form A
- Chapter Review Form B
- Assessment Portfolio
    Mechanics Pretests
    Mechanics Mastery Tests

CHAPTER OVERVIEW

This chapter contains rules for using end marks and commas. The first section reviews the use of end marks and their role as indicators of the purpose of sentences, as well as the use of periods in abbreviations. The remainder of the chapter deals with the use of commas to set off items in a series, adjectives preceding a noun, independent clauses, certain introductory elements, non-essential phrases, clauses, and interrupters. Comma usage in conventional situations is also covered. The **Writing Application** challenges students to apply their knowledge of end marks and in the creation of instructions for an original game. You may wish to refer to the chapter throughout the year and make individual assignments as students' writing reveals their needs.

USING THE DIAGNOSTIC TEST

If students are having problems with using end marks or commas correctly in writing, you can use the results of this test to pinpoint error patterns and specific strengths and weaknesses. You can then assign practice accordingly.

MECHANICS

MECHANICS

5. The Great Pyramid of Cheops, in Egypt, dates back to 2680 BC.

6. Vendors sold T-shirts, buttons, caps, and pennants to the sports fans outside the stadium.

7. Listening to my friend's grandfather talk about the Mexican Revolution, I realized that I'm proud to be Mexican American.

8. The hikers munched on unsalted sunflower seeds and quenched their thirst with ice-cold, refreshing spring water.

9. Their address, I think, is 1042 Cleveland Ave, Enid, OK 73703.

10. Marian Anderson, a contralto, was the first African American to become a permanent member of the Metropolitan Opera Company.

11. Rita did not call me this morning, nor did she call in the afternoon.

12. We rushed to the airport, stood in line, bought our tickets, and then heard that the flight would be delayed for three hours.

13. Norm has had an incredible run of bad luck, yet he still says that tomorrow will be a better day, for he prides himself on being an optimist.

14. The Ming vase, wrapped in cotton and packed in a crate, was delivered to the museum today.

15. If we're late for practice again, however, Ms. Stubbs will kick us off the team.

16. How lucky I was that my sister had taught me how to swim, for I could have drowned when the boat tipped over!

17. Early in the eighteenth century, Chikamatsu Monzaemon wrote the first Japanese tragedies to focus on the lives of common, ordinary people.

18. Nowadays the Sioux, generally speaking, make their living as farmers and ranchers.

19. Jan Matzeliger, an inventor in Lynn, Massachusetts, revolutionized the shoe industry in 1883 with his machine that joined the top of a shoe to its sole.

20. These four students should report to the auditorium after lunch: Bob Wilcox, Amalia Gibson, Cora Mall, and Phil Assad, Jr.

END MARKS Rules 25a–25e

OBJECTIVE

• To correct sentences by adding appropriate end marks

In speaking, your tone of voice, your pauses, and your gestures and facial expressions help you express yourself. In writing, punctuation marks help you communicate these elements.

End Marks

End marks—periods, question marks, and exclamation points—indicate the purpose of a sentence. Periods are also used in many abbreviations.

☞ REFERENCE NOTE: For information on how sentences are classified according to purpose, see pages 565–566.

25a. A statement (*or* declarative sentence) is followed by a period.

EXAMPLES Margaret Walker's poems celebrate the trials and triumphs of African Americans.
Barb asked who could give her a ride home.

As the second example above shows, a declarative sentence containing an indirect question is followed by a period.

25b. A question (*or* interrogative sentence) is followed by a question mark.

EXAMPLES What score did you get on the road test?
Weren't you nervous?

A direct question should be followed by a question mark even if its word order is like that of a declarative sentence.

EXAMPLES You got what score on the road test?
You weren't nervous?

NOTE: Be sure to distinguish between a declarative sentence that contains an indirect question and an interrogative sentence, which asks a direct question.

INDIRECT QUESTION She asked me who nominated him.
[declarative]
DIRECT QUESTION Who nominated him? [interrogative]

MECHANICS

Teacher's ResourceBank™

RESOURCES

END MARKS
• Using End Marks

🦉 **QUICK REMINDER**
Write on the chalkboard the following sentences, omitting the end marks:

1. The parachute failed to open!
2. Please be calm.
3. Are you all right?

Ask students to identify the purposes of these sentences (to state, to question, to exclaim, or to command or request) and to suggest end marks that convey these purposes.

MEETING
INDIVIDUAL
NEEDS

LEP/ESL

Spanish. Exclamation points and question marks are used somewhat differently in Spanish than they are in English. In Spanish these marks are used at the beginnings of sentences as well as at the ends and are inverted at the beginnings of sentences. Students who have been in the United States for a lengthy period of time will probably already be familiar with the English format, but newly arrived students may need additional practice in making this shift in punctuation.

MECHANICS

COOPERATIVE LEARNING
Divide the class into groups of three or four and have the members of each group collaborate to write a very short story. Students should omit end marks of any kind in their final drafts. Have groups exchange papers to supply end marks. Encourage students to try to create sentences that invite various interpretations when not punctuated.

INTEGRATING THE LANGUAGE ARTS
Punctuation and Capitalization. Exercise 1 asks students to write the first words of the sentences that follow the end marks they add. You could take this opportunity to remind students of the punctuation rule requiring that the first words of sentences be capitalized.

25c. An exclamation is followed by an exclamation point.

EXAMPLES   Great shot!
Oh, no! Not again!

Declarative and interrogative sentences that express strong emotion may be followed by an exclamation point instead of a period or a question mark.

EXAMPLES   There you are!
Why are you always late!

25d. An imperative sentence is followed by either a period or an exclamation point.

EXAMPLES   Open the door, please.
Open the door!

An imperative sentence may be stated in the form of a question. However, since its purpose is to give a command or make a request, it should be followed by a period or an exclamation point.

EXAMPLES   May I have your attention, please.
Will you pay attention!

▶ EXERCISE 1   **Correcting Sentences by Adding End Marks**

For each of the following paragraphs, write each <u>word that should be followed by an end mark,</u> and add the appropriate end mark. Then, if a sentence follows the end mark, write the first word of that sentence.
Triple underscores indicate capitalization.

EXAMPLE   [1]   What striking costumes the musicians on the next page are wearing they're members of *Campanas de América,* a mariachi group in San Antonio, Texas

1.   *wearing! They're; Texas.*

[1] Have you ever heard mariachi <u>music</u>?<u>t</u>his lively, infectious music originated in central <u>Mexico</u>.
[2] Before the nineteenth century, Mexican music was played by string ensembles or wind <u>bands</u>?around 1800 the two types of groups <u>merged</u>?the resulting sound came to be known as <u>mariachi</u>.

[3] As social gatherings became larger, brass instruments such as cornets and trumpets were <u>added</u>.adding the brasses made the music easier to hear above the sounds of <u>dancing</u>.usually only the lyrics of the songs were written <u>down</u>.younger players learned the melodies by <u>ear</u>.did you know that some schools now offer courses in Mexican folk music and award academic credit for playing in a mariachi <u>ensemble</u>**?**colleges, junior and senior high schools, and even elementary schools are incorporating mariachi music into the <u>curriculum</u>.

[4] Now young mariachi players are studying music theory and writing their own mariachi music, sometimes adding instruments such as trombones, fluegelhorns, and <u>accordions</u>.consequently, mariachi is <u>changing</u>.some older players dislike the <u>changes</u>.most people, however, applaud the music's new <u>flexibility</u>.they ask how mariachi can grow if it doesn't <u>change</u>.

[5] And growing is just what mariachi's <u>doing</u>.it's becoming more popular each <u>year</u>.in fact, the annual mariachi festival filled California's eighteen-thousand-seat Hollywood Bowl when the festival was launched in <u>1990</u>.<u>w</u>hat an exciting event that must have <u>been</u>**!**

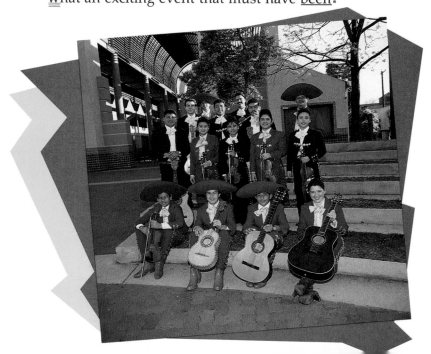

MECHANICS

MECHANICS

**VISUAL CONNECTIONS
Ideas for Writing.** Mariachi music's growing popularity is just one example of new interest in the rich and varied contributions of diverse ethnic groups to United States culture.

Have students write expressive/descriptive paragraphs about their favorite contributions to culture in the United States by ethnic groups other than their own. For example, students could write about a type of food that they enjoy, such as Vietnamese food; a type of music, such as Jamaican reggae; or a holiday, such as St. Patrick's Day.

COMMON ERROR

Problem. Students might confuse abbreviations with acronyms.

Solution. Explain that while an abbreviation is usually a shortened form of one word and is followed by a period, an acronym is a shortened form of a series of words and is not followed by a period.

Examples of acronyms are *NASA* (National Aeronautics and Space Administration) and *radar* (radio detecting and ranging).

Tell each student to list five acronyms and to give the series of words represented by each.

INTEGRATING THE LANGUAGE ARTS

Mechanics and Dictionary Skills. Explain to students that abbreviations like *Mr.* are alphabetized as if they were unabbreviated. For example, *Mr.* would be alphabetized with words beginning with *mi* rather than *mr.*

REVIEW A
OBJECTIVE
• To write original sentences that correctly use the three types of end marks

792 *Punctuation*

25e. An abbreviation is usually followed by a period.

TYPE OF ABBREVIATION	EXAMPLES		
Personal Names	W.E.B. Du Bois Susan B. Anthony W. H. Auden N. Scott Momaday		
Organizations and Companies	Assn. Co.	Corp. Inc.	Ltd. Org.
Titles Used with Names	Mr. Ms.	Mrs. Jr.	Dr. Ph. D.
Units of Measure	oz. lb.	in. ft.	cu. yd. sq. mi.
Time of Day	A.M.	P.M.	
Years	B.C. (written after the date) A.D. (written before the date)		
Addresses	Ave. Blvd.	St. Rd.	Pkwy. P.O. Box
States	Calif. Ind.	Tex. Fla.	Mass. N.Y.

NOTE: Two-letter state codes are used only when the ZIP code is included. Two-letter state codes are not followed by periods.

EXAMPLE   Nashville, TN 37201

When an abbreviation that ends with a period comes at the end of a statement, do not add another period as an end mark. *Do* add a question mark or an exclamation point if one is needed.

EXAMPLES   The history of Egypt dates back to before 3000 B.C.
When did she move to St. Louis, Mo.?

Some common abbreviations are often written without periods.

EXAMPLES   TV, OK, VCR, CD, DNA, NAACP, UN, IQ, YWCA, COBOL, mph, km, cm, ml, kg, hp, lb, rpm, cc, psi

NOTE: Most abbreviations are capitalized only if the words they stand for are capitalized. If you're not sure whether to use periods with an abbreviation or whether to capitalize it, look it up in a dictionary.

SEGMENT 3 *(pp. 793–811)*
COMMAS Rules 25f–25m

OBJECTIVES

- To proofread sentences and to add commas to separate items in a series and to separate two or more adjectives preceding a noun
- To proofread sentences and to add commas to separate independent clauses joined by coordinating conjunctions

Commas **793**

25 e–f

REVIEW A   Using End Marks

This chart shows the results of a 1990 *TV Guide* poll that asked people what types of TV shows they'd be willing to pay to see. Write five sentences expressing your reactions to the poll's results. Use each type of end mark—period, question mark, and exclamation point—at least once.

EXAMPLE   **1.** *Why didn't the poll ask about science fiction shows?*

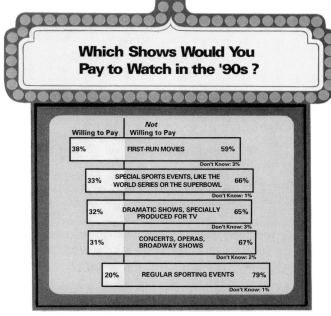

Commas

Items in a Series

25f. Use commas to separate items in a series.

EXAMPLES   The camp counselor distributed baseballs, bats, volleyballs, tennis rackets, and bandages. [words]

We have a government of the people, by the people, and for the people. [phrases]

I know I will pass the test if I take good notes, if I study hard, and if I get a good night's sleep. [clauses]

ANSWERS
Review A

Students' sentences should express their reactions to the poll's results. Be sure that students have used the three types of end marks correctly.

MECHANICS

MECHANICS

Teacher's ResourceBank™
RESOURCES

COMMAS
- Commas and Items in a Series
- Commas to Separate Adjectives
- Commas to Join Clauses
- Commas with Nonessential Elements
- Commas with Introductory Elements
- Commas with Elements That Interrupt
- Other Uses of Commas

793

- To proofread sentences and to add commas to set off nonessential phrases and clauses
- To proofread sentences and to add commas after certain introductory elements
- To proofread sentences and to add commas to set off nonrestrictive appositives and appositive phrases
- To proofread sentences and to add commas in certain conventional situations
- To write a dialogue that uses end marks and commas correctly

QUICK REMINDER

Write the following sentences on the chalkboard and have students tell you where commas should be inserted:

1. I met Bette who lives next door yesterday.

2. Bette knows the names biographical dates and accomplishments of the leaders of the Civil Rights movement.

3. She has a photo of Martin Luther King Jr. but she also wants a poster of him.

MEETING
INDIVIDUAL
NEEDS

LEP/ESL

General Strategies. ESL students typically retain those aspects of the English language that they can use immediately, especially those aspects that best support their ability to communicate needs and desires. Knowing when and where to insert commas may not seem particularly useful or meaningful to them. When introducing students to standard punctuation, it is important to keep in mind the very different sets of learning priorities that they bring to the classroom.

When the last two items in a series are joined by *and,* you may omit the comma before the *and* if the comma isn't needed to make the meaning clear.

CLEAR WITHOUT COMMA   The entertainers sang, danced and juggled.

NOT CLEAR WITHOUT COMMA   John, Sue and Mary went fishing.
[Did John go fishing, or is he being addressed?]

CLEAR WITH COMMA   John, Sue, and Mary went fishing.

NOTE: Some words—such as *macaroni and cheese* and *law and order*—are paired so often that they may be considered one item in a series.

EXAMPLE   For lunch we could order a sandwich, macaroni and cheese, or soup.

(1) If all items in a series are joined by *and, or,* or *nor,* do not use commas to separate them.

EXAMPLES   We ran **and** walked **and** even limped to the finish line.

Neither poverty **nor** discrimination **nor** lack of encouragement prevented Alice Walker from becoming an accomplished writer.

(2) Independent clauses in a series are usually separated by semicolons. Short independent clauses, however, may be separated by commas.

EXAMPLES   To prepare for the race, we swam twenty-five laps in the pool; we jogged four miles around the lake; and we exercised with workout equipment.

We swam, we jogged, and we exercised.

☞ REFERENCE NOTE: Also see rule 25h on page 796.

25g.   Use a comma to separate two or more adjectives preceding a noun.

EXAMPLE   I've had a long, hectic, tiring day.

When the last adjective before a noun is thought of as part of the noun, omit the comma before the adjective.

EXAMPLE   I mailed the package at the main post office.

For lunch we had smooth, creamy broccoli soup.

25g

Compound nouns such as *post office* and *broccoli soup* are considered single units rather than two separate words.

You can use two tests to determine whether an adjective and a noun form a unit.

TEST 1: Insert the word *and* between the adjectives. If *and* fits sensibly between them, use a comma. In the first example above, *and* cannot be logically inserted: *main and post office.* In the second sentence, *and* sounds sensible between the first two adjectives (*smooth and creamy*) but not between the second and third (*creamy and broccoli*).

TEST 2: Change the order of the adjectives. If the order of the adjectives can be reversed sensibly, use a comma. *Creamy, smooth broccoli soup* makes sense, but *broccoli creamy soup* and *post main office* do not.

▶ EXERCISE 2 **Correcting Sentences by Adding Commas**

Write each word that should be followed by a comma, and then add the comma. If a comma may or may not be used, circle the word and the comma. If a sentence is correct, write *C.*

EXAMPLE **1.** The singer wore a red vest blue shoes and white jeans.
　　　　1. vest, shoes,

1. I was late because my alarm clock didn't go off, we were out of milk, and the school bus had a flat tire.
2. The river overflowed again and filled our basement and our neighbors' basements. **2.** C
3. Coriander, cumin, and saffron are three spices widely used in traditional Mexican cooking.
4. I took a flashlight, a sleeping bag, extra tennis shoes, a pocket knife, and a parka on our camping trip.
5. Magic Johnson, Michael Jordan, Larry Bird, and Julius Erving have received Most Valuable Player Awards.
6. At the gymnastics meet Les performed on the parallel bars, the rings, and the high bar.
7. A little blond child in faded blue jeans emerged from the shrubbery to stare at the mail carrier. **7.** C

MECHANICS

MECHANICS

INTEGRATING THE LANGUAGE ARTS

Literature Link. Students often become confused when they read literature in which authors seem to disregard punctuation rules like the ones in this segment. Have students read a story in which the standard rules for comma usage are not always followed. "The Genuine Mexican Plug" by Mark Twain is a good choice. Ask students to find at least two examples of comma usage in the story that contradict the rules in this segment. Students should be prepared to name the rules that are contradicted by their examples.

Point out to students that creative writers often experiment with punctuation, and that, possibly as a result of such experimentation, the rules for punctuation change over time. Remind students that the English language is not static; it changes to meet the communication needs of a changing world. See **Chapter 14: "English: Origins and Uses"** for more information about the dynamic nature of the English language.

8. Gwendolyn Brooks, Toni Morrison, and Alice Walker have each won a Pulitzer Prize for their writing.
9. Have you read any of the novels by Jane Austen or the Brontë sisters or Virginia Woolf? **9.** C
10. With a quick, powerful leap, the stuntman bounded over the burning balcony.

Independent Clauses

25h. Use a comma before *and, but, or, nor, for, so,* and *yet* when they join independent clauses.

EXAMPLES   Patrick brought the sandwiches, and Cindy brought the potato salad.
We got there on time, but Jeff and María were late.

NOTE: Always use a comma before *yet, so,* or *for* joining independent clauses. The comma may be left out before *and, but, or,* and *nor* if the independent clauses are very short or if the sentence cannot be misunderstood.

EXAMPLE   I applied for the job and I got it.

Don't confuse a compound sentence with a simple sentence that has a compound verb.

SIMPLE SENTENCE   Bob brought charcoal and lighter fluid but forgot matches. [one independent clause with a compound verb]

COMPOUND SENTENCE   Bob brought charcoal and lighter fluid, but he forgot matches. [two independent clauses]

 REFERENCE NOTE: For more information about simple sentences and compound sentences, see pages 467 and 610–611. For a discussion of compound subjects and compound verbs, see pages 466–467 and 554–555.

EXERCISE 3   **Correcting Compound Sentences by Adding Commas**

If a comma should be used before the conjunction, write the <u>word preceding the needed comma</u>, the comma, and the <u>conjunction</u>. If a sentence is correct, write C.

EXAMPLE   **1.** Uncle Phil carefully steered the boat through the narrow channel and Lynn began baiting the hooks.
       1. *channel, and*

1. All students must arrive on <u>time</u>‸<u>for</u> no one will be admitted late.
2. The movie review complimented all the <u>performers</u>‸ <u>but</u> the leading actress received the strongest praise.
3. A few spectators tried to climb over the <u>fence</u>‸<u>but</u> the police ordered them back.
4. The Japanese actors in Kabuki plays do not <u>speak</u>‸ <u>but</u> they pantomime lines chanted by narrators on the stage.
5. Most people today work fewer hours than their grandparents <u>did</u>‸<u>yet</u> for many there never seem to be enough hours in a day.
6. The cost of living is <u>rising</u>‸<u>for</u> consumers pay higher prices for gasoline and other products.
7. Our guide led and we followed closely.   **7.** C [*or* <u>led, and</u>]
8. When two groups of Hopis disagreed about running the town of Oraibi, they settled the matter with a tug of <u>war</u>‸<u>and</u> the losers moved away and founded the town of Hotavila.
9. She said she did not like the story in the science fiction <u>magazine</u>‸<u>nor</u> did she enjoy the illustrations.
10. High school graduates may go on to college or may begin working immediately.   **10.** C

Nonessential Clauses and Phrases

25i. Use commas to set off nonessential clauses and nonessential participial phrases.

A *nonessential* (or *nonrestrictive*) clause or participial phrase is one containing information that isn't needed to understand the main idea of the sentence.

NONESSENTIAL CLAUSES   Emilia Ortiz**, who lives across the street from me,** won a scholarship to Stanford University.
         The capital of Massachusetts is Boston**, which is sometimes called the Athens of America.**

MECHANICS

LEARNING STYLES

Kinetic Learners. If students are having trouble deciding whether a clause or phrase is essential or nonessential, suggest that they try the following strategy:

1. Copy the sentence onto a slip of paper.
2. With scissors, cut the clause or phrase out of the sentence.
3. Piece the remaining halves of the sentence together. If the resulting sentence retains the same meaning as the original sentence, the clause or phrase is nonessential.

Visual and Auditory Learners. The activity can also be adapted for other learning styles. Visual learners could write a sentence and then bracket or mark out the clause or phrase in question. Auditory learners could read a sentence aloud, omitting the clause or phrase. In both instances, if the sentence retains its meaning without the clause or phrase, the clause or phrase is nonessential and should be set off by commas.

| NONESSENTIAL PHRASES | Kelly, **waiting outside the stage door,** got the band leader's autograph. |
| | Robert Hayden, **born in Detroit,** was educated at the University of Michigan and later became a distinguished professor there. |

Each nonessential clause or phrase in the examples above can be left out without changing the main idea of the sentence.

EXAMPLES	Emilia Ortiz won a scholarship to Stanford University.
	Boston is the capital of Massachusetts.
	Kelly got the band leader's autograph.
	Robert Hayden was educated at the University of Michigan and later became a distinguished professor there.

An *essential* (or *restrictive*) phrase or clause is one that can't be left out without changing the meaning of the sentence. Essential clauses and phrases are *not* set off by commas. Notice how leaving out the essential clause or phrase would change the meaning of each of the following sentences.

| ESSENTIAL PHRASES | Students **planning to try out for a role in the play** should sign up no later than Friday afternoon. |
| | Two poems **written by Lorna Dee Cervantes** are included in our literature book. |

| ESSENTIAL CLAUSES | The sophomores **who made the Honor Roll** were listed in the paper. |
| | Library books **that are lost or damaged** must be paid for. |

NOTE: Adjective clauses beginning with *that*, like the one in the example above, are nearly always essential.

Some clauses and participial phrases may be either essential or nonessential. The presence or absence of commas tells the reader how the clause or phrase relates to the main idea of the sentence.

| NONESSENTIAL CLAUSE | Marla's sister, **who attends Stanford University,** sent her a sweatshirt. [Marla has only one sister. She sent the sweatshirt.] |

ESSENTIAL CLAUSE	Marla's sister **who attends Stanford University** sent her a sweatshirt. [Marla has more than one sister. The one at Stanford sent the sweatshirt.]
NONESSENTIAL PHRASE	My former lab partner**,** **now living in Chicago,** visited me last week. [I have only one former lab partner. That person visited me last week.]
ESSENTIAL PHRASE	My former lab partner **now living in Chicago** visited me last week. [I have more than one former lab partner. The one from Chicago visited me last week.]

👉 **REFERENCE NOTE:** See Chapter 18 for more information on clauses and pages 582–583 for more on participial phrases.

▶ EXERCISE 4   **Correcting Sentences by Adding Commas**

For each of the following sentences, write each <u>word that should be followed by a comma</u>, and place a comma after it. If a sentence is correct as it is written, write *C*.

EXAMPLE   **1.** Gigantic supermarkets like the one on the next page which offer a stunning variety of goods and services developed from much smaller stores that first opened in the nineteenth century.
     1. *page, services,*

1. The stores that became the world's first supermarkets were designed by Clarence Saunders. **1.** C
2. <u>Saunders,</u>who lived in Memphis, <u>Tennessee,</u>named his stores Piggly Wiggly.
3. He got the idea for the name when he saw a fat pig wiggling under a fence. **3.** C
4. The Piggly Wiggly store that Saunders developed had only one long aisle. **4.** C
5. Customers who shopped there saw all the products before they came to the exit. **5.** C
6. Albert <u>Gerrard,</u>who noticed that people often had difficulty finding <u>products,</u>opened his own grocery store.
7. All of the items that were for sale were arranged alphabetically. **7.** C

MECHANICS

 INTEGRATING THE LANGUAGE ARTS

Mechanics and Writing. Tell students that they can make their writing more interesting by varying the lengths and structures of their sentences. To demonstrate the value of variation, write the following choppy paragraph on the chalkboard:

Pocahontas was a Native American. She was a princess. Captain John Smith said that she rescued him. He had been taken prisoner by Native Americans. Later, she was taken prisoner. Colonists took her prisoner. She became a Christian. She was called Rebecca. She married a colonist. In 1616 she was taken to England. In 1617 she died. She was twenty-two years old.

Have students revise the paragraph by combining some of the sentences so that sentence structures and lengths are more varied. Remind students to pay careful attention to comma usage as they combine sentences.

MECHANICS

8. The name that Gerrard selected for his store was Alpha-Beta. **8.** C
9. George <u>Hartford</u>‸who founded the Great Atlantic & Pacific Tea Company in <u>1859</u>‸nicknamed his stores A & P.
10. The model for today's huge <u>supermarkets</u>‸which was developed by Michael <u>Cullen</u>‸opened in an abandoned garage in Queens, New York, on August 30, 1930.

Introductory Elements

25j. Use a comma after certain introductory elements.

(1) Use a comma after words such as *well, yes, no,* and *why* when they begin a sentence. Interjections such as *wow, yikes,* and *hey,* if not followed by an exclamation point, are also set off by commas.

EXAMPLES **No,** I haven't taken the exam yet.
Sure, I'll go with you.
Wow, look at that car!

(2) Use a comma after an introductory participial phrase.

EXAMPLES **Calling for a timeout,** the referee blew her whistle and signaled.
Exhausted after a three-mile swim, Diana emerged from the water.

MECHANICS

MECHANICS

(3) Use a comma after two or more introductory prepositional phrases.

EXAMPLE   **By the light of the harvest moon in September,** we
went on an old-fashioned hayride.

A single introductory prepositional phrase does not require a comma unless the sentence could be misread or awkward to read without one.

EXAMPLES   In the book the writer develops a clever plot.
In the book, review pages 236–290.
In the book review, the critic praised the writer's
clever plot.

(4) Use a comma after an introductory adverb clause.

An introductory adverb clause may appear at the beginning of a sentence or before any independent clause in the sentence.

EXAMPLES   **When you've gone to this school as long as we have,**
you'll know your way around, too.
The first game of the season is Friday; **after we claim
our first victory,** we'll celebrate at Darcy's Deli.

▷ EXERCISE 5   **Correcting Sentences with Introductory Elements by Adding Commas**

If a sentence lacks a comma, write the <u>word that should be followed by a comma</u>, and place a comma after it. If a sentence is correct, write *C*.

EXAMPLE   **1.** Trying to reduce the amount of fat in their diets
many Americans are eating less meat.
   1. *diets,*

1. For many people in the <u>world,</u>meat is not a daily food staple.
2. Serving as a main source of <u>nutrition,</u>whole grains such as corn, oats, wheat, and rice feed millions.
3. In Mexico a favorite nutritious meal is a corn tortilla combined with beans. **3.** C
4. Because the soybean is high in <u>protein,</u>it has been a principal crop in Asian countries for more than five thousand years.

COOPERATIVE LEARNING

Divide the class into six groups. Have one group write at least five introductory participial phrases followed by commas; another, five interjections followed by commas; another, five adverb clauses followed by commas; and the three remaining groups, five independent clauses each—all on separate slips of paper. Mix the slips from the first three groups in one container and those from the second three in another. Have a student read an introductory element and then have another respond with an independent clause. You could then have students decide whether each combination expresses a complete thought.

COMMON ERROR

Problem. Students might have problems with introductory adverb clauses that are short enough to make pauses seem unnecessary, as in the sentence "When I moved here, I was very lonely."

Solution. Remind students that a dependent clause is always followed by a comma when it precedes an independent clause and have them memorize a simple formula: DC, IC.

5. If you'd like more variety in your <u>diet,</u>you may want to substitute unrefined whole grains for meat occasionally.
6. Offering healthful alternatives to <u>meat,</u>whole grains contain nutrients such as vitamins, proteins, amino acids, and starches.
7. In the process of making spoilage-resistant <u>products,</u> food manufacturers refine whole grains.
8. Refined for commercial <u>use,</u>the grains lose most of their food value because the nutritious outer hulls are stripped away.
9. If you take time in the <u>supermarket,</u>you should be able to find whole grains.
10. Since many cookbooks now include recipes for grain <u>dishes,</u>you can learn to use grains in many tasty snacks and meals.

▶ REVIEW B   **Using Commas**

For each of the following sentences, write all the <u>words that should be followed by a comma</u>. Place a comma after each one. If a comma may or may not be used after a word, circle the word and the comma.

EXAMPLE [1] Throughout history around the world people have used weapons for hunting for fighting and for defending themselves from wild animals.
　　　　　 1. *world, hunting,(fighting,)*

[1] Many weapons that we<u>re produced</u> in early times were similar in <u>appearance,</u>(function,)and design. [2] The English word *weapon* is related to the Old English <u>*wæpen,*</u> the Dutch <u>*wapen,*</u>the German (*Waffe,*)and an earlier common root. [3] <u>Sticks,</u>(stones,)and natural <u>poisons,</u>such as the toxic sweat of these Central and South American <u>frogs,</u>were probably the first weapons. [4] Among those varieties of weapons,the stick thrown by hand became one of the most heavily specialized. [5] As you can <u>see,</u>the <u>dart,</u>the <u>arrow,</u>the <u>spear,</u>the (lance,)and the javelin were all developed from the stick thrown by hand. [6] Another kind of weapon, the sling, was used all over the <u>world,</u>for it was

REVIEW B
OBJECTIVE
• To proofread a paragraph and correct it by adding commas

REVIEW B
Teaching Note

The optional commas in sentences seven and eight in **Review B** could provide a good departure point for discussion. Discuss with students the subtle variations in meaning caused by the presence or absence of commas after *sling* and *artillery*.

Commas **803**

easy to make and not too difficult to master. [7] According to the Biblical account, when the Hebrew king David was just a boy, he killed the Philistine giant Goliath with a simple handmade sling, like the one shown here. [8] An unusual weapon similar to the sling is the bola, which is a cord or thong with heavy balls of stone or wood or metal at the ends. [9] In some parts of South America, gauchos like this one still hunt with bolas, which entangle the quarry without inflicting pain, injury, or death. [10] Over the centuries these simple weapons have been developed into highly sophisticated artillery, like these missiles used in Operation Desert Storm.

MECHANICS

MECHANICS

WRITING APPLICATION

Using Commas in Writing Instructions for a Game

When you talk, you punctuate your speech with pauses. When you write, you use commas to show where such pauses should occur. Commas, like pauses, indicate how parts of a sentence are related to one another. Making such relationships clear is especially important when you give directions. If commas are left out or used incorrectly, the result is an awkward or confusing sentence.

WRITING APPLICATION
The **Writing Application** could be done cooperatively. Divide the class into groups of three or four. You may wish to group students according to their interests. For example, you could group students interested in science together to create a game involving science.

Each member of the group should participate in the creation of the game and should submit a written version of the rules and procedures.

CRITICAL THINKING
Synthesis

This assignment requires students to synthesize previous knowledge of games with information from a subject area to create a game. To help them get started, you may want to suggest that they use the structure of a familiar game and simply change its focus. For example, the focus of a board game could be changed from acquiring money and property to saving endangered species studied in science class.

WRITING

Point out to students that their knowledge of end marks and commas will be most useful in the proofreading stage. Students should not worry overmuch about correct punctuation during the writing stage but should focus instead on using their prior knowledge of games and their interesting facts from a subject area to produce a flow of good ideas.

---

804 *Punctuation*

AWKWARD	In the game players travel to Mars fly through the rings of Saturn and race back to Earth. [Because the sentence lacks commas, a reader may mistakenly run together *game player* or *Mars fly*.]
REVISED	In the game, players travel to Mars, fly through the rings of Saturn, and race back to Earth.
CONFUSING	The first player, who returns to Earth, wins the game. [The commas make it appear that the clause *who returns to Earth* is not essential—in other words, that the player who has the first turn always wins.]
REVISED	The first player who returns to Earth wins the game.

▶ WRITING ACTIVITY

Create an educational board game or computer game, and write instructions explaining how to play it. In your game, include information from at least one of your school subjects, such as math, science, history, or a foreign language.

 Prewriting Choose a subject area that interests you. Then decide what the object of the game will be. Jot down notes about the number of players, the kinds of supplies or equipment each player will need, and other rules of the game. Give your game a catchy title, and then arrange the instructions in an order that will be easy for players to follow.

Writing Keep in mind that your instructions will be the players' only source of information. Try to anticipate their questions, and aim for an informal, conversational tone, as if you were explaining the game in person.

Evaluating and Revising Ask some of your friends to play the game. As you watch them, note any problems they have with understanding the instructions. Then add, delete, change, or rearrange information to make the instructions easier to understand and the game more fun to play.

Proofreading and Publishing Proofread your instructions carefully, paying special attention to your use of end marks and commas. Then input your instructions on a computer or photocopy them. You could offer copies of your game to your school's media center, to a local hospital, or to one of the agencies or organizations that serve your community.

Interrupters

25k. Use commas to set off elements that interrupt a sentence.

(1) Appositives and appositive phrases are usually set off by commas.

An *appositive* is a noun or pronoun that follows another noun or pronoun to identify or explain it.

EXAMPLES   Nancy Landon Kassebaum, a **senator** from Kansas, was the principal speaker.
Do you know him, the **boy** wearing the blue shirt?

When you set off an appositive, be sure to include all the words that modify it.

EXAMPLES   I read *At Home in India,* **a book by Cynthia Bowles.**
Neil Armstrong, **the first person to walk on the moon,** took his historic step on July 20, 1969.

Sometimes an appositive is used to specify a particular person, place, thing, or idea. Such an appositive is called a *restrictive appositive.*

EXAMPLES   My brother **James** helped me. [The writer has more than one brother. The appositive *James* specifies which brother.]
Have you ever seen the movie ***Home Alone***? [The appositive *Home Alone* specifies the particular movie.]

☞ REFERENCE NOTE: See pages 590–591 for more information on appositives and appositive phrases.

▶ EXERCISE 6   **Correcting Sentences with Appositives and Appositive Phrases by Adding Commas**

Correctly punctuate the appositives in the following sentences. If a sentence is correct, write C.

1. Leonardo da Vinci's painting *Mona Lisa* is a prized possession of the Louvre in France.   **1.** c
2. The painting₍a portrait of a young Florentine woman₎ is slightly cracked as a result of temperature changes.

25k

MECHANICS

LEARNING STYLES

Auditory Learners. Have students read the following sentences aloud, first without pausing for commas, then with the appropriate pauses. Ask students to discuss the differences in meaning they perceive.

1. My sister, Susan, talks on the phone incessantly.
2. My sister Susan, who talks on the phone incessantly, is in her room.
3. My, Susan talks on the phone incessantly!

MECHANICS

3. In 1911 an Italian house painter‸Vincenzo Perugia‸ stole the painting from its frame.
4. For two years the Paris police‸some of the world's cleverest detectives‸were baffled by the crime.
5. Since its recovery the painting‸one of the most valuable portraits in the world‸has been closely guarded.

(2) Words used in direct address are set off by commas.

EXAMPLES   **David,** please close the door.
Did you call me, **Mother**?
Yes, **Mr. Ramos,** I turned in my paper.

(3) Parenthetical expressions are set off by commas.

Parenthetical expressions are remarks that add incidental information or relate ideas to each other.

Commonly Used Parenthetical Expressions		
after all	however	nevertheless
at any rate	I believe	generally speaking
consequently	in fact	on the contrary
for example	that is	on the other hand
for instance	meanwhile	in the first place
of course	moreover	therefore

EXAMPLES   You are, **I hope,** planning to arrive on time.
Gwendolyn Brooks, **in fact,** is my favorite poet.

Some expressions may be used both parenthetically and not parenthetically.

EXAMPLE   Long-distance calls are a bargain, at any rate.
[parenthetical, meaning "in any case"]
Long-distance calls are a bargain at any rate.
[not parenthetical, meaning "at any cost"]

 REFERENCE NOTE: Parentheses and dashes are sometimes used to set off parenthetical expressions. See pages 862–864.

NOTE: A contrasting expression introduced by *not* or *yet* is parenthetical and should be set off by commas.

EXAMPLE   Emily Brontë, **not her sister Charlotte,** wrote *Wuthering Heights.*

▶ REVIEW C

Correcting Sentences by Adding Commas

For each of the following sentences, write each <u>word that should be followed by a comma</u>, and place a comma after it.

Optional commas are circled.

EXAMPLE [1] Artist Faith Ringgold painstakingly hand-letters her beautiful unique story quilts.

1. *beautiful,*

[1] Continuing the ancient tradition of <u>quilting,</u> Ringgold combines <u>printed,</u> <u>dyed,</u> and pieced fabric with acrylic paintings or photoetchings. [2] By placing the tradition in a new <u>context,</u> the artist gives it new meaning.

[3] <u>Ringgold,</u> whose earlier works include <u>landscapes,</u> <u>murals,</u> <u>masks,</u> and soft <u>sculptures,</u> began making story quilts in 1980. [4] Titled *Echoes of Harlem,* the first one was a collaboration between the artist and her <u>mother,</u> dress designer Willi <u>Posey,</u> who learned quilting from her own <u>grandmother,</u> who had learned it from her <u>mother,</u> a slave.

[5] Most of Ringgold's story quilts are designed to be viewed as parts of a <u>series,</u> not as separate <u>pieces,</u> and many include portions of a narrative linking the works in the series. [6] This <u>work,</u> *Double Dutch on the Golden Gate,* lacks an accompanying text and is from the *Woman on a Bridge* <u>series,</u> which includes five works. [7] Capturing the excitement of a childhood <u>game,</u> it depicts a pastime cherished by generations of African Americans. [8] <u>However,</u> the work speaks to more than a single culture and appeals to all people who recognize in it joyful moments from their childhood.

[9] Ringgold still lives and works in <u>Harlem,</u> the section of New York City where she was born. [10] One of her story <u>quilts,</u> which sell for <u>$40,000,</u> is in the permanent collection of the city's Guggenheim <u>Museum,</u> a major gallery of modern art.

Faith Ringgold, *Double Dutch on the Golden Gate Bridge,* 1988
Private Collection, Courtesy Bernice Steinbaum Gallery, NYC.

MECHANICS

VISUAL CONNECTIONS

About the Artist. Faith Ringgold's art is boldly political, focusing on the discrimination and repression facing African Americans and women in American society. Born in Harlem in 1934, she attended City College of New York and received her Bachelor of Science degree in 1955 and her Master of Fine Arts degree in 1959.

In 1972, Ringgold helped to found the Women Students and Artists for Black Liberation, an organization that ensured that exhibitions of black artists' works gave equal space to art by both men and women. Later, she donated to the Women's House of Detention in Manhattan a large mural that depicts the roles of women in American society.

MECHANICS

AT-RISK STUDENTS

Point out to students that adherence to **Rule 25l** is very important in job applications and résumés. To help students to recognize the importance of understanding the comma usage discussed in the **Conventional Situations** section, have students write letters of application for jobs that appeal to them. Students might need to refer to **Chapter 35: "Letters and Forms"** for the correct form for a business letter. Finally, have students trade letters and evaluate one another's letters for standard punctuation.

PICTURE THIS

Before asking students to complete the **Picture This** assignment, you may want to discuss the meaning of *closed captions* and *hearing-impaired* so that students clearly understand the activity's objective.

You may wish to put students in groups or pairs for the preliminary part of this activity so that they can discuss the picture. Then have students write their paragraphs individually. Ask them to circle each comma and end mark, citing beside it the rule that dictates its use.

808

Conventional Situations

25l. Use commas in certain conventional situations.

(1) Use a comma to separate items in dates and addresses.

EXAMPLES On Saturday, June 21, 1991, Robert moved to Miami Beach, Florida, with his parents.
His new address is 814 Georgia Avenue, Miami Beach, FL 33139.

Notice that no comma separates the month from the day, the house number from the street name, or the ZIP code from the two-letter state code.

If the day is given before the month or if only the month and the year are given, no comma is used.

EXAMPLES The British forces at Pensacola Bay surrendered to Bernardo de Gálvez on 10 May 1781.
The hottest month on record here was July 1962.

(2) Use a comma after the salutation of a friendly letter and after the closing of any letter.

EXAMPLES Dear Marcus,   Dear Aunt Meg,
Affectionately yours,   Sincerely yours,

(3) Use a comma after a name followed by an abbreviation such as *Jr., Sr.,* or *M.D.* and after the abbreviation when it is used in a sentence.

EXAMPLES Elena Moreno, M.D.
Russell E. Davis, Jr., has been elected mayor.

PICTURE THIS

You're a writer for a company that prepares the closed captions that hearing-impaired viewers see on their television screens. Write a page of dialogue that might be shown with this scene from the *I Love Lucy* show, starring Lucille Ball and Desi Arnaz. Use a variety of end marks, and include commas where they are needed.

Subject: a scene from *I Love Lucy*
Audience: hearing-impaired viewers
Purpose: to entertain

Unnecessary Commas

25m. Do not use unnecessary commas.

Too many commas can be as confusing as too few. Don't use a comma unless a rule requires one or unless the meaning would be unclear without it.

CONFUSING   On Friday, after school, my friend, Rita, and I played badminton at her house until her dog, Ruffles, a frisky, golden retriever, joined us and ran off with the shuttlecock, clenched in its teeth.

CLEAR   On Friday after school, my friend Rita and I played badminton at her house until her dog Ruffles, a frisky golden retriever, joined us and ran off with the shuttlecock clenched in its teeth.

▶ EXERCISE 7   **Correcting Sentences by Adding Commas**

For each of the following sentences, write each <u>word that should be followed by a comma</u>, and place the comma after it.

MECHANICS

MECHANICS

810 *Punctuation*

EXAMPLE   **1.** On our way to Birmingham Alabama we stayed overnight in Chattanooga Tennessee.
       1. *Birmingham, Alabama, Chattanooga,*

1. On August 1₎1991₎we moved from Eureka₎California₎ to 220 Tuxford Place₎Thousand Oaks₎California.

2. We left Tampa₎Florida₎on Monday₎June 15₎and arrived in Albuquerque₎New Mexico₎on June 17.

3. The hotel on Gulfport Road was destroyed by fire on Tuesday₎March 13₎1984.

4. My brother received a letter that started, "Dear John₎ There's something I've been meaning to tell you."

5. We interviewed Franklin R. Thomas₎M.D.₎at his emergency clinic on Wilson Road.

REVIEW D   **Revising Paragraphs by Adding Commas**

For each sentence in the following paragraphs, write each <u>word that should be followed by a comma</u>, and place the comma after it. If a sentence is correct, write C. [Note: If a comma may or may not be used, circle the word and the comma.]

Optional commas are circled.

[1] As early as the sixth century <u>B.C.</u>₎plays were performed in this <u>amphitheater</u>₎the Theater of <u>Dionysus</u>₎in <u>Athens</u>₎Greece. [2] The Theater of Dionysus is located on the south slope of the <u>Acropolis</u>₎an <u>elevated</u>₎fortified section of Athens. [3] The plays presented in ancient Greece marked the beginning of drama in the Western world. [4] In <u>fact</u>₎the English word *theater* comes from the Greek word *<u>theatron</u>*₎which means "a place for seeing."

3. C

[5] Wearing masks to show which characters they were <u>portraying</u>₎the actors in ancient dramas often played several different roles. [6] In <u>addition</u>₎all <u>roles</u>₎including those of female <u>characters</u>₎were performed by men.

OBJECTIVES

- To correct sentences by adding end marks and commas
- To correct paragraphs by adding end marks and commas

🙏 COOPERATIVE LEARNING

Have students write short informative paragraphs about topics that interest them. Then pair students and have them dictate their paragraphs to each other. When they have finished, have pairs compare comma usage in both versions of each paragraph. If there are any discrepancies, have students decide cooperatively which version is correct.

[7] Although records show that Greek playwrights wrote hundreds of <u>tragedies</u>⊙ fewer than thirty-five of these plays survive. [8] The earliest Greek <u>dramatist</u>⊙ <u>Aeschylus</u>⊙ wrote the *Oresteia*⊙ a powerful story of <u>murder</u>⊙ <u>revenge</u>⊙ and divine mercy. [9] <u>Sophocles</u>⊙ often regarded as the greatest dramatist of all <u>time</u>⊙ is credited with writing more than one hundred plays. [10] Among the surviving works of <u>Aristophanes</u>⊙ whom the ancient Greeks considered the greatest comic <u>playwright</u>⊙ are the three satires *The Clouds*⊙ *The Wasps*⊙ and *The Frogs*.

Review: Posttest

A. Correcting Sentences by Adding End Marks and Commas

Write the following sentences, adding end marks and commas where they are needed. [Note: If a comma may or may not be used, circle the comma.]

Optional commas are circled.

EXAMPLE **1.** When is the bus coming or has it already left

　　　　1. *When is the bus coming, or has it already left?*

1. On June 1⊙ 1992⊙ I wrote to the Wisconsin Department of Development at 123 Washington Ave⊙ Madison⊙ WI 53702⊙
2. Federico Peña⊙ mayor of Denver⊙ Colorado⊙ from 1983 to 1991⊙ was born in Laredo⊙ Texas⊙ in 1947.
3. Wow⊙ Bill⊙ what a great save you made in last night's game!
4. Water transports nutrients throughout the body⊙ aids in digestion⊙ and helps regulate body temperature⊙
5. I⊙ M⊙ Pei⊙ who was born in China⊙ has designed many buildings in the United States⊙ for example⊙ the Dallas⊙ Texas⊙ City Hall and the Government Center in Boston⊙ Massachusetts⊙
6. The chief crops grown in Trinidad⊙ one of the most prosperous islands in the Caribbean⊙ are sugar⊙ coffee⊙ cocoa⊙ citrus fruits⊙ and bananas⊙
7. Did you know that Navajo Community College⊙ located in Tsaile⊙ Arizona⊙ was founded in 1968?

MECHANICS

MECHANICS

COOPERATIVE LEARNING

Divide the class into groups of four and assign each group the task of writing a test that covers each of the rules in this chapter. Each group should provide an answer key.

Then have groups exchange the tests they have created and complete the tests they are given.

8. If I finish my report, if I do the laundry, and if I promise to be home by eleven, may I go to the concert?
9. After staying up so late, I was exhausted, of course, yet I couldn't fall asleep right away.
10. In the mail last Wednesday a large, heavy package, addressed to Phyllis M. Saunders, M.D., was delivered to our house by mistake.

B. Correcting Paragraphs by Adding End Marks and Commas

For each sentence in the following paragraphs, add end marks and commas where they are needed. [Note: If a comma may or may not be used, circle the comma.]

EXAMPLE   [1] As soon as I got home I called my best friend Stephanie to tell her about my vacation

     1. *As soon as I got home, I called my best friend, Stephanie, to tell her about my vacation.*

[11] Stephanie, have you ever visited Cody, Wyoming? [12] Well, if you do, be sure to stop by the Buffalo Bill Historical Center. [13] Opened in 1927 in memory of William "Buffalo Bill" Cody, an army scout who later had his own Wild West show, the Center is actually four museums in one. [14] Under one roof are the Buffalo Bill Museum, the Whitney Gallery of Western Art, the Winchester Arms Museum, and the Plains Indian Museum. [15] All of the museums are interesting, but the best one, I believe, is the Plains Indian Museum, which has artifacts from Native American cowhands, settlers, and roving artists. [16] Of all the treasures in the museum's collections, the highlight is an exhibit on Tatanka Yotanka, better known as Sitting Bull, the mighty Sioux warrior, holy man, chief, and statesman. [17] The exhibit includes a dozen drawings that Sitting Bull, who was born about 1831 and died in 1890, made while he was a prisoner at Fort Randall, an army post in the Dakota Territory. [18] Depicting some of his many battlefield conquests, the drawings reveal his talent for design and composition. [19] Other displays show weapons, clothing, and accessories of the Cheyenne, Shoshone, Crow, Arapaho, Blackfeet, and Gros Ventre peoples. [20] What a journey back through time the museum offers!

SUMMARY OF THE USES OF THE COMMA

25f Use commas to separate items in a series.

(1) If all items in a series are joined by *and*, *or*, or *nor*, do not use commas to separate them.

(2) Independent clauses in a series are usually separated by semicolons. Short independent clauses may be separated by commas.

25g Use commas to separate two or more adjectives preceding a noun.

25h Use a comma before *and*, *but*, *or*, *nor*, *for*, *so*, and *yet* when they join independent clauses.

25i Use commas to set off nonessential clauses and nonessential participial phrases.

25j Use commas after certain introductory elements.

(1) Use a comma after words such as *well*, *yes*, *no*, and *why* when they begin a sentence.

(2) Use a comma after an introductory participial phrase.

(3) Use a comma after two or more introductory prepositional phrases.

(4) Use a comma after an introductory adverb clause.

25k Use commas to set off elements that interrupt a sentence.

(1) Appositives and appositive phrases are usually set off by commas.

(2) Words used in direct address are set off by commas.

(3) Parenthetical expressions are set off by commas.

25l Use commas in certain conventional situations.

(1) Use a comma to separate items in dates and addresses.

(2) Use a comma after the salutation of a friendly letter and after the closing of any letter.

(3) Use a comma after a name followed by an abbreviation such as *Jr.*, *Sr.*, or *M.D.*

25m Do not use unnecessary commas.

MECHANICS

OBJECTIVE

• To locate semicolon and colon errors in sentences

Teacher's ResourceBank™
RESOURCES

FOR THE WHOLE CHAPTER
• Chapter Review Form A
• Chapter Review Form B
• Assessment Portfolio
   Mechanics Pretests
   Mechanics Mastery Tests

CHAPTER OVERVIEW

This chapter stresses the idea that semicolons and colons can help writers achieve clarity when they are presenting complex ideas. It also links that complexity to maturation of the thought processes of students.

Semicolons are treated first, followed by a treatment of colons. The **Writing Activity** has each student planning an itinerary and writing a letter to procure tickets for a trip. The chapter concludes with a **Posttest** for determining students' mastery of these two punctuation marks.

USING THE DIAGNOSTIC TEST

The **Diagnostic Test** requires students to edit sentences for correct use of colons and semicolons. Most of the errors are omissions of correct punctuation. This test should indicate which students need additional help with the rules for using semicolons and colons.

MECHANICS

26 PUNCTUATION

Semicolons and Colons

Diagnostic Test

Correcting Sentences by Using Semicolons and Colons

Most of the following sentences have a comma or no punctuation mark where a semicolon or a colon should be used. Write the <u>word preceding each error</u>; then, add the needed punctuation mark. If a sentence is correct, write C.

EXAMPLE   **1.** The Arthurs are not home, they've left for work.
       1. *home;*

1. Native Americans inhabited North America long before any other human <u>beings;</u>however, many Native Americans weren't recognized as citizens of the United States until 1924.
2. The meeting is scheduled for 3<u>:</u>30 this <u>afternoon;</u> please don't be late.

3. The following committees will report at that time⌃ budget, membership, awards, and programs.

4. Every morning when I get up, I read a Bible verse⌃ this morning I read John 14⌃27.

5. We left some food out for the stray dog⌃it looked so forlorn huddled in the doorway.

6. Our modern literature class has read these poems⌃ "Incident" by Countee Cullen, "The Love Song of J. Alfred Prufrock" by T. S. Eliot, and "Ars Poetica" by Archibald MacLeish.

7. When she transferred to Barton Academy, Millie joined several clubs, helped in planning the Spring Carnival, and worked at a food bank for the needy⌃ nevertheless, it took her months to make some new friends.

8. While campaigning to become mayor of San Antonio, María Antonieta Berriozábal summed up her point of view in these words⌃ "Our greatest resource is our people. We have to deal with business interests and human needs simultaneously."

9. Conrad Aiken was a correspondent for *The New Yorker* and also wrote essays and short stories⌃he is best known, however, for his poetry.

10. The Bering Strait links the Arctic Ocean with the Bering Sea⌃ both the strait and the sea are named for Vitus Bering, a Danish explorer.

11. S. I. Hayakawa made this statement⌃"It is not true that we have only one life to live⌃ if we can read, we can live as many more lives and as many kinds of lives as we wish."

12. The winners in the Douglas Fun Run last Saturday morning were Otis Williams, a sophomore⌃ Janice Hicks, a senior⌃ and Rodrigo Campas, a junior.

13. They opposed every motion that came before the meeting⌃in addition, they said they would circulate petitions if any of the proposals were passed.

14. At first the children were afraid, believing that they were lost⌃only after their teacher reassured them that she knew the way did they settle down.

15. This design will be applied to the following types of machines⌃commercial, manufacturing, military, and agricultural.

OBJECTIVE

- To use semicolons correctly between independent clauses and between items in a series

16. Jennifer Lawson became programming chief of PBS in <u>1990;</u>she is a former civil rights activist, film professor, and producer.
17. In addition to the imaginative, eerie tales for which Shirley Jackson is known, she wrote *Life Among the Savages* and *Raising <u>Demons;</u>*these autobiographical novels are amusing accounts of her own household.
18. In the past twelve years, Justin has lived in Tucson, <u>Arizona;</u>Dallas, <u>Texas;</u> Shreveport, <u>Louisiana;</u> and Tulsa, Oklahoma.
19. For the golf tournament seasoned players were paired with players new to the <u>game;</u>consequently, the experienced players were frustrated and the novices were confused.
20. When Hernando Cortes invaded Mexico in 1519, he burned his <u>ships;</u>as a result, his troops were unable to return to Cuba.

Semicolons

26a. Use a semicolon between independent clauses in a sentence if they are not joined by *and, but, or, nor, for, so,* or *yet.*

EXAMPLE Everyone else in my family excels in a particular sport**;** I seem to be the only exception.

When the thoughts of two short sentences are very closely related, a semicolon can take the place of the period between them.

EXAMPLE The river is rising rapidly. It's expected to crest by noon. [two simple sentences]
The river is rising rapidly**;** it's expected to crest by noon.

26b. Use a semicolon between independent clauses joined by conjunctive adverbs or transitional expressions.

QUICK REMINDER

Write the following pairs of sentences on the chalkboard and ask students to combine them by using semicolons:

1. The bell rang as I hurried toward the classroom I was tardy again. [classroom; I]
2. Mr. Scott frowned as I tried to slip into my seat he was not pleased with me. [seat; he]
3. I have no explanation in my life, lateness is a state of being. [explanation; in]

Ask the students why semicolons might be better punctuation here than periods. [Although separating the clauses with periods would make them grammatically correct sentences, the clauses are very closely related, and semicolons help indicate this close relationship.]

MECHANICS

MECHANICS

EXAMPLES Leonor is planning to become an engineer**;** **however,** she is also interested in commercial art.
Only two people registered for the pottery lessons**;** **as a result,** the class was canceled.

Notice in the examples above that the conjunctive adverb and the transitional expression are followed by commas.

Commonly Used Conjunctive Adverbs

accordingly	however	moreover
besides	indeed	nevertheless
consequently	instead	otherwise
furthermore	meanwhile	therefore

Commonly Used Transitional Expressions

as a result	for example	for instance	that is
in spite of	in conclusion	in other words	in fact

NOTE: When a conjunctive adverb or a transitional expression appears *within* one of the clauses instead of *between* the clauses, it is usually set off by commas. The two clauses are still separated by a semicolon.

EXAMPLE Ralph Ellison is best known for his 1952 novel, *Invisible Man***;** he has also**, however,** written short stories and essays.

 EXERCISE 1 ### Correcting Sentences by Adding Commas and Semicolons

For each of the following sentences, write all the <u>words that should be followed by a semicolon or a comma</u>. Place the needed punctuation mark after each one.

EXAMPLE **1.** The clever carvings shown on the next page were handmade in southern Mexico they're sold all over the world.
1. *Mexico;*

1. The carvings come from the Oaxaca (pronounced wä hä' kä) <u>Valley</u>ˬin <u>fact</u>ˬ90 percent of the two hundred families who make them live in three villages.

MECHANICS

MECHANICS

COOPERATIVE LEARNING

Send students in groups of three to the library to find semicolons in professional writing. Assign groups to search in different types of texts: magazine articles, novels, nonfiction books, encyclopedias, dictionaries, and so on. Have the students appoint a spokesperson in each group who is to report not only the rule of use, but also what the group thinks was the writer's reason for using a semicolon instead of some other punctuation mark.

To ensure that all group members participate, make one member responsible for turning in a written version of the report and appoint another to write samples of the group's sentences on the chalkboard.

2. Carving has been a tradition among Oaxacans for hundreds of <u>years</u>;only <u>recently</u>,<u>however</u>,have the artists sold their work outside the valley.
3. In many families the fathers and older sons do the actual <u>carving</u>;meanwhile,the other members of the family sand and paint the figures.
4. The artists find inspiration for their creations in everyday <u>life</u>;for <u>example</u>,religion and nature are rich sources of ideas.
5. Even those carvers whose works have won worldwide acclaim have chosen to continue living in the <u>valley</u>;their ties to their families and communities are very strong.

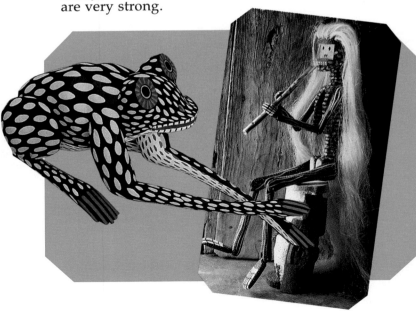

> **26c.** A semicolon (rather than a comma) may be needed to separate independent clauses joined by a coordinating conjunction if commas appear within the clauses.

CONFUSING June sat with Tony, Pat, and me, and Josh sat with Flora, Zack, and Geraldo.

CLEAR June sat with Tony, Pat and me; and Josh sat with Flora, Zack, and Geraldo.

**26
c–d**

CONFUSING   Searching for my house key, I found a dime, a nickel, and a penny, and, putting them into my wallet, I realized that my key had been in there all along.

CLEAR   Searching for my house key, I found a dime, a nickel, and a penny; and, putting them into my wallet, I realized that my key had been in there all along.

👉 REFERENCE NOTE: For information on using a comma to separate independent clauses joined by a coordinating conjunction, see page 796.

26d. Use a semicolon between items in a series if the items contain commas.

EXAMPLES   There are four home stations for the Goodyear blimps: Long Beach, California; Houston, Texas; Miami, Florida; and Rome, Italy.

You may turn in your book reports on Thursday, September 14; Friday, September 15; or Monday, September 18.

▶ REVIEW A   **Correcting Sentences by Adding Commas and Semicolons**

For each of the following sentences, write all the <u>words that should be followed by a semicolon or a comma</u>. Place the needed punctuation mark after each one. If a sentence is correct, write *C*.

EXAMPLE   **1.** The diagram on the next page shows the typical seating plan of a symphony orchestra the conductor occupies the podium.

   1. *orchestra;*

1. All of the instruments in a symphony orchestra are divided into classes based on how they produce <u>sound</u>;many musicians can play several instruments within a class.
2. The four classes are the stringed instruments, the woodwinds, the brasses, and the percussion instruments. **2.** C
3. Woodwinds, which include the flute, the clarinet, and the saxophone, were once made solely of <u>wood</u>; but today they may be made of metal or plastic instead.

INTEGRATING THE LANGUAGE ARTS

Technology Link. If your students have access to word processors, you may want to have them correct comma splices or combine short, choppy sentences by using the insert function to add semicolons. You could enter sentences of your own for students to correct, or you might use those in **Review A.**

MECHANICS

MECHANICS

COMMON ERROR

Problem. After becoming acquainted with the list of commonly used conjunctive adverbs (p. 817), some students might over-apply **Rule 26b** (p. 816) by using semicolons every time they encounter one of the words in the list. *Furthermore, however,* and *therefore* seem to be the words that most often get this type of treatment.

Solution. Stress that semicolons are used when these words join independent clauses, and make sure everyone understands that independent clauses have both a subject and a verb and could, in fact, be sentences by themselves. When this type of erroneous use of semicolons occurs, have the students try to find the subject and verb in each word group on either side of the semicolon. When they see that a word group is not an independent clause, they should have a better understanding of **Rule 26b** and how to apply it.

4. Some of the stringed instruments are played with a <u>bow</u>,some are plucked with the fingers or with a <u>pick</u>,and some are operated by means of a keyboard.

5. Most brass instruments, such as the trumpet, tuba, and cornet, have valves that regulate the <u>pitch</u>,but the trombone has a sliding section for this purpose.

6. Kettledrums, or timpani, are percussion instruments that can be tuned to a specific <u>pitch</u>,most other kinds of drums, the cymbals, and the <u>triangle</u>,however, cannot be tuned.

7. The conductor's job is to coordinate the sounds produced by these different <u>instruments</u>,however,this task is only one of a conductor's responsibilities.

8. Conductors must study the history and theory of music for many <u>years</u>,furthermore,they must be skilled at playing at least one instrument.

9. Many people think that a conductor just establishes and maintains the tempo of the <u>music</u>,they don't realize that he or she also selects the music, interprets the composer's meaning, and brings out the best in each of the musicians.

10. The goal of every conductor is to lead a major orchestra such as one of those in London, <u>England</u>, Mexico City, <u>Mexico</u>,Boston, <u>Massachusetts</u>,or Chicago, Illinois.

OBJECTIVE

• To use colons before lists and in certain other conventional situations

Colons

26e. Use a colon to mean "note what follows."

(1) Use a colon before a list of items, especially after expressions such as *as follows* and *the following [items]*.

EXAMPLES In Washington, D.C., we visited four important national sites: the White House, the Washington Monument, the Vietnam Veterans Memorial, and the Lincoln Memorial.

The only articles allowed in the examination area **are as follows:** pencils, compasses, rulers, and protractors.

During summer vacation, Juanita read biographies of **the following people:** John Ross, Annie Wauneka, and María Martinez.

NOTE: Do not use a colon before a list that immediately follows a verb or a preposition.

INCORRECT At the new amusement park we rode: the roller coaster, the Ferris wheel, the bumper cars, and the water slide.

CORRECT At the amusement park we rode the roller coaster, the Ferris wheel, the bumper cars, and the water slide.

INCORRECT Our family has lived in: California, Arizona, North Carolina, and Texas.

CORRECT Our family has lived in California, Arizona, North Carolina, and Texas.

(2) Use a colon before a long, formal statement or quotation.

EXAMPLE Thomas Paine's first pamphlet in the series *The American Crisis* starts with these famous words:

These are the times that try men's souls. The summer soldier and the sunshine patriot will, in this crisis, shrink from the service of their country; but he that stands it *now* deserves the love and thanks of man and woman.

☞ REFERENCE NOTE: See pages 838–839 for more information on using long quotations in a composition.

MECHANICS

Teacher's ResourceBank™
RESOURCES.

COLONS
• Using Colons

🦉 **QUICK REMINDER**
Write the following sentences on the chalkboard:

1. When I come to school, I always bring my glasses, my textbook, a stack of papers, and a sandwich.
2. When I come to school, I always bring four things: my glasses, my textbook, a stack of papers, and a sandwich.

Ask why one sentence has a colon and the other doesn't. [In the second sentence, the reader's attention is directed to the list instead of to the idea of coming to school in the morning.]

MECHANICS

PICTURE THIS

Remind students that journal entries typically are examples of free writing and therefore don't have to be grammatically correct. However, because this exercise is designed to give students practice in the use of the colon, they should concentrate on making sure that colons appear in the correct places in their entries.

LEP/ESL

General Strategies. The Picture This exercise may be difficult for some students to complete. Although mainstream students have grown up with television, movies, books, and history lessons about the western frontier and the pioneers who settled it, many ESL students might not share this frame of reference.

Give students the option of writing about leaving their native countries or of writing about when their parents or ancestors left their native countries. Students' journal entries can tell what happened during the journey or, more specifically, what happened the day they or their families arrived. Their lists can detail what in the United States is different from their native countries.

PICTURE THIS

The year is 1878. Responding to this poster, your family sold its home in Tennessee, and now you're on your way to Kansas with this wagon train. The land, the people, the chores—everything is different from the life you left behind. You've decided to keep a journal so that you'll always remember this difficult but exciting journey. Write a journal entry telling what happened today on the trail. In your entry, use at least three semicolons and two colons.

Subject: traveling to Kansas with a wagon train
Audience: yourself some time in the future
Purpose: to record

26f. Use a colon in certain conventional situations.

(1) Use a colon between the hour and the minute.

EXAMPLES   **6:15** P.M.   **9:55** tomorrow morning

MECHANICS

MECHANICS

26f

(2) Use a colon between chapter and verse in referring to passages from the Bible.

EXAMPLES   Psalms 8:9   Luke 10:27

(3) Use a colon after the salutation of a business letter.

EXAMPLES   Dear Ms. Weinberg: Dear Sales Manager:
            Dear Sir or Madam: To Whom It May Concern:

NOTE: Use a comma after the salutation of a friendly letter.

        EXAMPLE   Dear Suzanne,

▶ EXERCISE 2   **Correcting Sentences by Adding Colons**

Correct the following sentences by adding colons where they are needed. If a sentence is correct, write C.

EXAMPLE   **1.** I began my acceptance speech as follows "Fellow
              students, thank you for your votes!"
           1. *follows:*

1. My family often enjoys the humor of the following cartoonists: Garry Trudeau, Charles Schultz, Cathy Guisewite, and Lynn Johnston.
2. Sometimes the paper comes at 6:15 A.M., but other times it doesn't hit the driveway until 7:00.
3. My little sister has several items embossed with Garfield's picture: a poster, a nightgown, a notebook, and a clock.
4. Bruce Barton made this perceptive comment: "Many a man who pays rent all his life owns his home, and many a family has successfully saved for a home only to find itself at last with nothing but a house."
5. Sherry's favorite artists are Jacob Lawrence, Romare Bearden, and Margaret Burroughs. 5. C
6. The story of Moses and Pharaoh's daughter is told in Exodus 2:5–10.
7. The directions were as follows: cover with plastic wrap, place in oven, and microwave for at least ten minutes.
8. I prefer my bicycle to a car for three reasons: I don't pay for gasoline, I don't pay for insurance, and it's all mine.

MECHANICS

COOPERATIVE LEARNING
Pair advanced students with less-advanced students for an editing exercise when they have finished the **Picture This** activity. Less-advanced students benefit doubly from the input of their partners and from seeing the exercise done well, and the better students will be required to verbalize their understanding of the writing process.

COMMON ERROR
Problem. Invariably, some students confuse the colon and the semicolon or think they are interchangeable.
Solution. Allowing a time lapse between the introduction of semicolons and that of colons is often all that is needed to prevent confusion. Explain that a colon is a kind of pointer to something that a writer wants to emphasize. A semicolon provides clarity (in setting off a list with internal commas) or accentuates a close relationship between two independent clauses.

MECHANICS

9. In Cuba, which is a Spanish-speaking country, most of the people are of Spanish, African, or Spanish-African descent. **9.** C

10. Mr. Wise asked us to bring the following items to biology class: a deciduous leaf, a coniferous needle or branch, and wax paper.

▶ REVIEW B **Correcting Sentences by Adding Semicolons and Colons**

For each numbered sentence in the following letter, write each <u>word that should be followed by a semicolon or a colon</u>. Place the needed punctuation mark after each word. [Note: A sentence may need more than one punctuation mark.]

EXAMPLE [1] Hampton University was founded in 1868 it was originally named Hampton Institute.

1. *1868;*

1238-C Landon Street
Kansas City, MO 64105
October 17, 1993

Director
George Foster Peabody Collection
Hampton University
Hampton, VA 23668

[1] Dear Sir or <u>Madam:</u>

[2] The media coordinator at Central High School suggested that I write to <u>you;</u>she explained that Hampton has an extensive collection of materials on African American history. [3] For my history class I am preparing an oral report on the August 28, 1963, March on <u>Washington;</u>and, to make my report more interesting, I would like to display pictures of the march.

[4] I am particularly interested in pictures of the following <u>speakers:</u>Floyd <u>McKissick,</u>John <u>Lewis,</u>Roy <u>Wilkins,</u> and, of course, Martin Luther King, Jr. [5] I would also like pictures showing the size and diversity of the <u>crowd;</u>for example, a shot of the marchers filling the area around the Reflecting Pool between the Lincoln Memorial and the

Washington Monument would be especially effective. [6] Either prints or slides will be <u>useful</u>;however, I would prefer slides if they are available.

[7] My grandfather, who took part in the march, remembers it <u>vividly</u>;in fact, he considers it one of the high points of his life. [8] He took several rolls of film himself that <u>day</u>;unfortunately, the pictures were lost in a fire a few years ago.

[9] Please send me information on ordering copies of suitable <u>pictures</u>;a stamped, self-addressed envelope is enclosed. [10] Thank you for your <u>help</u>;I look forward to hearing from you.

Sincerely,

Jesse Fletcher

Jesse Fletcher

WRITING APPLICATION

Using Semicolons and Colons in a Business Letter

As you grow older, your knowledge and your thoughts expand and become more complex. To express what you know and think, you begin using longer, more complex sentences. When you write, semicolons and colons can help you make these sentences easier to understand. Compare the following examples.

IMMATURE	I'd like to visit three cities. The cities are in the Southwest. One is Santa Fe, New Mexico. One is Phoenix, Arizona. One is Los Angeles, California. I can't afford to. That's unfortunate.
MATURE	I'd like to visit three cities in the Southwest: Santa Fe, New Mexico; Phoenix, Arizona; and Los Angeles, California; unfortunately, however, I can't afford to.

STUDENTS WITH SPECIAL NEEDS

To help learning disabled students gain a sense of the function of the colon, use scrambled sentences. Have students write sentences containing colons. Then have them cut out the words and punctuation marks with scissors. The students should then exchange work and put the words and punctuation back together.

Another activity is to choose a paragraph of high interest to the students and make incorrect changes in colon usage. Inform the students of the number of errors and have them locate and correct the errors.

 WRITING APPLICATION

Writing this letter gives students an opportunity to use what they've learned about semicolons and colons. They will also gain experience in using a formal tone and in developing planning skills.

MECHANICS

MECHANICS

CRITICAL THINKING
Analysis

Remind students that the person reading the letter is not responsible for having awarded the prize. Effusive thanks are inappropriate. The point of the letter is to establish an itinerary, not to express gratitude or to say how much the prize winner anticipates enjoying the trip. Brevity is an asset in business correspondence.

PREWRITING

Have students make lists of the places they'd most like to visit. You may need to have maps in class to help them calculate distances and travel times between destinations.

EVALUATING AND REVISING

Have students exchange papers to take turns role-playing the ticket agent to see if the drafts are complete and coherent enough to get them where they want to go when they want to go there.

▶ WRITING ACTIVITY

You have just won the grand prize in Blue Star Airlines' Fly-by-Night Sweepstakes. For one week, you can travel free to anywhere that Blue Star flies in the United States—just so long as your flights depart between 8 P.M. and 4 A.M. You can remain in one location for the whole week, or you can travel to as many places as you'd like. To use your prize, you must give Blue Star Airlines a detailed itinerary of your trip at least two weeks before you plan to take it. Write a letter to the airlines, giving the specific information needed to prepare your tickets. Use semicolons and colons to make your information easy to understand.

 Prewriting First, decide where you would most like to go. (If you plan to include more than one destination, remember that the trip is to last only one week from start to finish; be as realistic as you can about the travel time required.) Then, arrange the information in an order that will be easy for the ticket agent to understand.

 Writing As you write your first draft, remember that the accuracy and completeness of your letter could make the difference between an enjoyable trip and a disastrous one. Stick to the point, and try to make the information as clear as possible.

 Evaluating and Revising Put yourself in the ticket agent's place as you evaluate the letter. Have you included all the necessary flight information? Have you arranged the details in an order that's easy to understand? Add, delete, change, or rearrange information to make the letter clearer and more useful. Also make sure that you use the correct form for a business letter (see pages 941–943).

 Proofreading Proofread your letter carefully, paying special attention to your use of semicolons and colons. Check pages 822–823 to be sure that you have followed the rules for using colons in conventional situations. Also make sure that you have correctly spelled the names of the places you wish to visit.

REVIEW: POSTTEST

OBJECTIVE

- To correct sentences by adding semicolons and colons

Review: Posttest

Correcting Sentences by Adding Semicolons and Colons

For each of the following sentences, write the <u>word preceding each punctuation error</u>; then write the semicolon or colon needed. If a sentence is correct, write *C*.

EXAMPLE **1.** Please bring the following items books, pencils, and newspapers.
    1. *items:*

1. If you want to send fragile items through the mail, the post office recommends that you pack them in fiberboard <u>containers</u>;use foam, plastic, or padding to cushion <u>them</u>;and then seal the package carefully, reinforcing it with filament tape.
2. In 1904, Mary McLeod Bethune founded a school for girls in Daytona Beach, <u>Florida</u>;that school is now Bethune-Cookman College.
3. Psalms <u>23:1–6</u> is one of the best-known passages in the Bible.
4. Richard is working hard to improve his grades this <u>year</u>;he wants his record to show that he's college material.
5. If I had a million dollars, I'd visit London, <u>England</u>; Cairo, <u>Egypt</u>;Buenos Aires, <u>Argentina</u>;and Tokyo, Japan.
6. We have to write reports for gym class on one of the following <u>athletes</u>:Jesse Owens, Sonja Henie, Jim Thorpe, Althea Gibson, or Babe Didrikson Zaharias.
7. Our neighbor's cocker spaniel barked on and off all night <u>long</u>;as a result, I didn't sleep well.
8. Candice will take Sandra's place in tonight's <u>performance</u>;unfortunately, Sandra sprained her ankle and cannot walk.
9. My Aunt Pam loves to play backgammon and <u>chess</u>; however, she rarely has time because she works at two jobs.

TIMESAVER

When students have completed the **Posttest**, you can save time by letting them help you grade their performances. Distribute colored pens, pencils, or fine-point markers to the class and, as you call out the answers, have the students correct their papers by writing the correct responses over any errors. The corrections in color will be more vivid to visual learners, and hearing the answers given orally will benefit auditory learners.

MECHANICS

MECHANICS

10. Asia has both the highest and the lowest points on earth‸Mount Everest, the highest, soars 29,028 <u>feet</u>‸ the Dead Sea, a salt lake, lies 1,300 feet below sea level.

11. Instructed to be prompt, we arrived at school at <u>7‸15</u>, but the doors were <u>locked</u>‸consequently, we had to wait until <u>7‸30</u> to get in the building.

12. Indira Gandhi, who served for many years as the prime minister of India, grew up in the world of politics and <u>government</u>‸for her father, Jawaharlal Nehru was the first prime minister of India, from 1947 to 1964.

13. My friends Ruth and Cindy disagree about the role of fate in <u>life</u>‸Ruth believes that people can control their own destiny, but Cindy insists that people are simply pawns of fate.

14. I don't like to prepare <u>outlines</u>‸nevertheless, the highest grade I ever received was for a report that I wrote from an outline.

15. Mr. Kowalski has always regretted that he didn't learn to speak Polish when he was a <u>child</u>‸now he is taking conversational Polish.

16. The computer software industry is an enormous, growing <u>business</u>‸for instance, people can buy software for everything from balancing budgets to plotting biorhythm charts.

17. Every morning Lonnie rises at <u>5‸00</u>, jogs until <u>5‸30</u>, showers and eats breakfast by <u>6‸15</u>, and catches the <u>6‸35</u> bus.

18. Red Cloud, leader of the Oalala Sioux, was a military <u>genius</u>‸he successfully defended Sioux lands against settlers who wanted to build a trail from Laramie, Wyoming, to Bozeman, Montana.

19. Gates of the Arctic National Park, which is located in northern Alaska, is known for its large populations of certain <u>animals</u>‸caribou, grizzly bears, moose, and wolves.

20. I have ridden bicycles, horses, and <u>motorcycles</u>‸and I have traveled in trains, buses, and <u>planes</u>‸someday I hope to ride in a hot-air balloon.

⇨ DIAGNOSTIC TEST

OBJECTIVE

- To correct sentences by adding italics (underlining) and quotation marks where needed

Teacher's ResourceBank™

RESOURCES

FOR THE WHOLE CHAPTER
- Chapter Review Form A
- Chapter Review Form B
- Assessment Portfolio
   Mechanics Pretests
   Mechanics Mastery Tests

27 PUNCTUATION

Italics and Quotation Marks

Diagnostic Test

Correcting Sentences by Adding Italics and Quotation Marks

Write each letter, word, title, or sentence that should be in italics (underlined) or in quotation marks. Then supply the needed underlining or quotation marks.

EXAMPLES
1. Can you tell me the way to Logan Street? she asked.
1. *"Can you tell me the way to Logan Street?"*

2. Tekeda Izumo, Namiki Senryō, and Miyoshi Shoraku wrote the Kabuki play cycle known in English as The Treasury of the Loyal Retainers or as The League of the Loyal Ronin.
2. *The Treasury of the Loyal Retainers; The League of the Loyal Ronin*

1. Carlos Chávez, Mexican composer and conductor, wrote the symphony <u>Sinfonia Antigona</u> in 1933.
2. We have subscribed to the <u>Orlando Sentinel</u> ever since we moved here.

CHAPTER OVERVIEW

This chapter is divided into a section on italics (underlining), followed by a section on quotation marks. The quotation-mark section has two parts: punctuating titles, and punctuating direct and indirect quotations, including dialogue.

The rules concerning the punctuation of titles and quotations will be most useful as students write literary analyses and research papers. The punctuation rules for dialogue will be helpful in expressive and creative writing.

USING THE DIAGNOSTIC TEST

The **Diagnostic Test** contains items for most of the twelve rules in the chapter. Many students will not be familiar with some of the rules, and the **Diagnostic Test** will help you discover which rules students need help with most.

MECHANICS

3. "Are you going to help me," he asked, "or shall I look for someone else?"

4. James Dickey wrote the novel <u>Deliverance</u>, which was made into a movie featuring the song "Dueling Banjos."

5. In modern Spanish the letters that occur with the greatest frequency are <u>a</u> and <u>s</u>.

6. Clarita served a delicious appetizer called <u>pulpo</u>; when I asked her what it was, she told me that I'd just eaten octopus.

7. For our homework assignment we have to define <u>ionization</u>, <u>electrolyte</u>, <u>quark</u>, and <u>neutrino</u>.

8. During the Civil War, the <u>Merrimack</u>, on the Confederate side, and the <u>Monitor</u>, on the Union side, fought to a draw in the first battle between ironclad ships.

9. "I never should have agreed to be on that committee," wailed Ellie. "When I asked Mary to help, she said, 'Not on your life!' Now I'm stuck doing all the work."

10. "Where have you been, Ramón?" asked Leroy. "The bus leaves in three minutes."

11. Announcing the scholarship winners, the principal called the following students "Elwood High's finest scholars": Daphne Johnson, Michael Lewis, Ruben Perez, and Winsie Chung.

12. One of my favorite TV shows, <u>Disaster Chronicles</u>, ran an episode called "Volcanoes in Italy," which had some interesting facts I used in my report on ancient Rome.

13. Sam, who's originally from Boston, tends to drop the <u>r</u>'s at the ends of words.

14. Politicians still quote Abraham Lincoln's phrase "government of the people, by the people, for the people."

15. During lunch we discussed the magazine article "Michael Jackson's Perfect Universe."

16. "Indians Today, the Real and the Unreal" is the opening chapter in Vine Deloria's book <u>Custer Died for Your Sins</u>.

17. My mother has never liked the term <u>baby boomer</u>.

18. Many articles about Emily Dickinson's poems contain the term <u>paradox</u>.

OBJECTIVES

- To correct sentences by adding underlining (italics) where appropriate
- To write sentences containing titles of works

Italics **831**

27a

19. When the players came onto the field, the fans shouted, "Go for it!"
20. Have you seen the sculpture <u>Young Shadows</u>, by Louise Nevelson?

Italics

Italics are printed letters that lean to the right, like this:

These words are printed in italics.

When you are writing or typing, indicate italics by underlining. If your composition were printed, the typesetter would set the underlined words in italics. For instance, if you typed

All sophomores in our school read <u>The Good Earth</u>, by Pearl Buck.

the sentence would be printed like this:

All sophomores in our school read *The Good Earth*, by Pearl Buck.

> **NOTE:** If you use a personal computer, you can probably code in italics to appear on the printout. Most word-processing software and many printers are capable of producing italic type.

27a. Use italics (underlining) for titles of books, plays, films, periodicals, works of art, record albums, long musical compositions, television series, ships, aircraft, and so on.

TYPE OF TITLE	EXAMPLES	
Books	*The Red Badge of Courage*	*A Fire in My Hands* *Black Elk Speaks*
Plays	*A Raisin in the Sun*	*Julius Caesar*
Films	*Dances with Wolves*	*High Noon*

(continued)

MECHANICS

Teacher's ResourceBank™
RESOURCES

> **ITALICS**
> - Italics and Underlining

QUICK REMINDER

Take a survey of students' votes for the best movie, book, and television series for the year. Write the titles on the chalkboard, underlining each. Ask students what they notice about how you wrote the titles [underlining]. Have them brainstorm other types of works whose titles receive special treatment in writing [plays, works of art, poems, songs].

RULE 27a

Individual newspapers and magazines may have house styles that affect the punctuation of titles. For example, some publications use quotation marks instead of italics for movie titles.

MECHANICS

LEP/ESL

General Strategies. Students are likely to perform more successfully on tasks like **Exercise 2** if they are paired with native English-speakers. Collaboration rather than competition will facilitate their understanding of how italics are used and may also expose students to useful cultural information.

Both students should be required to submit written responses to the exercises, but completing those responses together can help both students' comprehension.

LESS-ADVANCED STUDENTS

Some students might have a difficult time with the lists in **Rules 27a** and **27k** because the items in the lists might not seem to have any connection with each other. Students might benefit from an overall characterization of the rules governing the lists—that italics are usually used for long works, and quotation marks are used for parts of works and for short works.

You may wish to put the lists on a large poster as a handy reference in the classroom and as an aid to visual learners, or you can let the students make posters for themselves.

MECHANICS

832

MECHANICS

832 *Punctuation*

TYPE OF TITLE	EXAMPLES	
Periodicals	*Ebony* *Kansas City Times*	*Women: A Journal of Liberation*
Works of Art	*The Three Musicians*	*Agrarian Leader Zapata*
Long Musical Compositions	*Peter and the Wolf*	*Black, Brown, and Beige*
Television Series	*All Creatures Great and Small*	*Soul Train* *The Wonder Years*
Ships, Trains	*Lusitania* *Flying Cloud*	*Orange Blossom Special*
Aircraft, Spacecraft	*June Bug*	*Pioneer 11*

NOTE: Italicize the title of a poem long enough to be published in a separate volume. Such poems are usually divided into titled or numbered sections, such as cantos, parts, or books. The titles of these sections are enclosed in quotation marks.

EXAMPLE Longfellow's *Evangeline* opens with a section titled simply "Prelude."

The words *a, an,* and *the* before a title are italicized only when they are part of the title. However, they're not italicized (or capitalized) before the titles of newspapers even if they appear that way in the publication.

EXAMPLES John Hersey's *The Wall* recounts the destruction of the Jewish ghetto in Warsaw during World War II.
In Shakespeare's play *A Midsummer Night's Dream,* Bottom, a weaver, and his friends perform a play-within-a-play.
The article in the *Wall Street Journal* mentioned that among his other accomplishments, Frederick Douglass founded the *North Star,* a newspaper he published for seventeen years.

 REFERENCE NOTE: Use quotation marks, not italics, for chapter headings and the titles of magazine articles, short poems, short stories, short musical compositions, and single episodes of television series. See page 840 for this rule.

27b. Use italics (underlining) for words, letters, and figures referred to as such and for foreign words.

27b

EXAMPLES The first *o* in *zoology* is pronounced with a long *o* sound.

On my typewriter, the lowercase letter *l* is also used to type the numeral *1*.

Montana's state motto is *oro y plata,* the Spanish phrase for "gold and silver."

 EXERCISE 1 ### Correcting Sentences by Adding Underlining (Italics)

Identify all the <u>words and word groups that should be italicized</u> in the following sentences.

EXAMPLE **1.** In 1988, Toni Morrison won the Pulitzer Prize for her novel Beloved.
   1. *Beloved*

1. Did you know that the <u>B</u> in <u>Cecil B. De Mille</u> stands for <u>Blount</u>?
2. The first full-length animated film, Walt Disney's <u>Snow White and the Seven Dwarfs</u>, used two million drawings.
3. Among the items that the Pilgrims brought with them on the <u>Mayflower</u> were apple seeds.
4. James Earle Fraser, best known for his painting <u>End of the Trail</u>, designed the U.S. Indian-head nickel.
5. In the late eighteenth century, Edward Gibbon wrote the influential book <u>The History of the Decline and Fall of the Roman Empire</u>.
6. In <u>Voyage to the Bottom of the Sea</u>, an old TV series, the submarine <u>Seaview</u> was commanded by Admiral Nelson.
7. <u>Daktari</u> is Swahili for the English word <u>doctor</u>.
8. The first U.S. space shuttle was named <u>Columbia</u>.
9. Richard Sears met Alvah Roebuck through an ad in the <u>Chicago Daily News</u>.
10. The three <u>M</u>'s in <u>3M Company</u> stand for <u>Minnesota Mining</u> and <u>Manufacturing</u>.

 EXERCISE 2 ### Writing Sentences Containing Titles of Works

You probably recognize at least some of the awards on the next page. Now you've been appointed to the nominating

MECHANICS

 ## INTEGRATING THE LANGUAGE ARTS

Literature Link. If your students' literature book contains the excerpt from T. H. White's *The Once And Future King*, titled "Arthur Becomes King," ask the students to read the excerpt and find examples of the use of italics. In a discussion, have the students explore why the italics were used. [Italics are used in a synopsis of material left out to distinguish the synopsis from the text of the story. Italics are also used to emphasize the difference between the words *able* and *ought* and to give special emphasis to the word *after*.]

Technology Link. Many software programs have print controls or print-option menus that allow users to choose roman (standard), italic, or boldface type. Explain to students using such programs that print choices remain in effect until they are changed, so if italic type is activated for a title, students must remember to deactivate it after the title. If italic type is not available, students can use underlining, just as they would when writing by hand.

MECHANICS

SEGMENT 3 *(pp. 834–844)*

QUOTATION MARKS Rules 27c–27l

OBJECTIVES
- To correct sentences by adding quotation marks where needed
- To write a persuasive dialogue that is punctuated correctly

ANSWERS

Exercise 2

Responses will vary, but nominations should include five correctly capitalized and punctuated titles, one from each category. The supporting reasons for the nominations should be clear and persuasive.

Teacher's ResourceBank™

RESOURCES

QUOTATION MARKS
- Using Quotation Marks A
- Using Quotation Marks B
- Using Quotation Marks C
- Using Quotation Marks D
- Using Quotation Marks E

MECHANICS

QUICK REMINDER

To emphasize how quotation marks facilitate a reader's understanding of a text, write the following dialogue between two students, Julio and Martha, on the chalkboard as a single paragraph with no quotation marks. Have students read the passage and ask them to figure out who is saying what. Then show them where the divisions occur. Have them talk about the conventions for making dialogue easier to read and understand.

["Hello," said Julio, "where are you going? I'm going to gym class."

"I'm going to study hall. Have you done your algebra homework?"

"Sure."

"When did you do it?" Martha asked. "I finished it this morning."]

834

MECHANICS

834 *Punctuation*

committee for a new award, the Golden Guppy, which will be presented for an outstanding work in each of these categories:

- a book
- a musical recording
- a television program
- a work of art (painting, sculpture, or some other form)
- a magazine

In a sentence or two, nominate a work in each category and explain why you think it should win one of the awards.

Quotation Marks

27c. Use quotation marks to enclose a ***direct quotation***—a person's exact words.

Do not use quotation marks for an *indirect quotation*.

DIRECT QUOTATION	Joan said, **"My legs are sore from jogging."** [Joan's exact words]
INDIRECT QUOTATION	Joan said that her legs were sore from jogging. [not Joan's exact words]

NOTE: Remember to place quotation marks at both the beginning and the end of a direct quotation.

INCORRECT	"I'm taking the road test tomorrow, said Reed.
CORRECT	**"I'm taking the road test tomorrow,"** said Reed.

27d. A direct quotation begins with a capital letter.

EXAMPLE Bianca asked, **"When do we get our uniforms?"**

NOTE: If a direct quotation is obviously only a fragment of a sentence and is not intended to stand alone, use a lowercase letter.

EXAMPLE   Christine promised that she would be here "as soon as possible."

27e. When a quoted sentence is divided into two parts by an interrupting expression such as *he said*, the second part begins with a lowercase letter.

EXAMPLES   "I hope," said Diego, "that it doesn't rain during the fiesta."
"I'm not sure," remarked Annette, "if I'll be able to attend the meeting."

If the second part of a divided quotation is a new sentence, a period (not a comma) follows the interrupting expression. The second part begins with a capital letter.

EXAMPLE   "The date has been set," said Greg. "We can't change it now."

NOTE: An interrupting expression is not part of a quotation, so it should never be inside the quotation marks.

INCORRECT   "Where, I inquired, have I seen you before?"
CORRECT   "Where," I inquired, "have I seen you before?"

When two or more of the same speaker's sentences are quoted together, use only one set of quotation marks.

INCORRECT   Tamisha suggested, "Let's donate the profits from the car wash to Project Day Care." "It provides help for many low-income working parents in this area."
CORRECT   Tamisha suggested, "Let's donate the profits from the car wash to Project Day Care. It provides help for many low-income working parents in this area."

27f. A direct quotation is set off from the rest of the sentence by commas or by a question mark or an exclamation point.

EXAMPLES   Mrs. Castaneda announced, "Remember that your research reports are due Monday," just as the bell rang.

MECHANICS

MECHANICS

COMMON ERROR

Problem. When a direct quotation appears in a sentence that begins with an attribution, students might fail to capitalize the first word of the quotation.

Solution. Have students read each direct quotation in their writing without the attribution. This will help them to decide whether the quotation needs capitalization.

This technique can also help students make better judgments about the flow of dialogue in their writing, and it can also help them decide whether attributions are necessary in the dialogue.

Elwyn asked, "On what date does the Ides of March fall?" when it was his turn to quiz the others in his study group.
"That's easy! It's March fifteenth!" Dot exclaimed.

27g. When used with quotation marks, other marks of punctuation are placed according to the following rules.

(1) Commas and periods are always placed inside the closing quotation marks.

EXAMPLE   "The concert tickets are sold out," Mary said, "and I had really hoped to go."

(2) Colons and semicolons are always placed outside the closing quotation marks.

EXAMPLES   The following students have been named "most likely to succeed": Corey Brown and Sally Ling.
Paka quoted a Cameroonian proverb, "By trying often, the monkey learns to jump from the tree"; it reminded me of the expression "If at first you don't succeed, try, try again."

(3) Question marks and exclamation points are placed inside the closing quotation marks if the quotation is a question or an exclamation. Otherwise, they are placed outside.

EXAMPLES   "What time is the game tomorrow?" Maria asked.
Why did you answer, "It doesn't matter"?

On the last lap Vicky said, "Do your best!"
Don't say, "I quit"!

▶ EXERCISE 3   **Writing Sentences with Direct and Indirect Quotations**

Add quotation marks where they are needed in the following sentences. If a sentence is correct, write *C*.

EXAMPLE   **1.** When I saw this ad in the paper, I said to Grandmother Hsu, T'ai chi is Chinese, isn't it?
1. *When I saw this ad in the paper, I said to Grandmother Hsu, "T'ai chi is Chinese, isn't it?"*

27g

1. She seemed pleased that I'd asked and replied,"Yes, it's short for t'ai chi ch'uan."
2. She explained that t'ai chi ch'uan was developed in ancient China as a system of self-defense and as an aid to meditation.   **2.** C
3. "But the ad says that it's for health and relaxation,"I pointed out.
4. "Yes,"she said,"it's that, too; it improves coordination and flexibility. In fact, in China people of all ages practice it."
5. "You see,"she went on,"its postures and movements are all based on those of animals such as monkeys, birds, and snakes."
6. "Snakes!"I exclaimed.
7. "Why do you twist your face so?"Grandmother asked. "If you observe a snake closely, you'll see how gracefully it moves."
8. "That's true,"I admitted.
9. "Maybe,"I said, thinking aloud,"I'll check out this grand opening."
10. Imagine my surprise when Grandmother replied with a wide smile,"I'll see you there. I'm one of the instructors."

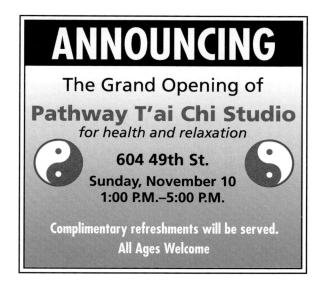

ANNOUNCING

The Grand Opening of

Pathway T'ai Chi Studio
for health and relaxation

604 49th St.
Sunday, November 10
1:00 P.M.–5:00 P.M.

Complimentary refreshments will be served.
All Ages Welcome

MECHANICS

MEETING
INDIVIDUAL
NEEDS

LESS-ADVANCED STUDENTS

Some students might have difficulty completing **Exercise 3**, which requires them to identify quoted words (if any) and to punctuate them properly. You may wish to make mimeographed copies of the exercise for students to write on, and then give them the following guidelines:

1. Find the attribution (the words that tell who was talking) in each sentence. Circle them. Find the part that is an indirect quotation—it is after the attribution and begins with *that*.
2. Direct quotations may come before the attribution, after the attribution, or both. Have students go through the exercise and underline all the words they think are direct quotations. Then have them read aloud the words that they think are direct quotations. Does the dialogue make sense? If not, have them recheck the words they underlined—they may have underlined too few or too many. (Students might need help with number 3, which contains an indirect quotation within a direct quotation.)
3. Have students add quotation marks to the sentences on their papers. Remind them to put quotation marks both before and after the quotation. Also remind them that commas and periods always go within quotation marks, while exclamation points and question marks are placed inside only when they are part of the quotation.

MECHANICS

27h. When you write dialogue (a conversation), begin a new paragraph every time the speaker changes.

EXAMPLE A man of Merv, well known as the home of complicated thinkers, ran shouting one night through the city's streets. "Thief, Thief!" he cried.

The people surrounded him, and when he was a little calmer, asked: "Where was the thief?"

"In my house."

"Did you see him?"

"No."

"Was anything missing?"

"No."

"How do you know there was a thief then?"

"I was lying in bed when I remembered that thieves break into houses without a sound, and move very quietly. I could hear nothing, so I knew that there was a thief in the house, you fool!"

Niamat Khan, "The Thief"

27i. When a quoted passage consists of more than one paragraph, put quotation marks at the beginning of each paragraph and at the end of the entire passage. Do not put quotation marks after any paragraph but the last one in the passage.

EXAMPLE The saleswoman told my mother, "Now, this car is one of our hottest sellers. It has bucket seats, a CD player, and alloy wheels.

"It's also one of the safest cars on the road because of its heavy suspension and anti-lock brake system. It gets good mileage, too.

"All in all, I think this would be the perfect car for you."

NOTE: A long passage (not dialogue) quoted from a book or some other source is usually separated from the rest of the text in one of several ways. The entire passage may be either indented or set in smaller type. Sometimes the passage is single-spaced rather than double-spaced; however, Modern Language Association guidelines call for double-spacing. When a quoted passage is set off in one of these ways, no quotation marks are necessary.

MECHANICS

EXAMPLE   The Sauk chief Black Hawk had this to say in his
                speech after his last battle against the whites:

> I fought hard. But your guns were well
> aimed. The bullets flew like birds in the
> air, and whizzed by our ears like the
> wind through the trees in winter. My
> warriors fell around me; it began to
> look dismal. I saw my evil day at hand.
> The sun rose dim on us in the morning,
> and at night it sank in a dark cloud, and
> looked like a ball of fire. That was the
> last sun that shone on Black Hawk. His
> heart is dead, and no longer beats quick
> in his bosom. He is now a prisoner to
> the white men; they will do with him as
> they wish. But he can stand torture, and
> is not afraid of death. He is no coward.
> Black Hawk is an Indian.

PICTURE THIS

It's 1870, somewhere on the plains of Nebraska. On your
way back to camp, you and two friends stop to warm your
hands at the chimney of this dugout built by a settler. One
of your companions admires the comforts the dugout provides; the other scorns it because it can't be moved, as
your own dwellings can. Write a short dialogue in which
you side with one of your friends and the two of you try to
convince your other friend to agree with you.

Subject: dwellings
Audience: your
               companions
Purpose: to persuade

National Cowboy Hall of Fame
Oklahoma City, OK

MECHANICS

COOPERATIVE LEARNING
Have students work together in
groups of three to complete the **Picture
This** assignment. Each student should
assume the role of one of the three
friends and create and record the characterization and dialogue for that persona.
Remind students that at least one of
them has to admire the dugout, and at
least one has to scorn it. Have groups
work through the stages of the writing
process as described in the feature.
Make it clear that all three students are
responsible for carrying out each stage in
the process.

PICTURE THIS

Begin prewriting by having students create appropriate personas for
themselves and their friends. Students
might imagine themselves as Native
Americans, ranchers, farmers, gold rush-
ers, cattle hustlers, Pony Express employees, robbers, and so on.

Have students complete the
prewriting part of this assignment by
making a chart showing each character's
occupation, actual dwelling place, preferred style of dwelling, and reasons to
be used in the argument.

When students revise, they should
check each persona's statements to make
sure they are consistent and have a persuasive aim. When they proofread, they
should check the punctuation, indenta-
tion, and capitalization of the dialogue.

MECHANICS

OBJECTIVE

- To correct sentences by adding underlining (italics) and quotation marks where needed

TIMESAVER

To save teaching time and make assimilation of rules for punctuating titles easier for students, have them make charts of the materials covered in **Rules 27a** and **27k.** You and they can use the charts for easy reference.

STUDENTS WITH SPECIAL NEEDS

Students with learning disabilities often have poor levels of intrinsic motivation. To help them master the use of quotation marks, assign one or more of the following activities:

1. Choose an article that contains quotation marks and make incorrect changes. Have the students correct the errors.

2. To help students learn the difference between direct and indirect quotations, give them an article and have them make changes so that all direct quotations become indirect quotations.

840

---

840   *Punctuation*

 27j. Use quotation marks to enclose titles of articles, short stories, essays, poems, songs, individual episodes of TV series, and chapters and other parts of books and periodicals.

EXAMPLES   I chose to memorize "Pueblo Winter," by Bernice Zamora.
"The Unicorn in the Garden" is my favorite Thurber short story.
For tomorrow, read Chapter 8, "Twentieth-Century Playwrights."

☞ REFERENCE NOTE: Remember that the titles of long poems and long musical compositions are italicized, not enclosed in quotation marks. See the examples on page 832.

 27k. Use quotation marks to enclose slang words, technical terms, and other unusual uses of words.

EXAMPLES   What's "in" one year is often "out" the following year.
The salesperson said that we should buy a "mouse" to operate the art software on our computer.

NOTE: It is best to avoid using slang words and technical terms whenever possible, except in dialogue, informal writing, technical writing, and other special contexts. If you're not sure whether a word is appropriate, look it up in a dictionary.

27l. Use single quotation marks to enclose a quotation within a quotation.

EXAMPLES   Ron said, "Dad yelled, 'No way!'"
Val asked, "Did you like my arrangement of 'America the Beautiful'?"

 REVIEW A   **Correcting Sentences by Adding Underlining (Italics) or Quotation Marks**

In the following sentences, write all the words that should be underlined (italicized) or placed in quotation marks, and add the appropriate markings.

EXAMPLE **1.** He read aloud The Tell-Tale Heart from The Collected Stories of Edgar Allan Poe.
   1. *"The Tell-Tale Heart"; The Collected Stories of Edgar Allan Poe*

1. Mr. Croce used the word <u>denouement</u> in discussing Rudolfo Anaya's novel <u>Bless Me, Ultima</u>.
2. By next Thursday I have to read the following works: "The Medicine Bag," a short story by Virginia Driving Hawk Sneve; <u>Crown of Shadows</u>, a play by Rodolfo Usigli; and "Daisy Bates: First Lady of Little Rock," an article by Lerone Bennett, Jr., in <u>Ebony</u> magazine.
3. Have you read this article, "El Niño, Global Weather Disaster"?
4. Karen asked me how many <u>m</u>'s are in the word <u>accommodate</u>.
5. Oswald Rivera's 1990 novel <u>Fire and Rain</u> is about the Vietnam War.
6. My favorite plant is <u>Saintpaulia ionantha</u>, commonly called the African violet.
7. We had <u>risotto alla milanese</u> for dinner.
8. The short story "Luke Baldwin's Vow" deals with conflicts in values.
9. The counselor's use of outdated slang terms such as <u>cool</u> and <u>right on</u> amused the campers.
10. She crossed the <u>t</u> with such a flourish that she obliterated the letters above it.

▶ REVIEW B

Correcting Sentences by Adding Underlining (Italics) and Quotation Marks

For each of the following sentences, add underlining (italics) or quotation marks where they are needed. If a sentence is correct, write C.

EXAMPLE **1.** Look at this intriguing painting, said Marshall.
   1. *"Look at this intriguing painting," said Marshall.*

1. He told us that he'd found the painting in <u>Mexican American Artists</u>, a book by Jacinto Quirate; the painting is in the chapter called "The Third Decade."
2. "The painting is by that man on the left, Emilio Aguirre," he explained, "who titled it <u>Alpha 1</u>."

MECHANICS

MECHANICS

3. "What do you see when you look at it?" he asked.
4. "You can't miss the <u>Y</u> on the left and the <u>T</u> on the right," he said.
5. "But," he went on, "can you make out the profile of a person sitting on the ground to the left of the <u>T</u>?"
6. Laura said, "Yes, the head is an <u>O</u>," but I objected, saying that it looked more like a <u>Q</u> to me.
7. "I guess you're right," she said. "Anyway, the <u>G</u> outlines the front of the body."
8. Ben asked, "Do you think that the <u>B</u> is supposed to be the person's sunglasses? And," he added, "isn't that an <u>M</u> in the background, behind the <u>T</u>?"
9. "Look at this!" exclaimed Marlene. "If you turn the painting ninety degrees to the left, the body looks like a question mark."
10. Can you see why we all agreed when she said, "<u>Intriguing</u> really is the word for <u>Alpha 1</u>"?

WRITING APPLICATION

Writing an Interior Dialogue

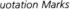

Like many people, you probably carry on running conversations with yourself, especially when you have a decision to make. Expressing your ideas and feelings—even to yourself—can help you analyze a situation and arrive at a conclusion. Such interior conversations can involve two, three, four, or more points of view. If you were to write out one of these conversations, you would probably give each point of view a name and use quotation marks to reproduce the dialogue exactly.

▶ WRITING ACTIVITY

You're scheduled to give an oral report on a short story of your own choosing. Write an interior dialogue recording your thoughts as you decide which of two stories to use.

Prewriting List the titles of several short stories you've read. Then choose the two that, for whatever reason, you feel most strongly about. Next, determine how you'll distinguish between your different points of view as you decide which story to choose. For example, you could use your first name for one side, your middle name for another, and other names for as many different points of view as you have.

Writing Write down your thoughts as you consider the pros and cons about using the two stories. (You may want to skim both stories first, but remember, at this point you're not analyzing them, you're just deciding which one to use.) Keep writing until you reach a decision. Don't worry about grammar, mechanics, and usage, but do try to keep track of where you are in the decision-making process.

Evaluating and Revising As you reread your dialogue, check whether your diction (word choice) and sentence structure sound authentic to you. Can you tell at all times which story you're referring to? Is it clear which one you decided to report on, and why? Revise your writing to make it express your thinking process more accurately.

MECHANICS

This exercise focuses students' attention on the conversations that go on in their minds when they make decisions. Some students might have difficulty distinguishing their internal voices, and some might find it difficult to transcribe their thoughts while they are thinking.

You may wish to have students speak their thoughts into a tape recorder as they arrive at their decisions. Students can then identify the voices and transcribe the dialogue afterwards.

CRITICAL THINKING
Analysis

Classification of the statements made in their decision-making processes might help students distinguish points of view and help them organize their prewriting material.

The concepts of classification and organization might seem complicated to students, so you may need to remind them that in most cases, these processes can be very simple. For instance, the statements for this assignment could be classified as those for story 1, those for story 2, those against story 1, and those against story 2. Organization can then be a matter of grouping statements for each story, grouping statements against each story, or grouping statements about story 1 and grouping statements about story 2.

MECHANICS

REVIEW: POSTTEST

OBJECTIVE

- To correct sentences by adding underlining (italics) and quotation marks where needed

LESS-ADVANCED STUDENTS

Remind students that context clues in the sentences—words like *said, asked,* and *replied*—will help them identify dialogue requiring quotation marks.

Also, titles will often have an accompanying clue to help students know what should be italicized. The thing the title refers to will usually appear somewhere within the sentence.

844 *Punctuation*

 Proofreading and Publishing As you proofread, pay special attention to your use of quotation marks and to the capitalization and punctuation before and after them. Then, photocopy your dialogue or input it on a computer. You and your classmates could tape-record your dialogues or act them out for one another in person or on film. Then you could discuss your responses to writing an interior dialogue to help in decision making.

Review: Posttest

Correcting Sentences by Adding Italics or Quotation Marks

For each of the following sentences, add italics (underlining) or quotation marks where they are needed. If a sentence is correct, write C.

1. "Why did you buy another sleeping bag?" she asked.
2. In his surrender speech, Chief Joseph of the Nez Percé said that he would never fight again. **2. C**
3. The dance company is performing <u>Swan Lake</u>, a ballet by Tchaikovsky.
4. Anita asked, "Why did he say, 'I won't go to the game?'"
5. <u>The Boston Cooking School Cookbook</u>, now known as <u>The Fannie Farmer Cookbook</u>, was first published in 1891.
6. The first word my baby brother said was <u>bird</u>.
7. "There's an article in this issue of <u>Newsweek</u> that I'd like you to read," said Joan.
8. Wendell B. Harris wrote, directed, and starred in the 1991 movie <u>Chameleon Street</u>.
9. "Her street address has four <u>4</u>'s in it," said Rose. "Did you know that?"
10. "Susan drove one hundred miles," he replied, "to see you on your birthday."

11. My art teacher subscribes to <u>Godzilla</u>, a periodical about Asian artists working in New York City.
12. "Please write to me," Joyce requested. "I want to keep in touch with you."
13. In my report I wrote, "One reviewer praised Dee Brown's book <u>Bury My Heart at Wounded Knee</u> in these words: 'an important and angry book; but I forgot to cite the <u>New Republic</u> magazine as the source of the quote.   **13.** book'";
14. As we ran down the street, Charles shouted, "Faster! Faster!"
15. Sally said, "John just whispered, 'I'll be at the game tonight.'"
16. Our next history assignment is Chapter 14, "Great Ideals in the Constitution."
17. Did you read the article "The Costs of College Today"?
18. My aunt asked, "What did your friend mean when he said that you look 'rad' in your new glasses?"
19. <u>The Novelist</u> is in a collection of W. H. Auden's shorter poems.
20. "You often use the French expression <u>au revoir</u>," said Hannah.

COMMON ERROR

Problem. Students are sometimes confused as to where a question mark or an exclamation point is placed when the mark is used with a quotation that is part of a larger sentence.

Solution. Tell students to replace the quotation with the letter *x* and ask themselves if the question mark or exclamation point is proper punctuation for the remaining sentence. If it is, the punctuation mark goes outside the quotation marks. If not, the punctuation goes inside. The placement can be double-checked by removing the quotation from the sentence and reviewing the quotation by itself. If the question mark or exclamation point seem to be proper end punctuation for the quotation, it goes inside the quotation marks. If not, it goes outside.

OBJECTIVE

- To add apostrophes, hyphens, dashes, or parentheses, as needed, in given sentences

MECHANICS

CHAPTER OVERVIEW

A review of this chapter can aid students in the correct use of often-tricky punctuation marks. This chapter presents fifteen rules involving apostrophes, hyphens, dashes, and parentheses. The chapter will show students how to use these less-common marks correctly and effectively. In addition, the **Writing Application** offers an opportunity for students to practice using one of these marks, the dash, by writing poetry.

Have students refer to this chapter during the proofreading and publishing stages of writing. The rules contained in this chapter cover the most-common errors made with these punctuation marks.

USING THE DIAGNOSTIC TEST

This test will help teachers to gauge students' knowledge and ability in applying the punctuation rules for apostrophes, hyphens, dashes, and parentheses. **Part A** examines students' ability to use apostrophes and hyphens. **Part B** focuses on using dashes and parentheses correctly.

MECHANICS

28 PUNCTUATION

Apostrophes, Hyphens, Dashes, Parentheses

Diagnostic Test

A. Using Apostrophes and Hyphens Correctly

Add apostrophes and hyphens where they are needed in the following sentences. [Note: Some sentences contain more than one error.] Hyphens are indicated by the $_\wedge$ symbol.

EXAMPLE   **1.** The childrens boots were lined up outside the door.
   1. *children's*

1. The town's record on supporting youth projects has been good.
2. We hope to see some Aztec and Mayan ruins during our three-week vacation in Mexico.
3. The police officer said that everyone's house should be searched for the missing child.
4. Only fifty-three people went to our ballet recital, and thirty of them were our relatives.
5. I bought four pairs of gloves as my two sisters' birth-day presents.

6. Judo, a Japanese martial art that is popular with both men and women, calls for strength, skill, and self-discipline.
7. Christopher's writing is hard to read because his *a*'s look like *o*'s.
8. We're going on a field trip to the art museum to see the exhibit of post-Impressionist art.
9. The women's basketball team, which is coached by an ex-Laker, has run up quite an impressive string of victories.
10. Sampson and Smith's Bakery, which displays its pastries in the window, is around the corner from my house.

B. Using Dashes and Parentheses Correctly

Add dashes or parentheses where they are needed in each of the following sentences. (Do not add commas or colons.) Answers may vary. Carets indicate placement of dashes.

EXAMPLE **1.** The school's volunteers freshmen, sophomores, and juniors were honored during the assembly.
  1. *The school's volunteers—freshmen, sophomores, and juniors—were honored during the assembly.*

11. My cousins like many of Charlie Pride's songs his "Crystal Chandeliers" is their favorite.
12. When we met my chemistry teacher at the mall, my little sister's question "Why doesn't that man have any hair on his head?" embarrassed me so much I wanted to hide.
13. This report contains information about agriculture in three South American countries Brazil, Argentina, and Colombia.
14. Crystal's time for the fifty-yard dash the fastest time of anyone on the team qualified her for the regional track meet.
15. I read the wrong chapter for my history homework a disastrous mistake!
16. Mary Ellen Jefferson, a former district attorney, will speak at Thursday's assembly (I'll have to miss gym class) and will address the topic of student rights.

MECHANICS

OBJECTIVES

- To form the singular and plural possessive cases of words in a list of nouns and pronouns
- To proofread given phrases and to add necessary apostrophes
- To correct errors in a paragraph by forming possessives
- To identify and to use correctly the possessive forms of words

848 *Punctuation*

17. Our newspaper, the *Sexton High Chronicle* (it used to be called the *Weekly Warrior*) won the highest award in the state.
18. Bessie Coleman (I read an article about her) was the first licensed African American pilot.
19. Rushing to catch the bus, I dropped my books in the mud (I never should have overslept!) and then lost the heel of my shoe.
20. He works nearly all day in his garden (he retired last year) and is always weeding, mulching, and pruning.

 QUICK REMINDER

Write the following words on the chalkboard:

1. their, they're, there
2. theirs, there's
3. who's, whose
4. we're, were
5. it's, its
6. you're, your

Have volunteers use these words correctly in a sentence. Ask students to explain how these words are different. [They can be classified into two groups: possessive pronouns and contractions.]

Apostrophes

Possessive Case

The possessive case of a noun or a pronoun shows ownership or relationship.

OWNERSHIP	**Jorge's** calculator has a solar battery. Where did she buy **her** bracelet?
RELATIONSHIP	**Pam's** aunt is a plumber. The mother birds had fed **their** young.

Many writers are not always sure about when an apostrophe should be used. Whenever you are in doubt about whether or not to use an apostrophe, try an "of" phrase in place of the word. If the "of" phrase makes sense, then an apostrophe is needed.

EXAMPLE: **yesterdays news** [Should there be an apostrophe in *yesterdays*?]
news "of yesterday" [Because this makes good sense, an apostrophe should be used.]
ANSWER: **yesterday's news**

Nouns in the Possessive Case

28a. To form the possessive case of a singular noun, add an apostrophe and an *s*.

EXAMPLES Barbara's house   one boy's uniform
          a week's salary   that stereo's speakers

A proper name ending in *s* may add only an apostrophe if

- the name has two or more syllables
  and
- the addition of *s* after the apostrophe would make the name awkward to pronounce.

    EXAMPLES   Xerxes' army
               Moses' law
               Sophocles' plays

However, most proper names that end in *s* form the possessive case by adding an apostrophe and an *s*.

EXAMPLES James's idea
          Dickens's stories
          Dr. Seuss's books

Singular common nouns ending in *s* need both the apostrophe *and* the *s* if the added *s* is pronounced as a separate syllable.

EXAMPLES the princess's slipper
          my boss's orders
          a bus's wheels

28b. To form the possessive case of a plural noun ending in *s*, add only the apostrophe.

EXAMPLES cats' owners   cities' problems
          coaches' records princesses' duties

The few plural nouns that do not end in *s* form the possessive case by adding an apostrophe and an *s*.

EXAMPLES geese's migration   children's stories

☞ REFERENCE NOTE: For more examples of irregular nouns, see page 878.

NOTE: Don't use an apostrophe to form the *plural* of a noun.

    INCORRECT   The four horse's pulled the wagon
    CORRECT   The four horses pulled the wagon.

MEETING INDIVIDUAL NEEDS

LEP/ESL

Spanish. Spanish has a possessive form for pronouns but not for nouns; therefore, there may be much confusion about the use of apostrophes. For example, in Spanish, the possessive form would be "the book of José." Students will need extra practice in using the possessive case. You may want to give the students a series of statements that they change by using a possessive form of the noun. An example is "This book belongs to José. It is ____." [José's book]

COMMON ERROR

Problem. Students become confused with the use of the apostrophe in contractions and personal pronouns.

Solution. Tell students that a rule to remember is that none of the personal pronouns use 's to form a possessive case.

MECHANICS

MECHANICS

MECHANICS

ANSWERS
Exercise 1

1. governor, governor's; governors, governors'
2. secretary, secretary's; secretaries, secretaries'
3. bird, bird's; birds, birds'
4. deer, deer's; deer, deer's *or* deers, deers'
5. woman, woman's; women, women's
6. picture, picture's; pictures, pictures'
7. pencil, pencil's; pencils, pencils'
8. class, class's; classes, classes'
9. chief, chief's; chiefs, chiefs'
10. mouse, mouse's; mice, mice's

COOPERATIVE LEARNING

A scrambled-sentence game using familiar homonyms could be a successful way to teach apostrophes to students.

There should be three students on each team, and each team receives two sets of homonyms. Members can each write a scrambled sentence, or the entire team can compose one. Students must place one of the homonyms correctly in their sentences. Or they can work together on the sentences, and the class can have a relay race in which a student from each team must work on one sentence at a time.

 EXERCISE 1   **Writing the Possessive Forms of Nouns**

Make four columns headed *Singular, Singular Possessive, Plural,* and *Plural Possessive*. Write those forms of each of the following words. If you don't know how to spell a plural form, check a dictionary.

	Singular	Singular Possessive	Plural	Plural Possessive
EXAMPLE				
1.	*temple*	*temple's*	*temples*	*temples'*

1. governor	3. bird	5. woman	7. pencil	9. chief
2. secretary	4. deer	6. picture	8. class	10. mouse

Pronouns in the Possessive Case

28c. Possessive personal pronouns and the relative pronoun *whose* do not require an apostrophe.

> **Possessive Personal Pronouns**
>
> my, mine   our, ours
> your, yours   their, theirs
> his, her, hers, its

My, your, her, its, our, and *their* are used before a noun. *Mine, yours, hers, ours,* and *theirs* are used as subjects, complements, or objects. *His* is used in both ways.

EXAMPLES   This is **my** desk. This desk is **mine**.
I borrowed **your** pencil. I borrowed a pencil of **yours**.
Her work is excellent. **Hers** is the best work.
Clara is **our** captain; Dena is **theirs**.

☞ REFERENCE NOTE: Don't confuse the possessive forms of pronouns with contractions, such as *whose* and *who's, its* and *it's, their* and *they're,* and *your* and *you're.* See pages 890, 865, 889, and 890.

28d. Indefinite pronouns in the possessive case require an apostrophe and an *s.*

EXAMPLES   anyone**'s** choice   either**'s** idea

☞ REFERENCE NOTE: See page 517 for a list of indefinite pronouns.

Compounds in the Possessive Case

28e. In compound words, names of organizations and business firms, and words showing joint possession, only the last word is possessive in form.

COMPOUND WORDS	someone **else's** problem sister-in-**law's** office
ORGANIZATIONS	board of **directors'** report Urban **League's** membership
BUSINESS FIRMS JOINT POSSESSION	Acosta and **Rivera's** law firm Bob and **Jim's** canoe Kimi and **Tanaki's** plan aunt and **uncle's** photograph

However, when one of the words showing joint possession is a pronoun, both words should be possessive in form.

EXAMPLE **Sean's** and her conversation

NOTE: To avoid forming a possessive that sounds awkward, use a phrase beginning with *of* instead.

AWKWARD the Samuel H. Scripps American Dance Festival Award's winner

BETTER the winner of the Samuel H. Scripps American Dance Festival Award

28f. When two or more persons possess something individually, each of their names is possessive in form.

EXAMPLES **Michael's** and **Lila's** wallets
Denise's and **Mark's** books

 EXERCISE 2 **Correcting Phrases by Adding Apostrophes**

Proofread the following phrases, adding apostrophes where they are needed. If a phrase is correct, write C.

 INTEGRATING THE LANGUAGE ARTS

Mechanics and Writing. Ask students to look around the classroom or to think about their neighborhoods and to write paragraphs that each contain at least ten examples of apostrophes used to show possession or the possessive forms of personal and relative pronouns. As in **Exercise 4**, students should read each other's paragraphs to find apostrophe errors.

Technology Link. Have students use the spell-checking part of a word-processing program, if available, to aid in proofreading their writing. You might remind students that this helpful feature will not detect incorrectly spelled homonyms. For example, in the sentence "Their going to the movies," the personal pronoun would go unnoticed.

MECHANICS

MECHANICS

INTEGRATING THE LANGUAGE ARTS

Literature Link. One use of apostrophes is often found in literary writing. Authors omit letters and substitute apostrophes to make words sound more like normal speech patterns.

In a selection such as "Mother to Son" by Langston Hughes, students can see how apostrophes are used to create a conversational tone. You could have students rewrite the poem without contractions and then read their versions aloud. Ask students to describe how their versions are different from the original.

EXAMPLE   **1.** the cameras lens
          1. *the camera*'s lens

1. a week's pay
2. Ann's and my project   **3.** C
3. two pairs of tennis shoes
4. my father-in-law's boat
5. a good night's sleep

6. Socrates'oration
7. Lynn's and Mike's shoes
8. the seconds ticking by   **8.** C
9. the two balloonists'feats
10. a citizen's rights

 EXERCISE 3   **Correcting Paragraphs by Adding Apostrophes**

For each sentence in the following paragraphs, write each <u>word that should be in the possessive case</u>, and add the missing apostrophe.

EXAMPLE   **[1]** Last week I followed my parents suggestion and enrolled in an amateur photography class offered by our citys art center.
          1. *parents'; city's*

[1] I shared my mom and <u>dad's</u> exasperation when, once again, I spent a whole <u>week's</u> allowance on disappointing pictures. [2] I had borrowed Uncle <u>Fred's</u> expensive camera; but even with all that <u>camera's</u> extra features, my photographs looked like <u>children's</u> smudged finger paintings.

[3] My pictures of Bob and <u>Ruth's</u> wedding reception, our <u>family's</u> social event of the year, were destroyed when I fell into the pool with my camera. [4] Last summer I also took pictures during our <u>month's</u> vacation in <u>Arizona's</u> famous Painted Desert. [5] Unfortunately, I did not understand enough about the <u>sun's</u> strong light at midday, and most of my photographs had that washed-out look.

[6] My <u>life's</u> most embarrassing moment occurred when I took a picture of my class for the <u>school's</u> yearbook and discovered that I had forgotten to put film in the camera. [7] Another time, I took my camera to <u>Tom's</u> party but could not get <u>anyone's</u> attention long enough to set up the shots that I wanted. [8] As a result, I gave up on people and tried to take my <u>pets'</u> pictures; however, a <u>dog's</u> will and a <u>parakeet's</u> wings are hard to control. [9] After all these bad experiences, I knew that I needed a <u>professional's</u> advice. [10] I'm pleased to report that during the very first

MECHANICS

photography class, the instructor raised all the <u>students</u>′ confidence, including mine.

▶ EXERCISE 4   **Proofreading for Errors in Possessive Forms**

Most of the following sentences contain at least one incorrect possessive form. For each error, give the correct form of the word. If a sentence is correct, write *C*.

EXAMPLE   **1.** The island nation of the Philippines bears the marks of both Spains and the United States occupations.
      1. *Spain's; United States'*

1. The ~~countrys~~ national language is Pilipino, but ~~it's~~ people also speak Spanish, English, and other regional languages.   **1.** country's/its

2. In the United States, Filipino immigrant Pedro ~~Flores~~ invention, the yo-yo, became a popular toy.   **2.** Flores'

3. My ~~mothers~~ boss was visiting the Philippines when Corazon Aquino became president in 1986.   **3.** mother's

4. He took this picture of Mrs. Aquino and some of her supporters dressed in yellow, the color identified with their campaign.   **4.** C

5. ~~Tina's~~ and Phil's plan to visit the Philippines was postponed when Mount Pinatubo erupted in 1991.   **5.** Tina

6. The ~~Philippines~~ capital and largest city is Manila, which is on the big island of Luzon.   **6.** Philippines'

MECHANICS

👁 **VISUAL CONNECTIONS**
Ideas for Writing. The picture of Corazon Aquino may allow you to discuss other women who are leaders. Students can generate a list of important women in government and politics. The objective of the lists is to illustrate shared and individual traits and to illustrate how the possessive forms of the women's names should be written; for example, some traits (in possessive form) are Ann Richards' and Barbara Bush's love of reading, Barbara Jordan's impressive career, and Sandra Day O'Connor's historic appointment to the Supreme Court.

CONTRACTIONS Rule 28g

OBJECTIVES

- To use contractions correctly to write captions
- To choose either a contraction or a word in the possessive case to complete a sentence
- To write a short critical review that uses five contractions correctly

854 *Punctuation*

7. Both˰K̶i̶m̶ and Marta's lunches came with delicious Filipino custard. **7.** Kim's
8. It's ˰a̶n̶y̶o̶n̶e̶s̶ guess how many islands actually make up the Philippines, though there are certainly more than seven thousand islands. **8.** anyone's
9. The Spanish monarch˰w̶h̶o̶'̶s̶ soldiers named the Philippines was King Philip II. **9.** whose
10. ˰C̶h̶i̶l̶d̶r̶e̶n̶s̶ pastimes in the Philippines include kite flying and swimming. **10.** Children's

Contractions

28g. Use an apostrophe to show where letters, words, or numerals have been omitted in a contraction.

A *contraction* is a shortened form of a word, a figure, or a group of words. The apostrophes in contractions show where letters, words, or numerals have been left out.

Common Contractions	
who is .... who's	she will ...... she'll
there is .... there's	I am .... I'm
could have ..... could've	you are ..... you're
1993 .... '93	we had........ we'd
of the clock ..... o'clock	she has........ she's
let us .... let's	Lisa is .... Lisa's

The adverb *not* is often shortened to *n't* and added to a verb without any change in the verb's spelling.

EXAMPLES	is not .... isn't	were not .... weren't
	are not ...... aren't	has not .... hasn't
	does not .... doesn't	have not .... haven't
	do not .... don't	had not ...... hadn't
	did not ...... didn't	would not .. wouldn't
	was not ..... wasn't	should not .. shouldn't
EXCEPTIONS	cannot .... can't	will not .... won't

Make sure that you don't confuse contractions with possessive pronouns.

MECHANICS

Teacher's ResourceBank™
RESOURCES

CONTRACTIONS
- Apostrophes in Contractions

QUICK REMINDER

Some students need to be reminded of the correct placement of the apostrophe and spacing of the letters in a contraction. Write these two pairs of words on the chalkboard:

does'nt   wouldn't
doesn't   would'nt

Ask students to tell you which words are correct. Explain that the two incorrect words illustrate a common misuse of the apostrophe in contractions.

854

REVIEW A

OBJECTIVE

- To identify words that need apostrophes in given sentences and to insert the apostrophes where they belong

28g

CONTRACTIONS	POSSESSIVE PRONOUNS
Who's next? [who is]	**Whose** turn is next?
It's purring. [It is]	Listen to **its** purr.
You're late. [You are]	**Your** report is late.
There's a mule. [There is]	That mule is **theirs.**
They're healthy pets. [They are]	**Their** pets are healthy.

EXERCISE 5   **Using Contractions**

You are learning how to draw these cartoon figures in action. Using these sketches as models, make five original drawings of characters in motion. Then write captions to go with your drawings. In your captions, use at least five of the following expressions correctly as contractions.

1. should not
2. they have
3. of the clock
4. they would
5. were not
6. she will
7. he is
8. let us
9. who is
10. does not

Running

Kicking

Jumping

Back kick

Diving

Graceful fall

Awkward fall

Cartoons from *Drawing and Selling Cartoons* by Jack Markow, copyright © 1964 by Grosset & Dunlap, Inc. Reprinted by permission of Grosset & Dunlap, Inc.

REVIEW A   **Correcting Sentences by Adding Apostrophes**

Identify each <u>word that needs an apostrophe</u> in the following sentences. Then insert the apostrophes correctly.

ANSWERS
Exercise 5

Answers will vary. The sketches can be rudimentary and the captions need not be very amusing. The main objective is to have students use the contractions correctly.

MEETING
INDIVIDUAL
NEEDS

LEP/ESL

    General Strategies. To give students more practice in using contractions, have them write dialogues to present in class. Give them a situation on which to base their writing. For example, a ten-dollar bill has been found in the classroom. Whose is it and what should be done with it? Tell students that they must each include a specified number of contractions (six). Then have them work in pairs or small groups to write their dialogues. Students can then present the dialogues to their classmates. You could even use one of the dialogues for a class exercise to recapitulate.

MECHANICS

MECHANICS

COMMON ERROR

Problem. Students might confuse the apostrophe showing a contraction with the apostrophe showing possession.

Solution. Tell students to take away the apostrophe and to read the sentence without the contraction. Most students will hear their mistakes.

MEETING
INDIVIDUAL
NEEDS

LEP/ESL

General Strategies. For the **Picture This** writing assignment, you may first want to brainstorm about the topic of art, because the vocabulary for this subject may be quite difficult for LEP/ESL students. The students could begin discussing what they like or dislike in art. Then they could describe the sculpture objectively. The discussion could then lead to whether the *Geometric Mouse* sculpture is good or bad. It is important that key words be written on the chalkboard for students to copy so that students can refer to the words as they write their assignment.

EXAMPLE   **1.** Werent you the one who said you didnt like eggplant?
         1. *Weren't; didn't*

1. <u>Who's</u> going to be at Leon and <u>Josh's</u> party?
2. <u>Let's</u> hide and see if <u>they'll</u> look for us.
3. I <u>can't</u> find the calamata olives and the feta cheese for the Greek salad.
4. Is her <u>doctor's</u> appointment at nine <u>o'clock</u>?
5. Cleve doesn't have time to mow both his and <u>Ray's</u> lawns.
6. <u>That's</u> the best idea <u>you've</u> had in two days.
7. <u>We're</u> lucky that that <u>dog's</u> barking didn't awaken them.
8. <u>I'm</u> trying to follow <u>Paul's</u> map to <u>Jean's</u> house.
9. <u>It's</u> hailing; therefore, I <u>don't</u> think you should go skiing.
10. Elise <u>couldn't</u> remember the characteristics of the tiger in the Chinese zodiac.

EXERCISE 6   Recognizing the Correct Use of Apostrophes

Choose the <u>correct word</u> in parentheses in each of the following sentences.

EXAMPLE   **1.** (*It's, Its*) never too late to learn something new.
         1. *It's*

1. (*You're, Your*) sure that (*you're, your*) allowed to bring (*you're, your*) book to the exam?
2. (*Whose, Who's*) idea was (*you're, your*) trip to the National Civil Rights Museum in Memphis?
3. (*They're, Their*) trying to sell (*they're, their*) house.
4. (*It's, Its*) the best choice.
5. Do you know (*who's, whose*) responsible for (*they're, their*) confusion?
6. I hope the dog can find (*it's, its*) way home.
7. (*It's, Its*) Philip (*who's, whose*) always late.
8. Although (*it's, its*) been snowing all day, (*they're, their*) still planning to go.
9. (*Who's, Whose*) the designer of (*they're, their*) float for Galveston's Mardi Gras parade?
10. I know (*you're, your*) upset with the plan, but (*it's, its*) the only way to solve the problem.

SEGMENT 4 *(pp. 857–858)*

PLURALS Rule 28h

OBJECTIVE

- To identify words that need apostrophes in given sentences and to add the apostrophes correctly

PICTURE THIS

You are an art critic for *ARTnews* magazine. Write a short review of this modern sculpture. In your review, try to convince readers that *Geometric Mouse* either is or is not good art. In writing the review, rely on your own taste, as well as your understanding of art. Begin by stating your opinion of the sculpture, and then give reasons to support that opinion. Include five different contractions in your review. When you finish writing, compare your review with those of your classmates. Can your class agree on the artistic value of this work?

Collection Walker Art Center, Minneapolis, Intended gift of Mr. and Mrs. Miles Q. Fiterman, 1974

Subject: a sculpture
Audience: *ARTnews* readers
Purpose: to persuade

MECHANICS

Apostrophes **857**

28h

PICTURE THIS

You could ask an art teacher to discuss criticism and some of the vocabulary that is associated with it, such as *form, texture, depth, interpretation*. This activity integrates the curriculum and introduces students to what possibly is an unfamiliar subject.

Or you could have students create their own three-dimensional interpretations of a mouse.

Teacher's ResourceBank™
RESOURCES

PLURALS
- Apostrophes in Plurals

MECHANICS

QUICK REMINDER

Give students the following letters and words, and have the students identify which need apostrophes to make them plural:

a, b, c, and, or, m
[*A, b, c,* and *m* require an *'s*, but *and,* and *or* do not.]

Next, you can have students volunteer example sentences that use each of these words or letters.

Plurals

28h. Use an apostrophe and an *s* to form the plurals of some letters and some words referred to as words.

As a rule, only an *s* is added to form the plurals of most letters and most words used as words.

EXAMPLES   Make your uppercase *W*s higher so that they don't look like lowercase *w*s.
Mr. Carr suggested that I replace some of the *and*s in my paper with other words that are more exact.

However, in some cases both an apostrophe and an *s* are added to prevent confusion.

857

LEP/ESL

Spanish. In many Spanish dialects, a word's final *s* is often not pronounced. As a result, the students have problems hearing the plural *s* even when it is clearly spoken. To give the students practice in hearing the plural forms, as well as practice in using apostrophes to form plurals of letters and of words used as words, give the students a number of dictations that use both types of plural forms. Have students write the sentences on the chalkboard and discuss the words with the class.

A DIFFERENT APPROACH

Students could work in small groups of three for this assignment. Their objective is to write a children's book about a world made up of letters and words. Each student could create a different part of the book. Students are to use as many plural letters and plural words referred to as words as they can. Encourage the use of illustrations.

REVIEW B

OBJECTIVE

• To identify words that need apostrophes and to add apostrophes where needed in given sentences

858 *Punctuation*

EXAMPLES **There are four *s*'s and four *i*'s in *Mississippi*.** [Without an apostrophe, the plural of *i* would look like the word *is*. Since an apostrophe and *s* are used to form the plural of one letter, an apostrophe and *s* are also used with the other letter for consistency.]
Mr. Carr suggested that I replace some of the *so*'s in my paper with other words that are more exact. [Without the apostrophe, the plural of *so* could be confused with the acronym *sos*.]

NOTE: Using both an apostrophe and an *s* is never wrong. If you have any doubt about whether or not to use the apostrophe, use it.

☞ **REFERENCE NOTE:** For more information about forming these kinds of plurals and the plurals of numerals, see pages 879–880.

▶ REVIEW B **Correcting Sentences by Adding Apostrophes**

For each of the following sentences, write all the <u>items needing apostrophes</u>, and add the apostrophes.

EXAMPLE **1. You may agree with the school boards decision, but I dont.**
1. *school board's; don't*

1. <u>Arent</u> you familiar with the expression "<u>Threes</u> a crowd"?
2. <u>Youve</u> forgotten that there are two <u>I</u>s in *llama*.
3. The <u>countrys</u> first African American on the Supreme Court was Justice Thurgood Marshall, who was appointed in 67 and resigned in 91.
4. Lewis <u>Carrolls</u> novel *Alices Adventures in Wonderland* was originally called *Alices Adventures Underground*.
5. <u>Whos</u> going to change the <u>babies</u> diapers?
6. After school <u>were</u> going to visit <u>Pams</u> brother; <u>hes</u> in St. <u>Marys</u> Hospital.
7. Rochelle thinks that <u>shell</u> get <u>A</u>s in both biology and English this term.
8. <u>Its</u> been six weeks since I checked the <u>cars</u> oil and its tires.
9. Your story would be better if <u>youd</u> remove about thirty *verys*.
10. She learned the Hawaiian <u>alphabets</u> twelve letters, but Max didn't.

SEGMENT 5 *(pp. 859–862)*
HYPHENS AND COMPOUND WORDS
Rules 28i–28j
OBJECTIVES

- To divide words that come at the end of a line by adding hyphens correctly
- To identify compound words in given sentences and to hyphenate them correctly

28i

Hyphens

Word Division

28i. Use a hyphen to divide a word at the end of a line.

EXAMPLE   Even with today's modern technology, scientists can ac▪count for only about 10 percent of the universe.

As the example shows, a word at the end of a line is always divided between syllables. If you're not sure about a word's syllables, check a dictionary. Also, keep in mind the following rules for dividing words.

(1) Do not divide one-syllable words.

INCORRECT   After a long journey, the Spanish explorers reach▪ed their destination.

CORRECT   After a long journey, the Spanish explorers reached their destination.

(2) Words containing double consonants should usually be divided between the double consonants.

EXAMPLES   cor▪rect   begin▪ning

 REFERENCE NOTE: See rule 28i (3) for exceptions like *tell-ing* and *call-ing*.

(3) Words with a prefix or suffix can usually be divided between the prefix and the root or the root and the suffix.

EXAMPLES   pro▪mote   peace▪ful   tell▪ing   de▪pend▪able

(4) If a word is already hyphenated, divide it only at the hyphen.

INCORRECT   My stepsister Melissa plans to take a course in self-de-fense.

CORRECT   My stepsister Melissa plans to take a course in self▪defense.

INCORRECT   Ms. Malamud always seems to have such a hap-py-go-lucky attitude.

CORRECT   Ms. Malamud always seems to have such a happy▪go-lucky attitude.

Teacher's ResourceBank™
RESOURCES

HYPHENS AND COMPOUND WORDS
- Hyphens and Compound Words

 QUICK REMINDER
Write these nouns on the chalkboard:

oil slick	oilskin
lee shore	leeward
push button	push-pull

Some are open compounds [lee shore], some closed [leeward], and some hyphenated [push-pull]. Tell students that the use of the hyphen is favored for less-commonly known compound words. As a compound noun becomes part of everyday usage, the hyphen is usually dropped and the compound becomes closed or open. An example is the word *notebook*.

LEP/ESL

General Strategies. English differs from Romance languages in that its speakers often create new words by inventing compound adjectives. This allows writers quite a bit of freedom.

You may want to point out that compound adjectives, like compound nouns, may be joined by hyphens. Give students an example and then have them think of some other examples that they may have heard in informal speech or in the mass media.

MECHANICS

(5) Do not divide a word so that one letter stands alone.

INCORRECT   In the gloomy twilight, we had caught a momentar-y glimpse of them.

CORRECT   In the gloomy twilight, we had caught a momen▪tary glimpse of them.

INCORRECT   The other driver suddenly changed lanes to go a-round the line of cars.

CORRECT   The other driver suddenly changed lanes to go around the line of cars.

▶ EXERCISE 7   **Using Hyphens to Divide Words at the Ends of Lines**

Write each of the following words, adding a hyphen where you would divide the word at the end of a line. If a word should *not* be divided, write *no hyphen*. If you are unsure where to divide a word, look it up in a dictionary.

Carets indicate possible word divisions.

EXAMPLE   **1.** harmonious
             1. *har-mo-ni-ous*

1. Olympic
2. algebra
3. toast **3.** no hyphen
4. pemmican

5. drummer
6. alert **6.** no hyphen
7. someone
8. Honduras

9. reservation
10. Johnny‸come‸ lately

Compound Words

Some compound words are written as one single word (*blueberry*); some are hyphenated (*blue-collar*); and some are written as two or more words (*blue jay, Blue Ridge Mountains*).

Whenever you are not sure about the spelling of a compound word, look up the word in a recently published dictionary.

28j. Use a hyphen with compound numbers from *twenty-one* to *ninety-nine* and with fractions used as adjectives.

EXAMPLES   twenty▪seven students
                   a two▪thirds majority [but *two thirds* of the class]

COMMON ERROR

Problem. Open compounds used as adjectives can be misleading.

Solution. Hyphenate the words that are closely related or that are ambiguous without hyphens. For example, *free form sculpture* should be *free-form sculpture*.

MECHANICS

28 j–l

28k. Use a hyphen with the prefixes *ex–, self–,* and *all–,* with the suffix *–elect,* and with all prefixes before a proper noun or proper adjective.

EXAMPLES
ex-president   mid-December
self-control   pro-American
all-purpose   anti-Stalinist
secretary-elect   pre-Civil War

28l. Hyphenate a compound adjective when it precedes the noun it modifies. Do not use a hyphen if one of the modifiers is an adverb ending in *–ly.*

EXAMPLES   a well-organized trip [But *The trip was well organized.*]
an after-school job
a perfectly good answer

NOTE: Some compound adjectives are always hyphenated, no matter whether they precede or follow the nouns they modify.

EXAMPLES   full-scale
down-to-earth

If you have any doubt about whether a compound adjective is hyphenated or not, look up the word in a dictionary.

▶ EXERCISE 8 **Hyphenating Words Correctly**

For each of the following sentences, write and hyphenate the <u>compound words that should be hyphenated</u>. Hyphens are indicated by the ⌃ symbol.

EXAMPLE   **1.** The host of that late night show interviewed an^ expert on America's pre Civil War years.
     1. *late-night; pre-Civil War*

1. <u>Ex‑students</u> were not allowed at the festively decorated <u>post‑prom</u> party.
2. His <u>self‑confidence</u> faded when he forgot his <u>well‑planned</u> speech.
3. <u>Twenty‑five</u> students said they had never heard of the <u>well‑traveled</u> Overland Trail to California.
4. Two thirds of the class voted, but the proposal was defeated by a <u>seven‑tenths</u> majority.

INTEGRATING THE LANGUAGE ARTS

Literature Link. Shakespeare used many compound adjectives in his plays and poems. In *The Tragedy of Julius Caesar,* Cicero states, "Indeed, it is a strange-disposed time . . ." (Act I, Scene iii). Discuss the meaning of "strange-disposed time." Are there any other words that would describe the situation as well as "strange-disposed"? Students could look for more compounds in the play and show how the blending of two words adds to the clarity of the meaning.

Some examples of other compound words found in the play are "live-long day" (1.1.46), "sleek-headed men" (1.2.193), "noblest-minded Romans" (1.3.122), "once-commended beauty" (2.1.271), and "barren-spirited fellow" (4.1.36).

Mechanics and Library Skills. Have each student find five compound words in a dictionary. Then have students research in the library to find the etymologies of the compounds; they can present this information to the class. Students should explain how the separate meaning of each word in a compound adds to the meaning of the compound word.

MECHANICS

MECHANICS

DASHES AND PARENTHESES Rules 28m–28o

OBJECTIVE

- To add dashes and parentheses where needed in given sentences

COOPERATIVE LEARNING

Have each student write a dream sequence or a dialogue with a specified number of dashes in a stream-of-consciousness style. You may want to review this technique with the class first. Group students either into pairs or groups of three. One person will start the dream or dialogue, and the others will write the thoughts and prompt the next thought or sentence. After these samples are completed, you could display them in the classroom.

Teacher's ResourceBank™
RESOURCES

DASHES AND PARENTHESES
- Dashes and Parentheses

QUICK REMINDER

Parentheses with other punctuation create problems that plague many writers. Here are a few sample sentences that employ parentheses. See whether students can tell you where other punctuation belongs with the parentheses—either inside or outside the closing one.

1. The salad tastes wonderful (even though it contains my least favorite food, spinach) [).]
2. Our drama club (the award-winning one) practiced for the fall competition. [no other punctuation]
3. Watermelons (when they are in season) pears, and apples are all combined in this delicious dessert. [),]

862

5. Our new <u>governor-elect</u> was once an <u>all-American</u> football player.
6. In our last debate, some students were <u>pro-United</u> Nations, but others were <u>anti-UN</u>.
7. General Colin Powell, who is a former resident of the Bronx, spoke quite eloquently about the importance of <u>self-determination</u>.
8. We all had to memorize a list of <u>twenty-five</u> <u>well-known</u> writers and their works.
9. You must turn in your reports by <u>mid-November</u>.
10. Christopher's <u>achievement-test</u> scores ranked in the <u>eighty-eighth</u> percentile.

Dashes

Most parenthetical elements are set off by commas or parentheses.

EXAMPLES   Felipe, **however,** had a better idea.
Her suggestion **(that we serve fruit and cheese instead of junk food)** was approved unanimously.

Sometimes, though, such elements call for a sharper separation from the rest of the sentence. In such cases, dashes are used.

NOTE: On a typewriter or a computer, indicate a dash by typing two hyphens. Do not leave a space before, between, or after the hyphens.

28m. Use a dash to indicate an abrupt break in thought or speech or an unfinished statement or question.

EXAMPLES   The party—I'm sorry I forgot to tell you—was not changed to next week.
When Jiffy was born—he was the last puppy—we weren't sure he would survive.
"Why—why won't you believe me?" Ronnie asked pleadingly.
"What I meant was—" Vonda began as the doorbell rang.

28n. Use a dash to mean *namely, that is, in other words,* and similar expressions that come before an explanation.

EXAMPLES   Our family owns two vehicles—a station wagon and a pickup truck. [*namely*]
The weather was unseasonably warm—in the low eighties—which was a welcome change. [*that is*]

NOTE: Either the dash or a colon is acceptable in the second example above.

Parentheses

28o. Use parentheses to enclose material of minor importance in a sentence.

EXAMPLES   The Pyramid of the Magician (never thought I'd actually see it in person) rose majestically against the purple sky of Uxmal, in the Mexican Yucatán.
My grandmother (she's only fifty) swims three miles every day.

Material enclosed in parentheses may range from a single word to a short sentence. A short sentence in parentheses may stand by itself or may be included in the main sentence.

When punctuation marks belong with the parenthetical materials, place them inside the parentheses. When they belong with the sentence as a whole, place them outside the parentheses.

EXAMPLES   Mark your answers with a lead pencil. (Do not use ink.) [The parenthetical sentence stands by itself.]
The child's question ("What inning is it?") tickled the rest of us watching the football game. [The parenthetical sentence is a quoted question included in the main sentence.]
When we reached Shaker Heights (it's just outside Cleveland), we met our cousins for dinner. [The parenthetical sentence is a statement included within the main sentence. Notice that no period is used at the end of a parenthetical declarative sentence included within another sentence.]

LEP/ESL

    General Strategies. The placement of punctuation marks inside or outside the parentheses is a major problem for ESL students. You could give sentences that require students to identify correct placement of the punctuation marks. Have students work in pairs or in small groups, and place lower-ability students with those who have more proficiency in English.

MECHANICS

MECHANICS

INTEGRATING THE LANGUAGE ARTS

Literature Link. Have students scan the poetry section of their literature books to discover poems that include several dashes. For example, in the poem "Theme for English B" by Langston Hughes, students will find nine dashes and parentheses. Ask students to describe the implication of each.

[The dashes emphasize the goal of the instructor's assignment, the poet's connection to his community, his self-examination, his tastes in music, the teacher-student relationship, and the student's role as teacher. The parentheses enclose an additional comment by the poet explaining that he should listen not only to the voices from his black heritage but also to the voices of all people.]

GUIDELINES FOR PUNCTUATING PARENTHETICAL MATERIAL

Commas, dashes, and parentheses are all used to enclose parenthetical material. In general, follow these guidelines for determining when to use the three different types of punctuation marks.

1. Remember that only material that can be omitted without changing the sentence's basic meaning is considered parenthetical.
2. Use commas to set off elements that are closely related to the rest of the sentence.
3. Use dashes to emphasize an abrupt change in thought.
4. Use parentheses to minimize the importance of the enclosed material.
5. Don't confuse your reader by using too many parenthetical elements.

EXAMPLES   We rehearsed for the show, a wonderful musical comedy.

We rehearsed for the show—the musical event of the year!

We rehearsed (at least those of us who managed to remember our lines did) for the show.

 EXERCISE 9   **Correcting Sentences by Using Dashes and Parentheses**

Write the following sentences, adding dashes and parentheses where they are needed. If a sentence is correct, write C.   Answers may vary. Carets indicate placement of dashes.

EXAMPLE   **1.** The Oak Ridge Boys and Alabama I have every one of their albums have won many awards.

       1. *The Oak Ridge Boys and Alabama (I have every one of their albums) have won many awards.*

1. "Yankee Doodle" (it was the unofficial United States anthem at the time) was played after the signing of the Treaty of Ghent.
2. While standing at the top of Pikes Peak, Katherine Lee Bates wrote the words to the song "America the Beautiful." **2.** C

3. Gloria Estefan(I love her songs!)gave a concert here, and it was sold out.
4. There were three original members of the Sons of the Pioneers₍Roy Rogers(his real name is Leonard Slye), Bob Nolan, and Tim Spencer.
5. Linda Ronstadt has recorded many different kinds of music, including rock, songs from the 1930s and '40s, and Mexican tunes. **5.** C
6. The Beatles used several names₍Foreverly Brothers, the Cavemen, the Moondogs, and the Quarrymen₍ before they settled on Beatles.
7. Bob Dylan's real name₍Robert Allen Zimmerman₍ isn't commonly known.
8. Cathy agreed to listen to Mozart's concertos(what a surprise!)if her parents would listen to one of Paula Abdul's tapes.
9. Last night's concert was about average₍the beat was good, but the singers were uninspired.
10. Whitney Houston had a hit song(Wouldn't Francis Scott Key be pleased?)with her version of "The Star-Spangled Banner."

▶ REVIEW C   **Proofreading for Errors in Punctuation**

Each of the following sentences contains at least one error in punctuation. Correct these errors by adding apostrophes, hyphens, dashes, or parentheses where they are needed. Answers may vary. The ₍ symbol indicates placement of hyphens; carets indicate placement of dashes.

EXAMPLE   **1.** Dont you ever wonder I frequently do about who invented different kinds of machines and tools?
          1. *Don't; —I frequently do—*

1. Both Trish's and Robert's reports(the ones required for social studies)were about the shoe industry.
2. Trish joked that she chose the subject because at least seventy₍five percent of the world's students wear shoes.
3. I thought the other report₍the one that Robert gave on the invention of the lasting machine₍was better written, though.
4. The lasting machine(its many parts are numbered in the intricate patent drawing on the next page)changed the shoe industry's future.

MECHANICS

MECHANICS

REVIEW C

Teaching Note. In sentence 10, students may forget to use an apostrophe for *United States*. Explain that it is a proper adjective. This would provide an opportunity to review or to introduce the subject of proper adjectives.

VISUAL CONNECTIONS

Exploring the Subject. Jan Matzeliger was offered fifteen hundred dollars for his model machine, but he refused to sell it. He was not satisfied with it and worked five more years to perfect it. With this machine, income from shoe manufacturing increased 350 percent in New England within a few years.

WRITING APPLICATION

You could have students skim through the poetry section of their literature textbook to find a poem that contains dashes or parentheses. In addition, students should be able to describe how the dashes or parentheses are used in their own poems or be able to comment on the effectiveness of this punctuation in their poems.

866

MECHANICS

WRITING APPLICATION

OBJECTIVE

- To use four dashes correctly in a poem

5. The machine's inventor, the distinguished-looking young man pictured below, was Jan Matzeliger.
6. He came to the United States from Dutch Guiana (now Suriname) in the 1870s and found work as a shoemaker's apprentice.
7. Matzeliger wasn't happy with the amount of workers' time that was spent putting shoes together.
8. Within ten years' time, he perfected a machine that shaped leather for the upper shoe and attached it to the sole.
9. Matzeliger's patent for this all-important machine was granted in 1883.
10. The United Shoe Manufacturing Company's decision to buy the machine gave that company control of the United States' shoe market.

WRITING APPLICATION

Using Dashes in Poetry

Have you ever noticed that many poems contain dashes? Poets use dashes not only to indicate sharp separations of thoughts but also to emphasize particular words or phrases. Notice how John Ciardi uses dashes in the following poem.

> How Time Goes
>
> How old am I? I really don't know,
>   But I can tell you I have spent
> My whole life—up to a minute ago—
>   Being younger than I am now. I meant
> To keep it that way, I suppose,
> But that's how it is with time—it goes.

Which use of the dash in the poem signals a break in thought? Which use of the dash means *namely*?

▶ WRITING ACTIVITY

You've decided to enter a local poetry contest for high school students. The name of the contest is Poetry for Our Time, and all the poems have to reflect students' ideas about current subjects. For the contest, write a poem that uses at least four dashes.

Prewriting Start by making a list of some subjects that interest you. You might list abstract subjects, such as love and peace, or concrete ones, such as environmental or school issues. Choose a subject from your list, and then freewrite about it. List as many sensory details as you can to describe your subject. Then start grouping these details to create a loose structure for your poem. Before you begin writing your poem, decide on a rhyme scheme and rhythm.

Writing Use your freewriting notes to write your first draft. As you form your ideas into lines of poetry, keep in mind your rhyme scheme and rhythm pattern. Choose words carefully, paying attention both to their sound and to the images they create.

Evaluating and Revising Read your poem silently to be sure that it says what you want it to. Add, cut, or rearrange details to express your ideas more effectively. Then read your poem aloud and listen to the sound and rhythm of the words you've used. Make any changes that are necessary to create the rhyme scheme and rhythm you chose in your prewriting. Be sure that you've used at least four dashes in your poem.

MECHANICS

CRITICAL THINKING
Synthesis

Have students discuss what kind of subject would allow a dash to be used appropriately [a dream, for example, in which thoughts are unsettled]. Next, have students move into small groups to create scenes with dialogue in which it is appropriate to use dashes. An argument might serve as a starting point. Set a very limited time period for this collaborative creation and encourage students to write dialogues or arguments based on topics of concern to them.

PREWRITING

You could brainstorm some topics by using the front page of the newspaper. If the topics don't spark interest, ask students what issues concern them. List some of their responses on the chalkboard.

STUDENTS WITH SPECIAL NEEDS

This activity may overwhelm learning disabled students, as some have difficulty with expressive language.

Have students write poems that use words and phrases from magazines and newspapers. Tell each student to choose a theme and to cut out words pertaining to this theme. Students should arrange the words on the page, and add dashes for emphasis and separation of idea.

MECHANICS

REVIEW: POSTTEST

OBJECTIVES

- To add apostrophes or hyphens in order to correct errors in given sentences
- To rewrite given sentences, adding dashes or parentheses where needed

PROOFREADING AND PUBLISHING

Have students combine their poems in the form of a booklet. Copies could be made and students would then have a collection of poems on topics that were of concern during their tenth-grade school year.

 Proofreading and Publishing   Now, check the spelling and punctuation in your poem. If you've typed your poem or input it on a keyboard, check to see that the spacing around hyphens and dashes is correct. You could publish your poem by submitting it to a school newspaper or literary magazine, or by reading it aloud to the class.

TIMESAVER

Listed below are the applicable chapter punctuation rules for each question in **Part A** of the **Review: Posttest**. For example, the answer to question one is *armies'* and **28b** states the punctuation rule on the possessive case of plural words. If a student does poorly on the **Posttest**, the cross-reference may help you focus on what rules have not been mastered by the student.

1. b	**6.** b	**11.** g
2. g	**7.** k	**12.** g
3. j	**8.** l	**13.** k; i
4. g; h	**9.** a	**14.** g
5. g	**10.** j; e	**15.** g; h

Review: Posttest

A. Correcting Sentences by Using Apostrophes and Hyphens

For each of the following sentences, write the <u>word or words that should have an apostrophe or a hyphen</u>, and add the appropriate punctuation mark. If a sentence is correct, write C.   Hyphens are indicated by the ∧ symbol.

EXAMPLE   **1.** Michaels stamp collection contains thirty two rare stamps.
     1. *Michael's; thirty-two*

1. Because of the sudden blizzard, the <u>armies'</u> supplies were cut off.
2. <u>It's</u> frustrating when the car <u>won't</u> start because its battery is dead.
3. After hours of discussion, the decision is that we need a <u>two-thirds</u> majority to pass new rules in the student council.
4. Even though Li moved here from Korea last year, <u>she's</u> making <u>A's</u> in most of her classes.
5. If you go to the game on Saturday, <u>who's</u> going to watch the children?
6. Miranda had the flu this past week, and now she has five <u>days'</u> worth of homework to do this weekend.
7. Rodney interviewed the <u>treasurer-elect</u> of the Honor Society for the "Personality Profile" column in the school newspaper.

8. James Berry, who was born in Jamaica, wrote the <u>well-received</u> collection of short stories *A Thief in the Village.*

9. One of my <u>aunts'</u> favorite expressions is "Never let the sun set on your anger."

10. My <u>brother-in-law</u> Murray works at a resort in New <u>York's</u> Catskill Mountains.

11. If we return the tape recorder by five <u>o'clock</u>, the store clerk said she would refund our deposit.

12. The alarm clock <u>hasn't</u> worked since the morning I knocked it off the night stand.

13. Last week, the senator presented as evidence the <u>anti-American</u> pamphlets distributed by the terror-ist group.

14. You have such a wonderful singing voice that <u>I'm</u> sure <u>you'll</u> get a part in the school musical.

15. <u>Don't</u> be alarmed, Brian; the red <u>+'s</u> on your paper indicate correct answers.

B. Correcting Sentences by Using Dashes and Parentheses

Rewrite the following sentences, adding dashes or parentheses where they are needed. (Do not add commas or colons to these sentences.) Answers may vary. Carets indicate placement of dashes.

EXAMPLE **1.** The books on that table they are all nonfiction are on sale today.

       1. *The books on that table—they are all nonfiction—are on sale today.*

16. The discovery of gold at Sutter's Mill brought floods of people settlers, miners, prospectors, and mer-chants to California in their covered wagons.

17. The old white house on Tenth Street it was once a governor's mansion is a landmark in our town.

18. Answer the ten questions on this English quiz be careful, they're tricky! and then write a couplet or a limerick for extra credit.

19. My mom's Persian cookbook has a recipe I'm not making this up for eggplant pickles.

20. The Atacama Desert the driest region on the earth receives so little rainfall that it cannot be measured.

Teacher's ResourceBank™

RESOURCES

FOR THE WHOLE CHAPTER
- Chapter Review Form A
- Chapter Review Form B
- Assessment Portfolio
    Mechanics Pretests
    Mechanics Mastery Tests

CHAPTER OVERVIEW

This chapter focuses on strategies for learning how to spell correctly and on specific spelling rules, and it clarifies the distinctions between words whose spellings are often confused. In addition, the chapter provides lists titled **100 Commonly Misspelled Words** and **Three Hundred Spelling Words** that students can study over the course of a semester or year.

The material in this chapter can serve as a useful reference for students when they are studying dictionary skills, the principal parts of verbs, or any of the writing chapters.

MECHANICS

29 SPELLING

Improving Your Spelling

MECHANICS

Good Spelling Habits

The following techniques can help you become a better speller.

1. *To learn the spelling of a word, pronounce the word, study it, and write it.*

    - First, pronounce the word.
    - Second, study the word, noting especially any parts that might be hard to remember.
    - Third, write the word from memory. Check your spelling.
    - If you misspelled the word, repeat the process.

2. *Use a dictionary.* Don't guess about correct spelling. Look up any words you misspell. In the dictionary, you can often find other, related words that may help you remember the correct spelling. For example, it may be easier to spell *denomination* after you see its kinship with the words *nominate* and *denominator*.

3. **Spell by syllables.** A *syllable* is a word part that can be pronounced by itself.

> EXAMPLES   **pul´•sate** [two syllables]
> **bul´•le•tin** [three syllables]
> **en•vi´•ron•ment** [four syllables]

4. **Pronounce words carefully.** If you say *suprise* instead of *surprise*, you'll likely misspell the word. When you look up the spelling of a word in a dictionary, notice how the word is pronounced. Knowing the correct pronunciation of a word will usually help you spell it correctly.

> EXAMPLES   **ath***l***etic** [not atha letic]
> **es cape** [not ex cape]
> **heigh***t* [not heigh*th*]

5. **Proofread for careless spelling errors.** Reread your writing carefully, correcting any mistakes and unclear letters.

6. **Keep a spelling notebook.** Divide each page into four columns:

> COLUMN 1   Correctly spell the word you missed. (Never enter a misspelled word.)
> COLUMN 2   Write the word again, dividing it into syllables and accenting the stressed syllable(s).
> COLUMN 3   Write the word a third time, circling the part(s) that cause you trouble.
> COLUMN 4   Jot down any comments that will help you remember the correct spelling.

Correct Spelling	Syllables and Accents	Trouble Spot	Comments
February	Feb´•ru•ar•y	Feb(ru)ary	Pronounce correctly.
disapproval	dis´•ap•pro´val	di(sa)ppro(val)	Study rules 29d and 29f.

GOOD SPELLING HABITS

Here are some additional spelling strategies that you could suggest to students:

1. Generate mnemonic aids. For example, students might use the sentence "*We* are *weird*" to remember how to spell *weird*.
2. Write particularly troublesome spelling words on index cards and post them in prominent places.
3. Visualize correctly spelled words or visualize writing correctly spelled words.
4. Periodically review spelling notebooks for duplicate entries. Duplicate entries might suggest that particular spelling rules should be studied.

MECHANICS

MECHANICS

OBJECTIVES

- To proofread a paragraph to correct spelling errors
- To correctly add prefixes and suffixes to words
- To correctly spell the plurals of nouns

Teacher's ResourceBank™

RESOURCES

SPELLING RULES
- Proofreading for Spelling Errors
- Using Spelling Rules
- Adding Prefixes and Suffixes
- Forming Plurals of Nouns
- Spelling Numbers

QUICK REMINDER

Each of the misspelled words in the following sentences violates one of the spelling rules in this segment. Write the sentences on the chalkboard and have students identify and correct the misspelled words.

1. Carmen's soccer team had to forfiet its last game of the season. [forfeit]
2. Councilwoman Ortega's opponent conceeded the election at 2:30 A.M. [conceded]
3. High school achievment tests will be given Tuesday morning. [achievement]
4. In many offices, computers are prefered. [preferred]
5. James and Thomas are brother-in-laws. [brothers-in-law]

MECHANICS

MECHANICS

872 *Spelling*

Spelling Rules

The following rules can help you remember how to spell many words.

ie and *ei*

29a. Write *ie* when the sound is long *e*, except after *c*.

EXAMPLES **chief, believe, niece, deceive, perceive, receipt**
EXCEPTIONS **either, leisure, neither, seize, weird**

29b. Write *ei* when the sound is not long *e*.

EXAMPLES **forfeit, freight, height, neighbor, veil, weigh**
EXCEPTIONS **friend, mischief**

–cede, –ceed, and *–sede*

29c. The only English word that ends in *–sede* is *supersede*. Only three words end in *–ceed: exceed, proceed,* and *succeed.* All other words with this sound end in *–cede.*

EXAMPLES **con*cede*, pre*cede*, re*cede***

⊳ EXERCISE 1 **Proofreading a Paragraph to Correct Spelling Errors**

Proofread the following paragraph, correcting the ten misspelled words.

1. superseded/
   preceded

2. achieved/
   leisure-time

3. height

4. their

[1] During the 1920s, one craze ~~superceded~~ another, each one weirder than the one that ~~preceeded~~ it. [2] Pictured on the next page is fifteen-year-old Avon Foreman, who ~~acheived~~ fame in Baltimore for his bizarre ~~liesure-time~~ activity. [3] In 1929, he spent ten days, ten hours, ten minutes, and ten seconds perched atop a hickory sapling, at a ~~hieght~~ of eighteen feet. [4] The people craning ~~thier~~

4. friends/received   **5.** succeeded

necks to look up at him are just a few of the hundreds of ∧freinds and neighbors from whom he∧recieved encouragement. [5] He even ∧succeeded in attracting the attention of the mayor, William F. Broening, who wrote to him that his "grit and stamina . . . show that the old pioneer spirit of early America is being kept alive by the youth of today." [6] Evidently the mayor∧beleived that Avon was indeed someone to look up to.   **6.** believed

MEETING
INDIVIDUAL
NEEDS

LEP/ESL

General Strategies. Not all languages form plurals by adding suffixes, as in English. In Swahili, for example, plurals are formed by changing prefixes. If you have students in your class who speak other languages, involve them in this lesson by asking them how plurals are formed in the other languages they speak.

Adding Prefixes

29d. When a prefix is added to a word, the spelling of the original word remains the same.

EXAMPLES   mis + spell = **mis**spell   dis + advantage = **dis**advantage
un + likely = **un**likely   il + legible = **il**legible

Adding Suffixes

29e. When the suffix –*ly* or –*ness* is added to a word, the spelling of the original word usually remains the same.

EXAMPLES   nice + ly = nice**ly**   mean + ness = mean**ness**
usual + ly = usual**ly**   same + ness = same**ness**

EXCEPTIONS   1. Words ending in *y* usually change the *y* to *i* before –*ness* and –*ly*.
steady—steadily, sloppy—sloppiness
2. However, most one-syllable adjectives ending in *y* follow rule 29e.
shy—shyness, dry—dryly

ANSWERS
Exercise 2

1. heaviness
2. dissatisfied
3. illegal
4. unnerve
5. sincerely
6. ordinarily
7. immature
8. suddenness
9. specially
10. overrate

 INTEGRATING THE LANGUAGE ARTS

Mechanics and Vocabulary.
To help students build vocabulary, categorize for them prefixes that modify the meanings of words. The following prefixes are grouped according to meaning:

Prefixes that show quantity:

half   *semi*circle
one   *uni*cycle

Prefixes that show negation:

not, lack of,   *un*happy, *dis*respect
against   *anti*war

Prefixes that show time:

before   *fore*cast, *pre*date
after   *post*war
again   *re*view

Prefixes that show direction or position:

above, over   *super*vise
across, over   *trans*port
together   *co*exist

You may want to ask students to generate lists of words that include these prefixes.

▶ EXERCISE 2   **Spelling Words with Prefixes and Suffixes**

Add the prefix or suffix given for each word, and spell the new word formed.

1. heavy + ness
2. dis + satisfied
3. il + legal
4. un + nerve
5. sincere + ly
6. ordinary + ly
7. im + mature
8. sudden + ness
9. special + ly
10. over + rate

29f. Drop the final silent *e* before a suffix beginning with a vowel.

EXAMPLES   dine + ing = dining   safe + er = safer
            sense + ible = sensible   hope + ed = hoped
            use + able = usable   nice + est = nicest
EXCEPTIONS 1. Keep the final silent *e* in words ending in *ce* or *ge* before a suffix that begins with *a* or *o*.
               servi**ce**able, mana**ge**able, advanta**ge**ous
            2. To avoid confusion with other words, keep the final silent *e* in some words.
               dyeing and dying   singeing and singing

29g. Keep the final silent *e* before a suffix beginning with a consonant.

EXAMPLES   use + ful = useful
            advertise + ment = advertisement
EXCEPTIONS true + ly = truly
            argue + ment = argument
            judge + ment = judgment

▶ EXERCISE 3   **Spelling Words with Suffixes**

Add the suffix given for each word, and spell the new words formed.

1. courage + ous   **1.** courageous
2. nine + ty   **2.** ninety
3. advance + ing   **3.** advancing
4. hope + ful   **4.** hopeful
5. approve + al   **5.** approval

29h. If the final *y* is preceded by a consonant, change the *y* to *i* before any suffix except one beginning with an *i*.

EXAMPLES lively + ness = liveliness   rely + ed = relied
bury + al = burial   funny + er = funnier
study + ing = studying   hasty + est = hastiest

▶ EXERCISE 4   **Spelling Words with Suffixes**

Add the suffix given for each word, and spell the new words formed.

1. happy + est **1.** happiest   **6.** spy + ing **6.** spying
2. marry + ing **2.** marrying   **7.** pity + ing **7.** pitying
3. delay + ed **3.** delayed   **8.** try + ed **8.** tried
4. shiny + er **4.** shinier   **9.** pretty + ness **9.** prettiness
5. beauty + ful **5.** beautiful   **10.** busy + ly **10.** busily

29i. Double the final consonant before a suffix that begins with a vowel only if the word

—has only one syllable or is accented on the last syllable

and

—ends in a *single* consonant preceded by a *single* vowel.

EXAMPLES glad + est = gladdest
[one-syllable word]
begin + ing = beginning
[accent on the last syllable]

differ + ence = difference
[accent on the first syllable]
droop + ed = drooped
[single consonant preceded by a *double* vowel]

©John Caldwell 1986.

NOTE: In some words, the final consonant may or may not be doubled. Both spellings are acceptable.

EXAMPLES travel + ed = traveled *or* travelled
stencil + ing = stenciling *or* stencilling

MEETING
INDIVIDUAL
NEEDS

LESS-ADVANCED STUDENTS
Students might feel defeated by the number of rules in this segment and the number of exceptions to them. Have students make flashcards with spelling rules and exceptions on one side and examples on the other. Stress to students that they should focus on one rule at a time.

LEARNING STYLES
Auditory Learners. Auditory learners will benefit from hearing words pronounced and spelled aloud. Invite students to make up rhymes about particular spelling rules. You could provide the following rhyme, used to explain the order of *i* and *e*, as an example:

Write *i* before *e*
Except after *c*
Or when sounded like *ay*
As in *neighbor* and *weigh*.

TIMESAVER

Provide a key for **Exercises 1–7** and allow students to check their answers independently. Have students enter any misspelled words in their spelling notebooks. You can then use **Reviews A–C** for assessment purposes.

REVIEW A

OBJECTIVE

• To proofread a paragraph and to correct spelling errors

876 *Spelling*

EXERCISE 5 **Spelling Words with Suffixes**

Add the suffix given for each word, and spell the new words formed.

1. mad + er   **1.** madder   6. confer + ed   **6.** conferred
2. propel + er   **2.** propeller   7. suffer + ance   **7.** sufferance
3. shovel + ing   **3.** shoveling   8. hop + ing   **8.** hopping
4. refer + al   **4.** referral   9. shop + ed   **9.** shopped
5. repel + ent   **5.** repellent   10. remit + ance   **10.** remittance

REVIEW A **Proofreading a Paragraph to Correct Spelling Errors**

Proofread the following paragraph, correcting the misspelled word in each sentence.

1. committed

2. seizing

3. forfeit

4. succeeded

5. living

6. their

[1] The Shawnee war chief Tecumseh was ~~commited~~ to the goal of uniting Native Americans. [2] He believed that unification was the only way to prevent white settlers from ~~siezing~~ and taking over the land that his people lived on. [3] Opposed to treaties that forced Native Americans to ~~forfiet~~ their land, Tecumseh believed that the land was owned by no one. [4] After much hard work, he ~~succeded~~ in convincing some midwestern Native American peoples to join together. [5] With his brother, known as the Shawnee Prophet, Tecumseh urged his people to preserve their traditional ways of ~~liveing~~ and not to surrender the land. [6] Tecumseh and the Shawnee Prophet (shown below) led ~~thier~~ followers in building Prophetstown at

the location indicated on this map of Indiana. [7] In 1811, while Tecumseh was delivering a speech in a neighboring village, the governor of the Indiana Territory, William Henry Harrison,~easyly attacked Prophetstown. [8] Against Tecumseh's wishes, the Shawnee Prophet proceeded to counterattack, but he finally had to~consede defeat in the Battle of Tippecanoe. [9]~Overrun by Harrison, Tecumseh's people scattered, leaving the town in ruins and bringing an end to twenty years of Tecumseh's work. [10] Tecumseh had~planed to start over, but his death in 1813 at the Battle of the Thames ended all hopes of uniting the various Native American nations.

7. easily
8. concede
9. Overrun
10. planned

Forming Plurals of Nouns

29j. To form the plural of most English nouns, simply add *s*.

SINGULAR	dog	kite	pencil	video	organization
PLURAL	dog**s**	kite**s**	pencil**s**	video**s**	organization**s**

29k. To form the plurals of other nouns, follow these rules.

(1) If the noun ends in *s, x, z, sh,* or *ch,* add *es*.

SINGULAR	glass	waltz	suffix	bush	trench
PLURAL	glass**es**	waltz**es**	suffix**es**	bush**es**	trench**es**

NOTE: Proper nouns usually follow this rule, too.

EXAMPLES   the Barnes**es**, the Gómez**es**

(2) If the noun ends in *y* preceded by a consonant, change the *y* to *i* and add *es*.

SINGULAR	city	enemy	spy	penny
PLURAL	cit**ies**	enem**ies**	sp**ies**	penn**ies**

(3) If the noun ends in *y* preceded by a vowel, add *s*.

SINGULAR	alloy	turkey	essay	Sunday
PLURAL	alloy**s**	turkey**s**	essay**s**	Sunday**s**

MECHANICS

MECHANICS

A DIFFERENT APPROACH

Students might be wondering why there has been no attempt to make English spelling more consistent. Tell students that several campaigns have been mounted to simplify English spellings. One of the most famous proponents of a simplified spelling system was George Bernard Shaw. Challenge interested students to find out more about Shaw's ideas for reform. Students could then present their findings orally to the class.

(4) For some nouns ending in *f* or *fe*, add *s*. For others, change the *f* or *fe* to *v* and add *es*.

Add *s*:

SINGULAR	belief	roof	fife	cliff
PLURAL	beliefs	roofs	fifes	cliffs

Change *f* or *fe* to *v* and add *es*:

SINGULAR	wolf	thief	knife	leaf
PLURAL	wolves	thieves	knives	leaves

(5) If the noun ends in *o* preceded by a vowel, add *s*. If the noun ends in *o* preceded by a consonant, add *es*.

SINGULAR	patio	rodeo	tomato	hero
PLURAL	patios	rodeos	tomatoes	heroes

EXCEPTIONS
1. Nouns for musical terms that end in *o* preceded by a consonant form the plural by adding only *s*.

SINGULAR	alto	soprano	piano	solo
PLURAL	altos	sopranos	pianos	solos

2. A few other nouns that end in *o* preceded by a consonant form the plural by adding only *s*.

SINGULAR	photo	memento
PLURAL	photos	mementos

NOTE: In some cases, the plural of a word ending in *o* may be formed by adding either *s* or *es*.

SINGULAR	mosquito	cargo
PLURAL	mosquitos *or* mosquitoes	cargos or cargoes

(6) The plurals of some nouns are formed in irregular ways.

SINGULAR	child	ox	woman	tooth	mouse	foot
PLURAL	children	oxen	women	teeth	mice	feet

(7) Some nouns have the same form in both the singular and the plural.

SINGULAR AND PLURAL   Chinese   scissors   salmon   sheep

(8) For most compound nouns, make the main word plural.

The main word is the noun that is modified.

SINGULAR	editor in chief	son-in-law	looker-on	runner-up
PLURAL	editor**s** in chief	son**s**-in-law	looker**s**-on	runner**s**-up

The plurals of a few compound nouns are formed in irregular ways.

SINGULAR	drive-in	lean-to	two-year-old
PLURAL	drive-in**s**	lean-to**s**	two-year-old**s**

(9) Some nouns borrowed from other languages form their plurals as they do in the original language.

SINGULAR	PLURAL
alumnus [male]	alumni
alumna [female]	alumnae
vertebra	vertebrae
parenthesis	parentheses
datum	data

NOTE: A few nouns borrowed from other languages have two plural forms. Check a dictionary to find the preferred spelling of such plurals.

SINGULAR	formula	index
PLURAL	formulae *or*	indices *or*
	formulas [preferred]	indexes [preferred]

(10) To form the plurals of numerals, most capital letters, symbols, and words used as words, add either an *s* or an apostrophe and an *s*.

EXAMPLES　His **7**s [or **7**'s] look like **T**s [or **T**'s].
　　　　　Do not write **&**s [or **&**'s] for *and*s [or *and*'s].
　　　　　Phillis Wheatley wrote during the **1700**s [or **1700**'s].

To prevent confusion, always use both an apostrophe and an *s* to form the plurals of lowercase letters, certain capital letters, and some words used as words.

EXAMPLES　Mind your *p*'s and *q*'s.
　　　　　His note is filled with *I*'s. [Without an apostrophe, the plural of the pronoun *I* would look like the word *Is*.]
　　　　　Make sure that each one of your *her*'s has a clear antecedent. [Without the apostrophe, the plural of the word *her* could be confused with the possessive pronoun *hers*.]

INTEGRATING THE LANGUAGE ARTS

Mechanics and Dictionary Skills. Have students look up the etymologies of the words *alumnus, vertebra, parenthesis,* and *datum.* [Three of these words have Latin origins, and one of the words, *parenthesis,* entered English via Latin.] Students might also be interested in looking up the etymologies of some other groups of words to see if they can detect any patterns. For example, students might look up the etymologies of the nouns listed as forming their plurals in irregular ways—*child, ox, woman, tooth, mouse,* and *foot*—and find out whether any of these words have similar origins.

MECHANICS

MECHANICS

879

MECHANICS

> **NOTE:** In your reading, you may notice that some writers use an apostrophe and an *s* to form the plurals of *all* capital letters and words used as words. Using both an apostrophe and an *s* is never wrong. Therefore, if you have any doubt about whether or not to use an apostrophe, use it.

☞ **REFERENCE NOTE:** For more information on forming these kinds of plurals, see pages 857–858.

▶ EXERCISE 6   **Spelling the Plurals of Nouns**

Write the plural form of each of the following nouns.

1. girl
2. valley
3. sky
4. coach
5. Japanese
6. sister-in-law
7. solo
8. self
9. loaf
10. hero

▶ EXERCISE 7   **Proofreading a Paragraph to Correct Spelling Errors**

Proofread the following paragraph, correcting the five misspelled words.

1. cities
2. structures/drive-ins
3. children

[1] This shoe repair shop in Bakersfield, California, is one of many businesses in ~~citys~~ across the United States whose shapes advertise the goods or services they offer. [2] Most of these eye-catching ~~structurs~~, many of them originally ~~drives-in~~, were built between the 1920s and the 1950s. [3] They appeal not only to ~~childs~~ but also to teenagers and adults who enjoy the offbeat. [4] Watch for restaurants and stores shaped like foods and other objects when you're traveling: photos of them make good mementoes of a trip.

MECHANICS

OBJECTIVES
- To give the spelling rules that apply to certain words
- To proofread a paragraph and to correct spelling errors

▶ REVIEW B   **Applying Spelling Rules**

Explain the spelling of each of the following words.

1. crises
2. deceive
3. writing
4. believe
5. sopranos
6. misstep
7. meanness
8. noticeable
9. relief
10. countries

Spelling Numbers

29l. Always spell out a number that begins a sentence.

EXAMPLE   **One hundred twelve** sea lions were spotted in the bay.

29m. Within a sentence, spell out numbers that can be written in one or two words; use numerals for other numbers.

EXAMPLES   We drove **four hundred** miles in **seven** hours.
Edie weighs **110** pounds.
EXCEPTION   If you use some numbers that are written with one or two words and some written with more than two words, use numerals for all of them.
*The final vote was **201 to 90.***

29n. Spell out numbers used to indicate order.

EXAMPLE   My brother placed **third** [not *3rd*] in the race.
EXCEPTION   Use numerals for dates when you include the name of the month.
*Cinco de Mayo is celebrated on **May 5** [not *5th*].*
Writing *the fifth of May* is also correct.

▶ REVIEW C   **Proofreading a Paragraph to Correct Spelling Errors**

Proofread the following paragraph, correcting the misspelled words.

1. fortieth

[1] Last Saturday my mom's parents, Grandma and Grandpa Reyes, celebrated their ~~fortyeth~~ anniversary by repeating their wedding vows in a beautiful ceremony at

MECHANICS

ANSWERS
Review B

1. *crises:* Some nouns borrowed from other languages form their plurals as they do in the original language. **Rule 29k**

2. *deceive:* Write *ie* when the sound is long *e*, except after *c*. **Rule 29a**

3. *writing:* Drop the final silent *e* before a suffix beginning with a vowel. **Rule 29f**

4. *believe:* Write *ie* when the sound is long *e*, except after *c*. **Rule 29a**

5. *sopranos:* Nouns for musical terms that end in *o* preceded by a consonant form the plural by adding only *–s*. Exception to **Rule 29k**

6. *misstep:* When a prefix is added to a word, the spelling of the original word remains the same. **Rule 29d**

7. *meanness:* When the suffix *–ly* or *–ness* is added to a word, the spelling of the original word usually remains the same. **Rule 29e**

8. *noticeable:* Keep the final silent *–e* in words ending in *–ce* or *–ge* before a suffix that begins with *a* or *o*. Exception to **Rule 29f**

9. *relief:* Write *ie* when the sound is long *e*, except after *c*. **Rule 29a**

10. *countries:* If the noun ends in *–y* preceded by a consonant, change the *y* to *i* and add *–es*. **Rule 29k**

MECHANICS

WORDS OFTEN CONFUSED

OBJECTIVE

- To distinguish between words often confused

---

882 *Spelling*

2. learner's	St. Teresa's Church. [2] Since I have my ~~learnner's~~ permit now and it was light out when we went to the church, Mom let me drive. [3] My aunts and uncles on Mom's side
3. wives	of the family were there with their husbands and ~~wifes~~. [4] In addition, all of my cousins except Ernesto, whom I'd
4. hoping	been especially ~~hopeing~~ to see, attended the ceremony. [5] Unfortunately, the flights from Denver, where Ernesto goes to college, had been canceled because it had snowed
5. heavily	~~heavyly~~ there the night before. [6] Although I missed
6. eighty-five	Ernesto, I enjoyed visiting with many of the ~~85~~ friends and family members who had come to the celebration.
7. unnecessary	[7] Grandma and Grandpa had insisted that anniversary gifts were ~~unecessary~~, but this time they were overruled.
8. truly	[8] You could tell that they were ~~truely~~ stunned when they opened the gift from their children. [9] Mom and her sis-
9. chipped	ters and brothers had ~~chiped~~ in to buy them plane tickets to Mexico City, where they were born. [10] Everyone had
10. planning/fiftieth	such a good time that we've already started ~~planing~~ for Grandma and Grandpa's ~~50th~~ anniversary.

Words Often Confused

affect	[verb] *to influence* How did that sad movie *affect* you?
effect	[verb] *to accomplish;* [noun] *consequence; result* Head Start centers can *effect* an improvement in the lives of underprivileged children. What *effect* did the rain have on the lawn?
all ready	*all are ready* We were *all ready* to leave.
already	*previously* We have *already* painted the sets.
all right	This is the only acceptable spelling. The spelling *alright* is not standard usage.

QUICK REMINDER

Write the following sentences on the chalkboard and have students choose the word in parentheses that correctly completes each sentence. The correct choices are italicized.

1. Young children sometimes have trouble (adopting, *adapting*) to new environments.
2. On his eighteenth birthday Calvin said, "Hooray! I'm no longer a (*minor*, miner)."
3. The seventh-grade class traveled to Jackson to see the (capital, *capitol*) building.
4. The cacti and other plants in the (*desert*, dessert) burst into bloom after the thunderstorm.
5. Hortense's tooth was so (lose, *loose*) she feared she would (*lose*, loose) it.

MECHANICS

all together	*everyone in the same place* The players were *all together* in the gym.
altogether	*entirely* I'm not *altogether* convinced.
brake	[verb] *to slow down or stop;* [noun] *a device used to slow down or stop something* Georgia *braked* the speeding car. The worn *brakes* couldn't stop the car.
break	[verb] *to violate; to fracture;* [noun] *the fracture itself* Don't *break* the speed limit. The doctor says it isn't a bad *break*.
capital	Correct spelling for all uses except when the word means *government building*. What is the *capital* of Zimbabwe? You need *capital* to start a business. Begin every sentence with a *capital* letter. Do you believe in *capital* punishment?
capitol	*government building* We could see the *capitol* from our hotel.
choose	[verb, present tense] We *choose* partners today.
chose	[verb, past tense of *choose*] Each of us *chose* a partner.
coarse	*rough; crude* Burlap is a *coarse* fabric.
course	*a part of a meal; a program of study;* or *a playing field;* also used with *of* to mean *naturally* or *certainly* She skipped the first *course* at dinner. The speech *course* helped my diction. A new golf *course* opened last week. Of *course*, you're always welcome.

MECHANICS

LEP/ESL

General Strategies. Because these words might be especially confusing to LEP/ESL students, allow the students to focus on the words that they are most likely to use in their daily lives. For example, students are probably more likely to use the words *brake* and *break* than the words *consul* and *council*.

MECHANICS

883

complement	[verb] *to make whole or complete;* [noun] *that which makes whole or complete* That scarf *complements* your outfit nicely. The *complement*, or full crew, is six hundred people.
compliment	[noun] *a courteous act; a flattering statement;* [verb] *to express these qualities* He received many *compliments* on his cooking. I *complimented* her on her success.
consul	[noun] *a representative of a foreign country* The Chinese *consul* returned to Beijing.
council	[noun] *a group charged with taking official actions*
councilor	[noun] *a member of such a group* Four of the *councilors* on the Security Council voted for the resolution.
counsel **counselor**	[noun] *advice;* [verb] *to advise* [noun] *an adviser* Sue followed her aunt's *counsel*. Sue's aunt *counseled* her to take judo lessons. Ask your guidance *counselor*.
des′ert	[noun] *a dry region* The car crossed the *desert* at night.
desert′	[verb] *to leave* The rats *deserted* the sinking ship.
dessert	[noun] *the last part of a meal* For *dessert* we had cheese and fruit.

EXERCISE 8   **Distinguishing Between Words Often Confused**

Choose the <u>correct word</u> of the pair in parentheses.

1. The Epstein family was (*all together*, *altogether*) last week for the Hanukkah celebration.

ADVANCED STUDENTS

Some of the pairs of words often confused have similar origins. *Counsel* and *council,* for example, both come from the Latin word *concilium,* meaning "group of people," or "meeting." Students might enjoy using a dictionary to find out which of the pairs or groups of words have similar etymologies and which do not. Afterward, ask students if they could have predicted the results.

MEETING **INDIVIDUAL** NEEDS

MECHANICS

2. The illness has had a strange (*affect*, *effect*) on everyone who has caught it.
3. My cousin knows the (*capitol*, *capital*) city of every state.
4. If you don't have your car's (*brakes*, *breaks*) inspected each year, you may be (*braking*, *breaking*) a state law.
5. The British (*council*, *consul*) (*counciled*, *counseled*) the reporter to leave the country.
6. After all his worry, everything turned out (*all right*, *alright*).
7. The two fast guards on our basketball team are (*complimented*, *complemented*) by our towering center.
8. The actors were (*all ready*, *already*) for the audition.
9. My uncle had either flan or sopapillas for (*desert*, *dessert*).
10. Did you (*choose*, *chose*) that topic for your essay?

formally	*in a formal manner* Do you plan to dress *formally* for the party?
formerly	*previously* This lake was *formerly* a valley.
hear	*to receive sound through the ears* Please speak up—I can't *hear* you.
here	*this place* Let's sit *here*.
its	[possessive form of *it*] The town hasn't raised *its* tax rate in years.
it's	[contraction of *it is* or *it has*] *It's* cold, and *it's* started to snow.
lead	[verb] *to go first* Who will *lead* the Juneteenth parade?
led	[verb, past tense of *lead*] He *led* us five miles out of the way.
lead	[noun, pronounced "led"] *a heavy metal;* *graphite in a pencil* A pencil *lead* is not made of *lead*.

MECHANICS

MECHANICS

885

VISUAL CONNECTIONS
Related Expression Skills.
Students might enjoy creating cartoons that feature puns with the words in this segment. For example, a student might draw a cartoon of someone lost in a *dessert* or of a car *breaking* for a stoplight.

MECHANICS (left margin)

MECHANICS (inner margin)

loose	[adjective, pronounced "loos"] *free, not connected tightly* Put all your *loose* papers in a folder. My little brother has two *loose* teeth.
lose	[verb, pronounced "looz"] *to suffer loss* Don't *lose* your tickets.
miner	[noun] *worker in a mine* The trapped *miners* were finally rescued.
minor	[noun] *person under legal age;* [adjective] *of small importance* The curfew applies only to *minors.* He received *minor* injuries in the accident.
moral	[adjective] *good;* [noun] *a lesson of conduct* We admire a *moral* person. The story's *moral* is "Look before you leap."
morale	*mental condition, spirit* After three defeats, the team's *morale* was low.
passed	[verb, past tense of *pass*] We *passed* our papers to the front.
past	[noun] *the history of a person, group, or institution;* [adjective] *former;* [preposition] *farther on than* Sitting Bull told his son Crow Foot many stories about the *past.* Adele read the minutes of the *past* meeting. The dog walked right *past* the cat.

Rubes   By Leigh Rubin

Miner surgery.

RUBES by Leigh Rubin. By permission of Leigh Rubin and Creators Syndicate.

REVIEW D

OBJECTIVE

- To proofread an article and to correct spelling errors

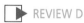 EXERCISE 9 **Distinguishing Between Words Often Confused**

Choose the <u>correct word</u> of the pair in parentheses.

1. Where did you (*here*, <u>*hear*</u>) that Kiowa legend?
2. If you (<u>*lose*</u>, *loose*) the directions, we'll never get there.
3. The mail from home improved the troops (*moral*, <u>*morale*</u>).
4. The estate is being held in trust until the heir is no longer a (<u>*minor*</u>, *miner*).
5. My horse (*lead*, <u>*led*</u>) the parade.
6. In only a few minutes, the guest speaker will be (*hear*, <u>*here*</u>).
7. After he went on a diet, his clothes were too (*lose*, <u>*loose*</u>).
8. (<u>*Formerly*</u>, *Formally*), Gloria Estefan performed with the Miami Sound Machine.
9. (*Its*, <u>*It's*</u>) not every day that her parents let her use the car.
10. After taking French I twice, John (<u>*passed*</u>, *past*) the course.

 REVIEW D **Proofreading an Article to Correct Spelling Errors**

Proofread the following article, correcting the misspelled word or words in each sentence. If all words in a sentence are spelled correctly, write *C*.

NHS MEMBERS MEET GOVERNOR
by Cornelia Charnes, Staff Writer

[1] One of the advantages of living in the state ~~capitol~~ is having the opportunity to see state government up close. [2] Last Friday, twenty-seven members of our school's National Honor Society chapter toured the nearby ~~capital~~ building. [3] Tour guide Floyd Welty, who ~~lead~~ the group, outlined the workings of the government's three branches and pointed out many of the building's architectural features. [4] The students ate lunch in the underground cafeteria and even got to meet Governor (~~formally~~ U.S. Senator) Iola Jones.

1. capital
2. capitol
3. led
4. formerly

STUDENTS WITH SPECIAL NEEDS

Students might feel overwhelmed by the task of proofreading blocks of text for an unknown number of errors. To help students to succeed, suggest that they proofread each sentence in isolation and inform them of the number of misspelled words in **Reviews C, D,** and **E,** and in **Exercise 12** (**Review C**—11, **Review D**—10, **Review E**—20, **Exercise 12**—10).

MECHANICS

MECHANICS

MEETING INDIVIDUAL NEEDS

LEARNING STYLES

Auditory Learners. Students might benefit from intentionally mispronouncing and then pronouncing correctly some of these words as they study them. Students could mispronounce the words to exaggerate the spelling differences among homonyms. Exaggerating the spelling differences aloud may help students recall them.

888 *Spelling*

5. all ready
6. C
7. minors/ hear
8. it's
9. counselor/ past
10. C

[5] The group met Governor Jones just as they were ~~already~~ ⋀already to leave the building. [6] Said student Botan Park, "Governor Jones shook hands with each of us and complimented us on being honor students. [7] Even though we're still ⋀~~miners~~, she told us, 'I want to ⋀~~here~~ from you whenever you have a concern with my administration's policies.'" [8] "Of course," added student Elena Cruz, "⋀~~its~~ her first term as governor, and we'll be eligible to vote when she comes up for reelection."

[9] The group's sponsor, guidance ⋀~~councilor~~ Diego Vargas, said, "I've been taking groups there for the ⋀~~passed~~ ten years, but I've never met a governor before. [10] That had a big effect on me and on the students."

personal	*individual* The store manager gave us her *personal* attention.
personnel	*a group of people employed in the same place* The management added *personnel* to handle the increased workload.
principal	[noun] *head of a school;* [adjective] *main; most important* The *principal* of our school is Mr. Osaka. The *principal* export of Brazil is coffee.
principle	*a rule of conduct; a main fact* or *law* Her *principles* are very high. Martin Luther King, Jr., supported the *principle* of nonviolence.
quiet	*silent; still* I need complete *quiet* to study.
quite	*wholly; rather; very* Are you *quite* sure this is the right path?
shone	[past tense of *shine*] The stars *shone* brightly last night.
shown	[past participle of *show*] The slides were *shown* after dinner.

stationary	[adjective] *in a fixed position* Are these desks movable or *stationary*?
stationery	[noun] *writing paper* Purple *stationery* isn't appropriate for business letters.

than	[a conjunction, used for comparisons] She is smarter *than* I.
then	[an adverb or a conjunction] *at that time; next* I didn't know you *then*. We swam for an hour; *then* we ate.

their	[possessive of *they*] *Their* apartment has a view of the river.
there	[adverb] *in that place;* [expletive, used to fill out the meaning of a sentence] I haven't been *there* in a long time. *There* is too much pepper in my soup.
they're	[contraction of *they are*] *They're* reading a book by Virginia Driving Hawk Sneve.

 EXERCISE 10 **Distinguishing Between Words Often Confused**

Select the correct word of the choices in parentheses.

1. I'm learning some of the (*principals*, *principles*) of physics.
2. The gold ring (*shone*, *shown*) with a warm glow.
3. He acts much older (*than*, *then*) he is.
4. The bookstore is having a big sale on (*stationery*, *stationary*).
5. You ask too many (*personnel*, *personal*) questions.
6. Soon after the strange uproar, all became (*quite*, *quiet*) again.
7. The *pad thai* they serve here is (*quite*, *quiet*) good.
8. Several Pueblo artists are displaying (*there*, *their*, *they're*) work.

COOPERATIVE LEARNING

All of the often-confused words on this page are homophones—they sound alike but have different spellings and meanings. Have students work in groups of three or four to generate as many homophones as possible in a given period of time. Then have groups compare lists and delete any homophones that two or more groups have in common. The group with the greatest number of homophones remaining wins.

890 *Spelling*

9. If you see the (*principle*, *principal*) in the hall, tell her she's wanted in the main office.
10. (*Their*, *They're*, *There*) parents may not let them go.

to	[preposition; also part of the infinitive form of a verb] Please return these books *to* the library. He began *to* whistle.
too	[adverb] *also; more than enough* Ruben Blades is a musician and an attorney, *too.* You're *too* young to drive.
two	*one plus one* I will graduate in *two* years.
waist	*the midsection of the body* At the Japanese restaurant, the server wore an obi around her *waist.*
waste	[verb] *to use foolishly;* [noun] *a needless expense* *Waste* not; want not. Waiting in line is a *waste* of time.
weather	[noun] *conditions outdoors* The *weather* has been perfect all week.
whether	[subordinating conjunction; indicates alternative or doubt] They don't know *whether* or not they'll go.
who's	[contraction of *who is* or *who has*] *Who's* there? *Who's* been wearing my socks?
whose	[possessive of *who*] *Whose* book is this?
your	[possessive of *you*] *Your* coat is in the closet.
you're	[contraction of *you are*] *You're* never on time.

EXERCISE 11 **Distinguishing Between Words Often Confused**

Select the <u>correct word</u> of the choices in parentheses.

1. Around his (*waste*, <u>*waist*</u>) he wore a handmade leather belt.
2. (*You're*, <u>*Your*</u>) mother made a delicious Korean dinner of *bulgogi* last night.
3. There was (<u>*too*</u>, *to*, *two*) much traffic on the road (*too*, <u>*to*</u>, *two*) enjoy the ride.
4. (*Whose*, <u>*Who's*</u>) going to use that ticket now?
5. It really doesn't matter (<u>*whose*</u>, *who's*) fault it is.
6. You, (*to*, *two*, <u>*too*</u>), can be a better speller if you try.
7. (*Weather*, <u>*Whether*</u>) it rains or not, we'll be there.
8. This is fine (*whether*, <u>*weather*</u>) for a softball game.
9. (*Your*, <u>*You're*</u>) sure Ms. Thompson wanted to see me?
10. I don't know (*whose*, <u>*who's*</u>) taller, Hakeem Olajuwon or Buck Williams.

EXERCISE 12 **Proofreading a Paragraph to Correct Spelling Errors**

Proofread the following paragraph, correcting the misspelled words.

[1] The face on the postage stamp on the next page is that of Benjamin Banneker, considered ~~too~~ be the first African American man of science. [2] First issued on February 15, 1980, this stamp honors a man ~~who's~~ contributions in the areas of mathematics and astronomy are impressive. [3] Banneker grew up on a farm in Maryland in the 1700s, a time when life was particularly difficult for African American people ~~weather~~ they were slaves or not. [4] Although free, Banneker, ~~to~~, faced prejudice and discrimination. [5] However, a neighbor who was interested in science gave some astronomy equipment ~~too~~ Banneker. [6] Banneker ~~waisted~~ no time in using it to determine when the sun and moon rose and set, when the brightest stars set, and when eclipses occurred. [7] All of this information was very helpful to a variety of people, including sailors who needed to chart courses and farmers who needed to know the ~~whether~~. [8] Banneker compiled his data into an

1. to
2. whose
3. whether
4. too
5. to
6. wasted
7. weather

MECHANICS

 INTEGRATING THE LANGUAGE ARTS

Mechanics and Vocabulary. **Exercise 12** discusses a commemorative postage stamp. Tell students that the practice of collecting stamps can also be called *philately*. Then challenge students to match the following words with the hobbies they describe:

1. numismatics
2. spelunking
3. equitation
4. angling
5. bibliophilism

A. horseback riding
B. collecting books
C. exploring caves
D. collecting coins
E. fishing with hook and line

MECHANICS

891

OBJECTIVE

- To proofread an essay and to correct spelling errors

892 *Spelling*

8. two   almanac, and after‸too or three attempts, he succeeded in getting his almanacs published each year for several years. [9] These popular books received widespread attention, and Benjamin Banneker became a symbol of what African Americans could do if their lives

9. wasted   were not‸~~waisted~~ in slavery. [10] If

10. you're   ‸~~your~~ someone who collects commemorative postage stamps, you'll likely want this one, which celebrates the achievements of this gifted scientist.

▷ REVIEW E

Proofreading an Essay to Correct Spelling Errors

Proofread the following essay, correcting the misspelled words in each sentence. If all the words in a sentence are spelled correctly, write *C*.

[1] One of my most embarrassing moments‸~~occured~~ the day I took the road test‸~~too~~ get my driver's license. [2] Since one of the branches of the Motor Vehicle Department is near my dad's office, I met him‸~~their~~ after school. [3] He ‸~~tryed~~ to calm me down by telling me that the world wouldn't end if I didn't pass the first time. [4] Still, my hands were‸~~shaking‸noticably~~ when I got behind the wheel.

[5] The examiner, Mrs. Ferro, was very patient. [6] She assured me that the‸~~coarse~~ was a‸~~peice~~ of cake and that she wouldn't ask me to do anything‸~~ilegal~~ to try to trick me. [7] She said I'd be fine if I just‸~~proceded‸steadyly~~ and didn't‸~~overeact~~ to her instructions.

[8] Everything went surprisingly well until we reached the end of the course and Mrs. Ferro told me to stop the car and turn off the ignition. [9] I stopped,‸~~alright—I acci-dentaly‸slamed~~ on the‸~~breaks~~ so hard that we both went lurching forward against our seat belts. [10] Luckily, ‸~~niether~~ of us‸~~sustainned~~ any‸~~injurys~~, and I succeeded in passing the test despite‸~~mistakeing~~ the end of the course for the edge of a cliff.

ANSWERS

Review E

1. occurred; to
2. there
3. tried
4. shaking; noticeably
5. C
6. course; piece; illegal
7. proceeded; steadily; overreact
8. C
9. all right; accidentally; slammed; brakes
10. neither; sustained; injuries; mistaking

MECHANICS

MECHANICS

100 Commonly Misspelled Words

ache	could	happiness	raise	tonight
again	country	having	read	too
always	dear	hear	ready	trouble
among	doctor	here	said	truly
answered	does	hoarse	says	Tuesday
any	done	hour	scene	two
been	don't	instead	seems	very
beginning	early	knew	separate	wear
believe	easy	know	shoes	Wednesday
break	enemy	laid	similar	week
built	enough	loose	since	where
business	every	lose	straight	whether
busy	existence	making	sugar	which
buy	February	meant	sure	whole
can't	finally	minute	tear	women
chief	forty	none	their	won't
choose	friend	often	there	would
color	grammar	once	though	write
coming	guess	piece	through	writing
cough	half	probably	tired	wrote

300 Spelling Words

absence	analyze	bulletin
absorption	angel	calendar
abundant	annual	category
acceptable	apparatus	changeable
accidentally	appearance	characteristic
accommodation	application	chemistry
accompaniment	appropriate	circumstance
accurate	approximately	civilization
accustomed	arousing	cocoon
achievement	arrangement	commencement
acquaintance	ascend	commissioner
actuality	association	committed
adequately	athlete	comparative
administration	bankruptcy	comparison
adolescent	basically	competition
aggressive	beneficial	conceivable
agriculture	benefited	confidential
amateur	bicycle	confirmation
ambassador	breathe	conscientious
analysis	brilliant	consciousness

ADVANCED STUDENTS

Some students will not have any problems with spelling the words in the **100 Commonly Misspelled Words** list. Allow such students to work as a group to compile a list of words that they have encountered in their reading and have difficulty spelling. Students can then study words from the list they have compiled instead of spending time studying words they already know how to spell.

MECHANICS

MECHANICS

A DIFFERENT APPROACH

Challenge each student to write a paragraph that includes one of the groups of ten words from the **300 Spelling Words** list. Here is a sample paragraph that includes the first group of ten words:

His *absence* is due to the *absorption* of an *abundant* amount of hardly *acceptable* soup. He ingested the soup *accidentally*—quite an *achievement*—and was not *accustomed* to its potency. If my predictions are *accurate,* we will not have the pleasure of his *accompaniment* to our songs tonight at our *accommodations.*

consequently
considerable
consistency
continuous
controlled
controversial
cordially
corps
correspondence
criticize

curiosity
curriculum
definition
delegate
denied
develop
difference
disastrous
disciple
dissatisfied

distinction
distinguished
dividend
dominant
dormitory
earnest
easily
ecstasy
eighth
eliminate

embroidery
endeavor
enormous
equipment
especially
essential
estimation
etiquette
exaggeration
examination

exceedingly
exceptional
excitable
executive
exercise
exhaustion
exhibition
expense
experience
extension

extraordinary
fallacy
fantasies
favorably
fiery
financial
foreigner
forfeit
fragile
fulfill

fundamentally
gasoline
gentleman
grammatically
grateful
guidance
gymnasium
handkerchief
heroic
hindrance

humorist
hygiene
hypocrisy
illustrate
imitation
immense
inability
incidentally
indispensable
influential

innocence
inquiry
institute
intellect
interference
interpretation
interruption
interval
irrelevant
irresistible

island
jealousy
journal
laborious
liability
lightning
likelihood
liveliest
locally
luxury

magnificence
maintenance
maneuver
mansion
martyr
maturity
medical
merchandise
merit
miniature

mischievous
missile
misspelled
monotony
mortgage
municipal
narrative
naturally
neighbor
noticeable

MECHANICS

MECHANICS

nuisance
obstacle
occasionally
occupy
odor
offensive
omitted
opinion
opposition
optimism

ordinary
organization
ornament
pageant
pamphlet
parachute
parallel
pastime
peaceable
peasant

peril
permanent
persistent
perspiration
pertain
phase
picnic
pigeon
playwright
pleasant

poison
politician
positively
possibility
practically
practice
precede
precisely
predominant
preferred

prejudice
preliminary
preparation
primitive
priority
prisoner
procedure
proceedings
procession
prominent

proposition
prosperous
prove
psychology
publicity
purposes
qualities
quantities
questionnaire
readily

reference
referring
regard
register
rehearsal
religious
remembrance
representative
requirement
resistance

resolution
responsibility
restaurant
ridiculous
satisfactorily
security
senator
sensibility
sheer
sheriff

significance
simile
situated
solution
sophomore
souvenir
specific
specimen
spiritual
strenuous

stretch
substantial
subtle
successful
sufficient
summarize
superintendent
suppress
surgeon
suspense

syllable
symbol
symphony
technique
temperature
tendency
tournament
traffic
twelfth
tying

tyranny
unanimous
undoubtedly
unforgettable
unpleasant
unusually
vacancies
varies
vengeance
villain

MECHANICS

PART THREE

RESOURCES

SPEAKING *(pp. 898–910)*

OBJECTIVES

- To explain how problems involving speaking on the telephone could be solved
- To provide directions for given situations
- To explain social introductions for given situations
- To prepare and give speeches with note cards and visual aids

RESOURCES

CHAPTER OVERVIEW

This chapter provides basic instruction in both formal and informal speaking situations. After a brief discussion of the communication cycle and nonverbal communication, the chapter continues with attention to such informal speaking situations as impromptu speaking, speaking on the telephone, giving directions, and making introductions. Aspects of formal speaking such as preparing a speech, analyzing audiences, gathering materials, organizing speech notes and materials, speaking expressively, and delivering the speech are then considered. Instruction on group discussion, including roles and parliamentary procedure follows. The chapter concludes with instruction in adapting and presenting material as oral interpretation.

RESOURCES

30 SPEAKING

Skills and Strategies

A good speech requires careful thought and thorough preparation. To communicate effectively, you should think about your purpose, your topic, and your audience.

The Communication Cycle

Oral communication is a process that you take part in when you communicate your feelings or ideas to another person. In turn, this person responds to your message. This response is called *feedback.*

- To write announcements for suggested events
- To prepare and deliver introductions for guest speakers
- To present group discussions on suggested topics
- To present a five-minute oral interpretation based on a scene from a piece of literature

Nonverbal Communication

In addition to words (verbal signals), you communicate meaning with *nonverbal* (unspoken) signals. How you stand, move about, and gesture can communicate a variety of messages.

NONVERBAL SIGNALS	EXAMPLES
Gestures	thumbs up (approval, encouragement), shrugging (uncertainty), nodding head (yes), shaking head (disagreement)
Facial expressions	smiling, raising an eyebrow, smirking, frowning, grimacing, pouting, grinning, (meanings vary depending on context)
Body language	turning away (rejection), stroking the chin (puzzlement), crossing arms on chest (reluctance, uncertainty)
Sounds	laughing, groaning, giggling (meanings vary depending on context)

Speaking Informally

Speaking Impromptu

An *impromptu speech* is one you make on the spur of the moment. The ideas you express have not been prepared in advance. When an impromptu speech is required, consider the following suggestions.

1. *Consider your purpose.* Impromptu speeches are often informative (telling what you know about a subject) or persuasive (giving your opinion or trying to convince your listeners).
2. *Consider your topic.* Cover the main ideas and add details to support or explain your main points.
3. *Consider your audience.* Think about the specific speaking occasion and consider the interests and knowledge of the audience.

RESOURCES

QUICK REMINDER

Pair the students and give them ten minutes to interview each other. Students should endeavor to discover what makes their partners unique and interesting. Then have each pair go to the front of the class, where each partner will introduce the other.

MEETING INDIVIDUAL NEEDS

LEP/ESL

General Strategies. Students may worry about using correct grammar in front of an audience of native English speakers. They should be relieved to find out that listeners focus more on message than on form. Advise ESL students that if they suddenly realize they have made a mistake, it is better to keep going than to back up and draw attention to an error that few are likely to have noticed. Listeners prefer uninterrupted content to perfect grammar.

STUDENTS WITH SPECIAL NEEDS

Students with emotional disabilities may find speaking in front of the class stressful, and this may result in inappropriate behavior. To help the students learn to participate with the appropriate behavior, formulate a contract with each student. The focus of the contracts should be on mutually agreed upon assignments that the students will complete.

RESOURCES

INTEGRATING THE LANGUAGE ARTS

Technology Link. Because many homes have answering machines, you may wish to stress to students the importance of leaving messages that are concise, clear, and complete.

TIMESAVER

You can save time by having students generate topics for impromtu speaking. Have each student write a topic on a slip of paper, preferably in the form of a question. Students can then draw topics and, by using their existing knowledge and experiences, give impromptu speeches. Before students draw topics, you may wish to review the topics to weed out unsuitable or unnecessarily difficult topics.

COMMON ERROR

Problem. Many people have difficulty remembering a person's name after being introduced.

Solution. You might share with students common techniques used to remember names. These include paying close attention when being introduced and observing the person closely for distinguishing characteristics.

Other techniques include matching the name with a similar word or words and associating the name with a characteristic of the person.

Communicating Effectively

The most important part of speaking in many social situations is to remember that you need to speak clearly and courteously. The following are common social situations where you can practice communicating effectively by working on your speaking skills.

Speaking on the Telephone

1. Call people at a reasonable hour.
2. Identify yourself and state your purpose for calling.
3. Be polite and speak clearly.
4. Keep your call to an appropriate length.

Giving Instructions or Directions

1. Divide the information into clear, logical steps.
2. Give the steps in order.
3. Check to be sure your listeners understand all the steps.
4. If necessary, repeat the steps in the same order.

Making Social Introductions

1. Take the initiative; introduce yourself if no one else does.
2. When introducing others, identify them by name.
3. It is customary to address first
   - a person of higher status
   - an older person before a younger person
   - the person you know better

Speaking Formally

Preparing a Speech

When you are required to give a speech, you must choose a suitable subject and determine your purpose for speaking. You need to limit your subject to a manageable topic so that it can be adequately treated in your speech and so that it reflects a definite purpose.

PURPOSE	DESCRIPTION OF SPEECH	EXAMPLES OF SPEECH TITLES
To inform	gives facts *or* explains how to do something	Animals That Live on the Ocean Floor How to Avoid Snakebite
To persuade	attempts to change an opinion *or* attempts to get listeners to act	Senior Citizens Are Important to the Community You Should Eat a Low-fat Diet
To entertain	relates an amusing story or incident	My First Job as a Baby Sitter

Analyzing Your Audience

Your audience is the group of people who are going to listen to your speech. You will need to think about the needs, background, and interests of your audience if you expect them to understand and respond to your speech topic.

AUDIENCE CONSIDERATIONS		
QUESTIONS ABOUT AUDIENCE	EVALUATION	YOUR SPEECH WILL NEED
What does the audience already know about this subject?	very little	to provide background or details to better inform your listeners
	a little	to include some background details
	a lot	to focus on interesting aspects or issues
How interested will the audience be in this subject?	very interested	to maintain their interest
	somewhat interested	to focus on aspects that most interest them
	uninterested	to focus on persuading your listeners that this topic is important

A DIFFERENT APPROACH
Speech material drawn on personal experience is usually vivid and adds to the speaker's credibility. Suggest that while speeches shouldn't consist of personal experience only, they should contain personal experience if possible.

RESOURCES

RESOURCES

COOPERATIVE LEARNING
Before students give their speeches, you may wish to assign a partner to each speaker who will have the task of announcing that speaker.

 COMMON ERROR
Problem. Beginning speakers will often prepare visual aids too small to be easily seen past the first row of the audience.

Solution. Tell students to check that their visual aids can be seen at a distance. Remind the class that audience members in the back row are just as important as the ones in the front row.

Gathering Material

After you've chosen a topic for your speech, you'll need to plan how you want to develop your topic. Then you'll need to brainstorm or do research to find material that supports your ideas or opinions. Try the following strategies for gathering interesting information.

1. *Explore your own background.* Ask yourself what you already know about the topic. Explore your own knowledge and experience.
2. *Observe.* Keep an eye out as you look through newspapers and periodicals for material related to your topic. Speeches or radio and television broadcasts may provide you with additional information.
3. *Read.* Go to the library. Use reference sources, magazines, and books to research your topic.
4. *Reflect.* Review the material you have gathered and take time to become familiar with it.

Organizing Speech Notes and Materials

The most effective type of speech to give is often an *extemporaneous speech.* An extemporaneous speech is one that is carefully developed and organized, but not memorized.

To develop an extemporaneous speech, you usually prepare a complete outline of your main points. Then use your outline to prepare note cards that can be used while delivering your speech to help you remember main ideas and supporting details.

Here are some suggestions for preparing your note cards.

1. Include one key idea (and possibly an example or detail) for each card.
2. Make a special note card for a quotation or a series of dates or statistics that you plan to read word for word.
3. Make a special note card to indicate when you plan to show a chart, diagram, graph, drawing, model, or other visual.
4. Number your completed cards to help you keep them in the appropriate order.

Speaking Expressively

Have you ever listened to a speaker who put you to sleep? You don't want that to happen to your audience. To speak expressively, you should practice using good verbal and nonverbal communication signals. Follow these suggestions.

1. *Stand confidently.* Be alert, be interested in what you're saying, and use natural gestures.
2. *Speak clearly.* Speak loudly enough so everyone in the audience can hear you. Pronounce your words slowly and carefully.
3. *Look at your audience as you speak.* Make direct eye contact as you focus on the faces of your listeners.
4. *Choose your words carefully.* Use specific rather than general words. Also, use vivid words that appeal to the senses to reinforce meaning.
5. *Use variety in speaking.* Vocal variety helps emphasize your message.
   - *Volume:* Speak loudly enough to be heard, but raise or lower your sound volume for emphasis.
   - *Pitch:* Use the rise and fall of your voice to emphasize various ideas and avoid a monotone.
   - *Stress:* Emphasize important words.
   - *Rate:* Speak at a comfortable, relaxed pace.

Giving Your Speech

Most speakers feel nervous before giving a speech. In fact, a little nervousness can help you by keeping you alert and focusing your energy. The following suggestions will help you avoid excessive nervousness.

1. *Relax.* Realize that your audience wants you to do well. They aren't waiting for you to make mistakes.
2. *Be prepared.* Organize and practice with your note cards and visual aids.
3. *Practice your speech.* Rehearse as if you're giving the actual presentation.
4. *Focus on your purpose.* Remember what you want to accomplish. Instead of focusing on yourself, think how your speech will affect your audience.

RESOURCES

LESS-ADVANCED STUDENTS

To combat the problem of nervousness before and during a speech, you may wish to relieve some pressure by not grading the first few speeches students give. Also, a frank and open discussion of the common symptoms of stage fright may help students realize that it is a natural phenomenon.

COMMON ERROR

Problem. Student speakers sometimes spoil the spontaneity of their delivery by preparing detailed notes.

Solution. Tell students to use note cards that contain just enough to jog the memory. Signal words or short phrases are all that are normally needed.

A DIFFERENT APPROACH

When a student is making an announcement, it is all too easy for the student to leave out vital information. You may wish to instruct your students to answer these five traditional questions when preparing announcements: *When? Where? Who? Why?* and *How?*

Special Speaking Situations

Making an Announcement

The purpose of an announcement is to provide general information to an audience. Follow these suggestions for making an effective announcement.

1. When preparing your announcement, include all the necessary facts and add interesting details that will capture your listeners' attention.
2. Get your audience's attention and then announce your message slowly, clearly, and carefully.
3. Repeat information if necessary to be sure it is clear to your listeners.

Making an Introduction to a Presentation

An introduction is often given before a speaker's presentation or before a short performance. This type of an introduction focuses the audience's attention. It also provides listeners with important information about the speaker, the players, the subject, the dramatic work, or the author of the work being presented.

A good introduction fills in details that the audience might need to know before the main presentation begins. But don't provide too many details. A good introduction is short and to the point.

Group Discussions

Establishing a Purpose

Group discussions or cooperative learning groups work best when the group has a specific purpose to accomplish. This purpose may be

- to share ideas and cooperate in group learning
- to suggest solutions for solving a problem
- to make an evaluation, a recommendation, or a decision

To establish the purpose for the group, first decide what specific task the group needs to accomplish. Then the group can determine a plan of action, depending on how much time is allowed to reach this goal.

Assigning Roles for a Discussion

Each participant in a group discussion takes a role with specific responsibilities. Sometimes a group selects a chairperson who will help keep the discussion moving along smoothly. Another group member may be chosen to be secretary or reporter (recorder), with the responsibility of taking notes during the discussion.

Frequently, a group establishes an *agenda,* or outline of the order that they will follow in their discussion. Setting the agenda is often the responsibility of the chairperson, but the agenda may sometimes be agreed upon by all the members.

A Chairperson's Responsibilities

1. Announce the topic and establish the agenda.
2. Follow the agenda.
3. Encourage each member to participate.
4. Manage group conflict.

A Secretary's or Reporter's Responsibilities

1. Record significant information and developments.
2. Prepare a final report.

A Participant's Responsibilities

1. Take part in the discussion.
2. Cooperate and share information.
3. Listen carefully to others.
4. Be considerate.

Parliamentary Procedure

Groups such as clubs or committees often follow the principles of *parliamentary procedure* to make sure meetings are run smoothly and fairly.

RESOURCES

A DIFFERENT APPROACH

In parliamentary procedure, motions should be stated in the affirmative rather than the negative. Negative motions tend to confuse the voting. For example, "I move the class picnic be held in the city park" is better than "I move we don't hold the picnic on campus."

Also, you may wish to explain to students how a motion can be modified through amendments. If an amendment is proposed, it must be seconded before discussion, just like a motion. Amendments are voted on before the motion.

RESOURCES

RULES OF PARLIAMENTARY PROCEDURE

The meeting follows a step-by-step agenda.

1. The chairperson calls the meeting to order.
2. The secretary reports details of the last meeting.
3. The treasurer makes a report.
4. Unresolved issues or actions are discussed.
5. New issues or proposed actions are discussed.
6. The chairperson ends the meeting.

The meeting has specific procedures for discussions.

1. Anyone wishing to speak must raise his or her hand until recognized by the chairperson.
2. A participant may introduce a motion by saying, "I move that . . .".
3. To support a motion or suggestion, a participant other than the one who made the motion must say, "I second the motion." If no one seconds it, the motion is then dropped.
4. If a motion is seconded, it is discussed by the group.
5. After discussion, the group votes on the motion. The chairperson usually votes only in case of a tie.

INTEGRATING THE LANGUAGE ARTS

Reading and Speaking. Students might enjoy staging an oral interpretation recital. Each member of the class could read a short poem, or the class could read poems in chorus, with one or two students acting as narrators to link each poem with the next.

Oral Interpretation

Oral interpretation is like an acting performance. You use vocal techniques, facial expressions, body language, and gestures to indicate the meaning of the literary work you are interpreting.

Adapting Material

When you adapt material for an oral interpretation, you usually have a specific purpose, audience, and occasion in mind. Every situation has its own requirements. Be sure you have thought about factors such as the length of time for your presentation and your audience's interests. Most oral readings rely on the audience's imagination and not on props or costumes.

You will often need to make an abbreviated version, or *cutting,* of a work of fiction, nonfiction, a long poem, or a play. Here are some suggestions.

HOW TO MAKE A CUTTING

1. Follow the story line in time order.
2. Delete dialogue tags such as *she said softly.* Instead, use these clues to indicate how you should act when you interpret the character's words.
3. Take out any passages that don't contribute to the overall impression that you intend to create with your oral interpretation.

Presenting an Oral Interpretation

You may need to write an introduction to your interpretation to set the scene, tell something about the characters, give some background details about the author, or provide some necessary details about what has already taken place in the story.

To be effective in presenting an oral interpretation, you will need to prepare a reading script. A ***reading script*** is usually typed (double-spaced) and is marked to assist you in your interpretive reading. For example, you may underline words for emphasis or mark a slash (/) to indicate a pause.

After you have developed a reading script, rehearse the material several different ways until you are satisfied that you have chosen the most effective manner of interpreting the passage.

Use your voice in a manner that suits your presentation. Be sure to pronounce your words carefully. You can use your body and your voice to show that you are portraying different characters. Use body language and gestures to emphasize your meaning or to reveal traits of the major characters in the story as you act out what they say and do.

Literature Link. Before students perform their oral interpretations, you may want to have them read and discuss several poems such as Langston Hughes' "Dreams" and E. E. Cummings' "i thank You God for most this amazing." Topics for discussion could include how such diverse poetic aspects as theme and punctuation influence interpretation.

LEP/ESL

General Strategies. Exercises 1–3 can be especially helpful to LEP/ESL students because these execises focus on language that is appropriate in conveying a specific meaning or message. Give students plenty of opportunities to role-play the situations. Encourage improvisation, spontaneity, and as much active involvement with the material as possible.

ANSWERS
Exercise 1

Responses will vary. Here are some possibilities:

1. Excuse me, I'm really interested, but my father needs to use the phone now. Could I call you back later?
2. Hello, this is ____. Yesterday, I bought an AX10 tape player from your Morganville store, but after looking at the receipt, I think I was charged for the more expensive AX20 model. Can you help me?
3. Hello, this is ____. I have an appointment with Dr. Lynch at 3:00 today, but I can't make it. Could I please reschedule?

ANSWERS
Exercise 2

Responses will vary, but the directions should be given in clear, understandable steps.

ANSWERS
Exercise 3

Responses will vary. Here are some possibilities:

1. Hi. Doesn't ____ give great parties? My name's ____. I was in English class with ____ last year. What's your name?
2. Hello, my name's ____. I have a job interview with Ms. Torres at 2:15.
3. Mom, I'd like you to meet my science teacher, Ms. Nanez. Ms. Nanez, this is my mother.

908

Review

▶ EXERCISE 1 **Exploring Telephone Speaking Situations**

For each of the following situations, explain how you might handle the problem. What would you say to be polite but clear?

1. A caller is talking too long, and you need to get off the phone because your father wants to make a call.
2. You call the headquarters of a department store chain to complain about a billing error for a purchase that was charged at one of the chain's local stores.
3. You call a dentist's office at the last minute to reschedule an appointment.

▶ EXERCISE 2 **Giving Directions**

Provide directions for each of the following situations. Make sure your directions are simple and easy to follow.

1. You are having a party Friday night. Explain to a classmate how to get from your school to your house.
2. A new student needs to know how to get from the cafeteria to the gymnasium.
3. Explain to a visitor how to get from your school to another school in the area. Be sure to point out any helpful landmarks.

▶ EXERCISE 3 **Making Social Introductions**

In each of the following situations, explain what you would say.

1. You are at a party and the host doesn't seem to be around. Introduce yourself to another person who is standing alone.
2. You have an interview scheduled with Ms. Torres at the Youth Employment Center. Introduce yourself to the receptionist.
3. You are introducing your mother (or father or other relative) to your science teacher.

Responses will vary. Each speech should be of the appropriate length, should include suitable body language, and should be delivered clearly. Eye contact should be maintained with the audience.

▶ EXERCISE 4 **Preparing and Giving a Speech**

Choose a topic for a short, three- to five-minute speech to give to your English class. Consider your audience and purpose when choosing your speech topic. First, gather appropriate material. Next, prepare note cards for your speech. Include one visual, such as a chart, diagram, time line, or drawing, and prepare a note card to indicate at what point in your speech you should pause to explain and incorporate this item. Finally, deliver your speech, using effective speaking techniques and appropriate non-verbal signals.

ANSWERS
Exercise 5

Responses will vary. Here are some possibilities:

1. The sophomore class's annual carwash to benefit the Special Olympics will be held Saturday from noon until 6:00 P.M. in the Goodwill parking lot at 334 Main Street.

2. An election to choose the next student body president will be held Friday. Voting booths are in the auditorium, and students should vote during lunch break or study hall.

3. The annual sports award banquet has been scheduled for the last Saturday in March at the City Convention Center. It begins at 8:00 P.M. Tickets are five dollars each and can be purchased in the principal's office. Nominations for outstanding athletes in all sports should be delivered to the athletic director's office.

▶ EXERCISE 5 **Making an Announcement**

Write an announcement for one of the following events. Supply specific details wherever they are needed.

1. A car wash will be held by the sophomore class with the proceeds to benefit Special Olympic participants.
2. A special election will be held to choose the next student body president.
3. This year's sports award banquet has been scheduled. All students desiring to attend should bring the fee for tickets. Nominations for outstanding athletes in each school-sponsored sport are encouraged.

▶ EXERCISE 6 **Introducing a Speaker**

Prepare and deliver in class an introduction for your state or national representative or senator, your mayor, your county commissioner, a school board member, or a famous person from history.

ANSWERS
Exercise 6

Responses will vary. Each speech should be reasonably brief, delivered with confidence, and should include highlights from the speaker's career.

▶ EXERCISE 7 **Conducting a Group Discussion**

Select a group chairperson and present a discussion about any of the following topics or one of your own choosing. Establish an agenda and determine how much time you will have for your discussion.

1. Radio and television advertising
2. Comic books and their characters
3. Teenage crime

ANSWERS
Exercise 7

Responses will vary. The success of the discussion should be gauged on the ability of the chairperson and the participants to fulfill their roles and on the group's ability to cover the topic in the time available.

RESOURCES

RESOURCES

4. How to achieve a goal
5. The impact of the young voter
6. The ideal school
7. Choosing a career
8. Job opportunities in your city
9. Ways to prevent war
10. Our local environment

EXERCISE 8 **Presenting an Oral Interpretation**

Select a portion of a short story, a scene from a play, or a section of a novel that contains a scene for one or two characters. Prepare a script for a five-minute oral interpretation to present to your classmates. Write a brief introduction that tells the title and author of the selection and gives enough background information about the characters and the setting so that your audience can understand the meaning of the scene.

ANSWERS
Exercise 8

Responses will vary depending on the literature chosen to be interpreted. Each interpretation should have a suitable introduction, be delivered within the time limit, and retain narrative coherence. Students should deliver the interpretations in a way that conveys the different characters.

OBJECTIVES

- To give a list of instructions and to listen to the lists of others' instructions
- To listen critically to a short speech
- To analyze a magazine or newspaper to identify purposes in mass media
- To identify persuasive techniques employed in various statements

Teacher's ResourceBank™
RESOURCES

LISTENING
- Listening for Details
- The LQ2R Method
- Conducting an Interview
- Critical Listening
- Persuasive Techniques in the Media
- Chapter Review Form A
- Chapter Review Form B

31 LISTENING

Strategies for Active Listening

Listening is not the same thing as hearing. If you are able to detect sounds, hearing just happens. However, listening is an active process that requires you to think as well as hear.

Listening with a Purpose

You can become a more effective listener if you keep your purpose in mind as you listen. People hear things differently depending on what they are listening for. Common purposes for listening are

- for enjoyment or entertainment
- to gain information
- to understand information or an explanation
- to evaluate or form an opinion

CHAPTER OVERVIEW

This chapter leads students through such basic skills as listening with a purpose, listening for details, listening to instructions, and listening politely. The LQ2R study method is explained, and students are taught how to conduct an interview, how to listen critically, and how to take lecture notes. Finally, students are introduced to an understanding of the impact of mass media on their lives.

QUICK REMINDER

Ask students to discuss the things they listen to on a daily basis and why they listen to those things. Ask them to provide examples of things they listen to that satisfy the common purposes for listening. Then ask students to name the six basic *5W-How?* questions [*Who? What? When? Where? Why? How?*].

RESOURCES

RESOURCES

LEP/ESL

General Strategies. Of the four basic skills (listening, speaking, reading, and writing), it might seem that listening would be the most passive, and therefore the easiest for students. However, listening can prove difficult for several reasons. First of all, it is especially difficult to control the listening experience. One can ask the speaker to slow down, but often that leads to embarrassment, especially in the classroom. Second, it is often difficult for ESL students to remember what they are listening to because they are trying to determine the meaning of new vocabulary. Additionally, listening skills are based on prior knowledge and knowledge of the language and the cultural context, which includes non-verbal clues. A native speaker comes equipped with this prior knowledge and can therefore understand a great deal without actively listening. The ESL student does not have the same equipment, and is therefore rarely listening without anxiety.

Listening for Information

Listening for Details

When you listen for information, you are listening for details that answer the six basic *5W-How?* questions: *Who? What? When? Where? Why?* and *How?*

For example, when you are asked to take messages on the telephone, you will need to listen to important details that the caller tells you, such as

- the caller's name
- who the call is for
- the caller's message
- the caller's telephone number

Using the LQ2R Method

The LQ2R study method is especially helpful when you are listening to a speaker who is giving information.

L *Listen* carefully to material as it is being presented. Focus your attention on the speaker.

Q *Question* yourself as you listen. Make a list, mentally or in your notes, of questions that occur to you.

R *Recite* in your own words the information as it is being presented. Summarize information in your mind or jot down notes as you listen.

R *Re-listen* as the speaker concludes the presentation. Major points may be reemphasized.

Listening to Instructions

Instructions are usually made up of a series of steps. When you listen to instructions, be sure you understand everything you are required to do.

1. *Listen for the order of steps.* Listen for words that tell you where each step ends and the next one begins, such as *first, second, next, then,* and *last.*

2. *Identify the number of steps in the process.* Take notes if the instructions are long and complicated.
3. *Visualize each step.* Imagine yourself actually performing each step. Try to get a mental image of what you should be doing at every step in the process.
4. *Review the steps when the speaker is finished.* Be sure you understand them.

Listening Politely

When you are listening to someone speak, you are taking part in the communication cycle. People who are speaking usually respond to you as a listener, depending on how well it appears you are paying attention. Here's how to be a more courteous and encouraging listener.

1. *Respect the speaker.* Be tolerant of individual differences. Show respect for the speaker's cultural background, such as customs, race, or religion.
2. *Don't interrupt.* Wait until the speaker finishes.
3. *Pay attention.* Don't distract others.
4. *Keep an open mind.* Try to understand the speaker's point of view. Also, be aware of how your own point of view affects the way you evaluate the opinions and values of others.
5. *Don't judge too soon.* Wait to hear the speaker's whole message before you begin to make judgments about the content of the speech.

Conducting an Interview

An interview is a special listening situation. Most often an interview takes place between two people, and inter-viewer and the person being interviewed (called the *interviewee*). Follow these suggestions to conduct an effective interview.

Before the Interview
- Decide what information you really want to know.
- Make a list of questions.
- Make an appointment and be prompt.

COMMON ERROR
Problem. Even after students listen carefully to instructions, they may forget a crucial step.

Solution. Tell students that after listening to instructions, they should repeat the instructions aloud to ensure that all steps have been remembered. If there are more than three steps, students should write them down.

A DIFFERENT APPROACH
You may wish to read a short story to your students to encourage them to listen using the LQ2R method. When the story is over, ask your students to write down short answers to questions about the story. Students should then compare their answers. Suitable short stories are Saki's "The Storyteller" or Kate Chopin's "A Pair of Silk Stockings."

COOPERATIVE LEARNING

For practice with conducting interviews and listening, students can be put in pairs, either by allowing them to select their own partners or by assigning partners randomly. The members of each pair can then take turns interviewing each other. Interviewers should be given a purpose, such as discovering favorite hobbies or pastimes, or obtaining opinions on aspects of school life. Interviewers should prepare some questions in advance and should take notes during the interviews. You may wish to have the students make brief verbal reports after the interviews are completed.

INTEGRATING THE LANGUAGE ARTS

Literature Link. Responding effectively to an essay read aloud tests all aspects of critical listening. Annie Dillard's "In the Jungle," Harry Crew's "The Hawk is Flying," and Edward Abbey's "Desert Images" are all suitable for such an exercise. After reading the essay to your students, ask them for written responses to questions. These responses (which you may or may not wish to collect) can provide a basis for class discussion.

914

During the Interview

- Be patient, giving the interviewee time to answer each question.
- Pay attention and ask questions if you're not sure you understand what the interviewee means.
- If you are planning to quote the person directly, it is best to ask permission.
- Respect the interviewee's opinion. You can ask the other person to explain an opinion, but be polite even you disagree.
- Conclude courteously. Thank the person for allowing the interview.

After the Interview

- Check your notes to be sure they are clear.
- Write out note cards or a summary of your impressions while you still remember the interview clearly.

Critical Listening

When you listen critically, you think carefully about what you hear. You can't remember every word a speaker says. But if you listen critically, you'll be able to find the parts of the speaker's message that are most important.

GUIDELINES FOR LISTENING CRITICALLY	
Find main ideas.	What are the most important points? Listen for clue words a speaker might use, such as *major, main, most important,* or similar words.
Identify significant details.	What dates, names, or facts does the speaker use to support the main points of the speech? What kinds of examples or explanations are used to support the main ideas?

(continued)

GUIDELINES FOR LISTENING CRITICALLY *(continued)*	
Distinguish between facts and opinions.	A fact is a statement that can be proved to be true. An opinion is a belief or a judgment about something. It cannot be proved to be true.
Identify the order of organization.	What kind of order is the speaker using to arrange his or her presentation—time sequence, spatial order, order of importance?
Note comparisons and contrasts.	Are some details compared or contrasted with others?
Understand cause and effect.	Do some events that the speaker mentions relate to or affect others?
Predict outcomes and draw conclusions.	What can you reasonably conclude from the facts and evidence you have gathered from the speech?

 REFERENCE NOTE: For more information about interpreting and analyzing information, see pages 955–956.

Taking Lecture Notes

When you listen to a speaker, don't rely entirely on your memory. Take notes to help you remember information. You can take notes by writing the most important words or phrases the speaker says. Other note taking techniques include paraphrasing and summarizing.

Paraphrasing. When you *paraphrase* material, you express the ideas of others in your own words. Translate complex terms or examples that the speaker uses into your own words and write your paraphrase in your notes.

Summarizing. When you *summarize,* you condense material by restating it in fewer words. As you listen to the speaker, sum up the major points of the lecture. Write these statements in your lecture notes.

RESOURCES

A DIFFERENT APPROACH
Arrange for a guest lecturer to speak to your class and ask your students to take careful notes. At the following class meeting, ask your students, with the aid of their notes, to reconstruct on paper the lecturer's main points in order. You may then wish to quiz your students on these main points.

MEETING INDIVIDUAL NEEDS

STUDENTS WITH SPECIAL NEEDS
The activities in this chapter may boost the confidence level of many learning disabled students since many are auditory learners. However, students may require structure to adequately utilize their abilities.

Many students need help understanding cause and effect. Thus, have them fill out a chart representing cause-and-effect relationships. Have them look in the media for examples of false cause and effect. For example, advertisements may imply that if people purchase a particular product, they will gain many friends. Have the students relate this to their own lives.

RESOURCES

A DIFFERENT APPROACH

Exposure to the mass media is so pervasive that students often fail to recognize how great it is. After discussing with your students the ways in which they are exposed to the mass media, ask them to keep a 24- or 48-hour log of what they see or hear. Remind them to include fleeting glimpses, such as messages on billboards or headlines on tabloids in a rack in a market. Students should be encouraged to compare logs.

Understanding the Impact of Mass Media

The *mass media* are forms of communication that affect you and millions of other people every day. The mass media include

- television
- radio
- newspapers
- magazines
- movies
- video cassettes
- some compact discs

The mass media give you contact with the whole world. Today's mass media make all types of information available to just about everyone. Television and radio bring you information about world happenings almost instantly. Newspapers and magazines bring you detailed accounts and analyses of worldwide events within a short time after the occurrence.

Since the mass media distribute a great deal of information quickly, people often assume that the media's only purpose is to inform. However, the mass media also entertain. Today you can see and hear performances of your favorite music, television, and film stars even if you never attend their performances in person. You can also tour great cities, view natural wonders, and visit historic landmarks without leaving home. When you view the media, you usually have a purpose in mind—to find information or to be entertained.

A primary goal of the broadcast and print media is to build a successful business and earn profits. Radio and television stations must find listeners and viewers. Magazines and newspapers must find readers. To do this, the media need your attention and loyalty.

The media produce programs designed to interest and entertain you so that you will continue watching, listening, or reading. Just as you have a purpose in watching or listening to the media, the media have their own purposes for you, their audience.

Both the media and the media audience have specific purposes and responsibilities. A media product may be intended by its creators to entertain you, to inform you, or to persuade you. Media products may also serve more than one purpose. For example, an editorial cartoon in a newspaper may entertain you as well as persuade you to agree with the cartoonist's opinion.

THE MEDIA		
PURPOSE	MEANS	RESPONSIBILITIES
To attract a loyal audience To sell advertising time and increase profits	broadcasting or printing informative, entertaining, or persuasive presentations	presenting factual information in a truthful, fair, and unbiased manner striving for accuracy of information
THE AUDIENCE		
PURPOSE	MEANS	RESPONSIBILITIES
To receive information To be entertained	watching, reading, or listening to various media presentations	responding to the media actively through evaluating and assessing presentations choosing whether or not to watch, read, or listen to a presentation; or responding by writing letters or otherwise demonstrating an opinion

Persuasive Techniques

Advertisers, politicians, and others frequently buy media time to sell their products or ideas. To convince you, they may use *persuasive techniques.* Knowing about persuasive techniques will help you evaluate the factors that are used in the media to influence you in various ways.

COMMON PERSUASIVE TECHNIQUES FOUND IN THE MEDIA	
Bandwagon	Those who use this technique urge you to "jump on the bandwagon" by suggesting that you should do or believe something because everyone (or everyone admirable or worthwhile) is doing it.
Testimonial	Experts or famous people sometimes give a personal "testimony" about a product or idea. However, the person offering the testimonial may not really know much about that particular product or idea.
"Plain folks"	Ordinary people (or people who pretend to be ordinary) are often used to persuade others. People tend to believe others who seem to be similar to themselves.
Emotional words	This technique uses words that appeal to your emotions rather than to your ability to reason.

Review

EXERCISE 1 **Listening to Instructions**

Give a list of instructions explaining how to do or make something. Be sure to organize the steps of the process in a specific order. After giving your instructions to the class, allow your classmates a chance to ask questions. Then call on classmates to repeat your instructions to be sure that everyone understands all of the steps.

EXERCISE 2 **Listening Critically**

Take brief notes while listening to a short speech presented by your teacher in class. Then answer the following questions about the speech.

ANSWERS

Exercise 1

Responses will vary. Steps of processes should be given in the correct order. Students responding to instructions should be able to repeat them accurately and in order. If students have been instructed in a physical skill, they should be able to perform that skill correctly.

1. What are the main ideas expressed in the speech?
2. What details are used to support the main points in the speech? Identify several of these supporting details.
3. Identify one fact and one opinion mentioned in the speech. What reasons does the speaker give that support this opinion?
4. What is the order of the speech's organization?
5. Draw a conclusion about the ideas presented in the speech. Did you find the speech convincing? Explain why or why not.

▶ EXERCISE 3   **Identifying Purpose in Mass Media**

Work in small groups to analyze a copy of a magazine or your local newspaper. List examples of regular features or columns. Which features are primarily for entertainment? for information? for persuasion? Prepare a brief report, and be ready to compare your conclusions with those of other groups in class.

▶ EXERCISE 4   **Recognizing Persuasive Techniques**

Identify the persuasive technique used in each of the following items.

1. "Join the millions of satisfied customers who buy our product." **1.** bandwagon
2. "He's a greedy politician who will steal every taxpayer's money." **2.** emotional words
3. "Don't be left out! Hurry, hurry, hurry! Join the new club that everyone's talking about." **3.** bandwagon
4. "As an Olympic champion, I can tell you this investment is solid gold." **4.** testimonial
5. "I'm just an 'average Joe,' but I know she's got the right stuff to be a great mayor." **5.** "plain folks"

RESOURCES

ANSWERS
Exercise 2

Responses will vary. Students should be able to discover main ideas, identify supporting material, distinguish between a statement of fact and one of opinion, list the main points in order, identify the type of organizational patterns used, and evaluate the overall message of the speech.

ANSWERS
Exercise 3

Responses will vary. Students should be able to present, with justification, examples of mass media used to entertain, inform, and persuade. Students may find examples that seem to fall in more than one category. You may wish to encourage class discussion in order to determine what the primary category of those examples might be.

RESOURCES

THE LIBRARY/MEDIA CENTER *(pp. 920–926)*

OBJECTIVES

- To use the card catalog in the school library to find the subjects, titles, authors, and call numbers of books
- To use the *Readers' Guide to Periodical Literature* to find the titles, authors, magazines, dates, and page numbers of articles about selected topics

CHAPTER OVERVIEW

This chapter provides students with the basic information they will need to use the library. The chapter opens with a discussion of how information is classified and arranged, and then it describes the card catalog. A description and a discussion of various reference materials follow. Review exercises at the end of the chapter can be used to discover how much students have learned about the library.

QUICK REMINDER

To open the lesson on the library, bring to class a stack of notecards with book titles on them, put the cards on a volunteer's desk, and ask the volunteer to find a particular card. After the student has struggled for a few minutes, you can call a halt to the search. Tell the class that without organization finding a book in the library would be virtually impossible—students would have to examine every book until they found what they were looking for the way the volunteer had to examine every card.

Tell students that the Dewey decimal system, the Library of Congress system, and classification by author or subject are all tools designed to help them find the books they need.

RESOURCES

RESOURCES

32 THE LIBRARY/ MEDIA CENTER

Finding and Using Information

You can find the answers to a great number of questions by consulting the resources available in a library or media center. To take advantage of these resources, however, you must know how to find out what information sources your library contains and how the library's contents are arranged.

Classifying and Arranging Information

Libraries arrange books by classifying them according to the Dewey decimal or the Library of Congress system. These systems assign a number and letter code—a *call number*—to each book. The call number tells you how the book has been classified and where it can be found in the library.

Most school libraries use the Dewey decimal system. Using this system, works of nonfiction are assigned a number according to their subjects.

DEWEY DECIMAL CLASSIFICATION		
NUMBERS	SUBJECT AREAS	EXAMPLES OF SUBDIVISIONS
000–099	General Works	encyclopedias, handbooks
100–199	Philosophy	psychology, ethics
200–299	Religion	bibles, theology, mythology
300–399	Social Science	government, economics, education
400–499	Languages	dictionaries, grammars, languages
500–599	Science	science, mathematics
600–699	Technology	engineering, business, health
700–799	The Arts	music, painting, theater, recreation
800–899	Literature	poetry, drama, essays
900–999	History	history, biography, geography

Dewey Decimal Arrangement of Fiction

According to the *Dewey decimal system,* works of fiction are grouped in alphabetical order according to their authors' last names. When a library has several novels by the same author, they are arranged alphabetically by the first word of their titles (not counting *A, An,* or *The*). Sometimes, collections of short stories are grouped separately.

The Card Catalog

The *card catalog* is a cabinet of small drawers that contains cards. These cards list books by title, author, and subject. For each book in the library, there are at least two cards—a *title card* and an *author card.* If the book is nonfiction, there is a third card—a *subject card.* You can tell what type of card it is by what is printed on its top line. Occasionally, you may find "see" or "see also" cards. These are cross-reference cards that tell you where additional information on this subject may be found.

An *on-line catalog* is a computerized version of the card catalog. It contains the same information found on the title, author, subject, and the "see also" cards.

LEP/ESL

General Strategies. You may want to introduce ESL students to the library by taking them on a tour of the fiction section and letting them select books from the appropriate reading levels. You could also allow the students to read for the first ten minutes of class to reinforce the idea that leisure reading is as important as required reading. Stress that reading is a good way to become familiar with a second language, and that reading will also help students improve their writing.

LEARNING STYLES

Kinetic Learners. Some students will better internalize the information on the library if they are lead through the process of finding a book.

COMMON ERROR

Problem. When working on research projects, students may neglect to record information about each source they use.

Solution. Have students make note cards for each source they use. The cards should contain the following information: author or authors (complete names as listed on the title page), complete title (including subtitle), city where the publisher is located, publisher's name, and date of publication.

COOPERATIVE LEARNING

Have students compete in teams of three in a hunt for the call numbers of the following books:

A travel book
A novel by Mark Twain
A book about geology
A book about Madam Curie
An astronomy book
A book about Albert Einstein
A biography of Abraham Lincoln
A book about art
A music book
A sports book

INTEGRATING THE LANGUAGE ARTS

Technology Link. To familiarize students with the on-line catalog, help them develop a simple step-by-step list of instructions. When they see how easy it is to use the on-line catalog, they might develop an interest in learning more about computers.

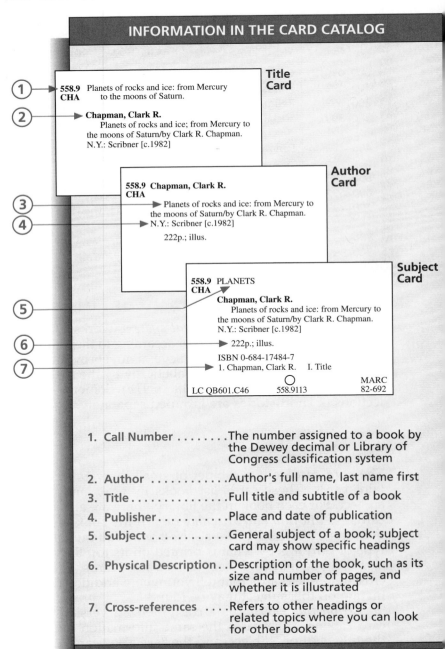

INFORMATION IN THE CARD CATALOG

Title Card

(1) 558.9 CHA Planets of rocks and ice: from Mercury to the moons of Saturn.

(2) **Chapman, Clark R.**
Planets of rocks and ice; from Mercury to the moons of Saturn/by Clark R. Chapman.
N.Y.: Scribner [c.1982]

Author Card

558.9 CHA **Chapman, Clark R.**
(3) Planets of rocks and ice: from Mercury to the moons of Saturn/by Clark R. Chapman.
(4) N.Y.: Scribner [c.1982]

222p.; illus.

Subject Card

558.9 CHA PLANETS
Chapman, Clark R.
(5) Planets of rocks and ice: from Mercury to the moons of Saturn/by Clark R. Chapman.
N.Y.: Scribner [c.1982]
(6) 222p.; illus.
ISBN 0-684-17484-7
(7) 1. Chapman, Clark R.   I. Title
LC QB601.C46   558.9113   MARC 82-692

1. Call Number . . . . The number assigned to a book by the Dewey decimal or Library of Congress classification system

2. Author . . . . Author's full name, last name first

3. Title . . . . Full title and subtitle of a book

4. Publisher . . . . Place and date of publication

5. Subject . . . . General subject of a book; subject card may show specific headings

6. Physical Description . . Description of the book, such as its size and number of pages, and whether it is illustrated

7. Cross-references . . . . Refers to other headings or related topics where you can look for other books

Using Reference Materials

The *Readers' Guide*

To find a magazine article, use the *Readers' Guide to Periodical Literature.* The *Readers' Guide* indexes all the articles, poems, and stories from more than 150 magazines. In the *Readers' Guide,* magazine articles are listed alphabetically by author and by subject. These headings are printed in boldfaced capital letters.

Entries may contain abbreviations. Use the key at the front of the *Readers' Guide* to find the meanings of these abbreviations. You can see how *Readers' Guide* items are arranged by looking at the following excerpt.

① **SHORT STORY**
② *See also*
Fiction in periodicals and newspapers
The new flowering of the American short
story. B. Oliver. il *USA Today (Periodical)*
118:82–4 Mr '90
Bibliography
③ The glory of the story. il *Newsweek* 115:56–7+
Ap 2 '90
SHORTWAVE RADIO
The future of shortwave broadcasting. S. Leinwoll.
④ il *Radio-Electronics* 61:73+ Ja '90
**SHOSTAKOVICH, DMITRII DMITRIEVICH,
1906–1975**
about
⑤ The young Dmitri. P. Kennicott. il *Dance Magazine*
64:70–1 F '90
⑥ **SHOUSE, DEBORAH**
Why aren't my children like the ones on TV? il
Good Housekeeping 210:200+ Mr '90
SHOW BUSINESS *See* Entertainment industry
⑦ **SHOWER BATHS**
Showers for bath people. il *Mademoiselle* 96:26 F '90
SHOWERS, MARGI
about
⑧ Saga of a business start-up (II). L. Washer. il pors
Working Woman 15:37–8+ Ja '90
SHRADY, NICHOLAS
The alpine retreat of a musical legend. il pors
⑨ *Architectural Digest* 47:262+ Mr '90
Spanish acquisitions: a Madrid couple celebrate
their country's art. il *Architectural Digest*
47:166–71+ Mr '90

① **Subject entry**
② **Subject cross-
reference**
③ **Title of article**
④ **Name of magazine**
⑤ **Volume number
of magazine**
⑥ **Author entry**
⑦ **Page references**
⑧ **Author of article**
⑨ **Date of magazine**

LEP/ESL

General Strategies. Some students might be overwhelmed by the number of reference tools available. They might even become frustrated and give up. To keep this from happening, schedule a special trip to the library. Carefully show and explain to students how each reference tool is used. You may want to stress that they won't necessarily need to use all of these tools for each assignment—for most assignments, two or three reference tools will serve nicely.

STUDENTS WITH SPECIAL NEEDS

To help students with attention-deficit disorder remain focused on their work, vary their library activities and allow them to explore non-print media.

Another effective strategy is to help students evaluate their own behavior. Make a chart listing desired behavior, such as being on time, being polite, completing assignments, and so on. Have the students fill in the chart with a " + " or a "–," depending on their behavior for the day. Provide positive feedback for good behavior and accurate assessments.

RESOURCES

RESOURCES

SELECTION AMENDMENT
Description of change: excerpted
Rationale: to focus on the concept of using the *Readers' Guide*
presented in this chapter

INTEGRATING THE LANGUAGE ARTS

Literature Link. Before students read *Julius Caesar*, have them read about it in *Masterplots* to prepare for reading the play itself. *Masterplots* gives information about the play's setting, major characters (in alphabetical order), and plot, and also includes a brief criticism. The information supplied in *Masterplots* might help students keep from getting lost in a long and complex play such as *Julius Caesar*.

COOPERATIVE LEARNING

Divide the class into four or five groups and have each group make up a list of subjects. These can be anything from favorite authors or sports heroes to possible professions or hobbies. Each group member should supply one item for the list.

When the lists are complete, have groups trade lists and go to the library to find one book, one magazine article, and one newspaper article about each item on their new lists. They should list the title, author(s), call number, publisher, place published, and date of publication for each book; title, author, magazine, date, and page numbers for each magazine article; and title, byline (if given), newspaper, date, and page number(s) for each newspaper article.

Special Information Sources

The *vertical file* contains up-to-date materials such as pamphlets, newspaper clippings, and pictures. These materials may include government, business, and educational information.

Microforms are newspaper and magazine articles that have been photographically reduced in size. The two most common types are *microfilm* (a roll or reel of film) and *microfiche* (a sheet of film). A special projector enlarges the microscopic images to a readable size.

Increasingly, libraries are storing many of their reference sources on computer. The kind of information you can find on computer in a library depends on what database systems the library has. A *database* is the body of information that is stored on computer for easy retrieval.

Reference Works

There are many types of reference books that you can use to find specific kinds of information.

REFERENCE WORKS	
TYPE	**DESCRIPTION**
ENCYCLOPEDIAS *Collier's Encyclopedia* *Compton's Encyclopedia* *The Encyclopedia Americana* *The New Encyclopaedia Britannica* *The World Book Encyclopedia*	■ multiple volumes ■ articles arranged alphabetically by subject ■ best source for general information ■ may have index or annuals
GENERAL BIOGRAPHICAL REFERENCES *Current Biography* *Dictionary of American Biography* *The International Who's Who* *Webster's New Biographical Dictionary*	■ information about birth, nationality, and major accomplishments of prominent people

(continued)

REFERENCE WORKS *(continued)*	
TYPE	**DESCRIPTION**
SPECIAL BIOGRAPHICAL REFERENCES *American Men and Women of Science* *Mexican American Biographies* *Contemporary Authors* (series)	▪ information about people noted for accomplishments in a specific field or for membership in a specific group
ATLASES *Atlas of World Cultures* *National Geographic Atlas of the World*	▪ maps and geographical information
ALMANACS *The World Almanac and Book of Facts* *Information Please Almanac, Atlas and Yearbook*	▪ up-to-date information about current events, facts, statistics, and dates
BOOKS OF QUOTATIONS Bartlett's *Familiar Quotations* *The Oxford Dictionary of Quotations*	▪ famous quotations indexed or grouped by subject ▪ often tells author, source, and date
BOOKS OF SYNONYMS *Roget's International Thesaurus* *The New Roget's Thesaurus in Dictionary Form* *Webster's New Dictionary of Synonyms*	▪ lists of exact or more interesting words to express ideas
REFERENCE BOOKS ABOUT LITERATURE *Granger's Index to Poetry* *Subject Index to Poetry* *Essay & General Literature Index* *Short Story Index* *Play Index*	▪ condensed information about various literary works

RESOURCES

 A DIFFERENT APPROACH

Most students won't realize how many reference tools libraries have to offer. To introduce students to the reference tools, write the following items on the chalkboard:

1. magazine articles
2. pamphlets
3. back issues of periodicals
4. databases
5. documentaries

Then write the following list of reference tools on the chalkboard:

a. the vertical file
b. recorded materials
c. the *Readers' Guide*
d. microforms
e. computers

Ask students to match the tool with the type of material it can help a student find. [1—c; 2—a; 3—d; 4—e; 5—b]

RESOURCES

ANSWERS
Exercise 2

Answers will vary. Here are some possibilities:

1. Title: "Great Games for Kids"
   Author: J. A. Flagg
   Magazine: *Good Housekeeping*
   Date: June '90
   Page Numbers: 92 +

2. Title: "Is the Brain's Mind a Computer Program?"
   Author: J. R. Serle
   Magazine: *Scientific American*
   Date: 31 January '90
   Page Numbers: 267–76

3. Title: "Songs of Exile [South African Exiles M. Makeba and H. Makeba]"
   Authors: H. Bordowitz and W. Kinnelly
   Magazine: *American Visions*
   Date: April '90
   Page Numbers: 30–4

4. Title: "The Family Funny Bone"
   Author: R. S. Shanok
   Magazine: *Parents*
   Date: March '90
   Page Number: 188

5. Title: "Drinking in America: Portrait of a Teenage Alcoholic"
   Author: A. N. LeBlanc
   Magazine: *Seventeen*
   Date: March '90
   Page Numbers: 179–83

926

Review

EXERCISE 1   Using the Card Catalog

Use the card catalog or on-line catalog in your library to find the following information. If the information cannot be found, write "not in our library."   Information will vary.

1. List the title of one book by each of the following authors.
   1a. *The Yearling/Cross Creek/ The Sojourner*
   a. Marjorie Kinnan Rawlings
   b. Toni Cade Bambara   **1b.** *Gorilla, My Love/ The Salt Eaters*

2. Find the title card for each of the following books. Give the author's full name.
   a. *The House on Mango Street*   **2a.** Sandra Cisneros
   b. *Johnny Tremain*   **2b.** Esther Forbes

3. Find a book on each of these subjects. List the title, author, and call number of each book.
   a. Eskimos   **3a.** Chance, Norman A.; *The Eskimo of North Alaska;*
   b. Martin Luther King, Jr.   **3b.** Lerone, Bennett;   E 99 E7 C5
   What Manner of Man: A Biography of Martin Luther King, Jr.; 92 K5853B

EXERCISE 2   Using the *Readers' Guide*

In the *Readers' Guide*, find one entry listed for each of the following subjects. For each entry, give the title, author or authors (if given), magazine, date, and page numbers.

EXAMPLE   Subject: greenhouse effect
   Readers' Guide entry: Global Warming Trends
   P. D. Jones and T.M.L. Wigley
   bibl il Scientific American 263:84–91
   Ag 90

ANSWER   *Title: "Global Warming Trends"*
   Authors: P. D. Jones and T.M.L. Wigley
   Magazine: Scientific American
   Date: August 1990
   Page Numbers: 84–91

1. games
2. artificial intelligence
3. African popular music
4. family
5. health

THE DICTIONARY *(pp. 927–930)*

OBJECTIVES

- To look up words in a dictionary and to check for alternative spellings
- To divide words into syllables
- To use the pronunciation key in a dictionary to pronounce words correctly ☞

Teacher's ResourceBank™
RESOURCES

THE DICTIONARY
- Types of Dictionaries
- The Dictionary Entry A
- The Dictionary Entry B
- The Dictionary Entry C
- Chapter Review Form A
- Chapter Review Form B

33 THE DICTIONARY

Types and Contents

Types of Dictionaries

There are many different types of dictionaries. They vary in the kinds of information they contain and in the arrangement of their contents.

TYPES OF DICTIONARIES		
TYPES OF DICTIONARIES	**NUMBER OF ENTRIES**	**NUMBER OF PAGES**
Unabridged *Webster's Third International Unabridged Dictionary*	460,000	2,662
College or Abridged *Webster's Ninth Collegiate Dictionary*	160,000	1,563
Paperback *The Random House Dictionary*	74,000	1,054

CHAPTER OVERVIEW

This chapter offers a brief description of the types of dictionaries available and a ten-part treatment of the standard dictionary entry. Review exercises at the end of the chapter offer students the opportunity to test their mastery of dictionary use.

QUICK REMINDER

Most students are familiar with ordinary English dictionaries, but few know that specialized dictionaries exist on a wide variety of subjects. To introduce students to the idea of specialized dictionaries, write the following items on the chalkboard and ask students where they would look for the information. If possible, bring several specialized dictionaries into the classroom for students to examine.

1. the meaning of an Italian word [Italian-English dictionary]
2. words that rhyme with *love* [rhyming dictionary]
3. a seven-letter word that means "to rest" [crossword puzzle dictionary]
4. the abbreviation *AFL-CIO* [college dictionary]

RESOURCES

RESOURCES

- To use a dictionary to identify the parts of speech certain words can be used as
- To use a dictionary to find the etymologies of words
- To use a dictionary to find synonyms for words

LEP/ESL

General Strategies. Some students may have already learned the usefulness of bilingual dictionaries, but others may not know such dictionaries exist. If your ESL students don't know how to use a bilingual dictionary, work with them individually or in small groups to show them.

You may want to set up a kind of game in which the ESL students give a word in their first language and the non-ESL students look that word up in a bilingual dictionary and give its meaning in English. The game can also work in reverse, with the non-ESL students giving a word in English for the ESL students to look up.

STUDENTS WITH SPECIAL NEEDS

Learning disabled students are often poor decoders and may need extra time to complete assignments. You may want to shorten the word lists in the exercises for them and include words with which they have experienced difficulties. Teaching the students to use a thesaurus also may help them overcome problems with expressive language.

SELECTION AMENDMENT
Description of change: numbers added
Rationale: to provide references for the contents of a dictionary entry as presented in this chapter

A SAMPLE ENTRY

From *Webster's New World Dictionary.* © 1986 by Merriam-Webster Inc., publisher of Merriam-Webster ® Dictionaries. Reprinted by permission of Merriam-Webster Inc.

1. **Entry word.** The entry word shows how the word is spelled and how it is divided into syllables. The entry word may also show capitalization and provide alternate spellings.
2. **Pronunciation.** The pronunciation is shown using accent marks and other phonetic respellings or diacritical marks. A pronunciation key is provided as a guide to diacritical marks or phonetic symbols.
3. **Part-of-speech labels.** These labels (usually in abbreviated form) indicate how the entry word should be used in a sentence. Some words may be used as more than one part of speech. In this case, a part-of-speech label is given in front of each of the numbered (or lettered) series of definitions.
4. **Other forms.** These may show spellings of plural forms of nouns, tenses of verbs, or the comparative forms of adjectives and adverbs.
5. **Etymology.** The etymology is the origin and history of a word. It tells how the word (or its parts) came into English.
6. **Definitions.** If there is more than one meaning, definitions are numbered or lettered.
7. **Special usage labels.** These labels identify words that have special meaning or are used in special ways in certain situations.

8. **Examples.** Phrases or sentences may demonstrate how the defined word is to be used.
9. **Related word forms.** These are various forms of the entry word, usually created by adding suffixes or prefixes.
10. **Synonyms and antonyms.** Synonyms and antonyms may appear at the end of some word entries.

Review

EXERCISE 1   Looking Up the Spelling of Words

Look up the following words in your dictionary and write any alternate spellings listed. If the word has only one spelling in your dictionary, write the word *single* as your answer. Answers may vary according to the dictionary used. These are from *Webster's New World Dictionary,* Third College Edition.

EXAMPLE   **1.** judgment
        1. *judgement*

1. encyclopedia   1. encyclopaedia   **4.** skeptic   4. *single*
2. fledgling   2. fledgeling   **5.** yogurt   5. yoghurt/yoghourt
3. theater   3. theatre

EXERCISE 2   Dividing Words into Syllables

Divide the following words into syllables. Check with the dictionary to see how well you have done.

1. ostentation   4. particularize
2. environment   5. distinction
3. conservation

EXERCISE 3   Using the Pronunciation Key

Pronounce each of the following words using the pronunciation key in your dictionary.

1. legerdemain   4. indigent
2. parquet   5. Portuguese
3. theocracy

COOPERATIVE LEARNING

Have students work in groups of three to look up the same word in an unabridged dictionary, a college dictionary, and a paperback dictionary. Ask the students to compare the information given in each type of dictionary by making a comparison chart of the elements each dictionary contains.

TEACHING NOTE
Exercise 2

Point out to students that some dictionaries use vertical lines in syllable divisions to indicate places where words should not be divided if they come at the end of a line of text. The proper places for dividing words when they come at the end of a line are those syllable divisions indicated by a raised dot.

ANSWERS
Exercise 2

1. os•ten•ta•tion
2. en•vi•ron•ment
3. con•ser•va•tion
4. par•tic•u•lar•ize
5. dis•tinc•tion

ANSWERS
Exercise 3

Answers may vary according to the dictionary used.

Answers may vary according to the dictionary used. These are from

EXERCISE 4   **Identifying Part-of-Speech Labels**

Webster's New World Dictionary, Third College Edition.

Look up the following words in a dictionary and write the part-of-speech labels given for each of their meanings.

1. objective   **1.** adj./n.
2. dry   **2.** adj./v.
3. still   **3.** adj./n./adv./conj./v.

4. branch   **4.** n./v.
5. no   **5.** adv./adj./n.

EXERCISE 5   **Exploring the Etymology of a Word**

Use a college or unabridged dictionary to find the etymology of the following words. For each word, tell what language the word came from.

1. rodeo
2. kindergarten
3. palm

4. tea
5. kayak

EXERCISE 6   **Finding Synonyms**

Come up with as many synonyms as you can for each of the following words. Then, using your dictionary, check your list and add to it.

1. famous
2. error
3. legal

4. old
5. beautiful

ANSWERS

Exercise 5

Answers may vary according to the dictionary used. These are from *Webster's New World Dictionary,* Third College Edition:

1. The word *rodeo* originally came from a Spanish word meaning "a going around, cattle ring" from the Latin *rotare,* "to turn."

2. The word *kindergarten* comes from the German words *kinder,* meaning "children," and *garten,* meaning "garden."

3. The word *palm* comes through Middle English from the Latin word *palma*— "the palm of the hand."

4. The word *tea* comes from the Mandarin Chinese word *ch'a.*

5. The word *kayak* comes from the Eskimo language.

ANSWERS

Exercise 6

Answers may vary according to the dictionary used. These are from *Webster's New World Dictionary,* Third College Edition:

1. renowned, celebrated, noted, distinguished, eminent, illustrious

2. mistake, blunder, slip

3. lawful, legitimate, licit

4. ancient, antique, archaic

5. lovely, handsome, pretty, comely, fair, good-looking

VOCABULARY *(pp. 931–940)*

OBJECTIVES

- To use context clues and the general context to determine the meanings of words
- To use roots, prefixes, and suffixes to determine the meanings of words

Teacher's ResourceBank™

RESOURCES

VOCABULARY
- Using Context Clues A
- Using Context Clues B
- Using Context Clues C
- Choosing the Right Word
- Word Roots
- Prefixes
- Suffixes
- Chapter Review Form A
- Chapter Review Form B

34 VOCABULARY

Learning and Using New Words

CHAPTER OVERVIEW

The chapter discusses two methods for determining the meanings of new words: using context clues and using word parts, including roots, prefixes, and suffixes. Review exercises at the end of the chapter give students the opportunity to test their mastery of these methods.

A good way to learn new words is by building your vocabulary as you read books, newspapers, and periodicals. You can also increase your vocabulary by analyzing an unfamiliar term, looking at how it's used in the sentence or paragraph. You can also discover the meaning of words by learning frequently used word parts and how they are combined to form new words.

Creating a Word Bank

One good way to increase your vocabulary is to start a word bank. Your word bank can be a notebook or simply a section of a notebook that you use for recording vocabulary words. When you encounter an unfamiliar word, write the word and its definition in your work bank. Check your dictionary to see if you have understood the meaning of each word.

RESOURCES

RESOURCES

QUICK REMINDER

Write the following sentence on the chalkboard:

Scientists say that the giant otter, an animal whose numbers are decreasing because it's still killed for its fur, is an endangered or threatened species.

Ask students these questions:

1. If you did not already know, how could you tell from reading the sentence what a giant otter is? [It is defined as "an animal" which has "fur".]

2. What clue to the meaning of *endangered* do you find in the sentence? [The word is equated in the sentence with "threatened."]

Tell students that they have used context clues to find the answers; that is, they have looked at the words surrounding *giant otter* and *endangered* to help themselves understand the meaning of those words.

932 *Vocabulary*

Using Context Clues

Sometimes you can figure out the meaning of a word by examining the context in which it is used.

HOW TO USE CONTEXT CLUES	
TYPE OF CLUE	EXPLANATION
Definitions and Restatements	Writers may sometimes restate a word in order to define it. ■ When Henry B. Gonzalez was elected to Congress, many of his Spanish-speaking *constituents,* the voters in his district, felt that he would fight for their rights.
Examples	Examples used in context may help reveal the meaning of an unfamiliar word. ■ The scientist was accused of several acts of *espionage,* such as photographing secret documents and taping private conversations.
Synonyms	Look for familiar words that may be synonyms of words you don't yet know. ■ The club's *coffers* were so low that the members had to ask for donations to refill the treasury.
Comparisons	An unknown word may be shown to be similar to a more common word. ■ As in so many polluted cities, the air in our community is sometimes too *contaminated* to breathe.
Contrast	An unfamiliar word may be contrasted to a more familiar word or phrase. ■ The team's uniforms were *immaculate* before the game, but by the end of the first quarter they were filthy.
Cause and Effect	Look for clues that indicate that an unfamiliar word is related to the cause or the result of an action, feeling, or idea. ■ Will Rogers was considered to be a *humanitarian* because he worked to improve people's lives.

Determining Meanings from the General Context

Context clues are not always obvious. Sometimes you have to read an entire passage to understand the meaning of an unfamiliar word. However, you can draw on what you already know about the subject of the passage as well as your own experiences. Your own knowledge and resources can frequently help you determine the meanings of many unfamiliar terms.

Choosing the Right Word

Sometimes context clues are not enough to help you figure out a word's meaning. At times, the best way to determine the meaning of an unfamiliar word is to look up the word in the dictionary.

Very few words in English have a single meaning. Most have several meanings that vary depending on the context in which the word appears. Therefore, when you're looking in a dictionary for the meaning of a word, read *all* the definitions given, keeping in mind the context in which you originally read or heard the word.

To help you, dictionaries often provide sample contexts. These are usually several words surrounding the word being defined. They help you see how the word generally appears in a sentence. When sample contexts are given, compare them with the original context in which the word occurred to make sure you've found the meaning that fits.

Synonyms are words that have the same or nearly the same meaning. Use a dictionary or thesaurus to make sure you understand the exact differences in meanings between synonyms.

It is also important to understand that two words may have the same *denotation,* or dictionary definition, but a different *connotation,* or emotional overtone. For example, the words *slender* and *skinny* both mean "thin." However, the word *slender* has a more positive connotation than *skinny,* which suggests a bony or gaunt appearance.

RESOURCES

MEETING INDIVIDUAL NEEDS

LEP/ESL

General Strategies. A question often asked by ESL students when they are trying to improve their English vocabulary is how two similar English words differ. Such questions indicate that students might be having problems discerning subtleties in meaning from the contexts of the words.

When explaining the differences between similar words, remember that the emphasis should be on how the words are used, not on the words' denotations. You may want to have students find examples of how the words are used be-fore you begin explaining their differences.

STUDENTS WITH SPECIAL NEEDS

Students with learning disabilities often have limited vocabularies. To help students build vocabulary, it is important to use many strategies.

Make sure the students are familiar with all the words in a passage in question. Help them also with the background knowledge needed to understand the words.

Help students learn to generalize parts of familiar words. After they become familiar with a word, have students write definitions. Check their definitions and discuss the word with them. Relate the word to ideas with which the students are familiar to integrate it into their knowledge base.

RESOURCES

INTEGRATING THE LANGUAGE ARTS

Literature Link. Have students read and discuss W. W. Jacobs' "The Monkey's Paw," and then have them build a list of unfamiliar words they encounter in the story. From that list, have them extract the words with prefixes and suffixes listed in this chapter. See if they can deduce the meanings of those words from the meanings of the prefixes and suffixes.

Using Word Parts

If you know the meanings of some commonly used word parts, you will be better able to guess the meanings of many unfamiliar words.

Many English words are made up of word parts that come from other languages or that have been inherited from earlier forms of English. A complete word, one that can stand independently and alone, is called a ***base word.*** Word parts, such as prefixes and suffixes, may be added to base words to form new words. Look at the examples in the following chart. They show how word parts can be combined with base words to create new words.

PREFIX	BASE WORD	SUFFIX	NEW WORD
dis–	continue	–ous	discontinuous
in–	compare	–able	incomparable
mis–	judge	–ment	misjudgment

Unlike base words, word parts are not complete and cannot stand alone. Word parts must be combined in some way to create a complete word. The three types of word parts are

- roots
- prefixes
- suffixes

Roots

The main part of a word is called the ***root.*** The root carries the word's basic meaning. Other word parts can be added to a root to create many different words.

For example, the root *–port–* means "to carry." This root can be combined with other word parts to make new words, such as *portable, transportation,* or *importer.* For another example, the root *–vis–* means "to see." This root can be combined with other word parts to make new words, such as *invisible, visor, visualize, visionary,* or *television.*

COMMONLY USED ROOTS		
ROOTS	MEANINGS	EXAMPLES
GREEK		
–anthrop–	human	anthropology, misanthrope
–chrono–	time	chronology, chronometer
–cycl–	circle, wheel	cyclone, bicycle
–dem–	people	demography, democracy
–graph–	write, writing	autograph, biography
–hydr–	water	hydrant, hydrate
–log, –logy	study, word	biology, monologue
–morph–	form	metamorphosis, polymorph
–phon–	sound	phonograph, symphony
LATIN		
–cis–	cut	decision, concise
–cred–	believe	incredible, discredit
–dic–, –dict–	say, speak	dictate, predict
–fac–, –fact–, –fec–, –fic–	do, make	deface, manufacture, defective, efficient
–fid–	belief, faith	confident, fidelity
–frag–, –fract–	break	fragment, fraction
–ject–	throw	eject, trajectory
–junct–	join	conjunction, juncture
–magn–	large, grand	magnate, magnificent
–mal–	bad	malice, dismal
–mit–, –miss–	send	missionary, transmit
–ped–	foot	biped, pedestrian
–pend–, –pens–	hang, weigh	pendant, pensive
–pon–, –pos–	place, put	exponent, position
–scrib–, –script–	write	inscribe, postscript
–solv–	to loosen, accomplish	solvent, resolve
–ven–, –vent–	come	convention, prevent
–vers–, –vert–	turn	reverse, convertible
–voc–, –vok–	call	vocal, provoke
–volv–	roll, turn around	revolve, evolve

MEETING INDIVIDUAL NEEDS

LEP/ESL

Spanish. Remind Spanish speakers that many English words have the same Latin roots as do corresponding or similar words in their native language. Although some definitions may deviate from that suggested by the Latin root, most will be closely related, and if students understand the context in which the word is used, recognizing and knowing the meaning of the Latin root will help students determine the word's meaning.

You may want to have each of your Spanish speakers compose a list of ten to twenty English words and Spanish counterparts that share the same Latin roots.

RESOURCES

RESOURCES

Prefixes

A *prefix* is a word part that is added before a base or root word. When a prefix is added, the new word combines the meanings of the prefix and the base or root word.

COMMONLY USED PREFIXES		
PREFIXES	MEANINGS	EXAMPLES
GREEK		
anti–	against, opposing	antimissile, antisocial
hyper–	over, above	hyperactive, hyperventilate
mono–, mon–	one	monologue, monarch
para–	beside, beyond	parallel, parasail
psych–	mind	psychology, psychosomatic
LATIN AND FRENCH		
contra–	against	contraband, contraposition
de–	away, from, off, down	depart, deplane, descend
dif–, dis–	away, not, opposing	differ, dismount, dissent
ex–, e–, ef–	away from, out	excise, emigrate, efface
il–, im–, in–, ir–	not, in	illogical, impolite, incite, irrational
post–	after, following	postpaid, postwar
pre–	before	prejudge, preview
pro–	forward, favoring	proceed, pro-American
re–	back, backward, again	return, reflect, reforest
OLD ENGLISH		
be–	around, about	beset, behind
mis–	badly, not, wrongly	misbehave, misfire, mispronounce
un–	not, reverse of	untrue, unfold

 REFERENCE NOTE: For guidelines on spelling when adding prefixes, see page 873.

Suffixes

A *suffix* is a word part that is added after a base or root word. Often, adding a suffix changes both a word's part of speech and its meaning.

COMMONLY USED SUFFIXES		
SUFFIXES	**MEANINGS**	**EXAMPLES**
GREEK, LATIN, AND FRENCH *NOUNS*		
–ance, –ence	act, condition	forbearance, excellence
–cy	state, condition	accuracy, normalcy
–er, –or	doing, actor	singer, conductor
–ion	action, result, state	union, fusion, dominion
–ism	act, state, manner	baptism, socialism
–tude	quality, state	fortitude, magnitude
–ty, –y	quality, state, action	novelty, surety, jealousy
ADJECTIVES		
–able, –ible	able, likely	washable, divisible
–ate	having, characteristic of	animate, collegiate
–ive	tending to, given to	reflective, pensive
–ous	marked by, given to	glorious, nervous
–ulent	full of, characterized by	turbulent, fraudulent
ADJECTIVES OR NOUNS		
–al	doer, pertaining to	rival, autumnal
–ary	belonging to, one connected with	primary, adversary, auxiliary
–ent	doing, actor	confident, adherent
–ic	dealing with, caused by, person or thing showing	classic, choleric, workaholic
–ite	formed, showing	finite, favorite

A DIFFERENT APPROACH

Let students use the lists of prefixes and suffixes in the chapter to make up a story. Choose a student to begin with the first prefix on the list of prefixes, *anti–*. That student must use the prefix in a word in a sentence that starts the story. Then each student in turn provides a sentence that helps to elaborate the story. The catch is that the sentence must contain the prefix or a suffix that is next on the list. See how far down both lists the students can get. Allow them to use example words from the lists.

RESOURCES

RESOURCES

COMMONLY USED SUFFIXES *(continued)*		
SUFFIXES	**MEANINGS**	**EXAMPLES**
VERBS		
—ate	become, cause	evaporate, irate
—esce	become, grow, continue	convalesce, acquiesce
OLD ENGLISH ADJECTIVES OR ADVERBS		
—ly	like, characteristic of	friendly, cowardly
—ward	in the direction of	backward, upward
VERBS		
—en	cause to be, become	deepen, darken

☞ REFERENCE NOTE: For guidelines on spelling when adding suffixes, see pages 873–875.

Review

▶ EXERCISE 1 **Using Context Clues to Find Meanings**

See how well you can figure out the meanings of words from the way they are used in a sentence. Write the letter of the definition that best fits each italicized word.

a. large structure   e. celebrity
b. coloring   f. lawmaker
c. amiable   g. worsening
d. profitable   h. emotional displays

1. Lars often uses *histrionics* such as wailing and crying to get his way.   **1.** h   **2.** d
2. Unlike our money-losing ventures, selling popcorn at soccer games has been a *lucrative* project for our club.
3. The towering *edifice,* like many buildings in New York, seems to reach to the clouds.   **3.** a

MEETING INDIVIDUAL NEEDS

LEARNING STYLES

Auditory Learners. You may want to read aloud some sentences from **Exercises 1** and **2** and ask students to listen for context clues about the italicized words. After you read each sentence, ask students to tell you the context clues.

✈ TIMESAVER

When students have finished **Exercise 1,** have them exchange papers. Ask volunteers to supply the answers. The students can indicate any incorrect answers on the papers, and the class can discuss the context clues that lead to the correct answers.

938

4. Because the empty building is *deteriorating* so rapidly, it will soon be beyond repair. 4. g
5. Former Congresswoman Barbara Jordan was one of the first African American women to become a *legislator*. 5. f

▶ EXERCISE 2 **Using the General Context to Determine Meaning**

For each italicized word, write your own definition or synonym. Then check the dictionary's definitions of each word. If you guessed incorrectly, check the context again to look for clues you might have missed.

Most jobs available to students are found in the service [1] *sector*, in places such as department stores and fast-food restaurants. This type of work is often [2] *menial* and [3] *monotonous*—regarded as servile and offering little or no variety. Federal laws [4] *curtail* the number of hours students under sixteen can work for pay, but some employers [5] *exploit* students by demanding that they work longer. Rather than disagree and lose their jobs, many students [6] *comply*. Working may also [7] *impede* learning, as time spent on the job [8] *encroaches* on time needed for homework. Even good students may find their grades [9] *degenerating* from A's to B's or from B's to C's or D's. In addition, officials [10] *cite* hazardous conditions in some workplaces, mentioning numerous injuries to young people who work around large or dangerous machines.

▶ EXERCISE 3 **Using Roots to Determine Meanings**

Use the list of commonly used roots on page 935 to identify the root or roots in the following words. Then guess each word's meaning. Check your answers with a dictionary.

EXAMPLE **1.** vocation
  1. *–voc– (call);* vocation *means "a calling or summoning, especially in the sense of a chosen career"*

1. junction
2. contradiction
3. demographic

4. subvert
5. genealogy

ANSWERS
Exercise 2

Answers may vary but should be similar to the following examples:

1. sector — group, area, section
2. menial — easy, servile, low
3. monotonous — boring, tedious, tiresome
4. curtail — limit, reduce, cut short
5. exploit — use, abuse, manipulate
6. comply — obey, follow, go along with
7. impede — hinder, obstruct, delay
8. encroaches — trespasses, moves in, takes up
9. degenerating — declining, deteriorating, falling
10. cite — mention, point out, make known

ANSWERS
Exercise 3

1. *–junct–* means "join"; *junction* means "a joining or point of intersection"
2. *–dict–* means "say," or "speak"; *contradiction* means "speaking against"
3. *–dem–* means "people"; *–graph–* means "write" or "writing"; *demographic* means "relating to written statistics about people"
4. *–vert–* means "turn"; *subvert* means "to undermine or corrupt"
5. *–gen–* means "birth" and *–logy–* means "study"; *genealogy* means "study of birth or descent"

RESOURCES

RESOURCES

939

ANSWERS

Exercise 4

Answers may vary. Here are some possibilities:

1. hypercritical — too critical
2. disclose — uncover
3. except — not including
4. paramedic — medical worker
5. besides — in addition to

ANSWERS

Exercise 5

1. *–or;* one who puts money away
2. *–ency;* the state of being lenient
3. *–able;* able to be drawn back
4. *–ism;* in the manner of the military
5. *–ate;* make active

ANSWERS

Exercise 6

1. *e–* (away from); *–miss–* (send); *–ary* (one connected with doing); someone sent to do something
2. *hydr–* (water); *–logy* (study of); study of water
3. *de–* (away, from); *–pend–* (hang, weigh); *–able* (able, likely); able to hang away from
4. *re–* (again); *–volv–* (turn around); *–er* (doing, actor); something that turns around again
5. *pro–* (forward, favoring); *–pon–* (place, put); *–ent* (doing, actor); one who puts something forward or favors (an idea)

▶ EXERCISE 4 **Identifying Words with Prefixes**

Give an example of a word containing each of the following prefixes. (Do not use any of the words given as examples in this chapter.) Then tell what each word means. Use a dictionary if necessary.

EXAMPLE **1. pre–**
       1. prehistoric—existing in times before written history

1. hyper–
2. dis–
3. ex–
4. para–
5. be–

▶ EXERCISE 5 **Identifying Suffixes and Defining Words**

For each word, identify the suffix. Then guess what the whole word means. Use a dictionary to check your answers.

EXAMPLE **1. privacy**
      1. –cy; the state or condition of being private

1. depositor
2. leniency
3. retractable
4. militarism
5. activate

▶ EXERCISE 6 **Using Word Parts to Determine Meaning**

Identify the roots, prefixes, and suffixes in each of the following words. Then try to guess what the words mean. Use a dictionary to check your answers.

EXAMPLE **1. anthropomorphous**
      1. –anthrop– (human); –morph– (form); –ous (marked by, given to)
      marked by human form or appearance

1. emissary
2. hydrology
3. dependable
4. revolver
5. proponent

- To write letters of request, complaint, appreciation, and application
- To write a thank-you letter
- To address a business envelope

Teacher's ResourceBank™
RESOURCES

LETTERS AND FORMS
- The Parts of a Business Letter
- Types of Business Letters
- Types of Personal Letters
- Addressing an Envelope
- Completing Printed Forms
- Chapter Review Form A
- Chapter Review Form B

35 LETTERS AND FORMS

Style and Contents

CHAPTER OVERVIEW

Students need to know how to write letters and complete forms correctly if they are to function effectively in society. This chapter can be used either for reteaching basic concepts or as a reference for students who have not been exposed to this material.

Tenth-grade students have studied basic composition skills and can apply what they have learned about descriptive, informative, and persuasive writing (**Chapters 5, 7,** and **9**) to the material in this chapter. Even though instruction focuses on the formal elements of letter writing, students will also provide information, give descriptions, and express opinions in their letters.

You write letters for a variety of purposes. Clearly and concisely written letters will get results and create a favorable impression. Following accepted business procedures and using the correct style will give your letters a professional look. You should also follow a few simple guidelines in completing printed forms.

The Appearance of a Business Letter

- Use white, unlined $8\frac{1}{2}'' \times 11''$ paper.
- Type your letter if possible (single-spaced, leaving an extra line between paragraphs). Otherwise, neatly write the letter by hand, using black or blue ink. Avoid cross-outs, smudges, erasures, and inkblots. Check for typing errors and misspellings.
- Center your letter on the page with equal margins on the sides and at the top and bottom.
- Use only one side of the paper. If your letter won't fit on one page, leave a one-inch margin at the bottom of the first page and carry over at least two lines onto the second page.

RESOURCES

RESOURCES

QUICK REMINDER

You may choose to begin this chapter by drawing two rectangles on the chalkboard to represent business stationery. Label one "Block Form" and the other "Modified Block Form." Draw lines to show the block and modified block arrangements of a business letter. Then ask volunteers to name the six parts of a business letter and to tell where they are placed on the page.

MEETING
INDIVIDUAL
NEEDS

LEP/ESL

General Strategies. Many students have difficulty punctuating items such as salutations, closings, dates, and addresses. The reasons for this vary. Some Asian languages, for example, use word groupings rather than special marks for punctuation.

Before students work **Exercise 1**, you may want to discuss the conventional uses of commas in English. Then give students a short letter that has no punctuation and let them add the correct marks.

942

Writing Business Letters

The Parts of a Business Letter

A business letter contains six parts:

(1) the heading
(2) the inside address
(3) the salutation
(4) the body
(5) the closing
(6) the signature

There are two common styles for arranging the parts of a business letter. For the *block form,* begin each of the parts of the letter at the left margin and don't indent any paragraphs. However, for the *modified block form,* align the heading, the closing, and your signature with an imaginary line down the center of the page. The other parts of the letter begin at the left margin. Paragraphs are indented.

Block Style

Modified Block Style

The Heading. The heading usually has three lines:

- your street address
- your city, state, and ZIP code
- the date the letter was written

The Inside Address. The inside address gives the name and address of the person you are writing. Use a courtesy title (such as *Mr., Ms., Mrs.,* or *Miss*) or a professional title (such as *Dr.* or *Professor*) in front of the person's name. After the person's name, include the person's business title. The name of the company or organization and the address follow.

The Salutation. The salutation is your greeting. If you are writing to a specific person, begin with *Dear,* followed by a courtesy title or a professional title and the person's name. End the salutation with a colon (*Dear Mr. Jones:*).

If you don't have the name of a specific person, you can use a general salutation, such as *Dear Sir or Madam* or *Ladies and Gentlemen.* You can also use a department or a position title, with or without the word *Dear.*

The Body. The body, or main part, of your letter contains your message. It begins beneath the salutation. If the body of your letter contains more than one paragraph, leave a blank line between paragraphs.

The Closing. The closing should end your letter courteously. There are several closings that are often used in business letters, such as *Sincerely yours, Yours truly,* or *Regards.* Capitalize only the first word.

The Signature. Your signature should be written in ink, directly below the closing. Type or print your name neatly below your signature.

GUIDELINES FOR THE CONTENTS OF A BUSINESS LETTER

There are a few simple guidelines to follow in writing business letters that get results.

- *Use a polite, respectful, professional tone.* A courteous letter will be much more effective than a rude, angry, or sarcastic one.
- *Use formal, standard English.* Avoid slang, contractions, and abbreviations. Informal language that might be acceptable in a personal conversation or letter is often inappropriate in a business letter.
- *Explain the purpose of your letter quickly and clearly.* Keep in mind that the person reading your letter is busy. Include only necessary details.
- *Include all necessary information.* Be sure your reader can understand why you wrote and what you are asking.

COOPERATIVE LEARNING

Have students work in groups of four to create business letters. Students in each group should first brainstorm names and products for imaginary business firms. Next, they should select a reason for writing a letter of request, appreciation, application, or complaint to one of the firms. Then have them develop the letter together. One group member might act as the recorder, another might check the form of the letter, a third might edit the letter for any errors in capitalization and punctuation, and the fourth might volunteer to read the letter aloud to the class.

MEETING INDIVIDUAL NEEDS

STUDENTS WITH SPECIAL NEEDS

Students with learning disabilities often have difficulty expressing themselves.

It may be helpful to show an example of a letter and to provide a list of vocabulary words. For example, for a letter inquiring about a job, you may want to give students a list such as the following: employment, experience, education, information, and requirements.

Types of Business Letters

Request or Order Letter

In a *request letter,* you're asking for something. You might request information about a product, or you might ask for someone's time or services. An *order letter* is a special kind of request letter asking for something specific, such as a free brochure advertised in a magazine. You might also write an order letter to purchase, by mail, a product for which you don't have a printed order form. In a request or order letter, the most important consideration is to be clear about exactly what you want.

19 Brookside Drive
Latham, NY 12110
September 2, 1993

Mr. Stuart Reinhardt, Manager
Rollerama Skating Rink
2008 Route 9
Latham, NY 12113

Dear Mr. Reinhardt:

    Shaker High School's sophomore class has voted to hold a class get-together at Rollerama. As class secretary, I am writing to ask if we could plan this event for Saturday, November 20, from 7:30 to 10:30 p.m. We expect about 85 students.

    Could we rent the rink on the same terms you gave the senior class last spring? The sophomore class can guarantee a minimum attendance of 75 students. Students will pay at the door an admission price of $4.50. Skate rental will be a separate $2.00 charge.

    Our class is looking forward to an enjoyable evening at Rollerama.

Yours truly,

Linda O'Connell

Linda O'Connell
Class Secretary
Shaker High School
Class of '96

When you are writing a request or order letter, remember the following points.

1. State your request clearly.
2. If you're asking someone to send you information, enclose a self-addressed, stamped envelope.
3. If you're asking someone to do something for you, make your request well in advance.
4. If you're ordering something, include all important information, such as the size, color, brand name, or any other specific information. If there are costs involved, add the amount correctly.

Complaint or Adjustment Letter

If you are dissatisfied with a service or product, you might wish to write a *complaint* or *adjustment letter.* The purpose of this type of letter is to identify what's wrong and how you think it should be corrected. Here is the body of a sample adjustment letter.

> I have noticed that there are only two litter cans in Edgemont Park. I think that the litter situation would improve if the Parks Department would get more litter cans for the park. I think these cans should be placed so that they are convenient to the field, the picnic area, and the creek. More people might pick up their litter if there were trash containers located close to where they are needed.
>
> Please give your attention to this suggestion. I think Edgemont Park is a wonderful neighborhood resource that should be kept clean for everyone in our community to enjoy.

When you write a complaint or adjustment letter, remember these suggestions.

1. Register your complaint promptly.
2. Mention specifics. Necessary details might include the following:
   - how you were affected (lost time or money)
   - how you want the problem to be resolved
3. Keep the tone of your letter calm and courteous.

RESOURCES

RESOURCES

LESS-ADVANCED STUDENTS

Determine how much students remember about the appropriate ways to express themselves in social correspondence. Construct an example of a thank-you letter, a letter of regret, or an invitation. Include errors in basic structure, tone, and mechanics. Put this letter on an overhead projector and ask students to identify the problems and to suggest solutions.

INTEGRATING THE LANGUAGE ARTS

Literature Link. In Shakespeare's play, *The Tragedy of Julius Caesar,* Caesar received a warning before he went to the Senate on the Ides of March. Ask students to think about what might have happened if a friend of Caesar's had written him a letter describing the details of the assassination plot. Students could also write such a letter. They should include names of those who are plotting against Caesar, what they are planning to do, and why.

Appreciation or Commendation Letter

An *appreciation* or *commendation letter* is written to express your appreciation or to encourage a person, group, or organization to continue doing good work. When you write an appreciation or commendation letter, it is important to tell the person or organization exactly why you are pleased. Here is the body of a sample appreciation letter.

> I am writing to congratulate all of you at WQBK on your change in format from oldies to Top 40.
>
> Although I enjoy listening to oldies, I am more interested in hearing what musicians are recording today. Even my parents are getting tired of hearing nothing but '50s and '60s music.
>
> I hope you succeed with your new format. I know my friends listen to your station, and sometimes my parents do, too. Good luck!

Letter of Application

The purpose of a *letter of application* is to provide a selection committee or possible employers with enough information about you so that they can make a decision about whether you are a good choice for a position, such as a scholarship or summer job. When you are writing a letter of application, remember the following points.

1. Identify the job or position you are applying for and tell how you heard about it.
2. Tell about yourself. Depending on the position you are applying for, you might include
   - your age, grade in school, or grade-point average
   - your experience, or your activities, awards, and honors
   - personal qualities or characteristics that make you a good choice for the position
   - the date you can begin work

3. Offer to provide references. References are usually two or three responsible adults (generally not relatives) who can speak from experience about your character or qualifications and will give you a good recommendation. Be prepared to give the addresses and telephone numbers of your references when you are asked to provide them.

Here is a sample of an application letter.

1437 Windy Ridge Rd.
Milwaukee, WI 53224
January 23, 1993

Ms. Veronica Fong, Director
Spanish Student Exchange Program
P.O. Box 3001
New York, NY 10001

Dear Ms. Fong:

I am writing to apply for the summer exchange program to Barcelona, Spain, advertised in the January 14, 1993 edition of <u>Student Voice.</u>

I am a sophomore at Lanier High School in Milwaukee, Wisconsin. My grade point average is 3.3. I have studied Spanish for three years. Last semester I won an award for my work in this class.

I would be proud to be selected for this program. I am aware of the responsibility this involves. I would feel privileged to gain a new understanding of the Spanish language and culture and, on my return, to share this information with others in my school and community.

I will gladly furnish references who can tell you more about my qualifications for this program. My parents, too, are supportive of my interest.

Please let me know if there is any other information I need to give you before you can consider me as a candidate for this program.

Sincerely yours,

Brody Collins

Brody Collins

MEETING INDIVIDUAL NEEDS

LEP/ESL

General Strategies. In many countries, the return address is always written on the back of the envelope. You may want to point out that this practice is considered nonstandard in the United States and should never be used for business letters. Explain to students that the U.S. Postal Service prefers the standard address format given in the textbook. Provide extra practice with address abbreviations if some students are not familiar with them. Write a list of words on the chalkboard and ask volunteers to write abbreviations. Some examples are Lane — Ln., Boulevard — Blvd., Avenue — Ave., Street — St.

LEP/ESL

General Strategies. A birthdate sequence of day/month/year is used in many countries. Remind students that the standard date sequence in the United States is month/day/year. Also, many Hispanic last names are hyphenated, such as, Perez-Lopez (sometimes the hyphen is omitted). The first part is the father's last name and the second is the mother's. When a form asks for the last name, the father's name is used rather than the complete last name if there is not space for both.

RESOURCES

RESOURCES

Writing Informal or Personal Letters

Personal messages are often best expressed in the form of letters. Often a written message is more effective—and more appreciated—than a telephone call or other form of communication. The most common types of informal or personal letters are thank-you letters, invitations, and letters of regret. Personal letters are less formal than business letters and don't follow a rigid style.

Thank-you Letters. These are informal letters of appreciation that you send to tell someone that you appreciate his or her taking time, trouble, or expense on your behalf. Try to think of something about the person's effort or gift that made it special.

Invitations. An informal invitation should contain specific information about a planned event, such as the occasion, the time and place, and any other special details your guests might need to know.

Letters of Regret. Send a letter of regret if you have been invited somewhere but are unable to go. A written reply is especially appropriate if you were sent a written invitation with the letters *R.S.V.P.* (in French, these letters stand for "please reply").

Addressing an Envelope

Your return address (your name and complete address) goes in the top left-hand corner of an envelope. Just to the right of center, place the name and address of the person or organization to whom you are writing. The addressee's name and address should exactly match the inside address on your letter. Be sure to include correct ZIP codes.

Completing Printed Forms

There are many types of printed forms, but there are certain common techniques that will help you fill out any form accurately and completely.

Read all of the directions carefully. Follow the instructions on the form exactly.

Type or write neatly, using a pen or pencil as directed. When you type or print your information on the form, avoid cross-outs or smudges if possible.

Proofread your completed form. Make sure you have given all the information requested on the form. Check for errors and correct them neatly before you give the form to the appropriate person or mail it to the correct address.

Review

▶ EXERCISE 1   **Writing a Request Letter**

Choose one of the following situations to practice writing a request letter. Use your own return address and today's date, but make up any other information you need to write the letters.

1. You are the president of a school club. Write a letter to a local business asking it to sponsor club members in a sports competition for charity.
2. You are working on a History Day project. Write a letter to your state historical society requesting information on early political campaigns or facts about the settlement of your region of the state.
3. You want to buy a sweatshirt that displays the name of your favorite college football team. Write a letter to that school's varsity bookstore requesting information about the item.

ANSWERS
Exercise 1

Each part of the business letter should correctly follow either the block or the modified block form. The body of the letter should be courteous in tone and should contain a specific, reasonable request.

RESOURCES

ANSWERS
Exercise 2

All letters should correctly follow the block or the modified block form. The complaint letter should be courteous in tone and should contain all necessary information, such as a specific complaint and a suggested adjustment. Examples of specific complaints may be that the wrong item was sent, that the item was the wrong color or size, or that the wrong number of items was sent.

ANSWERS
Exercise 3

All letters should correctly follow either the block or the modified block form, should be courteous in tone, and should contain all necessary information.

ANSWERS
Exercise 4

All letters should correctly follow the block or the modified block form. Letters need to identify the position being applied for and include all important personal information. Students should include a statement explaining why they are a good choice for the position. They should also provide at least two suitable references that can be attached on a separate page.

ANSWERS
Exercise 5

Students should use the modified block form and maintain a polite, friendly tone in their letters.

ANSWERS
Exercise 6

Return addresses will vary.

Mahalia Hamlin
32 Rio Vista Avenue
Alamogordo, New Mexico 88310

EXERCISE 2 Writing a Complaint or Adjustment Letter

Practice writing a letter of adjustment or complaint. Write a letter to your local town council complaining about a proposed curfew for teenagers. Be specific in suggesting alternate solutions to the problems that led the council to consider the curfew. Use your own return address but make up any other information you need.

EXERCISE 3 Writing a Letter of Appreciation or Commendation

Practice writing a letter of appreciation or commendation. Write a letter to the author of a book you enjoyed. Explain how his or her writing has changed, inspired, or simply entertained you. Use your own return address and today's date, but make up any other information you need to write the letter.

EXERCISE 4 Writing a Letter of Application

Practice writing a letter of application. Think about a part-time or summer job that you are interested in and for which you feel qualified. Use the classified ad section of a newspaper to find the name of an organization or company that might offer this kind of position. Write a letter of application that states your interest and qualifications.

EXERCISE 5 Writing a Thank-you Letter

Write a thank-you letter to someone you know. Express your appreciation for a specific comment, gift, or action.

EXERCISE 6 Addressing Business Envelopes

Draw a rectangular outline to represent an envelope. Then address the envelope to Mahalia Hamlin, who lives at 32 Rio Vista Avenue, Alamogordo, New Mexico (ZIP code 88310). Use your own return address.

36 STUDYING AND TEST TAKING

Using Skills and Strategies

Are you using your study time to your best advantage? When you learn how to organize your study time, you can finish your work by the due date without agony at the last minute. You can learn strategies to make your study time and your test performance more effective.

Planning a Study Routine

If you want to study effectively, you need to be committed to a realistic study schedule. Here are some suggestions.

1. *Know your assignments.* Keep an assignment planner or a calendar for recording your assignments and noting when they are due. Make sure you understand all the instructions for each assignment.
2. *Make a plan.* Break your big assignments into small steps. Make deadlines for completing each step.
3. *Concentrate when you study.* Set aside a specific time and place for studying. Then focus your attention solely on your assignment. Avoid distractions.

Teacher's ResourceBank™
RESOURCES

FOR THE WHOLE CHAPTER
- Chapter Review Form A
- Chapter Review Form B

CHAPTER OVERVIEW

Since the information in this chapter can prove immediately useful to students and can help them to grasp the material covered in other chapters, you may want to cover this section during the first week or two of class. In addition to helping students academically, a review of study skills and test-taking strategies can give you insight into students' abilities and attitudes and can provide an opportunity for you to become better acquainted with the class.

The chapter discusses and reinforces reading strategies, writing as a tool for learning, critical thinking skills, interpretation of graphic aids, study methods such as outlining and paraphrasing, and strategies for standardized tests and essay tests.

RESOURCES

RESOURCES

SEGMENT 1 *(pp. 952–967)*

STRENGTHENING STUDY SKILLS

OBJECTIVES

- To choose appropriate reading rates for given situations
- To use the SQ3R study method to formulate and answer questions about reading material
- To analyze details in a reading passage

Teacher's ResourceBank™
RESOURCES

STRENGTHENING STUDY SKILLS
- Reading Rates
- The SQ3R Method
- Stated and Implied Main Ideas
- Making Inferences
- Analyzing Graphics
- Taking Notes
- Classifying
- Formal and Informal Outlines
- Paraphrases and Summaries

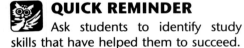 **QUICK REMINDER**
Ask students to identify study skills that have helped them to succeed.

---

952 *Studying and Test Taking*

Strengthening Study Skills

Reading and Understanding

You will find it easier to keep focused and to remember what you read if you read with a purpose. Some common purposes for reading are

- to find specific details
- to find main ideas
- to understand and remember

When you need to deal with a variety of materials, adjust your rate of reading to suit your purpose.

READING RATES ACCORDING TO PURPOSE		
READING RATE	**PURPOSE**	**EXAMPLE**
Scanning	Reading for specific details	Searching a history chapter for the date on which a specific treaty was signed
Skimming	Reading for main points	Reviewing chapter headings in your health textbook the night before a quiz
Reading for mastery	Reading to understand and remember	Reading a new chapter in your science book before writing an outline

Writing to Learn

Your writing can be a very useful tool for learning. Writing helps you focus your thoughts, discover new ideas, record your observations, and plan your work. Although there are many forms of writing, the following chart shows how you might use your writing as a method of learning.

- To identify evidence or reasoning used to make inferences and draw conclusions
- To interpret graphic information
- To create a graph
- To use graphic information to draw conclusions and predict outcomes
- To analyze note-taking methods
- To identify classifications

TYPE OF WRITING	PURPOSE	EXAMPLE
Freewriting	To help you focus your thoughts	Writing to connect ideas from today's history lecture and yesterday's reading
Autobiographies	To help you examine and express ideas about important events in your life	Writing about the day you learned an important lesson
Diaries	To help you recall impressions and express your feelings	Writing about a person you admire and want to emulate
Journals and Learning Logs	To help you record your observations, descriptions, solutions, and questions	Writing to keep a record of the progress of a Spanish writing project
	To help you present a problem, analyze it, and propose a solution	Writing about the way you plan to organize a history project

Using a Word Processor as a Writing Tool

The word processor can eliminate many repetitive tasks. Though the word processor can't do the work for you, it can offer benefits at every step of the writing process.

Prewriting. Typing is fast on a word processor. Revisions of rough notes or outlines can be made without retyping.

Writing First Drafts. You can revise as often as you want. If you like, you can use the printer to produce a hard copy (or printout) with each new revision.

Evaluating. The word processor lets you compare and evaluate different versions of your writing. Just save a copy of your document under a different name, and type your changes on this copy. Then, if you don't like the revisions, you still have the original.

INTEGRATING THE LANGUAGE ARTS

Studying and Writing. You may want to point out to students that many of the examples listed in the **Writing to Learn** chart are expressive in aim. Tell students that they can also learn by writing for other aims. For example, writing an informative piece on the Civil War might help students memorize facts about the war, and writing a persuasive essay might help students decide where they stand on a particular issue. Have students generate examples of informative, descriptive, and persuasive writing that can help them to learn.

LEP/ESL

General Strategies. The information concerning word processors might need to be addressed more thoroughly. It is unlikely that most students have access to this equipment at home. Many students will not be familiar with personal computers. Therefore, you may want to plan a field trip either to the school's computer lab or to a nearby facility (perhaps a community college). Students should be guided individually through the procedures of opening a new file and naming it, creating a short document and saving it, and printing out hard copy.

- To create a graphic organizer
- To paraphrase a poem

Revising.   Changes can be typed in easily and a clean copy printed out without having to repeat steps.

Proofreading.   Some word processors offer a feature that checks your spelling. Some have features that evaluate sentence structure and punctuation.

Writing the Final Version.   Final revisions are easy to make on a word processor. After proofreading the last version, it's simple to print a final copy. You can even print multiple copies on your printer.

Using the SQ3R Method

Francis Robinson, an educational psychologist, developed a method of study called SQ3R. There are five steps to using this SQ3R study method.

S   *Survey* the entire study assignment. Look at all of the headings, scan material in boldface and italics, and take note of the information in the charts, outlines, and summaries.

Q   *Question* yourself. What should you know after completing your reading? Make a list of questions that you want to be able to answer after finishing your reading.

R   *Read* the material section by section. Think of answers to your questions as you read.

R   *Recite* in your own words answers to each of the questions you have identified.

R   *Review* the material by rereading quickly, looking over your questions, and recalling the answers.

The SQ3R method can help you convert routine assignments into more interesting and active reading sessions. If you respond actively to what you read, it will be easier for you to recall what you have read.

 REFERENCE NOTE: For study techniques to help with listening skills, see page 912.

 CRITICAL THINKING
Evaluation

There are variations of the SQ3R study method. The PQ6R method, developed by Francis Robinson and adapted by Norma Kahn in *More Learning in Less Time,* includes the following steps: preview, question, read, recite, write, review, reflect, and review. Have students compare the two methods and decide which one they think would be more helpful to them.

RESOURCES

RESOURCES

Interpreting and Analyzing Information

The information in every essay, article, or textbook chapter that you read is organized into a logical pattern in which the ideas are related to one another. If you interpret and analyze these relationships, you will find it easier to think critically about what you read.

Stated Main Idea. When you are looking for the main idea, you want to find the most important point that the writer makes. When the main idea is stated, the author expresses the major point clearly and directly. A stated main idea can often be found in one specific sentence in a written passage.

Implied Main Idea. The main idea is sometimes implied, or suggested, rather than directly stated. To find an implied main idea, you will need to analyze the relationship of the details you are given. Then decide what general meaning is expressed by these combined details.

HOW TO FIND THE MAIN IDEA

- Skim the passage. (What topic do all of the sentences have in common?)
- Identify the general topic. (What's the passage about?)
- Identify what the passage really says about the topic. (What is the message of the passage as a whole?)
- Sum up the meaning of the passage in one clear sentence.
- Check back over the passage. If you have correctly identified the main idea, the details will support it.

 REFERENCE NOTE: For additional information on finding the main idea, whether stated or implied, see page 67.

Recognizing Relationships Among Details

To understand the meaning of a reading passage, you'll need to learn to identify details and understand how they are related to each other and to the main idea.

MEETING INDIVIDUAL NEEDS

AT-RISK STUDENTS

Students may have difficulty applying themselves to looking for main ideas when they find reading material boring or irrelevant. Give students photocopies of high-interest, relevant articles to read, and tell them to write sentences that express the main ideas of the articles. You could also have students identify facts and opinions presented in the articles.

RESOURCES

RESOURCES

FINDING RELATIONSHIPS AMONG DETAILS	
Identify specific details.	What details answer specific questions such as *Who? What? When? Where? Why?* and *How?*
Distinguish between fact and opinion.	What information can be proved true or false (fact)? What statements express a personal belief or attitude (opinion)?
Identify similarities and differences.	Are there any details that are shown to be similar to or different from one another?
Understand cause and effect.	Is there any event that happened before and had an impact or effect on another?
Identify an order of organization.	In what kind of order are the details arranged—chronological order, spatial order, order of importance, or any other organizing pattern?

Reading Passage

On February 4, 1913, Rosa Parks was born in Tuskegee, Alabama. Her family later moved to Montgomery. Growing up, Ms. Parks saw the inequality in the treatment of African Americans in Montgomery. For instance, they had to sit in the back of a shoe store to try on shoes, even if every seat in the front of the store was vacant. Blacks also had to sit in the back section of buses or to stand if a white person wanted a seat. As an African American, Ms. Parks hated this injustice. In December of 1955, her feelings translated into action.

Sample Analysis

DETAIL: What are some places where African Americans encountered unfair treatment?
ANSWER: The passage cites examples from shoe stores and buses.

FACT: When did Rosa Parks refuse to be treated unfairly on the bus?
ANSWER: She refused to give up her seat in December of 1955.

LEARNING STYLES

Visual Learners. Visual learners might benefit from color-coding this or another reading passage. Students could color-code main ideas and details, facts and opinions, similarities and differences, or causes and effects.

Auditory Learners. Some students will benefit from hearing the reading passage read aloud. Pause after each paragraph to discuss the annotations in the students' textbook.

Kinetic Learners. Students might enjoy dramatizing this fateful incident. Have students act as Rosa Parks, the man who wanted her seat, the bus driver, and the police, while another student uses the reading passage to narrate.

Ms. Parks was working at a tailor shop. One evening on the bus, wearily heading home, Ms. Parks refused to give up her seat for a white man. She was arrested for her refusal. After this incident, Ms. Parks decided to stop using the bus. She was soon joined in her boycott by thousands of African Americans in Montgomery. Many workers bravely risked their jobs by joining the boycott. Some white employers, however, preferred to give rides to their African American employees rather than do without their services.

The boycott lasted for 381 days and sparked the civil rights movement in America. The impact of this one incident spread like a pebble that starts a landslide. Because she led the boycott, Ms. Parks was fired from her tailoring job, but she was soon hired in Detroit as a special assistant to Congressman John Conyers. She worked at this position for twenty-five years. In 1988, she founded the Rosa and Raymond Parks Institute for Self-Development.

Rosa Parks can be cited to refute those who say that the actions of one person cannot make a difference. Rosa Parks's actions took courage as well as faith that her demand for justice would not be in vain.

OPINION: How did Rosa Parks feel about the unfair treatment of blacks?
ANSWER: She hated the injustice of this treatment.

SIMILARITY: How was the response of African Americans in Montgomery similar to the reaction of Rosa Parks?
ANSWER: Many black people in Montgomery also refused to ride the bus.

CAUSE AND EFFECT: What was the effect of this boycott?
ANSWER: The civil rights movement began in America.

ORDER: In the course of her life, where did Rosa Parks live?
ANSWER: She was born in Tuskegee, Alabama; later she lived and worked in Montgomery, Alabama; and finally, she worked for a congressman in Detroit, Michigan.

Applying Reasoning Skills

It's important to interpret and evaluate the evidence and facts that you gather from your reading. When you draw *conclusions,* you come to a decision by reasoning from clearly expressed facts and evidence.

When you make *inferences,* you arrive at decisions by reasoning from evidence that is only suggested.

MEETING INDIVIDUAL NEEDS

LESS-ADVANCED STUDENTS

Setting aside time each day for independent reading will show your students that you think reading is important, and it will also give students time to practice their reading skills. Allow students to bring reading materials to class each day and allot ten minutes of class time for independent reading. You will probably want to have plenty of high-interest selections available for those who forget to bring something to read.

RESOURCES

RESOURCES

A DIFFERENT APPROACH

You may want to compare the process of drawing conclusions to the experiments students perform in their science classes. Ask a student volunteer to describe an experiment and the conclusion that was reached through the experiment.

For example, based on your analysis of the reading passage on pages 956–957, you might make the following conclusions or inferences about Rosa Parks.

> Many people shared Parks's hatred of the unequal treatment of African Americans. (Evidence: Thousands joined her in her boycott of the bus system—a protest that might have cost them their jobs.)

> Americans today benefit from Rosa Parks's act of courage. (Evidence: Rosa Parks's action marked the beginning of the civil rights movement, which had the goal of fairer treatment for all people, regardless of race, creed, or gender.)

A *valid* conclusion is a conclusion that is firmly grounded in facts, evidence, or logic. An *invalid* conclusion is one that doesn't follow reasonably or logically from the evidence. For example, it is invalid to conclude that Rosa Parks refused to give up her seat because of a sudden impulse. This conclusion is not consistent with facts stated in the reading passage about her lifelong hatred for the injustice in the treatment of black people.

When you draw conclusions and make inferences, you are doing what a detective does to solve a mystery.

HOW TO DRAW CONCLUSIONS OR MAKE INFERENCES	
Gather all the evidence.	What facts or details have you learned about the subject?
Evaluate the evidence.	Do you know enough to judge information without jumping to conclusions or making invalid assumptions?
Make reasonable connections.	Based on evidence you have gathered and evaluated, what connections can you make? What conclusions can you draw?

Analyzing Graphics and Illustrations

Many of your textbooks—as well as articles from newspapers and magazines—include diagrams, maps, graphs, and illustrations. Visuals such as these make information clear and easy to understand.

Paragraphs full of detailed information can be difficult to read and to remember. Graphs or diagrams are often much easier to understand. Graphics and illustrations help you understand the relationships between one set of facts and another. For example, the bar graph below shows the percentage of the U.S. population between ages five and seventeen from 1900 to 1980.

Percentage of U.S. Population Aged 5 to 17

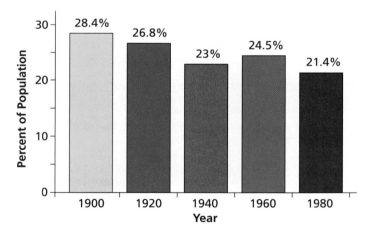

From this graph you can quickly compare the percentage of school-age children, measured in twenty-year periods, in the United States over the course of this century.

Suppose you were a television producer who was trying to decide whether to plan for an increase or decrease of programming for school-age children over the years after 2000. By looking at the graph, you could quickly see that the percentage of people of school age has shown an overall decrease over this century. You could reasonably assume that this trend would continue, and so you could plan for programming that focuses on other age groups.

Graphs such as the one above can help you make decisions more easily. They help you to see the relationship among items of data.

RESOURCES

INTEGRATING THE LANGUAGE ARTS

Studying and Writing. Compare the study methods described here—taking notes, classifying, and outlining—to the prewriting process by emphasizing the similarities between organizing information for writing and organizing information for study. Organization helps writers to understand and communicate what they are writing about. It also helps students to learn and recall new information.

LEP/ESL

General Strategies. Taking lecture notes can prove difficult and frustrating for many students. First of all, it is especially difficult to control the listening experience. Except in an interview situation, students cannot ask speakers to slow down, and they are therefore likely to miss important information. Second, it is often difficult for students to understand main ideas because they have to determine the meaning of new vocabulary. They will often try to record verbatim the information they hear, which often results in further frustration. Depending on the students' proficiency levels, note-taking skills could be practiced and reinforced, or students could be encouraged to tape-record lectures.

Applying Study Methods

Study methods are simply different ways of organizing and handling information. Some of the most common are

- taking notes
- classifying
- organizing information visually
- outlining
- paraphrasing
- summarizing
- memorizing

Taking Notes

If you take careful notes when you read or listen to a lecture, your information will be better organized when you study, take tests, or write research papers.

HOW TO TAKE STUDY NOTES	
Recognize and record main points.	Set off main points as headings in your notes. ■ In a lecture, key words and phrases such as *major* or *most important* and similar clues may indicate key points. ■ In a textbook, chapter headings and subheadings are usually reliable clues about main ideas.
Summarize.	Don't write down every detail. Instead, summarize or abbreviate, using key words or phrases to note main ideas. Indent supporting points.
Note important examples.	Make notes of a few meaningful examples. They can help you remember the main ideas.

On page 961 are sample study notes that a careful student might make about the reading passage on pages 956–957. Note that the main points in the passage are identified and then arranged in groups. Each of these groups of main points is given a heading that identifies the key idea.

Rosa Parks

Biography

- *African American, born Feb. 4, 1913—Tuskegee, Ala.*
- *grew up in Montgomery, Ala.*
- *despised injustice in treatment of blacks*
- *incident in Dec. 1955 started bus boycott*
- *fired from her tailoring job because of boycott*
- *hired by congressman in Michigan—worked as his asst. 25 years*
- *1988—founded Rosa and Raymond Parks Inst. for Self-Development*

Examples of Inequality in Treatment

- *had to sit at back of shoe stores*
- *had to sit at back of buses*
- *had to stand if white person wanted seat on bus*

Details of Montgomery Bus Boycott

- *Ms. Parks refused to give up seat to white man*
- *Ms. Parks arrested for her refusal*
- *Ms. Parks stopped using the bus*
- *thousands joined her boycott of bus system*
- *many risked jobs*
- *many employers gave rides instead of losing workers*
- *boycott lasted 381 days*
- *sparked American civil rights movement*

MEETING INDIVIDUAL NEEDS

LEARNING STYLES

Visual Learners. You may want to suggest that students use color-coding in their notes to organize ideas or to emphasize important points. For example, they might highlight anything a speaker repeats or otherwise indicates is important.

RESOURCES

RESOURCES

Classifying

Classification is organizing information by arranging items into categories. You use classification when you make an outline, deciding which supporting ideas fit together under a major heading. In order to group things, you need to identify relationships among them.

EXAMPLE   What do the following people have in common?
            Dolly Madison, Bess Truman, Betty Ford, Rosalyn Carter
ANSWER   They are all former first ladies of the United States.

You also use classification when you identify patterns in data. For example, look at the relationship of the following items.

ANSWER   The pattern is for even-numbered columns (columns 2 and 4) to be double the height of the columns that precede them (columns 1 and 3), while odd-numbered columns (1, 3, and 5) increase by one unit in height. The next column, column 6, should be double the height of column 5, or fourteen units high. Column 7 would then be eight units high.

Organizing Information Visually

Mapping, diagramming, and charting organize new information so that it is visually presented. This makes the information easier to understand.

For example, the passage that follows is full of literary terms. It contrasts two types of sonnets.

> A sonnet is defined as a poem containing fourteen lines, usually written in rhymed, iambic pentameter. Sonnets are generally classified into two types: the Petrarchan, or Italian, sonnet and the Shakespearean, or English, sonnet. Originating in Italy in the fourteenth century, the Petrarchan sonnet has two parts, an octave (eight lines) and a sestet (six lines). Often, the octave raises a poetic question that the sestet answers. This type of sonnet is usually rhymed *abba abba cdecde*. The second type of sonnet, the Shakespearean sonnet, consists of three stanzas of four lines each and a concluding couplet. This type of sonnet usually uses the rhyme scheme *abab cdcd efef gg*. Often the final rhyming couplet provides a statement that summarizes or concludes the poem by making an emphatic point about its theme.

It would be difficult to remember all the details in this reading passage. However, if you organize the information visually by mapping the details, you will find the information easier to remember.

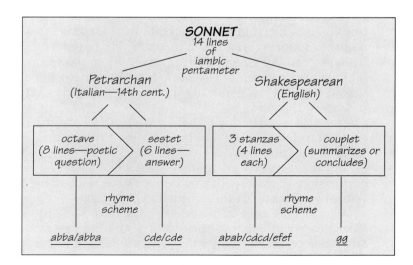

INTEGRATING THE LANGUAGE ARTS

Literature Link. You may want to take this opportunity to review the sonnet form. Have students read a sonnet, such as "Shall I Compare Thee to a Summer's Day?" by William Shakespeare, and ask them to identify it as either an Italian or an English sonnet. Then ask students if the poem conforms to all of the conventions given in the passage for that type of sonnet.

RESOURCES

RESOURCES

Outlining

An *outline* organizes ideas and information. When you make an outline, you identify the most important information and ideas in a passage. Then you group all these ideas into an organized pattern that shows their order and their relationship to one another.

Sometimes, however, as with lecture notes, you may want to use an informal outline form. This method of arranging notes allows you to organize information very quickly. (See an example in the study notes on page 961.)

FORMAL OUTLINE FORM

1. Main Point
  A. Supporting Point
    1. Detail
      a. Information
        or detail

INFORMAL OUTLINE FORM

Main Idea
  Supporting detail
  Supporting detail
  Supporting detail

Paraphrasing

When you *paraphrase,* you restate someone else's ideas in your own words. Paraphrasing is a good way to check your understanding of what you read, especially if the original is written in poetic or elaborate language (such as complex wording in a poem or poetic language in a scene from a play by Shakespeare). A written paraphrase is usually approximately the same length as the original, so this technique is generally not used for very lengthy passages of writing.

As you read things that you think are difficult to understand, paraphrase what you read by putting these ideas into your own words in your study notes. Your paraphrased version might include dialect or slang expressions if you feel more comfortable with these than with the wording of the original expressions.

Or, in language arts classes, you may sometimes be asked to write a paraphrase of a short literary passage, such as a poem. Use the following guidelines to help you paraphrase.

HOW TO PARAPHRASE

1. Be sure you understand what the material means. Look up any unfamiliar words.
2. Identify the main idea of the selection. Keep it in mind while you write your paraphrase.
3. Identify the speaker in fictional material. (Is the poet or author speaking, or is it a narrator or a character?)
4. Write out your paraphrase in your own words, remembering to use complete sentences and traditional paragraph form.
5. Check to be sure that your paraphrase expresses the same idea as the original.

Here is an example of a poem to be paraphrased.

Sick Leave
by Po Chü-i[1] (translated by Arthur Waley)

Propped on pillows, not attending to business;
For two days I've lain behind locked doors.
I begin to think that those who hold office
Get no rest, except by falling ill!
For restful thoughts one does not need space;
The room where I lie is ten foot square.
By the western eaves above the bamboo twigs,
From my couch I see the White Mountain rise.
But the clouds that hover on its far distant peak
Bring shame to a face that is buried in the World's dust.

[1] Po Chü-i (pō′chōō′ē)

Following is one possible paraphrase of the poem.

A Chinese government official is home, sitting up in bed. He is thinking about all of his work that is not getting done. The official has been sick for two days, and he has apparently locked himself in his room to remain undisturbed. He states that he believes getting sick is probably the only way that people who have official responsibilities ever get any time off.

 INTEGRATING THE LANGUAGE ARTS

Literature Link. To give students practice in paraphrasing, have them paraphrase a poem as a class. Then have a student read the paraphrase aloud and have another student present the poem. Lead a discussion of how the students' paraphrase differs from the poem. Students might notice that their paraphrase does not convey the same mood, tone, or even meaning as the poem. Help students see how the poet's choice and placement of words affects the poem.

Studying and Writing. Point out to students that the ability to paraphrase will be useful to them when they are taking notes for research papers. Remind students that even when they paraphrase information, they must always give credit for other people's ideas.

RESOURCES

RESOURCES

His room is very small, only ten feet by ten feet, but he comments that since all he is doing is resting and thinking, he does not need a large room. His room is on the west side of a house high enough to be above the growing bamboo. From his window, he can see the White Mountain rising above the clouds. He contemplates the contrast between the mountain, as it rises high above the pressures of life, and his own life, as it is burdened down by these pressures.

You will use paraphrasing when you write research reports. Remember, however, that you must cite your sources when you use someone else's ideas.

 REFERENCE NOTE: For more about paraphrasing in research reports, see pages 420–421.

Summarizing

A *summary* restates the main points of a passage in condensed form. A summary, or a *précis*, helps you identify and remember the most important points of the material you are studying. When you write a summary, it is necessary for you to analyze the material in order to decide what is most important and should be included in the summary, and what can be left out.

HOW TO SUMMARIZE
1. Skim the material and identify the main ideas.
2. Review the passage and look for supporting details.
3. Write a sentence in your own words about each main idea. Write approximately one sentence for each paragraph of the original.
4. Use your list of sentences to write your summary in standard paragraph form. Use transitional words between the ideas to show how the ideas are related.
5. Evaluate and revise your summary, checking to see if your summary covers key points. Make sure the reader can follow your ideas.

CRITICAL THINKING
Evaluation

You may want to illustrate the differences between a summary and an evaluation. Write the two words on the chalkboard. Then have the class choose a well-known movie to discuss. Ask a volunteer to very briefly summarize the movie. Then ask a volunteer to evaluate the movie, giving reasons for her or his views. Discuss with students the differences between the summary and the evaluation. Are there any value judgments included in the summary? Does the evaluation include a description of the movie's plot?

Here is a sample summary of the article on pages 402–403.

> Astronomy was closer to religion than science to many Native American peoples. They believed the planets and the stars were gods. Since they thought these gods affected every aspect of human life, these early astronomers struggled to learn the exact patterns of the movements of heavenly bodies. Then they recorded their findings. In some places, calendars were made of wood, stone, or string. In others, astronomical observances were written on folded, book-like forms made of hide or bark. In some places, buildings and cities were aligned with planetary sightlines. The earth, too, was believed to be a sacred being. Certain routes were thought to be holy. Lines, such as the Nazca Lines in Peru, may also have had religious significance.

Memorizing

Frequent, short, focused sessions of practice are best when you are trying to memorize material. It is not very efficient to cram, because you will not retain the information well.

HOW TO MEMORIZE	
Condense the information, if possible.	If you're studying reading material, such as a chapter, passages can often be summarized or condensed.
Rehearse the material in several different ways.	Use several different senses. Copy or write the material so you can see it as well as touch it. Say it out loud so you can hear it.
Play memory games.	Make a word out of the initials of key terms or use other creative ways to make the information more memorable.

A DIFFERENT APPROACH

Ask students to think about a time when they read a novel or a short story and visualized its characters and scenes. Then ask students to speculate about whether the same kind of visualization and sensory involvement might help them learn new material. [When studying science material, a student might visualize an experiment, perhaps recalling the smell of a chemical. When studying history notes, a student might visualize the events being studied, as if she or he were watching a movie. When studying any subject, the student can practice recalling a teacher's instruction by visualizing the classroom, replete with sounds, smells, and sights.]

RESOURCES

RESOURCES

OBJECTIVES

- To complete analogies
- To identify key verbs in essay questions and to state the kinds of information needed to answer those essay questions

QUICK REMINDER

Ask students to brainstorm ideas for overcoming test anxiety. Then have students give you their ideas orally. Write the ideas on the chalkboard. Discuss with students which ideas work best for them and which ideas they would like to try.

MEETING INDIVIDUAL NEEDS

LEP/ESL

General Strategies. One way to begin this segment on test-taking skills is to initiate class discussion. How do students feel about taking tests? What kinds of past experiences have contributed to these feelings? LEP/ESL students need to be encouraged to examine and express their feelings and to trust that the classroom environment is a safe place to do so. An open class discussion often serves as an icebreaker and underscores the fact that you, as a teacher, believe all of your students have something valid to contribute.

968

---

968 *Studying and Test Taking*

Improving Test-Taking Skills

Preparing Yourself

Your attitude is an important factor in doing well on a test. It's normal to feel nervous before a big test. However, you can channel this nervous energy productively if you concentrate on your test performance.

HOW TO PREPARE FOR A TEST

Analyze your preparedness. Decide early what you need to study most, then study thoroughly.

Focus on the test. During the test, as you read and answer the questions, concentrate on what you know, not anything else. Don't allow yourself to be distracted.

Make a commitment. Keep trying until you find the right study method for you.

Preparing for Standardized Tests

A *standardized test* is one in which your score is evaluated in comparison with a "standard" that is compiled from the scores of many other students nationwide who have taken the same test. There are two common kinds: achievement and aptitude tests.

Achievement tests are designed to measure how much you know about specific subjects, such as biology or Spanish. Aptitude tests evaluate your basic skills in various areas of study, such as reading comprehension or vocabulary skills.

Standardized tests often cover material you have learned during many years of study. To prepare for most standardized tests, it's best to improve your overall study habits: read often, write frequently, increase your vocabulary steadily, and use the study skills described earlier in this chapter. In addition, there are some short-term preparations you can make to improve your performance.

HOW TO PREPARE FOR STANDARDIZED TESTS

Learn what skills will be tested on the specific test you plan to take. Information booklets may be provided that tell about the types of questions and how the test is scored. Practice with these or with published study guides available through bookstores or libraries.

Know what materials you need for the test. For the test, you may need to bring specific materials, such as number 2 pencils or pens and a prepared examination booklet of lined paper for an essay answer.

Determine how this test scores answers. If there is no penalty for wrong answers, you should make your best guess on all questions possible. If wrong answers are penalized, make guesses only if you are fairly sure of your answer.

Objective Tests

Two basic types of tests are *objective* and *essay tests.* Certain strategies can help you with each type.

There are many types of objective tests. They may include multiple-choice, true/false, matching, reasoning or logic, or short-answer questions. Although they appear in many forms, all objective questions have one characteristic in common: There is usually only one correct answer.

HOW TO STUDY FOR OBJECTIVE TESTS

1. Review the study questions in your textbook, and skim class notes to identify important terms or facts.
2. Review the information in more than one form. For example, if you are responsible for knowing a list of important terms, test yourself on how well you can define each one of the terms without looking at your book or notes.
3. Practice and repeat factual information. Use flashcards to see if you can remember the correct terms. Identify difficult items and review them.

RESOURCES

MEETING INDIVIDUAL NEEDS

AT-RISK STUDENTS

Students may be discouraged by a history of poor performances on tests, and they may think that their past poor performances mean that they are incapable of academic success. You may want to let students know that even people who are famous for their intelligence and ability have received poor evaluations at some time in their lives. Winston Churchill, for example, failed the sixth grade, and Albert Einstein had poor grades in mathematics when he was in high school.

RESOURCES

A DIFFERENT APPROACH

To help students to develop self-confidence and reduce stress before a test, teach them the following positive imaging exercise:

Close your eyes and imagine your teacher distributing the test. Take a deep breath through your nose and then exhale slowly through your mouth. Imagine that the test is on your desk. You glance through it and find no surprises. Remember, you have prepared for the test. Imagine picking up your pencil and marking or writing correct answers. Now, move forward in time. Imagine your test being returned to you with an "A" on it.

Tell students that they can do this positive imaging exercise before any test that they feel anxious about.

Adapt your study strategies to suit the specific type of objective test you will be taking. For example, if your test includes a map you'll have to label, test yourself by labeling a practice version.

Taking Different Kinds of Objective Tests

At the beginning of an objective test, scan the test quickly to count the number of test items. Then decide how to budget your time. For each type of objective test question, use the following specific, effective strategies.

Multiple-Choice Questions. Multiple-choice questions ask you to select a correct answer from among a given number of choices.

EXAMPLE **1.** After she was arrested for refusing to yield her seat on a bus, Rosa Parks

(A) decided to stop using the bus system.
B was elected to Congress.
C moved to Tuskegee, Alabama.
D married her husband, Raymond.

HOW TO ANSWER MULTIPLE-CHOICE QUESTIONS	
Read the initial statement carefully.	■ Make sure you understand this statement before examining the choices. ■ Look for qualifiers such as *not* or *always* since these—and other, similar terms—limit the answers.
Read all the answers before making a choice.	■ Narrow the choices by eliminating incorrect answers. Some answers may be clearly wrong, while others may only be somewhat related to the correct answer. ■ Seek the most correct choice. Some choices (such as "Both A and B" or "All of the above") affect your other choices.

True/False Questions. You are asked to determine whether a given statement is correct.

EXAMPLE   **1.** T (F) The percentage of school-age children in the United States has increased over this century.

HOW TO ANSWER TRUE/FALSE QUESTIONS	
Read the statement carefully.	■ If any part of the statement is false, the whole statement is false.
Check for qualifiers.	■ Words such as *always* or *never* qualify or limit a statement. ■ A statement is true only if it is wholly and always true.

Matching Questions. In matching questions, two lists are placed near each other so that you may match items on one list with those on the other.

Directions: Match the term in the left-hand column with its description in the right-hand column.

___D___ **1.** Shakespearean sonnet   **A** group of eight rhymed lines of a sonnet
___C___ **2.** couplet   **B** Italian sonnet
___A___ **3.** octave   **C** group of two rhymed lines in a sonnet
___B___ **4.** Petrarchan sonnet   **D** English sonnet

HOW TO ANSWER MATCHING QUESTIONS	
Read the directions carefully.	Sometimes answers may be used more than once.
Scan the columns and match items you know first.	You can gain more time to evaluate items you are less sure about.
Complete the matching process.	Make your best reasoned guess on remaining items.

COMMON ERROR

Problem. Some students worry that they must be wrong if they end up with a pattern of true-false answers or have marked too many of one or the other kind.

Solution. You may want to advise students to ignore any pattern that develops, to rely on their knowledge, and, if necessary, to make informed guesses.

TIMESAVER

You may want to survey students to find out which types of test questions are most difficult for them, so that you can focus primarily on those types of questions.

RESOURCES

RESOURCES

Since logic questions are increasingly used on standardized tests, you may want to give students plenty of practice with them. Bring to class a book of brain teasers and have students work in pairs to complete them.

Reasoning or Logic Questions. Some questions (especially on standardized tests) may test your reasoning abilities more than your knowledge of a specific subject. These questions often ask you to identify the relationship between several items (such as words, pictures, or numbers), or they may ask you to predict what the next item in a series should be.

Reasoning questions might ask you to identify a pattern in a number sequence (for example: 3, 9, 27, 81—these are squares of the number 3). Or, you might be asked to predict the next item in a sequence of drawings.

What comes next?

In this sequence of drawings, the two white dots are pointed outwards, moving counter-clockwise around the configuration of dots. Therefore, in the fourth frame the white dots should point toward the bottom right.

HOW TO ANSWER REASONING OR LOGIC QUESTIONS	
Be sure you understand the instructions.	On standardized tests, reasoning or logic questions are usually multiple-choice. On some other tests, you may need to write a word or phrase, write out a number sequence, or draw your answer.
Analyze the relationship implied in the question.	Look at the question carefully to gather information about the relationship of the items.
Draw reasonable conclusions.	Evaluate the relationship of the items as a basis for your decision.

Analogy Questions. Analogy questions are special types of reasoning and logic questions that ask you to analyze the relationship between one pair of words and to identify or to supply a second pair of words that has the same relationship.

Analogy questions usually appear on standardized tests in multiple-choice form, but sometimes they appear as fill-in-the-blank questions.

EXAMPLE **1.** Directions: Select the appropriate pair of words to complete the analogy.

DRESS : CLOTHING :: _____

A wheel : car
B page : read
C bicycle : vehicle
D world : round

EXAMPLE **2.** Directions: Complete the following analogy.

SHOWER : CLEAN :: mud : *dirty*

HOW TO ANSWER ANALOGY QUESTIONS	
Analyze the first pair of words.	Identify the relationship between the first two items. (In Example 1, a *dress* is a kind of *clothing*; this is an analogy of classification. See the Analogy Chart on pages 974–975.)
Express the analogy in sentence or question form.	Example 1 could be read as "A *dress* is a kind of *clothing*, just as . . . (what other pair of items among the choices given?)."
Find the best available choice to complete the analogy.	▪ If choices are given, select the pair of words with the same relationship between them as the first pair. ▪ If you must fill in a blank to complete an analogy, you may be asked to supply the final word. (Using Example 2, a *shower* makes you *clean*. What would *mud* make you? You would be *dirty*.)

RESOURCES

INTEGRATING THE LANGUAGE ARTS

Literature Link. Point out to students that metaphors and similes are figures of speech that draw analogies — they describe or explain things by comparing them to other things. Write the definitions of *metaphor* and *simile* on the chalkboard.

Then have students read a poem, such as "Courage" by Anne Sexton, that contains several metaphors and similes. Ask students to list the comparisons made in the poem and to identify each as either a metaphor or a simile. ["Courage" includes the following comparisons: the child's first step — earthquake (simile), courage — small coal (metaphor), love — shaving soap (simile), heart — sock (simile), spring — sword (metaphor).]

You might want to challenge students to create original metaphors and similes. If students have read "Courage," you could have them write alternate comparisons for *the child's first step, courage, love, heart,* and *spring.*

RESOURCES

A DIFFERENT APPROACH

Students may be unaware of how diet can affect test performance. Remind students to avoid caffeine and sugar in general and especially on the day of a test. You might also want to tell students to make sure they are getting plenty of protein for energy (found in milk, fish, meat, nuts, eggs, and in legumes combined with whole grains), vitamin B complex for memory and concentration (found in peanuts, green vegetables, and bran), iron for memory and energy (found in green leafy vegetables, whole grains, molasses, and dried fruit), and calcium and magnesium to reduce restlessness and hyperactivity (found in dairy products).

974 *Studying and Test Taking*

ANALOGY CHART		
TYPE	EXAMPLE	SOLUTION
Synonyms	ROUND : CIRCULAR :: strong : muscular	*Round* is similar in meaning to *circular*, just as *strong* is like *muscular*.
Antonyms	PATRIOT : TRAITOR :: loyal : unfaithful	A *patriot* is the opposite of a *traitor*, just as *loyal* means the opposite of *unfaithful*.
Cause	VIRUS : SICKNESS :: water : dampness	A *virus* causes *sickness*, just as *water* causes *dampness*.
Effect	TEARS : SORROW :: smiles : joy	*Tears* are the effect of *sorrow*, just as *smiles* are the effect of *joy*.
Part to Whole	DROPLETS : SEA :: grains : desert	*Droplets* (of water) make up a *sea*, just as *grains* (of sand) make up a *desert*.
Whole to Part	WALL : BRICKS :: deck : cards	A *wall* contains *bricks*, just as a *deck* contains *cards*.
Classification	BAGEL : BREAD :: pork : meat	A *bagel* is a type of *bread*, just as *pork* is a type of *meat*.
Characteristics	PUPPIES : FURRY :: fish : slippery	*Puppies* feel *furry*, just as *fish* feel *slippery*.
Degree	COLOSSAL : LARGE :: microscopic : small	*Colossal* means *very large*, just as *microscopic* means *very small*.
Use	DESK : STUDY :: bed : sleep	A *desk* is used to *study*, just as a *bed* is used to *sleep*.

(continued)

ANALOGY CHART *(continued)*		
TYPE	**EXAMPLE**	**SOLUTION**
Measure	BAROMETER : AIR PRESSURE :: scale : weight	A *barometer* is used to measure *air pressure,* just as a *scale* is used to measure *weight.*
Action to Performer	TEACHING : PROFESSOR :: cleaning : maid	*Teaching* is the action performed by a *professor,* just as *cleaning* is the action performed by a *maid.*
Performer to Action	AUTHOR : WRITE :: chef : cook	An *author's* profession is to *write,* just as a *chef's* profession is to *cook.*
Place	SPACE NEEDLE : SEATTLE :: Lincoln Memorial : Washington, D.C.	The *Space Needle* is in *Seattle,* just as the *Lincoln Memorial* is in *Washington, D.C.*

Short-Answer Questions. Answers to short-answer questions should show your knowledge of the subject. Like other objective questions, short-answer questions usually have only one correct answer. However, you do not have a choice of answers: You have to write out your response.

Some short-answer questions (such as a diagram, a map, or a fill-in-the-blank question) can be answered with one or a few words. In another type of short-answer question, you are asked a question and you must write a full response, usually one or two sentences in length.

EXAMPLE   Describe briefly the comparison made at the end of Po Chü-i's poem "Sick Leave."

ANSWER   *The speaker contrasts himself with the mountain he sees from his sickroom window. The mountain is above the world's cares, while he is buried beneath them.*

RESOURCES

RESOURCES

A DIFFERENT APPROACH
Have students bring their science or history textbooks to class. Ask them to use material in chapters they are currently studying to create short-answer quizzes that will help them review for an upcoming test.

HOW TO RESPOND TO SHORT-ANSWER QUESTIONS	
Read the question carefully.	Some questions have more than one part, and you will have to include an answer to each part to receive full credit.
Plan your answer.	Briefly, decide what you need to include in the answer.
Be as specific as possible in your answers.	Give a full, exact answer.
Budget your time.	Begin by answering all of the questions you are certain about. Return later to the questions you are less sure about.

Essay Tests

Essay tests ask you to think critically about material you have learned and to express your understanding of that material in an organized way. You will be expected to write at least a full paragraph, if not several paragraphs, in answer.

HOW TO STUDY FOR ESSAY TESTS
1. Review your textbook carefully.
2. Make an outline, identifying main points and key details.
3. Make a practice set of possible questions on your own and practice writing out the answers.
4. Evaluate and revise your practice answers, checking your notes and textbook for accuracy and the writing chapters of this textbook for help in writing.

Taking Essay Tests

Before you start writing on an essay test, scan the questions quickly. Make sure you know how many answers you are expected to write. If you have a choice between several items, decide which one or ones you think you can answer best. Then plan how much time to spend on each answer, and stay on this schedule.

Read the question carefully. There may be several parts to the answer.

Pay attention to important terms in the question. Essay questions usually ask you to perform specific tasks. A verb expresses each one of these tasks. It helps to become familiar with each key verb. Each one identifies the tasks that you will need to accomplish in a good essay response.

ESSAY TEST QUESTIONS		
KEY VERB	TASK	SAMPLE QUESTION
argue	Take a viewpoint on an issue and give reasons to support this opinion.	Argue whether or not your school should require all students to participate in extra-curricular activities.
analyze	Take something apart to see how each part works.	Analyze the central character in Edgar Allan Poe's "The Tell-Tale Heart."
compare	Point out likenesses.	Compare George Washington Carver and Thomas Edison as inventors.
contrast	Point out differences.	Contrast the economic conditions in the South and in the North at the end of the Civil War.
define	Give specific details that make some-thing unique.	Define the term *colonialism* as it applies to America's early history.
demonstrate (also illustrate, present, show)	Provide examples to support a point.	Demonstrate that a line intersecting parallel lines produces equivalent angles.
describe	Give a picture in words.	Describe the eulogy scene in *Julius Caesar.*

STUDENTS WITH SPECIAL NEEDS

Students with learning disabilities may need to see the meanings of these key verbs illustrated in concrete terms. Bring an apple and an orange to class and use these fruits to illustrate each verb. For example, to illustrate *argue,* take a viewpoint as to which fruit is better and give reasons to support your opinion. To illustrate *analyze,* cut the apple and the orange in half to examine the parts that make up the whole fruits. To illustrate *compare,* point out the similarities between the apple and the orange. Continue this process for each key verb.

RESOURCES

RESOURCES

A DIFFERENT APPROACH

You may want to give students practice in composing their own essay questions. This activity is especially useful for the study of supplementary reading material. To spark their interest, let students write essay questions on materials they are reading independently or for another class.

ESSAY TEST QUESTIONS *(continued)*		
KEY VERB	**TASK**	**SAMPLE QUESTION**
discuss	Examine in detail.	Discuss the term *manifest destiny.*
explain	Give reasons.	Explain why the United States entered World War II.
identify	Point out specific persons, places, things, or characteristics.	Identify the leaders of the Confederacy and their importance in the Civil War.
interpret	Give the meaning or significance of something.	Interpret the role of Cesar Chavez in organizing the farm labor movement.
list (also outline, trace)	Give all steps in order or all details about a subject.	List the events leading up to the Montgomery bus boycott.
summarize	Give a brief overview of the main points.	Summarize the plot of Bernard Malamud's short story "A Summer's Reading."

Take a moment to use prewriting strategies. After considering the key verbs in the question, make notes or a simple outline to help you decide what you want to say. Write the notes or outline on scratch paper.

Evaluate and revise as you write. You probably will not be able to redraft your whole essay. However, you can edit your essay to strengthen it.

QUALITIES OF A GOOD ESSAY ANSWER

- The essay is well organized.
- The main ideas and supporting points are clearly presented.
- The sentences are complete and well written.
- There are no distracting errors in spelling, punctuation, or grammar.

Review

▶ EXERCISE 1 **Choosing an Appropriate Reading Rate**

Identify the reading rate that best fits each of the given situations.

1. You are looking through a list of ZIP codes to find the code for Scranton, Pennsylvania. **1.** scanning
2. You are looking through a library book to see if it would be a good resource for a research paper on Pedro **2.** scanning
   Menéndez de Avilés, founder of St. Augustine, Florida.
3. You have a 100-question, multiple-choice test tomorrow on a chapter in your science textbook that you have already read but need to review. **3.** skimming
4. You are reading a chapter in your literature book for a class discussion tomorrow and a test in two weeks.
5. You are reading instructions on a standardized test to see how much time is allowed for a section of the test.
   4. reading for mastery **5.** scanning

▶ EXERCISE 2 **Applying the SQ3R Method**

Use the SQ3R method while reading a newspaper article or a chapter that you need to read for a class. List at least five questions that you might be asked on a test about the material and write brief answers to each one.

▶ EXERCISE 3 **Analyzing Details in a Passage**

Answer the following questions about the reading passage on pages 956–957.

1. Give two facts about Rosa Parks (other than those already noted in the sample analysis).
2. What was the reaction of other African Americans to Rosa Parks's actions?
3. What were the effects of the Montgomery bus boycott— good or bad—on Rosa Parks's life?
4. What is the impact of the Montgomery bus boycott compared to?
5. What order is used to arrange the details of the first three paragraphs of the passage?

ANSWERS
Exercise 2

Questions and answers will vary. Students should ask pertinent questions that could serve as useful study guides.

ANSWERS
Exercise 3

Answers may vary. Here are some possibilities:

1. Rosa Parks was born in Tuskegee, Alabama.
   Rosa Parks was born on February 4, 1913.

2. Thousands of African Americans joined Rosa Parks in the bus boycott and participated in the civil rights movement sparked by her actions.

3. Ms. Parks, as a result of starting the boycott, was fired from her tailoring job but was hired for a much better job as an assistant to a congressman.

4. The impact of the boycott is compared to a pebble that starts a landslide.

5. Chronological order is used to arrange the details of the first three paragraphs.

RESOURCES

ANSWERS
Exercise 4

Answers may vary. Here are some possibilities:

1. The bus driver had her arrested. Her boss fired her.

2. The passage states that she was weary after work.

3. The boycott sparked the civil rights movement in the United States.

4. Many employers took time to give rides to their employees rather than hire someone who would ride the bus.

5. Rosa Parks faced opposition from members of the white community who had the power to arrest her and fire her, but she eventually overcame these obstacles.

▶ EXERCISE 4 **Drawing Conclusions and Making Inferences**

Using the reading passage on pages 956–957, identify the evidence or reasoning that you might use in order to make the following inferences or to draw the following conclusions.

1. Some people disagreed with Rosa Parks's refusal to obey the segregation laws.
2. Rosa Parks's job at the tailor shop was tiring.
3. People outside of Montgomery, Alabama, were aware of the bus boycott.
4. The services of many black employees were valued by their white employers.
5. Since a hero can be defined as someone who faces obstacles but manages to overcome them, Rosa Parks is a hero.

▶ EXERCISE 5 **Interpreting Graphic Information**

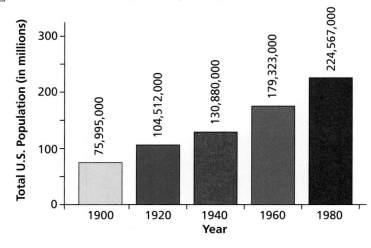

Historical Summary of Total U.S. Population

Look at the graph above, and then compare with the graph on page 959. Review both graphs to answer the following questions.

1. Did the percentage of the population between the ages of five and seventeen increase or <u>decrease</u> between 1920 and 1940? By how much? **1. by 3.8%**
2. Did the percentage of the population between the ages of five and seventeen <u>increase</u> or decrease between 1940 and 1960? By how much? **2. by 1.5%**
3. Compare the percentage of the population between the ages of five and seventeen in the years 1960 and 1980. How much did this portion of the population increase or <u>decrease</u>? **3. by 3.1%**
4. Did the percentage of the population between the ages of five and seventeen increase or <u>decrease</u> between the years 1900 and 1980? **4. by 7%**

▶ EXERCISE 6   **Evaluating Graphic Information**

Study the numbers in the table below. Then follow the numbered instructions.

PERCENTAGE OF POPULATION ATTENDING HIGH SCHOOLS				
1900	1920	1940	1960	1980
3.3%	10.2%	26.0%	23.5%	32.9%

1. Using the graphs on page 959 and page 980 as models, create a graph from the information in the table above.
2. Write a list of at least four conclusions you can draw from a point-by-point comparison of each of these three graphs. (You might look at your answers to Exercise 5 to suggest the type of questions you could ask.)
3. For each of the three graphs, make a prediction about the population figures for the year 2000.
4. Write a brief paragraph in which you discuss the observations and conclusions you have made. Cite specific information or identify evidence from the three graphs to support your findings.

RESOURCES

ANSWERS
Exercise 6

Graphs may vary.

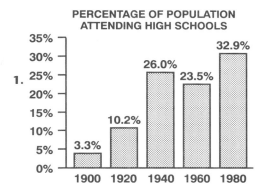

PERCENTAGE OF POPULATION ATTENDING HIGH SCHOOLS

2. Answers may vary. Here are some possibilities: **1.** Although the total U.S. population increased, the number of people between the ages of 5 and 17 did not increase as much as the number of people in other age groups. **2.** Either the percentage of the population under 5 or the percentage over 17, or both, increased. **3.** Although the percentage of young people aged 5 to 17 decreased, the percentage of the population attending high school increased. **4.** Either the percentage of young people attending high school increased, or people from other age groups began attending high school.

3. Answers may vary. The percentage of the United States population that is aged 5 to 17 will be less than 20%; the total United States population will be over 250,000,000; the percentage of the United States population attending high school will be greater than 35%.

4. Paragraphs will vary. They should include the conclusions students have drawn and evidence to support the conclusions.

RESOURCES

ANSWERS
Exercise 7

Paragraphs will vary. Students should compare, contrast, and evaluate the note-taking methods. You might want to specify a length for students' paragraphs.

ANSWERS
Exercise 8

Answers may vary. Here are some possibilities:

1. devices to look through or devices that have lenses
2. different cuts of meat
3. prime numbers
4. forms of entertainment
5. ocean birds
6. books by Mark Twain
7. numbers separated by eleven
8. yellow things
9. sports
10. palindromes

▶ EXERCISE 7   **Analyzing Your Note-Taking Method**

For one day, take notes in all of your classes by using the techniques suggested on pages 960–961. Write a paragraph, comparing and contrasting your usual method and this new method. Be sure to address these points: How are the two methods similar? How are they different? Which works better? Why?

▶ EXERCISE 8   **Identifying Classifications**

For each of the following groups of items, describe the category.

1. telescope, binoculars, microscope, camera, periscope
2. T-bone, hamburger, filet mignon, pot roast, prime rib
3. 1, 2, 3, 5, 7, 11
4. television, movies, plays, concerts, musicals
5. albatross, pelican, seagull, penguin, sandpiper
6. *The Adventures of Tom Sawyer, Huckleberry Finn, Innocents Abroad, The Prince and the Pauper*
7. 12, 23, 34, 45, 56, 67
8. butter, banana, blonde, canary, life raft
9. soccer, golf, tennis, field hockey, polo
10. tot, nun, deed, radar, pip

▶ EXERCISE 9   **Completing Analogies**

Consider the first relationship, then write the word that best indicates the second relationship so that it parallels the first. There may be more than one correct answer.

EXAMPLE   **1.** CARPENTER : WOOD :: potter : _____
          1. *CARPENTER : WOOD :: potter : clay*

1. SHEEP : FLOCK :: cattle : ____ 1. herd
2. BOSTON : MASSACHUSETTS :: Reno : ____ 2. Nevada
3. DUCK : QUACK :: turkey : ____ 3. gobble
4. OWL : WISE :: fox : ____ 4. sly, crafty, or cunning
5. TROT : GALLOP :: jog : ____ 5. run
6. LIZARD : REPTILE :: whale : ____ 6. mammal
7. KEY : LOCK :: combination : ____ 7. safe
8. THUNDERSTORM : RAIN :: blizzard : ____ 8. snow
9. HAMMER : HIT :: saw : ____ 9. cut
10. ARTIST : PAINT :: weaver : ____ 10. thread *or* yarn

▶ EXERCISE 10   **Applying Visual Organization**

After reading the paragraph below, draw a visually organized representation of its contents. Then use your graphic to answer the numbered questions that follow the reading passage.

> There are four layers of the atmosphere above the earth's surface. The lowest layer is the troposphere. This layer touches the earth's surface and extends to about seventeen kilometers above sea level. Within this layer are all the known living things, almost all the air and moisture, and almost all the weather conditions of our planet. The stratosphere extends from the upper limit of the troposphere to approximately fifty kilometers above sea level. This layer is important because it contains almost all the ozone in the atmosphere. Ozone protects the inhabitants of the earth from the harmful effect of the sun's rays. Since very little weather occurs in the stratosphere, airplane pilots like to fly there to avoid storms at low altitudes. The mesosphere extends from about fifty kilometers to about eighty kilometers above sea level. The mesosphere has greatly varying temperatures. At its lower level, it drops to about 0°C, but at its upper level it drops to about −100°C. Meteor trails, those hot gas streaks left behind by extraterrestrial debris, occur in the mesosphere. The thermosphere extends from approximately eighty kilometers above sea level into outer space. The upper limit of the thermosphere may extend to a thousand kilometers above sea level. In the upper limits of the thermosphere the air is especially thin. This is the region of the atmosphere where artificial satellites orbit the earth.

1. What is the temperature range of the mesosphere?
2. How many kilometers above sea level is the top of the thermosphere?
3. Why is the stratosphere important?
4. Which sphere has the least air?
5. Where in the atmosphere does most weather occur?

RESOURCES

ANSWERS
Exercise 10
Distance Above Sea Level

above 1000 km	outer space
80–1000 km	thermosphere (very little air at upper limits; here, satellites orbit earth)
50–80 km	mesophere (greatly varying temperatures: upper level, −100 degrees C; lower level, 0 degrees C)
17–50 km	stratosphere (almost all of the ozone in the atmosphere)
0–17 km	troposphere (all known living things; almost all air, moisture, and weather)
sea level	earth

1. −100 degrees to 0 degrees C
2. 1000 km
3. The stratosphere contains ozone, which protects the earth from the harmful rays of the sun.
4. the thermosphere
5. the troposphere

RESOURCES

ANSWERS
Exercise 11

Paraphrases will vary. Here is a possibility:

The speaker is a cloud talking about its various activities. It says it waters the thirsty flowers, taking the moisture from various bodies of water. It brings shade for plants when the sun is at its highest and hottest point. It drops dew on flowers that have closed during the night, when the earth spins around the sun. The cloud also brings hail whipping to the ground, making the ground white. Then it melts the hail with rain, and thunders as it goes by.

ANSWERS
Exercise 12

Answers may vary. Here are possibilities:

1. Identify the abilities of each man and show how their abilities are similar by referring to two crises.
2. Give reasons for your views on mandatory education.
3. Use words to create a picture of what happens during a major earthquake.
4. Point out likenesses between the characters of the two men.
5. Identify changes in Pip's character, listing them in the order in which they occur (chronological order).
6. Give examples of how the setting affects the action in the play.
7. Give the steps of the water cycle in order, beginning with rain.
8. Tell how it is significant.
9. Examine at least three factors of economic conditions that played a part in causing the Civil War.
10. Identify the traits of a good mayoral candidate.

SELECTION AMENDMENT
Description of change: excerpted
Rationale: to focus on the concept of paraphrasing presented in this chapter

RESOURCES

RESOURCES

EXERCISE 11 **Paraphrasing a Poem**

Read the following excerpt from a poem by Percy Bysshe Shelley. Then write a paraphrase of the poem.

from The Cloud
by Percy Bysshe Shelley

I bring fresh showers for the thirsting flowers,
  From the seas and the streams;
I bear light shade for the leaves when laid
  in their noonday dreams.
From my wings are shaken the dews that waken
  The sweet buds every one,
When rocked to rest on their mother's breast,
  As she dances about the sun.
I wield the flail of the lashing hail,
  and whiten the green plains under,
And then again I dissolve it in rain,
  And laugh as I pass in thunder.

EXERCISE 12 **Analyzing Essay Questions**

Identify the <u>key verb</u> that states the specific task in the following essay questions. Do not write an essay. Just state briefly what you would need to do to answer the question.

1. <u>Compare</u> the leadership abilities of Richard M. Nixon and John F. Kennedy, citing two specific crises.
2. <u>Explain</u> your beliefs about mandatory education.
3. <u>Describe</u> the events of a major earthquake.
4. <u>Compare</u> the characters of Romeo and Tybalt in *Romeo and Juliet.*
5. <u>Trace</u> the changes in the character of Pip in Charles Dickens's novel *Great Expectations.*
6. <u>Show</u> how the setting affects the action in the play "The Third Man."
7. <u>List</u> the steps in the water cycle, starting with rain.
8. <u>Interpret</u> the importance of the Bill of Rights to the American democratic system.
9. <u>Analyze</u> the economic conditions that helped cause the Civil War, including at least three factors.
10. <u>Give</u> the characteristics of a good mayoral candidate.

DIAGRAMING SENTENCES

A *sentence diagram* is a picture of how the parts of a sentence fit together and how the words in a sentence are related.

Subjects and Verbs (pages 546–555)

Every sentence diagram begins with a horizontal line intersected by a short vertical line, which divides the subject from the verb.

EXAMPLE   Alice Walker wrote *The Color Purple.*

Understood Subjects (page 554)

EXAMPLE   Answer the phone, please.

Nouns of Direct Address (page 554)

EXAMPLE   Pass me the picante sauce, **Gina.**

Compound Subjects (page 554)

EXAMPLE   **Arturo** and **Patsy** are dancing the conga.

Compound Verbs (page 555)

EXAMPLE   Roger **swims** and **dives**.

Here is how a compound verb is diagramed when the helping verb is not repeated.

EXAMPLE   Sally Ann **was reading** and **studying**.

Compound Subjects and Compound Verbs
(page 555)

EXAMPLE   **Kittens** and **puppies can play** together and **become** friends.

When the parts of a compound subject or a compound predicate are joined by a correlative conjunction, diagram the sentence this way:

EXAMPLE   **Both** Norma **and** Lisa will **not only** perform **but also** teach.

Modifiers (pages 518–521, 529–531, and 714–715)

Adjectives and Adverbs (pages 518–521 and 529–531)

Adjectives and adverbs are written on slanting lines beneath the words they modify.

EXAMPLE **The blue** car **quickly** swerved **left.**

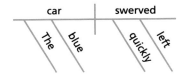

When an adverb modifies an adjective or an adverb, it is placed on a line connected to the word it modifies.

EXAMPLE The Neville Brothers performed **exceptionally** well.

Here, There, and *Where* as Modifiers
(page 553)

EXAMPLES **Here** come the astronauts!

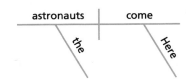

There goes the new Mohawk chief.

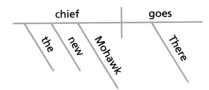

Where will the balloonists land?

NOTE: Sometimes *there* begins a sentence but does not modify the verb. When used in this way, *there* is called an *expletive.* It is diagramed on a line by itself.

EXAMPLE   **There** are seven stars in the Pleiades.

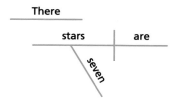

Subject Complements (page 560)

A subject complement is placed on the horizontal line with the simple subject and the verb. It comes after the verb. A line *slanting toward the subject* separates the subject complement from the verb.

Predicate Nominatives (page 560)

EXAMPLE   Some dogs are good **companions.**

Predicate Adjectives (page 560)

EXAMPLE   That cockatiel is **friendly.**

Compound Subject Complements (page 560)

EXAMPLE   Martin Yan is both a **chef** and a **comedian.**

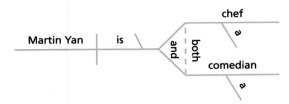

Objects (pages 562–563)

Direct Objects (page 562)

EXAMPLE   Cathy led the **band.**

Notice that a vertical line separates the direct object from the verb.

Compound Direct Objects (page 563)

EXAMPLE   We heard **cheers** and **whistles.**

Indirect Objects (page 563)

The indirect object is diagramed on a horizontal line beneath the verb.

EXAMPLE   They gave **her** a present.

Compound Indirect Objects (page 563)

EXAMPLE   Mr. Stephens lent **Karen** and **Shanna** *The Fire Next Time.*

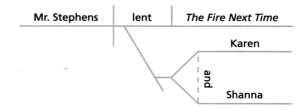

Phrases (pages 573–591)

Prepositional Phrases (pages 574–576)

The preposition is placed on a slanting line leading down from the word that the phrase modifies. The object of the preposition is placed on a horizontal line connected to the slanting line.

EXAMPLES   **The steep slopes of the mountains are covered with forests.** [adjective phrase modifying the subject; adverb phrase modifying the verb]

They sailed late in the fall. [adverb phrase modifying an adverb]

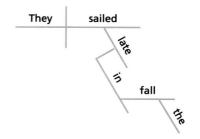

Nina read this Chinese folk tale to Aaron and Joey.
[compound object of preposition]

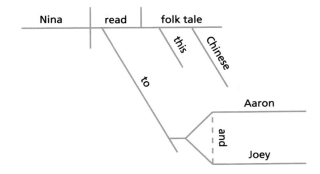

Down the valley and **across the plain** wanders the river. [two phrases modifying the same word]

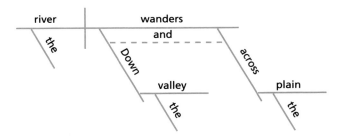

The princess lived **in a castle on the mountain.** [phrase modifying the object of another preposition]

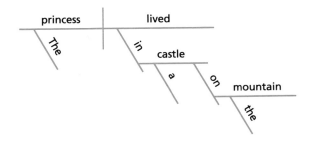

Participles and Participial Phrases (pages 579–583)

EXAMPLES I heard them **laughing.**

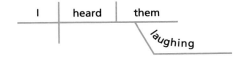

Waving her hat, Sara flagged the train **speeding down the track.**

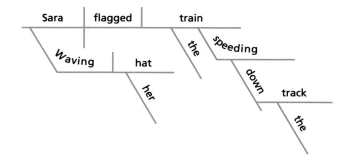

Gerunds and Gerund Phrases (pages 584–585)

EXAMPLES **Waiting** is not easy. [gerund used as subject]

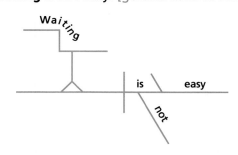

Waiting patiently for hours is usually a sure means of **observing wild animals.** [gerund phrases used as subject and as object of a preposition]

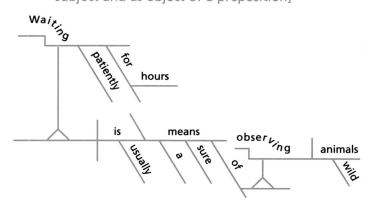

Infinitives and Infinitive Phrases (pages 586–588)

Infinitives and infinitive phrases used as modifiers are diagramed in the same way as prepositional phrases.

EXAMPLE   **He plays to win.** [infinitive used as adverb]

Infinitives and infinitive phrases used as nouns are diagramed as follows.

EXAMPLES   **To choose the right career** takes careful consideration. [infinitive phrase used as subject]

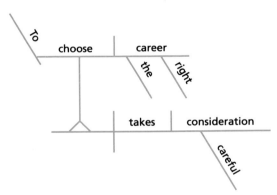

She is hoping to visit Morocco soon. [infinitive phrase used as direct object]

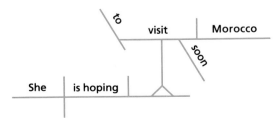

My brother watched me prune the tree. [infinitive with subject, *me,* and with *to* omitted]

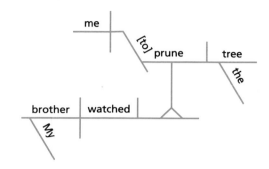

Appositives and Appositive Phrases (pages 590–591)

Place the appositive in parentheses after the word it identifies or explains.

EXAMPLES   My cousin **Bryan** is a carpenter.

Mohammed Tahir, **our newest classmate,** comes from Yemen, **a country near Saudi Arabia.**

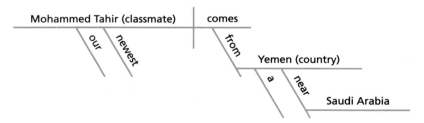

Subordinate Clauses (pages 598–606)

Adjective Clauses (pages 600–602)

An adjective clause is joined to the word it modifies by a broken line leading from the modified word to the relative pronoun.

EXAMPLES   The coat **that I wanted** was too expensive.

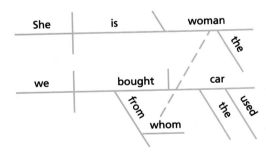

The box, **which contained the treasure,** was missing.

She is the woman **from whom we bought the used car.**

Adverb Clauses (pages 603–604)

Place the subordinating conjunction that introduces the adverb clause on a broken line leading from the verb in the adverb clause to the word the clause modifies.

EXAMPLE   **Before a hurricane strikes,** ample warning is given.

Noun Clauses (page 606)

Noun clauses often begin with relative pronouns, such as *that, what, who,* or *which.* These relative pronouns may have a function within the dependent clause or may simply connect the clause to the rest of the sentence. How a noun clause is diagramed depends on its use in the sentence and whether or not the relative pronoun has a specific function in the noun clause.

EXAMPLES   **What she said** convinced me. [The noun clause is used as the subject of the independent clause. *What* functions as the direct object in the noun clause.]

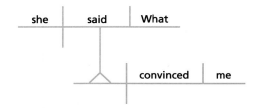

We know that you won the prize. [The noun clause is the direct object of the independent clause. *That* has no specific function in the noun clause.]

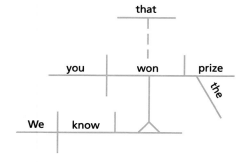

If the relative pronoun were omitted from the preceding sentence, the diagram would look like this.

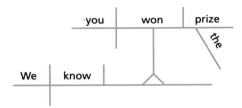

Sentences Classified According to Structure

(page 610)

Simple Sentences (page 610)

EXAMPLE   The Hudson is a historic waterway. [one independent clause]

Compound Sentences (page 610)

EXAMPLE   A strange dog chased us, but the owner came to our rescue. [two independent clauses]

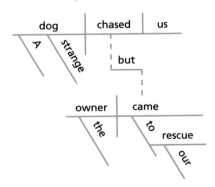

If the compound sentence has a semicolon and no conjunction, a straight broken line joins the two verbs.

EXAMPLE Phillis Wheatley wrote poetry in the 1700s; she was the first published African American poet.

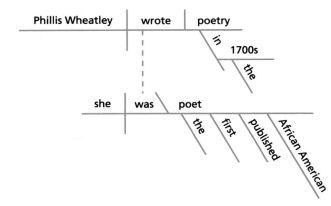

Notice that the compound adjective *African American* is written on one slanted line.

If the clauses of a compound sentence are joined by a semicolon and a conjunctive adverb (such as *consequently, therefore, nevertheless, however, moreover,* or *otherwise*), place the conjunctive adverb on a slanting line below the verb it modifies.

EXAMPLE Dylan works part time after school; consequently, he can afford to buy a new bike.

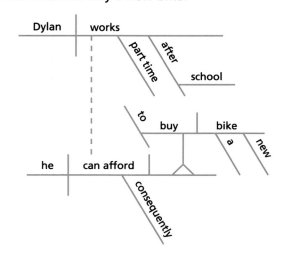

Complex Sentences (page 611)

EXAMPLE   **As night fell, the storm grew worse.** [one independent clause and one subordinate clause]

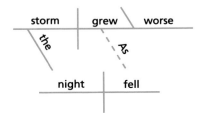

Compound-Complex Sentences (page 611)

EXAMPLE   **The room that Carrie painted had been white, but she changed the color.** [two independent clauses and one subordinate clause]

Glossary of Terms

Abstract noun Names an idea, a feeling, a quality, or a characteristic. (See page 515.)

Action verb Expresses physical or mental activity. (See page 524.)

Active voice The voice a verb is in when it expresses an action done *by* its subject. (See page 694.)

Adjective Modifies a noun or a pronoun. (See page 518.)

Adjective clause A subordinate clause that modifies a noun or a pronoun. (See page 600.)

Adjective phrase A prepositional phrase that modifies a noun or a pronoun. (See page 574.)

Adverb Modifies a verb, an adjective, or another adverb. (See page 529.)

Adverb clause A subordinate clause that modifies a verb, an adjective, or an adverb and tells *when, where, why, how,* or *to what extent*. (See page 603.)

Adverb phrase A prepositional phrase that modifies a verb, an adjective, or another adverb. (See page 576.)

Agreement The correspondence, or match, between grammatical forms. (See Chapter 19.)

Aim One of the four basic purposes, or reasons, for writing. (See page 7.)

Ambiguous reference Unclear phrasing that occurs when a pronoun can refer to either of two antecedents. (See page 669.)

Analyzing Looking at the parts of a whole and their relationships. (See pages 379 and 423.)

Anecdote An extended example, or story, used to support a main idea. (See pages 74 and 123.)

Antecedent The word to which a pronoun refers, usually preceding the pronoun and giving the pronoun its meaning. (See page 637.)

Appositive A noun or a pronoun placed beside another noun or pronoun to identify or explain it. (See pages 450 and 590.)

Appositive phrase Consists of an appositive and its modifiers. (See pages 450, 464, and 590.)

Article *A, an,* or *the,* the most frequently used adjectives. (See page 519.)

Audience The person(s) who reads or listens to what a writer or speaker says. (See pages 35 and 899.)

Base word A word that can stand alone, without prefixes or suffixes. (See page 934.)

Block method A way of arranging details in a comparison/contrast essay by discussing all the features of the first subject, then the same features of the second subject in the same order. (See page 262.)

Body States and develops a composition's main points in one or more paragraphs. (See page 128.)

Brainstorming A technique for finding ideas by using free association: recording every idea about a subject that comes to mind, without stopping to evaluate any of the ideas. (See page 27.)

Business letter A formal letter in which a writer might request or order something, complain or seek the correction of a problem, or express appreciation for someone or something. (See Chapter 35.)

Call number A number and letter code a library assigns to a book, which tells how the book has been classified and where it has been placed on the shelves. (See page 920.)

Case The form of a noun or pronoun that shows how it is used in a sentence. (See page 649.)

Cause-and-effect essay A form of writing in which a writer examines and explains the reasons for a situation or event and its results. (See Chapter 8.)

Chronological order A way of arranging ideas in a paragraph or composition according to when events happened. (See pages 39 and 82.)

Classification A strategy of development: looking at a subject as it relates to other subjects in a group. (See pages 97 and 962.)

Clause A group of words containing a verb and its subject, used as part of a sentence. (See pages 451 and 597.)

Cliché An overused, worn-out figure of speech. (See page 508.)

Climax The high point of a story plot; the tense or exciting scene that settles the main conflict. (See page 376.)

Clincher sentence The concluding sentence of a paragraph: pulls all the details together by restating or summarizing the main idea. (See page 76.)

Clustering A visual technique for finding writing ideas and gathering information: breaking a large subject into its smaller parts to create a visual map of one's thoughts. (See page 28.)

Coherence A quality achieved when all the ideas in a paragraph or composition are clearly arranged and connected. (See pages 82 and 128.)

Collective noun A noun that names a group of persons or things. (See page 629.)

Colloquialism An informal, colorful expression of conversational language. (See page 501.)

Comma splice A run-on sentence with only a comma to separate complete sentences. (See page 456.)

Common noun Names a member of a group of persons, places, or things; it is not capitalized. (See pages 515 and 764.)

Comparative degree The form a modifier takes when comparing two things. (See page 722.)

Comparison/Contrast essay A form of writing in which a writer discusses similarities or differences (or both) between two subjects. (See Chapter 7.)

Complement A word or group of words that completes the meaning of a predicate. (See page 557.)

Complex sentence Has one independent clause and at least one subordinate clause. (See pages 469 and 611.)

Compound-complex sentence Has two or more independent clauses and at least one subordinate clause. (See page 611.)

Compound sentence Has two or more independent clauses but no subordinate clauses. (See pages 467 and 610.)

Compound word Consists of two or more words used together as a single word. (See page 860.)

Compound subject Consists of two or more subjects that are joined by a conjunction and have the same verb. (See pages 554 and 627.)

Compound verb Consists of two or more verbs that are joined by a conjunction and have the same subject. (See pages 555 and 627.)

Conclusion (1) Reinforces a main idea and brings a composition to a definite close. (See page 130.) **(2)** A decision or determination reached by reasoning from clearly expressed facts and evidence found in a reading passage or other materials. (See page 957.)

Concrete noun Names an object that can be perceived by the senses. (See page 515.)

Conflict The central problem a character faces in a story. (See pages 226 and 376.)

Conjugating Listing all forms of a verb in all tenses. (See page 684.)

Conjunctive adverb An adverb used as a connecting word between independent clauses in a compound sentence. (See page 457.)

Conjunction Joins words or groups of words. (See page 536.)

Connotation The emotional meanings suggested by or associated with a word. (See pages 504 and 934.)

Context The way a word is used in a reading passage. (See page 932.)

Contraction A shortened form of a word, a figure, or a group of words, written with an apostrophe to indicate where letters or numerals have been omitted. (See page 854.)

Coordinating conjunction Joins parallel words, phrases, or clauses. (See page 536.)

Correlative conjunctions Are used in pairs (*either . . . or, not only . . . but also,* and so on). (See page 536.)

Creative writing Aims at creating literature: stories, poems, songs, and plays. (See page 7.)

Critical analysis A form of writing in which a writer analyzes the elements, or parts, of a work such as a poem, a play, a novel, or a short story. (See Chapter 10.)

Dangling modifier A modifying word, phrase, or clause that does not clearly and sensibly modify a word or a group of words in a sentence. (See page 728.)

Declarative sentence Makes a statement and is followed by a period. (See page 565.)

Denotation The direct, plainly expressed meaning of a word—the meaning a dictionary lists. (See pages 504 and 934.)

Description A strategy of development: using sensory details and spatial order to describe individual features of a specific subject. (See pages 94 and 179.)

Dialect A distinct version or variety of a language used by a particular group of people; may be **ethnic** or **regional.** (See page 496.)

Dialogue The "talk," or conversation, in a story. (See page 229.)

Direct object A noun or pronoun that receives the action of the verb or shows the result of the action, answering the question *Whom?* or *What?* after a transitive verb. (See page 562.)

Direct quotation A reproduction of a person's exact words, enclosed in quotation marks. (See pages 427 and 834.)

Direct reference Connects ideas in a paragraph or composition by referring to a noun or pronoun used earlier. (See pages 88 and 128.)

Double comparison The use of both *–er* and *more* (*less*) or *–est* and *most* (*least*) to express the comparison forms of modifiers. (See page 724.)

Double negative The use of two negative words when one is sufficient. (See page 756.)

Double subject The use of an unnecessary pronoun after the subject of a sentence. (See page 744.)

Dramatic irony A device used by a writer to heighten readers' interest by letting the reader know something the main character in a story does not. (See page 378.)

E

Early plan An **informal** or **rough outline** for a composition in which a writer groups and orders information. (See page 117.)

Emotional appeal A strategy used to support a writer's opinion and to persuade an audience by appealing to readers' feelings. (See page 339.)

Emphasis The focus of a description, designed to create a specific impression for the reader. (See page 187.)

End marks Punctuation marks (periods, question marks, exclamation points) used to indicate the purpose of a sentence. (See page 789.)

Essay test Requires a student to think critically about material learned and to express his or her understanding of that material in an organized piece of writing. (See page 976.)

Essential clause/Essential phrase Also called **restrictive:** is necessary to the meaning of a sentence; not set off by commas. (See page 798.)

Ethnic dialect A distinct version of a language used by people who share the same cultural heritage. (See page 498.)

Etymology The origin and history of a word. (See page 928.)

Euphemism An agreeable term that stands for a more direct, less pleasing one. (See page 505.)

Evaluating A stage in the writing process: making judgments about a composition's strengths and weaknesses in content, organization, and style. (See pages 6, 23, and 47.)

Evaluation A strategy of development: making judgments about a subject in an attempt to determine its value. (See page 100.)

Example A specific instance, or illustration, of a general idea. (See page 73.)

Exclamatory sentence Expresses strong feeling and is followed by an exclamation point. (See page 566.)

Expressive writing Aims at expressing a writer's feelings and thoughts. (See page 7.)

Extemporaneous speech A speech for which a speaker researches and prepares notes, then delivers the rehearsed but not memorized speech. (See page 902.)

F

Fact Can be checked and proved to be true by concrete information. (See pages 71 and 337.)

Fallacy An error in logical thinking that may lead a writer into a false or oversimplified discussion of cause-and-effect relationships. (See page 300.)

Feedback The reaction of a receiver to the message given by a sender during the communication process. (See page 866.)

Figurative language Also called a **figure of speech:** a word or a group of words that has a meaning other than its literal one. (See pages 193 and 507.)

5W-How? questions Questions (*Who? What? Where? When? Why? How?*) a writer uses to collect information about a subject. (See page 30.)

Foreshadowing A hint or suggestion of upcoming events in a story. (See page 377.)

Formal outline A highly structured, clearly labeled writing plan with a set pattern, using letters and numbers to label main headings and subheadings. (See page 118.)

Freewriting A technique for finding ideas: writing whatever thoughts occur, without regard to form. (See page 26.)

Fused sentence A run-on sentence with no punctuation separating the run-together sentences. (See page 456.)

General reference An error that occurs when a pronoun has no specific antecedent, but refers instead to a general idea. (See page 669.)

Gerund A verbal ending in *–ing,* used as a noun. (See page 584.)

Gerund phrase Consists of a gerund and its modifiers and complements. (See page 585.)

Idiom A word or phrase that means something different from its literal meaning. (See page 501.)

Imperative sentence Gives a command or makes a request and is followed by either a period or an exclamation point. (See page 565.)

Impromptu speech A short speech made on the spur of the moment, with little or no time for development or preparation of ideas. (See page 899.)

Indefinite pronoun A pronoun (*each, no one, anybody,* and so on) that does not refer to a specific person or thing. (See page 622.)

Independent clause Expresses a complete thought and can stand by itself as a sentence; also called a **main clause.** (See pages 451 and 597.)

Indirect object A noun or pronoun preceding a direct object that usually tells *to whom* or *for whom* (or *to what* or *for what*) the action of a transitive verb is performed. (See page 563.)

Indirect quotation A rewording or paraphrasing of something another person has said. (See page 834.)

Inference A decision or determination reached by reasoning from evidence that is hinted at or implied in a reading passage or other materials. (See page 957.)

Infinitive (1) One of the principal parts of a verb. (See page 678.) **(2)** A verbal (verb form), usually preceded by *to,* used as a noun, an adjective, or an adverb. (See page 586.)

Infinitive phrase Consists of an infinitive and all of its modifiers and complements. (See page 587.)

Informative writing Aims at conveying information or explaining something. (See page 7.)

Interjection Expresses emotion and has no grammatical relation to the rest of the sentence. (See page 537.)

Interrogative sentence Asks a question and is followed by a question mark. (See page 566.)

Interview A special listening situation with the specific purpose of gathering information. (See page 913.)

Intransitive verb Expresses action (or tells something about the subject) without passing the action from a doer to a receiver. (See page 524.)

Introduction Begins a composition and should catch the reader's interest, set the composition's tone, and present the thesis statement. (See page 122.)

Invalid conclusion Is not reasonably or logically based on the available evidence. (See page 958.)

Irony A contrast between appearance or expectation and reality. (See page 378.)

Irregular verb Forms its past and past participle in some other way than by adding –d or –ed. (See page 679.)

Jargon Language that has a special meaning for a particular group of people; also wordy, puffed-up language called **gobbledygook.** (See page 506.)

Levels of usage The various forms of a language suitable for different situations. (See page 500.)

Linking verb Serves as a link between its subject and another word; may be a form of the verb *be.* (See page 525.)

Loaded words Words intended to provoke strong feeling, either positive or negative. (See page 505.)

Loanwords Words adopted from another language. (See page 487.)

Logical appeal A strategy used to support a writer's opinion and to persuade an audience by appealing to reason. (See page 337.)

Logical order A way of arranging details in a paragraph or composition according to what makes logical sense, such as grouping related ideas together. (See pages 39 and 84.)

Main idea The idea around which a paragraph or composition is organized. (See page 67.)

Mass media Forms of communication (television, radio, movies, newspapers and magazines) that reach a large audience daily. (See page 916.)

Metaphor A figure of speech directly comparing two things (without using the words *like* or *as*) by saying that something *is* something else. (See page 194.)

Misplaced modifier A word, phrase, or clause that makes a sentence awkward because it seems to modify the wrong word or group of words. (See page 730.)

Modifier A word, a phrase, or a clause that makes the meaning of another word more definite. (See pages 518 and 714.)

Narration A strategy of development: relating events or actions over a period of time, usually using chronological order. (See page 95.)

Nominative case The form a noun or pronoun takes as the subject or predicate nominative in a sentence. (See page 651.)

Nonessential clause/Nonessential phrase Also called **nonrestrictive:** adds information not necessary to the main idea in the sentence and is set off by commas. (See page 797.)

Nonverbal communication Sending a message—by gestures, facial expressions, and so on—without the use of verbal signals (words). (See page 899.)

Noun Names a person, place, thing, or idea. (See page 514.)

Noun clause A subordinate clause used as a noun. (See page 606.)

Noun of direct address Identifies the person spoken to or addressed in a sentence. (See page 554.)

Number The form of a word that indicates whether the word is singular or plural. (See page 618.)

Object A complement that does not refer to the subject. (See page 562.)

Objective case The form a noun or pronoun takes when used as a direct object, an indirect object, or the object of a preposition. (See page 655.)

Objective description Creates an accurate, thorough picture, using factual details without revealing a particular judgment or feeling about the subject. (See page 182.)

Objective test Requires a student to give a specific, limited response; may contain multiple-choice, true/false, matching, reasoning or logic, analogy, or short-answer questions. (See page 969.)

Object of a preposition The noun or pronoun that ends a prepositional phrase. (See page 534.)

Opinion A belief or attitude. (See page 333.)

Oral interpretation An expressive presentation of a literary work to an audience, using vocal techniques, facial expressions, body language, and gestures. (See page 906.)

Order of importance A way of arranging details, in a paragraph or composition, from least to most important or from most to least important. (See pages 39 and 84.)

Parallel structure The use of the same form or part of speech to express equal, or parallel, ideas in a sentence. (See page 473.)

Paraphrase To restate someone else's ideas in different words. (See pages 421 and 915.)

Parenthetical expression A remark that adds incidental information or relates ideas. (See page 806.)

Parenthetical citation A form of documentation that places source information in parentheses at the end of a sentence in which someone else's word or ideas are used. (See page 428.)

Parliamentary procedure A plan for following a priority of actions: sometimes used by groups to keep meetings running smoothly. (See page 905.)

Participial phrase Consists of a participle and its complements and modifiers. (See pages 464 and 582.)

Participle A verbal (verb form) used as an adjective. (See pages 464 and 579.)

Passive voice The voice a verb is in when it expresses an action done *to* its subject. (See page 694.)

Personal letter An informal letter in which a writer might thank someone for something, invite someone to a particular event or occasion, or reply to an invitation he or she has received. (See Chapter 35.)

Personal narrative A form of writing in which an author explores and shares the meaning of an experience that was especially important to him or her. (See Chapter 4.)

Personification A figure of speech giving human characteristics to nonhuman things. (See page 194.)

Persuasive essay A form of writing in which a writer supports an opinion and tries to persuade an audience. (See Chapter 9.)

Persuasive writing Aims at persuading people to change their minds about something or to act in a certain way. (See page 7.)

Phrase A group of related words used as a single part of speech; does not contain both a predicate and its subject. (See pages 449 and 573.)

Plagiarism Using someone else's words or ideas without giving credit for them. (See page 422.)

Plot The series of events in a story that follow each other and cause each other to happen. (See pages 226 and 376.)

Point-by-point method A way of arranging details in a comparison/contrast essay by discussing one feature of the first subject, then the same feature of the second subject, repeating in the same order for all features. (See page 262.)

Point of view The vantage point, or position, from which a writer tells a story or describes a subject. (See pages 183 and 377.)

Possessive case The form a noun or pronoun takes when used to show ownership or relationship. (See page 848.)

Predicate The part of a sentence that says something about the subject. (See page 546.)

Predicate adjective An adjective in the predicate that describes the subject of a sentence or clause. (See page 560.)

Predicate nominative A noun or pronoun in the predicate that identifies or renames the subject of a sentence or clause. (See page 560.)

Prefix A word part added before a base or root word. (See page 936.)

Preposition Shows the relationship of a noun or a pronoun to some other word in a sentence. (See page 534.)

Prepositional phrase A group of words beginning with a preposition and ending with an object (a noun or a pronoun). (See pages 450, 464, and 574.)

Prewriting The first stage in the writing process: thinking and planning, deciding what to write about, collecting ideas and details, and making a plan for presenting ideas. (See pages 6 and 23.)

Principal parts of a verb A verb's forms—the *infinitive,* the *present participle,* the *past,* and the *past participle*—used to form the verb tenses. (See page 678.)

Progressive form of a verb Used in all six tenses to show continuing action; made up of a form of *be* plus the verb's present participle. (See page 686.)

Pronoun Is used in place of a noun or more than one noun. (See page 516.)

Proofreading A stage of the writing process: carefully reading a revised draft to correct mistakes in grammar, usage, and mechanics. (See pages 6, 23, and 55.)

Proper adjective An adjective formed from a proper noun. (See page 764.)

Proper noun Names a particular person, place, or thing and is always capitalized. (See pages 516 and 764.)

Publishing The last stage of the writing process: making a final, clean copy of a paper and sharing it with an audience. (See pages 6, 23, and 57.)

Purpose A reason, or aim, for writing or speaking: to express yourself; to be creative; to entertain; to explain, inform, or explore; or to persuade. (See pages 35 and 899.)

▼ **R**

Regional dialect A distinct version of a language used by people in or from a particular geographical area. (See page 497.)

Regular verb Forms its past and past participle by adding *–d* or *–ed* to the infinitive. (See page 679.)

Relative pronoun A pronoun that relates an adjective clause to the word that the clause modifies, while also serving a function within the clause. (See page 601.)

Relevant features The specific details about a subject that are related to the main idea of a composition. (See page 260.)

Research report A form of writing in which a writer presents factual information discovered through exploration and research. (See Chapter 11.)

Revising A stage of the writing process: making changes in a composition's content, organization, and style in order to improve it. (See pages 6, 23, and 50.)

Root The base a word is built on, which carries the word's core meaning, but cannot stand alone. (See page 934.)

Run-on sentence Two or more complete sentences run together as one. (See page 456.)

Sensory details Precise bits of information observed, or collected, through any of the five senses—sight, sound, smell, touch, or taste. (See pages 71 and 191.)

Sentence A group of words that contains a subject and a verb and expresses a complete thought. (See pages 447 and 544.)

Sentence fragment A part of a sentence that does not express a complete thought. (See pages 446 and 545.)

Setting Where and when a story takes place; may provide background for understanding characters and events, establish the conflict, or create the mood in a story. (See pages 225 and 376.)

Simile A figure of speech comparing two basically unlike things, using the words *like* or *as*. (See page 194.)

Simple sentence Has one independent clause and no subordinate clauses but may have a compound subject, a compound verb, and any number of phrases. (See page 610.)

Situational irony A device used by the writer of a story: what is expected—by the character(s) and usually by the reader—is not what happens. (See page 378.)

Slang Informal language made up of newly coined words or of old words used in new ways. (See page 502.)

Source card An index card on which bibliographical information about a source for a research report is recorded. (See page 416.)

Spatial order A way of arranging details in a paragraph or composition according to how they are spaced—nearest to farthest, left to right, and so on. (See pages 39 and 83.)

Statistic A fact based on numbers. (See page 71.)

Story map A written plan of the essential elements of a story. (See page 228.)

Stringy sentence Has too many independent clauses strung together with coordinating conjunctions like *and* or *but*. (See page 474.)

Subject The part of a sentence that names the person or thing spoken about in the rest of the sentence. (See page 546.)

Subject complement A noun, pronoun, or adjective that follows a linking verb and describes or explains the subject. (See page 560.)

Subjective description Creates a selective picture, revealing the writer's thoughts and feelings about a subject. (See page 182.)

Subordinate clause Does not express a complete thought and cannot stand alone; also called a **dependent clause.** (See pages 452 and 598.)

Subordinating conjunction Introduces an adverb clause but does not serve a function in that clause. (See page 603.)

Suffix A word part added after a base or root word. (See page 937.)

Summarize To restate, in condensed form, the main points of a passage. (See pages 421 and 915.)

Superlative degree The form a modifier takes when comparing more than two things. (See page 722.)

Supporting sentences Give specific details or information to support the main idea. (See page 71.)

Suspense Unanswered questions in the plot development of a story that make a reader wonder what will happen next. (See page 227.)

Syllable A word part that can be pronounced by itself. (See page 871.)

Synonym A word that has a meaning similar to, but not exactly the same as, another word. (See pages 503 and 933.)

T

Tense The time indicated by the form of a verb: *present, present perfect, past, past perfect, future,* and *future perfect.* (See page 684.)

Theme The underlying meaning or message a writer wants to communicate to readers. (See page 378.)

Thesis statement Announces the limited topic of a composition and the main, or unifying, idea about that topic. (See pages 113 and 423.)

Time line A visual arrangement of information in chronological order. (See page 44.)

Tired word A word that has lost so much of its freshness and force through overuse that it has become worn-out and almost meaningless. (See page 507.)

Tone The feeling or attitude a writer conveys about a topic. (See pages 36 and 122.)

Topic sentence Expresses the main idea of a paragraph. (See page 68.)

Transitional expression A word or phrase that indicates relationships between ideas in a paragraph or composition. (See pages 89 and 129.)

Transitive verb Expresses an action directed toward a person or thing named in a sentence. (See page 524.)

U

Understood subject The unstated subject *you* in a request or a command. (See page 554.)

Unity A quality achieved when all the sentences or paragraphs in a composition work together as a unit to express or support one main idea. (See pages 77 and 128.)

V

Valid conclusion Is firmly grounded in facts, evidence, or logic. (See page 958.)

Verb Expresses an action or a state of being. (See page 524.)

Verbal irony A device used by the author of a story: what a character says is not what is meant. (See page 378.)

Verbals A word (participle, gerund, or infinitive) formed from a verb, but used as another part of speech. (See pages 449 and 579.)

Verbal phrase Consists of a verbal and its modifiers and complements. (See page 449.)

Verb phrase Consists of a main verb preceded by at least one **helping verb** (also called an **auxiliary verb**). (See page 527.)

Voice Writing in a way that sounds like oneself, using language to sound as natural and distinctive as possible. (See page 36.)

W

Weak reference Unclear phrasing that occurs when a pronoun refers to a suggested, but not clearly stated, word or idea. (See page 670.)

"What if?" questions A creative thinking technique used to help a writer draw upon his or her imagination to explore ideas for writing. (See page 34.)

Word bank A writer's storehouse of words to be used in writing. (See pages 192 and 931.)

Works Cited A list of all the print and nonprint sources used in a research report; the term **bibliography** means that only print sources were used. (See page 429.)

Writer's journal A written record of a person's experiences and observations, feelings and opinions, ideas and questions. (See page 25.)

Writing A stage in the writing process: putting ideas into words, following a plan that organizes the ideas. (See pages 6, 23, and 45.)

Writing process The series of stages, or steps, that a writer goes through to develop ideas and to communicate them clearly in a piece of writing. (See pages 6 and 22.)

Glossary

This glossary is a short dictionary of words found in the professional writing models in this textbook. The words are defined according to their meanings in the context of the writing models.

Pronunciation Key

Symbol	Key Words	Symbol	Key Words
a	asp, fat, parrot	b	bed, fable, dub, ebb
ā	ape, date, play, break, fail	d	dip, beadle, had, dodder
ä	ah, car, father, cot	f	fall, after, off, phone
e	elf, ten, berry	g	get, haggle, dog
ē	even, meet, money, flea, grieve	h	he, ahead, hotel
i	is, hit, mirror	j	joy, agile, badge
ī	ice, bite, high, sky	k	kill, tackle, bake, coat, quick
ō	open, tone, go, boat	l	let, yellow, ball
ô	all, horn, law, oar	m	met, camel, trim, summer
ᴏᴏ	look, pull, moor, wolf	n	not, flannel, ton
ᴏ̄ᴏ̄	ooze, tool, crew, rule	p	put, apple, tap
yᴏ̄ᴏ̄	use, cute, few	r	red, port, dear, purr
yᴏᴏ	cure, globule	s	sell, castle, pass, nice
oi	oil, point, toy	t	top, cattle, hat
ou	out, crowd, plow	v	vat, hovel, have
u	up, cut, color, flood	w	will, always, swear, quick
ᵘr	urn, fur, deter, irk	y	yet, onion, yard
ə	a in ago	z	zebra, dazzle, haze, rise
	e in agent	ch	chin, catcher, arch, nature
	i in sanity	sh	she, cushion, dash, machine
	o in comply	th	thin, nothing, truth
	u in focus	*th*	then, father, lathe
ər	perhaps, murder	zh	azure, leisure, beige
		ŋ	ring, anger, drink

Abbreviation Key

adj.	adjective	*pl.*	plural
adv.	adverb	*prep.*	preposition
conj.	conjunction	*vi.*	intransitive verb
n.	noun	*vt.*	transitive verb

abstracted [ab strak′tid] *adj.* Not paying attention; absent-minded.

adjacent [ə jā′sənt] *adj.* Next to or beside.

anna [än′ə] *n.* A former unit of money in India, equal to 1/16 of a rupee.

aquiline [ak′wə līn′] *adj.* Curved.

assimilate [ə sim′ə lāt′] *vt.* To absorb.

auspicious [ôs pish′əs] *adj.* Successful and deserving of respect.

befuddled [bē fud″ld] *adj.* Confused.

buffoonery [bə fōōn′ə rē] *n.* Clowning around.

careworn [ker′wôrn′] *adj.* Visibly exhausted by worrying.

carnivore [kär′nə vôr′] *n.* A meat-eater.

chauvinist [shō′vin ist] *adj.* Characterized by an unthinking loyalty toward a particular behavior.

cheroot [she root′] *n.* A square-tipped cigar.

contrivance [kən trī′vəns] *n.* A plan or device designed to produce a specific, intended result.

cowrie shell [kou′rē shel′] *n.* A shiny, bright-colored seashell once used as money in India.

curb [kurb] *vt.* To limit or restrain.

din [din] *n.* Loud and continuous noise.

dissipate [dis′ə pāt′] *vi.* To gradually disappear.

draw [drô] *n.* A deep ditch formed by rainwater drainage.

effigy [ef′i jē] *adj.* Symbolic.

electrodynamics [ē lek′trō dī nam′iks] *n.* The science of electricity and magnetic forces.

embolden [em bōl′dən] *vt.* To make bold.

émigré [em′i grā′] *n.* A person who has moved from his or her native country to live in another.

endue [en dōō′] *vt.* To give desirable qualities to.

eradicate [ē rad′i kāt′] *vt.* To do away with; to remove.

execute [ek′si kyōōt′] *vt.* To make or create.

exhilaration [eg zil′ə rā′shən] *n.* Happy excitement.

expertise [ek′spər tēz′] *n.* Highly qualified knowledge or skill.

franchise [fran′chīz′] *n.* A locally-owned business with a license to sell another company's product.

gnome [nōm] *n.* A mythological dwarf.

gulch [gulch] *n.* A deep, narrow riverbed.

guru [gōō′rōō′] *n.* A respected spiritual leader.

harbor [här′bər] *vt.* To keep in mind and remember frequently.

humor [hyōō′mər] *n.* Moisture.

hydrocarbon [hī′drō kär′bən] *n.* A poisonous chemical compound made of hydrogen and carbon.

hypothesis [hī päth′ə sis] *n.* A theory to be proved.

icon [ī′kän′] *n.* A symbol or easily recognized image.

illustrious [i lus′trē əs] *n.* Well-known and greatly respected.

imbue [im byōō′] *vt.* To give ideas or feelings to.

impetuous [im pech′ōō əs] *adj.* Impulsive; acting without prior thought.

implication [im′pli kā′shən] *n.* An unstated but expected result of an action or event.

incredulous [in krej′ōō ləs] *adj.* Not believing.

indifferent [in dif′ər ənt] *adj.* Uncaring; unaware.

jaggery [jag′ər ē] *n.* A dark-colored sugar made from palm-tree sap.

lorry [lôr′ē] *n.* A type of truck.

M

malevolent [mə lev′ə lənt] *adj.* Evil.

malicious [mə lish′əs] *adj.* Wishing harm.

maxim [maks′im] *n.* A statement generally accepted as true.

mesmerize [mez′mər īz′] *vt.* To capture the attention as if by magic; to hypnotize.

N

notoriously [nō tôr′ē əs lē] *adv.* In a well-known and undesirable manner.

O

ode [ōd] *n.* A long poem with short lines, usually in a specific rhyme pattern; it commonly expresses emotion in a formal manner.

ordnance [ôrd′nəns] *n.* Weapons, ammunition, parts, etc.

P

palmyra writing [pal mī′rə rī′tiŋ] *n.* Ancient writing on strips of the leaves of a palmyra palm tree.

paraphernalia [par′ə fər nāl′yə] *n.* A group of articles used for a specific purpose; tools or equipment.

parochial [pə rō′kē əl] *adj.* Narrow-minded; limited in the way one sees the world.

pie [pī] *n.* A former unit of money in India, equal to 1/192 of a rupee.

piqued [pēkt] *adj.* Irritated or displeased.

pontoon [pän tōōn′] *n.* A floating support for a temporary bridge.

porous [pôr′əs] *adj.* Having tiny holes to absorb moisture.

precipice [pres′i pis] *n.* A steep cliff.

procure [prō kyoor′] *vt.* To find and get.

proselytize [präs′ə li tīz′] *vi.* To argue in a persuasive manner.

purgatory [pur′gə tôr′ē] *n.* Temporary punishment.

R

rupee [rōō′pē] *n.* The basic unit of money in India.

S

saffron [saf′rən] *adj.* Orange-yellow.

scant [skant] *adj.* Limited in amount or quantity; not enough.

scapegrace [skāp′grās′] *n.* An unprincipled person; a rascal.

searing [sir′iŋ] *adj.* Causing a feeling of being marked or changed by an experience.

serried [ser′ēd] *adj.* In a tight formation, as soldiers.

siege [sēj] *n.* An attack in which the enemy is encircled and fired upon.

sodden [säd′′n] *adj.* Soaked.

spare [sper] *adj.* Minimal; using few words to describe.

stark [stärk] *adj.* Not softened; realistic.

stipulated [stip′yo͞o lāt′id] *adj.* Specific; set.

strut [strut] *n.* A metal brace to stiffen the leg.

subterranean [sub′tə rā′nē ən] *adj.* Underground.

succulence [suk′yo͞o ləns] *n.* Juiciness.

T

tapestry [tap′əs trē] *n.* A cloth or rug with designs and pictures.

tendency [ten′dən sē] *adj.* Relating to a habitual action.

tram [tram] *n.* A streetcar.

tramp steamer [tramp stēm′ər] *n.* A type of steam-powered ship.

trapezoid [trap′i zoid] *n.* A figure similar to a rectangle but with only two sides parallel.

V

vermilion [vər mil′yən] *n.* Bright red paint.

vigor [vig′ər] *n.* Energy.

virtually [vur′cho͞o ə lē] *adv.* Almost totally; for all practical purposes.

vociferousness [vō sif′ər əs nis] *n.* Loud, continuous talk.

Index

A

A, an, 519, 738
Abbreviations
  addresses, 792
  capitalizing, 765, 792
  organizations, 792
  personal names, 792
  punctuating, 792
  states, 792
  time of day, 792
  titles used with names, 792
  units of measure, 792
  years, 792
Abstract noun, defined, 515
Accept, except, 739
Action verb
  defined, 524–25
  distinguished from linking verb, 715
  and objects, 562
  in personal narrative, 166
Active listening, 911
Active reading, 369
Active voice, 694–96
Add, as revision technique, 50–51
Addresses
  abbreviations with, 792
  commas with, 808
  hyphenated street numbers, 768
Addressing envelopes, 948
Adjective, 518–21
  articles, 519
  commas and, 794–95
  comparison of, 719–25
  compound, 765, 861
  defined, 518
  diagramed, 987
  distinguished from pronoun, 520
  nouns used as, 521
  placement of, 519
  predicate, 560
  proper, capitalizing, 764–79
Adjective clause, 600–602
  beginning with *that*, 798
  and combining sentences, 470–71
  comma and, 471
  defined, 600
  diagramed, 994–95

  essential, nonessential, 600
  placement of, 600
  relative adverb, 602
  relative pronoun, 601
Adjective phrase
  defined, 574
  placement of, 575
Adjustment letter, 945
Adverb, 529–31
  comparison of, 719–25
  conjunctive, 817
  defined, 529
  diagramed, 987
  distinguished from preposition, 535
  modifying adjectives, 530
  modifying other adverbs, 531
  modifying verbs, 529
  relative, 602
Adverb clause, 603–604
  and combining sentences, 452, 471
  comma and, 471
  defined, 603
  diagramed, 995
  introductory, 471, 603, 801
  placement of, 452
  subordinating conjunction, 471,
    603–604
Adverb phrase
  defined, 576
  placement of, 576
Advertising, 359, 509
Affect, effect, 739, 882
Agenda, in group discussion, 905
Agreement, number, 618–34, 637–39
Agreement, pronoun-antecedent,
    637–39
  collective noun, as
    antecedent, 629
  compound antecedents, 639
  gender, 637–39
  indefinite pronouns, 638–39
  number, 637–39
  personal pronouns, 637–38
Agreement, subject-verb, 619–34
  collective nouns, 628–29
  and combining sentences, 468
  compound subjects, 627
  contractions, 631, 633

M

INDEX

INDEX

INDEX

INDEX

INDEX

INDEX

Acknowledgments

For permission to reprint copyrighted material, grateful acknowledgment is made to the following sources:

Emily R. Alling: Adapted from "Letter to the editor" by Emily R. Alling from *Newsweek,* July 30, 1990.

American Heritage: From "The Business of America: Financial Folklore" by John Steele Gordon from *American Heritage,* vol. 42, no. 1, February/March 1991. Copyright © 1991 by American Heritage, a Division of Forbes, Inc.

Atheneum Publishers, an imprint of Macmillan Publishing Company: "Hard Luck Stories" from *From Approximately Coast to Coast . . . It's the Bob and Ray Show* by Bob Elliott and Ray Goulding. Copyright © 1983 by Goulding-Elliott-Graybar Productions, Inc.

Margaret Atwood: Quotation by Margaret Atwood.

August House, Inc.: From *Moncrief: My Journey to the NBA* by Sidney Moncrief with Myra McLarey. Copyright © 1990 by Sidney A. Moncrief.

Basic Books, a division of HarperCollins Publishers Inc.: Eight ambigrams from *Metamagical Themas: Questing for the Essence of Mind and Pattern* by Douglas R. Hofstadter. Copyright © 1985 by Basic Books, Inc.

Susan Bergholz Literary Services, NYC, NY: "Eleven" from *Woman Hollering Creek and Other Stories* by Sandra Cisneros. Published by Random House, Inc., New York, NY. Copyright © 1991 by Sandra Cisneros. First published in *El Saguaro,* vol. 3, 1986.

Gwenda Blair, Charles Mann, and Knapp Communications Corporation: From "Juan's Place" by Charles Mann and Gwenda Blair from *GEO,* vol. 6, no. 7, July 1984. Copyright © 1984 by Knapp Communications Corporation.

Gwendolyn Brooks: "The Bean Eaters" and "Home" from *Blacks* by Gwendolyn Brooks. Copyright © 1987 by Gwendolyn Brooks.

James Chiles: From "To break the unbreakable codes" by James R. Chiles from *Smithsonian,* vol. 18, no. 3, June 1987. Copyright © 1987 by James Chiles.

Michael Coe: From "Olmec and Maya: A Study in Relationships" by Michael D. Coe from *The Origins of Maya Civilization,* edited by Richard E. W. Adams.

Consumer Reports: "Audio and Video Come Together" from "CD Players: Single-Play and Changer Models" from *Consumer Reports,* March 1990. Copyright © 1990 by Consumers Union of United States, Inc., Yonkers, NY 10703.

Harold Courlander: From "Why No One Lends His Beauty" from *Olode: The Hunter and Other Tales* by Harold Courlander with Ezekial A. Eshugbayi. Copyright © 1968 by Harold Courlander.

Thomas Y. Crowell Company, a division of HarperCollins Publishers: From "To Work, Not to Weep" from *Voices from the Civil War: A Documentary History of the Great American Conflict,* edited by Milton Meltzer.

Current Health 2 Magazine, Weekly Reader Corporation: From "What's Your Type? Introverts and Extroverts" by Sandra R. Arbetter, M.S.W., from *Current Health 2,* March 1991. Copyright © 1991 by Weekly Reader Corporation.

Delacorte Press/Seymour Lawrence, a division of Bantam Doubleday Dell Publishing Group, Inc.: From "Where Have You Gone, Charming Billy?" from *Going After Cacciato* by Tim O'Brien. Copyright © 1978 by Tim O'Brien.

Ebony Magazine: From "The Fitness Craze" by Lynn Norment from *Ebony,* October 1988. Copyright © 1988 by Johnson Publishing Company.

Ann Elmo Agency, Inc.: From *Leiningen Versus the Ants* by Carl Stephenson.

Entertainment Weekly Inc.: From "New Dash for 'The Flash'" from "Rusty Steel" by Ken Tucker from *Entertainment Weekly*, March 29, 1991. Copyright © 1991 by Entertainment Weekly Inc.

Esquire and The Hearst Corporation: From "The Most Beautiful Girl in the World" by Stanley Bing from *Esquire*, January 1990. Copyright © 1990 by *Esquire*. From "Neil Armstrong's Famous First Words" by George Plimpton from *Esquire*, December 1983. Copyright © 1983 by *Esquire*.

Family Media, Inc.: From "Black Kings of Ancient America" by Boyce Rensberger from *Science Digest*, vol. 89, no. 8, September 1981. Copyright © 1981 by Family Media, Inc.

Farrar, Straus and Giroux, Inc.: From "Clean Fun at Riverhead" from *The Kandy-Kolored Tangerine-Flake Streamline Baby* by Tom Wolfe. Copyright © 1965 by Tom Wolfe.

Harcourt Brace Jovanovich, Inc.: From "Spring" from *Marcovaldo* by Italo Calvino. Copyright © 1963 by Giulio Einaudi editore s.p.a., Torino; English translation copyright © 1983 by Harcourt Brace Jovanovich, Inc. and Martin Secker and Warburg Limited. From *The Name of the Rose* by Umberto Eco. Copyright © 1980 by Gruppo Editoriale Fabbri-Bompiani, Sonzogno, S.p.A. English translation copyright © 1983 by Harcourt Brace Jovanovich, Inc. and Martin Secker and Warburg.

HarperCollins Publishers: From *A Browser's Dictionary* by John Ciardi. Copyright © 1980 by John Ciardi. From *An American Childhood* by Annie Dillard. Copyright © 1987 by Annie Dillard.

Harvard University Press: From *One Writer's Beginnings* by Eudora Welty. Copyright © 1983, 1984 by Eudora Welty.

Harvard University Press and the Trustees of Amherst College: "I'll Tell You How the Sun Rose" from *The Poems of Emily Dickinson,* edited by Thomas H. Johnson, Cambridge, Mass.: The Belknap Press of Harvard University Press. Copyright 1951, © 1955, 1979, 1983 by the President and Fellows of Harvard College.

Henry Holt and Company, Inc.: From *My Life with Martin Luther King, Jr.* by Coretta Scott King. Copyright © 1969 by Coretta Scott King.

Houghton Mifflin Company: "How Time Goes" from *Doodle Soup* by John Ciardi. Copyright © 1985 by Myra J. Ciardi. All rights reserved. From *The Street* by Ann Petry. Copyright 1946 and renewed © 1974 by Ann Petry.

Alfred A. Knopf, Inc.: From "White Tigers" from *Memoirs of a Girlhood Among Ghosts* by Maxine Hong Kingston. Copyright © 1975, 1976 by Maxine Hong Kingston. "Sick Leave" by Po-Chü-i, translated by Arthur Waley, from *Translations from the Chinese* by Arthur Waley. Copyright 1919 and renewed 1947 by Arthur Waley.

The Ledger, A New York Times Co. Newspaper: From "Two tornadoes damage airport, Miami school" (Retitled: "Tornadoes Damage School") from *The Ledger*, January 16, 1991. Copyright © 1991 by The Lakeland Ledger Publishing Company.

Life Magazine: From "The Surprises of the Mail" by Shana Alexander from *Life*, June 30, 1967. Copyright © 1967 by Time Warner Inc. From "Reopening the Gateway to America" by Doris G. Kinney from *Life*, vol. 13, no. 11, September 1990. Copyright © 1990 by Time Warner Inc.

1044 *Acknowledgments*

Little, Brown and Company: From *Mythology* by Edith Hamilton. Copyright 1942 by Edith Hamilton. Copyright renewed © 1969 by Dorian Fielding Reid and Doris Fielding Reid. From *Blue Highways: A Journey into America* by William Least Heat Moon. Copyright © 1982 by William Least Heat Moon. From *Nisei Daughter* by Monica Sone. Copyright 1953 and renewed © 1981 by Monica Sone. From *Blooming: A Small-Town Girlhood* by Susan Allen Toth. Copyright © 1978, 1981 by Susan Allen Toth.

Los Angeles Times: From "Time Out! Is Baseball Finnished?" by Bob Secter from *Los Angeles Times Service.* Copyright © 1990 by Los Angeles Times. Published August 3, 1990.

David Low: From "Winterblossom Garden" by David Low from *Ploughshares,* vol. 8, no. 4, 1982. Copyright © 1982 by David Low.

Macmillan Publishing Company: From "The Sun: The Star We Know Best" from *Private Lives of the Stars* by Roy A. Gallant. Copyright © 1986 by Roy A. Gallant. From *The Elements of Style* by William Strunk, Jr. Copyright 1918, © 1959, 1979 by William Strunk, Jr.

Madison Press Books: From "The Fateful Night" from *Exploring the Titanic* by Robert D. Ballard, edited by Patrick Crean. Copyright © 1988 by Ballard & Family. A Scholastic/Madison Press Book.

Marshall Editions Limited: From "How are spiders different from insects?" from *Do Animals Dream? Children's questions about animals most often asked of The Natural History Museum,* answered by Joyce Pope. Copyright © 1986 by Marshall Editions Limited.

N. Scott Momaday: "The Eagle-Feather Fan" from *The Gourd Dancer* by N. Scott Momaday.

Harry A. Moneyhun: Agayuh chart by Harry A. Moneyhun.

Daniel Morrison, and American Way, inflight magazine of American Airlines: From "Date with Dracula" by Daniel D. Morrison from *American Way,* October 15, 1990. Copyright © 1990 by American Airlines.

William Morrow & Company, Inc.: From "Covering the News" from *Behind the Headlines at a Big City Paper* by Betty Lou English. Copyright © 1985 by Betty Lou English. From "The War-Horse" from *Once Upon a Horse: A History of Horses - And How They Shaped Our History* by Suzanne Jurmain. Copyright © 1989 by Suzanne Jurmain.

National Geographic Society: From "America's Ancient Skywatchers" by Robert B. Carlson from *National Geographic Magazine,* March 1990. Copyright © 1990 by National Geographic Society. From "Japanese Americans: Home at Last" by Arthur Zich from *National Geographic,* vol. 169, no. 4, April 1986. Copyright © 1986 by National Geographic Society.

The New York Times Company: From "3 Scientists Say Travel in Time Isn't So Far Out" by Malcolm W. Browne from *The New York Times,* November 22, 1988. Copyright © 1988 by The New York Times Company. From "School for Homeless Children: A Rare Experience" by Timothy Egan from *The New York Times,* November 17, 1988. Copyright © 1988 by The New York Times Company. From "A Thirsty California Is Trying Desalination" by Lawrence M. Fisher from *The New York Times,* November 18, 1990. Copyright © 1990 by The New York Times Company. From "At Rye High, Students Not Only Must Do Well, They Must Do Good" by Lisa W. Foderaro from *The New York Times,* April 30, 1990. Copyright © 1990 by The New York Times Company. From "For Young and Old, a Pocket Paradise" by Kathleen Teltsch from *The New York Times,* April 30, 1989. Copyright © 1989 by The New York Times Company.

The New Yorker: From "Driving Miss Daisy" (review) by Pauline Kael from "Goings On About Town" from *The New Yorker*, March 26, 1990. Copyright © 1990 by Pauline Kael.

Newsweek, Inc.: Quotation by Elmore Leonard from *Newsweek*, April 22, 1985. Copyright © 1985 by Newsweek, Inc.

W. W. Norton & Company, Inc.: From the Editors' Introduction to "The Origin of Diseases" by Mourning Dove (Hum-ishu-ma) from *The Norton Anthology of Literature by Women: The Tradition in English*, edited by Sandra M. Gilbert and Susan Gubar. Copyright © 1985 by Sandra M. Gilbert and Susan Gubar.

The Octagon Press Ltd.: "The Thief" from *Caravan of Dreams* by Idries Shah. Copyright © 1968 by Idries Smith.

Omni Publications International, Ltd.: From "Pioneers Underfoot" by Sherry Baker from "Continuum" from *Omni*, vol. 12, no. 1, October 1989. Copyright © 1989 by Omni Publications International, Ltd. From "Can Bicycles Save the World?" by Jane Bosveld from "Continuum" from *Omni*, vol. 11, no 5, February 1989. Copyright © 1989 by Omni Publications International, Ltd. From "Quasi-Humans" by R. A. Deckert from *Omni*, vol. 12, no. 5, February 1990. Copyright © 1990 by Omni Publications International, Ltd.

Oxford University Press, Inc.: From "Sky Dance" from *A Sand County Almanac, with other essays on conservation from Round River* by Aldo Leopold. Copyright © 1949, 1953, 1966, and renewed © 1977, 1981 by Oxford University Press, Inc.

Noel Petty: From "Charles Spencer ('Charlie') Chaplin" by Noel Petty from *How To Become Absurdly Well-Informed About the Famous and Infamous: A Collection of Brief Biographies*, edited by E. O. Parrott. Copyright © 1987 by Noel Petty.

Clarkson N. Potter, Inc., a division of Crown Publishers, Inc.: From *The Arapaho Way: A Memoir of an Indian Boyhood* by Althea Bass. Copyright © 1966 by Althea Bass.

The Progressive, 409 East Main Street, Madison, WI 53703: From "We Need Power, Program and Progress" by Jesse L. Jackson from *The Progressive*, vol. 54, no. 11, November 1990. Copyright © 1990 by The Progressive, Inc.

Publications International, Ltd.: "Frankenstein" (review) from *The Best, Worst, and Most Unusual: Horror Films* by Darrell Moore. Copyright © 1983 by Publications International, Ltd.

The Putnam Publishing Group: From "The Slow Train to Langxiang: Number 295" from *Riding the Iron Rooster* by Paul Theroux. Copyright © 1988 by Cape Cod Scriveners Co.

Random House, Inc.: From "Woman Work" from *And Still I Rise* by Maya Angelou. Copyright © 1978 by Maya Angelou. From *I know why the caged bird sings* by Maya Angelou. Copyright © 1969 by Maya Angelou. From "Blues Ain't No Mockin Bird" from *Gorilla, My Love* by Toni Cade Bambara. Copyright © 1971 by Toni Cade Bambara. Quotation by Truman Capote. Quotation by John Gardner. From "North Africa: November 1942–June 1943" from *Ernie's War: The Best of Ernie Pyle's World War II Dispatches*, edited with a biographical essay by David Nichols. Copyright © 1986 by David Nichols.

Running Press Book Publishers, 125 S. 22nd Street, Philadelphia, PA: Quotations by Anne Bernays, Willa Cather, Truman Capote, Ernest Hemingway, and Isaac Bashevis Singer from *Writers on Writing*, selected and compiled by Jon Winokur. Copyright © 1986, 1989, 1990 by Jon Winokur.

1046 *Acknowledgments*

The Saturday Evening Post Society: From "Arnold: The Pied Piper of Fitness" by Cory SerVaas, M.D. from *The Saturday Evening Post*, November/December 1990. Copyright © 1990 by *The Saturday Evening Post.*

Seventeen Magazine: From "Why I Choose to Veg Out" by Rebecca Moore from *Seventeen*, August 1988. Copyright © 1988 by News America Publishing. Distributed by Los Angeles Times Syndicate.

Ellen Ruppel Shell: From "Seeds in the bank could stave off disaster on the farm" by Ellen Ruppel Shell from *Smithsonian*, January 1990. Copyright © 1990 by Ellen Ruppel Shell.

Simon & Schuster, Inc.: From *Garbage! Where It Comes From, Where It Goes* by Evan and Janet Hadingham. Copyright © 1990 by WGBH Educational Foundation. From "Leonardo da Vinci Asks the Duke of Milan for a Job" from *A Treasury of the World's Great Letters*, edited by M. Lincoln Schuster. Copyright 1940, © 1968 by Simon & Schuster, Inc.

Gary Soto: From "Foreword" from *A Fire in My Hands: A Book of Poems* by Gary Soto. Copyright © 1990 by Scholastic, Inc.

Sports Illustrated: From "A Yen for Baseball Cards" by Rick Wolff from *Sports Illustrated*, March 4, 1991. Copyright © 1991 by The Time Inc. Magazine Company. All Rights Reserved.

Summit Books, a division of Simon & Schuster, Inc.: From "It's Only Make Believe" from *Rock of Ages: The Rolling Stone History of Rock & Roll* by Ed Ward, Geoffrey Stokes, and Ken Tucker. Copyright © 1986 by Rolling Stone Press.

Gary A. Taubes: From "Boxer with a Future" by Gary A. Taubes from *The Atlantic*, Magazine, vol. 254, no. 2, August 1984. Copyright © 1984 by Gary A. Taubes.

Tribune Media Services: Adapted from "Mo Better Blues" by Steve MacQueen from *Tallahassee Democrat*, August 10, 1990. Copyright © 1990 by Tribune Media Services.

United Press International, Inc.: From "Hayes: 'There Is So Much to Do'" by Helen Hayes.

University of California Press: From *The Olmec World* by Ignacio Bernal, translated by Doris Heyden and Fernando Horcasitas. Copyright © 1969 by The Regents of the University of California.

University of Nebraska Press: From "Grandmother's Land" from *Black Elk Speaks: Being the Life Story of a Holy Man of the Oglala Sioux* by John G. Neihardt. Copyright 1932, © 1959, 1972 by John G. Neihardt; copyright renewed © 1961 by the John G. Neihardt Trust.

Viking Penguin, a division of Penguin Books USA Inc.: Quotation by James Baldwin from "On Revising: Self-Evaluation" from *The Writer's Chapbook*, edited from *The Paris Review*, interview and with an introduction by George Plimpton. Copyright © 1989 by The Paris Review. From *Going Green: A Kid's Handbook to Saving the Planet* by John Elkington, Julia Hailes, Douglas Hill, and Joel Makower. Text copyright © 1990 by John Elkington, Julia Hailes, Douglas Hill, and Viking Penguin, a division of Penguin Books USA, Inc. From *Golden Lilies* by Kwei-li, adapted and with a foreword by Eileen Goudge. Copyright © 1990 by Eileen Goudge. From *The Pearl* by John Steinbeck. Copyright 1945 by John Steinbeck; copyright renewed © 1973 by Elaine Steinbeck, Thom Steinbeck and John Steinbeck IV.

David Wagoner: "Tumbleweed" from *Collected Poems 1956–1976* by David Wagoner. Copyright © 1976 by David Wagoner.

Wallace Literary Agency, Inc.: "An Astrologer's Day" from *Malgudi Days* by R. K. Narayan. Copyright © by R. K. Narayan. Published by Viking Press, 1982.

Webster's New World Dictionaries, a Division of Simon & Schuster, New York: The entry, "empty," and from the "pronunciation key" from *Webster's New World Dictionary*, Third College Edition. Copyright © 1988 by Simon & Schuster, Inc.

H. W. Wilson Company: From entries, "shortcake biscuits" through "Shrady, Nicholas" from *Reader's Guide to Periodical Literature*, May 1990, Vol. 90, No. 5, p. 563. Copyright © 1990 by H. W. Wilson Company.

Writer's Digest Books, an imprint of F & W Publications, Inc.: From quote by Ellen Goodman from *On Being a Writer*, edited by Bill Strickland. Copyright © 1989 by Writer's Digest Books.

Richard B. Zabel: From "The Swan" by Richard Zabel from *The Atlantic Monthly*, vol. 265, no. 5, May 1990. Copyright © 1990 by Richard B. Zabel.

PHOTO CREDITS

Pressfoto; 272, Johnny Johnson/Allstock; 273, Carol Boone; 278, James Newberry; 281(l), HRW photo by Eric Beggs; 281(r), Shelby Thorner/ David Madison; 283(tc), 283(tl), 283(bl), 283(br), 283(tr), Carol Boone; 286(l), 286(r), The Granger Collection; 287, Panhandle-Plains Museum, Photo by Scott Hyde.

CHAPTER 8: Page 298, Kevin Schafer/Martha Hill/Allstock; 304, Park Street; 305, Burke/Triolo Photographic Studio; 307, Steve Chenn/West-light; 309, HRW photo by Eric Beggs, 315(l), Donald Graham/Allstock; 315(br), Richard Hutchings/Photo Researchers; 315(tr), Phyllis Graber Johnson/Stock Boston; 319, "Book of How Things Work", Kingfisher Books, Courtesy of Grisewood and Dempsey Ltd.

CHAPTER 9: Page 326, FourByFive/SuperStock; 327(r), SuperStock; 327(l), 328, Archiv Fur Kunst und Geschichte; 332(t), Michael Baytoff/Black Star; 332(b), Bill Curtsinger/Photo Researchers; 338, Stephen Frisch/Stock Boston; 344, C. Bruce Forster/Allstock; 346, Jeff Spielman/The Image Bank; 348, Nick Gunderson/Allstock; 349, R.L. Kaylin/Allstock; 351, Washington Post Writer's Group; 353, FourByFive/SuperStock; 360, HRW photo by Lance Schriner; 361, Rob Nelson/Black Star.

CHAPTER 10: Page 364, 365, Everett Collection; 366, Nawrocki Stock Photo; 376(l), Jonathan T. Wright/Photographers Aspen; 376(r), SuperStock; 380, Dover Publications; 394, Everett Collection; 395, Skrebneski/The Dial Magazine./The Everett Collection; 397, Park Street.

CHAPTER 11: Page 403, SuperStock; 404(t), Wingstock/Comstock; 413, James Newberry; 430, 431, Donne Bryant/DDB Stock Photo; 433, Frid-mar Damm/Leo de Wys; 435, Donne Bryant/DDB Stock Photo; 439; James Newberry; 441, Art Resource; 443(l), 443(r), Archiv fur Kunst und Geschichte, Berlin; 445, James Newberry.

CHAPTER 12: Page 451, Gerry Ellis/The Wildlife Collection; 453, The Granger Collection; 453(i), Library of Congress; 455, Didier Givois/Vandys-tadt/Photo Researchers; 457(r), Joe Cavanaugh/ DDB Stock Photo; 457(l), SuperStock; 459, all photos by Lee Boltin; 460, Duomo.

CHAPTER 13: Page 462, Courtesy of the Stein-hart Aquarium, Tom McHugh/Photo Researchers; 466, Paul Conklin/PhotoEdit; 470, Robert Footho-rap; 472, all from The Granger Collection; 475, FourByFive/SuperStock; 480, SuperStock; 482, Lance Schriner.

CHAPTER 14: Page 491(r), Historical Picture Service; 491(l), Culver Pictures; 509; both photos by SuperStock.

CHAPTER 15: Page 516, both photos by Tom Jimison; 520, Smithsonian Institution; 527, Wal-ter Rawlings/Robert Harding Picture Library; 529, FourByFive/SuperStock; 532, Martha Swope; 540(cl), Luis Castaneda/The Image Bank; 540(br),

Robert Harding Picture Library; 540(tl), Eric Beggs; 540(cr), Robert Harding Picture Library; 540(bl), M. Bruce/Lightwave; 540(tr), Guido Alberto Rossi/The Image Bank.

CHAPTER 16: Page 546, Nebraska State Histori-cal Society; 549, Richard Laird/FPG; 551, Richard T. Nowitz; 556(tr),(cr),(tl),(bl), Culver Pictures; 556(br), HRW photos by Eric Beggs; 556(cl), HRW photo by Rodney Jones; 557, Scala/Art Resource; 559, M. Richards/PhotoEdit; 564, HRW Photo by Eric Beggs; 567(r), Steve McCutcheon; 567(l), Phil Degginger; 569, Ron Watts/WestLight.

CHAPTER 17: Page 577, Photo courtesy of the National Broadcasting Company; 583, Culver Pictures; 589, David Frazier; 591, Kent & Donna Dannen; 593, SuperStock.

CHAPTER 18: Page 599, Kennedy/TexaStock; 605(t), Alain Dejean/Sygma; 605(b), Ron Behrmann; 612(l), 612(c), Craig Aurness/West-light; 612(r), Burke/Triolo.

CHAPTER 19: Page 625, NASA; 626, Russ Kinne/ Comstock; 630, Adam J. Stoltman/Duomo; 635, The Peabody Museum of Salem, Photo by Mark Sexton; 637(tl), W.K. Fletcher/Photo Researchers; 637(tr), Kjell B. Sandved/Photo Researchers; 637 center (left to right), Fletcher & Bayliss/Photo Researchers, Kjell B. Sandved/Photo Researchers, Ray Coleman/Photo Researchers, Doug Wech-sler; 637(bl), J.H. Carmichael/Photo Researchers; 637(br), Lawrence Migdale/Photo Researchers; 640, George Skene/Orlando Sentinel; 643(l), 643(r), Circus World Museum, Baraboo, Wisconsin.

CHAPTER 20: Page 650(l), Giraudon/Art Resource; 650(c), People's Republic of Congo, Northeast Region, Mahongwe Ethnic Group, Mask, Musee Barbier-Mueller, Geneva; 650(r), Tate Gallery, London/Art Resource, N.Y.; 653(tl),(tr), Marcus Castro/Picture Group; 653(bl), Curtis Norman/Picture Group; 653(br), Marcus Castro/Picture Group; 655, Park Street; 660, Jo Browne/Mick Smee/Tony Stone World-wide; 667(l), Jeffrey W. Myers/Stock Boston; 667(c), Bernard Giani/Agence Vandystadt/Photo Researchers; 667(r), Richard Hutchings/Photo Researchers; 674, Kerrick James.

CHAPTER 21: Page 683, Hampton University Museum; 684, Bob Sebree; 691, Wide World Photos; 693, The Granger Collection; 702, HRW photo by Photo Art Commercial Studios, Inc.

CHAPTER 22: Page 716, all courtesy of McAllen International Museum, HRW photos by Eric Beggs; 719, Caroline Wood/Allstock; 723(l), The Bettman Archives; 723(r), Chad Slattery/Tony Stone Worldwide; 726, all photos courtesy of School of American Research, Indian Arts Research Center; 731, Joseph A. DiChello; 733, all from the Granger Collection.

CHAPTER 23: Page 742(r), Okanogan County Historical Society; 742(l), Historical Photograph

Collection, Washington State University Libraries; 759(l), Courtesy of Ya-Ya, Inc,; 759(r), Photo by Charles Nes, courtesy of Ya-Ya, Inc,; 759(c), Leo Touchet.

CHAPTER 24: Page 766(tr), Mary Ellen Mark/ Library; 766(br), John Dominis; 766(l), Gordon Parks, Jr.; 772, Walter Bibikow/The Image Bank; 775, Osceola, Chief of the Seminoles. Painting by Catlin. Courtesy of the Department of Library Services, American Museum of Natural History; 776, The Granger Collection.; 781, Christopher Magadini, HRW photo by Eric Beggs.

CHAPTER 25: Page 791, Al Rendon; 793, Schafle Associates, TV Guide, January 20, 1990; 800(l), Fernando Bueno/The Image Bank; 800(r), Peter Mauss/Esto; 802(r), Gary Retherford/Photo Researchers, Inc.; 802(tl), Bill McMackins/Unicorn Stock Photos; 802(bl), Tom McHugh/Photo

Researchers, Inc.; 803(r), Courtesy of Raytheon; 803(l), HRW Photo by Eric Beggs; 809, Photoworld/FPG; 810, Arthur Hustwitt/Leo de Wys, Inc.

CHAPTER 26: Page 818(l), 818(r), Vicki Ragan; 822(r), Courtesy of the Union Pacific Railroad; 822(l), Kansas State Historical Society.

CHAPTER 27; Page 834(l), Park Street; 834(cl), ATAS/NATAS; 834(r), Academy of Motion Picture Arts and Sciences.; 834(cr), FourByFive/ SuperStock; 842, HRW photo by Eric Beggs.

CHAPTER 28: Page 853, Christopher Morris/ Black Star; 866(r), The Granger Collection; 866(l), Courtesy of United Shoe Manufacturing Corp.

CHAPTER 29: Page 873, UPI/Bettmann Archive; 876, Library of Congress; 880, John Margolies/ ESTO, 892, HRW collection.

ILLUSTRATION CREDITS

Pierre Babasin—475, 480, 482

Brian Battles—564, 927

Kate Beetle—221

Linda Blackwell—21, 107, 112, 162, 167, 180, 294, 274, 358, 389, 426

Keith Bowden—298, 309, 466, 497, 559, 577

Stephen Brayfield—87, 193, 225, 621, 803

Rondi Collette—xxii, 26, 76, 81, 455, 485, 490, 608, 612, 657, 810, 820

Chris Ellison—371, 372, 374

Richard Erickson—xxi, 200, 239, 487, 525, 551, 589

Janice Fried—83, 145

Tom Gianni—72, 73, 80, 124, 149, 723, 731

John Hanley—451, 549

Tom Herzberg—197

Mary Jones—xxix, 215, 216, 217, 218, 501, 508

Linda Kelen—xix, 43, 97, 230, 356, 456, 488, 496

Susan Kemnitz—11, 13, 122 & 123, 206, 232, 235

Rich Lo—xiii, xvii, 50, 209, 317, 323, 430, 435, 470, 523, 625, 626, 749, 880

Pamela Paulsrud—64, 65, 66, 67

Precision Graphics—298, 653, 776, 853

Doug Schneider—91, 99, 182

Jack Scott—222, 489, 746

Steve Shock—30, 92, 290–291

Troy Thomas—464

Nancy Tucker—88, 173, 409, 447, 457, 729

Acknowledgments

For permission to reprint copyrighted material in the Annotated Teacher's Edition, grateful acknowledgment is made to the following sources:

American Association of University Women: Quotation by Rachel Carson from a speech given on June 22, 1956.

Arte Publico Press: From "The Jacket" from *Small Places* by Gary Soto. Copyright © 1986 by Gary Soto.

Bantam Books, a division of Bantam Doubleday Dell Publishing Group, Inc.: Adapted from "Because" from *Wild Mind: Living the Writer's Life* by Natalie Goldberg. Copyright © 1990 by Natalie Goldberg.

Dell Publishing Co., Inc., a division of Bantam Doubleday Dell Publishing Group, Inc.: From *The Problems of a Writer in War Times* by Ernest Hemingway. Copyright © 1942 by Ernest Hemingway.

Editions Gallimard: Quotation by Marcel Aymé.

Forbes, Inc.: Quotation by B. C. Forbes from *Epigrams*.

The Guardian: Quotation by Jean Renoir from *The Guardian*, 1961. Copyright © 1961 by The Guardian.

Harcourt Brace Jovanovich, Inc.: From "A Formative Clock" from *The Five Clocks* by Martin Joos. Copyright © 1961, 1962, 1967 by Martin Joos.

HarperCollins Publishers: From *Black Elk: The Sacred Ways of a Lakota* by Wallace H. Black and William S. Lyon. Copyright © 1990 by Wallace Black Elk and William S. Lyon. From *The News Business* by John Chancellor and Walter R. Mears. Copyright © 1983 by John Chancellor and Walter R. Mears.

Harvard University Press: From "The Raison d'Etre of Criticism in the Arts" has appeared in this country under the title of "On Criticism in the Arts, Especially Music" in *Music and Criticism: A Symposium*, edited by Richard Frederic French. Copyright 1948 by the Harvard University Press.

International Creative Management on behalf of Toni Morrison: Quotation by Toni Morrison from *Conversations with American Writers* by Charles Ruas. Copyright © 1984 by Charles Ruas. Published by Alfred A. Knopf, Inc.

Alfred Kazin: Quotation by Alfred Kazin.

Alfred A. Knopf, Inc.: From *Minority Report* by H. L. Mencken. Copyright © 1956 by Alfred A. Knopf, Inc.

Longman Group UK Limited: Quotation by John Henry Cardinal Newman from *Oxford University Sermons*. From *Wit and Wisdom of Dean Inge*, edited by William R. Inge and James Marchant. Copyright 1927 by Longman, Green & Co. Ltd.

The Metropolitan Museum of Art: Quotation by Richard A. Diehl from *Mexico: Splendors of Thirty Centuries*, introduction by Octavio Paz. Copyright © 1990 by The Metropolitan Museum of Art.

Marianne Craig Moore, Literary Executor of the Estate of Marianne Moore and Vogue: Quotation by Marianne Moore from *Vogue*, August 15, 1963. Copyright © 1963 by The Condé Nast Publications Inc.

The New York Times Company: Quotation by Robert Frost from *The New York Times*, November 7, 1955. Copyright © 1955 by The New York Times Company. Quotation by Theodor Geisel ("Dr. Seuss") from "On Becoming a Writer" from *The New York Times*, May 21, 1986. Copyright © 1986 by The New York Times Company. Quotation by Whitney Griswold from *The New York Times*, February 24, 1959. Copyright © 1959 by The New York Times Company. Quotation by Ernest Hemingway from a letter to book critic Charles

Poore from *The New York Times*, 1972. Copyright © 1972 by The New York Times Company. Quotation by Joyce Carol Oates from "The Emergence of Joyce Carol Oates" by Lucinda Franks from *The New York Times*, July 27, 1980. Copyright © 1980 by The New York Times Company. Quotation by Stephen Spender from *The New York Times*, March 26, 1961. Copyright © 1961 by The New York Times Company.

Harold Ober Associates, Incorporated: From "Call to Creation" from *The Life of Langston Hughes, Volume 1: 1902–1941, I, Too, Sing America* by Arnold Rampersad. Copyright © 1986 by Arnold Rampersad. Published by Oxford University Press.

The Observer: Quotation by Walter Gropius from *The Observer*, 1956. Quotation by Arthur Koestler from *The Observer*, 1973.

People Weekly: "Hell on Wheels" from the "Up Front" section of *People Weekly*, September 16, 1991, vol. 36, no. 10. Copyright © 1991 by People Weekly.

William Phillips: Quotation by William Phillips from *A Sense of the Present*, 1967.

Prentice Hall, Inc., Englewood Cliffs, NJ: From the Introduction and p. 26 of *Writing with style: Conversations on the art of writing* by John R. Trimble. Copyright © 1975 by Prentice-Hall, Inc.

Running Press Book Publishers: Quotations by E. M. Forster, Stephen Leacock, Marshall McLuhan, and Louis Untermeyer from *Writers On Writing*, selected and compiled by Jon Winokur. Copyright © 1986, 1987, 1990 by Jon Winokur.

St. Martin's Press, Inc.: Quotation by David Beaty from *Contemporary Novelists*, 1976. Copyright © 1976 by St. Martin's Press, Inc.

Charles Scribner's Sons, an imprint of Macmillan Publishing Company: From *Death in the Afternoon* by Ernest Hemingway. Copyright 1932 by Charles Scribner's Sons; copyright renewed © 1960 by Ernest Hemingway.

Straight Arrow Publishers, Inc.: Quotation by Richard Nixon from "The Global Assassins" by Mary Shivanandan and Montague Kern from *Rolling Stone*, 227:43, December 2, 1976. Copyright © 1976 by Straight Arrow Publishers, Inc. All Rights Reserved.

University of Nebraska Press: Quotation by Louise Erdrich from *Winged Words: American Indian Writers Speak* by Laura Coltelli. Copyright © 1990 by the University of Nebraska Press.

Van Nostrand Reinhold: From *Toward A Psychology of Being*, Second Edition, by Abraham H. Maslow. Copyright © 1968 by Litton Educational Publishing, Inc.

Viking Penguin, a division of Penguin Books USA Inc.: From *Stephen Vincent Benét on Writing*, edited and with comment by George Abbe. Copyright © 1964 by George Abbe. Published by The Stephen Greene Press. From *Dramatis Personae: A Retrospective Show* by John Mason Brown. Copyright 1929, 1930, 1934, 1938, 1940, 1944, 1947, 1948–1955 inclusive, © 1957, 1958, 1962, 1963 by John Mason Brown. From *Journal of a Novel* by John Steinbeck. Copyright © 1969 by the Executors of the Estate of John Steinbeck.

A. P. Watt Ltd. on behalf of The Trustees of the Robert Graves Copyright Trust: From *Difficult Questions, Easy Answers* by Robert Graves. Copyright © 1972 by Robert Graves.

Weekly Reader Corporation: Quotation by Ethel Grodzins Romm from "The Virtues of Variety" from *Writing!*®, vol. 10, no. 3, November 1987. Copyright © 1987 by Weekly Reader Corporation. Published by Weekly Reader Corporation.

The Writer, Inc.: From "Erasing the Blue-Pencil Blues" by David Petersen from *The Writer's Handbook*, edited by Sylvia K. Burack. Copyright © 1968 by The Writer, Inc.

Writer's Digest: Quotation by Virginia Woolf from *Writer's Digest*, vol. 58, no. 7, February 1978. Copyright © 1978 by Writer's Digest.

PHOTO CREDITS *(Annotated Teacher's Edition)*

ILLUSTRATION CREDITS: *(Annotated Teacher's Edition)*